East & Southern Africa

THE BACKPACKER'S MANUAL

Second Edition

Philip Briggs

Bradt Travel Guides, UK
The Globe Pequot Press Inc, USA

First published in 1998 by Bradt Publications.
This second edition published in 2001 by Bradt Travel Guides,
19 High Street, Chalfont St Peter, Bucks SL9 9QE, England
web: www.bradt-travelguides.com
Published in the USA by The Globe Pequot Press Inc, 246 Goose Lane,
PO Box 480, Guilford, Connecticut 06475-0480

British Library Cataloguing in Publication Data
A catalogue record for this book is available from the British Library
ISBN 1 84162 028 9

Library of Congress Cataloging-in-Publication Data
Briggs, Philip.
    East & southern Africa : the backpacker's manual / Philip
Briggs,—2nd ed.
        p. cm.
    Includes bibliographical references and index.
    Rev. ed. of: East and southern Africa. 1998.
    ISBN 1-84162-028-9
    1. Backpacking—Africa, Eastern—Guidebooks. 2. Backpacking—
Africa, Southern—Guidebooks. 3. Africa, Eastern—Guidebooks.
4. Africa, Southern—Guidebooks. I. title: East and southern
Africa. II. Briggs, Philip. Eastern and southern Africa. III. Title.
GV199.44.A35 B74 2001
917.7604'4—dc21
                                                                00-049031

Cover photograph Ariadne Van Zandbergen
Illustrations Annabel Milne
Maps Steve Munns

Typeset from the author's disc by Wakewing
Printed and bound in Italy by Legoprint SpA, Trento

Author/Contributors

AUTHOR

Philip Briggs is a travel writer and tour consultant specialising in sub-Saharan Africa. Born in Britain and raised in South Africa, Philip first travelled in East Africa in 1986, and since 1990 he has divided his time equally between travelling in Africa and writing about it. He is the author of Bradt guides to South Africa, Tanzania, Uganda, Ethiopia, Malawi, Mozambique and Ghana, as well as a South African-published guide to Kenya, the co-author of a soon-to-be-published Bradt guide to Rwanda, and has contributed to eight other travel guides covering diverse parts of Africa. In collaboration with his wife, the photographer Ariadne Van Zandbergen, Philip has contributed more than 50 articles to magazines such as *Travel Africa*, *Africa Environment & Wildlife*, *Africa Birds & Birding* and *Wanderlust*. Email: philari@hixnet.co.za.

CONTRIBUTORS

Chris McIntyre, who co-authored the chapters on Zambia, Namibia and Botswana for both editions of this guide, first starting travelling in Africa in 1987, during a three-year stint as a VSO teacher in Zimbabwe. On his return to London, Chris worked as a business analyst, but in 1994 he left the City to concentrate on what he enjoys: travel to southern Africa. The author of Bradt guides to Namibia and Zambia, as well as a forthcoming Botswana guide, Chris is a regular contributor to *Wanderlust*, *Travel Africa* and *BBC Wildlife*, and the managing director of Sunvil Discovery, a specialist Africa division of one of the UK's leading independent tour operators. Email: chris@sunvil.co.uk.

Johannesburg-born **Mike Slater**, who updated the Mozambique chapter for the second edition, started hitching in southern Africa at the age of 14, and has worked as a river-guide, voice-journalist, aid-worker, travel writer and tracher. He first visited Mozambique during a bicycle trip from Cape Town to Sudan, and has subsequently authored two guide books to the country. Mike lives in Johannesburg with his wife and son Daniel, where he divides his time between teaching geography at the Holy Family College, travelling to Mozambique every two months, and running a small advice centre for prospective visitors and investors to Mozambique. Email: slaterm@iafrica.com.

Contents

ACCOMMODATION PRICE BANDS

A	under US$2.50		**D**	from US$8.50 to US$12.50
B	from US$2.50 to US$4.50		**E**	from US$12.50 to US$17.50
C	from US$4.50 to US$8.50		**F**	from US$17.50 to US$25.00

LIST OF MAPS

Introduction

People often think of 'Africa' as one place. So it may be instructive, should you be preparing to visit that place, to imagine the composite picture you'd form of a place called 'Europe' based on a newsflash of a rock festival and a faithful production of a Shakespearian play, or of a place called 'North America' based on a postcards depicting Canada in midwinter and another of a sunny beach in Mexico.

Africa, to a greater extent even than Europe, is far from being a homogenous entity. It is near impossible to make *any* meaningful generalisation about a continent embracing 50 countries as divergent as, say, Libya and Lesotho, or Mali and Malawi, or Ethiopia and Zimbabwe, or Egypt and Mozambique.

The quarter of Africa covered by this guide book does in some respects form a reasonably cohesive unit. Geographically, East and Southern Africa is given some unity by the Rift Valley, the vast chasm that runs from the Red Sea in the north to the Zambezi Valley in the south. And in historical terms, much of the region has been bound together by the medieval Indian Ocean trade routes, by the spread of Bantu-speaking cultures south of Lake Victoria, and by the common British colonial experience.

And although the first image that comes to mind when mentioning individual countries may be vastly different – try, for starters, Rwanda, Ethiopia, South Africa and Kenya – there is no doubt that East and southern Africa as a region embodies the single most pervasive and compelling of the images associated with Africa. This is big game territory, where the world's greatest concentrations of wild animals are protected in more than 100 game reserves, a good dozen of which individually cover the area of a moderately sized European country. For backpackers, who often have more time than money, it is worth emphasising that for every big safari reserve, for every Maasai Mara, Serengeti, Okavango or Kruger Park, there are ten times as many more low-key reserves suited to gentle exploration on foot.

The bountiful diversity of Africa's wildlife never fails to astound: from mountain gorillas to elephants, from ungainly wildebeest to regal lions, from fleet-footed cheetahs to lumbering, earthbound white rhinos, from a warthog family darting off with tails comically erect to a troop of colobus monkeys with their plumed white tails trailing as they leap from tree to tree. East and southern Africa boasts the world's greatest numbers and variety of large mammals – not to say in excess of 1,500 bird species and all manner of small mammals, reptiles and butterflies.

If any single landscape characterises East and southern Africa, it is the one that old Africa hands refer to simply as 'the bush': the vast tracts of dry *acacia* and *brachystegia* woodland so memorably described in the book *Cry of the Kalahari* as 'miles and miles of bloody Africa'. Even as it is today, often depleted of game outside designated reserves, there is something timeless, compulsive, even mesmerising about the African bush. It is a landscape that thrills me more than could any high mountain, tropical beach or beautiful lake. And what, ever, could compare to the awe one experiences when the bush, still but for the mild cooing of doves and strident piet-my-vrou call of the red-chested cuckoo, is suddenly shattered by a blood-curdling trumpeting as a herd of elephants emerges ghostlike from its depths?

But even with the unifying tracts of bush, East and southern Africa is a study in contrasts. Its attractions range from the snow-capped volcanic peak of the world's highest free-standing mountain to the sweltering tropical humidity of the palm-lined Indian Ocean coast; from the barren red dunes of the Namib and Kalahari to the lush, primate-laden rainforests of Uganda; from the rolling grasslands of the Serengeti to freshwater lakes as vast as inland oceans; from the cactus-enclosed stick-and-mud *manyattas* of Maasailand to the astonishing rock-hewn churches of northern Ethiopia; from the stately Old World charm of Stellenbosch or Ilha de Mozambique to the bustling modernity of downtown Nairobi or Addis Ababa.

It is when confronting Africa's human variety that media-generated images make the greatest mischief with one's expectations. Superficially, when it comes to things like dress and urban lifestyles, Africa often seems remarkably Westernised. In a million more subtle ways, however, perceptive travellers will realise that beneath the cast-off jeans and ragged *Bon Jovi Tour 1989* T-shirts, Africa remains intrinsically itself, not least in the atmosphere of cheerful chaos, as intoxicating as it can be frustrating, that seems to surround every aspect of travel in the region.

The message for first-time travellers is simple: arrive with as few preconceptions as possible. Too many tourists recognise only the Africa they seek: a 'Real Africa' burdened with dubious notions of authenticity. It would be absurd to visit Africa and not go on safari, and a great shame not to encounter people living reasonably traditional liftstyles. But, equally, it pays to recognise that this sort of stuff is as peripheral to the day-to-day life of most Africans as fox hunts and Morris Dancers are to the average Londoner. Those travellers who are prepared to embrace the modern reality in all its complexity and variety will find an Africa more engaging, more dynamic – more inherently *African* – than any prescribed one could possibly be.

ABOUT THIS GUIDE

The aim of this book is quite simple: it is to provide backpackers with a thorough, compact and long overdue one-volume travel guide to a group of countries that together form a cohesive and largely self-contained backpacking circuit.

The contents of this book have been distilled from a decade of African travel, during which time I've written comprehensive travel guides to South Africa, Tanzania, Uganda, Kenya, Ethiopia, Malawi and Mozambique, all but one of which was the first dedicated practical guide to that country. My chief frustration throughout this period has been that these one-country guides, packed solid as they are with 'new' off-the-beaten-track information, have been bought mostly by short-stay visitors who simply don't have the time to explore away from the established tourist spots. The publication of the Backpackers Manual will, I hope, set this right, by finally bringing the information that I've gathered over the last few years to the attention of its natural audience: the adventurous backpacker.

A few words of explanation may help readers make the most of this guide, especially as the biggest difficulty I've faced in its compilation has been to chisel away at my own painstakingly constructed one-country guides to decide which information should be retained and which get the chop. Firstly, and with much regret, I've kept background information to the minimum. Secondly, since the guide is aimed specifically at backpackers, I've generally omitted places that are inaccessible without private transport and I've restricted my coverage of accommodation and other practical information to the more affordable options.

I've also tried to avoid including what might be termed 'cosmetic information' – the sort of stuff that looks impressive on paper but in reality dates quickly and/or can easily be checked out on the spot. I don't, for instance, see any value in listing a whole pile of restaurants in Johannesburg when the choice is endless and any hostel will have up-to-date knowledge of the best options in their immediate vicinity. On the other hand, were you to bus into a small town in Tanzania, you would certainly want to be pointed to any decent Indian or Western restaurant that happened to exist. In the same vein, all you really need to know about public transport between, say, Moshi and Arusha in Tanzania, is that there's plenty of it. Why waste words on something so straightforward when there's a thesis waiting to be written about the time-consuming complexities of public transport in northern Mozambique?

A central aim in compiling this guide has been to supply the essential information for as many places as possible, as opposed to giving a vast amount of detail on a selected few spots. Many backpackers would claim that the difference between the traveller and the conventional tourist is a matter of budget. In my opinion, it would be truer to say that the tourist simply wants to travel as quickly as possible between the established tourist sights, whereas the traveller is just as interested in experiencing what lies between them. By this definition, the hop-between-hostel style of backpacking that has emerged recently in many parts of the region is, in spirit, a form of budget tourism. And this book, emphatically, is a travel guide. My job, as I see it, is to dazzle the reader with choices and options, to instil in the first-time visitor to Africa an explorative, interactive and self-motivated approach to travel, not merely to recycle where most travellers sleep and what most travellers do in the same few established places that most travellers visit.

The guide is structured country by country starting with Ethiopia in the north and finishing with South Africa in the south. Each country has been broken down into several modules, each of which covers a cluster of nearby places or a logical route. Within reason, each module is as long or as short as circumstance dicates: the north coast of Kenya, for instance, would form a logical, self-contained travel module whether it required one page or six to describe.

Each module follows a similar format. First up is an introductory overview of the region covered by the module, with a description of every main town and other places of interest that lie within it. This is followed by a section on *Access and getting around*, in which details of the main public transport options are generally followed by directions to places that lie remote from the main routes. Next is the section on *Where to stay and eat*, which lists cheap hotels and sometimes a few restaurants for each town or other place of interest. Finally, most modules contain at least one 'box', and this generally gives expanded information about one particular place or aspect of the region – for instance arranging a Kilimanjaro climb or a historical background to Great Zimbabwe – that would have broken the flow had it been included in the main introductory section.

There are several reasons why I elected to use this modular format, not the least of which is that it discouraged waffle and repetition. Most significant to readers, however, is that a modular structure will save them a great deal of paging around, and it makes it unlikely that they will bypass a places of interest because the information is tucked away somewhere under a different heading. Should you, for instance, be travelling from Dar es Salaam to Mbeya, then you can be sure that all information about every stop or excursion from this route is included in logical order over the space of a few pages.

A large portion of the average practical travel guide is comprised of accommodation information, and while this is perfectly acceptable, even desirable, in the relaxed context of a one-country guide, it feels like a waste of space in a guide covering a dozen countries. When you travel to a new place, what you really need to know is that affordable accommodation exists, and then ideally to be pointed to a couple of decent places. In this context, a comment such as 'good value' or 'recommended' ultimately says as much as a rambling discourse about the friendly management, the fresh paint, the exact price of a plate of meat and rice on a March afternoon in 1997, and the wit and wisdom of a barman called Fred. In my experience, no aspect of African travel is as reliably unreliable as the minutae of budget accommodation, for which reason I've tried to keep to the point and to restrict my recommendations to a few obvious standouts, favouring places that have offered good value over several years or that form part of a cluster of budget hotels. I would always encourage travellers to explore beyond the recommendations made in any travel guide, particularly in countries such as Ethiopia and Tanzania where there are frequently up to 50 small lodgings in any given town.

Two final points. The first is that I could find no logical method of integrating border crossings into country chapters, so to save repetition I have placed all the information on all border crossings in a discrete chapter entitled *Crossing between Countries*. The second is that all mentions of the Congo in this book refer to the Democratic Republic of the Congo, or Zaire as it was known before May 1997. There is, of course, an African country called simply the Congo, but as it doesn't border the region covered by this guide, no serious room for confusion exists.

ACKNOWLEDGEMENTS

First and foremost, boundless love and gratitude to my wife and tireless travel companion Ariadne, whose opinions, thoughts and research are scattered throughout this book. Also on the personal front, many thanks to my parents Roger and Kay Briggs; my brothers Anthony and Matthew; Unusual Destinations and Wild Frontiers in South Africa; Hoopoe Adventure Tours in Tanzania; Gametrackers in Kenya; Jaco Rautenbach of the Word of Mouth Hostel; and David Hartley and Dorette Boshoff, who picked my brain before setting off on a trip through Africa, and repaid me with comprehensive update notes from all over.

On the editorial front, this book – and I – owe much to the encouragement of Hilary Bradt, the hard work of typesetter Sally Brock, the ongoing support and patience of Tricia Hayne and others at Bradt HQ, and the following for their contributions to various regional chapters: Chris McIntyre (Zambia, Namibia and Botswana), Mike Slater (Mozambique update), Edward Paice (Eritrea), David Else (Simien Mountains and Zanzibar) and Janice Booth (Rwanda).

I'd also like to express my gratitude to the many people who have written to me or sent emails with invaluable new information: Enrico Ferrari, Tracey Riddle, Lucy Bailey, Christian Wenaweser, Arthur Gerfers, William Jones, Henk Klaassen, Dave Brown, Patrick Bartz, Jozef Serneels, Katrien Holvoet, Michael Rakower, Donna Hardy, Mark J Smith, Kristin Higgins, Tom Heffer, Antonia Hamilton, Annalinda and Tobin Robinson, Daniel Gorman, Robert H Lindley, Paul Norrish, Richard Franks, Arie van Oosterwyk, Marian Liebmann, Mike Coldham, Jonathan Trigg, Larry Gillen, Professor Hans and Mrs Jane Bode, Gert and Jana Myburgh, Cathy Cooke, John Tuson and Nicola Cornforth, Roger Davidson, Steve Newton-Howes, Morten P Broberg, Mark Moore, Mike Matthews, Dr K Deggeller, J E Clarke, Rosalind Lister, Bev Whiteside, Howard & Avril Gibson, A D H Wilson, Bill Derrett, Erik-Jan Kappers, Michael Santanelli, Iain Jackson, Alex Nuth, Norman V Quinnell, Raoul Boulakia, Emmet Soper, Steven Owad-Jones, Bob Mein, Yves Jackson, Patrick Wesner, Janet Booth, Kenneth Head, Leon Mascini, Marijn Swarte, Richard King, F W Hodgson, Lia de Wilde, R K White, Nigel Francis, and Aulden and Rachael of the Cardboard Box in Windhoek.

Part One

General Information

TELL US ABOUT YOUR TRIP

The readership of any travel guide will collectively experience far more aspects of the countries it covers than the author, and will personally test a far greater number of hotels, campsites, restaurants and safari operators. So, whether you want to make my day with a blow-by-blow account of your off-the-beaten-track adventures, or spoil it by letting me know that I'm wrong about absolutely everything, your time and effort in writing to me about your trip will be greatly appreciated. Every letter will help make for a better third edition, which will in turn enhance the experiences of those who follow in your footsteps. The more detail the better, though even one hot tip about a new hostel or restaurant will not only help me, but be of benefit to the owners of the establishment, and to future travellers.

Every correspondent will be acknowledged in the next edition, so do print your name clearly. Letters can be addressed to Philip Briggs, Bradt Travel Guides, 19 High Street, Chalfont St Peter, Bucks SL9 9QE, England. Alternatively you can email me at philari@hixnet.co.za with a copy to info@bradt-travelguides.com – the best contributors will receive a Bradt travel guide of their choice.

The Historical Framework

The modern political map of Africa took shape little more than a century ago; it would be difficult, if not downright misleading, to view the bulk of events that occurred in the region prior to 1890 in the isolated context of any one African state. To give one example of this, Kilwa is now part of Tanzania, but in medieval times it had stronger links to Sofala in Mozambique or Karangaland in Zimbabwe, even to Iran or India, than to a modern Tanzanian town such as Dodoma or Lushoto. What follows in this chapter, then, is a reasonably detailed overview of regional history which, even if you allow for the generalisations and simplifications that are unavoidable in such a broad context, should give readers a broad picture of events prior to the colonial era. Individual country histories are included in the main body of the guide and, in order to avoid repetition and space wastage, they stress the unique aspects of each country's history and place emphasis on the modern era.

Human evolution

A strong body of archaeological evidence suggests that not only modern humans but the entire chain of hominid ancestry evolved in East Africa. Early hominid species are generally divided into two genuses: the extinct *Australopithecus*, and *Homo*, of which modern man *Homo sapiens* is the only living species. It was long assumed that all *Australopithecus* species were ancestral to modern humans. However, fossils discovered in the 1960s by Louis and Mary Leakey at Olduvai Gorge in Tanzania demonstrated that late australopithecines such as *A. robustus* had far less in common with modern man than did their more lightly built ancestor *A. africanus*. Then, in 1972, the discovery of a two-million-year old *Homo habilis* fossil near Lake Turkana in Kenya proved conclusively that various *Australopithecus* and *Homo* species had cohabited in the region for some time – perhaps until 500,000 years ago – and that the two genuses were discrete evolutionary lines with an unidentified common ancestor.

In 1974, the known timescale of human evolution extended dramatically with the discovery of a 3.5-million-year-old female hominid skeleton in Ethiopia's Danokil Desert. Nicknamed Lucy, this fossil turned out to belong to a previously undescribed species, *A. afarensis*, which was probably ancestral to both hominid evolutionary lines and, with its long arms, would have been as happy swinging through the trees as it would have been jogging. As more *afarensis* fragments came to light, some palaeontologists argued that the wide divergence in skull and body size indicated the presence of several different australopithecine species in the Danokil at this time – any one, perhaps none, might be ancestral to modern man. Only in 1994, when the first complete male *afarensis* skull was uncovered, did it become clear that size differences were simply because males were much larger than females. Based on our present knowledge, it would be difficult to argue that *afarensis* – a remarkably successful species, since its fossil remains span a period of one million years – was anything but the common ancestor of all later hominids.

DNA evidence shows that modern man and chimpanzees are remarkably closely related, with evolutionary lines that diverged from a common ancestor only five million years ago. The Danokil has recently turned up fossils that could well belong to this so-called missing link: the incomplete bones of 17 individuals which would have lived about 4.4 million years ago, when the Danokil was a forest. The dentition of these specimens – tentatively dubbed *A. africanus*, but likely eventually to be placed in a new genus – is closer to that of a chimp than any known hominid, yet the fossils also have several hominid features.

Ethiopia, Kenya and Tanzania all lay claim to the title 'Cradle of Mankind', but the specifics of human evolution remain too controversial for any one country to make this boast confidently. Furthermore, the only certainties to be drawn from the discovery of hominid fossils in one place and not another are that contemporary conditions favoured fossilisation, that current conditions favour fossil recovery, and that palaeontologists were looking for fossils. What does seem reasonably certain is that human evolution, from the emergence of the first bipedal primate to the evolution of our own species from its immediate forebear *Homo erectus*, took place in Africa. Palaeontologists have focused on the East African Rift Valley, but it's interesting to note that in 1997 the oldest known footprints of modern man were discovered at Saldhana Bay near Cape Town, while in 1994 the earliest known proto-hominid fossil, about 12 million years old, was found in the Namibian desert.

The populating of the interior

East Africa entered the Stone Age at least one million years ago, according to implements found by archaeologists at a number of sites. It is in fact probable that this earliest human technology arose there. The earliest identifiable inhabitants of the region were hunter-gatherers, often remembered by the name Batwa, and similar in both culture and physique to the so-called 'Bushmen of South Africa' and pygmies of the Congolese rainforest. These hunter-gatherers, who lived in family bands throughout sub-equatorial Africa, left an enduring memorial in the form of thousands of paintings and engravings, scattered throughout the region in caves and rock shelters, but particularly prolific in South Africa and Zimbabwe. By the time that Europeans arrived in the region it would seem that the hunter-gatherers had been displaced by agriculturalists and pastoralists everywhere but in the driest parts of southern Africa. Today, the only hunter-gatherers left in the region are a few thousand San (or Bushmen) who live in the deserts of Botswana and Namibia.

The vast majority of the modern peoples of eastern and southern Africa speak a language of the Bantu group. The spread of Bantu languages from West Africa is widely associated with that of iron-age technology, on which basis they had reached Lake Victoria by 200BC and modern-day Zululand by AD500. You may read elsewhere that Bantu-speakers reached South Africa only 500 years ago, a widely repeated fiction which South Africa's Nationalist government cited as proof that black South Africans had no greater historical claim to the country than the Afrikaners! What is open to debate is the mechanism of this linguistic colonisation – often described as a migration, but now thought to have been a more gradual process driven by each new generation's search for land to plant or graze. It is difficult to know, as well, whether the new arrivals tended to integrate with or to drive away existing inhabitants.

Bantu-speakers predominate in Tanzania and further south, and probably also account for a good half of the population of Kenya and Uganda, but several other linguistic groups occur in the region. The most widespread of these is that of the

Nilotic-speakers, originally from Sudan and split into two broad groups: the Luo of Lake Victoria, who followed the Nile south into Uganda in the 15th century, and the Maasai and Samburu, who moved down the Rift Valley to end up in the Serengeti region in the 18th century. Another important group are the Cushitic speakers of northern Kenya and southern Ethiopia, such as the Rendille and Oromo. Many other Ethiopians, for instance the Amhara and Tigreans, speak Semitic languages related to Arabic.

For those who read further about African history, it's worth stressing the difference between linguistic, cultural and ethnic distinctions. Terms such as Bantu, Nilotic and Cushitic denote a group of related languages, and the very reason that they are used so often when discussing Africa is because linguists can chart prehistoric movements with a degree of precision unavailable to other disciplines. It is often impossible to determine the extent to which linguistic relationships reflect cultural or ethnic ones – as a clear example, most African Americans are English-speakers, but would not be described as English in a cultural or ethnic context. A semantic point, perhaps, but one which is often misunderstood in an African context, where it has fuelled more than its share of racist pontificating.

Until the 19th century, social structures in the interior of eastern and southern Africa tended not to be highly centralised. The region supported many thousands of clans or chiefdoms and, while neighbouring clans enjoyed a loose political affiliation, systems of government were fundamentally decentralised. A glaring exception to the above is northern Ethiopia, where the Axumite Kingdom was an international trade force from the days of Ancient Egypt through to early medieval times. Another area subject to centralised structures was that around Great Zimbabwe, where from AD1000 the Karanga prospered as a result of the lucrative gold trade with the coast. Centralised government was established in much of Uganda by AD1100, where the legendary Batembuzi and Bacwezi rulers left behind striking earthworks in the vicinity of Mubende and Ntusi.

The coast until 1500

The east coast of Africa has long attracted international maritime trade. The ancient Egyptians evidently entered into spasmodic trade with a port they knew as Punt, while from 600BC the Phoenicians and Romans traded for ivory and tortoiseshell with a port called Rhapta. Little is known about trade in this era, which ended with the collapse of Rome, but Ptolemy's 4th-century *Geography* and the 1st-century Phoenician *Periplus of the Erythrean Sea* point to Rhapta having been on a river mouth in Tanzania, possibly the Pangani or Rufiji. Tantalisingly, Ptolemy mentions that a Greek explorer called Diogenes had seen two snow-capped mountains 25 days upriver from Rhapta, and had been told that a vast lake lay further inland, indicating that 4th-century trade routes penetrated the interior to Mount Kenya and Kilimanjaro, possibly even to Lakes Victoria and Tanganyika.

The rise of Islam marked the beginning of a more enduring Indian Ocean trade epoch: the Shirazi or Swahili Era. The origins of this trade are rather mysterious: 9th-century Islamic ruins on Kenya's Manda Island are probably the oldest on the African coast, and there is little evidence suggesting that Arabs penetrated south of Zanzibar prior to the 10th century, yet one reliable source claims that an 8th-century Islamic cemetery has been discovered at Chibuene in southern Mozambique!

Ivory and slaves were initially the most important items of trade. After AD1000, their place was taken by gold, mined in Karangaland (Zimbabwe), transported by caravan to Sofala (near Beira in Mozambique) and then shipped to Kilwa (Tanzania), the most southerly port that could be reached by an Arab ship wishing to sail home in the same season. The 12th-century geographer Al Idrisi refers to Sofala as an important source of iron, gold and animal skins, and he indicates that by this time China and India were both trading with East Africa, an assertion supported by a mass of archaeological evidence. Trade patterns with the east were so well established by 1414 that the Emperor of China received a shipment of a giraffe courtesy of the Sultan of Malindi.

At this time, the Swahili Coast supported some 30 cities, notably Mogadishu, Malindi, Mombasa, Pangani, Zanzibar, Kilwa and Sofala, many of which were on islands and thus relatively easy to defend. Many of these cities have survived into modern times, but our best idea of their contemporary appearance comes from the extensive ruins of those that didn't, for instance Kilwa and Gedi. The rag coral architecture and obvious Islamic influences have led many popular accounts to treat these cities as Arabic implants, but most historians today agree there was a high level of integration between Arab settlers and indigenous Africans. Islam was widely adhered to, it is true, but the Swahili language is clearly Bantu in origin and the adoption of some Arabic words occurred during the Omani Era, in the 18th century.

The Swahili traders appear to have had little interest in the African interior. There is, for instance, no evidence to suggest that any Muslim ever set foot in Great Zimbabwe, even though this remarkable stone city lay only 20 days' walk from Sofala, for centuries the port that fed gold to the rest of the coast. Arab vessels do appear to have explored the Zambezi as far as Cahora Bassa, and they established some settlements along this river well before the arrival of the Portuguese. Compelling evidence of this comes from a 12th-century Arab document which mentions a town called Seyouna near the confluence of two rivers and a large mountain – the name and geographical details point to this being the same as the later Portuguese port of Sena.

The Portuguese era

Portugal was not the first European power to recognise that it might be possible to sail to the East by circumnavigating Africa – as early as 1291 a Genoese fleet tried to explore this possibility, only to disappear, last sighted off the west coast of Morocco. Portugal was, however, the first European kingdom to make a sustained effort at seeking out this sea-route, an epic of discovery that began with the capture of the Moroccan port of Ceuta in 1415 and culminated when Vasco da Gama sailed around the Cape of Good Hope in 1498 to visit Mozambique Island, Mombasa and Malindi and then to cross the Indian Ocean to Goa.

The Portuguese arrived in the Indian Ocean with many motives: the lure of the lucrative Indian spice and African gold trades, the desire to outdo Spain's American colonial adventure, and not least the opportunity to convert the heathens to Catholicism and (even more piously satisfying) to slaughter and rob the hated Muslim foe. Whichever of these motives dominated, Portugal's superior European firepower meant it had little difficulty taking decisive control of the region. In 1505, Kilwa and Sofala were captured, in theory giving Portugal control of the gold trade at its source. This was followed with vicious raids on several large ports further north – the island town of Mombasa was razed and looted after more than 1,500 residents were killed and the rest fled to the mainland. Only friendly Malindi was spared, to become Portugal's base on the northern part of the African coast. Elsewhere, Portugal seized Goa, the most strategically important Indian port, and it blockaded the Persian gulf to prevent boats from leaving Oman, the main maritime sultancy of the era.

By 1530 Portugal was firmly entrenched in the region, albeit due less to any clear strategy than to its possession of bigger and better guns. The Portuguese administration was shambolic, exploitative and characterised by an extraordinary level of infighting, at the very heart of which lay the personal profit to be extracted from levies by those in high position. Sofala, the main source of gold over the previous 500 years, proved a disappointment to Portugal, in part due to the northward shift in the gold trade that followed the abandonment of Great Zimbabwe in 1450 and in part because Muslim traders set up clandestine trade routes to circumvent Portuguese-held ports. To counter this, the Portuguese launched several military expeditions into the interior, but they generally met with little success and Portugal exerted some measure of control over the goldfields only for a 66-year period starting in 1632.

The one part of the interior to boast a sustained Portuguese presence prior to the 19th century was the Zambezi Valley, where the Muslim settlements at Sena and Tete had been occupied by Portuguese traders by 1550. In the same area, armed Portuguese renegades known as *mazungos* moved into the countryside and usurped the role of local chiefs to create their own mini-fiefdoms, a situation that gained official sanction only in the mid-17th century when the Crown introduced the formal prazo land grant system. It is from Tete in the Zambezi Valley that a trader called Gasper Bocarro launched a 1,000km (620 miles), seven-week march to Kilwa, crossing the Shire River near Chiromo, passing Lake Chilwa, and referring to 'a lake which looks like the sea, from which issues the River Nhanha, which flows into the Zambezi below Sena and there it is called the Chiry'. It's uncertain whether Bocarro actually saw this lake, but if he did then it would seem that David Livingstone, generally regarded to be the first European to reach Lake Malawi, was pipped by a matter of two centuries. All in all, the most lasting Portuguese influence on the African interior was the spread of introduced crops such as maize and cassava (and even on this count their influence was no greater than that of the Waqwaqs of Madagascar, who inadvertently introduced such crops as rice, bananas and mangoes to Africa in the 10th century AD).

Portugal's hold on the African coast north of Cabo Delgado was never as strong as it was further south. In the 16th century it used Malindi, with its friendly sultan, as a base on the north coast, launching occasional but often devastating naval raids on the rival Sultan of Mombasa. Tensions between Mombasa and the Portuguese culminated in a crippling naval attack in 1589, one that was made worse for the people of Mombasa by coinciding with the arrival on the facing mainland of the cannibalistic Zimba. The well-documented and grisly migration of this mysterious tribe up the coast had already been punctuated by a sojourn at Kilwa, where the townsfolk were captured, herded into a stockade, and then killed at a rate dictated by their captors' hunger pangs. The Zimba were eventually halted by the Portuguese near Malindi, but not before they had completed what Portugal started in Mombasa. Portugal in turn seized the opportunity to occupy Mombasa permanently, to which end they built the imposing Fort Jesus in 1593.

Something of an aside to all this was Portugal's belief that the legendary kingdom of Prester John lay in East Africa. Rumours of this remote and wealthy Christian kingdom had been circulating through Europe for 400 years before Portugal reached East Africa, and had been linked to the real, if altogether more humble, Christian Kingdom of Ethiopia since 1306 when an Ethiopian delegation visited the Pope seeking protection from Muslim attacks. The urgency with which the Portuguese Crown sought to contact its fellow Christians can be measured by the fact that Ethiopia was the target of the only extensive trips into the interior officially undertaken by Portugal in the 15th century.

The first of these, documented by the priest Francisco Alvarez in the book *A True Relation of the Lands of Prester John*, was an exploratory six-year mission which reached the court of the young Ethiopian king Lebna Dengel in 1520. This meeting fuelled Muslim fears of a united Christian attack from Ethiopia, and it is at least part of what motivated the Muslim leader Ahmed Gragn to capture the Ethiopian city of Harer. Supported and supplied with arms by the Turks, Gragn launched a largely successful campaign on Christian Ethiopia, resulting in immense loss of life, the destruction of many churches, and the death of Lebna Dengel. In 1541, 400 Portuguese troops under Christopher da Gama marched into Ethiopia; more than half, including da Gama, had been killed in battle by the time they made contact with the Ethiopian forces, but once they did so the combination of Portuguese firepower and Ethiopian numbers eventually proved too much for Gragn's army, which collapsed after its leader was killed in battle. Any nascent ties between Portugal and Ethiopia were doomed after the priest Pedro Paez persuaded Emperor Susenyos, who seized power in 1608, to convert to Catholicism. The result was a civil war between Orthodox Ethiopians and Catholic converts which ended in 1632 when Susenyos abdicated in favour of his son, Fasilidas. The new emperor reinstated the Orthodox Church and banned foreigners from his empire. From the 1640s until James Bruce's journey in 1770, only one European, a French doctor, was permitted to enter Ethiopia.

The Indian Ocean from 1600 to 1810

At the end of the 16th century, Portugal ruled the Indian Ocean beyond question, but its hold over this vast empire was in fact rather fragmented and tenuous, depending as it did on the absence of challenge from another similarly armed European power. By the end of the 17th century, Portugal's influence had been all but restricted to what is now the coast of Mozambique. It might well have been squeezed out of the region altogether were it not for the impregnable stone-walled Fortress of São Sebastião that protected its capital on Mozambique Island.

Not one but two major European naval powers first sailed into East African waters during the closing years of the 16th century. A British boat reached Zanzibar in 1589 before sailing on to India. The Dutch followed in 1596. Within a decade, the British East India Company (BEIC) and Dutch East India Company (VOC) had been formed. Portugal had competition, as it would discover quickly enough. In 1607 and again in 1608, the Dutch occupied Mozambique Island for longer than a month, but were unable to capture the Fortress of São Sebastião, and razed the town in revenge.

The BEIC, meanwhile, focused its attention on India, encouraging British traders to settle at important ports. With Dutch assistance, British ships blockaded Portugal's Indian stronghold at Goa during the outgoing monsoon season for many years. In 1622, Britain and Oman combined forces to drive Portugal from the entrance to the Persian Gulf, an action which removed a crucial plug in the Portuguese defence, allowed the resumption of free trade between Oman and India, and paved the way for a tacit but enduring Anglo-Omani alliance. For the beleaguered Portuguese, this was merely the beginning. In 1658, the VOC captured the Portuguese colony of Ceylon. Ten years later, the BEIC crowned the success of its more surreptitious takeover of India with the purchase of Bombay for a pittance.

It was the Dutch who inadvertently founded the Cape Colony, now part of South Africa. In 1647, the crew of a Dutch shipwreck was stranded at Table Bay for a year, and found it agreeable in every sense. In 1652, after hearing the reports of the Cape's healthy climate, good soil and friendly locals, the VOC sent Jan Van

Riebeeck there to establish a small fuelling station. The VOC never intended this to become a colony – on the contrary they were determined it shouldn't – but an excellent climate and convenient location on the sea-route to India ensured a high level of settlement at the Cape. Within 50 years, Cape Town was an impressive city with a settler population of 2,000.

Portugal's hold on Mombasa remained tenuous. In 1631, the Swahili residents of the island captured Fort Jesus, killing every Portuguese and reinstalling the sultan, who quickly recognised the futility of holding out against Portuguese firepower and returned the fort to its builders. In 1698, however, Portugal lost the fort again, following a two-year Omani siege, and its influence on the coast north of Cabo Delgado (the modern boundary of Tanzania and Mozambique) was effectively over.

During the 17th century, Portugal's ranking in the Indian Ocean had sunk below that of Britain, Holland, Oman and arguably France, soon to capture the abandoned Dutch colony on Mauritius and rename it Île de France. In the 18th century, Britain consolidated its standing in the Indian Ocean at the expense of every other European power. France's Indian Ocean challenge lost impetus when Britain won the Seven Year War in 1763, while the Dutch, dealt a drastic blow when France occupied Holland in 1789, faded altogether after the BEIC captured Ceylon and the Cape in 1795. By the end of the 18th century, if one is to disregard the motley assortment of pirates, slave traders and other racketeers who operated from the Île de France (a threat to ships but of little political significance), Britain had only one potential rival for regional dominance: its long-standing ally the Sultan of Oman.

The early 19th century

From 1794 to 1832, the southeast coastal belt of Africa, home of the Nguni people, was gripped by a terrible succession of droughts. During these severe years, many Nguni came to rely upon cattle raids for food; the ensuing arms race between what had previously been loosely allied clans was probably the prime cause of an increased political centralisation in the region. By 1815, the Nguni were consolidated into three kingdoms: the Zulu, Swazi and Ndandwe. It was the first of these, led by the innovative military tactician Shaka, that emerged as the most powerful force in the region. In a murderous purge remembered as the *Mfecane* ('The Crushing'), Shaka's Zulu army raided and looted vast tracts of the South African *highveld*, killing perhaps as many as one million people and leaving the survivors little option but to flee.

The *Mfecane* had effects far beyond the borders of South Africa. Refugee Nguni war bands swept northwards to mutate into unstoppable roving armies which attacked every village in their path and slaughtered all those who were too young or old to be added to their ranks. Some Nguni leaders settled relatively close to home. Shoshangane, for instance, founded the Gaza Kingdom in southern Mozambique, the major political entity in this region until it was conquered by Portugal in 1895. At Bulawayo, in what is now western Zimbabwe, Mzilikazi founded the Matabele Kingdom on the ashes of the Rozvi Empire (a centuries-old offshoot of the Karonga of Great Zimbabwe). Other war bands ranged north to Lake Tanganyika, not only creating short-term havoc but also having a more lasting effect, as astute local clan leaders mimicked Nguni military methods to expand their own influence.

It is perhaps stretching coincidence to suggest that the advent of the *Mfecane* was entirely unrelated to growing pressure on the Nguni from external sources. In the expanding Cape Colony, the population of which stood at around 15,000 in 1795,

Dutch settlers had enslaved, killed or driven out practically every last indigenous Khoisan person. The eastern border region of the colony was embroiled in an ongoing territorial conflict with the southern Nguni (now the Xhosa), and a steady trickle of European visitors had made its way to Zululand. The late 18th century also saw a sudden increase in the demand for slaves, particularly from the Île de France; many historians believe that a significant slave trade between Nguni chiefs and Portuguese traders could have provided a decisive economic impetus for political centralisation among the Nguni.

At sea, Britain continued to dominate. In 1798, Ceylon was formally made a Crown Colony, as was the Cape in 1815. In 1810, the troublesome Île de France was captured by Britain and reverted to the name Mauritius. For all Britain's efforts, however, the pivotal figure to events in the first half of the century was Seyyid Said, the Sultan of Oman from 1804 to 1854, during which time he radically reshaped the politics of the Indian Ocean. In 1827, Said captured Mombasa from the upstart Mazrui dynasty, giving him full control over the coast north of Cabo Delgado. He then sailed on to Zanzibar, which he selected as his East African base for its proximity to Bagamoyo (the terminus of a caravan route to Lake Tanganyika since 1823) and planted with cloves, giving scant regard to the land claims of the existing inhabitants. By 1840, when Sultan Said moved his capital from Muscat in Oman to Zanzibar, commerce on the island was dominated by the Omani.

Britain had an ambiguous attitude to Said. The BEIC gave the Omani Sultan a great deal of support, in exchange for which they had a practical trade monopoly in the Sultanate without any of the burdens of maintaining a colony. For the British government, however, lending support to Said stood in direct contravention of the Abolition of Slavery Act of 1807. Under Said's rule, the slave trade out of East Africa, once negligible by comparison with that in West Africa, increased exponentially to the point where as many as 50,000 slaves were being sold in Zanzibar annually by 1839.

Britain made genuine efforts to stall the slave trade. In 1822, Sultan Said signed a treaty forbidding the sale of slaves to Christian countries. In 1845, he signed another treaty outlawing the export of slaves beyond the coast between Kilwa and Lamu. Neither treaty was easy to enforce. Britain persuaded Portugal to abolish the slave trade out of Mozambique in 1836, with the effect of driving it underground – the volume of slaves shipped out annually in the 1850s was probably greater than it had been 20 years earlier.

One reason why Britain failed to close down the slave trade was that the coast was merely a transit point. It was easy for traders to use obscure ports to escape detection, and Britain had no influence whatsoever along the caravan routes through the interior. Of these, there were three: the northern route between Pangani and Lake Victoria, the central route between Bagamoyo and Lake Tanganyika, and the southern route between Kilwa and Lake Malawi. The effects of the slave trade on the interior were manifold. Tribes such as the Nyamwezi of central Tanzania and the Yao of Malawi became very powerful, serving as porters along the caravan routes and organising slave raids and ivory hunts deep into the interior. Their weaker neighbours were devastated as villages were ransacked, able-bodied men and women were taken away, and the young, old and infirm were brutally murdered.

How does one calculate the combined effect of the slave trade and *Mfecane* on the interior of eastern and southern Africa? The figures alone are chilling. It is unlikely that the region supported a population as great as ten million when the first slave caravans rolled in, yet for several decades as many as 50,000 slaves were sold annually at Zanzibar's slave market and probably twice as many died on the long march to the coast. A great many more met a brutal end in their village at the hand of slave raiders and Nguni war bands. The level of social disruption caused by such wholesale random slaughter over a period of several decades is, quite simply, incalculable. Above all, what should never be forgotten is that it was this Africa, one cowed and brutalised by decades of slave raids, that was encountered by the first Europeans to penetrate its interior and document the lifestyles of its people. We can only speculate about how the interior might have appeared to outsiders 50 years earlier.

European exploration of the interior

Europeans knew little more about the East African interior in 1850 than they had when Portugal first landed on the coast 350 years earlier. It is remarkable that as recently as 1846 and 1849 the German missionaries Rebmann and Krapf sent reports to Europe describing Mount Kilimanjaro and Mount Kenya, only to be ridiculed for suggesting there might be snow on the Equator. Even more remarkable, perhaps, that 40 years later Africa in its entirety had been partitioned off to the various European powers. Ironically, the kink in what is now the border between Kenya and Tanzania is a result of the Kaiser's insistence on owning the larger of the two great mountains mentioned above.

The most renowned of Africa's Victorian explorers was David Livingstone, an impoverished Scot who left school at the age of ten and educated himself to become a medical doctor and a missionary. Livingstone arrived at the Cape in 1841 to work in the Kuruman Mission, but decided that the greatest service he could perform would be to open up the continent for other missionaries. From 1853 to 1856 he became the first to cross Africa from west to east, 'discovering' and naming Victoria Falls on the way, and in 1859 he sailed up the Shire River and walked to Lake Malawi.

In 1855, a German missionary, James Erhardt, produced a map of Africa which, based on third-hand Arab reports, depicted a slug-shaped lake in the heart of the continent. This map fanned interest in a mystery that had tickled geographers since Roman times – the location of the source of the Nile. Attempting to solve this mystery, Richard Burton and John Speke marched along the caravan route from Bagamoyo to Lake Tanganyika in 1858, making them the first Europeans to see this lake. In the same year, while Burton recovered from fever in Tabora, Speke became the first European to set eyes on Lake Victoria. Speke returned to Lake Victoria in 1863, and concluded that Ripon Falls (near Jinja in Uganda) was the source of the Nile. Burton ridiculed this conclusion; and in 1864, on the eve of a public debate on the subject between the two men, Speke died of a self-inflicted gunshot wound. His death was described by the coroner as a shooting accident, but it seems just as likely he took his own life deliberately.

Livingstone, too, gave much thought to the Nile question. In 1867, he walked inland from Mikindani to spend the last six years of his life wandering between the great lakes, concluding that the most likely source of the Nile was the Lualaba River, which flowed out of Lake Bangweulu in Zambia. In 1872, Livingstone's wanderings were interrupted when he himself was 'discovered' at Ujiji by Henry Stanley, whose alleged greeting, 'Dr Livingstone, I presume', is the most famous phrase spoken in Africa. Livingstone died of fever near Lake Bangweulu in 1873. His heart was removed and buried by his porters, and his cured body was carried 1,500km to Bagamoyo. In 1875, Stanley returned to Livingstone's stomping ground, to ascertain not only that the Lualaba was a source of a large river, but also that the river in question was the Congo and not the Nile. Speke, it transpired, had been right all along.

Like most explorers of his era, Livingstone had ample opportunity to witness the slave trade at first hand, and he became perhaps its most outspoken critic. He believed the trade could be halted only by opening Africa up to the three Cs: Christianity, Commerce and Civilisation. Livingstone's quest to end the slave trade met with little success during his lifetime, but his highly emotional funeral at Westminster Abbey acted as an important catalyst. Missions were built in his name all over Malawi, while industrialists such as William Mackinnon and the Muir brothers invested in schemes to open Africa to commerce. In the year that Livingstone died, John Kirk – who had travelled with Livingstone on his 1856–62 trip to Malawi – was made British Consul in Zanzibar. In 1873, the British navy blockaded the island and Kirk offered Sultan Barghash (the son of Said) full protection against foreign powers if he banned the slave trade. Barghash agreed. The slave market was closed and an Anglican Church built over it. The trade continued on the mainland for some years – 12,000 slaves were sold at Kilwa in 1875 – and was fully eradicated only in 1918. Within ten years of Livingstone's death, however, the volume was a fraction of what it had been in the 1860s. Caravans reverted to ivory as their principal trade, while many coastal traders started rubber and sugar plantations, which turned out to be just as lucrative as their former trade.

The partitioning of East Africa

The so-called 'scramble for Africa' was entered into with mixed motives, erratic enthusiasm and an almost total lack of premeditation by the powers involved. Nevertheless, it had the result of dividing an entire continent into territories which frequently split unified ethnic groups (the Maasai across Kenya and Tanzania, for instance) and even more frequently united two or more groups with a long history of conflict. It was an act of European whimsy for which Africa is still paying today.

The colonial division of eastern Africa was particularly arbitrary. Before the scramble began, the British government enjoyed a degree of influence on Zanzibar which amounted to informal colonialism; not only was it content to maintain this mutually agreeable arrangement, but it was actively opposed to the direct acquisition of African colonies. Two events changed this: the decision of King Leopold of Belgium to colonise the Congo Basin, and an about-face by Germany, which had shown no previous interest in colonies and developed one largely in order to acquire negotiating chips against Britain and France in Europe.

In 1884, a young German metaphysician called Carl Peters arrived in Zanzibar, then made his way to the mainland to sign a series of treaties with local chiefs. The authenticity of these treaties is questionable but when Bismarck announced claims to a large area between the Pangani and Rufiji rivers, it rocked Britain's plans to expand the Sultanate of Zanzibar to include the fertile lands around Kilimanjaro. Worse, large parts of the area claimed by Germany were already part of the Sultanate. Not only was Britain morally bound to protect these, but it didn't want to surrender control of Zanzibar's annual import-export turnover of two million pounds.

Britain was left with little option but to negotiate with Germany, and in 1886 a partition of interest was agreed, identical to the modern border between Kenya and Tanzania. No other boundaries were defined at this time, and by 1890 Germany had claimed the Lamu area and was developing an interest in the rich agricultural land around Lake Victoria. Carl Peters forced the issue in May 1890, when he signed a treaty with the King of Buganda entitling Germany to most of what is now southern Uganda. Peters' plan was frustrated when Bismarck resigned and his successor decided to maintain good relations with Britain. In any case, Stanley had signed a similar treaty in Buganda in 1888, and Germany was far more interested in Heligoland, a North Sea island that had been occupied by Britain since 1807. In 1890, Britain and Germany knocked out an agreement delineating the modern borders of mainland Tanzania (a German territory from 1890 until World War I). In exchange for a North Sea island less than 1km² in area, Germany relinquished any claims to Zanzibar and much of what is now Kenya, Uganda and Malawi.

The partitioning of southern Africa

The process by which southern Africa was divided into colonial territories was somewhat more organic than the carve-up of East Africa. It was set in motion when Britain colonised the Cape, antagonising the Dutch settler population by making English the official language in 1828 and outlawing the recruitment of slaves in 1833. In response, many Boers (Dutch farmers) packed their families and possessions into ox-wagons and headed into the unknown on a mass migration later known as the Great Trek. The Boers trekked north to the Limpopo River and east to Delagoa Bay (the site of modern Maputo): a migration marked by a series of bloody altercations with the Zulus and by the foundation of several short-lived Boer Republics, often in areas that had been depopulated in the *Mfecane*.

By 1860, there were essentially two Boer republics in the interior of southern Africa, the Orange Free State (OFS) and Transvaal, while Britain had added the colony at Natal to its established one at the Cape Colony. So it might have remained but for the discovery of the world's richest diamond vein at Kimberley (then in the OFS, almost immediately afterwards annexed by Britain to its Cape Colony) and then, in 1886, of the immense vein of gold that lay beneath the soil of what is now Johannesburg. Britain was keen to acquire territorial rights to this wealthy region, no less so because it feared a Boer alliance with the Germans, who had announced their interests in the region with the annexation in 1884 of what is now the coast of Namibia.

In 1800, Portugal established a permanent presence at Lourenço Marques (Maputo) on the north shore of Delagoa Bay. Twenty years later, Britain raised its flag on the south shore of the same bay, initiating a protracted dispute between Britain, Portugal and the Boers over a strategic natural harbour that is perhaps the finest in southern Africa. The Boers and Portugal settled their differences in 1869, signing a treaty that not only designated the modern border between Mozambique and South Africa south to Swaziland, but also provided for the building of a railway which would bring business to the Portuguese and end the reliance of the Boers on British ports. The dispute over possession of Delagoa Bay was resolved in 1875, when a French arbitrator awarded the whole bay to Mozambique and drew the line that now forms the Mozambique–South Africa border east of Swaziland.

As the scramble reached its climax in southern Africa, a pivotal figure emerged in the form of Cecil John Rhodes, an Englishman who made his fortune in the Kimberley diamond rush, invested hugely and successfully in the goldfields around Johannesburg, served for several years as prime minister of the Cape, and was prepared to go to practically any lengths to further his two life goals: forging a British Empire that stretched from the Cape all the way to Cairo, and making lots and lots of money. In 1885, with Rhodes pulling the strings, the British government signed a treaty with the Tswana king, effectively driving a wedge between Boer and German territories with the Bechuanaland Protectorate (now Botswana). From 1888 to 1890, using the combination of fraudulent treaties and superior firepower, Rhodes' British South African Charter (BSAC) took control of the territories that would later bear his name: Southern and Northern Rhodesia (now Zimbabwe and Zambia).

The Beira Corridor became a battleground between Rhodes and Portugal, though for once the British government was disinclined to indulge Rhodes, and its treaty with Portugal, signed in 1891, gave Mozambique its modern shape. The northern boundary followed one that had been informally established two centuries earlier when Portugal lost Mombasa to Oman. Other borders were settled in favour of the power which had the higher presence in any given area – hence northern Mozambique was and still is bisected by the Scots-settled area that is now southern Malawi.

The colonial era

The delineation of the colonial boundaries that form the basis of Africa's modern political borders can be regarded as the point where the histories of the countries covered in this guide start to diverge on purely national lines. Nevertheless, there was a strong communality to many aspects of the colonial experience: for starters, most parts of the continent were colonised over the course of a decade, a process that was reversed at a similar pace 60 to 70 years later. It's also the case that only Mozambique, Rwanda, Burundi, Congo, Namibia and Ethiopia, of the countries covered in this guide, were not at some point administered by Britain, so that many aspects of policy were very similar throughout.

All the same, even British territories had vastly different experiences in some respects. At one extreme, take Malawi, a country that suffered terribly at the hands of the slave traders and Nguni war bands, and had the good fortune to be settled by benevolent Scots missionaries who were heavily influenced by Livingstone's idealism. Frankly, I'd defy any intelligent being to read an account of a slave raid on a Malawian village and argue that colonialism, even at its worst, was anything less than a blessing for this country. At the other extreme is Uganda, where short-sighted British administrators laid the foundation for post-independence tragedy by pursuing a divide-and-rule policy that exploited and exacerbated the tensions between the different kingdoms, between Catholic, Protestant and Muslim, and between north and south.

The most widespread means by which the colonial administrations exerted control were the gun and the hut tax. With few exceptions, however, overt military oppression lasted perhaps a decade after formal colonisation, and in most regions it amounted to a one-off beating into submission of tribes that didn't take naturally to colonisation. Between 1900 and 1950, rebellions were few and far between, though not unheard of: the Maji-Maji rebellion in Tanzania and Chilimbwe revolt in Malawi being obvious examples. It is also worth mentioning a fascinating and largely forgotten phenomenon of this period, the Ethiopianist churches which emerged in America and South Africa in the wake of Ethiopia's decisive victory over Italy in 1896. Infusing Christianity with traditional African customs and beliefs, Ethiopianism was distinctly African, with a strongly Baptist flavour, and to some degree the progenitor of the modern Zionist churches as well as the Rastafarian religion of the West Indies. By taking a pro-African stance at a time when few people of African descent had a political say, Ethiopianism was inherently political, and it became strongly aligned with the 'Africa for the Africans' philosophy of the Jamaican visionary Marcus Garvey.

Hut tax proved to be the most insidious means of control, since it made it impossible for villagers merely to subsist and forced them into the cash economy which has yet to work anywhere in Africa. A small proportion of local farmers got around the need to find work by growing cash crops. A great many more had to go to the cities or the mines to find work, or they had to work for the European farmer who in many cases had been granted the very land that their 'employees' had always lived on. In southern African countries such as Malawi and Mozambique, taxation was used to persuade Africans to become migrant labourers: they were forced to leave their homes to work in miserable conditions for puny wages in the mines of the Rhodesias and South Africa. In Malawi, for instance, it has been estimated that some 20% of the male population spent a part of any given year working outside the country in the 1930s. Throughout the region, villages were robbed of their most able workers for months at a stretch, and traditional family structures collapsed under the stress of long periods of separation, giving rise to the startling levels of prostitution which are still in evidence today.

World War II initiated a new wave of protest against colonialism throughout Africa. Thousands upon thousands of African conscripts had been shipped around the world to fight for the freedom of their colonisers; those who returned home found their own liberty as restricted as ever. The first major uprising against colonialism took place in February 1948 in the Gold Coast, when a group of returned war veterans started a riot in Accra. As a result, Britain granted the Gold Coast self-government in 1953 and full independence in 1957, when the country was renamed Ghana. Kwame Nkrumah, Ghana's first president, declared the moment to be 'the turning point on the continent'. It was. In 1957, Ghana had joined Ethiopia and Liberia as one of only three African countries with black rule. By 1968, only three of Africa's 50 countries (those colonised by Portugal, which had been neutral during the war) remained European dependencies, and three others (South Africa, South West Africa, and UDI Rhodesia) remained under white rule.

Planning and Preparation

WHEN TO GO

There's little to stop you travelling in any part of East and southern Africa at any time of year, though seasonal factors might have some bearing on exactly where you go and what you do once you're there. For backpackers spending some time in the region, a greater factor than climate might well be main tourist seasons, which is when prices in resort areas go up, beaches and reserves become more crowded, and accommodation is most likely to be full. The main influx of international tourists is during the European winter, particularly around Christmas and New Year. This is a lesser concern in countries such as Malawi or Uganda which see little fly-in tourism.

In southern Africa, every resort area is packed during the South African summer school holiday, which runs from the first week of December to early January. For backpackers, however, this isn't the problem it was a few years ago, due to the recent mushrooming of backpackers' hostels, most of which are closed to South African residents. One area to be avoided during *all* South African school holidays is the Mozambican coastal resorts south of Vilankulo – you'll struggle to find camping here at these times of year, and hostels are few and far between.

As for climatic factors, most of East Africa lies close enough to the equator that seasonal temperature variations are relatively insignificant, though the coast, which is hot and humid throughout the year, becomes uncomfortably so between December and March. In theory, East Africa has two rainy seasons, but neither personal experience nor rainfall charts suggest that the so-called 'short rains' (mid-October to mid-December) ought to be a factor in anybody's planning. The main rainy season in East Africa, the 'long rains', occurs in April and May, varying by a few weeks from region to region and year to year. Ethiopia has a different rainy season, starting in late June or early July and running through to late September.

Southern Africa has more distinct seasons than East Africa, with the southern African summer coinciding with the European winter and vice versa. The coldest months in southern Africa are June to August and the hottest months November to March. Most of the region experiences an emphatic summer rainfall pattern, the exception being Cape Town and the south coast roughly as far east as Port Elizabeth, where the bulk of the rain falls during the winter months. Depending on altitude, latitude and the rainy season, some parts of southern Africa are more pleasant in winter and others in summer. Hotter areas like Zimbabwe, Malawi and the Indian Ocean coastal belt north of Durban are distinctly more comfortable in the dry, warm winter months. Lying much further south, and with a different rainfall pattern, Cape Town and the Garden Route are quite splendid during the dry summer months and potentially most unpleasant during winter. Both seasons have their advantages in higher areas of South Africa and Zimbabwe such as Johannesburg, the Drakensberg and Zimbabwe's eastern highlands, where chilly winter nights are compensated for by the warm, clear days, and moderate to hot summer conditions are compromised by frequent and often unexpected storms.

Bearing in mind that short-lived storms are more normal than days of protracted drizzle, I wouldn't be unduly concerned about when you travel, though there are certainly disadvantages to travelling during the rainy season. Public transport might stop running on a few rough routes (for instance the coast of Tanzania between Dar es Salaam and Lindi), there's an increased risk of sensitive photographic equipment being damaged in a storm, and camping can be miserable. Healthwise, the risk of contracting malaria and other mosquito-borne diseases is far greater during the rains. In terms of game viewing, the dry season is better because the grass is lower, thereby improving visibility, and animals tend to be more concentrated in the vicinity of perennial rivers and waterholes – though the rainy season has its compensations in the form of greener scenery, more breeding and calving activity, and the huge number of migrant bird species that are present in the region from October to March.

PAPERWORK

Check well in advance that your **passport** hasn't expired and will not do so for a while, since many countries refuse entry on a passport that's due to expire within six months. Make sure, as well, that there are enough pages in your passport for entry and exit stamps for every country as well as any visas you require – allow half a page for each country you'll be visiting, and at least one more page for every country where you'll require a visa (bearing in mind that in some countries such as Ethiopia a monthly visa extension needs a new page).

A **visa** is a permit that must be stamped in your passport in order for you to enter a particular country. Not everybody needs a visa in order to visit every country – British nationals, for instance, can enter most of the relevant countries without one (although since 1996 Zambia, Tanzania and Kenya have required visas for British nationals, and other countries may follow suit). Rulings vary from country to country, but typically you can enter a country at any time for up to three months after the relevant visa is issued, so it's probably worth buying visas for the first few countries that you plan to visit before you fly to Africa. You can also buy your visas as you travel, since all countries covered in this book have diplomatic representation in the capital city of their neighbours. If your nationality means you'll need to buy several visas, bring a stock of passport-sized photos. Countries for which practically everybody requires a visa are Mozambique and Ethiopia (as well as Burundi, Rwanda and the Congo). Nationals of the USA, South Africa and most EU, Scandinavian and Commonwealth countries don't require visas for most countries in the region, but there are several exceptions, rulings do change, and you often cannot get a visa at the border. Check the latest situation at a High Commission or embassy. Backpackers who fly into Kenya from a territory where there is no diplomatic representation should note that it is possible to buy a visa at the airport. On the other hand, arrive at many other land borders without a visa (assuming that you require one) and you will be refused entry. Arrive by air and you may literally be put on the next plane home!

Should there be any possibility you'll want to drive or hire a vehicle while you're in Africa, do organise an **international driving licence** (any AA office in a country in which you're licensed to drive will do this for a nominal fee). You may sometimes be asked at borders for an **international health certificate** showing you've had a yellow fever vaccination.

For security reasons, it's advisable to detail all your important information on one sheet of paper, photocopy it, and distribute a few copies in your luggage, your money-belt, and amongst relatives or friends at home. The sort of things you want to include on this are your travellers' cheque numbers and refund information, travel insurance policy details and 24-hour emergency contact number, passport number, details of relatives or friends to be contacted in an emergency, bank and credit card details, camera and lens serial numbers, etc.

Should your passport be lost or stolen, it will generally be easier to get a replacement if you have a photocopy of the important pages.

GETTING THERE
By air
Nairobi (Kenya), Johannesburg (South Africa) and Harare (Zimbabwe) are the most popular points of arrival. In Europe, the best place to find cheap tickets to Africa is London, where you should be able to pick up a one-way ticket to Nairobi for the equivalent of around US$350 one-way or US$500 return. Bearing in mind that a Virgin Airways flight from some parts of the USA to London costs as little as US$250, North Americans with more time than money may find it advantageous to fly to London and organise a ticket to Africa from there. There are many travel agents in London offering cheap flights to Africa, and it's worth checking out the ads in magazines like *Time Out* and *TNT* and phoning around before you book anything.

Established UK **tour operators** that are well worth contacting are Absolute Africa (tel: 020 8742 0226; web: absoluteafrica.com), Acacia Expeditions (tel: 020 7706 4700), African Trails (tel: 020 8742 7724), Africa Travel Centre (4 Medway Court, Leigh Street, London WC1H 9OX, tel: 020 7387 1211, fax: 020 7383 7512; web: www.africatravel.co.uk), Art of Travel (tel: 020 7738 2038), Bukima Africa (tel: 01234 871329; web: www.bukima.com), Economic Expeditions (tel: 020 8995 7707; web: www.economicexpeditions.com), Hoopoe Adventure Tours (tel: 020 8428 8221; web: www.hoopoe.com), Oasis Overland (tel: 01258 471155; web: oasis-overland.co.uk), Phoenix Expeditions (tel: 01509 881818; www.phoenixexpeditions.com), Truck Africa (tel: 020 7731 6142; web: www.truckafrica.com) and Wildlife Worldwide (tel: 020 8667 9158; web: www.wildlifeworldwide.com). If money is not too tight, try Sunvil (tel: 020 8232 9777; email: africa@discovery.itsnet.co.uk). Two reputable agents specialising in cheap round-the-world type tickets, rather than Africa specifically, are Trailfinders (42–48 Earls Court Road, London W8 6EJ, tel: 020 7938 3366) and STA (117 Euston Road, London NW1 2SX, tel: 020 7361 6262, fax: 020 7937 9570). There are STA branches in Bristol, Cambridge, Oxford and Manchester.

There are several types of ticket you could buy in order to visit East and southern Africa, for instance a one-way ticket, a straightforward return ticket to one city, an open-jaw ticket that allows you to fly into one city and out of another, or a round-the-world-ticket that includes at least one stopover in Africa. Unless your plans are impossibly vague or you think you'll stay in Africa for longer than a year, I'd advise against a one-way ticket. Not only could it create problems with immigration officials when you arrive (most countries require an onward ticket as a condition of entry) but you'll almost certainly lose out when you buy another one-way ticket home. You can safely reject any plan that would involve buying a ticket between any two African countries once you are actually in Africa, since this will be prohibitively expensive (the cheapest return flight between Johannesburg and Addis Ababa, for example, is twice the price of the cheapest return between either of these cities and Europe). One thing that might be worth looking at, at least if you have thoughts of visiting Ethiopia, would be an open-jaw or return Ethiopian Airlines ticket that includes a stopover in Addis Ababa. Ethiopian Airlines flies to most European capitals as well as to Nairobi, Lilongwe, Harare and Johannesburg.

Overland from Europe

There are two overland routes between Europe and the region covered by this travel guide. The longer route, and the one that has been used by overland truck companies over the last decade, is through West Africa, starting in Morocco, crossing the Sahara desert via either Algeria or Mauritania and Mali, and then continuing through Burkina Faso, Ghana, Togo, Benin, Nigeria, Cameroon, Central African Republic (CAR) and the Democratic Republic of the Congo (known as Zaire until early 1997) to Uganda. This route has effectively been closed since early 1996, most recently due to the Zairian civil war, but it will probably become safe again in the not-too-distant future, assuming that the recent restoration of peace to the Congo is lasting. For readers based in the UK, the best way to gauge the current situation would be to get in touch with the many overland truck companies that advertise in magazines such as *TNT* and *Time Out*. And, frankly, one of these six-month overland truck trips is almost certainly the best way of doing this otherwise very difficult route.

The shorter Nile Route involves heading southwards along the Nile through Egypt to Khartoum in Sudan, from where it is possible to cut east to Eritrea or, in theory at least, continue following the Nile southwards to northern Uganda. For several years now, travel in southern Sudan has been forbidden due to the ongoing civil war, a situation which is unlikely to change in the foreseeable future, meaning that you can forget about the route through southern Sudan to Uganda. The route from Khartoum to Eritrea, on the other hand, has been open to travellers most of the time over the last few years, though anybody attempting it should realise that this part of Africa is prone to sudden and unpredictable change.

The broad outline of the Nile Route is to take a ferry from Aswan in Egypt across Lake Nasser to the Sudanese border town of Wadi Halfa. From Wadi Halfa, you'll have to use a combination of buses, trucks, trains and possibly ferries to get to Khartoum – at least three torrid days of dusty travel which can be broken up with stops at Dongola and Karima, both of which are close to important ancient ruins and pyramids. The situation for crossing between Sudan and Eritrea is very fluid, and you should check with an embassy of either or preferably both countries in advance. The last I heard you could get through to Asmara by bus from Khartoum, changing vehicles at Kassala, or failing this there is the possibility of paying for a lift with a boat heading between Port Sudan and Asmara. The best place to check out the current situation is the youth hostel in Khartoum. If you can't get through overland, Ethiopian Airlines flies from Khartoum to Addis Ababa for around US$250.

WHAT TO TAKE

There are two simple rules to bear in mind when you decide what to take with you on a backpacking trip in the developing world. The first is to bring with you *everything* that you could possibly need that mightn't be readily available when you need it. The second is to carry as little as possible. Somewhat contradictory rules, you might think, and you'd be right – so the key is finding the right balance, a personal decision that probably depends on experience as much as any advice. What is perhaps worth stressing is that most genuine necessities are surprisingly easy to get hold of in Africa, and most of the ingenious gadgets you can buy in camping shops are unlikely to amount to much more than dead weight on the road. In fact, you could easily travel through Africa with little more than a change of clothes, a few basic toiletries and a medical kit.

Carrying luggage

Almost everybody who travels in Africa using public transport carries their luggage in a proper backpack or a suitcase that converts into a backpack. Which of these you choose depends mainly on your style of travel. If you intend doing a lot of hiking, you will definitely be best off with a proper backpack. If, on the other hand, you'll be doing things where it might be a good idea to shake off the sometimes negative image attached to backpackers, there are obvious advantages in being able to convert your backpack into a conventional suitcase. The important thing is that you can carry your luggage on your back, since even if you're not specifically hiking you'll spend a lot of time walking between bus stations and hotels.

My current preference is for a robust 35cl daypack. The advantages of keeping luggage as light and compact as possible are manifold. For starters, you can rest it on your lap on bus trips, thus avoiding complications such as extra charges for luggage, arguments about where your bag should be stored, and the slight but real risk of theft if your luggage ends up on the roof. A compact bag also makes for greater mobility, whether you're hiking or looking for a hotel in town. The sacrifice? Leave behind camping equipment and a sleeping bag. Do this, and it's quite possible to fit everything you truly need into a 35cl daypack, and possibly even a few luxuries – I refuse to travel without binoculars, a bird field guide and at least five novels, and can still normally keep my weight down to around 8kg.

If you find that your luggage won't squeeze into a daypack, a sensible compromise is to keep a large daypack in your rucksack. That way, you can carry a tent and other camping equipment when you need it, but at other times reduce your luggage to fit into a daypack and leave what you're not using in storage. This makes sense only if you'll be travelling a fair bit in circuits from a central base.

Clothes

Take the minimum, bearing in mind that you can easily and cheaply replace worn items along the way. In my opinion, what you need is one or possibly two pairs of trousers and/or skirts, one pair of shorts, three shirts or T-shirts, at least one sweater or similar, a light waterproof windbreaker, enough socks and underwear to last five to seven days, one solid pair of shoes or boots for walking, and one pair of sandals, thongs or other light shoes.

When you select your clothes, remember that jeans are heavy to carry, hot to wear, and slow to dry. Far better to bring light cotton trousers and, if you intend spending a while in montane regions, tracksuit bottoms which will provide extra cover on chilly nights. Skirts are best made of a light natural fabric such as cotton. For reasons of protocol, it's advisable to wear skirts that go below the knee in Muslim coastal regions of Kenya, Tanzania and Mozambique.

T-shirts are lighter and less bulky than proper shirts, though the top pocket of a shirt (particularly if it buttons up) is a good place to carry spending money in markets and bus stations, since it's easier to keep an eye on than trouser pockets. For general purposes, one warm sweater or sweatshirt should be adequate, especially if you have a light windbreaker as extra cover, but obviously you will need more substantial clothing to hike in the Alpine zone of the region's major mountains. Bear in mind that the massive used clothing industry in East Africa means that most markets have stalls selling jumpers of dubious aesthetic but impeccable functional value for next to nothing – you might consider buying such clothing on the spot and giving it away afterwards.

Socks and underwear must be made from natural fabrics. Remember that re-using sweaty undergarments will encourage fungal infections such as athlete's foot, as well as prickly heat in the groin region. Socks and underpants are light and compact enough that it's worth bringing a week's supply. As for footwear, genuine hiking boots are worth considering only if you're a serious off-road hiker, since they are very heavy, whether on your feet or in your pack. A good pair of walking shoes, preferably made of leather and with good ankle support, is a good compromise.

Camping equipment

The case for bringing camping equipment to Africa is as compelling as the case against. It's an individual decision, one that will be strongly influenced by how you think you're likely to travel, and you should accept that either way you'll regret your decision at times. An important argument in favour of carrying a tent, assuming that you make reasonable use of it, is that it saves money on accommodation, though those who have to buy camping equipment specifically for the trip might want to weigh this against the initial outlay. More important to many travellers will be that a tent increases their flexibility when they go to places where other accommodation is limited or non-existent. Combined, these will be persuasive arguments to any backpacker who is on a very tight budget or who has a strong interest in hiking and/or off-the-beaten-track travel, particularly in southern Africa where cheap local lodgings are not available.

The main argument against carrying camping equipment is that it will increase the weight and bulk of your luggage by up to 5kg, all of which is dead weight except for when you camp (this includes organised camping safaris, since the company that you go with should provide all gear). There are, in fact, very few instances where backpackers who stick to reasonably well-trod travel circuits will truly need camping equipment, and in countries such as Ethiopia or Tanzania there are few opportunities to camp.

If you decide to carry camping equipment, the key is to look for the lightest available gear. It is now possible to buy a lightweight tent weighing little more than 2kg, but make sure that the one you buy is mosquito proof. Other essentials for camping are a sleeping bag and a roll-mat, which will serve as both insulation and padding. You might want to carry a stove for occasions when no firewood is available, as is the case in many montane national parks where the collection of firewood is forbidden, or for cooking in a tropical storm. If you do carry a stove, it's worth knowing that Camping Gaz cylinders are readily available only in southern Africa (which is where you're most likely to do most of your camping and open-air catering). A box of firelighter blocks will get a fire going in the most unpromising conditions. It would also be advisable to carry a pot, plate, cup and cutlery.

Other useful items

Most backpackers, even those with no intention of camping, carry a **sleeping bag**. A light bag will be adequate in most conditions, but not for high-altitude hikes. Non-campers who carry a sleeping bag will mostly use it in hostels, many of which don't provide bedding, in which case they could save a considerable amount of bulk and weight by carrying a sheet sleeping bag and supplementing it with heavy clothes in cold weather. You might meet backpackers who, when they stay in local lodgings, habitually place their own sleeping bag on top of the bedding provided. Nutters, in my opinion, and I'd imagine that a sleeping bag would be less likely to protect against fleas than to be infested by the things. I could be wrong.

I wouldn't leave home without **binoculars**, which some might say makes me the nutter. Seriously, though, if you're interested in natural history, it's difficult to imagine anything that will give you such value-for-weight entertainment as a pair of light compact binoculars, which these days needn't be much heavier or more bulky than a pack of cards. Binoculars are essential if you want to get a good look at birds (Africa boasts a remarkably colourful avifauna even if you've no desire to put a name to everything that flaps) or to watch distant mammals in game reserves. For most purposes, 7x21 compact binoculars will be fine, though some might prefer 7x35 traditional binoculars for their larger field of vision. Serious birdwatchers will find a 10x magnification more useful.

In East Africa, it's a good idea to carry your own **padlock**, since practically all rooms have padlockable latches but a smaller number supply the actual lock. In any case, put on your own padlock or perhaps better a combination lock and you have added protection against any staff member who might happen to have a spare key.

Your **toilet bag** should at the very minimum include soap (secured in a plastic bag or soap holder unless you enjoy a soapy toothbrush!), shampoo, toothbrush and toothpaste. This sort of stuff is easy to replace as you go along, so there's no need to bring family-sized packs. Men will probably want a **razor**. Women should carry enough **tampons** and/or **sanitary pads** to see them through at least one period (pads and to a lesser degree tampons are readily available in southern Africa, but only in large cities elsewhere), more if they're going to be off the beaten track. If you wear **contact lenses**, be aware that the various fluids are not readily available in East Africa – bring enough to last you through to Zimbabwe or, bearing in mind that many people find the intense sun and dry climate irritates their eyes, revert to glasses. Nobody should forget to bring a **towel**, or to have reasonably handy a roll of **toilet paper**, which although widely available at shops and kiosks throughout the region, cannot be relied upon to be present where it's most urgently needed in countries north of the Zambezi.

Other essentials include a **torch**, a **penknife** and a compact **alarm clock** for those early morning starts. If you're interested in what's happening in the world, you might also think about carrying a **short-wave radio**. Some travellers carry **games** – most commonly a pack of cards, less often chess or draughts or travel Scrabble. A light, plastic **orange-squeezing device** gives you fresh orange juice as an alternative to fizzy drinks and water.

You should also carry a small **medical kit**, the contents of which are discussed in *Health*.

Photographic equipment

An inexpensive point-and-shoot camera with a 50mm lens should produce reasonably satisfactory photographs of people and scenery, though a 28-70mm zoom lens allows for greater flexibility. You can forget about taking even halfway decent wildlife photographs with anything much less than 200x magnification; a 70-300mm or similar zoom lens would be perfect for anything less than professional purposes. Low-speed 50, 64 or 100 ASA films are ideal in most circumstances, and far less grainy than 400 ASA film. Except in South Africa, where most types of film are available (though at inflated prices), don't rely on being able to get anything but 400 ASA print film. If you want to use colour print film of other speeds, or any slide or black-and-white print film, bring it with you.

MONEY
Organising your finances

There are three ways of carrying money: hard currency cash, travellers' cheques, or a credit card. My advice is to bring at least as much as you think you'll need in the combination of cash and travellers' cheques, but if possible also carry a credit card to use in an emergency. I would strongly urge any but the most denominationally chauvinistic of backpackers to bring their cash and travellers' cheques in the form of US dollars, and to learn to think and budget in this currency, since it's by far the most widely recognised one throughout the region.

PHOTOGRAPHY
Ariadne Van Zandbergen
Your Africa trip will most likely be a once-in-a-lifetime experience, and while photography might seem like a minor detail among your other preparations, a small amount of forethought will help you take the best advantage of the many photographic opportunities that will come your way.

Equipment The simpler the camera, the less there is to go wrong – complex electronic gadgetry can be sensitive to rain, dust and heat. For landscapes and portraits, a solidly built manual-focus camera will be adequate. An auto-focus camera will, however, focus with greater precision than any person can hope to on a regular basis, which is particularly useful for moving subjects, such as animals.

For most purposes, the combination of 28-70 and 70-300 or similar magnification zoom lenses will be ideal. A higher magnification than 300 is useful for wildlife but very expensive; for a small loss of quality, teleconverters are a cheap way to get around this: a 300 lens with a 1.4x converter becomes 420mm, and with a 2x it becomes 600mm.

It is possible to buy one lens that covers the full range from 28-300, but such lenses are generally of inferior quality and bulky by comparison to a 28-70 when shooting at low magnifications.

The best way to protect equipment from dust, heat, water, vibrations and bumps is to store it in a Pelican case (any camera shop can order one). On foot, a backpack-style camera bag is more convenient and less likely to attract attention than a normal camera bag. A tripod will allow you to photograph on foot in low light conditions. I cannot overstate the importance of supporting your camera on a beanbag when you photograph wildlife from a car – you can make this yourself from strong fabric, and fill it with beans or rice.

Film Print film is the preference of most casual photographers, slide film of professionals, serious amateurs, and anybody else who hopes to have pictures published. Slide film is the more expensive, but is much cheaper to develop.

Most serious photographers working outdoors in Africa favour Fujichrome slide film, in particular Sensia 100, Provia 100 (the professional equivalent to Sensia) or Velvia 50. Slow films (ie: those with a low ASA (ISO) rating) produce sharper and less grainy images than fast films. Velvia 50 is extremely fine grained and shows stunning colour saturation; it is the film I normally use in soft, even light or overcast weather. For hand-held photography in low light, Sensia or Provia 100 is preferable because it allows you to work at faster shutter speeds. 100 ASA film is more tolerant of contrast, and thus preferable in harsh light.

For print photography, a combination of 100 or 200 ASA film should be ideal. It is advisable to stick to recognised brands. Fujicolor produces excellent print films, with the Superia 100 and 200 recommended.

It is important that you try to develop your film as soon as possible, but avoid developing print film outside major cities, and slide films anywhere but South Africa and Nairobi. One solution is to post or courier film home every few weeks.

Some basics The automatic programmes provided with many cameras are limited in the sense that the camera cannot think, but only make calculations. A better investment than any amount of electronic wizardry would be to buy or borrow a photographic manual for beginners and get to grips with such basics as the relationship between aperture and shutter speed.

Beginners should also note that a low shutter speed can result in camera shake and therefore a blurred image. For hand-held photographs of static subjects using a low magnification lens (eg: 28–70), select a shutter speed of at least 1/60th of a second. For lenses of higher magnification, the rule of thumb is that the shutter speed should be at least the inverse of the magnification (for instance, a speed of 1/300 or faster on a 300-magnification lens). You can use lower shutter speeds with a tripod or beanbag.

Most modern cameras include a reliable built-in light meter, and give users the choice of three types of metering: matrix, centre weighted or spot metering. You will need to understand how these different systems work to make proper use of them.

Dust and heat Dust and heat are a constant problem in Africa. Keep your equipment in a sealed bag, stow films in an airtight container (such as a small cooler bag) and avoid changing film in dusty conditions. Bring a cleaning kit and take care of your equipment. Regularly clean the inside of your camera with a small brush or air blower. A small grain of dirt inside your camera can scratch a whole film.

Light The light in Africa is much harsher than in Europe or North America, which is why the most striking outdoor photographs are often taken during the hour or two of 'golden light' after dawn and before sunset. Shooting in low light may enforce the use of very low shutter speeds, when a tripod or beanbag will be required to avoid camera shake. With careful handling, side-lighting and backlighting can produce stunning effects in soft light and at sunrise or sunset.

Generally, however, it is best to shoot with the sun behind you, which means most buildings and landscapes are essentially a 'morning shot' or 'afternoon shot'. If you spend a bit of time in one place, you'll improve your results by planning the best time to take pictures of static subjects (a compass can come in handy).

When photographing people or animals in the harsh midday sun, images taken in light but even shade are likely to look better than those taken in direct sunlight or patchy shade, since the latter conditions create high contrast. Avoid photographing a shaded subject against a sunlit background, which also creates contrast. Fill-in flash is essential to capture facial detail of dark-skinned people in harsh or patchy light.

Protocol Attitudes to photography vary greatly from one country to the next, and travellers should take heed of local sensibilities. As a rule, it is considered offensive to photograph people without asking first. Some people will refuse, some will agree enthusiastically, while others will expect a small payment. Even the most willing subject will often pose stiffly when a camera is pointed at them; relax them by making a joke, and take a few shots in quick succession to improve the odds of capturing a natural pose.

In most parts of Africa, official attitudes towards photographing government installations have relaxed over the last decade, but this too varies from one country to the next – be circumspect about pulling out your camera at border posts, near military installations and on bridges.

From a security point of view, it's advisable to bring the bulk of your money in the form of travellers' cheques, which can be refunded if they are lost or stolen. Best to use a widely recognised type of travellers' cheque such as American Express or Thomas Cook, and to keep your proof of purchase separate from the cheques, as well as noting which cheques you use, in order to facilitate a swift refund should you require one. Buy your travellers' cheques in a healthy mix of denominations, since you may sometimes need to change a small sum only, for instance when you're about to cross into another country. On the other hand, you don't want an impossibly thick wad of cheques. A suitably flexible mix might be about five US$10 cheques, five US$20 cheques, five US$50 cheques, and the remainder in US$100 cheques. Whatever your bank at home might say, currency regulations and other complications make it practically impossible to break down a large denomination travellers' cheque into smaller ones in most African countries, or to exchange a travellers' cheque for anything but the local currency – so don't bring cheques of US$500 or larger.

You should definitely also bring a proportion of your money in hard currency cash, say around US$300 to US$500, since you are bound to hit situations where travellers' cheques won't be accepted. It would be pretty pointless to bring cash in any currency other than US dollars, though the South African rand is almost as good as far north as Lusaka or Lilongwe. It's advisable to bring most of your cash in small denomination bills, bearing in mind not only the sort of circumstance in which they're likely to come in handy, but also that US$100 bills can be difficult to dispose of after several forgery scares since 1992. It's worth noting that in many countries cash will get you a significantly better rate than travellers' cheques, since banks don't normally charge commission on cash and many private bureaux de change offer better rates than banks and don't accept travellers' cheques at all. None of which would be much consolation if all your money were to be stolen, so don't decide to bring cash only, but do save the cash you bring for situations where it will buy you a real advantage.

Carry your hard currency and travellers' cheques as well as your passport and other important documentation in a moneybelt – one that can be hidden beneath your clothing rather than the sort of fashionable externally-worn codpiece which in some circumstances will serve as a beacon rather than protection. Your moneybelt should be made of cotton or another natural fabric, and everything inside the belt should be wrapped in plastic to protect it against sweat.

Credit cards are widely accepted in southern Africa (except for Mozambique) but elsewhere they're generally of use only in main cities and at upmarket hotels. You can normally draw up to US$150 daily in local currency against a Visa card at any main branch of Barclays Bank (or First National Bank in South Africa), though north of the Zambezi I wouldn't rely on this except in major cities. The American Express representative in any capital city will be able to issue their cardholders with up to US$2,000 in travellers' cheques. For all that, it strikes me that every time I've travelled recently I've bumped into at least one person who's strayed a bit too far off the beaten track with only a credit card for support. I would tend to carry a credit card as a fallback more than anything, and to be conservative in my assumptions about where I'll be able to draw money against it. Two other advantages of carrying a credit card: border officials regard it as equivalent to the 'sufficient funds' that are technically required to enter most countries in the region, and if carried elsewhere in your luggage it would be more than useful if your moneybelt was stolen.

No matter how long you are travelling, do make sure that you are set up in such a way that you won't need to have money transferred or drafted across. Except in South Africa, this can be a notoriously tedious process, and there is a small but real risk the money will never arrive. You will battle to have a draft issued in anything but the currency of the country to which it is drafted.

Most countries in the region levy an airport departure tax on international flights, generally payable only in hard currency cash. The travel agent that sells you your ticket should be able to tell you what tax you'll have to pay, and you'd be safest having the correct amount ready in US dollars. Of the more normal ports of entry and exit, the current airport tax out of Kenya and Tanzania is US$20 and out of Ethiopia it's US$10. The departure tax on tickets out of South Africa is included in the ticket price.

Costs and budgeting

The costs involved in your trip, not to say your daily budget, will depend on so many factors that it is practically impossible to do anything here but make the vaguest generalisations. Not only do costs vary greatly from country to country, but they will be heavily dependent on your style of travel and the sort of activities you undertake. A five-day climb of Kilimanjaro will cost at least US$400, a sum that might reasonably support a frugal traveller camping at Cape Maclear on Lake Malawi for two months.

It is difficult to discuss budgeting without first separating day-to-day costs from those relating to one-off activities. Tanzania, as an illustration, has a reputation among backpackers as an expensive country, but it would be truer to say that it is a cheap country in which many backpackers indulge in expensive activities. Taking day-to-day expenses, then, which basically amount to accommodation, food, drink and transport, there's little doubt that East Africa is cheaper than southern Africa, or that the cheapest countries in the region are Malawi and Ethiopia, where a single traveller could get by comfortably on under US$10 per day and a couple on under US$15. Not necessarily a great deal more expensive are Kenya and Tanzania, where you could get by on a similar amount away from the main tourist areas. In heavily touristed parts of Kenya and throughout Uganda, a minimum daily budget of US$15 for a single traveller and US$20 for a couple might be more realistic. But even this depends greatly on what you're doing. My experience is that day-to-day expenses invariably double when you're on the move for several days in a row, especially if this involves a couple of changes of country. Equally, you could find that they drop to as little as US$5 per head daily if you spend a week camping and cooking for yourself at somewhere like Lake Naivasha in Kenya.

Day-to-day expenses are considerably higher in southern Africa, though you do get a lot more for your money. The most expensive country in the region is almost certainly South Africa, where a dorm bed in a hostel alone costs around US$7 per head daily, and food and transport costs are also relatively high. Unless they stuck exclusively to camping and self-catering, it is difficult to imagine that anybody could travel in South Africa at a daily average of significantly less than US$20 per head. Botswana, Namibia and Zambia are no cheaper. Zimbabwe is generally cheaper, and standards are such that it ranks up there with Malawi and Ethiopia in terms of value for money, but a few days at Vic Falls will probably nullify any saving you make elsewhere in the country! Costs in Mozambique are wildly variable – it could well work out very cheaply if you focus your time there around an extended period of camping at Vilankulo or Barra Reef, but otherwise travel expenses might most aptly be described as East African standards at South African prices.

In summation, then, a realistic day-to-day budget might be as follows. If you'll mostly be camping and self-catering, bank on at least US$10 per day in East Africa (US$15 for a couple) and US$20 per day in southern Africa (US$30 for a couple). If you're not going to camp but will take the cheapest bed available, you should get by on the same in East Africa, but should allocate around US$5 more per person in southern Africa. And if you want to travel reasonably cheaply but to stay in self-contained rooms and eat at proper restaurants where possible, expect to spend US$15–20 per person per day in East Africa, double that in southern Africa.

For most backpackers, the sort of expenses catered for above form only one part of their budget. An organised safari or mountain climb in any East African national park, for instance, will set you back between US$50 and US$80 extra per day. A day's gorilla tracking in Uganda will add around US$250 to your budget for the day, while chimp tracking in the same country's Kibale Forest will cost independent visitors US$20 in park fees. In this respect, East Africa is very expensive – two people spending a week in practically any Tanzanian or Kenyan national park would together spend around US$400 in park entrance and camping fees alone, whereas they would spend around US$40 for the same in any South African national park, perhaps US$70–80 in Zimbabwe or Namibia, and around US$120 in Malawi or Ethiopia.

If you are on a relatively tight budget, it will help regulate your expenditure to split your budget to reflect this – if for instance you were spending around 100 days in the region, you might allow US$1,500 for day-to-day expenses and then keep whatever is left for safaris and other one-off treats. And if there isn't much left, don't fret – buy a tent, adjust your plans so that you concentrate on cheaper countries and regions such as Ethiopia, Malawi, southern Tanzania or western Kenya, and remember that the region (not to say this guidebook) is bursting with exciting and inexpensive possibilities for resourceful travellers!

ITINERARY AND ROUTE PLANNING

You might reasonably expect any itinerary through a region as vast as East and southern Africa to be a very personal thing. But the reality is that most backpackers stick to much the same route and indulge in only a few minor detours or variations. Three factors have helped to shape what might be termed the standard route through East and southern Africa – the best roads, the location of well-known travel highlights, and a certain amount of self-reinforcing feedback between travellers who stick mostly to places that are included in travel guides, and travel guides that emphasise the places most travellers visit.

The most popular route through the region at present usually sees travellers exploring Kenya and possibly Uganda following a fairly loose pattern centred out of Nairobi. From Nairobi, the established backpackers' trail south goes through Arusha, Moshi and Dar es Salaam (diverting to Zanzibar) in Tanzania, then via Mbeya to Malawi. After spending some time on the shore of Lake Malawi, most backpackers bus from Blantyre in Malawi to Harare in Zimbabwe via Mozambique's Tete Corridor. From Harare, everybody heads up to Victoria Falls. It's normal then to head on down to South Africa, using Johannesburg or Pretoria as a first base and then continuing to Durban and following the coast southwest to Cape Town.

With the exception of Ethiopia, Namibia and Mozambique, and allowing for a visit to Uganda's mountain gorilla reserves as a round trip from Kenya, the above route passes through most of the region's popular travel highlights, or at least brings you within easy striking distance of them. Although all major points along this route tend to be very busy with backpackers, there exists a remarkable number of easy excursions for those who want to get away from the beaten track. A great number of more significant variations are possible – for instance travelling between Uganda and Dar es Salaam via Lake Victoria, or down western Tanzania along Lake Tanganyika, or between Harare and Johannesburg via the south coast of Mozambique. And there are also a few radically different routes, some of them very little used by independent travellers, for instance the thousands of kilometres of coast separating Dar es Salaam from Beira in Mozambique, or the Namibian route between Victoria Falls and Cape Town, or the main road from the Tanzania border through Zambia to Victoria Falls. It's all a question of what you want.

I think the best way of deciding your basic route is to pick out a few highlights and use them as the basis. Having done this, the strongly route-based nature of this guide will make it easy to pick out other places that interest you along the way. Try to avoid taking on too much – public transport in this part of the world tends to be slow and draining, so that you ideally should limit your heavy travelling to perhaps one in three days. I would regard three months to be the realistic minimum to get the most out of travelling between East and southern Africa, bearing in mind that any one of Kenya, Tanzania, South Africa or Ethiopia could easily be explored on its own over several months. As a rule of thumb, I'd restructure any itinerary that doesn't allow for an absolute minimum of two weeks, and preferably three weeks, in each country visited (excluding transits such as the six-hour flit through Mozambique entailed in getting from Blantyre to Harare, or a short gorilla-tracking excursion into Rwanda or Zaïre). Above all, assuming that time permits, be flexible – while you don't want to miss the projected highlights of your trip, it would also be silly to stick to a rigid plan when mood, events or word-of-mouth information point you in another direction.

Some highlights

The following list of possible highlights for each country is by no means exhaustive. I have tried to give a balanced overview of what's on offer, focusing on places that are reasonably accessible to budget travellers, but a certain amount of subjectivity is inevitable. The list does, however, include most places that are likely to be considered unmissable either for the general traveller or for those who have more specific interests.

Ethiopia

Axum Capital of the 2,000-year-old Axumite Empire and home of the Ethiopian Church.
Bahir Dar Lake Tana monasteries, a great overnight ferry, and the Blue Nile Falls.
Bale National Park Lovely hiking amongst rare mountain nyala, Simien wolf and many endemic birds.
Gonder Seventeenth-century castles and the painted Church of Birhan Selassie.
Lalibela Famed for its astounding complex of medieval rock-hewn churches. Unmissable.
Rift Valley A string of beautiful lakes of which Ziway and Awasa offer amazing birdwatching.
Simien National Park Spectacular hiking country, Africa's fourth-highest peak, endemic gelada baboon.
Wukro Springboard for exploring the many rock-hewn churches of Tigre.

Kenya

Amboseli National Park Where elephants sweep the plains in the shadow of Kilimanjaro.
Kakamega Forest Reserve Low-key, low-cost antidote to safari circuit. Lots of monkeys and rare birds.
Lake Naivasha Classic setting, hippos, birds, walking amongst big game at Hell's Gate.
Lake Nakuru National Park Flamingoes in tens of thousands, good place to see rhino and leopard.
Lake Turkana Vast desert-fringed lake, visited by few, but raved about by all who get there.
Lamu The infinitely laid-back gem of the Swahili coast, unchanged in shape for centuries.
Maasai Mara Nature Reserve Kenya's smaller and over-touristed extension of Tanzania's Serengeti.
Mombasa East Africa's most compelling large city. Atmospheric old town, beaches to south

Mount Kenya National Park Africa's second highest peak, popular with hikers, cheaper than Kilimanjaro.

Samburu Nature Reserve Desert reserve bisected by river. Supports many localised large mammals.

Watamu Wonderful snorkelling on the reefs, in easy reach of Gedi Ruins and Sokoke Forest.

Uganda

Bwindi National Park Biologically diverse forest, supporting half the world's wild mountain gorillas.

Budongo Forest Reserve Affordable chimpanzee tracking, possibly the best forest birdwatching in East Africa.

Kibale Forest National Park Chimps, rare monkeys, swamp walk, many crater lakes nearby.

Murchison Falls National Park Launch to the waterfall, prolific hippos and crocs, the rare shoebill.

Queen Elizabeth National Park Uganda's best game viewing. Excellent launch trip.

Ruwenzori National Park Tough hiking up to 4,000m in bizarre Afro-alpine vegetation.

Ssese Islands Forested islands in Lake Victoria. One of East Africa's top chill-out spots.

Virunga Volcanoes Mountain gorilla tracking on the Rwanda and Congo border.

Tanzania

Kilwa Little-visited but compelling ruins of Africa's medieval gold-trading emporium.

Lake Manyara National Park With Serengeti and Ngorongoro a highlight of the northern safari circuit.

Lake Tanganyika Ferry The region's best public transport ride and loveliest body of water.

Mount Kilimanjaro National Park Africa's highest peak and most expensive hiking.

Mount Meru Africa's fifth-highest peak, underrated and cheaper alternative to Kilimanjaro.

Ngorongoro Crater Intact volcanic caldera teeming with game, simply not to be missed.

Serengeti National Park All it's cracked up to be and more, this is arguably Africa's finest game reserve.

Tarangire National Park An underrated reserve known for its dense baobab and elephant population.

Tukuyu At the heart of the low-key, inexpensive walking country of the Poroto Mountains.

Usambara Mountains Great views, hikes and birdwatching, especially near Amani and Lushoto.

Zanzibar Lively old town, atmospheric ruins, picture postcard beaches, spice tours.

Zambia

Lake Bangweulu Vast marshy area known for its abundant wildlife and shoebill population.

South Luangwa National Park One of Africa's finest reserves. Accessible to persistent backpackers.

Victoria Falls An unmissable sight, and less commercialised than the Zimbabwe side.

Malawi

Elephant Marsh A remote birdwatchers' nirvana best explored by dugout canoe.

Lake Malawi Snorkel, learn to dive, or relax at resorts like Cape Maclear and Nkhata Bay.

Livingstonia Victorian mission perched on the Rift Valley escarpment above Lake Malawi.

Liwonde National Park Elephants and hippos in their hundreds on the palm-lined Shire River.

Mulanje Southern Africa's highest mountain, Malawi's top hiking area, and very cheap.

Nyika National Park Hiking and rambling in montane grasslands rich in large mammals and birds.
Vwaza Marsh Game Reserve Accessible and inexpensive, good guided game walks.
Zomba The country's nicest large town, springboard to the hiker-friendly Zomba Plateau.

Mozambique

Bazaruto Islands Outstanding marine life; a good place to see the rare *dugong*.
Ilha de Mozambique Former Portuguese capital boasting many 16th-century buildings.
Lago Niassa Mozambique's part of Lake Malawi, better sunsets and reportedly less bilharzia.
Querimba Islands Off-the-beaten-track island hopping based out of atmospheric Ibo Town.
Vilankulo The main backpackers' congregation point on the sun-drenched south coast.

Zimbabwe

Eastern Highlands Low-key region offering some excellent hiking, walking and birdwatching.
Great Zimbabwe Revelatory ruined city that gave the country its name. Not to be missed.
Hwange National Park One of Africa's best reserves, noted for its dense elephant population.
Kaburi Wilderness The more accessible though tamer alternative to Mana Pools (below).
Mana Pools National Park Walk as you like among big game on the Zambezi. Access a problem.
Matobo National Park Memorable rock formations, good rock art, black rhino common, good hiking.
Victoria Falls Africa's biggest falls, centre for every activity from bungee jumps to rafting.

Botswana

Chobe National Park Highly rated reserve on the Chobe River, densely populated by elephant.
Okavango Swamp Game viewing from a mokoro dugout in this unique inland delta.

Namibia

Lüderitz Like a Bavarian village transplanted to the desert.
Etosha National Park Widely regarded to be southern Africa's finest game reserve. Access a problem.
Sossusvlei The massive red dunes seen in every photo essay on Namibia.
Walvis Bay Southern Africa's largest concentrations of migrant waders and flamingoes.
Waterberg Walking and hiking on the game-rich Waterberg Plateau.

South Africa

Cape Town One of the most beautiful cities in the world, a place to settle into for weeks.
Drakensberg The country's largest mountain range, an experienced hiker's haven.
Garden Route The coast between Jeffrey's Bay and Mossel Bay, as beautiful as it is varied.
Hermanus Whale-watching on the coast east of Cape Town.
Kalahari Gemsbok National Park Amazing game-viewing among the red dunes of the Kalahari.
Kruger National Park The major African reserve that's best suited to an affordable self-drive safari.
St Lucia Lush estuary and village at the heart of Zululand's excellent game reserves.
Stellenbosch Beautiful and historic university town in the heart of the Cape Winelands.
Wild Coast Stunning coastal scenery and hikes based out of Port St John or Coffee Bay.

32

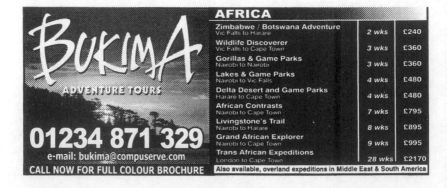

On the Road

3

GETTING AROUND

Roads and public transport facilities throughout the region have improved considerably over the last decade. Backpackers will have few problems getting to most places of interest other than national parks (where there is generally no public transport), though in some more remote regions the only option might be very slow and uncomfortably crowded buses. As a rule, you'll find that roads become better and public transport is quicker, safer and more expensive as you head further south.

Coaches, buses and other road transport

Coach services comparable with those in Europe or the USA are largely restricted to the main through routes in southern Africa. Within South Africa itself, well-established operators such as Greyhound, Translux and Intercape can ferry you in comparable comfort at around 120kph. Between them, these companies also run international services to Windhoek in Namibia and Harare, Bulawayo and Victoria Falls in Zimbabwe. There are also regular coach services connecting major centres in Zimbabwe and Blantyre and Lilongwe in Malawi. The main problem with coaches is that they are relatively expensive (around US$5 per 100km) and inflexible about where they stop. For this reason, most backpackers in South Africa prefer to use a service such as the Baz Bus, which caters specifically to backpackers. It's worth noting, incidentally, that little of what follows applies to travel in South Africa.

A step down from coaches, genuine **express buses** cover major routes such as Nairobi to Mombasa in Kenya, Arusha to Dar es Salaam in Tanzania, Mzuzu to Lilongwe to Blantyre in Malawi, and Blantyre to Harare in Zimbabwe via Tete in Mozambique. A genuine express bus will usually fill all or most seats at the point of departure, stop only at a few scheduled spots, and travel at a speed of around 80–100kph. Fares are generally around double those of ordinary buses, which is still cheap. If you want to go by express bus, make enquiries a day before you travel, since they practically always leave at a set time and normally have an office selling tickets with fixed seating in advance. If you just arrive at a bus station, you may well be told that some or other half-full bus is an 'express' service. That doesn't mean it is.

Then there is the standard African **bus**, a ponderous, densely laden beast of burden with an insatiable appetite for one thing: more passengers! At their worst, for instance in many parts of Tanzania away from the main road connecting Arusha to Mbeya via Dar es Salaam, bus rides can take on nightmarish proportions, as the vehicle becomes so crammed that nipping off for a meal or toilet break is near impossible even when the bus is held up for an hour, and an already slow rate of progress is exacerbated as the bus stops for the slightest reason – to take on board yet another passenger, to drop off the passenger it picked up 500m back, to collect a piece of luggage that's fallen off the roof, so that the driver can visit his mother… In remote parts of Tanzania, you'll be doing well to cover 20km in an hour with stops; I once memorably spent 14 hours on a bus travelling 200km from Iringa to Dodoma. Fortunately, ordinary buses in most other areas aren't quite that bad, though it would be remarkable to cover an average distance at more than 40kph on anything but an express bus.

The other important form of public transport on the African road is the broad and nebulous category of mostly **light vehicles** that includes the Kenyan *matatu*, the Tanzanian *dala-dala*, the Malawian *matola*, the South African taxi and the Mozambican *chapa*. We're talking about anything that moves, carries paying passengers and isn't a bus – it could be one of the comfortable but manically driven minibuses that whizz along surfaced roads in Uganda, South Africa and to a lesser degree Kenya and Malawi, or the customised tarpaulin-covered trucks that bounce between potholes in northern Mozambique, or the dangerously overcrowded pick-up trucks that heave and skid along muddy backroads impassable to buses, or a saloon car driven by a businessman who picks up a few people to subsidise his petrol costs. Wherever you go in East and southern Africa, buses are supplemented by a variety of light vehicles, and these take two broad forms. There are express vehicles such as minibuses, which are quicker and slightly more expensive than the equivalent bus, and often manned by cavalier drivers. And then there are the plodders, such as the jam-packed covered pick-up trucks that crawl and wobble around western Kenya, which you're only likely to want to use on poorly maintained backroads where little else is available.

Public transport between any two towns will generally run to one of two **scheduling systems**. The first is that vehicles leave when they are full (or should that be adequately overcrowded?). The other system is a fixed departure time, generally first thing in the morning. For obvious reasons, the first system tends to have developed where the travelling time between two towns is relatively short (less than four hours, say) and vehicles are plentiful, whereas the second system tends to apply on long hauls. In compact countries such as Malawi, Uganda and Kenya, it's generally the case that you can pitch up at the bus station at any reasonable hour and find a vehicle heading in your direction. In larger countries such as Tanzania or Ethiopia, major towns tend to be hundreds of kilometres apart and so public transport normally leaves at approximately fixed times in the early morning. That said, even in these countries you can expect to find a more casual system of light vehicles plying back and forth between any two significant towns that are within 100km or so of each other – Arusha and Moshi in Tanzania, for instance, or Dire Dawa and Harer in Ethiopia.

In Ethiopia and to a lesser extent elsewhere you'll find that **early starts** are the norm. Just about all buses covering more than 200km leave at 05.00 – or more accurately they start thinking about preparing to leave at some time shortly after 05.00, actually get going at around 06.30, and then are held up for another hour at the police check 1km out of town. In Mozambique, by contrast, when people say that a bus is leaving at 05.00 the chances are that it will have set off at 04.55!

In most African towns and cities there is one central **bus station** from where practically all public transport leaves. Important exceptions include most large towns in Zimbabwe, where buses often leave from a depot situated in a township some distance from the city centre, and just about anywhere in the north of Mozambique, where vehicles tend to pick up passengers from a point along the road out of town, sometimes a 20-minute walk from the town centre. There are also some large cities – Nairobi and Dar es Salaam are cases in point – with many public transport departure points, and in such places it's often worth stopping a taxi and asking the driver to drop you at the right stop for your destination.

I've not normally given specific bus **fares** in this guide, since road transport throughout most of the region is very cheap (you can bus halfway across many

African countries for the price of a return ticket between central London and Heathrow Airport!) and the combination of exchange-rate fluctuations and fare increases makes it impossible to give figures precise enough to counter the occasional instance of overcharging. Throughout the region, using any road transport except coaches, expect fares to work out at around US$1 per 50–100km, depending on the country, the type of transport, the duration of the trip, road conditions and the level of competition. The only time when you might legitimately be asked a higher fare is along rough back routes where there is very little transport and vehicles are likely to spend several hours on the road and to receive a real battering.

In some countries, the **overcharging** of foreigners is commonplace on public transport, a major irritant even when the sum you're talking about is meaningless in the big picture. The best insurance against this is to know the fare in advance: watch what other people pay, or ask a fellow passenger. After a time in any country you'll quickly know when you're being charged too much. The worst culprit is Uganda (where it's confined to light vehicles rather than buses), but it also happens quite a bit in Kenya and northern Tanzania. It's also in Kenya and Uganda that minibus drivers customarily fill an empty vehicle with their buddies in order to lure customers – what happens is that you step into what appears to be a full vehicle, raring to go, but then after paying your fare you find that you're stuck in an empty minibus while several three-quarter-full ones come past! One simple way to get around this is to insist that you'll pay only when the vehicle has left town.

Hitchhiking
The only countries where there's enough private traffic for hitching to be a reliable way of getting around are South Africa and, to a lesser degree, Zimbabwe. The problem with this is that hitching in South Africa can't really be recommended due to the combination of violent crime and the risk of encountering the sort of nutter you might find when hitching in any Western country. Elsewhere in the region, hitching is oddly unpredictable, and it's probably not worth making the effort when you're leaving a large city. In small towns, there's no reason why you couldn't wander out along the road until you find a suitable spot to stick out your thumb – or in East Africa, where that might be interpreted as a rude gesture, follow the local convention of waving your arms round like a scarecrow in a hurricane – but I wouldn't get fixated on the idea of a free lift, rather see it as a bonus if it happens.

In most African countries it's customary for local drivers to pick up passengers and charge them the standard bus fare. This means the distinction between hitching and public transport is somewhat fuzzy. From time to time I've met backpackers who have become highly indignant when a local asked them to pay for a lift. I should stress, therefore, that if and when this happens you're almost certainly not being 'ripped off' or discriminated against – on the contrary, you're being treated as any local 'hitcher' would be.

One argument against hitching is that there's a good chance you'll end up boarding a bus for your efforts but, since all the seats will have been taken by the time the bus gets to the outskirts of town, you may have to stand for several hours.

Rail and ferry
Where they exist, a train or boat would normally be my first choice of public transport in East Africa, and particularly in Tanzania, if only because it wouldn't force me to be cramped in a seat for hour upon bum-numbing, bladder-straining

hour with a chicken squawking at my feet, a child bawling in my ear, and a neighbour who hasn't washed in months insisting that all the windows are kept closed.

Most rail and ferry services run overnight, which is a good time to travel. First- and second-class cabins generally consist of two- and six-berth sleepers respectively, and third class consists of large seated carriages. Third class is cheaper than a bus, but it's very cramped and uncomfortable, and the risk of theft is often unacceptably high. First- and second-class fares are generally around 100% and 50% higher than the equivalent bus fare, a bit more in Kenya, but there isn't too much in it when you take into account that the fare effectively includes a night's accommodation. To give one example, the roughly 600km train trip between Moshi and Dar es Salaam in Tanzania costs around US$20/15/6 first/second/third class whereas the equivalent express bus costs around US$11. One instance where trains are the only realistic option is the central line in Tanzania, which connects Dar es Salaam to Kigoma on Lake Tanganyika and Mwanza on Lake Victoria. Trying to get between any of these towns by bus would be sheer madness.

The most important ferry service in the region is the one connecting Dar es Salaam to Zanzibar, since there's no overland alternative for obvious reasons, but you might also want to make use of the wonderful ferry service on Lake Tanganyika and the more utilitarian one connecting Uganda and Tanzania across Lake Victoria.

Internal flights

Most important towns in any country in the region will be linked to the real or commercial capital of that country by regular flights. Few travellers use these flights, however, since they tend to be prohibitively expensive. The one exception is Ethiopia, where a five-leg air ticket around the northern historical circuit is a real bargain at well under US$200.

Car hire

Hiring a vehicle for part of your trip is an attractive option, not least because it gives you the freedom to explore game reserves independently. Vehicles can be hired in any country, though rates are high by international standards, particularly as you head further north, where your options would become increasingly limited without paying the added expense involved in hiring a 4x4 vehicle. The best way to keep down costs when hiring a vehicle is to get together a like-minded group, at least one member of which will need to have brought an international driving licence from their home country.

I'd be reluctant to advise anybody to hire a car in East Africa. At the bottom end of the price scale you're unlikely to end up with a completely reliable vehicle, so you might easily break down on the poor roads that are characteristic of the region's game reserves. It makes far more sense to visit East Africa's game reserves on an organised safari, since vehicle problems on safari are not the customer's responsibility, and a huge proportion of the costs of a safari these days comprises fees which you will pay whether or not you drive yourself.

Southern Africa, by contrast, is well suited to self-drive trips, as both roads and vehicles are generally of a high standard. In South Africa, the Kruger National Park and Zululand reserves offer some wonderful and relatively inexpensive game-viewing in an ordinary saloon car, and it is practically impossible to do justice to Namibia and Botswana without your own transport. Any hostel in Pretoria, Johannesburg, Durban, Cape Town or Windhoek will be able to put you in touch with a cheap and reliable car hire company – expect to pay around US$250 per week for an unlimited-kilometre deal.

Organised safaris

There are few realistic alternatives to going on an organised camping safari if you want to see something of East Africa's finest game reserves, and increases in park fees over the last few years mean that this is not as affordable as it once was. Expect to pay around US$65–80 daily per person for the most basic all-inclusive safari package out of Nairobi or Arusha, the respective 'safari capitals' of Kenya and Tanzania. It's worth noting that safaris in southern Africa are much, much cheaper than those in East Africa: there are companies offering a four-day safari to the Kruger Park from Johannesburg for well under US$150 per person.

Overland truck and minibus trips

Quite a number of people who buy this guide will consider joining an overland truck trip, either coming down overland from Europe to Kenya via West Africa over six months or so, or else flying into East or southern Africa to join an existing truck trip, probably one heading between Nairobi and Harare over six to ten weeks. I've no wish to discourage those who genuinely feel that an overland truck is right for them. Having said that, I've spoken to a great many people over the years who, through a combination of fear and ignorance, booked a truck trip in London and later came to regret their decision. I must urge anybody who is hanging in the balance to examine their motives honestly.

There is much to be said for using an overland truck to get between Europe and East Africa, since it's the only reliable and affordable way of doing this most daunting journey without private transport. But unless you actually want to travel as part of a large group, I can see few advantages in travelling between Harare and Nairobi in this way. It's a question of temperament. An overland truck trip will probably be great fun if you are naturally gregarious, have no desire for autonomy and primarily want to see the sights. It will be a nightmare if you are strongly individualistic, need your privacy, relish the unexpected, and have any desire to mix with Africans on a one-to-one basis. The worst reason to take an overland truck would be because you are nervous about travelling independently in this part of Africa – aside from malaria, to which you are vulnerable whether you travel on your own or in a truck, there is really very little to fear, even for single women (once you're on the road, it'll be easy enough to find another backpacker heading in your direction).

There is a strong case for joining a short overland truck or minibus trip to visit specific areas. A few companies do three-week jaunts from Nairobi to the mountain gorilla reserves of Uganda, returning via the Serengeti, which effectively amounts to an extended safari but at much cheaper daily rates. In southern Africa, meanwhile, quite a number of companies now do very affordable two-week minibus trips to Namibia out of Cape Town, and there's also a company running ten-day minibus trips through Botswana out of Victoria Falls. In both cases, these would be by far the cheapest means of seeing something of these otherwise rather difficult countries. Rather less compelling, incidentally, are the minibus tours which I've seen advertised out of Zimbabwe and South Africa to Mozambique, since their itineraries focus largely on places that are perfectly accessible to independent travellers.

SLEEPING, EATING AND DRINKING
Accommodation

As a rule, it's easy to find affordable accommodation in the countries covered in this guide, though the type of accommodation available varies greatly from country to country, as do costs.

Local lodgings

In East Africa, backpackers will probably spend most of their nights in simple local lodgings, often known as guesthouses or resthouses, and typically consisting of several cell-like rooms squared around a courtyard. Most such lodgings have communal toilets and washing facilities, which you might want to look at before you take a room, bearing in mind that in many areas running water is a luxury and a hot shower even more so – usually you'll be brought a bucket of washing water on request.

Lodgings in East Africa can be anything from noisy dumps which serve primarily as brothels to quietly respectable family-run establishments, but most places fall somewhere between these extremes. In many towns, several lodgings are clustered in one place (typically near the bus station), and in such cases it's often worth looking around before you settle on a room – standards tend to vary more than prices and a slack attitude to maintenance means that the newest lodge will often be the best choice. However, no matter how dirty or raucous the lodging, there is generally little reason for concern about personal safety or items left in a padlocked room.

To give some idea of what to expect in different countries, local lodgings form the bulk of budget accommodation in Ethiopia, Tanzania, Kenya and Malawi, where any but the smallest of villages can be relied upon to have at least one lodging, and most towns of any substance have a dozen or more. In these countries, it's almost always possible to find an acceptable room in the US$2–4 range, perhaps double the price in capital cities and other places which attract a high volume of tourists. Accommodation in Uganda and Mozambique is similar, but most towns have fewer lodgings, standards are lower, and prices are considerably higher, particularly in Mozambique.

Backpacker hostels

Local lodgings as described above don't feature on the southern African travel circuit, where the last five years have witnessed an incredible mushrooming of backpacker hostels. At least one hostel aimed specifically at backpackers exists in practically every tourist centre and major town in South Africa, Zimbabwe and to a lesser extent Namibia and Malawi. In South Africa, you're typically looking at around US$7 per person for a dormitory bed in a hostel, around US$15–20 for a double room, and US$3–4 per person to pitch a tent. Elsewhere in the region, such as in Zimbabwe, hostels are generally a bit cheaper. If the hostel can't easily be reached on foot, give them a ring and they'll most often fetch you from the town centre.

Most backpacker hostels are run by travellers or former travellers. As a rule, they avoid the restrictive atmosphere that characterises institutional hostels such as youth hostels and church-run places, and they often act as an important source of information for travellers on a budget. However, while a night or two in a hostel provides welcome reprieve from the more grinding aspects of African travel, it could be argued that things have become a little too cosy when many backpackers find it normal to spend several months bouncing from one hostel to the next, exposing themselves as little as possible to any aspect of Africa other than tourist sights, hostel owners and other backpackers.

Camping

The question of whether to bring camping equipment to Africa is discussed in detail in *Planning and Preparation*. Assuming that you do bring camping equipment, you'll not only save a lot of money in countries where accommodation is relatively expensive, but you'll also have the flexibility to stay in many small reserves that you might otherwise be unable to visit. In southern

Africa, camping is the only affordable way of breaking away from the arguably rather restrictive backpackers' circuit.

Up-to-date information
It's inevitable that the accommodation information in this or any other travel guide will become dated during the lifespan of an edition. This is of no great concern in East Africa, where finding a cheap room is rarely a problem – in most places accommodation tends to be clustered in one part of town, and you'll easily find an alternative to any place recommended in a travel guide. In southern Africa, however, the situation is different in that many towns have only one affordable option, often some distance from the town centre, so you definitely want to know about changes. (See Chapter 18, pages 539–40.)

Food
Ethiopia is the only country in the region to boast a distinctive cuisine, covered in Chapter 7. Elsewhere, local food is at best dull. The staple source of carbohydrates throughout the region is a stiff porridge made of ground maize and known variously as *ugali*, *nsima*, *shima* and *mieliepap*, though this is supplemented in Uganda, western Tanzania and western Kenya with a boiled banana porridge known as *matoke* or *batoke*. In local restaurants you can often order rice, potato chips or occasionally boiled potatoes (known in Uganda as Irish potatoes) as an alternative to the maize or banana porridge. Whatever starch you order, it will generally be accompanied by a stew, typically a few gristly lumps of meat or a bony portion of chicken flavoured with nothing much but salt. In coastal regions and near lakes, the best dish to order in local restaurants is grilled or fried fish. The sole virtue of local restaurants in East Africa is that they are very cheap – in many parts of the region you can eat substantially for little more than US$1.

This sort of food soon palls for most travellers, so it's fortunate that most large towns in East Africa have at least one Westernised restaurant – often attached to an

ACCOMMODATION PRICES
These are coded alphabetically in ascending bands of **A** to **F** indicating prices as follows:

A under US$2.50
B from US$2.50 to US$4.50
C from US$4.50 to US$8.50
D from US$8.50 to US$12.50
E from US$12.50 to US$17.50
F from US$17.50 to US$25

Prices are given as in the following examples

Dorm **A** pp	= **A** per person for a dormitory bed
Room **B** sgl	= **B** for a single room
Room **C** dbl	= **C** for a double room
Room **B**/**C**	= **B** for a single room and **C** for a double room
Room **D** s/c dbl	= **D** for a self-contained double (ie: with en-suite toilet and shower)
Room **E** a/c dbl	= **E** for a double with air conditioning

upmarket hotel and typically serving dishes like grilled chicken and steak for US$3–5. There is a substantial Asian population in East Africa, and it's always worth looking out for Indian restaurants, as these tend to serve the most interesting meals.

Restaurants in southern Africa are generally much more Westernised. The combination of restaurants and take-aways in South Africa and Zimbabwe particularly is comparable to that in most European countries, with the predictable transatlantic fare widely supplemented by Italian, Greek, Portuguese and (in Namibia only) German dishes. Throughout southern Africa, a main course in a restaurant costs around US$5, though in South Africa itself take-away pizzas and burgers go for as little as US$2–3.

The alternative to eating out, especially attractive to vegetarians (who are poorly catered for by most restaurants), is to cook for yourself. In East Africa, self-catering can be hampered by the lack of variety in ingredients – the only vegetables you can normally get outside the cities are onions, tomatoes and potatoes, while supermarkets stock only the basics. If you think you'll be doing a lot of cooking, bring plenty of spices, stock cubes and other lightweight condiments, as well as your own stove. It's easier in southern Africa, where most hostels have kitchen facilities, supermarkets are well stocked, and a wide variety of fresh produce is available.

Drink

Tap water is OK to drink in South Africa, unless you are specifically told otherwise. This is also generally the case in Zimbabwe, Namibia and Botswana. Elsewhere in the region, except perhaps in a few large cities, it would be wise to assume the opposite, in other words to work on the basis that tap water is potentially contaminated, and be sceptical about any claims to the contrary. Unless you are prepared to take the trouble to boil your drinking water, this means you should stick to mineral water, which is cheap and widely available, except in Mozambique where a bottle can cost in excess of US$2.

Otherwise, the cheapest drinks throughout the region are the usual brand name fizzy drinks. These generally come in 300ml bottles and cost next to nothing; though a bottle of soft drink can cost more than US$1 in northern Mozambique, and tin cans are more normal than bottles in South Africa. A few South African companies produce an outstanding range of pure fruit juices: these are generally packaged in one-litre cartons and cost around US$1 in South Africa, more in the other countries in the region to which they are exported.

The main alcoholic drink in the region, if you exclude the ubiquitous locally brewed millet beer which most travellers will probably try once and never again, is lager beer, which is generally cheap and of a high quality. In off-the-beaten-track parts of East Africa, the concept of chilled lager hasn't really caught on, so it might be worth checking whether your hotel barman can pop a couple of bottles in the fridge. South Africa produces an excellent range of red and white wines to suit all budgets. Locally produced wine in Ethiopia and Zimbabwe tends to be a bit rough, but it's certainly affordable and drinkable. South African wines are excellent, and affordable enough in South Africa, but when exported to other parts of the region they sell at prices that are unlikely to tempt most backpackers. Imported spirits are available throughout East and southern Africa.

OTHER DAY-TO-DAY PRACTICALITIES
Books and newspapers

Bookshops in South Africa and to a lesser extent Zimbabwe and Kenya are comparable with those in most Western countries, though more expensive.

Elsewhere, it's generally difficult to get hold of anything but school textbooks and religious tracts. Unless you are flying directly into South Africa, bring field guides and other background literature with you. For novels, your best bet is to swap with other travellers as you go along. There are secondhand bookshops in Zimbabwe and South Africa, and excellent secondhand bookstalls in the Piassa area of Addis Ababa, central Dar es Salaam, and the River Road area of Nairobi.

Most countries in the region have an English language press, though the combination of a small readership and in many cases a high degree of censorship makes many local rags of greater interest for what they say about the country than for their inherent news content. Kenyan papers such as the *Daily Nation* and weekly *East African* are good on regional and international news, as are most South African papers. A particularly good weekly paper, offering a balanced mix of local, African and international news, the South African *Mail & Guardian* is affiliated to the British *Guardian* and available at good bookshops as far north as Kenya. Also widely available are the American weekly news magazines *Time* and *Newsweek* and from Britain the staid but informative *Weekly Telegraph* and more gossipy *International Express*.

Money and foreign exchange

You can change your hard-currency travellers' cheques and cash into local currency at any bank or private bureau de change, though the latter may accept US dollars cash only. You must normally show a passport as proof of identity when you change money, but otherwise the bureaucracy surrounding foreign exchange transactions in most countries has declined greatly in recent years. Aside from sometimes having to wait in a long queue, you should normally be in and out of a bank in less than ten minutes; although if you leave your foreign exchange transactions until you get to a small, little visited town, chances are it will be a much slower process than in a large city. In some countries, the largest banknote available is worth no more than one US dollar, which means that you want to make sure the bank has an adequate stock of large bills before you proceed with your transaction.

The question of black markets is often given undue attention in travel guides to African countries, a hangover of the not-so-distant days when absurd official exchange rates made it practically impossible to get around the region without extensive use of the black market. These days, official exchange rates throughout the region are favourable to tourists, and a high level of financial deregulation has encouraged a blossoming of private bureaux de change (often called forex bureaux), which generally offer better rates than banks. In effect, the black market has been marginalised, except to an extent in Ethiopia and Mozambique where street rates rarely stand at more than 10% higher than the best rate offered by a bank or forex bureau. In such circumstances, using the black market arguably amounts to squeezing the last cent from an already fragile economy. In any case, backpackers who heed the whispered calls of 'change money' that will follow them through many African capitals are more likely to end up being conned than to make a bit extra. Of course, there are bound to be instances where you need to change money outside banking hours (see also *Changing money at borders* in Chapter 6) – in such circumstances, change no more than you need, and ideally undertake the transaction through a shop owner, hotel manager or waiter rather than somebody on the street.

Prices throughout this guide are given in US dollars, largely because of the frequency with which African currencies have undergone sudden and rapid devaluations over the last decade. However, contrary to what you may read elsewhere, day-to-day expenses such as restaurant meals, accommodation and public transport can be and normally are best paid for in local currency. The one exception to this is Tanzania, and even there so far as backpackers need be concerned it is only government charges (for instance national park fees, airport and port taxes) that must be paid for in hard currency, preferably US dollars.

You'll soon realise that getting change is often a major mission in Africa; I sometimes feel that the continent might yet take over the world if only the amount of energy its people expended on running about looking for change could be channelled more productively. It's worth carrying a selection of small bills on you at all times. In Mozambique the apparent attitude of many people is that if they can't find change then you don't get change! The simple way to inject some urgency into this scenario is to refuse to pay until change is produced. Taxi drivers are the one class of people who, throughout the region, habitually 'don't have change' – if you get in a taxi at night without the appropriate banknotes, you're pretty much setting yourself up!

Public holidays
Individual public holidays are noted in the country chapters. Worth pointing out here is that banks, government departments and many shops and offices are closed on such days. Christmas and Boxing Day are taken as public holidays throughout the region, as is the Easter weekend, when all banks and bureaux de change will be closed for four days, except in the few countries where they open on Saturdays. The Easter weekend falls over April 13–16 in 2001, March 29 –April 1 in 2002 and April 18–21 in 2003; except in Ethiopia, where the Orthodox dates (and calendar) differ and should be checked separately.

Post
Postal services in Africa are generally cheap and slow, which is great if you want to post home a large box of curios, not so good if you're hoping a letter home will arrive quickly. I wouldn't rely on a letter posted to or from any African country reaching its destination in less than two weeks. Postal services in South Africa are more expensive but as slow as elsewhere in the region, though letters posted overseas via the private *Postnet* chain of shops, represented in most large shopping malls countrywide, should get to their destination within a week.

Poste restante can be collected from the main post office in any large city. Have your post addressed as in the following example, though do check under both your first and last name as letters are occasionally misfiled:

Philip Briggs
Poste Restante
Maputo
Mozambique

Telecommunications
If anyone from home is expecting a weekly phone call, you're in for a stressful and often frustrating time battling with what are for the most part inefficient telecommunications systems – frankly, you'd do well to impress on everybody concerned the advantages of communicating by post. Phone systems in South Africa, Namibia, Botswana and Zimbabwe are up to international standards, though international calls from public offices in Zimbabwe are time consuming and inefficient. Contrary to expectations, perhaps, the next best international phone system is the one in Ethiopia, and making an international call from the telecommunications centre in Addis Ababa is very straightforward. At the bottom of the pile is Tanzania, where you should avoid relying on international phone lines at all costs.

Time

The region covered by this guide, vast though it may be, is confined within a relatively small variance of longitude. The only time when you'd need to reset your watch within the region is upon crossing between Tanzania and Zambia or Malawi at any time of year, or upon crossing between Namibia and any neighbouring territory during the winter months. The good news for backpackers who arrive in East or southern Africa from Western Europe is that they'll have to reset their watch by no more than three hours, which means that jet-lag isn't a consideration (though travellers who arrive in Addis Ababa, Nairobi or Johannesburg may be tired out by the increase in altitude – these cities all lie above 1,800m!)

South Africa, Swaziland, Lesotho, Mozambique, Zimbabwe, Botswana, Namibia, Zambia and Malawi are all on Central African Time, two hours ahead of GMT/UT. The other countries in the region are on East African Time, one hour ahead of Central African Time. The only country in the region to run on daylight saving time is Namibia, where the clocks are set back one hour on the first Sunday of April and return to Central African Time on the first Sunday of September.

If this all seems too straightforward, then read the section on Swahili and Ethiopian time in Appendix Two.

Tourist information offices

With few exceptions – the Tigrean tourist office in the Ethiopian town of Mekele springs to mind – tourist offices in East Africa seem to serve as little more than an exercise in job creation, which is very nice but hardly justifies making an effort to pop by. By contrast, local tourist offices in most South African towns are generally very helpful and well informed, as are those in Zimbabwe and Namibia.

Health and Safety

4

This is the chapter which always gives me the creeps when I read a travel guide, and I'm quite sure that some readers will question the sanity of travelling to Africa by the time they finish it. Don't let it get to you – with a few precautions against theft, the right injections, and a sensible attitude to malaria prevention, the chances of serious mishap are small. It may help put things in perspective to point out that your greatest concern while travelling in Africa should not be the combined exotica of venomous snakes, stampeding elephants, gun-happy soldiers and the Ebola virus, but something altogether more mundane: a road accident.

HEALTH
Written in collaboration with Dr Jane Wilson-Howarth, with thanks to Dr Vaughan Southgate of the Natural History Museum, London, for up-to-date information on bilharzia transmission
A great number of tropical diseases are present in eastern and southern Africa but, although most travellers who spend a while in the region will become ill at some point, the chances are that it will be nothing more dangerous than diarrhoea or a cold. Provided that you have had the necessary immunisations before you travel, the biggest dangers are accidents, then malaria, a risk that can be minimised, though not eliminated, by using prophylactic drugs and taking precautions against mosquito bites.

Preparations
In addition to considering the points made directly below, do read this entire section before you leave, since subjects such as malaria prevention are discussed under a separate heading.

Travel insurance
Don't think about travelling without a comprehensive medical travel insurance policy, one that will fly you home in an emergency. The ISIS policy, available in Britain through STA (tel: 020 7361 6160), is inexpensive and has a good reputation. Pack a good insect repellent, at least one long-sleeved cotton shirt and one pair of long trousers, a hat and sunscreen; these are important insurance measures.

Immunisations
You must have a yellow fever immunisation, and may be required to show an international immunisation certificate as proof of this at some borders. It is also wise to be up to date on tetanus (10-yearly), polio (10-yearly), diphtheria (10-yearly). For many parts of Africa immunisations against meningococcus, rabies and hepatitis A are also needed. If your trip is a short, one-off visit you could have hepatitis A immunoglobulin, which is short-lived but cheap; it gives some protection for a couple of months and costs around £5. For most travellers, Hepatitis A immunisation with Havrix is better – it costs about £40 but protects for

ten years. Typhoid immunisation is rather ineffective; it needs boosting every three years unless you are over the age of 35 and have had four or more courses, in which case no further immunisation is required. Immunisation against cholera is no longer required anywhere. If you need several immunisations, it is best to go to a travel clinic a month or two before departure. British Airways Travel Clinics, now situated in 35 towns in the UK and three in South Africa (UK tel: 01276 685040 for the nearest), sell malaria tablet memory cards, bednets and a variety of treatment kits, as well as providing an immunisation service.

Medical kit

Take a small medical kit. This should contain malaria prophylactics, as well as a cure for malaria and a thermometer (the latter is crucial should you need to diagnose yourself), soluble aspirin or paracetamol (good for gargling when you have a sore throat and for reducing fever and pains), plasters (Band-aids), potassium permanganate crystals or another favoured antiseptic, iodine for sterilising water and cleaning wounds, sunblock, and condoms or femidoms. Some travel clinics in Britain will try to persuade you to buy a variety of antibiotics as a precaution. This is not necessary: most antibiotics are widely available in Africa, and you should be hesitant about taking them without medical advice. Restaurant meals in East Africa tend to be based around meat and carbohydrate, so you might like to carry vitamin pills.

Further reading

Self-prescribing has its hazards, so if you are going anywhere very remote consider taking a health book. For adults there is *Bugs Bites & Bowels*, the Cadogan guide to healthy travel by Jane Wilson-Howarth. If travelling with children look at *Your Child's Health Abroad: a manual for travelling parents* by Jane Wilson-Howarth and Matthew Ellis, published by Bradt.

Medical institutions
UK

British Airways Travel Clinic and Immunisation Service 156 Regent St, London W1, tel: 020 7439 9584. This place also sells travellers' supplies and has a branch of Stanford's travel book and map shop. There are now BA clinics all around Britain and three in South Africa. To find your nearest one, phone 01276 685040.

MASTA (Medical Advisory Service for Travellers Abroad) Keppel St, London WC1 7HT; tel: 09068 224100. This is a premium-line number, charged at 50p per minute.

Nomad Travel Pharmacy and Vaccination Centre 3–4 Wellington Terrace, Turnpike Lane, London N8 0PX; tel: 020 8889 7014.

Thames Medical 157 Waterloo Rd, London SE1 8US; tel: 020 7902 9000. Competitively priced, one-stop travel health service. All profits go to their affiliated company InterHealth which provides health care for overseas workers on Christian projects.

Trailfinders Immunisation Centre 194 Kensington High St, London W8 7RG; tel: 020 7938 3999. Also 254–284 Sauchiehall St, Glasgow G2 3EH; tel: 0141 353 0066.

NHS travel website, www.fitfortravel.scot.nhs.uk, provides country-by-country advice on immunisation and malaria, plus details of recent developments, and a list of relevant health organisations.

USA

Centers for Disease Control 1600 Clifton Road, Atlanta, GA 30333; tel: 877 FYI TRIP; 800 311 3435; web: www.cdc.gov/travel. This organisation is the central source of travel information in the USA. Each summer they publish the invaluable *Health Information for International Travel* which is available from the Division of Quarantine at the above address.

Connaught Laboratories PO Box 187, Swiftwater, PA 18370, tel: 800 822 2463. They will send a free list of specialist tropical-medicine physicians in your state.
IAMAT (International Association for Medical Assistance to Travelers) 736 Center St, Lewiston, NY 14092. A non-profit organisation which provides lists of English-speaking doctors abroad.

Australia
TMVC tel: 1300 65 88 44; website: www.tmvc.com.au. TMVC has 20 clinics in Australia, New Zealand and Thailand, including:
Brisbane Dr Deborah Mills, Qantas Domestic Building, 6th floor, 247 Adelaide St, Brisbane, QLD 4000; tel: 7 3221 9066; fax: 7 3321 7076
Melbourne Dr Sonny Lau, 393 Little Bourke St, 2nd floor, Melbourne, VIC 3000; tel: 3 9602 5788; fax: 3 9670 8394.
Sydney Dr Mandy Hu, Dymocks Building, 7th floor, 428 George St, Sydney, NSW 2000; tel: 2 221 7133; fax: 2 221 8401.

South Africa
There are four British Airways travel clinics in South Africa: *Johannesburg*, tel: (011) 807 3132; *Cape Town*, tel: (021) 419 3172; *Knysna*, tel: (044) 382 6366; *East London*, tel: (0431) 43 2359.

Travellers' diarrhoea
Most travellers to the tropics suffer a bout of travellers' diarrhoea during their trip. The newer you are to tropical travel, the more likely you are to suffer. Travellers' diarrhoea comes from getting other people's faeces in your mouth, which most often happens from cooks not washing their hands after a trip to the toilet, but even if the restaurant cook does not understand basic hygiene you will be safe if your food has been properly cooked and arrives piping hot. As for what food is safe to eat, any fruit or vegetable that you've washed and peeled yourself should be fine, as should hot cooked food. Raw food and salads are risky, as is cooked food that has gone cold or been kept lukewarm in a hotel buffet. Avoid ice-cream which is often not kept adequately frozen due to power cuts. Ice may have been made with unboiled water or deposited by the road on its journey from the ice factory.
It is less common to get sick from drinking contaminated water, but it can happen, so try to drink from safe sources. Tap water in South Africa, Namibia, Botswana and Zimbabwe is normally OK. Elsewhere, avoid drinking tap water where possible (mineral water is cheap and widely available in most countries). Any dodgy water should be brought to the boil (even at altitude this is all that's needed), passed through a good bacteriological filter or purified with iodine. Chlorine tablets (eg: Puritabs) are less effective and taste nastier.
By taking precautions against travellers' diarrhoea you will also avoid typhoid, cholera, hepatitis, dysentery, worms, etc.

Treatment
Dehydration is the reason you feel awful during a bout of diarrhoea, so the most important part of treatment is to imbibe lots of clear fluids. Sachets of oral rehydration salts give the perfect biochemical mix, but any dilute mixture of sugar and salt in water will do you good. Try a solution of a four-finger scoop of sugar with a three-finger pinch of salt in a glass of water, with a squeeze of lemon or orange juice to improve the taste and provide necessary potassium which is lost in diarrhoea and vomiting. If no safe drinking water is available, then Coke or similar with a three-finger pinch of salt added to each glass will do the trick. Drink two large glasses

after every bowel action, more if you are thirsty – if you are not eating you need to drink three litres a day **plus** the equivalent of whatever is pouring into the toilet.

With most diarrhoea attacks, medication will be less effective than simply resting up and forsaking greasy foods and alcohol. If you are hungry stick to dry biscuits, boiled potatoes or rice. The bacteria responsible for diarrhoea and related symptoms normally die after 36 hours. Avoid the use of blockers such as Imodium, Lomotil and Codeine Phosphate unless you have no access to sanitation, for instance if you have to travel by bus, since these blockers keep the poisons in your system and make you feel bad for longer. It is dangerous to take blockers with dysentery (evidenced by blood, slime or fever with the diarrhoea). Should diarrhoea or related symptoms persist beyond 36 hours, or you are passing blood or slime or have a fever, then consult a doctor or pharmacist. Chances are you have nothing serious but you may have something treatable, for instance giardia (indicated by severe flatulence, abdominal distension, stomach cramps and sulphurous belching), which is cured by taking 2g of Flagyl (Metronidozale) daily for three days and avoiding alcohol. If you can't get to a doctor, a three-day course of an antibiotic such as ciprofloxacin or norfloxacin or nalidixic acid is effective against dysentery and severe diarrhoea.

Malaria

Malaria kills a million Africans annually, and (after accidents) it poses the single biggest serious threat to the health of travellers to tropical Africa. Visitors to most countries covered in this guide should assume they'll be exposed to malaria. The main exceptions are South Africa, Swaziland and Lesotho, where malaria is restricted to the far north and the eastern coastal belt, and even then only in summer. Malaria is absent or less likely in areas above an altitude of 1,800m, most notably the vast Ethiopian Highlands. The *Anopheles* mosquito which transmits malaria is most abundant near the marshes and still water in which it breeds. In short, the risk of contracting malaria is greatest in low-lying wet areas such as the East African coast north of Durban, the hinterland of the great lakes, along large rivers such as the Zambezi and Shire, and in swampy areas such as the Okavango Delta. It is unwise to travel in malarious parts of Africa whilst pregnant or with children: the risk of malaria in many parts is considerable and such travellers are likely to succumb rapidly to the disease.

Prophylactic drugs

There is no vaccine against malaria, but various prophylactic drugs offer a level of protection against the disease. A specialised travel clinic will give the best advice on which drug is most appropriate. If *Mefloquine* (Larium) is suggested start this two weeks before departure to check that it suits you; stop it immediately if it seems to cause vivid and unpleasant dreams, mood changes or other changes in the way you feel. Anyone who is pregnant, who has suffered fits in the past, has a close blood relative who is epileptic or has been treated for depression or psychiatric problems should avoid *Mefloquine*. The usual alternative is *Chloroquine* (Nivaquine) and *Proguanil* (Paludrine): two tablets weekly and two tablets daily, respectively. Otherwise daily doxycyline can be useful.

Once in a while, I meet travellers who refuse to take prophylactics, either because they want to acquire resistance to malaria or else because they believe there is a homeopathic cure for this killer disease. Unfortunately, they think they're being very clever. For the record, travellers to Africa can't acquire effective resistance to malaria, and the medical profession would leap on any viable homeopathic cure for the disease. Travellers who don't use prophylactic drugs risk their life in a manner that is both foolish and unnecessary.

Equally important as taking malaria pills is making every reasonable effort not to be bitten by mosquitoes between dusk and dawn – see *Insects*.

Diagnosis and cures

Even those who take their malaria tablets meticulously and do everything possible to avoid being bitten may contract a strain of malaria that is resistant to prophylactic drugs. Untreated malaria is likely to be fatal, but even strains resistant to prophylaxis respond well to prompt treatment. You should visit a doctor or hospital as soon as you experience malarial symptoms: any combination of a headache, flu-like aches and pains, a rapid rise in temperature, a general sense of disorientation, and possibly nausea and diarrhoea.

It is preferable *not* to attempt self-diagnosis. Local doctors regularly deal with malaria, and any laboratory or hospital will be able to give you a quick malaria test. Nevertheless, you may be some distance from a doctor and could go from feeling healthy to having a high fever in the space of hours, in which case the risk associated with not treating malaria promptly should outweigh that of taking an unnecessary cure. Expert opinion is that the most safe and effective cure at present is to take two quinine tablets every eight hours until the fever subsides for a maximum of three days, then a single dose of three Fansidar tablets. Provided you follow this procedure before the symptoms have become chronic, it is practically 100% effective. Be warned that you must drink a lot of water after you take Fansidar, and that you should carry Fansidar, quinine and a thermometer with you since these are not always available locally. It could be that a better cure emerges during the lifespan of this edition, so seek advice from a travel clinic or another reliable source before you leave for Africa. And be warned that another popular cure called Halfan has been banned as dangerous and is not recommended for anyone any more, particularly if you are using Larium as a prophylactic.

Malaria symptoms take at least one week to become obvious, but can take much longer. Continue prophylaxis for at least four weeks after returning home and, if you display possible malaria symptoms up to a year later, then get to a doctor and be sure to mention that you have been exposed to malaria.

Finally, if you have a fever and the malaria test is negative (which does not completely exclude malaria), you may have typhoid, which should also receive immediate treatment. Where typhoid-testing is unavailable, a routine blood test can give a strong indication of this disease.

Bilharzia

Bilharzia or schistosomiasis is a common debilitating disease afflicting perhaps 200 million people worldwide. Those most affected are the rural poor of the tropics who repeatedly acquire more and more of these nasty little worm-lodgers. Infected travellers and expatriates generally suffer fewer problems because symptoms will encourage them to seek prompt treatment and they are also exposed to fewer parasites. But it is still an unpleasant problem, and worth avoiding.

When someone with bilharzia excretes into freshwater, the eggs hatch and swim off to find a pond snail to infest. They develop inside the snail to emerge as torpedo-shaped cercariae, barely visible to the naked eye but able to digest their way through human or animal skin. This is the stage that attacks people as they wade, bathe or shower in infested water. Lakes Victoria, Tanganyika and Malawi carry a risk of bilharzia, as do many other freshwater bodies. In a recent study of Malawi expatriates who were blood tested for bilharzia antibodies, two-thirds showed evidence of exposure to the parasites. In 1995, 75% of a group of people scuba diving off Cape Maclear for only about a week acquired the disease.

The snails which harbour bilharzia are a centimetre or more long and live in still or slow-moving fresh water which is well oxygenated and has edible vegetation (water-weed, reeds). The risk is greatest where local people use the water in any way, bearing in mind that wind can disperse cercariae up to 100m from where they entered the water. Scuba-diving off a boat into deep offshore water should thus be a low-risk activity. Showering in lake water or paddling along a reedy lake shore near a village carries a high risk of acquiring bilharzia.

Water which has been filtered or stored snail-free for two days is safe, as is water which has been boiled or treated with Cresol or Dettol. Some protection is afforded by applying an oily insect repellent like DEET to your skin before swimming or paddling.

Cercariae live for up to 30 hours after they have been shed by snails, but the older they are, the less vigorous they are and the less capable of penetrating skin. Cercariae are shed in the greatest numbers between 11.00 and 15.00. If water to be used for bathing is pumped early in the morning from deep in the lake (cercariae are sun-loving) or from a site far from where people excrete there will be less risk of infestation. Swimming in the afternoon is riskier than in the early morning. Since cercariae take perhaps 10–15 minutes to penetrate, a quick shower, or a splash across a river, followed by thorough drying with a towel should be safe. Even if you are in risky water longer, towelling off vigorously after bathing will kill any cercariae in the process of penetrating your skin.

Only a proportion of those cercariae which penetrate the skin survive to cause disease. The absence of early symptoms does not necessarily mean there is no infection, but symptoms are normal about two or more weeks after penetration: typically a fever and wheezy cough. A blood test, which should be taken six weeks or more after likely exposure, will determine whether or not parasites are going to cause problems. Treatment is generally effective, but failures occur and retreatment is often necessary for reasons that aren't fully understood but which may imply some drug resistance. Since bilharzia can be a nasty illness, avoidance is better than waiting to be cured and it is wise to avoid bathing in high-risk areas.

Other diseases
Sleeping sickness
This is carried by tsetse flies, which look like oversized houseflies and have a painful bite. Tsetse flies commonly occur in low-lying game reserves throughout tropical Africa; they bite in daylight and are attracted to blue clothing. Sleeping sickness has a patchy distribution within a small limit of the tsetse fly's range; it is a minor threat to travellers and treatable.

AIDS and venereal disease
HIV and other sexually transmitted infections are widespread in the region to a degree that is unimaginable in Western countries, and AIDS-related deaths in many of the countries covered in this guide have reached epidemic proportions. The risk attached to having unprotected sex with anybody but a regular partner is prohibitively high. Condoms and femidoms offer a high level of protection against HIV and other other sexually transmitted infections. The additional use of spermicides and pessaries further reduces the risk of transmission. If you notice any genital ulcers or discharge, seek prompt treatment.

Hospital workers in Africa deal with AIDS victims on a regular basis. Contrary to Western prejudices, health professionals do realise the danger involved in using unsterilised needles, and you are unlikely to be confronted with one in a town hospital or clinic. If you need treatment in a really remote area where supplies are a problem, you might be glad to be carrying a few needles and hypodermic syringes in your medical kit.

Meningitis

This is a particularly nasty disease as it can kill within hours of the first symptoms appearing. The telltale symptom is a combination of a blinding headache and usually high fever. A vaccination protects against the common and serious bacterial form in Africa, but not against all of the many kinds of meningitis. Local papers normally report localised outbreaks. If you show symptoms, get to a doctor immediately.

Rabies

Rabies can be carried by any mammal. Monkeys who are used to being fed in parks may carry rabies, village dogs must also be assumed to be rabid, and so should any wild animal behaving in an unusually tame manner. Any suspect bite should be scrubbed under running water for five minutes and then flooded with local spirit or dilute iodine. A post-bite rabies injection is needed even in immunised people and those who are not immunised need a course of injections. These should be given within a week if the bites are to the face. If the bites are further from the brain the incubation period is longer and you probably have more time, but do make sure you get the injections even if you are a very long way from civilisation. The incubation period for rabies can be very long, so never say that it is too late to bother – rabies cannot be cured once symptoms appear and death from rabies is probably one of the worst ways to go!

Tetanus

Tetanus is caught through deep, dirty wounds, including animal bites, so ensure that such wounds are thoroughly cleaned. Immunisation gives good protection for ten years, provided you do not have an overwhelming number of tetanus bacteria on board. If you haven't had a tetanus shot in ten years or you are unsure, get a tetanus toxoid injection and a tetanus booster as quickly as possible. Keep immunised and be sensible about first aid.

Insects and ticks

Even if you take malaria tablets, do all you can to avoid mosquito bites. The imperative reason for this is the increasing level of resistance to preventative drugs, while of lesser concern are several other mosquito-borne viral fevers which could be present in low and medium-altitude parts of the region. The *Anopheles* mosquito which spreads malaria emerges at dusk, as do most other disease-carrying mosquitoes, so you will greatly reduce your chances of being bitten by wearing long trousers and socks after dark and covering exposed parts of your body with insect repellent, preferably a DEET-based preparation such as Jungle Jell. Sprays or roll-ons of this sort are not available in most countries north of the Zambezi, so bring one with you. The *Anopheles* mosquito hunts mostly at ground level, so it is worth putting repellent on your ankles, even if you wear socks. When walking in scrub and forest areas by day, you should also cover and spray yourself, since the *Aedes* mosquito which spreads dengue and yellow fever is a day-biter (solid shoes, socks and trousers will in any case protect you against snakes, sharp thorns and harmless but irritating biters like midges).

Like many insects, mosquitoes are drawn to direct light. If you are camping, never put a lamp near the opening of your tent, or you will have a swarm of mosquitoes and other insects waiting to join you when you retire. In hotel rooms, be aware that the longer you leave on your light, the greater the number of insects with which you are likely to share your accommodation.

Once you are in bed, the best form of protection is a net. Mosquito coils, widely available in all countries, except for Ethiopia, will also reduce the biting rate, and even though strains of mosquito have evolved that are skilled at flying in turbulent air, so will a fan. Far better, though, is to carry your own *permethrin*-impregnated net, which will protect you against everything. Nets and impregnation kits are available from MASTA at the London School of Tropical Medicine and Hygiene, and from British Airways Travel Clinics (see page 46).

Minute pestilential **blackflies** spread river blindness in parts of Africa between 19°N and 17°S. You're at risk only near fast-flowing rivers and rapids, where they breed. The flies bite in daylight. Long trousers tucked into socks will help keep them at bay. Citronella-based repellents don't work against them.

Tumbu flies or *putsi* occur in hot, humid climates, where they often lay eggs on drying laundry. When a person puts on clean clothes or sleeps on a fresh sheet, the eggs hatch and bury themselves under the skin to form a crop of 'boils', each of which hatches a grub after about eight days before the inflammation settles down. In putsi areas, you should dry clothes and sheets in a screened house, or in direct sunshine until they are crisp, or iron them.

Jiggers or **sandfleas** latch on if you walk barefoot in contaminated places; these parasites set up home under the skin of the foot, usually at the side of a toenail where they cause a painful, boil-like swelling. They need picking out by a local expert and, if the flea bursts during eviction, then douse the wound in spirit, alcohol or kerosene – otherwise more jiggers will infest you.

There are several unpleasant illnesses which can follow a **tick bite** in Africa, including Lyme Disease, but the good news is that, even if a tick is carrying disease organisms, it will not inevitably infect you. You are less likely to be infected if you get the tick off promptly and do not damage it. Remove any tick as soon as you notice it on you – it will most likely be firmly attached to somewhere you would rather it was not – by grasping the tick as close to your body as possible and pulling steadily and firmly away at right angles to your skin. The tick will then come away complete as long as you do not jerk or twist. If possible douse the wound with alcohol (any spirit will do) or iodine. Spreading redness around the bite and/or fever and/or aching joints after a tick bite imply that you have an infection which requires antibiotic treatment, so seek advice.

To balance the warnings, it should be stressed that the overwhelming majority of insects don't bite people and, of those that do, the vast majority are entirely harmless. Mattresses quite often contain bedbugs and fleas, both of which are essentially harmless.

Skin infections

Any insect bite or small nick gives an opportunity for bacteria to foil the body's defences. It will surprise many travellers how quickly skin infections start in warm, humid climates, and it is essential to clean and cover the slightest wound. Creams are not as effective as a good drying antiseptic such as dilute iodine, potassium permanganate (a few crystals in half a cup of water) or crystal (or gentian) violet. One of these should be available in most towns. If the wound starts to throb, or becomes red and the redness starts to spread or the wound oozes, antibiotics will probably be needed: *flucloxacillin* (250mg four times a day) or *cloxacillin* (500mg four times a day) or, for those allergic to penicillin, *erythromycin* (500mg twice a day) for five days should help. See a doctor if it does not start to improve in 48 hours.

Fungal infections also get a hold easily in hot moist climates so wear 100% cotton socks and underwear and shower frequently. An itchy (often flaking) rash in the groin or between the toes is likely to be a fungal infection which will need treatment with an antifungal cream such as Canesten (*clotrimazole*) or if this is not available try Whitfield's ointment (*compound benzoic acid ointment*) or crystal violet (although this will turn you purple!).

Marine dangers

Don't swim or walk barefoot on the beach, or you risk getting coral or urchin spines in your soles or venomous fish spines in your feet. If you tread on a venomous fish soak the foot in hot (but not scalding) water until some time after the pain subsides; this may be for 20–30 minutes in all. Take the foot out of the water to top up otherwise you may scald it. If the pain returns, re-immerse the foot. Once the venom has been heat inactivated, get a doctor to check and remove any bits of fish spine in the wound.

Sharks are common in the Indian Ocean and attacks, although extremely rare, do occur from time to time. There is not much you can do about this, except to stick to beaches that are protected by coral reefs or shark nets.

Sun and heat

The equatorial sun is vicious. Although it is impossible to avoid some exposure to the sun, it would be foolish to incur it needlessly. Tanning ages your skin and it can cause skin cancer. If you are coming to Africa from a less harsh climate, let your body get used to the sunlight gradually or you will end up with sunburn. Take things too far and sunstroke – a potentially fatal condition – may be the result. Wear sunscreen and build up your exposure gradually, starting with no more than 20 minutes a day. Avoid exposing yourself for more than two hours in any day, and stay out of the sun between 12.00 and 15.00.

Be particularly careful of sunburn when swimming or snorkelling. A shirt will protect your shoulders and a pair of shorts will protect the back of your thighs.

In hot areas, you may sweat more than normal. To counter the resultant loss of water and salt, you should drink more than normal and eat extra salt if you develop a taste for it (salt tablets are useless). Prickly heat, a fine pimply rash caused by sweat trapped under the skin, is a harmless but highly uncomfortable and common problem when people first experience a humid tropical climate, such as on the coast. It helps to wear 100% cotton clothing, splash regularly with water (avoiding excessive use of soap), dab (don't rub) the area with talc powder and sleep naked under a fan. If it's really bad, check into an air-conditioned hotel room or head for a higher, cooler place.

Mountain health and safety

Mount Kilimanjaro is one of the highest mountains in the world accessible to a fit adult without special equipment, and East Africa has several other regularly ascended peaks topping 4,000m. Southern Africa boasts no peaks of comparable loftiness, but there are many montane hiking areas in the region, from Mulanje in Malawi to the Chimanimani range in Zimbabwe and the Drakensberg in South Africa.

Several climatic factors should be taken into consideration when you prepare to hike on a mountain. An increase in altitude is typically accompanied by a drop in temperature and, on clear days, by an increased ferocity in the sun's rays. Even in the tropics, many mountains are seasonally prone to fog, snow and blizzards, conditions which may descend with little warning. The highest peaks of Mount Kenya, Kilimanjaro and the Ruwenzoris have a permanent snow cap and temperatures fall below freezing at night.

Before you hike in any mountainous area, it is advisable to ask locally about potential weather conditions and to ensure that you are equipped for the worst. At the minimum, this means plenty of warm clothes, a windproof rain jacket, a warm sleeping bag, an insulation mat, a pair of thick socks, and solid shoes or preferably boots. Where sub-zero conditions are a possibility, you ideally want a pair of gloves and a balaclava as well. Less obviously you should bring sunglasses to counter glare, sunscreen, water bottles and an adequate first-aid kit. For most of East Africa's major mountains such equipment can be hired locally, though often it won't be in very good condition.

If you notice foggy conditions building up as you climb a mountain, you should consider turning back, depending on where you are in relation to overnight huts or shelters. If you are unfortunate enough to be trapped in foggy or blizzard conditions, you will have to decide whether visibility is such that you can safely attempt to descend. If in any doubt, stay put. In such conditions, you will be glad of a generous food supply, even more pleased if you've made the effort to find out what rescue services exist, and delighted if you registered your name and intended route.

Hypothermia is a lowering of body temperature usually caused by a combination of cold and wet. Mild cases generally manifest themselves as uncontrollable shivering. Put on warm dry clothes and get into a sleeping bag; this will normally raise your body temperature sufficiently. Severe hypothermia is potentially fatal: symptoms include disorientation, lethargy, mental confusion (including an inappropriate feeling of well being and warmth) and coma. In severe cases, a rescue team should be summoned if possible.

Nobody should attempt to climb East Africa's highest peaks unless they are reasonably fit, have no known pre-existing heart or lung condition, and are currently in good health. At altitudes of above 4,000m, you may cease to feel hungry but you should still try to eat. Carbohydrates and fruit are recommended, rich or fatty foods are harder to digest. You should drink plenty of liquids, and will need enough water bottles to carry several litres of water. Dress in layers so you can reduce water loss by taking off clothes before you sweat too much.

Depending to some degree on speed of ascent and individual susceptibility, most people who climb to an altitude of 3,500m to 4,000m will start to feel symptoms of altitude sickness: headaches, nausea, fatigue, sleeplessness and swelling of the hands and feet. The best way to limit these symptoms is to give yourself time to acclimatise by taking the ascent slowly (you are, for instance, less likely to suffer extreme effects of altitude if you climb Kilimanjaro over six days rather than five), eating and drinking properly, and trying not to push yourself – it's worth noting that very fit people are more prone to altitude sickness because they tend to ascend too quickly. While a certain level of discomfort is normal at high altitudes, severe symptoms require an immediate descent – even going down 300m is enough to start recovery. On mountains like Kilimanjaro, Kenya and the Ruwenzoris, follow the advice of your guide, who will almost certainly be able to distinguish between an acceptable level of discomfort and the initial stages of severe altitude sickness.

Pulmonary and cerebral forms of mountain sickness can be rapidly fatal if you do not descend. Symptoms of the former include shortness of breath when at rest, coughing up blood, and gurgling sounds in the chest. Symptoms of the latter are headaches, a general lack of co-ordination, disorientation, stumbling, poor judgement and even hallucinations. The danger is that the sufferer often doesn't realise how sick he/she is and may argue against descending. Once again, you are far less likely to have such problems if you ascend slowly.

Snakebite

Poisonous snakes are widespread but rarely encountered since they generally slither away when they sense the seismic vibrations made by a walking person. You should be most alert to snakes on rocky slopes and cliffs, particularly where you risk putting your hand on a ledge that you can't see. Rocky areas are the favoured habitat of the puff adder, potentially lethal and unusual in that it won't always move off in response to human foot treads. Wearing good boots when walking in the bush will protect against the 50% of snakebites that occur below the ankle, and long trousers will help deflect bites higher up on the leg, reducing the quantity of venom injected. Snakes rarely attack people unless provoked and most snakes are harmless; even venomous species will only dispense venom in about half of their bites. In South Africa, where venomous snakes are widespread, fewer than ten snakebite fatalities are recorded annually – more people die from being struck by lightning!

In the event of a snakebite, be aware that most first-aid techniques do more harm than good. Cutting into the wound is harmful, tourniquets are dangerous, and suction and electrical inactivation devices do not work. The victim must be taken to a hospital which has antivenin. While being transported, remember that the venom will spread more slowly if the victim stays calm, and if the bitten limb is splinted and kept below the height of the heart. If you have a crepe bandage, bind up as much of the bitten limb as you can, but release the bandage every half hour.

NEVER give aspirin; you may offer paracetamol which is safe.
NEVER cut or suck the wound.
DO NOT apply ice packs.
DO NOT apply potassium permanganate.

If the offending snake can be captured without risk of someone else being bitten, take it to show the doctor, but be aware that a severed head can dispense venom in a reflex bite.

Medical facilities

There are private clinics, hospitals and pharmacies in most large towns, and except in Mozambique doctors generally speak fluent English. In East Africa, consultation fees and laboratory tests are remarkably inexpensive when compared with those of most Western countries, so if you do fall sick it would be absurd to let financial considerations dissuade you from seeking medical help.

Commonly required medicines such as broad spectrum antibiotics and Flagyl are widely available and cheap throughout the region, as are malaria cures and prophylactics. Chloroquine, Fansidar and to a lesser extent quinine tablets can be bought in just about any town, but it is not always so easy to get hold of Paludrine and Larium. Generally, it's far better that you carry all malaria-related tablets with you, and rely on their availability locally only if you need to restock your supplies – for instance if you have to use your Fansidar and quinine tablets to cure yourself or a travelling partner who has malaria.

If you are on any medication prior to departure, or you have specific needs relating to a known medical condition (for instance if you are allergic to bee stings or prone to attacks of asthma), then you are strongly advised to bring any related drugs and devices with you.

In South Africa, medical facilities and pharmacies are of equivalent standard to those of other Western countries, but prices of treatment and medication tend to be very high.

SAFETY
Wild animals

The dangers associated with African wild animals have frequently been overstated in the past by the so-called 'Great White Hunters' and others trying to glamorise their chosen way of life. Contrary to such fanciful notions as rampaging elephants and man-eating lions, most wild animals fear us more than we fear them, and their normal response to human contact is to flee. On the other hand, many travel guides have responded to exaggerations about the dangers associated with wild animals by being overly reassuring – the likelihood of a tourist being attacked by an animal is indeed very low, but it can happen, and there have been a number of fatalities caused by such incidents in recent years, particularly in southern Africa.

The need for caution is greatest near water, particularly around dusk and dawn, when **hippos** are out grazing. Hippos are responsible for more human fatalities than any other large mammal, not because they are aggressive but because they tend to panic when something comes between them and the safety of the water. If you happen to be that something, then you're unlikely to live to tell the tale. Never consciously walk between a hippo and water, and never walk along riverbanks or through reed banks, especially in overcast weather or at dusk or dawn, unless you are certain that no hippos are present. Watch out, too, for **crocodiles**. Only a very large croc is likely to attack a person, and then only in the water or right on the shore. Near towns and other settlements, you can be fairly sure that any very large crocodile will have been disposed of by its potential prey, so the risk is greatest away from human habitation. It is also near water that you are most likely to unwittingly corner a normally placid terrestrial animal – the waterbuck on Crescent Island in Lake Naivasha have acquired a nasty reputation for attacking on close approach, and the riverine-forest-dwelling bushbuck are reputed to be the most dangerous African antelope.

There are areas where hikers might still stumble across an elephant or buffalo, the most dangerous of Africa's terrestrial herbivores. Elephants almost invariably mock charge and indulge in some hair-raising trumpeting before they attack in earnest. Provided that you back off at the first sign of unease, they are most unlikely to take further notice of you. If you see them before they see you, give them a wide berth, bearing in mind they are most likely to attack if surprised at close proximity. If an animal charges you, the safest course of action is to head for the nearest tree and climb it. Black rhinos are also prone to charging without apparent provocation, but they're now very rare except in a few reserves where walking is forbidden.

Elephants are also potentially dangerous if you are in a vehicle, and much the same advice applies – if an elephant evidently doesn't want you to pass, then back off and wait until it has crossed the road or moved further away before you try again. In general, it's a bad idea to switch off your engine when you are close to an elephant or to let yourself get boxed in between an elephant and another vehicle.

There are campsites in Africa where **vervet monkeys** and **baboons** have become a pest. Feeding these animals is highly irresponsible, since it encourages them to scavenge and may eventually lead to their being shot. Vervet monkeys are too small to progress much beyond being a nuisance, but baboons are very dangerous and have often killed children and maimed adults with their vicious teeth. Do not tease or underestimate them. If primates are hanging around a campsite and you wander off leaving fruit in your tent, don't expect the tent to be standing when you return. The great **apes** are also potentially dangerous but are unlikely to be encountered except on a guided forest walk, when there is little risk provided that you obey your guide's instructions at all times.

The dangers associated with large **predators** are often exaggerated. Most predators stay clear of humans and are likely to kill accidentally or in self-defence rather than by design. Lions are an exception, but it is uncommon for a lion to attack a human without cause – should you encounter one on foot, the important thing is not to run, since this is likely to trigger the instinct to give chase. Of the other cats, cheetahs represent no threat and leopards attack only when cornered. Hyenas are often associated with human settlements, and can potentially be very dangerous, but in practice they aren't aggressive towards people and will most probably slink off into the shadows when disturbed. A slight but real danger when sleeping in the bush without a tent is that a passing hyena or lion might investigate a hairy object sticking out of a sleeping bag and decapitate you through predatorial curiosity. In areas where large predators are still reasonably common, sleeping in a sealed tent practically guarantees your safety – but don't sleep with your head sticking out and don't at any point put meat in the tent.

Crime
One of the most difficult things to write about in this context is crime. Dwelling on the subject must inevitably fuel paranoia in first time visitors to Africa, yet glossing over it can only place inexperienced backpackers at greater risk of being robbed. Simplistically, I think Westerners in Africa need to recognise two things about crime. The first is that African society is inherently far more law-abiding than our own, to the extent that criminals are frequently stoned to death in many countries (in Nairobi, I once saw an entire bus-load of people stand to applaud a policeman apprehend a petty thief, a scene that would be unimaginable in the capital of most European countries). The second is that thieves are present in Africa, as they are everywhere, and they often target Westerners, who are not only reliably wealthy relative to most Africans but who also generally have a conspicuously different skin colour, manner and style of dress.

A degree of discrimination and caution is appropriate when you travel in Africa, but only a degree. Bear in mind that people with a criminal intent make up a tiny fraction of 1% of the population of the countries in question, so that an attitude of indiscriminate paranoia can only divert your attention away from genuinely suspicious characters. If this section seems inordinately lengthy, it's not because crime is a greater problem here than in many other parts of the world, but because experience suggests that the vast majority of crimes against tourists in Africa occur in one of a few specific places and/or reasonably predictable circumstances. It is my hope that, by highlighting where the risks lie, this section will not only help readers to be alert to dodgy scenarios but, just as important, also help them to relax for the rest of the time.

Securing your money
Keep all important documents and most of your money and travellers' cheques in a leather or cotton money-belt, one which can be worn beneath your clothing in a manner that makes it invisible to casual observers. It's advisable to protect the contents against sweat by wrapping them in a plastic bag. You should avoid disclosing the presence of your money-belt in public, so keep some spending money in a pocket or elsewhere on your person – it would be preferable to lose a few US dollars-worth of local currency to a pickpocket a couple of times a week than to lose your full complement of foreign currency along with your passport, credit card and vaccination certificate even once during your trip. It is probably also advisable to keep a reasonable amount of currency hidden away in your luggage, so you've something to fall back on should you lose your money-belt.

Most travellers carry their money-belt on them at all times. I'm not quite sure of the rationale behind this, since it will almost certainly be removed if you are actually mugged, and only one of the hundreds of thefts I've heard about first- or second-hand in Africa occurred from a locked room. For myself, where the choice is between carrying valuables on my person or locking them in a room, I generally favour the latter option. Since no course of action completely guarantees the safety of your valuables, it's a question of balancing the risks. On the one hand, I'd leave my money-belt practically anywhere in preference to walking with it through downtown Nairobi or Johannesburg after dark. On the other hand, if I were staying in a small town and my room didn't strike me as being completely secure, I'd definitely take my money-belt with me. It isn't a bad idea to carry your own padlock, preferably a combination lock because it's more difficult to pick – you'll often be able to use it in addition to the one provided in most local guesthouses in East Africa, and you may occasionally stay at a guesthouse where no padlock is provided. Frankly, though, I'd have far greater reservations about leaving valuables in a serviced room in an upmarket hotel than I would about locking them behind the flimsiest padlock in a small-town family-run guesthouse. A final factor to be considered is that some travellers' cheque companies will not refund cheques which were stolen from a room.

The best place to leave any jewellery of financial or sentimental value is at home.

Mugging and armed theft

This variety of crime is mainly restricted to large cities. The two hottest mugging spots in the region are central Nairobi and Johannesburg city centre, but several other places have a bad reputation: Addis Ababa, Mombasa and nearby beaches, Dar es Salaam, Bagamoyo, Nkhata Bay, Harare, Lusaka, Pretoria, Durban and Cape Town. Inevitably, this list will get longer with time, so keep an ear to the travellers' grapevine.

You can go a long way to avoid being mugged by applying the same sort of judgement you might in any large city. Don't flaunt your wealth, which in an African context doesn't mean dressing down so much as not wearing any jewellery and avoiding touristy trappings such as a daypack, camera bag or external money-belt. You should use taxis to get around city centres and other obvious trouble spots, particularly at night. If you do have to walk after dark, then avoid unlit roads, parks and quiet alleys, and use the centre of the road rather than the pavement. When you go out to drink or eat, don't carry significantly more money than you need for the evening.

I would also recommend that you use a taxi to take you to a hotel when you first arrive in any large city – wearing a backpack is tantamount to advertising that all your valuables are somewhere on your person, and in somewhere like Nairobi or Johannesburg it's more than likely that somebody will take up the challenge. And it's really asking for trouble to arrive in a large city after dark, particularly one where the budget accommodation is dispersed – if you're on a bus and think you're likely to arrive at your destination late, then get off at a smaller town on the way, spend the night there, and continue your journey the next morning.

Pickpocketing and casual theft

Most casual thieves and pickpockets operate in busy markets and bus stations, so you should keep a close watch on your possessions in such places. When you go to catch a bus, pack your luggage as compactly as possible, since this makes it more manageable, and always avoid having valuables or large amounts of money loose in your daypack or pocket.

One time when you should particularly watch out for pickpockets is in the human crush that often accompanies boarding a bus just about anywhere in Ethiopia as well as in a few other cities, such as Dar es Salaam. Another favourite trick is the twin-pronged approach whereby one person distracts you while the other rifles your pocket on the other side. This approach is particularly popular in Ethiopia (and part of the daily routine in Addis Ababa), where you are most likely to be distracted by somebody bumping into your side and then apologising profusely or pretending to be disabled – if this happens, turn around quickly and check out what's happening on your other side. In Addis Ababa, stuffing your most readily pickable pocket with a decoy such as a wad of scrunched-up tissue paper or an empty cigarette box is one way to keep the pickpockets amused while you get on with your life.

When you arrive in a town, aim to get out of the bus station as quickly as possible, since dithering around is likely to attract the attention not only of any stray pickpockets and thieves but also of the sort of self-proclaimed 'guides' who can become quite difficult to shake off once they've taken it upon themselves to befriend you. Ideally, take a look at the map as you enter the town to get your bearings so that you can walk out of the bus station with confidence in the right direction. If you forget to do this or there is no map for the town, then walk out confidently in any direction and wait until you've cleared the crowds before you stop to ask somebody for directions or pull out your travel guide.

On public transport

Generally speaking, you've little to be concerned about once you're on a bus or train. Theft from luggage is most unusual, even when it is placed on the roof, and the handful of instances I've heard of where something's been taken from a backpack in this sort of situation all occurred on overnight buses in Tanzania. What you should be alert to is theft through a bus or train window, again something that seems to be particularly commonplace in Tanzania. On trains in this country, you must keep windows closed at night (blocks of wood are provided for this purpose) or somebody may literally leap into the window to grab your luggage. On trains anywhere, I would tend to jam my rucksack under the lower bunk and avoid having things lying about loose. On buses in Tanzania, people who wear glasses should watch out for little hands snaking through the window as the bus starts moving. Little hands are also quite likely to take an interest in anything sitting on your lap.

Something you hear about from time to time is a backpacker being given drugged food or drink by a fellow bus passenger, only to awaken several hours later without a passport, money or any other possession. At present, the one area where you most definitely ought to be alert to this sort of thing is on the Kenyan coast, specifically on buses between Mombasa, Malindi and Lamu, but I have also heard of instances on overnight buses between Arusha and Dodoma and overnight buses between Dar es Salaam and Mbeya.

Confidence tricks

This is another predominantly urban phenomenon, with Nairobi once again being the main area of risk, followed closely by Addis Ababa, though in most instances the worst that's likely to happen is you lose U$10 or so and gain a degree of wisdom. In Nairobi, common tricks range from the relatively innocuous (a 'refugee' or a 'student' with a bogus sponsorship form trying to shame you out of a few dollars) to the more sinister (bogus policemen offering you the option of a fine or jail for illegally giving a few dollars to a 'refugee'). The sensible approach is to ignore *anybody* who approaches you in the street on the assumption that they're after something. In Addis Ababa, approaches tend to be along the lines of 'Do you remember me?' or 'I'm the gardener at your hotel'. A particularly common trick is to invite you for a drink of *tej* (honey wine) then produce a bill for the equivalent of US$50 (anybody who tries to charge you more than US$1 for a bottle of *tej* is chancing it!). In Addis Ababa, as in Nairobi, and as in any large city in Africa or elsewhere, people don't approach strangers on the street unless they are lost or mad or after something!

An area of ambiguity surrounds the youngsters who act as a self-appointed 'meet 'n' greet' agency at some bus stations. In a few places – Lamu, Arusha, Zanzibar town – these guys perform a fairly genuine hotel-finding service for which the hotel, not you, is expected to pay their commission. In other cases, they've little more to contribute to your life than a few banal questions and a request for an absurdly high 'guide' fee. Characters such as these aren't guides so much as confidence tricksters, even if they probably don't see it that way themselves, and I'd avoid getting into conversation with them on the basis that they become more difficult to shake off the longer you spend with them. This sort of behaviour occurs most frequently and persistently in Ethiopia, which is also where you'll encounter the highest level of skill when it comes to manipulating your emotions and tweaking Western guilt. After a month dealing with Ethiopian 'guides', you'll easily handle their more low-key, amateurish counterparts in other countries.

Other travellers
After trawling through all the above, it might just be worth mentioning that I've only twice been separated from a significant amount of cash while travelling in Africa, in both instances when the spare US dollars that I usually keep buried in my pack were removed in a dormitory in a backpackers' hostel!

Banditry, unrest and war
There are a few parts of eastern and southern Africa which carry a real risk of being held up at gunpoint by bandits and/or political dissidents. Car hijacking is a serious problem in South Africa (particularly around Johannesburg) and to a lesser extent in Nairobi and southern Mozambique, but the risk to somebody spending a short time in any of these places is negligible and for obvious reasons it is unlikely to affect backpackers. On public transport, the only areas where there is currently a significant risk of being involved in an armed hold-up are the remote and little-visited semi-desert regions of northern Kenya, northern Uganda and eastern Ethiopia. The countries covered in detail in this guide are generally stable and seem likely to remain so under present circumstances. One exception to the above is Ethiopia, which has been at war with Eritrea for some time, though a ceasefire was signed in mid-2000 and even at the height of the conflict it had little impact on parts of the country removed from the Eritrea border area. Zimbabwe, meanwhile, has suffered a great deal of internal conflict over the course of 2000, but this has largely been confined to farming districts away from the main tourist centres. Media coverage of the unrest has caused a marked decrease in tourism to Zimbabwe, but recently returned travellers report that the country is safe, provided you stick to recognised tourist centres.

The Interlacustrine region – Uganda, Burundi, Rwanda and the western part of the Democratic Republic of the Congo – has been subject to repeated bouts of instability ever since independence. Most of Uganda has been considered safe since the mid-1980s, and Rwanda has re-emerged as a stable travel destination since the first edition of this guide was published. The brutal murder of a group of tourists in Uganda's Bwindi National Park in 1999 is widely regarded to have been an isolated incident, unlikely to be repeated now there is increased security for tourists going gorilla tracking, but it does underline the volatility of this region, particularly while the Democratic Republic of the Congo remains in a state of civil war.

Cultural Considerations

This chapter looks briefly at cultural considerations in a variety of circumstances where travellers and local people interact. It's not an exposition on African culture or perspectives, subjects that are easily misrepresented even by 'objective' qualified observers and that tend to be reduced to culture-bound nonsense when framed in the platitudinous topicality beloved of travel writers. All I've set out to achieve in this chapter is to 'guide' backpackers through the uncertainty that follows first exposure to a different culture, since I believe this will make life easier both for travellers and for the locals they encounter. My approach is pragmatic rather than moral or judgmental – if it happened to be the case that Tanzanians found it rude for women to wear blue clothing on a Tuesday, then my duty would be to alert travellers to this custom, not to point out how silly or sexist I happen to find it. And it is to be expected that I bring my own prejudices to an area of discussion that is less than scientific. There are possibly (all right, probably) points about which I am quite wrong – you're welcome to write to me about them!

Travellers who want to espouse current African issues (and why is it that Africa is always discussed by Westerners on a single-issue basis rather than with the holistic overview we have of our own society?) should set about making sure that they actually are reasonably well informed – read some reliable source material and talk to the broadest possible spectrum of Africans. For my side, I'd rather travellers be unaware of any given issue than have them espouse an 'informed opinion' about a complex subject derived solely from one of those pithy three-paragraph 'boxes' that increasingly litter the pages of travel guides. If you're British, imagine meeting a tourist whose opinions on the relevant subjects were based on a guidebook to Britain written by a foreigner and containing 'authoritative' and politically correct 200-word boxes entitled 'The Royal Family: Should they stay or should they go?' or 'Ebony and Ivory: Racial Attitudes in Inner London' or 'Everything Must Go: The Destruction of traditional Welsh mining village culture by MTV' – perhaps then you'll understand the sort of humbug that I'm trying to avoid.

So, for the record, it would be easy enough in this guide to argue the case for maintaining the CITES ivory ban, just as easy to put forward the case for ending it. To do either, in my opinion, would be an abuse of my position. Likewise, I'm not certain whether the critical point about those Maasai warriors who pose professionally for snapshots is that tourism is hastening the 'commercialisation' and eventual destruction of an already fragile culture, or that tourism is playing a constructive role by offering employment to a people whose lifestyle is unviable given modern population pressures. And, yes, like most readers. I would like to see international pressure placed on countries that continue the abhorrent practice of female 'circumcision', but I'm not sure how this squares with my broader view that Westerners have some difficulty in recognising that those internal African matters are simply none of their business. Meet me in a bar, and I'll expound at length on whatever issue takes my fancy. In the context of this guide, however, I'd rather not add to that list of things on which the final word for many backpackers is 'But it says in the book...'.

Cultural expectations

Many people arrive in Africa with wildly romantic expectations about its people and feel completely let down by cities where everybody is dressed in Western clothing and villages where people in ethnic dress are only interested in selling them something. Disillusionment of this sort is most extreme on safaris, when you should expect the Maasai villages to which you are ferried to be contrived. But to complain, as tourists do, that Africans are 'commercialised' is somewhat absurd. Semi-professional posers and dancers are meeting a demand, doing a job, and have every right to expect payment.

By its very nature, independent travel allows for greater intermingling with ordinary citizens, the vast majority of whose livelihoods are not intertwined with tourism. Backpackers are fortunate in that they have the chance to see something of rural Africa, where they will discover that most Africans, even the poorest, are disarmingly open and hospitable. I strongly urge all readers to spend at least a few days exploring off the beaten track – for obvious reasons it would be counterproductive to recommend individual places, but virtually any small town or village will present the opportunity to meet local people in uncontrived conditions.

It is the new millennium in Africa as much as it is anywhere else in the world, and to go there expecting an entirely traditional society would be as unrealistic and parochial as going to the USA expecting to walk into the set of a cowboy film. Too many visitors arrive in East Africa with absurd preconceptions: that the culture of the villager is somehow more valid than that of the urbanite, or that African cultural purity is tainted by any trace of Westernisation. Far healthier to recognise that Africa has been a cultural melting-pot since prehistoric times (the Maasai and Samburu, to many visitors the archetypal people of East Africa, only arrived in the Kenyan Rift Valley at around the time the Dutch first colonised the Cape) and that the very notion of cultural purity has little historical basis. Much of the fascination of modern Africa lies in the vibrant interchange between traditional and exotic cultures: an evening in a small town bar will probably teach you more about African realities than any number of camera-based exchanges in tourist-orientated villages.

The only sensible attitude to Africa is to accept it and try to understand it on its own terms.

Culture shock

Most travellers experience a degree of culture shock during their first week or two in Africa. Obviously this will be marginal if you start your trip in South Africa and spend most of your time in hostels in the company of other backpackers, and rather more extreme if you fly into Addis Ababa and bus straight on to Gambela. Factors you have to adapt to in East Africa include the much higher level of dirt and noise than you're used to at home, the feeling that you're something of a target for crime, being unable to follow the language, and putting up with accommodation and public transport that is at times very rudimentary and uncomfortable.

Above all, the adaptation to be made when you arrive in East Africa is to being a constant focus of attention: at home, you are most conscious of yourself as an individual and used to walking down the street without attracting any special attention. In parts of East Africa, you start to feel like you're first and foremost a representative of that odd breed *mazungu* or *faranji*, and that by merely walking down a street you often attract the attention of dozens of hysterically yelling children.

The main thing to be said about any reaction you have to all this is that it's perfectly normal, and after a month in Africa you'll be completely used to it. Still, there will be days when it gets you down, in which case the best response is to put yourself in the most familiar environment possible. An afternoon in a British Council reading room will be enough to recharge your batteries, as will reading a novel in the grounds of an upmarket hotel. Failing that, if you've been travelling off the beaten track for a while, then try to get yourself to somewhere you're likely to meet other travellers.

Bargaining

This subject is in my opinion often misrepresented by travel writers, who like to assert that every price in Africa is negotiable. This is a half truth, almost always applicable to curio-sellers, taxi drivers and bus conductors, but not in many other situations. The problem that faces travellers going from town to town and country to country is knowing when they're being asked a fair price, and thus to hit the right balance between politely paying up and indulging in a certain amount of aggressive posturing to establish whether they're being ripped off.

A further fog factor is the notion of a fixed price, since in markets specifically there often isn't one and bargaining is normal even between locals. The best approach in markets is to visit a few stalls and feel out prices before you buy anything – walking away will almost always be enough to lower a ridiculously inflated price. But do keep things in perspective. In my experience, small stalls in areas with a low tourist volume will rarely ask an absurd price and, if the stall owner is reluctant to negotiate, I would tend to assume that the price is fair in the first place.

Curio stalls practically always ask an inflated price, and they are whimsical to an extent that makes nonsense of any rules of thumb; for instance that you should counter-offer half of what you are first asked and settle at around two-thirds. Pricing similar items at a few different stalls is a better approach. But even when buying curios, it is possible to take bargaining too far. In Nkhotakota, I watched two travellers bargain with a Malawian who was selling a couple of home-carved statues for a not unreasonable price of MK15 (around US$1). The Malawian dropped his price to MK8, obviously as low as he was prepared to go, but still the travellers weren't happy and they spent a full quarter of an hour beating him down to MK7, a price which was eventually accepted through sheer desperation for cash. Frankly, I find this sort of behaviour disgraceful. When dealing with individual curio- or fruit-sellers, as opposed to large stalls, I see no harm in recognising the situation for what it is (somebody scraping a living in difficult circumstances) and being a little generous in your dealings. One argument you'll hear against this is that travellers have an ethical duty to bargain prices as low as possible, otherwise they risk triggering an inflation rate that will eventually put goods out of the reach of locals. This might just be the case in a few extreme cases, for instance when you go shopping for woven baskets in Arusha or Nairobi. On the whole, though, it strikes me as drivel of the most obnoxiously self-serving sort.

Public transport works on a fixed fare, and overcharging tourists is commonplace in western Kenya and Uganda, less so elsewhere. The ideal is to be philosophical about this. Nobody likes being ripped off, but why let the loss of a few cents spoil your day? Where philosophy fails (and it doesn't work for me), a scientific approach is better than losing your temper. Ask other passengers what they are paying, or gently query the price and prevaricate about whether you like the look of the bus. A diplomatic bluff will usually do the trick, and it's far better all round than becoming aggressive or accusatory.

Bribery, bureaucracy and corruption

You often read about travellers having to bribe their way out of a testing situation, or having to pay a hefty tip to get a railway ticket or some other service. In reality, the eastern Congo is the only country in the region where backpackers regularly encounter this sort of problem these days (though it is true that motorists are frequently expected to pay 'fines' for no good reason to traffic officers in Kenya and Mozambique, although this doesn't affect backpackers). In the unlikely event that a bribe is being hinted at in any other country, your best response is probably to smile inanely and completely miss the point. As for more serious concerns about being put through the ropes by gun-wielding officials, they probably have as much substance as worries about man-eating lions – it could happen, true enough, but you really would have to be in the wrong place at the wrong time.

My experience with African bureaucrats has largely been positive, certainly by comparison with the carping that I've come across in many other travel guides. It goes without saying that some African bureaucrats are difficult, but such is the nature of the beast anywhere in the world, and I really don't think that Western visitors to Africa have much justification for complaint by comparison with African visitors to Western countries. If anything, tourists to all of the countries covered in detail in this book (except perhaps South Africa) will most often be subjected to positive discrimination, in that officials will deal with them far more courteously than they would the poorer citizens of their own country. That said, many officials are as incapable of speed or efficiency as they are fond of paperwork and rubber stamps – you're strongly advised to approach any bureaucratic encounter with plenty of time and infinite patience.

Something that should be pointed out, at least to that small but significant minority of travellers who evidently feel that their Western passport or white skin places them above African law, is that there is a difference between mindless bureaucracy and somebody who is simply doing his job. For instance, a backpacker who is validly arrested for climbing Kilimanjaro without paying the national park fees has no greater cause for complaint than if arrested for shoplifting at home. By the same token, travellers who arrive at a Mozambique border without a visa will be refused entry and, while they might query the thinking that lies behind the legal requirement to buy a visa in advance, it is hardly the fault of an individual immigration official who is quite properly and not unreasonably enforcing the laws he is paid to enforce.

One thing that backpackers ought to bear in mind when dealing with officials who don't speak fluent English is the ample room for misunderstanding. It is, for instance, standard in many African languages and cultures to greet a stranger with a list of questions – 'what is your name?', 'where have you come from?', 'what is your home country?' 'what is your mission in this country?' – that might easily take on a different cast coming from a policeman or customs officer. It is also easy to see how a traveller who has been primed to expect bureaucratic problems might respond to innocent questioning of this sort in a manner that could actually provoke trouble. If an official approaches you in the street, no matter what the pretext, I would tend to work on the assumption that he has no motive more sinister than friendliness and the desire to show off his English! In the unlikely event that things get nasty, your goal should not necessarily be to prove you are right but to defuse the situation, which is unlikely to happen if you take an aggressive, combative stance – far better to be friendly and deferent, explain your position slowly and simply (though possibly rather firmly) and avoid eye contact (which is considered to be rude in many African cultures).

Greetings

Elaborate formal greetings are an important form of social nicety in many African cultures – it is, for instance, quite normal for a couple of rural Swahili speakers to spend the first ten minutes of a conversation establishing the mutual good health of their spouses, parents, children, brothers, sisters, cows, goats and chickens. Travellers should be aware of this, first because they might otherwise find that people seem peculiarly nosy, but more important because they should at least go through a few rudimentary English greetings before asking a stranger the time of day or which way a bus is heading or whatever.

Gifts

I have little time for those travellers who carry around sweets or trinkets which they then hand out indiscriminately to African children. First of all, the motivation for this sort of thing is entirely selfish, in that it makes the giver feel good about him or herself. Secondly, there is something nauseatingly paternalistic about dewy-eyed tourists who adopt a beatific smile at the sight of 'adorable' African children scambling in the dirt for small change. Finally, and admittedly a selfish concern, is whether you really want to encourage children to beg from the next traveller who passes through. There are towns in Africa where children will ask you for money or sweets or a pen perhaps 100 times in an hour, others where the children are genuinely friendly and never ask you for things, and I'm convinced that it would need only one naïve tourist and a bag of sweets to transform the latter to the former.

The practice of handing out gifts is presumably a response to the guilt instilled by the visible gulf in wealth that separates most Westerners from most Africans. It is a perfectly understandable response, but not in my opinion an appropriate one. Consider why this gulf exists, and you'll recognise that the most constructive role tourism can play in a depressed economy is not to provide random handouts but to encourage legitimate and sustainable local business. Bearing in mind that a high proportion of the money earned by package tours to Africa stays in the hands of foreign investors, backpackers have a particularly high level of control over where their money goes. Collectively, the readers of this book can make a difference, not by salving their consciences with a few ultimately meaningless donations to beggars or children but by thinking about how and where they spend their money, and whenever possible lending their support to locally owned businesses and community projects.

The type of situation where a gift would be appropriate is when you've stayed with a local family or are similarly indebted. I don't personally see any need to carry around a selection of gifts for such eventualities – depending on their circumstances, you could take the family out for a meal, buy a chunk of meat for a special treat, bring back a crate of beer, or ask if there's something that they'd specifically like from your country and send it when you get back.

A final aside on the subject of giving is that a great many African children are aware that Westerners are far more likely to accede to a request for something that is perceived to be self-improving than they are to a request for money. It is one of life's little ironies that children who ask tourists for 'one pen' are not, as you might assume, worthier souls than those who ask for 'one shilling'. They're just more sussed!

Homosexuality

In most parts of Africa, homosexuality retains the status of a sin that dare not speak its name. It is, for instance, quite normal for heterosexual African men to hold hands while in conversation or walking together, and (unless I've grossly missed the point) it simply wouldn't occur to anybody to see a sexual undertone in this act. Refreshing as this attitude might be in another context, it doesn't change the fact that homosexual behaviour is not only illegal in most of the countries concerned, but as unacceptable as it was in Victorian Britain. For all that, you'd have to act with outrageous indiscretion for your sexuality to become an issue in most parts of Africa.

One country where homosexuals ought to be particularly discreet is Zimbabwe, where the issue of sexual orientation has gained high currency as a result of President Mugabe's frequent public expressions of staunch anti-gay sentiment.

The legal status of homosexuals in South Africa is ambiguous, since the new constitution guarantees sexual freedom, but laws against homosexual acts have yet to be scrapped. In practice, South Africa is the one country in the region where there is an open and active gay scene in all large cities and in general attitudes are comparable with those in the West, though on the whole more conservative.

Photography etiquette

Attitudes to photography vary widely, from Muslim parts of Tanzania where it would be highly offensive to pull out a camera without asking permission to Mozambican markets where merely setting off a flash can cause hundreds of kids to come trailing after you for the rest of the day in the hope you'll get them in the frame at some point. The basic rule of thumb is never to take a portrait without first asking the subject's permission. In Muslim areas, you should also be discreet about taking street or market shots.

In parts of Kenya and Tanzania, people like the Maasai and Samburu expect payment in exchange for having their photo taken, and some even make a living from hanging around a suitable spot wearing appropriately photogenic dress or by putting on dancing shows at tourist lodges. A large proportion of tourists have a problem with this but, for all the hot air that's been expounded on the matter of authenticity and commerciality, it strikes me that dancers, actors, musicians and models receive some financial reward for their efforts in the West, and that even the most debased of African dances boasts a level of cultural integrity that's entirely lacking from – just one example – the gung-ho crap that Hollywood thrusts at Africans. Take photos and pay, or don't take photos and don't pay – either way, you're no more being ripped off than when you buy a new CD or go to the cinema.

Religion

East and southern Africa supports a mixture of religions. Islam is well represented, particularly on the Indian Ocean coastline, and Christian denominations range from the idiosyncratic Orthodox Church of Ethiopia through the more familiar Protestant and Catholic churches to the celebratory and very Africanised Zionist Church of South Africa. Minority religions include a significant Jewish population in South Africa, a substantial Hindu presence throughout the region, and all manner of indigenous religions that are gradually being eroded by exotic faiths. There is generally a high level of tolerance between Islamic people and the various Christian denominations, and the surest way of giving offence to most Africans is to announce that you are an atheist.

Tipping

Tipping is not customary between Africans, nor is it expected from foreigners who use local restaurants, hotels and public transport – which doesn't mean that somebody who provided good service wouldn't appreciate a something. Tipping is customary at more Westernised hotels and restaurants, with 5–10% being the accepted norm. In South Africa, you would tip in any situation where you would at home. Throughout the region, South Africa included, catering and hotel workers are very poorly paid relative to those in Europe or the USA.

On organised safaris and mountain climbs it is customary to tip guides, porters and cooks, who generally derive most of their income from this source. As a rough guideline, around US$3 per group member per day to each employee feels right, depending obviously on performance. I would tend to ask the advice of the company with which you arrange your safari or climb. Should you make private arrangements with a guide, it would not be normal to give a tip over and above the negotiated fee, though again there would be nothing stopping you from doing so if it felt appropriate. What you should definitely avoid is being adopted by a self-professed 'guide' without negotiating a fee – invariably some sort of 'tip' will be expected and there's far less room for bad feeling when this has been negotiated in advance.

Women travellers

Most female travellers regard sub-Saharan Africa to be among the safest parts of the world when it comes to dangers that specifically relate to being female. On the whole, it's a region where a woman can travel alone with as much confidence as a man. The rape of tourists is extremely unusual, and you're probably at no greater risk travelling in this part of Africa than you would be at home – provided you don't leave your survival instincts at home and start wandering down dark alleys at night. The obvious exception to the above is South Africa, where armed robbers frequently rape their female victims, and female travellers should be far more concerned about hitchhiking than their male peers.

Women who travel alone in Africa won't be wanting for the attention of the opposite sex. A lot of this attention will come from African men, whose directness in such matters – 'We can fuck?' – fortunately extends to their capacity to shrug off a 'no' with good humour. Only perhaps in Ethiopia are you likely to feel threatened by this sort of thing. Putting aside political correctness for a moment and facing the reality that you're alone in an unfamiliar culture, definitely avoid giving off ambiguous signals, particularly in places such as Lamu and Watamu where a gigolo element feeds off tourists. Basically, avoiding ambiguous signals amounts to nothing more than dressing reasonably conservatively and nipping any unwanted flirtation firmly in the bud. In any case, many women travellers find they get less hassle from Africans than from other travellers, who also tend to be more persistent.

Women travellers will find that dressing skimpily gives offence in most rural areas, particularly strongly Muslim areas, a category that includes the east coast all the way from Lamu, south to Beira and much of eastern Ethiopia. The high level of religious tolerance in East Africa means that Western women, no matter how they dress, are unlikely to be subject to any serious hassle. However, you risk giving offence and may occasionally be greeted by catcalls or other unpleasantries if you don't wear a skirt or sarong that covers your knees, or if you wear a singlet that reveals significant expanses of breast or bra. Strictly speaking, women should not wear trousers of any sort in Muslim areas. In practice, trousers are unlikely to offend, and trousers that cover your knees would be preferable to a skirt that doesn't. As a rule, dress codes should be adhered to most strictly in areas that see few tourists – you can dress much as you choose in, for instance, Dar es Salaam or Mombasa, but you should dress very conservatively if you visit the south coast of Tanzania.

Foreign women are generally exempt from the numerous customs which combine to make African women, particularly those still living in villages or small towns, second-rate citizens. Many such customs are invisible to travellers, but you'll notice the constraints in bars and restaurants, where it's unacceptable for a woman to drink alcohol or smoke cigarettes and any woman who does so is assumed to be a prostitute. The only way you're likely to gain any real insight into the experience of African women is if you happen to be a black woman, in which case, judging by the experience of an Afro-American woman I met in Zimbabwe and another who wrote to me after travelling in Ethiopia, you might get rather closer to the situation than you'd like. Both received an unusually high level of harassment, and both indicated that dress played an important role in how they were perceived. Leave any African-looking clothing at home, along with anything that is at all revealing or that might appeal to a 16-year-old going to a disco, and make every possible effort to dress in a way that looks American. Something very preppy, such as pale cotton trousers or jeans and a golf shirt, might be right – or to put it another way, dress in such a way that you would recognise yourself as a foreigner if you saw yourself.

Finally, many women experience unusually heavy or prolonged periods when they first travel in the tropics. Nothing to worry about, but something to be prepared for, given that sanitary pads and tampons are only generally available in large cities.

Crossing between Countries

FORMALITIES

There was a time when African border posts were characterised by a level of bureaucracy that inspired dread in the most unflappable of travellers. These days, however, crossing between the countries covered in this book is generally straightforward, provided that you have a valid passport and (unless your nationality exempts you) a visa. Entry requirements for different countries in the region are detailed in the individual country chapters. Most technically require visitors to have an onward ticket and sufficient funds, but only when crossing into Zimbabwe or South Africa is this likely to become an issue at an overland border.

Currency declaration forms

In the days when black markets were rife, most of the countries in the region required visitors to declare all their foreign currency upon arrival by filling in a currency declaration form. All legal foreign exchange transactions were then recorded on this form and customs officials would check that the figures tallied when you left. These days, however, only Malawi and Ethiopia still use currency declaration forms and in both cases they are rarely, if ever, checked. One thing you should be alert to when crossing between countries in the region is that many still have restrictions on the import and export of local currency. If you declare that you have any excess currency, it will be confiscated by customs officials. In practice, you may be asked if you are taking any local currency out of the country, but you won't be searched.

Changing money at borders

The crossing of any international border in East and southern Africa will be accompanied by a change in currency. This can be a nuisance, since there's often no formal opportunity to buy local currency at the border. Instead, you'll normally have to deal with individuals who provide an informal money-changing service, one that's not always strictly legal but usually condoned for a lack of a practical alternative. As a matter of course, you should change at least enough money at the border to see you through to the next town – the equivalent of around US$10 or US$20 should be ample, unless you're unlikely to make it to a bank that day, in which case change enough to last you until the next banking day (taking into account that banks in most countries are closed on Saturdays, Sundays and public holidays). There are two reasons for this: you may not be able to find somewhere to change money in the next town and, even if you can, you'll be more comfortable and in some instances at considerably less risk seeking it out after you've found a room, had a meal, or whatever.

There are several things to bear in mind when you change money at a border. The first is that there will almost certainly be a few crooks hanging about, and you don't want them to see you digging in your moneybelt or flashing a wad of hard currency. It would be safer to put aside the amount of money you want to exchange some time before you arrive at the border, noting that most private dealers will accept only US dollars cash or the currency of the country you're leaving (though as far north as the southern borders of Zambia and Malawi, the South African rand is as useful as the dollar). As for rates, you should expect to be offered a poor deal initially, and it will be easier to negotiate a better one if you already have a rough idea of the exchange rate. Of course, at most borders you won't be dealing with the type of big city black marketeer who pays above the going rate to accumulate hard currency, but with a local who makes a living from trading back and forth the currencies of two neighbouring countries – so while you should ensure that you get the going rate, recognise too that this sort of trader can survive only by making a slight profit on transactions in both directions. When it comes to it, the reason for changing a sum of US$20 or so at the border is convenience and, given that quite a number of dodgy characters tend to hang around borders, it might be wiser to act quickly and decisively, even if it means losing a dollar on the deal, than to risk getting into a protracted and heated bickering session with an ever-growing group of hustlers.

In most instances, the border will be the last opportunity you have to get rid of excess currency from the country you're leaving.

Smuggling

Baggage searches are to be expected when crossing between countries and, although they are generally cursory, you'll be in serious trouble if you are caught with an illegal substance in your luggage. Grass is dirt cheap everywhere in the region; if you have some left over before crossing between countries then throw it away and buy some more on the other side of the border. Should you be caught carrying even the smallest amount across a border, the authorities will regard you as a drug smuggler and you'll probably spend a long, long time in an African jail.

THE CROSSING POINTS
Ethiopia to Kenya

The overland route between Addis Ababa and Nairobi will take the best part of a week. It's a rough trip, but the reward is that you pass through some of the most remote parts of East Africa. Starting in Addis Ababa, your first goal should be Dila, and at least one bus does this ten-hour trip daily, leaving at around 06.00. Alternatively, plenty of buses run throughout the day from Addis Ababa to Shashemene and Awasa, where you'll find regular transport along the last 100km to Dila. There are a number of cheap lodgings in Dila; the Mesera and Laie hotels are recent recommendations.

From Dila, the 420km road and 12-hour bus ride south to Moyale pass through an arid landscape where you can expect to see Guenther's dik-dik, Grant's gazelle and with a bit of luck larger animals such as giraffe and lesser kudu. Buses to Dila leave from Moyale at the relatively civilised hour of 05.00, though they're often held up for hours at the police check just outside Moyale. Buses to Moyale leave Dila at the bizarre hour of 02.00! Travellers heading this way from Arba Minch or Omo National Park will connect with the bus at Yabelo, halfway between Moyale and Dila, where the Borena Hotel, with rooms in the **A** range, has recently been recommended for its attractive gardens. Buses from Yabelo to Moyale leave at 05.30 and take about five hours.

Moyale itself is effectively two different towns straddling the border. The Ethiopian town is universally agreed to be more pleasant than its Kenyan counterpart, and it has a good selection of hotels, including an acceptable Bekele

Mola Hotel with s/c rooms in the **C** range, the Tewodros Hotel in the **B** range, and several **A** lodgings of which the Tropical Hotel is recommended. Make sure you try the local speciality of pancakes. Convoys south leave Moyale about three times a week, so check when the next one is leaving before you cross the border, otherwise you may end up stuck in Kenyan Moyale for a few days!

From Moyale, it's easy to find a lift with a truck heading south to Isiolo or Nairobi. The cost will be negotiable, but expect to pay US$10–15. Trucks travel in convoy due to periodic outbreaks of banditry in the area, so you may want to ask about recent incidents, though the risk to backpackers travelling on this main route as part of a convoy is minimal. The trip takes two hot, dusty days, with only the occasional large mammal and an overnight stop in the montane oasis of Marsabit to break the tedium. There is plenty of accommodation in Marsabit and you may want to stay here a couple of days before heading on south. Travellers crossing in the opposite direction should note that the best place to pick up transport to Moyale is Isiolo.

A more expensive but more comfortable way of travelling south from Moyale is to try for a ticket on a charter flight direct to Nairobi. These don't operate to any fixed schedule; the Yeta Agency in the Kenyan town will normally know about any flights. Prices vary, but you'd be doing well were you to secure a seat for less than US$100.

Kenya to Uganda

The train service which once connected Nairobi and Kampala was suspended in 1998 and seems unlikely to resume in the immediate future. There are, however, direct road links between the two capitals, of which the Akamba bus has been a reliable bet for several years now. This leaves twice daily in either direction, at 07.00 and 14.30, and takes between 12 and 15 hours. The bus costs US$18 one way, and it leaves Kampala from the Akamba bus depot on De Winton Street. Also worth checking out might be the new Silverstar Express, a daily shuttle between Nairobi and Kampala which costs US$20 one way (tel: Nairobi 240218 or 221839) for details.

It is cheaper to do the trip between Nairobi and Kampala in stages, using the Busia or Malaba border post. This is a more logical approach for those who want to explore parts of Kenya or Uganda which lie between the countries' respective capitals. There is plenty of local public transport all the way, and all major towns are covered in the appropriate country chapters.

Kenya to Tanzania

The most popular crossing point is Namanga, which lies about halfway between Nairobi and Arusha. The most straightforward way of getting across this border is to take one of the tourist minibus shuttles between Nairobi and Arusha run by Devanu and Riverside. These leave in either direction twice a day, at 08.00 and 14.00, and take about four to five hours depending on how long is spent at the border posts. In theory, these cost US$20 per person for non-residents, a price which is generally enforced when the ticket is booked through a hotel or travel agent. Based on our recent experience (we used the shuttle four times in 1999 and 2000), Riverside will normally agree to give you the resident rate (which works out to about US$12) if you book with them directly at their desk in the Stanley Hotel in Nairobi or at the Mount Meru Novotel or office next to the Chinese Restaurant in Arusha. This is a really good price, especially as the shuttle will normally collect and drop off passengers at the hotel of their choice in both towns, while also protecting you from the hustlers at the border post.

The same trip can be done more cheaply in stages, taking around seven hours and at a total cost of US$7 in fares – catch a minibus to Namanga from Ronald Ngala Road in Nairobi (ignoring any jokers who try to persuade you to buy Tanzanian shillings on the basis that you cannot enter the country without local currency) then, after crossing on foot (once again ignoring the money-changers who will almost certainly rip you off given half the chance), you can pick up a shared taxi directly to Arusha. There is a bank on either side of the Namanga border post, the best place to change money during normal banking hours. At other times you'll have to change money with private individuals; here you are far less likely to be cheated if you are changing Kenyan money to Tanzania (or vice versa) than if you try to change US dollars. One of the favourite tricks at Namanga at the time of writing is to change your US dollars then for some reason to make the transaction go sour, at which point you are given back counterfeit dollars.

Another quite popular border crossing is between Mombasa and Tanga or Dar es Salaam – straightforward enough, as a couple of buses do this run daily. You are strongly advised against taking a bus all the way from Mombasa to Dar es Salaam, since it will arrive at around midnight, when you run an unacceptably high risk of being mugged. Get off at Tanga and continue the next day.

A third route connects Voi on the Nairobi–Mombasa road to Moshi via Taveta, which lies in Kenya. By road, this is a fairly slow route, involving a change of vehicles at Taveta, but you should get through in a day. That's if you want to – there are plenty of cheap lodgings in Taveta, and about 90 minutes' walk down the Oloitokitok road lies Lake Chala, a beautiful and little-visited crater lake spectacularly positioned on the Kenyan foot slopes of Kilimanjaro. There is between Moshi and Voi, part of a service that connects Dar es Salaam to Mombasa and Nairobi.

The final option is to go between Kisumu and Mwanza. There are several buses daily along this route, leaving in the early morning and taking around 12 hours.

Uganda to Tanzania

For the moment, the only viable route between these countries is from Masaka to Bukoba. Regular minibuses run from Masaka to Kyotera, where the odd pick-up truck leaves for the Mukukulu border. At Mutukulu you can pick up a Land Rover to Bukoba, from where there are regular ferries to Mwanza. I've done this trip once in each direction and, despite the number of vehicle changes, I got through easily in a day.

The ferry service between Port Bell in Uganda and Mwanza in Tanzania was discontinued after the MV *Bukoba* sank in May 1996. Despite persistent rumours to the contrary, I've heard nothing to suggest that ferries will resume this route in the foreseeable future. The best places to check will be the Backpackers Hostel in Kampala or the ferry office in Mwanza.

Tanzania to Zambia

There are two main crossing points between Tanzania and Zambia: the Lake Tanganyika ferry and the Tunduma–Nakonde border on the main road and railway line between Dar es Salaam and Lusaka.

The ferry trip between Kigoma in Tanzania and Mpulungu in Zambia is among the most enjoyable public transport rides in East Africa. The MV *Liemba*, a ship that dates to World War I, leaves Kigoma at 16.00 on Wednesday and arrives in Mpulunga at 10.00 on Friday. The MV *Mongosa* leaves Kigoma on Saturday afternoon and arrives in Mpulungu on Monday morning. Both boats start the return trip on the same day that they arrive in Mpulungu, and after reaching

Kigoma 36 hours later they normally sail on to Bujumbura in Burundi. Tickets for sleeping cabins cost US$23 first class and US$18 second class.

The best way to get between Dar es Salaam and Lusaka is by the Tazara railway line. Trains to Kapiri Mposhi leave Dar es Salaam every Tuesday and Friday at 16.55, and take 36 hours. Trains heading in the opposite direction leave Kapiri Mposhi on Tuesday and Friday at 13.00. Tickets for sleeping carriages cost around US$50 first class and US$30 second class.

Tanzania to Malawi

The normal entry point from the north is the Songwe border post, and with an early start you can cross between Mbeya and Karonga in one day. Regular buses and *matatus* from Mbeya to Kyela take about three hours, and they stop at the turn-off to the Malawi border post 5km before Kyela. It's about 6km from this turn-off to Songwe, and more than likely you'll end up catching a bicycle taxi. Once across the border, several pick-up trucks ply back and forth all day between Songwe and Karonga, taking about an hour.

Tanzania to Mozambique

The only viable route, crossing the un-bridged Rovuma River between Mtwara and Palma, was until recently one of the most challenging and unpredictable borders in this part of Africa. This should have changed, however, with the installation of a motor ferry across the Rovuma in June 2000 and projected construction of a bridge in the not-too-distant future.

Before the ferry was installed, travellers had to catch a Land Rover from Mtwara to Mwambo, where they got an exit stamp, then walk for 5km to the village on the north bank of the Rovumu River, where dugout canoes crossed to Mozambique. From the river, it was another 2km on foot to the immigration office at Namiranga, then 50km to Palma – a distance which many travellers also ended up walking.

I have had no reports of public transport between Mtwara and Palma since the ferry started up, but over the last couple of years most travellers coming this way were able to catch a lift from Namiranga to Palma with the border officials, who travelled this road every morning and evening. The installation of a ferry service might well encourage more formal public transport along this route, and it should certainly mean that trucks will start heading this way, which will improve the odds of hitching a lift.

Zambia to Malawi

The only reason you're likely to be crossing between northern Zambia and Malawi is if you've taken the Lake Tanganyika ferry to Mpulunga. In theory you can cross from Mpulungu to Karonga via Nakonda, the Nyala border and the remote highland town of Chitipa, but transport as far as Nyala is slow and erratic. Once you've crossed the Nyala border post, it's easy enough to find a pick-up truck to Chitipa, where you'll probably have to spend a night or two before catching a bus to Karonga – there are several resthouses. Buses from Chitipa to Karonga leave at 06.00 on Tuesday, Thursday and Saturday and take five hours.

The alternative route between Lake Tanganyika and Malawi is to get off the ferry before it enters Zambian waters at Kasanga, where there is a basic resthouse. A few vehicles run daily between Kasanga and Sumbawanga, a large town with several resthouses. From Sumbawanga there are regular buses to Mbeya.

Buses from Lusaka to Chipata, 30km from the Malawi border, leave until around midday, though buses leaving much after 08.00 are unlikely to reach Chipata before nightfall. If you're still trundling along after dark, you might think about stopping over at Patauke or Betete, both of which have basic hotels costing around US$4. It's easy enough to pick up local transport from these towns on to Chipata (plenty of accommodation), and then a shared taxi to the border. Once you cross into Malawi, it's only a few minutes' walk to **Mchinji**, where there are several basic resthouses, and the Andrew's Motel has s/c **C** rooms with hot showers. Chipata is the best base for visiting Luangwa National Park in Zambia – see box *Chipata and South Luangwa National Park* on page 360).

It's worth noting that the Yellow Chicken Hostel near Chipata intends to start running a Baz Bus type minibus service connecting Lilongwe to Lusaka via Chipata. This should be operational by the time this book is published. Ask at Kiboko Lodge in Lilongwe or Chachacha Backpackers in Lusaka for news about this service.

Zambia to Zimbabwe

The two main crossings are at Victoria Falls and at Chirundu on the main road between Lusaka and Harare. Both are relatively straightforward. At Victoria Falls, most people cross on foot using the Victoria Falls bridge, but it's also quite easy to hitch a lift and a local rail service runs the 20km or so between Livingstone in Zambia and Victoria Falls in Zimbabwe twice daily in either direction. Crossing at Chirundu, the easiest option is to use a direct bus between Harare and Lusaka. The only drawback with this is that quite a bit of smuggling goes on across this border and buses are sometimes held up for hours while they searched. For this reason I would tend to catch a bus to the border, cross on foot, and then catch the next bus or hitch from the other side.

Travellers heading from Victoria Falls to Livingstone should take note that Fawlty Towers Hostel in Livingstone offers an irresistible package inclusive of transfer from Victoria Falls, Zambian visa, one night's accommodation, a meal, and a drink – all for US$10 per person.

Zambia to Botswana

The only border crossing is the Kazangulu vehicle ferry across the Chobe River, which runs regularly from 06.00 to 18.00. Coming there from Livingstone in Zambia, there is no public transport, but it's quite easy to hitch a lift to the border from the outskirts of Livingstone. From the Botswana side of the ferry, you should have no problem hitching the roughly 3km to Kubu Lodge or the 12km to Chobe Safari Lodge in Kasane. Alternatively, if you're heading on southwards, chances are your lift from Livingstone will be too, and there are a couple of buses daily from Kasane to Nata and Francistown.

Zambia to Namibia

The only direct border crossing between Zambia and Namibia is the motor ferry across the Zambezi which connects the small Zambian town of Sesheke, about 150km and five hours by bus from Livingstone, to Katima Mulilo in the Caprivi Strip. This is a very straightforward, quick crossing, since Sesheke and Katima Mulilo are less than 5km apart and locals regularly move between the two towns to do their shopping. The alternative to this route, quicker by road but probably more complicated for backpackers, is to use the Kazangulu ferry between Zambia and Botswana and then to cross into Namibia as you normally would from Kasane in northern Botswana.

Malawi to Mozambique

Four options are open to travellers who intend to visit northern Mozambique from Malawi. The most straightforward is the road crossing between Mangochi and

Mandimba. Regular transport to the border leaves Mangochi at the bus station a few hundred metres from the PTC supermarket, stopping on route at Namwera, a small town with plenty of resthouses. If you can't get a lift along the 7km road between the two border posts, your options are walking or hiring a bicycle-taxi – and if you opt for the latter you won't regret splashing out on a separate bike for your luggage. Mandimba lies on the main road between Lichinga and Cuamba – arrive before 14.00 and you should find transport in either direction, but there is a basic resthouse should you get stuck.

Also worth considering is the train service connecting Liwonde to Cuamba via Nayuchi border. Trains to Nayuchi leave Liwonde at 08.00 on Monday and Thursday and take about three hours. In Interlagos on the Mozambican side of the border there's a restaurant and resthouse, though if everything runs to schedule you should pick up the train to Cuamba on the same day; a four-hour trip which might take twice as long on a bad day.

More remote is the crossing between Likoma Island and Cobue on Lake Malawi. From Likoma, fishing dhows operate as a ferry service to Cobue, taking roughly one hour to cover the 10km stretch of water.

The Milange border between Mulanje and Mocuba is only worth considering if you're determined to visit Quelimane. It's easy to get a bus from Mulanje to Milange, where there's basic accommodation at Pensao Esplanada. Transport on to Mocuba is more erratic.

Those who are confining their Mozambican travels to the south must use the Zobue border post between Blantyre and Tete. Buses to Harare leave Blantyre at 06.00 daily, and they'll drop you in Tete, though they do charge the full fare of roughly US$15. Alternatively, local buses connect Blantyre to the border town of Mwanza. At Zobue on the Mozambican side there are at least two hotels and regular *chapas* on to Tete.

Malawi to Zimbabwe

Many travellers cross directly between Blantyre in Malawi and Harare in Zimbabwe using the Tete Corridor through Mozambique. Several bus services cover this route every day, leaving Blantyre from the bus station in front of Doogle's Backpackers' Hostel at around 05.00. The government Stagecoach bus is recommended over private operators because it is the fastest and should be the first to arrive at the border – with four lots of immigration and customs to go through, and up to five buses crossing daily, it is perfectly possible that a five-minute gap at the first border post will have translated into two hours by the time you reach your final destination. The trip between Blantyre and Harare can be done in stages, but there is no good reason to do this unless you plan to spend time in Mozambique, so this is covered in the relevant part of the Mozambique chapter. Note that you must have a transit visa in order to travel through the Tete border – these can be issued on the day of application at the Mozambique Consulate in Blantyre or the Embassy in Harare.

Mozambique to Zimbabwe

The most useful border crossing is along the Beira Corridor. The border post here lies about 10km east of Mutare in Zimbabwe and about 20km west of Manica in Mozambique. Regular buses run along this route, and hitching is a possibility. Trains between Beira and Mutare take about 12 to 15 hours and they run in either direction every other day, stopping at Manica and Chimoio. Travellers who are thinking of crossing into Mozambique from Mutare late in the day should bear in mind that there is no accommodation in Manica town. There is, however, a campsite and chalet complex about 20km further towards Beira at the Chicamba Real Dam, and a selection of hotels in Chimoio another 50km towards Beira.

I've never heard of a backpacker using Mount Selinda border post, though on paper at least it's the obvious crossing between the popular backpackers' haunts of Vilankulo and Chimanimani. If you're thinking of going this way, it's easy to travel between anywhere in Zimbabwe and Espungabera on the Mozambican side of the border: regular buses go from Chimanimani to Chipinge to Chirinda Forest, from where you can hitch the 10km to the border and walk the remaining 6km to Espungabera. More of a problem is finding transport from Espungabera further into Mozambique – the border officials say there's a daily bus from Espungabera to Muchaze, but from there you'd have to hitch the 80km or so to Mushungwe on the main Beira–Inhassoro road. If my information is correct, there's no accommodation anywhere between Chirinda Forest and Inhassoro.

It's difficult to see why anybody would want to use the Nyamapanda border post between Harare and Tete unless they were crossing directly to Malawi via the Tete Corridor.

Mozambique to South Africa/Swaziland

The normal crossing is the Komatipoort/Ressano Garcia border post between Johannesburg and Maputo. A train service runs three times a week between Johannesburg and Maputo, leaving Johannesburg at 17.45 on Tuesday, Thursday and Saturday, and Maputo at 18.00 on Monday, Wednesday and Friday. The journey takes about ten hours and tickets cost about US$30 first class and US$20 second class.

The Panthera Azul coach between Johannesburg and Maputo costs roughly US$35 one way. Coaches leave Johannesburg from the corner of Kerk and Polly Streets at 07.30 Monday to Saturday and at 08.30 and 09.00 on Sunday. There is also an overnight bus on Saturday leaving Johannesburg at 21.00. In the opposite direction, buses to Johannesburg leave Maputo from the Panthera Azul office on Avenida Mao Tse Tung at 08.00 Monday to Friday and at 09.00 on Saturdays and Sunday. On Sunday and Monday, a second bus leaves from Maputo at 12.00. The journey in either direction takes around ten hours.

Panthera Azul also runs a thrice-weekly bus service between Durban and Maputo. Buses leave Durban at 07.00 on Tuesday, Friday and Sunday, and Maputo at 07.30 on Monday, Thursday and Saturday. The trip takes about 12 hours and costs US$45 one way. Buses out of Durban leave from the main bus station.

Contact Panthera Azul on: Johannesburg 331-7409, Maputo 49-4238 and Durban 309-7798.

The Chillage establishment in Mbabane (the capital of Swaziland) runs a regular shuttle connecting Johannesburg to Maputo via Mbabane.

Zimbabwe to Botswana

The most popular route with backpackers is between Victoria Falls and Maun, which is covered by Route 49's twice-weekly door-to-door shuttle service, costing around US$50 per person one way. The shuttles leave from Maun every Wednesday and Sunday morning and from Victoria Falls every Monday and Friday morning. Any hostel or campsite in either town can make bookings and arrange tour pick-ups.

Another route between Zimbabwe and Botswana is from Bulawayo to Francistown via Plumtree. Plenty of buses cover this route daily, leaving Bulawayo from in front of the City Hall. Hitching between Bulawayo and Francistown is easy, and there is also a daily overnight train service continuing to Gaborone.

Zimbabwe to Namibia

There is at least one coach per week connecting Victoria Falls in Zimbabwe to Windhoek via Kasane (Botswana), Katima Mulilo, Rundu and Otavi. The coach takes two days with an overnight stop in Rundu, and it costs around US$50 one way. Ask at the UTC office in Victoria Falls for the current timetable. The cheaper alternative is to hitch to Kasane in Botswana from the junction 1km south of Victoria Falls and then cross from Kasane to Katima Mulilo in stages. It is also worth asking about Air Namibia flights between Victoria Falls and Katima Mulilo – these are less expensive than you might expect and generally include a free aerial trip over the falls!

Zimbabwe to South Africa

Route 49 operates two useful and popular door-to-door cross-border services for travellers, avoiding the slow and often difficult Beitbridge border in favour of travelling through Botswana. The first service is a twice-weekly service from Cape Town to Victoria Falls with an overnight stop in Bulawayo. Tickets cost around US$110 one way between Cape Town and Victoria Falls and US$100 between Cape Town and Bulawayo, inclusive of refreshments and a continental breakfast at a game lodge on the Botswana border. The total travelling time is 24 hours, with two drivers on board. The buses leave from Victoria Falls at 14.00 on Monday and Wednesday outside the Backpackers Bazaar, and from Cape Town on Tuesday and Thursday at 08.00.

The other service is Johannesburg or Pretoria to Victoria Falls, which costs around US$55 per person one way, including refreshments and a continental breakfast. Travelling time varies from 14 to 17 hours, and two drivers are on board. Buses leave from Johannesburg and Pretoria on Tuesday and Saturday (pick-ups commence from 23.30) and from Victoria Falls on Monday and Friday (pick-ups commence from 07.00).

All coach and rail services between Zimbabwe and South Africa pass through the Beitbridge border post. The overnight Greyhound coach service between Johannesburg and Harare leaves in either direction daily except on Saturday, and there are also four Greyhound coaches weekly between Johannesburg and Bulawayo. Translux run a few coaches weekly between Johannesburg and Harare, Bulawayo and Victoria Falls. All coaches stop at Pretoria and cost around US$50 one way.

The weekly train service to Harare leaves Johannesburg every Friday at 08.30, stops at Pretoria an hour later, reaches the border at 21.45 and arrives in Harare at 09.55 on Saturday. In the opposite direction, it leaves Harare every Sunday at 07.00, crosses the border at around 18.30, and arrives in Pretoria at 07.45 and Johannesburg at 09.00. The train to Bulawayo leaves Johannesburg every Tuesday at 15.25, passes through Pretoria an hour later and arrives in Bulawayo on Wednesday at 16.20. In the opposite direction, the train leaves Bulawayo every Thursday at 09.00 and arrives the next day in Pretoria at 07.11 and Johannesburg at 09.00. It's also worth noting that an overnight train service runs daily in either direction between Johannesburg and Messina, 15km south of Beitbridge.

Botswana to Namibia

Audi Camp runs a shuttle service connecting Maun in northern Botswana to Windhoek in Namibia via the recently surfaced Trans-Kalahari highway. This leaves from Maun on Monday and Friday, from Windhoek on Saturday and Wednesday, costs US$50 one way, and takes approximately nine hours. Tickets should be pre-booked though Audi Camp in Maun or any backpackers' hostel in Windhoek.

The main border crossing from northern Botswana into Namibia is at Ngoma Bridge on the Chobe River between Kasane and Katima Mulilo. This border lies about 60km from Kasane along a road that leads through Chobe National Park, and there is no public transport to the border. You'll have to hitch from outside Kasane, and you could be in for a wait – in fact, bearing in mind that most vehicles heading out in the direction of the border will merely be going to the national park, this will be one of those occasions when writing your destination on a piece of paper is indisputably a good idea. Once across the border, there are occasional buses to Katima Mulilo, though the odds are that whatever vehicle brought you to the border will be heading the same way.

Botswana to South Africa

The Greyhound coach service between Gaborone and Johannesburg has been discontinued. There is only a train service, which leaves Johannesburg every Tuesday at 13.30 and arrives in Gaborone at midnight. In the opposite direction, the train leaves Gaborone at 00.25 on Thursday and arrives in Johannesburg ten hours later.

Another option is the Route 49 bus detailed under *Zimbabwe to South Africa*.

Namibia to South Africa

An Intercape coach service connects Windhoek to Cape Town; phone Cape Town 386-4400 or Windhoek 22-7847 to make a reservation. Coaches leave from Windhoek at 18.00 on Monday, Wednesday, Thursday, Friday and Sunday and from Cape Town at 13.00 on Tuesday, Thursday, Friday and Sunday. The journey costs roughly US$70 one way and takes 18 hours, stopping at Clanwilliam and Springbok in South Africa and at Mariental and Keetmanshoop in Namibia. There is a connecting service to Johannesburg.

Part Two

The Guide

80

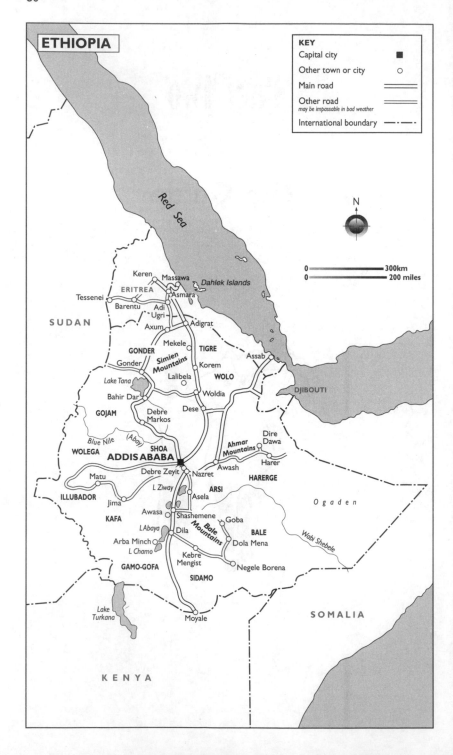

Ethiopia 7

Everything about Ethiopia is different. It is the one country in sub-Saharan Africa where tourism revolves around culture and history rather than beaches and wildlife, and it was the only part of the continent to emerge uncolonised from the 19th-century 'Scramble for Africa'.

Culturally, Ethiopia falls halfway between Africa and the Judaeo-Christian world. In several respects, it is unique: the spicy food, the Arabic-looking script, the music, the dancing, and, pivotally, the Ethiopian Orthodox Church which, since its foundation in the 4th century, has evolved in practical isolation from other denominations.

Few visitors would want to miss the northern historical circuit, highlights of which include the rock-hewn churches at Lalibela, the myriad ruins and stelae surrounding the ancient capital of Axum, the 16th-century castles at Gonder, and the Lake Tana island monasteries and Blue Nile Falls near Bahir Dar. Ethiopia also has much to offer natural history enthusiasts. In addition to the consistently dramatic scenery, it boasts more endemic bird species than any African country except for South Africa. There are also several endemic large mammals – the mountain nyala, Simien fox, gelada baboon and walia ibex – best seen in the Bale and Simien Mountains, which also offer excellent, inexpensive hiking possibilities.

Ethiopia is rich in off-the-beaten-track pickings – Lalibela, for instance, is merely the apex of a chiselling tradition which has resulted in more than 300 rock-hewn churches scattered around the country. Of great interest for birds and scenery is the string of Rift Valley lakes, while the walled city of Harer in the east has for centuries been the spiritual home of Ethiopia's Islamic population. Finally, those who cling to the perception that Ethiopia is just desert can enjoy dispelling that myth by undertaking a loop through the rainforests of the western highlands to the steamy river port of Gambela.

FACTS AND FIGURES
Area: 1,104,300km² (tenth largest in Africa)
Capital: Addis Ababa
Largest towns: Addis Ababa, Dire Dawa, Nazret, Dese, Mekele, Jima, Bahir Dar, Gonder
Population: 50–60 million
Official language: English
Other languages: Amharigna, Tigrigna, Oromigna and many others
Currency: Ethiopian birr
Head of State: President Meles Zanawi

Most visitors to Ethiopia agree it ranks close to being the most fascinating and rewarding country in Africa. But novice travellers should be aware that it can also be among the most frustrating, not because travel conditions are especially difficult, but because your every move is likely to be accompanied by the attentions of yelling kids, wannabe guides and other minor nuisances – nothing very threatening, but over the course of a few weeks somewhat exhausting.

BACKGROUND INFORMATION
Geography and climate
At the centre of Ethiopia lies a mountainous plateau, roughly twice as big as Great Britain, bisected by the Rift Valley and isolated on three sides by desert. Frequently referred to as the Ethiopian Highlands, the plateau has an average altitude of above 2,000m and has 20 peaks topping 4,000m. Particularly dramatic are the Simien Mountains to the north of Gonder, and the Bale Mountains southeast of the Rift Valley. The highlands are the source of four major river systems, including the Blue Nile, which rises at Lake Tana in the northwest. Other major river systems are the Wabe Shebele, Omo and Awash.

At one extreme, Ethiopia encompasses peaks in Bale that receive periodic snowfall; at the other is the Danokil Desert, with regular daytime temperatures of over 50°C. As a rule, however, the country has a pleasant, temperate climate, particularly the highlands and Rift Valley lake region, the areas most often explored by backpackers. The lowlands in the east are dry and hot, while the moist western lowlands around Gambela are one part of the country to feel truly tropical. The rainy season in the highlands runs from late June to early October. The northeastern highlands are prone to rainfall failure (such as the one which caused the notorious famine of 1985), but in normal years roughly 1,000mm falls over three months.

History
Ethiopia is the only country in the region with historical remnants stretching back to ancient times. As long ago as 1000BC, northern Ethiopia supported an urbanised agricultural civilisation of some magnitude, and there are more than 30 references to Ethiopia in the *Old Testament*. It has been ascertained that the extant town of Axum was occupied as early as 500BC, at which time it had strong cultural links with the Sabaean civilisation of Yemen.

The Ethiopian tradition is that a great-great-grandson of Noah called Aksumai was the founder of Axum as well as the progenitor of a ruling dynasty that survived for 50 generations. The last of this dynasty was Queen Makeda, the Biblical Queen of Sheba, who travelled to Jerusalem to visit King Solomon and returned home carrying the king's child, whom she named Menelik. As a young man, Menelik travelled to Jerusalem to learn the law of Moses; he returned home with the holiest of Judaic artefacts, the Ark of the Covenant, which Ethiopians insist is still locked away in the Church of St Mary Zion in Axum. Menelik is also credited with founding the Solomonic Dynasty which ruled Ethiopia for 237 generations until 1974 when Emperor Haile Selassie was murdered following a coup. Most Ethiopians accept the above version of events without question, but it is not taken very seriously by Western historians.

That Ethiopia has some very ancient Judaic links is not disputed. The Orthodox Church is unique in its Jewish influence, while the Felasha of the Lake Tana region (who were airlifted to Israel in 1991) clearly split from the Jewish mainstream before 640BC. Graham Hancock, in his book *The Sign and the Seal*, suggests that the Ark reached Axum via another route – that it was held in a temple on the Egyptian Nile for some time before being transported to a Lake Tana island monastery in 400BC and held there for 800 years. It's difficult to know how seriously to take a book that also drags in Freemasons and Atlantis, but it is certainly a good read and one of the few readily accessible books on Ethiopia.

The Axumite Empire was a major force in world trade from the 1st to the 7th centuries AD, when it stretched from modern-day Port Sudan south to Berbera and west almost to the Nile. The main port was Adulis in modern-day Eritrea. A 3rd-century Persian writer listed Axum as one of the world's four great powers, along with Persia, China and Rome, while Roman sources imply Axum was able to resist two attempts at incorporation into their empire. The Axumites were skilled masons, but their most impressive technological achievement was the erection of several solid granite stelae, the largest of which was taller even than the similar granite obelisks of Egypt.

The most influential Axumite king was Ezana, whose conversion to Christianity in AD341 was documented by the Romans and is attested to by the fact that Axumite coins minted after that date bear a cross rather than the pagan symbols found on older coins. Another important Axumite king was Kaleb, who took the throne in the early 6th century and ruled for 30 years; it is probably his palace described by the Byzantine traveller Cosmos in AD525 as having statues of unicorns on its corners and tame elephants and giraffes in the grounds. Kaleb's son is remembered for his patronage of Saint Yared, who invented the notation of Ethiopian religious music and wrote many songs, poems and chants still used today. Axum's decline is probably linked to the rise of Islam and subsequent usurping of its Red Sea trade routes. By AD750, Adulis was a ghost town, and Axum had sunk into global obscurity.

Ethiopian traditions relating to the end of the first millennium are dominated by the memory of Queen Yodit, who is credited with uniting the Felasha into a cohesive military unit that reduced many of Axum's finest buildings to rubble. There is little reason to doubt that Yodit was a real historical figure, but discrepancies in dating and the vividness of the legends suggest her memory may express a longer period of internal warfare and Felasha rule.

The Zagwe Dynasty captured the throne in around 1100, bringing a new stability and unity to Ethiopia. It was under the Zagwe King Lalibela that Ethiopian Christianity reached the peak of its physical expression in the form of rock-hewn churches carved at his capital. Zagwe rule ended when a Solomonic descendant called Yekuno Amlak took the throne in 1270. It was almost certainly under the Solomonic rulers of the 13th to 15th century that much of the mythologising surrounding Ethiopian history took place.

The Islamic presence in Ethiopia dates to AD615, when several of Mohammed's followers, including his wife, were offered protection by the Axumite king. For centuries, an uneasy peace existed between Christian Ethiopia and the Islamic world. However, in 1528, possibly as a result of a Portuguese expedition to Ethiopia in 1520, the Muslim leader Ahmed Gragn launched several destructive raids on the Christian kingdom from Harer (many rock-hewn churches throughout Ethiopia bear the scars of this campaign today). By 1535, Gragn held most of Shoa, Lasta, Amhara and Tigre – the heart of Christian Ethiopia – and were it not for the intervention of the Portuguese in 1543, it is likely that Ethiopian Christianity would have disappeared altogether.

This foundation of the modern Ethiopian state is generally accredited to three unifying emperors: Tewodros (1855–69), Yohannis IV (1872–89) and Menelik II (1889–1913). It was Menelik II who led a force of 100,000 men to victory over Italy at Adwa in 1896, and who founded the modern capital Addis Ababa. Menelik's attempts at modernisation and unification did not extend to reforming the deeply feudal nature of Ethiopian society; on the contrary, his period of rule saw a great increase in the slave trade. Menelik's chosen successor, Iyasu, turned out to be a natural progressive who tried to curb the slave trade, did much to woo the neglected Muslim population, and showed little regard for the ageing and self-serving government he inherited. In 1916, Iyasu was overthrown and Zauditu, the sheltered daughter of the dead emperor, was installed in his place. In 1930, Zauditu's husband was killed in murky circumstances, and the empress herself succumbed two days later to that most Victorian of maladies, heartbreak. A young prince from the Harer region, Ras Tafari, was crowned under the name Haile Selassie.

In October 1935, the Italian army crossed from their Eritrean colony into Tigre. After superior Italian air power and use of prohibited mustard gas decided the Battle of Maychew on March 31 1936, Mussolini decided to amalgamate Ethiopia, Eritrea and Italian Somaliland into one large territory he called Italian East Africa. The Italian Occupation was to be short-lived as a result of World War II: in January 1941 the Allies liberated Ethiopia and Haile Selassie returned from exile to claim the throne. After the war, Britain and the USA cynically urged the UN to federate the former Italian territory of Eritrea to Ethiopia. Ethiopia lacked access to the ocean, and the Allies, who had a good relationship with Haile Selassie, wanted Eritrea as a Red Sea base. In exchange, the USA developed a military training and armoury programme for Ethiopia which, by 1970, absorbed more than half the national budget for military aid to Africa. The world barely noticed when Ethiopia formally annexed Eritrea and placed it under military rule, initiating a war for self-determination that lasted three decades; claimed more than 100,000 Eritrean lives; and never once figured on the UN agenda.

On September 12 1974, following seven months of strikes, demonstrations, local peasant revolts and military mutinies, Emperor Haile Selassie was arrested by members of the military and murdered. Power was handed to a socialist military committee known as the Dergue, which proved to be even more ruthless than its imperial predecessor. The Dergue's attempts at collectivisation, villagisation and resettlement met neither with popular support nor with any significant success. Local and national opposition groups mushroomed, notably the Tigrean People's Liberation Front (TPLF) which allied itself to the cause of Eritrean self-determination while demanding democracy for Ethiopia. This outbreak of dissent was exploited mercilessly by Mengistu Haile Maryam, who undertook a purge of the Dergue which left him the uncontested leader of Ethiopia.

Ethiopia leapt into the world spotlight in 1985 with the worst famine in living memory. Initiated by three successive rainfall failures in Tigre and Wolo, the famine was a natural phenomenon exacerbated by the West's refusal to send aid to a socialist country and then by Mengistu's unwillingness to help food reach the troublesome province of Tigre. One in five Ethiopians were affected by the famine. One million died. It was entirely preventable.

The collapse of European Socialism in 1990 resulted in a cutback in military aid to Mengistu, and his weakened army was driven from Tigre and Eritrea. In May 1991, the EPRDM captured Addis Ababa and Mengistu jetted to safety in Zimbabwe. The new transitional government established by the EPRDM abandoned Mengistu's failed socialist policies, and allowed the EPLF to set up a transitional government in Eritrea. After a referendum in which Eritreans voted overwhelmingly in favour of secession, Eritrea was granted full independence in April 1993.

The future of both Ethiopia and Eritrea seemed highly promising until May 1998, when a border dispute over the Badme area erupted into a full-scale war which had claimed the lives of an estimated 40,000 soldiers by the end of 1999.

Such wholesale carnage, not to mention the wider economic cost of war to a relatively poor country, might seem disproportionate to what, in essence, is a squabble over a small piece of barren land. Indeed many commentators believe that the disputed border was the catalyst which forced to the surface the deeper malaise in trade relations between the two countries. Put simply, an independent Eritrea has left Ethiopia without a sea port of its own, creating an uneasy economic interdependence between the two territories. A ceasefire between the two countries has been signed, but there are still indications that further hostilities between the two countries might yet nullify this ceasefire.

PRACTICAL INFORMATION
Accommodation
You'll never have a problem finding a cheap room in Ethiopia, though many lodgings double as brothels. Most towns have in excess of 20 lodgings and even the smallest village can be relied upon to have something. With accommodation so abundant, I've restricted recommendations to a few standouts. You're advised to keep your eyes open for new places, which are often the best, and to be aware that in Ethiopia more than elsewhere in the region covered by this guide hotels tend to view a recommendation in a travel guide as licence to raise prices and neglect maintenance.

Books and newspapers
Except in Addis Ababa, you're unlikely to see anything in a script you can read.

Crime and safety
Pickpocketing is rife in Addis Ababa, where the worst spots are the Mercato, crowded bus ranks and the vicinity of government hotels in the city centre. The normal method is for one person to distract you by bumping into you or grabbing your arm or leg while a second person slips his fingers in your pocket. Elsewhere, the risk is largely confined to bus stations, where you are most likely to be pickpocketed in the surge of people getting on to a bus. Armed violence against tourists is a spasmodic risk in the east (Bale, Harer and Dire Dawa), so you are advised to ask around before heading out that way.

The recent border war with Eritrea has caused tourist arrivals to Ethiopia to plummet, and at one point in 1999 all domestic flights were cancelled so that planes could be used for military purposes. Aside from that, however, military activity has largely remained confined to the immediate border area, and the danger to tourists elsewhere is minimal. At the time of writing, flights to Axum have been suspended for some time, though I've heard from several travellers who've visited Axum by bus. It might be prudent, under the circumstances, to ask current advice before travelling to Ethiopia, but as things stand the country is perfectly accessible to backpackers.

Entrance fees
National parks in Ethiopia are among the cheapest in Africa, with an entrance fee equivalent to US$8.50 per 48 hours. In Gonder and Axum, a ticket costing US$8.50 covers entry to all secular sites for one day only. Most churches countrywide ask an entry fee, typically around US$3, though the main church in Axum now asks US$8.50. A blanket fee equivalent to US$12 is charged at Lalibela, covering all ten churches and valid for as long as you spend in town. Always get a receipt for fees paid to church officials, and be prepared to negotiate if you think you're being asked a silly price.

Entry requirements

Practically everybody needs a visa, which must be bought in advance at an embassy or high commission. Be aware that the Ethiopian Embassy in Nairobi has had an erratic attitude to granting visas for years: sometimes it issues them without fuss, while at other times it won't issue visas at all or will do so only on production of an air ticket to Addis Ababa. Ideally, buy your visa in your home country before you fly to Africa. When you arrive in Ethiopia, you will normally be given one month only, extendable for a month at a time to a total of three months. Extensions can be granted only in Addis Ababa, which forces you to plan your trip in such a way that you return there every month – though one week's grace is allowed on expired visas.

Faranji hysteria

A *faranji* is what Ethiopians call a foreigner, and hysteria is the characteristic response of an Ethiopian child or teenager upon sighting one. People yelling *'faranji'* or 'you' is an indelible part of travel in Ethiopia and, while it hardly constitutes a threat, it can become enervating after a while. The whole thing appears to disturb some travellers more than others, and it is probably more oppressive for those travelling alone, particularly women who'll almost certainly have some explicitly lewd suggestions yelled at them by some very brave gangs of teenage boys. The most effective response to *faranji* hysteria is to feign indifference or respond with humour – if a kid shouts 'you', then yell 'you' back, and if somebody shouts *'faranji'*, respond with *'habbishat'* (highlander). To be realistic, only a saint could travel in Ethiopia for a long time and not get slightly impatient with that section of the population whose behaviour, once all the patronising excuses have been made, is quite simply rude, racist and cowardly.

Flying there

I've never met a backpacker who used Ethiopia as the starting point of his or her overland journey through Africa, but if Ethiopia is on your planned itinerary it would make a great deal of sense to fly into Addis Ababa, if for no other reason than that it would save you the long, dusty overland trip between Nairobi and Addis Ababa in two directions. Assuming that the price is right, you might want to check out the possibility of buying an Ethiopian Airlines ticket to Nairobi and stopping over in Addis Ababa for a few weeks. Note that a departure tax of US$20 (payable in hard currency only) is levied for international departures from Ethiopia.

Food and drink

Most travellers find Ethiopian food refreshingly tasty after the bland stews that are the staple elsewhere in the region, but there are those who dislike it. In my experience, you'll enjoy the food more if you know the names of the more common dishes, otherwise you're likely to suffer for the widespread Ethiopian conceit that *faranjis* cannot handle food as spicy as theirs. Unless you are vegetarian, it helps if you're not there during Lent (late March and early April) when you can only get vegetarian food except in tourist hotels.

The staple is *injera*, a vast sour pancake made of fermented *tef* dough (a grain unique to Ethiopia) and served with a bowl of *wat* (stew). *Kai wat* is red in colour and very hot, while *alicha wat* is yellowish and bland. Most *wat* is made from meat (*siga*) such as lamb (*bege*), goat (*figel*), beef (*bure*) or fish (*asa*). The official national dish, *doro wat*, is to be avoided if you are hungry, since it's traditional to serve only a lonely chicken drumstick or wing in a bowl of sauce. Vegetarian *wat* is served on Wednesday and Friday, the Orthodox fasting days. It can be made from pureed beans (*shiro*), halved beans (*kik*) or lentils (*misr*).

Fried meat (*siga tibs*) and boiled meat (*siga kekel*) are popular. *Tibs kai wat* is where the meat is fried before the *kai* sauce is added. Other dishes are crumbed fish cutlets (*asa kutilet*), roast meat (*siga arosto*), steak (*stek*) and a mildly spicy brown stew (*gulash*). *Kitfo* is a very bland form of fried mince. *Kitfo special* is the same thing raw, so avoid it for health reasons. A popular breakfast dish is *inkolala tibs* – scrambled eggs cooked on request with onion (*shinkuts*), green pepper (*karia*) and tomato (*tamatim*). Another common breakfast dish is *yinjera firfir*, which consists of pieces of *injera* soaked in *kai* sauce.

Menus are normally printed in Amharigna script so you'll have to ask what's available (*migib min aleh*). If you don't understand the reply, suggest a few possibilities. The way to phrase this is to start with the type of meat or vegetable (prefaced with *ye*), then the type of dish. In other words, fried goat is *yefigel tibs*, fish cutlet is *yasa kutilet*, *kai wat* made with lentils is *yemisr kai wat*, and *alicha wat* made with beef is *yebure alicha wat*. If all else fails, *sekondo misto* consists of small portions of everything on the menu, replaced on fasting days by *atkilt bayinetu*, dollops of various vegetarian dishes heaped on the *injera*.

Many restaurants serve pasta (with variant spellings such as *spiggttii* or *makarronni*) and even in the smallest villages you'll usually find fresh bread (*dabo*). Hotels in Addis and government hotels elsewhere serve Western fare at reasonable prices. Pastry shops, found in most large towns, are great for inexpensive breakfasts – freshly baked cakes, biscuits and bread, along with coffee, tea and fruit juice.

Ethiopians are coffee-mad. The espresso-style coffee (*buna*) served with two spoons of sugar is rich, sweet and addictive. Coffee with milk is *buna watat*. In a traditional coffee ceremony the grains are roasted over charcoal, ground while the water is boiled, then used to make three successive pots of coffee – it's not advisable to accept an invitation if you're in a rush, but you should experience it at least once in your trip.

The usual brand name soft drinks (*leslasa*) are widely available and very cheap. So is carbonated mineral water – ask for *Ambo* in central, south and western Ethiopia, and *Babile* in the east. Pureed fruit juice is served at many pastry shops – most commonly banana, avocado, papaya, orange and guava – ask for *espris*, which consists of layers of everything. *Tej* is a mead-like drink made from honey (*mar*) or sugar (*isukalama*). *Mar tej* is OK, and dirt cheap, but avoid *isukalama tej*. Acceptable lager is sold throughout Ethiopia, at around US$0.50 for a 350ml bottle. Cheap draught lager is available in Addis Ababa and other large towns. Local wine is indifferent but affordable, especially if bought directly from a shop.

Getting around
By air
Ethiopian Airlines runs a useful network of inexpensive internal flights between Addis Ababa and most major tourist destinations. It is certainly worth thinking about flying between the main tourist centres on the northern historical circuit – a circular ticket out of Addis Ababa taking in Bahir Dar, Gonder, Lalibela and Axum costs less than US$200 and saves the best part of ten days of bus travel. If you're flying into the country with Ethiopian Airlines, ask them about special offers for internal flights. Air tickets must be paid for in hard currency, and each individual leg *must* be confirmed at the point of departure, ideally as soon as you arrive there.

By lake
There are two ferry services on Lake Tana, a daily service between Bahir Dar and Zege, and a weekly overnight service between Bahir Dar and Gorgora (see *Access and getting around*, pages 99–100).

By road

Cheap, reasonably efficient and uncrowded bus services cover all main roads. Expect to cover 30km per hour on dirt and up to 50km on surfaced roads. On longer trips, there are organised breakfast and lunch stops. Bear in mind the long distances when you plan your trip: travelling the northern historical circuit amounts to 3,000km of roads, which at an average progress of 30km per hour means 100 hours or the bulk of ten waking days on buses. Long-distance buses mostly leave in the morning – typically you'll be told to be at the bus station at 05.30, only to wait around for up to two hours while the conductors and luggage loaders do their stuff. Be warned, though, that buses do occasionally leave as early as 05.30.

The best buses, where they are available (and so far as I'm aware this includes the main loop through the historical circuit, from Bahir Dar to Gonder to Axum to Adigrat, as well as Nazret to Dire Dawa) are the recently introduced Iveco/ Cacciamla ones known by everybody in Ethiopia as *Katchamale*.

Ethiopians believe that opening a bus window is desperately unhealthy. No matter how stuffy the bus gets, or how many of your fellow passengers are puking their guts out with motion sickness, any attempt to open a window even a crack will be greeted with a swell of panicked tut-tutting. Then somebody will reach over and close the window. Quite why a nation that accepts defecating or urinating in the middle of the road as perfectly acceptable should be so terrified of fresh air is inexplicable, but you'll have little choice but to accept it.

By taxis and garis

Taxis can be found in many larger towns. Except in Addis and towns with a high tourist turnover (for instance Gonder) they are very cheap, but foreigners are frequently asked higher prices and you should expect to bargain. In towns with a cool climate, taxis are replaced by the horse-drawn cart or *gari*. These are even cheaper than taxis and very useful for reaching places a few kilometres out of town.

By bicycle

You can rent bikes very cheaply in most towns in Ethiopia, and they are often the easiest way of making short out-of-town trips. There is no fixed rate, of course, and an acceptable offer will probably vary from one town to the next, but something in the region of US$1–2 per day would feel about right. Do test drive the bike (particularly the brakes!) before you head off anywhere or pay anything, and insist on a pump.

Health

Malaria is largely absent from the historical circuit and from Addis Ababa. Sanitation-related diseases such as giardia, typhoid and hepatitis appear to be a greater threat in Ethiopia than they are in other parts of eastern and southern Africa. Fleas and bedbugs commonly occur in basic hotels, though they are more of a nuisance than a serious health threat.

Language

English is spoken only by the educated, and rarely with the fluency of educated Malawians or Ugandans. Amharigna remains the *lingua franca*, and it's important to know a few Amharigna phrases (see *Appendix 2*) if you plan to travel away from tourist centres. And do note a couple of linguistic oddities that create room for misunderstanding. Firstly, when Ethiopians ask you to play with them, they aren't proposing a grope but a conversation – many Ethiopians use the English word 'play' as a synonym of 'talk'. Secondly, the Amharigna word 'no' signals assent or agreement, which means that when somebody who speaks no English rattles off at you and you respond with a 'no', they may well think you are agreeing with them.

Money
The unit of currency is the birr, often referred to as the *dux* or (confusingly) the dollar. The exchange rate had hovered at around US$1=birr 6.3 for some years prior to 1998 but since it has devalued to around US$1=birr 8. Foreign currency can be changed at any Commercial Bank of Ethiopia (CBE), a straightforward and reasonably speedy procedure in Addis Ababa and to a lesser degree in the main tourist centres on the historical circuit, though not necessarily elsewhere – and certainly not in Lalibela where there is no bank. Banking hours in Addis are from 09.00 to 16.00 on weekdays, with a lunch break from 12.00 to 14.00. The CBE branch at Bole Airport is open every day of the week. There's a black market in Addis for US dollars cash, with rates 5–10% better than the banks. Ethiopia is very cheap.

Music
Bars are the best place to hear Ethiopian music which, like most aspects of Ethiopian culture, takes a little getting used to. The most widely played music emulates Western pop but with decidedly Arabic melodies and, in the hands of female vocalists like Aster Aweke and Hana Shenkute, the eerie, quavering pitch cuts right through the saccharine backing. Traditional and regional music also receives a fair amount of play. Music from the southwest is reminiscent of Zairian guitar pop, while some Tigrean music is not unlike the rural blues in structure. And if Ethiopian music is unusual, then the dancing defies succinct description. Several government hotels in Addis have resident bands and dancers – well worth visiting as they'll demonstrate a variety of styles. In local bars you're unlikely to remain an observer for long, since you'll be expected to provide amusement by attempting to emulate the moves.

Post and telephone
Ethiopia has a good internal and international post service. Mail between most parts of Europe and Addis Ababa takes around a week. The poste restante service in Addis seems reliable. Ethiopia has a good telephone service when compared to most parts of Africa. There are telecommunications centres in most towns, but it's best to make international calls from the one on Churchill Avenue in Addis Ababa. Expect to wait anything from ten minutes to an hour for your call to be placed. International rates are cheap.

Public holidays
7 January	Ethiopian Christmas	28 May	Downfall of the Dergue
19 January	Ethiopian Epiphany	29 August	Moulid
2 March	Adwa Day	11 September	Ethiopian New Year
6 April	Patriots' Victory Day	17 September	Meskel
Moveable	Ethiopian Easter	Moveable	Start of Ramadan
1 May	Labour Day		

Tourist information offices
The Ethiopian Tourist Commission office on Meskel Square in Addis Ababa sometimes stocks useful free booklets on Bale, Simien and Lalibela. There is a regional tourist office in every provincial capital, ranging from the impressively

organised Tigre Tourist Board in Mekele, through the helpful if slightly disorganised offices in Bahir Dar and Awasa, down to the utterly pointless offices in Harer and Gambela.

Addis Ababa

Situated at an altitude of 2,400m, Addis Ababa is the third-highest capital city in the world, with an encouragingly temperate climate that rapidly dispels media-derived images of Ethiopia as an endless desert. In other respects, however, Addis can be rather overwhelming on first contact, as a steady stream of beggars, cripples, taxi-drivers and street-hawkers clamour for the visitor's attention, while con artists and pickpockets do their best to divert it. By comparison with, say, Nairobi or Johannesburg, Ethiopia's capital is probably more bark than bite, with little real risk to life or limb. All the same, few would regard this chaotic city to live up to the name – Addis Ababa means *New Flower* – which was given to it by its founder Menelik II in 1887.

Addis Ababa does at least offer some good sightseeing. The Piazza is an obvious focus for backpackers, notable for its old buildings, which include the Taitu Hotel and St George's Cathedral (built in 1896 to commemorate the victory at Adwa), and dotted with cheap hotels, restaurants, pastry shops, all-night bars, good secondhand bookstalls and most other things a traveller would want. Within walking distance of the Piazza, the National Museum at Arat Kilo is a must-see. Of special interest is the replica of Lucy's skull – the 3.5-million-year-old fossil of a female *Australopithecus afarensis* – and a number of large stone statues of seated female figures (thought to have been a fertility symbol of a pre-Judaic religion), a sphynx from Yeha, and a cast of a Gragn stone from Tiya. The nominal entrance fee covers the services of a good guide. Near the museum, the Lion House at Sidist Kilo houses a group of lions with flowing black manes (these recently caused a stir when a South African biologist decided that they must be members of the extinct Cape or Barbary races of lion but, since the flowing black mane is regarded to be an adaptation to cool, open habitats, it strikes me as more likely they are simply members of the race confined to the Ethiopian highlands).

Less central, the Mercato is reputedly the largest market in Africa. Wistfully described elsewhere as boasting 'pungent aromas of incense and spices... [that]... make a stunning impact on the senses', the Mercato struck me more for the pungency of rotting vegetables and human excreta. Whiffy or not, Mercato *is* the real commercial hub of Addis, a vast grid of roads lined with stalls, kiosks and small shops where you can buy just about anything you want, from the latest local cassette to a traditional Ethiopian cross or enough chat to keep you chewing into your infirmity. Be warned, when you explore, that pickpockets and bag-snatchers are rife.

The Intoto Hills around Addis Ababa are said to be where the Axumite royal family took refuge during the reign of Queen Yodit, and medieval links between Intoto and Lalibela are suggested by the presence of two disused rock-hewn churches of the Lalibela style within 10km of the modern city centre. One of these churches, Kidus Raguel, lies very close to the site of Menelik's capital prior to his move into the valley of Addis Ababa, marked by the late 19th-century Intoto Maryam Church and the Menelik Museum. More accessible on foot, the rock-hewn church of Washa Mikael is a three-quarter monolith excavated entirely from below the ground, and a most impressive structure even if its roof has caved in.

Access and getting around

Backpackers who fly to Ethiopia will arrive at Bole Airport, 5km from central Addis Ababa. Taxis to the city centre can be hired at the NTO Kiosk in the airport building. Fares are fixed at US$3–6 depending on where exactly you're heading. There are also minibuses which run between the airport and city centre at a minimal cost – no significant risk of theft is attached, bearing in mind that you're unlikely to be at your most alert after a long flight. All internal flights leave from Bole Airport.

The two main bus stations in Addis are the Autobus Terra near the Mercato (Market) and the smaller terminal near the railway station on Ras Makonen Road. Buses to Nazret and Debre Zeyit leave from Ras Makonen Road; all other buses leave from the main Autobus Terra.

Addis Ababa is served by a cheap and efficient bus and minibus network, which starts up at around 05.30 and peters out at around 20.30. Buses are crowded and attract pickpockets, but minibuses are comfortable and safe. The main minibus stop in the Piazza area is opposite De Gaulle Square, while important stops in the city centre are on Churchill Avenue opposite the post office and Ras Makonen Road opposite the Stadium. Other stops likely to be used by travellers are at Arat Kilo near the National Museum, opposite the Autobus Terra (intercity bus station) near the Mercato, and in the airport car park. Minibuses connect all of these stops, and you'll rarely wait more than a few minutes for a ride.

To get to the rock-hewn church of Washa Mikael, catch a minibus from Arat Kilo to Yeka Park. A side road to the left immediately east of the park leads uphill to Kidus Mikael Church, from where it's about 5km to Washa Mikael by road or half that distance using a short cut through the eucalyptus forest. There are plenty of kids around who'll want to guide you, and several recent reports of unguided travellers being robbed along the way make a guide more-or-less mandatory. Agree on a fee in advance. Entrance to the church costs US$5.

To get to Intoto Maryam, catch a bus from Arat Kilo past Sidist Kilo to the foot slopes of the Intoto Hills, then follow the main road uphill on foot for about 3km. Kidus Raguel lies about 2km past Intoto Maryam.

Crime

Watch out for pickpockets, especially around the ETC office, the Ghion, Ras, Harambee and Ethiopia Hotels and the Mercato. Be alert to the twin-pronged attack where one person bumps into you or grabs your legs or otherwise distracts you, while a second fishes in your pocket – the cigarette and newspaper vendors around Churchill Avenue sometimes play the distracting role. Con artists hang out around the ETC office, on Churchill Avenue and in front of the Ghion Hotel. A request for money will be the outcome of any conversation that begins with somebody asking how you like Ethiopia or whether you remember them, or who claims to be the waiter or gardener at your hotel, or who wants to take you to an event that is only happening that day. If a friendly student asks you to join him for a drink, expect to be presented with a bill of US$50 or thereabouts.

Where to stay

Abyssinia Hotel Off Bole Rd behind Addis Ababa Museum. A good bet if you want to be near the city centre rather than the Piazza. Clean rooms **B**/**C** using communal hot showers.

Baro Hotel Muniyem St, Piazza. Opposite Wutma, and worth trying if that's full, though it's not as good value. Rooms 8–13 are the best. Safe luggage storage. Good place to make phone calls and send emails (non-residents welcome). Room **C**/**E** s/c with hot water.

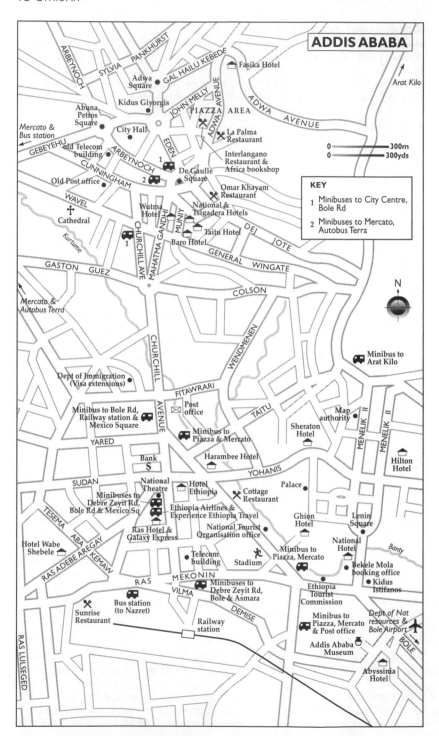

ADDIS ABABA

Arat Kilo

Fasika Hotel

Adwa Square

Kidus Giyorgis

PIAZZA AREA

Mercato & Bus station

Abuna Petros Square

City Hall

old Telecom building

Old Post office

De Gaulle Square

La Palma Restaurant

Interlangano Restaurant & Africa bookshop

Omar Khayam Restaurant

Cathedral

Wutma Hotel

National & Tsigadera Hotels

Taitu Hotel

Baro Hotel

0 ———— 300m
0 ———— 300yds

KEY

1 Minibuses to City Centre, Bole Rd

2 Minibuses to Mercato, Autobus Terra

Mercato & Autobus Terra

GASTON GUEZ

GENERAL WINGATE

COLSON

N

WENDMENEN

Minibus to Arat Kilo

Dept of Immigration (Visa extensions)

FITAWRARI

Post office

Map authority

Minibus to Bole Rd, Railway station & Mexico Square

Minibus to Piazza & Mercato

Sheraton Hotel

Hilton Hotel

YARED

Bank $

Harambee Hotel

YOHANIS

SUDAN

National Theatre

Hotel Ethiopia

Cottage Restaurant

Palace

Minibuses to Debre Zeyit Rd, Bole Rd & Mexico Sq

Ethiopia Airlines & Experience Ethiopia Travel

Ghion Hotel

Lenin Square

Ras Hotel & Galaxy Express

National Tourist Organisation office

National Hotel

Hotel Wabe Shebele

Telecom building

Stadium

Minibus to Piazza, Mercato

Bekele Mola booking office

Kidus Istifanos

RAS

MEKONIN

VILMA

Minibuses to Debre Zeyit Rd, Bole & Asmara

Ethiopia Tourist Commission

Sunrise Restaurant

Bus station (to Nazret)

DEMISE

Minibus to Piazza, Mercato & Post office

Dept of Nat resources & Bole Airport

Railway station

Addis Ababa Museum

Abyssinia Hotel

Banty

BOLE

Hawi Hotel Debre Zeyit Rd. Very clean, good value mid-range place. Rooms **E** s/c dbl with hot water.
Jerusalem Hotel Recommended mid-price hotel on Patriot's Street. Good snacks and pastries. **F** dbl.
National and **Tsigadera Hotels** 50m from the Taitu Hotel. The least brothel-like of a dozen cheap places that line the road between De Gaulle Square and the Taitu Hotel. Rooms in **A** to **B** range. The National has hot communal showers which non-residents can use for a fee.
Tensae Birhan Clean, quiet lodge on an alley behind the British Council (turn off Adwa Avenue at the Jolly Shop). **B** dbl.
Wutma Hotel Muniyem St, Piazza. Very popular and highly recommended. Safe luggage storage. Spotless rooms **C** s/c dbl (hot water). Good restaurant.

Where to eat
Piazza area
La Palma Restaurant Burgers, steak, roast chicken US$2.50.
Berhan Restaurant Mahatma Gandhi Rd. Italian dishes US$2.
Pizzeria Mahatma Gandhi Rd. Best pizzas in town US$2.
Omar Khayam Restaurant Excellent Ethiopian and Arabian dishes US$1–2.
Soul Kid Patisserie Perhaps the best of several good pastry shops on the Piazza, and strategically placed opposite British Council reading room.

City centre and Bole Road
Wabe Shebele Hotel Good buffet and Ethiopian dancing Thursday and Saturday. US$4.
Karamara Restaurant Bole Rd. Ethiopian cuisine in a traditional atmosphere. Meals cost US$2-3, or just have a draught beer and enjoy the live traditional music.
Sunrise Restaurant Tigrean-run place in large old house. Ethiopian dishes, steaks, chicken, pasta accompanied by a plate of salad, chips, rice and vegetables US$2–3.
Blen House of Sweets Churchill Av. Cakes, mini-pizzas, milkshakes, ice-cream cones.
Post Rendezvous Next to post office – read your mail over a creamy cake or spicy burger.
Connecticut Pastry Espris fruit juice to kill for. Good fruit salad, cakes and coffee.
Saay Pastry Bole Rd. Excellent cakes, cappuccino, ice-cream and other odds and ends.

Practical listings
Airlines Ethiopian Airlines branches are on Churchill Av near the Ras Hotel, on the Piazza near De Gaulle Square, in the Hilton Hotel and in the UN Building. Tel: 61 6161 or 61 6666. Also Air France (51 9044); Alitalia (51 4400); Kenya Airways (51 3018); Lufthansa (51 5666) and Saudi Airways (51 7746).

Books and newspapers Secondhand novels can be bought or exchanged cheaply at several bookstalls in the Piazza area. For non-fiction titles try the bookshop under the German Cultural Institute between Arat Kilo and the National Museum. The British Council on Adwa Road has recent copies of English newspapers.

Embassies Austria (71 2144); Belgium (61 1813); Canada (71 3022); Djibouti (61 3006); Egypt (55 3077); Eritrea (51 2940); France (55 0066); Germany (55 0433); Holland (71 1100); Ireland (61 3361); Israel (61 0999); Italy (55 1565); Kenya (61 0033); Sweden (51 6699); Switzerland (71 0577); UK (61 2354); USA (55 1002).

Maps The 1:2,000,000 map of Ethiopia produced by the Ethiopian Tourist Commission (ETC) is available from the curio kiosks in several of the government hotels in Addis. The Ethiopian Mapping Authority (EMA) opposite the Hilton Hotel is open during normal shopping hours on weekdays. It stocks good 1:50,000 maps covering most of the southern, central and western highlands, as well as 1:250,000 maps covering the whole country. These maps can be bought for US$1, but only with a letter of authority from the ETC.

National parks National parks and other reserves fall under the control of the Department of Natural Resources, which has a smart new office on Bole Road. Pamphlets are available for several of the national parks. Tel: 51 5970.

Post office On Churchill Av. Collecting poste restante is straightforward. No proof of identity is required, nor is there a charge.

Tourist information office Ethiopia Tourist Commission headquarters is on Abiot Square.

Visa extensions Department of Immigration, Churchill Av. Extensions are generally given a month at a time, and they can be processed on the day of application provided that you specify this and apply in the morning. A passport-sized photograph is required (there's a photo kiosk outside) and a fee of approximately US$20 must be paid in local currency.

Northern Ethiopia
ADDIS ABABA TO BAHIR DAR

A large and attractive town situated on the southern shore of Lake Tana, **Bahir Dar** is the established first port of call for those who fly around the historical circuit. It is notable for an outstanding market, and a moist tropical character typified by palm-lined avenues and pretty lake-side vistas. Bahir Dar lies a mere 2km from the source of the Blue Nile, the river that linked Ancient Ethiopia to the Mediterranean civilisations, and visitors will almost certainly see the papyrus *tankwa* boats that bear such a striking resemblance to those used in Ancient Egypt.

The most popular tourist attraction in the region is the **Blue Nile Falls** or **Tis Isat** – *The Smoke of the Nile* – which lies next to the village of Tis Abay 30km from Lake Tana and Bahir Dar. Although not particularly high at 45m, Tis Isat is regarded to be the second most spectacular waterfall in Africa after the incomparable Victoria Falls, and it is certainly the only comparably sized African waterfall which you can take a shower in – provided that your guide shows you the right spot and the water is reasonably low. Another very popular excursion from Bahir Dar is to one of the **island monasteries** on Lake Tana; see box *Zege and beyond* on page 97.

Bahir Dar lies only an hour from Addis by air, but it's two days away by bus, passing through some thrilling scenery which backpackers might want to break their trip to explore. The first good opportunity to do this is the **Muga River Gorge**, a spectacular and accessible 100m-deep canyon notable for the waterfall that plunges over its edge at the leafy village of **Durba**, which is also a good place to see the endemic gelada baboon and a variety of raptors, including the lammergeyer. Next up, near the town of Fiche, the 13th-century monastery of **Debre Libanos**, tucked away in a small wooded gorge above a much larger canyon, has a peaceful and devout atmosphere, and the surrounding countryside is quite stunning. Further north, the kilometre-deep **Blue Nile Gorge** has been compared in scale to America's Grand Canyon. The 30km-long Italian road through the gorge is an awesome feat of engineering, and one you'll have plenty of time to appreciate since the gradient forces buses to slow to around 10kph. If you want to explore a bit on foot, or you've had enough of sealed windows at low altitude and lower speed, then you could hop off at **Dejen** near the northern lip of the gorge. Past Dejen, the road splits, with one fork going directly to Bahir Dar and the other using a longer route via **Debre Markos**, the unremarkable capital of Gojam province.

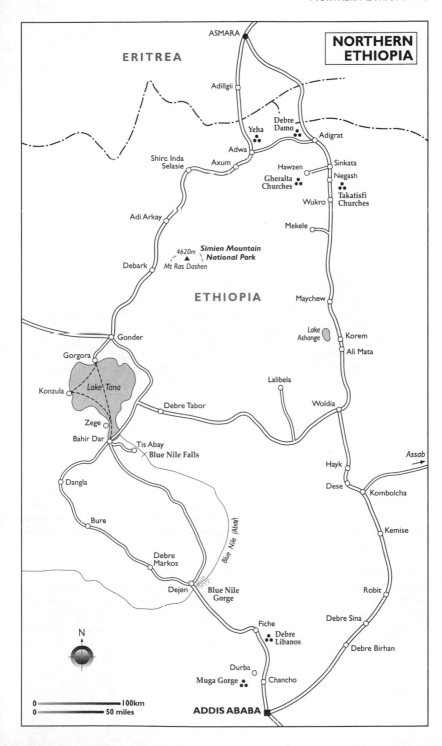

NORTHERN
ETHIOPIA

ERITREA

ASMARA

Adillgii

ETHIOPIA

Yeha
Debre
Damo
Adigrat

Adwa
Axum
Shirc Inda
Selasie

Sinkata
Hawzen
Negash
Gheralta
Churches
Takatisfi
Churches
Wukro

Adi Arkay

Mekele

4620m
Mt Ras Dashen
Simien Mountain
National Park

Debark

Maychew

Gonder

Lake
Ashange
Korem
Ali Mata

Gorgora

Lake Tana

Lalibela

Woldia

Konzula

Zege

Debre Tabor

Bahir Dar

Tis Abay
Blue Nile Falls

Hayk
Assab

Dangla

Dese
Kombolcha

Bure

Kemise

Blue Nile (Abay)

Debre
Markos

Dejen
Blue Nile
Gorge

Robit

Fiche
Debre Sina

Debre
Libanos

Debre Birhan

N

Durba
Muga Gorge
Chancho

0   100km
0   50 miles

ADDIS ABABA

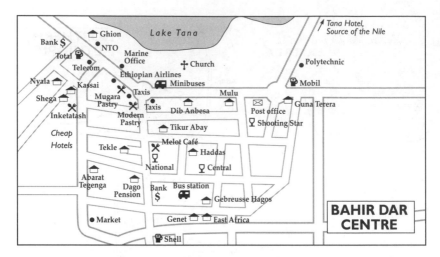

Bank $ · Ghion · NTO · Lake Tana · Tana Hotel, Source of the Nile · Total · Telecom · Marine Office · Ethiopian Airlines · † Church · Polytechnic · Nyala · Kassai · Taxis · Minibuses · Mobil · Shega · Mugara Pastry · Taxis · Dib Anbesa · Mulu · Post office · Guna Terera · Inketatash · Modern Pastry · Tikur Abay · Shooting Star · Cheap Hotels · Tekle · Melot Café · Haddas · Abarat Tegenga · National · Central · Dago Pension · Bank $ · Bus station · Gebreusse Hagos · Market · Genet · East Africa · Shell

BAHIR DAR CENTRE

Access and getting around

Direct buses between Addis Ababa and Bahir Dar take two days and leave at 06.00 daily in either direction. The journey involves an overnight stop at one of the villages on the way, and different drivers appear to favour different villages. It's possible to take control of matters and do the trip in two stages, by catching a bus from Addis to Debre Markos and then another the next morning to Bahir Dar.

The Muga River Gorge lies 20km west of the main Bahir Dar road, and the turn-off at Chancho is roughly 40km north of Addis. Regular local transport runs from the Autobus Terra in Addis Ababa to Chancho itself and, while there is no formal public transport on to Durba, you should be able to find a lift of some sort.

At least one bus daily connects Addis Ababa to Debre Libanos, leaving Addis between 05.00 and 06.00 and reaching Debre Libanos by around 10.00. Alternatively, you could visit Debre Libanos from Fiche, which lies 15km further north and has a better range of accommodation. Local buses connecting Addis Ababa and Fiche run throughout the morning and take four hours. From Fiche, at least one pick-up truck goes to Debre Libanos every morning. However you get to Debre Libanos, when you're ready to leave you should expect to walk the 4km from the monastery to the junction with the main road (allow a couple of hours because it's very steep). From the junction, you should have little difficulty finding a ride back to Fiche or Addis Ababa.

Four buses daily run between Bahir Dar and Tis Abay village. These leave Bahir Dar bus station at roughly 06.00, 09.00, 12.00 and 13.00. At Tis Abay, you must pay an entrance fee of US$2.50 to visit the waterfall. You should be supplied with a useful leaflet and map showing the 30-minute walking trail to the viewpoint, which crosses a 17th-century Portuguese bridge. A guide is optional but worthwhile if you want to continue to the swimming point below the falls and return by a different route that involves crossing the Nile by *tankwa* boat. The last bus out of Tis Abay leaves at 14.00.

Where to stay and eat
Bahir Dar

Betel and Haddas Hotels Multi-storey hotels next door to each other. Among the better of several clean places with rooms in the **B**–**C** range.

ZEGE AND BEYOND

Lake Tana is dotted with islands, many of which support monasteries, most notably perhaps the highly inaccessible Tana Kirkos, which some claim housed the Ark of the Covenant for 800 years. The most accessible and regularly visited 'island monastery', the 14th-century Kidane Mihiret, doesn't actually lie on an island but on a lovely forested peninsula near the village of Zege. A cheap ferry service connects Bahir Dar to Zege, leaving Bahir Dar from the Marine Authority compound at 07.30 daily and taking one hour, but at present tourists are forbidden to use this, largely so that the Marine Authority can charge enormous sums for foreigners to travel in their special tourist boat. Should this change, however, Zege is a pleasant place to while away a few days – the surrounding forest supports plenty of monkeys, birds and butterflies, Kidane Mihiret is covered in colourful 16th-century murals and line drawings, and the little-visited and disused churches of Mehal Giorgis and Bete Maryam on the same peninsula are also worth a look.

Zege is connected to Bahir Dar by a reasonably flat 20km road, impassable even in a 4x4, but manageable by bicycle. It's a fairly tough two-to three-hour trip, due to the rocks and sand (you'll probably have to carry your bike over one set of rocks), but an affordable option since bicycles can be hired in Bahir Dar for around US$1 per day. The road to Zege forks from the tar road between the town and the airport, more-or-less as the air traffic control tower comes into sight.

Many travellers get around the Marine Authority's restrictions and heavy prices by arranging a private trip to the monasteries. Companies that provide this service include Oasis Tours and Nile Tours (based in the Ghion Hotel), which should work out at around US$80 for a group of up to ten people and take in three monasteries (though I have a very recent report of a traveller arranging a similar trip out of the Ghion hotel for US$5 per head). It might also be worth asking around at the upmarket Tana Hotel on the outskirts of town; a lot of truck companies camp here and you might be able to join them on a boat trip which cuts the individual cost.

Two words of caution about private trips. The first is that concerns have been expressed about the safety of the boats, though it's difficult to judge how valid these are. The second is that a great many monasteries won't allow women to set foot on the island, and the guys who sell these tours tend not to divulge whether this is the case unless you specifically ask (Kidane Mihiret, incidentally, does allow women in).

I've recently heard of the Ghion Hotel arranging trips to the monasteries for as little as US$5 per person.

Blue Nile Springs Hotel Pleasant mid-range place 2km out of town. Rooms **D**/**E** s/c with hot water. Camping **B** pp.

Central Pastry Cakes, biscuits, fruit juice and coffee near the bus station.

Enkutatash Hotel New place five minutes' walk from the Ghion Hotel along the airport road. Clean s/c dbl room with running cold water **B**.

Genet Pension Popular **A**–**B** hotel in the road behind the bus station. The similarly-priced Axum and East Africa hotels next door are also reliable; the former has some s/c rooms, the latter serves good food.

Ghion Hotel Centrally-located former government hotel, where you can negotiate rooms to as low as **C** pp out of season. Camping **B** pp. OK food, great grounds, good place to arrange cheap boat trips to the monasteries.
Inketatash Restaurant Behind Telecommunications. Excellent local dishes. US$1.50.
Mango Bar Pleasant lakefront garden bar close to the Marine Office (next to signposted Mexico Hotel).
Zinc Pub good drinking hole with excellent traditional music.

Debre Libanos
A very basic lodging on the road uphill from the church has waterless **A** rooms, look out for the 'Pepsi/Miranda/Seven-up' signs. There are a few more commodious hotels in Fiche.

Debre Markos
Yenegatt Kobeb Hotel Well-run **A** hotel with hot showers next to the bus station.
Shebel Hotel New hotel to the left as you enter town coming from Addis. Clean, comfortable s/c rooms in **B** range.

GONDER AND THE SIMIEN MOUNTAINS
The former capital city of **Gonder** was founded in 1635 by Emperor Fasilidas after a tumultuous century during which the Christian Empire virtually collapsed under the onslaught of the Muslim leader Ahmed Gragn and then suffered great upheavals due to the influence of the Catholic Portuguese. Gonder is famous for its walled Royal Enclosure, which contains several 17th-century buildings, most impressively the three-storey and 32m-high castle constructed by Fasilidas. On the Bahir Dar road, 2km from the town centre, is the large sunken bathing pool built by Fasilidas, now used to host the Timkat Festival every January. A similar distance out of town in the direction of Debark, the church of Debre Birhan Selassie is famed for its roof mural of 80 cherubic faces, and for walls depicting dozens of separate scenes, the work of the 17th-century artist Haile Meskel. Entrance to the Royal Enclosure costs US$5 per day (English-speaking guide provided) and the ticket is good for Fasilidas' pool. An entrance fee of US$2 is charged to visit the church.

To the north of Gonder, **Simien Mountain National Park** is one of East Africa's most exciting and affordable hiking and mule-trekking destinations. The

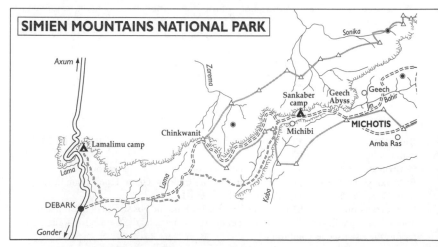

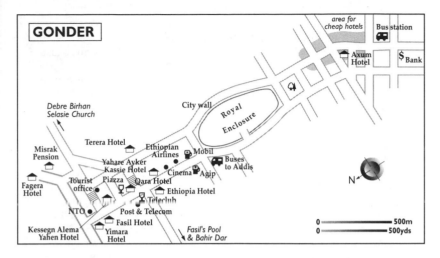

extensive Simien Range is topped by Mount Ras Dashen, which at 4,620m is the highest point in Ethiopia and the fourth highest in Africa. Few who travel along the main road between Gonder and Axum would disagree with the Edwardian traveller Rosita Forbes, who described the Simiens as 'the most marvellous of all Abyssinian landscapes'. In addition to the scenery, the park supports the world's only population of the walia ibex, as well as two other Ethiopian endemics, the gelada baboon and Simien fox, and more widespread species such as klipspringer, bushbuck, spotted hyena and golden jackal. (See box *Hiking in the Simien Mountains* overleaf).

Access and getting around

Buses between Bahir Dar and Gonder leave in either direction at around 06.00 and take half a day. An attractive alternative is the MV *Tananich*, which sails once a week in either direction between Bahir Dar and Gorgora, leaving Bahir Dar on Sunday morning and Gorgora on Thursday morning. The boat stops at Zege and overnights at Konzula, where you should disembark promptly to find a room in a

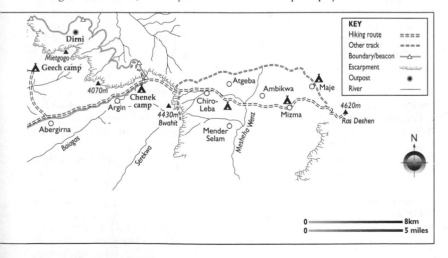

HIKING IN THE SIMIEN MOUNTAINS

The base for hikes is Debark, 90km north of Gonder on the Axum road, a three-hour trip covered by two buses daily leaving Gonder at roughly 06.00 and 10.00. The established place to stay in Debark is the Simien Hotel, which has **B** rooms and a restaurant serving good local food, though the more expensive Simien Park Hotel probably represents better value for money at **B/C**.

The national park office in Debark is the place to pay your entrance fees, to arrange for the mandatory armed ranger, and to make contact with one of the registered guides (who are excellent and work on a fixed rates and a rota system). Costs compare favourably to East Africa's other montane national parks – you're looking at around US$20–25 per person per day inclusive of entrance and overnight fees, a guide and an armed ranger, and a mule and driver. There is no formal accommodation on the trails, but if you are not equipped for camping, your guide can arrange rooms in local villages, or you can hire a tent and sleeping bag in Debark. Hikers must supply their own food, but a good stove can be hired inexpensively in Debark.

Some people visit the park for just two days, doing a short walk and staying one night at Sankaber Campsite. Other people spend ten days or more in the mountains, trekking to the top of Ras Dashen and diverting to several smaller peaks. In between these extremes lie several options, such as a four-day hike sleeping at Sankaber, Geech, then Sankaber again; a five-day hike sleeping at Sankaber, Chenek for two nights (with a day hike to the summit of Bwahit or the viewpoint on the way to Ras Dashen), then Sankaber again; or a seven day hike sleeping at Sankaber, Chenek, Ambikwa for two nights (with a day hike to the summit of Ras Dashen, then back to Chenek and Sankaber. The hikes mostly follow local trails, so conditions underfoot are reasonably good. Hikers should, however, be reasonably fit – the campsites are separated by four to eight hours' walking, and the high altitude can be tiring.

An increasingly popular way of setting up a Simien hike is with one of the 'fixers' in Gonder who will phone your exact requirements through to Debark and have your bus met. This is no more expensive than setting up the hike yourself from scratch, more efficient, and from all accounts thoroughly reliable. Since you don't pay for anything until you get to Debark, there's also no risk attached. A five-day hike set up like this will cost around US$100 per person inclusive of equipment.

lodge. A first-class ticket costs US$20. Bring food and drinking water, even though the ferry does stop for an hour or so at several ports selling wat, sodas and tea. Once at Gorgora, the medieval church is worth a look; there's a **D/E** hotel in the Marine Authority compound and a **B** dump right outside the compound gate. Buses from Gorgora to Gonder take about two hours.

Heading north from Gonder, there are a couple of buses every morning to Debark, the base for hikes into the Simiens.

Where to stay and eat
Gonder
Blue Nile Hotel Several recent recommendations for this newish hotel behind the Ethiopia Hotel. Rooms in **C–D** range. Good restaurant and terrace bar. Constant hot water.

Ethiopia and **Yahare Ayker Kassie Hotel** The best of a dismal selection of **A** lodges. The bar below the Ethiopia is a good place for a beer.

Fasil and **Yimara Hotels** Near NTO Office. Pick of a cluster of overpriced but basically decent places near the NTO office. **B**–**C**.

Fresh Pastry Excellent juice and pastry between the Piassa and Fagera Hotel.

Piazza Pastry Cakes, biscuits, coffee and fruit juice.

Misrak Pension Popular with travellers. S/c rooms with hot water **C**–**D**.

Qara and **Terera Hotels** Centrally located former government hotels where you can normally negotiate a room down to the **C**–**D** range.

Tana Snacks Popular place to eat on the main road next to the cinema.

Teleclub Good breakfast place below Telecommunications centre.

AXUM AND SURROUNDS

The oldest town in Ethiopia, most holy city of the Ethiopian Orthodox Church and former capital of one of the world's greatest empires, **Axum** is smaller than you might expect and rather inauspicious on first impression. On closer inspection, however, it is a treasure trove of compelling antiquities, well worth devoting at least two days to (see box *Exploring Axum*, pages 102–3). A mere 25km east of Axum, the relatively modern town of **Adwa** is of limited interest to tourists but of tremendous significance to Ethiopians, since it was on the granite hills surrounding the town that Emperor Menelik II defeated the Italian army in March 1896, crushing Italy's attempt to colonise Ethiopia.

Lying off the 100km road that connects Adwa to Adigrat are several fascinating historical sites and religious retreats. Foremost amongst these are the ruins of **Yeha**, a city which is thought to have rivalled Axum in importance between 2,700 and 2,200 years ago. Yeha's most remarkable antiquity is a well-preserved stone temple, dating to 500BC and apparently linked to the pagan faith of the Sabaen civilisation of South Arabia. Further east, the monastery at **Debre Damo** is notable for the 6th-century stone Church of Abuna Aregawi, presumed to be the oldest in Ethiopia, and for its impregnable position on a 3,000m-high table surrounded by sheer cliffs which can only be ascended by rope.

Access and getting around

Travellers heading to Axum from Gonder or Debark will have to take a bus as far as Shire-Inda Selasie, from where regular buses to Axum take at most three hours.

Transport along the main roads through Tigre is straightforward enough: a daily bus leaves in either direction between Axum and Mekele at 06.00, stopping at Adigrat and Wukro on route, and there are a few local buses daily between the larger towns on this route. On the road between Axum and Adigrat, light vehicles run throughout the day between Axum and Adwa, Adwa and Enticcio, Enticcio and Biset, and Biset and Adigrat.

The Yeha Ruins are about an hour's walk from a signposted turn-off which lies about 25km past Adwa on the Adigrat road. Light vehicles travelling between Adwa and Enticcio will be able to drop you at the turn-off and to pick you up later in the day, but an early start is recommended to ensure you don't get stuck on the roadside.

Debre Damo lies 11km north of the Adigrat road. The turn-off is 6km west of the village of Biset. No public transport goes to the monastery, but the occasional 4x4 heads out there during the dry months. You could visit on foot but, bearing in mind that it's a 22km round trip from the main road with a challenging rope-climb in the middle, you would need to catch the first bus from Adigrat towards Enticcio in the morning and pick up the last one back at about 15.00. Women are absolutely forbidden to visit the monastery.

EXPLORING AXUM

The best place to start a tour of Axum is the site museum next to the main stelae field, where you can see several multilingual stone tablets; an array of Axumite household artefacts including a set of Egyptian drinking glasses; a large collection of Axumite crosses and coins; and a 700-year-old Ge'ez Bible. The main stelae field is dominated by a 23m-high granite stele accredited to King Ezana, the third-highest stele to have been erected in Axum. Another 33m-high stele, the largest monolith erected in the ancient world, lies shattered on the ground next to it, while a 26m-high stele was looted by Italy and now stands on the Piazza in Rome. Also near the museum, the St Mary of Zion Church was founded by King Ezana in the 4th century. The original 12 temples were destroyed, probably by Ahmed Gragn, but the foundations of one temple have been left undisturbed. The most interesting of the standing churches is a stone building similar in age and appearance to the castles of Gonder. Axum's most famous religious artefact, the supposed Ark of the Covenant, is kept in a sanctified outbuilding near this church, but there's zero chance of being allowed to see it!

There are two major historical sites within the modern town, both of which cost nothing to visit. King Ezana's Park houses a 4th-century tablet inscribed in Sabaean, Ge'ez and Greek, as well as the pillars of a ruined palace, a large stele, a tomb, and an innocuous-looking slab of stone formerly used for cleaning corpses. This site, like several others which have been fenced off around the

Where to stay and eat
Between Gonder and Shire Inda-Selassie
Debark and Adi Arkay both have a few **A** hotels.

Shire-Inda Selassie
Africa Hotel Large clean s/c rooms **C** dbl.
Atse Kaleb Guesthouse Basic but acceptable **A** rooms.
National Hotel Clean s/c rooms with hot shower **C** dbl. Behind bus station.

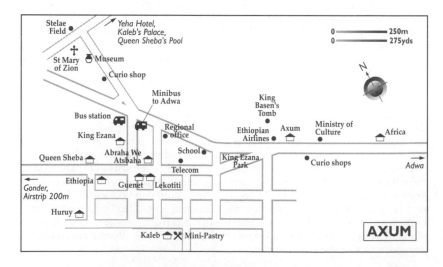

town, has never been excavated. Not far from the park, marked by the customary stele, King Basen's Tomb consists of a large rock-hewn tunnel and chamber dating to around the time of Christ.

On a hill about 2km out of town, little remains of the 6th-century palace of King Kaleb, though the burial vaults are in excellent condition and notable for their precise masonry. On the way to Kaleb's Palace, you pass a dam known locally as Queen Sheba's Pool and a trilingual tablet inscribed at the time of King Ezana. Another important site that lies outside the modern town is a ruined palace associated by locals with the Queen of Sheba, though in fact only about 1,500 years old. Nearby, a field of small, plain stelae is traditionally considered to mark the Queen of Sheba's grave.

The Pentaleon Monastery has one of the oldest churches in the country, and it is said to have been founded by King Ezana. Pentaleon lies on an isolated hill about 3km out of town – walk along the Adwa road for about five minutes, then take one of the footpaths to your left and you can't really miss it. There's also a short cut there from Kaleb's Palace, but you need a guide to find it.

A ticket covering all the secular sites in and around Axum costs US$8.50 and can be bought at the site museum. Official English-speaking guides can be organised at the museum, and they should be tipped. A separate fee of US$8.50 is charged to enter the Church of St Mary Zion – women can enter the grounds but not the old church.

Tewelde Hotel On the Gonder side of town. Clean s/c rooms in the **B–C** range, parking space, friendly staff.

Axum
Africa Hotel Perennially popular hotel with ordinary rooms **B**/**C** and s/c rooms **C**/**D**. Good food.
Axum Hotel Centrally situated government hotel serving Western meals.
Ghenet Hotel Reliable cheapie for several years. Rooms in **B–C** range.
Kaleb Hotel Popular mid-range hotel with attractive grounds **D**.
Mini-Pastry Next to Kaleb Hotel. Great pastries and breakfasts.

Between Axum and Adigrat
Adwa, Enticcio and Biset all have **A** hotels, the best selection being in Adwa.

EASTERN TIGRE
Adigrat, the second largest town in Tigre, lies on the junction of the main roads east to Axum, south to Mekele and north to Eritrea. Bustling and friendly, Adigrat has a distinctively Tigrean character and a wonderful mountain setting that make it an easy place to settle into for a few days. The market is a good place to buy Tigrean coffee pots and cloth. Nearby, Adigrat Chirkos is covered in fine 19th-century paintings and offers a great view over the town. The Catholic Church bears a strong resemblance to a church in Florence.

The part of Tigre immediately south of Adigrat boasts Ethiopia's densest concentration of **rock-hewn churches**, fewer than ten of which were known outside their immediate parishes until 1966, when Dr Tewelde Medhin read a paper at the Conference of Ethiopian Studies listing 123 churches carved into the sandstone cliffs and outcrops of the region. Two of these churches lie very

THE CHURCHES AT TAKATISFI

Three very different rock-hewn churches can be visited over the course of a few hours at Takatisfi. The first church, and the only one not in use, is Petros and Paulos Melehayzenghi, a large cavern extending out to a ledge with some fascinating line paintings of angels and saints. Below the ledge, a new church, also called Petros and Paulos, is fifteen years into the process of being carved by a recipient of a Godly vision. The second church, Mikael Melehayzenghi, is said to date to the 8th century; it has been hollowed from a large granite dome, and the tiny entrance opens into a finely-carved domed interior almost 3m in height. The third church is Medhane Alem Adi Kasho, dated by local tradition to the 4th century and described as 'one of the truly great churches of the Tigre'. It has an imposing exterior, cut free from the rock behind, and with four columns and two large doors, while the cathedral-like interior boasts a magnificent roof dense with patterned etchings.

To visit Takatisfi, ask a vehicle heading between Sinkata and Wukro to drop you at Shwadini School. It's cheap to arrange a guide at the school, and will save the inevitable mucking around associated with locating the priests who keep the keys. That said, if you want to head out independently, anybody can point you in the right direction and you'll soon enough see Petros and Paulos on the cliff to the east of the main road. Reaching this church involves a vertiginous scramble up ancient footholds, one which will test anybody who doesn't have a head for heights. From the base of the cliff below Petros and Paulos, it's a 20-minute walk south across relatively flat fields to the prominent euphorbia-studded rock outcrop that houses the church of Mikael Melehayzenghi.

To reach Medhane Alem from Mikael, continue south towards a low rocky hill until you come to a rough semi-motorable track. Follow the track to your left over the low hill to the base of a larger hill covered in olive and juniper trees. From here, it's a steepish hike along a clear footpath to the top of the hill and the church. From Medhane Alem, you can use a short cut back to the main road, following the motorable track back over the low hill, then taking the left fork and continuing along it for about ten minutes until you come to a marshy stream. Follow the footpath that runs roughly parallel to the stream until, after about ten minutes, you cross a rocky ridge. The main road is clearly visible from here, as is the dam on the opposite side of it. You shouldn't have a problem picking up a lift from here to Wukro or Sinkata.

close to Adigrat. **Mikael Kirsaba** is a stone church built over an older rock-hewn church in the village of Kirsaba about 5km from Adigrat on the Asmara road. To the south of Adigrat, 1.5km east of the Mekele road between Idaga Hamus and May Megelta, **Gebriel Tsilalmao** is a larger church with cruciform columns, neatly cut arches, Axumite windows, and two hermit's caves in its wall.

Sinkata is a quiet stone village on the Mekele road 60km south of Adigrat. Less than 30 minutes' walk to its east, following a path through the fields that starts at the Ghenet Hotel, Adi Chewa has the largest domed ceiling of any rock-hewn church in Tigre, as well as a whitewashed entrance and several strange red and yellow stencil-like figures painted on the interior columns. Sinkata also marks the

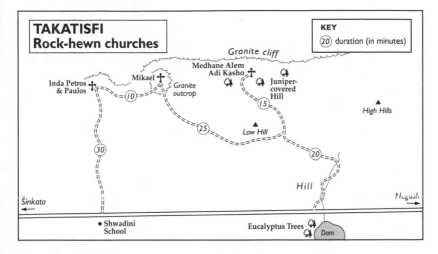

turn-off to **Hawzen**, a small town lying 22km west of the main road, where the tiny and very ancient rock-hewn church of Tekla Haymanot is enclosed within a more modern building. The group of four ancient stelae that formerly stood in Hawzen were destroyed in 1988, when Mengistu's air force bombed the market, killing an estimated 2,500 people. Hawzen is also the starting point for trips into the more remote cluster of 30-odd churches in the **Gheralta** region. The Gheralta churches are only accessible in a private vehicle or on foot – experienced hikers who are interested in exploring them should speak to Experience Ethiopia Travel in Addis Ababa or the Tigre Tourist Board office in Mekele, both of which are knowledgeable, enthusiastic and helpful.

The most accessible cluster of rock-hewn churches in Tigre is the **Takatisfi Cluster**, 2km east of the main road between Sinkata and Wukro (see box *The Churches at Takatisfi* opposite). About 5km south of Takatisfi, the small hilltop village of **Negash** is said locally to have been founded by Islamic refugees during Mohammed's lifetime with the permission of the King of Axum. The mosque, reputedly built on the site of the 7th-century original, hosts an important annual pilgrimage and festival. A further 15km south, **Wukro** is the most substantial town between Adigrat and Mekele. Only 500m out of town, the rock-hewn church of Wukro Chirkos is a three-quarter monolith, thought to date from the 8th century. The lovely line drawings on the ceiling must date to the 15th century as they were partially destroyed when the church was burnt by Ahmed Gragn. The external roof and raised porch were added in 1958 due to seepage.

To the east of Wukro, the church of Abraha-Atsbeha is widely regarded to be the finest of all the rock-hewn churches in the Tigre. Legend has is that the church dates to the 4th century AD and holds the bodies of Axum's first Christian kings, while archaeologists believe it was probably excavated in its present form in the 10th century AD. Until recently very difficult to reach, Abreha-Atsbeha is now connected to Wukro by a well-defined dirt road, and is easy enough to visit as a day trip using a hired bicycle.

The capital of Tigre, **Mekele**, is one of Ethiopia's fastest growing towns, with good facilities, lively nightlife, and the welcoming air typical of Tigre. Worth a look is the large market, where you may see camel-borne salt-traders recently arrived from the Danokil Desert. The Yohannis IV Museum, housed in the

ERITREA

Africa's most newly independent nation shares
with the bordering Ethiopian province of Tigre a
common Axumite heritage. The defunct port of
Adulis, some 30km south of modern Massawa,
was the main Red Sea trading centre of the
Axumites for several centuries prior to its abandonment
in about AD700. The modern state of Eritrea dates to
1890, when it became an Italian colony. After World War II,
the UN ignored the popular will of Eritreans by allowing
their country to become an appendage to Ethiopia. The
resulting liberation war endured for three decades, claimed 150,000 lives and
destroyed the country's infrastructure. Eritrea finally became an independent
country in 1993, the result of a referendum in which more than one million
Eritreans voted in favour and fewer than 2,000 against.

For backpackers travelling through Ethiopia an excursion to Eritrea is a
straightforward option, while those coming to East Africa via Sudan must pass
through Eritrea, assuming that border closures don't force them to fly between
Khartoum and Addis Ababa. Visas are required by all, must be bought in
advance, and cost around US$50. There are embassies in Addis Ababa (tel: 51
4302), Khartoum (tel: 73165) and Nairobi (tel: 44 3164) as well as in Yemen,
Djibouti, China, Canada, Australia, Belgium, Italy, Sweden and the UK and USA.
The Ethiopian birr remains the official currency at the time of writing, but this
will almost certainly change. The only dedicated travel guide is Edward Paice's
Guide to Eritrea, the second edition of which was published by Bradt in 1996.

Asmara

Eritrea's safe, attractive and culturally diverse capital lies at the comfortable
altitude of 2,347m, barely half a day's bus ride from Adigrat in northern
Ethiopia. There's not much in the way of historical sightseeing in Asmara – the
modern town dates to the 1880s – but the bustling street cafés and markets
repay relaxed exploration and the National Museum offers an excellent
introduction to Eritrea past and present. The choice of budget hotels is
practically limitless. The Legese Hotel off Liberty Ave (tel: 12 5054 – **C/D**) is
central and popular, as is the similarly priced Diana Hotel (tel: 12 1529) nearby.
In the **B** range, try the Zegereda Hotel (behind the Impero Cinema on Liberty
Ave), Mitzlal Hotel (near Zeray Deres Square behind the post office) and Maeza
Pension (Zeret Deres Square facing the police station).

Massawa

This is the country's main port, situated 115km from Asmara, a scintillating
descent from breezy highland to sweaty coast that takes five hours by bus,

castle that two Frenchmen built for the emperor in 1873, is dominated by some
esoteric displays of royal paraphernalia, but the combination of the rooftop view
and the photographic display of various rock-hewn churches justifies the
nominal entrance fee. Based in Mekele, the Tigre Tourist Bureau (tel: 03
400769) is an excellent source of practical information about visiting historical
sites.

Note that most rock-hewn churches in Tigre charge an entrance fee equivalent
to US$2.50.

offering some wonderful views and passing through the pretty towns of Embatcala, Ghinda and Dongollo along the way. Massawa is spread across the mainland and two small islands, which are linked together by causeways. It is an attractive port with diverse architecture, undergoing rapid restoration despite the extensive damage that occurred during the war. The islands have more character than the mainland. The first island coming from the mainland is Taulad, which has more of an Italian influence, while Port Island is more Islamic in feel and well worth exploring. There are several hotels in the **B** to **C** range on Port Island – try the Savoia, Torino, Ghenet, Massawa or Asmara. Massawa is the best base from which to visit the Dahlek Islands – contact the Ministry of Marine Resources for details of dives and other points of interest.

From the Ethiopian border to Asmara
This is the one route covered by practically every backpacker in Eritrea. The most important towns on this road, at least from a visitor's point of view, are **Sanafe** and **Adi Qayeh**, since both lie close to major Axumite sites. According to legend, the ruined city of Metara is linked by a tunnel to Axum, and it is probably the city referred to by contemporary sources as Kaloe. Metara lies east of the Adigrat road 2km south of Senafe, and it is notable for a 5m-high stele bearing 3rd-century inscriptions as well as numerous ruined compounds. There are two important sites near Adi Qayeh: Taconda is the more accessible on foot, since it lies only 4km out of town, whereas the more impressive relics at the larger site of Qohaito are some 11km from the main road. There is plenty of basic, cheap accommodation in both Senafe and Adi Qayeh.

From the Sudan border to Asmara
The first substantial Eritrean town passed through by travellers coming overland from Sudan will be **Tessenei**, a typical border town with all sorts of shady dealings going on and at least three hotels of which the Gelhafi is the best and the Selam the cheapest. Assuming that the border is open, Tessenei should be connected by bus to Khartoum, the Sudanese capital, though you may have to change vehicles at Kasala. The best route from Tessenei to Asmara is via **Barentu**, **Agordat** and **Keren**. There are buses all along this route and budget hotels in all three towns – the Asmara Hotel in Barentu and Barka Hotel in Agordat are about the best, with rooms in the **B** range. Keren is particularly attractive, ringed by mountains and lying at the heart of a rich agricultural area, and the Turko-Egyptian Tigu Fort and baobab shrine outside town justify an overnight stop. There are a great many cheap hotels in Keren; the pre-World War II Sicilian Hotel is recommended in the **B** range.

Access and getting around
In addition to a daily bus between Axum and Mekele, several buses daily connect Adigrat to Mekele and quite a number of light vehicles connect the various small towns and villages along the road between them. A few light vehicles head out daily from Sinkata to Hawzen.

Note that the 'old bus station' shown on the map of Mekele remained in use in November 1999 and there are no signs that the 'planned bus station' (which I heard about in 1994) will ever materialise.

Where to stay and eat
Adigrat
Ethiopia Hotel Rooms at top of **A** range. Warm shower. Residents' lounge. Restaurant.
Sweetcake Pastry Cakes, bread, juice and coffee.
Yohannis IV Hotel About the best of a dozen or so cheaper places. **A**.

Between Adigrat and Mekele
Sinkata, Hawzen, Negash and Wukro all have a few **A** hotels. The **Fasika Hotel** in Wukro is the obvious standout in the area, and good value at **A** including use of a hot shower.

Mekele
Axumamit Restaurant Good place to eat on circle opposite museum.
Ambassador and **Green Hotels** Recommended. Rooms **C** s/c dbl with cold water.
Anuwa and Sunrise Hotel Basic, clean rooms. **B**.
Lemlem and **Nyala Hotels** Adequate basic lodges. **A**.
National and **Seti Hotels** Excellent rooms **D** s/c dbl with hot water.
Queen Sheba Hotel Opposite bus station. Decent rooms with communal hot showers on cusp of **A–B** ranges.
Rendezvous Restaurant Superb roast lamb.

MEKELE TO ADDIS ABABA VIA LALIBELA
The pivotal town on the road from Mekele to Addis Ababa is **Woldia**, which lies at the junction of the road to Lalibela. The road from Mekele to Woldia passes through stunning scenery and, although it can easily be covered in a day, there are several places where you might choose to spend a night or two – **Maychew** and **Korem** offer good access to Lake Ashenge, while **Ali Mata** has a rather compelling wild west atmosphere, situated on a dusty plain below a quite majestic escarpment. Woldia itself is a moderately sized town set amongst pretty rolling hills – potentially good walking country, but mostly of interest as a springboard.

Perched at an altitude of 2,630m in the wildly scenic mountains of Lasta, **Lalibela** is a strange, somewhat isolated town, immediately set apart from elsewhere in Ethiopia by the two-storey circular stone houses that huddle in an amorphous mass over its steep slopes. Above all, Lalibela is famous for its rock-hewn churches, several of which are in excess of 10m in height and enclosed by wide subterranean trenches and courtyards. Inherently awesome as they are, what really makes Lalibela's churches special is that they remain an active Christian shrine, the spiritual centre of a village's religious life – to wander between the churches in the thin light of morning mass, as white-robed hermits emerge Bible-in-hand from their cells and the chill highland air is warmed by eucharistic drumbeats and gentle swaying chants, is to witness a scene little different from what has been enacted here every morning for eight centuries. See box *The churches of Lalibela* on page 110.

Heading south of Woldia towards Addis Ababa, the towns of **Hayk**, **Dese** and **Kombolcha** are separated by about 50km of wildly scenic road. Hayk is the first of these towns that you'll pass through, and also the smallest and most inherently attractive, since it is situated only 2km from the mountain-ringed and papyrus-fringed Lake Hayk where there is good birdwatching, as well as Hayk Istifanos, a very old male-only monastery that lies on a thickly wooded peninsula about an hour's walk from town. Dese is the capital of Wolo, notable for its rather decrepit town centre, an attractive montane setting, and little else. Kombolcha is similar in size to Dese, and arguably more attractive, but it too suffers from a distinct lack of character. To the east of Dese, keen hikers might think about

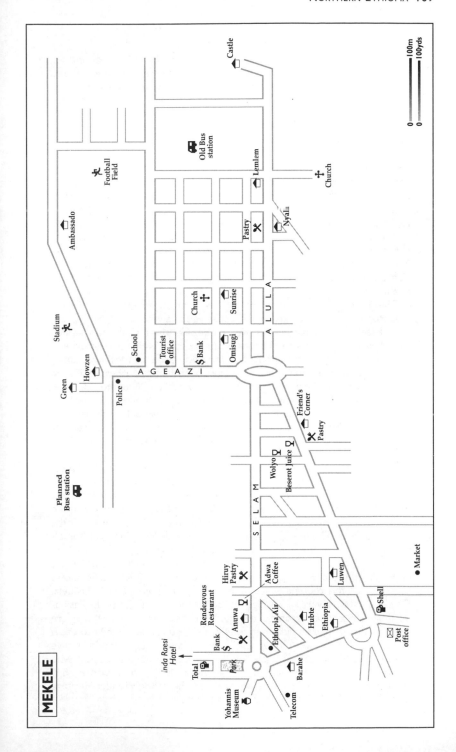

MEKELE

THE CHURCHES OF LALIBELA

The rock-hewn churches of Lalibela date to the 12th century AD. According to legend, their excavation was instigated by King Lalibela under divine instruction. The easterly cluster of churches is dominated by Bet Medhane Alem, which at 11.5m in height and with a ground area of 800m² is said to be the largest rock-hewn monolith in the world. Supported by 36 pillars on the inside and another 36 on the outside, Bet Medhane Alem has a classical nobility which has led some experts to think it was modelled on the original St Mary Zion Church at Axum. Several graves and hermits' cells have been carved into the walls of the courtyard. From Bet Medhane Alem, a short tunnel leads to a second courtyard which contains three churches. Bet Maryam is the largest of these, with a double-storey interior, and it is said to be oldest church in Lalibela. The tiny chapels of Bet Meskel and Bet Danaghel are carved into the walls of the courtyard. The third courtyard in the eastern cluster contains the twin churches of Bet Debre Sina and Bet Golgota, which share an entrance and together form a three-quarter monolith. There is a legend that King Lalibela is buried beneath a slab on the floor of these churches.

The eastern cluster of churches has a strong sense of cohesion, suggesting that the entire group was conceived as a whole, but the western cluster feels more hotch-potch in design. Bet Gebriel-Rufael is surrounded by a moat-like rock trench of perhaps 5m in depth, which has led experts to think that it was originally built as a fortified residence for King Lalibela. Bet Abba Libanos is said to have been built overnight by Lalibela's wife and a group of angels. The pink-tinged facade shows strong Axumite influences in its arched and cruciform windows, and it lies under an overhang reminiscent of certain churches in Tigre. Bet Emanuel is a 12m-high monolith considered by art historians to be the finest and most precisely worked church in Lalibela, possibly because it was the private church of the royal family.

The isolated cruciform monolith of Beta Georgis is the tallest and most majestic of Lalibela's churches. Legend has it that it was the last of the churches to be carved – the story is that St George was so offended that none of Lalibela's churches was dedicated to him that he personally visited the king, who promised he would build the finest of all his churches for the aggrieved saint. The holes in the stone tunnel walls are Georgis's horse's hoof-prints – or so they'll tell you in Lalibela.

Tours of the churches generally start at the eastern cluster, which lies downhill from the Seven Olives Hotel. A ticket costing US$12.50 allows access to all the churches over as many days as you spend in Lalibela. Official guides are very knowledgeable about the churches, but they ask as much as US$30 per person per day, and may become petulant if they are not tipped over and above the agreed price! You can get a child to show you around for a lot less money, but he won't know much and won't have the sway of the official guides when it comes to locating the priest who keeps the key for each church. If you go with a child or on your own, buy the informative, inexpensive booklet Lalibela: The World Wonder Heritage on sale at the Roha Hotel and possibly elsewhere.

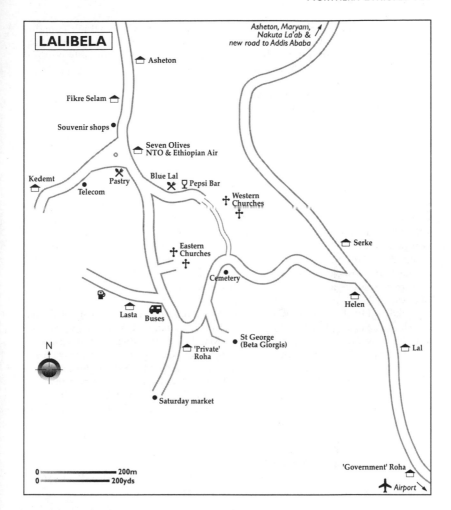

visiting the castle on **Makdela Hill** where Emperor Tewodros retreated in 1867, eventually to commit suicide rather than face defeat by a British force of 32,000 troops under Lord Napier.

A popular excursion out of Dese and Kombolcha is the fantastic Tuesday market at **Bati**. Only 40km from Kombolcha, Bati lies on the fringe of the Afar desert and is descended on by hordes of nomads on camelback as well as traders from the cities. It's easy to get to Bati and back for the occasion, though a couple of small lodgings do offer basic accommodation should you prefer to spend the night, and there's a decent restaurant (painted light blue)in the small town.

The long bus trip between Dese or Kombolcha and Addis Ababa is yet another that can be done in one fell swoop or drawn out over several days, depending on your temperament. About 50km south of Kombolcha, there is potentially some excellent birding in the seasonal wetlands that lie along the main road about 3km to the north and 5km to the south of **Kemise**. Further south, **Debre Sina** is a more significant town with a colourful market, and the sort of mountain setting that may give you itchy hiking boots – a worthwhile but reportedly rather elusive goal in this area is Menz Cave, which contains several mummified bodies. Lying about 130km northeast of Addis Ababa, **Debre Birhan** is a friendly highland town of some antiquity, the only physical evidence of which is the 15th-century church.

Access and getting around
Daily bus services connect Mekele, Woldia, Dese, Debre Birhan and Addis Ababa. You can use these buses to stop at other towns along the main road, or alternatively take advantage of the local transport which operates with varying degrees of efficiency and regularity between smaller towns.

One bus daily now runs between Woldia and Lalibela, leaving in either direction at 06.00 and taking around eight hours. Tickets are generally in high demand, so try to book one when the bus arrives in Woldia the afternoon before your departure. There are also sometimes Land Cruisers connecting the two towns, but these tend to get very crowded and uncomfortable. Road access to Lalibela can be difficult during the rainy season, so you might have to fly, which is now possible all year round due to the recent opening of an asphalt airstrip about 20–25km out of town. The cheapest place to fly to Lalibela is from Gonder; this costs around US$50 each way. The NTO bus between the airport and town charges a reputedly non-negotiable fare equivalent to around US$4 one way or US$6 return.

Makdela Hill lies to the northeast of Dese, near the remote town of Tenta, which can be reached by bus via Wegel Tena. The police at Tenta may require that you have written permission to visit Makdela from their counterparts in Kombolcha or Dese (easy enough to obtain, but do so in advance). They may insist that you take an armed guide – last I heard this cost around US$5, worth the outlay if only because you'll be shown several short cuts and points of interest that you might otherwise miss. The half-day walk from Tenta to Makdela passes through grand mountain scenery. You're advised to carry a tent and food, and to bank on camping overnight on the hill.

Where to stay and eat
Between Mekele and Woldia
There are **A** hotels in Maychew, Korem, Ali Mata and Hayk. The **Theodros Belai Hotel** in Ali Mata is a very good hotel that nudges into the **B** range.

Woldia
Colel Hotel Central location. Excellent s/c room with hot water. **B**.
Roha Hotel New, reasonably clean **A** hotel opposite bus station.

Lalibela
Asheton Hotel Popular though marginally overpriced. Shabby s/c room with hot shower **D**. OK food.
Blue Lal Restaurant Western dishes by advance order. Popular with travellers.
Firke Selam Hotel Popular cheap lodging. In **B** range.
Helen Hotel Decent family hotel on outskirts of town. Good food. Room **B/C**.
Kedemt Hotel Simple but clean rooms. Functional outside shower. Friendly owner. **B**.
'Private' Roha Hotel Not to be confused with mid-range government Roha Hotel. Popular cheapie. Rock-hewn toilet, reliable shower, fair meals. Rooms **B–C** negotiable.
Seven Olives Hotel Former government hotel and notable landmark in the town centre. Serves Western food. Rooms overpriced.

Dese

Ambaras Hotel Opposite Dessie Hotel. Large clean room with hot shower **C**–**D**. Good restaurant.

Dessie Hotel Large s/c rooms **B**. Basic rooms **A**.

Fasika Hotel Similar to Dessie Hotel, and nearby. Good meals.

Shamrock Pastry Fresh bread every morning.

Kombolcha

Hikma Hotel On roundabout 1km up hill from bus stop. Good restaurant. Large s/c room. **B** dbl. Recommended.

Sinay Hotel Near Hikma Hotel. Good s/c room. **B**.

Abraha Medhin Hotel 100m from bus station. Clean rooms **B** s/c dbl with hot shower. Good food.

Between Kombolcha and Addis Ababa

There are **A** hotels in Kemise, Debre Sina and Debre Birhan. The Helen Hotel in Debre Birhan is outstanding.

Western Ethiopia

The loop through the forested highlands of western Ethiopia to the river port of Gambela near the Sudanese border is one of East Africa's most invigorating off-the-beaten-track trips, though you would need to set aside the best part of two weeks to do it at a comfortable pace. The loop is described here running anti-clockwise from Addis Ababa, but it could as easily be done in reverse.

The outward leg of the loop to Gambela goes through two largish towns, Ambo and Nekemte. On the way to Ambo, you'll bypass **Gefersa Reservoir**, a reliable place to see the endemic blue-winged goose, and pass through **Addis Alem**, founded in 1900 as the projected capital of Menelik II. Also known as Agere Hiwot, **Ambo** is a small, rather scruffy town known for a hot-spring resort complete with murky swimming pool. The Ambo mineral-water factory can be visited 5km out of town along the Nekemte Road. About 13km past Ambo, a short walk from the small town of Guder, the **Guder Waterfall** carries an impressive volume of water in the rainy season, and the surrounding riverine forest is rattling with monkeys and birds. About 30km south of Ambo, **Mount Wenchi** is a 3,386m-high volcano with an extensive forest zone, areas of heather moorland, and several nested calderas enclosing a large crater lake and a field of mineral springs. **Nekemte** is the capital of Wolega Province, a leafy and pretty town with a good museum displaying a vast collection of Oromo artefacts

Gambela is a most appealing oddity. Lying at an altitude of 450m in the swampy, mosquito-ridden lowlands near the Sudanese border, this former British port is more what you'd expect of a Congo river port than of anything in Ethiopia. The lush vegetation and almost unbearable humidity exude an atmosphere of tropical languor that is only underscored by the lazy brown waters of the Baro River, a tributary of the Nile that is navigable as far as Khartoum. The spaciously laid-out town boasts several colonial buildings, and birds and monkeys are everywhere. In the market, you can buy the woven baskets and bubble pipes made by the town's Anuwak and Nuer inhabitants – people whose near black complexion and distinctive homesteads immediately set them apart from their highland neighbours.

The first major town on the return leg is **Matu**, the capital of Illubador Province and despite its pretty surrounds an unremarkable place – if you feel like a short

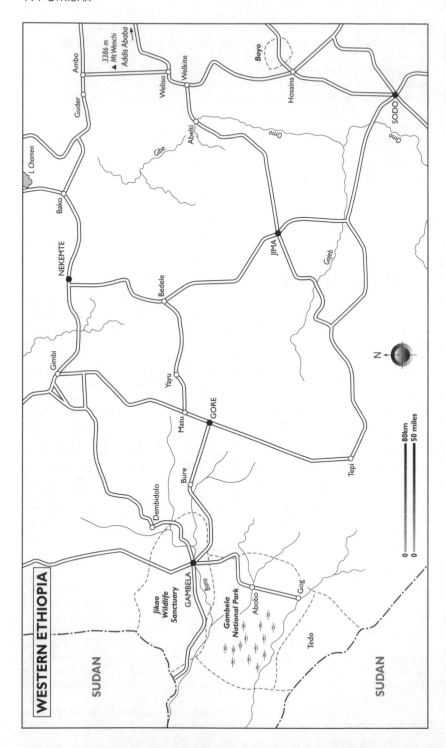

walk, the Sor River 2km northeast of the town centre lies in a wooded area where guereza monkeys are common. The road east from Matu leads through dense forest, crosses several large rivers and passes a few attractive waterfalls; potentially good walking country, best explored from **Yayu**, 40km from Matu. Next up is **Bedele**, where you can do a tour of Ethiopia's newest and best beer factory on presentation of your passport.

Jima is the largest town in Western Ethiopia and the capital of Kafa Province, Ethiopia's major coffee-growing region. The town lacks any notable tourist attractions, but you couldn't hope for a friendlier, greener or better equipped place to rest up between bus trips. The patch of woodland near the (waterless) public baths is worth investigating – guereza monkeys and silvery-cheeked hornbills appear to be resident. The nearby Jima Museum has several interesting ethnological displays and a good collection of musical instrument displays; the knowledgeable and enthusiastic English speaking caretaker will happily take you on a guided tour. More energetically, you could hire a bicycle opposite the minibus park and pedal around the surrounding countryside, which is very pretty and densely forested in patches. A group of hippos is said to be resident in a reservoir out of town along the Addis road.

Access and getting around

Buses to Ambo leave from the main Autobus Terra in Addis throughout the day and take two or three hours. There is regular transport between Ambo and Guder, but getting to Mount Wenchi could be problematic. The occasional 4x4 which serves as public transport between Ambo and Weliso will be able to drop you at a junction 3km from Wenchi, but it may be difficult to get a lift back out. At weekends, ask at the Ethiopia Hotel for a lift to Wenchi.

There are direct buses between Addis Ababa and Nekemte. Leaving from Ambo, you may find it difficult to get a seat on one of these. Instead, catch a bus from Ambo to Bako, where you can pick up another bus to Nekemte before around 13.00 – there are hotels in Bako if you get stuck. On paper, the obvious route between Nekemte and Gambela passes through Gimbi and Dembidolo, but this road may be impassable after the rains and it can involve lengthy delays at any time of year. There is normally a daily bus between Nekemte and Dembidolo, a 10–15-hour trip, longer when the bus breaks down (a regular occurrence), and even on a good day is memorable less for the lush scenery than for the general level of discomfort. The transport situation between Dembidolo and Gambela is even less encouraging: there is certainly no bus, but I recently heard from a traveller who caught a passenger minibus heading from Gambela to Dembidolo, and more recently from another traveller who waited in Dembidolo for three days before hitching a lift with a truck. Assuming that you do find some transport, it's advisable to stock up on mineral water for this long, hot ride. The easier and more reliable alternative route between Nekemte and Gambela takes you via Bedele and Matu – the 06.00 bus from Nekemte to Bedele takes three to four hours, and from there you should easily find transport on to Matu, where buses depart every morning for Gambela.

On the return trip, the daily bus covering the dramatic road between Gambela and Matu leaves in either direction at 06.00 and takes seven hours. Direct buses between Jima and Nekemte leave at 06.00 and take about eight hours with stops at Yayu and Bedele. A number of buses leave Jima for Addis Ababa throughout the morning, but only those that leave early will cover the 350km road in one day. Later buses will probably stop over at Welkite or Weliso, both of which have several lodgings.

Where to stay and eat
Ambo, Guder & Wenchi
Jibat and Mecha Hotel Ambo. Clean s/c rooms at bottom of **B** range. Restaurant.
Guder Hotel The smartest place in Guder. **A**.
Mount Wenchi No accommodation. Camping safe.

Nekemte
Wolega Ethiopia Hotel Agreeable government hotel. Rooms **D** s/c dbl. Good restaurant.
Wagugan Hotel Best private hotel but ridiculously overpriced at **D**.
Sissay Mammod and **Diribee Hotels** Pick of the **A** hotels 200m past the Agip Garage.

Dembidolo
Birhan Hotel Hotel opened in 1998 recommended not only for the comfortable rooms in the **A** range, but also for the friendly bar with satellite television.

Gambela
Ethiopia Hotel Government hotel on Baro River. Rooms **C** s/c dbl. OK meals US$1.50.
Opena Hotel Reader consensus has this as clear winner among the several mostly run-down local lodgings in Gambela. Clean **B** s/c rooms with nets and running water opposite the bus station.

Matu
Lusii Hotel Clean s/c rooms with hot shower in lower **B** range. Good restaurant.

Yayu
Shofeerootuu Hotel As cheap and scruffy as you'd expect. OK food. **A**.

Bedele
Menasha Hotel Spotless rooms **B** s/c dbl with hot water. Good food.

Jima
Goje's Minch Hotel Creaky 1930s hotel. Atmosphere better than rooms. **B**.
Nameless blue hotel Opposite the Mobil Garage. Rooms **B** s/c. Good food.
Wolde Argaw Hotel Mural-covered multi-storey building behind bus station. Spotless rooms with balcony and hot shower. **B**. Cheaper rooms at back. Good restaurant.

Eastern and southern Ethiopia
NAZRET AND DEBRE ZEYIT
Nazret is a pretty and sizeable town situated about 100km southeast of Addis Ababa on a plateau above the Rift Valley. An important route focus, Nazret lies on or near the junction of roads west to Addis Ababa, southeast to Asela and Bale, east to Harer and Dire Dawa, and south through the Rift Valley to Moyale on the Kenya border. There isn't much to see in Nazret, but the town has good facilities, and the hot springs resort 25km away at Sodore offers access to the forest-fringed Awash River – vervet monkeys and crocodiles, the odd hippo, and superb birdwatching.

Sprawling along the main road about halfway between Addis Ababa and Nazret, **Debre Zeyit** lies at the heart of one of the most accessible crater-lake fields in Africa. The most central lake is Bishoftu which, denuded of vegetation, has the appearance of a sunken quarry. Lake Hora, which lies 2km out of town (follow signposts to the Hora Ras Hotel) is the largest and most attractive of the lakes,

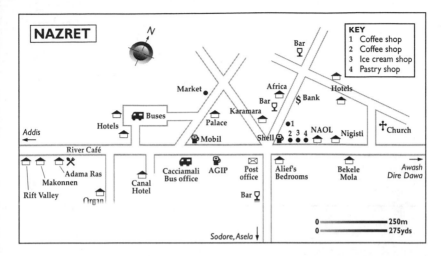

circumnavigated by a footpath with views over its thickly wooded slopes. About 2km past the Hora Ras, a right fork in the road (look out for the ILCA signpost) brings you to the Catholic Galilee Mission, where Lake Koriftu lies to the right of the road and Lake Bishoftu Guda to the left. You can return to town by a different route – walk back to the ILCA signpost, take the fork you missed out on first time and follow it for about 1km to the floodplain of Lake Chelelaka, which supports a variety of waterfowl and waders.

Access and getting around

Buses run throughout the day between Addis Ababa and Nazret, taking about two hours and stopping at Debre Zeyit on the way. There are buses from Nazret to most parts of southern Ethiopia, and regular minibuses between Nazret and Sodore.

Where to stay and eat
Nazret

Alief's Bedrooms Central and good value. Rooms **D** s/c dbl with hot water.
Bekele Mola Hotel Flowering grounds. Bungalow **C** s/c dbl. Good food. Recommended.
Organ and Franco's Hotel Basic clean rooms **C** s/c dbl.
River Café Good juice and pastry shop next to government Ras Hotel.
Sunshine Hotel Next to River Café. Basic s/c room **A** pp.

Sodore

Sodore Hot Springs Resort Rooms US$40. Attractive rambling campsite **A** pp (own tent) or **B** pp (standing tent). Lockers with keys in swimming pool enclosure.

Debre Zeyit

Bekele Mola Hotel Unsignposted faded yellow building. Rooms **C** s/c dbl. Restaurant.
Bishoftu Hotel Overlooking Lake Bishoftu. Good rooms **C** s/c dbl with hot water.
Main Grill Near Veterinary College. Recommended garden restaurant.
Hora Ras Hotel No longer functions as a hotel, but the patio overlooking Lake Hora remains a great spot for a meal or drink.
Terminal Hotel Opposite bus station. Rooms **B** s/c dbl.

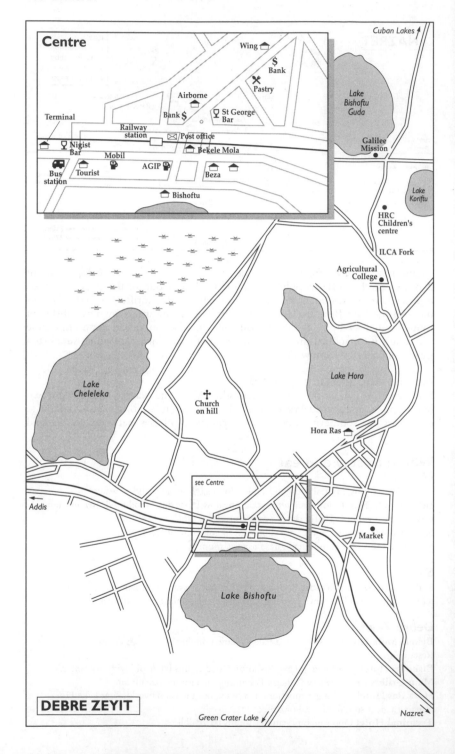

DEBRE ZEYIT

EAST TO HARER

The Muslim city of Harer, probably Ethiopia's most popular travel destination after the northern historical circuit, can be reached by bus in a day from Nazret, but as always there are plenty of possible diversions and stops.

Roughly 100km east of Nazret, **Awash National Park** is bisected by the road to Harer. Awash cannot easily be explored by backpackers, but you're quite likely to see some game from the road and you could do worse than to stop at one of the towns that border the park. The first of these, **Metahara**, is only 1km from Lake Beseka, beautifully situated at the base of Fentalle Volcano, and crossed by a causeway from where you can see a profusion of waterbirds as well as the odd hippo or crocodile. Lake Beseka lies just outside the park, so you can walk around its shore freely, but be warned that attempting to stray far from the road could antagonise any roaming park official. The town of **Awash** lies a mere 500m from the Awash River Gorge, the drama of which is accentuated by a row of low volcanic hills above the opposite cliff. A footpath leads to the base of the gorge, and there's some interesting looking riverine woodland a kilometre or so back towards the park boundary – but again, be aware that the park begins about 3km west of Awash town, and there's no telling what official attitudes would be if you crossed the line.

East of Awash, the road crosses the Awash River into a rather bleak and desolate landscape, brightened up by parties of colourfully dressed Oromo women who appear from nowhere to board the bus in an excited gossipy clatter. After three or four hours, the bus pulls in to **Abse Teferi**, tucked away in the Arba Gugu foothills and rescued from anonymity by some balconied double-storey legacies of the Italian occupation. The road then climbs into the Arba Gugu Mountains, where **Hirna** is an exceptionally cheerful and colourful little town surrounded by glistening green hills and fertile valleys – fantastic walking potential. Finally, shortly before hitting the T-junction with the main road connecting Dire Dawa and Harer, you pass the hilltop church of **Kalubi Gebriel**, founded by Ras Makonen after Ethiopia trounced Italy at Adwa in 1896, and the focus of a pilgrimage on July 26 and December 28 when over 100,000 Ethiopians from all over the country gather there.

The walled city of **Harer**, the world's fourth most holy Islamic city, rose to prominence after it was captured by Ahmed Gragn in 1520. The old town, enclosed by 5m-high walls that date to the 15th century, is strongly Muslim in character (its 99 mosques are said to be the largest concentration in the world), while the part of town outside the city walls is mainly Christian. For a city of such devout pedigree, Harer has a remarkably tolerant and somewhat hedonistic atmosphere – the compulsive chewing of mildly narcotic chat leaves dominates public life, and preconceptions about fundamentalism can be washed down at one of the bars which come close to outnumbering the mosques within the city walls. It would be easy to spend a week in Harer without doing anything very constructive, but it would be a pity not to have a guided tour of the old town – among the more interesting buildings are the 16th-century tomb of Emir Nur, the 12th-century al-Jami Mosque, the former home of Ras Makonen (where Haile Selassie spent much of his childhood) and the house in which the French poet Rimbaud is said to have lived during his time in Harer. Not to be missed are the legendary hyena-men of Harer, a bunch of nutters who will feed the wild hyenas that roam the city's outskirts with their hands and mouths – eerie stuff, easily organised through any tout, but don't pay more than around US$3 per person.

About 100km from Harer, **Dire Dawa** is the second most populous city in Ethiopia. Originally called Addis Harer (*New Harer*) it was founded in 1902 to service the rail link from Djibouti to Addis Ababa. In the first edition of my *Guide*

BALE NATIONAL PARK

Bale National Park protects the higher reaches of the Bale Mountains, including the 4,377m Tullo Deemtu, Ethiopia's second highest peak. Bale is the place to see animals endemic to Ethiopia – the mountain nyala is abundant near the park headquarters, while the 4,000m-high Saneti Plateau supports the largest remaining population of Simien wolf. More than half of the 30 birds endemic to Ethiopia have been recorded in Bale.

The park headquarters lie 2km from the village of **Dinsho**. The excellent self-catering resthouse at the headquarters has double rooms for **C** and dormitory beds at **A** per person, and there are a few **A** hotels in Dinsho itself. A two-hour walking trail through the juniper forest around the park headquarters is a certain place to see mountain nyala, as well as Menelik's bushbuck, bohor reedbuck, warthog and rare forest birds. Hikes and horse treks deeper into the park can be arranged for around US$15 per person per day, including fees and horse hire but not food.

The two main towns in the Bale area are **Roba** and **Goba**. In Roba, the Bekele Mola Hotel has large s/c rooms with hot showers in the **C** range, while the unsignposted Metaforak Hotel is the best of several **A** hotels. In Goba, the Yilma Hotel has outstanding s/c rooms in the **B** range as well as more basic **A** rooms and excellent food. The adjacent Nyala Pastry has fresh bread on sale and a coffee machine whirring at the unusually early hour of 06.00.

Bale can be approached from several directions. Coming from Addis Ababa or Nazret, the best route is via **Asela**, about three hours from Nazret by bus. Asela has several good lodges (try the Hanna, Tinsayye or Kutal Hotel) and you can eat well at the government Asela Ras Hotel. South of Asela, the wonderfully scenic road to Dinsho must be covered in stages. You may have to change vehicle at **Bekoji**, **Asasa**, **Dodola** and **Adaba**, all of which have at least one very basic hotel. Coming from the Rift Valley, the obvious option is to take a direct bus from Shashemene to Goba – several leave in either direction every morning, stopping at Dinsho and Roba.

The most exciting route out of Goba crosses the Saneti Plateau then descends through the stunning Harena Forest to the scrubby plains around **Dola Mena**. A pick-up truck seems to cover this road on most days, leaving at 06.00, taking seven hours, and charging US$3.50 for a perch in the back or US$5 for a seat. The scenery on this road is superlative, as can be the game viewing: in addition to Simien wolf, you stand a good chance of seeing klipspringer, giant mole-rat, golden jackal, bushbuck, bushpig and a variety of monkeys and birds – and one reader recently wrote to say he'd seen three African hunting dogs racing alongside the car!

After spending the night in one of three **A** hotels in Dola Mena (the unsignposted Rolo Hotel on the Goba side of town has been recommended), you should be able to find a pick-up truck heading south to **Negele Borena**. During the dry season, at least one truck normally covers this road every day, taking about ten hours. In the rainy season, transport is less regular. At the worst, there is always the possibility of returning to Goba via the Saneti Plateau. Once there, Negele Borena is a fascinating frontier town that shows a mixture of Oromo, Somali and Borena influences. There are a dozen or so **A** and **B** lodgings in Negele Borena, and jumping up a notch there is also the Green Hotel, with good s/c rooms in the **C** range and a decent restaurant.

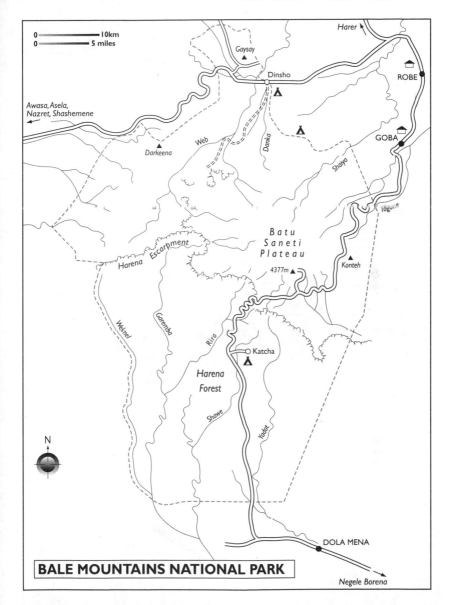

0 ——————10km
0 ——————5 miles

Harer

Gaysay

Dinsho

ROBE

Awasa, Asela,
Nazret, Shashemene

Web

Danka

GOBA

Darkeena

Shaiya

Ioguna

*Batu
Saneti
Plateau*

Escarpment

Harena

4377m

Konteh

Wehnel

Garemba

Rira

Katcha

*Harena
Forest*

Shawe

Yadot

N

DOLA MENA

BALE MOUNTAINS NATIONAL PARK

Negele Borena

to Ethiopia, I described Dire Dawa as 'hot, sweaty and entirely without charm', a dismissal which has been countered by the enthusiasm of some readers who regard its architecture, cleanliness and sense of order as 'a refreshing change from other towns in Ethiopia, or Africa for that matter'.

Access and getting around

In addition to the erratic train service between Addis Ababa and Dire Dawa (see box *The Djibouti Train* page 124), direct buses connect Addis Ababa to both Harer and Dire Dawa, leaving at 05.00 and arriving towards dusk. If you prefer to travel

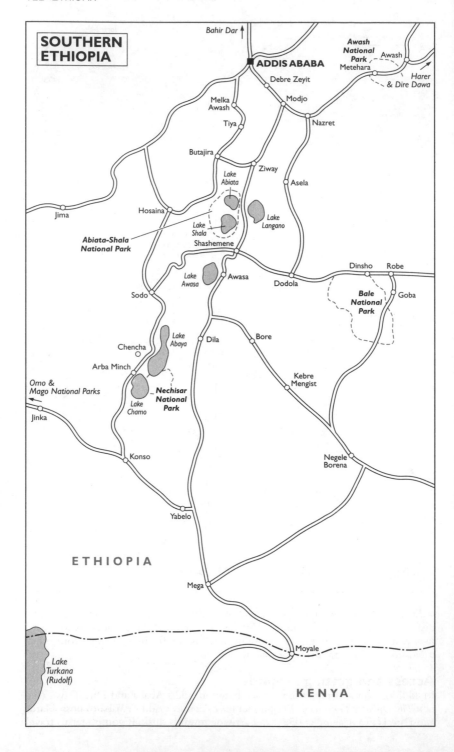

SOUTHERN
ETHIOPIA

Bahir Dar ↑

■ ADDIS ABABA

Debre Zeyit

Awash
National
Park
Metehara

Awash

Harer
& Dire Dawa

Melka
Awash

Modjo

Tiya

Nazret

Butajira

Ziway

Lake
Abiata

Asela

Jima

Hosaina

Lake
Shala

Lake
Langano

Abiata-Shala
National Park

Shashemene

Dinsho

Robe

Lake
Awasa

Awasa

Dodola

Bale
National
Park

Goba

Sodo

Lake
Abaya

Dila

Bore

Chencha

Arba Minch

Omo &
Mago National Parks

Nechisar
National
Park

Kebre
Mengist

Jinka

Lake
Chamo

Konso

Negele
Borena

Yabelo

ETHIOPIA

Mega

Moyale

Lake
Turkana
(Rudolf)

KENYA

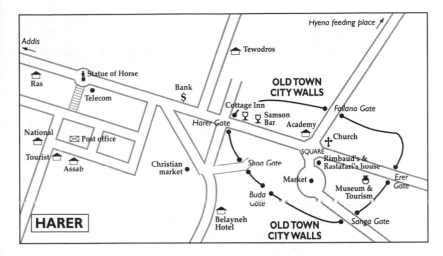

in stages, local buses connect the various towns along the way. Regular minibuses cover the 100km surfaced road between Dire Dawa and Harer.

Where to stay and eat
Awash
Buffet D'auche Hotel Attractive old hotel next to railway station. **B**.

Harer
Ali Baba Good pasta and fruit juice accompanied by non-stop CNN. On the main square in the walled town. Signposted in Amharic only.
Belayneh Hotel Near bus station. Rooftop restaurant. Rooms from **C** s/c dbl. Very popular with travellers.
Tewodros Hotel Reliable gem among the generally sleazy budget options. S/c rooms **B**. Basic rooms **A**. Good roast chicken.

Dire Dawa
Addis Ababa Hotel Good views and clean rooms with communal showers in the old town. You face the hotel directly as you cross the bridge into the old town. **A**.
Hotel Sai Basic but clean **B** rooms on the Piazza facing the railway station. Great patio bar draped with creepers next door.
National Hotel Clean, quiet and friendly. Rooms **C** s/c or **B** basic.
Paradiso Hotel Good restaurant.
Ras Hotel Government hotel. Pricey rooms. Of interest for the good food and swimming pool (nominal fee charged for day use).
Wagda Hotel Basic, clean rooms. **A**.

Other towns
There are **A** hotels in Metehara, Abse Teferi and Hirna.

THE RIFT VALLEY FROM ZIWAY TO AWASA
This stretch of the Rift Valley that bisects southern Ethiopia is covered in acacia woodland and dotted with a string of natural lakes reminiscent in feel if not facilities of the more publicised lake region of the Kenyan Rift Valley. The northernmost of these lakes is **Ziway**, fringed by the synonymous town and ringed by steep volcanic

THE DJIBOUTI TRAIN

This box is based extensively on a lengthy letter from Christine Wenaweser and Luca Zanetti, with input from Arthur Gerfers and Iain Jackson.

The cargo and passenger trains which connect Addis Ababa to Djibouti via Dire Dawa are used by relatively few travellers, but those who do travel this way invariably regard it as a highlight of their time in Ethiopia (with hindsight, anyway). Most sensibly viewed as an experience in its own right rather than a mode of public transport, the train runs to a notoriously unreliable timetable and is given to inexplicable stops of several hours' duration, most of which seem to be linked to the huge amount of smuggling between Ethiopia and Djibouti. Christine reckons that cargo trains are more comfortable than passenger trains, and tend to get from A to B more quickly, though you might need to improvise to make the most of the possibilities on the cargo train (she spent much of her time on the back of a pick-up truck being carried by the train).

In theory, one train leaves Addis Ababa daily at around 14.00 and arrives in Dire Dawa roughly 15–20 hours later. In practise, you are best off heading to the train station in Addis on a daily basis to check out the current situation – the railway staff are helpful and speak good English and French. Conditions on the train can be cramped due to habitual overbooking, but there is no longer a serious security problem and it's good value at around US$8 second class to Dire Dawa (first-class tickets cost US$12 but are not often available).

Christine and Luca travelled by train all the way to Djibouti (and back). This tiny Francophone country, named after its main port and capital, has assumed great strategic significance to Ethiopia following the recent closure of all borders with Eritrea. It's debatable whether the additional two to three days on the train this entails in either direction would be justifiable to anybody but serious rail buffs or passport-stamp collectors. Djibouti town reportedly has little to recommend it; the kindest epithet I've come across is 'likeable dump'. Also be warned that costs are high: accommodation starts at US$30 per room (the Djibouti Palace Hotel near the Assemblee Nationale has been recommended for offering reasonably priced rooms with air-conditioning, TV and running water). In addition to buying a Djibouti visa in Addis Ababa you'll need to fork out another US$60 for a fresh Ethiopian visa once in Djibouti (assuming that you want to return to Ethiopia). Then again, it is such obscure, difficult journeys such as the Djibouti Train that often result in the most memorable travel experiences. If you decide to give it a go, let me know how it went...

hills. Ziway offers great birdwatching: I saw around 60 species in two hours from a jetty 500m from the main road (turn off near the Bekele Mola Hotel). On the island of Tullo Guddo opposite the jetty, the 9th-century Debre Tsion monastery is said to have been founded by Axumite priests during the reign of Queen Yodit, when it offered sanctuary to the Ark of the Covenant for 70 years. The Fish Corporation in Ziway can arrange boat trips to the island for a negotiable fee.

About 50km north of Shashemene, the main road cuts between **Lake Langano** and **Abiata-Shala National Park**. Langano is arguably a bit overrated, particularly at weekends when it fills up with Addis residents and takes on a slightly manic, ghettoblasting Club Med-type atmosphere. During the week, things are a lot more tranquil, and the acacia-lined shore is of some interest to bird enthusiasts. The main attraction of Abiata-Shala National Park is the two lakes after which it is named and their attendant waterbirds – much of the land is densely settled and wildlife populations are low. A guided 12km round hike from the main entrance gate costing US$8 per person will allow you to see most places of interest, including a viewpoint over the two lakes and the hot springs on the shore of Lake Shala.

The sprawling town of **Shashamene** is the major transport hub in the Rift Valley, lying at the junction of the north–south highway and the main roads east to Bale National Park, west to Arba Minch, and southeast to Negele Borena. Shashemene is also amorphous, ugly and brash; the sort of place where you'd want to spend a night only if your public transport needs dictate it. Altogether more attractive is the resort at **Wondo Genet** in the forested hills 20km southwest of Shashemene. The nominal attraction here is the swimming pool fed by the springs just outside the entrance of the government hotel, but the area is perhaps of greater interest for the surrounding forest, home to a wide variety of forest birds as well as guereza monkey, Anubis baboon and bushbuck. Also of interest is swampy Lake Dabashi, 4km off the road to Wondo Genet, and home to hippo and crocodiles.

The large and attractively laid-out town of **Awasa**, capital of Sidamo province, lies on the eastern shore of the synonymous lake 20km south of Shashemene. With its mountainous background, Lake Awasa matches any of the Kenyan Rift Valley lakes for scenery. The fringing vegetation of dense scrub and fig woodland is teeming with birds and guereza monkeys, best explored from a raised footpath that starts about 1km north of the first Wabe Shebele Hotel and follows the shore southwards almost as far as the second Wabe Shebele Hotel. Hippos can be seen by organising a fishing boat to take you out from the small beach near the Unique Park Hotel. For a good view over the lake, climb the small but steep hill behind the second Wabe Shebele Hotel.

Access and getting around

There is plenty of transport along the main road between Addis Ababa and Shashemene. Buses take about six hours and they all stop at Ziway. The turn-off to the Bekele Mola Hotel on Lake Langano and the main entrance to Abiata-Shala National Park are signposted opposite each other between Shashemene and Ziway. The Bekele Mola Hotel lies about 30 minutes' walk from the turn-off.

Regular minibuses cover the 20km between Shashemene and Awasa. A few buses daily connect Shashemene to Wondo Genet (ask to be dropped at the village at the turn-off to the Wabe Shabele Hotel, 5km before Wondo Genet itself). From Shashemene, there are also regular buses heading west to Arba Minch via Sodo, and there is at least one bus daily east to Goba via Dinsho, as well as a daily bus to Negele Borena via Kebre Negist.

Where to stay and eat
Ziway
Bekele Mola Hotel Behind Agip Garage. Good food, nice grounds. Rooms **B** s/c dbl.
Brothers Hotel Clean rooms **A** s/c dbl with cold water only.
Jemeneh Hotel At minibus stop. Rooms **B**/**C** s/c dbl/suite with hot water. Fair food.
Selam Hotel New, clean, good value. Rooms **B** s/c dbl with hot water.
Tourist Hotel Best rooms in town only **C** s/c dbl with hot water. Definitely the place to eat.

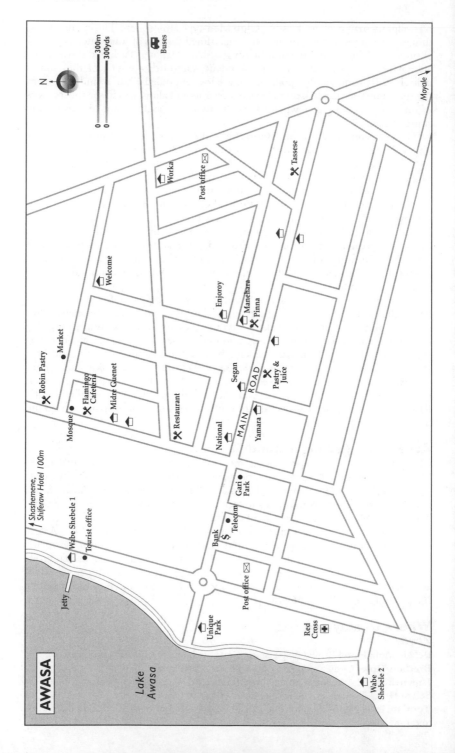

AWASA

Lake
Awasa

N

300m
300yds
0
0

Buses

Moyale

Worka
Post office

Tassese

Welcome

Enjoroy
Manehara
Pinna

Robin Pastry
Market

Flamingo
Cafeteria
Midre Guenet

Mosque

Restaurant

National

Segan

MAIN   ROAD

Yamara

Pastry &
Juice

Shashemene,
Shiferaw Hotel 100m

Wabe Shebele 1
Tourist office

Jetty

Bank

Telecom

Gari
Park

Post office

Unique
Park

Red
Cross

Wabe
Shebele 2

ADDIS ABABA TO ZIWAY: THE SCENIC ROUTE

It's easiest to travel between Addis Ababa and Ziway via Modjo, but there is a more interesting route between these towns. This takes you through the small town of Tiya, where barely 500m from the main road lies a field of roughly 40 engraved stelae, the most accessible and northerly of the 2,000-odd so-called 'Gragn Stones' that form a belt through southern Ethiopia. Erected to mark the mass graves of soldiers, the origin of these stelae is something of a mystery: local tradition links them to the 15th-century Muslim leader Ahmed Gragn, but archaeological evidence suggests that they predate Gragn by two or three centuries.

Lying to the west of the Addis Ababa road about 25km north of Tiya, and also worth visiting, the subterranean three-quarter monolith of **Adadi Maryam** is the most southerly rock hewn church in Ethiopia, traditionally associated with King Lalibela's visit to Mount Zikwala in AD1106. Adadi Maryam must be roughly contemporaneous with the non-Christian Gragn stones of Tiya, suggesting that the two sites effectively mark the southern boundary of Christian influence in medieval Ethiopia.

Public transport in this area is relatively scarce, though a few vehicles do run from Addis to Butajira daily, stopping at Tiya, and there is also some public transport between Butajira and Ziway. Adadi Maryam lies 12km west of the main road, with the turn-off clearly signposted 25km north of Tiya and 5km south of Melka Awash, the village on the northern lip of the Awash River gorge. The best days to visit Adadi are Thursday and Saturday (market days) when pick-up trucks head there from Melka Awash between 07.30 and 09.00; on other days you'll have to walk. There are **A** hotels in Butajira, Tiya (the Stelae Hotel is a recent recommendation) and Melka Awash, but I couldn't find one in Adadi.

Langano and Abiata-Shala

Bekele Mola Hotel On Langano, only 3km from Abiata-Shala entrance gate. Fair meals. Rooms **D** s/c dbl. Camping **A**.

Shashemene

Bekele Mola Hotel Rooms **C** s/c dbl. Good inexpensive meals.
Fasika Pastry Outstanding bread and pastries. Coffee and juice.
Rift Valley Hotel Very pleasant. Good meals. Rooms from **C** small s/c dbl with hot water.
Warka, **Bekela** and **Langano Hotels** Among the better of a great many **A** hotels.

Wondo Genet

Wabe Shebele Hotel Good food. Expensive rooms. Camping **C** per tent. At turn-off about 2km before Wabe Shabele hotel are several **A** hotels.

Awasa

Pinna Restaurant On main road. Excellent inexpensive restaurant.
Shiferaw Hotel Clean rooms **C** s/c dbl with hot water. Good value.
Unique Park Hotel On main road near the lake. Nice grounds. Good value rooms. **B** s/c dbl.
Wabe Shebele Hotel #2 Government hotel in wonderful forested grounds on the lakeshore 1.5km from town. Prolific monkeys and birds in the gardens. Swimming pool.

Good food. Friendly, helpful management. Rooms **D** s/c dbl with erratic hot water. A reader comments that 'if any hotel in the whole country merits a splurge it is this' and I can only agree.

Yamara Hotel Clean little place on main road. Rooms **B** dbl or **C** s/c dbl. Hot water.

ARBA MINCH AND THE OMO VALLEY

The capital of Gamo-Gofa province, Arba Minch is one of the most beautifully situated towns in Africa, lying amongst the foothills of the Rift Valley escarpment, with mountains rising to almost 4,000m to the west, and views over the mountainous sliver that separates the Rift Valley lakes of Chamo and Abaya. Fringing Arba Minch, **Nechisar National Park** protects parts of the two Rift Valley lakes as well as the grassy Nechisar plains to their east. Although much of the park is difficult to visit without private transport, backpackers can walk freely along the public road which connects the town to a group of forest-fringed hot springs lying just within the national park. Also of interest near Arba Minch is the crocodile farm, which lies about 6km out of town off the Sodo Road, and 500m from a stretch of the Lake Abaya shore where hippos and crocs are frequently seen in their natural state.

The former capital of Gamo-Gofa, **Chencha** lies only 40km from Arba Minch along a road that switchbacks dramatically during an altitude hike of 1,600m. The Guge Mountains around Chencha are notable for supporting substantial patches of bamboo and juniper forest, for the spectacular views over the Rift Valley Lakes, and for the Dorze people whose beehive bamboo huts measure up to 12m in height and may be used for 40 years or longer.

To the south of Arba Minch, the **Omo Valley** is home to the so-called 'Omotic' people, a closely linked group of small animist tribes whose cultural background is vastly different from that of other Ethiopians and who indulge in a variety of ritual practices which, to Western eyes at least, makes the Christian highlanders seem somewhat conventional. Based around the town of **Konso**, the largest and least isolated of these ethnic groups is the Konso, whose eerie funeral totems are readily seen at a few smaller villages within 15km of the town.

Past Konso, Jinka is the largest town in the region and the best base for visits to **Omo** and **Mago National Parks**. These vast wilderness areas are inhabited by a variety of remote Omotic groups, for instance the Mursi (noted for inserting large, circular clay plates behind the lower lips of the women) and the Karo (who take the Omotic custom of body-scarring and body painting to garish extremes), but they are rather difficult to reach unless you're prepared to hire a private vehicle from Jinka.

Access and getting around

There are a couple of buses daily between Shashemene and Arba Minch, though you may find it easier to get there by changing vehicles at Sodo-Wailita. Arba Minch is divided into two separate entities, a dusty commercial centre (Sikela) and a more attractive administrative centre (Shecha), linked by a 2km surfaced road and regular minibuses. The main bus station is in Sikela.

The most straightforward route from Arba Minch to the hot springs is to follow the Sodo road for about 1km out of town, then to turn right into the road next to the training college. After another 1km, you'll hit a fork in the road. The left fork is signposted for the park headquarters, but you should take the right fork, which follows the base of a cliff for about 3km, passing through low dense scrub then true forest before reaching the springs. No park entrance fee is charged for walking along this public road. If you actually want to explore the national park (beautiful

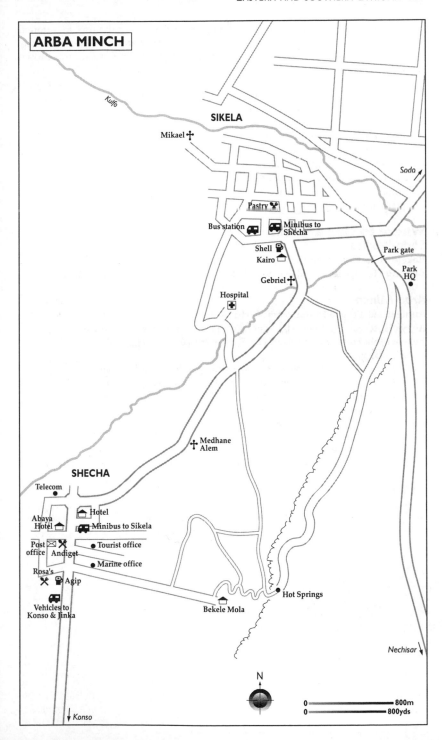

ARBA MINCH

Kulfo

SIKELA

Mikael ✝

Soda

Pastry ♟

Bus station 🚐

Minibus to Shecha 🚐

Shell 🏪
Kairo 🏠

Park gate

Park HQ ●

Gebriel ✝

Hospital ✚

✝ Medhane Alem

SHECHA

Telecom ●

Hotel 🏠

Abaya Hotel 🏠

Minibus to Sikela 🚐

Post office ✉ ✗
Andiget

● Tourist office

● Marine office

Rosa's
✗ 🏪 Agip

Vehicles to Konso & Jinka 🚐

Bekele Mola 🏠

● Hot Springs

Nechisar ↓

N

0 ────────── 800m
0 ────────── 800yds

↓ Konso

scenery and plenty of game), the park headquarters is just past the fork mentioned above and the warden will help you arrange vehicle hire at around US$50 for a day trip. To get to the crocodile farm, you need to follow the Sodo road out of town for 4km, where the 2km turn-off is clearly signposted to your right.

A couple of 4x4 vehicles run from Arba Minch to Chencha daily, leaving from the bus station in Sikela and taking around two hours. A daily bus now connects Arba Minch to Jinka via Konso, though it may not run after heavy rain. The bus leaves from Sikela at the crack of dawn. A couple of private pick-up trucks leave Arba Minch for Konso on most days, waiting for passengers in front of the Agip Garage in Shecha at around 06.00. Konso can also be reached from Yabelo (on the main road between Addis Ababa and Moyale) by pick-up truck, though you may have to wait a day or two for a lift.

Ethiopian Airways flies between Addis Ababa, Arba Minch and Jinka. Fares are not prohibitively expensive.

Where to stay and eat
Sodo-Wailita
Bekele Mola Hotel Comfortable s/c rooms **C**.
Birhanu Hotel The best value in town. Clean s/c rooms **B**. Restaurant attached.

Arba Minch
Andiget and **Teruye Restaurants** Shecha. Wonderful *asa kutilet* for less than US$2.
Abaya Hotel Shecha. Rooms **B** s/c or **A** with communal showers. Good food.
Bekele Mola Hotel 1km from Shecha. View over lakes. Room **D** s/c dbl.
Camping **A** pp.
Hotel Roza Scecha. This popular restaurant now also has a few **A** rooms.
Kairo Hotel Sikela. Similar standard and prices to Abaya. Next to Shell Garage.
Soma Restaurant Shecha. New restaurant rivalling Roza's in popularity.
Zebib Pastry Sikela. Good snacks and drinks.

Jinka
Hotel Orit Regularly recommended as the best lodge in town. S/c and non-s/c rooms in the **A**–**B** range. The **Omo** and **Goh Hotels** are smaller but similar in price and standard.

Other towns
Chencha, Konso and Yabelo all have **A** hotels.

Kenya

In many eyes Kenya is East Africa, and – even though a peek at a map reveals that many of the more evocative place-names associated with the region lie in neighbouring Tanzania – there is no doubt that Kenya, with its compact tourist circuit and fine range of facilities, remains one of the region's most attractive destinations for travellers of all persuasions and budgets.

Kenya is best known for its game reserves, particularly the Maasai Mara, which is too small and heavily touristed to stand comparison with Tanzania's Serengeti, but still offers superlative game viewing, and makes for a much cheaper safari objective than its Tanzanian neighbour. My nomination for Kenya's finest reserve – and one that's commonly included in safari packages – is Samburu in the deserts north of Mount Kenya.

Closely following the game reserves in the popularity stakes is the Indian Ocean coastline, the highlight of which is Lamu, a richly atmospheric and remarkably laid-back Swahili island town that's barely changed its shape in centuries. The old town of Mombasa is also atmospheric and notable for the Portuguese Fort Jesus, while to the south of Mombasa, on Tiwi Beach, Twiga Lodge is one of Africa's truly legendary backpackers' hangouts. The Watamu and Malindi area is a haven for snorkellers and divers, with the added attraction of the jungle-bound Gedi ruins on their doorstep.

Ignore anybody who tells you Kenya is too touristy – they simply haven't made the effort. The west of the country is rich in low-key, low-cost beauty spots ranging from the incomparable Kakamega Forest to the wonderful string of lakes dotting the Rift Valley, from Thomson's Falls outside Nyahururu to the camel safaris that run out of Maralal.

Tourism to Kenya has dropped in recent years owing to the high crime rate in Nairobi and along the coast, and more recently to the political instability linked with protest against the unpopular and seemingly interminable Moi

FACTS AND FIGURES
Area: 582,645km^2 (22nd in Africa)
Capital: Nairobi
Largest towns: Nairobi, Mombasa, Nakuru, Kisumu, Eldoret
Population: 27–28 million
Official languages: English and KiSwahili
Other languages: 70 including Kikuyu, Luo, Akamba and Maa
Currency: Kenya shilling
Head of State: President Daniel arap Moi

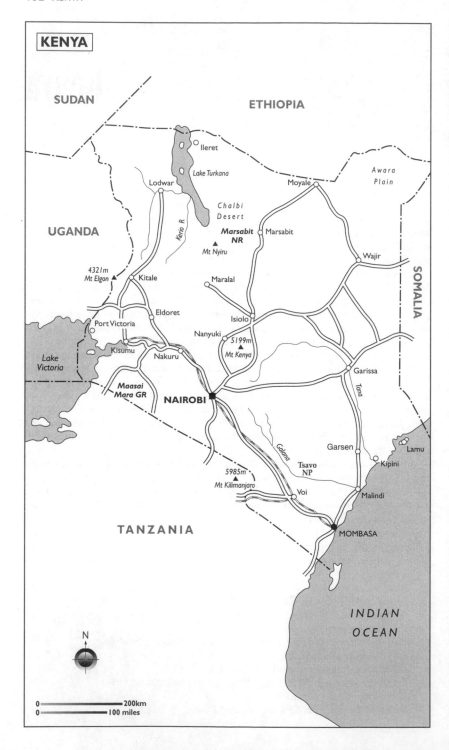

KENYA

SUDAN

ETHIOPIA

Ileret

Lake Turkana

Lodwar

Chalbi Desert

Moyale

Awara Plain

UGANDA

Kerio R

Marsabit NR

Marsabit

▲ Mt Nyiru

Wajir

SOMALIA

4321m
Mt Elgon ▲

Kitale

Maralal

Eldoret

Isiolo

Port Victoria

Nanyuki

5199m
▲ Mt Kenya

Kisumu

Nakuru

Garissa

Lake Victoria

Maasai Mara GR

NAIROBI

Tana

Garsen

Lamu

Goluna

Kipini

Tsavo NP

5985m
▲ Mt Kilimanjaro

Voi

Malindi

TANZANIA

MOMBASA

INDIAN OCEAN

N

0 ——— 200km
0 ——— 100 miles

regime. In late 1997, the coast around Mombasa and Malindi has been rendered unsafe by violence and, while there is no reason to think that this situation will persist indefinitely, you would be advised to check it out before heading to affected areas.

BACKGROUND INFORMATION
Geography and climate
Kenya is a country of geographical and climatic extremes. Essentially, eastern Kenya consists of low-lying coastal belt. In the south, this rises to the central highlands around Mount Kenya and Nairobi and the western highlands around Eldoret and Kitale. The central and western highlands are separated from each other by a dramatic stretch of the Rift Valley, the dusty, flat floor of which is studded with a string of lakes and extinct volcanoes. Mount Kenya is, at 5,199m, the second highest mountain in Africa. On the border with Uganda, the 4,321m-high Mount Elgon is the highest peak in the western highlands. The largest bodies of water in Kenya are Lake Victoria in the southwest and Lake Turkana in the north. With a few exceptions, the part of the country to the north and east of Mount Kenya is very dry and inhospitable.

The coast of Kenya is very hot and moist, with temperature and humidity peaking from December to March and rainfall figures peaking from April to June. The Lake Victoria basin is a bit cooler but has a similar rainfall pattern and humidity levels. Nairobi and other highland areas are far cooler than you'd expect of a region straddling the equator, with a main rainy season from March to May. The Rift Valley is hot and dry. The north is a desert, with soaring midday temperatures and an average annual rainfall of well under 250mm.

History
Kenya has long been something of a migrational crossroads, a status reflected today in its great cultural and linguistic diversity. Cushitic, Nilotic and Bantu speakers are well represented in the interior, and each language group has arrived in more than one set of migrations from elsewhere. The coast of Kenya, meanwhile, supported perhaps the greatest concentration of Swahili cities in medieval times, and many of these ports – notably Mombasa, Malindi, Lamu and Pate – have survived into the modern era.

In 1498, when Vasco da Gama arrived in East Africa, Mombasa was the wealthiest port between Mogadishu and Kilwa; its sultan was not disposed to be friendly to Christian intruders. The hostile reception that awaited Da Gama in Mombasa paved the way for the weaker Sultan of Malindi to forge an alliance with Portugal, which set up a base in Malindi and over the course of the sixteenth century conducted several destructive naval raids on Mombasa.

In 1589, Mombasa rose against Portugal. The rebellion was brutally quashed, Mombasa was placed under the jurisdiction of the Sultan of Malindi, and Portugal set to work on building Fort Jesus. For a century, Fort Jesus allowed Portugal to maintain tenuous control over Mombasa. In 1698, however, the fort was captured by Oman at the end of a two-year siege. Mombasa was restored to its former importance after the Mazrui Dynasty was founded there by an Omani family in 1729. The Mazrui eventually took control over the coast from Lamu to Tanga, and became the main rival to the *bona fide* Sultan of Oman in Zanzibar.

With the exception of a German Mission founded in the Taita Hills in the 1840s, the interior of Kenya remained unexplored for several decades after that of Tanzania. This is partly because the slave caravan routes followed by most European explorers left from Zanzibar-held ports south of Pangani, partly because of the ferocity of the Maasai. Several of the lakes in Kenya's Rift Valley were first seen by Europeans only in the late 1880s.

In 1888, Sir William McKinnon's Imperial British East Africa Company (IBEA) established a series of fortified trading posts 80km apart between Mombasa and the fertile Lake Victoria basin. Several IBEA forts, notably Machakos and Mumias, have since developed into towns. Following the collapse of the IBEA, Britain declared Protectorateship over Kenya and Uganda. The Maasai, weakened by smallpox, rinderpest and drought, were happy to sign a treaty with Britain if it helped them in the more important business of raiding their neighbours to replenish their rinderpest-affected cattle stocks. Between 1896 and 1901, Britain set about constructing the 'Uganda Railway' (a somewhat deceptive moniker to the modern reader, since the railway only reached Kisumu, part of Uganda until 1902), with the loss of thousands of lives to malaria and, with greater publicity, man-eating lions.

Decisive in shaping modern Kenya was Lord Elgin's pledge in 1907 that the fertile highlands around Mount Kenya and the Aberdares, traditional home of the Kikuyu, would be reserved for white settlers. Inevitably, it was the 'White Highlands' which suffered the first militant anti-colonial action. The Kenya African Union (KAU) was a fundamentally Kikuyu institution founded in 1945 and from 1947 led by Jomo Kenyatta, who had recently returned from a decade in the UK with a degree from the University of London. Following an attack on a white farm near the Aberdares in 1952, a State of Emergency was declared, KAU was banned, and Kenyatta and other African leaders were imprisoned. The attack also marked the beginning of the four-year-long Mau-Mau Rebellion, which, for all the publicity it received in the international press, resulted in the deaths of only 32 settlers and some 60 British troops as compared with roughly 20,000 Kikuyu.

Increasing internal pressure for self-determination led to the Lancaster House talks in 1960, where it was agreed that a democratic election would be held in 1961 prior to the granting of independence in 1963. Shortly after this, the KAU split into two parties, KANU and KADU, the former officially led by Kenyatta who was at that time under house arrest. KANU won the 1961 election with 19 seats to KADU's 11, and it refused to assume power until Kenyatta was released. On December 12 1963, Kenyatta became the first president of an independent Kenya, a position he held until his death in August 1978.

Contrary to the expectations of a great many doomsayers, the Kenyatta era was marked by a high degree of racial reconciliation and steady economic growth, the latter driven by the agricultural and tourist sectors (largely nullified by a correspondingly high birth rate which has seen Kenya's population quadruple since independence). Politically, the country rapidly became a one-party state, in effect if not in law, and Kenyatta's opponents tended to be jailed. In 1969, the assassination of Tom Mboya, the popular Luo Vice President who was hotly tipped as Kenyatta's successor, brought to the fore the tension between Kikuyu and Luo that has underscored Kenya's politics. Public faith in KANU was not improved in 1975 when the Kikuyu radical J M Kariuki called Kenya a nation of 'ten millionaires and ten million beggars'. He was arrested and weeks later found dead on the hills outside Nairobi.

Kenyatta's successor as president, Daniel arap Moi, gained some initial popularity by releasing all political prisoners and launching a campaign to stamp out corruption. It was all to be rather short-lived, however, as Moi realised that an atmosphere of open political debate was not entirely to his taste. The prominent Luo leader Odinga Odinga was expelled from KANU, academics and politicians were arrested, and in 1982 Kenya was officially declared a one-party state. Later that year, a failed coup attempt by the improbable combination of the airforce and students resulted in 150 deaths and extensive looting in Nairobi. From this time up until the end of the Cold War, Moi ran Kenya as a 'benign' dictator on the lines of Malawi's Banda, and he profited greatly from the backing of Western governments and businesses.

The 1990s have seen Moi under increasing pressure to introduce political reform. After large amounts of Western aid were cut off in 1991, Moi called a multi-party election for December 1992. Contrary to expectations KANU won a comfortable majority of seats, a result which can be attributed to the combination of superior funding (banknotes totalling US$250 million in Kenya shillings were printed just before the election for campaigning purposes), a hopelessly divided opposition (a mere 30% of the votes cast were actually for KANU) and some sophisticated gerrymandering (there isn't space   ) The 1992 election left Kenya in an uncomfortable political limbo, one that has resulted in a great deal of ethnic violence: most recently the well-publicised and murderous riots in and around Mombasa and Malindi. The election in late 1997 was again won by Moi amid considerable controversy.

PRACTICAL INFORMATION
Accommodation
Kenya has a good range of accommodation. In most towns you'll find a basic room for US$3 or a slightly smarter room for under US$10. Hotels are more expensive in Nairobi, where you are likely to stay at one of several official or unofficial hostels. As in Tanzania, be aware that the term *hoteli* means restaurant – local budget hotels are generally referred to as 'Boarding and Lodgings'. A tent will come in useful, especially in the Rift Valley.

Books and newspapers
There are several excellent bookshops in Nairobi and to a lesser extent Mombasa. The secondhand bookstalls in the River Road part of Nairobi are good, but be alert while you browse. A good range of international newspapers is available in Nairobi and Mombasa. The *Daily Nation* boasts good local news commentary, some coverage of international events, an obsession with road fatalities, and a quite remarkable letters page.

Crime and safety
It is difficult to overstate the risk of being mugged, pickpocketed or conned in Nairobi, particularly when you're still adjusting to travelling in Africa. Many travellers are relieved of valuables on the bus between the airport and the city centre, or taken in by bogus 'refugees', 'plain-clothes police' or 'students' on their first walkabout. Nairobi's criminal element has an uncanny knack of picking out new arrivals and you'll help their cause greatly if you wander around looking lost, wear a giveaway daypack or external money-belt, or pay any attention to anybody who approaches you in the street. I personally think that the best approach for those who fly into Nairobi, assuming that their flight arrives before mid-afternoon, is to take a taxi straight to the bus station and hop on to the first vehicle to somewhere like Naivasha.

Nairobi aside, the only part of Kenya where tourists are regularly targeted by criminals is along the coast, particularly around Mombasa and Malindi. In other parts of the country, the usual light fingers are to be found in bus stations and markets, but a modicum of commonsense and luck should see you through safely.

Entrance fees

Entrance fees to national parks and reserves are very high. Amboseli, Aberdares, Lake Nakuru, Samburu, Buffalo Springs, Shaba and Maasai Mara charge US$27 per 24 hours. Tsavo East and West charge US$23 per 24 hours, while Meru, Nairobi and Shimba Hills charge US$20 per 24 hours. More affordable at US$10 per 24 hours are Mount Kenya and Mount Elgon, reserves that are of interest mostly to hikers. All marine national parks levy a fee of US$5 per 24 hours. All other national parks charge US$15 per 24 hours. The rationale behind these different rates is that they encourage tourists to visit less publicised, cheaper parks. Frankly, US$15 per 24 hours still is a lot for low-key national parks such as Saiwa Swamps, Lake Bogoria and Hell's Gate, especially when you add on the US$8 daily camping fee. If these reserves are so little visited, then surely everybody would benefit were a one-off fee to be charged, allowing visitors to stay as long as they like?

It's worth emphasising that many beautiful parts of Kenya charge a nominal entrance fee or no fee at all – Lakes Naivasha, Baringo, Turkana and Victoria leap to mind, as do the Cherangani Hills, Olorgasailie, Gedi Ruins and Kakamega and Arabuko-Sokoke Forests.

Entry requirements

Visas are not generally required by nationals of Commonwealth and European Union countries, but there are several noteworthy exceptions (Britons, New Zealanders and Australians, for instance, do require visas) so check your status in advance. Visas can be bought in advance at any Kenyan Embassy or High Commission, or if you don't mind queueing after a long flight you can simply buy one for US$20 at Jomo Kenyatta Airport on arrival. All visitors are issued with a free visitor's pass when they enter Kenya, normally valid for up to three months on request and easily extended for up to six months once you're in the country. You are unlikely ever to experience problems regarding onward tickets or funds if you enter Kenya by a land border. If you arrive by air without an onward ticket, you may be put through the paces but it's extremely unlikely that you'll be refused entry, especially if you look reasonably smart and have a substantial sum of money or a credit card on your person.

Flying there

Nairobi's Jomo Kenyatta Airport is the most popular point of entry for backpackers travelling between eastern and southern Africa. Most major European airlines fly to Nairobi – for further details see *Getting there* in Chapter 2. If you fly to Nairobi, do not under any circumstances use public transport from the airport to the city centre – you will almost certainly be robbed. Catch a taxi directly to whichever hotel you want to stay at.

Food and drink

Local restaurants serve the usual bland fare accompanied by *ugali* (maize porridge), lumpy rice or *chapati*. A feature of Kenya's larger towns is the excellent Indian restaurants, many of which serve good vegetarian dishes. Those who cook for themselves will find that fruit and vegetables are generally very cheap, and that most markets have a good selection of pulses and spices. Fresh bread and a decent cup of coffee are scarce commodities in Kenya. Local lagers are inexpensive and good. Tap water in Kenya is not generally good to drink, but mineral water is widely available.

Getting around
By road
Kenya's roads are serviced by a chaotic array of buses and *matatus*. The *Nation* newspaper reports a fatal *matatu* accident practically on a daily basis so, if getting home alive features high on your list of priorities, stick to buses where possible. KBS Stagecoach and the Akamba Bus Company are recommended and seats on these are generally best booked a day in advance. Hopping between towns, especially to the west of Nairobi, you'll probably have to use *matatus* from time to time. Nissan minibuses are the fastest and least crowded form of *matatu* while converted pick-up trucks are a complete nightmare.

Hitching is quite easy on main roads, but remember that many local drivers routinely pick up passengers and expect payment for a lift. The psycho-type dangers associated with hitching in the West aren't a real cause for concern – certainly not by comparison with the far greater risk of being involved in a *matatu* smash or catching a lift with a drunk.

By rail
Kenya's trains are relatively expensive, but where they exist they form a safe and comfortable alternative to road transport. The most popular rail trip, highly recommended if you can afford it, is the overnight run from Nairobi to Mombasa. This costs around US$50/35/6 first/second/third class. As with all other trains in Kenya, first class is a two-berth cabin, second class is a four-berth cabin, and third class is free-for-all bunks that make no concessions to comfort or the safety of your possessions. First- and second-class ticket prices include bedding and all meals. It's advisable to book two to three days ahead, although in my experience persistence will reward you with a last-minute ticket. There are also overnight trains from Nairobi to Kisumu, Eldoret and Malaba in Western Kenya. The train between Nairobi and Kampala is covered in Chapter 6.

By ferry
The limited ferry services out of Kisumu on Lake Victoria are infrequently used by travellers, but offer some interesting off-the-beaten-track options.

By air
The only internal flights likely to be of interest to backpackers are those connecting Lamu to Malindi, Mombasa or Nairobi, since the road from Malindi to Lamu has become unsafe in recent years. The cheapest place from which to fly to Lamu is Malindi, and it's easy enough to organise a flight at short notice.

Health
The health risks attached to travelling in Kenya are similar to those in neighbouring countries. Malaria is most prevalent on the coast and to a lesser degree in the Rift Valley and Lake Victoria region. Nairobi should be free of malaria as a result of its high altitude, but infected mosquitoes do find their way there on public transport.

Maps
A selection of commercially produced maps of Kenya and its most important game reserves and hiking areas can be bought in most bookshops in Nairobi.

Money
The Kenya shilling has dropped drastically in value since the mid-1980s, but over recent years it has hovered at around US$1=Ksh 70–75. Banking hours are 09.00 to

14.00 Monday to Friday and 09.00 to 11.00 on the first and last Saturday of the month. Private forex bureaux keep normal shopping hours during the week. In an emergency, you can change money at any time of day at Nairobi's Jomo Kenyatta Airport. Except at borders, there has never been a notable black market in Kenya, for which reason travellers who arrive overland are strongly advised to change enough money to see them through to a town before they leave the border. In cities, anybody who approaches you hissing 'Change money?' is a con artist (in Nairobi you'll hear some amazing litanies of dodgy services – 'Change money? Safari? Cocaine?').

It is easy to keep down day-to-day costs in Kenya, especially if you camp and cook for yourself at places like Tiwi Beach, the Rift Valley lakes, and Kakamega Forest. Even by staying in cheap local lodges and eating in local restaurants you could still keep ordinary expenses to under US$10 per day in many parts of the country. Nairobi, on the other hand, tends to be expensive, as are visits to national parks and reserves.

In most large towns, Kenya shillings can be drawn using a Visa card at any ATM attached to a Barclays or Standard Bank. This is a straightforward procedure, and should work out more favourably than exchanging hard currency or travellers' cheques at a bank (though you will be charged the same commission you would be charged by Visa for a credit card withdrawal anywhere in the world). Suitable ATMs are dotted around Nairobi and Mombasa, and they can also be found in Nyeri, Diani Beach, Kisumu, Nakuru, Malindi and Voi. Avoid using ATMs after dark, when there is a small but real risk of being observed by aspiring muggers.

Post, telephone and internet

Post out of Kenya is cheap and reasonably reliable. Poste restante can be collected in all large towns, and Nairobi is the most popular post collection point in East Africa. The best place from which to make international phone calls is Nairobi. The international dialling code into Kenya is +254. Area codes include Nairobi (02), Kisumu (035), Malindi (0123), Mombasa (011) and Nakuru (037).

Internet cafés are scattered all around Nairobi, and there are also a few in central Mombasa, Nakuru and Diani Beach. Elsewhere, even in large towns such as Nyeri, no internet facilities exist. Erratic lines and power failures combine with slow servers to make internet use in Kenya very slow, and prices are triple what you would pay in neighbouring Tanzania.

Public holidays

In addition to the Easter weekend, the following public holidays are officially recognised in Kenya:

1 January	New Year's Day	20 October	Kenyatta Day
1 May	Labour Day	12 December	Independence Day
1 June	Madaraka Day	25 December	Christmas Day
10 October	Moi Day	26 December	Boxing Day

On the coast in particular, the 30-day Islamic fast of Ramadan is widely observed, to the extent that most restaurants not catering specifically to tourists are closed until the evening during this period. Ramadan falls on different dates every year, because the Islamic calender is only 354 days long: in 2001 it will fall over mid-November to mid-December, dropping back 11 days on each successive year. Other Islamic holidays are observed on the coast, but they won't generally affect travellers.

Tourist information offices

There is no tourist office in Nairobi and the one in Mombasa isn't up to much.

Nairobi and surrounds
NAIROBI

Kenya's cosmopolitan capital city is in several respects East Africa's answer to Johannesburg. Both cities are economic and social hubs with a sphere of influence that extends far beyond national boundaries to meet, almost tangibly, at the distant border of Tanzania and Zambia. Like Johannesburg, Nairobi is little more than a century old: it has a somewhat rootless feel, the combination perhaps of a compressed sense of history and a rather improbable setting (in Nairobi's case, this is not due to any great mineral wealth but to its midway position on the railway line between Uganda and the coast). From a backpacker's perspective, the two cities in question have long been the main entry points into the region, but – despite sharing a pleasant high altitude climate – neither boasts much in the way of tourist attractions and they vie with each other for the dubious status of sub-equatorial Africa's crime capital.

Nairobi is a study in contrasts. The part of the city centre to the southwest of Tom Mboya Street contains what must be the largest concentration of high-rise buildings in East Africa, and its smart, cosmopolitan, even Westernised feel is underscored by a surprising number of posh hotels, restaurants, boutiques and safari operators. Cross Tom Mboya Street, however, and you're confronted by the altogether more chaotic underworld of the River Road district, a degraded equatorial Soho that may exude squalor and dirt and noise and lawlessness, but is also distinctly, vibrantly, even buoyantly African in character. Similarly, suburban Nairobi ranges from the transatlantic shopping mall nirvana of Westland and the wild, forested gardens of Karen to corrugated-iron shanty towns that rank among the largest and poorest on the continent. Most remarkable of all, only a few kilometres from the city centre, Nairobi National Park extends unfenced in one direction on to the vast, animal-rich Athi Plains while in the other direction offering the timeless sight of a lion or a cheetah or even a rhino pacing the savannah, but with a most anomalous backdrop supplied by East Africa's tallest skyscrapers.

Nairobi can be an overwhelming introduction to East Africa. Few travellers spend much longer there than they have to, and I can think of no convincing reason why any backpackers should prolong their first encounter. It is undeniable that a high proportion of newcomers – whether overseas visitors or rural East Africans – fall prey to the city's almost Dickensian cast of pickpockets, muggers, 'refugees', slimeballs and con artists. And even those backpackers who escape the attention of Nairobi's criminal classes will have to contend with the persistent plague of safari touts and curio-sellers who prowl the city centre. This aspect of Nairobi is enough to reduce the most phlegmatic soul to a paranoid wreck, and anybody whose first night in Africa is spent trying to sleep in one of the countless budget hotels that line the backstreets around River Road is likely to start the next day with their most romantic expectations severely dashed.

Once you get to know Nairobi, however, it is not all bad – on the contrary, it is one of my favourite African cities. The point is not that backpackers should avoid Kenya's capital, rather that they might do well to delay a prolonged period of exposure until such time as they have acquired something of a tan, picked up a few Swahili phrases, put a couple of travel highlights behind them, and generally adapted to the mood of East Africa. Once you are tuned in, Nairobi's curio-sellers and safari touts can easily be deflected with a touch of humour, and even the risk of being mugged or pickpocketed can be minimised by a bit of good judgement and common sense, faculties that tend to be cast adrift or difficult to apply on first exposure to another culture. What tends to come to the fore then is the cavalier good humour and

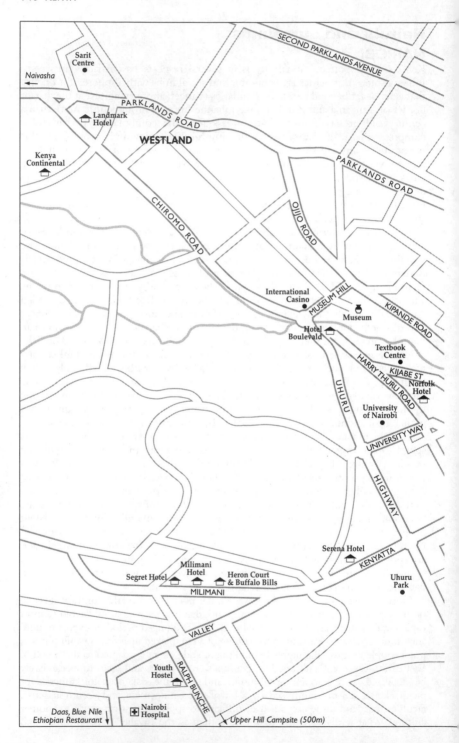

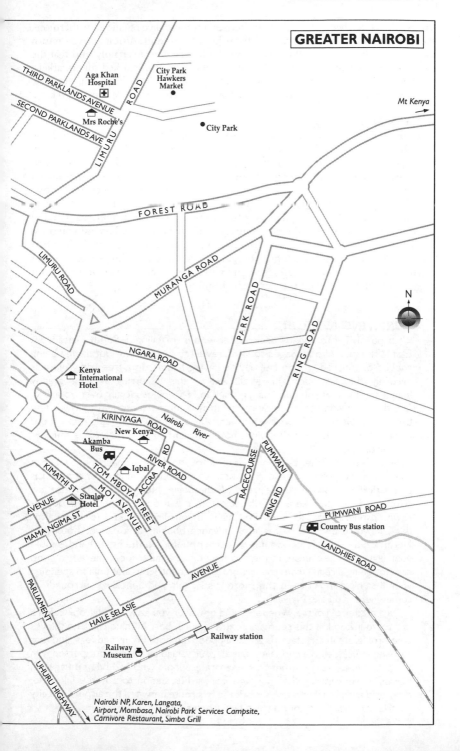

GREATER NAIROBI

Aga Khan Hospital

City Park Hawkers Market

Mt Kenya

THIRD PARKLANDS AVENUE

LIMURU ROAD

City Park

SECOND PARKLANDS AVE

Mrs Roche's

LIMURU ROAD

FOREST ROAD

MURANGA ROAD

PARK ROAD

N

RING ROAD

NGARA ROAD

Kenya International Hotel

KIRINYAGA ROAD

Nairobi River

New Kenya

Akamba Bus

RIVER RD

Iqbal

ACCRA RD

RIVER ROAD

RACECOURSE

PUMWANI

RING RD

KIMATHI ST

TOM MBOYA STREET

MOI AVENUE

Stanley Hotel

AVENUE

MAMA NGIMA ST

PUMWANI ROAD

Country Bus station

LANDHIES ROAD

PARLIAMENT

AVENUE

HAILE SELASIE

Railway station

Railway Museum

UHURU HIGHWAY

Nairobi NP, Karen, Langata,
Airport, Mombasa, Nairobi Park Services Campsite,
Carnivore Restaurant, Simba Grill

irresistibly relaxed hedonism that characterises this most alive of cities. Furthermore, those who come to Nairobi overland from Europe or South Africa, or even return there from a dusty safari or Mount Kenya climb, will almost certainly find that the glitter – the excellent restaurants, ubiquitous cold beers, well-stocked supermarkets, the bookshops and cinemas – outweighs the squalor. Nairobi is a great city. The message? Get out just as quickly as you can after you arrive in Africa. But do go back.

Access and getting around

The Jomo Kenyatta International Airport is situated 15km out of town off the Mombasa road. There is a municipal bus service between the airport and city centre, the number 34, but you run a high risk of being distracted and then robbed if you use it. There is also a regular shuttle bus, but it isn't much cheaper than a taxi (in fact, at around US$7 per person, it will probably be more expensive for two people) and it will drop you at the Barclays Plaza, a long way from any budget accommodation. The best option is quite simply to get a taxi: metered London taxis cost around US$15 to the city centre, unmetered taxis a bit less but you must negotiate the fare in advance. Once the haggling is over, you'll generally find that Nairobi taxi drivers are an obliging bunch – if you intend to bus straight out of town, they'll know where to take you and will probably ensure that you and your luggage are safely placed on the next vehicle going.

SURVIVING NAIROBI

It's probably fair to say any backpacker who is travelling to South Africa from East Africa and who manages to say farewell to Nairobi without having been robbed or mugged will be halfway to having had a crime-free trip. And it is certainly the case that the likelihood of this occurring will be greatly influenced by how you conduct yourself in Nairobi, especially over your first few days. Provided that you apply a bit of common sense and follow a few basic rules, Nairobi is probably not nearly as dangerous as people make it out to be. Throw caution to the wind, however, and you are sure to be mugged sooner or later.

Whatever the merits and demerits of downtown Nairobi, I cannot overstress the point that the right time to go about seeing it for yourself is emphatically not when you're fresh off the plane. New arrivals to Africa are strongly advised to take a taxi directly from the airport to one of the out-of-town hostels, at least for their first night. If your flight is likely to arrive after dark, it would be wise to make an advance booking at a proper hotel (the Heron Court Hotel is a good, inexpensive option). On the other hand, should your flight land at Nairobi in the morning or early afternoon, there is a good case for going directly from the airport to the country bus station and spending your first night in Africa in the more rustic, safe and appealing surrounds of somewhere like Lake Naivasha.

As a matter of course, whenever and however you arrive in Nairobi, catch a taxi to your hotel. If this seems an extravagance, bear in mind that the thieves who proliferate in bus stations are equipped with both brains and legs, and that carrying a rucksack is a sure sign that all your valuables are on your person. On a recent trip to Kenya, I met three separate people who had been mugged in Nairobi while carrying their luggage from a bus station to a hotel. Likewise, pickpockets and snatch thieves work the bus route between the airport and city centre, and they'll pick out a fresh face like a shot.

If you want to catch a bus to destinations within 100km or so of Nairobi, the best place to head for is the Country Bus Station about 1km from the city centre on Landhies Road, where buses leave to just about everywhere on a fill-up-and-go basis. For destinations further afield, the **Akamba Bus Line** is very reliable and it has the most extensive network of services, most of which have fixed departure times and leave from in front of their centrally located office on Lagos Road. A number of other reliable bus operators have offices near the junction of River and Accra Roads, about 300m from the Akamba office. Minibuses and *matatus* to various parts of the country all leave from different spots. In general, it's advisable to check where vehicles to your next destination leave from the afternoon before you go, so that you don't wander around looking lost with your luggage. Better still, a taxi within the city centre won't cost more than US$2–3, and the drivers, again, will often take care of you beyond the call of duty. The main concentrations of taxis are found outside the Sixeighty, Norfolk, New Stanley and Hilton Hotels, as well as at the airport and most bus stations. Taxis also hang around outside the railway station, which is situated at the southeastern end of Moi Avenue, a good ten-minute walk from most of the budget hotels.

Numbered buses and *matatus* cover every conceivable route in Nairobi. The driving is as lunatic as you'd expect, at least in intent, but fortunately the ponderous traffic means that bumps and dings are more likely than serious accidents. What

While such things are difficult to quantify, anecdotal evidence suggests that the worst area for muggers and pickpockets is the triangle of streets between Moi Avenue and River Road. Many budget travellers are drawn to this area for the cheap accommodation and earthy atmosphere, and a high proportion get mugged. Walking around this area after dark verges on asking for trouble, certainly until you've settled into East Africa and have acquired some judgment about what is and isn't safe, and you would have to be crazy to go out with more money than you need to buy a meal and a few drinks. Your best security in this area is probably not to walk around alone – muggers are most unlikely to attack a group of three or more people, and it should be easy enough to find other backpackers who want to accompany you to a restaurant or bar.

There are plenty of con artists in Nairobi, most blatantly the money changers who work the area around the New Stanley Hotel and the many 'refugees' and 'students' from whichever nearby country is currently most newsworthy. Avoid getting into discussions with these guys. A more underhand genre of trick involves bogus policemen offering you the option of arrest or a large fine. In any situation like this, demand to be taken to a police station to sort it out – but not via a quiet alley. In fact, much as I hate to encourage distrust, Nairobi is one place in East Africa where there is cause to be suspicious of anyone who approaches you on the street – and remember that a successful con artist must appear to be trustworthy, so you should perhaps be more wary of a smooth-talker in a business suit than a drunk in rags.

Finally, bear in mind that looking like a tourist will mark you out as a target for crime. You'll be hassled less if you're mistaken for an expatriate, something that's more likely to happen if you are not dressed in shorts and a T-shirt, you don't wander around with a daypack or external money-belt, and you can deflect hawkers with Swahili rejoinders such as *sitaki* (I don't want) and respond to the 'tourist greeting' of *Jambo* with a more correct one (see *Appendix 2*).

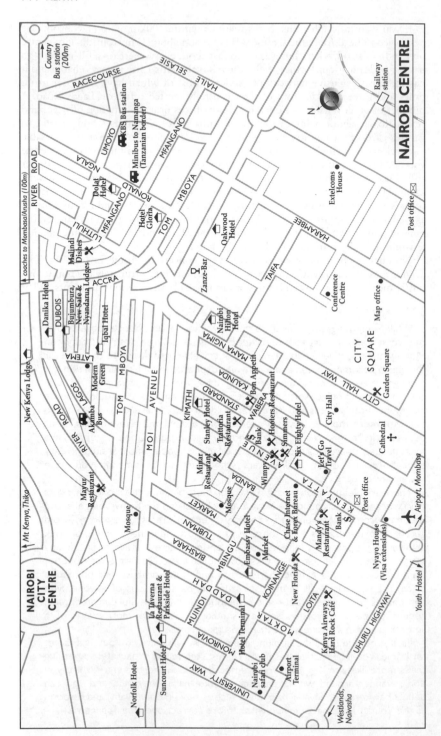

NAIROBI CENTRE

Country Bus station (200m)

RACECOURSE

HAILE SELASIE

Railway station

N

KBS Bus station

Minibus to Namanga (Tanzanian border)

UMOYO

NGALA

RONALD

MFANGANO

MBOYA

Extelcoms House

RIVER ROAD

Dolat Hotel

MFANGANO

TOM

Oakwood Hotel

coaches to Mombasa/Arusha (100m)

LUTHULI

Hotel Gloria

HARAMBEE

Post office

Malindi Dishes

ACCRA

Danika Hotel

DUBOIS

Bujumbura, New Safe & Nyandarua Lodges

Iqbal Hotel

LATEMA

Modern Green

MBOYA

TOM

AVENUE

Zanze-Bar

TAIFA

Conference Centre

Map office

Nairobi Hilton Hotel

MAMA NGIMA

KAUNDA

Bon Appetit

CITY SQUARE

Garden Square

New Kenya Lodge

RIVER ROAD

LAGOS

Akamba Bus

KIMATHI

STANDARD

Stanley Hotel

Trattoria Restaurant

WABERA

Hooters Restaurant

Bank

Simmers

Six Eighty Hotel

City Hall

CITY HALL WAY

Cathedral

MOI

TOM

Mayur Restaurant

Minar Restaurant

BANDA

Wimpy

VENUE

Let's Go Travel

KENYATTA

Mosque

Mosque

MARKET

TUBMAN

Chase Internet & Forex Bureau

Mandy's Restaurant

Post office

Bank

Nyayo House (Visa extensions)

Airport, Mombasa

BIASHARA

Embassy Hotel

Market

MBINGU

New Florida

KOINANGE

LOITA

NAIROBI CITY CENTRE

Mt Kenya, Thika

La Taverna Restaurant & Parkside Hotel

MUINDI

DADDAH

Hotel Terminal

MONROVIA

MOKTAR

Kenya Airways, Hard Rock Café

UHURU HIGHWAY

Norfolk Hotel

Suncourt Hotel

Nairobi safari club

Airport Terminal

UNIVERSITY WAY

Youth Hostel

Westlands, Naivasha

SIGHTSEEING IN AND AROUND NAIROBI

One of the few places in Nairobi that's definitely worth a visit is the **National Museum**, which has a good prehistory section including reproductions of rock art from Tanzania, a fairly unremarkable natural history section, and good ethnographic displays. The Lamu Gallery covers 1,000 years of coastal history. The adjoining snake park and aquarium outside are utterly missable. The **Railway Museum**, ten minutes' walk from the Railway Station, has displays relating to the building of the Uganda Railway in the late nineteenth century.

Emphatically worth visiting, the 117km² **Nairobi National Park** may lie a mere 7km from the city centre but it's no more artificial than any other game reserve. The park is fenced only on the city-facing perimeter, so wildlife moves freely across the other boundaries to the adjacent Athi Plains. Almost every species of plains animal apart from elephant is found here, more than 400 bird species have been recorded, and it is rated the best park in the country for seeing lion kills and black rhinoceros. The main entrance to the park, the Kenya Wildlife Services headquarters on Langata Road, can be reached on a number 24 or any other bus heading from the KBS terminal to Langata, and hitching is feasible, particularly at weekends. Alternatively, half-day tours cost around US$40–50, or you could think about hiring a car for a day – an inexpensive safari for a group.

Continuing out of town towards Langata and Karen is a cluster of rather more artificial attractions, often lumped together as an afternoon tour by Nairobi safari companies, but easy enough to get to by the number 24 bus. The **Bomas of Kenya** is packaged ethnic authenticity: a collection of traditional huts representing the building styles of most of Kenya's main ethnic groups, boosted by dancing extravaganzas every afternoon. The **Langata Giraffe Centre** is a breeding centre for the rare Rothschild's giraffe, which visitors can feed by hand. And there is, of course, the **Karen Blixen Museum**, the former dwelling of the Danish Baroness and author Karen Blixen, restored and furnished in period style during the shooting of *that* film. Self-evidently a must for *Out of Africa* cultists, but the unconverted might be more amused by the coffee shop, restaurant and rather good nature trail through the immaculate grounds.

The **Ngong Hills** south of the city centre support substantial areas of forest, large mammals including buffalo, bushbuck and leopard, and a good variety of birds. The highest peaks (2,459m) offer great views back to Nairobi and across the Rift Valley. Sadly, mugging has become a serious problem in the area and what used to be a popular unescorted day walk can no longer be considered safe. The good news is that the police station in Ngong village will generally provide an armed escort for walkers – take a bus number 111 or 126 to Ngong.

you should be concerned about, and in direct proportion to the value and conspicuousness of the possessions on your person, is pickpockets and snatch thieves. If you're only carrying a smallish sum of local currency, safely tucked away somewhere, then buses and *matatus* are a cheap, efficient and recommended way of getting around. When you're weighed down with a heavy rucksack and carrying all your cash and your passport, I'd stick to taxis.

Where to stay
Out of town
Heron Court Hotel Milimani Rd; tel: 72-0740/3; fax: 71-1698. Comfortable and reasonably priced mid-range accommodation. Swimming pool, sauna, laundry, restaurant and bar. Self-catering flatlets **E**/**F**.

Ma Roche's Third Parklands Ave. Legendary overlanders' haunt in a private garden in the suburb of Parklands, known for its relaxed if somewhat time-warped atmosphere. To get there, take a *matatu* to Aga Khan Hospital from Latema Road (in front of the Iqbal Hotel). When rooms are full, you'll be allowed to crash on the balcony. Use of kitchen but no restaurant – the staff will point you to a few local bars and restaurants. Theft from tents and rooms has become a problem in recent years. Dorm **B** pp. Camp **A** pp.

Nairobi Park Services Campsite Tel: 890325; email: shling@net2000ke.com or allk@form-net.com. Situated along the Magadi Road 2km past the junction with Langata Road, this excellent campsite runs along similar lines to the backpacker hostels of southern Africa. Facilities include two bars, a restaurant, hot showers, internet and email, pool table, satellite TV and a variety of day trips out of Nairobi. Access from the city centre on a number 125 *matatu* or 126 Stagecoach bus. Camping and dorm accommodation both in the **B** range.

Nairobi Youth Hostel Ralph Bunche Rd; tel: 72-3012. Once a claustrophobic one-storey compound, the rebuilt youth hostel now straddles three floors. Lockers, kitchen, hot showers, luggage storage. No alcohol. Near shopping mall and banks. Regular *matatus* between Kenyatta Av in the city centre and Ralph Bunche Rd. Inexpensive meals and cold beer around the corner at Silver Springs Hotel. Dorm **C** pp.

Upper Hill Campsite Off Hospital Rd, 1km from the youth hostel; tel: 72-3788. Popular with overland trucks. Very secure. Restaurant, bar, hot showers. To get there, take any bus from Kenyatta Av heading to Nairobi Hospital and get off at the junction of Ngong and Hospital Roads. Rooms from **D**. Dorm **B** pp. Camp **A** pp. Tents for hire.

Wildlife Clubs of Kenya Hostel Langata Rd; tel: 89-1904. On bus route 24, about 1km past entrance to Nairobi National Park. Dorm **C** pp.

City centre
Danika Lodge Dubois Street. Friendly, safe and comfortable guesthouse with reliable hot water. S/c room **D** dbl.

Dolat Hotel A reliable favourite for many years. Clean s/c rooms with a constant supply of hot water **C**/**D**.

Embassy Hotel Tubman Rd; tel: 22-4087. A good bet if you arrive at the Terminal to find it's full. Rooms **E** s/c dbl.

Hotel Terminal Moktar Daddah St; tel: 22-8817. Very central and good value, though noisy on Sunday nights when there is live music downstairs. This has been my Nairobi standby for years. Large, clean s/c rooms with net and hot showers **D**/**E**.

Hotel Gloria Cnr Ronald Ngala and Tom Mboya Rd; tel: 22-8916. Around the corner from the Dolat, this is another well established haunt of budget travellers. Noisy area but good, clean s/c rooms with hot showers. If it's full, try the slightly cheaper Terrace Hotel a couple of doors up on Ronald Ngala Rd **D**/**E**.

Iqbal Hotel Latema Rd; tel: 22-0914. A long-standing favourite with backpackers: clean, convenient and secure, with good facilities such as cheap laundry, baggage storage and hot showers. Avoid the noisy rooms facing the street. Expect to put your name on a waiting list for a day or two. Rooms **B**/**C**.

New Kenya Lodge Cnr River and Latema Rd; tel: 22-2202. Another popular backpackers' haunt, but decidedly more downmarket than the Iqbal. Security can be a problem. Rooms **B**/**C**.

Where to eat

Blue Nile Ethiopian Restaurant Argwings Kodhek Rd. Out of town, 1km from the youth hostel. A must if you've yet to try Africa's most distinctive cuisine – the *secondo misto* (a bit of everything) is a safe bet and good value at around US$3.

Bon Appetit Cnr Kaunda and Wabera. The curries and grills are nothing exceptional in culinary terms but the portions are large and it's cheap even by Nairobi's standards.

Carnivore A visit to Nairobi's most famous restaurant, 5km along Langata Road, is a popular way of tailing off a safari. The main draw is the all-you-can-eat game meat buffet, which costs US$15. Surprisingly the non-meat dishes have received a thumbs-up from several vegetarians I've spoken to. More moderately priced food and a cosmopolitan disco are to be found at the Simba Grill next door. Plenty of taxis hang about outside.

Daas Restaurant Out of town (you need a taxi). Good Ethiopian restaurant in a private house. The prices will seem absurd if you've just come from Ethiopia. Great dancing, though.

Hooters Standard St. New, very trendy eatery serving slightly overpriced sandwiches, burgers, etc. The upstairs bar and pool tables are a greater attraction than the food.

La Scala Restaurant Standard St. Meat, pizza and pasta for comfortably under US$5 per main course. Recommended.

La Taverna (formerly the Curry Pot) Monrovia St. Despite the name, essentially a downmarket Indian restaurant, serving tasty, filling and inexpensive curries and grills. Busiest over lunch. Popular with locals and travellers alike.

Lord Delamere Terrace In the Norfolk Hotel, Moi Av. Worth visiting as much for the swanky atmosphere as the food. That said, the pizzas are as good as you'll get in Nairobi, and they're surprisingly moderately priced. Draught beer on tap.

Malindi Dishes Gaberone Rd. Long-standing source of good, cheap Swahili cooking. Meals in US$2–3 range.

Mandy's Koinange Rd. Central and incredibly popular with local office workers, this place dishes up large plates of curry and stew at very affordable prices.

Mayur Restaurant Supreme Hotel, Keekorok Rd. Superb Indian vegetarian buffet, US$3.

Minar Restaurant Banda St. Varied Indian menu, consistently good food and generous portions over several visits the last decade. Not cheap, but nor is it dauntingly expensive.

Pesara Sandwich Market Lonhro House, Standard St. The best coffee in central Nairobi, wholewheat sandwiches and good salads.

Steak House Ltd Chester House, Koinange St. The 1.2kg T-bones are likely to set alight the eyes of any hardened carnivore.

Thorn Tree Café Stanley Hotel. Popular central meeting point, and a good place to stop for cake and coffee, but the meals are overpriced and the service tardy.

Trattoria Standard St. Very popular Italian restaurant, with a varied menu and excellent food at ever-escalating but still not unreasonable prices.

Wimpy Kenyatta Av. Exactly as you'd expect, but with extra grease! Cheap burgers and French fries.

Bars and clubs

Bombax Club About 3km out of town on Ngong Rd; tel: 56-5691. Good live music, easy to get to by bus, though you'll want to get a taxi home.

Buffalo Bill's Heron Court Hotel, Milimani Rd. Tacky beyond belief, this is an unabashed pick-up joint, close to the youth hostel. You probably don't want to miss it, but are advised not to brave it alone – even though there are usually plenty of other tourists. The open-air bar is relatively sedate.

Florida 2000 Moi Av. Loud and brash, though some relief from the sound system can be found at an open-air bar and restaurant behind the dance floor.

Garden Square Restaurant City Hall Way. A popular central venue with live music at weekends.

Hard Rock Café Barclays Plaza, Loita St. As you'd expect. Most people agree it's worth a visit.

Modern Green Day and Night Club Latema Rd. One of several bleary dives in the River Road area, this place has acquired a slightly self-perpetuating reputation as a 'must-visit' with budget travellers. A friendly, boozy, frantic and arguably rather voyeuristic experience.

New Florida Koinange St. Even louder and sleazier than its sister club the Florida 2000. Great for a reggae mind-blast perhaps, but conversation is impossible.

Simba Grill Next to the Carnivore Restaurant. Loud and lively venue attracting a mixed crowd of well-to-do locals, expatriates and tourists. Live music once in a while but mostly a disco. Plenty of taxis waiting outside when you want to leave.

Simmers Opposite the Six Eighty Hotel, this new open-air cluster of bars and cheap eateries has a bustling atmosphere throughout the week and gets seriously crowded on Friday night. Cheap draught or bottled beer, *nyama choma* (grilled meat), take-away kiosks, pool tables and lots of lively conversation.

Six Eighty Hotel Kenyatta Av. The rooftop bar of this upmarket hotel lacks atmosphere, but it's pleasant enough and remains one of the few places for a drink in the city centre that's free of both cover charges and hassle. Pool table.

Zanze-Bar Moi Av. Lively, noisy, central place for cheap food, cold beers and as often as not live music.

Practical listings

Airlines Aeroflot (22-0746); Air France (21-6954); Air India (33-4788); Air Madagascar (22-5286); Air Malawi (33-3683); Air Tanzania (21-4936); Air Zimbabwe (33-9524); Alitalia (22-4361); British Airways (33-4362); EgyptAir (22-6821); El Al (22-8123); Ethiopian Airlines (33-0387); Gulf Air (82-2934); Kenya Airways (21-0771); KLM (33-2637); Lufthansa (22-6271); Olympic (33-8026); Qantas (21-3221); Sabena (22-2185); South African Airways (22-9663); Swissair (25-0288); Uganda Airlines (22-1354).

Books, newspapers and maps A good selection of novels is available from the two bookshops on the corner of Kimathi and Kenyatta Avenue, which also stock a good range of field guides, travel guides to Kenya and neighbouring countries, and maps of the more popular game reserves and mountains. Street vendors along Kimathi Road sell foreign newspapers. The Public Map Office will only sell survey sheets with written authority from the Survey of Kenya office, which can be an involved and lengthy process.

Curio shopping The largest concentration of curio kiosks is around the city market; take your time, bargain, and you can get curios here very inexpensively. The Maasai Market every Tuesday on the corner of Uhuru Highway and Kenyatta Avenue is recommended.

Embassies Australia (44-5034); Belgium (74-1567); Burundi (21-8458); Canada (21-4804); Congo (22-9771); Denmark (33-1088); Egypt (21-1560); Ethiopia (72-3027); France (33-9978); Germany (71-2527); Ireland (22-6771); Israel (72-4021); Japan (33-2955); Madagascar (22-6494); Malawi (44-0569); Netherlands (58-1125); New Zealand (72-2467); Rwanda (33-4341); South Africa (21-5616); Spain (33-5711); Sweden (22-9042); Switzerland (21-5616); Tanzania (33-7618); Uganda (33-0801); United Kingdom (33-5944); USA (33-4141); Zambia (72-4796); Zimbabwe (72-1049).

Foreign exchange There are banks dotted all over the city centre. Larger branches are open from 09.00 to 16.00 on weekdays, and the main branch of Barclays on Kenyatta Avenue is open from 09.00 to 13.00 on Saturday. There is no black market worth talking about in Nairobi, and you can take it that anybody who approaches you to change money is a crook. The only place where you can reliably exchange money outside banking hours is the 24-hour foreign exchange counter at Jomo Kenyatta Airport – you could ask at tourist class hotels but they'll generally only change money for hotel residents. For better rates and faster service than the banks, visit any of several Forex Bureau dotted around the city centre and suburban malls. Not all will take travellers' cheques. Recommended is the Chase Forex Bureau on Kenyatta Avenue – it's efficient, free of lurking eyes, offers top rates, and travellers' cheques are accepted at no commission.

International phone and fax These can be made with an acceptable degree of success from Extelcomms House on Haile Selasie Avenue or more expensively but with less fuss at any tourist class hotel.

Internet There are dozens of internet cafés dotted around the town centre and in the Westlands area, though rates are uniformly high (typically around US$2 for 15 minutes' access) and servers are generally very sluggish. The Chase Internet Café on Kenyatta Avenue is probably the best, with plenty of terminals and an above average chance of seeing a bit of on-screen motion.

Medical For blood tests, visit the Nairobi Laboratories in Pioneer House on Moi Avenue. The Nairobi Hospital on Argwings Kodhek Road (tel: 72-2160) is regarded as the best in the city. Well stocked pharmacies are dotted all over the city centre.

Post restante This should be collected at the main post office on Haile Selassie Avenue.

Safari companies Nairobi is the best place for organising safaris to Kenya's popular game reserves. The following companies are reputable and geared towards hikers and backpackers: *Gametrackers* Kenya Cinema Plaza, Moi Ave; tel: 33-8927; fax: 33-0903; email: game@africaonline.com; web: www.gametrackers.com. Established and reliable camping safaris plus camel-trekking, cycling trips, climbing on Mt Kenya and the Aberdares. Their eight-day trip up to Lake Turkana via Marsabit and the Chalbi Desert (see box *Turkana by overland truck*, page 179) is particularly recommended).
Hiking & Cycling Kenya Arrow House, Koinange St; tel: 21-8336; fax: 21-4212. As the name suggests, and very reasonably priced.
Kenia Safaris Jubilee Insurance Building, Kaunda St; tel: 22-3699; fax: 21-7671. Reliable, well-priced camping safaris on all the standard itineraries.
Let's Go Travel Caxton House, Standard St; tel: 34-0331; fax: 33-6890; email: info@letsgosafari.com; web: www.letsgosafari.com. A useful first stop for most requirements. Wide range of itineraries gives a good feel for current prices and options. Agency for dozens of operators and hotels, for Bike Treks (a good company specialising in bicycle trips), and offer their own reliable budget camping safaris.
Safari Camp Services Cnr Koinange and Moktar Daddah St; tel: 22-8936; fax: 21-2160. Best known for their seminal Turkana Bus, which has been running for close on two decades and remains good value. Their Wildlife Bus is also highly rated.
Savuka Safaris Pan-Africa Insurance Building, Kenyatta Ave; tel: 51-5256; fax: 21-5016. Recommended first port of call for standard itineraries. Daily departures on several routes, well-organised tented camp in the Maasai Mara, and rates that compete with anyone.
Tour Africa Safaris Cnr Kimathi and Mama Ngima St; tel: 33-6767. Good twice-daily tours to Nairobi National Park on the Big Simba bus.
Worldwide Adventure Ltd Nginyo House, cnr Koinange & Moktar Daddah St; tel: 21-0024; fax: 33-2407. In addition to the usual itineraries, specialises in Turkana trips and 14–35-day mountain gorilla safaris.
Yare Safaris Moi Av; tel: 21-4099; fax: 21-3445. Specialists in trekking in northern Kenya. Excellent seven-day camel safari in the Maralal district leaving from Nairobi Saturdays.

Visa and visitor's pass extensions These take anything from five minutes to a couple of hours at Nyayo House on the corner of Kenyatta Avenue and Uhuru Highway, depending on the length of the queue. A punctual 08.30 early arrival helps.

THE MAGADI ROAD

The one Rift Valley lake that makes no concessions to tourism is, oddly enough, the closest one to Nairobi. And in truth, the bizarre and inhospitable apparition known as **Lake Magadi** is not so much a lake as a sludge bed of blindingly white salt and soda deposits, commercially exploited since before World War I and host to large flocks of water birds including flamingoes. Magadi township is strictly a mining concern, and travellers are few and far between. As much an attraction as the lake itself is the road there which, almost as soon as you're out of Nairobi, descends into a harshly beautiful part of the Rift Valley where there are no settlements other than Maasai villages and large mammals such as giraffe still occur with some frequency.

In the middle of this austerity, **Olorgasailie Prehistoric Site** overlooks what was once a vast shallow lake, frequented by roving bands of the hunter-gatherer *Homo erectus*. Excavated by the Leakey family in the 1940s, Olorgasailie Gorge holds a wealth of stone-age tools which can be seen on a short guided trail along with a fossilised pachyderm leg bone that dwarfs the equivalent modern elephant one placed alongside it. Olorgasailie is also a wonderfully scenic spot, and the surrounding bush is rich in wildlife (there's a good chance of seeing giraffe, baboon, gerenuk and eland – the latter regularly stroll into the campsite after dark – and hearing the calls of hyenas, jackals and sometimes even lions at night) and dry country birds, notably the resident and very tame red-and-yellow barbets that punctuate the calm with their absurd, clockwork-like display and call. If you speak a bit of Swahili, Olorgasailie is an easy place to get chatting to the local Maasai (or at least those who also speak some Swahili), bearing in mind that, in a rural area like this, it would probably be foolish and certainly be rude to produce a camera without first feeling out the situation.

Access and getting around

Two Akamba buses cover the 94km surfaced road between Nairobi and Magadi daily, leaving Nairobi at 13.00 and 15.00 and returning at 06.00 the next day. Olorgasailie lies 1km from the Magadi Road, about 60km from Nairobi, and it's clearly signposted.

Where to stay and eat

Olorgasailie

Prehistoric Site Four basic double bandas with mattresses but no bedding. Firewood and drinking water. A limited range of foodstuffs as well as warm beers and sodas can be bought at Oltopesi village about 45 minutes' walk away, but you're advised to bring a stock of food with you. *Banda* (African hut) **C** dbl. Camp **A** pp. Entrance US$3pp. Rarely full, but it might be safer to book bandas through the National Museum in Nairobi (tel: 74-2161).

Magadi

Lower Guesthouse Only accommodation in town, opposite hospital. **C** dbl.

The safari circuit

Practically all budget safaris to Kenya's main game reserves run from Nairobi, and since few backpackers visit these reserves independently it seems sensible to break with the normal format of this book and cover these reserves together rather than in regional sections. Exceptions are **Nairobi National Park** (see page 145) and **Lake Nakuru National Park** (see page 180), the former because it is most often visited as a day trip from the capital and the latter – even though it follows Maasai Mara as the most common fixture on camping safari itineraries – because it is easy to visit as a day trip from nearby Nakuru town.

Most safaris start with at least two nights in the renowned **Maasai Mara National Reserve**, the 1,680km² northern extension of Tanzania's much larger Serengeti National Park. The gentle hills of the Maasai Mara are covered in open savannah, with patches of acacia woodland and riparian forest, and the reserve is best visited between late July and October when the famous wildebeest migration crosses the border from the Serengeti. That said, game viewing is good at any time of year: on a two-day visit you can be reasonably assured of seeing lion, cheetah, spotted hyena, black-backed jackal, elephant, hippo, Maasai giraffe, Burchell's zebra, buffalo, wildebeest, impala, Thomson's and Grant's gazelles, topi, Coke's hartebeest, bushbuck, waterbuck and Bohor reedbuck. The few black rhinos that survived the poaching onslaught of the 1980s are seen with surprising frequency. If you can only afford to visit one major African game reserve, then the Maasai Mara should probably be that one – even if the relatively small size and high tourist volume make it congested by comparison with the neighbouring Serengeti.

A common fixture on camping safari itineraries of five days or longer, **Samburu National Reserve** together with the adjoining Buffalo Springs and Shaba National Reserves forms a contiguous 844km² block on either side of the Uaso Nyiro River. Not the least of Samburu's attractions is the drive there, culminating in a spectacular descent from the grassy, rolling Mount Kenya foothills to the skeletal acacia scrub of Kenya's northern semi-desert. Samburu itself is a study in vegetational contrasts: the best roads follow the river, which means it's normal to have lush riparian forest to your one side and desert to the other. Samburu is the best place to see dry-country animals such as Grevy's zebra, reticulated giraffe, Beisa oryx, Rainey's gazelle, Guenther's dik-dik, gerenuk, eland, greater kudu and unstriped ground squirrel, while the riverine forest supports buffalo, lesser kudu, impala, waterbuck, bushbuck, warthog, hippo, elephant, baboon and vervet monkey. Cheetah and lion are the most frequently seen predators. Samburu has a remarkably varied bird life and it's the place to see dry country 'specials' such as the vulturine guineafowl, identified by its brilliant cobalt chest feathers. The reserve is still inhabited by Samburu people, pastoralists who diverged from the closely affiliated Maasai in the seventeenth century and who are frequently seen in their characteristic red blankets bringing their livestock to the river.

To the east of Mount Kenya, **Meru National Park** has never featured strongly on safari itineraries, and its popularity has waned since the late 1980s when poachers claimed not only its famous white rhino herd, but also the lives of several rangers, two tourists and the 83-year-old conservationist George Adamson. Meru has been safe to visit since 1990 and, should the first camping safaris start trickling back there during the lifespan of this edition, you're unlikely to regret joining one of them. Meru is characterised by lush green grassland, which makes the animals relatively difficult to locate, but they are there: large herds of elephant and buffalo, prides of 20 or more lion, Grevy's and Burchell's zebra, impala, Grant's gazelle, reticulated giraffe, Coke's hartebeest, lesser kudu, bushbuck, waterbuck, gerenuk, Beisa oryx and the usual range of large predators. With its wild and intimate landscapes, Meru boasts a meditative ambience enhanced by the lack of other tourists.

Lying on the Tanzanian border southeast of Nairobi, **Amboseli National Park** is epitomised by the classic picture of an elephant herd sweeping across a dusty plain below the snow-capped peak of Kilimanjaro. Unfortunately, Amboseli is rather dense with tourist minibuses, and its naturally bleak landscape has been seriously degraded by the high level of off-road driving. Scenically, Amboseli excels towards dusk, when the harsher aspects of the landscape are softened by a reddish glow filtered through the dust and a will-they, won't-they shroud of clouds offers tantalising glimpses of Kilimanjaro. Whatever else, Amboseli provides excellent game-viewing – abundant elephant, zebra, buffalo, waterbuck, Thomson's gazelle, wildebeest, giraffe, hippo and warthog – though large predators have been hunted close to extinction by the Maasai whose livestock they attack.

Straddling the Nairobi-Mombasa highway and railway line, **Tsavo East and West National Parks** together form one of Africa's largest conservation areas, a combined spread of more than 20,000km². Tsavo East was until the early 1990s the focus of Kenya's elephant poaching war. For several years the two-thirds of the park north of the Galana River was closed to tourism, and even south of the river you'd regularly encounter tuskless elephant carcasses left to rot where they had been shot. The war is over now, and tourists are gradually returning, but Tsavo East retains a harsh and remote character, its dry red earth supporting a thin cover of acacia scrub broken only along the wooded banks of the Galana and Voi rivers. It's a good place to see large herds of elephant and buffalo, as well as the normal predators and dry country antelope. Tsavo West, by contrast, protects an attractively undulating volcanic landscape, covered in tall grass and dense bush, and criss-crossed by an established and well-defined tourist circuit. The full range of large predators is present here, as are elephant, buffalo, giraffe, zebra and various antelopes. Tsavo West is reasonably well developed for tourism, but the wildly rutted roads and dense foliage ensure that a visit never feels like a milk-run. The one must-see in Tsavo West is Mzima Springs, a pair of transparent pools fed by underground water filtered by the volcanic rock of the Chyulu Hills and fringed with riparian forest and raffia palms. A submerged viewing tank allows you to watch hippos from a fishy perspective.

Access and getting around
Organised safaris
The simplest and cheapest way of getting to see something of Kenya's game reserves is to join an organised camping safari. The most popular itineraries out of Nairobi are a three- to four-day trip to the Maasai Mara only, and a six- to seven-day trip to the Maasai Mara and Samburu with an overnight stop at Lake Nakuru. The latter itinerary offers an excellent introduction to Kenya's wildlife: even somebody with no previous knowledge of African fauna could reasonably expect to see up to 40 mammal species. Organising a safari along these lines is simple and straightforward, and there's no need to pre-book since several companies offer daily departures from Nairobi.

Competition between budget safari companies in Nairobi is fierce, so shop around to feel out the situation before you pay for anything. Be wary of companies that act as agencies for other companies, and assume that any company offering a safari at a significantly cheaper rate than the reputable cheapies will be a fly-by-night operation. That said, you should attempt to haggle down the first price that you're asked, and if you're reasonably flexible you might want to do your safari shopping late in the day when it's often easy to get a discounted price to make up numbers on a safari that's scheduled to leave the next morning. At the time of writing, the lowest price you'll pay for a budget safari with a reputable operator is around US$60–70 per day inclusive of everything but drinks and a driver's tip of around US$2–3 per client per day. There are several alternatives to the conventional camping safari – see Safari companies on page 149 for a list of recommended operators and their specialities.

Self drive

The alternatives to an organised safari are to hire a vehicle and put together your own trip or to attempt to hitch into the reserves. The main advantage of hiring a vehicle is that it gives you full autonomy and allows you to visit more untrammelled reserves such as Meru and Tsavo. It will not be any cheaper than an organised safari, and it will be up to you to deal with any mechanical problems. On the whole, a self-drive safari makes more sense in South Africa or Zimbabwe, where reserves are more geared to independent visits, and roads and rental vehicles are in better condition.

Hitchhiking

Hitching into the parks isn't impossible, but it's a hit-and-miss approach, and the recent hike in entrance fees has made the possibility of getting stuck in a reserve for a few days without necessarily seeing a lot of game an expensive one.

Of the most popular reserves, Amboseli is probably the most hitchable. There is reasonably affordable accommodation as well as good game viewing at Ol Tukai village in the centre of the park, and there is only one approach road from Nairobi. Samburu offers fair prospects to tent-carrying hitchers, since practically any lift will be able to drop you at the campsite next to Samburu Lodge; from there you'll see plenty of game and you should have little difficulty getting a lift out. The Maasai Mara is too remote and its facilities too dispersed for hitching to be advisable. The best places from which to hitch to these reserves would be Namanga (for Amboseli), Narok (for Maasai Mara) and Isiolo (for Samburu), all of which have a few cheap lodges and can be reached from Nairobi directly on public transport.

Meru National Park is a very difficult hitch. Step one would be to hop on a *matatu* from Meru town to Maua, 30km before the park entrance gate. The junction 3km before Maua is the road to the park, and there's a small but convenient lodge right there. When you give up on that elusive lift, the green Nyambeni Mountains – covered in tea plantations, the mildly narcotic miraa plant and small forest patches – could offer up some pleasant walking.

The main gates to Tsavo East and West are accessible on public transport. The Voi Gate to Tsavo East is only an hour's walk from Voi town on the Mombasa road, and the Mtito Andei gate to Tsavo West is right on the Mombasa Road at Mtito Andei. The campsite at Voi Gate is probably worth the entrance fee in its own right, since quite a bit of game passes through and you should be allowed to make use of the staff bus to the nearby Voi Safari Lodge, where for the price of a meal or a soda you can spend several hours looking over a waterhole which attracts numbers of elephant and buffalo. Hitching into Tsavo West from Mtito Andei isn't too difficult, but you'll have to refuse a lift with the majority of vehicles since they'll be heading for an upmarket lodge – however, you don't have much to lose by waiting outside the gate, since you can always get a room in town if you fail to get a lift.

Where to stay and eat

People who do an organised budget safari will almost invariably camp at a spot designated by the safari company. Those who visit the parks independently, whether in a hired vehicle or by thumb power, are advised to carry camping equipment and should give some thought to what food they need to carry. If driving, the relevant Macmillan or Surveys of Kenya maps and perhaps a more detailed guidebook to Kenya would be a good idea.

Maasai Mara National Reserve
The only affordable option is to camp. The sites at the Olooloo, Musiara, Talek, Sekenani, Ololaimutiek or Sand River gates have no facilities other than water and they cost **C** per person. Musiara is a particularly attractive and popular campsite and you can normally eat at a nearby upmarket lodge called Governors Camp. You can also camp at the basic Riverside Camp less than 1km from Talek Gate and close to a trading centre where you can buy a few basic foodstuffs. It may be possible to make discrete arrangements to camp near some of the upmarket camps, especially out of season.

Samburu National Reserve
The most convenient place to pitch a tent, particularly for hitchers, is at the main campsite next to Samburu Lodge. The absence of facilities here is compensated for by the abundant bird and animal life along the river, and you can walk to the lodge for a meal or cold beer. Hitchers who don't have any luck with lifts around the park can organise game drives from the lodge and excellent bird walks within its grounds. For hitchers, it might also be worth noting that there is a basic guesthouse in Archer's Post, the small town on the main Marsabit Road about 2km from the park entrance – if nothing else, a stay here should yield excellent contacts with the Samburu people.

Meru National Park
The National Parks campsite is situated about 15km from the entrance gate in a patch of acacia woodland bounded by a small stream near the park headquarters. A fair amount of wildlife passes through, and there are plenty of birds. Bandas **E** per person. Camping **C** per person.

Amboseli National Park
If you hitch into the park, you're almost certain to end up at Ol Tukai village in the centre of the park, where the only option for backpackers is to ask about an unofficial room at the Drivers' Bandas which will cost around **B** per person. You can eat well at the three upmarket lodges in Ol Tukai, and should certainly spend some time in their attractive grounds, but it's much cheaper to eat at the excellent canteen in the Drivers Lodge. For those with private transport, there's an under-utilised fenced campsite in an acacia thicket verging Amboseli's southern boundary, 15km from Ol Tukai – individually cleared sites, running water and longdrop toilets, all for **B** per person.

Tsavo East National Park
More attractive than staying at one of the several basic lodges in Voi town, you can pitch a tent at Voi Gate for **C** per person. This is a great little site in a patch of acacia woodland which is teeming with birds and visited daily by elephant and more sporadically cheetah and lion – it might be advisable to use one of the bat-infested bandas in the campsite (no extra charge). Basic provisions and sodas are sold at the staff canteen. Those with vehicles can drive to Voi Safari Lodge for meals, even after dark. Backpackers can use the staff bus to take them there for a late breakfast or lunch. The alternative to camping at the gate is to stay in Voi town, which has a number of affordable hotels – the Ghana Guesthouse, five minutes' walk from the bus station just past Barclays Bank, is particularly recommended for its rooms with net and hot shower at **C** s/c sgl or dbl, while the more upmarket Tsavo Park Hotel serves quality Western and Indian meals in the US$3–5 range.

Tsavo West National Park

There are self-catering cottages at around US$30 per unit at Ngulia Safari Camp and Kitani Lodge, bookable through Let's Go Travel in Nairobi. Ngulia is on a small cliff above a waterhole which, judging by the well-worn animal paths, should produce excellent nocturnal game-viewing. Kitani's setting may seem rather more ordinary until the clouds lift and you realise that the overgrown white-capped molehill on the horizon in front of your verandah is none other than Kilimanjaro. The little-used campsite at junction three, about 2km from the park headquarters, has showers, running water, and a water tank which bodes well for nocturnal animal visits. The campsite at Chyulu Gate isn't as nice. Travellers without a vehicle may be allowed to camp at Mtito Andei Gate, and there are also a few cheap lodgings in Mtito Andei. About 50km south of Mtito Andei, a five-minute walk from the Mombasa road, there is a free campsite (no facilities) on the Tsavo River near Tsavo Gate.

The coast

MOMBASA AND SURROUNDS

Mombasa is the second largest city in Kenya and most important port in East Africa. You might reasonably expect it to be a major tourist magnet, but in fact Mombasa serves as something more like a funnel for tourists. Practically everybody first reaches the coast at Mombasa, but few people linger for any longer than they have to before heading directly on to one of the nearby beaches. My advice is to give Mombasa a bit more attention: it's a fascinating city, enveloped by a rich sense of historical continuity and a cultural integrity that might well be described as invigorating were it not neutralised by the sticky tropical languor of the coastal climate.

The labyrinthine alleys of Mombasa's **old town** invite slow exploration, punctuated with frequent stops at the many roadside coffee stalls and juice shops. The earliest extant building in the old town is Mhandry Mosque, erected in 1570, though some might claim this title should go to Basheikh Mosque which was reputedly built over the foundations of a 14th-century mosque. Most of the old town's buildings are relatively recent, dating to the turn of the century, and they show a strong Zanzibari influence in their ornate balconies and carved wooden doors. One old town landmark fitting this description is Ali's Curio Market opposite Fort Jesus, which was built in 1898 and has served as a police station and bar in its day. Otherwise, the old town is characterised by a mix of residential buildings and small family businesses (at least one of which, the scent emporium on Bachuma Street, has been run by the same family since 1850) which makes it feel more like a self-contained village than the suburb of a large city.

The Portuguese-built **Fort Jesus**, now a national museum, is situated on the edge of the old town at the end of Nkrumah Avenue. Despite several renovations and additions over the years, Fort Jesus has largely retained its original 1593 plan, and it deserves a couple of hours exploration. Clambering around the fortifications is great fun, and your understanding will be enhanced by reading the booklet which is normally on sale at the gate. A museum displays indigenous and imported pottery discovered at various coastal archaeological sites, and there are some restored Omani living quarters in a turret overlooking the old town. After leaving the fort, wander around the corner to view the sheer 16m-high walls of the seaward projection.

The most popular beaches with backpackers lie to the south of Mombasa. About 20km out of town, the beautiful palm-fringed **Tiwi Beach** is extremely popular

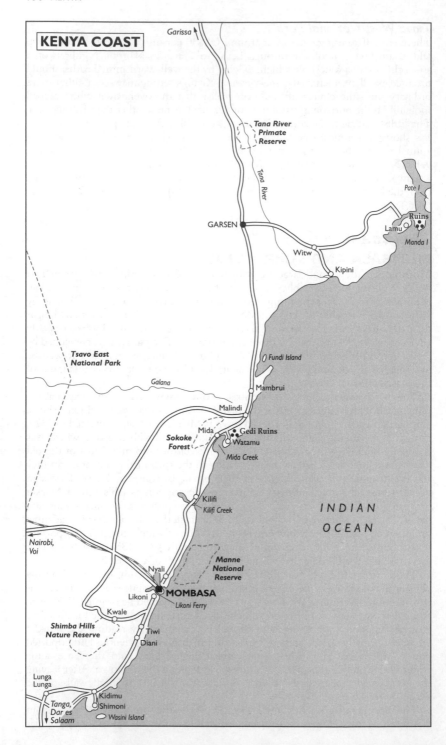

KENYA COAST

Garissa

Tana River Primate Reserve

Tana River

GARSEN

Witw

Kipini

Pate I

Lamu

Ruins

Manda I

Tsavo East National Park

Galana

Fundi Island

Mambrui

Malindi

Mida

Gedi Ruins

Sokoke Forest

Watamu

Mida Creek

Kilifi

Kilifi Creek

INDIAN OCEAN

Nairobi, Voi

Nyali

Manne National Reserve

Likoni

MOMBASA

Likoni Ferry

Kwale

Shimba Hills Nature Reserve

Tiwi

Diani

Lunga Lunga

Kidimu

Tanga, Dar es Salaam

Shimoni

Wasini Island

with budget travellers, largely because of Twiga Lodge which has served as a budget travellers' hangout since the hippy era. There's good snorkelling on the reef, and it's easy to arrange snorkel hire.

To the south of Tiwi, **Diani Beach** boasts about 20 upmarket hotels and several restaurants, banks, curio shops and supermarkets. Yet despite it being perhaps the most developed beach in East Africa, Diani still offers access to remnant forest patches where you can see typical lowland forest birds and primates. The Tiwi River at the north of the beach near the Indian Ocean Beach Club is rich in birds, and the disused 16th-century Kongo Mosque is hidden in the baobab forest near the river. If you want to explore by bicycle, try Glory Car Hire in the Diani Shopping Centre. Most of the upmarket hotels hire out equipment for windsurfing, sailing, snorkelling and diving.

Wasini Island and the nearby mainland village of **Shimoni** lie north of the Tanzania border near the Pemba Channel, an area renowned for game fishing and snorkelling. Wasini has supported a minor Swahili settlement for centuries and the modern village is built around old ruins. The Shimoni Caves, in a patch of forest near the jetty, are thought to be over 20km long and they were used in the 19th century for storing slaves. The forests near Shimoni and mangroves on Wasini support a range of forest birds and monkeys. The market in Shimoni is built over an old British colonial outpost.

Access and getting around

There is plenty of road transport between Nairobi and Mombasa, including several express coach services taking six to eight hours. Recommended bus lines include Akamba and Coast. More evocative than the buses, but also much more expensive, the overnight train service between Nairobi and Mombasa is regarded to be one of the world's great rail trips. The trains leave daily in either direction at 19.00 and arrive the next morning at 08.30. Tickets cost around US$50/32 first/second class inclusive of bedding and a good dinner and breakfast. First- and second-class compartments sleep two and four people respectively, and they are single sex unless booked as a unit. You're advised to buy a ticket as far in advance as possible, though it is often possible to get one at the last minute.

Two major train crashes on this line in the 1990s, together resulting in hundreds of fatalities, might put some people off using the rail service, though it's difficult to quantify whether this makes it any less safe than the corresponding road route.

The road that runs parallel to the south coast is connected to Mombasa Island by the Likoni Ferry, which runs in either direction every 10–15 minutes or so. From Mombasa city centre, regular *matatus* to the ferry terminal leave from in front of the post office on Digo Road. Once across the ferry, you'll find plenty of southbound buses and *matatus* leaving from the opposite ferry terminal. Tiwi Beach lies 17km south of the ferry terminal, and it's reached via a signposted 2km turn-off – muggings are so commonplace here that you're strongly urged to wait at the junction for a lift or taxi.

The turn-off to Diani is about 10km past Tiwi Beach at the village of Ukundu. Regular *matatus* run between the ferry terminal and Ukundu, where you can pick up another *matatu* to the beach (depending on which part of Diani you are heading to, check whether the *matatu* will be following the beach road northwards or southwards). Again, due to the high incidence of mugging, you are advised against walking between Ukundu and the beach.

There are frequent buses from Mombasa to Shimoni, which is 14km off the main tar road to Tanzania. You'll have no problem finding a boat to carry you from Shimoni to Wasini Island.

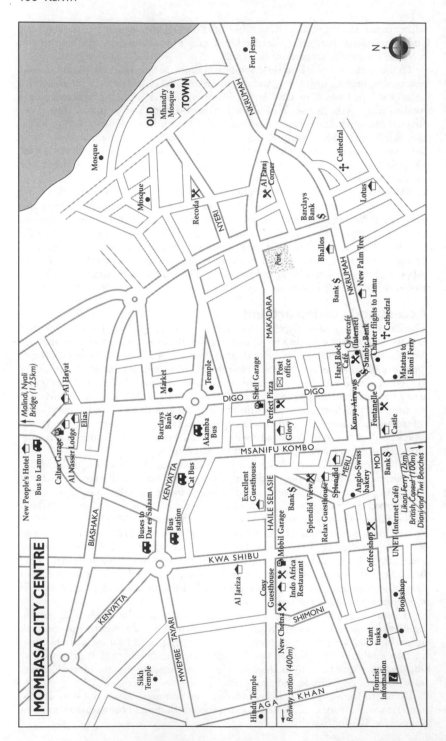

MOMBASA CITY CENTRE

N

Malindi, Nyali
Bridge (1.25km)

New People's Hotel
Bus to Lamu

Caltex Garage
Al Nasser Lodge
Al Hayat
Elias

Mosque

Mosque

Recoda

NYERI

Al Faraj
Corner

OLD
TOWN

Mhandry
Mosque

Fort Jesus

NKRUMAH

Cathedral

Barclays
Bank $

Lotus

Bhallos

New Palm Tree

Bank $

NKRUMAH

Charter flights to Lamu

Cathedral

Park

Temple

MAKADARA

Hard Rock
Café

Cybercafé
(Internet)

Stanbic Bank

Matatus to
Likoni Ferry

Markt

Shell Garage

Post
office

Kenya Airways

Fontanelle

Castle

Barclays
Bank $

DIGO

Perfect Pizza

DIGO

Glory

BIASHAKA

KENYATTA

Akamba
Bus

Cat Bus

MSANIFU KOMBO

MERU

Anglo-Swiss
bakery

MOI

Bank $

Buses to
Dar es Salaam

Bus
station

Excellent
Guesthouse

HAILE SELASIE

Bank $

Splendid View

Relax Guesthouse

Splendid

Coffeeshop

UNET (Internet Café)

Likoni Ferry (2km)
British Consul (100m)
Diani and Tiwi Beaches

KENYATTA

MWEMBE TAYARI

KWA SHIBU

Al Jariza

Cosy
Guesthouse

Mobil Garage

Indo Africa
Restaurant

New Chetna

SHIMONI

Bookshop

Sikh
Temple

Hindu Temple

AGA

KHAN

Railway station (400m)

Giant
tusks

Tourist
information

Where to stay
Central Mombasa

Al Nasser Hotel & Lodge Digo Rd. Noisy but otherwise acceptable local lodgings close to the Lamu bus station. Reasonable s/c room **C** dbl with net and fan.

Cosy Guesthouse Haile Selassie Rd; tel: 31-3064. An established backpackers' haunt, somewhat decrepit but reasonably friendly and secure. As is generally the case in the city's cheaper lodgings, rooms are no more than acceptable, running water is a bonus, and single women should don a stony veneer from the outset. Rooms **B** sgl or dbl with fan and balcony.

Elias Hotel Digo Rd. Very run down but affordable, friendly and apparently secure. Ground floor restaurant serves cheap Indian dishes. Rooms **B** dbl with fan but no net.

Excellent Guesthouse Haile Selassie Rd; tel: 45-1926. Aptly named, this is arguably the best budget option in town. Clean, well-maintained s/c rooms **D/E** with net and fan.

New Palm Tree Hotel Nkrumah Rd; tel: 31-1756. This pleasantly time-warped colonial relic, with its grandly proportioned reception area, is not new by any means, but the clean, spacious rooms, inviting first-floor courtyard and central location make it a good choice assuming that your budget runs to it. Ground floor bar with cheap Spanish wine and pool table. Rooms are s/c with net, fan, and hot water, and just creep into the **E/F** brackets.

New People's Hotel Abdul Nassir Rd; tel: 31-2831. A sprawling multi-storey hotel, this makes the exaggerated claim of being the 'most economical and simply the best in town'. It's OK, though its popularity with travellers rests on its convenient location for catching an early morning bus to Lamu and Malindi. Rooms **B** sgl or dbl with fan (communal showers) or **B/C** s/c sgl/dbl with fan and occasional hot water.

Relax Guesthouse Quiet, comfortable local lodgings around the corner from the Splendid Hotel. **C** dbl with net and fan.

Splendid Hotel Meru Rd. Functional if less than splendid multi-storey block located at the heart of the commercial centre. Large, clean s/c rooms for **E** sgl or dbl with fan, net, hot water. Decent value.

Tiwi Beach

Twiga Lodge This has been a popular backpackers' hangout for as long as anybody cares to remember, and more recently it has become an established starting point for overland truck trips to South Africa and elsewhere. The congenial atmosphere is hard to fault, and you'll probably end up spending time in Twiga's sensibly priced restaurant and lively bar even if you do stay elsewhere on the beach. There is similarly priced and better accommodation at Coral Cove Cottages and Minilets, which flank Twiga Lodge to the north and south respectively. Four-bed dorm **B** pp. Private rooms **D/E**. Camping **A** pp.

Diani Beach

Southfork Cottages With the apparent closure of Dan's Camping, this is the most (only?) affordable option on Diani, a cluster of unpretentious s/c cottages charging **E** dbl with net and fan. Meals and drinks available. To get there, catch a minibus from Ukunda heading south along the beachfront road and ask to be dropped at the post office, where you must turn right into a dirt track signposted Malibu Cottages. After about 500m, turn right at a fork opposite a quarry; Southfork is to your left a further 500m along this road.

Shimoni and Wasini

Mpunguti Lodge Wasini Island. Good Swahili cooking. Simple bandas **E/F** including meals. Camping **A** pp. Bring drinking water if possible.

Mwazaro Beach Camp 8km before Shimoni along turn-off from Mombasa road. Camping **A** pp.

Where to eat

Al Faraj Corner Restaurant Makadara Rd. Cheap, tasty biriani lunches near the old town.

Anglo Swiss Bakery Chembe Rd. Good pastries, cakes and bread.

Hard Rock Café Nkrumah Rd. Not exactly traditional, but if you've been in Africa a while, it may be difficult to resist the combination of chilled draught beer, air-conditioning, splendidly tacky decor, pop videos interspersed with muted wildlife documentaries, and – assuming the televised animals tearing each other to shreds doesn't dull your appetite – very good Western meals in the US$5–7 range.

New Chetna Restaurant Haile Selassie Av. Cheap Indian fare a few doors up from the popular Cosy Guesthouse.

Recoda Restaurant Nyeri St. Established in 1942 and long regarded to be the best Swahili eatery in the old town. It's cheap too – you'll eat well for well under US$3.

Splendid View Restaurant Msanifu Kombo St. One of my favourite eateries anywhere in Kenya. Good Indian food mostly under US$3 per head. The chicken tikka and naan bread is a highlight of the menu. No alcohol served, but you can follow your meal with a drink at the rooftop bar of the Splendid Hotel opposite.

Mombasa listings

Books and newspapers There are several book shops dotted around the junction of Digo Road and Moi Avenue, selling the usual travel guides and coffee-table tomes, but with a limited selection of novels. A good place to pick up cheap secondhand beach reading is the book stall next to the Excellent Guesthouse. The reading room at the British Council on Digo Rd has plenty of recent UK newspapers and offers cheap temporary membership (well under US$1 per day).

Curios Don't expect the selection you will find in Nairobi, but there are several curio shops along Moi Avenue.

Foreign exchange The best place to change hard currency cash is at any of several Forex Bureaux dotted around the town centre. Most private bureaux will not accept travellers' cheques, so with these expect less favourable rates (and a longer wait) at a bank.

Internet There are quite a few internet cafés in Mombasa, though many were practically non-functional in mid-2000 due to daily electricity cuts. Two which seem reliable and well organised are U-NET on Moi Avenue and the Cyber Café next to the Hard Rock Café.

Post restante Collect at the main post office on Digo Avenue.

NORTH OF MOMBASA

A suggested first stop north of Mombasa is **Watamu**, a small fishing village that's become something of a sideshow to the string of tourist class hotels emanating from it – it's difficult to know whether to laugh or cry at the misplaced Maasai warriors who strut photogenically through Watamu's odd mix of mock German beer halls, flashy curio stalls and traditional homesteads. Watamu is the most tacky and contrived of Kenya's resorts, but it overlooks a beach of singular memorability – an idyllic stretch of white sand rescued from anonymous perfection by a group of ragged coral formations which mushroom dramatically from the bay. Further in its favour, Watamu is ideally positioned to explore a diverse concentration of low-key attractions, not the least of which is **Watamu Marine National Park**, a maze of underwater coral gardens overrun by all manner of dazzlingly colourful fish. The beach at Watamu is lined with glass-bottomed boats, most of which are equipped with snorkelling equipment, and you can negotiate with the owner to be taken out for a few hours.

The ruined city of **Gedi**, a short walk from the synonymous village at the turn-off to Watamu, is among the most intriguing and atmospheric historical sites on the East African coast, not to say one of the most accessible. Gedi was evidently founded in the 13th century, when it would have housed 2,500 people. The city appears to have been evacuated in the 17th century, for reasons that remain unclear – it's very possible that many of its residents ended up in the tummies of the cannibalistic Zimba. Gedi is surrounded by thick jungle, giving it the feel of the archetypal lost city. The main ruins include a fluted pillar tomb, a less ornate tomb dating to 1399, and a 15th-century mosque and palace. Clear footpaths lead through the forest to the city wall, where there are several small mosques and discrete houses. At the entrance gate, you can buy an excellent booklet about the ruins, visit the small site museum devoted to artefacts unearthed during excavations – and ask about the nearby butterfly farm, which welcomes visitors.

The jungle that gives Gedi much of its atmosphere forms part of the **Arabuko-Sokoke Forest**, the last significant expanse of lowland forest on the Kenyan coast. Isolated from similar habitats, this forest supports several endemic and localised animals, of which Ader's red duiker and the golden-rumped elephant shrew are most likely to be seen on the footpaths through Gedi, where they are relatively used to people. In order to see some of the forest's rare birds, such as Sokoke scops owl, Sokoke pipit, Clarke's weaver and Amani sunbird, you'd be better off visiting the forest reserve headquarters about 2km south of Gedi. Another spot that's of interest to birders is **Mida Creek**, the wader-rich northern shore which is a short walk along one of several footpaths leading from the main Mombasa–Malindi road near the forest headquarters. The entrance of Mida Creek

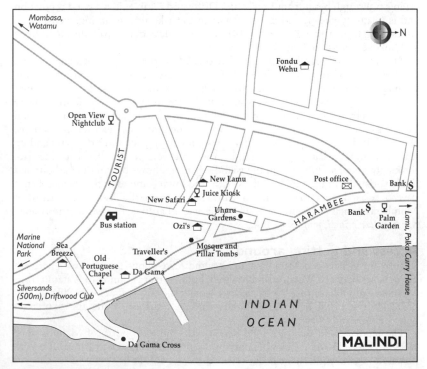

SABAKI RIVER MOUTH

A reader recently wrote to recommend a visit to the Sabaki River Mouth, 8km north of Malindi, a spot renowned for the thousands of birds that gather there, including flamingos. In addition to the estuary, there are ponds, marshes, dunes and diverse bush. Accommodation can be found at the Sabaki River Cottage on a hill overlooking the estuary. The two large rooms have private showers and flush toilets and costs US$30 per double. Meals can be arranged, and safe camping is available.

To reach the cottage, catch a taxi north from Malindi for about 8km and cross the large Sabaki River bridge. On the north side of the bridge, turn right through the village, and ask directions for the track to the home of the cottage's owner, Rodgers Karabu, who is well known locally. The cottage is signposted to the right about 1km out of the village.

can also be reached directly from Watamu by following the beach road for about 3km past Hemingways Hotel.

Malindi was an important medieval trading city, and it was the 16th-century base for Portuguese operations on this part of the coast. Today, it is first and foremost a resort town. The nominal old quarter is rather small and it contains few buildings that date to much before World War II. Of interest is the cross erected by Vasco da Gama in 1499 at the southern end of the beach, the small 16th-century Portuguese church and graveyard on the beachfront, and the old mosque and pillar tombs facing Uhuru Gardens. Scuba-diving and game fishing excursions can be arranged through beachfront hotels (the Driftwood Club enjoys a good reputation and is relatively cheap) and it's easy enough to make private arrangements to go snorkelling from a glass-bottomed boat. If the seaside activities pall, the Gedi Ruins and Sokoke Forest are both feasible day trips.

The undoubted highlight of the Kenya coast, **Lamu** is a small but ancient island town, separated from Malindi by 200km of dusty roads. Not touristy in any normally accepted sense of the word, Lamu has nevertheless been a popular congregation point for backpackers since the 1960s, and it has a unique atmosphere determined by the fascinating dynamic between the traditional Islamic and Swahili lifestyles of its occupants and the influence of generations of backpackers. Lamu is, above all, laid back – if you arrive here expecting to stay for three days and end up leaving a month later, you won't be the first person this has happened to. Strikingly, there are no cars on the island – fishing dhows bob in the harbour and donkeys dawdle in the cobbled alleys of the old town – and even the touts in Lamu have a relaxed aura that seems a world apart from the hysterical energy of Mombasa's beach boys and Malindi's taxi drivers. Lamu is, in a word, unmissable. See box *Exploring Lamu*, page 164.

Access and getting around

Regular buses between Mombasa and Malindi take about four hours. There are direct buses between Watamu and Malindi, but if you are coming to Watamu from Mombasa you'll have to ask a bus to drop you at the turn-off at Gedi, 20km south of Malindi – you'll have no difficulty finding transport along the 5km road between Gedi and Watamu.

The regular incidence of armed banditry on the road north of Malindi since 1992 has caused several bus operators to discontinue services to Lamu. If you're prepared to take your chances, however, there are still at least two buses daily to

Lamu, leaving Mombasa at around 07.00 and arriving at Mokowe, from where motorboat taxis transfer passengers to Lamu, in the late afternoon. Far safer than the bus, however, is to take one of Air Kenya's daily flights to Lamu from Mombasa via Malindi – the price isn't too prohibitive (about US$120 return from Malindi to Lamu) and any travel agent can book you a ticket. Motorboat taxis transfer passengers from the airstrip on Manda Island to Lamu town.

Where to stay and eat
Watamu
Adventist Youth Centre Overlooking lagoon 1km from village. Run down, but cheap rates and location compensate. Dorms sometimes available. Camping permitted any time **A** pp.
Arabuko-Sokoke Forest Headquarters On the Mombasa–Malindi road 2km south of the Watamu turn-off. Nature trail nearby. Guided bird walks. Basic campsite **A** pp.
Dante Hotel Bordering the village 200m from Barclays Bank. Lacks atmosphere but clean and comfortable enough. Rooms **C** s/c dbl with fan. Reasonable food.
Villa Veronika Facing the Dante, and similar, though it has a better garden and a more welcoming atmosphere. Rooms **C** s/c dbl with fan and net.

Malindi
Bawaly and Sons Opposite Uhuru Gardens. Excellent Halwa jellies and coffee.
Da Gama Inn The rooms aren't up to much for the price, but the restaurant serves large, tasty burgers and steaks at reasonable prices.
Fondo Wehu Guest House Deservedly popular, this family run hostel 10 minutes' walk from the bus station is arguably the best place of its kind in East Africa. Rooftop dorm with nets **B** pp. Rooms **C** / **D** with net and fan.
Juice Bar Anonymous kiosk next to bus station does fruit juice surpassing even that in Lamu.
New Lamu and **New Safari Lodges** Very basic but adequate lodgings with good local restaurants, both within 100m of bus station. Rooms straddling **A** and **B** range.
Open View Nightclub Cheap Swahili dishes served to predominantly local clientele.
Ozi's B&B One of the best lodges in Malindi, and close to the bus station and beach. Good Indian food, too. Rooms **C** / **D** with net and fan.
Palm Garden Restaurant A popular rendezvous, the seedy atmosphere is compensated for by a reliable supply of cold beer and cheap if unexceptional curries and Western dishes.
Polka Curry House Good vegetarian dishes.
Sea Breeze Guest House A short walk from the town centre. Excellent value for money. Rooms **B** sgl or **C** s/c dbl with fan.
Silversands On the beach 2km south of town, this place has been popular with backpackers for years. The campsite lacks shade, but the rooms and covered standing tents are good value. Facilities include bicycle hire and an inexpensive restaurant. You shouldn't walk between Silversands and town with valuables at any time of day. Standing tent **B** dbl. Chalet **C** dbl. Camping **A** pp.

Lamu
There are dozens of acceptable budget hotels in Lamu, and when you first arrive you must expect to be surrounded by touts offering to find you the 'best' room. There is little you can do to resist the touts and, all things considered, they're more of a help than a hindrance – Lamu town is confusing on first arrival, the touts know where rooms are available, and it's up to the hotel owner, not you, to pay their commission. When you are shown a room, check it has a fan and net and test the water pressure. Be prepared for some gentle but protracted negotiation – rates in Lamu depend on season, quality of room, whether it's self-contained, the number

EXPLORING LAMU

For many, the most attractive option in Lamu is to do nothing. The sticky heat induces a physical and mental torpor, so that days slip by in a dream-like state in which you wander aimlessly through the cobbled alleyways of the old town, punctuating your meanderings with regular stops for fruit juice, or beer, or idle conversation.

You'll quickly familiarise yourself with the main north–south thoroughfare, Harambee Avenue, which was the waterfront until the 1830s but now lies about 50m inland. The older part of town is the northern sector, known as Mkomani, and is notable more for its anachronistic atmosphere and street layout, than for any particular historical landmark (though you should try to see the medieval pillar tomb and nearby Riyadha Mosque, as well as the 14th-century Pwani Mosque and early 19th-century fort). The waterfront Lamu Museum gives visitors a good overview of Lamu's history.

Lamu has its own distinctive architectural style, a feature of which is the rooftop 'verandas' you'll find at the top of many hotels. The rooftop is the place to catch a breeze while you view the town from an unusual, panoramic angle. After dark, it can be hauntingly beautiful, as you look down on palm trees swaying below a pristine night sky, and listen to the insane braying of the island's manifold donkeys.

Several good day trips can be undertaken from Lamu town. **Shela Beach** is a 12km stretch of perfect white sand situated an hour's ambling distance south of town. The start of the beach is marked by a small village, also called Shela, notable for a mosque dating to 1829. Cold drinks and meals are to be found at Peponi's Hotel and Bahari Restaurant. There's no shade on the beach, so take along sunblock and a hat. Shela has the reputation of being a danger spot for rapes and muggings and it would be inadvisable to go much beyond the village unless you're in a group. Walking between Lamu and Shela is safe enough, though you may prefer to use one of the regular motorboat taxis in one direction.

On the opposite side of Lamu island, **Matondoni** is an industrious little village, noted as a dhow building centre. The gracious village headman runs a *duka* that stocks sodas but little else, and he'll find a room for anyone who wishes to stay overnight. The best way to visit (easily organised through any of the touts in Lamu) is on the back of a donkey – a two-hour trip each way, dependent to a large degree on the stubbornness of the individual beast. A hat and long trousers offer essential protection against the sun, not to say the vicious acacia trees to which Lamu's donkeys are irresistibly attracted.

The other popular day excursion is a **dhow trip**. One option is to head to the reefs around Mandatoto island, which are teeming with fish and offer good snorkelling. Another combines fishing and a lunchtime barbecue with an afternoon trip to the Takwa Ruins on Manda Island. Either way, you'll have to negotiate the price, which drops as the group becomes larger, and you must clarify who is to organise food, drinks and snorkelling equipment. Overnight camping is permitted at Takwa Ruins, but you must be self-sufficient and you will pay extra to retain the services of a dhow for a second day.

Pencil-shaped **Kiwaiyu Island**, a three-hour motorboat-taxi ride from Faza, is notable for its idyllic beach, excellent snorkelling and total sense of isolation, also for Kasimu's camp which has bandas in the **C** range and camping for **A** opposite.

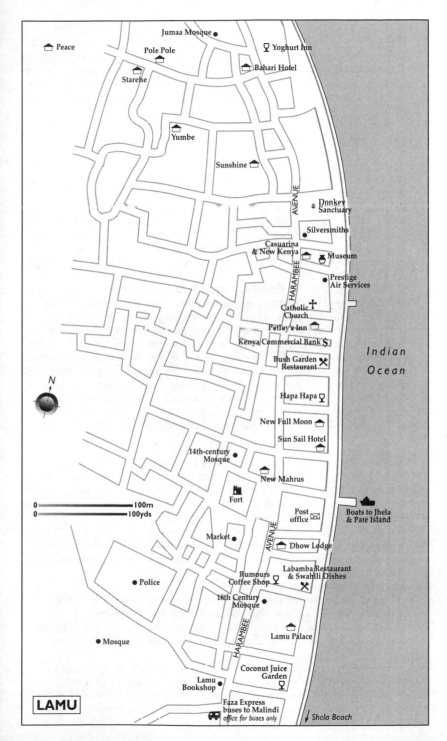

Peace

Jumaa Mosque

Yoghurt Inn

Pole Pole

Bahari Hotel

Starehe

Yumbe

Sunshine

AVENUE

Donkey Sanctuary

Silversmiths

Casuarina & New Kenya

Museum

HARAMBEE

Prestige Air Services

Catholic Church

Petley's Inn

Kenya Commercial Bank

Indian Ocean

Bush Garden Restaurant

Hapa Hapa

New Full Moon

Sun Sail Hotel

N

14th-century Mosque

New Mahrus

Fort

0   100m
0   100yds

Post office

Boats to Jhela & Pate Island

Market

AVENUE

Dhow Lodge

Police

Rumours Coffee Shop

Labamba Restaurant & Swahili Dishes

18th Century Mosque

HARAMBEE

Mosque

Lamu Palace

Coconut Juice Garden

Lamu Bookshop

LAMU

Faza Express buses to Malindi
office for buses only

↓ Shela Beach

PATE

Few travellers ever reach Pate, the largest island in the Lamu Archipelago, yet it forms an enticing onward trip from Lamu town, with much to offer those with a strong interest in Swahili architecture or a penchant for getting way off any beaten track into a part of Kenya that feels largely untouched by the modern world.

Pate's main attraction, the eponymous town, is a bizarre anachronism, quite unlike any settlement I've seen in East Africa. Despite supporting a population of no more than 3,000, Pate feels like the centre of a much larger city: a time-warped huddle of tall coral buildings, interwoven by dark, narrow alleys, and enclosed by swaying coconut plantations and low mangroves. The 'modern' stone town is thought to be around 150 years old, but the surrounding tobacco fields are studded with overgrown mosques, ancient tombs and crumbling walls, the legacy of the much older and larger city that flourished here in medieval times. In Pate, more even than in Lamu, we felt a deep sense of cultural and historical continuity, heightened by the realisation that most of the modern homes have been constructed phoenix-like from the ruins of the older city.

About an hour's walk from Pate town, **Siyu** is another former boom town which has been relegated to backwater status. Until 100 years ago, Siyu was regarded to be one of the region's main centres of Islamic scholarship and craft, and, as with Pate, the modern town is surrounded by the crumbling relics of its glory days, most prominently a substantial and largely intact Arabic fort built around a well. The houses of Siyu are very different to those in Pate, mostly only one storey, yet their arched interiors are strikingly reminiscent of the ground plan of houses at medieval ruins such as Gedi. There is no electricity on Pate, only one motorised vehicle, no alcohol, and in Siyu not even a Coke bottle. The recently installed public telephone in Siyu is the pride of the town. We were taken to see this technological marvel by four different

---

of nights you want to stay, and your bargaining abilities. Out of season, expect to pay a rate in the upper **C** or lower **D** bracket for a s/c double with fan, net and breakfast included. You'll pay in the lower **C** bracket for a basic double, and a bit less for a single. Prices tend to increase when the demand for rooms is high (December, July and August).

Bahari, **Sunshine**, **Casuarina** and **Pole Pole Guesthouses** Well-established, popular lodgings with good rooftop verandas and s/c rooms boasting a fan, net and relatively reliable water supply. In **C** to **D** bracket.
Coconut Juice Garden Good fruit juice.
Hapa Hapa and **Bush Garden Restaurants** The best of several affordable Swahili seafood restaurants on the seafront. The Bush Garden also does good curries.
Peace Guesthouse On the outskirts of town, 10 minutes from the waterfront. The only place with dorms **B** pp and camping **A** pp. It also has s/c rooms with fans at the usual rates.
Petley's Inn The rooms at Lamu's oldest hotel are well beyond the reach of budget travellers, but the rooftop bar is recommended for the view over the harbour, the atmospheric decor, as one of only two places in town where beer is officially sold – not to mention excellent meals and snacks which are (unexpectedly) no more expensive than those served at more established backpacker eateries.

villagers, and several children pointed at Ariadne's camera and shouted 'telephone'.

Any visit to Pate should be approached in a spirit of flexibility. That said, contrary to what the touts in Lamu might tell you, there is regular public transport to the island: a motorised dhow which travels between Lamu and Pate once daily in either direction except on Friday. Departure times are determined by the tide, so you are advised to ask around on the day before you want to travel, and to pitch up a couple of hours in advance to be sure of not missing the boat. The ferry doesn't go directly to either Pate or Siyu town, so you will need to disembark at Mtangawanda Port. On a good day, the ferry will be met by a customised safari vehicle which now serves as an open-topped, breakdown-prone *matatu*. On a bad day, you'll have to walk the 3km to Pate or 8km to Siyu – a straightforward enough prospect, with plenty of other passengers to point out the right footpath to Pate town.

There is a guesthouse of sorts in Pate town, a four-storey building which locals say was built 120 years ago by a Portuguese settler. The hospitable caretaker, Abala Hussein, maintains three room for travellers, charging around US$3 per person per night. He can also arrange inexpensive, tasty meals, best eaten on the marvellous shaded rooftop – this is the highest point in the town and offers excellent stargazing on a clear night.

There is no formal accommodation in Siyu. We stayed at the house of Auni Mahomed, a very friendly and obliging man who regularly puts up the few travellers who make it to Siyu, and can also arrange good meals. There is no fixed price for staying here, nor will Auni suggest one – it would be reasonable to pay what you would for a cheap room and meal in Lamu.

Pate may not be for everybody, but it was a highlight of our recent travels, a rare escape to a genuinely unaffected part of Kenya, where tourist relations are dictated by traditional Swahili hospitality rather than modern business. We loved it!

Sun Sail Hotel The newest addition to Lamu's beachfront accommodation, already proving very popular as it bridges the considerable gap between the town's many cheap guesthouses and two genuine upmarket hotels. Large, clean s/c rooms **D** dbl with net and fan, breakfast included.

Rumours Coffee Shop Cappuccino, espresso and delicious confectionery.

North of Nairobi
THE CENTRAL HIGHLANDS

The lush and fertile central highlands to the north of Nairobi are home to the Kikuyu, Kenya's most populous ethnic group. Heavily settled by colonials, the central highlands were the setting of the notorious 1930s Happy Valley scene and later of the anti-colonial Mau-Mau rebellion.

The physical focus of the central highlands is **Mount Kenya**, the second highest mountain in Africa, with a snow-capped peak rising to 5,199m. When it was formed volcanically around three million years ago, the cone of this mountain probably topped 7,000m, but it has since been eroded by intense glaciation. The 600km² area above the forest line is protected in a national park, which protects rain and bamboo forest to an altitude of 3,000m and above that the characteristically surreal Afro-alpine landscape of giant heather, lobelia and groundsel. The forest contains an outstanding variety of birds as well as typical large African mammals such as elephant, buffalo, black-and-white colobus, blue monkey, lion, black rhinoceros, bushpig, Harvey's red duiker and bushbuck. It also protects the most easterly populations of the scarce bongo antelope and giant forest hog. (See box *Climbing Mount Kenya* below.)

Mount Kenya is circled by a surfaced road which starts about 100km north of Nairobi. Most of the region's main towns lie close to this road. Starting in the south (as you do coming from Nairobi), and following the road that runs to the east of the mountain, the first town you'll pass through is **Embu** which, despite being a reasonably substantial and attractive local administrative centre, holds very little of interest to travellers. Next up is **Chogoria**, much smaller than Embu, but of greater interest since it's the starting point of the increasingly popular Chogoria route up Mount Kenya. Then, almost immediately after crossing into the northern hemisphere, you reach **Meru**, which sprawls along the road for a couple of kilometres. Aside from a small and worthwhile museum containing ethnographic displays on the Meru people, this rather sizeable town offers little in the way of

CLIMBING MOUNT KENYA

Mount Kenya vies with Kilimanjaro as the most popular climb in East Africa. The 4,985m-high Point Lenana can be reached without specialised climbing equipment by several routes. Climbs can be arranged independently at the entrance gate or through most Nairobi tour operators and local hotels such as the Naro Moru River Lodge. Mount Kenya is far cheaper to climb than Kilimanjaro: a self-organised four- or five-day hike should work out at less than US$200 inclusive of porters, guides and park and hut fees. With a professional operator, expect to pay around double that.

The climb to Lenana is essentially an extended uphill hike, but the mountain should not be underestimated. Sudden weather changes are normal and there is a danger of getting lost in blizzard conditions or suffering altitude sickness, or hypothermia in mist and drizzle. These risks will be heightened should you succumb to the temptation to cut costs by skimping on guides and porters, or spend less than three nights on the mountain before ascending Lenana. If time permits, a week allows a full day to explore each of the forest and moorland zones from a base, and it minimises the effects of altitude.

Andrew Wielochowski and Mark Savage's *Mt Kenya Map and Guide* includes a good 1:50,000 map and detailed information on ecology and geology as well as tips on equipment and health. It is available for a couple of dollars from most Nairobi booksellers and is highly recommended. Climbers who wish to tackle the higher peaks or to explore the peak area over a longer period of time are pointed towards the Mountain Club of Kenya's *Guide to Mount Kenya and Kilimanjaro*.

The two most popular routes start at Naro Moru on the western side of the mountain and at Chogoria on the eastern side.

Naro Moru Route This route leads from Naro Moru on the main ring road. The Naro Moru River Lodge organises packaged hikes on this route, and you can hire their equipment even if you wish to make private arrangements. The Youth Hostel is the place to make independent arrangements and to meet with other hikers to form a party.

There are two main overnight stops on the Naro Moru Route. The Met Station (3,050m) has bandas, standing tents, and a campsite. It is 26km from the prescribed tourist attractions, but the surrounding dense forest could yield some good walking.

Following the circular road in an anti-clockwise direction, you'll pass its most northerly point – the departure point for the Trans-Africa Highway to Isiolo, Samburu National Reserve, Marsabit and eventually Ethiopia – before curving back southwards towards **Nanyuki**, an important military town, settled by colonials in 1907, and practically on the equator but otherwise of little inherent interest. Then, back in the southern hemisphere, **Naro Moru** is little more than a village, but it's perhaps the most popular base from which to climb Mount Kenya.

The busy, compact market town of **Nyeri**, the main administrative centre of Central Province, lies about 10km to the west of the circular road en route to Nyahururu. Nyeri was the final resting place of Baden-Powell (of scouting and Mafeking fame), who is buried at the north end of town. Less esoterically, the upmarket Outspan Hotel 1km out of town ranks among the most atmospheric tourist-class hotels in Kenya, built in 1932, with beautifully landscaped grounds facing Mount Kenya, and worth visiting if only to do the guided walk along the

main road, and it's often possible to get a lift some of the way. Before reaching the Met Station, it's possible to overnight at the youth hostel or camp at the entrance gate (2,400m) 17km from the ring road. If you catch a lift to the Met Station and arrive early in the day, do not continue any higher on the same day as this would virtually guarantee ill-effects from altitude.

Mackinder's Camp, six hours from the Met Station, consists of a bunkhouse and several standing tents. Ideally you should spend two nights at Mackinder's – there's no shortage of good walking in the area – before taking on Lenana. The hike from Mackinder's to Lenana takes three to four hours; an 03.00 start is recommended so that you will get there around sunrise for maximum visibility. An alternative to climbing Lenana is to spend two or three days circling the peak area in an anticlockwise direction.

Chogoria Route This is the most scenic route up the mountain and it seems to have taken over from Naro Moru as the most popular with independent travellers. Guides and porters can be arranged through one of the lodgings in Chogoria village, as can a lift along the 30km road to Chogoria Gate (2,950m) or to the road head (3,250m), a further 10km up. If you take a lift up, bargain hard and don't think about ascending higher without spending a night or two at the entrance gate or road head to acclimatise.

There's no problem whiling away a couple of days around the gate, since it's in the forest zone and there's plenty of wildlife to be seen, including elephants. You can camp either at the gate itself, at Parklands Campsite about 1.5km further along the road, or even at the road head. Alternatively, there's attractive and inexpensive *banda* accommodation at the Meru Mount Kenya Lodge close by the entrance gate. The actual park boundary is at the road head, not the entrance gate, so you need not pay park fees when you wait.

When you come to ascend further, your first goal, a six-hour walk past the road head, should be Minto's Hut (4,200m), which is run down but attractively situated near a group of tarns (note that the water here should be purified before you drink it). As with Mackinder's, it's advisable to spend a day here acclimatising before ascending further. Lenana is three to four hours away; again, a 03.00 start is recommended.

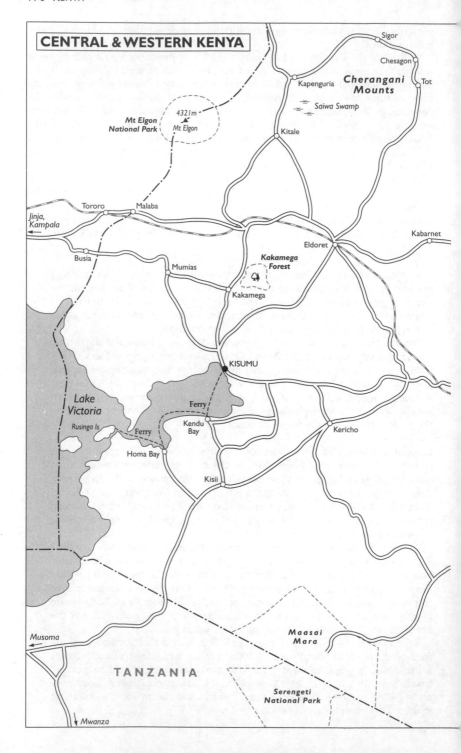

CENTRAL & WESTERN KENYA

Sigor
Chesagon
Kapenguria
Tot
Cherangani Mounts
Saiwa Swamp
Kitale
Mt Elgon National Park
4321m
Mt Elgon
Tororo
Malaba
Jinja, Kampala
Eldoret
Kabarnet
Busia
Mumias
Kakamega Forest
Kakamega
KISUMU
Lake Victoria
Rusinga Is
Ferry
Ferry
Kendu Bay
Ferry
Kericho
Homa Bay
Kisii
Musoma
Maasai Mara
TANZANIA
Serengeti National Park
Mwanza

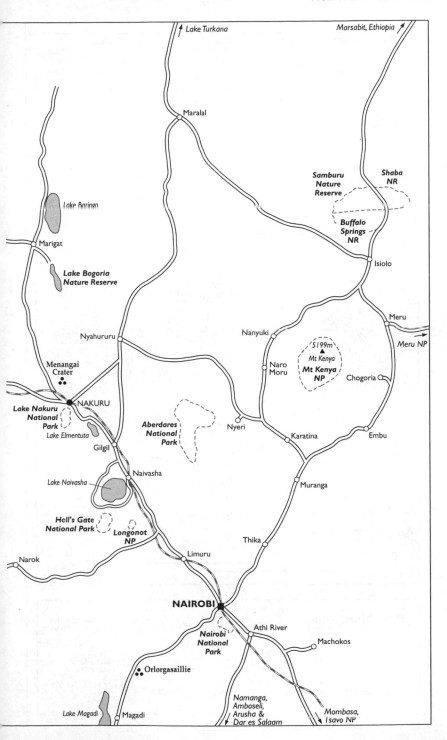

MOUNT KENYA

KEY

Circuit
— Trail
▲ Camp
⇧ Hut
≈ Pass

Routes
═ Road
= = = Trail
▲ Camp
⇧ Hut

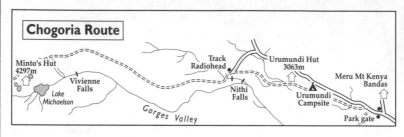

Chogoria Route

Minto's Hut
4297m
Vivienne
Falls
Lake
Michaelson
Track
Radiohead
Nithi
Falls
Urumundi Hut
3063m
Urumundi
Campsite
Meru Mt Kenya
Bandas
Park gate
Gorges Valley

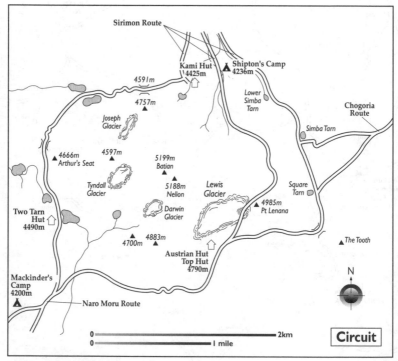

Sirimon Route

Kami Hut
4425m
Shipton's Camp
4236m
Lower
Simba
Tarn
Chogoria
Route
4591m
4757m
Simba Tarn
Joseph
Glacier
4666m
Arthur's Seat
4597m
5199m
Batian
5188m
Nelion
Lewis
Glacier
Square
Tarn
Tyndall
Glacier
Darwin
Glacier
4985m
Pt Lenana
Two Tarn
Hut
4490m
4700m
4883m
Austrian Hut
Top Hut
4790m
The Tooth
Mackinder's
Camp
4200m
Naro Moru Route

N

0 ———————————— 2km
0 ———————————— 1 mile

Circuit

Naro Moru Route

Two Tarn Hut
4490m
Teleki Valley
Northern Naro Moru
Meteorological
station
3050m
Mackinder's
Camp 4200m
Vertical Bog

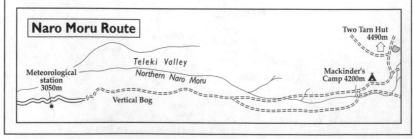

Chania River (US$5) which should produce sightings of the usual monkeys as well as two dozen or more highland birds.

Nyeri is also the base for visits to the Aberdares National Park, which protects the forested slopes and moorland of the Aberdares Mountains, home to a diverse range of large mammals including elephant, lion, rhino and bongo antelope, and known for its melanistic leopards (black panthers). The only realistic way of seeing this park is to spend a night at one of the so-called 'tree hotels', Treetops and The Ark, an option that few backpackers will be in a financial position to consider. Should you decide to treat yourself, the place to check out current rates is in Nairobi: be aware that Treetops, for all its romantic appeal (if you do visit, you might just be reminded that a certain Elizabeth went to bed here a princess and woke up a queen), offers significantly inferior game viewing to The Ark. In fact, while you're about it, ask about rates at the relatively under-hyped and probably cheaper Mountain Lodge on Mount Kenya, which has larger rooms, better food, and far superior game viewing – there's even a realistic chance of seeing giant forest hog!

About 50km northwest of Nyeri, Nyahururu at 2,360m is Kenya's highest town, and it has a cool coniferous setting that belies its position virtually on top of the Equator. Aside from being a route focus for those crossing between the central highlands and Nakuru in the Rift Valley, Nyahururu is best known for Thomson's Falls, which lies 2km out of town, and is the third-highest waterfall in Kenya. The waterfall is very pretty and the forested gorge below, reached by a slippy footpath, holds black-and-white colobus monkeys and some good birds. More birds and a few hippo can be seen at a papyrus-fringed pool 2km upstream; the staff at the lodge can direct you.

Access and getting around
There is plenty of public transport from Nairobi to all the towns in this region, and between all towns on the road circling Mount Kenya, though buses are generally preferable to *matatus* when travelling to towns east of Mount Kenya due to the high incidence of fatal accidents. There are also regular minibuses from Nyeri through to Nyahururu, and then from Nyahururu north to Maralal and south to Nakuru in the Rift Valley.

Where to stay and eat
Embu
Al Aswad Lodging One of the better of several basic lodgings near the bus station. Fair restaurant. Rooms **C** dbl.

Chogoria
Cool Inn Cheap, friendly, central place with clean rooms **C** dbl.
Transit Motel 3km out of town. A good place to organise Mount Kenya climbs. Rooms **C** s/c dbl. Camping **A** pp.

Meru
Castella Hotel Similar to the Continental Hotel (see below) but further from the bus station.
Continental Hotel Popular basic lodge around the corner from the bus station. Rooms **B** dbl.
Ivory Springs Restaurant Good meals and snacks a few doors up from the Castella.
New Milimani Hotel Nairobi side of town, about 2km from bus station. Good food. **C/D** s/c room with hot water.

Nanyuki
Equator Café Opposite the Kenya Commercial Bank, decent s/c rooms in the **C** range.

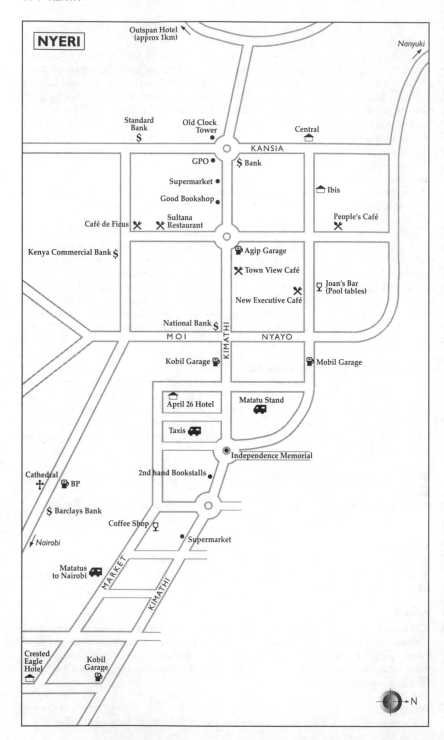

NYERI

Outspan Hotel
(approx 1km)

Nanyuki

Standard
Bank $

Old Clock
Tower ■

Central

KANSIA

GPO ●

$ Bank

Supermarket ●

Ibis

Good Bookshop ●

People's Café ✗

Café de Ficus ✗

Sultana
✗ Restaurant

Kenya Commercial Bank $

Agip Garage

Town View Café ✗

Joan's Bar
(Pool tables) ♀

New Executive Café ✗

National Bank $

MOI

KIMATHI

NYAYO

Kobil Garage

Mobil Garage

April 26 Hotel

Matatu Stand

Taxis

Independence Memorial

Cathedral
✝

BP

2nd hand Bookstalls ●

$ Barclays Bank

Coffee Shop ♀

Nairobi

Supermarket ●

Matatus
to Nairobi

MARKET

KIMATHI

Crested
Eagle
Hotel

Kobil
Garage

N

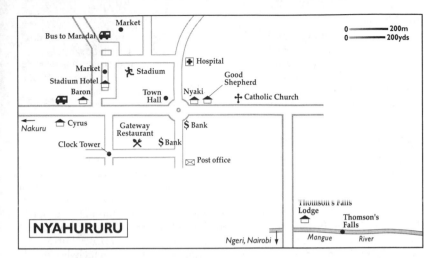

Highlife Bar Acceptable and reasonably priced s/c rooms on the main road 500m from the *matatu* station. **B** dbl.

Marina Grill Popular restaurant and bar on the main road opposite the post office.

Nanyuki River Lodge Tel: 32523. Probably the best cheap accommodation in town. Rooms are quiet, clean and secure, with hot showers, and cost **C** s/c sgl or dbl.

Nanyuki Youth Hostel Emmanuel Parish Centre, Market Rd. Rooms are basic and very cramped, but affordable enough at **B** pp.

Simiron Guesthouse About the best of several basic lodges dotted around the *matatu* station. Rooms **B**/**C**.

Naro Moru

Mount Kenya Youth Hostel This is the traditional base for budget travellers climbing Mount Kenya. Unless you're lucky with a lift, the hostel is a 9km walk from Naro Moru along the road to Mount Kenya National Park. It's a good place to put together a group to climb the mountain, but also worth visiting in its own right for the wonderful walking, birdwatching and mammal spotting in the surrounding forest. Dorm **B** pp. Camp **A** pp.

Naro Moru Hotel 86 One of several basic lodgings in the village, all of which are in the **B**/**C** range.

Naro Moru River Lodge Pleasant mid-range hotel 15 minutes' walk from Naro Moru village on forested banks of the Naro Moru River. Swimming pool, tennis courts, restaurant, good trout fishing and abundant birds. The management has a vast experience of organising Mount Kenya climbs. Dorm **C** pp. Camp **B** pp.

Nyeri

April 26 Hotel Acceptable local lodgings in the **B** range.

Bahati Lodging On Kimathi Way next to the bus station. Clean, basic rooms. **A**/**B**.

Café de Ficus Good meals for around US$2–3.

Central Hotel Faded colonial-era hotel with good value s/c rooms with hot water. Opposite Barclays Bank. Restaurant. **D**/**E**.

Greenleaf Restaurant Good local restaurant.

Ibis Hotel Unexpectedly smart five-storey block with popular ground floor restaurant, offering s/c accommodation with hot showers at a reasonable **C**/**D** sgl/dbl.

Outspan Hotel Both the rooms and meals at this lovely out-of-town hotel are out of reach of most backpacker budgets, but the grounds are a great place for a wander and expensive beer.

Nyahururu

Good Shepherd Lodging On the road to the falls about 500m from the bus station, this is about the best of a dozen or so cheap hotels in the town centre. Rooms **A** sgl.

Thomson's Falls Lodge Underpatronised and atmospherically creaky colonial hotel built 1km out of town above the falls in 1931. Nice place to eat, even if you stay in town. Rooms around US$30/40 (open to negotiation). Camping **D** per site (hot showers).

Stadium Hotel Opposite the stadium, about 200m from bus station. Good rooms **B**/**C** s/c with hot water.

THE NORTHERN DESERTS

The northern half of Kenya is an arid, thinly populated region visited by few backpackers and (at least to the east of the Isiolo–Moyale road) frequently rendered unsafe by Somali bandits. Increasingly, the few backpackers who do visit northern Kenya are simply travelling along the Isiolo–Moyale road to get to or from Ethiopia. There are, however, two other interesting routes through the north: those leading from Nyahururu in the central highlands and Kitale in the Uganda border region to, respectively, the eastern and western shores of Lake Turkana.

The springboard for overland travel to Ethiopia is **Isiolo**, which lies barely 30km to the north of the central highlands yet could be another world. In contrast to sedate, orderly highland towns such as Nyeri and Nanyuki, Isiolo is the archetypal frontier town, situated at the end of the tarmac, supporting a weird and colourful ethnic mix of Somali, Boran, Meru, Samburu and Turkana peoples. The dusty air of Isiolo is seemingly infused with the mildly narcotic *miraa* leaves that are chewed religiously wherever you look. Even if you're not heading further north – no, especially if you're not heading further north – Isiolo makes for a fascinating diversion from travelling in the central highlands.

From Isiolo, the Trans-African Highway continues for another 270km, skirting Samburu National Reserve, crossing the flat Kaisut Desert, before it reaches the town of **Marsabit**. Something of an oasis, Marsabit is situated on an isolated volcanic range, dotted with briny crater lakes, covered in montane grassland and lush forest, and supporting a varied ethnic mix similar to Isiolo. Surrounding the town, the 2,090km^2 Marsabit National Reserve supports mammals and birds you wouldn't normally associate with northern Kenya. The forest on the outskirts of town (entry to which is permitted only by vehicle) is home to elephant, black-and-white colobus, blue monkey, buffalo, bushbuck, leopard and lion. More open parts of the reserve may be explored on foot, and they offer the chance of seeing cheetah, reticulated giraffe, greater kudu, Grevy's zebra and striped hyena – try the walk to Gof Redo Crater, 5km north of town near the junction of the North Horr and Moyale Roads.

Maralal is the gateway town to the eastern shore of Lake Turkana and the unofficial capital of the Samburu people. A pleasant, interesting town, Maralal is worth a visit in its own right – it's not a long minibus ride from Nyahururu, with the added incentive that elephants are commonly seen along the road. The town itself lies within the little-visited Maralal Wildlife Sanctuary, and a 30-minute walk north of town brings you to the Safari Lodge, where you can do your game viewing from the bar. Another good reason to visit Maralal is the camel trips run by Yare Safaris.

The gem of northern Kenya is **Lake Turkana**, alternatively known as the Jade Sea. Covering an area of 6,400km^2, Turkana is the largest desert lake in the world, and the Turkana region has long been Kenya's most talked-about off-the-beaten-track destination: a dry and inhospitable lunar landscape offset by the changeable blue-green waters of the vast lake. Turkana is a wildlife sanctuary of sorts, supporting a staggering 22,000 crocodiles, a large hippo population and a profusion of birds, particularly migrant waders. The main breeding sites, South and Central Island, have been declared national parks.

The only tourist centre on the eastern shore of Turkana, **Loiyangalani**, was founded in the 1960s around a palm-fringed freshwater spring. The surrounding area is home to a variety of ethnic groups, notably the Elmolo: Cushitic-speaking fishermen who are regarded to be the lake shore's earliest remaining inhabitants, and who are possibly the smallest ethnic group in the world, numbering a mere 500. Turkana's other tourist centre is **Ferguson's Gulf** on the west shore, once famed for its bird life, large crocodiles and game fishing (Nile perch and tiger fish), but now dried up for several years. The Ferguson's Gulf area does, however, remain the best base for visits to Central Island, an extinct volcano with three crater lakes and, in April and May, the world's largest breeding population of crocodiles.

Access and getting around
There is regular public transport to Isiolo from Nairobi and most other towns in the central highlands. There are normally a few buses between Isiolo and Marsabit every week, though these are sometimes suspended after outbursts of banditry, in which case you should wait at the police barrier for a lift with a truck – the convoy to Moyale on the Ethiopian border leaves Isiolo at dawn, takes about ten hours to get to Marsabit, and then another 12 to 20 to reach Moyale on the border. Once you're in Marsabit, the entrance gate to the national reserve is about 2km from the town centre and the lodge is 3km into the park. You can walk to the entrance gate, or catch a lift with the staff vehicle which runs between the town and the lodge at least once every day.

Minibuses between Nyahururu and Maralal leave every hour or two. If you're doing a camel safari, Yare Safaris can include the transfer to Maralal in their package, so discuss this with them in Nairobi. Hitching to Turkana from Maralal is erratic, so many travellers opt to do a one-to-two-week camping safari to the lake – a few operators (see *Safari companies* on page 149) run these trips and departures are coordinated so that you will normally end up with whichever company heads up next. If you do try to make it there on your own, there will be the occasional *matatu* from Maralal to Baragoi, possibly even to South Horr, but there's no public transport whatsoever beyond that.

It's a lot easier to get to the western shore of the lake, though unfortunately this is a much less interesting route. At least one bus every morning leaves Kitale for Kalekol on Ferguson's Gulf, a hot, dusty trip which you might want to break up at Lodwar, the capital of the Turkana people. At one time, Kalekol was practically lapped by Turkana's waters, but these days it's a two-hour walk to Longech, the nearest lake shore village. The nearby Lake Turkana Fishing Lodge, once the best place to organise a boat trip to the crocodile breeding colony on Central Island, has closed.

Where to stay and eat
Isiolo
Jamhuri Guesthouse A long-standing favourite, situated behind Barclays Bank, and good value if you don't mind the Somali hustlers who tend to hang around and swarm newly arrived travellers. Hot communal showers in the morning. Clean but basic rooms **A**/**B** sgl/dbl. S/c rooms likely to be operational by the end of 2000.
Madina Classic Lodge The gaudy yellow-and-blue exterior makes it easy to pick out this new place situated about 200m down the road from the Jamhuri. Clean, quiet and good value at **A**/**B** sgl/dbl.
Silent Inn Practically next to the Jamhuri, and similar in standard, but quieter and scruffier. **A**/**B** sgl/dbl.

Marsabit

Al-Nasser Guesthouse Quiet, secure, hot bucket-showers. **A** sgl.
Catholic Mission. Free camping. Limited facilities.
Jey Jey Boarding and Lodging Clean s/c rooms, reputed to have hot water showers in the morning. **B**/**C** sgl/dbl.
Marsabit Lodge Former government hotel in stunning location overlooking a crater lake in the park. Regularly visited by elephants, plenty of water birds to be seen. Camping **B** pp. Access could be a problem unless you can hitch a lift (some wealthy locals like to head up there for a drink).
Marsabit National Reserve Gate On the outskirts of town. Cleared sites in forest, popular with baboons. Showers. Longdrop toilets. Camping **A** pp. Park entrance fees must be paid.
Kisatu Hotel Clean rooms with hot showers, just off the main road next to the market. **B**/**C**.

Maralal

Buffalo Hotel A long-standing travellers' favourite, but growing increasingly shabby with each passing year. The noise from the bar can be disruptive unless you intend joining in! Basic rooms **B**, communal showers haven't functioned in years.
Impala Lodge New, central lodge with clean rooms and working showers. Recommended. **B** dbl.
Yare Safaris About 3km out of town on Nyahururu road; tel: Nairobi 72-5610. A friendly place and the resident Samburu are very approachable. Good restaurant and bar. Bandas **E**/**F** dbl. Camping **B** pp. Tent hire.

Loiyangalani and stops along the road from Maralal

There are a few possible stops on route. The largest town en route is **Baragoi**, 97km north of Maralal, which has a few **B** lodgings. A more attractive proposition is **South Horr**, which lies in a forested valley a further 40km towards Loiyangalani. Again, there are a few cheap lodgings here, and there is also an attractive and practically free campsite next to a stream near the Catholic Mission. About 10km further north, you can pitch a tent for next to nothing at the isolated **Kurungu Camp**, where the staff can arrange guided walks on the forested slopes of nearby Ngiro Peak (2,848m), a refuge for many types of bird as well as large mammals including elephant. In **Loiyangalani** itself, you have the choice of pitching your own tent at Sunset Camp or Elmolo Lodge for **A** pp, or taking a basic room at the Cold Drink Inn for **B** pp.

Ferguson's Gulf and Lodwar

There are several places to stay in Lodwar, of which the Turkwel Hotel is about the best bet, with rooms for **C** s/c dbl with fans. There are a couple of basic lodgings in Kalekol, neither of which is anything out of the ordinary. Closer to the lake shore, there used to be a campsite at the Lake Turkana Fishing Lodge, but the lodge has been closed for some time now, and your only option is to ask around for a room in a private house in the nearby village of Longech.

Western Kenya
THE RIFT VALLEY

To the west of Nairobi, the Rift Valley cuts between the highlands of western and central Kenya to dramatic effect. The dusty Rift Valley floor is delineated by cliffs up to one kilometre high, and broken up by a string of gem-like lakes and the evocative outlines of extinct volcanoes. The grand scale of the scenery seems to

TURKANA BY OVERLAND TRUCK

Lake Turkana is one of those alluring but virtually inaccessible destinations for which even the most staunchly independent of travellers might think seriously about joining an organised trip. We did this in 1999, travelling on an eight-day overland safari arranged by Gametrackers, and can recommend it highly as an exciting, off-the-beaten-track alternative to the more conventional safaris through the southern reserves .

The route followed by Gametrackers allows for plenty of game viewing, starting as it does with two nights at a permanent tented camp in Samburu Game Reserve. This is followed by a dusty, spine-jarring drive northwards along the laughably mistitled 'Trans-Africa Highway' to the montane oasis of Marsabit, where you camp on the edge of the national reserve after spending an afternoon at Marsabit Lodge, which overlooks a crater lake teeming with birds and regularly visited by elephants.

From Marsabit, the truck passes through the remote Chalbi desert, passing through stunningly empty vistas where you can drive all day without encountering another vehicle – here, even the domestic camel are skittish at the approach of a truck. The overnight stop is at a mission in Kachula, a traditional Gabbra village notable for its church, decorated in mediaeval Ethiopian style. From Kachula, another hot, bumpy drive leads to the Rift Valley Escarpment and the first glimpse of Lake Turkana, it sshimmering green waters enclosed by a primal landscape of extinct volcanoes and solidified lava flows.

Two nights are spent on the lakeshore at a private permanent camp outside Loiyangalani, a one-street settlement whose status as the largest settlement on the 250km eastern lakeshore provides some perspective on what a desolate region this actually is. A boat ride on the lake provides good birdwatching, and probable sightings of some of the lake's enormous crocodiles, before visiting Elmolo Island, home to what is reputedly the world's smallest tribe.

While it is the lake that provides the nominal incentive for doing this trip, it is the people of northern Kenya that make the most lasting impression, nomadic pastoralists such as the Gabbra, Turkana and Samburu whose adherence to a strictly traditional lifestyle and dress is practically unique in modern East Africa. In small villages such as North Horr or Kachula, even in the, um, city of Loiyangalani, you could be forgiven for thinking that the whole human spectacle is being put on for tourists – except that practically no tourists pass this way aside from the fortnightly Gametrackers truck. As we returned to Nairobi from Turkana, we felt as if we had travelled not only through space but through time, to be granted a vision of Africa as it must have been a hundred years ago. That this ancient human landscape still exists in a country as relatively developed as Kenya simply defies belief!

epitomise East Africa and, with ample opportunity to see large mammals on foot, it is an area that begs gentle exploration by backpackers.

The main string of Rift Valley Lakes lies northwest of Nairobi. **Lake Naivasha** is the closest of these lakes to Nairobi, and arguably the most attractive, making it an ideal first stop for backpackers in Kenya. One of only two freshwater lakes in this part of the Rift Valley, Naivasha is given to large fluctuations in water level, for which reason the shape and environment of the shore is in a constant state of flux. In recent years, the lake has been fringed by dense stands of papyrus and yellow fever woodland, a marked contrast to the dusty euphorbia scrub of the surrounding plains. Naivasha supports a large hippo population and it is rightfully regarded as one of the finest birding areas in East Africa, with over 400 species recorded in the immediate vicinity. There is also some terrestrial game around, easily seen if you take a day trip to Hell's Gate National Park, Crescent Island or the Green Crater Lake Reserve (see box *Day trips in the Naivasha area* on page 182).

To the west of Naivasha, **Nakuru** is the capital of Rift Valley Province and Kenya's fourth largest town. A dusty, rather nondescript place, Nakuru is of interest mostly as a major transport hub, though there are a couple of worthwhile day trips in the area. About 4km out of town along the Nairobi road, Hyrax Hill has been a site of human habitation for at least 3,000 years, and is of interest for several ancient pit dwellings, a ruined fort, and ritual burial sites, all of which are described in detail in a booklet available at the on-site museum. The extinct Menangai Volcano, the large mountain which rises unobtrusively behind Nakuru, is notable for its partially collapsed 90km² crater, which can be seen from a spectacular viewpoint about 10km from the town centre.

The most important tourist attraction in the Nakuru area, **Lake Nakuru National Park** is reasonably accessible to independent travellers. The centrepiece of this small national park is Lake Nakuru, a shallow soda pan given to unpredictable fluctuations in water level. When the water level is suitable, Nakuru supports flocks of up to two million greater and lesser flamingoes – a daunting sight from up close, and one of East Africa's great wildlife spectacles as seen from Baboon Cliff viewpoint, where the flamingoes appear as a shimmering pink fringe around the lake. Even when the flamingoes aren't around (and this has most often been the case in recent years), Lake Nakuru always offers delightful birdwatching and reliably good game viewing – waterbuck, warthog and buffalo are prolific, particularly in the yellow fever forest that lines the northern shore, and the reserve offers a good chance of seeing leopards, rhinos and the rare Rothschild's giraffe.

Following the B4 north from Nakuru, grassy farmland gives way to an altogether harsher landscape of baked red soil, dry watercourses and tangled acacia scrub. About 60km along this road, at the base of the Rift Valley escarpment, hidden behind a range of low hills, the little-visited but immensely spectacular **Lake Bogoria National Reserve** protects the brackish lake after which it is named. Regarded as the best place in Kenya to see the rare greater kudu, and supporting a fluctuating flamingo population which at times outnumbers that of Lake Nakuru, Bogoria is primarily of interest for its scenery. Nestled in a mountainous bowl, the lake has a primeval quality that is epitomised by the geysers at Maji ya Moto, some of which leap 2m into the air from a grassy field on the western shore.

Lake Baringo is the most northerly of Kenya's small Rift Valley lakes, and after Naivasha it is probably the most budget friendly and accessible to backpackers. Lying in arid acacia scrub at the base of the Rift Valley escarpment, Baringo is lined with papyrus beds and well-developed acacia woodland. Hippos, crocodiles and monitor lizards are easily seen from the shore, as is a wonderful array of water birds. It's also worth walking back towards Nakuru to the cliffs 2km from the lake shore, where you are likely to see rock hyrax, baboon and the distinctive black eagle. Climb a footpath up the cliff for a great view back to the lake. Boat trips can be organised by asking around at Kampi Ya Samaki, the largest village on the lake shore.

Access and getting around

Public transport along the surfaced road connecting Nairobi to Naivasha and Nakuru runs regularly throughout the day. From Naivasha town, Lake Naivasha is most easily approached along the Moi South Lake Road, which branches from the old Nairobi–Naivasha road about 2km out of town. The first 30km of the South Lake Road is surfaced and serviced by regular *matatus* from Naivasha town.

Nakuru town is a major transport hub, connected by buses, minibuses and/or *matatus* to Nairobi, Naivasha, Nyahururu, Kisii, Kisumu, Marigat and Eldoret. Travellers heading north along the B4 should be able to find a bus to Kampi ya Samaki on Lake Baringo. If not, catch a minibus to Marigat, from where there are a few *matatus* daily to Lake Baringo. The entrance gate to Lake Bogoria National Reserve lies about 20km east of the B4 by road – there is the occasional *matatu* there from Marigat, or you could ask to be dropped at the signposted turn-off to the gate 3km south of Marigat and hitch from there. The hot springs lie 11km from Loboi Gate; there are no restrictions on walking within the national reserve.

To reach Menangai Crater from Nakuru, follow the Nairobi road out of town for 2km, turn left into the road marked 'Hill Climb' and then take the second right turn. Once out of suburban Nakuru, a dirt road leads through eucalyptus plantations and grassland for 8km till it reaches the viewpoint. It's a five-to-six-hour round trip by foot, or you can hire a taxi from town. Hitching isn't a viable option, except perhaps at weekends.

Lake Nakuru National Park is visited on a high proportion of organised safaris, but it is also one of the easier national parks to visit independently, not least because the main entrance gate lies about 30 minutes' walk from Nakuru town centre. Hitching from outside the gate is not impossible, though you should check that your lift isn't staying overnight at one of the upmarket lodges. If you prefer not to leave things to chance, organise a day trip through any travel agency in Nakuru or, more cheaply, make your own arrangements with a taxi driver (the roads are fine for a saloon car and many taxi drivers know the park well).

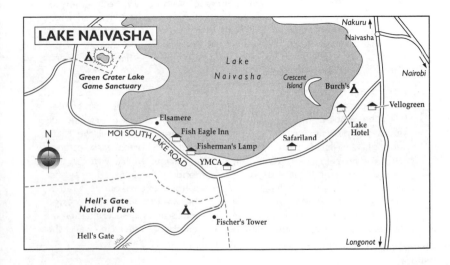

DAY TRIPS IN THE NAIVASHA AREA

The area around Lake Naivasha offers several opportunities for seeing wildlife on foot. Running along the South Lake Road coming from Naivasha town, these are:

Crescent Island

Opposite Lake Naivasha Country Club. The island supports large herbivores such as giraffe and some rather aggressive waterbuck, as well as a wide range of birds. It can only be visited from the club. The entrance fee of around US$10 includes a motorboat ride across.

Hell's Gate National Park

Named after the impressive sandstone gorge it protects, Hell's Gate is one of the few accessible places in East Africa where you can walk or cycle unaccompanied amongst a wide variety of plains animals – most commonly Thomson's gazelle, Coke's hartebeest, klipspringer, zebra and buffalo, but also sometimes lion, leopard, cheetah or elephant (though you can forget about the heavily hyped pair of lammergeyers, since they disappeared more than a decade ago). Near the entrance to the park, Fischer's Tower is a striking volcanic plug overrun with rock hyrax. The Elsa Entrance Gate is 1.5km from the South Lake Road, and clearly signposted just past the YMCA. The most attractive way to visit is on foot or by bicycle (hire at Fisherman's Camp). The gorge is very hot during the day, so an early start is recommended – and carry plenty of water.

Elsamere

The former home of Joy Adamson, this lies on the lake shore 2km past Fisherman's Camp. It is open to day visitors between 15.00 and 17.00, when an elaborate afternoon tea is served and you can look out for the troop of black-and-white colobus monkeys that is resident in the grounds.

Green Crater Lake Sanctuary

This crater lake lies in the extinct Songasoi volcano, where a variety of reintroduced plains animals can be seen along with the black-and-white colobus monkeys, buffaloes and birds that naturally inhabit the forested rim. The entrance is on the South Lake Road 6km past the end of the tarmac. The best way to get there is to hire a bicycle from Fisherman's Camp. A small entrance fee is charged.

Longonot National Park

Mount Longonot is the distinctive ragged-edged volcano which can be seen from the South Lake Road. The perfect volcanic caldera offers fantastic views in all directions, and it can be climbed from Longonot village 15km south of Naivasha town on the old Nairobi road. The normal park entrance fee must be paid at the KWS office in the village, where you can also organise an armed guide (highly recommended for protection against thieves if nothing else). The ascent takes an hour or two, and it is rather steep towards the end. Once at the top, the view down to the forested floor of the crater makes a dramatic contrast to the sparse vegetation on the old lava flows which you've just climbed. You can walk the circumference of the crater rim in about three hours.

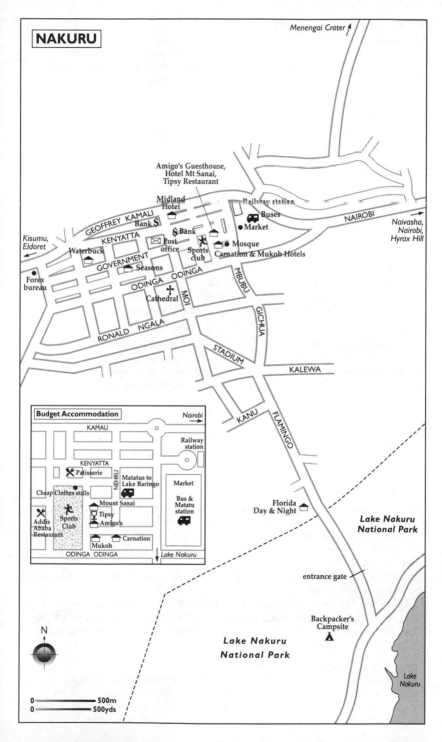

NAKURU

Menengai Crater

Amigo's Guesthouse,
Hotel Mt Sanai,
Tipsy Restaurant

Midland
Hotel

Railway station

GEOFFREY KAMALI

Bank $

Buses

NAIROBI

Naivasha,
Nairobi,
Hyrax Hill

Kisumu,
Eldoret

KENYATTA

$ Bank

● Market

Post
office

Waterbuck

Sports
club

● Mosque

Carnation & Mukoh Hotels

GOVERNMENT

Seasons

MBUBU

Forex
bureau

ODINGA ODINGA

Cathedral

MOI

GICHUA

RONALD NGALA

STADIUM

KALEWA

Budget Accommodation

Nairobi

KAMAU

Railway
station

KENYATTA

KANU

FLAMINGO

Patisserie

NEHRU

Matatus to
Lake Baringo

Market

Cheap Clothes stalls

Mount Sanai

Bus &
Matatu
station

Florida
Day & Night

**Lake Nakuru
National Park**

Addis
Ababa
Restaurant

Sports
Club

Tipsy

Amigo's

Mukoh

Carnation

ODINGA ODINGA

Lake Nakuru

entrance gate

N

Backpacker's
Campsite
▲

**Lake Nakuru
National Park**

Lake
Nakuru

0 ——— 500m
0 ——— 500yds

Where to stay and eat
Naivasha
There's little reason to overnight in Naivasha town, unless perhaps you arrive towards nightfall, in which case you can bed down at any number of indifferent lodgings in the **B** bracket. The **Naivasha Silver Hotel** is the pick of the accommodation, and you can have an exceptional meal at the cosy **La Belle Inn**.

Lake Naivasha
There is a good selection of accommodation along the South Lake Road, catering to most tastes and budgets. In the order that you'll pass them coming from Naivasha town, with rough distance from the start of the South Lake Road in brackets:

Burch's Farm (3km) Family-run place. Highly recommended during the week, when it's blissfully quiet except for regular nocturnal hippo visits and prolific birds. It can get crowded when the Nairobi boat owners roll in at weekends. The entrance is next to a dilapidated blue building signposted Thitavo Shop & Hotel. Chalets **C** dbl. Camping **A** pp.

YMCA (15km) Run-down dorms and cramped campsite some distance from the water. The cheapest place to stay near the lake. Ideally positioned for walking to Hell's Gate. Dorm **B** pp. Camping **A** pp.

Fisherman's Camp (20km) Situated in a stand of yellow fever woodland that's rustling with birds and visited by hippos, this is the established backpackers' hangout on the lake. Bicycle, boat and tent hire available. Cold beer and sodas on site. Meals at the adjacent Fish Eagle Inn. Reed huts **E** dbl. Dorm or standing tent **B** pp. Camping **A** pp.

Nakuru
Addis Ababa Restaurant Good and reasonably priced Italian and Ethiopian food, a welcome change from the usual chips with everything Kenyan menu.

Amigo's Guesthouse The best in a cluster of cheap hotels off Mosque road, a block or two west of the bus station, and a long-standing favourite with budget travellers. Hot showers. Rooms **B** sgl or dbl.

Carnation Hotel Good, quiet, relatively mid-range hotel close to the bus station. Rooms **C/D** s/c with hot water.

Joska Hotel New, central lodge, just off Kenyatta Av, clean and quiet with a good restaurant. **B/C** s/c sgl/dbl.

Lake Nakuru Backpackers' Campsite Immediately inside the park entrance gate and accessible on foot. No entrance fee is charged to backpackers unless they get a lift further into the park. Once a quiet retreat with plenty of game passing through, this site is now generally overrun by budget safari companies and the only wildlife you're likely to encounter are the resident and very aggressive troops of baboon and vervet monkey. Camping **C** pp.

Midland Hotel Mid-range hotel of interest to backpackers mainly for its busy bar, affordable courtyard grill (good chicken) and row of pool tables – all of which make it deservedly popular with local office workers.

Mount Sanai Hotel New hotel offering clean, good value accommodation with s/c singles and doubles both in the **C** range.

Mukoh Hotel This vast but conveniently located block serves as a useful fallback if the competition is full. Otherwise seems a bit musty and run down for rooms in the **C** range.

Tipsy Restaurant Next to Amigo's, this is another established favourite serving Indian and Western dishes for around US$2. Recommended.

Lake Bogoria National Reserve
Loboi Gate Campsite Basic site without any facilities worth mentioning. **B** pp.

Papyrus Inn Hotel Immediately outside Loboi Gate. Clean but basic rooms seem overpriced at **C/D** , though you should be able to negotiate a better rate. Smart restaurant, TV lounge and bar with fridge.

Lake Baringo

Bahari and **Lake View hotels** The best of a few scruffy **B** lodges in Kampi ya Samaki.
Roberts Campsite The established place to stay at Baringo for a couple of decades,
Roberts has wonderfully lush lakeshore grounds adjacent to the upmarket Lake Baringo
Club and about 1km from Kampi ya Samaki village. The site is teeming with birds and a
favoured haunt of hippo. Firewood. Shop selling cold sodas and canned food. Meals
available at the club next door. Camping **B** pp. Bandas **C** pp.

THE UGANDA BORDER AREA

Dominated by the densely populated and fertile highlands which rise around the
Lake Victoria basin, the far west of Kenya is largely undeveloped for tourism and
its main attractions have a low key, off-the-beaten-track feel that might come as
something of a revelation to backpackers who arrive from the coast or the major
game reserves.

The main regional route focus is **Kisumu**, Kenya's third largest town and
probably the most populous port anywhere on the Lake Victoria shore. With its
languid, tropical character and somewhat run-down air, Kisumu has an engaging
atmosphere, vaguely reminiscent of the less touristed parts of the Tanzanian coast.
The extensive Kisumu Museum and attached snake park on the Nairobi road
about 500m past the bus station are certainly worth a look. To see something of the
lake, you can walk along the main road south of town for about 30 minutes to
Hippo Point, which still occasionally lives up to its name, and then for another half
hour or so to the small Luo fishing village of Dunga.

Kisumu is connected by ferry services to several smaller lake ports, of which
Kendu Bay is perhaps the most obvious target for a day trip or overnight
excursion. The papyrus beds around the jetty are teeming with birds, and it should
be possible to negotiate with local fishermen to take a small boat out to see hippos.
Only 4km from the small town centre, flamingoes are resident on Simbi Crater
Lake, which is said to have been formed by an angry old lady who brought down
a massive flood to kill the residents of a village that annoyed her.

Travellers who approach Kisumu from the Rift Valley have the option of coming
through the highlands to the east of Lake Victoria and the town of **Kericho** in the
heart of Africa's most important tea-growing region. It's an extraordinarily attractive
area, with orderly tea plantations stretching over rolling hills interrupted by forested
valleys and enhanced by occasional glimpses over the Rift Valley. On the Nakuru
road, 8km out of Kericho, the Chagaik Arboretum consists of a variety of endemic
and exotic trees sloping down to a small dam ringed by lush indigenous forest – a
good spot to see forest birds and black-and-white colobus monkeys. Between
Kericho and Lake Victoria, **Kisii** is a rather frenetic small town surrounded by
fertile hills and noted for its fine soapstone carvings, most of which are produced
25km out of town at a co-operative near Tabaka.

The largest town in the highlands to the north of Lake Victoria, and unique
among Kenyan towns in that it was founded by Afrikaners, **Eldoret** is of interest
to travellers mostly as a transport hub – unless you arrive late in the day there's
little reason to explore beyond the off-puttingly chaotic bus station. Much the
same can be said of the smaller but still substantial town of **Kakamega**, which
would barely warrant a mention were it not for its proximity to the renowned
Kakamega Forest: one of Kenya's most alluring destinations for anyone with
more than a passing interest in natural history, and a readily accessible and
affordable target for backpackers (see box *Kakamega Forest* on page 186–7).

The most northerly and arguably the most attractive town in the western
highlands, **Kitale** is a useful base for further exploration, though the town itself

boasts only one notable attraction in the form of the Kitale Museum, where you can see detailed displays on the ethnic groups of northwestern Kenya as well as walk the short nature trail through a strip of riverine forest. About 15km northeast of Kitale, the tiny and infrequently visited **Saiwa Swamp National Park** boasts a compact network of walking trails and rickety viewing platforms making it particularly well suited to pedestrian visits. Saiwa Swamp is the one place in Africa where visitors are practically guaranteed a clear sighting of the otherwise elusive sitatunga antelope, and it's also a good place to see bushbuck, a variety of primates including the localised De Brazza's monkey, and several unusual forest and swamp birds.

To the east of Saiwa Swamp, the metamorphic **Cherangani Mountains** rise to an altitude of 3,581m, where they form a barrier between the lush highlands around Kitale and the arid desert of the north. The area below the mountains offers a striking contrast in scenery, particularly around Marich Pass and along the dirt road towards Tot, while the forested slopes protect typical forest birds and monkeys as well as the shy bongo antelope. Walking in the area is unrestricted, there are no prohibitive park fees to pay, and the range is crossed by a number of dirt roads – the possibilities are endless. For further details of hiking routes, get hold of David Else's *Mountain Walking in Kenya* (Robertson McCarta) or speak to the staff at the Marich Pass Field Studies Centre.

Access and getting around

Heading directly to western Kenya from Nairobi, plenty of public transport runs via Nakuru directly to Kisumu and Eldoret, with the Akamba bus being the most

KAKAMEGA FOREST

This large forest is a serious contender for East Africa's best-kept game-viewing secret, and it is highly attractive to backpackers for the combination of inexpensive accommodation, relative accessibility on public transport, and limitless walking opportunities in the company of some of the most skilled and knowledgeable wildlife guides in the country.

Kakamega Forest is renowned by naturalists for supporting isolated populations of numerous typically West African species. The most visible large mammals are monkeys, of which baboon, black-and-white colobus, red-tailed monkey and blue monkey are common and De Brazza's monkey is resident in the part of the forest protected by Kaseri Nature Reserve. Most of Kakamega's other mammalian 'specials' are nocturnal and unlikely to be seen without some effort – the large sloth-like potto, loosely related to the lemurs of Madagascar, is quite easy to pick up at night with a powerful flashlight or torch. Bushbaby, tree pangolin, leopard and several types of squirrel are also present. Over 320 bird species have been recorded in and around the forest, 16 of which are found nowhere else in Kenya. The bird checklist compiled by Udo Savali in 1989 is sometimes available at Udo's Bandas. Enthusiastic birdwatchers and those wishing to enter the heart of the forest are advised to take a guide, at least on their first outing. There are, however, many opportunities for self-guided exploration.

There are two places to stay in the forest, situated about 15km apart as the crow flies. Udo's Bandas lies in the northern part of the forest, an area protected by the small and relatively recently proclaimed Kakamega National Reserve, run by KWS. Udo's is a good place to see black-and-white colobus and red-tailed monkeys and to familiarise yourself with the relatively common forest birds such reliable and speedy service. Train services covering the same routes are slow and overpriced. All the main towns in western Kenya are connected to each other by a regular stream of minibuses and/or *matatus*.

A daily ferry links Kisumu to Kendu Bay, leaving Kisumu at 09.00 on Tuesday, Friday and Sunday and arriving two hours later before continuing to Homa Bay. The ferry returns to Kisumu on the following day, passing through Kendu Bay at around 14.00. There are also frequent *matatus* between Kisumu and Kendu Bay. To reach Simbi Crater Lake from Kendu Bay, follow the Homa Bay road for about 2km. Immediately after the first bridge, turn right and continue walking for about 1km.

From Kitale there are regular *matatus* between Kitale and Kapenguria, stopping at the turn-off to Saiwa Swamp and Sirikwa Safaris. The entrance to Saiwa Swamp lies about an hour's walk from the signposted turn-off. If you are continuing northwards, a few *matatus* daily leave Kapenguria for Ortum and Sigor daily. The early morning bus from Kitale to Lodwar can drop you at Marich Pass.

The most accessible part of the Kakamega Forest is Udo's Bandas, 2km from the main road between Kakamega and Webuye road – any *matatu* to Webuye can drop you at the turn-off 17km from Kakamega town. Note that there are two signposted turn-offs 50m apart here – take the southerly one, which is signposted 'Kakamega National Reserve Headquarters'. Isecheno Rest House lies in a separate part of the forest, about 5km past Shinyalu along a dirt road running from Kakamega town to Kapsabet. The once-daily *matatu* service connecting Eldoret to Kakamega via Shinyalu can drop you 1km from the rest house. Alternatively, catch a *matatu* from Kakamega town to Shinyalu and walk the last 5km to the resthouse.

as Luhder's bush shrike, snowy-headed robin-chat, blue flycatcher, great blue touraco, grey-headed barbet, black-and-white casqued hornbill, joyful greenbul, and white-headed woodheap. Two self-guided round trips, both around 5km long, start at the path marked 'Hiking Trail' near the toilet at Udo's. The routes diverge about 1km along this trail. The left fork leads through a well developed stand of forest, where red-tailed and colobus monkeys are common, to an excellent viewpoint near a quarry. The right fork leads through light forest interspersed with open grassland before emerging at a grassy car park from where it descends through riparian forest to a small waterfall – a good place to see mountain wagtail and Ross's touraco. From the waterfall, you can return to Udo's via a motorable track that passes through a heath-like area where flowering plants attract a good range of sunbirds, finches and seedeaters.

The Isecheno Resthouse faces the dense stand of forest where Dale Zimmerman undertook the first detailed ornithological study of the area. The stunning great blue touraco is common around the resthouse, and a troop of black-and-white colobus comes swinging past most evenings. The Zimmerman Plot is criss-crossed by a labyrinth of footpaths, which cannot easily be explored without a guide, and there are no formal trails in this part of the forest. However, the main road towards Kapsabet passes through patches of dense forest, where there is excellent bird and monkey viewing. About 8km along this road, there is a bridge over the Ikuywa River – the footpaths that follow this stream pass through an area that's reckoned to hold the greatest variety of bird species in the forest.

Serious hikers will be interested to hear that KWS has cut an overnight hiking trail from Bunyunga to Isecheno, which will open to the public once bridges have been built over the rivers – for an update, contact the KWS office in Nairobi.

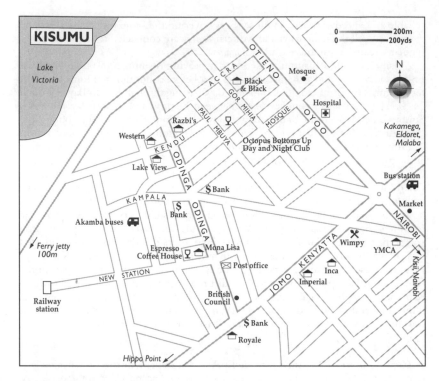

Where to stay and eat
Kisumu

Dunga Refreshments Near Hippo Point 5km out of town. Great position and good Indian and western food. Dorm **B** pp. Camping **A** pp.

Espresso Coffee House Inexpensive fruit juices, curries, steaks and burgers in the city centre.

Octopus Bottoms Up Day and Night Club One of Kenya's most outrageous discos.

Razbi's Guesthouse One of the best and most popular basic lodges in the town centre. Clean rooms **A**/**B**.

Safari Hotel About the best of a few cheapies near the bus station. Rooms **B** dbl.

Western Hotel Comfortable, good value rooms **C** s/c sgl with net and shower.

YMCA Off Nairobi Road 100m from bus station. Basic triple rooms **A** pp.

Kendu Bay

A few cheap lodges on the main road.

Kericho

Embassy Hotel Acceptable basic lodge near bus station. **B**.

Kericho Garden Lodge On the outskirts of town next to the upmarket Tea Hotel. The large, leafy grounds are nicer than the rooms, but it's still about the best deal in town. Rooms **B**/**C**. Camp **A** pp.

Kericho Lodge and Fishing Resort Overlooking forested stream about 1km out of town on Nairobi Road. Good s/c rooms **D**/**E**. Camping **B** pp. Restaurant and bar.

Tea Hotel Colonial era upmarket hotel, of interest to backpackers for the large grounds, cosy lounge with log fire, and affordable Western meals.

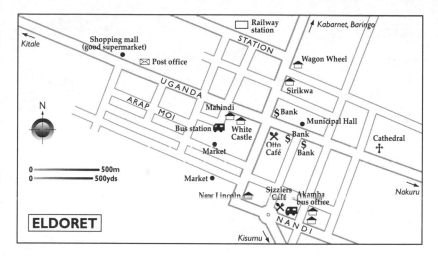

ELDORET

Kisii

Kisii Hotel Run-down state compensated for by attractive grounds and mild period charm. Rooms **C**/**D** s/c.

Safe Lodge and Njua Guesthouse Reasonable local lodges in **B** range.

Eldoret

Mahindi Hotel About the best of a few lodges near the bus station. **B**/**C** s/c sgl/dbl.

Naiberi River Campsite In forested area 20km out of town near Kaptagat. Popular with overland trucks, and has something of the atmosphere of the backpackers' hostels in southern Africa. Dorm **B** pp. Bandas **F** dbl. Camping **A** pp. Phone Eldoret 32644 for a lift there before 17.00 on weekdays.

Otto Café Good varied menu at reasonable prices.

Wagon Wheel Hotel Popular mid-range hotel. Allows camping in the grounds.

Kakamega

Bendera Hotel 500m from bus station, next to BP garage. Large, clean rooms **C** s/c dbl.

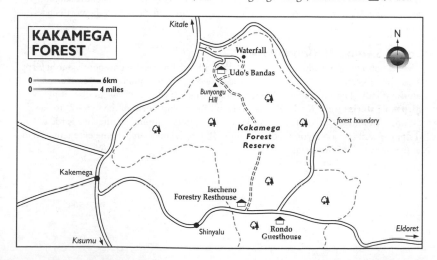

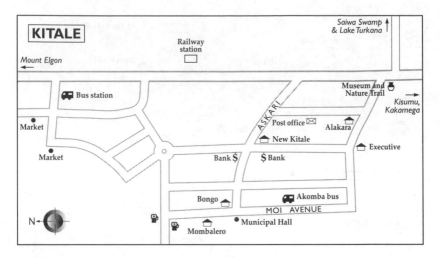

Golf Hotel Upmarket hotel, of interest to backpackers for its good restaurant and lush grounds.

Salama Boarding Reasonable cheapie near bus station. **A**/**B**.

Kakamega Forest

Isecheno Rest House PO Box 88 Kakamega. Four s/c double bedrooms excellent value at **B** pp. Booking for rooms advisable over weekends. Camping permitted and no booking required. Canteen prepares basic meals and tea, but advisable to bring food with you.

Udo's Bandas & Campsite KWS site near reserve headquarters. Huts with bed/mattresses but no bedding **B** pp. Camping **A** pp. Communal cooking area, free firewood, longdrop toilets. Water for washing and drinking from nearby stream. Bring all your own food, though a limited selection of foodstuffs can be bought from the village on the main road between Kakamega and Webuye, 1km north of the turn-off to the campsite.

Kitale

Bongo Hotel Comfortable clean rooms from **C** sgl to **D** s/c dbl. Excellent restaurant.

Star Lodge About the best of several **B** lodges near the roundabout on the north end of Moi Avenue.

Saiwa Swamp National Park

The beautiful but unfacilitated campsite at the park headquarters seems poor value at **C** pp. That said, it's certainly worth spending at least one night there in order to get in an early morning walk. The alternative is to visit as a day trip, either from Kitale or else from **Sirikwa Safaris** on the Kitale–Kapengoria road about 5km north of the turn-off to Saiwa Swamps. Run by a pleasant family, Sirikwa Safaris offers camping in attractive gardens (**B** pp) as well as good accommodation in the **E** range, and there is some excellent walking in the surrounding farmland.

Uganda

In a subcontinent plagued by drought and famine, Uganda seems wonderfully moist and fertile. Flanked by the twin forks of the Great Rift Valley, this is where the eastern savannah meets the western rainforest. The first thing that's likely to strike anybody who arrives in Uganda from elsewhere in the region is how overwhelmingly tropical it looks – the one country in this guide that will fulfil expectations of Tarzan's jungle.

Uganda's charm as a travel destination lies in the combination of lushly intimate landscapes and a compact travel circuit. Nowhere else in Africa can you see such a wide variety of primates with so little effort, from mountain gorillas and chimpanzees, through over ten types of monkey down to the tiny wide-eyed bushbaby. Uganda is also one of the top birdwatching countries in Africa, with over 100 West African rainforest species at the eastern limit of their range. And the opportunities for off-the-beaten-track rambling and hiking are practically without limit.

Uganda has yet to completely rehabilitate an international image formed by the highly publicised reigns of terror of Idi Amin and Milton Obote. In fact, it is one of the safest countries in the region: since the current regime took power in 1986, political stability and economic growth have been high and the incidence of crime against tourists has been remarkably low. No less remarkable is the friendliness of ordinary Ugandans, an estimated million of whom met a violent death between 1966 and 1986, and who are now victims of the worst AIDS epidemic in the world.

BACKGROUND INFORMATION
Geography and climate
Uganda lies on an elevated basin between the eastern and western branches of the Great Rift Valley. Most of the country is rather flat and lies at an altitude of above

FACTS AND FIGURES
Area: 235,796km² (32nd in Africa; similar to Great Britain or Oregon)
Capital: Kampala
Largest towns: Kampala, Jinja, Mbale, Fort Portal, Kabale
Population: 16,582,000 (1991)
Official language: English
Other languages: KiSwahili (widely spoken but not indigenous), Luganda, Runyoro
Currency: Uganda shilling
Head of State: President Yoweri Museveni (since 1986)

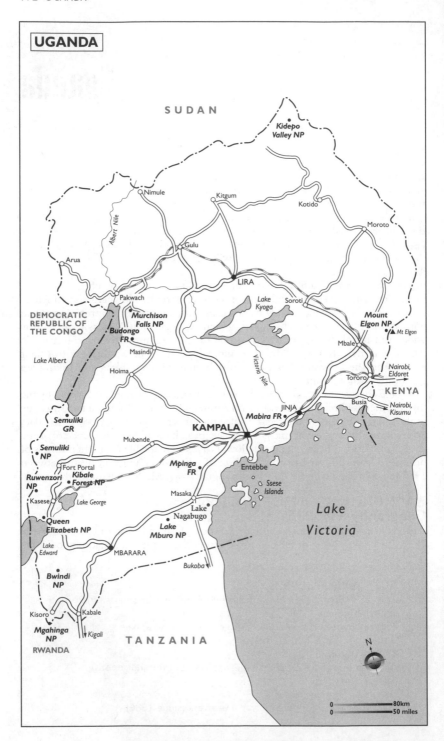

UGANDA

1,000m, though the Kigezi region in the southwest is very mountainous and the Ruwenzori Mountains on the Congolese border reach 5,119m, an altitude exceeded in Africa only by Mount Kenya and Kilimanjaro. Other large mountains in Uganda include the Virungas on the border with the Congo and Rwanda, and Mount Elgon on the Kenya border. Important bodies of water include Lakes Victoria, Albert, Edward, George and Kyoga. The Owen Falls (submerged by a dam near Jinja) is regarded as the official source of the White Nile, the world's longest river.

Uganda's equatorial climate is tempered by its elevated altitude. In most parts of the country, the daily maximum is between 20°C and 27°C and the minimum is between 12°C and 18°C. The highest temperatures in Uganda occur on the plains immediately east of Lake Albert, while the lowest temperatures have been recorded on the glacial peaks of the Ruwenzori. Except in the dry north, where annual rainfall may be as low as 100mm, most parts of Uganda receive between 1,000mm and 2,000mm annually. There is wide regional variation in rainfall patterns, but as a rough guide the wet seasons are from mid-September to November and from March to May.

History

Archaeological evidence suggests that a centralised political entity, which oral traditions remember by the name of Bunyoro-Kitara, had emerged in central Uganda by AD1100. Legend has it that the first rulers of this kingdom were the Batembuzi Dynasty, founded by supernatural beings who arrived from elsewhere (historians think Sudan or Ethiopia) to integrate culturally and linguistically with the Bantu-speakers over whom they ruled for at least ten generations.

Legendary accounts claim that Ndahura, a grandson of the last Batembuzi King, was the founder of a new dynasty called Bacwezi. Ndahura is thought to have been a genuine historical figure, another migrant from further north, who came to power before 1400. Tradition places Ntusi and Mubende at the heart of Bunyoro-Kitara during the Bacwezi era and casts Ndahura as a militant expansionist who led successful raids into parts of western Kenya, northern Tanzania and Rwanda. The Bacwezi ruled for only two generations, yet their influence on Uganda is immense. Most subsequent royal dynasties claim Bacwezi roots, and the Nakayima Tree near Mubende and Bigo Earthworks near Ntusi remain shrines for Bacwezi cultists to this day. Historians link the collapse of Bacwezi to the arrival of the Luo in around 1450, after which Bunyoro-Kitara splintered into smaller kingdoms, notably Bunyoro, Buganda, Ankole and Rwanda.

By the mid-19th century, Buganda was the largest and most influential kingdom in the region. Under the rule of Kabaka Mutesa, who died in 1884, the Buganda capital at Kampala became a hotbed of religious rivalries. First Islamic slave traders, then French Catholics and British Protestants settled in Kampala and converted various clan chiefs from their traditional beliefs. In 1888, after Mutesa's son and successor Mwanga convinced the traditionalists to expel all converts from Buganda, the Muslims and Christians joined forces to overthrow Mwanga. A dummy Kabaka was installed but, when his traditionalist leanings became apparent, the Muslims rebelled and Buganda exploded into civil war. In 1889, the Christians drove the Muslims from the capital, and Mwanga was re-installed.

Following the expulsion of the Muslims, tensions between Catholic and Protestant were exploited by Captain Lugard of the IBEA in a way that left Mwanga no viable option but to sign a treaty recognising the IBEA in 1892. On returning to Britain, Lugard persuaded the British government to consider colonising Buganda. Sir Gerald Portal was dispatched to Uganda; swayed by the enthusiasm of missionaries of both persuasions, he raised the Union Jack over

Kampala and signed a treaty with an unwilling Mwanga in May 1893, offering British Protectorateship over Buganda in exchange for the right to collect and spend taxes.

Britain swiftly set about extending its protectorate by signing treaties with the kings of Ankole and Toro. It then attacked Bunyoro, forcing Omakuma Kabalega to hide in the Budongo Forest, from where he was able to lead several attacks on British forts. Kabalega was a thorn in Britain's side, but he was unable to prevent Bunyoro from being unilaterally annexed to Uganda, or his 12-year-old son from being installed on the Bunyoro throne. Back in Kampala, Britain deposed Mwanga in favour of *his* one-year-old son. In 1897, Mwanga and Kabalega joined forces, but to little avail. They were captured in 1899 and exiled to the Seychelles, never again to set foot in Uganda.

Britain ruled Uganda by deploying educated Protestant Baganda in a sub-imperialistic role. In return, Buganda was run as a privileged state within a state right up until independence. The area that suffered most under British rule was the north, deliberately underdeveloped so it might serve as a reliable source of cheap labour and recruits to the police and army. Writing before Amin ascended to power, the Ugandan historian Samwiri Karugire commented that 'the full cost of this neglect has yet to be paid, not by the colonial officials, but by Ugandans themselves'. Milton Obote and Idi Amin both hailed from north of the Nile.

At independence in 1962, Uganda was deeply fragmented along both religious and ethnic lines. The prime minister, Milton Obote, inherited a bizarre constitution awarding Buganda full federal status and other traditional kingdoms semi-federal status, but linking the rest of the country directly to central government. Obote's majority depended on a marriage of convenience between two Protestant parties which disagreed on everything but religion, and he was compelled to recognise Kabaka Mutesa II of Buganda as head of state. In 1966, Obote scrapped this constitution. Mutesa was stripped of his presidency, to die impecunious in London three years later. Obote made himself life president and abolished the kingdoms in 1967, after which time the maintenance of political stability was dependent largely on the use of force.

On January 25 1971, while Obote was out of the country, a coup orchestrated by the Commander of the Army, General Idi Amin, was greeted with incautious but short-lived jubilation. By late 1973, half of the 23 officers who held a rank of lieutenant-colonel or higher at the time of the coup were dead, as were eight of the 20 members of Obote's last cabinet. In mid-1972, Asians were expelled from the country and Amin 'Africanised' their businesses and commandeered their money and possessions for state use. So began a reign of terror in which as many as 300,000 Ugandans died, many as a result of horrific torture.

African leaders closed ranks behind Uganda's despotic ruler. Incredibly, Amin was made president of the OAU in 1975, with Tanzania's Julius Nyerere offering the sole voice of dissent as he asserted the hypocrisy of African leaders criticising the white regimes of southern African while ignoring similarly cruel regimes elsewhere. Nyerere gave exile to several of Amin's opponents, and he refused to attend the OAU summit in Kampala. In 1978, Amin declared war on Tanzania, bombing the towns of Bukoba and Musoma. The Tanzanian army and a number of Ugandan exiles retaliated by invading Uganda. In April 1979, Amin was driven out of Kampala and into an exile from which he has yet to return.

When Amin departed in 1979, it was seen as a fresh start. Instead, it was to be Uganda's third false dawn in 17 years. In a climate of intrigue which resulted in three different stand-in presidents taking office in two years, a rigged general election returned Obote to power in December 1980, initiating a reign of terror that many

Ugandans regard as worse even than what came before. In 1982 another returned exile, Yoweri Museveni, formed the National Resistance Movement (NRM), an army of orphans left behind by the excesses of Obote and Amin. Obote's response was characteristically brutal: his troops waded into the NRM heartland in the Luwero Triangle killing civilians by their thousands. The Commander of the Army, Tito Okello, suggested that Obote might negotiate to stop the slaughter. Obote refused and in July 1985 he was for the second time in his career forced into exile by the commander of his own army. The NRM entered into negotiations with Okello, but these broke down and Museveni returned to the bush. On January 26 1986, the NRM entered Kampala, Okello surrendered tamely, and Museveni was sworn in as president – Uganda's seventh head of state in as many years.

To the outside world, the NRM takeover appeared to be just another instalment in an apparently endless succession of coups and civil wars. But Museveni was no Amin or Obote. He shied away from retribution, appointed a government that crossed party and ethnic lines, re-established the rule of law and press freedom, appointed a Human Rights Commission, and encouraged the return of Asians and other exiles. On the economic front, his pragmatic policies have encouraged foreign investment and tourism to an extent that the country has enjoyed an average growth rate of 10% in the last decade. In 1993, he restored the monarchies of Buganda, Bunyoro, Toro and Ankole, a healing gesture and a potent symbol of how far Uganda had come in seven years.

Museveni has been tardy in establishing Western-style democracy, arguing that stability should take precedence. Western criticisms of this are countered somewhat by the fact that he won 74% of the vote in a presidential election in May 1996. Uganda is not a multi-party democracy, but nor is it a one-party state. Any Ugandan is free to join the NRM or to stand for government, and the NRM in turn has no powers to evict anybody from its ranks. In short, Uganda is officially a no-party state – pedantry, perhaps, from some sources, but who would argue with a man who has initiated and overseen arguably the greatest political and economic 'miracle' to have occurred in independent Africa. Any serious criticism of the NRM's broad policies should be seen in the light of where Uganda would be today without Museveni.

BANTU PREFIXES

Bantu languages use prefixes to form words in a manner that can become rather confusing when discussing Uganda's kingdoms. The prefixes of mu-, ba- and bu- respectively refer to an individual, the people collectively and the land they occupy – in other words, a Muganda is a member of the Baganda who live in Buganda. The language of the Baganda is Luganda and their religion and customs are Kiganda. To use another example, the Banyoro live in Bunyoro where they speak Runyoro and follow Kinyoro customs.

The reason why the British protectorate came to be known as Uganda not Buganda is because Europe had its initial contact with the region through Swahili-speakers, for whom the prefix u- is the equivalent of the Luganda bu-. Many Baganda writers have complained that their country has been misnamed in this way, but it helps create a distinction between Uganda the country and Buganda the kingdom.

The title of Kabaka is bestowed on the Baganda king, the title Omakuma on the Bunyoro king, and Omugabe on the Ankole king.

PRACTICAL INFORMATION
Accommodation
Budget accommodation consists primarily of the local lodges found throughout East Africa, except that there's generally less choice in Uganda, standards are lower, and prices are higher. There's a good backpackers' hostel in Kampala. Organised campsites are mostly restricted to national parks and reserves, though a number of community-run campsites have opened in recent years, particularly in the Fort Portal region.

Books and newspapers
There are a couple of bookshops in central Kampala. Uganda has a lively English-language press – the *New Vision* and weekly *Monitor* offer the best international coverage. The weekly *East African* and American *Time* and *Newsweek* are sold at street stalls in Kampala.

Crime and safety
Of the countries covered in this guide, Uganda is probably more free of crime and con-tricks aimed at tourists than any other – apply some common sense and you've little to worry about. Northern Uganda is prone to periodic outbreaks of political unrest and banditry, and a couple of national parks in the west are closed at the

CRIME AND SECURITY
Of the countries covered in this guide, Uganda quite probably presents the least cause for concern when it comes to petty theft, muggings and con-tricks aimed at tourists. While a degree of caution is advisable in any city, even the capital Kampala is essentially a very safe place with few of the problems travellers might encounter in places such as Johannesburg, Nairobi, Addis Ababa and to a lesser extent most other large African cities.

Sadly, the same cannot be said for general security. Uganda itself is by-and-large a stable country, and has been for 15 years, though the little-travelled north has been prone to periodic outbreaks of political unrest and banditry, and any traveller heading that way should make advance enquiries.

Of far greater concern to the average traveller will be the potential instability in the west and in the capital, which is largely attributable to incursions from Congolese and Rwandan elements. In 1998, a number of bombs went off in and around Kampala, including one in the backpacker hostel which fortunately claimed no lives. At the same time, the Ruwenzori area was the scene of numerous grisly attacks on locals by the ADF, a rather mysterious organisation with probable Congolese links and whose aim is evidently plain destabilisation. As a result of this, the Semuliki and Ruwenzori national parks have been closed for several years, and are unlikely to re-open as long as the government considers there is any threat to tourists.

In August 1998, a group of travellers were kidnapped in neighbouring Congo after having crossed from Uganda to go gorilla tracking, a tragic event which at the time seemed to have little bearing on the safety of travel within the borders of Uganda. Six months later, tragedy struck again when the park headquarters at Bwindi were attacked by Rwandan rebel troops, and two rangers were shot and eight tourists bludgeoned or hacked to death. If, as seems probable, the goal of the rebels was to strike a blow at the heart of Uganda's small but steadily growing tourist industry, then it could not have

time of writing following the civil war in the Congo – you can check the current situation at the backpackers' hostel in Kampala.

Entrance fees
The Uganda Wildlife Authority, the body responsible for all national parks and wildlife reserves, introduced a new fee structure in late 1998. Most national parks and reserves now charge a visitation fee of US$7 per 24 hours to foreign nationals, payable in US dollars or local currency. Exceptions are Bwindi, Mgahinga, Queen Elizabeth and Murchison Falls, which charge US$15 per 24 hours, and Mount Elgon and Ruwenzori, which respectively charge a one-off visitation/ mountaineering fee of US$90 and US$250 for a five-day trek. Entrance fees to museums, historical sites, forest reserves and other conservation areas not administered by the UWA are nominal.

Entry formalities
Nationals of the UK, USA, Canada, Australia, New Zealand, European Union and Scandinavian countries no longer require a visa, but rulings have changed several times in recent years, so do seek advance confirmation.

Most other nationals, including South Africans, do require a visa, which can be bought in advance at a Ugandan Embassy or High Commission. If you do this,

been better calculated. For 15 years, it had been mountain gorillas more than anything that had helped Uganda overcome the negative international image generated by the barbarities of the Amin and Obote regimes. Suddenly, the country's premier gorilla-tracking reserve was making headlines as the site of perhaps the most shocking and unexpected attack on tourists in Africa in a decade.

Prior to March 1999, Bwindi was considered safe by almost everybody who knows Uganda. The attack on the unprotected park headquarters came as a total shock, and in hindsight could probably have been averted by a greater military presence. Soldiers have been installed at Bwindi since the park re-opened in May 1999, and in addition to protecting the headquarters they accompany visitors on all walks. Tourists are starting to come back, and the general consensus is that they are now well protected.

Readers who are thinking of visiting Uganda will presumably be asking themselves whether a similar event is likely to happen again, at Bwindi or elsewhere in the country. The honest answer is that nobody knows. Away from the Congolese and Rwandan border areas, Uganda is probably as safe as anywhere in Africa, and Bwindi itself is so well protected now that it must be regarded as an unlikely target for a similar attack. The official line, followed by most tour operators, is that this attack was a one-off tragedy, and that adequate precautions have been taken to prevent a repeat incident. A recent edition of *Travel Africa* magazine reports that military attachés from three continents have surveyed the whole country and concluded that the increased security makes travelling safe for visitors. For my part, I expect to visit Uganda in 2001 and, assuming that nothing newsworthy happens in the interim, I don't expect to approach this trip with any particular trepidation. But I think it would be irresponsible to state categorically in print that the Bwindi massacre was definitely a one-off event. The decision to travel in Uganda, and the responsibility, belongs ultimately to the individual traveller.

dates of travel must be given, and visas may not be extended, so it makes sense to do this in a neighbouring country (there are Ugandan embassies in Nairobi, Dar es Salaam and Addis Ababa). It is also possible to buy a visa on arrival for US$30.

Land borders to Uganda are generally very relaxed, and provided that your papers are in order there's no serious likelihood of being asked about onward tickets, funds or vaccination certificates. When you enter Uganda, a free 30-day visitor's pass will be stamped into your passport, extendable at any immigration office a few days before it expires.

Flying there

Uganda's international airport is at Entebbe on the Lake Victoria shore 30km from Kampala. It is difficult to get discounted tickets from Europe directly to Uganda, for which reason you're unlikely to meet budget travellers who started their African trip in Uganda.

Food and drink

Uganda is the land of *matoke*, a cooked banana dish eaten with the usual bland meat or bean stew or groundnut sauce. Rice and potatoes (for some reason just about always referred to as Irish potatoes) are also available at many local restaurants. Most larger towns have at least one more Westernised restaurant. Local beers such as *Nile Special*, *Pilsner* and *Bells* come in 500ml bottles and cost round US$1 in local bars and up to US$3 in tourist class hotels.

Getting around
By rail

The services connecting Kampala to Kasese and to Pakwach via Tororo and Gulu have been discontinued, though the latter has recently resumed according to the UTB website. (See box *A loop through the far northwest* on page 243.)

By road

Buses cover all main routes. They are the cheapest and safest way of getting around, and remarkably quick by African standards. Most buses have fixed departure times, so make enquiries in advance. All major routes are covered by a regular stream of white minibuses, which leave when full and race along at a reckless 100kph. It is customary on minibuses to pay the fare shortly before you arrive at your destination, which minimises the risk of being overcharged provided you take note of what other passengers pay.

By boat

Boats connect Port Bell, Kansenyi and Masaka to the Ssese Islands in Lake Victoria. There are also boats between Wanseko and Panyimur on Lake Albert, and from Masindi Port to Apoch and Shengebe to Namisole on Lake Kyoga.

Health

Malaria is present in most of Uganda throughout the year, with the Lake Victoria hinterland and Nile River being particularly bad. Lake Victoria also has a bad reputation for bilharzia. Except in Kampala, tap water is unsafe to drink.

Money

The unit of currency is the Uganda shilling. At the time of writing the exchange rate is roughly US$1=Ush 1,300/-. Banking hours are from 09.00 to 14.00 on weekdays, while forex bureaux generally stay open till 17.00 and on Saturday morning. As a rule, forex bureaux offer more favourable rates than banks, especially in Kampala.

Maps

The best general map is probably the Nelles 1:700,000 Uganda. Also recommended is the 1:800,000 Uganda published by International Travel Maps (ITMB) of Vancouver, the only major error on which is a latitudinal displacement that causes the equator, for instance, to be shown as 1°north. The second edition of the multilingual Macmillan *Uganda Travellers Map* is very up to date and accurate. Detailed survey maps and town plans can be bought from the Department of Land and Surveys map sales office in Entebbe.

Post and telephone

Post from Uganda is very slow. The formerly convoluted poste restante system in Kampala has recently been streamlined. The telephone system is good, and Uganda is one of the few African countries you'll normally get through to first try. The international code is +256. Area codes include Entebbe (042), Fort Portal (0493), Jinja (043), Kabale (0486), Kampala (041), Kasese (0493), Masaka (0481), Mbale and Tororo (045) and Mbarara (0485).

Public holidays

In addition to Easter, Christmas Day, Boxing Day and New Year's Day, Uganda recognises the Muslim Idd el Fitri and the following public holidays:

January 26	NRM Anniversary Day	June 3	Martyrs' Day
March 8	Women's Day	June 9	Heroes' Day
May 1	Labour Day	October 9	Independence Day

Tourist information offices

The Uganda Tourist Board is very helpful and well informed at PO Box 7211 Kampala; tel: 041 242196; fax: 041 242188; email: utb@starcom.co.ug.

Eastern Uganda
THE KENYA BORDER AND MOUNT ELGON

Most backpackers coming from Kenya arrive in Uganda at **Busia** or **Malaba** and, although both these border towns have a lodging or two, it would be a rare soul who felt inspired to spend a moment longer in them than was necessary. The more substantial town of **Tororo**, only 10km from the Malaba border, is rescued from total anonymity only by Tororo Rock, the steep and climbable hill which dominates its skyline, but otherwise it isn't much of an improvement on the border town.

Eastern Uganda offers little of interest when compared with the west; if you're in a rush, you can minibus straight through to Kampala from Tororo or Busia in five hours. For those with the urge to linger, the attractive town of **Mbale**, 45km north of Tororo, offers a few worthwhile excursions. The most popular of these is **Sipi Falls**, a series of four waterfalls set on the foot slopes of Mount Elgon and offering spectacular views across to the plains around Lake Kyoga. There is a footpath to the bottom of Sipi Falls and to the caves on the opposite side of the river, starting in Sipi trading centre behind the post office. A rather less well-known excursion from Mbale, the **Nyero Rock Paintings** near Kumi are regarded to be among the finest examples of geometrical paintings in East Africa.

The Kenya border east of Mbale is straddled by the 4,321m Mount Elgon, the Ugandan portion of which was gazetted as a 1,145km² national park in 1993. Like

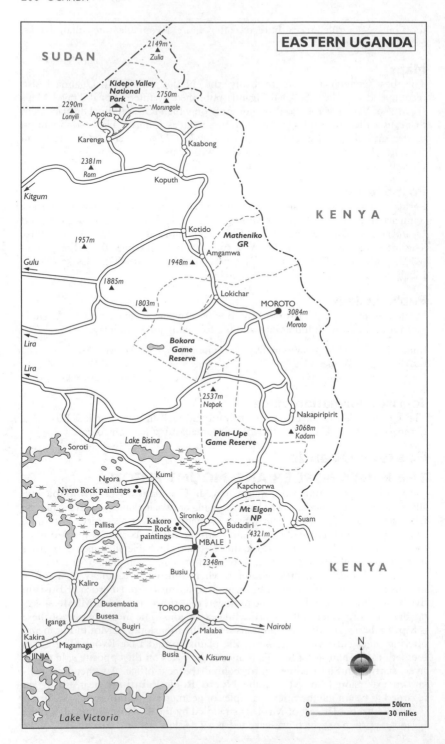

EASTERN UGANDA

SUDAN

2149m ▲
Zulia

Kidepo Valley
National Park

2750m ▲
Morungole

2290m ▲
Lonyili

Apoka

Karenga

Kaabong

2381m ▲
Rom

Koputh

Kitgum

KENYA

Kotido

1957m ▲

Matheniko GR

Amgamwa

1948m ▲

Gulu

1885m ▲

Lokichar

MOROTO ●
3084m ▲
Moroto

1803m ▲

Lira

Bokora Game Reserve

Lira

2537m ▲
Napak

Nakapiripirit
3068m ▲
Kadam

Soroti

Lake Bisina

Pian-Upe Game Reserve

Ngora

Kumi

Nyero Rock paintings ●●

Kapchorwa

Sironko

Mt Elgon NP

Suam

Pallisa

Kakoro Rock paintings ●●

Budadiri

4321m ▲

MBALE

Kaliro

Busiu

2348m ▲

Busembatia

Busesa

TORORO

Iganga

Bugiri

Malaba

Nairobi →

Kakira

JINJA

Magamaga

Busia

Kisumu →

KENYA

N

Lake Victoria

0 ___ 50km
0 ___ 30 miles

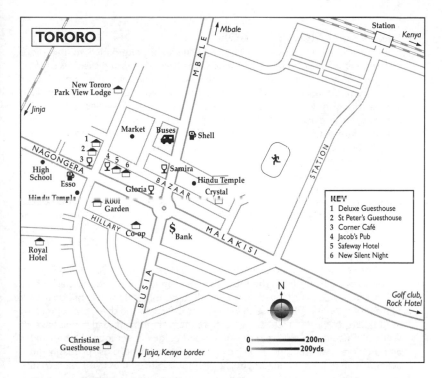

most other large mountains in East Africa, Elgon is an extinct volcano, active until about ten million years ago, at which time it was almost certainly higher than Kilimanjaro is today. The main peaks circle the jagged but largely intact caldera, one of the largest in the world and filled with crater lakes formed by glacial activity in the Pleistocene era. Mount Elgon was a sensitive area throughout much of the 1980s, but the situation has improved greatly in recent years and climbs can be organised at Budadiri trading centre or the national park office in Mbale (see box *Hiking on Mount Elgon* on pages 202–3).

Access and getting around

Regular minibuses whizz between Mbale, Tororo, Busia, Jinja and Kampala, typically travelling at a hair-raising 100kph. You shouldn't wait more than half an hour for a minibus to leave between any two of the above towns. Buses cover the same routes, and are almost as quick and a lot safer.

From Mbale, *matatus* covering the 20km road to Budadiri (the base for Mount Elgon hikes) leave from the Kumi road about 300m out of town from the clock tower. Sipi Falls lies about 40km from Mbale on the Kapchorwa road. There is one bus daily from Mbale to Kapchorwa. Pick-up trucks to Kapchorwa leave Mbale every hour or so from the junction of Perryman and Kumi Roads. The Nyero rock shelters lie 7km from Kumi along a side road to Ngora. Any minibus heading between Mbale and Soroti can drop you at Kumi, where you can organise a bicycle taxi to Nyero.

Where to stay and eat
Tororo

Corner Café Some OK snacks (pies, samosas), meals nothing special.

HIKING ON MOUNT ELGON

Elgon makes an attractive and relatively affordable alternative to the more popular and expensive hikes on Mount Kilimanjaro, Kenya and the Ruwenzoris. The vegetation is characteristic of large East African mountains, with distinct forest, bamboo, heath and Afro-alpine zones, the latter consisting of moorland dotted with giant lobelias and groundsels. Large mammal species known to be resident in the park include blue and De Brazza's monkeys, black-and-white colobus, leopard, elephant, bushpig, buffalo, sitatunga and common duiker. Elgon's bird checklist numbers 305 species, several at the most westerly extreme of their range.

Elgon is a relatively easy mountain to climb. No special skills are required, making the peaks accessible to ordinary hikers, and the mountain is not high enough for there to be any great risk of being affected by the altitude-related illnesses which regularly force people who hike up Mount Kilimanjaro or Kenya to turn back before they reach the peak. Elgon can be climbed at any time of year, though the dry seaons (June to August and December to March) are best.

Hikes can be organised at the national park office in Mbale, which lies out of town about 100m from the Mount Elgon Hotel, or the national park office in Budadiri, which is situated next to the Wagagai Hotel, or the national park office at Kapkwata. The office in Mbale is more organised than its counterpart in Budadiri, but since trekkers who start their climb at Budadiri will have to visit the office there to organise porters and guides (the Mount Elgon Guides and Porters Association is based in this office), there is probably little advantage in making arrangements at the Mbale office unless you want to hire equipment there or plan to ascend the mountain using the Piswa Route from Kapkwata.

There are several possible hiking routes within the park, of which the most popular is the four-day round trip from Budadiri to Wagagai Peak via the Sasa Trail. Other possibilities include a five-day round hike from Budadiri taking in Wagagai and the hot springs, and a five- or six-day hike between Budadiri and Kapkwata via Wagagai and the hot springs. Although most trekkers ascend the mountain via the Sasa Route out of Budadiri, Brad Weltzien (who spent two years working as a Peace Corps volunteer on Elgon) suggests that trekkers consider using the Piswa Route from Kapkwata. This is because Kapkwata lies 1,000m higher than Budadiri, so the ascent is more gradual and far less strenuous.

The first three days of all hikes out of Budadiri follow the same route. On the first day, the Sasa Trail involves a stiff six- to eight-hour walk from Budadiri (1,250m) via the village of Bumasifwa to a Sasa River Camp (2,900m). This is followed on the second day by a four- to five-hour walk Mude Caves (3,500m). Many people use the spare afternoon at Mude Caves to ascend Jackson's Summit (4,165m), a round trip that takes around five hours. On the third day, you will ascend from Mude Caves to Wagagai (4,321m) and back, an eight- to nine-hour trip. Hikers doing the four-day route will descend from Mude Caves back to Budadiri on the fourth day. Hikers doing the full trek to Kapkwata will on the fourth day walk from Mude Caves to Hunters Cave Camp (3,870m) via the hot springs, a trek of at least ten hours. On the fifth day, they will descend to Piswa Camp, a five-hour trek, and on the sixth day to Kapkwata, a further four hours. It is possible to combine the last two days into one, thereby cutting the duration of the trek to five days. As already noted, hikers who want to do the full route should consider starting at Kapkwata rather than Budadiri.

Hiking prices are very reasonable when compared to most other mountains in East Africa. Park fees for non-residents are currently US$90 for up to five days. Other fixed costs are for guides and porters. Each group must take at least one guide at $7 per day (divisible by the number of people in the group) and each person in the group must take at least one porter at $5 per day. There are no huts on the mountain, so hikers must either bring their own tent and sleeping bag, or hire equipment from the national park office in Mbale. Elgon is below the snow line, but it can be very cold at night and in windy weather. You must be sure to bring enough warm clothing. It is not high enough for altitude sickness to be a major cause of concern, but you may experience headaches and other altitude-related symptoms near the peaks. Water on the mountain should be purified or boiled before drinking. The ascent of the escarpment via a tricky path known as the Wall of Death is not recommended if you are afraid of heights. It is currently mandatory for trekkers visiting the hot springs area between Mude and Hunters Cave to be escorted by an armed ranger.

For those who don't have the time or money for an extended hike, the **Mount Elgon Forest Exploration Centre** is a good alternative, lying within the national park boundaries roughly one hour on foot from Sipi (see page 199). Three connecting circular day trails emanate from the exploration centre. The 7km, four-hour Mountain Bamboo Loop leads past a cave before climbing to the main viewpoint (from where, on a clear day, the peaks of Mount Elgon can be seen), and then follows a ridge northwards through montane forest to a large bamboo forest. The popular 5km, three- hour Chebonet Falls Loop passes the eponymous waterfalls as well involving a climb up a rock chimney and passing through areas of montane and bamboo forest leading to the main viewpoint. The 3km, two-hour Ridge View Loop involves a relatively easy ascent of the ridge, passing through areas of colourful wild flowers, where it connects with the other trails at the main viewpoint. In addition to passing through areas of regenerating forest and extensive bamboo stands, people who walk these trails are likely to see black-and-white colobus and blue monkey as well as several bird species associated with bamboo and montane forests.

The centre lies roughly 12km from Sipi by road, and you can drive there in a solid 4x4 vehicle, following the road towards Kapchorwa for 6km before taking the signposted feeder road to your right. Without private transport, you could either catch a *matatu* as far as the turn-off and walk the final 6km, or – better – ask one of the guides at Sipi to show you the shorter walking trail from Sipi to the exploration centre. It is possible to visit the centre as a day trip out of Sipi, but you may also want to spend a night or two there. A bed in the dormitory costs $11 per person whether resident or non-resident, and camping costs $10 per person for non-residents and $5 per person for residents. To this must be added the park entrance fees. Simple meals can be prepared on request, or you can bring food with you – there is a cooking hut with a stove. Before heading this way, you might want to pop in to the national parks office in Mbale, where you can confirm bed availability and pick up a copy of the excellent pamphlet and map of the exploration centre.

FROM SIPI TO THE SAUM BORDER

The northern footslopes of Mount Elgon are known to travellers mostly for Sipi Falls, but it possible to continue from Sipi to the Saum border and on to Kitale in western Kenya, a little-used but increasingly attractive-looking border crossing now that this formerly unstable area has been safe for some years. The first stop on the way is **Kapchorwa**, 13km past Sipi on a road that offers some wonderful views north towards Lake Kyoga and the 2,068m high Mount Kadam, which consists of little more than one main road flanked by a few untidy buildings. An altitude of almost 2,000m ensures that Kapchorwa has a breezy climate, and there must be plenty of walking opportunities in the area. The Paradise Lodge evidently offers the only accommodation in town – basic rooms in the **B** range – as well as reasonable local food and chilled beers and sodas. Coming from Sipi, any truck or *matatu* heading between Mbale will give you a lift to Kapchorwa, assuming that it has space.

Kapkwata trading centre lies about 30km from Kapchorwa along the road to Saum. It is of interest as the trailhead for the Piswa Trail up Mount Elgon, a little-used route with many advantages over the more popular Sasa Trail. In addition to being a trailhead, Kapkwata offers travellers heading to Saum a good excuse to break up the journey in the form of an obscure forestry resthouse, complete with solar-powered hot shower, bang in the middle of a plantation at the rangers' post roughly 500m past the trading centre. The resthouse has three rooms and costs **D** per person. No park entrance fees are charged, because the resthouse lies in a forestry reserve, not the national park, and camping is permitted for a small fee. The resthouse can cook meals to order, or you can eat in one of the small restaurants in the trading centre. Free tea is served in the morning. There are several good day walks from the resthouse to local viewpoints.

Saum lies at an altitude of 2,070m on the Kenya border, and it is only likely to be passed through by travellers crossing between Kitale and Mbale north of Mount Elgon. A few trucks run between Kapchorwa and Saum daily, taking roughly four hours when the road is dry and a great deal longer in wet conditions. If the uncomfortable hour I spent on the back of a truck covering the 13km between Sipi and Kapchorwa is anything to go by, this is likely to be a pretty hairy trip, so it would be worth trying to secure a seat in the front. There are a couple of basic lodgings in Saum, or you can continue directly across the border – which is connected to Kitale by a reasonable surfaced road and regular minibuses.

Crystal Hotel The smartest place in town. Comfortable rooms with private balcony **E** s/c dbl. Good inexpensive meals.
Deluxe Guesthouse New hotel with clean s/c rooms **B**/**D**.
Jacob's Bar Fun drinking hole with courtyard, serves substantial snacks.
New Silent Night Lodge Cheapest rooms in town, but a dump. **B** sgl.
Royal Hotel Spartan but clean rooms using communal showers. **C** sgl or dbl.
St Peter's Hotel Large rooms with clean communal showers. **C** sgl or dbl.

Mbale

Mount Elgon View Hotel The best place to stay if you're not too strapped for cash. Spacious, clean doubles with netting, fan, table and chairs **D**. Clean communal showers and rooftop where you can sit.

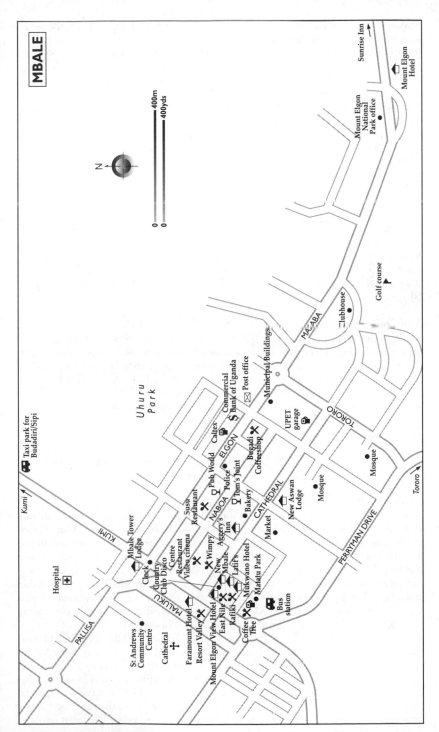

MBALE

N

0 400m
0 400yds

Uhuru Park

Kumi

Taxi park for
Budadiri/Sipi

Hospital

St Andrews
Community
Centre

Cathedral

PALLISA

KUMI

MALUKU

Mbale Tower
Lodge

Clock

Country
Club Disco

Centre
Restaurant
Video cinema

Wimpy

New
Aggrey's
Inn

Paramount Hotel

Mount Elgon View Hotel

Resort Valley

East Nile

Rafiki

Mbale
Inn

Latif's

Coffee
Tree

Mitkwano Hotel

Mafatu Park

Bus
station

Susu
Restaurant

Pub World

NABOA

Tom's Joint

Bakery

Market

Police

Caltex

ELGON

Commercial
Bank of Uganda

Brigadi
Coffeeshop

CATHEDRAL

New Aswan
Lodge

Post office

Municipal buildings

UPET
garage

Mosque

PERRYMAN DRIVE

TORORO

Mosque

MACABA

Clubhouse

Golf course

Mount Elgon
National
Park office

Sunrise Inn

Mount Elgon
Hotel

Tororo

Mukwano Hotel (formerly the New Michaelsworth) Absurdly overpriced at **D**/**E** for a scruffy s/c room using bucket showers.

Salem Brotherhood Rustic accommodation 10km from Mbale and 10 minutes' walk from Nakaloke trading centre on the Soroti Road. All proceeds go to orphan support. Vegetarian food. Car, bicycle and climbing equipment rental. Good source of current information about travel in Karamoja and Kidepo. Rooms **E** dbl. Dorm **B** pp. Camping **A** pp.

Sunrise Inn Private mid-range hotel 2km out of town past the Mount Elgon Hotel. Of less interest to most backpackers for the rooms (around US$35) than the excellent, inexpensive outdoor bar and restaurant.

St Andrews Church Community Centre Pallisa Rd. Reliable and sensibly priced. Dorm **B** pp. Room **C**/n/D sgl/dbl. **E** s/c dbl.

Tom's Joint and **Pub World** Popular drinking holes facing each other on Naboa Road. Both serve substantial snacks.

Wimpy Tasty steak rolls for around US$1.50.

Budadiri

Lawla Paradise Hotel Basic singles **B**.

Roses Last Chance Recommended new guesthouse opposite national park office. Basic but clean accommodation, friendly staff, good local food. Camping or room **B** pp.

Wagagai Hotel Smarter rooms **B**/**C**. Camping free for those climbing Elgon, otherwise **C** per tent.

Sipi Falls

Crows Nest Owned by local people but built with the help of two former Peace Corps volunteers, this backpacker resort lies on a small hill about 500m before Sipi trading centre coming from Mbale; look for the signpost to your left. The camp has a grandstand view over all four waterfalls to Mount Elgon. Meals and drinks available. Rooms **D** dbl. Camping **B** pp. Tents and sleeping bags can be hired cheaply.

Elgon Maasai Resthouse Friendly locally run place in Sipi village near falls. Adequate rooms with double bed **C**.

Sipi Falls Resort Former governor's residence above falls. Used to be popular with backpackers but now aimed at upmarket tourists with rooms in the US$100-plus bracket. Travellers staying elsewhere are welcome to enjoy the view and partake of the best meals and only refrigerated drinks in Sipi for a US$2.50 entrance fee.

THE ROAD TO KIDEPO

The remote Karamoja region of northeastern Uganda is home to the nomadic Karamojong people, whose love of cattle has an obsessive quality rivalling that of the Maasai of Tanzania and Kenya. The Karamojong are apparently something of an embarrassment to more westernised Ugandans – when I discussed visiting Karamoja's capital town Moroto with people in Tororo and Mbale, I was repeatedly warned about the backward people who run around half-naked. Aside from the ethnicity exposed by such accusations, they are also rather unfair – you won't see too many flashers in Moroto itself, though it is true that in rural areas most Karamojong people still dress in skimpy traditional attire.

The obvious goal of any trip to the northeast is **Kidepo Valley National Park**, the well vegetated plains of which are isolated from the rest of the country by the sparsely populated badlands of Karamoja. The fact that Kidepo is so rarely visited by tourists only adds to its alluring wilderness atmosphere. Surprisingly, it also protects a greater variety of large mammals than any other reserve in Uganda, including 28 species found nowhere else in the country, while the bird checklist of almost 500 species includes more than 60 recorded in no other Ugandan national park. Among the more interesting mammals are patas monkey, African hunting dog, bat-eared fox, striped hyena, aardwolf, cheetah, leopard, lion, Beisa oryx, elephant, Burchell's zebra, warthog, buffalo and Rothschild's giraffe.

If you're thinking of heading this way, a more realistic cause for concern than glimpsing the occasional bared breast is the spasmodic armed fighting to which the area is prone. Ethnic rather than directly political in nature, this violence mostly takes the form of cross-border cattle rustling, for which reason a tourist would have to be unlucky to get involved. That said, you should make advance enquiries about the current situation (allowing for the fact that many Ugandans will warn you off simply because of the 'backward' tag, which is neither here nor there), and resist any temptation to bring along your private herd of cattle!

Access and getting around

It's not easy to hitch up to Kidepo, but nor is it impossible, provided that you're prepared to spend at least two or three days travelling in each direction, with the possibility of being stuck in the park for a week You can get from Mbale to Moroto in a day. Regular minibuses between Mbale and Soroti take around two hours, so with an earlyish start you'll be in plenty of time to connect with the bus which leaves Soroti for Moroto at around 12.00. From Moroto bus station, you should find a vehicle of some description heading along the 95km road to Kotido. From Kotido, you shouldn't have too much difficulty finding transport to Kaabang, a further 95km north. Beyond Kaabang, transport is very unpredictable, and your best chance is with one of the park vehicles that do this run once or twice a week.

Where to stay and eat
On the road

There are several cheap lodgings in Soroti and Moroto. In Kotido, the Paradise Lodge has basic **A** singles. Comfortable rooms at the mission in Kaabang cost **D** dbl. There is no formal accommodation between Kaabang and the national park.

Kidepo National Park

A bed at the normally empty Students' Hostel costs **F** pp, or you can pitch your tent at the nearby campsite at **D** pp. Guided game walks cost US$7pp. Game drives are US$1/km. Dry foods are sometimes but not always available, so bring food along. There's a reliable beer and soft drink supply.

JINJA AND SURROUNDS

On the Lake Victoria shore roughly half-way between Tororo and Kampala, Jinja is Uganda's second-largest town, with a lazy, tropical ambience that rewards gentle exploration. Thirty minutes' walk from the town centre, the plaque which has for years marked the spot where Speke became the first person to correctly identify the source of the Nile in 1862 has recently been joined by a restaurant and gaudy view-obscuring information board (on which Speke's name is incorrectly spelt). Otherwise, Jinja itself has little in the way of compelling sightseeing, but the roads lined with fading Asian and colonial architecture make for an atmospheric introduction to Uganda for travellers coming from Kenya.

Roughly 7km from Jinja, the **Bujagali Rapids** make for an attractive day trip or overnight camping excursion, and this stretch of the Nile is lined by thick riparian woodland that harbours many birds and monkeys. Regrettably, nothing has been heard in years of Mr Bujagali who, according to a yellowing tourist handout, 'occasionally sits on the water in a bark-cloth mat'. These days, the falls are somewhat better known as the setting off point for the excellent white-water

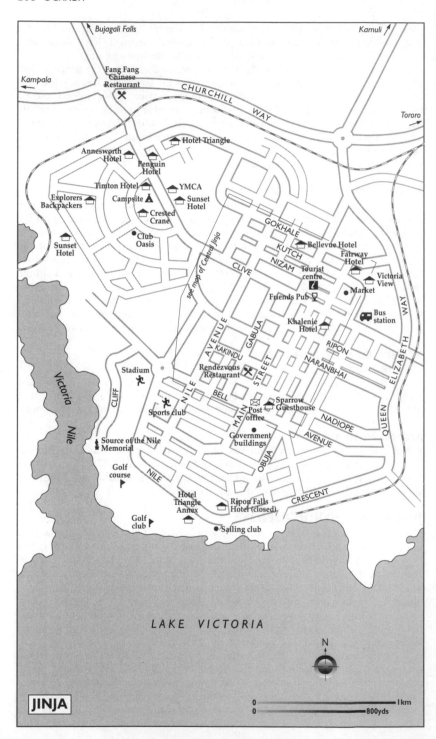

Bujagali Falls

Kamuli

Kampala

CHURCHILL WAY

Tororo

Fang Fang Chinese Restaurant

Hotel Triangle

Annesworth Hotel

Penguin Hotel

Timton Hotel

YMCA

Explorers Backpackers

Campsite

Sunset Hotel

Crested Crane

Club Oasis

Sunset Hotel

GOKHALE

KUTCH

Bellevue Hotel

Fairway Hotel

NIZAM

CLIVE

Tourist centre

Victoria View

Market

Friends Pub

Bus station

Khalenie Hotel

RIPON

AVENUE

GABULA

NARANBHAI

KAKINDU

Stadium

STREET

Rendezvous Restaurant

CLIFF

NILE

BELL

MAIN

Sports club

Post office

Sparrow Guesthouse

Source of the Nile Memorial

Government buildings

NADIOPE

AVENUE

ELIZABETH WAY

QUEEN

Golf course

NILE

Hotel Triangle Annex

Ripon Falls Hotel (closed)

OBUJA

CRESCENT

Golf club

Sailing club

Victoria Nile

See map of Central Jinja

LAKE VICTORIA

N

JINJA

0 ——————— 1km
0 ——————— 800yds

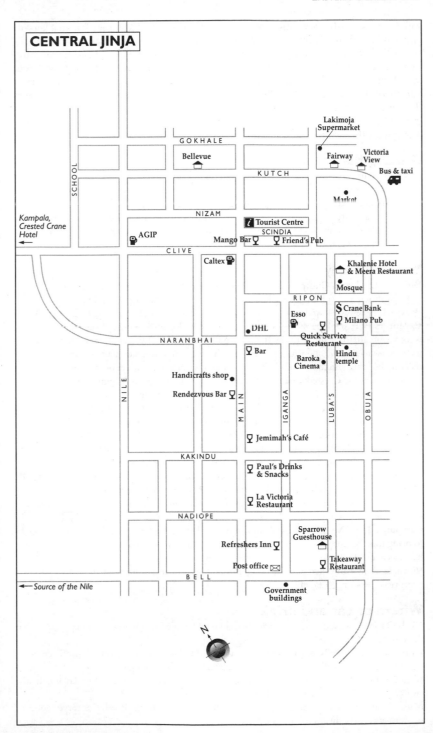

CENTRAL JINJA

GOKHALE

Lakimoja Supermarket

Bellevue

Fairway

Victoria View

Bus & taxi

KUTCH

SCHOOL

Market

NIZAM

Kampala, Crested Crane Hotel

Tourist Centre

SCINDIA

AGIP

Mango Bar

Friend's Pub

CLIVE

Caltex

Khalenie Hotel & Meera Restaurant

Mosque

RIPON

Crane Bank

Milano Pub

Esso

DHL

Quick Service Restaurant

NARANBHAI

Hindu temple

Bar

Baroka Cinema

Handicrafts shop

NILE

Rendezvous Bar

MAIN

IGANGA

LUBA'S

OBUIA

Jemimah's Café

KAKINDU

Paul's Drinks & Snacks

La Victoria Restaurant

NADIOPE

Sparrow Guesthouse

Refreshers Inn

Takeaway Restaurant

Post office

BELL

Source of the Nile

Government buildings

N

rafting trips run by Nile River Explorers, based out of Explorers Backpackers in Jinja and Adrift in Kampala (see box *White-water rafting on the Nile* opposite).

Only 20km from Jinja, straddling the main Kampala Road, bandas, camping facilities and guided trails are to be found in the 306km² **Mabira Forest Reserve**, which protects one of the best-preserved forests in eastern Uganda and supports a variety of monkeys as well as 287 bird species, including numerous forest specials. This is a little-visited spot, but very accessible and rewarding to nature lovers, with a plethora of colourful sunbirds and raucous hornbills frequenting the campsite, along with the familiar African grey parrot and red-tailed monkeys.

Getting there and around

Regular minibuses connect Jinja to Mbale, Tororo, Busia and Kampala. Buses cover the same routes, and are a lot safer. From Jinja, any minibus or bus heading to Kampala can drop you at the signposted entrance to Mabira Forest Reserve. The Bujagali Falls are signposted from the roundabout where the Nairobi–Kampala road meets the road going into Jinja – there's not much transport to the falls, but it's within easy walking or cycling distance of Jinja.

Where to stay

Bujagali Explorers Campsite Landscaped camping terraces in large, leafy, secure site next to Bujagali Rapids. Run by the rafting company Nile River Explorers (see Explorers Backpackers below). Popular with overland trucks. Bar and meals available. Camping **B** pp.

Explorers Backpackers 41 Wilson Av; tel: 043 120236; email: rafting@starcom.co.ug; web: www.raftafrica.com. Run by the rafting company Nile River Explorers (see box *White-water rafting on the Nile* opposite), this popular hostel, formerly called Paddlers Inn, has recently been relocated; ask minibuses entering town from the direction of Kampala to drop you near the Crested Crane Hotel, then follow the signposts. Facilities include a pool table, table tennis, satellite TV, large gardens, a well-stocked bar, hot showers, email and laundry. In addition to rafting on the Nile (US$65 full-day inclusive of light lunch, evening barbecue and one night free accommodation), they organise kayak school (US$40 per lesson), sunset cruises (US$25pp, US$5 off if you raft), car hire (from $30 per day plus fuel) and gorilla bookings at no extra charge.

Fairway Hotel Nothing special, but newly renovated and central. **C** dbl.

Khalenie Hotel Consistently clean, pleasant s/c rooms for years, but now overpriced at **D/E**.

Mabira Community Campsite Mabira Forest Reserve. Borehole water, hot showers, firewood. Day trails from 30 minutes to four hours in duration. Entrance US$6/24 hours or US$10/48 hours. Guided walks US$3pp. Bicycle hire US$5/day. Bandas **D/E**. Camping **B** pp. Five minutes' walk and signposted from the Kampala–Jinja road. No need to bring food because the village at the junction has a market selling grilled chickens, bananas and cold drinks to passing *matatu* passengers!

Victoria View Inn Once popular budget hotel that now feels very tired and a bit overpriced. Rooms **C** s/c dbl.

Where to eat and drink

Club Oasis Pleasant bar with big gardens, pool table, satellite TV and good pizzas, close to the Crested Crane Hotel.

Fang Fang Chinese Restaurant A short walk from the town centre on the traffic circle with the Kampala road. Serves great Chinese food in US$7–8 range.

Jinja Sailing Club Fair meals and cold beer on the lush lake shore. The Sunday lunch all-you-can-eat buffet is recommended at around US$10.

Munch Corner 2000 Recently relocated to a house on Madhvani Road, this serves good western and Asian dishes for around US$2–3.

WHITE-WATER RAFTING ON THE NILE

In 1996, the international rafting company **Adrift** started operating on the Nile below Bujagali Falls, since when white-water rafting has become one of the most popular activities with travellers in Uganda. The section of the Nile in question is said to offer more exhilarating rafting than even the famous Zambezi Gorge below Victoria Falls, with several grade five rapids, but it is also very safe because there is little danger of hitting a rock should you fall off the boat, and the distance between the rapids means that you are unlikely to be underwater at any point for longer than 20 seconds.

Adrift runs full-day rafting trips out of Kampala, starting at Bujagali Falls, a short way north of Jinja, and finishing at Itanda about 20km further north. The trip takes in nine major rapids, four of which are classed as grade five, namely Total Gunga, Big Brother, Overtime and Itanda. The price of US$95 per person covers all rafting equipment, return transportation from Kampala (the pick-up points are the Backpackers' Hostel and the Sheraton Hotel), an excellent cold buffet lunch on a small island, and as much beer as you can drink on the ride back to Kampala. While on the river, you'll get to see a lot of different birds, and to swim in the calm stretches of water between the rapids. The entire day is recorded on video and screened on the following evening; you can buy a personal copy of the video for US$30. Bookings can be made through the Backpackers' Hostel in Kampala or through most tour operators in the city centre. Alternatively, contact Adrift direct at PO Box 8643 Kampala, tel/fax: 041 268670, back-up fax: 041 341245, cellphone: 075 707668, email: adrift@starcom.co.ug.

Adrift has recently started operating an overnight rafting trip which covers the 45km stretch of the Nile between Njeru (near Jinja) and Nabuganyi. The first day of this trip covers the same rapids as the one-day excursion, with one extra rapid called Novocaine tagged on at the end of the day. Rafters camp on an island where they will be treated to a big barbecue. On the second morning, four rapids are traversed: Hair of the Dog, Kula Shaker, Nile Special and Malalu. After lunch the going is smoother, though the day culminates with one last rapid called Weleba. The price of US$230 per person covers all rafting equipment, tents, food, water and drinks – all you need to bring is a sleeping bag and mat, and a change of clothes.

A company called **Nile River Explorers** has recently started running white-water rafting trips directly out of Jinja. These start a short way upriver of Bujagali Falls, which means the trip involves a slightly different combination of rapids to those run by Adrift, but otherwise the experience offered by the two different companies is much the same. Nile River Explorers is based out of the Explorers' Backpackers in Jinja, and the trips cost US$75 per person inclusive of a free night's accommodation at the hostel. You can contact Nile River Explorers at PO Box 2155 Jinja, tel: 043 22381, fax: 043 22050, email: rafting@starcom.co.ug. Alternatively, visit the hostel or wait for their truck at around 09.30 at the pick-up point in front of the Fang Fang Restaurant at the Kampala roundabout outside Jinja.

The future of rafting trips on this part of the Nile is uncertain, pending a governmental decision as to whether a proposed dam and hydro-electric power scheme should be constructed at Bujagali Falls. Even if this dam does go ahead, it seems likely that enough rapids will be left untouched upriver of the falls for rafting trips to continue, albeit following a different itinerary.

Rangoli Restaurant Good Indian meals. On main road.

Source Café Formerly Jemima's Café, this is a non-profit set-up which funds a resource centre providing library services and a computer centre for use by local people. Not only is the venture worth supporting, but the food – pizzas, sandwiches, ice-cream – is both good and reasonably priced.

Speke's Camp This recently built stilted restaurant near the Source of the Nile serves good food and cold beers. The setting is superb, and evening booze cruises can be organised.

Central Uganda

KAMPALA AND ENTEBBE

Spread over seven hills, Kampala is a remarkably green and attractive capital, and even before the colonial era formed the political centre of the Kingdom of Buganda. The city's name derives from the Luganda expression *Kosozi Kampala* (Hill of Antelope), a reference to the domestic impala which grazed the lawns of the Kabaka's court. At independence, Kampala was the showpiece of the East African Community, but its status deteriorated dramatically under Amin. By the time Museveni took power, in 1986, Kampala was in chaos: skeletal buildings scarred with bullet holes dotted the town centre, shops and hotels had been boarded up after widespread looting, public services had ground to a halt, and the streets were crowded with war orphans and refugees from rural areas.

Kampala today is practically unrecognisable from its war-scarred incarnation of the mid-1980s. The main shopping area along Kampala Road could be that of any African capital, and the area immediately to its north, where foreign embassies and government departments rub shoulders with renovated tourist hotels, is smarter than any part of Nairobi or Dar es Salaam – an image compromised comically by the scavenging marabou storks which flop gracelessly from the trees and lampposts. For all this renovation, a walk through the overcrowded, run-down back streets and inner city slums south of Kampala Road reveals the Kampala that most of its residents know.

Uganda's only international airport is at **Entebbe** on the Lake Victoria shore about 30km from Kampala. Entebbe Airport achieved instant immortality in July 1976, when a hijacked Air France airbus flying from Israel landed there, prompting

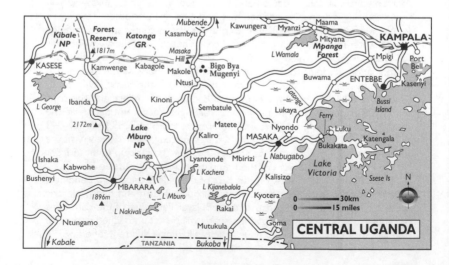

Israel to send a group of paratroopers to storm the airport in a daring surprise raid which resulted in all the hostages being freed. For backpackers, the small town is of interest for its excellent botanical garden and animal orphanage.

Situated in Lake Victoria, 23km offshore of Entebbe, the **Ngamba Island Chimpanzee Sanctuary** was recently established as a facility for 19 orphaned chimpanzees. The chimps range freely on the 40ha island, which is covered in natural forest and supports more than 50 plant species utilised by chimps. A raised viewing platform at the edge of the sanctuary allows visitors to view chimps from a few metres away at supplementary feeding times (11.00 and 15.00). Half-day, full-day and overnight trips to Ngamba can be arranged out of Entebbe or Kampala, starting at US$36 per person for groups of more than ten people – for further details, contact G & C Tours at 041 321479 or 077 502155/403482.

Access and getting around

Regular buses and minibuses connect Kampala to most large towns in Uganda, including Mbale, Tororo, Busia, Jinja, Masaka, Mbarara, Kabale, Kisoro, Kasese, Fort Portal, Hoima, Masindi and Pakwach. Minibuses to or from most places west of Kampala terminate at the new taxi park, while minibuses to Entebbe, Port Bell and destinations east of Kampala leave from the old taxi park, 200m away from the new one. The bus station is close to both taxi parks.

Most travellers heading directly between Kampala and Nairobi use the twice-daily Akamba bus service or the weekly train service (see *Kenya to Uganda* on page 71). Two internal rail services terminate at the railway station on Kampala Road: a weekly service between Kampala and Kasese, and a weekly service connecting Kampala and Pakwach via Tororo. Neither is used by backpackers with any regularity, since they're both very slow and crowded.

Ferries to Mwanza and the Ssese Islands leave from Port Bell, about half an hour's minibus ride from the old taxi park. Entebbe International Airport lies on the Lake Victoria shore about 3km from Entebbe town. There are cheap shared taxis between the airport and Entebbe town, and regular minibuses between Entebbe and the old taxi park in Kampala.

Where to stay
Kampala
Backpackers Hostel & Campsite Tel: 041 272012; email: backpackers@infocom.cu.ug. Excellent and long-standing hostel, founded in 1993 and set in large rambling grounds 3km from city centre along Masaka Road. Take a minibus to Natete from the new taxi park – the touts will tell you which minibus to catch (ask for 'Backpackers'). All profits fund permaculture (sustainable agriculture) training scheme. Good meals and bar. Useful 'travellers tips' book. Best source of current information about gorilla tracking. S/c rooms **F** dbl. Bandas **E** dbl. Rooms **D** dbl. Camping or dorm **B** pp.
Entebbe Resort On the lakeshore 15 minutes' walk from Entebbe town centre. Camping **B** pp.
Kidepo Hotel Cheapest rooms in Entebbe, but not exactly a bargain at **E**/**F** for a scruffy sgl/dbl. Just off the road between the town centre and the airport road.
Namirembe Guesthouse Clean, friendly church-run place on minibus route to Backpackers Hostel. Rooms arguably overpriced at **E**/**F**.
Red Chilli Hideaway Tel/fax: 041 22 3903. New backpacker campsite 3km out of town off the Port Bell Road. Ask any minibus heading from old taxi park to Bugolobi, Luzira or Nakawa to drop you at Silver Springs Hotel, then turn left off Port Bell Road and then take second right (Sunderland Av). Facilities include bar and meals. Camping **B** pp, dorms and rooms under construction.

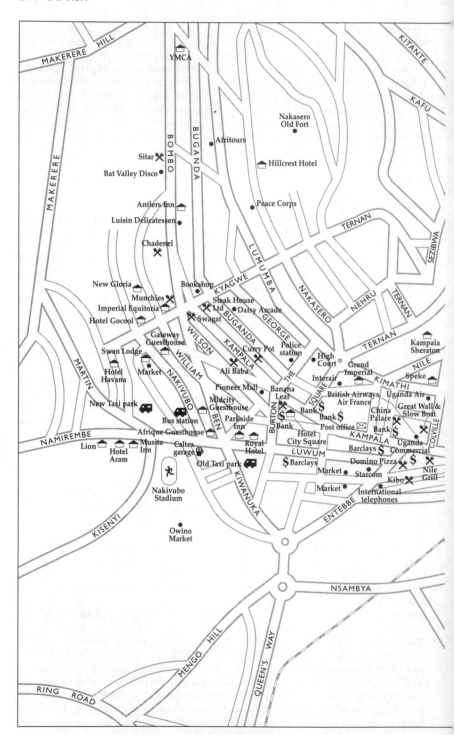

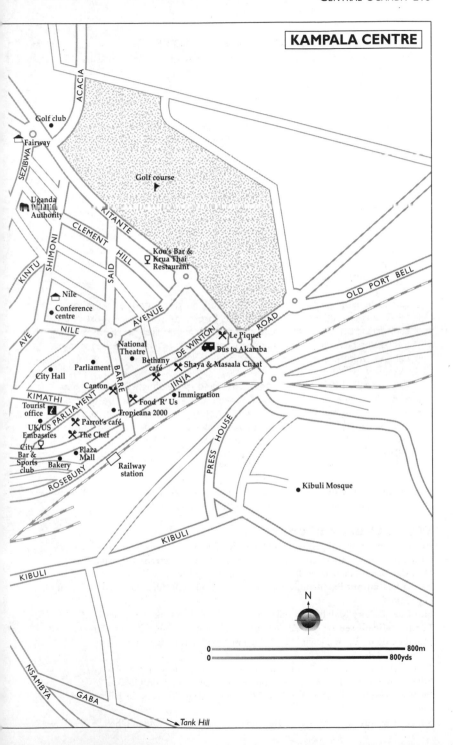

SIGHTSEEING IN KAMPALA AND ENTEBBE

National Museum Established 1908, moved to present site 1954. Stimulating displays on the Nakayima Tree, Ntusi and Bigo Bya Mugenyi. Collection of musical instruments from all over Africa. About 2km out of town on Kira Road – catch minibus from new taxi park to Kamwocha.

Kasubi Tombs Kasubi Hill, capital of Kabaka Mutesa from 1881. Mutesa buried here, as are three successors: Mwanga II (ruled 1884–1897), Chwa II (1897–1939) and Mutesa II (1839–1966). Tomb is enormous domed structure made of poles, reeds and thatch, maintained and guarded by Baganda clanspeople. Open daily 08.00 to 18.00. Catch a minibus to the market on the corner of Hoima and Kimera roads, then 500m walk up hill (signposted).

Kabaka Mwanga's Lake Completed in 1888, this was the product of Kabaka Mwanga II's somewhat hare-brained scheme of linking his capital to Lake Victoria via a water channel. It's a popular day walk from backpackers' hostel.

Entebbe Botanical Garden Established on the Entebbe lake shore in 1902, this attractive mix of indigenous forest, cultivation and horticulture supports troops of black-and-white colobus monkey as well as many interesting birds, including yellow-throated leaflove, slender-billed weaver, palmnut vulture, great blue touraco and pied hornbill.

Entebbe Wildlife Orphanage Often and misleadingly referred to as a zoo, this place offers sanctuary for animals which would be unable to fend for themselves in the wild, notably a number of orphaned chimpanzees. The aviary is your best chance of getting a good photo of the elusive shoebill. A nominal entrance fee is charged, plus US$2 for a camera.

Uganda Students Christian Hostel Clean and secure. 2km out of town off Balintuma Road. Catch minibus to Kasubi, get off Nakulabye Market. **D/E**.

Where to eat and drink

Al's Bar One of several good pubs on Gaba Road. Good music, cheap snacks.
Chippers Kampala Rd opposite Hotel Equatoria. Great ice-cream and shakes.
DV8 Bar Behind Pioneer Mall. Pool tables and cheap beers.
Fasika Restaurant Excellent Ethiopian food on Tank Hill Rd, a short taxi ride from the city centre.
Hot Loaf Bakery Mall behind Nile Grill. Good bread and take-away snacks.
Luisin Delicatessen Next to Antlers Inn. Cold meats, cheese, fresh bread, pizza.
Masala Chaat House Dewington Rd opposite National Theatre. Cheap, filling Indian dishes.
Music Club In National Theatre. Impromptu jam sessions Monday 19.00.
Nile Grill Kampala Rd. Popular meeting place. Unexciting food US$5.
Parkside Inn Next to Old Taxi Park. Watch Kampala go by from the balcony over a cold beer.
Shagut Restaurant Kampala Rd. Indian vegetarian dishes less than US$5.

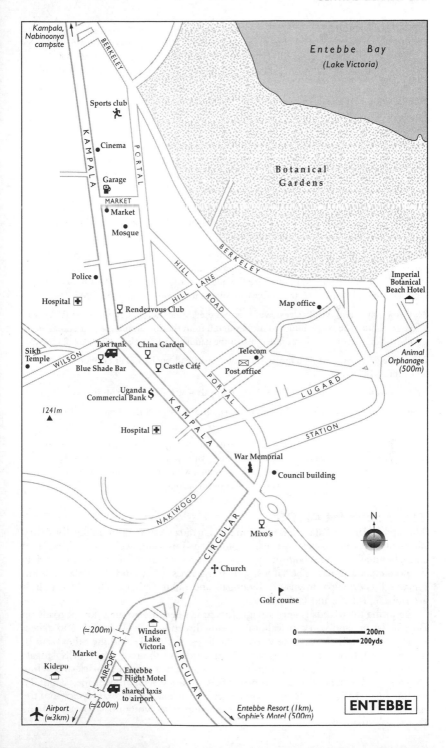

Kampala, Nabinoonya campsite

BERKELEY

KAMPALA

PORTAL

Sports club

Cinema

Garage

MARKET

Market

Mosque

Entebbe Bay
(Lake Victoria)

Botanical Gardens

BERKELEY

Police

Hospital

HILL LANE

HILL ROAD

Rendezvous Club

Map office

Imperial Botanical Beach Hotel

Sikh Temple

WILSON

Taxi rank

China Garden

Blue Shade Bar

Castle Café

Telecom

Post office

PORTAL

LUGARD

Animal Orphanage (500m)

Uganda Commercial Bank

1241m

KAMPALA

STATION

Hospital

War Memorial

Council building

NAKIWOGO

CIRCULAR

Mixo's

N

Church

Golf course

| 0 | 200m |
| 0 | 200yds |

(≈200m)

Windsor Lake Victoria

Market

AIRPORT

Kidepo

Entebbe Flight Motel

shared taxis to airport

(≈200m)

CIRCULAR

Airport (≈3km)

Entebbe Resort (1km),
Sophie's Motel (500m)

ENTEBBE

Practical listings

Airlines Air France (23-3495); Air Tanzania (23-4631); Alliance (24-4011); British Airways (25-7414/5/6); EgyptAir (23-4740); Ethiopian Airways (25-4796/7); InterAir (25-5508); Kenya Airways (23-3068); Royal Swazi (24-5597); Sabena (25-4200/1); Uganda Airlines (23-2630/1/2/3).

Books and newspapers Foreign newspapers at Daisy's Arcade. The Aristoc Book Shop on Kampala Road opposite the main bank has a selection of novels, travel guides, field guides and books on Ugandan history. Reading room at British Council on Parliament Avenue.

Embassies Burundi (22-1697); Congo (Philip Rd, 23-3777); Denmark (25-0398); France (24-2176); Germany (23-6421/2); Italy (25-0442); Kenya (26-7368); Rwanda (next to National Museum, 24-4045); South Africa (25-9156); Tanzania (25-6271/2) UK (Parliament Rd, 25-7054-9); USA (Parliament Rd, 25-9791/2/3).

Foreign exchange Private forex bureaux concentrated along Kampala Road. Open from 09.00 to 17.00 weekdays, some also on Saturday morning. Rates vary greatly. At other times, can exchange money at bank in Entebbe International Airport.

Internet As in most other African capitals, Kampala now has a number of internet cafés. One that has been recommended is the Cyberworld Café, across from Fido Dido in the Park Royal Building. The computers are fast and cost around US$2 for 15 minutes. On Saturday from 21.00 to 24.00 they offer unlimited internet use for around US$5.

National parks and wildlife reserves Contact the Uganda Wildlife Authority (UWA) head office on Kintu Road, a few hundred metres uphill from the Sheraton Hotel, for enquiries, gorilla-tracking permits, and pamphlets about the national parks. Tel: 34 6290; fax: 23 6291.

Nightlife There are several popular clubs on Gaba Road, such as Half London, Al's Bar and Buffalo Bill's.

Poste restante The main post office is on Kampala Road in the heart of the city centre.

Tourist information office Helpful information office in IPS Building behind British Council.

Tour operators No tour operators in Kampala particularly cater to backpackers, but most overland truck companies in Kenya run regular trips passing through Uganda. A recommended tour operator in Kampala is Afritours, whose office is on Lumumba Avenue. Tel/fax: 041 344855/714; email: afritour@swiftuganda.com.

THE SSESE ISLANDS

This archipelago in Lake Victoria is one of Uganda's prime destinations for casual rambling and off-the-beaten-track exploration. Lush and well-watered, with an annual rainfall of over 2,000mm, it supports extensive areas of forest and a variety of monkeys and birds. The largest and most accessible island, Buggala, is 43km long, and its principal towns are Kalengala and Luku. Other easily visited islands are Bubeke, Bukasa and Bufumira.

Exploring the islands is very straightforward. There are about 50km of roads on Buggala Island, and you can walk out in any direction from Kalengala and expect to be greeted with pleasing views over the forest to the lake and the other islands. Travellers tend to concentrate on the Luku road, but the road south of Kalengala is also worth exploring. Forest animals such as vervet monkey, black-and-white colobus and a variety of birds and butterflies are often seen all over the island. To explore further afield on Buggala you can either backpack or hire a bicycle from the Andronica Lodge – a popular cycling excursion is to Mutambala Beach off the Kalengala–Luku road.

If you decide to explore the other islands, the only real limits are your time and imagination. Bukasa, the second largest island, is even more attractive than Buggala. It is extensively forested, birds and monkeys are profuse, and there is a fair network of roads which you can explore on foot. Individual points of interest on Bukasa include an attractive beach at Misenyi Bay, 20 minutes' walk from Agnes' Guest House, and a plunge-pool ringed by forest below a waterfall one hour's walk from the guesthouse. For monkeys and views, the walk along the road to Rwanabatya Village has been recommended.

Access and getting around
The ferry MV *Barbus*, which used to do a twice-weekly run from Port Bell near Kampala to Bubeke, Bukasa, Bufumira and Buggala Islands, and was the most popular and easiest way to get between the islands, ceased operating in 1997. I do, however, have definite confirmation that a new passenger ferry started operating between Port Bell and the islands in early 2000, crossing at least three times a week. No details of the exact timetable are available, but the backpackers' hostel in Kampala should have current information.

Assuming that bus services have not been rendered redundant by the new ferry service, Kalengala and Luku on Buggala Island are connected to Kampala and Masaka by a bus service which leaves Kampala at 09.00 on Monday, Wednesday and Friday, passes through Masaka at about 14.00 and arrives at Kalengala after 17.00, the exact time of arrival depending on the efficiency of the ferry crossing between Bukakata and Luku. Buses for Kampala and Masaka leave Kalengala at 06.00 on Tuesday, Thursday and Saturday. You can get between Masaka and Kalengala in stages, by catching a shared taxi from Nyondo to Bukakata and taking the next ferry to Luku.

A cheap and quick way of getting to most of the islands is to use a fishing boat from Kasenyi on the Entebbe Peninsula. Unfortunately this is also rather risky – overloaded boats frequently capsize and should absolutely be avoided in windy or stormy weather. The boats sail from Kasenyi at 16.00 and 18.00 daily except Sunday, and take about six hours to reach the island they're heading for. Boats to Kasenyi leave the islands at around 07.00. There are minibuses between Kasenyi and the old taxi park in Kampala. Fishing boats connect most of the larger islands on a daily basis.

Where to stay and eat
Agnes' Guesthouse Bukasa Island, close to ferry jetty. Friendly. Spectacular sunsets. Room **B** pp. Camping **A** pp. Meals served, but bring some food with you.
Father Christopher's Guesthouse Bukasa Island, 30 minutes from jetty. Rooms **B** pp. Camping **A** pp.
Hornbill Campsite Superb location on forested lakeshore a steep 1km walk from Kalengala. Meals available. Rooms from **B**/**C**. Dorm **C** pp. Camping **A** pp (cheap tent hire).
Panorama Lodge Behind Hornbill Camp. Indifferent setting but good rooms. **E** dbl.
People's Bar In Kalengala, close to Andronica Lodge. The only refrigerated drinks in town.
PTA Andronica Lodge Kalengala. Once popular but now tired and overpriced. Rooms with sagging beds and mice **C** pp. Camping **A** pp. Meals.
Ssese Scorpion Lodge About 1km from Luku ferry jetty, Buggala Island. Rooms **B** pp. Camping **A** pp.

THE MBARARA ROAD
The town of **Mbarara** is 283km east of Kampala by road. It is the gateway to southwestern Uganda, lying at the junction of the main road southeast to Kabale and the road north to Kasese and Fort Portal. Mbarara is a dull little town, despite having

been the pre-colonial capital of the Ankole Kingdom, but there are several spots worth investigating along the road there from Kampala. First up is the 450ha **Mpanga Forest** near Mpigi, a remnant of the medium-altitude rainforest which once extended over much of the Lake Victoria hinterland, and criss-crossed by an extensive network of public footpaths from which a variety of monkeys and birds can be seen. Visitors are welcome, and entrance is free, but you must check in at the forest station.

The major town along the Mbarara road, **Masaka**, is a reasonably important route focus: the place to pick up road transport towards Bukoba in Tanzania and buses to the Ssese Islands in Lake Victoria. Only 16km from Masaka, and altogether more alluring, **Lake Nabugabo** is separated from Lake Victoria by a forested sand bar, and ringed by patches of forest interspersed with grassy clearings and cultivated smallholdings. The lake shore supports squirrels, vervet monkeys and a variety of lizards and birds, and it can be explored along any of several roads and footpaths.

Lying south of the main road between Masaka and Mbarara, the 260km² **Lake Mburo National Park** is centred around Lake Mburo, part of a cluster of 14 lakes, all of which are fed by the Ruizi River and connected by seasonal swamps. The predominant vegetation type is acacia savannah. The park supports a wide variety of large mammal species including impala, eland topi, bushbuck, sitatunga, common duiker, klipspringer, oribi, Defassa waterbuck, Bohor reedbuck, Burchell's zebra, buffalo, warthog, bushpig, hippopotamus, leopard, spotted hyena and side-striped jackal. More than 310 bird species have been recorded. Lake Mburo is not so easy to reach without a private vehicle, but once you get there it's relatively easy to explore via guided walks and boat trips on the lake. The 72-page *Lake Mburo National Park Guidebook* (African Wildlife Foundation, 1994) contains bird and mammal checklists, and a detailed historical and ecological background.

Access and getting around

This road between Kampala and Mbarara is quite probably the busiest in Uganda, and public transport runs along it in all shapes and forms. Regular minibuses connect Kampala to Masaka, and Masaka to Mbarara, and buses heading to destinations in western Uganda can drop passengers at any town along the road.

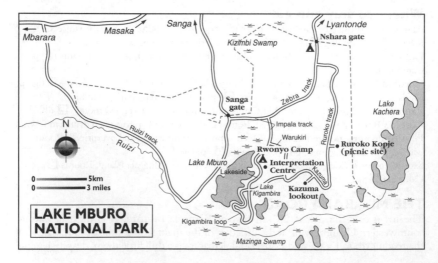

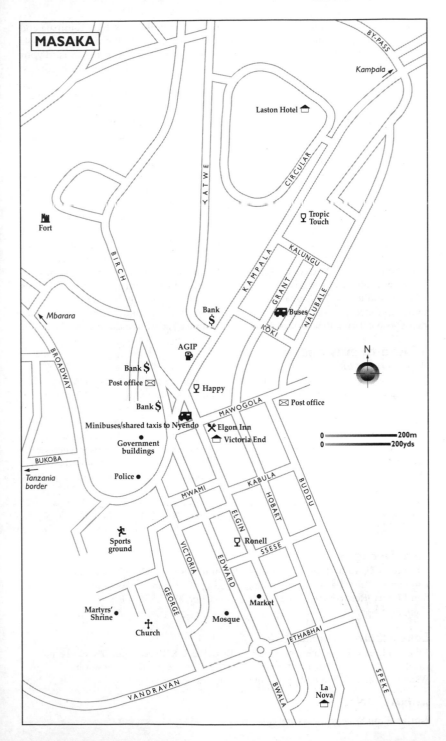

MASAKA

To get to the Mpanga Forest, your best bet is a minibus between Kampala and Masaka. The forest station lies 500m off the Mbarara road, 40km from Kampala and 3km west of Mpigi township – coming from Kampala, the turn-off is to your right immediately after the road passes through a dip flanked by the southernmost tip of the forest.

The resort on Lake Nabugabo lies 16km from Masaka. The cheapest way to get there is to pick up a shared taxi to Bukakata at Nyondo trading centre, 2km from Masaka on the Kampala road, and ask to be dropped at the signposted turn-off to the resort. It's a 4km walk from the turn-off to the resort. Alternatively, it's possible to arrange a special hire from Masaka directly to the resort for around US$15.

There are two turn-offs to Lake Mburo park, one at the 50km marker which lies 13km from Lyantonde on the Mbarara road, and one at Sango about 25km before Mbarara. On weekdays, park vehicles often travel between Mbarara and the rest camp, and they'll give you a lift if there's room. Rather than try to locate the vehicle in Mbarara, go to Sango and, if you can establish that a park vehicle has left for Mbarara earlier in the day, you can assume that it will return. At weekends, Lake Mburo may be visited by Kampala residents, so the turn-off at the 50km marker is the best place to wait. If you don't want to leave things to chance, a special hire from Mbarara will cost about USS$50. You could also ask the Uganda National Parks office in Kampala to radio through a day in advance to arrange for a vehicle to meet you at Sango – this will cost about US$40. With an early start, you could also walk the 13km from Sango to the entrance gate – it's reasonably flat most of the way – and organise for a ranger to escort you along the 6km road from the entrance gate to the camp.

Where to stay and eat
Mpanga Forest
A basic campsite has been cleared in the forest and more formal tourist accommodation is reportedly under construction. There are guesthouses 3km from Mpanga in Mpigi town.

Masaka
Masaka Backpackers' Cottage and Campsite Great and sadly under-utilised set-up 5km out of town on the Bukoba Road. Facilities include meals, bar, book swap, cheap laundry, visitors' book. Dorm **B** pp. Camping **A** pp. To get there, catch a shared taxi towards Kyotera and asked to be dropped at the signposted junction, from where it's a five-minute walk.
Tropic Touch Restaurant Indian meals, steaks, spaghetti dishes US$3–5.
Victoria End Resthouse Popular as much as anything for a lack of central alternatives. Rooms **C**/**D**.

Lake Nabugabo
Church of Uganda Resort Tel: 041 272900 for reservations. Great location and good atmosphere. *Banda* **E** dbl. Dorm or camping **B** pp. Cheap meals. Soft drinks.
Sand Beach Resort New place 500m from the Church of Uganda Resort. Camping **A** pp.

Lake Mburo National Park
Rwonyo Rest Camp Guided walks US$7. Boat trips US$10 per group. Bandas **F** pp (booking advisable). Camping **D** pp. Basic meals, beer, soft drinks. Hot showers. Waterbuck, warthog and bushpig wander through camp at night.

Mbarara
Coffee Shop Spaghetti, steak and chicken dishes. US$4.

Mayoba Inn Decent and reasonably priced, but avoid the noisy street-facing rooms. ◙ dbl (communal shower) or ◙ s/c dbl.
Memory Lodge One of the better cheapies. Basic rooms ◙ single.
Pan-Afric Motel Pretty, rural retreat at Ndija on Kabale road 35km past Mbarara. Ringed by steep hills. Rooms ◙ dbl. Camping ◙ pp. Meals. Bar. Day excursions US$5–10pp (monkey and bird walks, fishing, herbal medicine tour).

Kabale and the mountain gorilla reserves

In the far southwest of Uganda, set amongst the terraced hills of the Kigezi region, **Kabale** is the gateway to the popular mountain gorilla reserves of Uganda, Rwanda and the Congo. It's a town with a most equable atmosphere and excellent backpacker facilities, and it lies in an area with some great walking potential. Only 6km from Kabale, the beautiful, island dotted **Lake Bunyonyi** has been a mandatory day trip with travellers for years, and its popularity can only grow now that a number of campsites have been opened on its shore and islands.

Nestling close to the Congo border, **Kisoro** is smaller and scruffier than Kabale, but the setting compensates. The volcanic peaks of the Virunga Mountains tower over Kisoro's southern skyline, while green hills roll out of town in every direction. The area around Kisoro is, once again, great walking country, with the most obvious goals being Lakes Mutanda and Mulehe, around 6–8km out of town along the Mushangiro road, though under present circumstances wandering unguided in this volatile border area might be considered unduly risky.

The world's 600 remaining wild **mountain gorillas** are concentrated around Kabale and Kisoro, where they are split all but evenly into two separate populations. One population lives entirely within Uganda, on the forested slopes protected by the **Bwindi Impenetrable National Park** to the north of Kabale. The other lives in the Virunga Mountains, the volcanic range straddling the borders of Uganda, Rwanda and the Congo, where it is protected respectively in the Mgahinga Gorilla National Park, Parc National des Volcans and Parc National des Virungas. In the past, all four of these reserves have offered gorilla tracking, and they are all most easily and normally approached from Uganda (see *Gorilla tracking* and *The eastern Congo* on pages 225 and 230). At present, however, only the parks in Uganda and Rwanda are open to tourists, and only Bwindi offers reliable gorilla tracking throughout the year.

The emphasis on gorilla tracking means the other attractions of Uganda's so-called mountain gorilla reserves are often neglected. **Mgahinga National Park** protects part of the majestic Virunga Mountains, including three extinct volcanoes, Muhabura (4,127m), Sabinyo (3,645m), and Gahinga (3,475m), all of which could be ascended on guided day hikes until recently, but are now practically inaccessible. Half-day nature trails through the forest zone or to Rugezi Swamp offer the opportunity to see some of the 76 mammal species recorded in the park (most commonly golden monkey, bushbuck and various duikers, with a fair chance of seeing elephant and giant forest hog near the swamp), as well as 12 bird species endemic to the Albert Rift.

The vast rainforest protected within Bwindi Impenetrable National Park harbours 93 mammal species, more than any Ugandan national park except Queen Elizabeth, as well as 300 butterfly and 350 bird species (a bird checklist is available at Buhoma). The forest can be explored along five day-trails, which range from 30 minutes to eight hours in duration. The 30-minute Muyanga River Trail lies just outside the national park, so it can be walked unguided without paying park fees.

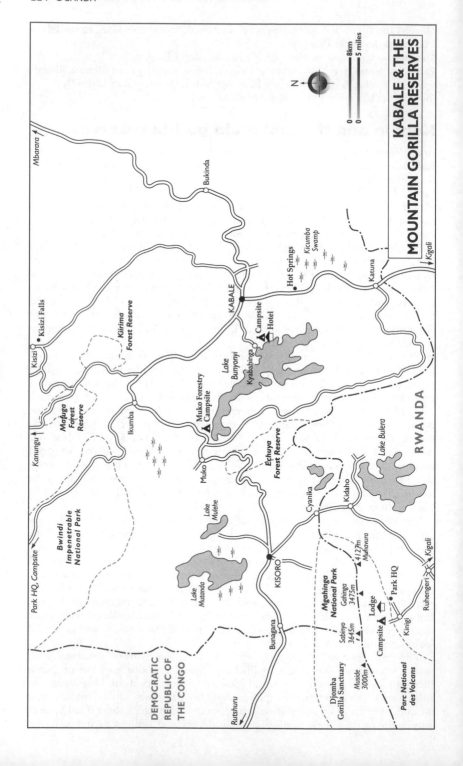

KABALE & THE
MOUNTAIN GORILLA RESERVES

GORILLA TRACKING

The comparative costs of gorilla tracking in the different reserves break down as follows:

Bwindi National Park Gorilla tracking US$250. Park entrance US$15 per 24 hours.

Mgahinga National Park Gorilla tracking US$250. Park entrance US$15 per 24 hours.

Parc des Virungas (Congo) Gorilla tracking US$125. No entrance fee. Visa US$40–80. (1998 prices.)

Parc des Volcans (Rwanda) Gorilla tracking US$250. No entrance fee. Visa US$50. Car hire from Ruhengeri town to the car park at the base of the mountains can cost anything from US$30–60 per vehicle.

Buying a gorilla-tracking permit

Bwindi National Park Six permits issued for any given day, to be booked in advance through UWA in Kampala. No standby permits are available any more, and permits are often booked up months in advance.

Mgahinga National Park Habituated gorillas spend only part of the year in Mgahinga, typically March to May and September to December. Tour operators don't use Mgahinga, due to the unpredictability of gorilla movements, and permits can no longer be bought in advance from UWA in Kampala but are available on-site only.

Parc des Virungas Effectively closed to tourism mid-2000.

Parc des Volcans Since the park re-opened to tourists in mid-1999, up to 32 permits (eight each for four different groups) have been available daily. As of mid-2000 there are still free permits available on most days, something that is likely to change as Rwanda attracts more travellers. Permits can be booked in advance through the ORTPN office in Kigali (the capital of Rwanda), or on the day before visiting the gorillas at the ORTPN office in Ruhengeri) the closest Rwandan town to the park).

What to take

When gorilla tracking, take with you all the food and water you'll need for the day, and a waterproof daypack for binoculars and camera. You may need ASA 800 or 1600 film to photograph gorillas successfully with a high magnification lens. In the forest, wear your heaviest trousers, a long-sleeved shirt, socks, solid walking shoes and a hat.

Illness

Apes are susceptible to many airborne human diseases, for which reason visitors are asked to keep 5m distance from the gorillas – difficult in Rwanda and Congo, where young gorillas frequently leap on to tourists – but strictly enforced in Uganda. Bear in mind that if you are ill, even just with the sniffles, you could transmit a contagious and possibly fatal virus to a gorilla population where there is no immunity. In Uganda, ill permit holders who withdraw voluntarily before the trip leaves the headquarters are offered a full refund. Should your guide notice any symptoms of illness once you're in the forest, you'll be forced to withdraw without a refund.

Of the guided trails within the park, the three-hour Waterfall Trail is particularly good for monkeys and birds; the Mazubijiro Loop Trail and Rushara Hill Trail both take about three hours and offer good views across to the Virunga Mountains; while the eight-hour Ivo River Walk leads to the southern boundary of the park, and offers a good opportunity for seeing monkeys, duikers and a variety of birds. For more details, buy a copy of Phenny Gongo's inexpensive booklet *Agandi Bwindi: A Visitor's Handbook to the Impenetrable Forest* from the canteen opposite the community campsite.

Access and getting around

Buses between Kampala and Kabale leave throughout the morning and they take around six hours, stopping at Mbarara. A daily bus travels directly between Kampala and Kisoro, leaving in either direction at 08.00. Buses from Kampala to Kisoro stop in Kabale at about 14.00. There are also a few pick-up trucks running between Kabale and Kisoro every day.

To get to Lake Bunyonyi from Kabale, follow the Kisoro road out of town for about 1km past the Highlands Hotel, then turn into the first road to your left. The road reaches the lake shore after about 5km, near the shell of a hotel (owned by the Vice Chancellor of Makarere University before he was murdered by Amin), from where it's another 1km to Kyabahinga village. At the campsite in Kyabahinga, you can organise a dugout on to the lake – a return trip to Bwama Island costs around US$2.50pp and takes 25 minutes each way.

Mgahinga National Park lies 14km from Kisoro along a signposted dirt road. Ask at the National Park office in Kisoro whether any official vehicles are heading to the gate – if not, you can hire a park vehicle for US$15, or walk. The road is quite hilly, but it shouldn't take more than three hours by foot, and you can get a free route map at the park office.

Bwindi Park Headquarters are at Buhoma Entrance Gate, 108km from Kabale and 17km from Butogota trading centre. Coming from Kabale, ask around at the bus station for a pick-up truck heading directly to Butogota. If nothing's heading that way, you may be able to persuade a pick-up truck heading to Kihihi to divert to Butogota for an extra US$10, or else you can arrange a special hire, though this is very expensive. A better option is the daily Silverline bus which leaves Kampala

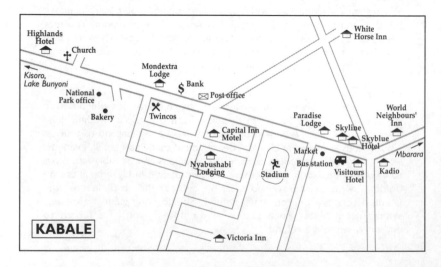

at 06.00 and passes through Mbarara at around midday before arriving at Butogota in the late afternoon. Whatever way you get to Butogota, you will probably have to spend a night there (see *Where to stay and eat* below) before looking for a pick-up truck to Buhoma the next morning. For a group, it's worth considering a special hire from Butogota to the gate (expect to pay around US$15). You could also walk – the terrain is hilly, but the gradients are reasonably gentle and it shouldn't take more than five hours.

Where to stay and eat
Kabale
Bakery Near National Park office. Fresh bread, pies and pastries.
Capital Inn Motel Run-down relic of 1960s tourist boom. Spartan rooms **B** dbl.
Kadio Hotel New place. Good restaurant. Clean rooms **C** dbl.
Skyblue Hotel Good restaurant. Clean rooms **D** pp.
Visitours Hotel As good value as there is in Uganda. Wonderful restaurant. Rooms **B** pp.

Lake Bunyonyi
Bushala Island Camp Small island facing Bwama. Camping **B** pp. Standing tent **E/F** sgl/dbl.
Bwama Island Rest House On the largest island, which was formerly a leper colony but is now a craft centre for the disabled.
Kalibuni Campsite At Kyabahinga on the lake shore. Beer, soft drinks, meals. Camping **A** pp.
Kyahuge Island Campsite Camping **A** pp.

Kisoro
Rugigana Campsite 1km along road to Congo. Clean rooms **B** dbl. Camping **A** pp. Meals. Highly recommended.
Skyblue Hotel A relation of its longer-established namesake in Kabale. Comfortable rooms **D** dbl.

Mgahinga Gorilla National Park
Amanjambere Iwacu Campground Spectacular setting just outside Ntebeko Gate. Guided ascent of volcanoes US$18pp. Guided nature trail US$7pp. Rooms **B** pp. Camping **B** pp. Tent hire. Basic meals, beer, soft drinks. No park entrance fee charged unless you enter the park. The campground offers an inexpensive pick-up service from Kisoro; ask the wildlife office in town to radio them to make arrangements.

Butogota
Travellers Resthouse Clean and pleasant rooms **B/C**. Restaurant.

Bwindi National Park
Buhoma Community Campsite Just outside Buhoma Gate on slope facing forest gallery. *Banda* **C** pp. Camping **B** pp. Canteen. Guided forest walks US$7pp.

The Ruwenzori border area
KASESE AND SURROUNDS
Lying in the foothills of the Ruwenzori Mountains, **Kasese** has a dusty, dour atmosphere that contrasts oddly with its beautiful setting. Kasese boasts few attractions – if you have a spare afternoon, you could hire a bicycle to cycle along the 11km road to Kilembe Copper Mine, passing a colony of thousands of fruit

HIKING THE RUWENZORIS

The Ruwenzoris are arguably the most challenging of all East African mountains, and the six-day Ruwenzori loop trail is widely regarded to be a tougher hike than the ascents of Mount Kilimanjaro or Kenya. Hikers will require above average fitness and stamina to enjoy the muddy trails – in parts, you may literally be wading through waist-high mud.

The Ruwenzori National Park had been closed to tourists for about three years in 2000, due to the activities of the ADF. There are no indications that the park will re-open in the immediate future, but it could happen during the lifespan of this edition. Prior to the closure of the park, hikes and climbs had to be organised through the Ruwenzori Mountain Service (RMS) in Kasese. The six-day loop trail cost US$300 per person, inclusive of park fees, porters, guides, transport to and from the trail head, food and equipment. Many travellers opted for a shorter three-day hike, which follows the loop trail for two days before descending via the same route. Shorter hikes cost US$50–60 per person per day. The RMS office was semi-permanently closed when I was last in Kasese, and there is no saying whether it will still exist when and if the national park re-opens. Contact details used to be PO Box 33, Kasese; tel: 0493 4115; fax: 0483 4235.

Hikers should be prepared for cold, wet conditions in the Ruwenzoris. Bring plenty of warm clothing for the nights. The drier seasons are from December to early March and from late June to early September, but it can rain at any time of year. The paths are incredibly muddy after rain, particularly around the Bigo Bog and Lake Bujuku, and between Kitandara and Guy Yeoman Huts. It is advisable to wear gumboots and a waterproof jacket and trousers. Before you climb, waterproof your matches and seal changes of clothes in plastic.

Altitude sickness is unlikely to be a major cause for concern on the loop trail, which reaches a maximum altitude of 4,372m, though you can expect to feel some effects especially around Scott Elliot and Freshfield Passes. Guides are trained to recognise altitude-related symptoms, and they will force you to turn back if they feel it is unsafe for you to continue. Only experienced mountaineers should attempt to climb the peaks – the guides have a reputation for losing their way once they're off the standard loop trail.

The definitive *Guide to the Ruwenzori* (Osmaston and Pasteur, 1972), recently updated for 1997 republication, can be ordered by mail from Stanfords (12–14 Long Acre, London, WC2E 9LP; tel: 020 7836 1321).

bats on the way – but it does see a fair amount of travellers on account of being the base for hikes into the Ruwenzori Mountains.

Protected in the 996km² **Ruwenzori National Park**, the extensive Ruwenzori Mountains are widely identified as the source of the legend of the Mountains of the Moon, the snow-capped range documented in AD150 by the Roman geographer Ptolemy. The loftiest peak, Margherita (5,109m) on Mount Stanley, is the third highest in Africa. Four other glacial peaks reach an altitude of over 4,600m: Mount Speke (4,890m), Mount Emin (4,791m), Mount Gessi (4,715m) and Mount Luigi da Savoia (4,627m). The Ruwenzoris have a fascinating biology, in particular the open heather and alpine zones, which span an altitude of 3,000m to 4,500m, and are renowned for their otherworldly vegetation: forests of giant

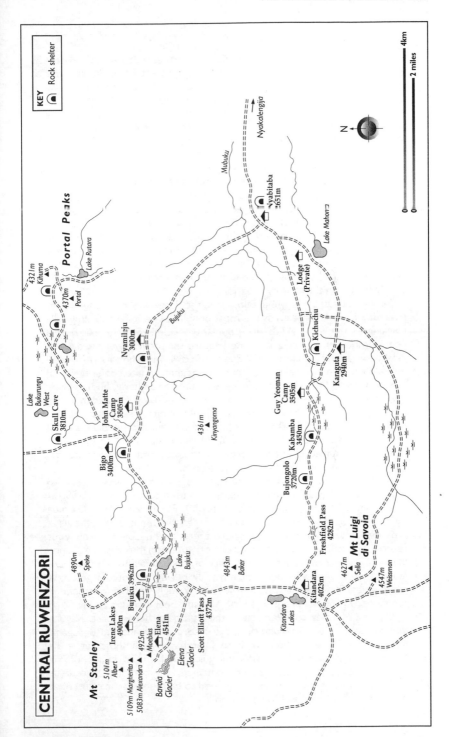

CENTRAL RUWENZORI

KEY
🏠 Rock shelter

N

0 — 2 miles
0 — 4km

Mt Stanley
5101m Albert ▲
5109m Margherita ▲ 5083m Alexandra ▲
4925m Moebius ▲
Elena 4541m ▲
Bavoia Glacier
Elena Glacier
4890m Speke ▲
Irene Lakes 4900m
Bujuku 3962m 🏠
Lake Bujuku
4843m Baker ▲
Scott Elliott Pass 4372m
Kitandara Lakes
Kitandara 4023m
4627m Sella ▲
Mt Luigi di Savoia
4547m Weissman ▲
Freshfield Pass 4282m
Bujongolo 3720m 🏠
Kabamba 3450m
Guy Yeoman Camp 3505m
Karaguta 2940m 🏠
Kichuchu 🏠
Lodge (Private) 🏠
Lake Mahoro
Nyabitaba 2651m 🏠
Nyakalengija
Mubuku
Bujuku
4361m Kinyangoma ▲
Nyamileju 3000m 🏠
John Matte Camp 3505m 🏠
Bigo 3400m 🏠
Lake Bukurungu West
Skull Cave 3810m 🏠
4370m Portal 🏠
4321m Kihuma ▲
Portal Peaks
Lake Rutara

THE EASTERN CONGO

The former Belgian territory of the Congo (formerly Zaire) has in recent years been one of the most unstable and war-prone parts of Africa. After suffering years of exploitative dictatorship at the hands of Mobutu Sese Seko, the country was captured by Laurent Kabila's ADFL with the strong support of Rwanda and Uganda in May 1997. Despite initially promising signs, the country has been in a constant state of civil war more-or-less since Kabila took power, and the part of the country bordering Uganda and Rwanda has been a no-go area for some years now.

The eastern Congo has always been particularly popular with travellers, and the few who did visit in happier times generally crossed over briefly with the sole aim of seeing mountain gorillas in the Parc National des Virungas (the Congolese section of the Virunga Mountains). To do so would be highly inadvisable, if not downright suicidal, at the moment, and while things might change during the lifespan of this edition, it would be foolhardy to venture into this area without first obtaining current information from other travellers, or from somewhere such as the Kampala Backpackers Hostel. The embassy in Kampala should also be able to advise you on the security situation.

To give a bit of background, Djomba in the Parc des Virungas took over Rwanda's Parc des Volcans as the most popular place for mountain gorilla tracking in the early 1990s. Its popularity waned in 1996 following a poaching incident involving habituated gorillas the previous year, and it was closed for several months in 1997 due to the civil war. The park re-opened in late 1997. Within weeks, the situation was thrown into confusion when the exclusive rights to sell permits were granted to an Italian businessman. Park officials, whose sole income was often the money generated by selling permits, refused to acknowledge the official permits. Just as this situation was resolved, four tourists were kidnapped en route to the park, two of whom are presumed to have been killed. Since late 1998, the Parc des Virungas has effectively been closed to tourists, and crossing into the Congo has been regarded as highly dangerous.

In the event that Parc des Volcans should again be considered safe to visit, a visa will probably be mandatory (this used to cost a stiff US$80 at the Congo Embassy in Kampala or Nairobi). For those visiting Djomba only, the alternative was to pay US$40–50 to the immigration officials at the border and leave your passport there to be collected on your return. The quite incredible level of corruption in the eastern Congo places any concerns about the morality of doing this into the realms of fantasy, and I've never heard of anybody having a problem getting a passport back. There's always a first time, though, and being trapped in the Congo without a passport simply doesn't bear thinking about.

Djomba Hut lies only 7km from the Bunagana border post. Regular *matatus* cover the 11km road between Kisoro in Uganda and Bunagana, from where it's a two-hour walk to Djomba along a short cut – the children hanging around the border will guide you for US$1 or so. In 1998, you could camp at the hut, which contained four beds that had to be shared by however many people happened to be there on the night. Basic meals and soft drinks used to be available.

heather plants, and lobelias and groundsels growing up to 10m in height. (See box *Hiking the Ruwenzoris*, page 228.)

Kasese is also the closest town to Uganda's most popular and accessible game reserve, the **Queen Elizabeth National Park** (rather confusingly known as Ruwenzori National Park during the Amin era, and still marked as such on some maps). This park protects the entire Ugandan shore of Lake Edward, the northern and western shores of Lake George, and an acacia and euphorbia-dotted area of 1,978km^2 between the two lakes. Over 550 bird species and 95 mammal species have been recorded in the park. Mammals which are regularly seen by visitors include vervet monkey, baboon, Uganda kob, bushbuck, topi, Defassa waterbuck, elephant, buffalo, hippopotamus, warthog, side-striped jackal, spotted hyena, lion and leopard. The main focus of tourist activity in Queen Elizabeth, Mweya Lodge, is situated on a peninsula overlooking the Kazinga Channel where it enters Lake Albert – see box *Around Mweya* on page 232.

Mweya Lodge is reasonably accessible to backpackers but, if you can't get a lift or the cumulative accommodation and entrance fees are beyond your means, then the small and monumentally run-down town of **Katwe** should prove a worthy alternative. Katwe has a superb situation on a grassy rise separated from the Mweya Peninsula by Lake Edward and flanked by two saline crater lakes to the north. Hippos are common, flamingo flocks occur on the crater lakes, and you've a fair chance of seeing elephants on the facing lake shore. Katwe is easy to reach and there is accommodation. No park entrance fee is charged for travelling along the road to Katwe, or along other public roads through the park, for instance the main Mbarara–Kasese Road and the Katanguru–Ishasha road.

Access and getting around

Plenty of road transport connects Kasese to Mbarara, Kabale and Fort Portal. Direct buses between Kampala and Kasese leave in both directions throughout the morning, taking around six hours. Large herds of Uganda kob are likely to be seen from the

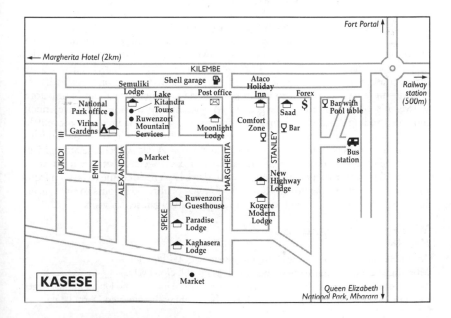

AROUND MWEYA

Mweya is a lovely place, with a village-like atmosphere. On a clear day, the lodge grounds offer spectacular views across the channel to the glacial peaks of the Ruwenzori Mountains. There must be about 10km of walkable roads running through the village, the bird life is prolific, and you are likely to see plenty of animals from vantage points overlooking the channel and Lake Edward.

The most popular and compelling activity run out of Mweya is the twice-daily launch trip down the Kazinga Channel, which normally offers close encounters with elephant, buffalo, waterbuck, Uganda kob, large numbers of hippo and crocodile and an abundance of water birds. Launch trips costs US$90 per group for up to nine people, and US$10 per person for larger groups.

A group of chimpanzees from the animal orphanage in Entebbe was recently released on to a small island near Mweya. The idea is not to attempt to rehabituate the animals to living in the wild, but to confine them in the natural sanctuary of an island rather than in the artificial one of a cage. Boat trips from Mweya Lodge run to a viewing platform alongside the island twice a day. The round trip takes one hour and costs US$15 per person.

There are daily chimp tracking walks through the Chambura (or Kyambura) Gorge, on the eastern border of the national park and the Chambura Game Reserve. The chimps here are reasonably well habituated to people, and the confined nature of the gorge means that they are easier to locate than in some other reserves. The walk costs US$40 per person. The only problem is that unless somebody else who is doing it can offer you a lift, you'll have to hire a park vehicle to take you to the gorge, at a cost of US$1/km.

All activities can be booked at the office outside Mweya Lodge.

main tar road as it passes through Queen Elizabeth National Park. The rail service between Kampala and Kasese is very slow and unreliable. If you're heading to the Ruwenzoris from Kasese, packages with the RMS include transfer to the trail-head.

A few jam-packed pick-up trucks run between Mweya and Katwe daily, usually leaving Kasese at around 11.00. There's often good game-viewing on the way. If you want to hitch to Mweya, ask to be dropped at the entrance gate about 5km before Katwe. It's only 6km from the gate to Mweya, and you shouldn't have much difficulty finding a lift. At the worst, the ranger at the gate can radio for a park vehicle to fetch you – at a cost of US$12, irrespective of group size. The other option is to hire a vehicle in Kasese to take you directly to Mweya. A taxi will charge around $25 (highly negotiable) irrespective of the number of passengers. Ask the taxi driver in advance if he is prepared to stop for animals – there is plenty of game to be seen from the road. Most tour operators in Kampala do two- or three-day tours to the Queen Elizabeth National Park, and the RMS in Kasese can organise day visits.

Where to stay and eat
Kasese
Ataco Holiday Inn Adequately clean rooms with nets. **C/D** sgl/dbl.
Moonlight Lodges Large clean rooms with nets **C** dbl. Good value.
Saad Hotel Long standing and well-managed travellers' haunt, but no longer in the budget category. Good, inexpensive restaurant. Rooms **E** s/c dbl with hot water. Dorm **C** pp.

Virina Gardens Campsite The best cheap lodging in town. Thatched huts 🅲 sgl. Camping 🅱 pp.

Queen Elizabeth National Park and surrounds
Katwe The Lake View Hotel is cleaner than the flaking exterior might suggest and good value at 🅱 pp.

Maramagambo Forest A recently opened and relatively accessible campsite lies in this beautiful stand of rainforest in the south of Queen Elizabeth. The site lies about 9km from the main Kampala–Kasese road (you'll either have to walk or arrange a bike), and you will have to bring your own food (firewood and water are available). Camping costs 🅲 pp plus the usual park entrance fees.

Mweya Peninsula The cheapest rooms are at the Student Camp, but they are very scruffy and often full. 🅳 pp. Camping costs 🅳 pp, but watch out for hippos at night. The Institute of Ecology Hostel, near Mweya Lodge, has comfortable but overpriced rooms for 🅵 pp. Mweya Lodge serves good and relatively affordable meals.

FORT PORTAL AND KIBALE FOREST
The attractive town of **Fort Portal** lies in the northern Ruwenzori foothills, some 50km north of Kasese and 320km west of Kampala. The surrounding hills offer excellent views to the Ruwenzori Mountains, and the town itself has a pleasant atmosphere and relatively smart appearance, barely recognisable from the run-down 'Fort Pothole' of a few years back. Fort Portal is the unofficial capital of the Toro Kingdom: the circular shell of the palace built by King Rukidi III in the 1960s is perched on a hill outside town, and two former Toro kings, Kasagama and Rukidi III, are buried at the Karambi Tombs, 5km along the Kasese road.

About 30km southeast of Fort Portal, the 766km^2 **Kibale Forest National Park** supports 13 primate species, the highest total for any East African forest. The national park's outstanding attraction is the habituated chimpanzees which can be seen on guided forest walks leaving from Kanyanchu Camp at 07.30 and 15.00 daily. Morning walks offer the better likelihood of seeing chimps, but on either walk the guides will identify various monkeys, medicinal plants, bird calls and animal spoor.

Just outside the national park boundary, looping out of Bigodi trading centre 6km from Kanyanchu Camp, the guided **Magombe Swamp Walk** is not only one of the best guided bird trails in East Africa, but also provides reliably good monkey-viewing, with an excellent chance of seeing the rare red colobus. Better still, the US$7pp fee goes directly towards funding community projects such as the construction and maintenance of a new secondary school. The walk starts at 15.00 from the library in Bigodi, where you can also hire gumboots for a nominal fee

MUBENDE
Travellers heading directly between Fort Portal and Kampala might think about breaking up the trip with an overnight stop at **Mubende**, a town of great significance in Bunyoro traditions. Mubende's main claim to posterity – standing on the top of a hill about an hour's walk from town – is the 40m-high Nakayima Tree, a fantastic piece of natural sculpture and an active shrine said to hold the spirit of the sixteenth-century Bacwezi king Nduhura. Also worth exploring, the forested Old Kampala Road out of Mubende supports a variety of birds, butterflies and monkeys. The Nakayima Hotel in Mubende has rooms from 🅲 and allows camping at 🅱 per tent. There are cheaper rooms at the nearby Kisekende Lodge.

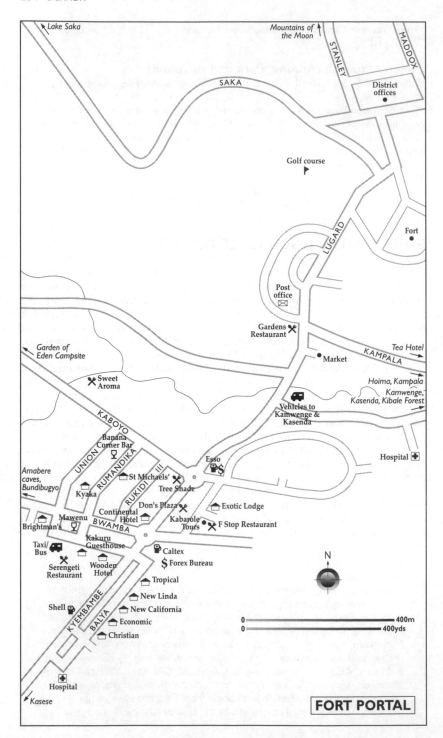

Lake Saka

Mountains of
the Moon

STANLEY

MADDOX

SAKA

District
offices

Golf course

LUGARD

Fort

Post
office

Gardens
Restaurant

KAMPALA

Tea Hotel

Garden of
Eden Campsite

Market

Hoima, Kampala

Kamwenge,
Kasenda, Kibale Forest

Sweet
Aroma

KABOYO

Vehicles to
Kamwenge &
Kasenda

Hospital

Banana
Corner Bar

Amabere
caves,
Bundibugyo

UNION

RUMANDIKA

RUKIDI

St Michaels'

Tree Shade

Esso

Kyaka

Don's Plaza

Exotic Lodge

Mawenu

BWAMBA

Continental
Hotel

Kabarole
Tours

F Stop Restaurant

Brightman's

Kakuru
Guesthouse

Caltex

Taxi/
Bus

Forex Bureau

N

Serengeti
Restaurant

Wooden
Hotel

Tropical

Shell

KYEMBAMBE

BALYA

New Linda

New California

Economic

Christian

| 0 | | 400m |
| 0 | | 400yds |

Hospital

Kasese

FORT PORTAL

(you'll be glad of them). The guides are knowledgeable, and they should be armed with binoculars and a bird field guide. Note that Magombe Swamp, Bigodi and the Safari Motel lie outside the national park, and that the main road between Fort Portal and Bigodi is public, so you must pay the daily entrance fee only if you stay at Kanyanchu Camp or when you do the guided forest walk.

If you're looking to spend a few quiet, inexpensive days in beautiful surrounds, it's difficult to think of a more suitable area than the **Bunyuruguru Crater Lakes** (see box *Exploring Bunyuruguru* on page 237) – the field of roughly 30 volcanically formed lakes that lies to the west of Kibale Forest about 20km south of Fort Portal. Bunyuruguru offers practically limitless walking opportunities, and the lush cultivation and forest patches of the region support a profusion of monkeys and birds with the Ruwenzoris providing a dramatic backdrop.

Further information and tours
Kabarole Tours on Moledina Street in Fort Portal (tel: 0483 22568, fax: 0483 22636, email: IUCNKSCD@infocom.co.ug) is committed to catering to the needs of backpackers, and it has been a driving force behind the creation of several community-run tourist projects around Fort Portal. Their 35km bicycle tour takes in a variety of crater lakes, caves and waterfalls and costs US$5pp inclusive of map and bicycle. Vehicle tours such as a chimp-tracking trip in Kibale Forest or a Crater Lake Tour cost a very reasonable US$40 for up to four people, exclusive of park fees. They will gladly supply independent travellers with current information about the Fort Portal area.

Access and getting around
Regular buses and minibuses cover the 50km road between Fort Portal and Kasese. Direct buses and minibuses covering the 320km road between Kampala and Fort Portal via Mubende take about seven hours. Direct minibuses to Mubende leave Kampala from the new taxi park and take about two hours.

To get from Fort Portal to Kibale Forest, go to the intersection of Lugard Road and the road to Kamwenge. Pick-up trucks to Kamwenge leave from here at around 10.00 daily except for Sunday, and they reach the Kanyanchu Camp and Bigodi at around midday. Kibale Forest can also be approached from the south, using the daily bus between Kampala and Kamwenge. You'll have to spend the night in Kamwenge, before jumping on a pick-up truck towards Fort Portal at around 05.00 the next morning – these normally reach Kanyanchu in time to do the morning forest walk, though I wouldn't stake my life on their punctuality. Watch out for overcharging on these pick-up trucks.

Pick-up trucks to Kamwenge also pass the Crater Valley Resort, about half-way between Fort Portal and Kanyanchu. To get to Lake Nkuruba, a more convenient base for extended exploration, you need a pick-up truck heading to Rwaihamba or Kasenda – at least three leave daily from the junction of Lugard Road and the Kamwenge road, one in the early morning, one at around noon, and one at 15.00.

Where to stay and eat
Fort Portal
Amabere Caves Campsite Rural retreat above cave and forest-fringed waterfall, and near two crater lakes. 8km from Fort Portal, turn-off signposted 6km along Bundibugyo road. Rooms **B** pp. Camping **A** pp. Tent hire. Sodas and meals.
Brightmans Executive Lodge Comfortable accommodation on Bundibugyo Road. Rooms **C** sgl or dbl.

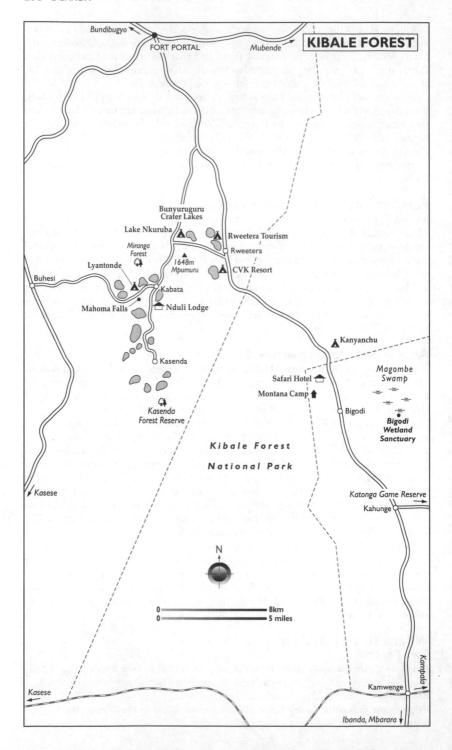

KIBALE FOREST

Bundibugyo

FORT PORTAL

Mubende

Bunyuruguru
Crater Lakes

Lake Nkuruba

Rweetera Tourism

Miranga
Forest

Rweetera

Lyantonde

1648m
Mpumuru

CVK Resort

Buhesi

Kabata

Mahoma Falls

Nduli Lodge

Kanyanchu

Kasenda

Magombe
Swamp

Safari Hotel

Montana Camp

Bigodi

Bigodi
Wetland
Sanctuary

Kasenda
Forest Reserve

Kibale Forest

National Park

Kasese

Katonga Game Reserve

Kahunge

N

0 ──────── 8km
0 ──────── 5 miles

Kasese

Kampala

Kamwenge

Ibanda, Mbarara

EXPLORING BUNYURUGURU

This field of crater lakes is one of the most exciting areas for unstructured rambling anywhere in East Africa, and the strong level of community involvement in developing its low-key tourist sites deserves the support of travellers.

An attractive and easy walk takes you along a motorable track which leaves the Kamwenge Road at Rweetera trading centre, roughly 1km north of Crater Valley Resort, and emerges on the Kasenda Road a few hundred metres south of Lake Nkuruba. The walk takes two to three hours at a relaxed pace, and on the way you'll see Lakes Nyamirima, Nyinabulita and Nyamibere, as well as Mpurumu Peak.

From the campsite at Lake Nkuruba, it's about an hour's walk along the Kasenda road to the first of the cluster of lakes around Kabata trading centre. Lakes Nyimuanbuga and Kifuruka are visible from the Kasenda road about 500m before Kabata, at the junction with a road leading to Buhesi. Turn right into the Buhesi road, and after about 500m you'll see Lake Lyantonde to your right, then after another 2km Lakes Katanda and Mwegenyi. From Kabata, you can also visit the powerful Mahoma Falls, passing en route a forested crater and Lake Rukwanzi. The waterfall lies about 3km off the main road. Guides can be arranged for a nominal fee at the community office in Kabata.

Further afield, at least six crater lakes lie along the 8km road between Kabata and Kasenda, and another group of five lakes forms an arc about 2km south of Kasenda. The one obstacle to visiting these lakes is the absence of organised accommodation around Kasenda – though you could ask permission of the village chairman to camp at Kasenda, which shouldn't be a problem. If you're heading to Kasenda, you'd do well to buy the 1:50,000 map of Kuhenge (map no 66/2) from the Department of Lands and Surveys in Entebbe.

Continental Hotel About the best value of the cheaper lodgings, with clean rooms in the **C**–**D** range. Hot showers and pleasant courtyard bar.
Don's Plaza Pleasant, centrally situated bar. Snacks available.
Exotic Lodge Clean if a little run down. Rooms **B**/**C**.
F-Stop Restaurant Tasty Italian food and burgers in US$3–4 range. Slow service. Next to Kaberole Tours.
Garden of Eden Campsite set on a riverbank about 1km out of town along Kaboyo Rd. Run by Kabarole Tours. Camping **A** pp.
Kakuru Guesthouse Similar in price and standard to Brightman's. Excellent Indian restaurant on ground floor. One of the few places in Fort Portal with a generator.
Ruwenzori View Guesthouse Popular place run by an Anglo-Dutch couple. Falls a bit outside the budget range but still used by many backpackers. Rooms cost US$23/30.
Tree Shade Restaurant Predictable local fare. US$2–3.
Wooden Hotel Formerly smart and popular lodge that's become very run down and overpriced. **C** ordinary dbl. **E** s/c dbl.

Kibale Forest National Park
Kanyanchu Camp In forest clearing. Camping **D** pp. Standing tents **E** pp. Toilets, showers, drinking water and firewood. Guided forest walk US$7. Beer, soft drinks. No food.
Mucuso Lodge Near Bigodi, 6km from Kanyanchu. Similar set-up and prices to Safari Hotel.

Safari Hotel Rustic family hotel 3km from Kanyanchu towards Bigodi. Rooms and camping **B** pp. Free laundry. Great atmosphere and food. Padlock your room.

Bunyuruguru Crater Lakes
Kibale CVK Resort Kamwenge Rd; Tel: 0483 22035; email: kabogoza@starcom.co.ug. Overlooking Lake Nyabikere. Monkeys and birds on trail circling lake. Partly furnished huts **C** pp. Furnished huts **E/F**. Camping **B** pp. Restaurant. Bar.
Lake Nkuruba Nature Reserve Kasenda Rd, 5km before Kabata. Community-run campsite on forest-fringed lake, rustling with birds and monkeys, perfectly situated for exploration. Camping **A** pp. Tent hire. Canoes and bicycles. Simple meals. Beer, soft drinks.

THE SEMULIKI VALLEY
To the west of Fort Portal, the lush Semuliki Valley is reached by a dramatically scenic road that clings tightly to the steep curves of the northern Ruwenzori foothills. About 50km along this road, **Semuliki National Park** protects the eastern extension of the vast and faunally diverse Ituri rainforest in the Congo. Despite its small size, Semuliki supports almost 400 bird species (roughly 10% of which occur nowhere else in Uganda), a healthy chimpanzee population (not yet habituated to humans), seven other diurnal primate species and elephant, bushpig, water chevrotain, buffalo and hippo. The most popular attraction in Semuliki National Park, **Sempaya Hot Springs**, can be reached from the Bundibugyo Road via a short walking trail that starts at the Sempaya park office roughly 50km from Fort Portal. Guided day walks, costing US$7 per person and offering a good opportunity to see various forest birds and mammals, can also be arranged at this office. Note that no national park fee is charged for driving or walking along the public road to Bundibugyo, or for visiting places that lie to the south of the road, for instance the campsite at Sempaya or the pygmy village at Ntandi.

The largest town in the Semuliki Valley, **Bundibugyo**, sprawls attractively over lushly vegetated hills below the peaks of the Ruwenzoris. **Nyahuka** trading centre lies roughly 40 minutes' drive from Bundibugyo towards the Congolese border, and it offers even better views of the Ruwenzori peaks. From Nyahuka, it's possible to visit the beautiful Nyahuka and Ngite Falls – reached by rigorous three-hour hikes that are best undertaken with a local guide (the guides are good and the fee will be minimal).

About 30km along the Bundibugyo road, at **Isoja**, another road branches northeast through the **Semuliki Game Reserve** (formerly the Toro Game Reserve and a discrete entity from the synonymous national park), a 500km² area of open savannah interspersed with patches of rain forest and swamp. Despite heavy poaching during the civil war, Uganda kob are still common in the reserve, and it has viable elephant, buffalo and chimpanzee populations. The road through the game reserve terminates at Ntoroko fishing village on Lake Albert, an inexpensive and potentially rewarding place to spend a few days. You can walk freely in the game reserve or hire a boat to explore the lake and its islands. Hippos are common, and the prolific bird life includes a resident population of shoebill. The entrance fee is a refreshingly affordable US$3 per day.

Note *The Semuliki Valley has mostly been unsafe for travel during the last few years. This might change during the lifespan of this edition, but the facilities listed below and transport details essentially reflect the situation as it was when I last visited the area in 1996. I would advise travellers to chat to Kabarole Tours before heading this way.*

Access and getting around

A few pick-up trucks cover the 72km road between Fort Portal and Bundibugyo daily, leaving Bundibugyo before 08.30 and starting the return trip from Fort Portal at around 13.00. These vehicles can drop passengers at Sempaya and Ntandi in Semuliki National Park, and they will stop at Karugutu, the village at the junction of the 40km road through Semuliki Game Reserve to Ntoroka on Lake Albert. From Karugutu, pick-up trucks go to Ntoroka most days.

Hikers can cross between Fort Portal and Bundibugyo using the 'Ruwenzori mini-trek' which takes about eight hours if you are driven to the trail-head, and up to twelve hours if you walk all the way from Fort Portal. The hike can be broken up with an overnight stay at the Mountains of the Moon Campsite, a recently-opened community project situated in Kighomu trading centre. For maps and further information, speak to Kabarole Tours, who have played an advisory role in developing this campsite.

Where to stay and eat
Karugutu
Anonymous lodge at the village at the junction of Bundibugyo and Ntoroka Roads.

Semuliki Game Reserve
Ntoroka Informal camping at house near Lake Albert shore. Kabarole Tours will be able to update you on planned community-run campsite.

Semuliki National Park
Sempaya Campsite Opposite Sempaya Hot Springs office. Standing tent **B** pp. Camping **A** pp. No food.

Bundibugyo
Picfare Guest House By far the best of several basic lodges. Clean room **C** dbl.

Nyahuka
Holiday Inn Clean rooms. **B**.

Northwest Uganda

The northwest of Uganda sees relatively little backpacker traffic, but it is an interesting area, dominated by the vast Murchison Falls National Park (Uganda's largest) and Budongo Forest Reserve. For travellers coming from the direction of Fort Portal, the gateway town to the region is the pleasant if unmemorable town of **Hoima**. About 4km from Hoima, the domed Mparo Tombs were built on the site of the former capital of the Bunyoro King Kabalega, who died in involuntary exile in 1923. Similarly constructed to the Kasubi Tombs in Kampala, Mparo is well worth a look and it houses many of Kabalega's personal effects.

The regional route focus and its largest town is **Masindi**, a charmless grid of erratically surfaced roads, dusty or muddy depending on when it last rained. About 40km east of Masindi, **Masindi Port** lies in the marshy area where the Nile River exits Lake Kyoga. Hippos and birds abound, there's a small rest house in Apoch on the opposite bank, and you'd be unlikely to have problems hiring a dugout to explore the lake or river.

For backpackers, the round trip from Masindi to Murchison Falls is something of an adventure, best allocated at least five days. If you are carrying a tent, an essential stop on route is the beautiful Busingiro Tourist Site in the heart of the **Budongo Forest Reserve**. The largest mahogany forest in East Africa, Budongo

NTANDI PYGMY VILLAGE

On the southern fringe of the Bundibugyo road, 5km past Sempaya, this village stands in depressing contrast to the healthy community-based tourist projects that otherwise characterise the Fort Portal area. Far from offering an insight into another lifestyle and culture, a visit to the Ntandi pygmies amounts to little more than spending good money to be harassed by a bunch of shorter-than-average dopeheads who spend the day hanging around their banana-leaf huts waiting for the next bunch of tourists to arrive. I've yet to meet anyone who left Ntandi without feeling disturbed but, since the good folk of the village appear to be locked into a cycle of dependency which would now be difficult to break, it could be argued that visiting Ntandi will offer you an instructive insight into the potential consequences of irresponsible cultural voyeurism. If nothing else, Ntandi should present backpackers with an irrefutable argument for leaving be any 'uncommercialised' pygmy communities that they might happen to hear about elsewhere in Uganda or Eastern Congo.

supports around 900 chimpanzees, and the guided chimp walks which leave from Busingiro at 07.00 and 15.00 are the cheapest in Uganda. More than 330 bird species are present in the forest, several of which have a restricted distribution in East Africa. From Busingiro, you can arrange guided walks along the road through the forest – a good place to see such localised birds as the chocolate-backed kingfisher and white-tailed hornbill, as well as red-tailed, samango and black-and-white colobus monkeys.

Backpackers heading up to Murchison Falls will almost certainly have to spend a night at **Bulisa**, an unremarkable little village boasting one of the most unpleasant guest houses I've stayed at in Africa. On the way back from the national park, you'll be faced with the prospect of an extra day and night in Bulisa before catching a vehicle out the following morning. Instead, walk or hitch the 6km to Wanseko, a fishing village on Lake Albert. With something of a wild-west feel, Wanseko may not have much intrinsic appeal, but this is compensated for by the impressive views across the lake and the nearby Nile estuary, where you can see hippos, crowned cranes, and with a bit of luck a shoebill.

The 3,840km² **Murchison Falls National Park** is bisected by the Victoria Nile, flowing in a westerly direction between Lake Kyoga and Lake Albert. The park's most striking geographical feature is the 43m-high waterfall which gives it its name, notable not so much for its size as for its immense power, caused by the 50m-wide Nile being funnelled into a 7m-wide cleft in the rocks and then virtually shooting out from the other side. It is an important game sanctuary, although it will be some time before it recovers from the heavy poaching of the Amin years and civil war, with the most common large mammals being elephants, buffalo, vervet monkey, olive baboon, Jackson's hartebeest, bushbuck, Uganda kob, Defassa waterbuck, Rothschild's giraffe, hippopotamus, warthog and lion. Over 460 bird species have been recorded. The park headquarters and tourist focal point is at Paraa, from where excellent launch trips can be arranged to the base of the waterfall (see box on page 242).

Security

As recently as 1996, roads between Masindi and Murchison Park were subject to occasional bouts of banditry, and the park itself was briefly closed in March 1996

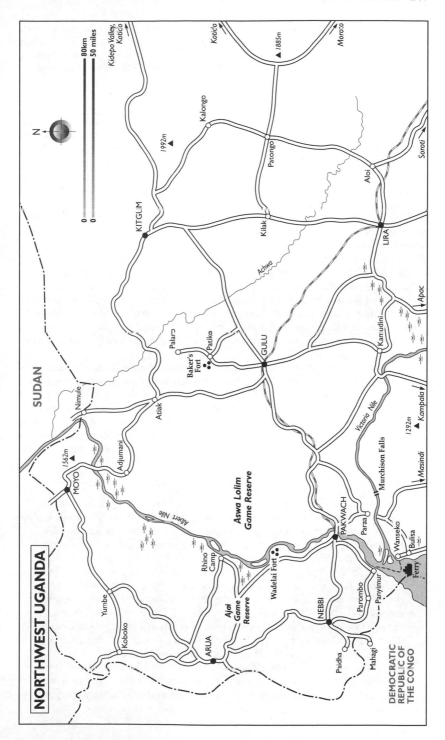

due to clashes between rebels and the military. Since then, the area has been stable, and Murchison Falls is now visited on most upmarket safari itineraries through Uganda. Nevertheless, following reports that a goods truck was attacked by bandits in March 2000, travellers might want to check with the UWA office in Masindi or Tourist Office in Kampala before heading this way.

Access and getting around

Masindi is the best staging post for trips to Murchison Falls and the Budongo Forest. Coming directly from Kampala, there are regular buses and minibuses to Masindi throughout the day, taking roughly five hours. Coming from Fort Portal via Hoima isn't quite so straightforward – public transport is erratic as far north as Hoima and the probability is that you'll have to change vehicles at Kagadi trading centre (where there's a basic guest house). Once at Hoima, regular minibuses to Masindi take around three hours.

There isn't much transport between Masindi town and Masindi Port – you'll have to ask around at the bus station in Masindi. At Masindi Port, an erratic but free ferry service crosses the Nile to Apoch on the opposite bank, taking about ten minutes. When it's not running, you can hire a dugout to take you across for next to nothing.

The shorter route to Murchison Falls heads almost directly north from Masindi and it's the route most often used by private vehicles. There's no public transport, and hitching is a matter of luck – the place to wait is at the signposted junction next to the Masindi Hotel. If you are lucky with a lift, the Kanyiyo Pabidi Tourist Site offers chimp tracking, camping and similar facilities to Busingiro at an identical price – except that you also have to pay the national park entrance fee of US$15 per 24 hours.

The longer route to Murchison Falls goes via Bulisa on the Wanseko road. This is the more scenic route, with some great views across to Lake Albert, and it allows for stopovers at Busingiro Tourist Site in Budongo Forest and the Bugungu Wildlife Reserve, both of which are within a few minutes' walk of the main road and are clearly signposted. Bulisa trading centre lies 6km before Wanseko and it can be reached in several ways. A bus to Wanseko leaves Kampala at around 06.00 every other day, passing through Masindi at around 13.00, arriving at Bulisa

LAUNCH TRIP TO MURCHISON FALLS
The highlight of any visit to Murchison Falls is likely to be the twice-daily three-hour launch trip between Paraa and the base of Murchison Falls. Game viewing from the boat is superb – hippos and crocodiles are everywhere, you're almost certain to see elephant, buffalo, waterbuck, bushbuck and giraffe, and with luck you may even get a glimpse of a lion or leopard. But the real prize of any launch trip will be a sighting of the shoebill, a large slate-grey bird which sports an imbecilic Cheshire cat grin and has the overall demeanour of something designed by a committee of camels and science fiction cartoonists. Not only is the papyrus-dwelling shoebill one of Africa's most bizarre natural creations, but it is also among the most localised large birds on the continent – and the probability of seeing it around Paraa is arguably better than anywhere else.

The launch trip costs US$100 per group. At least 20 people would fit in the boat, so it's not too expensive if there are a few of you. For an extra US$5 per group, the boat can moor at the base of the waterfall while you follow a footpath to the top, where its full force is most evident.

A LOOP THROUGH THE FAR NORTHWEST

If you're heading from Kampala to Wanseko or Murchison Falls, you may want to try the following off-the-beaten-track route through the far northwest. Before heading this way, be aware that the area is prone to periodic unrest and banditry, and the situation has deteriorated since 1995, so make advance enquiries and keep an eye on local newspapers.

The loop can be done using a combination of buses and ferries but, if you're in the right place at the right time, it could be amusing to use the unreliable but dirt cheap train service between Kampala and Pakwach to hop between any two towns. This train leaves Kampala at 16.00 Wednesday and arrives in Tororo at midnight. On Thursdays, the train leaves Tororo at 04.00, passes through Lira in the mid-morning, and arrives in Gulu at 16.00. On Friday, it does a return trip between Gulu and Pakwach, leaving Gulu at 07.00 and Pakwach at 13.30. On Saturdays, the train leaves Gulu at 08.00, passes through Lira at midday, and reaches Tororo at 20.30. It leaves Tororo for Kampala at 07.00 on Sunday.

The first town on the loop, **Lira** can be bussed to from Kampala or Masindi, but the more interesting option is to ferry across Lake Kyoga between Shengebe and Namasale. To do this, ask a minibus running between Kampala and Masindi to drop you at Nakasongola, where a pleasant lodge on the Kampala side of town has basic rooms in the **A** range. A few minibuses run between Nakasongola and Shengebe every morning – best to get the earliest one since the ferry might go at any time after 08.00. If you miss the ferry, Lwampanga police station, 2km from Shengebe, will probably let you sleep on the floor or pitch a tent in the compound. The crossing to Namasale takes one hour and costs US$1. Pick-up trucks from Namasale to Lira leave in the early morning, but there's a good little lodge in the **B** range in Namasale. There are several basic lodgings in Lira.

Several buses leave Lira every morning for **Gulu**, the largest town in northern Uganda, and one which still bears scars from the civil war. If you need to spend the night in Gulu, the Church of Uganda Hostel is recommended. From Gulu, minibuses to **Pakwach** leave every morning. Pakwach is a one-street town perched on the west bank of the Albert Nile – you can explore the riverbank from town, but be aware that walking and photography are forbidden on the large bridge across the Nile. Guest houses in Pakwach include the Dreamers Lodge (**C** dbl) and Executive Lodge (**B** dbl). The best food is at the Family Hotel.

From Pakwach, you need to get to **Nebbi** and then **Panyimur**, from where you can pick up a ferry to Wanseko. There's plenty of transport from Pakwach to Nebbi, and a few local lodgings once you arrive. You should find transport between Nebbi and Panyimur on most days, but expect to change vehicles and aim for an early start. There's a lot more traffic between Nebbi and Panyimur on Wednesdays (Nebbi's market day). The ferry between Panyimur and **Wanseko** takes one hour, costs US$2, and crosses at least twice a day in either direction. The ferry consists of a crowded fishing boat – in the event of high winds or signs of an oncoming storm, you're strongly advised to overnight at the Lake View Lodge at the jetty and try in better weather.

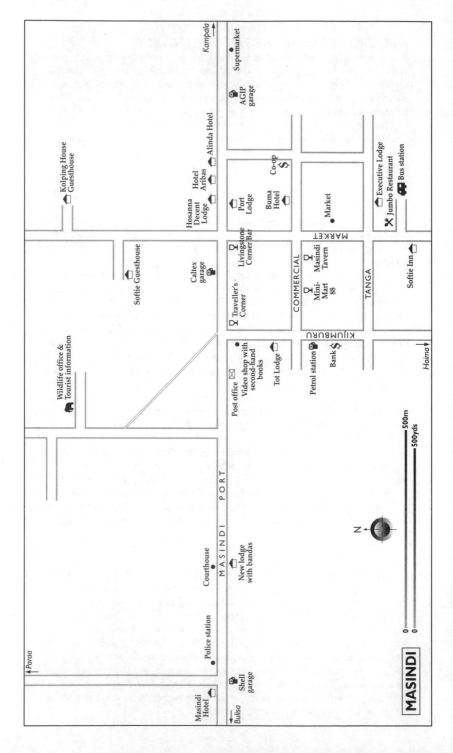

MASINDI

Paraa
Bulisa
Kampala
Hoima

Masindi Hotel
Shell garage
Police station
Courthouse
New lodge with bandas

MASINDI PORT

Wildlife office & Tourist information
Kolping House Guesthouse

Softie Guesthouse
Caltex garage

Post office
Video shop with second-hand books
Tot Lodge

Traveller's Corner
Livingstone Corner Bar

Hosanna Decent Lodge
Hotel Aribas
Port Lodge
Alinda Hotel

AGIP garage
Supermarket

COMMERCIAL
KIJUMBURU

Petrol station
Bank

Mini-Mart 88
Masindi Tavern

MARKET
Market
Buma Hotel
Co-op

Executive Lodge
Jumbo Restaurant
Bus station

TANGA
Softie Inn

N

0 500m
0 500yds

towards dusk, and then starting the return trip from Wanseko at 05.30 the next day. A few pick-up trucks leave Wanseko at 05.30 daily and arrive in Masindi at around 09.30, starting the return trip before 10.30. Finally, Bulisa can be approached directly from Hoima: at least two pick-up trucks leave Wanseko for Hoima at 05.30 daily and start the return trip at around 10.00.

There's no public transport from Bulisa to the national park, and hitching isn't easy since most private vehicles use the direct route from Masindi. The best option is to hire a bicycle through Bulisa Corner Guest House (negotiable, but around US$5/day feels right). The 28km road from Bulisa to the park entrance gate is sandy in stretches but reasonably flat. The 7km road from the entrance gate to Paraa involves a steep descent – check that both of your brakes are working before you attempt this, and if they're not, then walk. Nile Safari Camp lies 11km from the Bulisa–Paraa road, and the turn-off is signposted to the left about 5km before the entrance gate. All going well, you should get through in two to three hours, but I would advise an overnight stay in Bulisa or Wanseko before you cycle out – tyres can be repaired at a village a few kilometres before the entrance gate, but you could still be in for a long walk if you have a puncture, and you don't want to arrive after dark.

Budongo Forest can be visited as a self-contained round trip from Masindi or en route to Murchison Falls. Any vehicle heading between Masindi and Wanseko can drop you right at the Busingiro Tourist Site (40km from Masindi) or at the start of the signposted 2km side-road to Nyabyeya Forestry College (10km closer to Masindi). Note that it is difficult to find transport from Busingiro to Masindi after 09.00.

Where to stay and eat
Hoima
BA & Family Lodge Quiet, family-run place. Spotless rooms **B**.
Classic Inn Bright, clean rooms **B**/**C**.
Nsamo Hotel Smartest place in town. Rooms **B** sgl or **D** s/c dbl. OK food.

Masindi
Alinda Hotel Two-storey hotel with spotless rooms and communal hot showers. Reasonable meals served in the courtyard bar. From **C** pp.
Hotel Aribas Quiet, clean and very reasonably priced. **B** sgl.
Kolping House Guesthouse Clean, secure, friendly. **C** pp using communal showers. **D** pp s/c room.
Softie Guesthouse Basic but very pleasant rooms with net. **B** pp.
Supermarket Kampala road, 100m past Agip Garage. Good place to stock up if you're heading off to camp for a day or two.
Travellers Corner Restaurant Pizzas, roast chicken, steak, burgers, pasta US$4–6. Eat indoors or on the balcony.

Apoch
Anonymous lodge On opposite bank of Nile to Masindi Port. Fish meals. Rooms **B** sgl.

Budongo Forest
Busingiro Tourist Site Wanseko Road. Plenty of birds and monkeys. Entrance fee US$6 pp (valid for up to a week). Guided walks US$4–6pp. Facilities include hot showers. Beers and soft drinks normally available, but must bring food. One room **E** dbl. One four-bed dorm **C** pp. Camping **B** pp.
Nyabyeya Forestry College **D** pp. Water. Firewood. Bring food.

Bugungu Wildlife Reserve

Camping No charge for camping at the headquarters, provided you pay the park entrance fee of US$7 pp. Basic provisions can be bought 30 minutes' walk away. An inexpensive rest camp may soon be constructed. Guided walks into the reserve available at a negotiable fee.

Bulisa

Bulisa Corner Guesthouse Squalid. From **B** pp (negotiable). Basic meals.

Wanseko

Wanseko Lodge Cheaper and better than lodge in Bulisa. Meals available.

Murchison Falls National Park

Nile Safari Camp Upmarket lodge with separate campsite on wooded riverbank facing southern boundary of national park. Elephant, hippo and good birds. Camping **D** pp. No park entrance fee. Phone 041 25-1211 for more details.
Paraa Camp At park headquarters on south bank of Nile. Basic huts with bedding and nets **F** pp. Camping **D** pp. Meals and cold drinks available. Park entrance fee must be paid.

Rwanda

In the 1980s, Rwanda was known in African travel circles as *the* place to track mountain gorillas, and was affectionately referred to by the 30–40,000 tourists who visited it annually as The Land of a Thousand Hills or the Switzerland of Africa on account of its thrillingly scenic landscapes. Then, in 1991, this tiny Central Africa republic erupted into a civil war which culminated in a genocide that is estimated to have claimed a million lives and forced twice as many Rwandans into temporary exile. A tenuous peace was restored in 1995, since when Rwanda has gradually re-established itself as a safe and stable destination – admittedly one whose notoriety ensures it still sees very few visitors, whether backpackers or fly-in tourists.

For most backpackers, the single best reason to visit Rwanda today is the mountain gorillas. Up to 32 permits are available daily, as compared to a dozen in Uganda and none in the DRC, and at the time of writing it is easy to obtain a permit without prior notice. It is also the case that the quality of gorilla contacts in Rwanda far exceeds that in the DRC or Uganda – particularly the Susa Group of 33 individuals, by far the largest gorilla group that can be visited anywhere in Africa.

If gorillas are what brings travellers to Rwanda, there are plenty of other attractions that make it worth prolonging a stay in this spectacularly scenic land of mountains, lakes and forests. Foremost among these attractions is Nyungwe Forest, the largest tract of montane forest in East and Central Africa, and probably the most accessible – transected by a surfaced road, and boasting two inexpensive resthouses and a campsite. Nyungwe is renowned for its diversity of primates, with chimpanzee, Angola colobus, L'Hoest's monkey, silver monkey and grey-cheeked mangabey all being common. The forest is also highly alluring to birdwatchers and botanists, with more than 275 bird and 100 orchid species recorded.

Lake Kivu is a large Rift Valley lake hemmed in by steep hills and serviced by the atmospheric ports of Gisenyi, Cyangugu and Kibuye. The historic university town of Butare, altogether different in atmosphere, is noted for its fine national museum,

FACTS AND FIGURES
Area: 26,340 km²
Capital: Kigali
Largest towns: Kigali, Butare, Gisenyi, Cyangugu, Ruhengeri, Gitarama
Population: 8 million
Official languages: Kinyarwanda, French, English.
Currency: Rwanda franc
Head of State: President Paul Kagame

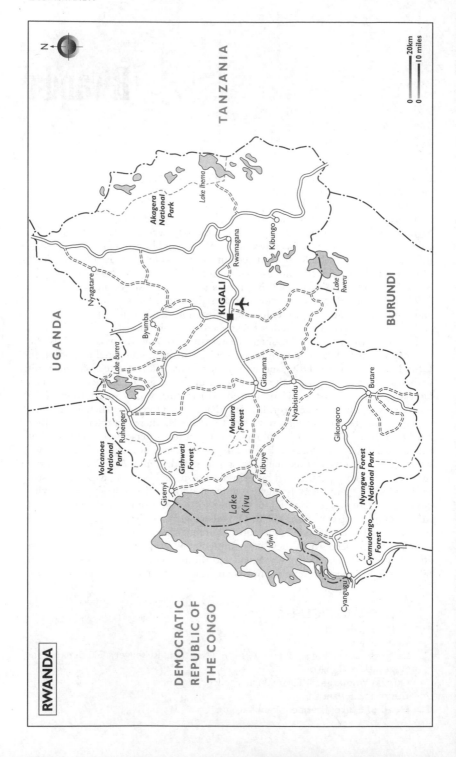

which houses possibly the best ethnographic collection in East Africa. For those who want to get right off the beaten track, there are a number of smaller but equally scenic lakes: Burera and Ruhondo being the best examples, rarely visited by tourists yet only a few kilometres from the gorilla tracking base of Ruhengeri.

Since 1995, the main instigators of the genocide have been brought to trial. The refugees have mostly returned to their homeland. Rwanda today functions as normal, and is as safe as anywhere in Africa. Yet the horrors of the genocide still cast a heavy shadow over Rwanda's present. The Genocide Sites which dot the countryside pay testament to the madness of the recent past: most of these sites consist of mass graves covered in bleak slabs of concrete, but at others the skeletons have been left where they fell. There is nothing much one can say about these chilling memorials, except perhaps that they are indicative of the spirit of a nation unafraid of confronting events which it believes should never be forgotten – or repeated.

But the genocide *is* history, and Rwanda, at the start of the new millennium, comes across as a nation emerging from post-traumatic stress towards a brighter future. Tourism has a big role to play in that future: as a primary impetus for the economic growth which is a vital ingredient in maintaining political stability. For backpackers, there is no better time to visit Rwanda, while tourist numbers are low, and gorilla tracking permits are readily available. What's more, Rwanda is a beautiful country, whose compact and varied tourist circuit is complemented by a hassle-free atmosphere and genuine desire to welcome back tourists back after the long years in the wilderness.

PRACTICAL INFORMATION
Accommodation
Finding a decent room is never a problem in main centres and most small towns. Accommodation tends to be a bit more expensive than in some countries covered by this guide, but is generally good value at the price. Organised campsites are few and far between: camping is the best option in Nyungwe Forest (though accommodation exists on the edge of the forest), and the only one in Akagera.

Books and newspapers
There are a couple of book shops in Kigali, but little is available in English. Two English-language weeklies are printed: *The New Times* toes the government line and *Newsline* is more independent. Ugandan dailies can be bought on the street in Kigali and Butare.

Crime and safety
Crimes levels against tourists are very low by comparison to some neighbouring countries, but it would be wise to take the usual precautions. All of Rwanda is secure at the time of writing, though given the instability of this part of Africa, you might want to check the situation with other travellers.

Entrance fees
These are low by East African standards: Nyungwe costs US$10 daily, while at Akagera there is a one-off entrance fee of US$9. There is no entrance fee as such to the Parc des Volcans, but gorilla tracking permits cost US$250.

Entry formalities
A valid passport is mandatory. Visas, required by all visitors except nationals of the USA, Uganda, Tanzania, Kenya, Burundi and the Democratic Republic of the

Congo, cost US$35 upwards depending on place of issue. Nationals of countries without an embassy can obtain a visa on arrival by prior arrangement with their hosts, who can arrange a *facilité d'entrée*.

Flying there

Alliance Express flies directly to Kigali from Entebbe (Uganda), Johannesburg (South Africa), Nairobi (Kenya) and Bujumbura (Burundi). Other international flights are with Sabena (Brussels), Kenya Airways (Nairobi), Ethiopian Airlines (Addis Ababa), Air Tanzania (Dar es Salaam) and Air Burundi (Bujumbura). All international flights arrive at Kanombe Airport, 10km from central Kigali. An airport tax of US$20 is levied upon departure.

Food and drink

Kigali boasts a good range of restaurants representing international cuisines such as Indian, Italian, Chinese and French. In most other towns, a couple of hotels or restaurants serve uncomplicated Western meals – chicken, fish or steak with chips or rice. Possibly as a result of the Belgian influence, restaurant standards seem to be far higher than in most East Africa countries (the chips are probably the best on the continent!). Servings tend to be dauntingly large, and prices very reasonable – around US$5 for a main course.

Wherever you travel, local restaurants serve Rwandan favourites such as goat kebabs, grilled or fried tilapia, bean or meat stews. These are normally eaten with *ugali, matoke, chapatti*, boiled potatoes (somewhat mysteriously referred to as Irish potatoes in Rwanda as in Uganda) – not to mention the ubiquitous chips. At local restaurants, you should be able to fill yourself adequately for US$2 or less.

Brand name soft drinks such as Pepsi, Coca Cola and Fanta are widely available and very cheap by international standards. Tap water is debatably safe to drink in larger towns; bottled mineral water is widely available if you prefer not to take the risk. The local beers, brewed near Gisenyi, are *Primus*, which comes in 700ml bottles and costs anything from US$0.75 in local bars to US$2 in Kigali's swankiest hotels, and *Mutzig*, which tastes little different, costs about 30% more, and comes in 700ml or 350ml bottles.

Getting around

All main roads in Rwanda are serviced by regular minibus taxis.

Health

Malaria is present, but not at higher altitudes, which means the risk of contracting it in Rwanda is less than in neighbouring countries. Bilharzia may be present in some of the lakes, though a greater concern at Lake Kivu at least is underwater currents which have caused many people to drown – ask before you swim.

Money

The unit of currency is the Rwanda franc (Rfr). In September 2000, the exchange rate against the dollar varied from Rfr 390 to Rfr 455, depending on whether the transaction involved cash or travellers' cheques, and where it took place. In Rwanda more than most African countries, US dollars are by far the most widely recognised foreign currency, and, except in Kigali, US dollars cash is the only foreign currency likely to be exchangeable outside of banks.

Post, telephone and internet

International post is slow. The international dialling code for Rwanda is +250 and there are no area codes – all land line numbers are on the same code and consist of five numerals. Cell phones are very popular and numbers can be recognised by the 08 prefix. At the time of writing, internet facilities are available in Kigali and Butare only.

Public holidays

In addition to New Year's Day, Christmas Day and Boxing Day, Rwanda recognises Good Friday and Easter Monday, which fall on different dates from one year to the next. Other holidays are as follows:

January 28	Democracy Day	August 15	Assumption Day
April 7	Genocide Memorial Day	September 8	Culture Day
May 1	Labour Day	September 25	Republic Day
July 1	Independence Day	October 1	Heroes Day
July 5	National Liberation Day	November 1	All Saints' Day
August 1	Harvest Festival		

Tourist information

The Office Rwandais du Tourisme et des Parcs Nationaux, more commonly referred to as ORTPN (*Or-ti-pen*), doubles both as tourist office and national park authority. The ORTPN tourist offices in central Kigali and at the airport both stock a fair range of booklets and maps, and are the best place to seek out current information relating to national parks and other reserves. The central Kigali office is also where you need to go to make advance bookings for gorilla tracking permits in the Parc des Volcans (depending on availability, these permits can also be bought on the spot at the ORTPN office in Ruhengeri). Contact details for the ORTPN head office are BP 905, Kigali, tel: 76514/5 or 73396; fax: 76512.

Northern Rwanda

The main tourist centre in northern Rwanda is **Ruhengeri,** the closest town to the Parc National des Volcans and most convenient base from which to track mountain gorillas in the Virungas. Aside from its superlative setting, Ruhengeri offers little that couldn't be experienced in a hundred other small African towns, but it is an agreeable travel base, with some accommodation and food bargains, and a friendly mood. A good pretext for stretching your legs while in Ruhengeri is the **Musanze Cave and Natural Bridge**, which lies in school grounds 2km out of town along the Gisenyi Road; take a left turn opposite the large steel *Entrepôts Opravia Musanze* and follow the road for about 100m.

Situated only 15km from Ruhengeri, the **Parc des Volcans** protects the Rwandan portion of the Virunga Mountains, a range of steep volcanoes on the border with Uganda and the DRC. The Parc des Volcans is where Dian Fossey did all her research into gorilla behaviour, and is where the film *Gorillas in the Mist* was shot. This park currently protects about half the gorilla population of the Virungas, and it offers the best mountain gorilla tracking in East Africa, with up to 32 permits available daily, and no waiting lists – though this might well change as more people become aware of it (see box *Gorilla tracking in the Parc des Volcans* pages 252–3). In addition to the gorillas, the Virungas harbour elephant and buffalo – whose spoor are regularly seen on the trails – and the rare golden monkey as well as many different birds. The hiking trails to the peaks of the volcanoes have been closed for some years and are unlikely to re-open in the immediate future.

GORILLA TRACKING IN THE PARC DES VOLCANS

Gorilla tourism was initiated in the Parc des Volcans (Volcanoes National Park) in 1978, and by the mid-1980s it raised up to US$10 million dollars annually, making it Rwanda's third highest earner of foreign revenue. It came to an abrupt halt in 1991, when the country erupted into civil war, but resumed in July 1999. Today, a gorilla tracking permit costs US$250, and it can be bought in advance through the ORTPN office in Kigali, or bought on the day at the ORTPN office in Ruhengeri (situated on the first floor of the municipal buildings on Avenue du 5 Juillet; tel: 546645 or 085 19874). Either way, it is advisable to visit or ring the ORTPN office in Ruhengeri on the afternoon before you intend to go tracking to make arrangements.

Eight permits per day are issued for each of the habituated groups. At the time of writing, two habituated groups stay within tracking range on a permanent basis, another one spends most of its time in the Parc des Volcans but occasionally crosses the border in Uganda or the DRC, as does a fourth semi-habituated group. This means that between 16 and 32 permits can be issued daily. In mid-2000, advance booking was rarely necessary, but that might easily change during the lifespan of this edition.

The more difficult to reach of the two permanent groups is the **Susa Group**, which lives on the slopes of Mount Karisoke and consists of 33 individuals, including two silverbacks – the second largest group of mountain gorillas in the world. The Susa Group is the first choice of most fit visitors, but be under no illusions about the severity of the hike. The ascent from the car park to the forest boundary is gaspingly steep, and will take the best part of an hour. On a good day, it might take 20 minutes to reach the gorillas from the boundary; on a bad day you might be looking at two hours in either direction.

A far less strenuous prospect is the **Sabinyo Group**, resident on a lightly forested saddle between Mount Sabinyo and Mount Gahinga. Depending on exactly where the gorillas are, the walk from the car park to the forest boundary is flat to gently sloping, and will typically take 20-30 minutes. Once in the forest, the gorillas might take anything from ten minutes to an hour to reach, but generally the slopes aren't too daunting. The Sabinyo Group consists of 12 individuals, again with two silverbacks. **Group Thirteen** spends most of its time on the same saddle as the Sabinyo Group, but its territory crosses into neighbouring countries, so it is not permanently in the Parc des Volcans. When it is around, however, it is normally just as easy to reach as the Sabinyo Group. Although Group Thirteen numbers only seven gorillas, the silverback is more relaxed than those in other groups. If no permits are available for these groups, ask about the **Amahoro Group**, which consists of 19 animals, and is reasonably habituated, though the silverbacks are very jumpy.

Getting there

No public transport connects Ruhengeri to any of the points where one enters the forest to track gorillas, all of which lie about 10–15km from town. At the time of writing, the ORTPN people in Ruhengeri are usually happy to squeeze single permit-holders or couples into the vehicle they use to transport the guides and trackers, but this is likely to change as tourist volumes increase. For larger groups, the only option is to hire a vehicle and driver for the morning. In the rainy season, a 4x4 is necessary and should cost around US$50-70 for the round trip. The ORTPN office in Ruhengeri can put you in touch with reliable drivers and vehicles. In the dry season, an ordinary taxi should be adequate, and will cost approximately half the price of hiring a 4x4. Before doing this, however, consider that the cost of hiring a vehicle is minimal relative to the cost of a gorilla permit: should you make private arrangements, and the vehicle breaks down or isn't sturdy enough for the roads, you risk not being able to use your permit.

Hiking conditions

Depending on which group you visit, and your own level of fitness, the trek to see the gorillas will be at best taxing and at worst exhausting, due to the steep slopes, thick vegetation, and muddy conditions underfoot. The hike takes place at elevations of between 2,500m and 3,000m above sea level, not high enough for altitude sickness to be a concern, but sufficient to knock the breath out of anybody – no matter how fit – who has just flown in from a low altitude. For this reason, try to avoid coming to the Virungas directly from somewhere low-lying – a couple of days hiking at Nyungwe, where the campsite lies at 2,300m, would be great preparation. If you are uncertain about your fitness, *don't* visit the Susa Group. Once on the trail, drink plenty of water, and carry some quick calories – biscuits and chocolate can both be bought at supermarkets in Ruhengeri. The good news is that in 99% of cases, whatever exhaustion you might feel on the way up will vanish with the adrenalin charge that follows the first sighting of a silverback gorilla!

Put on your sturdiest walking shoes for the trek, and wear thick trousers and a long-sleeved top as protection against vicious stinging nettles. Whatever clothes you wear to go tracking are likely to get very dirty as you slip and slither in the mud, so if you have pre-muddied clothes, you might as well wear them!

Carry as little as possible, ideally in a waterproof bag of some sort. During the rainy season, a poncho or raincoat might be a worthy addition to your daypack, while sunscreen, sunglasses and a hat are a good idea at any time of year. Especially during the rainy season, make sure your camera gear is well-protected – if your bag isn't waterproof, seal your camera and films in a plastic bag; it might be worth taking along some 400ASA or 800ASA film in case the gorillas are deep in the forest.

Visitor protocol

Note that tourists are permitted to spend no longer than one hour with the gorillas, and it is forbidden to eat or smoke in their presence. It is also forbidden to approach the gorillas within more than 5m, a rule that is difficult to enforce with curious youngsters (and some adults) who often approach human visitors. Gorillas are susceptible to many human diseases, and it has long been feared by researchers that one ill tourist might infect a gorilla, resulting in the possible death of the whole troop should they have no immunity to that disease. For this reason, you should not go gorilla tracking with a potentially airborne infection such as flu or a cold, and are asked to turn away from the gorillas should you need to sneeze in their presence. To the best of my knowledge, no tourists have ever been seriously hurt by habituated gorillas, but there is always a first time. An adult gorilla is much stronger than a person, and will act in accordance with its own social codes. For this reason, it is vital that you listen to your guide at all times regarding correct protocol in the presence of gorillas.

In addition to the gorillas, the Ruhengeri region boasts several lovely lakes, of which the smallest but most accessible is **Lake Karago**, only a 20-minute walk from the junction town of Mukamiira on the Gisenyi Road. The much larger **Lake Ruhondo**, ringed by cultivated mountains and offering great views to the Virungas, is more time-consuming to reach, but makes for an enticing overnight trip with the Foyer de Charitié offering good accommodation. Most alluring of all, the vast and stunningly beautiful **Lake Burera** is reminiscent of Lake Bunyonyi in Uganda; it has little in the way of organised transport or accommodation, but could be appealing to enthusiastic hikers (see box *Lake Burera*).

Only an hour by minibus-taxi from Ruhengeri, **Gisenyi** is the most northerly port on the Rwandan part of Lake Kivu, and well worth a visit. Gisenyi is split into an upper and lower town, the former an undistinguished grid of busy roads centred around a small market area, the latter a more spacious and atmospheric conglomeration of banks, government buildings, old colonial homesteads and hotels lapped by the waters of Rwanda's largest lake. The waterfront, with its red sandy beaches, pleasing mismatch of architectural styles, and shady palm-lined avenues, has the captivating air of a slightly down-at-heel tropical beach resort. Indeed, Gisenyi could be easily be mistaken for a sweaty West African or Indian Ocean backwater, except that the relatively high altitude of 1,500m means it has a refreshing climate at odds with its tropical appearance. Gisenyi offers little in the way of formal sightseeing, but it is the sort of town which you could easily settle into for a few days. Further afield, the 6km walk or *matatu* drive to **Rubona** port offers some lovely lake views; once at Rubona you can easily arrange to explore the immediate vicinity in a dugout canoe or pirogue.

Access and getting around

The regional transport hub is Ruhengeri, where the main bus and *matatu* stand is on Avenue de la Nutrition, within five minutes' walk of the more popular budget hotels. Kigali and Ruhengeri are only 96km apart, and connected by regular minibus taxis which charge a fare of around US$2 and take about 90 minutes. The 62km road between Ruhengeri and Gisenyi is also covered by regular minibus taxis which take about an hour and cost US$1.50. The minibus station in Gisenyi is next to the market in the old town centre. Any transport heading between Gisenyi and Ruhengeri can drop you at Mukamiira, from where it's a 20-minute walk along the Ngororero road to Lake Karago.

Heading south from Gisenyi, public transport towards Kibuye is rather infrequent, but a few minibus-taxis cover the route daily at a fare of US$2.50. You'll need to change vehicles at Kibuye if you are heading on to Cyangugu; with an early start this should be do-able in a day. In theory, the most appealing means of transport between the lake ports is by boat. The lake ferry which once covered this route hasn't operated in years, but small cargo boats run between the three ports and will take passengers for a negotiable fare (expect to pay around US$2.50). This is an informal arrangement, dependent on what boats are leaving and when; the best place to check things is Rubona port, 6km from Gisenyi and easily reached by minibus-taxi. Boats take about six to eight hours to travel to Cyangugu, half that time to Kibuye – make sure you have sun-block and a hat, as well as plenty of water and food.

Where to stay and eat
Ruhengeri
Centre d'Accueil d'Eglise Episcopale Good value church hostel with basic but clean rooms, some with nets, at ⬛pp. Communal hot showers. Meals available. Camping permitted for a nominal charge.

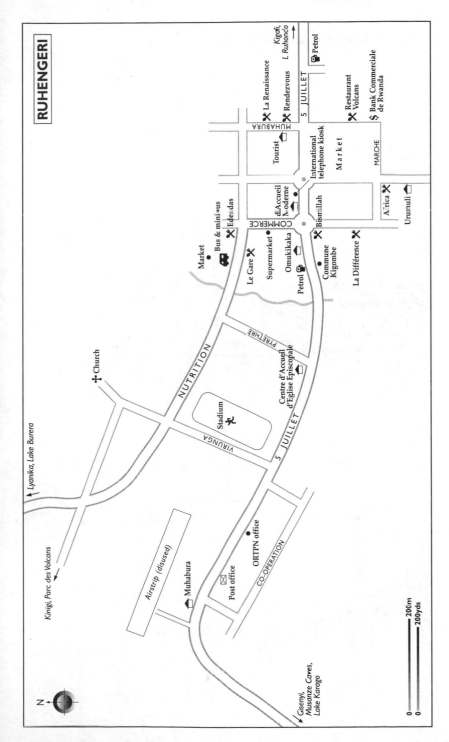

RUHENGERI

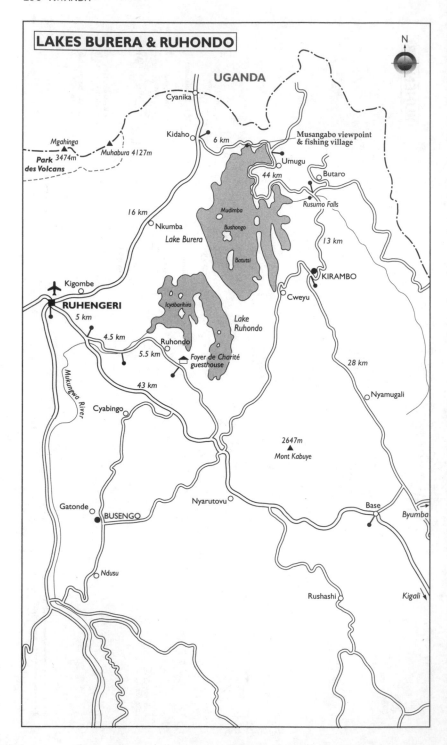

LAKES BURERA & RUHONDO

N

UGANDA

Cyanika

Mgahinga
Park
des Volcans
3474m

Muhabura 4127m

Kidaho

6 km

Musangabo viewpoint
& fishing village

Umugu

Butaro

44 km

Rusumo Falls

16 km

Nkumba

Lake Burera

Mudimba

Bushongo

Batutsi

13 km

Kigombe

KIRAMBO

RUHENGERI

Icyabarihira

Lake
Ruhondo

Cweyu

5 km

4.5 km

Ruhondo

5.5 km

Foyer de Charité
guesthouse

28 km

43 km

Cyabingo

Nyamugali

Mukungwa River

2647m
Mont Kabuye

Gatonde

BUSENGO

Nyarutovu

Base

Byumba

Ndusu

Rushashi

Kigali

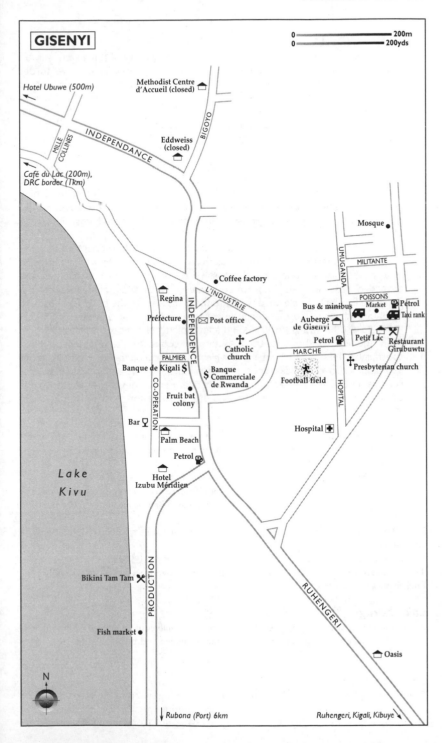

GISENYI

0 ——————— 200m
0 ——————— 200yds

Hotel Ubuwe (500m)

Methodist Centre
d'Accueil (closed)

MILLE COLLINES

INDEPENDANCE

BIGOYO

Eddweiss
(closed)

Café du Lac (200m),
DRC border (1km)

Mosque

UMUGANDA

MILITANTE

Coffee factory

L'INDUSTRIE

POISSONS

Regina

Bus & minibus   Market   Petrol
Taxi rank

INDEPENDANCE

Préfecture

Post office

Auberge
de Gisenyi

Petrol   Petit Lac   Restaurant
Girubuwtu

PALMIER

Catholic
church

MARCHE

Banque de Kigali $

Presbyterian church

Banque
Commerciale
de Rwanda

CO-OPERATION

Fruit bat
colony

Football field

HOPITAL

Bar

Hospital

Palm Beach

Petrol

Lake
Kivu

Hotel
Izubu Méridien

PRODUCTION

RUHENGERI

Bikini Tam Tam

Fish market

Oasis

N

↓ Rubona (Port) 6km

Ruhengeri, Kigali, Kibuye

LAKE BURERA

The largest and most beautiful of the lakes in the vicinity of Ruhengeri, Burera has until now been almost entirely neglected by travellers. Adventurous backpackers could, however, spend several days exploring the lake using a combination of motorcycle-taxis, boats, and their feet. No formal accommodation exists anywhere on the lake shore, but the area is dotted with small villages where it shouldn't be a problem to ask permission to pitch a tent.

The first – and easiest – stage in reaching the lake is to catch a minibus-taxi towards the Cyanika border and ask to be dropped at Kidaho. Here, you need to turn right into an unsignposted dirt road which, after six relatively flat kilometres, reaches the lake at a small fishing village (so far as we could ascertain, this is also called Kidaho) below the Musangabo Peninsula, which offer stunning views in all directions. You could walk this stretch over 60–90 minutes, or organise a bicycle-taxi in Kidaho (this should cost less than US$1).

Musangabo is a feasible target for a day trip from Ruhengeri. With an early start, you should also have time to catch a boat-taxi from the fishing village to Butaro, the largest centre on the eastern shore of the lake. At Butaro, the attractive Rusumo Falls (not to be confused with their namesake on the Tanzania border) tumbles over a cliff to the fields next to the lake. The boat taxi to Butaro takes 30–60 minutes in either direction, and costs around US$1.25. It should also be straightforward and affordable to hire a boat privately.

In addition to the boat-taxis, Butaro is connected to Musangabo by a spectacular 44km stretch of road which hugs the cultivated contours about 100–200m above the lake shore. Keen ramblers might ambitiously view this road as an unusually wide hiking trail: it offers great views the whole way, is used by very few vehicles, and follows the contours for most of its length. En

---

Home d'Accueil Moderne Tel: 54 6525; fax: 54 6904. Recommended central hotel with clean, freshly painted rooms **C** s/c dbl or twin with hot shower. Good courtyard bar/restaurant; try the fried fish.

Hotel Muhabura Tel/fax: 54 6296. Mid-range hotel on the outskirts of town along Avenue du 5 Juillet. Good restaurant and bar with Western and Indian meals at around US$5. Large s/c doubles with hot bath and shower are excellent value at the lower end of the **E** range.

Hotel Urumuli The scruffy rooms can't be recommended at **D** s/c dbl (cold water only). Great food though, and very reasonably priced.

Omikikaka Inn Eminently avoidable dump with rooms in the **C** range

Tourist Resthouse Clean but cramped rooms relatively overpriced at **C** sgl. Friendly English-speaking staff an asset.

Lake Karago

Anonymous Guesthouse Signposted *Bar Restaurant Chambres* in Mukamiira, 500m from Ngororero junction. Basic but friendly. Hot water provided and meals available. Rooms **A** sgl.

Lake Ruhondo

Foyer de Charité Tel: 085 10659. Religious retreat offering sweeping views across the lake to the Virungas. Lay visitors are very welcome except during special religious events, so ring to confirm availability. Comfortable rooms **D/E** sgl/dbl. Communal hot showers.

route, the road passes through the small market village of Umugu. Past Butaro, the road veers away from the lake, and the views are few and far between, which leaves you with the option of returning to Musangabo by boat. Alternatively, you could carry on to the next main settlement, Kirambo, which is also referred to as Cyeru, the district for which it is the headquarters. There is no public transport along the 13km road between Butaro and Kirambo, but a limited amount of transport does connect Kirambo to Base on the main Kigali–Ruhengeri road, from where it is easy to pick up a lift in either direction.

The absence of public transport along parts of this circuit make it inaccessible or challenging, depending on how one sees these things. Extended exploration would be practical only if you carry a tent and are prepared to ask permission to camp at the many villages and homesteads along the way. It would probably be advisable to carry some food (fish and potatoes should be easy to buy along the way). It is difficult to imagine that any serious security concerns are attached to hiking in this Uganda border area; you'll come across loads of local pedestrians for company, and travellers are still something of a novelty.

Lake Burera could also be explored more extensively by boat, once again an option suitable only for those with a tent and a pioneering spirit. The obvious place to start a trip of this sort would be Musangabo, though boats are the main form of transport throughout the area, so it should be easy enough to hire a boat and paddler anywhere. In addition to Rusumo Falls, there are at least four large islands in the southern half of the lake: Mudimba, Munanira, Bushongo, and Batutsi. In theory, it should be possible to hire a boat to the south of Lake Burera, hike across the narrow strip of hilly terrain that separates it from Lake Ruhondo, and then pick up another boat to the Foyer de Charitié guesthouse. I've never heard of a traveller who attempted anything like this, so drop me a line to let me know how it goes!

Solid meals cost US$2 (breakfast) or US$5 (lunch or dinner). Cold beers and soft drinks. The retreat lies 10km off the main Kigali road along a side road signposted for Remera, 5km south of Ruhengeri. If you are walking, take a left fork after 2.8km, then 2km further turn right across a bridge, from where the road ascends gently, with the lake becoming visible to the left after about 2.5km. Beyond the first viewpoint, the road continues to climb for 3km to Kadahero village, where a left turn leads after about 200m to the mission. A motorcycle taxi from Ruhengeri should cost around US$3–4 one-way.

Gisenyi

Anonymous Restaurant New place 500m from the harbour and brewery in Rubona port. The owner Odette Nyiramungi said travellers are welcome to pitch a tent for a small fee; phone 085 24293 to confirm this.

Auberge de Gisenyi Adequate local guesthouse opposite the bus station. Clean but cramped rooms **D** s/c dbl. Restaurant and courtyard bar attached.

Bar-Restaurant Bikini Tam-Tam Good sundowner spot on the lake shore, marred only by the smell from the adjacent fish market next door. Snacks and grills available. No camping permitted, despite the signposts indicating that it is.

Café du Lac Atmospheric and affordable colonial house in which two upstairs rooms are rented out at **D** dbl. Meals and drinks are served in the ground floor restaurant or on the large lawn.

Logement Petit Lac The cheapest option at **C** dbl, and close to the bus station, but otherwise short on virtues.

Palm Beach Hotel Tel: 085 00407. Atmospheric midrange hotel with art deco façade and stylish decor. Large rooms good value starting in the **F** range. Excellent restaurant and likeable beachfront bar.

Hotel Izubu Meridien Large modern monolith set in lovely wooded gardens running down to the lake shore. Too pricey for most backpackers, but an important landmark and a good place to eat.

Hotel Regina This colonial era waterfront hotel with period fittings would easily make my nomination list for Africa's best budget hotel. Large, airy rooms using communal hot baths and toilets **D/E** sgl/dbl.

KIGALI

Rwanda's attractively hilly capital sprawls across the hills of central Rwanda, within a few hours' minibus-taxi ride of all major tourist attractions. Despite being something of a garden city, and having an eminently agreeable climate and atmosphere, Kigali is of limited interest to travellers: it is the best place in the country to deal with practicalities such as changing money and catching up on your email, but there is no sightseeing worth speaking of. The compact, low-rise city centre is where most of the budget accommodation, banks and other facilities are to be found, but the main bus and minibus station lies 2km from the centre. Travellers who have no specific business to attend to in Kigali can easily pass through the city in a day en route between most places of interest in Rwanda.

Access and getting around

Kigali is connected to all other centres in Rwanda by minibus-taxis. These leave and arrive at Nyabugogo Bus Station, 2km from the city centre. There are regular minibus-taxis between Nyabugogo and Avenue de Commerce, near the market, in the city centre. Private minibuses run by Taxi Ponctuel and Volcano Express connect Kigali to Butare, leaving from the Avenue du Commerce bus station at 07.00, 10.00, 13.00 and either 16.00 or 17.00. There are also bus and/or minibus services between Kigali and Bujumbura (Burundi) and Kampala (Uganda).

Where to stay

Auberge la Caverne Tel: 74549. Pleasant new hotel set around a quiet courtyard on the Nyabugogo Road. Rooms **D** s/c dbl with hot water. Recommended.

Gloria Hotel Conveniently central hotel with adequate s/c rooms for **E/F** sgl/dbl. Cold water only (hot buckets on request).

Hotel Panafrique Run-down but agreeable old hotel with rooftop restaurant, nightclub and eight rooms at **D** s/c dbl with hot water.

Hotel la Vedette Tel: 73575. In Nyamirambo quarter, near the mosques, this is a friendly small place where guests 'live as family'. Rooms **D/E** sgl/dbl with clean communal showers. It's right by the taxi-minibus route up into town.

Logement Belle Vie Clean, central lodgings **D** dbl with communal showers, small restaurant.

New Modern Guesthouse Old Clapped-out Guesthouse would be closer to the mark; a possible fallback if the Belle Vie opposite is full. (rooms cost the same).

Where to eat

American Club Burgers, steaks, pizzas from US$6–8 in a clean courtyard close to the Hotel Mille Collines.

La Retrouvaille Good, cheap, central restaurant on the same road as the Lodgement Belle Vie. A plateful of rice, beans, vegetables, meat/chicken and salad costs US$1.50!

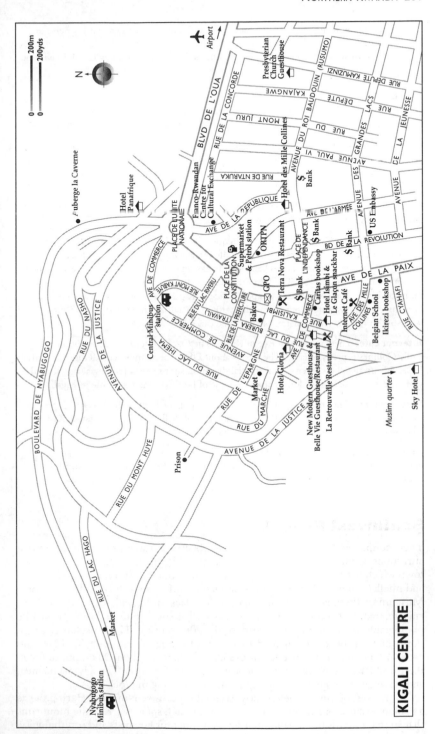

KIGALI CENTRE

Le Glaçon Friendly, functional place for snacks, chicken/rice, pasta etc with a menu in hilarious English.

Terra Nova Restaurant Opposite the Post Office. Highly rated buffets US$1.50 without meat, US$2.50 with meat.

Practical listings

Airlines Alliance Express (77777), Sabena (75290), Ethiopian Airlines (72712), Kenya Airways (77972), Rwanda Airlines (77103), Rwanda Airways (71176), Air Tanzania (72643).

Books and newspapers The best bookshops are Librairie Caritas next to the PO and Librairie Ikirezi on Avenue de la Paix. The ORTPN office stocks a wide range of books and maps relating to Rwanda. The Ugandan *New Vision* newspaper is available from street vendors on the day of publication.

Embassies Canada (73210) UK (84098/85771), USA (75601). For details of other embassies, contact the ORTPN office in Kigali.

Foreign exchange Cash and travellers' cheques can be changed into Rwandan francs at any main bank. Private forex bureaux generally offer better rates than banks for cash. Travellers' cheques can only be exchanged at banks; rates are very unfavourable and a hefty commission may be charged. The best rates for US dollars cash are offered by the private individuals who hang out around the post office in Kigali. I've not heard of any con tricks here, but the atmosphere is pretty fraught, with up to a dozen individuals clustering around you, so it's probably only a matter of time – be careful!

Internet cafés There are at least five in Kigali. The Ozone Internet Café in the Hotel Mille Collines is pretty reliable. The rate is about US$2 for 30 minutes. Membership costs US$2.50 and members receive a substantial discount, so it's worth looking at this should you expect to be online for longer than a couple of hours during your time in Kigali.

Poste restante Since the new 'main' post office has opened out in the government area, there are two possible addresses: Poste Restante, Kigali Ville and Poste Restante, Kacyiru. The first is more reliable and convenient.

Tourist information The main ORTPN stocks a good range of brochures, maps and books, and is the best place to check on developments in the national parks. Gorilla-tracking permits can be booked in advance here. Tel: 76514/5 or 73396; fax: 76512.

Southwest Rwanda

The mountainous southwest of Rwanda boasts a varied selection of tourist attractions. Coming from Kigali, the first regional highlight is **Butare**, a university town which lies 135km from the capital and is the country's second city and cultural and intellectual heart. The big tourist attraction in Butare is the excellent National Museum of Rwanda, with comprehensive displays on Rwanda's history, geology, culture, traditions, people, handicrafts… as well as some stunning black-and-white photographs dating to the early years of the 20th century. The museum is 1.5km north of town on the main road to Kigali. Opening hours are 09.00–12.00 and 14.00–17.00, and an entrance fee of US$2.50 is charged. About 20km out of town, the Royal Palace at Nyanza is also worth a day trip – it's been lovingly maintained, and can easily be visited as a day trip from Butare using minibus-taxis.

To the west of Butare, the recently gazetted **Nyungwe National Park** protects a 970km² expanse of Afro-montane rainforest which sprawls across the mountains that stretch towards the Burundi border. A magnet for botanists and ornithologists alike, Nyungwe is best known for the volume and variety of its primates – 13 species in all, including chimpanzee, L'Hoest's monkey and troops of 400-plus Ruwenzori colobus. Highly accessible, and serviced by two affordable resthouses and a campsite, Nyungwe is a must for any traveller with a strong interest in natural history, and worth dedicating three or four days to explore properly (see box *Nyungwe National Park*).

Continuing westwards from Nyungwe, the surfaced road leads to **Cyangugu**, the most southerly of Rwanda's Lake Kivu ports. Cyangugu is divided into a bustling but bland upper town called Kamembe, and a more intriguing lower town, Cyangugu proper, connected by a 5km road and a steady stream of inexpensive minibus-taxis. The lower town lies on the lakeshore, alongside a bridge across the Rusizi River, the border post between southern Rwanda and the DRC. Although it consists of little more than one pothole-scored main road, Cyangugu must once have been very prosperous. Today, however, many of the old multi-storey buildings have been reduced to shells – victims of one or other war, perhaps, or just decades of neglect – generating an aura of dilapidation which is less than invigorating, but somehow rather moving. Unless you are thinking of crossing into the DRC – at the time of writing, not an option that attracts many takers – Cyangugu has to be classed as something of a dead end in travel terms.

An off-the-beaten-track excursion from Cyangugu takes you to the **Bugarama Hot Springs**, 60km from Cyangugu by road and 5km from the Cimerwa Cement Factory. Set in a bed of limestone dotted by large sinkholes, the springs bubble up into a large green pool which is circled by a footpath. An even more remote excursion in this area is the 6km² **Cyamudongo Forest**, bisected by a rough dirt road, and reputedly still home to chimpanzee and L'Hoest's monkey, as well as a few rare forest birds no longer found in Nyungwe. There is some talk of protecting this pocket of forest as an isolated annexe of the mooted Nyungwe National Park.

Back on the Lake Kivu shore, halfway between Cyangugu and the northern port of Gisenyi, lies **Kibuye**, the most conventionally pretty of the lake ports, sprawling across a series of hills interwoven with the lagoon-like arms of the lake. Surrounded by hills planted with pines and eucalyptus, Kibuye has a pristine, almost Alpine appearance, in contrast to the atmosphere of fading tropical languor which to some extent afflicts the other ports. The church, one of the oldest European buildings in the country, was the site of a brutal massacre in which thousands were killed in 1994. The church is no longer used as a place of worship, but is preserved as a Genocide Site.

Access and getting around

The surfaced road between Kigali and Cyangugu via Butare and Nyungwe is serviced by regular minibus-taxis. The fare between Kigali and Cyangugu is around US$7 and the trip takes 4–5 hours. Between Butare and either Cyangugu or Kigali, the fare is around US$4 and the trip takes two hours. Minibus-taxis leave Kigali from Nyabugogo, 2km from the city centre. In Butare, you can be dropped at the minibus station on the northern edge of town or opposite the central market, but when you leave town you must go to the minibus station. All public transport in and out of Cyangugu terminates at the minibus station at Kamembe, where another minibus taxi must be taken to get to Cyangugu proper.

Private minibuses run by Taxi Ponctuel and Volcano Express connect Kigali and Butare, leaving the capital from near the Avenue du Commerce bus station at 07.00, 10.00, 13.00 and either 16.00 or 17.00 depending on the company. The fare is roughly the same as that of the minibus-taxis, and they are reputedly much safer.

Nyungwe Forest Reserve is transected by the main surfaced road between Butare and Cyangugu, and any minibus-taxi heading between the two will be able

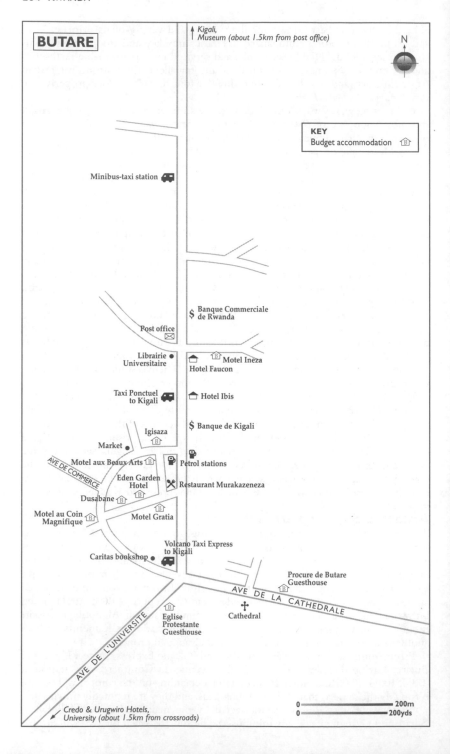

BUTARE

Kigali,
Museum (about 1.5km from post office)

N

KEY
Budget accommodation

Minibus-taxi station

Banque Commerciale
de Rwanda

Post office

Librairie ●
Universitaire

Motel Ineza
Hotel Faucon

Taxi Ponctuel
to Kigali

Hotel Ibis

Igisaza

Banque de Kigali

Market ●

Motel aux Beaux Arts

Petrol stations

Eden Garden
Hotel

Restaurant Murakazeneza

Dusabane

Motel au Coin
Magnifique

Motel Gratia

Volcano Taxi Express
to Kigali

Caritas bookshop ●

Procure de Butare
Guesthouse

AVE DE LA CATHEDRALE

Eglise
Protestante
Guesthouse

Cathedral

AVE DE L'UNIVERSITE

AVE DE COMMERCE

0 ━━━ 200m
0 ━━━ 200yds

Credo & Urugwiro Hotels,
University (about 1.5km from crossroads)

to drop you there (though you may be expected to pay the full fare). Uwinka Campsite lies alongside the main road 90km from Butare and 54km from Cyangugu. The ORTPN Resthouse is also on the main road, 18km closer to Cyangugu, on the right side of the road about 2km after you exit the western boundary of the forest reserve coming from Butare. The resthouse on the Gisakura Tea Estate is about 500m from the main road, along the dirt road to the tea estate signposted to your left and about halfway between the western boundary of the forest and the ORTPN Resthouse coming from Butare.

Public transport between Kamembe (Cyangugu) and Kibuye is restricted to one bus daily, leaving at 08.00 in either direction. There are also minibus-taxis from Kibuye direct to Kigali and northward to Gisenyi. Travelling by lake between Cyangugu and the more northerly ports is a definite possibility, though our hypothetical enquiries around the port left us little the wiser. We were initially told that a regular passenger boat runs up to Gisenyi, leaving at 10.00 daily, but were then asked a 'fare' of US$100, which suggests either that we had the wrong end of the stick or we looked indecently rich and stupid! What is certain is that cargo boats cover this route most days, and will often take passengers informally for a negotiable fare, perhaps US$2–3 to Gisenyi, and half that to Kibuye. It's one of those situations where interested travellers just have to ask around – especially as there is some talk of the ferry service between the main lake ports being resumed in the medium term.

To visit the Bugarama Hot Springs, there are minibus taxis between Kamembe and the town of Bugarama, which has one local guesthouse. The springs lie 16km from town, along a dirt road that passes through a series of small villages to Cimerwa Cement Factory. About 5km past the factory, immediately after a signpost reading *Secteur Nyamaranko*, you'll see a hillside quarry and a three-way fork to your left. Follow the leftmost fork for about 100m, then turn right onto a small dirt track, and after 100m or so you'll see the pool in front of you. If in doubt, ask for directions to the *Amashyuzaya*. It should be possible to hitch to the cement factory, but you might have to walk to the springs from there. Another possibility would be ask about a motorbike-taxi in Bugarama.

The closest town to Cyamudongo Forest is Nyakabuye, which lies about 20km from Bugarama town, and 5km past the hot springs. With patience, it should be possible to hitch to Nyakabuye on the back of a truck from Bugarama. According to locals, Nyakabuye is also serviced by some sort of public transport direct from Kamembe (Cyangugu) on Wednesday and Friday. From the town, a steep road leads uphill for 8km, past traditional homesteads, before it winds through the indigenous forest for 2km. You'll almost certainly have to walk this stretch. No formal accommodation exists in the area, but it is difficult to imagine that anybody would refuse permission to pitch a tent at one of the homesteads which line the road up to the forest, or that any significant risk would be attached to doing so.

Where to stay and eat
Butare
Dusabane Hotel Unprepossessing exterior, but clean shared facilities and good value at C dbl. The restaurant does a generous mixed plate of food. C dbl.

Eden Garden Hotel New place near the market with plain, clean rooms set around a central courtyard C pp.

Hotel Ibis Midrange hotel on main road with good and not particularly expensive patio bar and restaurant.

Igisaza Guesthouse Quiet cheapie near the market, with four twin en-suite rooms (cold water) at D sgl or dbl.

NYUNGWE NATIONAL PARK

Nyungwe is magnificent: the largest single tract of montane forest remaining anywhere in East or Central Africa, and a remarkably rich centre of biodiversity due to its great antiquity and altitudinal variation (1,600–1,950m). The forest harbours 75 mammal species, 275 birds, 120 butterflies, and more than 100 varieties of orchid. Nyungwe today is a fragment of what was once an uninterrupted forest belt covering the length of the Albertine Rift, the stretch of the western Rift valley running from the Ruwenzoris south to Burundi. Protected as a forest reserve since 1933, it is the only substantial tract of forest left in Rwanda.

The main attraction of Nyungwe is its rich variety of primates, 13 species in all, representing about 20% of the African checklist. The primates most likely to be seen by tourists are L'Hoest's monkey (often seen from the main road and the campsite), chimpanzee, Ruwenzori colobus (the troops of up to 400 at Nyungwe are the largest arboreal primate troops in Africa), silver monkey, red-tailed monkey, grey-cheeked mangabey and possibly Dent's mona monkey. Many other large mammals are present, including elephant, leopard, golden cat, giant forest hog, and various duikers.

The forest comprises at least 200 tree species. The upper canopy in some areas reaches 50–60m in height, dominated by slow-growing hardwoods such as African mahogany. Of the smaller trees, one of the most striking is the giant tree-fern *Cyathea mannania*, which grows to 5m high, and is seen in large numbers along the ravines of the Waterfall Trail. Also very distinctive are the 2–3m high giant lobelias, more normally associated with montane moorland than forest, but common in Nyungwe, particularly along the roadside.

Nyungwe is the most important birdwatching destination in Rwanda, with more than 275 bird species recorded, of which the majority are forest specialists and 24 are regional endemics, whose range is restricted to a few forests along the Albertine Rift. The more common regional endemics are handsome francolin, Ruwenzori turaco (a stunner!), stripe-breasted tit, red-collared babbler, red-throated alethe, Archer's ground robin, Kivu ground thrush, Grauer's rush warbler (confined to marshy areas), red-faced woodland warbler, Kungwe apalis, Grauer's warbler, yellow-eyed black flycatcher, Ruwenzori batis, blue-headed sunbird, regal sunbird and strange weaver. Birdwatching in Nyungwe can be rather frustrating, since the vegetation is thick and many birds tend to stick to the canopy, but almost everything you do see ranks as a good sighting, and you don't have to be an ardent twitcher to appreciate forest oddities like great blue turaco, a chicken-sized bird with garish blue, green and yellow feathers, often seen gliding between the trees along the main road.

A large selection of walking possibilities and other excursions are available within Nyungwe. The options for travellers without private transport will depend on whether they are based at Uwinka campsite or at one of the resthouses. From Uwinka, the main attraction is the Coloured Trails, a network of seven walking trails designated by a particular colour. These range in length from 1km to 10km, and the footpaths are well-maintained and clearly marked, but don't underestimate the steepness of the slopes or – after rain – the muddy conditions, which can be fairly tough going at this high altitude. The coloured trails pass through the territory of a habituated troop of 400 colobus monkeys. During the rainy season, a troop of chimpanzees often moves into this area. You can reasonably expect to see some primates along any of the coloured trails, as well as a good variety of forest birds – though the latter requires patience and regular stops where there are open views into the canopy. Unless you opt for a specific primate visit, chance will be the decisive factor in what you see, though the 2.5km Blue Trail is regarded to be especially good for primates and birds, while the 10km Red Trail is good for chimpanzees and passes four waterfalls. For those spending a bit of time in the forest, the Kamiranzovu Trail leads to a quite different ecosystem, a marshy area rich in orchids and swamp-associated birds. This used to be the best place to see Nyungwe's elephants, but none have been sighted here in recent years.

From the resthouses, the superb Waterfall Trail takes between three and six hours to cover as a round trip, passing through rolling tea plantations dotted with relic forest patches (worth scanning closely for monkeys and birds) then descending into the forest proper and crossing several streams, before arriving at the base of a pretty waterfall. Monkeys are often seen along the way (colobus seem to be particularly common within the forest) and the steep slopes allow good views into the canopy. I found this trail to be the most rewarding of those we walked for true forest interior birds.

A relic forest patch on the Gisakura Tea Estate, only 20 minutes' walk from the ORTPN Resthouse, and less than five minutes from the tea estate's guesthouse, supports a resident troop of 38 Ruwenzori colobus monkeys. This troop is very habituated, far more so than the larger troop at Uwinka, and easy to locate. Oddly, a solitary red-tailed monkey moves with the colobus – some of the guides say that it is treated as the leader. A visit to this forest patch is treated as a primate walk by the ORTPN office, but it is also an excellent birdwatching site, since it lies in a ravine and is encircled by a road, making it easy to see deep into the canopy. Most of what you see are forest-fringe or woodland species, but numerically this proved to be the most rewarding spot we visited in Nyungwe, with some 40 species identified in an hour.

Forest entrance fees are not expensive by comparison to national park fees in many neighbouring countries, but the system as it stands is somewhat confusing. A daily forest visitation fee of US$10 per person allows you to walk guided or unguided along any of the forest trails. This fee includes the camping charge of US$10 per person at Uwinka, which effectively means that no visitation fee is charged to campers. Although you are likely to encounter primates on any forest walk, a primate visit fee of US$20 per person is charged for any specific primate visit – which includes going to look for the Angola colobus troop close to Uwinka, visiting the colobus troop on the Gisakura Tea Estate, or tracking chimpanzees or grey-cheeked mangabey. So far as I could ascertain, the fees are charged per calendar day rather than per 24 hours. This means that for somebody camping in the forest, it would, on the basis of budget alone, make sense to leave specific primate visits until the morning of departure, since all other forest walks on other days would be covered by the camping fee.

A basic fact sheet about the Nyungwe is available from the ORTPN tourist office in Kigali. An excellent 60-page booklet entitled *Nyungwe Forest Reserve* is sold for around US$5 at the ORTPN office next to the resthouse. Mysteriously, the booklet is not for sale at Uwinka. Be warned, too, that it might take some urging to encourage the staff at the ORTPN office to offer you this booklet in preference to their range of faded old postcards, but do persist – a pile of several hundred copies was stashed away in the back room when we visited!

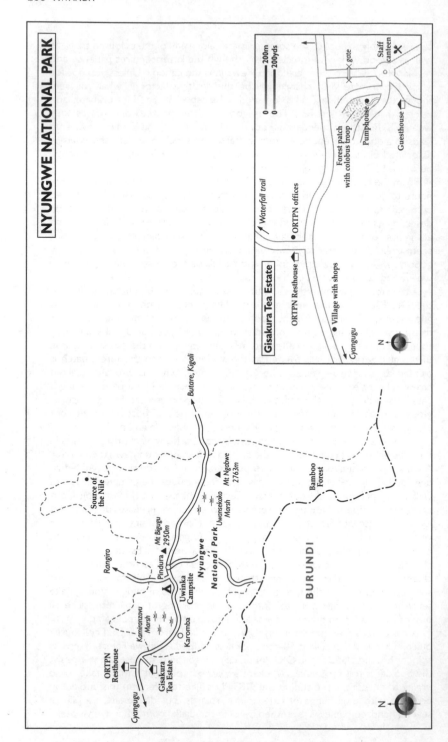

NYUNGWE NATIONAL PARK

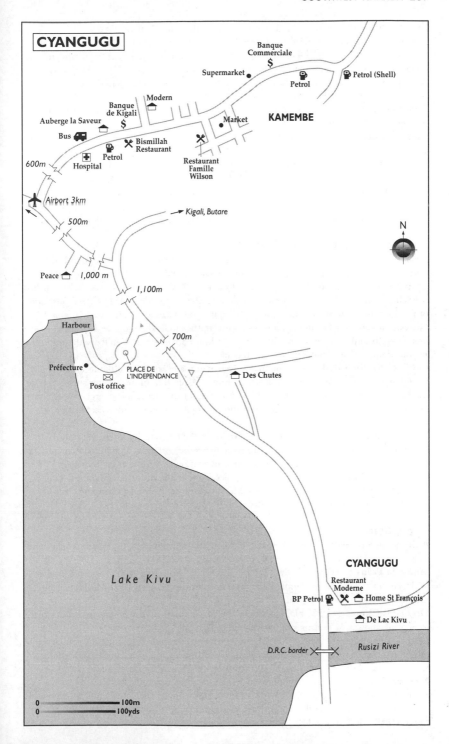

CYANGUGU

Banque Commerciale $
Supermarket ●
Petrol
Petrol (Shell)
KAMEMBE
Modern
Banque de Kigali $
● Market
Auberge la Saveur
Bus
Hospital
Petrol
Bismillah Restaurant
Restaurant Famille Wilson
600m
Airport 3km
500m
Kigali, Butare
Peace
1,000 m
1,100m
700m
Harbour
Préfecture ●
PLACE DE L'INDEPENDANCE
Post office
Des Chutes
N
Lake Kivu
CYANGUGU
Restaurant Moderne
BP Petrol
Home St François
De Lac Kivu
D.R.C. border
Rusizi River

0   100m
0   100yds

M16 Nightclub Lively bar with dancing later near the Hotel Faucon.

Motel aux Beaux Arts Smart two-storey hotel near the market with clean reasonably-priced s/c rooms in the **D**–**E** bracket. Restaurant with English menu serves a standard range of cheap snacks and main meals.

Motel Ineza Recommended cheapie offering small s/c rooms (cold water) set around a secluded garden at **C**/**D**. Relaxed garden restaurant.

Motel Gratia, Pleasant hotel with rooms set around a well-watered courtyard garden. Rooms span **D**–**E** ranges. Snacks and meals available.

Presbyterian Church Guesthouse. Friendly welcome but cell-like accommodation and grotty shared ablutions. At the crossroads en route to the university. **C** dbl.

Procure de Butare Guesthouse Clean, inexpensive accommodation opposite the cathedral. Rooms using shared facilities **C**/**D** sgl/dbl. Good value meals available.

Restaurant Murakazeneza Generous two-person mixed platter with salad for less than US$5.

Town Restaurant Standard Rwandan fare next to the Motel des Beaux Arts.

Nyungwe Forest National Park

Gisakura Tea Estate Guesthouse. Friendly and excellent value, with two four-bed dormitories available at **B** pp (unless it's full, female travellers or couples will probably be given private use of a room). Meals are great value at US$2 for a huge spread (whole grilled fish, chips, rice and fruit). The guesthouse is about 2km from the ORTPN Resthouse and office: from the main road, follow the dirt road into the tea estate (signposted *Usine à thé Gisakura*) for about 500m until you reach a large traffic circle, then follow the central road branching from this circle (at roughly two o'clock) for about 200m. You'll see the resthouse to your right, next to a concrete volleyball court.

ORTPN Resthouse Alongside the main Cyangugu road 2km west of the forest close to the Gisakura Tea Estate. Clean, comfortable rooms **C** pp. Intermittent water supply. Huge meals can be prepared with a couple of hours notice for the reasonable charge of US$5 per person. Good access to the Waterfall Trail and the colobus troop on the Gisakura Tea Estate.

Uwinka Reception Centre and Campsite Set in the heart of the forest, yet only a couple of hundred metres from the main road, the is the best option provided that you have a tent and are reasonably self-sufficient. Chilly at night. Monkeys pass through regularly. Drinks available but no food. Doubles as the trailhead for the Coloured Trails, making it the most convenient base from which to explore the forest. Camping costs US$10, but since this includes the US$10 forest visitation fee, it is effectively free.

Cyangugu

Auberge la Saveur Basic but acceptable local guesthouse alongside the minibus-taxi stand in Kamembe. Dbl with hot shower **D**. Lively restaurant and bar.

Home St Fransious Opposite the Hotel de Lac Kivu, this is one of the best budget places in the country. Rooms, communal toilets and hot showers **B**/**C** sgl/dbl. Meals available. Unmarried couples not accepted.

Hotel des Chutes Tel: 537405. Overlooks the lake 500m from the border post. Nice place for a drink and snack. Rooms a bit overpriced at **F** s/c dbl.

Hotel du Lac Kivu Tel: 085 27709. The smartest hotel in town, set among the row of semi-dilapidated buildings close to the border post. Riverfront bar and restaurant recommended. Rooms **E**/**F** s/c sgl/dbl with hot shower and balcony. May try to overcharge.

Modern Rest Lodge Last gasp option in Kamembe. **D** for a grotty double.

Peace Guesthouse Tel/fax: 61423. On a hill overlooking the lake between Cyangugu and Kamembe. Clean and friendly. Rooms using communal hot showers **C**/**D** sgl/dbl. S/c rooms **D**/**E**. Meals available.

Bugarama

Tripartite Bar Small lodge 50m from the main junction in the direction of the cement factory. Single rooms ◪.

Kibuye

Home St Jean Signposted down a rough track to the right of the memorial church, this has clean doubles with shared facilities at ◪ pp. No breakfast is provided, and it's a good 10-minute walk from town.

Kibuye Guesthouse The s/c chalets with hot water and TV will be too pricey for most backpackers at US$25/35 sgl/dbl, but the great lakeshore position and excellent meals in the US$4–6 range make it a good place to spend an afternoon.

Eastern Rwanda

The east of Rwanda currently holds little of interest to backpackers, though it is the main through route from Rwanda to Tanzania. Main towns in the region include **Rwamagana**, (60km from Kigali), **Kayonza** (on the major regional road intersection 80km from Kigali), and **Kibungu** (the largest town in the region and closest to Akagera National Park, 100km from Kigali). One scenic part of eastern Rwanda that is accessible to backpackers is **Lake Muhazi**, an erratically shaped body of water whose shores follow the contours of the surrounding hills, skirted by the surfaced road towards the Uganda border 8km north of Kayonza.

The Rusumo border with Tanzania, 60km southeast of Kibungu, is also the site of Rwanda's most impressive waterfall. **Rusumo Falls** couldn't be mentioned in the same breath as the Victoria or Blue Nile Falls, but it is a voluminous rush of white-water, facing the bridge between the two border posts. The Rwandan officials don't appear to have any objection to tourists wandering onto the bridge to goggle at the spectacle. If you are heading this way, **Nyakarimbi** is a large village straddling the Rusumo–Kibungu road in an area noted for its distinctive cow-dung 'paintings' – earthy, geometric designs which are mostly used to decorate the interiors of houses. In Nyakarimbi, an unsignposted building easily recognised by the black-and-white whorled pattern facing the main road, serves as a craft co-operative.

The theoretical highlight of eastern Rwanda is **Akagera National Park**, which runs along the Tanzania border and is named after the river which runs along its eastern boundary. In contrast to the rest of the country, Akagera is relatively warm and low-lying, and its undulating plains support a cover of dense broad-leafed and acacia woodland interspersed with an network of lakes, channels and papyrus swamps. Despite heavy poaching and resettlement since the war, Akagera harbours an impressive range of plains animals – elephant, buffalo, leopard, lion, giraffe, zebra and a dozen antelope species – while the wetlands support large numbers of hippo and crocodile and concentrations of waterbirds. In terms of game viewing, it would be misleading to compare Akagera to East Africa's finest savannah reserves, and access is a problem using public transport. Balanced against that, the reserve is very scenic, and it has a decidedly untrammelled quality. This, together with the relatively inexpensive park fees (a one-off payment of US$9, no additional camping charge) makes it worth checking out whether any backpacker-friendly development has taken place.

Access and getting around

The main centres in the region are connected to each other and to Kigali by regular minibus-taxis. Rusumo is about four hours from Kigali on public transport,

Kibungo is two to three hours, and Rwamagana about one hour. Minibus-taxis heading towards the Uganda border can drop travellers at Lake Muhazi.

In a private vehicle, Akagera can be reached from Kigali in a long two hours, and from Kibungo or Rwamagana in about one hour. The only usable entrance gate, 500m from the disused Hotel Akagera, is reached via a 27km dirt road which branches from the main surfaced road at Kabarondo, 15km north of Kibungo. To reach Akagera on public transport, any minibus-taxi travelling between Kayonza and Kibungu can drop you at Kabarondo junction, from where the only realistic option is a motorbike-taxi (assuming that you can find one). At the time of writing, travellers are permitted to travel by motorbike as far as Lake Ihema (where they can camp), but the options beyond that are limited – no walking is permitted with or without a guide, and no vehicle is available for game drives.

Where to stay and eat
Rwamagana
Dereva Hotel Tel: 67244. Set in large green grounds alongside the main road. Very reasonably priced at **D/E** for a suite-sized sgl/dbl with hot showers. The attached restaurant serves large meals in the US$3–5 range.

Kayonza
Greenland Guesthouse Decent local place offering small but clean rooms for **C/D** sgl/dbl. Tasty and inexpensive local food.

Lake Muhazi
Seeds of Peace Centre Tel: 67422. Attractive position, 8km north of Kayonza, overlooking the lake, with access to a small beach and boats. Camping permitted at a rather steep **D** per tent. Rooms should be available by early 2001. A second, similar-looking resort was under construction 500m further up the road in late 2000.

Kibungu
Umbrella Pine Guesthouse Tel: 66269 or 72567. Set on the main Kigali–Rusumo about 200m past the turn-off to Kibungu proper. Clean but rather gloomy rooms with en suite hot showers and nets **C/D** sgl/dbl. Good meals around US$5.

Rusumo
Fine Corner Guesthouse This lodge lies in Nyakarimbi, about 20km from the border, and is the closest accommodation to Rusumo. Clean but basic rooms **B** dbl (bucket showers only). Meals available.

Akagera National Park
Hotel Akagera Perched on a rise overlooking Lake Ihema, this upmarket hotel has been closed since 1994 but might well be re-opened at some point.
Gabiro Lodge This lodge in the north of the park has been seconded to the military and seem unlikely to return to civilian use.
Camping Permitted at the staff headquarters on the shore of Lake Ihema, from where baboons, crocs, hippos and various birds can easily be seen. Boat trips are sometimes available at a small charge. Water is available, but campers should otherwise be self-sufficient. A far nicer place to pitch a tent is Lake Shakani, a small forest-fringed body of water which lies about 4km from Lake Ihema, but this is inaccessible without private transport. At present, there is no charge for camping, but this is likely to change at some point.

Tanzania

It would be easy to reduce an introduction to Tanzania to a list of statistics: it contains Africa's highest mountain, most famous national park and largest game reserve, while along its borders lie the three largest lakes on the continent. It would be just as easy to reduce Tanzania to a list of evocative place names: Zanzibar, Kilimanjaro, Serengeti, Dar es Salaam, Ngorongoro Crater, Olduvai Gorge, Gombe Stream, Lake Victoria…

Tanzania really does embody the Africa of dreams, boasting everything from plains teeming with wild animals, rainforests alive with cackling birds and monkeys, snow-capped Kilimanjaro rising dramatically above the surrounding flat scrubland, colourful Maasai herding their cattle alongside herds of grazing wildebeest, and perfect palm-lined beaches lapped by the clear warm waters of the Indian Ocean stretching as far as the eye can see. Almost 25% of the country is given over to conservation areas which, together, protect an estimated 20% of Africa's large mammal population.

You might expect a country that can be described in such superlative terms to be crawling with tourists, especially when it has enjoyed an unparalleled level of political stability since independence in 1962. Yet Tanzania has traditionally attracted a mere fraction of the tourism of somewhere such as Kenya, South Africa or Zimbabwe. This is basically because the country was such an economic mess in the 1980s. But Tanzania is a mess no longer and the northern circuit – Serengeti, Ngorongoro Crater, Kilimanjaro, Zanzibar – is rapidly catching on with fly-in tourists.

For adventurous travellers who are prepared to put up with basic accommodation, slow transport and the need to learn some Swahili, Tanzania is one of the most rewarding and fascinating countries in Africa. Virtually anywhere south of the Dar es Salaam–Mwanza railway line is miles from any beaten tourist track, and there are some wonderful possibilities: the south coast, the Poroto Mountains, Lake Tanganyika, the Makonde Plateau…

Tanzania is the most underrated country in the region.

FACTS AND FIGURES

Area: 945,166km² (13th in Africa)
Capital: Dodoma recently displaced Dar es Salaam as the official capital
Largest towns: Dar es Salaam, Mwanza, Tanga, Arusha, Mbeya, Zanzibar, Iringa
Population: 28 million (1992 estimate)
Official languages: KiSwahili and English
Currency: Tanzanian shilling
Head of State: President Benjamin Mkapa

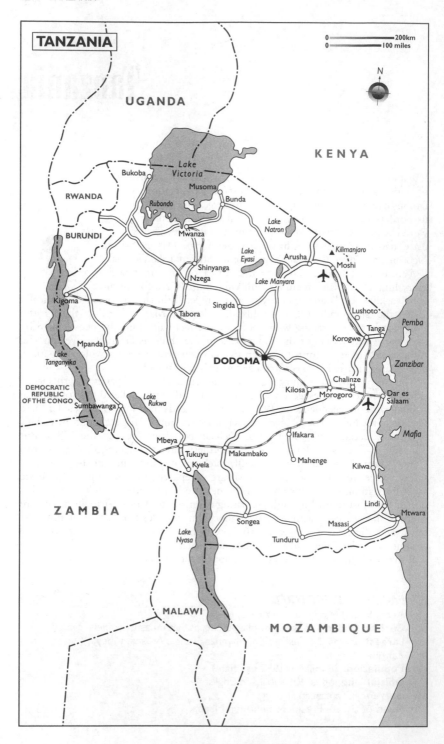

TANZANIA

0 ——————— 200km
0 ——————— 100 miles

N

UGANDA

KENYA

Lake Victoria

Bukoba

Musoma

Rubondo

Bunda

RWANDA

Lake Natron

Mwanza

BURUNDI

Lake Eyasi

Kilimanjaro

Arusha

Moshi

Shinyanga

Nzega

Lake Manyara

Kigoma

Singida

Lushoto

Tabora

Tanga

Pemba

Korogwe

Mpanda

Lake Tanganyika

Zanzibar

DODOMA

DEMOCRATIC REPUBLIC OF THE CONGO

Lake Rukwa

Kilosa

Chalinze

Morogoro

Dar es Salaam

Sumbawanga

Mafia

Mbeya

Ifakara

Tukuyu

Makambako

Kyela

Mahenge

Kilwa

ZAMBIA

Lindi

Mtwara

Songea

Masasi

Lake Nyasa

Tunduru

MALAWI

MOZAMBIQUE

BACKGROUND INFORMATION
Geography and climate

Tanzania is dominated by a vast, dry and thinly populated plateau which rises to an altitude of between 1,000 and 1,500m to the west of the moister, hotter coastal belt, and is bisected by the eastern arm of the Great Rift Valley. Predominantly flat and featureless, Tanzania somewhat paradoxically boasts an unparalleled wealth of superlative geographical landmarks: the 5,985m-high Mount Kilimanjaro and 4,565m-high Mount Meru are Africa's highest and fifth highest mountains respectively, while the interior of the coastal belt is dotted with isolated mountain ranges such as the Pare, Usambara, Uluguru, Udzungwa and Poroto. Also lying within Tanzania's territory are significant portions of Africa's three largest bodies of water, Lakes Victoria, Tanganyika and Malawi (the latter still known as Lake Nyasa, its colonial name, in Tanzania), and thus three of the world's eleven largest lakes.

Climatic conditions in Tanzania range from the sweltering humidity of the coast to the ice cap of Kilimanjaro. Broadly speaking, the coastal belt and hinterland of the great lakes is very hot and humid, while the interior is hot and dry, cooling off significantly at night at higher altitudes. The rainy season falls between November and April, which is also the warmest time of year by a matter of a few degrees. At the coast and in parts of northern Tanzania, the rainy season is spilt into the short rains in November and December and the long rains from March to May.

History

The Tanzanian coast has played an important role in maritime history. It is likely that the port of Rhapta, mentioned in ancient Roman and Phoenician documents, was on a river mouth in Tanzania, possibly the Pangani or Rufiji. In medieval times, the small island of Kilwa off the south coast of Tanzania lay at the centre of the Indian Ocean gold trade, and it boasted a mosque and palace that were the largest and finest on the Swahili coast. In the 19th century, Zanzibar Island became the capital of the Sultan of Oman, while the mainland ports of Bagamoyo, Pangani, Kilwa and Mikindani served as the gateways to the African interior for Omani slave trader and European explorer alike.

Mainland Tanzania was ceded to Germany in the Scramble for Africa. Under German rule, the southeast became the setting for one of the largest and most influential uprisings ever in Africa. The Maji-Maji rebellion was initiated by a prophet called Kinjikitile who claimed that anybody sprinkled with the water (maji) from a particular spring would be immune to bullets. In August 1905, after leading a raid on the German outpost at Kibatu, Kinjikitile was hanged by German troops. But news of his magic water spread. A group of missionaries was speared to death, several trading posts were burnt with their occupants inside, and the staff of the Ifakara garrison was killed. The rebellion lost momentum only after 1,000 warriors who attacked the Mahenge garrison discovered they most definitely weren't immune to machine guns. After the rebellion subsided, Germany burnt crops indiscriminately throughout the region; the resultant famine claimed 250,000 lives through disease or starvation. The Maji-Maji rebellion was the most important and tragic event during German rule, and of long-term significance in that it united several disparate tribes against European invaders. Many Tanzanians feel that Maji-Maji paved the way for the non-tribal mood of modern Tanzania, and it certainly affected the strategies used against colonial powers elsewhere in Africa.

At the end of World War I, the League of Nations granted Britain a mandate over Tanganyika (though the northwestern province of Ruanda-Urundi – now

Rwanda and Burundi – went to Belgium). Tanganyika was not heavily settled by Europeans, and the indigenous population had greater opportunity for self-reliance than in other colonies. Nevertheless, settlers were favoured when it came to land, as were Asians in commerce. The Land Ordinance Act of 1923 secured some land rights for Africans, who otherwise were repeatedly forced into grand but misguided agricultural schemes such as the Groundnut Scheme of 1947, a spectacularly ineffective and costly attempt to convert the southeast into mechanised groundnut production.

In the late 1950s, the British governor Sir Edward Twining put in place a multi-racial electoral system giving equal representation to whites, blacks and Asians. Candidates backed by Julius Nyerere's TANU party won 67% of the vote in this election, and Twining's successor Sir Richard Turnball decided to scrap multi-racialism in favour of full democracy. On December 9 1961, Tanganyika attained full independence with Nyerere and TANU at the helm. Not one life had been taken in the process. Britain granted Zanzibar full independence in December 1963, and only a month later the island's unpopular Arab government was toppled in a bloody rebellion. In April 1964, Tanganyika and Zanzibar united to become Tanzania.

TANU (later to be renamed CCM) came to power with no defined goal except the one it had attained. Tanganyika was the least developed country in East Africa, and Nyerere's first concern was to better the lot of rural Africans rather than to nurture a money-grabbing elite. In 1967, Nyerere embarked on the Ujamaa (familyhood) scheme, wherein rural people were to form collective farming communities; which would allow the government to provide civil amenities from a central point. The scheme met with some initial success, encouraging Nyerere to embark on an ill-considered policy of forcible resettlement. By late 1975, 65% of rural Tanzanians lived in Ujamaa villages. In many areas, however, water supplies were inadequate to support a village, and the resultant mess was exacerbated by drought; so the scheme ended. Ujamaa is often considered to have been an unmitigated disaster. It did not achieve what it was meant to, but most reliable sources feel that it allowed the government to improve education and health care, and did little long-term damage to agricultural productivity.

On the international front, Nyerere emerged as perhaps the only statesman among the first-generation leaders of independent Africa. In theory, Tanzania pursued a non-alignment policy, but Nyerere's outspoken socialist views alienated the West and bonds were forged with socialist powers, notably China. Relations with Britain soured after Nyerere condemned its tacit acceptance of UDI in Rhodesia. Nyerere supported liberation movements in South Africa, Mozambique and Angola, allowing the ANC and Frelimo to operate from Tanzania. Tellingly, he pulled out of the 1975 OAU conference in Amin's Uganda saying: 'The refusal to protest against African crimes against Africans is bad enough ... but ... by meeting in Kampala ... the OAU are giving respectability to one of the most murderous regimes in Africa'. In October 1978, Amin bombed the ports of Bukoba and Musoma. Tanzania retaliated by invading Uganda and toppling Amin. Bizarrely, Nyerere's actions were condemned by other African leaders and Tanzania received financial compensation neither from the West nor from another African country.

Nyerere may have been a statesman, but he was no pragmatist. By the late 1970s Tanzania was an economic disaster, and after re-election in 1980 Nyerere announced he would retire at the end of that term. In 1985 he was succeeded by Ali Hassan Mwinyi, under whom Tanzania moved away from socialism with remarkable results. The first multi-party election took place in October 1995, and the CCM was returned to power under Benjamin Mkapa with a 75% majority. Nyerere's great legacy to mainland Tanzania and the CCM is the tremendous sense of national unity he forged by making KiSwahili the national language, banning tribal leaders, forcing government officials to work away from the area in which they grew up, and his own example. The picture is perhaps less rosy on Zanzibar, where there are strong calls in some quarters for disintegrating the union forged in 1964, and the CCM candidate scraped home in the 1995 election with a disputed 0.4% majority. Tanzania remains one of the world's poorest countries, but most sources agree that the lot of the average Tanzanian has improved since independence, and the country's remarkable political stability and increasingly pragmatic economic policies bode well for future growth.

PRACTICAL INFORMATION
Accommodation
Every town in Tanzania has dozens of cheap lodgings, generally called guesthouses, and even the smallest village will have somewhere you can stay. Expect a basic room in an established tourist area (Arusha, Moshi, Zanzibar or Dar es Salaam) to cost around US$5–7. Elsewhere, it will cost well under US$5 and you can often get a self-contained hotel room for that sort of price. In towns with many guesthouses, don't be afraid to look beyond the listings in this guide. Bear in mind, however, that the Swahili word *hoteli* refers to a restaurant – ask for a guesthouse or *gesti*. Camping opportunities are few.

Books and newspapers
Most bookshops in Tanzania are appalling, but this is compensated for by the excellent secondhand bookstalls in Dar es Salaam. The main newspaper, the *Daily News*, is OK for local news, useless for international news. The *Kenyan Daily Nation* is available in Dar es Salaam, Arusha and Mwanza, as is the weekly *East African*.

Entrance fees
In 1997, Tanzania followed Kenya's lead in charging higher fees for popular parks: the old blanket entrance fee of US$20 per 24 hours was raised to US$25 for Arusha, Kilimanjaro, Lake Manyara, Serengeti and Tarangire national parks and dropped to US$15 for Katavi, Mikumi, Ruaha, Rubondo and Udzungwa. Entrance to Gombe Stream is US$100 per 24 hours and to Mahale Mountains US$50. Of other conservation areas, Selous Game Reserve charges US$15 per 24 hours and Ngorongoro Conservation Area US$25, a fee that applies if you just pass through the Ngorongoro on your way to or from the Serengeti, so that people who bus between Arusha and Mwanza via the Serengeti pay a total of US$50 in fees.

No entrance fee is charged for using public or private transport on public roads that pass through national parks, for instance the main Morogoro–Iringa road through Mikumi National Park or the Mpanga–Sumbawanga road through Katavi National Park.

Game reserves other than the Selous charge only US$3 per 24 hours inside. Fees to other places of interest, such as historical or archaeological sites, are non-existent or nominal.

Entry formalities
Visas are not required by nationals of most Commonwealth and Scandinavian countries and the Republic of Ireland, though do note that British nationals now require a visa at a cost of US$50. It is possible to buy a visa in advance at a Tanzanian embassy or high commission, but these days they can also be bought on

arrival, which is far simpler. Provided you have a valid passport, a 30-day visitor's pass will be stamped in your passport for free upon arrival, and this is easily renewed at any immigration office.

Flying there
Several major European and African airlines fly to Dar es Salaam, but it's much easier to find discounted tickets to Nairobi.

Food and drink
Tanzanian *hotelis* provide the usual unimaginative but filling meals. In coastal towns and near lakes, whole fried fish comes as a welcome change from tough stews. Larger towns normally have at least one Western or Indian restaurant, and there is considerable culinary variety in Dar es Salaam and Arusha. The main alcoholic beverages are lager beer (of which Pilsner is the best) and *konyagi*, a spirit made from sugar cane. The superior beers produced in neighbouring countries can be bought in towns near the appropriate border.

Getting around
By road
Good surfaced roads and quick buses connect Dar es Salaam to Arusha, Moshi, Tanga, Morogoro and Dodoma. The road from Dar es Salaam to Mbeya is in a fair state, as are the roads between Mbeya and Kyela, Mwanza and Musoma, Lindi and Mtwara, Chalinze and Songea, and Mombo and Lushoto. Buses on these roads typically cover 40–50km hourly. In more remote areas, road conditions range from bad to impassable, driving speeds from slow to comatose, vehicles stop every two minutes to collect or drop off passengers, and the concept of a full vehicle simply isn't recognised – use trains or ferries where possible.

By rail
Dar es Salaam is connected by rail to Kigoma, Mwanza and Mbeya (the service between Dar es Salaam and Moshi has been discontinued). The train services are slow and carriages are run down and whiffy, but trains are also surprisingly efficient and punctual, rarely leaving or arriving more than an hour behind schedule. For some odd reason, first- and second-class tickets for trains leaving Dar es Salaam generally need to be booked a couple of days in advance, but you can normally get tickets for trains heading towards Dar es Salaam on the day of departure. Two-bunk, first-class compartments and four- or six-bunk second-class carriages are single sex unless the whole carriage is booked by one mixed party. Details of individual rail services are included in the *Access and getting around* section of the relevant regional part of this chapter.

By ferry
Ocean-going ferries link Dar es Salaam to Zanzibar and Mtwara. There are useful ferry services on all the great lakes – see the relevant regional section for further details.

Crime and safety
Mugging is largely restricted to Dar es Salaam and Bagamoyo, but pickpockets and casual thieves hang out at markets and bus stations anywhere. On buses and trains, be alert to hands reaching through the window, and never leave a train window open at night. By repute, there is a risk of being drugged by fellow passengers or having your luggage tampered with on overnight buses between Arusha and

Dodoma or Dar es Salaam and Mbeya. Any bus trip that will land you in Dar es Salaam after dark should be avoided due to the high risk of being mugged while you are looking for a room.

Internet and email
The internet is booming in Tanzania, and rates are the best in Africa, dropping as low as US$1.50 for an hour. There are internet cafés scattered all over Tanzania and Arusha, and similar facilities can be found in most substantial towns in Tanzania (I recently heard that an internet café had opened in Mtwara, arguably the most remote town of any size in Tanzania).

Photography
Until recently, taking photographs outside of game reserves could land you in trouble. This ruling has since relaxed, but it remains illegal to photograph military installations or government buildings. Tanzanians tend to be more sensitive about having their photograph taken than most Africans, presumably because of the strong Muslim influence – ask first.

Language
Relatively little English is spoken in Tanzania by comparison with the other former British territories in the region. English-speakers will get by easily enough in the larger towns and established tourist areas, but elsewhere a few basic phrases of Swahili will go a long way. And do familiarise yourself with Swahili time (see *Appendix 2*), since bus times are often given that way.

Maps
The most useful map of Tanzania is the BP 1:1,125,000, available at some tourist hotels in Dar es Salaam. Town plans and 1:50,000 maps covering most of the country can be bought from the Department of Maps and Surveys in Dar es Salaam.

Post and telecommunications
Post from Tanzania is cheap and relatively reliable. Incoming post arrives more quickly than in many neighbouring countries, and the Poste Restante service in Dar es Salaam is very efficient, though there is a nominal charge for collecting letters.

Tanzania's international phone service is awful, but if you want to give it a go there's a TTC Extelcomms Centre in most large towns. Contrary to expectations, international calls from Dar es Salaam are more difficult than from Arusha or Moshi. The international code for Tanzania is +255 and main local codes include Arusha (027), Dar es Salaam (022), Moshi (027), Tanga (027) and Zanzibar (024).

Money
The unit of currency is the Tanzanian shilling. At the time of writing the exchange rate is in the region of US$1 = Tsh 700 with better rates offered at private bureaux than at banks. Banking hours are from 08.30 to 12.30 on weekdays, and 08.30 to 11.30 on Saturday. In larger towns, some banks stay open in the afternoon. Most forex bureaux stay open until 15.00 or 16.00.

Tanzania has a reputation as an expensive country, which it will probably live up to if you restrict your travels to the northern safari circuit, Kilimanjaro, Dar es Salaam and Zanzibar, then rush through the south as quickly as you can. In fact, away from the main tourist centres, day-to-day costs are among the cheapest in the region, and there are many areas where you'd struggle to spend more than US$10 per day.

Public holidays
Good Friday, Easter Monday, Idd-ul-Fitr, Islamic New Year and the Prophet's Birthday are recognised as public holidays. Fixed-date holidays are:

1 January	New Year's Day	7 July	Public Holiday
12 January	Zanzibar Revolution Day	8 August	Peasants' Day
26 April	Union Day	9 December	Independence Day
1 May	International Workers' Day	25 December	Christmas Day

Tourist information office
The main office of the Tanzania Tourist Corporation (TTC) is on Maktaba Street in Dar es Salaam opposite the New Africa Hotel.

Western Tanzania
LAKE VICTORIA
The lake port of **Mwanza** is the second largest town in Tanzania and the obvious regional focus for overland travellers. An atmospheric town, Mwanza is notable for the bizarre granite outcrops which surround it, the best known of which is the precariously perched Bismarck Rock at the harbour entrance. An inexpensive day trip from Mwanza is to **Saa Nane Island**, a game reserve and zoo that is primarily of interest for the variety of animals that occur there naturally – rock hyraxes, colourful rock agamas, metre-long monitor lizards, crocodiles, fish eagles and many localised birds. On the lake shore further out of town, the **Sukoma Museum** displays exhibits relating to the Sukoma, Tanzania's largest tribe. On Saturdays, the Sukoma Snake Dance is performed in tandem with a live python!

Ferry services out of Mwanza make it possible to explore several of the lake's larger islands. The closest and most accessible of these is **Ukerewe Island**, where ferries land at the small, rather scruffy town of Nansio, next to a pretty beach resort (reportedly free of bilharzia though I wouldn't stake my life on it) and a base for limitless walking possibilities. More adventurously, ferries visit **Kome** and **Maisome Islands**, both of which support a couple of small fishing villages and substantial areas of forest, and I've yet to hear of a traveller who's made it to either of them.

Ferries also go to **Nyamirembe**, the nearest port of call to **Rubondo Island National Park**, a little-visited 240km² island reserve where a combination of rainforest, grassland and papyrus swamp supports such large mammals as sitatunga, bushbuck, hippo, elephant and chimpanzee, not to say a rich variety of birds. Rubondo is backpacker friendly in that game viewing is only on foot or from a boat, but you would need to spend a full week in the area due to the ferry schedules, in which case national park fees are going to add up to quite a sum. That said, assuming that time isn't a worry, you could restrict yourself to two or three days on the island itself, and spend the rest of the week in a guesthouse in Nyamirembe. The Nyamirembe area could be worth exploring on foot since the port borders the remote **Biharamulo Game Reserve**, sanctuary to such large mammals as elephant, zebra, buffalo and hippopotamus.

Mwanza aside, there are two large ports on the Tanzanian part of the lake shore. **Musoma** is nothing special, and you're only likely to pass through it when you enter Tanzania from Kisumu in Kenya. **Bukoba** boasts a more attractive situation,

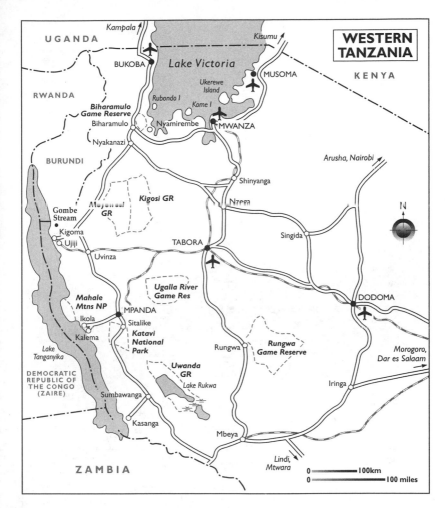

and several run-down Indian-style buildings give the town centre some character
– it is, nevertheless, of interest mostly as the first target for travellers coming
overland to Tanzania from Uganda.

Access and getting around

Mwanza is an important regional transport hub, connected by ferry services to
several ports on the lake. Ferries to Bukoba leave Mwanza at 21.00 or 22.00 daily
(except Wednesday and Friday), and return from Bukoba at a similar time on the
following day. The 12-hour trip costs US$14/10/5 first/second/third class. At least
one ferry daily in each direction runs between Mwanza and Nansio on Ukerewe
Island, a three-hour trip which costs US$3/2 second/third class, but times of which
vary from day to day. To get to Maisome or Kome Island, you want the ferry to
Nkome which leaves Mwanza at 08.00 Wednesday and Saturday and starts the
return trip at 08.00 on Thursday and Sunday, at a cost of US$4/3 second/third
class. In addition to the fare itself, a port tax of US$5 must be paid in hard currency
when leaving any Tanzanian port.

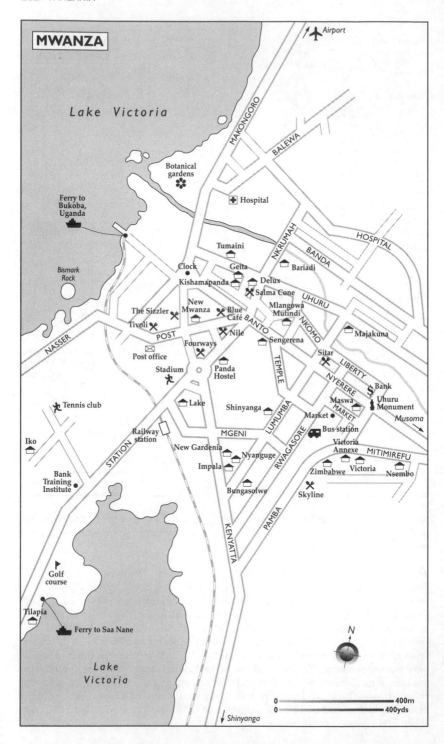

MWANZA

Lake Victoria

Airport

MAKONGORO

BALEWA

Botanical gardens

Hospital

Ferry to Bukoba, Uganda

Bismark Rock

Tumaini

NKRUMAH

BANDA

HOSPITAL

Clock
Kishamapanda

Geita
Bariadi

UHURU

Delux
Salma Cone

The Sizzler
New Mwanza
Blue Café
Tivoli

BANTO

Mlangowa Mutindi

NKOMO

Majakuna

POST
Nile

Fourways
Sengerena

Sitar

LIBERTY

Post office

Stadium

Panda Hostel

TEMPLE

NYERERE

Bank

MARKET
Uhuru Monument

Maswa

Musoma

Tennis club

NASSER

Lake

Shinyanga

LUMUMBA

Market
Bus station

Victoria Annexe

MITIMIREFU

Iko

Railway station

New Gardenia
Nyanguge

MGENI

Zimbabwe
Victoria
Nsembo

Bank Training Institute

Impala

STATION

Bungasolwe

RWAGASORE

Skyline

Golf course

KENYATTA

PAMBA

Tilapia

Ferry to Saa Nane

N

Lake Victoria

0   400m
0   400yds

Shinyanga

Getting to Rubondo Island on public transport is a trip suitable only for reasonably flexible and adventurous travellers. The straightforward bit is catching the weekly ferry which leaves Mwanza for Nyamirembe on Wednesday evening and arrives ten hours later, to start the return trip on Thursday morning. This ferry service is very cheap, would be an interesting trip in its own right, and there is at least one guesthouse in Nyamirembe should you need to spend a night there. From Nyamirembe, you can hire a private boat across to the island, but this might cost as much as US$120. A better idea would be to continue by road from Nyamirembe to Muganza (this is 25km trip and transport is light, so you might have to walk) where the Lutheran Mission Hospital, 3km from town, can radio the national park headquarters, who charge around US$30 for the return boat trip to Rubondo. The direct buses between Mwanza and Muganza are very cramped and slow, but since the alternative is spending eight days in the area between ferries, it would probably be worth bussing in one direction.

The jetty for Saa Nane Island lies 15 minutes' walk from Mwanza town centre. A motorboat makes the ten-minute crossing to the island every two hours from 11.00 to 17.00.

The Sukoma Museum lies 20km along the surfaced Musoma road, and any bus heading that way can drop you. Road transport elsewhere in this region is appalling, so travellers heading to Kigoma, Tabora or Dar es Salaam are advised to use the rail service (see *The Central Railway* on page 285).

Travelling between Mwanza and Arusha poses several problems. The comfortable option is to go directly across the Serengeti – at least three buses do this trip every week, as do a number of private Land Rovers which carry passengers – provided that you don't mind paying US$50 in park entrance fees. This is a waste of money if you plan to go on safari, but those who can't afford a safari might view it as a cheap way to see the Serengeti. Land Rover drivers (but not bus drivers) are reportedly happy to stop for the occasional photograph!

The cheapest way to cross between Mwanza and Arusha is by bus through Singida and Shinyanga, a hellish ride taking from 36 to 73 hours, with stops dictated by breakdowns and flat tyres as much as anything.

Where to stay and eat
Mwanza
Delux Hotel Slightly run-down but pleasant. Excellent cheap meals. Rooms **B**/**D** s/c.
Kishamapanda Guest House Superior local lodging opposite Delux. Rooms **B** dbl.
Kuleana Pizzeria Next to the New Mwanza Hotel. Excelleny pizzas in the US$3–6 range.
Lake Hotel Mid-range hotel near railway station. Rooms **D**/**E** s/c with nets, hot water.
Panda Hostel Centrally situated and good value. Rooms **B**/**C** with nets.
Pizzeria Mgahawa Fresh brown bread from bakery.
Salma Cone Great ice-cream sundaes and fresh popcorn at reasonable prices.
Sitar Restaurant Well established and popular with travellers. Food can be very greasy.
Sizzler Restaurant Outstanding Indian restaurant. Meals around US$5.
Szechwan Mahal Close to the Sizzler. World-class Chinese and Indian meals for around US$10.
Yacht Club Camping on lakeshore close to town. Clean showers and toilets. Price negotiable but expect to pay **B** pp.

Sukoma Museum
Campsite Facilities limited to running water and a toilet. Camping and bandas **B** pp.

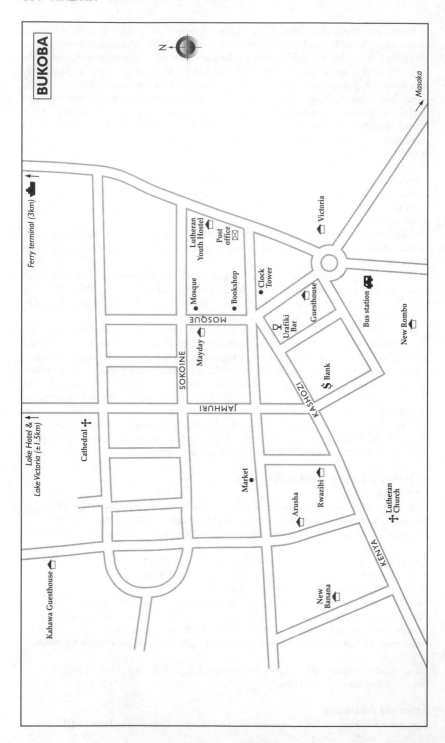

Nansio (Ukerewe Island)
Gullu Beach Hotel Lakeshore resort. Restaurant. Rooms **C**/**E**. Camping **C** pp.
Panda Hostel and **Island Inn** Best of a few guest houses on cusp of **A** and **B** ranges.

Musoma
Beach Hotel and Campsite Popular with overlanders for stunning location on lakeshore, but rooms rather run down at **D** dbl (negotiable) using communal showers. Good food, expensive bar. Camping permitted at negotiable rate.
Butata Lodge Best of the **A** lodgings. Nets.
Silver Sands Inn On lake shore 1km from town. Rooms **B** pp. Meals on request.

Rubondo Island National Park
National Park Camp Bandas and campsite **F** pp. Bring food.

Bukoba
Catholic Youth Centre Clean rooms **C** s/c. Fax, computer and secretarial services.
Lake Hotel Mid-range hotel near lake shore. Rooms **D**/**E** s/c. Camping **B** pp.
Lutheran Youth Hostel (Nyumba wa Vijina) Clean, secure four-bed dorms or dbl **A** pp.
New Banana Hotel Dingy rooms **D** dbl. Good restaurant – *tilapia* and chips for US$2.
Rwabizi Hotel Eccentrically shaped and brightly painted rooms **C** s/c dbl.

THE CENTRAL RAILWAY
The only sane form of public transport between the coast and western Tanzania is the 1,238km German-built railway that connects Dar es Salaam to Kigoma on Lake Tanganyika, and was extended by Britain to Mwanza on Lake Victoria in 1928.

The central line follows the old slave caravan route between the coast and Lake Tanganyika. The modern junction town of **Tabora**, where travellers crossing between Lakes Victoria and Tanganyika will swap trains and maybe spend a night, was an important slave trading post in the nineteenth century, visited by Burton, Speke, Stanley and Livingstone amongst others. Today, Tabora is a hot, dusty town, given some character by the shady mango and flame trees that line its avenues. The house that Livingstone occupied in 1871 is now a museum, 6km from the town centre. Tabora is a potential springboard for a couple of more adventurous expeditions – the thrice-weekly train service to Mpanga would set you on the road described in the box *The wild southwest* (on pages 286–7), while a ten-hour bus trip south to Rungwa village would offer you the chance of exploring the border of the **Rungwa Game Reserve**. Rungwa is a remote extension of the Ruaha ecosystem and, provided that you have a tent, food and the US$3 daily entrance fee, the head ranger should be willing to organise a guide to take you hiking in the reserve.

The other important town on the central railway is **Dodoma**. Aside from being the correct answer to a potential Trivial Pursuit question (how many of us could name the capital city of Tanzania?), there is really very little to be said about Dodoma, except to note that any plan which involves bussing there from anywhere but Dar es Salaam should instantly be dismissed as a bad idea. Unless you're on some sort of esoteric quest that involves 'collecting' capital cities, Dodoma is eminently missable.

Access and getting around
Trains to Kigoma and Mwana leave Dar es Salaam on Tuesday, Wednesday, Friday and Sunday at 18.00. There are trains in the opposite direction on Tuesday, Thursday, Friday and Sunday, leaving Mwanza at 19.00 and Kigoma at 16.00. The

THE WILD SOUTHWEST

The road that runs south of Kigoma roughly parallel to Lake Tanganyika, passing through Mpanda, Katavi National Park and Sumbawanga, must rank among the most untravelled in East Africa. I went this way in 1992, and have yet to hear of anybody who has followed in my footsteps, so the account below is a relatively subjective description of what happened to me.

I took the Lake Tanganyika ferry from Kigoma to **Kalema**, an important staging post during the slaving era, and later settled by the White Father missionaries. The church built by the White Fathers in 1890 is possibly the oldest extant building in this part of Africa, and the fortified mission, which has a slightly Mediterranean appearance, dates to 1893. There is nowhere to stay in Kalema – the police offered to let me pitch a tent in their compound – but instead I found a lift through to **Ikola**, 16km further north, from where it is supposed to be easier to get a lift through to **Mpanda**. There is nowhere to stay in Ikola either, but there's no problem finding somewhere to pitch a tent. The next day I got a lift on a truck to Mpanda, a quite large town that can also be reached by overnight train from Tabora (thrice-weekly in either direction taking 12 hours). There are a few basic, inexpensive lodgings in Mpanda – the City Guesthouse is the best bet, if only because it is favoured by truckies, on whom you'll be dependent to get a lift south towards Sumbawanga.

Katavi National Park, the entrance gate to which is on the Sumbawanga road, 1km south of Sitalike village and 35km south of Mpanda, must rank as Tanzania's most obscure national park – when I arrived, I had been preceded by only 18 parties of tourists in more than two years, and I was the first person to arrive without a vehicle. I organised for a park vehicle to run me the 18km to the rest camp – an empty cement hut overlooking Katavi flood plain – from where I saw more than 100 hippos grazing one evening, as well as a spotted hyena, a herd of 200 buffaloes and a group of 50 elephants. I also walked out on to the plain with an armed ranger. I see no reason why travellers arriving today shouldn't be able to do the same thing – in addition to an entrance fee, the hut costs US$30pp and you'll pay around US$20 for use of the vehicle and US$10 daily for an armed guide. Even if you can't afford or aren't permitted to do this, you have little to lose since the main road goes through the park for about 50km and no fee is charged for merely passing through.

full journey takes about 40 hours, and in my experience the trains are remarkably punctual. Note that there is no direct service between Kigoma and Mwanza – travellers crossing between these towns must first take a train as far as Tabora, where they must make an onward booking. Since extra carriages are added at Tabora, most people have no problem getting through.

Tickets can and should be booked a few days in advance at Dar es Salaam, Kigoma, Tabora and Mwanza. Tickets for the full trip between Dar es Salaam and either Kigoma or Mwanza cost US$35 first class (two-berth compartment) and US$25 second class (six-berth compartment). The compartments are very run down and they have a pervasive smell of sweat and urine. Third class consists of seated carriages, and is only worth thinking about if you value neither your comfort nor your possessions. Theft from train windows at night is not unusual, so close the windows securely when you turn the light off (a block of wood is provided for this purpose). The meals served on the trains are surprisingly good and reasonably priced. Beers and soft drinks are normally available.

At Sitalike, I waited five hours for a lift further south – as it happened, in a covered truck piled high with timber. After 200km of jolting about on planks in pitch darkness, I arrived in the nondescript town of **Sumbawanga**, relieved to be able to rest my battered body at an affordable mid-range hotel, the Upenda View Inn, which also had a good bar and restaurant. There is no shortage of **A** lodgings in Sumbawanga – try the Zanzibar Guest House. For something smarter, the new Forestry Country Club is excellent value with very comfortable s/c rooms in the **D**–**E** bracket inclusive of a big breakfast, and it also serves good meals for around US$3–4. Buses to Mbeya leave Sumbawanga at 05.00 every morning. There is also some transport between Sumbawanga and Kasanga, the most southerly ferry port on the Tanzanian shore of Lake Tanganyika.

Attractively situated on the lakeshore between Kitavi and Sumbawanga, the **port of Kipili** has recently been recommended as worthwhile by travellers. The MV *Liemba* stops at Kipili en route between Kigoma and Mpumulungu, and the port is also connected by a sideroad to the main Sumbawanga road, though matatus are somewhat thin on the ground. The Saint Benedict Catholic Mission in Kipili has a small guesthouse, where clean s/c double rooms with net fall in the **C** bracket, and camping is permitted for free (but please leave a donation).

I didn't explore the **Mbizi Mountains** east of Sumbawanga, but I've been told that you can reach Kijiji village by *matatu*, then walk to Mpondo village, from where there's a great view over Lake Rukwa. Maps suggest this road continues to the game rich shores of the lake itself, passing through some forest patches en route. With maps, camping equipment and a stock of food, this area could be rewarding for experienced hikers, though I'd suggest you get written permission from the district headquarters in Sumbawanga before you attempt it.

An interesting trip in this part of Tanzania is to the **Kalombo Falls** on the border with Zambia. At 221m high, this is the 12th-tallest waterfall in the world. The closest town is Kasanga on Lake Tanganyika, a major stop for the MV *Liemba* (there is even a jetty here!), with a few very basic lodgings and road transport links to Sumbawanga. Getting to the waterfall involves a short pick-up ride and a round trek of about eight hours. Mr Mapata, who lives in Kasanga-Muzi, 40 minutes' walk from Kasanga ferry jetty, is extremely helpful and speaks excellent English. A trustworthy young guide called Peter meets the ferry and can take you to the falls.

Dodoma's strategic position in the centre of Tanzania tempts many travellers to head south from Arusha via Dodoma, bypassing Dar es Salaam. It must be stressed that this idea only looks good on paper – the main road from Arusha to Iringa via Dodoma is in appalling condition and can require up to 30 hours of bus travel. There is, however, a good tar road connecting Dodoma to Dar es Salaam and Morogoro, covered by regular buses.

Where to stay and eat
Tabora
Fama Hotel Recently recommended new hotel with clean s/c rooms and nets. On the right side of the street that goes off the road opposite the school for the blind. Rooms **D** dbl.
Furaha School for the Blind and **Pentecostal Church Hostel** Clean rooms **B** dbl.
Tabora Hotel Renovated former Railway Hotel near station. Large room **D** s/c dbl with net.
Vatican and **Morovian Guesthouses** Among the best of a few dozen **A** lodgings.

Dodoma

CCT Hostel Close to railway station near domed church. Clean rooms in **B** to **C** range.

Climax Club Good bar on outskirts of town. Popular with ex-pats. Swimming pool, cold beers, meals.

Dodoma Hotel Good mid-range hotel opposite railway station. Fair meals US$4. Three-course set menu US$7. Live music. Rooms **E** s/c dbl.

Kilimanjaro Villa Guesthouse Leafy property 500m from station. Rooms **B**/**C** s/c.

LAKE TANGANYIKA

Lake Tanganyika is the longest and deepest lake in Africa, and it covers an area second only to that of Lake Victoria. Hemmed in by the mountainous walls of the western arm of the Rift Valley, Lake Tanganyika measures 675km from north to south and an average of 50km from east to west. Due to its extraordinary depth – over 1,400m in parts – the lake holds a volume of water seven times greater than that of Lake Victoria.

Kigoma is the largest settlement on the lake, an attractive, easy-going and cosmopolitan town, built around a mango-lined avenue that climbs uphill from the lake shore. Kigoma is a pleasant place to spend a few days waiting for the next train or ferry, but the older town of **Ujiji**, 10km away by road, is of greater historical interest as an important 19th-century trading post which still shows Swahili influences you wouldn't expect in this part of the country. Ujiji is where Stanley 'discovered' Livingstone: a plaque marks the spot where the phrase 'Doctor Livingstone, I presume?' was first spoken and an adjoining museum displays some gleefully inept and absurdly captioned paintings of the scene.

Another option out of Kigoma, albeit one that is rarely taken up by backpackers because it charges the highest national park fees in Africa, is **Gombe Stream National Park**, famous for its chimpanzees and the behavioural research initiated there by Jane Goodall in 1960. Chimpanzee tracking in Uganda is altogether simpler and more budget-friendly than in Tanzania, but another option would be to visit **Mahale Mountains National Park**, which protects a 1,613km² knuckle of land jutting into Lake Tanganyika south of Kigoma. Over 700 chimpanzees live in the lowland forest of Mahale, and a habituated 100-strong troop has been studied by Japanese researchers since 1961. Chimps are less readily seen at Mahale than Gombe Stream, but there's far more of a wilderness atmosphere, and the

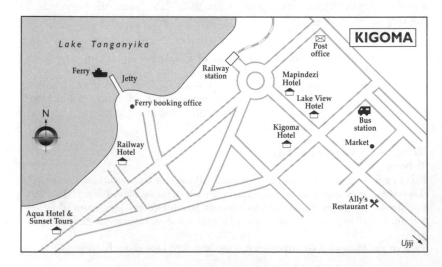

normal park fees are charged. All game viewing in both national parks is on foot, but you may not walk without a guide.

For those who don't have the time or money to visit Gombe or Mahale, the 120ha **Kitwe Point Sanctuary** makes for an easy and interesting day trip out of Kigome. Founded by the Jane Goodall Institute, this sanctuary is home to three orphaned chimpanzees as well as a few antelope, zebra and vervet monkey. It lies in an area of regenerating forest next to the lake, so should also be of great interest to birdwatchers. Visitors are welcome at feeding time (16.00 daily except for Wednesday, Sunday and the first Monday of the month) and can be dropped 20m from the entrance by *matatus* from Kigoma to Katonga.

Access and getting around

The Lake Tanganyika ferry, one of Africa's most memorable public transport rides, qualifies as an attraction in its own right. The boat that does the full run from Bujumbura in Burundi to Mpulungu in Zambia is the legendary MV *Liemba*, transported to Kigoma by rail and assembled there during World War I. Over the last couple of years, the boat has only travelled to Burundi when political conditions are stable. The *Liemba* departs from Kigoma at 16.00 Wednesday and arrives in Mpulungu at 10.00 Friday. It then turns back at 16.00 Friday and arrives in Kigoma at 10.00 Sunday. It leaves Kigoma at 16.00 Sunday and arrives in Bujumbura at 10.00 Monday. The return trip from Bujumbura departs at 16.00 Monday and arrives back in Kigoma at 10.00 Tuesday. A second boat, MV *Umoja*, operates entirely within Tanzania, though when the *Liemba* isn't running it does the full run from Bujumbura to Mpulungu.

Tickets for the MV *Liemba* from Kigoma to Mpumulungu cost US$60 first class, US$50 second class or US$45 third class. Fares includes port tax and non-residents must pay in hard currency (no travellers' cheques accepted). Both boats have a restaurant serving cheap meals and a bar serving beer and soft drinks.

The ferry stops at lake-shore villages such as Mugambo, Ikola, Kalema and Kasanga. If you don't want to go into Zambia, Kasanga is the place to get off, since it has a basic guesthouse and there is transport on to Sumbawanga and then Mbeya (see box *The wild southwest* on pages 286–7). For budget travellers, the only feasible way to get to Mahale Mountains is to radio the park headquarters from Kigoma to arrange to be picked up at Lagosa when the MV *Liemba* stops there on its way to and from Zambia. This can be arranged through Sunset Tours in Kigoma, a helpful set-up next to the Aqua Hotel.

To reach Gombe Stream, 16km north of Kigoma, you need to catch a lake-taxi from a village 3km from Kigoma at roughly 11.00. These take four hours to get to Gombe, and cost US$2. Lake-taxis returning to Kigoma pass Gombe Stream at around 05.45.

Kigoma is accessible by rail from the coast and Lake Victoria (see *The Central Railway* on page 000), but not by any remotely decent road.

Where to stay and eat
Kigoma
Ally's Restaurant Meals for around US$1. Good snack menu and fresh bread and pastries.
Kigoma Hotel Opposite Lake View. Similar in price and standard.
Lake View Hotel Clean, comfortable rooms **A**/**B** sgl/dbl with nets.
Stanley's Restaurant Reasonably priced Western dishes opposite the Lake View Hotel.

Gombe Stream National Park
National Park Camp *Bandas* US$30pp. Kitchen but bring food. Beware thieving baboons.

Mahale Mountains National Park
Kasiha Guest House & Campsite **F**pp. Bring all food.

Kasanga
Mwenya Resthouse Ten minutes from ferry jetty. Clean basic rooms **A**.

The northern safari circuit
ARUSHA AND SURROUNDS
Lying in lush farmland at the base of the 4,565m Mount Meru, **Arusha** is strategically located on the main Nairobi–Dar es Salaam road just south of the Kenya border, for which reason it serves as many backpackers' introduction to Tanzania. The undisputed capital of Tanzania's burgeoning safari industry, Arusha lies less than half a day's drive from the quartet of outstanding game reserves that comprise the northern safari circuit. Despite the fierce competition that surrounds the safari business, Arusha seems a relaxed and pleasant town. Unexpectedly, it is also one of the best places in East Africa to buy Makonde carvings, batiks, Maasai jewellery and other souvenirs (the curio shops are clustered between the clock tower and India Road).

Inevitably, it is lure of the big name reserves – Serengeti, Ngorongoro Crater, Lake Manyara and Tarangire – that dominates most people's minds when they arrive in Arusha. But the surrounding area is not without its more low-key points

CLIMBING MOUNT MERU
Mount Meru is the fifth highest mountain in Africa and just as interesting as Kilimanjaro from a biological point of view. Comparatively few people climb Mount Meru, which means that those who do are more likely to disturb shy forest animals than those who follow the well-worn path through Kilimanjaro's forest zone. In addition to this, big game species such as giraffe and buffalo are frequently seen by hikers on the slopes below the forest zone.

Meru can technically be climbed in two days, but three days is more normal, allowing time to explore Meru Crater and to look at wildlife and plants. Most people arrange a climb through a safari company in Arusha at a going rate of US$150–200 per person for three days inclusive of all park fees. It is also possible to make direct arrangements with park officials at the gate, but this won't be significantly cheaper. Meru is cold at night so you will need adequate clothing. In the rainy season, mountain boots are necessary.

The trail starts at Momella Gate (1,500m), from where it's a three-hour ascent to Miriakamba Hut (2,600m). The trail first passes through woodland, where there is a good chance of seeing large animals such as giraffe, then at an altitude of about 2,000m it enters the forest zone. With an early start, there will be ample time to explore Meru Crater in the afternoon. The second day of the climb consists of a three-hour hike to Saddle Hut (3,600m), passing through forest, then at about 3,000m the moorland zone, similar to the one on Kilimanjaro. It is not unusual to see Kilimanjaro peeking above the clouds from Saddle Hut. If you feel energetic, you can climb Little Meru (3,820m) in the afternoon, a two-hour round trip from Saddle Hut. On the final day, an early start is required to ascend the 4,566m peak, which takes four to five hours. It is then an eight- to nine-hour walk back down the mountain to Momella Gate.

of interest: the eminently visitable and strangely underpublicised **Lake Duluti**, for instance, a beautiful forest-fringed crater lake, rich in bird and monkey life, and situated barely 2km from the busy Moshi road (see also box *Community tourist projects around Arusha*, pages 296–7).

There is also **Arusha National Park**, which despite being the closest reserve to Arusha features on few tourist itineraries. Covering an area of only 137km2, this national park protects a remarkable diversity of habitats including the eastern slopes and peak of Mount Meru, the fully intact 3km-wide and 400m-deep Ngurdoto Crater, and the shallow alkaline Momella Lakes. Leopard, spotted hyena, buffalo, elephant, hippo, giraffe, zebra and a variety of antelope are regularly seen, while black-and-white colobus and blue monkey are common in forests. (See box *Climbing Mount Meru* opposite).

Access and getting around

Arusha is connected to Dar es Salaam, Moshi, Tanga and Nairobi by good tar roads, all of which carry regular public transport. If you're coming from Nairobi, check out *Kenya to Tanzania* on pages 71–2. Buses between Arusha and Moshi run throughout the day and take around two hours. Buses to and from Dar es Salaam and Tanga leave in the early morning only and – assuming you do the sensible thing and pay the extra for an express bus – take about 12 and seven hours respectively.

It's possible to visit Arusha National Park independently and relatively inexpensively, provided that you have a tent. Ask a vehicle heading to Moshi to drop you at the signposted turn-off near Usa River, from where you should be able to hitch along the 23km public road to Momella Lodge (the one place where you can camp without having to pay the park entrance fee). You could even walk from the turn-off to the lodge – locals do it, you'll certainly see some game, and no park fees are charged for using the public road.

Where to stay

Arusha By Night Annexe Best value in its price range. Rooms **F** s/c dbl with hot water.

Arusha National Park Campsites At foot of Tululusia Hill (2km from Momella Gate) and in the forest near Ngurdoto Gate. Drop toilets. Firewood. Near streams. Camping **D** pp. Cannot walk to these campsites unaccompanied.

Arusha Resort Centre Good value and very central. **E/F** s/c rooms with fan, nets and hot water.

Arusha Vision Campsite Central. Camping **A** pp. Tent hire. Basic tasty meals.

Duluti Club Little used but attractively rustic campsite on the Lake Duluti shore. Ablution block. Cafeteria. Camping **B** pp.

Maasai Campsite Tel/fax: 027 2548299; email: reservations@tropicaltrails.com; web: www.info@tropicaltrails.com. Popular and highly recommended site 2km out of town on old Moshi Road. Hot showers, good restaurant, reliable safaris and Kili climbs arranged on-site. Bandas **F** dbl. Camping **B** pp. Tent hire US$3 per night. A taxi here costs US$2.

Mashele Guesthouse Be warned that a lot of travellers are brought here by touts because it's recommended in all the guidebooks and it's one of the few guesthouses where the management allow the touts to hassle travellers on the premises. Facilities include regular bar-room brawls, occasional theft from the rooms, and door-to-door safari salesmen. Eminently avoidable.

Midway Hotel and **Williams Inn** Two quiet, unpretentious hotels, aimed at local businessmen rather than tourists, perched next to each other near the stadium. Rooms in the **D–E** range.

Monje's, **Kitundu** and **Hanang Guesthouses** Among the best of dozens of places dotted around the bus station and stadium, and Monje's in particular has been good value for

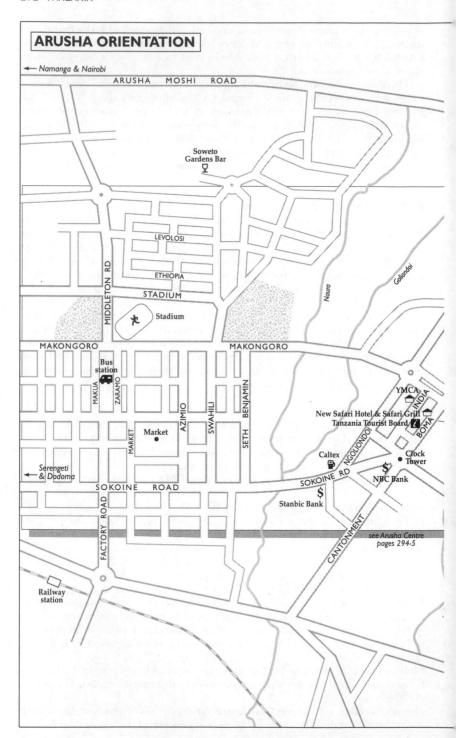

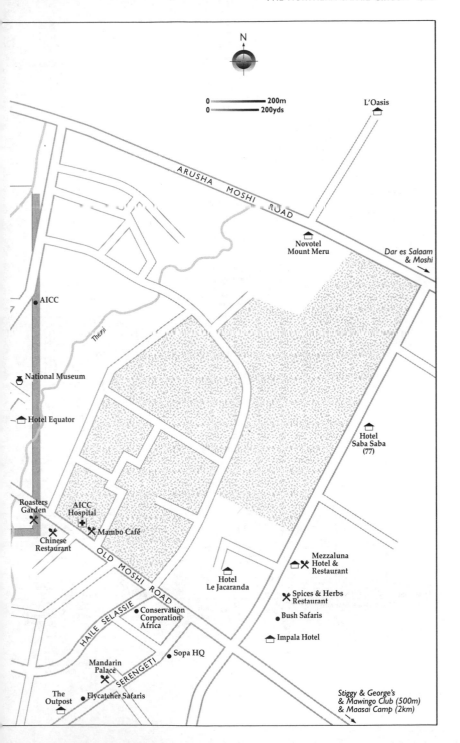

N

0 ———— 200m
0 ———— 200yds

L'Oasis

ARUSHA MOSHI ROAD

Thezi

Novotel
Mount Meru

Dar es Salaam
& Moshi

AICC

National Museum

Hotel Equator

Hotel
Saba Saba
(77)

Roasters
Garden

AICC
Hospital

Chinese
Restaurant

Mambo Café

Hotel
Le Jacaranda

OLD MOSHI ROAD

Mezzaluna
Hotel &
Restaurant

Spices & Herbs
Restaurant

Bush Safaris

Impala Hotel

HAILE SELASSIE

Conservation
Corporation
Africa

Sopa HQ

Mandarin
Palace

SERENGETI

The
Outpost

Flycatcher Safaris

Stiggy & George's
& Mawingo Club (500m)
& Maasai Camp (2km)

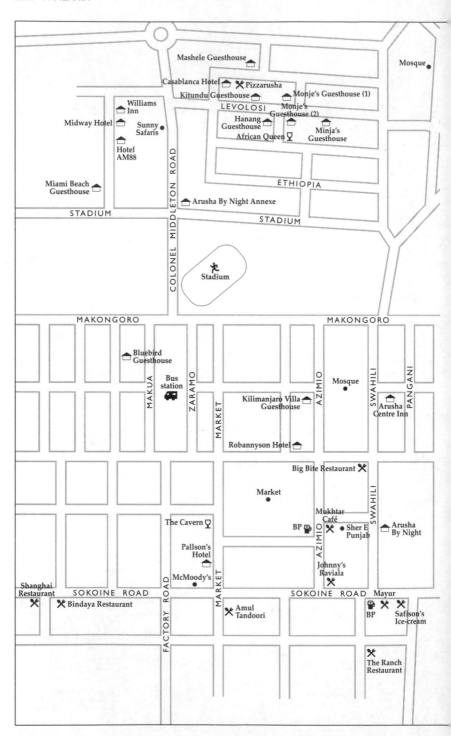

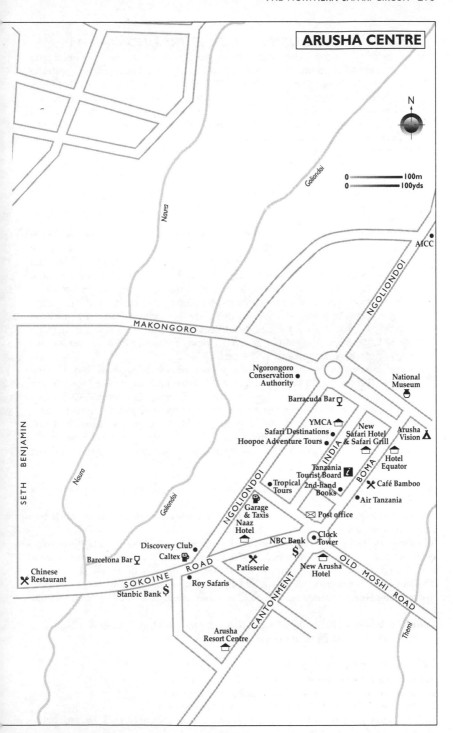

ARUSHA CENTRE

N

0 ——— 100m
0 ——— 100yds

Goliondoi

Naura

AICC

NGOLIONDOI

MAKONGORO

SETH BENJAMIN

Naura

Goliondoi

NGOLIONDOI

Ngorongoro
Conservation ●
Authority

National
Museum

Barracuda Bar ▽

YMCA
Safari Destinations ●   New
Hoopoe Adventure Tours ●   Safari Hotel
                        & Safari Grill

Arusha
Vision ▲

INDIA

BOMA

Hotel
Equator

Tanzania
Tourist Board
● Tropical 2nd-hand
  Tours   Books

● Café Bamboo

● Air Tanzania

⊠ Post office

NGOLIONDOI

Garage
& Taxis
Naaz
Hotel

NBC Bank   ● Clock
              Tower

Discovery Club ●
              Caltex
Barcelona Bar ▽

$

New Arusha
Hotel

OLD MOSHI ROAD

Chinese
✕ Restaurant

SOKOINE   ROAD

Stanbic Bank $

● Roy Safaris

✕
Patisserie

CANTONMENT

Themi

Arusha
Resort Centre

COMMUNITY TOURIST PROJECTS AROUND ARUSHA

An exciting recent development in northern Tanzania has been the establishment of about ten community tourist projects in conjunction with the Netherlands Development Agency (SNV) and Tanzania Tourist Board (TTB). The following are most easily visited as a day or overnight trip out of Arusha.

The traditional **Ng'iresi Village** is set on the slopes of Mount Meru 7km from Arusha town. The programmes here offer insights into the Wa-Arusha culture as well as walks in the surrounding Mount Meru foothills, with highlights being Lekimana Hill (views over the Maasai Steppe and on a clear day to Kilimanjaro) and Kivesi Hill (extinct volcano whose forested slopes support a variety of birds and small mammals). Three different 'modules' are available: half-day (US$16), full-day (US$21), and overnight (US$27), with all prices inclusive of meals, guided activities, and a US$4 donation to the local primary school.

Another cultural tourism programme situated in a village on the fertile footslopes of Mount Meru, **Mulala** lies at an altitude of 1,450m, close to the forested Marisha river, home to variety of birds and primates, and to Mazungu Lake, where it is said that a mazungu was once lured to his death by a demon. Another local place of interest is Mama Anna's dairy, which supplies cheese to several upmarket hotels in Arusha. The tourist programme here is run in conjunction with a women's group which provides guides, snacks and camping facilities. All visitors pay a village development fee of US$3, while a daily guide fee of US$4.50 is charged per group. Camping costs US$1.50 per person per night, and meals cost around US$4 each.

Of particular interest to more adventurous travellers is the **Mkuru Camel Safari**, based at Mkuru at the northern base of Mount Meru near a pyramid-shaped mountain known as 'Ol Doinyo Landaree'. Organised camelback trips range in duration from a short half-day excursion to a week-long camel safari though the dry plains which are rich in birds and still support small numbers of game animals. Other options include a bird walk on the plain, or a hike to the top of Ol Doinyo Landaree. Camel trips cost

years. These guesthouses have nets and showers, rooms in the **B**–**C** range, and forbid touts from hanging about in search of custom.

Naaz Hotel Popular, and a reliable, secure bet, but hardly great value for money at **F** for a very ordinary s/c dbl.

The Outpost The closest thing in Arusha to a backpacker hostel. Homely and highly praised, but it's ten minutes' walk out of town, on Serengeti Road just off the old Moshi Road. Space is limited so call 2548045 before heading out. Good food. Hot showers. Rooms **E/F**.

YMCA Popular but overpriced. Rooms **D/E** using communal cold showers.

Robannyson Hotel Recently renovated and now exceptional value at **C** s/c room with dbl bed.

Tanzanite Hotel Mid-range hotel at Usa River on Moshi road, close to Arusha National Park turn-off. Campsite **C** pp. Restaurant.

Where to eat and drink

Amul Tandoori Restaurant Good Indian food in US$5–7 range.

Barracuda Bar Lively, central drinking hole.

Big Bite Restaurant Excellent, reasonably-priced Indian food.

Café Bamboo Restaurant Filter coffee, fruit juices, home-cooked lunches. Daytime only.

roughly US$25 per person per night all inclusive. Visitors must provide their own tent. If you only visit the camel camp, this costs US$5 per person. For walks and hikes, you will pay a village development fee of US$2.50 per person as well as a guide fee of US$6 per group. A cottage is available for US$15/18 single/double.

Longido, one of the most accessible projects in the region, provides an excellent opportunity to spend time among the Maasai, since it is co-ordinated by a local Maasai who studied abroad as a sociologist before he was paralysed in an accident. Walking modules range from half a day to two days in duration, and include the ascent of Longido mountain (views to Mount Meru and Kilimanjaro on a clear day). On the overnight module you camp overnight in the Kimokouwa Valley, before visiting a dense rainforest which has buffaloes and monkeys. There is a fair amount of large game left in the plains around Longido, notably gerenuk, lesser kudu, giraffe, Thomson's gazelle and black-backed jackal. It is worth trying to be in Longido on Wednesday, when there is a busy cattle market. Longido straddles the main Namanga road roughly 100km from Arusha, so any Namanga-bound vehicle can drop you there. There are guesthouses in town, or you can pitch a tent for US$3 per person. A daily development fee of US7.50 is charged, to go towards the construction of a much-needed cattle dip. In addition to this, a co-ordination fee of US$7.50 per group per visit is charged, as well as a daily guide fee of US$6 per group, and a 'present' of around US$3–6 to any boma that you visit. Meals are available from the local women's group at US$4 (lunch or dinner) or US$2.50 (breakfast).

The TTB office on Boma Road in Arusha stocks informative pamphlets adequate to the needs of most tourists, while those with special interests are invited to contact SNV directly in room 643 of the Serengeti Wing of the AICC (tel/fax: 057 7515; email: tourinfo@habari.co.tz). About the only tour company that promotes visits to these cultural projects is the backpacker-friendly Safari Makers, whose office is near the Clock Tower (tel: 057 6013, email: safarimakers@habari.co.tz).

Chinese Restaurant A once-popular standby that's now well past its sell-by date – mentioned only for the live bands that occasionally play at the attached bar.

Discovery Bar Likeable 'sports bar' set-up with satellite TV and comfy decor.

Everest Chinese Restaurant A short distance from the town centre along the Old Moshi Road, many rate this as the best Chinese eatery in Arusha. Pleasant grounds. Around US$6 for a main course with rice.

Mayur Restaurant Indian vegetarian restaurant. Cheap snacks. Meals around US$7.

Patisserie Fresh bread, rolls and pastry, filter coffee, tasty light meals.

Pizzarusha A personal favourite, atmospheric and friendly, serving good curries, grills and pizzas for around US$3.

Roaster's Garden Chilled beers and grilled meat 200m from the Clock Tower along the Old Moshi Road.

Shamiara Restaurant Pallson's Hotel. Indian dishes US$5–7. Quality justifies slow service.

Soweto Gardens Relaxed and decidedly non-touristy garden bar normally hosting live music at weekends.

The Ranch New South-African owned complex with rooftop bar, pool tables, Western food.

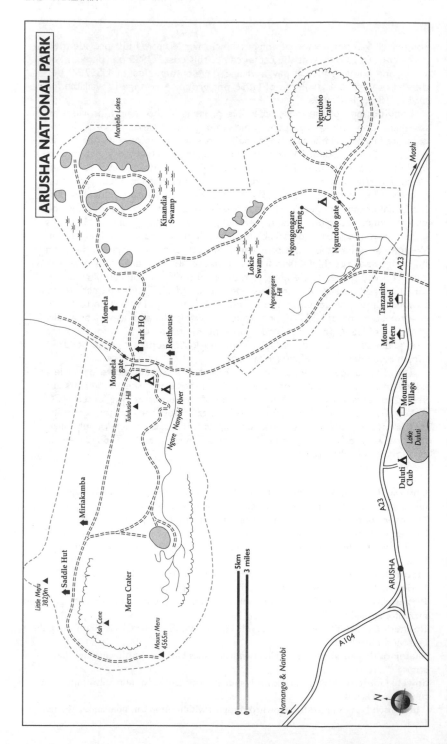

ARUSHA NATIONAL PARK

Momella Lakes

Ngurdoto Crater

Kinandia Swamp

Lokie Swamp

Ngongongare Spring

Ngurdoto gate

Ngongongare Hill

Momela

Park HQ

Resthouse

Momela gate

Tululusia Hill

Ngare Nanyuki River

Miriakamba

Saddle Hut

Little Meru 3820m

Ash Cone

Meru Crater

Mount Meru 4565m

Moshi

A23

Tanzanite Hotel

Mount Meru

Mountain Village

Lake Duluti

Duluti Club

A23

ARUSHA

A104

Namanga & Nairobi

5km
3 miles

N

Practical listings

Books and newspapers Secondhand book stalls are to be found on Boma Road and around the market area. Current international newspapers can be bought from the stalls opposite the Clock Tower.

Communications The post office is on Boma Road facing the clock tower. The telecommunications centre further up Boma Road is a good place to make international calls. For email and internet try the Cybernet Centre at the south end of India Road (US$6 per hour) or the cheaper business centre next to the Bamboo Café on Boma Road. Many safari companies offer free or reduced email rates to customers.

Foreign exchange We've found the NBC facing the Clock Tower to offer the best rate of exchange for travellers' cheques on all recent visits to Arusha. You'll generally get the best rate for US dollars cash at private forex bureaux, but it's worth shopping around. Never change money on the street in Arusha.

Tanzania Tourist Board Not only friendly and helpful, but perhaps the most genuinely well-informed tourist office I've visited in East Africa. It's worth picking up the informative pamphlets about community tourist projects in the Arusha area, and checking the list of registered (and therefore accountable) safari operators, as well as the blacklisted ones.

National Park Headquarters The National Park Headquarters in Arusha's International Conference Centre (PO Box 3134, tel: 027 3471 or 3181) is the cheapest and most reliable place to buy the excellent booklets which are available on all the national parks. An equally good booklet on Ngorongoro can be bought at the Ngorongoro Conservation Authority (PO Box 776, tel: 027 6091, fax: 027 3339) on the corner of Makongoro and Gollondoi roads.

THE MAIN NORTHERN RESERVES

Most safaris out of Arusha kick off with a stop at **Lake Manyara National Park**, a scenic reserve dominated by the shallow alkaline Rift Valley lake after which it is named. In the 1970s, the park was famous for its elephants, immortalised by Ian Douglas-Hamilton in the book *Amongst the Elephants* but vastly reduced in number in recent years due to poaching. Manyara is also notable for being one of the few places in Africa where lions are regularly seen climbing trees, and for supporting a population of giraffes so dark in colour that at a distance they appear melanistic. Other attractions are the lovely fig forest near the entrance gate (great birdwatching and a good place to see blue monkeys), the hippo pools (several dozen hippos can be seen soaking and yawning alongside a myriad of water birds), the hot springs (a good place to see buffaloes and elephants) and the large flocks of flamingoes that frequent Lake Manyara itself.

The village of **Mto wa Mbu** lies near the entrance gate to Lake Manyara and it sees a lot of tourist traffic. When you get out of your vehicle expect to be swarmed around by curio dealers and bear in mind that prices here are double what they would be in Arusha. Spend the night at one of the several lodges and campsites in Mto wa Mbu – *River of Mosquitoes* – and you'll be in no doubt as to why it acquired this name.

From Mto wa Mbu, a spectacular and bumpy ascent of the Rift Valley escarpment followed by a ride through the rich agricultural land surrounding the small town of Karatu brings you to the base of the extinct volcano in which lies the **Ngorongoro Crater**. The largest intact caldera in the world, and one of the most spectacular sights in Africa, this 260km^2, 600m-deep crater has been the subject of countless television documentaries and its status as a wildlife sanctuary barely needs stating. With the notable exception of impala and giraffe, just about every species of African plains mammal lives on the crater floor in abundance, and it's perfectly possible to see elephant, buffalo, lion and black rhino in the course of one

MOUNT HANANG

This 3,417m-high extinct volcano, the third-highest mountain in Tanzania, lies at the base of the Rift Valley escarpment to the west of Babati town on the A104 between Arusha and Dodoma. Hanang isn't protected within a national park, which means that it is relatively cheap to climb, and the peak affords excellent views over a part of the Rift Valley floor dotted with volcanic craters, as well as to the remote Lake Balangida.

The Hanang and Babati area supports several ethnic groups who have retained a largely traditional way of life. The Barbaig, for instance, are semi-nomadic pastoralists with cultural affiliations to the Maasai. The Iraqw, by contrast, claim to have migrated to the area from the Middle East, a tradition backed up by Arabic intonations in their language. Also of interest is Lake Babati, which lies within easy walking distance of Babati town centre, and supports a reasonable number of hippos as well as many water birds.

There is nothing preventing travellers from exploring this area independently, though I have yet to hear from anybody who has done so. A few buses daily connect Arusha to Babati, and at least one bus daily covers the three- to four-hour run from Babati along the B143 to the village of Katesh at the base of Mount Hanang. Several hotels and guesthouses can be found in Babati, and at least one guesthouse exists in Katesh. The mountain can be climbed in a day, taking roughly six hours each way. A knowledgable local guide is essential and can be arranged in Katesh for a negotiable fee.

The alternative is to contact Kahembe's Enterprises, a local company which has made a commendable effort to open up this little-known area to adventurous tourists. Based in Babati, Kahembe's arranges a four-day Hanang hike using the relatively easy Gendabi route for US$300 per person all-inclusive, and a three-day trip along the steeper Katesh route for US$240 per person. Other itineraries range from a three-day Barbaig walking trip to an eight-day hike that visits several local *bomas* and skirts the game-rich verges of Lake Manyara and Tarangire National Parks. The 16-day 'African rural life adventure' includes overnight stays in villages, an ascent of Mount Hanang, and game walks around Lake Burungi on the edge of Manyara National Park. I've heard no bad reports about the packages put together by Mr Kahembe; they are not luxurious, but they are well-organised and informative, and offer an unforgettable glimpse into a way of life that has vanished in many other parts of Africa. Interested readers are advised to contact Mr Kahenge in advance through his Arusha agent J M Tours (tel: 027 6773; fax: 027 2548801) or write directly to PO Box 366 Babati.

game drive. Large herds of grazers, mainly zebra and wildebeest, are resident on the crater floor, while the forested crater rim is the place to see bushbuck, leopard and a variety of monkeys.

Also lying within the Ngorongoro Conservation Area, **Olduvai Gorge** achieved a degree of fame in 1959 when Mary and Louis Leakey uncovered a 1.75-million-year-old *australopithecus* jawbone which provided the first conclusive evidence that hominids had existed for over a million years and that they had evolved in Africa. There is an interesting site museum at the gorge (though the important findings all reside in the National Museum in Dar es Salaam) and it's a good place to see dry country birds.

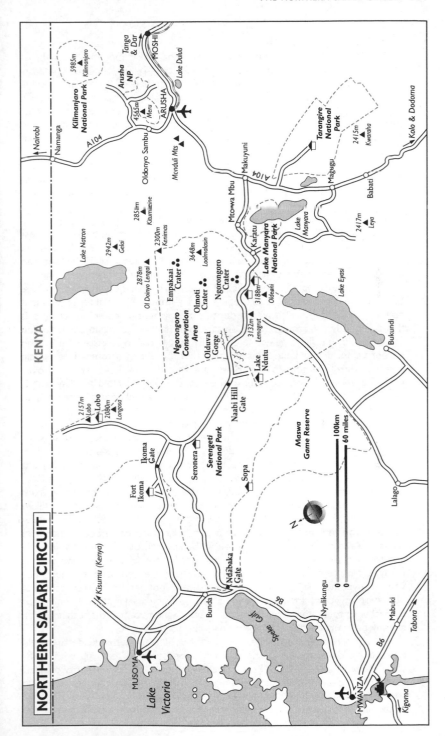

NORTHERN SAFARI CIRCUIT

ORGANISING A SAFARI

At least 100 safari companies operate out of Arusha. The competition is cut-throat and a high proportion of budget travellers are caught by unscrupulous operators who cut costs by using inadequate vehicles and inexperienced drivers, and provide substandard meals and services. At the time of writing, the cheapest rate for a camping safari with a reputable company is around US$80 per person per day for a group of four people. You can safely assume that any company offering a safari at a lower rate than the cheapest companies recommended below is simply not worth getting involved with.

To an extent, backpackers have themselves to blame for the way in which the budget safari industry in Arusha has developed. All the safari companies know that a substantial proportion of travellers will go on the cheapest safari that they are offered, thereby practically inviting small companies to do whatever must be done to undercut the rates offered by their established rivals. It is convenient to tag these companies rip-off artists; it would be more honest to recognise that they are providing the service that many travellers want, namely low-cost, high-risk safaris. If you take the cheapest safari that you can find, it is only reasonable to accept your own complicity if things go wrong.

While some companies are guilty of little more than incompetence, others do cross the line into plain crookedness, and it's not unheard of for fly-by-night operators to simply vanish with a deposit or payment. A common scenario is that somebody will arrange to go on safari with a 'new' company, only to find that they are actually going with a company they know to be disreputable. And it's normal for disreputable firms to show their potential customers the vehicle in which they'll be going on safari, except that the spanking new Landrover you'll be shown bears no resemblance to the battered old vehicle that is eventually used. The long and short of it is that you should not take anything at face value. And bear in mind that even if you realise you are dealing with crooks, there's no chance of a refund once you've paid.

The first and simplest advice I can give you is to allow a couple of days for shopping around, since it only takes a bit of common sense and a few conversations around town to pick out the dodgy operators. You certainly want to take time to check out the list of blacklisted companies in the tourist office, bearing in mind that being blacklisted doesn't prevent a company from operating under a new name. Remember, too, that many safari touts are skilled manipulators, and they will often try to pressure you into a decision by making you feel you've a one-off chance at a particularly attractive deal. When you arrive in Arusha by bus, you'll be greeted by several touts offering to find you accommodation and, while it does no harm to let one of them find you a room (it's in their interest to find you a good deal, and the onus is on the hotel not you to give them a commission), you should not let it create a sense of obligation on your part when it comes to organising a safari. If you don't want to deal with touts, they'll quickly lose interest when you tell them that you've already been on safari or that you don't want to go on one.

A group of two people will typically pay about 50% more per head than would four people doing the same trip, so it's a good idea to team up with other travellers to organise a safari. Bear in mind, however, that the majority of safari companies use 4x4 vehicles such as Landrovers: these get very cramped for group sizes of greater than four, and in any case the saving per head between four, five or six people isn't that significant. It's advisable to try to form a group before you look for a safari, or the touts will try to pressure you into going with an existing group, which means that you'll be using a company not of your choice.

Although there are a great many safari companies to choose from in Arusha (and new ones spring up and vanish all the time), it's more-or-less the case that those which can be recommended without reservation lie at the middle to upper end of the price spectrum. Two well-established exceptions to this rule are **Sunny Safaris** (Opp Golden Rose Hotel; tel: 027 7145; fax: 027 2548094; email: sunny@arusha.com) and **Roy Safaris** (Off Sokoine Road; tel: 027 2115; fax: 027 2548892; email: roysafaris@intafrica.com; web: www.intafrica.com/roysafaris), both of which have been offering reasonably priced and reliable camping safaris for longer than a decade. I've long regarded Sunny to be the benchmark for camping safari prices out of Arusha, and even though they'll be more open to negotiation when business is quiet, travellers on a strict budget can be pretty sure that anybody offering a significantly cheaper price will be dodgy. Roy Safaris tend to charge a few dollars more per day than Sunny, but their rates are less affected by season and their reputation is spotless (most overland trucks with foreign-registered vehicles use them). Roy also offers amazing deals on lodge safaris during the rainy season (when camping isn't much fun), while their recently opened subsidiary **Safari Destinations** specialises in Kilimanjaro climbs and other treks in northern Tanzania.

It's difficult to recommend newer companies with the absolute confidence one can a more established outfit, but we liked the feel of **Safari Makers** (office on India Street near the Clock Tower; tel/fax: 0812 400114 or 400112; email: safarimakers@habari.co.tz; web: www.whiteyellow.com/safarimakers). This American-Tanzanian venture, established in 1998, is one of the few registered companies that's prepared to slug it out with the pirate outfits and flycatchers for the backpacker trade; it offers competitively-priced budget camping safaris as well as more unusual trips to the various community tourist projects in the Arusha area.

If you're looking for something a bit more upmarket, for instance using the campsites within national parks rather than those at Kidatu or Mto wa Mbu, and providing extras such as portable showers at campsites, a recommended first port of call is **Hoopoe Adventure Tours** (India Street; tel: 027 7011; fax: 027 2548226; email: hoopoe@form-net.com). Hoopoe recently merged with **Tropical Tours** (India Street; tel: 027 2548353; fax: 027 2548907), a well-established German-run company which specialises in walking and mixed walking and driving tours on the edge of the Serengeti and other more remote parts of northern Tanzania. Not to be confused with this, **Tropical Trails** is a well-established and highly regarded lower- to mid-range safari and trekking company run out of Maasai Campsite (tel/fax: 027 2548299; email: reservations@tropicaltrails.com; web: www.info@tropicaltrails.com).

As for your itinerary, it is worth pointing out that a good part of your first and last days on safari will be spent on the road, so that you effectively get better value for money on a longer safari. Three to six days is the normal duration. A typical five- or six-day trip will take in Ngorongoro, Serengeti, Manyara and Tarangire, while a typical three-day trip takes in all these reserves except for the Serengeti. The distances between reserves are considerable, however, and the roads are poor, so you will have a more relaxed trip and probably see more game if you visit fewer reserves. On a five-day safari, I would drop either the Serengeti or Tarangire. To visit all four reserves, six days is just about adequate, and seven days would be better.

If there is one game reserve better known than Ngorongoro, it has to be the vast **Serengeti National Park**, in my opinion the finest game reserve anywhere in Africa. Covering an area of almost 15,000km², and lying at the heart of an unspoilt ecosystem more than double that in size, Serengeti National Park consists largely of open grassland broken by isolated granite koppies and patches of acacia woodland. The Serengeti ecosystem supports some of the most numerous mammal populations left anywhere on the planet: an estimated 1,300,000 wildebeest, 250,000 Thomson's gazelle, 200,000 zebra, 70,000 impala, 50,000 topi and 30,000 Grant's gazelle. These in turn feed a plethora of large predators. Close encounters with lions occur almost on an hourly basis in the Serengeti, while the Seronera Valley is one of the best places in Africa for leopards, and less exalted predators such as spotted hyena, cheetah, golden and black-backed jackals and bat-eared foxes are abundant. A well-publicised feature of the reserve is the annual wildebeest migration, which follows a fairly predictable pattern: first a dispersal into the southern part of the Serengeti during the rainy season (December to May), when it is normal to see herds of 10,000 animals; then an 800km migration to the western Serengeti and Maasai Mara in Kenya (sometime between April and June); and then the return trip to the southern plains in October to November.

The most obscure of northern Tanzania's large reserves, **Tarangire National Park** is, like the Serengeti, part of a wider ecosystem within which there is a great deal of migratory movement. In direct contrast to the Serengeti, however, Tarangire comes into its own during the dry season between June and November, when it is likely to provide the most rewarding game viewing in the region. A striking feature of the park is the profusion of palms and baobab trees, particularly along the Tarangire River, and it supports an impressive population of elephants as well as the localised fringe-eared oryx and gerenuk antelope. It's a good place to see three endemic birds: the ashy starling, rufous-tailed weaver and black-collared lovebird.

Access and getting around

The most realistic way to explore this area is with an organised safari (see box *Organising a safari* on pages 302–3). Trying to hitch into the reserves makes little sense, since there are few private vehicles and most safari companies forbid their drivers to pick up hitchhikers. Even if you do get a lift, you may find yourself stuck for a few days at a campsite seeing little game but having to pay the park entrance fee.

If you can't afford an organised safari, your best option for the Serengeti itself is one of the buses or Land Rovers that travel directly between Arusha and Mwanza skirting Ngorongoro Crater before passing through the Serengeti for about 100km. This trip will allow you a good look at the scenery and you should see plenty of game, but be prepared to pay US$50 in entrance fees.

Regular buses between Arusha and Karatu pass through Mto wa Mbu, where you can easily organise a day safari into Lake Manyara National Park. The Ngorongoro Conservation Authority runs a staff bus twice daily between Arusha and the crater rim, which travellers are free to use. If you're prepared to pay the entrance fee then a night on the Ngorongoro Crater rim will be a worthwhile experience in itself, but hitching any further in would remain problematic, and for the price of driving into the crater in a Conservation Authority Vehicle you might as well pay to do a proper safari out of Arusha.

Where to stay
Mto wa Mbu

Holiday Fig Camp Popular but overrated. Fair restaurant. Swimming pool normally empty. The place to arrange day trips to Manyara. Rooms **E** pp. Cramped campsite **C** pp.

Twiga Campsite & Lodge Rooms **F** s/c dbl. Large grassy campsite **B** pp. Restaurant.
Jambo Campsite Adequate rooms **C** dbl with net. Camping **B** pp.
Camp Vision Lodge Recommended. Bright little rooms **B** dbl with nets.

Kidatu
Safari Junction Spacious grounds 1km from town. Showers. Restaurant and bar. Log
cabins **C** pp. Camping **B** pp.

Ngorongoro Conservation Area
Simba Campsite Lovely situation on crater rim. Chilly at night. Basic facilities. **F** pp.

Serengeti National Park
Seronera Campsites 5km from Seronera Lodge. Long-drop toilets. **F** pp.

Tarangire National Park
Kigongoni Campsite About 5km outside park. Rooms **D** pp. Camping **B** pp. Ask a
vehicle heading to Dodoma to drop you at the junction with the turn-off to Tarangire,
from where it's 2km to the campsite. There is also a **B** guesthouse at the junction itself,
and several basic campsites within the park costing **F** pp.

From Moshi to Dar es Salaam
MOSHI AND KILIMANJARO
Situated at the heart of a major coffee-growing region, **Moshi** is an attractive if
intrinsically unremarkable small town, salvaged from anonymity by one of the
most imposing backdrops imaginable. Moshi lies at the base of Kilimanjaro; at
dusk or dawn, when the peaks most often emerge from their customary blanket of
cloud, they form a sight as stirring and memorable as any in Africa. Despite the
teasing proximity of snow-capped Kilimanjaro, Moshi is not the cool highland
settlement you might expect. Instead, lying at an altitude of below 1,000m, Moshi
has a surprisingly humid, sticky climate, reminiscent of the coast.

Lying only 8km south of the main gate to Kilimanjaro National Park, **Marangu**
has an alpine feel, with a babbling mountain stream running alongside the main
road. Even if you are not climbing the mountain, Marangu would be a pleasant
place to spend a few days as a base for day walks – if the high price of
accommodation doesn't put you off.

Mount Kilimanjaro is, at 5,895m (19,340ft), the highest mountain in
Africa. It is also the highest free-standing mountain in the world, rising 5,000m
above the surrounding plains, and it is the only one of its size that can be
climbed with comparative ease by non-mountaineers. The area of 756km² lying
above the 2,700m contour has been a national park since 1977, and parts of the
lower slopes are protected in forest reserves. In geological terms, Kilimanjaro is
a new mountain, formed by volcanic activity about one million years ago. The
first written reference to Kilimanjaro occurs in Ptolemy's 4th-century
Geography, but its existence was only confirmed to European geographers when
a German missionary called Johan Rebmann visited it in 1848. Rebmann's
observations were derided by European experts who thought it ludicrous to
claim there was snow so near the equator, and the mountain's existence was
only accepted in 1861 when it was surveyed by an experienced geologist, Von
der Decken. Local legends suggest that no local person ever successfully
climbed Kilimanjaro before Hans Meyer and Ludwig Purstscheller reached its
summit in 1889.

CLIMBING KILIMANJARO

The ascent of Kilimanjaro requires no mountaineering skills, since it is basically a long uphill slog that takes four or five days, followed by a more rapid descent. That said it is important not to underestimate the mountain. Adequate preparations are a prerequisite, as is an awareness of the potentially fatal health risks attached to being at altitudes of over 4,000m (see *Mountain health and safety*, pages 53–4). For many, however, the most daunting factor about climbing Kilimanjaro is the cost. The national park entrance, hut and rescue fees along with the obligatory guide and porter fees work out at a minimum of US$380 for a climb; most reliable operators will add well in excess of US$100 to this for food, equipment and services; and you're probably looking at another US$30–50 in tips.

The only sensible way to go about climbing Kilimanjaro is with a reputable tour company, which will offer a comprehensive package inclusive of a registered guide, two porters per person, all park fees, food and transport to and from the gate. If you are in a group, you must ensure that at least one porter is a registered guide, or the entire party will have to turn back if one person has to. The normal length for a climb is five days, but a sixth day is recommended in order to acclimatise at Horombo Hut, which will increase the likelihood of making the peak. Reliable climbs can be arranged through the following companies in Moshi: **Shah Tours** (Mawenzi Road; tel: 027 252370; fax: 027 251449); **Keys Hotel** (tel: 027 252250; fax: 027 250073; email: keys@intafrica.com); **Trans-Kibo** (YMCA; tel: 027 252017; fax: 027 254219; email: transkibo@habari.co.tz); and **Zara International** (Ground floor, Moshi Hotel; tel: 027 254240; fax: 027 253105; email: zara@form-net.com). In all cases, you are looking at around US$550–650 for a five-day climb on the popular Marangu Route, and an extra payment of US$100 for a sixth day. Climbs along other, more obscure routes generally cost around US$800.

In Marangu, the **Marangu** and **Kibo Hotels** (see *Where to stay*, page 310) also arrange very reliable Kilimanjaro climbs, and both have decades of experience to back them up, though their standard packages are a bit pricey for most backpackers. The Marangu Hotel does, however, put together what they call 'hard way' packages for self-caterers, probably the cheapest reliable way to climb the mountain. Finally, it's possible to arrange Kili climbs through any Arusha safari operator, though with a few exceptions – notably **Tropical Tours**, **Tropical Trails** and **Safari Destinations** – they will subcontract to a Marangu or Moshi operator, which pushes up the price.

The alternative to using one of the above companies is to take your chances with a small operator or private individual who approaches you in the street. These guys will offer climbs for around $100 cheaper than established operators, but the risks are greater and they have little accountability. A crucial point when comparing this situation to the similar one that surrounds arranging a safari out of Arusha is that you're not merely talking about losing a day through breakdown or being left out of pocket. On Kilimanjaro, you could die. I've heard several stories of climbers being supplied with inadequate equipment and food, even of people being abandoned by their guides mid-climb. If you make arrangements of this sort, the least you should do is verify that your guide is registered; he should have a small wallet-like document to prove this.

Two climatic factors must be considered when preparing to climb Kilimanjaro. The obvious one is the cold. Bring plenty of warm clothes, a windproof jacket, a pair of gloves, a balaclava, a warm sleeping bag and an insulation mat. During the rainy season, a rain jacket and rain trousers will come in useful. A less obvious factor is the sun, which is fierce at high altitudes. Bring sunglasses and sunscreen. Other essentials are water bottles, a first-aid kit, and solid shoes or preferably boots. Most of these items can be hired in Moshi or at the park gate, or from the company you arrange to climb with.

The Marangu Route

The vast majority of people who climb Kilimanjaro use the Marangu Route, because it is by far the cheapest and has the best facilities.

Day one: Marangu to Mandara Hut On an organised climb you will be dropped at the park entrance gate 8km past Marangu. The four-hour walk to Mandara passes through the forest zone, where there is a high chance of rain in the afternoon, so set off early. Foot traffic is heavy along this stretch, and the shy forest animals, though present, are rarely seen by hikers. Mandara hut (2,750m) is an attractive collection of buildings with room for 200 people.

Day two: Mandara Hut to Horombo Hut You continue through forest for a short time before reaching the heather and moorland zone at roughly 3,000m. There are good views of the peaks and of Moshi. The walk takes up to six hours. Horombo Hut (3,720m), which sleeps up to 120 people, lies in a valley surrounded by the giant lobelia and groundsel that is characteristic of this semi-alpine zone. If you do a six-day hike, you will spend a day at Horombo to acclimatise.

Day three: Horombo Hut to Kibo Hut The vegetation thins out as you enter the desert-like alpine zone at around 4,000m, and when you cross the saddle Kibo peak comes into view. This seven-hour walk should be done slowly: many people start to feel the effects of altitude. Kibo Hut (4,703m) is a stone construction which sleeps up to 120 people. Water must be carried there from a stream above Horombo. You may find it difficult to sleep at this altitude and, as you will have to rise at around 01.00 the next morning, many people feel it is better not to bother trying. This semi-desert zone receives an annual rainfall of under 250mm; the ground often freezes at night, but ground temperatures soar to above 30°C by day. Few plants other than lichens and grasses survive in these conditions.

Days four and five: Kibo Hut to the summit to Marangu The penultimate day starts at around 01.00, since it is easier to climb the scree slope to Gillman's Point on the crater rim when it is frozen, and an early start for the six-hour hike improves your chances of reaching the summit in time for sunrise. From Gillman's Point it is a further two-hour round trip along the crater's edge to Uhuru Peak, the highest point in Africa. From the summit it is downhill all the way to Horombo Hut where you will spend your last night on the mountain before descending to Marangu the next day.

Maps and further reading

A map is not generally considered necessary for the Marangu Route, but it is for any other. The *Walker's Guide and Map to Kilimanjaro* by Mark Savage (African Mountain Guides, 32 Sea Mill Crescent, Worthing, UK, tel: 01903 37565) is popular and reliable, and has useful information printed on the back. The 60-page national parks handbook, *Kilimanjaro National Park*, has detailed route descriptions and background information. It is available from the National Park office in Arusha for US$2.50.

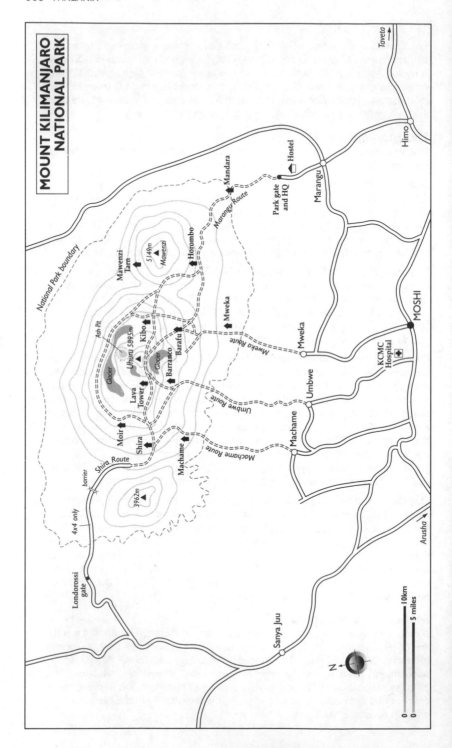

MOUNT KILIMANJARO NATIONAL PARK

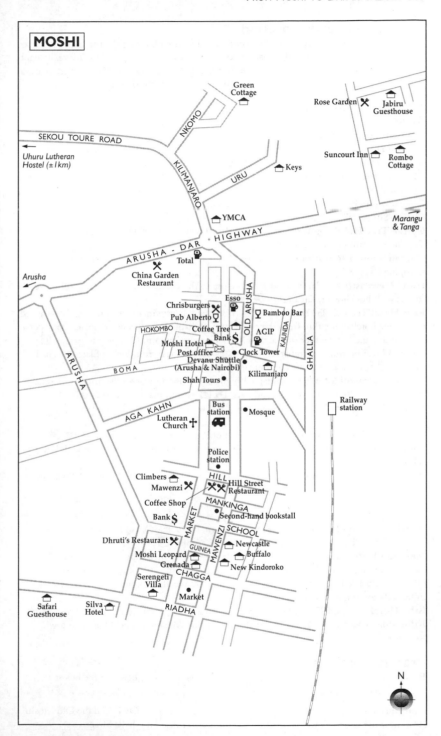

MOSHI

Green Cottage

Rose Garden ✗ Jabiru Guesthouse

NKOMO

KILIMANJARO

SEKOU TOURE ROAD

Uhuru Lutheran Hostel (±1km)

URU

Keys

Suncourt Inn   Rombo Cottage

Marangu & Tanga

YMCA

HIGHWAY

ARUSHA - DAR

Arusha

Total

China Garden Restaurant

Esso

OLD ARUSHA

Chrisburgers ✗   Bamboo Bar

Pub Alberto

KAUNDA

Coffee Tree

Bank $ AGIP

HOKOMBO

Moshi Hotel

Post office

Clock Tower

GHALLA

Devanu Shuttle
(Arusha & Nairobi)

ARUSHA

BOMA   Kilimanjaro

Shah Tours

Railway station

Bus station

AGA KAHN   Mosque

Lutheran Church ✝

Police station

Climbers

Mawenzi ✗   HILL   Hill Street Restaurant ✗✗

Coffee Shop   MANKINGA

Bank $ Second-hand bookstall

SCHOOL

Dhruti's Restaurant ✗   Newcastle

GUINEA

Moshi Leopard   Buffalo

MAWENZI

Grenada   New Kindoroko

CHAGGA

Serengeti Villa

Safari Guesthouse   Silva Hotel   Market

RIADHA

N

Access and getting around

There are no longer any trains between Moshi and Dar es Salaam. Express buses between Dar es Salaam and Moshi take eight to ten hours; several leave in each direction every morning. There are regular buses between Moshi and Tanga. Buses from Moshi to Marangu or Arusha leave regularly throughout the day.

Where to stay and eat

Moshi

Bar Alfredo Sports bar set-up near the Clock Tower.

Buffalo Hotel Popular with volunteers and probably the best budget option in Moshi. Bar and restaurant. Clean rooms with fans **C/D** using communal hot showers.

China Garden Restaurant CCM Building on Dar es Salaam road near YMCA. Decent Chinese food at reasonable prices.

Chrisburgers Eggburgers, samosas and excellent fruit juice.

Coffee Shop Hill Street. Good place for breakfast with filter coffee.

Coffee Tree Hotel Central Spacious but run-down rooms **C/D** s/c sgl/dbl with nets. Top floor restaurant has a commanding view of Kilimanjaro but uninteresting food.

Golden Shower Restaurant 2km along Marangu Road. Best food in town around US$5. Camping **B** pp.

Hotel Newcastle Similar in standard and close to the Buffalo and New Kinderoko. S/c rooms with hot shower, fan and net **C/D**.

Keys Hotel Tel: 027 252250; fax: 027 250073; email: keys@intafrica.com. Highly regarded mid-range hotel about 1km from the city centre. Reliable Kili climbs arranged, hikers get a free night at the hotel either side of the climb. Good restaurant. Camping in garden **C** pp.

Moshi Hotel Nominally upmarket hotel that's become very run down of late. Not bad value at **D/E** for rooms using communal showers.

New Kinderoko Hotel Has maintained high standards and reasonable prices. Good bar and restaurant. Rooms all have fan and nets: **C/D** (communal showers) or **D** pp s/c.

Rombo Cottage Inn Clean and quite popular, but not very central. Good, inexpensive meals. Rooms **C** s/c dbl.

Serengeti Villa Guesthouse About the best of the cheapies near the market. **B/C**.

Suncourt Inn Next to Rombo Cottage. Great value. Clean rooms **C** s/c dbl with hot showers.

YMCA Popular and secure but overpriced for what it is. Rooms **D/E** sgl/dbl. Swimming pool.

Marangu

Babylon Bar and Hotel Cheapest place in town, but still astonishingly overpriced at US$25/45 for a basic s/c sgl/dbl with hot water. Camping **C** pp.

Marangu Hotel Tel: 027 251307; fax: 027 250639; email: marangu@africaonline.co.ke. Family-run midrange hotel. The rooms, though good value at US$50, are outside the range of most backpackers. Their 'hard way' Kili climbs are worth looking at for those who don't mind self-catering on the mountain.

Kibo Hotel Tel/fax: 027 251308. Camping in attractive grounds of upmarket hotel. **D** pp.

Kilimanjaro Mountain Lodge Immediately outside Marangu Gate, 8km from town. Rooms **F** pp.

Practical listings

Books There's a good secondhand bookstall on Mawenzi Street between the bus station and the Hotel Newcastle.

Communications Internet and email facilities are available at EOLTZ on the Old Moshi Road near the Clock Tower and at KIT Technology House on Ghalla Street.

Foreign exchange Banks and forex bureaux generally offer significantly lower rates than in Arusha or Dar es Salaam.

Further information The inexpensive *Moshi Guide* compiled and sold by the people who run the Coffee Shop on Hill Street would be a valuable investment for those spending time in Moshi.

SOUTH TO DAR ES SALAAM

Most travellers heading south from Moshi jump on an express bus directly to Dar es Salaam, but the area between these towns offers several rewarding excursions, notably in the Usambara Mountains, a large range that lies to the east of the main road and north of Tanga.

The main town in the western Usambara, **Lushoto**, has a somewhat time-warped atmosphere. The main street has the east of an Alpine village, while the side roads and market, filled with colourfully-dressed Shambaa women, are pure Africa. The surrounding vegetation shows similar contradictions, with neat rows of exotic pines subverted by papaya trees and interspersed with patches of indigenous forest. The area around Lushoto is riddled with footpaths and winding roads – it's good walking country, with the two-to-three-hour round trip to Irente, where there is a stunning view over the vast Maasai Steppe, a popular option. The Usambara Mountains Tourism Project next to the Green Valley Restaurant can organise guided walks to Irente and elsewhere for US$4 per day for the guide plus US$4 per person. Profits are used for development projects, and use of their guides is recommended due to a number of recent thefts by private guides.

Several other towns in the Usambara are worth a visit. Lying about halfway between the main Moshi–Tanga road and Lushoto, **Soni** is notable for its attractive waterfall and pleasant colonial-era hotel. Deeper into the Usambara, and reached via a series of terrifying hairpin bends, **Mtae** village is perched on a ridge with a drop of several hundred metres on either side and stunning views across to Kenya and on a clear day Kilimanjaro. The larger settlement of **Mlalo** lies about 30km past Lushoto along a road that skirts Magambo Peak (2,230m) and passes through an extensive patch of indigenous forest. Mlalo has an insular, almost other-worldly atmosphere, and its two-storey mud houses with intricately-carved wooden balconies create the feeling of a misplaced Mediterranean kingdom which seems to show both German and Arab influences.

In 1902 the Germans established an agricultural research station and botanical garden at **Amani**, on the forested eastern slopes of the Usambara. Amani today has the genteel appearance of an English country village transplanted to the African jungle. Scheduled to become a nature reserve, the forest around Amani is a good place to see black-and-white colobus and blue monkey, as well as several localised birds such as the green-headed oriole. The East Usambara Catchment Forest Project, established in 1991 and funded by FINNIDA, has been charged with implementing a conservation plan to protect these forests, the source of fresh water to 200,000 people. The development of Amani for ecotourism is a definite priority of this project: nine trails have already been demarcated, ranging in length from 3km to 10km, and leaflets with trail descriptions are in preparation. Plans include the restoration of the German stationmaster's house as an information centre, and the training of guides – visit the office in Tanga for further details (tel/ fax: 027 26443820).

Tanga is the third largest town in the country, a relaxed, friendly place with a German-era town centre that's in an atmospheric state of decay. About 8km north of Tanga along the Mombasa road, you can take a guided tour through the vast limestone Amboni Caves, believed by locals to be inhabited by a fertility god. Also

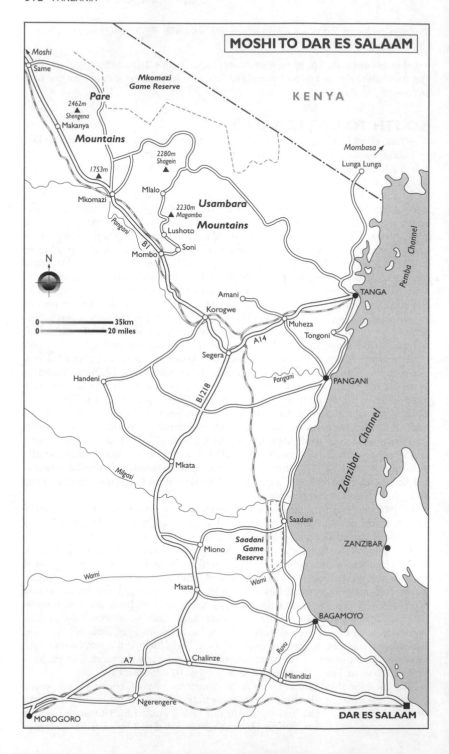

MOSHI TO DAR ES SALAAM

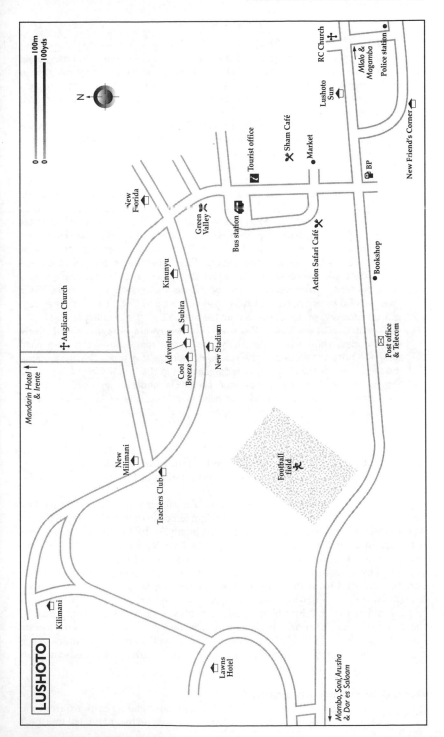

THE PARE MOUNTAINS

Situated between Kilimanjaro and the Usambara, the remote and little-visited North Pare and South Pare Mountains have recently been opened up to adventurous travellers through a pair of community tourist projects implemented with the help of the SNV and TTB (see box *Community tourist projects around Arusha* pages 296–7).

The main base for exploring the **North Pare** is **Usangi**, an attractive town ringed by 11 peaks, and particularly lively on market days (Monday and Thursday). Usangi lies roughly 25km east of the B1, where it is connected to the junction town of Mwanga by a few buses daily. A three-bedroom resthouse at Lomwe Secondary School puts up travellers for US$3 per person, and the teachers will find you a room for a similar fee (the headmaster is the co-ordinator of the tourism project). From the school, you can organise a number of excursions to nearby points of interest. A good half-day walk is the Mangatu Tour, which takes you through the Mbale Forest to a viewpoint towards nearby Kilimanjaro and Lake Jipe on the Kenya border. The half-day Goma Tour visits a set of caves which were dug by the Pare people in the 19th century as a hiding place from the slave raiders, and can be extended to a full-day walk to the forested upper slopes of Mount Kinderoko, home to a variety of birds and monkeys. Overnight hiking trails can also be arranged. All walks hikes cost around US$9 per group per day, with an additional village development fee of US$2.50 per person per day.

Tourist activities in **South Pare** are centred around **Mbaga**, an attractively well-wooded, semi-urban, electricity-free sprawl that follows the main road along the northern slopes of the range. Remote as it is today, Mbaga became the site of one of the earliest Lutheran missions in the interior in 1902, and the original church built by its founder Jakob Dannholz is an oddly Bavarian apparition in these remote African hills. In Mbaga, the Hilltop Tona Lodge consists of a few self-contained cottages in a jungle setting with great views over

of interest, 20km south of Tanga along the Pangani road, the Tongoni Ruins are what's left of a Shirazi town that peaked in the fourteenth and fifteenth centuries, and is now noted for having the largest concentration of historical tombs on the East African coast.

The port of **Pangani** on the mouth of the Pangani river has been described by one historian as 'the Bagamoyo of the first eighteen centuries of the Christian era'. The modern town centre was founded by Omani Arabs in around 1820 as the main terminus for slave caravans heading to the Lake Victoria region. Before that, the town was situated about 4km upstream and known as Muhembo. Pangani has been cited by some historians as the most probable location of Rhapta, the trading port first referred to in the *Periplus of the Ancient Sea*, largely because Ptolemy's Geography mentions that two snow-capped peaks lay some 25 days upriver from it. Pangani has a sleepy Swahili atmosphere, with several buildings dating back to the slave trade, and the nearby beach is very attractive. Also of interest is the forest-lined Pangani River, which offers good birding as well as the opportunity to see crocodiles and other game, though you'll have to make private arrangements with a boat captain to get up the river.

Access and getting around

All the places mentioned above are reached along roads heading eastward from the main road between Moshi and Dar es Salaam. Tanga is the main regional transport the Mkomazi Plains and a natural swimming pool in the river. Rates start at **B** per person for a roon, while camping costs **A** per tent and the basic restaurant serves meals in the US$1.50–4.50 bracket.

A number of guided activities can be arranged out of the Hilltop Tona Lodge at a cost of US$3 per group per day (plus a village development fee of US$3 per walk). These include a visit to a respected traditional healer (who also happens to be a Seventh Day Adventist, so don't bother visiting on Saturday), and hikes to the caves where the Pare hid from slave raiders in the 1860s and a rock where thousands of children were sacrificed before the 1930s. For natural history enthusiasts, the day walk to Ronzi Dam through patches of rainforest and montane moorland is recommended (there's an excellent cleared campsite at the dam) along with the walk to the legendary 'Red Reservoir'. Overnight hikes are also available.

The springboard for visits to Mbaga, **Same** is a dusty small town straddling the B1 between Moshi and Mombo, and of interest for its scenic location at the foot of the mountains as well as its traditional Maasai flavour. One daily bus and a couple of matatus run along the 35km road between Same and Mbaga daily, generally leaving Mbaga before 07.00 and embarking on the return trip from Same at around 11.00. Should you need to spend a night in Same, the Kambeni Guesthouse is an excellent local lodging, with standard rooms for **A**/**B** and s/c doubles in the **C** range. If it's full, try the similarly-priced Amani Lutheran Centre or Tumaine Guesthouse. The helpful tourist centre at the Sasa Kazi Hotel (which despite its name is only a restaurant) is the best place to ask for current advice about lifts to Mbaga, or about anything else for that matter.

Buses from Same continue for another 15km past Mbaga to **Gonja**, another scenic town set on the slopes of the South Pare and known locally for it large hospital. Should you be in the mood for a bit of exploration, cheap rooms are available at the Vuje Guesthouse.

hub, connected to both Moshi and Dar es Salaam by regular seven-hour express bus trips. From Tanga, a few buses daily travel to Pangani, but there is practically no transport from Pangani further south along the coast to Bagamoyo. A motorboat service connects Tanga to Pemba and Zanzibar every other day – contact the Bandorini Hotel for details.

To get to the western Usambara, your best bet is to catch an express bus between Moshi and Tanga, hop off at Mombo, and then pick up a local bus or *matatu* to Soni or Lushoto (there are several guesthouses in Mombo should you need to spend the night). Direct buses connect Lushoto to both Moshi and Tanga, but they are agonisingly slow. Lushoto is connected to Mlalo by two buses a day, both of which leave Lushoto at 14.00 and Mlalo at 07.00, a two-hour trip in either direction. Buses to Mtae also leave Lushoto in the early afternoon and take around two hours, and they return the next morning at 05.30.

The springboard for visiting Amani in the eastern Usambara is Muheza on the Moshi road 40km from Tanga. A daily bus to Amani leaves from Muheza at 14.00, taking around three hours, and it starts the return trip at 05.00 the next morning. The last 7km of the dirt road to Amani follows a spectacular series of hairpin bends through the forest, so I doubt that the bus would run after heavy rain. There are a few guesthouses in Muheza should you need to spend the night.

Where to stay and eat
Lushoto
Action Safari Café Cheap local food. In bus station.
Green Valley Hotel Sporadically serves meals. Chilled beers and *Saturday Night Fever* decor more reliable attractions.
Kilimani Guesthouse Popular travellers' hangout. Recently renovated. Good value at **C** dbl.
Lawns Hotel Colonial era hotel with a certain faded charm (emphasis on the faded) but reasonable value at **E** dbl. Good restaurant. Mountain bike hire and horseback excursions.
Lushoto Sun Hotel Central, comfortable and reasonably priced at **D** s/c dbl with hot showers. Meals around US$3.
Magamba Forest Reserve Only 15km from Lushoto off the Mlalo Road, Magamba supports several types of monkey and is one of the best places to seek out localised forest birds such as the Usambara akalat and weaver. Entrance fee US$4 per day. Camping **A** pp. The best way to get here is by taxi, which can be organised affordably through the UMTP office in Lushoto.
Muller's Mountain Lodge Tel: Lushoto 134. Atmospheric 1930s residence fringing Magamba Forest Reserve (see above). Despite the charge (**F** pp), a lot of backpackers stay here and reports are uniformly glowing. To organise a lift from Lushoto, the BP garage will know when the owner is next heading to town..
New Friends Corner Hotel Decent s/c rooms at bottom end of **C** range.
Teachers Club Superior cheapie. **A**/**B** sgl/dbl.

Soni
Kimulabe Hotel Accommodating family-run lodge about 1km before Soni coming from Mombo. Clean rooms **C** dbl. Bar and evening meals to order. Cold running showers and buckets of hot water on request. Better value than anything in Lushoto.
Soni Falls Hotel Clean, friendly colonial-era building overlooking the waterfall. Rooms **E** s/c dbl. Camping **A** dbl. Good food.

Mlalo
Afilex Hotel Best of a few **A** lodgings.

Mtae
Mwivano and **Kuna Manena Guest Houses** OK **A** lodges.

Amani
Amani Club and **IUCN Rest House**. Rooms **F** pp (full board). Camping **B** pp.

Tanga
Bandorini Hotel Once *the* budget hangout in Tanga, this closed in 1999, with no indication as to whether it will re-open. Rooms used to cost **B**/**C** with net and fan.
Food Palace Wonderful Indian restaurant, with evening barbecue and good meat and vegetarian dishes in the US$3–5 range. Closes over Ramadan.
Hotel Kolo Prieto Comfortable s/c rooms with fan and hot shower **D**/**E** Air-conditioned rooms **E**/**F**.
Inn by the Sea Beachfront location compensates for run-down state of this once-popular resort. S/c dbls **D** with fan or **E** with air conditioning. The nominally upmarket Mkongwe Hotel next door serves cold drinks and decent meals.
King Fish Restaurant The attraction of this reasonably priced fish-and-chip restaurant will depend on your tolerance for the overwhelming odour of greasy fried fish.
Patwas Restaurant A perennial favourite for samosas, snacks and passion-fruit juice. The owner is a good source of local travel information.

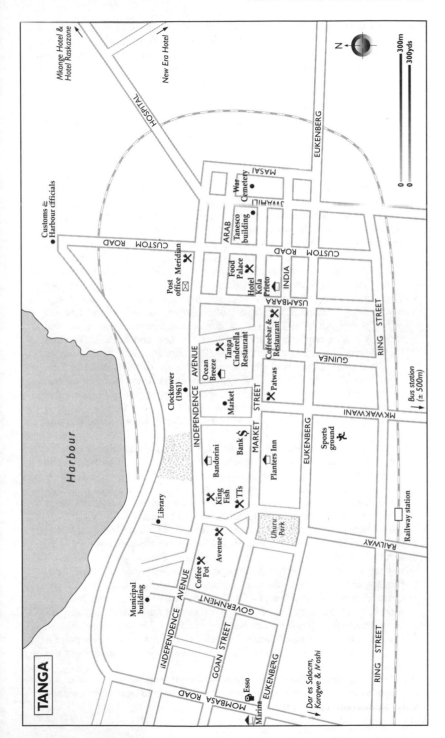

Ocean Breeze Hotel Central high-rise hotel. Exceptional value for money. Clean, comfortable s/c rooms with nets, fans, large beds and hot showers **C** dbl.
Planters Inn Early 20th-century building with wide creaky balconies and vast airy rooms. Fans. Unreliable showers. Run-down but atmospheric and affordable. Rooms **B** dbl.

MKOMAZI AND SADANI

Either of these little-known game reserves could be an interesting diversion for adventurous backpackers – and because neither is a national park, walking is permitted. However, the recent hike in fees from US$3 daily to US$20 makes them both less attractive prospects than they used to be.

Mkomazi Game Reserve, a southern extension of Kenya's Tsavo National Park, is practically undeveloped for tourism. Subject to much human pressure over the last 20 years, Mkomazi doesn't offer game viewing comparable with northern Tanzania's finest, but this is compensated for by the wild scenery and near certainty of not seeing another tourist. A recent Royal Geographical Society study has shown that most large mammal species found in Tsavo are resident in Mkomazi or at least regular visitors. Facilities are limited to a basic campsite about 2km from Zange Gate and another site about 20km from Zange overlooking Dindera Dam. The northeastern portion of the reserve near Zange Gate is very hilly – tough walking but great scenery – and there is a very real chance of encountering lion and buffalo. Nicholas McWilliam, who was attached to the RGS survey, says that the way to go about organising a walking trip would be to foot or hitch the 5km from **Same** on the Moshi–Tanga road to Zange Gate, where you can arrange with the warden to hire an armed ranger/guide. To see a fair range of large mammals, you need a few days in the reserve, so bring camping gear and enough food. (For more details about Same see box *The Pare Mountains*, pages 314–15.)

Bisected by the Pangani-Bagamoyo road, **Sadani Game Reserve** is the last place in East Africa where elephants can still be seen bathing in the Indian Ocean. As with Mkomazi, animal numbers have been depleted by poaching, but lion, leopard, elephant, zebra, roan antelope, giraffe, oryx and buffalo are still resident. Sadani is the nearest game reserve to Dar es Salaam, so you might reasonably expect it to be bustling with tourists. On the contrary, it is one of the least visited and most underpublicised reserves in Tanzania – a shame, since it would otherwise form part of an alluring coastal route between Tanga and Dar es Salaam. Getting to Sadani will require some initiative, at least if my fruitless attempts from both Pangani and Bagamoyo mean anything. A lucky hitch isn't out of the question, and you might even find a dhow. By road, the most reliable route is probably to catch a bus to Mioni (10km east of the Moshi road) and ask around there for a pick-up truck heading to Sadani. There is a government resthouse in the village of Sadani, a backwater which was at one point a serious rival to Bagamoyo for the dominant power on this stretch of the coast.

Visits to either reserve are recommended only to those who are prepared to take things as they come – and I'd love to hear from anybody who does get to one of them.

Pangani
New River View Lodge Basic but clean lodgings on the riverfront 300m from the bus stop. Running water and electricity. B/C.
Pangadeco Beach Hotel Run-down rooms compensated for by great beachfront location and bar with fridge. B dbl.

DAR ES SALAAM
Tanzania's largest city and most important port, Dar es Salaam was recently replaced as capital by Dodoma, but it seems likely to remain at the commercial and social heart of the country for the foreseeable future. Dar es Salaam draws extreme reactions from travellers, most of whom either love it or hate it. It is my favourite East African city, with all the hustle and bustle of Nairobi yet none of that city's underlying aggression.

Dar es Salaam's distinctive character comes from the cultural mix of its people and buildings, and a sloth-inducing coastal humidity that permeates every aspect of day-to-day life. By coastal standards, it is a modern city, dating to 1866 when Sultan Majid of Zanzibar built a palace there and named it Dar es Salaam (Haven of Peace). The town only acquired any real significance, however, when a German camp was established there in 1887. Four years later the fledgling city was made the capital of German East Africa.

Several relics of Dar es Salaam's early days survive. The **Old Boma** on the corner of Morogoro Road and Sokoine Drive is a rather austere whitewashed monolith, built by Sultan Majid as a hotel in 1867, and easily recognised by its inscribed Zanzibari door. Other early buildings include the **Hospital** on Ocean Road (1897), the nearby **State House** (restored in 1922 following war damage), the Bavarian-style **Lutheran Church** on the corner of Sokoine Drive and Maktaba Road (1898), the rather Gothic looking **St Joseph's Cathedral** (1897–1902) and the **City Hall** on Sokoine Road (opposite the Old Boma).

Dar es Salaam's **National Museum** is one of the best in Africa, housing some of the world's most important hominid fossils as well as exhibits dating from the era of European exploration and German occupation and an outstanding selection of artefacts found during excavations at Kilwa. Also of interest, about 10km along the Bagamoyo Road, the **Village Museum** consists of life-size replicas of huts built in architectural styles from all over Tanzania, while nearby **Mwenge Market** is a traditional Makonde carving community and one of the best places in East Africa to buy Makonde sculptures.

Oyster Bay is the closest swimming beach to the city centre. It is a reasonably attractive spot and very popular at weekends. The Oyster Bay Hotel, which overlooks the beach, is a pleasant place to have a drink. Another pleasant escape from the city is to take one of the cheap and regular ferries from Kivukoni to **Kigamboni**. After disembarking from the ferry, turn left into the road, and after about 2km you will come back to the coast at an attractive beach where there are a couple of bars and guesthouses.

Further afield, **Kunduchi Beach** is the main beach resort near Dar es Salaam. Aside from the obvious beach activities, the Kunduchi Ruins near the Kunduchi Beach Hotel consists of a 16th-century mosque and 18th-century graveyard set amongst a grove of baobab trees. About 100km north of Dar es Salaam, the historical town of **Bagamoyo** (see box *Bagamoyo* on pages 320–1) is definitely worth visiting.

Access and getting around
Dar es Salaam is the country's major transport hub. Several boats leave from the jetty off Sokoine Avenue daily for Zanzibar and there are also occasional boats to

Pemba, Mtwara, Tanga and Mombasa in Kenya. The main station, also on Sokoine Drive, is the terminus and booking office for trains to and from Moshi, Mwanza and Kigoma. The booking office for trains to southern destinations such as Ifakara and Mbeya is at the Tazara Station, 5km from the city centre and easily reached by bus from the Post Office on Maktaba Road.

Buses connect Dar es Salaam to most other towns in Tanzania. Buses to Arusha and Moshi mostly leave from the large bus station on the corner of Morogoro Road and Libya Street, as do buses to coastal destinations south of Kilwa. Buses to Tanga, Iringa, Mbeya and Songea generally leave from Mnazi Mmoja on UWT Street; buses to Bagamoyo, Morogoro and Kilwa leave from the backstreets around Kariakoo Market; and buses to western destinations such as Dodoma, Tabora and Mwanza leave from Msimbazi Street. The simplest way to find the bus you want is to hire a taxi: cab drivers are familiar with the system, they generally speak English, and they'll help cut through the waffle to make sure you get a seat on the next bus to leave. For long hauls, it's worth booking a ticket a day in advance, which not only guarantees you a seat but also allows you to choose one.

For getting around Dar es Salaam, there are taxis all over the place: the standard price for a ride within the city centre is about US$2, but you will have to bargain. The city bus system is good and most buses leave from in front of the post office on Maktaba Road – but do watch out for pickpockets. To get to Kunduchi Beach, the shuttle bus that leaves from the New Africa Hotel at 09.00, 12.00, 14.00 and 17.00 on weekdays, and every other hour between 09.00 and 17.00 over weekends, will take you right to the hotel you want. There are ordinary buses to Kunduchi village, but thefts and muggings are commonplace along the road between the village and the hotels.

The cheapest transport to the international airport, 13km from the city centre, is the Air Tanzania shuttle. This goes to the airport every other hour from 08.00 to

BAGAMOYO

The small port of Bagamoyo, some 70km to the north of Dar es Salaam, was the most important mainland terminus of the 19th-century slave trade (the name Bagamoyo is variously translated as meaning 'to lose hope' or 'where the heart lays down its burden'). Bagamoyo was visited at some point by just about every European explorer of note, including Burton, Speke, Grant, Stanley and Livingstone. In 1888, it became the capital of German East Africa, though it was abandoned when Germany realised its harbour was too shallow for modern ships.

Bagamoyo today has a fascinating museum-like quality. The old town centre is small, but several of the buildings have carved Zanzibar-style doors. The impressive former State House now serves as a customs office, and you can still see the double-storey building from which, in 1889, the Emin Pasha had a near-fatal fall during the party that followed his rescue from modern-day Uganda by Henry Stanley. Nearby, the so-called 'Hanging Tree' is where Germany's colonial masters hanged those Africans who were unfortunate enough to annoy them. The building which is now the police station used to be where slaves were held prior to being shipped to Zanzibar. On the beachfront, the former slave market is now used by fishmongers.

The Holy Ghost Mission, 3km out of town, was established in 1868 as a result of Livingstone's publicising the horrors of the slave trade. Fittingly, the mission church, the oldest on the East African mainland, held Livingstone's

16.00, leaving from in front of the New Africa Hotel, and it returns every other hour from 09.00 to 17.00. There is a taxi rank at the airport.

Where to stay

There are plenty of hotels in the city centre, but the cheaper places have a reputation for filling up early in the day, something that seems to be less of a problem today than it was a few years ago. Still, it is fortunate that budget accommodation is reasonably well clustered, with one group near the Morogoro Road Bus Station, another within a block or two of the Clock Tower, and the YMCA and YWCA a block apart on Maktaba Street. My experience is that the very cheap places around Morogoro Road and the Clock Tower still tend to fill up by early afternoon, but places in the **D** range upwards have always had rooms available on our recent visits to Dar.

Maktaba Road

Luther House Near Lutheran Church. Once very popular and booked up days in advance, but these days it's trading on its reputation and is rarely full. Run-down rooms seem very overpriced at **E/F** (using communal showers) and over **F** s/c.
YMCA Clean and secure. Rooms **C/D** dbl with net but no fan. Canteen.
YWCA Popular with couples and women. Clean rooms **C/D** sgl/dbl (fan, net). S/c flats **E**. Canteen.

Morogoro Road area

Econo Lodge Tel: 022 2116048; fax: 022 2116053; email: stepin@raha.com. Falls at upper end of backpacker price range but smart enough to be used by tour operators. Good place to book into should you be arriving in Dar after dark. **E/F** s/c sgl/dbl (or US$33 a/c dbl).
Jambo Inn Tel: 022 2114293; fax: 022 2113149. A perennial favourite. Not the cheapest but good value, central and reliable. The ground floor Indian restaurant is excellent value too. S/c rooms with fans and reliable hot water **D/E**.

preserved body after it had been carried by his porters all the way from Lake Bangweulu in Zambia. The small museum in the mission has fascinating displays on every aspect of Bagamoyo's past.

Also of interest are the ruins of the Shirazi town of Kaole, which lie on the beach less than 5km from Bagamoyo. In medieval times, Kaole was the largest trading centre between Kilwa and Mombasa. The main ruins date from the 13th century and include what is thought to be the oldest mosque on the East African mainland.

Regular buses to Bagamoyo leave Dar es Salaam from outside Kariakoo Market. The road to Bagamoyo used to be outrageously bad, and the trip took four hours, but the surface was completely re-graded in August 1999, cutting an hour off the trip. Expect the bus to take around two hours if, as expected, the road has been surfaced by the end of 2000. Another potentially interesting possibility are organised boat transfers from Bagamoyo to Zanzibar, following the route used by the slave traders in the 19th century. These are likely to start up in late 2000 and will be cheaper and quicker than boats from Zanzibar to Dar.

Arguably the best place to stay is the **Bagamoyo Beach Resort**, which in addition to more upmarket accommodation has a few basic beach bungalows in the **C/D** range and allows camping for **A** per person. Tel: 022 2440083; fax: 022 2116238. Another popular option is the **Badeco Beach Hotel** on the beachfront, where rooms with net cost **D** dbl. If that's too expensive, the **Alpha Motel** near the bus station has very basic but clean rooms in the **A** range.

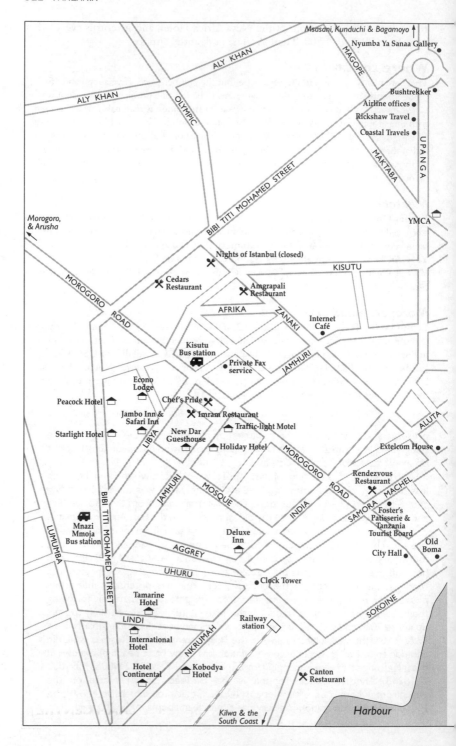

Msasani, Kunduchi & Bagamoyo ↑

Nyumba Ya Sanaa Gallery ●

ALY KHAN

MAGOPE

Bushtrekker ●
Airline offices ●
Rickshaw Travel ●
Coastal Travels ●

ALY KHAN

OLYMPIC

MAKTABA

UPANGA

BIBI TITI MOHAMED STREET

YMCA

Morogoro,
& Arusha
←

KISUTU

Nights of Istanbul (closed) ✕

Cedars ✕
Restaurant

Amgrapali ✕
Restaurant

AFRIKA

ZANAKI

Internet
Café ●

MOROGORO ROAD

JAMHURI

Kisutu
Bus station 🚌

Private Fax ●
service

Econo
Lodge 🏠

Chef's Pride ✕

ALUTA

Peacock Hotel 🏠

Imram Restaurant ✕

Jambo Inn & 🏠
Safari Inn

Traffic-light Motel 🏠

New Dar 🏠
Guesthouse

Extelcom House ●

Starlight Hotel 🏠

LIBYA

Holiday Hotel 🏠

MOROGORO ROAD

JAMHURI

Rendezvous ✕
Restaurant

MOSQUE

INDIA

SAMORA

MACHEL

Mnazi 🚌
Mmoja
Bus station

Foster's
Patisserie &
Tanzania
Tourist Board

LUMUMBA

AGGREY

Deluxe 🏠
Inn

City Hall ●

Old
Boma ●

BIBI TITI MOHAMED STREET

UHURU

Clock Tower ●

Tamarine 🏠
Hotel

SOKOINE

LINDI

Railway 🏠
station

International 🏠
Hotel

NKRUMAH

Hotel 🏠
Continental

Kobodya 🏠
Hotel

Canton ✕
Restaurant

Kilwa & the
South Coast ↓

Harbour

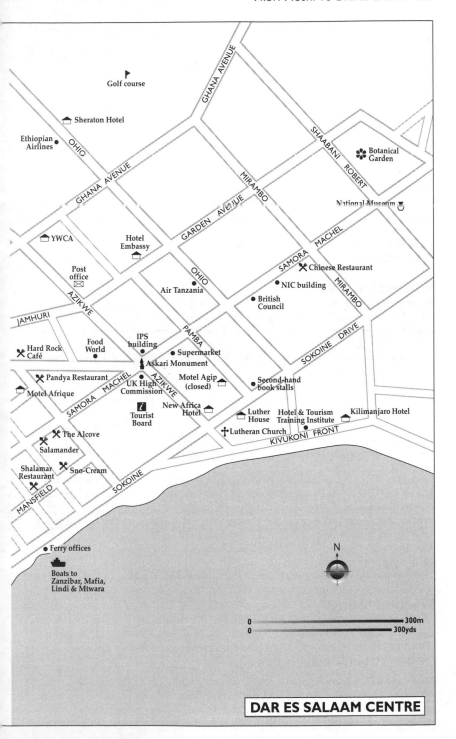

Golf course

Sheraton Hotel

GHANA AVENUE

SHAABANI ROBERT

Ethiopian
Airlines

OHIO

Botanical
Garden

GHANA AVENUE

MIRAMBO

GARDEN AVENUE

National Museum

YWCA

Hotel
Embassy

MACHEL

Post
office

OHIO

SAMORA

Chinese Restaurant

Air Tanzania

NIC building

MIRAMBO

AZIKWE

British
Council

JAMHURI

IPS
building

PAMBA

SOKOINE DRIVE

Hard Rock
Café

Food
World

Supermarket

Askari Monument

Pandya Restaurant

SAMORA MACHEL

AZIKWE

UK High
Commission

Motel Agip
(closed)

Second-hand
book stalls

Motel Afrique

New Africa
Hotel

Tourist
Board

Luther
House

Hotel & Tourism
Training Institute

Kilimanjaro Hotel

The Alcove

Lutheran Church

KIVUKONI FRONT

Salamander

Shalamar
Restaurant

Sno-Cream

SOKOINE

MANSFIELD

N

Ferry offices

Boats to
Zanzibar, Mafia,
Lindi & Mtwara

| 0 | 300m |
| 0 | 300yds |

DAR ES SALAAM CENTRE

New Dar Guesthouse and Holidays Popular cheapies with run-down rooms and erratic water supply. **C** dbl.
Safari Hotel Tel: 022 2119104; fax: 022 2116500. Similar in price and feel to the Jambo Inn, and literally around the corner. Also has air-conditioned rooms. **F** dbl.

Clock Tower area
Hotel Continental Multi-storey hotel with mid-range aspirations but no running water and general aura of decaying tropical torpor. Probably hasn't been full in a decade – a good place to head for if you arrive late in the day. Rooms **F** s/c dbl with fan.
Deluxe Inn, International and **Tamarine Hotels** Adequate. **C** dbl with net and fan.
Kobodya Hotel Clean, mid-range rooms **D** s/c dbl with hot water, fan and net. Good value.

Out of town
Salvation Army Mgulani Hostel Tel: 022 2851467; email: bamartin@maf.org. Little-used by travellers but rated highly by many volunteers. About 5km out of town along the Kilwa Road. Facilities include swimming pool and restaurant. Clean s/c rooms with net and fan **C/D**.
Rungwe Oceanic Hotel Comfortable mid-range rooms **F** dbl with fan, net, hot water. Camping **B** pp. Bar, restaurant and disco. Popular with overland trucks.

Where to eat and drink
Amgrapoli Restaurant Most backpackers staying in the Morogoro Road area end up eating here at some point. Basic but good Indian restaurant. Very cheap.
Chef's Pride Inexpensive and wide selection of mostly Western dishes, around the corner from the Jambo Inn.
Empire Restaurant Good Indian food above the Empire Cinema on Maktaba St. Should work out at US$10 per head.
Foster's Coffee, pastries, snacks and ice-cream on Samora Machel Av.
Hard Rock Café As you'd expect: international menu, chilled beers, pool tables and slot machines in air-conditioned trendy atmosphere.
Hong Kong Restaurant Regarded to serve the best Chinese food in the city centre.
Hotel and Tourism Training Institute Despite the unpromising name, this spot on Kivukoni Front (close to the Lutheran Cathedral) is one of earthiest drinking holes in the city centre.
Jambo Inn We rate the ground-floor restaurant to serve the best-value Indian food in Dar. The evening barbecue on the veranda is especially recommended. Great juices but no alcohol.
Pandya Restaurant Vegetarian Indian buffet dinner good value at US$3.25.
Salamander Restaurant Best lunches in town. Fish and chips, spaghetti bolognaise US$3.
Sno-Cream Parlour Best sundaes in the country around US$3.
The Alcove Well-established and classy Indian restaurant. Also serves Chinese dishes. Main course with rice around US$10.
The Cedars Lebanese restaurant. Filled pita bread around $1.50 each.

Practical listings
Airlines Air France (246653/4); Air Tanzania (246643); British Airways (244651/4); EgyptAir (246806); Ethiopian Airlines (220868); Kenya Airways (246875/7); KLM (246497); Lufthansa (246813/5); Sabena (250476); Swissair (246816); Uganda Airlines (246818/9); Zambia Airways (246662).

Books and newspapers A good range of secondhand novels can be bargained for at stalls around the Agip and New Africa Hotel. The British Council library and reading room has up-to-date British newspapers and magazines. You can sometimes buy recent European and American newspapers at the stalls on Samora Avenue near the Salamander Restaurant.

Embassies Belgium (246194); Britain (229601/5); Burundi (246307); Canada (246000); Congo (246350); Denmark (246318); France (246329); Germany (246334); Ireland (246852); Kenya (246362); Malawi (246673); Mozambique (246487); Netherlands (246391); Rwanda (246502); Uganda (246256); USA (266010); Zambia (246383).

Foreign exchange Numerous private forex bureaux on Samora Avenue and Zanaki Street keep normal shopping hours. Rates vary considerably, so shop around before you change large sums. Rickshaw Travel on UWT Street (PO Box 1889, tel: 229125/35079, fax: 246655) is the Tanzanian representative of American Express, and it can provide financial services such as emergency cashing of cheques and foreign exchange. Open from 08.00 to 17.00 Monday to Saturday.

Maps The Department of Lands and Surveys (on Kivukoni Front about 100m past the Kilimanjaro Hotel) stocks 1:50,000 maps of off-the-beaten-track hiking areas such as the Poroto, Usambara, Udzungwa and Mbizi Mountains. The accurate *Dar es Salaam City Map & Guide* is available at most tourist class hotels.

Tour operators Most tour operators in Dar es Salaam specialise in visits to the southern reserves, which are out of the price range of most backpackers. Coastal Travels (tel: 237479; fax: 246045) is a highly regarded company which serves as the main booking agent for many lodges and hotels in southern and central Tanzania, as well as for charter flights to Mafia and Zanzibar.

Tourist information The Tanzania Tourist Board (tel: 022 2131555; email: md@ttb.ud.or.tz) recently relocated its information office to the ground floor of Matasalamat Building on Samora Avenue. The helpful staff is knowledgeable about Dar and Zanzibar, but unreliable on more far-flung parts of the country. For current information about nightlife, restaurants and other activities an and around Dar, pick up a free copy of the bi-monthly *Dar es Salaam Guide* from any upmarket hotel or the office of the publisher, East Africa Movies Ltd, in Mavuno House on Azikiwe Street (tel: 022 2111529; email: eam@raha.com).

Internet and email There's a good internet café on Zanaki Street near the junction with Libya Street. Internet use costs US$3 per hour or US$57.50 per month.

Zanzibar
ZANZIBAR TOWN
Zanzibar is a separate state within Tanzania, consisting of Zanzibar and Pemba Islands as well as several smaller islets. Most people arrive at **Zanzibar Town**, the old quarter of which, usually called the Stone Town, is a fascinating maze of narrow streets and alleyways which lead the visitor past numerous old houses and mosques, ornate palaces, and shops and bazaars. The area outside the Stone Town is rather less attractive, dominated by ugly apartment blocks that were built by East German engineers as part of an international aid scheme.

You can spend many idle hours wandering through the fascinating labyrinth of narrow streets and alleyways of the old **Stone Town**, much of which dates from the 19th-century slave boom. Arab houses have plain outer walls and large front doors leading to an inner courtyard, while Indian houses have a more open façade and large balconies decorated with railings and balustrades. A striking feature of many houses is the brass-studded doors and elaborately carved frames. The size of a door and intricacy of its design was an indication of the owner's wealth and status. The use of studs probably originated in Persia or India, where they helped prevent doors being knocked down by war-elephants. In Zanzibar, studs were purely decorative.

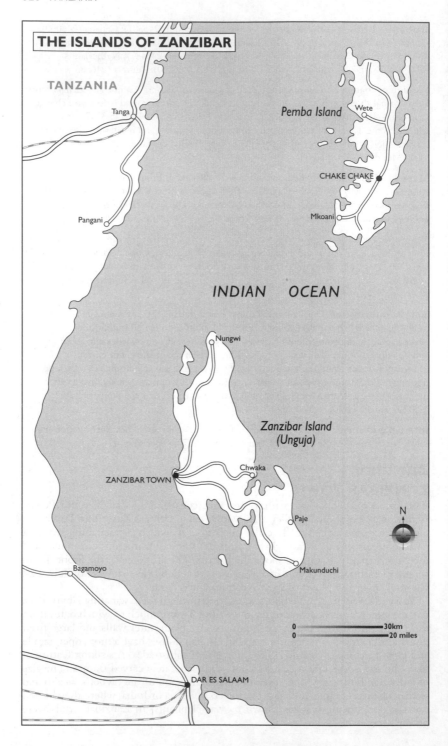

THE ISLANDS OF ZANZIBAR

TANZANIA

Tanga

Pangani

Pemba Island Wete

CHAKE CHAKE

Mkoani

INDIAN OCEAN

Nungwi

Zanzibar Island (Unguja)

Chwaka

ZANZIBAR TOWN

Paje

Bagamoyo

Makunduchi

N

0 ————— 30km
0 ————— 20 miles

DAR ES SALAAM

There are several historical buildings in the stone town. The **People's Palace** is the large white building with castellated battlements overlooking the sea at the west of the old town. Built in the late 1890s, it was the official residence of the Sultan of Zanzibar from 1911 until the 1964 revolution, after which it was renamed the People's Palace. It is now a government office and closed to the public. Photos are not allowed.

Next to the palace, the multi-storey **House of Wonders** is surrounded by tiers of impressive balconies and topped by a clock tower. Built as a ceremonial palace in 1883, it was the first building in Zanzibar to have electric lights, for which reason it became known as Beit el Ajaib – House of Wonders. You may not enter the building, but can see the huge carved doors and two old bronze cannons with Portuguese inscriptions from the outside.

The **Arab Fort** next to the House of Wonders is a large brown building with castellated battlements. It was built by the Omani in the early 18th century, and you can still reach the top of the battlements and go into some of the towers.

Tippu Tip's House, near the Africa House Hotel, was the residence of an influential 19th-century slave trader who knew the African interior well and helped explorers such as Livingstone and Stanley with supplies and route-planning. It is privately owned and closed to visitors, but the huge carved front door can be seen from the street.

The **Anglican Cathedral** on the eastern side of the stone town was built between 1873 and 1880 over the former slave market – tradition has it the altar stands on the site of the market's whipping block. Nothing of the slave market remains, though the cellar of the nearby St Monica's Guesthouse is said to be the remains of a pit where slaves were imprisoned before they were sold. Sultan Barghash, who closed the slave market, is reputed to have asked Bishop Steere, leader of the mission, not to build the cathedral tower higher than the House of Wonders. When the Bishop agreed, the Sultan presented the cathedral with its clock. The crucifix in the cathedral is said to be made from the tree under which Livingstone's heart was buried in present-day Zambia. The cathedral is open to visitors. You should leave a donation if you can.

The informative and well-organised **National Museum** at the southern end of the Stone Town has sections on archaeology, slavery, palaces, sultans, explorers, missionaries, traditional crafts, coins, and clove cultivation. In the annexe there is a library, and a natural history collection where dodo bones are exhibited. In the garden, a group of giant tortoises do their best to keep the grass short. The museum is open from 09.00 to 12.30 and 15.30 to 18.00 every day except Sunday. There is a small entrance charge. You may be asked to make an extra donation by the somewhat over-enthusiastic curator.

Access and getting around

A number of hydrofoils and catamarans run between Dar es Salaam and Zanzibar daily, taking from two to three hours and charging around US$30 one way (payable in hard currency). Tickets out of Dar es Salaam are sold at the kiosks near the main jetty on Sokoine Drive; you'll rarely wait longer than an hour for the next boat. All foreigners leaving Dar es Salaam by boat must pay a port tax of US$5 in hard currency. Because Zanzibar is a separate state to the mainland, you must complete an immigration card and show your visa on arrival.

You could probably get from Arusha to Zanzibar in a day by catching the Dar Express coach out of Arusha at 06.30, in time to connect with the 16.00 Sea Express ferry to Zanzibar.

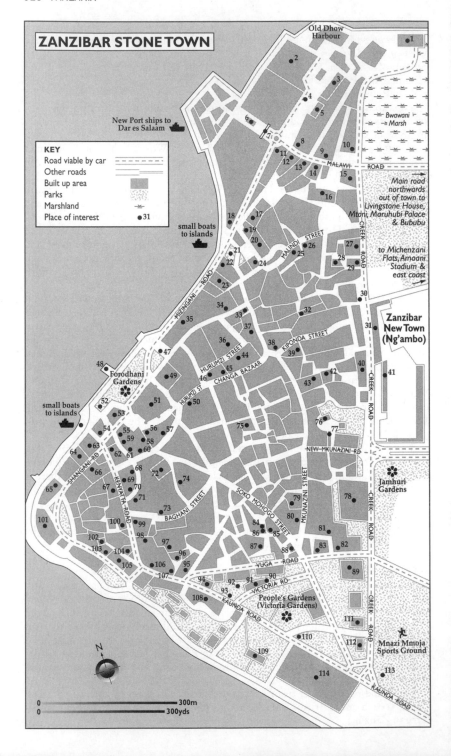

ZANZIBAR STONE TOWN

Old Dhow Harbour

New Port ships to Dar es Salaam

KEY
Road viable by car
Other roads
Built up area
Parks
Marshland
Place of interest ●31

small boats to islands

Bwawani Marsh

Malawi Road

Main road northwards out of town to Livingstone House, Mtoni, Maruhubi Palace & Bububu

to Michenzani Flats, Amaani Stadium & east coast

Zanzibar New Town (Ng'ambo)

Malindi Street

Mizingani Road

Hurumzi Street
Changa Bazaar
Hurumzi St

Forodhani Gardens

small boats to islands

Kiponda Street

Creek Road

New Mkunazini Rd

Shangani Rd
Kenyatta Road
Baghani Street
Soko Mohogo Street
Mkunazini Street

Jamhuri Gardens

Yuga Road
Victoria Rd
Victoria Rd
Kaunda Road

People's Gardens (Victoria Gardens)

Mnazi Mmoja Sports Ground

Kaunda Road

0   300m
0   300yds

N

Numerical key to Zanzibar Stone Town map opposite

1 Bwawani Hotel
2 Clove Distillery
3 Malindi Guesthouse
4 Fish market
5 Warere Guesthouse
6 Shipping company ticket offices
7 Port gates
8 Ciné Afrique
9 Mzuri Guesthouse
10 Petrol station
11 Hotel Marine
12 Malindi Bureau de Change
13 Zan Air
14 Passing Show Restaurant
15 Police station (main)
16 Zan Tours
17 Old Dispensary (Stone Town Cultural Centre)
18 Pychi's Restaurant
19 Gulf Air
20 Ijumaa Mosque
21 The Big Tree
22 Sea View Indian Restaurant
23 Old Customs House
24 Kenya Airways
25 Pyramid Hotel
26 Narrow Street Hotel
27 Zanzibar Tourism Corporation
28 Kokoni Hotel
29 BP petrol station
30 Taxi rank
31 Container shops
32 Narrow Street Annexe Hotel
33 Palace Restaurant
34 Hotel Kiponda
35 Palace Museum
36 Hindu Temple
37 Aga Khan Mosque
38 Spice Inn
39 Hotel International, Bureau de Change
40 Market
41 Bus & dala-dala station
42 Masumo Bookshop
43 Shamshuddin Cash & Carry Supermarket
44 Emerson & Green Hotel
45 Bottoms Up Guesthouse
46 Clove Hotel
47 Taxi rank
48 Blues (restaurant)
49 House of Wonders
50 Sama Tours
51 Arab Fort
52 Suna
53 Orphanage
54 Zanzibar Dive Centre
55 Radha Food House
56 People's Bank of Zanzibar
57 The Gallery
58 People's Bank of Zanzibar (Foreign Exchange)
59 Karibu Inn
60 Luis' Yoghurt Parlour
61 Coco de Mer Hotel
62 Galleromer (shopping mall)
63 Old British Consulate
64 Tembo Hotel
65 Starehe Club
66 Fisherman Restaurant, Bashasha Bar
67 Stone Town Inn, Garage Club
68 Shangani Hotel
69 Namaste Indian Restaurant
70 Post office
71 Blue Ocean Hotel
72 Dolphin Restaurant
73 St Joseph's Catholic Cathedral
74 Chavda Hotel
75 Chit-Chat Restaurant
76 Hamamni Baths
77 Anglican Cathedral
78 St Monica's Hostel
79 Haile Selassie School
80 Jambo Guesthouse
81 Flamingo Guesthouse
82 Zanzibar Medical & Diagnostic Centre
83 Kiswahili Language Institute
84 Air Tanzania
85 Manch Lodge (guesthouse)
86 Nyambani Restaurant
87 Haven Hotel
88 Florida Guesthouse
89 Fisherman Tours, Fernandes Tours
90 Maha Travel & Tours
91 Ben Bella School
92 Victoria House (guesthouse)
93 Zi-Bar & Restaurant
94 Two Tables Restaurant
95 Garden Lodge
96 Chemah Brothers Tours
97 Dr Mehta's Hospital
98 Afya Medical Hospital
99 Zanzibar Hotel
100 Dhow Palace Hotel, Baghani House Hotel
101 Sunrise Restaurant & Pub
102 Mazsons Hotel
103 Serena Inn
104 Tippu Tip's House
105 Jasfa Tours
106 Pagoda Chinese Restaurant
107 Africa House Hotel
108 Camlur's Restaurant
109 Maharaja Restaurant
110 High Court
111 State House
112 Zanzibar Milestone
113 Museum Annexe
114 Peace Memorial Museum
115 Old Cricket Pavilion
116 Mnazi Moja Hospital

Several direct ferry services between Mombasa (Kenya) and Zanzibar have been started up in the last few years, but none has lasted very long.

Walking is the best way to get around Zanzibar Town, though buses, pick-up vans (called *dala-dalas*) and taxis are available. All *dala-dala* routes start at the Darajani Bus Station on Creek Road. Maharouky Bicycle Hire between the market and the petrol station rents out bikes for US$0.50 per hour or US$4 per 24 hours. Nasor Aly Mussa Scooter Service near the cathedral rents motor scooters for around US$20 per day.

The agent for dhows out of Zanzibar has an office in the Malindi Sports Club on Malawi Road, almost opposite the police station.

Where to stay

Travellers arriving by boat will be met by a group of hotel touts. Some are quite aggressive, but others are friendly and will find you suitable accommodation. Touts get a commission from the hotel, so it's effectively a free service and it may save you a lot of walking.

Something that you don't want to do is pitch a tent anywhere on Zanzibar Island without making sure that it's permitted, at least not if you go by a 1997 newspaper report that a tourist was sentenced to two years in jail for camping in a 'restricted area'. He was released after three weeks, but still...

Africa Lodge Recommended new lodge to the left as you exit the harbour gates, directly opposite the fish market. Rooms **D** pp s/c inclusive of breakfast.

Bottoms Up Guesthouse Popular and cheap lodge in the alleys between the Spice Inn and House of Wonders. Book-swap service. Cheap lively bar. Rooms **C** pp (fan, net).

Flamingo Guesthouse Tel: 024 232850. Rooms with net and fan **C** pp.

Fuji Beach Guesthouse In Bububu, 9km north of the port, and 100m or so from Fuji Beach. Rooms using communal showers **E** dbl. S/c rooms **F** dbl. *Dala-dalas* on Route B terminate in Bububu 200m from this guesthouse.

Garden Lodge Tel: 024 233298. Pleasant and clean. **E** dbl.

Haven Hotel Tel: 024 233454. Clean rooms using communal hot showers. **D/E**.

Island View Hotel Tel: 024 232666. New high-rise hotel between the airport and town. Large s/c rooms with hot showers **F** dbl. Free lifts to town.

Malindi Guesthouse Tel: 024 230165. Good clean lodgings, consistently popular with travellers. **D** pp.

Pyramid Guesthouse Tel: 024 230045. Near the seafront behind Ijumaa Mosque. Recommended. Rooms **D** pp or **E** pp s/c.

Riverman Hotel Tel: 024 233188. Good facilities and clean rooms with net and fan. **D** pp.

St Monica's Guesthouse Clean, secure rooms near the Anglican Cathedral. **D** pp.

Stone Town Inn Tel: 024 233101. Mid-range hotel with a few rooms using communal showers **E** pp.

Victoria Guesthouse Tel: 024 232861. Unremarkable clean dbl rooms in the **E** range.

Where to eat and drink

Africa House Hotel Popular and well situated for sundowner drinks, but there's no food and the abundance of touts can be offputting.

Blues Restaurant This floating restaurant next to Forodhani Gardens has a great location and serves arguably the best food in the Stone Town (grills, pizzas and seafood US$8–10), though the trendy, trans-Atlantic atmosphere feels oddly detached from the Zanzibari setting.

Camlur's Restaurant Kenyatta Street. Goan dishes. US$5–10.

Cave Disco Vast open-air beachfront dancehall which was empty whenever we dropped in. Good place for a cold beer.

NUNGWI

This dhow-building and fishing village on the north end of Zanzibar Island lies on an attractive beach lined with palm and casuarina trees, while the surrounding waters offer good snorkelling and diving. Nungwi has emerged over the last few years as one of the more popular tourist retreats on Zanzibar, boasting a cluster of more low-key guesthouses which might collectively host up to 100 budget travellers on any given day. A short walk along the beach east of Nungwi brings you to the headland of Ras Nungwi, where there is an old lighthouse (photography forbidden) and the Mnarani Turtle Sanctuary (entrance US$1), which consists of a fenced-off saline natural pool hosting around 15 greenback and hawksbill turtles. The well-preserved 16th-century Fukuchani Ruins lie about 200m off the main road to Zanzibar Town, 10km south of Nungwi.

Erratic *dala-dalas* connect Zanzibar Town to Nungwi, but most travellers use a private minibus, which costs up to US$10 per person depending on group size and negotiating skills. The ideal would be to get a group together in Zanzibar when you want to head out here, then organise a transfer through a *papaasi*, a taxi driver or a tour company. Unless you have very rigid timings, there is no need to organise your transfer back to Zanzibar Town in advance, since several vehicles can be found waiting around for passengers in Nungwi in mid-morning.

Immediately southwest of Nungwi lies what is virtually a traveller village. The most established guesthouse here is **Amaan Bungalows** (tel: 0811 327747), but there are several others, of which we felt that the **Baraka Guesthouse** offered the best value for money. Prices are uniform, with ordinary rooms falling in the **D** range pp and s/c dbl in the US$25–30 range. There are several restaurants, and a diving centre offers single dives at US$30 per person and full five-day courses for US$300 per person, as well as renting snorkelling and watersports equipment. South of Nungwi, on the west coast, **Kendwa Rocks** is a relaxed backpackers' haunt where you can pitch a tent for **B** per person or rent a bungalow for **F** dbl. Their boat runs up to Nungwi a few times daily to collect passengers; ask at the diving centre about the current rates and timetables.

Dolphin Restaurant About the cheapest place for a sit-down meal in the south end of the Stone Town. Good curries and grills US$3. The jury's out on the psychotically muttering parrot, but otherwise firmly recommended.

Fisherman Restaurant Sea food and grills from US$5, close to the Serena Inn.

Forodhani Gardens This waterfront park opposite the House of Wonders offers one of Africa's most memorable eating experiences – stall after stall selling freshly grilled meat, chicken, fish and prawn kebabs, salads and naan bread to locals and tourists alike. Not to be missed – and you'd have to be seriously hungry not to leave with change from US$3.

Hotel Kiponda Good Zanzibari dishes and seafood in the US$5–10 range.

Le Pecheur Bar Lively pub atmosphere.

Old Arab Fort Great Swahili dancing displays and indifferent buffets at least three times weekly. US$10 pp (or US$5 to watch the dancing only).

Pychi's Another classic sundowner spot. Cold beers and wonderful fruit juices. Small, overpriced pizzas.

Sea View Indian Restaurant Near the People's Palace. Excellent vegetarian and meat curries in the US$7–10 range served on an atmospherically rickety old first-floor veranda.

Practical listings

Zanzibar Tourist Corporation ZTC is the state travel service. You can make bookings for all ZTC bungalows at the main office in Livingstone House (PO Box 216, tel: 232344) on the northeast side of town. The ZTC office on Creek Road, near Kenya Airways, sells good maps of Zanzibar.

Post and telephones The main post office in the new part of town has a post restante service. To make international phone calls, you can also use the old post office on Kenyatta Road, in the Shangani area.

SOUTHERN ZANZIBAR

Roughly 85km long and 25km wide, Zanzibar Island is flat and low lying, with a varied coastline boasting numerous rocky inlets, sandy beaches, lagoons, mangrove swamps and coral reefs. The popular **East Coast** of Zanzibar Island is where you will find the idyllic tropical beaches you dreamed about during those interminable bus rides on the mainland: clean white sand lined with palms and lapped by the warm blue water of the Indian Ocean. It's the sort of place where a planned two-night visit might easily extend itself over weeks. The most popular stretch of coast is between Bwejuu and Makunduchi, the area with the best range of accommodation, restaurants and fresh sea produce.

On the way to the East Coast beaches, you pass two places of interest. The **Bi Khole Ruins** are about 6km south of the village of Tunguu, to the west of the main road. Bi Khole was a daughter of Sultan Said and her house was used up to the 1920s. Only the main walls now stand. The main road there passes through a splendid boulevard of gnarled old mango trees, supposedly planted for Khole. The track to the ruins branches off about halfway down this.

DAY TRIPS OUT OF ZANZIBAR

Many travellers go on an organised tour to a spice plantation. Known as spice tours, these cost from US$10 per person upwards, and they often include a visit to one of the island's ruins. Spice tours can be arranged most cheaply though not always so reliably through independent guides, known locally as *papasi*. Spice tours cost roughly US$10.

For independent day trips, **Fuji Beach** is the nearest swimming beach to Zanzibar Town. Nearby is a small café where the staff will look after your gear while you swim. Fuji is just past Bububu village.

Several small islands lie near Zanzibar Town. Boat trips arranged with a tour company or independent guide will cost from $20 to $60, not too expensive if you can get together a group. The most popular of the islands is **Changuu** or **Prison Island**, the latter name is a reference to the prison built there in 1893. A path circles the island (an hour's easy stroll), where there is a small beach, a restaurant and a guesthouse. Several giant tortoises, probably brought from the Seychelles in the eighteenth century, inhabit the island. A fee of US$1 per person must be paid in hard currency.

Marahubi Palace lies on the coast 3km north of Zanzibar Town. It was built in 1882 for the concubines of Sultan Barghash, and at one time it housed 100 women. The palace was destroyed by fire in 1899, so all that remains are the great pillars which supported the upper storey and Persian bathhouse. The ruins of **Mtoni Palace** lie a short way north of Marahubi. Mtoni is the oldest palace on Zanzibar, built for Sultan Said in the 1840s. A book written

Also en route to the East Coast, **Jozani Forest Reserve** protects a remnant of the indigenous forest which once covered much of central Zanzibar. It is home to several rare mammals. Two endemic subspecies, Kirk's red colobus monkey and Zanzibar leopard, are found nowhere else, while Ader's duiker is restricted to Jozani and one forest in Kenya. A red colobus monkey troop is habituated to tourists and close sightings can be almost guaranteed! The entrance to Jozani is off the main road, a few kilometres south of Pete.

At the small settlement of **Dimbani**, near Kizimkazi village west of Makunduchi, are the remains of the oldest known mosque in East Africa. Kufic inscriptions date it to AD1107. Kizimkazi was then a large walled city, traditionally founded by a king called Kizi. Little of the city remains, but the mosque has been rebuilt several times, most recently in about 1800. The inscriptions, around the niche at the eastern end of the mosque (facing Mecca), are in the decorative floriated style. Similar inscriptions have been found in old buildings in Persia. The silver pillars on either side of the niche are decorated with pounded shells from Mafia Island. To see inside the mosque, now protected by a corrugated iron roof, you must find the caretaker who lives nearby. It is respectful to cover any bare limbs and take off your shoes when you enter.

Access and getting around

Tour companies can arrange day trips to Jozani Forest Reserve. Several tour companies and some independent guides arrange minibuses to the popular East Coast beaches costing US$3–5pp each way with an optional stop at the Bi Khole Ruins and Jozani Forest.

The Jozani Forest can easily be reached by taking a number 9 or 10 *dala-dala* from Zanzibar Town and asking to be dropped at the forest reserve entrance.

by his daughter Salme describes the palace in the 1850s. At one end of the house was a large bathhouse, at the other the quarters where Said lived with his principal wife. Gazelles and peacocks wandered around the large courtyard. Mtoni was abandoned before 1885, though it was used as a warehouse in World War I.

Further north, near Fiji Beach, the disused **Kidichi Persian Baths** were built in 1850 for Said's wife, Binte Irich Mirza, the grand-daughter of the Shah of Persia. A colony of bats seems to have taken up residence. The nearby **Kizimbani Persian Baths** were also built in the Persian style for Said, though they are less ornate inside. The plantations around Kizimbani originally belonged to Saleh bin Haramil, the Arab trader who imported the first cloves to Zanzibar.

A short walk from **Mangapwani**, 20km north of Zanzibar Town, is a large natural cavern and a man-made slave cave. The natural coral cavern has a narrow entrance and a pool of fresh water at its lowest point. The Slave Cave, a square cell cut into the coral, was used to hold slaves after the trade was abolished in 1873. The natural cavern may also have been used to hide slaves, but this is not certain.

Except for the islands, all the places listed below can be visited by scooter or bike, or by a combination of foot and public transport. *Dala-dalas* following Route B go past the Marahubi and Mtoni palaces to Bububu, from where you can walk to Fuji Beach or Kidichi. There are occasional buses to Mangapwani on Route 2.

Where to stay and eat
Chwaka
East End Guesthouse Basic lodge charging **D** pp.

Dongwe
Twisted Palm Popular guesthouse charging **D** pp bed only.

Bwejuu
Dere Guesthouse One of the most popular guesthouses on the Zanzibar coast, constantly expanding and offering a good restaurant and rental of snorkelling gear and bicycles. **C–D** pp.
Palm Beach Hotel Smarter place charging **E** pp for a s/c room or **F** for a dbl bungalow.

Paje
Ufukwe and **Amani Guesthouses** Rooms **C** pp with breakfast.

Jambiani
Horizontal Inn and **Oasis Beach Inn** Small family-run places **C** pp including breakfast. Meals US$2–3.
Jambiani Beach Hotel Rooms **D** pp. Good restaurant in US$3–6 range. Bar.

PEMBA
The island of Pemba lies to the northeast of Zanzibar directly east of Tanga. It is smaller than Zanzibar, about 75km long and between 15km and 20km wide, and has a more undulating landscape. It is also more densely vegetated, with both natural forest and plantation. Few tourists visit Pemba and facilities are limited. For many people, this is its main attraction. The island's largest town is **Chake Chake**, north of which lies the main port **Wete**. The smaller port of **Mkoani** is in the southwest.

Points of interest around the island include the 11th-century **Ras Mkumbuu Ruins**, on the end of the peninsula west of Chake Chake, where you can see the remains of a mosque and several pillar-tombs. **Mesali Island**, to the west of Chake Chake, is surrounded by a coral reef and there is good snorkelling from its idyllic beach.

The **Pujini Ruins** 10km southeast of Chake Chake are the remains of a 13th-century Swahili town known locally as Mkame Ndume (milker of men) after a despotic king who forced the inhabitants to carry large stones for the town walls while shuffling on their buttocks. The overgrown remains of the walls and ditches can be seen, as can a walkway which joined the town to the shore, some wide stairways that presumably allowed access to the defensive ramparts, and the site of the town's well.

Access and getting around
Pemba can be reached from Zanzibar town by motorboat or dhow. Unscheduled dhows between Tanga and Pemba take up to two days and are uncomfortable and dangerous, but there is a much quicker motorboat service that does this run every other day, continuing on to Zanzibar – ask the Bandorini Hotel in Tanga for details.

On the island, Chake Chake is linked to Wete by bus and *dala-dala* number 6, and to Mkoani by number 3. Bicycles can be hired through the ZTC Hotel in Chake Chake or Faizin Tours in Mkoani. Mr Nassour, contactable through the ZTC Hotel in Chake Chake, rents out a Suzuki 4x4 and driver for about US$20 per day (petrol is extra), and a motorboat for US$35 per day (including petrol and captain).

For day trips and other arrangements, the most switched-on agency in Pemba is **Partnership Tours** in Chake Chake. **Faizon Tours & Travel** in Mkoani is also recommended, and it has a branch office in Wete.

Where to stay

ZTC Hotels One each in Chake Chake, Wete and Mkoani. Run down but clean. Rooms **F** pp. Meals US$2–3.

Machakos Inn Chake Chake. Opposite the ZTC Hotel and a lot better. Rooms **D** pp.

Star Inn Chake Chake. 3km north of town near Gombani Stadium. Rooms from **D** sgl. Good food.

Jondene Lodge Mkoani. Good food and clean rooms **D**/**F**.

Sharook Guesthouse Wete. Simple family-run place near bus station. **C** pp.

Southern Tanzania
THE COAST SOUTH TOWARDS MOZAMBIQUE

The Indian Ocean coastline between Dar es Salaam and the Mozambican border is visited by few travellers at present, though interest in the area has been growing for some time now that crossing into Mozambique from southern Tanzania is a safe option. It could well be that this route starts to take off with backpackers' following the news that a motor ferry service across the Rovuma River on the border started operating in June 2000, soon to be followed (or so rumour has it) by a tar road connecting Dar es Salaam to Mtwara and the construction of a bridge over the Rovuma.

For the time being, however, the south coast remains something of a backwater, isolated in all directions by some of Africa's poorest roads, a fascinating, thought-provoking and often rather enchanting area whose towns are dotted with crumbling German and Arabic buildings, creating a mesmerising, time-warped atmosphere that is reinforced by the treacly humidity of the air and the gracious, slow pace of life in this most traditionally Swahili part of East Africa.

But be warned: the south coast is suitable only for those prepared to forsake creature comforts: accommodation is basic, few people speak even the most rudimentary English, organised tourist attractions are limited, and buses are overcrowded, uncomfortable and painfully slow.

Lying off the south coast, opposite the Rufiji Delta, **Mafia Island** has acquired a near-legendary status amongst travellers, largely because so few ever get to it. If what I saw from the *Canadian Spirit* is anything to go by, Mafia is pretty much all that you would expect a remote, densely vegetated and thinly populated Indian Ocean island to be. Sightseeing possibilities include Shirazi ruins at Ras Kisimani, Omani ruins on the nearby island of Juani and a turtle colony on another nearby island. In recent years, Mafia's upmarket lodge has been renovated, and quite a number of tourists visit the island using a charter flight. However, Mafia remains a difficult objective on a budget, unless you don't mind the possibility of waiting a week or two to get back to the mainland.

The definite highlight of any trip down the south coast is **Kilwa**, which lies about halfway between Dar es Salaam and the Mozambique border. Kilwa actually consists of three discrete settlements, the oldest of which is Kilwa Kisiwani (*Kilwa on the Island*). Lying 2km offshore, Kilwa Kisiwani is the site of the most impressive ruins on the East African coast, those of the medieval gold-trading city of Kilwa – the *Quiloa* of Milton's *Paradise Lost* and once thought to be the site of King Solomon's mythical mines. On the mainland, the modern town of Kilwa Masoko (*Kilwa of the Market*) is rather bland but very friendly and the obvious base from

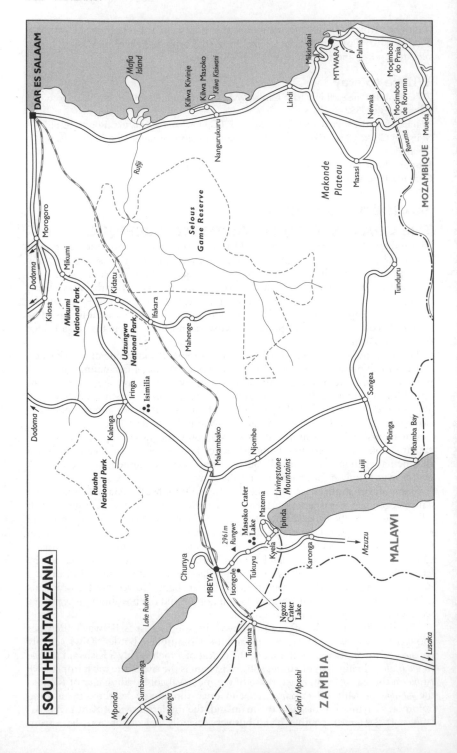

SOUTHERN TANZANIA

which to explore, since it directly faces the island ruins. Connected to Kilwa Masoko by 20km of good road, the 19th-century slave trading town of Kilwa Kivinje (*Kilwa of the Casuarina Trees*) is one of East Africa's most compelling backwaters. See box *Exploring the Kilwas* on page 338–9.

Like Kilwa Kivinje, **Lindi** was a 19th-century slave-caravan terminus, as evidenced by the chimney-like stone tower opposite the NBC club, said to have been used to hold prisoners. There is every indication Lindi was a prosperous town at one time. The sprawling town centre contains numerous posh colonial-era buildings, many of which are now ruined or heading that way. With one eye closed, you can imagine that Lindi's run-down beachfront was once a resort of sorts, possibly used by farmers living upcountry. Lindi doesn't exude a fascination comparable to that of Kilwa, but it's a stimulating town, and a sandy, palm-lined beach stretches for a couple of kilometres to either side. Further afield, there's reputedly a more secluded swimming beach at Ras Bura, perhaps 30 minutes' walk along the Kilwa Road, and regular ferries run from the pier next to the Lindi Beach Hotel to a small settlement in the wooded hills on the opposite side of Lindi Bay.

The largest and most southerly town on the south coast, and the springboard for crossing into Mozambique, **Mtwara** seems rather sprawling and nondescript after the compact old towns further north. The small grid of roads that comprises the nominal town centre lies about 1km inland, surrounded by open fields, and about 1.5km southwest of the harbour, 1km north of the main market and bus station, and about 2–3km south of the main swimming beach. If you get the feeling that Mtwara was intended for greater things, that's because it was purpose built as the port for the infamous Groundnut Scheme of 1946–51, a £30-million folly that was abandoned when it was discovered that the surrounding area was unsuitable for groundnuts.

The village of **Mikindani**, only 10km north of Mtwara, is far older than its larger neighbour and has considerably more character. Founded 1,000 years ago by Shirazi traders, Mikindani has variously been occupied by the Portuguese, Omani Arabs, Germans and British, and it is where Livingstone set off for his last expedition into the interior, an event commemorated by the predictable plaque. The alleys of the old quarter boast a few dilapidated Zanzibar-style buildings, as well as ruins dating back to the slave trading era (including the former slave market) and German colonial buildings. The disused seafront fort was built in the 16th century by the Portuguese and later renovated by Omani Arabs, who used it as a slave prison before it was occupied by Germany and bombarded by the British Navy in World War I. Formerly neglected even by the few travellers who made it to Mtwara, Mikindani has recently been the focus of exciting tourist developments and is arguably the more rewarding base in this part of Tanzania.

Another point of interest in the Mtwara area, also currently being developed for tourism, is **Msimbati**, one hour from Mtwara by bus and best known to travellers as the place to pick up dhow transport to Mozambique. But Msimbati is also a very beautiful spot in its own right, its unspoiled white beach lined with swaying palm trees. The beach shelves steeply, so swimming is good even at low tide, and the offshore reefs provide great snorkelling and diving.

Inland of Mtwara and Lindi, the **Makonde Plateau** is the home of East Africa's most renowned craftsmen, the Makonde carvers. Many of the carvings you see elsewhere in Tanzania come from the Makonde Plateau (many, too, are carved by Makonde who have settled in Arusha or Dar es Salaam), but you will need contacts to see any on the plateau itself, since those that are carved for sale are usually bought by dealers for distribution in the more touristy parts of the country. The main town on the plateau, **Masasi**, is ringed by large granite koppies reminiscent of parts of Zimbabwe, and its modern atmosphere and relatively fresh climate feel refreshingly healthy after the humid degeneracy of the coast. Also of interest is the smaller town of **Newala**, as much as anything for the drive there, which ascends the plateau through dense miombo woodland, passing through a number of the immaculately neat and orderly villages that are characteristic of the area.

Access and getting around
During the dry season, from April to October, daily buses connect Dar es Salaam to all the large towns covered in this section. As things stand, the road is poor as far south as Lindi and often impassable during the rainy season. Even when the buses do run, they are very slow: the 300km run from Dar es Salaam to Kilwa Masoko takes at least 12 hours and the 650km run between Dar es Salaam and Masasi 24

EXPLORING THE KILWAS
Kilwa Kisiwani is separated from Kilwa Masoko by a 2km-wide channel. A fishing dhow to the island can be arranged in the harbour, after you've obtained permission to visit the ruins from the Cultural Centre in Kilwa Masoko (a straightforward process, and no charge is made, but bring your passport).

Kilwa Kisiwani's rise to prominence started in about AD1150 and it prospered as a gold trading centre throughout the so-called Golden Age of Swahili (1250 to 1450), when it was the dominant political and economic entity on the East African coast. The source of Kilwa's gold, shrouded in mystery for centuries, gave rise to such myths as King Solomon's Mines, but is now known to have been Karangaland in what is now Zimbabwe. In 1331, Kilwa was visited by the medieval traveller, Ibn Battuta, who described the city as 'among the finest and most substantially built in the world'. At this time, Kilwa had a population exceeding 10,000, as well as the first coin mint in sub-equatorial Africa and an extensive system of wells which is still in use today.

Kilwa collapsed following the Portuguese takeover of the coast in 1505. Most of its residents were either killed or forced to flee when Portugal attacked the island, and the final death blow was dealt in 1589 when the town residents were captured and killed at a pace dictated by the need of the cannibalistic Zimba. Kilwa came briefly back to life in the late 18th century, after the Omani captured the coast north of Cabo Delgado from the Portuguese, but the traders relocated to the mainland town of Kilwa Kivinje in the early 19th century.

The first building that modern visitors will see is the **Gereza**, the squarish, partially collapsed fort which draws the eye as you sail across to the island. Built by Omani Arabs in about 1800, the fort incorporates the walls of a smaller Portuguese fort built in 1505. Walking uphill from the Gereza, you pass first through the small modern village before coming to the **Main Ruins**. There are a number of interesting buildings here; an ornate **Domed Mosque** and the so-called **Great House** stand out. West of these is the triangular **Mukatini Palace**, built in the 15th century and enclosed by a crumbling 18th-century wall built by the Omani. Also of interest are the remains of the ancient well system, still used by the villagers today.

The most impressive building in the main ruins is the multi-domed **Great Mosque**, the largest mosque of its period on the coast. Most of the building dates from the 14th century as an extension of an earlier 11th-century mosque. The Great Mosque would have been the focal point of community life in Kilwa,

hours. The entire south coast road is scheduled to be surfaced over the next couple of years, which means there is a reasonable chance that transport in this part of Tanzania will improve greatly during the lifespan of this edition.

Buses to most places along the south coast leave Dar es Salaam at around 05.00. Buses to Lindi and Mtwara leave from Morogoro Road bus station, while buses to Kilwa leave from in front of Kariakoo Market. Travelling between Kilwa and Lindi or Mtwara, you may have to change vehicles at Nangurukuru, the town at the junction of the main Dar es Salaam road and the 15km side road to Kilwa Masoko. Regular *matatus* connect Kilwa Masoko, Kilwa Kivinje and Nangurukuru. There is a guesthouse in Nangurukuru should you need to spend a night there.

Mtwara, Lindi and Masasi are connected by good surfaced roads. Regular buses, leaving every hour or so, connect Mtwara to Masasi and Lindi, and can

where Friday prayers were held. A few hundred metres to its south is a graveyard containing the tombs of many of Kilwa's sultans.

The most remarkable building on Kilwa lies about 1km east of the main ruins, on a low cliff overlooking the sea. Known locally as the **Husuni Kubwa**, it was described by the archaeologist Neville Chittick as 'the only attempt to go beyond the merely practical and approach the grand' in pre-colonial Africa. The Husuni Kubwa was built in the early 14th century by Sultan al-Hasan ibn Talutas, and it was used as both a dwelling place and a store house by three successive sultans. In some aspects it is a typical Swahili building, but its scale and complexity are unprecedented and many of its features are unique, for instance the sunken audience court and swimming pool. The Husuni Kubwa is in poor condition, but the main features are clearly discernible.

Further ruins dating to the Shirazi era can be found on **Songo Mnara Island**. There is supposedly a daily boat between Kilwa Masoka and Songo Mnara via Pande, but it doesn't always go. You can also arrange private transport in a local fishing dhow – a fisherman called Juma Meli has been recommended as 'a real gent'. The ruins on Songo Mnara don't match those on Kilwa Kisiwani, but it's an enjoyable day out, and a good reason to stay on an extra day at Kilwa before braving the public transport system.

Visitors to Kilwa should make the effort to reach **Kilwa Kivinje**. In fact, if you're not in a hurry, this small, run-down town, a living memorial to its more prosperous past, would be a fascinating place to settle into for a few days. Kilwa Kivinje came to prominence as an Omani slave-trading centre in the early 19th century. By the mid-19th century it was a very wealthy town, with up to 20,000 slaves passing through annually. Following the abolition of the slave trade in 1873, many of Kilwa's traders established rubber plantations, and the town continued to prosper. In 1886, Kilwa Kivinje became a German administrative centre, and it remained a town of regional importance during the first half of this century, since when it has been superseded by Kilwa Masoko. Today, it is dotted with the crumbling remains of Omani dwellings and fortifications: uninhabitable, but enough to convey what the town must have looked like 150 years ago. There is a large whitewashed German Boma on the waterfront, and a small common – complete with park benches! – between the Boma and the stone sea wall. The main street through town is lined with double-storey buildings boasting ornate balconies, as well as several small homesteads with Zanzibar-style doors and a few boarded-up shops decorated with steel advertising boards that must be forty years old. The covered market, still in use today, is said to have been built by the Germans.

drop you at Mikindani, which straddles the Lindi road 10km from Mtwara. About five buses daily connect Newala to Masasi, leaving between 05.00 and 12.00 and arriving four to six hours later. There is a bus every other day in either direction between Masasi and Dar es Salaam, leaving Masasi from in front of the Masasi Hotel.

Another way to visit the south coast is by boat from Dar es Salaam to Mtwara. For years, the only boat to cover this route was the *Canadian Spirit*, which always ran to a rather whimsical schedule and ceased operating altogether in 1998. In early 1999, a new boat called the MV *Safari* started a weekly run between Dar es Salaam and Mtwara, leaving Dar es Salaam at 12.00 every Wednesday and from Mtwara at 10.00 on Friday. The voyage takes roughly 24 hours and a first-class fare costs around US$15 one-way, to which must be added a US$5 port tax payable in hard currency. The latest news is that two other ferries, the MV *Zahara* and MV *Mandileo*, also started doing this run in early 2000; I have no details of timetables but all services can be booked from kiosks close to the market.

Where to stay and eat
Mafia Island
Aside from two very upmarket lodges, the only option is to camp on the beach, which is reportedly perfectly safe. You can buy fish locally, but bring anything else you might need from Dar es Salaam.

Kilwa Masoko
Mjaka Enterprises Old guesthouse with basic, clean rooms **A** sgl (net, fan). New guesthouse has larger rooms **C** s/c dbl.
Masoko Hilton Hotel New place near market. Spotless rooms **C** s/c dbl with fan and net.

Kilwa Kivinje
Savoy Guesthouse On the beach. **A** dbl (net, fan).

Lindi
Coast Guesthouse Basic. Good beachfront position. **B**.
Nankolawa Guesthouse Clean rooms with nets and fans, friendly staff, good meals by advance order. **C** dbl or **D** s/c dbl.
NBC Club Cold beer and good meals. May charge a nominal entrance fee.
Malaika Restaurant New restaurant recommended by travellers.
South Honour and **Town Guesthouses** Best of the cheapies near the bus station. Clean rooms with net and fan **B**.

Mikindani
The **Old Boma** has recently been converted to a resthouse by Trade Aid (UK tel: 01425 65 7774; fax: 01425 65 6684; email: tradeaid@netcomuk.co.uk). Rooms cost US$50 dbl but they also run a hostel aimed at budget travellers charging **C** pp. Another option is the small **Litingi Hotel**, which lies on an attractive stretch of coast along the Mtwara road 2km from Mikindani.

Msimbati
A *banda* complex is currently under construction. The bandas will be self-contained, with fans and nets, and should cost around US$25. In addition to a beachfront bar and restaurant, snorkelling and sailing equipment will be available for hire. The Trade Aid people at Mikindani are the best source of current information about these developments.

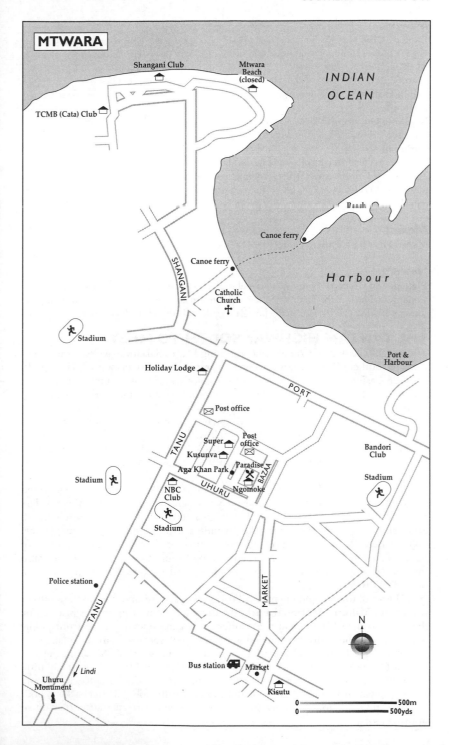

MTWARA

Shangani Club

Mtwara Beach (closed)

INDIAN OCEAN

TCMB (Cata) Club

Canoe ferry

SHANGANI

Canoe ferry

Catholic Church

Harbour

Stadium

Holiday Lodge

PORT

Port & Harbour

Post office

TANU

Super

Post office

Kusunva

Paradise

Aga Khan Park

Bandori Club

Stadium

Ngomoke

UHURU

NBC Club

Stadium

BAZAA

Stadium

MARKET

Police station

TANU

↙ Lindi

Bus station

Market

N

Uhuru Monument

Kisutu

| 0 | | 500m |
| 0 | | 500yds |

Mtwara

Bandari Club Near the harbour. Good place for a night out. Often has a live band.
CATA Club (pronounced like Carter). Near beach 3km out of town. Run-down rooms **C** dbl with net and fan.
Finn Club Good food, satellite TV, table tennis. Daily membership US$1.
Jagaju Holiday Lodge Reasonable rooms on the road between the town centre and beach. **B**.
Kapilima Guesthouse Good s/c rooms near the bus station **C** dbl. There are a few cheaper lodges scattered around the bus station.
Lutheran Mission Comfortable, well-equipped rooms **D** dbl. On your left as you approach the first roundabout coming from Lindi or Mikindani.
Tingatinga Guesthouse Highly recommended new guesthouse 2km from town centre towards CATA Club. Rooms **C** s/c dbl with nets and communal hot showers, inclusive of good breakfast.

Masasi

Masasi Hotel and **Panama Guesthouse** Clean, spacious rooms **B** dbl.

Newala

Plateau and Country Lodges Comfortable accommodation in the **D** range. The Country Lodge does the best food in town. There are also several basic lodges with bucket showers and local restaurants in the **A**-**B** range dotted around the bus station.

THE TANZAM HIGHWAY SOUTH TO MBEYA

The roughly 900km of road or rail connecting Dar es Salaam to Mbeya, the largest town in southern Tanzania, is travelled by practically every person who backpacks between East and southern Africa, but it is another of those routes that very few people take the time to explore. The first main town along the road, about 200km from Dar es Salaam, is **Morogoro**, a spacious and well-maintained place lying in the fertile foothills of the Uluguru Mountains. There are few tourist attractions around Morogoro, but the town has a healthy, lively feel, and it's a good place to see live music. A good day walk is to the Rock Garden Resort, a sort of botanical garden on the lower slopes of the Uluguru Mountains, about 3km out of town past the upmarket Morogoro Hotel.

The 2,646m **Uluguru Mountains** is yet another of the isolated forest-covered ranges that stretches down the eastern coastal belt of Tanzania.The range is less accessible than the Usambara or Udzungwa, but there is no reason why an experienced and self-sufficient hiker couldn't explore the area. One possible hiking base is the disused Morning View Camp, which is situated near a patch of natural forest about 8km from Morogoro along Boma Road. (Permission to camp must be obtained from the Department of Natural Resources, 2km out of town on Kingalu Road).

A cluster of three adjoining national parks and game reserves lies to the south of Morogoro. **Mikumi National Park**, the third-largest in Tanzania, is bisected by the main road to Mbeya, and it can offer good game-viewing even from public transport – I once counted ten different mammal species from the main road including large herds of elephants and eland. To the south of Mikumi, the vast **Selous Game Reserve** is the largest conservation area in Africa. As with Mikumi, part of the Selous can be seen from public transport – in this instance, the Tazara Railway between Dar es Salaam and Ifakara. Unfortunately for backpackers, both Mikumi and the Selous can only otherwise be visited in private transport or on an upmarket safari.

Altogether more accessible, **Udzungwa Mountains National Park** was opened to the public in October 1992. The Udzungwa Mountains are covered in extensive montane forests, and their isolation from similar habitats has resulted in a high degree of endemism. Two monkey races, the Uhehe red colobus and Sanje crested mangabey, are confined to the Udzungwa Mountains, and the forest also supports blue and red-tailed monkeys and black-and-white colobus monkeys. Still relatively unexplored, the Udzungwa Mountains have thrown up four previously undescribed birds in the last decade or so, including the presumably endemic Udzungwa partridge, which has been placed in its own genus. A short trail leads from the entrance gate to a small waterfall, where you should see plenty of monkeys including red colobus. You can also organise a four-hour guided walk to a waterfall deeper in the reserve, and several overnight trails are planned – you might want to check progress at the national parks office in Arusha before heading this way.

The first major town south of Morogoro is **Iringa**, an interesting and agreeable place with an attractive setting on a cliff above the Little Ruaha River and several period buildings in the old German quarter near the market (see box *Day trips from Iringa* on page 345). Iringa lies at the junction for the road to **Ruaha National Park**, the second largest national park in the country and widely regarded to be one of the wildest and best, with an elephant population of more than 12,000, as well as 30,000 buffalo, 20,000 zebra, and large numbers of leopard and lion. Unfortunately, as with the other game reserves in southern Tanzania, Ruaha is really only geared for visitors with private transport and for organised safaris. The only option for backpackers would be to hire a 4x4 in Iringa (Iringa Safari Tours on Uhuru Avenue between Benbella Street and Karume Road may be able to fix you up) and then to camp at one of the public campsites in the park.

Access and getting around

Travellers heading directly between Dar es Salaam and Mbeya are advised to use the Tazara Railway, which connects Dar es Salaam to Kapiri Mposhi via Mbeya. Two trains run every week between Dar es Salaam and Kapiri Mposhi, leaving Dar es Salaam on Tuesday and Friday at 16.55, and take 36 hours. Three additional slow trains run every week as far as Tunduma on the Zambian border. These leave Dar es Salaam on Monday, Thursday and Saturday at 11.00. All trains stop at Ifakara, Mbeya and Tunduma, and slow trains pass through the Selous Game Reserve during daylight hours, where there is usually plenty of game to be seen.

There is plenty of road transport connecting Dar es Salaam to Mbeya. Direct buses travel during the night, when there is a high risk of having your luggage tampered with, but you can hop between the larger towns using local buses. Hitching between towns is also a possibility, provided that you get yourself out on the main road before trying for a lift.

Buses between Dar es Salaam and Morogoro leave every hour or so and take about four hours. There is regular public transport between Morogoro and Iringa, with the best option being minibuses, which take around five hours.

Many travellers heading directly from Arusha to Mbeya opt to bus via Dodoma. This is one of the worst routes in the country, and it should definitely be avoided. If you want to travel between Arusha and Mbeya bypassing Dar es Salaam, the best thing to do is catch a bus from Arusha to Dar es Salaam and get out at the junction town of Chalinze, which lies about halfway between Dar es Salaam and Morogoro. Arriving in Chalinze early enough, you should be able to travel straight on to Morogoro, but if not there are a couple of basic guesthouses in Chalinze.

There are several ways of getting to Udzungwa Mountains National Park, the entrance to which lies roughly halfway between the small towns of Kidatu and

Ifakara on a road branching south from the main Mbeya road at Mikumi town. Coming from Morogoro, a daily bus leaving at 14.00 will take you to Kidatu. Coming from Iringa, you could use a bus heading to Morogoro to get to Mikumi town, where you can pick up the bus from Morogoro at around 15.30. The other option is to use the Tazara rail to get to Ifakara directly from Dar es Salaam or Mbeya. A few *matatus* cover the 40km road between Kidatu every day, stopping at Mangula opposite the entrance gate.

Where to stay and eat
Morogoro
Lukumba Family Guesthouse Best of a few **B** lodges near the bus station.
Luna Hotel Spacious rooms **C** s/c dbl with fan and net.
New Acropol Hotel New upmarket hotel serving excellent food.
Mama Pierina's Bright rooms **C/D** sgl/dbl (fan, net, hot shower). Good restaurant.
Masuka Village Hotel Ten-minute walk from bus station along Boma Rd. Attractive retreat in flowering gardens at base of Uluguru Mountains. Rooms **D** s/c dbl (net, hot shower).
New Green Restaurant Centrally positioned. Inexpensive, tasty Indian and Portuguese dishes.

Mikumi
Genesis Guesthouse New mid-range hotel in the junction town for Udzungwa and closest town to Mikumi National Park. S/c rooms **E** dbl. Good restaurant. Day trips to the national park. There are several cheaper lodgings in Mikumi.

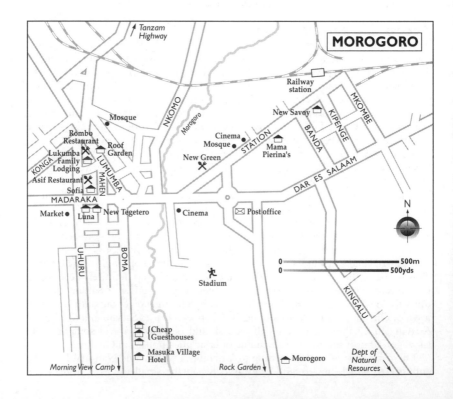

DAY TRIPS FROM IRINGA

There are a couple of good possibilities. The first is to **Kalenga**, the former capital of the Wahehe King Mkwawa, who was a major thorn in the side of the early German administration, refusing to allow their caravans to pass through his territory and defeating a troop of 1,000 Germans in 1891. Mkwawa's fortified capital was razed in 1894, when the Germans stood a battery of cannons along the ridge of the hill that is still known locally as Tosamagana ('Throwing Stones'). Mkwawa went on the run, and in 1898 he shot himself through the skull rather than be taken alive. His skull rests in the Mkwawa Museum in Kalenga, as do several of his personal artefacts. Ask the caretaker of the museum to show you around the village, and to point out several remnants of Mkwawa's fortifications. Pick-up trucks to Kalenga leave Iringa from the end of the surfaced road 200m past Samora Stadium. They stop at Kalenga's small market, from where it's a five-minute meander through the village to the museum.

Isimilia Stone Age Site lies in a dry river bed 22km south of Iringa. First excavated in 1957, Isimilia is littered with artefacts dating from its Stone-Age inhabitants 60,000 years ago. A small museum houses a number of tools, as well as the fossilised bones and teeth of the massive extinct *Hippopotamus gorgops*. In another gully, ten minutes' walk away, a group of fantastic 10m-high sandstone pillars, carved by a river which dried up years ago, might easily be the set for a Lilliputian western. Isimilia Stone Age Site is signposted from the Mbeya road 20km from Iringa. Any vehicle heading south can drop you at the turn-off, from where it's a 20-minute walk to the site. On the way you pass through a small group of huts where the caretaker lives – you might as well find him on your way past. You could also negotiate with a taxi driver to do a round trip to Isimilia – the caretaker at the site speaks no English, so an English-speaking taxi driver will be a definite asset.

Udzungwa Mountains and Ifakara

Maryland Lodge Best of a few **B** lodges in Kidatu. Spotless rooms with nets and fans.
Nshangu Guesthouse Recently recommended as an OK place in Ifakara.
Twiga Guesthouse 200m from park entrance gate. Rooms **D** s/c dbl. Canteen.
Udzunga Mountain View Hotel Under same management as Genesis Hotel in Mikumi. Close to entrance gate. S/c rooms **E**. Inexpensive camping. Good restaurant. Hikes organised.

Iringa

Hasty Tasty Too Inexpensive stews, juices, and Indian snacks.
Isimilia Hotel Small but clean rooms **C**/**D** s/c dbl with hot water.
Lutheran Centre Guesthouse Basic clean rooms **B**.
Mount View Hotel Clean and inexpensive. **B**/**C** s/c single/double. If this is too pricey there are dozens of cheaper guesthouses scattered around the bus station.
Kisolanza Farm Highly recommended stopover about 55km south of Iringa on the Mbeya Road. Fresh farm produce available at shop. Cottages US$30. Camping **B** pp.
Raj Hotel Iringa's top restaurant. Varied menu. Open long hours. Main courses around US$3.
Lantern Restaurant Great view over Majumba Street. Good food. Meals around US$2.

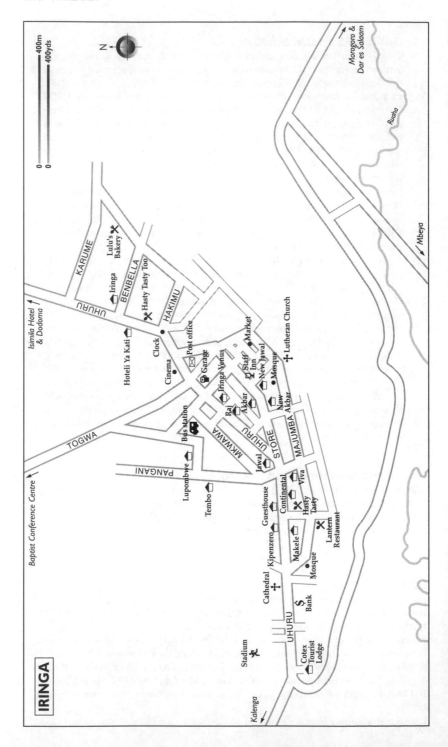

IRINGA

N

400m
400yds
0
0

Isimila Hotel & Dodoma
Morogoro & Dar es Salaam
Ruaha
Mbeya
Kalenga
Baptist Conference Centre

KARUME
UHURU
BENBELLA
HAKIMU
TOGWA
PANGANI
MKWAWA
UHURU
STORE
MAJUMBA
UHURU

Lulu's Bakery
Iringa
Hasty Tasty Too
Hoteli Ya Kati
Clock
Cinema
Post office
Garage
Market
Staff Inn
New Jawal
Mosque
Lutheran Church
Iringa Venus
Rai
Akbar
New Akbar
Bus station
Jawal
Lupombwe
Tembo
Guesthouse
Continental
Viva
Hasty Tasty
Lantern Restaurant
Makele
Kipenzero
Cathedral
Mosque
Bank
Stadium
Cotex Tourist Lodge

MBEYA AND SURROUNDS

Situated at the foot of the synonymous mountain range, **Mbeya** is the largest town in southern Tanzania and the normal springboard for crossings into Zambia and Malawi. Mbeya was founded in 1927 to service the Lupa goldfields near Chunya. Although the mines were boarded up in the 1950s, Mbeya's strategic position combined with the rich agricultural land surrounding it has ensured that the town has continued to prosper – today, it has an unusually Westernised, bustling feel and it shows few of the signs of neglect that characterise most Tanzanian towns. Travellers generally view Mbeya as no more than an overnight stop-off coming to or from Malawi – in fact, people who come from Dar es Salaam by train normally arrive early enough to bus on to the Malawi border the same day – but anybody who enjoys a bit of off-the-beaten-track walking or hiking should seriously consider devoting more time to the area.

The intriguing small town of **Chunya**, 70km north of Mbeya, was the epicentre of a major gold rush in the 1920s and 1930s. After mining became unprofitable in the 1950s, Chunya enjoyed a short-lived tobacco boom before degenerating into something approaching a ghost town. Many of the grander buildings are now boarded up and there is a general air of faded prosperity. You can still see local prospectors panning the river which runs through the town, and there is talk of working the gold again using modern methods.

The **Mbeya Mountains** that tower over Mbeya are of less biological interest than the more extensive mountains around Tukuyu, but the peaks offer good views over the Rukwa region, and wild flowers are abundant in the wet season. The most accessible peak, Kaluwe (2,656m), can be climbed in a few hours from

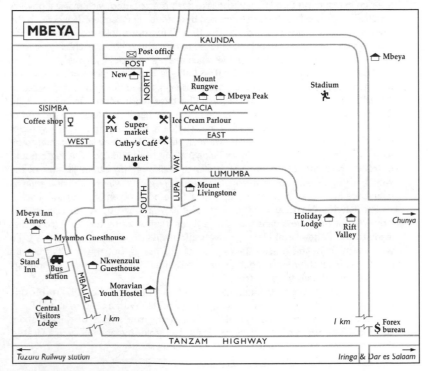

Mbeya by following a path which starts behind the hospital. The highest point in the range, Mbeya peak (2,834m), is most easily climbed from Luiji, a village about 20km from Mbeya town. If you want to do a longer hike in the area, you can cross from Mbeya Peak to Pungulume (2,230m) at the western extreme of the range. The Utengule Country Resort in Luiji is a good hiking base, and the staff can give you details of routes.

Straddling the main road roughly halfway between Mbeya and the Malawi border post, **Tukuyu** is a rather amorphous and run-down small town which

HIKING AND RAMBLING AROUND TUKUYU

The Poroto Mountains offer wonderful rambling, particularly in the dry months between May and October. The winding dirt roads pass through lovely scenery, supporting varied bird life and vegetation, and offering spectacular glimpses of Lake Nyasa almost 1,000m below. The area is home to the Nyakyusa, whose neatly painted homes were described by the explorer Joseph Thomson as 'perfect arcadia'. Rich volcanic soil and an annual rainfall of 1,500mm support a thriving subsistence economy based around bananas, mangos, tea and coffee. Even on by-roads there is a fair amount of traffic (expect to pay for lifts), which makes it easy to explore from one base. The following are some of the more accessible spots, most of which are easily visited as a day trip from Tukuyu. With time, initiative and 1:50,000 maps from the Department of Lands and Surveys in Dar es Salaam, you could easily explore further.

One of the Poroto's most spectacular sights is **Ngozi Crater Lake**, more than 2km in diameter and enclosed by 200m-high cliffs. The forested slopes of Ngozi are rich in plant and bird life, and the lake itself is attributed with magical powers locally. The turn-off to the lake is marked by a faded signpost near Isongole on the Tukuyu–Mbeya road. From the turn-off, a 5km motorable road leads to the footpath to the crater rim. The trip takes two to three hours each way by foot, and it is advisable to organise a guide, since the path is not always clear.

Closer to Tukuyu, **Masoko Crater Lake** is a pretty spot with interesting historical associations. The stone courthouse on the crater rim, constructed in 1912 to house a German garrison, was the base from which Germany fought British troops in neighbouring Nyasaland. Rumour has it that towards the end of the war, the Germans dumped a fortune in gold bars, money and military vehicles into the lake. Locals also claim that swimming in the 3km-deep lake is tantamount to suicide. Masoko lies 15km from Tukuyu along the Ipinda road. A fair amount of traffic heads there, but you may prefer to walk – gently downhill most of the way, with intimate cultivated slopes occasionally giving way to sweeping views over Lake Nyasa. With an early start, you'll have no problem getting a lift back.

The **Kiwira Natural Bridge**, formed 400 years ago by water-cooled lava from Mount Rungwe, spans the Kiwira River further along the same road that leads to the Pentecostal Holiness Association Mission (see Where to stay). To walk there from the mission takes a couple of hours, but the trucks that run most days from the main road to an army base near the bridge may give tourists a lift. Ask for details at the mission.

More ambitiously, fit walkers can ascend and descend the 2,957m **Mount Rungwe** in ten hours, preferably with a local guide. With a tent, map and food, you could also spend a couple of days exploring the slopes of this dormant volcano. The most popular ascent starts at Isongole, bypasses Shiwaga Crater, then takes you through extensive patches of forest.

boasts one of the most appealing settings in Tanzania. Ringed by the Poroto Mountains, Tukuyu lies at the base of Mount Rungwe, the second highest point in the southern highlands, and at the heart of one of East Africa's most accessible – and neglected – walking areas (see box *Hiking and Rambling around Tukuyu* below). Originally called Nieu Langenberg, Tukuyu is one of the oldest towns in Tanzania, founded as a German administration centre in the late 19th century after the first Langenberg, on Lake Nyasa near Ikombe Mission, was abandoned due to the high incidence of malaria.

For experienced wilderness hikers, the **Kipengere Mountains**, a westward extension of the Poroto stretching almost as far as Njombe, offer interesting possibilities. Foremost of these is the Kitulo Plateau, on which lies the highest peak in the southern highlands, Mtorwi (2,961m), as well as the 2,929m Chaluhangi Dome. The plateau is noted for the wild flowers which blanket it after the November rains, and for the pastoral Nji people who inhabit it. The **Livingstone Mountains** near Matema also have possibilities. The manager of the Langiboss Hotel in Tukuyu should be able to advise you about them.

The Department of Lands and Surveys in Dar es Salaam stocks 1:50,000 maps of this region, which you should definitely carry if you want to climb Rungwe unguided or do any wilderness hiking. Hikers should also carry camping equipment, be self-sufficient in food, and consider speaking to the police to get written permission to visit remote areas.

The following account, edited from a letter written by Gerhard Buttner in February 1998, gives some idea not only of the opportunities that are open to adventurous hikers in this remote corner of Tanzania, but also of how few travellers explore them:

We settled on a north-to-south route, starting at Izyonje near Lake Ngozi, via the Kitulo Plateau (where the Kitulo Government Farm rents out an entire three-bed guesthouse for US$3) through Mtorwi, Makete and Bulongwa to Matema Beach on the shores of Lake Nyasa. Hardly any English is spoken in these mountains. The area has some scenic spots, but many are highly populated farming settlements and finding isolated camping spots was not easy. People couldn't quite understand what we wanted in this area, but they were never unfriendly in spite of a rumour that we had come to plant bombs in the forest! Local people walk across parts of these mountains, but the last people before us to attempt crossing the whole area were two Germans who never completed their journey in the 1980s because they nearly landed in jail as suspected South African spies. A few times, villagers joined us for a few hours to show us the way, without ever asking for a guiding fee. We communicated with their few words of English and our limited Swahili. You will need your own food, but *ugali*, potatoes and some tomatoes and onions can occasionally be traded. The most spectacular part of the walk was the endless drop down to Matema Beach. Villagers walk this path once a week on market day, as a greater variety of products is available on the plains around Matema.

Unfortunately, Gerhard doesn't mention how many days it took them to hike this route. He does say that knowing the Swahili words listed in the language section of this guide without having to look them up is the minimum you'll need to get by. He also notes that the range which several maps call the 'Kipengere Mountains' are referred to by locals as the Livingstone Mountains, and that the name Kipengere is used locally to refer to the inhabited plains.

Access and getting around

Mbeya can be approached by rail or road from Dar es Salaam (see *The Tanzam Highway south to Mbeya*, page 342) or by road from western Tanzania (see box *The wild southwest*, page 286–7). The Tazara Railway Station is a few kilometres out of town on the road towards Zambia. Buses from Mbeya to more long-haul destinations generally only leave in the morning and seats should be booked in advance.

For those exploring around Mbeya, a few pick-up trucks ply the scenic road to Chunya every day, leaving from near the Mbeya Peak Hotel. To get to Luiji, ask any bus heading south from Mbeya to drop you at the turn-off near Mbalizi. It is 9km from Mbalizi to Luiji, and you may have to walk.

Buses from Mbeya to Kyela, Njombe and Tundumu leave when full throughout the day. Buses to Kyela take about four hours, stopping at Tukuyu as well as at the turn-off to the Malawi border 5km before Kyela (for details of crossing into Malawi see *Tanzania to Malawi*, page 73).

Where to stay and eat
Mbeya

Eddy's Restaurant On Sisimba Road. Good food at moderate prices.
Holiday Lodge Excellent clean guesthouse. Rooms in **B** range. Good value restaurant.
Mbeya Inn Annexe, **Myambo** and **Stand Guesthouses** Good **A** lodges near bus station.
Moravian Youth Hostel Five minutes' walk from town. Secure and popular. **B** dbl.
Mount Livingstone and **Rift Valley Hotels** Upmarket hotels with excellent restaurants.
Mount Rungwe Guesthouse Cheap cosy rooms **B**. Hot communal showers.
Ramji's Supermarket In THB Building near post office. Ice-cream, imported food and recent international newspapers.

Luiji
Utegele Country Resort On coffee farm. Rooms **F** s/c dbl. Camping **B** pp. Meals US$5.
Chunya
Moonlight and **Night Queen Guesthouses** **A**.

Tukuyu
Langiboss Hotel 1km out of town facing Mount Rungwe. Clean, comfortable rooms **B** dbl. Hot communal showers. Basic meals. English-speaking manager, well-informed about hikes in the area. Can leave excess gear while hiking.
Pentecostal Holiness Association Mission 30-minute walk from turn-off signposted 10km from Tukuyu on Mbeya road. Camping permitted.

LAKE NYASA

Lake Nyasa was the original colonial name applied to Lake Malawi, and it is still the name given to the Tanzanian portion of the world's 11th largest lake (ask a Tanzanian about Lake Malawi and they'll tell you to go to Malawi). Little explored by travellers, Tanzania's Lake Nyasa is, if anything, even more stunning than the more southerly part of the lake, with the Livingstone Mountains towering for a kilometre above its eastern shore and the Poroto Mountains rising less sharply above the plains to the west of the lake.

Lying a mere 5km past the turn-off to the Malawi border, **Kyela** is the epitome of scruffy, smalltown Africa, boasting as motley a collection of guesthouses as you'll encounter in East Africa. Kyela is also the gateway to Lake Nyasa, linked by road or ferry to **Matema Beach**. Situated at the northern tip of the lake, Matema is arguably more beautiful than any of the more publicised places on the Malawian part of the lake, boasting a perfect swimming beach, mountains towering on all

TRAVELLING FROM MTWARA TO SONGEA

Edited from notes made by Joe Williamson and Mike Wilks, who travelled from Mtwara to Mbamba Bay and back again in early 1999

The wild, scenic route between the south coast and Lake Nyasa is one of the most remote and least travelled in Tanzania. It is a trip that will take at least three days, longer if you want to break it up with a day's rest, and the road is mostly in poor condition. The journey is broken into three legs: Mtwara to Masasi (200km), Masasi to Tunduru (200km) and Tunduru to Songea (273km). The road degrades from Masasi onwards, but each leg can usually be done in a single day, though travel times depend greatly on the weather and availability of transport. Overall, 4x4 vehicles are the fastest option on the roads west of Masasi, especially in the rainy season, but they may not be as comfortable as buses, are often double the price, and don't have fixed departure times.

Except between Mtwara and Masasi, it's best to get to the departure area between 04.30 and 06.00 to have guaranteed transport. It also helps to catch the first available vehicle while there are people waiting to go, otherwise you may wait up to a day until there is a full vehicle ready to leave. The travelling times quoted are for the dry season; they might well double in the wet season.

Leg One: Mtwara/Mikindani to Masasi Transport starts in Mtwara or Mikindani, takes up to four hours on mostly tarmac or good-quality roads, and costs about US$3. The main stops en route are at Mnasi Moja (where the road forks to Lindi) and Ndanda. The first buses leave from the Indian section and then the main roundabout in Mtwara at about 05.30 and depart roughly every half hour until mid-afternoon. In Mikindani the buses stop by the Old Prison. A reasonable guesthouse can be found in Ndanda; for details of accommodation in Masasi see *Masasi* page 342.

Leg Two: Masasi to Tunduru This 200km trip takes upwards of eight hours by lorry (make sure you have a padded bag to sit on or use a grain sack if they are carrying them) with only one major stop for food and soft drinks. We had to pay in dollars (US$20) but the going rate is around US$6 per person in local currency. Coming in the opposite direction, there is a bus which leaves Tunduru at 04.30 most days, but it takes a long time and we found that Land Rovers were best for the return trip. In Tunduru, we stayed in the Naweka Guesthouse which was adequate and seemed to have running water in the early morning and electricity in the evenings. The cost is about US$3/single and US$4.50 s/c dbl with fan but no nets. The Yakiti Guesthouse is more basic, charging around US$2 for a single with a mosquito net. The Sunrise Guesthouse had self-contained rooms but no mosquito nets and cost US$4.50. Restaurants include the Greenland Bar and Al Jazira Hotel. Camping and cheap rooms are also available at the Catholic Convent.

Leg three: Tunduru to Songea This should ideally be covered in a Land Rover, as the road is much worse than the stretch between Masasi and Tunduru. The trip takes at least seven hours, passing through uninhabited areas which become rather tedious scenically. The cost is about US$9 for lorries and US$12 for Land Rovers. Namtumbo is a good place on the way for refreshment.

horizons, and breathtaking sunsets over the Poroto. The Matema Pottery Market, held every Saturday at the village 1km east of the resort, is renowned for the Kisi pots sold there. The rocky shore about 500m past the village is a good place to see colourful cichlids (though anybody swimming away from the main beach should make enquiries about crocodiles). Crocodiles are easily seen at the river mouth 3km west of Matema and hippo have been seen a short way upriver.

Kyela is also linked by a twice-weekly ferry to the small port of **Mbamba Bay**, which lies on a pretty, coconut-lined stretch of the western lake shore near the Mozambican border. In both directions, the ferry stops at several small villages, the most interesting of which is **Liuli**, set in an attractive natural harbour protected by a rocky peninsula, topped by the sphinx-like formation from which is derived the village's German name Sphinxhafen. Not only does Liuli boast the largest mission in this part of Tanzania, but it was also the site of the first naval encounter of World War I, a bloodless altercation between former drinking pals which *The Times* in London heralded with the headline 'Naval Victory on Lake Nyasa'! Liuli could be a lovely place to spend a few peaceful days, provided that you have a tent and don't mind waiting for the occasional mission vehicle heading to Mbamba Bay.

East of Mbamba Bay, a stunning ascent of the Rift Valley escarpment will bring you to **Songea**, a large, lively town and obscure route focus, lying at the junction of the road to Mbamba Bay, a good tar road to Chalinze on the main Dar es Salaam and Mbeya road, and a rough and little-used route to Mtwara on the south coast. Between Songea and Chalinze, **Njombe** is a quiet and pleasantly situated highland town, with good walking potential – there is an attractive waterfall on the Ruhidji River, next to the main road 2km north of the town centre.

Access and getting around

The ferry connecting Itungi Port to Mbamba Bay is the best way to see the spectacular northern Lake Nyasa shore. Ferries to Mbamba Bay leave Itungi at 07.00 on Monday and Friday, arriving at around midnight. They turn around more or less immediately to arrive back at Itungi at 17.00 the next day. Ferries to Mbamba Bay stop at Lupingu, Manda, Lundu, Nindai and Liuli. Another ferry leaves Itungi at 07.00 on Wednesday and arrives back on Thursday afternoon. This stops at most lakeside villages, including Matema Beach, but it doesn't go as far as Mbamba Bay.

Itungi Port lies 10km from Kyela, which is connected to Tukuyu and Mbeya by regular buses and *matatus*. There is no accommodation in Itungi, so travellers using the ferry must spend the night in Kyela then at 05.30 catch a *matatu* from in front of the TRC office, 1km out of town, to Itungi. The booking office at the TRC building serves no real function, since the ticket officer travels with the ferry – you can buy a ticket at Itungi before departure. There is one class, it is not overcrowded, and tickets cost US$4. Basic meals are available on board, as are soft drinks and beers.

The best way to get to Matema Beach is with the daily bus from Mbeya, which leaves at around midday and stops at Tukuyu, Kyela and Ipinda. You can also get to Matema in hops from Kyela via Ipinda, a large village 27km from Matema. Regular *matatus* connect Kyela and Ipinda, and there is even the odd pick-up truck to Ipinda from Tukuyu, going via Masoko Crater Lake. A few trucks travel between Ipinda and Matema daily, especially on Saturdays. Should you get stuck in Ipinda, there is a basic but adequate guesthouse behind the bank (US$1/2 single/double). The other way to get to Matema is with the ferry that leaves Itungi at 07.00 on Wednesday, arriving at Matema an hour later. This ferry also stops at Matema on Thursday afternoon on its way back to Itungi.

Travelling east of Mbamba Bay, a thrilling 60km dirt road winds its way up the Rift Valley escarpment through well-developed miombo woodland to the town of Mbinga. There is an erratic bus service between Mbamba Bay and Mbinga but, if the bus doesn't show up, you should be able to get a lift with a pick-up truck. I did this trip in the rain, a terrifying seven-hour ordeal. In dry conditions, it would probably take three hours. Once at Mbinga, there is plenty of transport along a well-maintained dirt road to Songea (even a thrice-weekly 'Special Video Bus' to Dar es Salaam!) as well as a few guesthouses and *hotelis* if you feel compelled to stick around.

From Songea you have two choices: the 300km tar road to Chalinze on the main Dar es Salaam–Mbeya road, or the wild, scenic road connecting Songea to Masasi on the Makonde Plateau and then Mtwara on the south coast (see box *Travelling from Mtwara to Songea*, page 351). Songea and Chalinze are connected by regular buses taking six to seven hours, and passing through Njombe after 237km (this distance is marked incorrectly on some maps). To get from Songea to Masasi, you'll be dependent on trucks and 4x4 vehicles, and can bank on an overnight stay at one of several guesthouses in the remote mining town of Tunduru.

Where to stay and eat
Kyela
Kyombo Guest House On main road towards Tukuyu. About the best of a fairly shoddy selection of cheap lodgings. Plenty more to choose from.
Mkoko's Restaurant Shady veranda. Well-stocked fridge.

Matema Beach
Lutheran Mission Resort On lakeshore. Spotless bandas with nets **D** dbl. Camping **B** per tent. Cold soft drinks, coffee/tea, enormous buffet meals US$2.50 per head.

Mbamba Bay
Neema Beach Decent low-key resort. S/c rooms **C** dbl. Bar, restaurant. Generator to combat frequent power cuts.
Nyasa View Lodge About the best of a few **A** lodges

Songea
Africa House Near the District Council office. Clean if a bit shabby. **C**.
Deluxe, **New Nipu** and **Mkomi Guesthouses** Clean, basic lodges in **A** to **B** range.
OK Hotel Clean rooms **C** s/c dbl. Lively bar. Good restaurant.

Njombe
Milimani Hotel Excellent two-storey hotel 250m from bus station towards Songea. Spacious rooms **B** s/c dbl with hot shower. Good restaurant.
Lutheran Centre Hostel Dormitory **A** pp. Canteen.

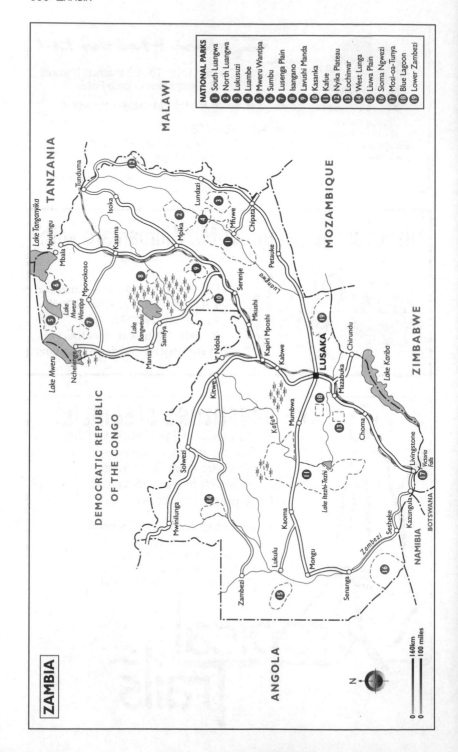

ZAMBIA

NATIONAL PARKS
1 South Luangwa
2 North Luangwa
3 Lukusuzi
4 Luambe
5 Mweru Wantipa
6 Sumbu
7 Lusenga Plain
8 Isangano
9 Lavushi Manda
10 Kasanka
11 Kafue
12 Nyika Plateau
13 Lochinvar
14 West Lunga
15 Liuwa Plain
16 Sioma Ngwezi
17 Mosi-oa-Tunya
18 Blue Lagoon
19 Lower Zambezi

Zambia

Philip Briggs and Chris McIntyre

Zambia is a large, landlocked country which, along with Malawi, forms something of a transitional zone between East and southern Africa. Despite boasting some of Africa's finest and most untrammelled game reserves, Zambia has never really caught on with backpackers, presumably due to the high day-to-day expenses and the difficulty of reaching the most alluring areas on public transport. Until a few years ago, Zambia attracted a fair amount of backpacker through-traffic, largely as a result of the risks attached to travelling through the Tete Corridor during the Mozambican civil war and the temporary closure of the direct border between Tanzania and Malawi. These days it is very unusual to meet somebody who has travelled through Zambia on public transport, with the exception of people who have crossed between Mpulungu on Lake Tanganyika and Karonga on Lake Malawi.

It is difficult to think of one wholly convincing reason why any backpacker would want to explore Zambia before, say, Malawi. Equally, it is difficult to find any single good reason not to spend some time in Zambia. My impression of this country on the several occasions I've travelled through it has always been dominated by its people – among the most friendly and articulate English-speakers on the continent. Zambia is emphatically not a cheap country by regional standards, but nor is it ludicrously expensive. And for those prepared to make the effort, many interesting parts of Zambia are accessible to backpackers: Lake Bangweulu, for instance, or the Zambezi River above Victoria Falls, or a number of accessible waterfalls in the northern regions. All in all, Zambia is probably the perfect country for anybody who isn't on a stringently tight budget and who wants to get completely away from the established backpacker circuits.

What follows is an overview of some of the more obvious travel options in a little-visited country. Those seeking greater substance are pointed to Chris McIntyre's *Guide to Zambia*, published by Bradt.

FACTS AND FIGURES
Area: 752,610km² (17th in Africa)
Capital: Lusaka
Largest towns: Lusaka, Ndola, Livingstone, Kabwe, Kitwe
Population: 9 million
Official language: English
Currency: Kwacha
Head of State: President Frederick Chiluba

PRACTICAL INFORMATION
Accommodation
There is little in the way of budget accommodation in Zambia, certainly when compared with neighbouring countries like Malawi and Tanzania. Aside from the backpackers' hostels or campsites in Lusaka, Mpulungu and Livingstone, the cheapest place to stay in most towns will be the government or council resthouse, where a room typically costs around US$10. Cheap motels and hotels tend to charge upwards of US$15 for a double room.

Crime and security
Lusaka has earned a bad reputation for muggings and pickpockets. You should never walk around Lusaka by night, and you are advised not to carry anything of value in an accessible place at any time of day, especially when you visit crowded areas such as markets and bus stations. Outside of Lusaka, Zambia is as safe as any country covered in this book.

Entry formalities
Visas are not required by nationals of most Commonwealth countries, Ireland and Denmark, but they are required by British passport holders and nationals of most other Western countries. The best place to buy a visa is at a Zambian embassy in the capital city of a nearby country such as Kenya, Tanzania, Malawi, Zimbabwe or South Africa. Visas are normally valid for up to three months and they are generally inexpensive, though British nationals are asked a fee of US$50. Seven-day transit visas can be issued at the Victoria Falls border. Provided that your papers are in order and you don't look ridiculously scruffy, you're unlikely to encounter any problems when you enter Zambia overland.

Food and drink
The regional staple of maize porridge is called *nshima* in Zambia. It is this or rice that you'll be served in most local restaurants, accompanied by a bland stew or possibly fish. In larger towns there are generally a few more Westernised restaurants serving steaks and chicken dishes for US$3–5.

The usual brand name soft drinks are widely available and cheap. The best of the local beers is a bottled lager called *Mosi* – derived from the local name for Victoria Falls *Mosi Oa Tunya*. Imported South African or Zimbabwean Castle beer is also available in many places.

Geography and climate
Zambia lies on the Central African plateau at an average altitude of between 1,000m and 1,600m above sea level. The country is incised by the Zambezi, Kafue, Luangwa and Luapala Valleys. Lakes Tanganyika and Mweru lie on its northern borders, the artificial Lake Kariba on the border with Zimbabwe and swamp-fringed Lake Bangweulu lies entirely within Zambia. The summer and main rainy season falls between November and April.

Getting around
Buses cover most major routes. The government UBZ buses are generally quicker than privately owned buses. Hitching is reasonably easy on main roads, though you will be expected to pay for most lifts with local drivers. There are internal ferry services on Lakes Mweru and Bangweulu, as well as an international service on Lake Tanganyika. Except for the Tazara line to Tanzania, which is very efficient, Zambian rail services are slow, crowded and unreliable.

Maps

Excellent detailed maps covering the whole of Zambia can be bought for around US$3 per sheet from the Ministry of Lands map office in the basement of Mulungushi House near the corner of Independence Avenue and Nationalist Road in Lusaka.

Money

The unit of currency is the kwacha, which has devalued dramatically over the last decade and currently trades at around US$1=K1,250. Foreign currency can be changed into kwacha at any bank and at most tourist class hotels, though US$ cash are often acceptable. Banking hours are normally from 08.15 to 14.45 Monday to Wednesday and Friday, and 09.00 to 11.00 on Thursdays (and on Saturday in Lusaka). There are 24-hour exchange facilities at the international airport outside Lusaka.

Public holidays

In addition to New Year's Day, the Easter weekend and Christmas and Boxing Day, the following public holidays are taken in Zambia:

12 March	Youth Day
1 May	Labour Day
25 May	Africa Freedom Day
First Monday and Tuesday of July	Heroes' and Unity Days
First Monday of August	Farmers' Day
October 24	Independence Day

Northern Zambia
MPULUNGU AND THE GREAT NORTH ROAD

Backpackers who pass through northern Zambia are generally heading to or from **Mpulungu**, a cosmopolitan small town on the southern tip of Lake Tanganyika which is notable not only as the terminal for lake ferries to Tanzania and Burundi, but also for being Zambia's largest port – draw your own conclusion about the other contenders for this exalted title. The main attraction at Mpulungu is the lake, which is very pretty and offers outstanding snorkelling. A worthwhile excursion is to the little-visited **Kalombo Falls**, where the Kalombo River plummets for 221m down the side of the Rift Valley escarpment to form the 12th highest waterfall in the world.

From Mpulungu, a surfaced road leads directly south for roughly 415km, passing through **Mbala** and **Kasama** before connecting with the main highway between Dar es Salaam and Lusaka at the junction town of **Mpika**. None of these towns is in any way out of the ordinary, though Mbala – 40km from Mpulunga but almost 1,000m higher – is worth stopping at for the Moto Moto Museum, an important collection of traditional Bemba artefacts that was originally assembled by a missionary. Near Kasama, there's a campsite at the reasonably accessible and attractive **Chisimba Falls**, the site of an unobtrusive hydro-electric plant.

Lying within walking distance of the Lusaka road about 180km south of Mpika, the 65m high **Kundalila Falls** is one of the most attractive waterfalls in the country. There's a campsite above the waterfall and a clear pool below (safe for swimming), while the fringing forest supports samango monkeys as well as a variety of birds. No more than 50km further south, the small town of **Serenje** is of limited interest to travellers except as the best place to pick up public transport towards Lake Bangweulu (see page 363).

For travellers with tents, the **Mkushi** area is one of the most attractive and accessible places to stop over along the Great North Road, with a couple of

CHIPATA AND SOUTH LUANGWA NATIONAL PARK

Few backpackers are likely to explore the part of Zambia lying east of Lusaka, unless they happen to be heading to or from Malawi. The main town in this part of eastern Zambia, Chipata, lies about 600km from Lusaka and 30km from the border with Malawi. Chipata also lies at the turn-off to South Luangwa National Park, one of Africa's best and most atmospheric game reserves. A highlight of South Luangwa are the night drives. Luangwa reputedly has the densest leopard population in Africa, and many individuals are habituated to spotlights and vehicles. It is also one of the best places I've visited for reliable sightings of smaller nocturnal creatures such as genet, civet, elephant-shrew and porcupine.

South Luangwa is an ambitious but by no means impossible goal for adventurous backpackers, best visited during the dry season (May to October) when large herds of elephant, buffalo and smaller herbivores accumulate along the banks of the Luangwa River. Daily buses connect Chipata to Lusaka, and there are regular shared taxis between Chipata and the Malawi border post. From Chipata, at least one minibus daily carries passengers to Mfuwe on the edge of South Luangwa National Park, and the driver will normally drop backpackers at Flatdogs on request. Hitching is also a distinct possibility, provided that you get an early start. A good place to wait is outside the Chipata Motel, but don't accept a lift unless it's going as far as Flatdogs.

The Chipata Motel is the best lodge in Chipata and close to the junction to South Luangwa – rooms cost **D** dbl. Cheaper accommodation is available at the Government Resthouse. At South Luangwa, Flatdogs (tel: 062 45074) is the only camp that's both affordable and reasonably accessible, situated 1km before the bridge over the Kafue River. Simple, clean chalets with net and shower cost **F** pp. Camping is **C** pp. The US$15 daily park entrance fee is payable only upon entering the park, so you don't need to pay it to stay at Flatdogs. Plenty of game passes through Flatdogs, notably elephants and hippos, and the camp also organises late afternoon game drives into the park, which continue for an hour or so after dark.

A new and welcome development in the Chipata area is **Yellow Chicken Camp** (email: roverift@hotmail.com), 10km from town along the road to the Malawi border. Run by experienced African travellers, the camp has an attractive location overlooking a dam rich in birdlife and regularly visited by small antelope. The ethos is environmentally friendly (solar power, biogas, efficient fuel use, coupled with a sustainable wood supply), and facilities include hot water, bar, *braai* pits, fishing, fresh farm produce, level camping sites, and twin and double A-frame chalets. By the end of 2000, these should be enhanced by dormitory accommodation, a restaurant serving home cooked meals and pizzas, mountain-bike trails, walking trails and cultural tours. Chalets cost US$20 dbl, camping US$3 pp, and dorm beds will cost US$6 pp.

By early 2001, Yellow Chicken intend to run a regular minibus connecting Lilongwe, Chipata, Lusaka and South Luangwa, a service which would do much to open up South Luangwa to backpackers. Kiboko Hostel in Lilongwe and Chachacha Backpackers in Lusaka are bound to be able to provide information about this service as soon as it is operational.

attractive guest farms and some reasonable possibilities for walking and mountain biking. Further south, **Kapiri Mposhi** is an important transport hub: not only is it the southern terminal of the Tazara Railway from Dar es Salaam, but it also lies at the junction of the Dar es Salaam–Zambia road and the road to the so-called 'Copperbelt'. Sad to report, Kapiri Mposhi is also a dump of the first order. Meanwhile, the Copperbelt towns of **Ndola**, **Kitwe** and **Chingola** are all pleasant enough as small African towns go, but there are no obvious reasons to visit them. There's also not too much to grab your attention along the 200km stretch from Kapiri Mposhi to Lusaka itself – the fact that **Kabwe** has thrown up the oldest human fossil yet found in south-central Africa (a 125,000-year-old skull known as 'Broken Hill Man') hardly justifies stopping over in this nondescript town.

Access and getting around

Regular buses run between all towns along the main road from the Tunduma/Nakonde border to Lusaka, as well as along the roads connecting Mpika to Mpulungu and Kapiri Mposhi to Chingola. Hitching is also a viable way of travelling along these trunk routes. There are two rail services in northern Zambia: the Tazara train between Dar es Salaam and Kapiri Mposhi (see *Tanzania to Zambia* on page 72) stops at Nakonde, Kasama, Mpika and Serenje; while the daily train between Ndola and Lusaka stops at Kapiri Mposhi and Katwe.

The best way to get to the Kolombo Falls is to hire a private water-taxi in Mpulungu. The river mouth lies 17km from Mpulungu, and taxis should be able to take you upstream towards the base of the waterfall. The walk to the top of the waterfall is steep and strenuous, and it should only be undertaken if you plan to camp there overnight – it's possible to arrange for the water-taxi to collect you on the following day.

To get to Chisimba Falls, take any transport heading from Kasama to Luwinga and ask to be dropped off at the turn-off to Mporokoso, 19km from Kasama. About 5km along the Mporokoso road you'll see the short track to the waterfall signposted to your left.

The Kundalila Falls lie 13km east of the main Lusaka road, along a dirt road that's reasonably well signposted from the village of Kanona.

Where to stay and eat
Mpulungu
Harbour Inn Tel: 04 455041. New place in the heart of Mpulungu. Good value. Dbl room with en-suite facilities **D**. Boat for hire. Next to Bantu Juu restaurant.

Lake Tanganyika Lodge Backpacker lodge reached by short boat-taxi ride. Chalet **D** pp. Camping **B** pp. Meals available. Swimming possible.

Mishembe Bay – Luke's Beach (two tents and a stone cottage and camping) contact via Thorn Tree Lodge, Kasama; tel: 04 221615; email : kansato@zamnet.zm. White sandy beach sheltered in its own bay. Reached by 30-minute water-taxi from Mpulungu. No food available. Good snorkelling. Camping **C** pp, cottage or standing tent **E** pp including guided walk to Kalambo Falls.

Nkupi Lodge Tel: 04 455166. Popular, long-serving backpackers retreat near the lake shore 500m from town. Bed with net **D** pp. Camping **A** pp. Meals sometimes available.

Mpika
DDSP Resthouse Tel: 04 370118. About 2km along road to Kasama. Clean rooms **D** per bed.

Government Resthouse and Musakanya Guesthouse Town centre. Basic rooms **C**.

Malashi Executive Guesthouse About 2km along road to Kasama. Good value. Dbl **D**.

Mkushi

Forest Inn Tel: 05 362188. Clearly signposted on the Great North Road 30km south of Mkushi. Comfortable guest farm with restaurant, bar, barbecue area, and farm produce for sale. Hiking trails. Mountain-bike hire. Rooms US$32/45. Camping **C** pp.
Sweetwater Guesthouse Tel: 05 362245; email: sweetwtr@zamnet.zm. Set on the Mkushi River about 1km from the Great North Road north of Mkushi. Rooms US$24/32. Camping **B** pp. Good meals available.

Kitwe

Edinburgh Hotel Tel: 02 222444; email: edin@zamnet.zm. Good s/c rooms starting at US$30.

Ndola

Travellers Lodge Tel: 02 621840; email: travell@zamnet.zm. Affiliated to the Edinburgh Hotel in Kitwe and of a similar high standard. S/c rooms from US$30.

Other towns and waterfalls

There is at least one resthouse in all the towns that appear in bold in the main text. Basic campsites charging **A** pp are to be found at the Kalombo, Chisimba and Kundalila Falls.

LAKE BANGWEULU

Lying to the east of the main Lusaka road, the **Lake Bangweulu** region first drew the attention of Europe in 1873 when David Livingstone, hopelessly misdirected in his search for the source of the Nile, died there at the village of Chitambo. Bangweulu is regarded to be one of Africa's great wilderness areas, and it is one of the few comparable places which is both accessible and budget-friendly to determined backpackers, who can easily reach the port of **Samfya** on the southwest shore and the inhabited island of Chilubi to its northeast.

Of greater interest than the lake itself, however, is the vast swampy region fringing its eastern shore: this area supports a thriving population of the endemic black lechwe antelope, as well as an estimated 10–20% of the global population of the shoebill (a large and unmistakeable papyrus dweller regarded by many birdwatchers to be Africa's ultimate 'megatick'). The Bangweulu swamps support many other large mammals, including elephant, buffalo, hippo, sitatunga and leopard, and the number and variety of birds is stunning.

A very adventurous onward option from Lake Bangweulu would be to follow the road from Samfya west to **Mansa**, then to continue north towards the Congolese border and the port of **Nchelenge** on Lake Mweru. This remote corner of Zambia still supports substantial crocodile and hippo populations, and the lake is rich in birds, with a number of localised papyrus species likely to be seen at the mouth of the Luapula River just outside Nchelenge. Better still, if you are seeking some serious off-the-beaten-track travel, Nchelenge may be to all intents and purposes the end of the road, but it is also the terminus for a thrice-weekly ferry service to two populated islands on Lake Mweru: Kilwa and Isokwe.

Also of interest in this part of Zambia are the succession of waterfalls along the Kalungwishi River close to **Chimpempe Pontoon** and the boundary of Lusenga Plain National Park. Affordable accommodation in this area is limited to the excellent Cascade Plantation Tourist Cottage (tel: 01 772052; email: zbu@zamnet.zm). This six-bed self-catering cottage lies about 2.5km from Chimpempe Pontoon, from where it is signposted, and within walking distance of Chimpempe, Lumangwe and at a push Kabweluma Falls – the caretaker can point out the footpaths.

Access and getting around

The surfaced road to Nchelenge, Mansa and Samfya branches to the west of the main Lusaka–Dar es Salaam highway between Serenje and Kanona. The best place to pick up buses along this road is at Serenje. The erratic 'post boat' service from Samfya will happily take paying passengers, and it connects to various points on Lake Bengweulu, including Chilubi Island, probably the best place for backpackers to organise dugouts to take them into the swamp. There is also a thrice-weekly ferry service between Nchelenge and various islands on Lake Mweru. It should be noted that backpacking in this area would really only be appropriate for flexible travellers with a pioneering sensibility; if any readers do take up the challenge I'd love to hear about it!

Where to stay and eat

Samfya

Unfortunately, there is no longer any formal accommodation in Samfya that we're aware of, though travellers who are waiting for the 'post boat' could always ask around for a room or, assuming they have a tent, pitch it on the beach. Swimming is not advisable due to the large numbers of crocodiles.

Mansa

Mansa Hotel Tel: 02 821606. Good value accommodation and meals. Rooms **F** dbl.

Nchelenge

Lake Mweru Water Transport Guesthouse Tel: 02 972029. Clean s/c rooms overlooking lake.

Nchelenge District Resthouse Run down but cheap.

Southwest Zambia

LUSAKA AND THE ZIMBABWE BORDER AREA

Lusaka is a modern capital city located at the crossroads to which all roads in Zambia seem to lead. It is difficult to avoid passing through Lusaka if you travel through Zambia, and few would want to spend more time there than they have to, but the city has recently become considerably more attractive to travellers than it was even two or three years ago due to a sudden eruption of relatively affordable accommodation options. Travellers who have spent a while bussing through northern Zambia might even find Lusaka's comfortable hostels, abundance of decent restaurants, and relatively westernised facilities a thoroughly welcome respite for a few days before they continue southwards.

People heading south from Lusaka are likely to follow one of two routes, crossing into Zimbabwe either near Lake Kariba or at Victoria Falls. These two routes split from each other about 50km south of Lusaka near **Kafue**, a rather nondescript small town that nevertheless serves as a good alternative to overnighting in the capital itself. The shorter but less popular option is to cross near Kariba, and travellers doing this can either go directly through **Chirundu** border-post, which crosses the Zambezi about 50km downstream of the Kariba dam wall, or divert southwards to **Siavonga**, which is the Zambian counterpart to the Zimbabwean town of Kariba near the dam wall.

The main route through southern Zambia, however, is the 475km road connecting Lusaka to Livingstone and the Victoria Falls via Kafue and **Choma**. The attractive and compact town of **Livingstone** is well geared to tourism, since it lies a mere 10km from Victoria Falls, and its low-key atmosphere comes as a refreshing contrast to the more explicitly tourist-orientated town on the Zimbabwean side of the waterfall. The

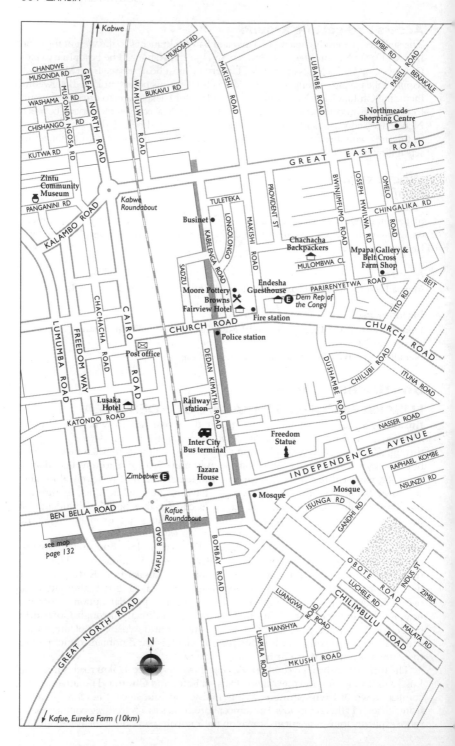

↑ Kabwe

CHANDWE
MUSONDA RD
WASHAMA
CHISHANGO
KUTWA RD
MUSONDA RD
NGOSA RD

GREAT NORTH ROAD

WAMULWA ROAD
MUKOSA RD
BUKAVU RD
MAKISHI ROAD

LUBAMBE ROAD

LIMBE RD
PASELI ROAD
BENAKALE

Northmeads
Shopping Centre

GREAT   EAST   ROAD

Zintu
Community
Museum

PANGANINI RD

KALAMBO ROAD

Kabwe
Roundabout

TULETEKA

Businet ●

KABELENGA ROAD

LONGOLONGO

MAKISHI ROAD

PROVIDENT ST

BWINJIMFUMO RD

JOSEPH MWILWA RD

OMELO ROAD

CHINGALIKA RD

Chachacha
Backpackers

MULOMBWA CL

Mpapa Gallery &
Belt Cross
Farm Shop

SADZU

Moore Pottery ●
Browns
Fairview Hotel 🏠

Endesha
Guesthouse

✕

🏠 Ⓔ Dem Rep of
the Congo

PARIRENYETWA ROAD

TITO RD

BEIT

Fire station

LUMUMBA ROAD

FREEDOM WAY

CHACHACHA ROAD

CAIRO ROAD

Post office ✉

CHURCH ROAD

DEDAN KIMATHI ROAD

● Police station

DUSHAMBE ROAD

CHILUBI RD

CHURCH ROAD

ITUNA ROAD

Lusaka
Hotel 🏠

KATONDO ROAD

Railway
station

Inter City
Bus terminal 🚐

Freedom
Statue ⚑

NASSER ROAD

INDEPENDENCE   AVENUE

RAPHAEL KOMBE

NSUNZU RD

Zimbabwe Ⓔ

Tazara
House ●

● Mosque

Mosque ●

ISUNGA RD

GANDHI RD

BEN BELLA ROAD

Kafue
Roundabout

KAFUE ROAD

BOMBAY ROAD

OBOTE ROAD

LUCHELE RD

INDUS ST

ZIMBA

see map
page 132

GREAT NORTH ROAD

LUANGWA ROAD

MANSHYA ROAD

LUAPULA ROAD

CHILIMBULU ROAD

MALATA RD

MKUSHI ROAD

N

↓ Kafue, Eureka Farm (10km)

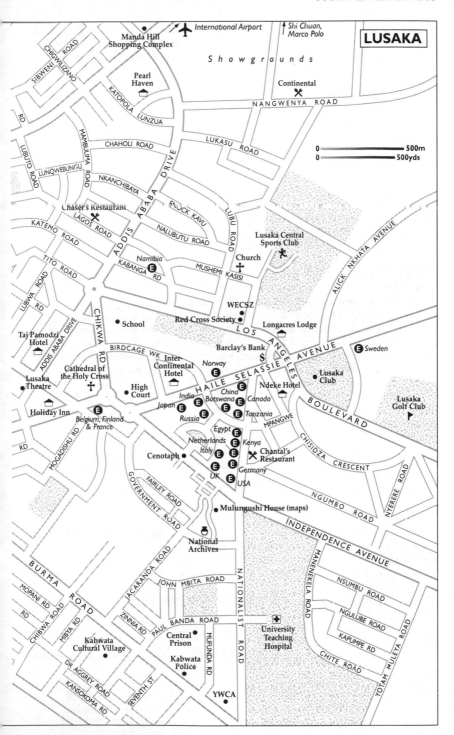

LUSAKA

International Airport

Shi Chuan,
Marco Polo

Manda Hill
Shopping Complex

CHIGWILIZANO ROAD
SIBWENI ROAD
LUBUTO ROAD
LUNQWEBUNGU ROAD
MAMBULIMA ROAD
KATOPOLA
LUNZUA

Pearl
Haven

Showgrounds

Continental

NANGWENYA ROAD

CHAHOLI ROAD

ADDIS ABABA DRIVE

LUKASU ROAD

0   500m
0   500yds

NKANCHIBAYA

Chaser's Restaurant

LAGOS ROAD
KATEMO ROAD
TITO ROAD
LUBWA RD

CHUCK KAVU
NALUBUTU ROAD

LUBU ROAD

Lusaka Central
Sports Club

Namibia
KABANGA RD

MUSHEMI KASISI

Church

WECSZ

ALICK NKHATA AVENUE

School

Red Cross Society

CHIKWA RD

Taj Pamodzi
Hotel

ADDIS ABABA DRIVE

BIRDCAGE WK

LOS ANGELES
Longacres Lodge

Barclay's Bank

Inter-
Continental
Hotel

Norway

HAILE SELASSIE AVENUE

Sweden

Cathedral of
the Holy Cross

Lusaka
Theatre

High
Court

India
Japan
Russia

China
Botswana
Canada
Tanzania

Ndeke Hotel

Lusaka
Club

BOULEVARD

Lusaka
Golf Club

Holiday Inn

MOGADISHU RD

Belgium, Finland
& France

Egypt

MPANGWE

CHISIDZA CRESCENT

NYERERE ROAD

Cenotaph

Netherlands
Italy

Kenya

Chantal's
Restaurant

UK
USA

Germany

NGUMBO ROAD

GOVERNMENT ROAD
FAIRLEY ROAD

Mulungushi House (maps)

INDEPENDENCE AVENUE

National
Archives

JACARANDA ROAD
JOHN MBITA ROAD

NATIONALIST ROAD

MANENEKELA ROAD

NSUMBU ROAD

NGULUBE ROAD

KAPUMPE RD

BURMA ROAD
MOPANI RD
CHIBWA RD
MBIYA RD
ZINNIA RD
PAUL BANDA ROAD
MUFUNDA RD

Kabwata
Cultural Village

Central
Prison

Kabwata
Police

University
Teaching
Hospital

CHITE ROAD

YOTAM MULEYA ROAD

DR AGGREY ROAD
KANSOKOMA RD
SEVENTH ST

YWCA

Victoria Falls, of course, need no introduction – suffice to say that this 1km wide, 100m deep waterfall ranks high on the list of the region's must-sees, and the Zambian side is these days perhaps more suitable for the budget-conscious traveller than the more developed and expensive Zimbabwean side.

Access and getting around

Daily buses connect Lusaka to Chipata, Siavonga, Chirundu and Livingstone. Travellers who are heading southwards from Lusaka will find that regular minibuses leave from Freedom Way in the city centre to Kafue town, which would be a far more attractive overnight option than the capital and also a good place from which to hitch to Chirundu or Livingstone. A number of relatively upmarket or backpacker-oriented coach and minibus services have covered the road between Lusaka and Livingstone in recent years. The best bet at the time of writing is the Virgin Lux Bus, which leaves from CR Carriers on Cairo Road in Lusaka, takes around seven hours to get to Livingstone, and costs about US$7 one-way. Any of the backpacker hostels or campsites in either town will be able to give you more details about this or any other recommended service.

Where to stay and eat
Lusaka

Chachacha Backpackers 161 Mulombwa Cl; tel 222257. Great and long-overdue backpacker hostel 10 minutes' walk from central Lusaka. Good meals, lively bar and up-to-date travel advice for elsewhere in Zambia. Email and internet facilities. Camping **B** pp. Dorm **C** pp. Room **E** dbl, chalet **F** dbl. Best place for backpackers.

Eureka Farm Kafue Rd 7km south of town; tel: 272351. Camping. **B** pp, A-frame chalets with 2 or 3 beds **F** per unit. Bar sells steak and pies on camping ground. Any minibus heading to Kafue can drop you.

Fringilla Farm About 50km north of Lusaka on Kabwe road; tel: 61 1199. Good option if coming to Lusaka from the north. Chalets and campsite with hot showers and clean toilets. Camping **B** per tent. Simple huts **D** dbl.

Kapini Village Traditional village two hours from Lusaka, with food available and rooms in the **B** bracket. To get there from Lusaka, catch a minibus from the Flash bus station to Mandavu, then a pick-up to a place called 15 Miles, from where it is a 2km walk. For more details, ask at Chachacha Backpackers (above).

Pioneer Campsite Cell 771936; email pioneer@zamnet.zm; 20 minutes' drive from Lusaka. On weekdays, a free shuttle leaves Lusaka at 16.30 from Businet Internet Café on Kabelenga Rd (off Church Rd). They also arrange transfers to/from town or the airport on request, costing US$2 + US$2pp. Facilities include a bar, restaurant, barbecue packs and satellite TV. Camping **C** pp. Dorm **C** pp. Chalet **F** dbl.

Lusaka Club Restaurant Near cnr Saddam Hussein and Haile Selassie. Excellent, inexpensive meals – around US$5 for the speciality, pepper steak. Just one of many, in middle of accommodation.

YWCA Nationalist Rd opposite teaching hospital; tel: 25 2726. Accepts both sexes. Basic rooms **C** pp.

Kafue

River Motel On main road. Clean s/c rooms **E/F** dbl. Cheaper resthouses also available.

Chirundu

Nyambandwe Motel About 200m from border post. Small, clean s/c rooms **E/F**.
Gwabi Lodge Tel: 01 515078. Used by overland trucks, 12km from Chirundu, and 3km from the Kafue River's confluence with the Zambezi. Camping **C**.

Siavonga

Eagle's Rest Chalets Tel: 51 1168; email: eagles@zamnet.zm. Self-catering chalets **E** pp. Camping **C** pp.

Mazabuka

Mazabuka Garden Motel Tel: 032 30284. Room **F**.

Choma

Mambushi Chalets c/o Gwembe Safaris; tel: 032 20169. Camping about 2km past Choma towards Livingstone **C** pp.
Choma Hotel Tel: 032 20189. Run down.
New Kalundo Motel Tel: 032 20028.
Hot Springs Guesthouse Tel: 032 20064 on northeast side of town, beyond the museum.
Tonga Craft Museum Good snack bar in town centre.

Livingstone and Victoria Falls

Fawlty Towers Lodge and International Backpackers Mosi-oa-Tunya Rd; tel 03 323432; email: ahorizon@zamnet.zm; web: www.adventure-africa.com. This popular backpackers' hostel is situated in a large, secure garden with massive mango trees on the main Victoria Falls road, two minutes from the centre of town. It offers free daily transfers to the Backpackers Bazaar, Shoestring Backpackers and Hitch Haven in Victoria Falls town (Zimbabwe) at 08.30 and 16.30, as well as free visas to pre-booked clients. Ask about the special 'first night' offer of US$10 for pick-up in Victoria Falls, a dorm bed, a meal, a drink and falls entry. Facilities include self-catering kitchens, vehicle workshops, restaurant, internet café, travel office, swimming pool, storage facilities and bicycle hire. Camping **C** pp. Dorm **D** pp. Air-conditioned dorm **D** pp. Rooms **F** dbl.
Gecko's Guesthouse Limulunga Rd, south of town, 10-minute walk from centre; tel: 03 322267; email gecko@zamnet.zm. Lovely residential place. Quieter than backpackers' places in the centre of town. Dorm for 6 people, 4 rooms and camping. Dorm **C** pp, dbl room **D** pp, single **D**. Camping **B** per tent.
Grubby's Grotto Tel: 03 324024. Used by overland trucks rather than independent backpackers. Swimming pool and bar. No food provided. Camping **B** pp.
Jolly Boys Hostel Mokambo Road; tel: 03 324299; email: jboys@zamnet.zm. Popular, central, long-serving backpacker hostel. Swimming pool, mountain-bike hire. Meals. Dorm **C** pp. Camp **B** pp.
Jungle Junction See *Victoria Falls* in Chapter 15 on page 486.
Maramba River Lodge and Campsite Tel: 32-4189. On tributary of Zambezi, next to main road between town and the falls. Clean facilities, friendly people, wildlife. Camping **C** pp. Chalet **F** dbl. Larger chalets available. *Braai* packs.
Thompson's Guesthouse Tel: 03 320565/324100. Beside main road as you approach Livingstone from Lusaka. Three double rooms and two singles, lounge and self-catering facilities. Away from town, but inexpensive alternative if hostels are full. Rooms **C/D**.

THE FAR WEST

The little-visited far west of Zambia is accessible enough to backpackers and not without its rewards. The main town, Mongu, is connected by bus to both Lusaka and Livingstone, making for an interesting off-the-beaten-track alternative to the direct route between these centres. The main attraction along the 600km surfaced road between Lusaka and Mongu is **Kafue National Park**, which doesn't cater to unmotorised travellers, but there's a good chance of seeing some wildlife from the main road since it skirts or passes through the park for close on 100km.

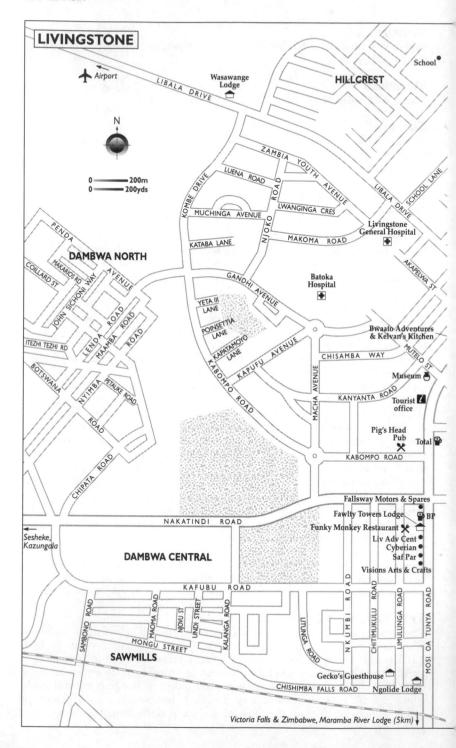

LIVINGSTONE

✈ Airport

LIBALA DRIVE

Wasawange Lodge

School ●

HILLCREST

N

0 ━━━ 200m
0 ━━━ 200yds

ZAMBIA YOUTH AVENUE

LIBALA DRIVE

SCHOOL LANE

KOMBE DRIVE

LUENA ROAD

NJOKO ROAD

LWANGINGA CRES

MUCHINGA AVENUE

Livingstone General Hospital ✚

PENDA

DAMBWA NORTH

MAKARIOS RD

COILLARD ST

JOHN SICHONI WAY

AVENUE

KATABA LANE

MAKOMA ROAD

AKAPELWA ST

GANDHI AVENUE

Batoka Hospital ✚

ITEZHI TEZHI RD

LENDA ROAD

MAAMBA ROAD

ROAD

YETA III LANE

POINSETTIA LANE

KAPATAMOYO LANE

KAPUFU AVENUE

Bwaato Adventures & Kelvan's Kitchen

MUTELO ST

BOTSWANA

NYIMBA

PETAUKE ROAD

ROAD

KABOMPO ROAD

MACHA AVENUE

CHISAMBA WAY

Museum ☕

KANYANTA ROAD

Tourist office ℹ

Pig's Head Pub ✕

Total ⛽

CHIPATA ROAD

KABOMPO ROAD

Fallsway Motors & Spares ●

Fawlty Towers Lodge 🏠

BP ⛽

NAKATINDI ROAD

Funky Monkey Restaurant ✕

Liv Adv Cent ●

Cyberian ●

Saf Par ●

←
Sesheke, Kazungala

DAMBWA CENTRAL

Visions Arts & Crafts ●

KAFUBU ROAD

NKUMBI ROAD

CHITIMUKULU ROAD

LIMULUNGA ROAD

MOSI OA TUNYA ROAD

SAMBONO ROAD

MAOMA ROAD

NJOVU ST

UNDI STREET

KALANGA ROAD

LITUNGA ROAD

MONGU STREET

SAWMILLS

Gecko's Guesthouse 🏠

Ngolide Lodge 🏠

CHISHIMBA FALLS ROAD

Victoria Falls & Zimbabwe, Maramba River Lodge (5km) ↓

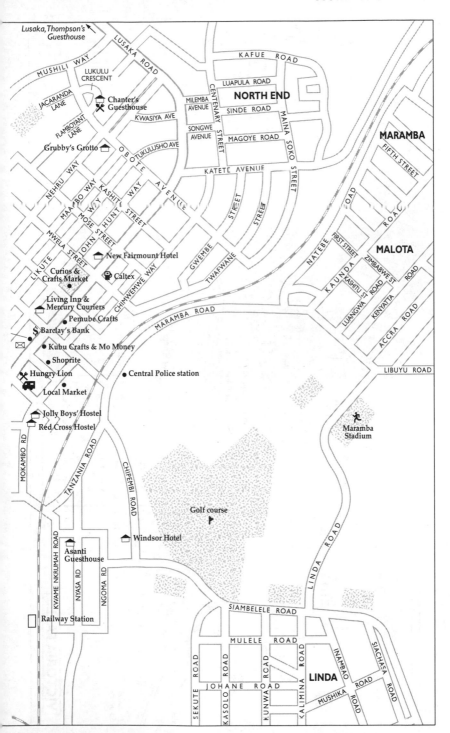

Lusaka, Thompson's Guesthouse

MUSHILI WAY

LUSAKA ROAD

KAFUE ROAD

LUAPULA ROAD

LUKULU CRESCENT

MILEMBA AVENUE

CENTENARY STREET

NORTH END

SINDE ROAD

MAINA SOKO STREET

MARAMBA

JACARANDA LANE

Chanter's Guesthouse

KWASIYA AVE

SONGWE AVENUE

MAGOYE ROAD

FIFTH STREET

FLAMBOYANT LANE

OBOTE TUKULUSHO AVE

KWASIYA AVE

Grubby's Grotto

KATETE AVENUE

NEHRU WAY

MAAPO WAY

KASHITU WAY

WAY AVENUE

STREET

STREET

GWEMBE STREET

TWAFWANE STREET

NATEBE ROAD

FIRST STREET

MALOTA

MOSE STREET

JOHN HUNT STREET

KAUNDA ROAD

KASHITU ST

ZIMBABWE ST

ROAD

MWELA STREET

LIKUTE

New Fairmount Hotel

CHIMWEMWE WAY

LUANGWA ROAD

KENYATTA ROAD

ACCRA ROAD

Curios & Crafts Market

Caltex

MARAMBA ROAD

Living Inn & Mercury Couriers

Pemube Crafts

Barclay's Bank

Kubu Crafts & Mo Money

LIBUYU ROAD

Shoprite

Hungry Lion

Central Police station

Local Market

Maramba Stadium

Jolly Boys' Hostel

Red Cross Hostel

MOKAMBO RD

TANZANIA ROAD

CHIPEMBI ROAD

Golf course

LINDA ROAD

KWAME NKRUMAH ROAD

NYASA RD

NGOMA RD

Windsor Hotel

Asanti Guesthouse

Railway Station

SIAMBELELE ROAD

MULELE ROAD

SEKUTE ROAD

KASOLO ROAD

KUNWA ROAD

CALIMINA ROAD

INAMBAO ROAD

LINDA

SIACHASA ROAD

JOHANE ROAD

MUSHIKA ROAD

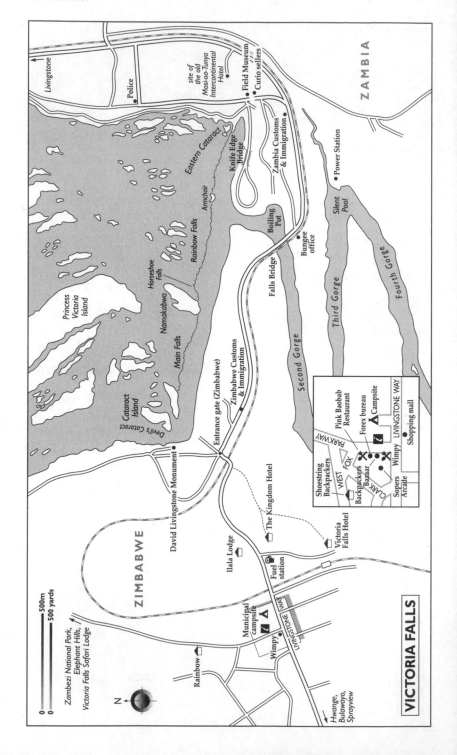

VICTORIA FALLS

Mongu was once the administrative centre of the British Protectorate of Barotseland, home to the Lozi people, who were granted far greater autonomy than other Zambians during the colonial era and whose cultural heritage and subsistence lifestyle has changed little since the beginning of the 20th century. Mongu sprawls along a ridge that offers excellent views across the Zambezi floodplain, and it is connected to the Zambezi itself by an 8km-long channel – it is possible to explore the surrounding waterways by hiring a dugout canoe. If you are travelling in western Zambia during February or March, do ask about when the Ku-omboka will take place – this colourful annual festival, which usually occurs on the last Thursday before a full moon, marks the moving of the Lozi king from the floodplain to higher ground.

There are a few potential stops between Mongu and Livingstone. **Senanga** is a small village with an attractive setting on the Zambezi 95km south of Mongu. A further 100km or so towards Livingstone, **Sioma** is situated within easy walking distance of the **Ngonye Falls**, a spectacular sight that would surely be a major tourist attraction were it not for the more impressive Victoria Falls downstream (ask at the NPWS office in Sioma for a reliable guide to the best viewing point and also to avoid the large crocodiles in the river downstream of the falls). Sesheke is the largest village between Mongu and Livingstone, straddling the river near the border crossing to Katima Mulilo in Namibia.

Access and getting around
Daily buses connect Lusaka to Mongu. Buses between Mongu, Sesheke and Livingstone are very slow and may not be running during the rains. There is also a 'post boat' that runs along the Zambezi to an erratic schedule and willingly takes passengers for a small charge. The best place to ask about its current movements is the District Council Offices in Mongu.

Where to stay and eat
Kafue National Park
Chunga Safari Village Superb site on bend in river next to National Park headquarters 22km south of main Mongu road; tel: 01 221681. Access a problem without transport, but very affordable if you can find a lift. Room **C** pp. Camping **B** pp.

Mongu
Mongu Lodge Most basic place in town. Rooms **E** pp.
Ngulu Hotel Reasonable s/c rooms **F** pp.
Lyamba Hotel Smartest rooms in town **F** pp.

Senanga
Senanga Safari Lodge Rondawels, overlooking river. May allow camping. Good bar and restaurant. Room **E** dbl.
Sioma and Ngonye Falls
Maziba Bay Safaris Signposted about 6km south of Sioma. Canoe hire. Boat trips to falls. Camping **D** pp.
National Parks Campsite Basic site near NPWS office in Sioma. Camp **B** pp.

Sesheke
Government Resthouse Basic rooms **D** dbl.
Soka Camp Tel: 032 20169/20021. Three s/c chalets, basic kitchen equipment, bring your own food. Rooms **D** pp. Might have been sold.

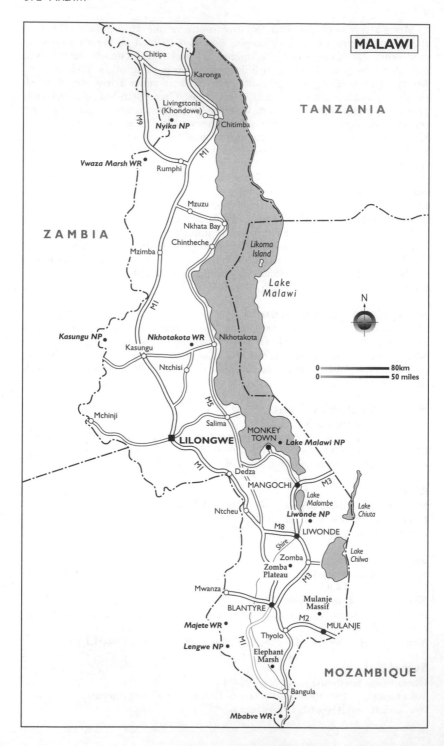

Malawi

13

Malawi lacks the high international profile enjoyed by many other countries in the region, but it is in many respects the perfect backpacking destination: compact, cheap, hassle-free and for the most part stunningly beautiful. Many travellers who fly into Africa are barely aware of Malawi's existence; an equally high proportion will have come to regard it as their favourite country by the time they fly home.

Travel in Malawi inevitably centres around Lake Malawi, the third largest body of water in Africa and, enclosed by the sheer walls of the Rift Valley escarpment, probably the most beautiful. Cape Maclear and Nkhata Bay in particular have become the most popular backpackers' congregation points between Zanzibar and the Victoria Falls, and there are dozens of low-key resorts scattered along the palm-fringed lake shore.

But there is more to Malawi than its lake. The country lacks the vast animal-rich plains found in several other African countries, but places like Vwaza Marsh and Nkhotakota Game Reserves and Nyika and Liwonde National Parks will reward adventurous travellers with some of the most affordable game viewing there is, while all the little-visited mountains, lakes and forest reserves add up to a vast, largely untapped, pool of off-the-beaten-track hiking and rambling opportunities.

BACKGROUND INFORMATION
Geography and climate
Malawi is dominated geographically by the Rift Valley. The 585km-long Lake Malawi is part of the Rift Valley, as is the Shire River, the largest in the country. Malawi is characterised by extremes of altitude – the surface of the lake lies at an altitude of 435m and the Shire River descends to 38m before it flows out of the country into Mozambique. The sheer Rift Valley escarpment rising to the west of Lake Malawi reaches an altitude of over 2,000m. The highest points in the country are Mulanje in the southeast and Nyika in the northwest.

FACTS AND FIGURES
Area: 118,484km² (35th in Africa)
Capital: Lilongwe (Zomba until 1975)
Largest towns: Blantyre, Lilongwe, Zomba, Mzuzu
Population: 10–11,000,000
Official language: English
Other languages: Chichewa, Yao, Ngoni, Nyanja
Currency: Kwacha
Head of State: President Bakili Muluzi

There are three seasons in Malawi: a hot, rainy season from November to April, a moderate, dry season from May to August, and a hot, dry season in September and October. Temperatures vary as much with altitude as they do with season. The lake shore and Shire valley are hot and humid throughout the year. Mid-altitude areas like Lilongwe and Blantyre are hot to moderate, depending on season. Mountainous areas such as Mulanje, Nyika, Viphya, Zomba and Dedza are warm to moderate by day and often quite chilly at night.

History

The name Malawi derives from the Maravi Kingdom, which was established in the central part of the country in the late fifteenth century and reached its peak in the early 17th century under Chief Masula, when it extended almost to Portuguese-held Mozambique island. By 1700, Maravi had collapsed, but many of Malawi's modern ethnic groups, notably the Chewa, share a common Maravi heritage.

The Lake Malawi region suffered greatly as a result of intruders in the 19th century. From the 1830s onwards, in the aftermath of the Mfecane in South Africa, the people of northern Malawi were terrorised by Nguni war bands. In 1845, an Omani trader called Jumbe settled at Nkhotakota, from where he shipped thousands of slaves annually to Metangula on the eastern lake shore in preparation for the three-to-four-month march to Kilwa on the coast. At around the same time, a tribe of Islamic converts called the Yao settled in southern Malawi, where they captured the local Maganja and Chewa in large numbers for sale to the Portuguese. Both the Yao and the Omani slave raids were ruthless affairs in which villagers unfit for shipment were brutally slaughtered.

In 1859, the missionary David Livingstone took a steamer up the Shire, the tributary of the Zambezi which flows out of Lake Malawi. Livingstone explored much of southern Malawi, and helped establish the short-lived UMCA mission at Chiradzulu Mountain near modern Blantyre. In late 1861, Livingstone reached the slaving emporium at Nkhotakota: 'an abode of bloodshed and lawlessness ... strewed with human skeletons and putrid bodies'. By 1863, the bloodshed had spread south: the Shire had, in the words of one member of the expedition, become 'literally a river of death' where the steamer's paddles had to be cleared of bloated corpses every morning.

Livingstone's descriptions of the slave trade in Malawi catalysed an influx of Scots missionaries. In 1874, the year of Livingstone's death, the Livingstonia Mission was established by Dr Robert Laws, followed shortly by the Likoma and Blantyre Missions, the latter named after Livingstone's birthplace. The Scots missionaries in Malawi were a happy exception to the 'Bible in one hand and gun in the other' breed. Inspired by Livingstone's humanitarianism, they risked their lives to end local wars and curb slavery, and provided an outstanding education to many thousands. In 1895, the first British Commissioner to the region, Sir Harry Johnston, dealt the final death blow to the slave trade in Malawi with the defeat of the last two Yao traders in the south and the execution of Mlozi, the self-styled Sultan of Nkondeland, at Karonga in the north.

Malawi was led to independence by the enigmatic Dr Hastings Kamuzu Banda. Born in Malawi in roughly 1897, Banda had worked and/or studied in South Africa, the USA, the UK and Ghana between 1915 and 1957, when he returned to the land of his birth at the request of local nationalist politicians. On July 6 1964, Nyasaland gained independence; Banda set out his stall three weeks later at the OAU summit in Cairo, stating that Malawi had 'one party, one leader, one government and no nonsense about it'. It's often been said that Banda was a benign dictator, but – while not in the murderous league of somebody like Amin – he was certainly ruthless in his quest for absolute power. At least 250,000 people were detained without trial during his rule, and his perceived political opponents tended to become road accident statistics or, as the man himself often boasted, 'meat for crocodiles' in the Shire River. Intolerant of criticism and keen on censorship, Banda's whimsical dictates covered everything from how people dressed (women were banned from wearing mini-skirts or trousers) to what they said about his 'Official Hostess' Mama Cecilia Tamanda Kadzamira. No episode illustrates the vanity, megalomania and paranoia of Banda better than his banning of a Simon and Garfunkel song, released during a rocky patch in Banda's love life. The lyric 'Cecilia, you're breaking my heart...' was more than he could bear.

Banda was perceived as benign for the simple reason that he was a conservative Anglophile in the prevalent mood of African socialism and nationalism. In 1989, Margaret Thatcher and the Pope both visited Malawi, and uttered not a word of criticism of what had become the longest-lived dictatorship of its sort in Africa; on the contrary, the British prime minister praised Banda for his 'wise leadership'. Two years later, by which time the Cold War had thawed and courting friendly dictators was out (unless they had vast reserves of oil sitting under their soil), Britain made the hypocritical gesture of withdrawing non-humanitarian aid to Malawi in belated protest at Banda's abuse of human rights.

By 1989, the 91-year-old tyrant was basically a puppet president, manipulated by his shadowy Official Hostess and her uncle John Tembo, neither of whom had Banda's charismatic grip on the peasantry. In March 1992, a group of Catholic bishops read out the so-called Lenten Letter, which documented in detail the failings and power abuses of the Banda administration. The letter was then faxed to the BBC. Banda placed the bishops under house arrest, but for once the world was watching, and for the first time since independence Malawi experienced a climate of open dissent culminating in the Lilongwe Riot of May in which 40 people were shot dead by police. A referendum in March 1993 drew an overwhelming majority of votes in favour of a multi-party election, which was held on March 17 1994 and won by a recently emerged party: the UDF under Bakili Muluzi.

In 1996, Banda (who subsequently died in 1999) as well as Tembo and Mama Cecilia were tried for the alleged murder of three cabinet ministers and an MP who had died in a car accident in 1983. Their acquittal said much about the new Malawi: a legal trial was a privilege given to few in the days of Banda.

PRACTICAL INFORMATION
Accommodation
Resorts or hostels specifically catering to backpackers exist in Lilongwe, Blantyre, Cape Maclear, Nkhata Bay and elsewhere on the lake shore. There is no shortage of local lodgings elsewhere, and you'll rarely pay more than US$3 for a basic room. In practically every town, reserve or resort, there's somewhere to pitch a tent at the fairly standard price of US$1pp.

Books and newspapers
Bookshops in Lilongwe and Blantyre sell a limited selection of novels at inflated prices. Since the advent of democracy, an extraordinary number of English-language newspapers are printed. International papers are sold at Times Book Shops in Blantyre, Lilongwe, Mzuzu and Zomba.

Crime and safety

Until recently, Malawi was widely regarded to be the safest travel destination in the region as far as crime against tourists was concerned. This has all changed, and while Malawi can hardly be compared to Nairobi or Johannesburg, travellers should be alert to the risk of casual and armed theft. Unusually for Africa, it is not the cities that are the main area of concern in Malawi: aside from the pickpockets who work the market areas, neither Lilongwe nor Blantyre has a reputation for crime against tourists, though a degree of caution would be advisable at night. Crime is a greater problem at the more popular lakeshore resorts, notably Nkhata Bay, Cape Maclear and Sengo Bay, and the pattern seems to be for a sudden spate of robberies in one or other resort which dies down once the perpetrators have been arrested or moved on. The best advice I can give is to keep your ear to the ground and be cautious wherever you've heard of recent robberies.

In Cape Maclear, be wary of offering anybody advance payment for a service (chances are you'll never see them again) and don't leave valuables in your pockets while you swim, even from a boat. Tent slashing has been reported at several lakeshore resorts.

Entrance fees

All national parks and game reserves charge an entrance fee equivalent to roughly US$6 per 24 hours. There is no entrance fee for forest reserves.

Entry formalities

A visa is required by all except holders of Commonwealth, European Union, USA or South African passports, and it must be bought in advance. All visitors will have a free visitor's pass stamped into their passport upon arrival, valid for up to 30 days and easily extended at any immigration office. For stays of longer than three months, a six-month temporary residence permit costs US$5. You may be required to complete a Currency Declaration Form at some borders – it'll be kept by the customs officials and you'll never hear about it again.

Food and drink

Maize porridge, called *nsima*, is served with a bland stew for around US$1. Near the lake shore, grilled and fried fish is the main diet – most often *chambo* (a pleasant, slightly bland member of the tilapia family) but sometimes *kampango* (mudfish) or *mpasa* (a large cichlid with dark flesh, also called lake salmon). In larger towns, 'proper' restaurants serve a limited range of Western dishes for US$2–5. Most large towns have at least one good supermarket, normally part of the PTC or Kandodo chain. Local lager beer is excellent; most travellers favour *Carlsberg 'Green'* over the sweeter *Carlsberg 'Brown'*.

Getting around
By road
Distances in Malawi are short by African standards, most main roads are surfaced and well-maintained, and buses tend to be relatively new. The Stagecoach Bus Company covers practically every conceivable route in Malawi. Express buses run daily between Lilongwe and Blantyre, taking five hours to cover 300km and stopping only at Dedza, Ntcheu, Balaka, Liwonde Barrage and Zomba. Express buses also connect Lilongwe and Karonga (stopping at Kasungu, Mzimba, Chikengawa, Mzuzu, Rumphi and Chilumba); Nkhata Bay and Blantyre (stopping at Chintheche, Kande, Nkhotakota and Salima); Blantyre and Mulanje (stopping at Thyolo); and Blantyre and Monkey Bay (stopping at Zomba, Liwonde

LAKE MALAWI FERRIES

The MV *Ilala II*, which has been plying the length of Lake Malawi since 1957, remains the only way to get between the mainland and Likoma and Chizamulu Islands, as well as a good if unusual way to cross between Tanzania and Malawi, and a great trip in its own right. Most backpackers travel first class on the upper deck, which is affordable, though not cheap, and has the advantage being very uncrowded by comparison to the dirty and sweaty (but very cheap) lower deck. There's a bar on the upper deck, and a restaurant serves good three-course meals which must be ordered a couple of hours in advance.

The main drawback to the *Ilala* is that the timetable is rather whimsical. The schedule reproduced below is less than strictly adhered to, in fact it is normal for the boat to run five to six hours behind, it has been known to run up to a day behind, and very occasionally it will skip a leg to catch up time and might actually arrive ahead of schedule!

In theory, two other ferries, the MV *Mtendere* and MV *Chauncy Maples* do a weekly run up and down the Malawian section of the lake, but both of these boats seem to have been in dry dock semi-permanently for the last few years. A more intriguing possibility is the Tanzanian MV *Songea* which normally leaves from Ituri Port in Tanzania on Thursday morning, stops at Mbamba between dusk on Thursday and dawn on Friday, then arrives at Nkhata Bay sometime on Friday before starting the return trip.

MV *Ilala*

	day	arrives	departs
Monkey Bay	Friday		08.00
Chilinda	Friday	10.30	12.20
Nkhotakota	Saturday	07.30	08.30
Likoma	Saturday	14.30	17.30
Chizumulu	Saturday	18.45	20.15
Nkhata Bay	Saturday	23.30	04.00 (Sunday)
Chilumba	Sunday	18.00	02.00 (Monday)
Nkhata Bay	Monday	16.30	01.00 (Tuesday)
Mbamba Bay (Tanz)	Tuesday	04.30	07.30
Nkhata Bay	Tuesday	11.00	13.00
Chizumulu	Tuesday	16.00	17.30
Likoma	Tuesday	18.45	21.45
Nkhotakota	Wednesday	03.00	04.00
Chilinda	Wednesday	21.00	22.30
Monkey Bay	Thursday	01.00	

Leaves Monkey Bay Friday for the north, arrives Nkhata Bay late Saturday night, leaves Sunday heading north.

Heading south arrives Nkhata Bay Monday lunchtime, heads to Mbamba bay Monday night.

Arrives Nkhata Bay Tuesday afternoon, leaves heading south Tuesday evening. *MV Songea* comes into Nkhata Bay Friday morning and leaves Friday evening for Mbamba Bay.

and Mangochi). Unlike express buses, country buses stop at designated bus stages every couple of kilometres, which makes them very slow but useful for reaching isolated resorts and forest reserves. Buses are supplemented (and on some minor routes replaced) by a semi-formal system of paid lifts known as *matola*. Hitching is possible on main roads.

By rail
Malawi's railways are rarely used by travellers, except for the line between Liwonde and the Mozambique border (see *The Crossing Points* in Chapter 6).

Health
The Lake Malawi shore and Shire Valley are among the worst parts of Africa for malaria, particularly during the wet season. Remember to cover up at night in these places!

Maps
A useful general-purpose map, printed in 1992, is the Ministry of Surveys' 1:1,000,000 *Malawi Road and Tourist Map* (though it erroneously marks Chilumba as Khondowe, and was printed before the lake shore road between Nkhata Bay and Nkhotakota and the M14 from Lilongwe to Salima were established). It can be bought at the map sales offices in Lilongwe, Blantyre or Karonga for US$2, as can 1:50,000 and 1:25,000 maps covering most of the whole country.

Money
Malawi is a very cheap country, even by African standards, and a daily budget of US$10 is more than achievable. The unit of currency is the Malawi , divided into 100 *tambala*. The exchange rate is approximately US$1=K16. Foreign currency can be changed at any branch of the Commercial Bank of Malawi or National Bank of Malawi, or at private forex bureaux in Lilongwe or Blantyre. Banking hours are from 08.00 to 13.00 Monday to Friday. The once thriving black market is now only of interest if you have to change money outside of banking hours. Street touts will only accept US dollars or South African *rand* cash. Note that there is no bank at Cape Maclear or Monkey Bay; the nearest one is in Mangochi.

Post and telephone
International post is very cheap, but also very slow and unreliable; allow at least three weeks for it to get through. Malawi is a good place from which to post curios inexpensively. All telephone numbers in Malawi have six digits. Assume that a number starting with a seven is in Lilongwe and that one starting with a six is in Blantyre. Malawi's telephone service is reasonably efficient by African standards. Phone booths can be found outside most post offices.

Public holidays
In addition to New Year, Easter, Christmas and Boxing Day, the following public holidays are recognised. If a public holiday falls on Saturday or Sunday, it's taken on the next Monday.

16 January	John Chilembwe Day
3 March	Martyrs' Day
1 May	Labour Day
6 July	Independence Day
Second Monday in October	Mothers' Day
Second Monday in December	National Tree-Planting Day

Tourist information offices

The tourist offices in Blantyre and Lilongwe are mostly of interest for the useful books that they stock.

Northern Malawi
FROM KARONGA TO MZUZU

The largest town on the northern lakeshore, **Karonga** is where most travellers arriving from Tanzania will spend their first night in Malawi. The lakeside setting aside, it's a rather dull town, with some slight historical interest provided by the Armstrong Gun guarding the District Commissioner's Office (used in 1888 in an attempt to capture the fort of a notorious slave trader) and the large baobab tree in front of the post office (a makeshift gun platform during hostilities between German East Africa and British Nyasaland in 1915). There's a well-stocked Map Sales Office on the road to the Marina Club.

South of Karonga, the dramatic Rift Valley mountains that enclose the northern lake shore tower above the sandy beaches of **Chombe Bay**. The most significant village on this bay, Chitimba, lies at the junction of the M1 and the road to the **Livingstonia Mission**, one of the most attractive spots in northern Malawi. Founded by Doctor Robert Laws, the Livingstonia Mission was sited first at Cape Maclear and then at Bandawe before it was relocated to its present site in 1894 due to the high incidence of malaria around the lake shore. The mission today is a fascinating anachronism, centred around an isolated and faintly absurd stone roundabout and clock tower, and it offers stunning views across the lake to the Livingstone Mountains in Tanzania. Also well worth seeing are the 300m-high Manchewe Falls 2km from the mission along the Chitimba road.

Further inland, and most easily reached from the small town of **Rumphi**, the 3,134km^2 **Nyika National Park** is Malawi's largest conservation area, protecting the undulating grasslands and remnant forest patches of the 2,000m-high Nyika Plateau on the border with Zambia. Particularly attractive to hikers, Nyika offers a rare opportunity to walk freely amongst large mammals such as Burchell's zebra, roan antelope, reedbuck, bushbuck and eland, as well as roughly 200 orchid and 400 bird species. (See box *Walking and hiking on the Nyika Plateau* on page 381.)

Nyika is relatively difficult to reach on public transport, for which reason it's tempting to label the less publicised **Vwaza Marsh Game Reserve** as a consolation prize for the unlucky. But why damn Vwaza Marsh with faint praise, when the affordable and accessible Kazuni Camp is arguably Malawi's best-kept game viewing secret? The camp overlooks Lake Kazuni, which has a resident population of hippos and crocodiles and is visited by a steady stream of impalas, greater kudus and buffalos. Two 100-strong elephant herds, resident around Kazuni since 1992, come past the camp on most days, generally in the mid-morning or late afternoon. And if the animals don't come to you, then ask the rangers at Kazuni to take you on a guided game walk – excellent value.

Despite its status as the capital of Malawi's Northern Province, **Mzuzu** has a sleepy, provincial atmosphere. The comfortable mid-altitude climate and fertility of the surrounding hills make Mzuzu an attractive enough city, and it has some useful facilities: four large PTC and Kandodo supermarkets, a Times Book Store, several banks and national park and tourist offices. A good new internet café called Easymail, next to the PTC supermarket, offers full Internet and email services (easymail@malawi.net). All the same, few backpackers do more than pass through Mzuzu en route to the lake.

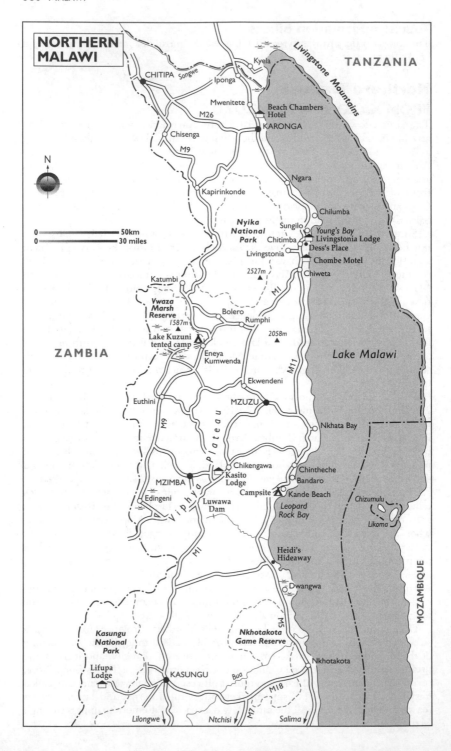

NORTHERN MALAWI

TANZANIA

Livingstone Mountains

Kyela

CHITIPA
Songwe
Iponga

Mwenitete

Beach Chambers Hotel

M26

KARONGA

Chisenga

M9

N

Ngara

Kapirinkonde

Chilumba

Nyika National Park

Sungilo
Young's Bay
Chitimba
Livingstonia Lodge
Dess's Place

Livingstonia

0 ——— 50km
0 ——— 30 miles

Chombe Motel

Chiweta

2527m

Katumbi

M1

Vwaza Marsh Reserve

1587m

Bolero
Rumphi

Lake Kuzuni tented camp

2058m

Eneya Kumwenda

Lake Malawi

Ekwendeni

ZAMBIA

M11

Euthini

MZUZU

M9

Nkhata Bay

Viphya Plateau

Chikengawa

Chintheche
Bandaro

MZIMBA

Kasito Lodge

Campsite
Kande Beach

Edingeni

Luwawa Dam

Leopard Rock Bay

Chizumulu

Likoma

M1

Heidi's Hideaway

MOZAMBIQUE

Dwangwa

M5

Kasungu National Park

Nkhotakota Game Reserve

Lifupa Lodge

Nkhotakota

KASUNGU

Bua

M18

Lilongwe
Ntchisi
M7
Salima

WALKING AND HIKING ON THE NYIKA PLATEAU

Chelinda Camp lies at the centre of the extensive network of roads and paths that cover the Nyika Plateau. An 8km round walk from Chelinda to two dams offers good game viewing, with frequent sightings of roan antelope and wattled crane. Another good short walk leaves Chelinda from behind Chalet Four, taking you to the Kasaramba turn-off, then left along Forest Drive and back to Chelinda through the pine plantation, where leopards are often seen towards dusk. Also recommended is the 16km round trip to Lake Kaulime, the only natural lake on the plateau. A private stable near Chelinda does horseback trails.

From the defunct Zambian Resthouse (which technically lies within Zambia, though there are no border formalities), you can visit the Zovo Chipola Forest and 4km walking trail through Chowo Forest, the best place to see the many forest birds on Nyika's checklist of 400-plus species, as well duikers and samango monkey.

Guided overnight hikes can be organised through the management of Chelinda Lodge, assuming you bring your own camping equipment and food. The popular three-day, two-night wilderness trail from Chelinda to Livingstonia costs US$80 for two people and US$10 for every extra person, inclusive of guide and camping fees and transport back for the guide. Other trails cost US$30 per night for two people and US$5 per night for every extra person inclusive of guide and camping fees. The four-night Jalawe and Chipome River Trail passes through the brachystegia woodland on the northern slopes of Nyika, where elephant, buffalo and greater kudu are reasonably common and lions are still present.

For further details of walks and trails, buy Sigrid Anna Johnson's comprehensive *Visitor's Guide to Nyika National Park* (Mbabazi Book Trust, Blantyre, US$4).

Access and getting around

The M1 south of Karonga runs roughly parallel to Chombe Bay as far as Chiweta, before climbing the escarpment towards Rumphi, Mzuzu and eventually Lilongwe. Express buses run along the M1 between Karonga, Mzuzu and Lilongwe, stopping at Chitimba, Chiweta and Rumphi. You need to use a country bus to be dropped at one of the resorts in between.

Livingstonia is connected to Chitimba by a steep 16km road that navigates 20 switchback bends. There's no public transport on this road, but a few *matola* pick-up trucks do the run daily. Quite a few travellers hike up, a four-to-five-hour walk that's best done in a group, since a few muggings have been reported.

The gateway to Nyika and Vwaza Marsh is Rumphi, connected by bus to Karonga and by regular minibuses to Mzuzu. The entrance gate to Nyika lies 60km west of Rumphi on the S10 to Chitipa, and the turn-offs to the Zambian Resthouse and Chitimba Camp lie another 45km past the gate. In the dry season, there's a daily bus between Rumphi and Chitipa which could drop you at either of these junctions, from where it would be a 2km walk to the Zambian Rest House or 15km to Chitimba. There's no public transport between Rumphi and Chitipa during the rains and, although a *matola* to Katumbi can drop you 8km from the entrance gate (where camping is permitted), you'd have to hitch to get further into the park, something that you might as well do from Rumphi.

Getting to Vwaza Marsh is easier. Kazuni Camp lies 25km from Rumphi along a back road to Mzimba. The daily bus which leaves Mzimba at 07.00 and starts the return trip from Rumphi at 11.30 stops at a village 1km from the camp – there's a dirt cheap council resthouse in Mzimba if you need to spend a night there. It's also possible to catch a lift from Rumphi to Kazuni with a pick-up truck heading to one of the tobacco farms in the Vwaza area – wait under the trees opposite the PTC supermarket in Rumphi.

Where to stay and eat
Karonga
Fukafukagha Resthouse Good, central cheap lodge. Rooms **A** dbl or **B** s/c dbl.
Marina Club On beach. Rooms **B**/**C** s/c with hot water. Camping. Good meals.
Mufwa Lakeside Centre On beach. Rooms **A** sgl or **C** s/c dbl.

Chitimba
Brothers-in-Arms Resthouse Best of a few **A** lodgings.
Chitimba Beach Campsite (formerly Dess's Place) Lakeside campsite with basic rooms coming, signposted 1km north of Chitimba. Meals are available, as are Landrover trips to Livingstonia. Camping **A** pp.

Livingstonia
CCAP Resthouses The Stone House, the former home of Dr Laws, is the nicer of two church resthouses. Basic meals. Good view from the veranda. Rooms **B** pp.
Lukwe Permaculture Camp This admirable eco-friendly set-up overlooks Manchewe Falls about 2km before you reach Livingstonia coming from Chitimba. Facilities include hot showers and toilets, the latter with breathtaking views over the Rift Valley. Organically grown meals, and bar facilities. Guided hikes to local places of interest. Proceeds go towards sustainable agricultural projects. Camping **A** pp.

Between Chitimba and Chiweta (north to south)
Namaishi Holiday Resort Nice beach setting. Large rooms **C** dbl with net. Camping.
Mbuta Lodge Next to Namaisha. Rooms **C** s/c dbl (hot water). Camping. Restaurant.
Nyathumbata Lodge 3km further along beach. Rooms **B** dbl. Camping. Basic meals.

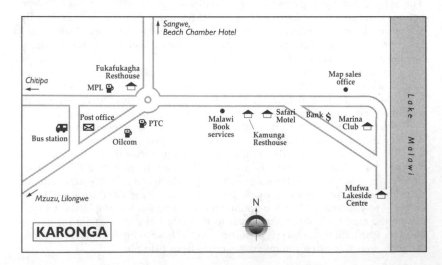

KARONGA

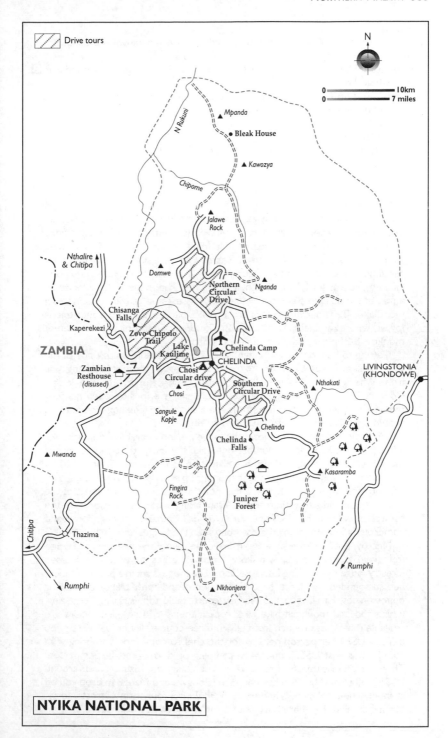

Drive tours

N

10km

7 miles

N Rukuni

Mpanda

● Bleak House

▲ Kawozya

Chipome

▲ Jalawe Rock

Nthalire ↑ & Chitipa

▲ Domwe

Northern Circular Drive)

▲ Nganda

Chisanga Falls

Zovo-Chipolo Trail

Lake Kaulime

Chelinda Camp

CHELINDA

Kaperekezi

ZAMBIA

Zambian Resthouse (disused)

Chosi Circular drive

Chosi

Sangule Kopje

Southern Circular Drive

LIVINGSTONIA (KHONDOWE)

▲ Nthakati

▲ Chelinda

Chelinda Falls

▲ Mwanda

Kasaramba

Fingira Rock ▲

Juniper Forest

Chitipa

Thazima

↙ Rumphi

↙ Rumphi

▲ Nkhonjera

NYIKA NATIONAL PARK

Rumphi

Kajiso Stopover Resort Riotous pick-up joint that's more downtown Nairobi than smalltown Malawi.
Luninya Motel Smartest place in town. Clean rooms with three-quarter bed and nets **B**; s/c dbl with hot water, net and fan **C**.
Mbakajiso Restaurant Currently rated the best place to eat in Rumphi.
Yangotha Hide-Away Best of several **A** lodgings.

Nyika National Park

Chelinda Lodge and Campsite Tel: 74 0848; fax: 74 0579; email: nyika-safaries@malawi.net. Beautifully located former government resthouse now under

---

THE VIPHYA PLATEAU

Barely an hour from Mzuzu by express bus, the little-known Viphya Plateau offers excellent rambling and birding, as well as a refreshingly breezy change of scene if you've spent a while on the humid lake shore. It is easily explored from the Department of Forestry's **Kasito Lodge**, a pair of former colonial residences with excellent facilities (fridge, fireplace, hot baths, equipped kitchen), rooms for **B** pp, and cheap camping. The lodge is surrounded by a mix of exotic pine plantation, indigenous forest and tangled brachystegia woodland. Birds and butterflies are prolific, particularly in the indigenous forest, where ramblers also stand a chance of encountering baboon, vervet monkey, bushpig, red duiker and even leopard.

Getting to Kasito is easy enough, since both lodges lie on the side of the M1. Express buses between Mzuzu and Lilongwe stop at Chikengawa, from where it's a 45-minute walk south along the M1 to the lodge. Country buses can drop you at Kasito bus stage opposite lodge number two. Soft drinks and basic foodstuffs are available at Chikengawa, but you should bring other food at Mzuzu or Mzimba.

While the walking options from the lodge are innumerable, you might like a few pointers. From lodge number one, take the footpath to the bottom of the valley, cross the stream into the plantation forest, and after about 200m you'll connect with a disused road that opens up several walking routes – turn left and after 2km you come to a five-point intersection in the heart of the forest. You could also walk to Kasito Dam along a track that leads from the M1 a short way south of lodge number two, or explore the riparian forest and numerous side-roads along the road between the lodges and Chikengawa.

Nearby, but less accessible and more expensive, **Luwawa Forest Lodge** (tel: (cell) 829725; email: wardlow@malawi.net) is a recently privatised forestry lodge overlooking Luwawa Dam. The lodge is set in a pine plantation, but surrounded by dense brachystegia woodland with plenty of walking opportunities. Facilities include squash court, table tennis, sailing, canoeing, fishing rod and mountain-bike hire, rock climbing and abseiling. Meals are available (breakfast or lunch from US$4, three-course dinner US$12) or you can pay US$3 per person per day for the chef to cook food you bring with you. Rooms cost US$30 dbl, while camping or dorms cost **C** per person. There is no public transport to Luwawa, but a taxi from Mzimba costs around US$12. Alternatively, ask a bus between Lilongwe and Mzuzu to drop you off at the junction to Luwawa and try to hitch with a tourist or a forestry lorry, bearing in mind that there is a risk of being stranded at the junction.

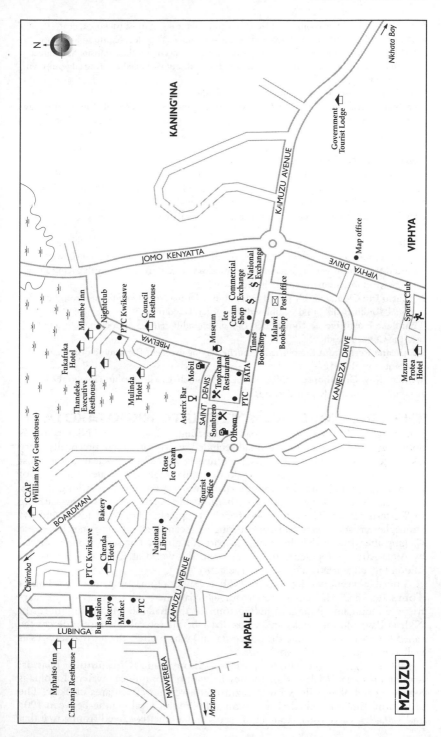

N

KANING'INA

Nkhata Bay

Government
Tourist Lodge

KAMUZU AVENUE

VIPHYA

JOMO KENYATTA

Map office

VIPHYA DRIVE

Mlambe Inn

Nightclub

PTC Kwiksave

Council
Resthouse

National
Exchange

Commercial
Exchange

Museum

Ice
Cream
Shop

MBELWA

Fukafuka
Hotel

Post office

Times
Bookshop

Malawi
Bookshop

Sports Club

Thandeka
Executive
Resthouse

Mulinda
Hotel

Mobil

SAINT DENIS

Tropicana
Restaurant

PTC

BATA

KANJEDZA DRIVE

Mzuzu
Protea
Hotel

CCAP
(William Koyi Guesthouse)

Asterix Bar

Sombreto

Olteam

BOARDMAN

Rose
Ice Cream

Tourist
office

Chitimba

Bakery

PTC Kwiksave

Chenda
Hotel

National
Library

KAMUZU AVENUE

MAPALE

Mphatso Inn

Chibanja Resthouse

LUBINGA

Bus station

Bakery

Market

PTC

MAWERERA

Mzimba

MZUZU

private ownership. The rooms are priced beyond the means of most backpackers at US$78/120 full-board single/double, while self-catering chalets sleeping up to four cost US$100. Set close to the lodge and under the same management, the campsite has a great location and good facilities (flush toilets, hot showers), but you need to bring all your own food. Camping **B** pp.

Thazima Entrance Gate Camping but no facilities.

Zambian Resthouse Closed 1997, unlikely to re-open in the foreseeable future. You may or may not be permitted to pitch a tent at the nearby scouts' camp, paying the US$5 Zambian entrance fee.

Vwaza Marsh Game Reserve

Kazuni Camp Tel: 74-0848; fax: 74-0579; email: nyika-safaries@malawi.net. Recently privatised, with attractive grass huts replacing old standing tents. New ablution block has hot showers and flush toilets. You need to bring all food with you, though the camp attendants might agree to cook for a small fee. Rooms **E/F**. Camping **C** pp.

Mzuzu

Chenda Hotel Quasi-mid-range hotel with smart rooms. **E** s/c dbl with hot shower.

Council Resthouse Very acceptable accommodation in the **A** range. Worth paying a few extra kwacha for a cleaner room in the new wing.

Mphatso Inn Clean, sensibly priced hotel on the Karonga road five minutes from bus station. **C** ordinary dbl or **D** s/c dbl with hot water. Good meals.

Thandeka Executive Resthouse Best of a dozen indifferent **A**/**B** lodgings clustered near the Council Resthouse.

Tropicana Restaurant Established favourite serving excellent Portuguese dishes and *chambo* at around US$2.

William Koyi Guesthouse Run by the CCAP Church, excellent value, close to the bus station, but often full. Rooms/dorms **A** pp.

THE LAKESHORE FROM MZUZU TO NKHOTAKOTA

The roughly 200km stretch of road connecting Nkhata Bay to Nkhotakota is dotted with attractive towns and small secluded resorts catering to practically every taste and budget. **Nkhata Bay** itself competes with Cape Maclear as the most popular backpackers' congregation point on Lake Malawi. Situated on a pair of pretty bays spilling into the wooded mainland and separated by a long narrow peninsula, Nkhata Bay is scattered with affordable hotels and restaurants catering to Western palates. There's a good beach at Chikela, 2km from town, and the atmosphere is addictively laid-back, though a recent spate of muggings has made walking after dark inadvisable except as part of a group. The scuba course offered by Aqua Africa is reputedly the cheapest in the world at US$130 for a week's tuition (email: aquaafrica@compuserve.com).

A notable recent development in Nkhata Bay is a tour company called **Tonga Tours** (tel: 352 341; email: tongatours@malawi.net) who set up backpacker-friendly mountain-biking and hiking tours of the Kandoli Mountains (north of Nkhata Bay) and the Nyika and Vwaza Marsh. There is also a bureau de change called Easy Money (opposite the police station) which offers the normal services as well as cash advances on credit cards.

Nkhtata Bay is the closest port to **Likoma** and **Chizumulu Islands**, territorially part of Malawi though they lie within Mozambican waters. Likoma is 8km long and 3km wide, while Chizumulu barely covers an area of 2km². The cruciform Anglican cathedral on Likoma, built with local granite between 1903 and 1905, has carved soapstone choir stalls and a crucifix carved from a tree that

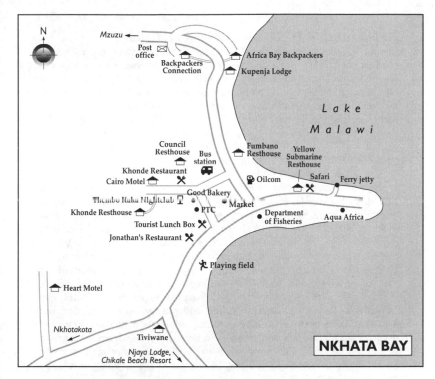

N

Mzuzu ←

Post office ✉

Backpackers Connection

Africa Bay Backpackers

Kupenja Lodge

Lake Malawi

Council Resthouse

Bus station 🚌

Fumbano Resthouse

Yellow Submarine Resthouse

Khonde Restaurant

Cairo Motel 🏠 ✕

Oilcom ⛽

Safari

Ferry jetty

🏠 ✕

Good Bakery

Thembo Huku Nightclub 🍸 ●

Market ●

Khonde Resthouse 🏠

● PTC

● Department of Fisheries

Aqua Africa

Tourist Lunch Box ✕

Jonathan's Restaurant ✕

🏃 Playing field

🏠 Heart Motel

Nkhotakota ←

Tiviwane 🏠

Njaya Lodge, Chikale Beach Resort ↘

NKHATA BAY

grew at Chitambo where Livingstone died. Likoma is rather barren, but it has a friendly, isolated atmosphere. Chizumulu is more lush, there's excellent snorkelling and fishing off its shores, and the sunsets are reputedly the most beautiful in Malawi.

The small trading centre of **Chintheche** straddles the lakeshore road about 40km south of Nkhata Bay. The surrounding paradisal beaches are rescued from chocolate-box anonymity by jagged rocky outcrops and patches of remnant forest. Chintheche lies at the widest part of the lake: with the Mozambican shore an indistinct blur on the horizon, it's easy to be lulled into the feeling you are at the ocean. About 10km from Chintheche, Bandawe was the site of the Livingstonia Mission from 1890 to 1894, but it was abandoned for the modern site due to its unhealthiness – notwithstanding Laws' practice of facing all buildings inland (he believed that malaria was caused by 'miasma' rising from the lake!). The original church and graveyard at Bandawe can still be seen on the headland south of Chintheche Inn.

Further south towards Nkhotakota are several isolated resorts, of which **Kande Beach Campsite** is rapidly establishing itself as one of Malawi's most popular backpackers' retreats, and **Heidi's Hideaway** deserves to. Before reaching Nkhotakota, the sugar-growing town of **Dwangwa** is relatively missable, unless perhaps the lingering smell of molasses turns you on.

Nkhotakota is often and somewhat euphemistically referred to as the oldest traditional market village in East and Central Africa. It was, in fact, the terminal from which as many as 20,000 slaves were shipped across the lake annually in the 19th century. Livingstone described Nkhotakota as an 'abode of lawlessness and bloodshed ... literally strewed with human bones and putrid bodies' after a futile

NKHOTAKOTA TO LILONGWE VIA NTCHISI

People travelling south from Nkhotakota generally follow the lakeshore road to Salima, then either cut west to Lilongwe or else continue south to Cape Maclear. An obscure alternative route is the dirt M7 which connects Nkhotakota and Lilongwe via Ntchisi. There's not much transport heading this way, but you should make it through easily enough if you're not in a rush. Buses reputedly run between Nkhotakota and Ntchisi during the dry season, while at other times a few trucks trundle back and forth daily – wait at the PTC supermarket in Nkhotakota – and at least one bus daily goes between Ntchisi and Lilongwe.

The road between Nkhotakota and Ntchisi bisects the scenic brachystegia-covered hills of **Nkhotakota Game Reserve**, home to a rich diversity of mammals including elephant, buffalo, sable antelope, warthog, lion and leopard. The undulating terrain and thick vegetation make animal-spotting difficult from the road, but the reserve can be explored on guided walks. The best base for this is Chipata Camp, where there are two double rondawels, a youth hostel and camping (all **A** pp). To get there, ask to be dropped at Mbobo Rangers Camp, 500m south of the junction of the M7 and the M18 to Kasungu, walk along the M18 for 3km, then turn left at the signpost reading Chipata Camp and Youth Hostel. The camp lies an hour's walk along this road, and you can walk it unguided, but if you're uneasy about encountering lions, elephants or buffalo, an armed escort from Mbobo will cost US$2. The best short walk from the camp is to the top of 1,638m Chipata Hill, a 6km round trip through evergreen forest. Entrance costs US$1.50 per 24 hours and guided walks cost US$2 per person per half-day.

Ntchisi town isn't much of a place, but it does at least have a couple of resthouses and a supermarket. Between Ntchisi and Lilongwe, **Ntchisi Forest Reserve** protects the extensive evergreen forest on the 1,655m Ntchisi Mountain, home to many unusual birds and butterflies as well as samango and vervet monkey, red and blue duiker, bushpig, porcupine, leopard – and even the occasional stray elephant from Nkhotakota Game Reserve. The walking possibilities are practically unlimited, and not restricted to the reserve. An excellent forestry resthouse with views to Lake Malawi is situated at the reserve entrance, with rooms for **B** pp and camping. To get there, ask a bus to Lilongwe to drop you at the turn-off to Ntchisi Forest Reserve, 12km from Ntchisi town. The bus stage is called Chindembwe, also the name of the small village about 5km along the road to the forest reserve. It shouldn't be difficult to find a *matola* ride to Chindembwe, but you'll probably have to walk the final 11km to the reserve entrance. There are signposts at all intersections.

attempt to convince its sultan, Jumbe, to abandon the slave trade. The 'magnificent fig tree' under which Livingstone and Jumbe met still stands in the attractive stone Mission compound; the modern market, thankfully, is quite unremarkable.

Access and getting around

Regular buses run the length of the road between Mzuzu, Nkhata Bay and Nkhotakota. Express buses stop at larger settlements such as Chintheche, Kande and Dwangwa, but only country buses stop at the turn-offs to some lake resorts (see *Where to stay and eat*). Many travellers make use of the direct overnight bus to Cape Maclear which leaves Nkhata Bay at around 21.00 daily.

Likoma and Chizumulu islands can be reached by lake ferry from Nkhata Bay. The trip to Chizumulu takes three hours and the trip to Likoma five hours (see ferry schedule on page 377 for further details). It's possible to arrange local boats between the two islands and to Cobue in Mozambique.

Where to stay and eat
Nkhata Bay

Africa Bay Backpackers Nicely positioned and popular, but suffers from regular changes of owner and intermittent theft problems. Bamboo huts or camping **A** pp. Restaurant attached.

Backpackers Connection The most central hostel, with a great view from a rise above the market over Nkhata Bay. Not the cheapest but very clean and secure, with good food, a pool table and hot showers. Rooms **B**/**C** with nets. Dorm **A** pp.

Butterfly Lodge New lodge next to the White-Fathers Beach run by a Malawian woman who used to work at Njaya.

Chikale Beach Resort Set on the same beach as Njaya Lodge, 2km from town, this is a relatively pricey but good value set-up. Chalets **E** dbl. Camping **A** pp.

Heart Motel This friendly, locally run place in the village has been going for as long as anybody can remember. Less popular than its trendier foreign-owned rivals, it remains great value. Room with nets **A** pp including breakfast.

Jonathan's Restaurant Western style dishes US$1.50. Memorable chocolate cake.

Mayoka Village New lodge on the road between Nkhata Bay and Chikale Beach. Similar prices to Njaya. Nice situation on a rocky stretch of the lakeshore.

Njaya Lodge PO Box 223, Nkhata Bay; tel 352342; email: njayalodge@compuserve.com; web: www.africanet.com/njaya/welcome.htm. The most trendy and popular of the backpacker lodges, with a beautiful position 2km from town on Chikale Beach. Excellent facilities include satellite TV, pool tables, good bar and restaurant. Credit cards accepted. Very secure, though do be conscious that people have been mugged walking between the lodge and town at night. Kayak safaris to Kande Beach or Likoma offered at US$40 pp daily all-inclusive. Diving courses likely to start up during the lifespan of this edition. S/c chalets **E** pp. Bamboo hut **C** pp. Camping **B** pp.

Safari Restaurant A recent and welcome addition to Nkhata Bay's eateries, serving steak and chips, pizzas and pasta for around US$3.

Yellow Submarine Resthouse Also relatively new, and next door to the Safari, this German-run hotel is good value at **A**/**B** .

Likoma

Akizuke Resthouse Popular resthouse five minutes' walk from jetty. Hot showers, flush toilets, bar with temperamental fridge, restaurant serving OK meals by advance order. Rooms with net **A** pp.

Hot Coconut Bar The closest thing on Likoma to a den of iniquity, this relaxed open-air bar with a reliable fridge lies ten minutes from town in the same direction as Kaya Mawa.

Kaya Mawa Blissfully chilled-out beach resort 45 minutes' walk from the ferry jetty (ferry passengers are normally met by a motorboat). Fun bar, good meals. Beach huts **B**/**C** Camping **A** pp.

Chizumulu

Wakwenda Retreat Backpacker-friendly lodge close to ferry jetty and about ten minutes from where the motorboats from Likoma arrive. Cheap meals. Diving course. Snorkel hire. Rooms **B** pp. Camping **A** pp.

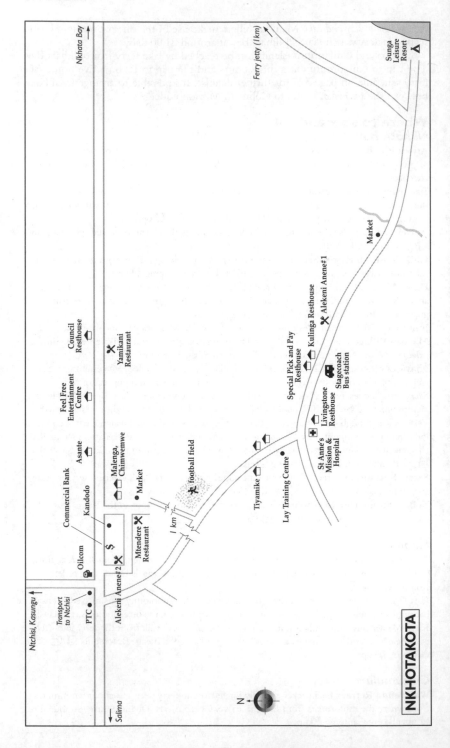

NKHOTAKOTA

Chintheche

Forestry Resthouse I loved this hideaway in a brachystegia grove near the beach, others have complained it's too run down. Ten minutes' walk and signposted from Chintheche town. Self-catering only; kitchen and fridge available. Good value at **A** pp s/c room with fan, hot shower.

Katoto Tourist Motel On beach 200m from Forestry Resthouse. The s/c rooms suffer from fantastically tacky decor but are fair value at **B/C**. Good meals US$2.

London Lodge Acceptable beachfront set-up, 500m from town, with a cheap restaurant. Rooms **B/C** and camping **A** pp.

South of Chintheche (north to south)

Flame Tree Lodge On forested peninsula 5km from Chintheche by road or ten minutes from Katoto Motel on beach. Rooms **D/E**. Camping **A** pp. Hot showers. Varied menu US$3 per meal.

Sambani Lodge 5km south of Chintheche, 20-minute walk from lakeshore road. In thickly forested area teeming with birds and monkeys. Rooms **D/E** with nets. Camping **A** pp.

Kande Beach Campsite Lively backpacker and overland truck hangout on beach 20km south of Chintheche, 40 minutes' walk along turn-off from Kande express bus stage. Sociable atmosphere, bar and basic meals. Scuba-diving courses US$150 pp. Snorkelling and watersport gear for hire. Camping only **A** pp though tents can be hired cheaply.

Mack's Lodge Basic but beautiful beach retreat signposted and 20 minutes' walk from *matate* bus stage about 10km south of Kande. Very peaceful and affordable. Camping and dorms **A** pp.

Mwaya Beach Lodge Attractive new resort 5km walk from *matate* bus stage. Run by foreigners, but strong community involvement (overnight trips with local fishermen, guided walks in a nearby forest reserve, guest participation in local football matches) and eco-friendly ethics make it a very different prospect from most backpacker-oriented lodges. Chalets with nets and private balcony **B** pp. Camping **A** pp. Inexpensive home-cooked meals.

Heidi's Hideout Lovely spot infrequently visited by travellers. Rooms with nets **D/E**. Camping **A** pp. Bar. Good meals US$3. Five minutes' walk from Ngala bus stage (country bus).

Nkhotakota

Alekeni Anene Restaurant The best restaurant in town, both by reputation and based on our experience, and close to the more popular resthouses. Fish and chips costs US$2.

Livingstone Resthouse In St Anne's Mission, opposite a historic church. Rooms **A/B** with nets and fan. Kitchen. Fridge. Recommended.

Pick and Pay and **Kulinga Resthouses** Opposite the bus station. Acceptable **A/B** rooms.

Sunga Leisure Resort Not as fancy as it sounds, this is a simple campsite with bar on the lakeshore towards the ferry jetty about 500m from the old town. Camping **A** pp.

Lilongwe and surrounds

LILONGWE

Lilongwe is the blandest of African capitals. The old town is indistinguishable from any number of small southern African towns, while the separate Capital City amounts to little more than a few shopping malls, restaurants and government buildings melting into leafy suburbia. That said, Lilongwe is an equable city – the climate is comfortable, getting in and out of town is simplicity itself, cheap

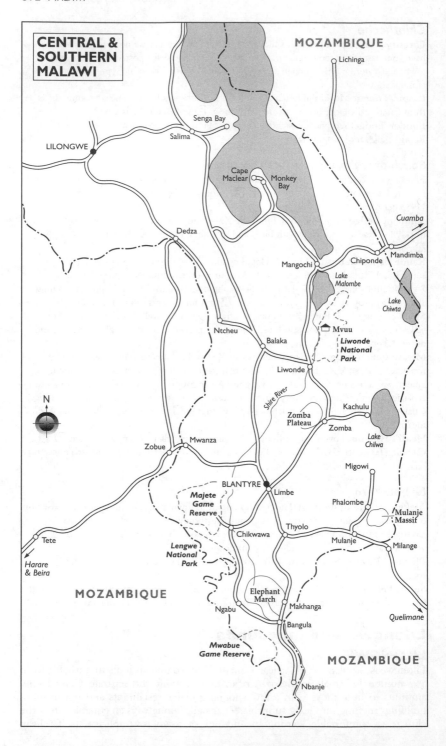

CENTRAL &
SOUTHERN
MALAWI

accommodation is abundant and conveniently situated, shops and markets are well stocked, and it's almost entirely free of crime targeted at tourists.

There's not much in the way of packaged entertainment in Lilongwe. The Capital City, built by President Banda with South African funding, is absurd enough to be worth a look, and the old town is a pleasant place to stroll around, particularly the market and nearby Asian quarter. Definitely worth exploring is Lilongwe Nature Sanctuary, situated between the new and old towns, where day trails through pristine brachystegia woodland and the riparian forest along the banks of the Lingadzi River offer the opportunity to see spotted hyena, otter, porcupine, bushpig, grey duiker, vervet monkey, bushbuck, crocodile and 150 bird species.

Access and getting around

Getting in and out of Lilongwe couldn't be more straightforward. All buses and minibuses to Lilongwe terminate at the large bus station in the old town. Buses to most destinations in Malawi leave throughout the morning until mid-afternoon. During daylight hours, cheap and regular minibuses connect the bus station in the old town to Capital City, stopping 100m from the entrance gate to Lilongwe Nature Sanctuary.

Where to stay

Annie's Coffee Pot Pleasant, clean and convenient. Room or dorm **B** pp.

Council Resthouse Opposite bus station. Rooms **A** dbl or **B** s/c dbl. Rooms in old wing very run down and noisy, rooms in new wing good. Same-day laundry. Cheap food.

St Peter's Church Near golf club. Clean rooms **B** dbl. Often full.

Kiboko Camp Tel: 82-8384; fax: 74-0135; email: kiboko@malawi.net; web: www.kiboko-safaris.com. Popular new suburban backpacker hostel within easy walking distance of the city centre. Restaurant and bar. Internet and email facilities. Backpacker tours to several parts of Malawi and Zambia (see tour operators below). Kiboko Camp lies off Glyn Jones Road about 1km past the golf club. To get here from the bus station, take a Likuni minibus and ask to be dropped at Likuni roundabout; the camp is the property with the high reed fence and hedge on the far left of the roundabout. Chalets, rooms and standing tents **D** pp. Dorms and camping **B** pp.

Outside Lilongwe

Safari Camp Ethnic Lodge Tel: 27 7406; email: safwag@malawi.net. Peaceful German-owned lodge 25km south of Lilongwe on the shore of Kamuzu Dam. Take a *matola* from Lilongwe to Malingunde (possibly changing vehicles at Likuni) then a 500m walk. Antelope roam the grounds and a great local band plays in the restaurant most nights. Chalets US$28pp. Camping **B** pp. German meals around US$5.

Dzalanyama Forest Lodge Bookings and transfers through Land and Lake Safaris (see *Tour operators* on page 394). Recently privatised and renovated self-catering lodge next to a stream in a remote brachystegia forest reserve 90 minutes' drive south of Lilongwe. Running hot water, equipped kitchen and refrigerator. Excellent hiking and on-site mountain bikes. Plenty of birds and small mammals. Rooms **E/F**. No public transport; transfers from Lilongwe US$22 pp (minimum two people) one-way.

Where to eat

Ali Baba Take-away Inexpensive Lebanese food and grills to eat on sidewalk tables or take away.

Annie's Coffee Pot Burgers, *piri-piri* chicken, *chambo* at around US$3. Disappointing when we last ate here. Dire coffee.

Bohemian Café Popular outdoor café serving filter coffee, cappuccino, fruit juice, toasted sandwiches. Closed at night and on Sunday.

Council Resthouse Canteen serving standard Malawian fare at around US$1 per plate.

Don Brioni's Bistro Recommended for steaks, pizzas and Italian dishes in US$6–8 range.

Gazebo Restaurant Sensibly priced if unmemorable curries and stews for around US$3.

Goodfellas Pleasant drinking hole with satellite TV tuned to major international sporting events. Pub meals.

Southern Fried Chicken Samosas, spring rolls, filled baked potatoes. Very cheap.

Modi's Restaurant A long-standing favourite. Steaks, grilled fish and prawns, excellent Indian dishes. US$4–6.

Korean Gardens Restaurant In Golden Peacock Hotel. Korean food US$5–8.

Lilongwe Hotel Good cakes and filter coffee. Lively bar at weekends.

Practical listings

Airlines Air Malawi (72-0966); Air Tanzania (78-3636); Air Zimbabwe (78-3804); Ethiopian Airlines (78-1308); KLM (78-1413); Kenya Airways (78-4227); South African Airways (see Blantyre).

Embassies China (78-3611); France (78-3520); India (78-0766); Israel (78-2933); Mozambique (78-4100); South Africa (78-3722); UK (78-2400); USA (78-3166); Zambia (78-2100); Zimbabwe (78-4988).

Foreign exchange Several banks and private forex bureaux in city centre plus 24-hour foreign exchange at the Lilongwe International Airport. Individuals offering kwacha for US dollars or South African *rand* cash can be found around the post office or council resthouse.

Immigration Off Chilambula Road, signposted from Lilongwe Hotel. Visa and visitor's pass renewals on the spot.

Map Sales Office In Old Town near golf club.

Poste restante Mail addressed to Lilongwe will be kept at post office in old town. To collect mail at Capital City post office, have it addressed to Lilongwe Capital City. No proof of identity required and no charge.

Books Times Book Shops in old town on Kamuzu Procession, in Capital City PTC, and in the Lilongwe and Capital Hotels.

Tourist information office Kamuzu Procession. Pamphlets, maps and books.

Tour operators *Kiboko Camp* offers a number of different packages aimed towards backpackers, including four-day safaris to South Luangwa in Zambia, five-day trips to Mulanje Mountain and Liwonde or to Nyika and Vwaza Marsh, and three-week safaris taking in large parts of Malawi and Zambia and overland trips between Nairobi and Lilongwe (see *Kiboko Camp* under *Where to stay* for contact details). *Central Africa Wilderness Safaris* is the agent for Mvuu Camp in Liwonde National Park (tel: 78-1393; fax: 78-1397; email: wildsaf@eo.wn.apc.org.). The *Nyika Safari Company* is the best source of information and the booking agent for all accommodation in Nyika National Park and Vwaza Marsh (tel: 74-0579; fax: 74-0848; email: nyika-safaries@malawi.net). Another reliable local tour operator is *Land and Lake Safaris*, PO Box 2140; tel: 743173 or 743213; fax: 744408; email: landlake@malawi.net.

Wildlife and national parks office Next to the immigration office. Accommodation reservations for national parks and game reserves. Tel: 72 3505; fax: 72 3089.

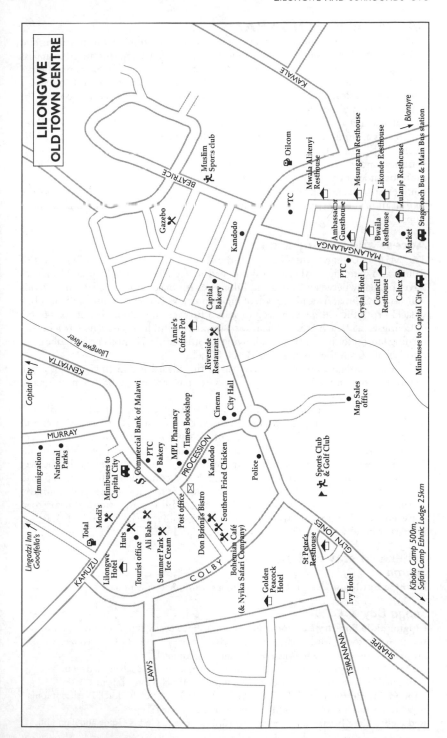

LILONGWE
OLD TOWN CENTRE

SALIMA AND SENGA BAY

Salima is an important route focus, lying at the junction of the northern and southern lakeshore roads and the M14 to Lilongwe. Few people do more than pass through Salima on their way to **Senga Bay**, attractively situated 15km away on the Lake Malawi shore. A popular day trip from Senga Bay, **Lizard Island** supports a dense population of gigantic monitor lizards and a breeding colony of white-breasted cormorants.

Worth a visit are the hippo pools on the seasonally marshy **Mpatsanjoka River** which arcs around the north of Senga Hill before it empties into Lake Malawi. The river is also attractive to birdwatchers – the colourful Boehm's bee-eater is common and it's a good place to look for the secretive rufous-bellied heron. Do be cautious: at least two people have been killed here by hippos in the last decade. The boulder-strewn and heavily wooded slopes of Senga Hill are worth exploring – the view from the top is excellent and klipspringers are commonly seen on the rocky slopes.

Access and getting around

The M14 to Lilongwe intersects with the southern lake road about 2km west of Salima and with the northern lakeshore road about 4km west of Salima. Minibuses travel regularly between Salima and Lilongwe. All buses along the lakeshore roads will stop at Salima. A steady stream of pick-up trucks connects Salima to Senga Bay village. From the village, you need to walk a further 2km along the tar road to get to Livingstonia Beach Hotel. The resorts towards Kambiri Point can be reached by turning left on to the beach and following it southwards. Kambiri point is about an hour's walk from the Livingstonia Beach Hotel.

It's easy enough to organise a day trip to the Lizard Island (inclusive of a fish barbecue) in Senga Bay village – expect to pay around US$5–8 per person, depending on group size.

The simplest way to reach the hippo pools is to pay a local child to guide you, but it's not difficult to go on your own. From the Forestry Resthouse, descend to the beach, follow it northwards for about 20 minutes until you reach the river mouth, from where it's about 3km upriver to the hippo pools (you've gone far enough when you connect with a dirt road that bridges the river). In the wet season, you could turn right across this bridge and continue north along the road for about 2km to a swampy rice paddy, where crowned crane and common pratincole are often seen. A path crossing Senga Hill is signposted from the road between the Forestry Resthouse and Livingstonia Beach Hotel (LBH), an upmarket hotel which is the best-known local landmark.

Where to stay and eat
Salima
Linthipe Resthouse Best of several **A** resthouses around bus station.

Senga Bay
Chigumukile Forestry Resthouse In woodland above beach 1km from Livingstonia Beach Hotel. Rooms have sporadic hot baths. Bar, kitchen, fridge. Gets mixed reviews but my first choice of cheapie in Senga Bay. Rooms or camping **A** pp.
God is Guide Resthouse Classic name, nice people, indifferent accommodation. Not frequented by touts. Between village and Livingstonia Beach Hotel. **A** pp.
Hippo Hide Resthouse In village 2km before Livingstonia Beach Hotel. Persistent touts might test your sense of humour. Basic rooms and camping **A** pp.
Red Zebra Café Inexpensive Western-style dishes close to God is Guide and Top Hill.

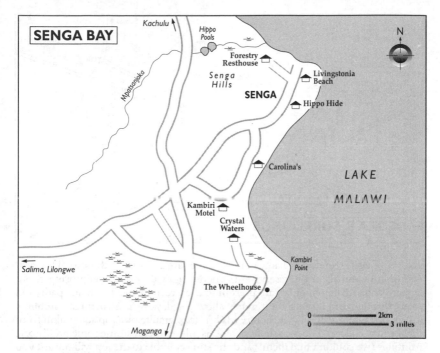

Steps Campsite Rated by many as one of the best campsites in Malawi. On beach next to Livingstonia Beach Hotel. Facilities include canteen/shop. Camping **B** pp.

Top Hill Restaurant On road between village and Livingstonia Beach Hotel. Rooms are par for the **A** pp range. Excellent meals for US$2, but order in advance. Semi-legendary banana pancakes.

Towards Kambiri Point (north to south)

Carolina's 45-minute walk from Livingstonia Beach Hotel. Rooms **E** s/c dbl. Camping. Excellent meals US$3.

Chimpango and **Baobab Chalets** Next to Carolina's. Chalets in **C** to **D** range.

Crystal Waters 20 minutes' walk from Carolina's. Rooms **D** s/c dbl (hot water). Camping. Good restaurant, bar, pool table.

The Wheelhouse Kambiri Point, ten minutes' walk from Crystal Waters. Camping. Raised wooden bar and restaurant.

DEDZA

The town of **Dedza** lies 84km south of Lilongwe at the southern foot of the 2,198m Dedza Mountain. Boasting a comfortable highland climate and an attractive setting, Dedza is the obvious base from which to explore a cluster of little-visited forest reserves – highly recommended to anybody with a taste for off-the-beaten-track rambling in beautiful surrounds.

An easy day walk from Dedza, the Dedza Mountain Forest Reserve is largely covered in plantation forest, but remnant patches of evergreen and riverine forest on the upper slopes support typical forest animals such as samango monkey, bushpig, baboon and leopard, as well as a variety of forest birds and epiphytic orchids.

The larger **Chongoni Forest Reserve**, the site of Malawi's forestry college, supports a mixture of plantation and brachystegia woodland, as well as small

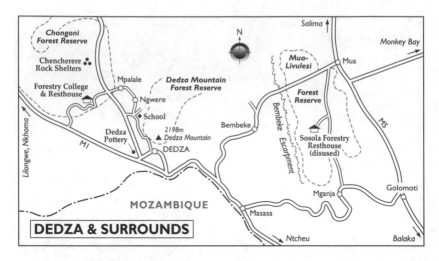

patches of evergreen forest. Large granite domes are a feature of the area. The most common mammals in the reserve are baboons, grey duiker and klipspringer, but leopard and samango monkey are present in evergreen forest. The many paths and roads through and around the reserve allow for days of unstructured rambling. One worthwhile goal is Chencherere Hill, a steep granite outcrop about 5km from the forestry college. The rock shelters on this hill reputedly house some prehistoric paintings (we couldn't find them!) and the stiff scramble to the top will reward you with a wonderful panoramic view over the forest to the surrounding hills.

The **Mua-Livulezi Forest Reserve** is another sizeable reserve. Lying at an altitude of around 800m, below the Bembeke escarpment, it protects medium-altitude brachystegia and bamboo woodland as opposed to the plantation and evergreen forest found at higher altitudes. Attractions include good bird-watching and an air of complete isolation, as well as great views down to Lake Malawi.

The Forestry Office in Dedza can give information and advice on the above reserves.

Access and getting around

Express buses along the M1 between Lilongwe and Blantyre stop at Dedza town. Dedza Mountain can be climbed as a day-trip from town using any of several converging and diverging paths which start from behind the Golf Club Resthouse. The peak is about 5km from Dedza and you pass a communication tower along the way.

The least complicated route to Chongoni is to bus or hitch to the signposted turn-off from the N1 about 10km north of Dedza, then walk the 6km to the college along a clear dirt road. A more scenic two-to-three-hour walk goes via the lower slopes of Dedza Mountain: leave town along the road that passes in front of the Golf Club Resthouse, take a right fork after 1km, then a left fork after 500m, and then keep going until you reach Dedza Secondary School. Here, a turn to the right takes you across a concrete bridge, through the school buildings, then after about 1km to a T-junction and a cluster of buildings including a *Chibuku* bar. Ask somebody at the bar to point out the footpath to Ngwere village (about 1km) and Mpalale (a further 2km), from where it's about 500m to a good dirt road. Turn left into the road, and after 200m you'll see the signposted turn-off to the forestry college.

If you're heading to Mua-Livulezi, your first objective should be Mganja, a small town on the winding dirt road between Masasa on the M1 and Golomoti near Lake Malawi. A few vehicles leave Masasa for Mganja before midday. There are also a few pick-up trucks daily between Mganja and Golomoti. From Mganja, it's a 10–15km walk to the resthouse, along the road signposted for Mua. After about 5km, the road enters the forest reserve, where cultivation gives way to thick brachystegia woodland. You'll soon reach a concrete bridge over the Namkokwe River. After 2km, the road crosses a second small bridge, and then after another 2km a third. Around 50m after the third bridge, turn left into an unsignposted and easily missed vehicle-width track, which leads through mixed plantation and bamboo woodland for about 3km before reaching the resthouse. Don't panic when you see the group of derelict buildings 500 metres before the resthouse – it isn't *that* run-down! When you're ready to leave Sosola, instead of returning to Mganja, you could continue to Mua on the M5 by retracing your steps for 3km back to the turn-off, then turning right. The distance to Mua is similar to that to Mganja, and from Mua you'll easily find transport on to Cape Maclear.

If you're exploring this area, it's worth buying the 1:50,000 map of Dedza (for Dedza Mountain and Chongoni) and the 1:50,000 map of Golomoti (for Mua-Livulezi) in Lilongwe or Blantyre. Sheet seven in the Malawi 1:250,000 series is a useful alternative.

Where to stay and eat
Dedza
CTC Mini-Motel Best of **A** lodges. Above-average restaurant.
Dedza Pottery Filter coffee, quiches, scones, fresh bread. Worth the 2km walk from town.
Golden Dish Clean rooms **B** s/c dbl. Best food in town.
Golf Club Large rooms **B**/**C**. Hot bath. Restaurant and bar.

Chongoni Forest Reserve
Forestry Resthouse In college grounds at base of Chiwawa Hill. Rooms **A** pp or **B** pp s/c dbl (hot bath, heater). Camping. Equipped kitchen and bar. Bring food. Can check room availability in advance with the Forestry Office in Dedza town.

Mua-Livulezi Forest Reserve
Sosola Forestry Resthouse Isolated, charming resthouse, with balcony looking over to Lake Malawi. Closed in late 1997 and no signs of re-opening, though you could check with the Forestry Office in Dedza.

From Salima to Blantyre
CAPE MACLEAR AND MANGOCHI
The most southerly ferry port on Lake Malawi and largest town on this part of the lake shore, **Monkey Bay** isn't of any great interest in itself. That it sees a huge amount of traveller through-traffic is largely because it's the springboard for visits to the legendary **Cape Maclear**, the busiest travellers' congregation point in Malawi, if not anywhere between Nairobi and Victoria Falls. Cape Maclear has been described as Africa's answer to Kathmandu or Marrakech, and backpackers flock here in their hundreds to enjoy a relaxed *chamba* and Carlsberg-enhanced atmosphere that is quite irresistible (though increasingly marred by crime and conmen) – even if you can't help but wonder what Doctor Robert Laws, who established the first Livingstonia Mission here in 1875, would make of it all!

UNDERWATER ACTIVITIES AT CAPE MACLEAR

Cape Maclear lies within Lake Malawi National Park which, in terms of the number of fish species it protects, must rank as the most important freshwater fish sanctuary in Africa, if not the world. Lake Malawi National Park offers great snorkelling and diving, and a wildlife viewing experience to match anything Malawi's terrestrial reserves have to offer. Kayak Africa, on the beach between Stevens' and Emanuel's, arranges overnight snorkelling and camping trips to a nearby island for US$30 per person inclusive of equipment, camping gear and food. The diving and water sports centre next to Stevens' does week-long scuba courses at US$150, and it hires out a variety of watersport and snorkelling equipment.

More informally, day trips to nearby West Thumbi Island can be arranged with local fishermen for around US$5 per person inclusive of food, snorkelling equipment and boat transport. The fish community around Mitande Point on West Thumbi is regarded to be one of the most diverse in the lake.

There is also good snorkelling at Otter Point, 20 minutes' walk from Chembe. The clear water here is teeming with cichlids of all colours, and the rocky point supports rock hyrax, baboon, klipspringer and a variety of lizards. Spotted necked otters are common in the area. To visit Otter Point, you need to pay the US$5 national park entrance. Snorkelling equipment can be hired from children in Chembe.

Lewis, Reinthall and Trendall's *Guide to the Fishes of Lake Malawi National Park* (WWF) includes good background information on the cichlids and other fishes of Lake Malawi.

Anybody who swims in the water around Cape Maclear is advised to test for bilharzia after returning home.

The simple fact that there is nowhere to change money near Cape Maclear forces quite a few travellers to make a flying visit to a bank in **Mangochi**. Formerly known as Fort Johnston and given township status in 1899, Mangochi was a river port and naval centre of some importance in the colonial era, and it remains one of the few Malawian towns with any character – sad to say, that of a colonial outpost going to seed. The old part of Mangochi, with its tangible Muslim influences, faded whitewashed buildings, sticky tropical atmosphere and leafy avenues is vaguely reminiscent of some of the more run-down towns on the East African coast. Sightseeing is limited to a few less than riveting national monuments: a war cemetery; a waterfront clock tower built in 1903, and the cannon from the HMS *Gwendolyn* (the ship which sank the German Hermann Von Wessman at Liuli in 1914). Possibly of more interest, but closed when I visited, is the Lake Malawi Museum.

Access and getting around

Monkey Bay and Mangochi are connected by regular buses to Blantyre, Zomba and Liwonde. The daily bus between Nkhata Bay and Monkey Bay stops at Nkhotakota and Salima. From the Dedza area, you can get to Monkey Bay via Mganja and Mua or Golomoti.

The turn-off to Cape Maclear is signposted from the Mangochi road 4km south of Monkey Bay. There is no public transport along the 18km road from the turn-off to Cape Maclear, but it's easy enough to find a lift. The vehicle at Stevens' Resthouse runs between Cape Maclear and Monkey Bay at least twice daily.

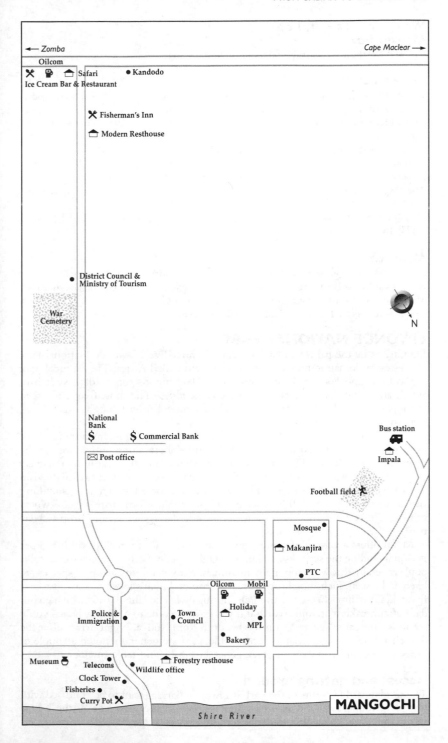

Where to stay and eat
Monkey Bay
Council Resthouse Acceptable **A** rooms in town centre.

Cape Maclear
Indaba Bar Large reed structure on Chembe Beach next to Stevens'. Chilled beer, good snacks by day, inexpensive vegetarian-friendly buffets in the evening.
Pizza Place Tasty pizzas cooked in a clay oven on the beach, only 20m from the Indaba Bar.
Stevens' Resthouse This Cape Maclear institution, set on Chembe Beach, has been hosting travellers for at least two decades, though many people feel its popularity these days leans heavily on its legendary status. Ordinary rooms **A**, s/c rooms **B/C**.
The Gap and **Emanuel's** On Chembe beach within 200m of Stevens'. Basic rooms with grass mat or camping **A** pp.
Top Quiet Resthouse Peaceful spot 100m from Stevens' and beach. Rooms **A/B**. S/c dbl **C**. Fair restaurant.

Mangochi
Holiday Motel Smart hotel with clean rooms **A/B** or **B/C** s/c. Good restaurant.
Ice Cream Bar & Restaurant At junction with Blantyre road. Curries, burgers, sundaes.
Makanjiro Resthouse Spotless rooms excellent value at **A** s/c dbl.
Press Bakery Fresh bread daily and a selection of pastries.

LIWONDE NATIONAL PARK
Dominated by the palm and baobab-fringed Shire River, Liwonde National Park evokes every romantic notion of primal, untrammelled Africa. The national park supports around 800 elephants, more than 2,000 hippos (on a 40km stretch of river!) and a healthy number of oversized crocodiles. The most frequently seen antelope are waterbuck, sable, impala and bushbuck. Birdwatching is exceptional, in terms of both variety and rarities.

Liwonde doesn't offer the best game viewing in Africa – lion, for instance, have been hunted close to extinction – but the atmosphere alone puts it among the continent's most compelling national parks. Mvuu, the main camp, is relatively easy and inexpensive to visit – if you camp and cook for yourself, a two-night visit, inclusive of the boat trips there and back, park fees, and a few activities, shouldn't run to more than US$100 per person. If you can't afford that, it's still worth thinking about doing the boat trip from Liwonde Barrage to Mvuu Camp as a day trip.

Mvuu offers a variety of game-viewing activities, all of which cost US$15 per person including the services of a knowledgeable guide. Early morning game walks don't generally throw up too many mammals, but several unusual bird species are likely to be seen, including brown-breasted barbet, Lilian's lovebird, Livingstone's flycatcher, Boehm's bee-eater and Pels' fishing owl. The launch trips which go out daily after breakfast are only worth it if you haven't come to Mvuu by boat – you'll see much the same species as on the boat trip from Kudya. Night drives offer the best chance of seeing predators: lion and leopard are generally noted a couple of times a week, and you may see civet, genet, bushbaby and sable antelope.

Access and getting around
The springboard for visits to the park is Liwonde Barrage (not to be confused with nearby Liwonde town), which straddles the M3 on the west side of the bridge across the Shire River, just south of the junction with the M8/M1 from Dedza.

Any bus heading between Blantyre and Mangochi can drop you at the bridge. Even if you have no intention of visiting the park, it's worth spending a night at Liwonde Barrage. This part of the Shire River exudes an atmosphere of tropical Africa – low wooded hills in the background, fishermen punting past in traditional dugouts, masses of hippos grunting and snorting, and thick reed beds rustling with birdlife.

The best way to get into the national park is by boat. Boat trips to Mvuu Lodge take around two to three hours each way, and they can be organised through private operators based at Kudya Discovery Lodge. Prices are to some extent negotiable, depending on group size and whether you want to return the same day, but expect to pay around US$30–40 per person for the round trip inclusive of park entrance fees. The boat trip is an unforgettable experience. Close encounters with hippos are guaranteed, and you can be confident of seeing elephants, waterbuck, impala and vervet monkeys. Birds are everywhere, and the vegetation – thick otando of borassus and wild date palms, ghostly baobab and yellow fever trees and dense beds of papyrus – creates the sort of tropical African atmosphere that is rarely seen outside of television documentaries.

Where to stay

Kudya Discovery Lodge Mid-range hotel 2km and signposted from the barrage. Good food US$2–3 and waterfront Bar. Hippos in grounds. Clean s/c rooms **D/E**. Camping **A** pp.

Liwonde Motel 100m from bus stop. Rooms **B** s/c dbl.

Liwonde Holiday Resort 500m along turn-off to Kudya. Clean, basic rooms **A**.

Mvuu Camp In National Park 25km by boat from Kudya. Standing tent or s/c room US$30pp. Camping **B** pp. Good meals US$10. Self-catering allowed. Book through **Central African Wilderness Safaris** in Lilongwe (see page 394). Last-minute bookings radioed from Kudya Discovery Lodge.

ZOMBA AND SURROUNDS

The town of **Zomba** was the capital of Malawi until 1975, and it has retained a sedate charm that's lacking entirely from the modern capital. It is still the site of Malawi's most important university, and there are several early colonial buildings including the State House, which dates from 1901.

Towering over the town, **Zomba Mountain** has been protected in a forest reserve since 1913. The extensive plateau is covered mostly in plantation forest, though there are still significant patches of indigenous riverine and montane forest, tangled scrub and brachystegia woodland. Circled by motorable roads and crossed by innumerable footpaths, the plateau is a hiker's paradise. Definitely worth doing is the short nature trail that starts about 2km from the campsite and runs past Mulunguzi Dam, the forested banks of the Mulunguzi River and the Mandala Falls, where you might see bushbuck, vervet monkey and various birds. Chingwe's Hole, rumoured to reach the bottom of the Rift Valley, is about two hours' walk from the campsite. A 3km circular nature trail leads from the hole past some good viewpoints, and through a patch of montane forest where samango monkeys and a variety of forest birds are likely to be seen. Dedicated walkers are pointed to the inexpensive 36-page booklet *Zomba Mountain: a Walker's Guide* by Martyn and Kittie Cundy.

A more unusual excursion from Zomba, **Lake Chilwa**, the most southerly of Malawi's large lakes, has a remote, captivating atmosphere. At dusk, with only Mulanje and Zomba punctuating the open horizon, the pink and orange-tinged sky is the picture of serenity. The lake is best explored from Kachula, a small, friendly village which might well benefit from a trickle of low-key tourism,

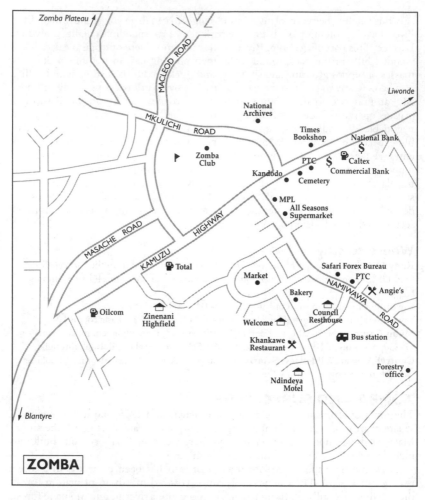

especially as dropping water levels have affected the local fishing industry. The shore around Kachula is worth investigating, especially if you're interested in birds. You can also take a boat-taxi to Chisi Island, which consists of a few baobab-studded hills, reputedly home to monkeys and hyenas. If you have ambitions to explore Lake Chilwa beyond this, bring a tent and the appropriate 1:50,000 or 1:250,000 maps.

Access and getting around
All buses between Blantyre and points north stop at Zomba town, and there are regular minibuses to Zomba from Limbe. The 13km road between Zomba town and the plateau, signposted for Ku Chawe Inn opposite the Kandodo Supermarket, splits half-way into a separate up road and down road. The easiest way to get up is to hire a private taxi from Zomba bus station (around US$10), though hitching is not impossible. And you could walk, though it's quite steep going towards the end, so leave your excess luggage at the Council Resthouse in Zomba for a nominal fee.

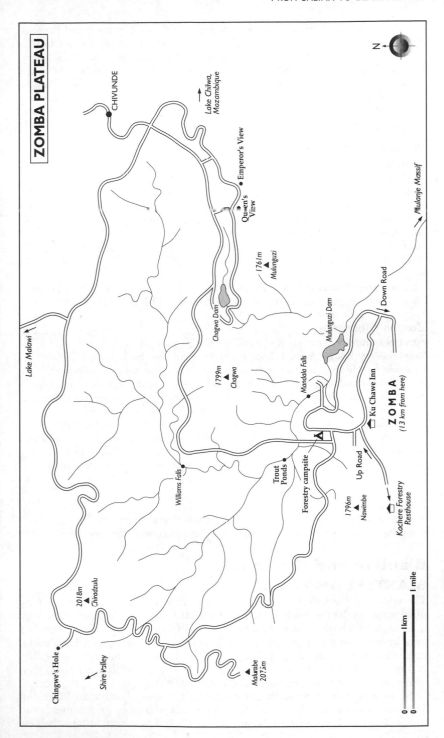

ZOMBA PLATEAU

CHIVUNDE

Lake Chilwa,
Mozambique

Emperor's View

Queen's
View

1761m
▲ Mulunguzi

Chagwa Dam

Lake Malawi

1799m
▲ Chagwa

Mulunguzi Dam

Mulanje Massif

Down Road

Mandala Falls

Williams Falls

Ku Chawe Inn

ZOMBA
(13 km from here)

Trout
Ponds

Forestry campsite

Up Road

1796m
▲ Nawimbe

Kachere Forestry
Resthouse

2018m
▲ Chiradzulu

Chingwe's Hole

Shire Valley

Malumbe
2072m

0 ———— 1km
0 ———— 1 mile

Getting to Lake Chilwa is more straightforward. Two buses travel between Zomba and Kachula daily, leaving Zomba at 13.00 and 16.00 and Kachula at 05.30 and 14.00. Boat-taxis from Kachula to Chisi take 30 minutes each way. Boat-taxis reputedly connect Kachula to some other points on the lake, but I couldn't get anybody to commit themselves as to where or how regularly they go. Even if they are mythical, there are plenty of willing boat owners in Kachula – bearing in mind that you shouldn't venture on to the lake without a local oarsman/guide.

Where to stay and eat
Zomba
Angie's Take-away Curries, burgers, etc for around US$2.

Council Resthouse Very run down and noisy with pungent communal toilets and showers, and a serious risk of theft from the rooms. Dorm or ordinary room **A**. S/c dbl **B**.

Golf Course Excellent meals US$2. Filter coffee. Day membership fee of US$2.

Khanaowe Restaurant Good meals. US$1–2 negotiable.

Ndindeya Motel The best compromise between cost and comfort in central Zomba, despite an isolated report of theft from rooms. Rooms **B/C** or **C/D** s/c. Inexpensive meals.

Zinenani Highfield Hotel New, acceptable-looking place about ten minutes' walk from bus station. No negative reports. Restaurant and bar. Rooms **B** sgl or **C** s/c dbl.

Zomba Mountain
Forestry Campsite 1km from Ku Chawe Inn. Camping only. Hot shower.

Zomba Forest Lodge (formerly Kachere Forestry Resthouse; book through *Land and Lake Safaris* in Lilongwe, see page 394). Situated in a secluded forest glade halfway up Zomba Plateau and signposted from the 'up-road', this well-equipped self-catering lodge consists of an old colonial building in spacious grounds with numerous forest birds and butterflies. A US$10 taxi ride or 12km hike from Zomba town. S/c rooms **E**.

CCAP cottage One of several private cottages dotted behind Ku Chawe Inn. Room availability can be checked at the CCAP headquarters opposite Zomba police station. The stables 1km from Ku Chawe Inn may also have rooms. Rooms around **B** or **C** pp.

Ku Chawe Inn Upmarket hotel with the only restaurant on the plateau. Meals from US$5.

Kachula
Anonymous resthouse Opposite bus park. Longdrop toilets. Basic rooms **A**.

Camping Several small villages on Chisi Island where you could ask to pitch a tent.

Blantyre and the south
BLANTYRE AND LIMBE
The unofficial commercial capital of Malawi, Blantyre was founded in 1876 by missionaries of the Established Church of Scotland, who named it after the village of Livingstone's birth. With its healthy climate and fertile soils, the mission proved to be attractive to European settlers, while its strategic position served as a useful communication centre for trade between Lake Malawi and the Zambezi Valley. Blantyre rapidly became the most important settlement in Malawi, a status it retains to this day, with a population of around 400,000.

Blantyre is more intrinsically attractive than Lilongwe, lying at an altitude of 1,038m in a valley ringed by low hills, and it is visited by a far greater number of backpackers simply because it's the springboard for bus transport through the Tete

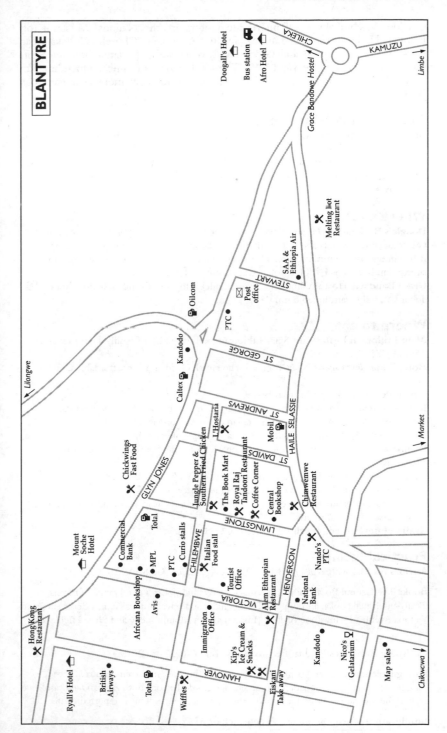

BLANTYRE

Lilongwe

CHILEKA

KAMUZU

Limbe

Grace Bandowe Hostel

Doogall's Hotel
Bus station
Afro Hotel

Melting Pot
Restaurant

SAA &
Ethiopia Air

STEWART

Oilcom

Post
office

PTC

ST GEORGE

Kandodo

Caltex

ST ANDREWS

Chickwings
Fast Food

L'Hostaria

Mobil

HAILE SELASSIE

GLYN JONES

Jungle Pepper &
Southern Fried Chicken

The Book Mart
Royal Raj
Tandoori Restaurant
Coffee Corner

ST DAVIDS

Central
Bookshop

Chimwemwe
Restaurant

Mount
Soche
Hotel

Commercial
Bank

MPL

PTC

Total

Curio stalls

CHILEMBWE

Italian
Food stall

LIVINGSTONE

Nando's

HENDERSON

PTC

Africana Bookshop

Avis

Tourist
Office

VICTORIA

Alem Ethiopian
Restaurant

National
Bank

Hong Kong
Restaurant

Ryall's Hotel

British
Airways

Total

Waffles

HANOVER

Immigration
Office

Kip's
Ice Cream &
Snacks

Eiskani
Take away

Kandodo

Nico's
Gelatarium

Map sales

Chikwcwa

Market

Corridor to Zimbabwe. Of interest to visitors are the National Museum (off Kamuzu Highway towards Limbe), and the All Angels Church (Chileka Road between the bus station and Grace Bandawe Hostel), the latter built by Scots missionaries between 1888 and 1891. The satellite town of Limbe, which lies 5km from Blantyre along Kamuzu Highway, has considerably more character than Blantyre.

Access and getting around

Blantyre is a major transport hub, with buses in every conceivable direction leaving from the bus station on Chileka Road (though be aware that buses coming from the direction of Zomba or Mulanje will stop in Limbe bus station before they proceed to Blantyre). Light vehicles heading to Zomba and Thyolo leave from near Limbe bus station.

Where to stay

Doogle's Backpacker Hostel Email: doogles@malawi.net. This popular private hostel next to the bus station is about the only place in Blantyre geared to backpackers. Good Italian meals, bar, swimming pool, TV lounge, notice board, hot showers, luggage storage, large grounds. Rooms **E** dbl. Dorms **C** pp. Camping **B** pp.

Grace Bandawe Hostel Church hostel on Chileka Rd, 1km from bus station. Rooms **D** dbl or **E** s/c dbl. Partitioned dorm **B** pp.

Where to eat

Alem Ethiopian Restaurant Spicy Ethiopian food served by a friendly Tigrean woman. Around US$4.

Hong Kong Restaurant Near Mount Soche Hotel. Good and very affordable Chinese food.

Jungle Pepper Popular take-away pizzas.

Kips Ice Cream & Snacks Hanover Av. Ice-cream. Inexpensive but greasy meals.

L'Hostaria Chilembwe Rd. Excellent Italian dishes and pizzas. US$5–10.

Mount Soche Hotel Blantyre's top hotel has a couple of good, but pricey restaurants. Popular with travellers during major sporting events for the Sportsman's Bar with satellite TV.

Nando's Haile Selassie Rd. Quarter *peri-peri* chicken with chips US$2.50.

Nico's Geletarium Victoria Av. Ice cream. Filter coffee.

Raj Tandoori Restaurant Excellent Indian food but not cheap at around US$10 for a main course with condiments.

Ryall's Hotel Very edible grill-type meals in US$3–4 range.

Practical listings

Airlines Air Malawi (62-0811); British Airways (62-4333) and SAA (62-0627/9).

Books The Central Book Shop on Livingstone Avenue stocks a good range of novels, locally-published books, and imported field guides and travel guides. Times Book Shops on Victoria Avenue, Livingstone Avenue (Limbe) and in Mount Soche and Shire Highlands hotels.

Carlsberg Breweries Popular free day tours. Tel: 67-0222 or 62-0133.

Foreign exchange Several banks and private forex bureaux in the city centre. Outside banking hours and at weekends, you can change US dollars or South African *rand* cash around the junction of Glyn Jones Road and Victoria Avenue. This is reportedly safe.

Immigration office On Victoria Avenue; tel: 62-3777.

Map sales office On the southern end of Victoria Ave; tel: 62-3722.

Mozambique Consulate Get there by 08.30 to collect a transit visa at 11.00. Minibuses between the city centre and Limbe pass the consulate – ask for Masalima Post Office.

Tourist information office Victoria Avenue. Pamphlets and books about Malawi. Tel: 62-0300.

MULANJE AND THYOLO
The pretty town of **Mulanje** lies amongst the tea estates at the base of the imposing Mulanje Massif. It is the largest urban centre in southeastern Malawi and

THE SHIRE VALLEY AND THE ELEPHANT MARSH
Although it is rarely visited by backpackers, the Shire Valley to the south of Blantyre is one of the most scenically evocative parts of Malawi, notable for the distinctively African aura that hangs over the sluggish, hippo-infested presence of the Shire River. Two of Malawi's game reserves lie in this region, as does Lengwe National Park, but none is easily visited without a private vehicle.

The Shire Valley does, however, boast at least one compelling and accessible attraction in the form of the 65km-long **Elephant Marsh**, a hyacinth- and lily-covered expanse fringing the eastern bank of the Shire River. Named by Livingstone, who recorded seeing a herd of 800 elephants on its edge, this lush marsh, thoroughly tropical in appearance, provides sanctuary to Malawi's largest crocodile population as well as a substantial number of hippos and a quite spectacular array of water birds – though, predictably, elephants were hunted out years ago.

To get from Blantyre to Makhanga, the nearest town to the marsh, catch a bus towards Nsanje and ask to be dropped at Bangula. Makhanga lies 10km from Bangula, and there is some *matola* transport. Alternatively, you could walk – the marsh laps the road in the rainy season, so you'll see plenty of birds on the way. There are two resthouses in Makhanga and several in Bangula.

To actually get out on to the marsh, you need to hire a boat at Mchacha James, 6km from Makhanga. To get there, follow the main road out of Makhanga towards Muona for about 20 minutes then turn left into an unsignposted track and after wandering through a sprawling village for about 45 minutes (keep asking directions – 'James' is the key word) you will reach the mosque where the boat owners hang out. Negotiating the rate for boat hire can be a tedious and comically furtive process, but you shouldn't pay more than US$5 per group per hour, and once on the water you'll find that the oarsmen are articulate guides, knowledgeable about every aspect of the marsh, and able to identify every bird you see.

Also of interest to backpackers exploring the Shire Valley is the waterfront Sports Club, a 6km walk from Nchalo town in the **Sucoma Sugar Estate**. Hippos and a variety of birds can be seen from the club, and if you stay the night you should be able to take the estate's motorboat out on to the river – you'll probably only be asked to cover fuel costs. Rooms at the club cost **C** s/c dbl, though be warned they are often fully booked over weekends, and there is a good restaurant and bar. There are also a few resthouses in Nchalo town.

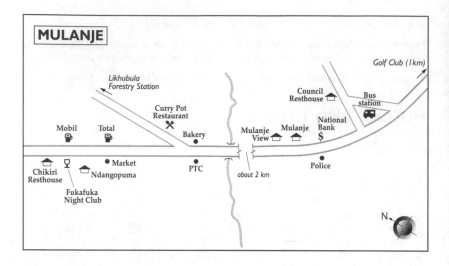

the gateway to a little-used route into Mozambique. The town is divided into two parts, which lie 2km apart along a flame-tree-lined road through a tea estate. The name Mulanje is generally used to refer to the leafy administrative centre, while the rather more scruffy commercial centre on the Blantyre side of the tea estate is called Chitikali. Travellers visit Mulanje to climb the **Mulanje Massif**, a vast granite outcrop towering more than 1,000m above the surrounding plains. The central plateau of Mulanje is 650km² in extent and it boasts 20 peaks topping 2,500m, of which Sapitwa is at 3,002m the highest point in Central Africa. Hikes and climbs can be arranged at **Likhubula Forestry Station** at the base of the massif – see box *Hiking on Mulanje* opposite.

Halfway between Blantyre and Mulanje, **Thyolo** (pronounced Cholo) is one of the oldest and most attractive towns in Malawi, set amongst rolling hills covered in tea plantations and patches of riparian forest. The leafy administrative centre of Thyolo consists of a cluster of colonial buildings around a pointless traffic circle, and it is separated from the busy market and bus station by a tea field. With something of the air of a European village, Thyolo would be an attractive town even without the splendid backdrop of Mulanje on the western horizon. If you're looking for the chance to limber up your legs before making an assault on Mulanje, the Thyolo area is riddled with dirt roads and would make for great rambling country. Of special interest is the 1,462m **Thyolo Mountain**, covered in well-preserved mahogany forest and regarded as *the* place in Malawi to see the green-headed oriole, as well as offering the opportunity to see a good variety of other forest species such as vervet and samango monkeys, bushbuck and leopard.

Access and getting around

Express buses to Mulanje town leave from Blantyre twice daily, taking three to four hours and stopping at Thyolo and Chitikali. Country buses to Mulanje take about an hour longer, and at least one daily continues to the Mozambique border. The trip to Mulanje can also be done in hops, using *matola* vehicles from Limbe to Thyolo.

Likhubula village lies 10km from Chitikali along the Phalombe road. A few buses run between Chitikali and Phalombe daily, as do *matola* vehicles. It's also an attractive walk. Likhubula Forestry Station is about ten minutes' walk and signposted from the village.

HIKING ON MULANJE

The plateau of Mulanje Mountain is similar in appearance to the alpine moorland on East Africa's larger mountains: a combination of heather, heaths and grasses, and supporting a wide array of wild flowers, including various helichrysums, irises, lobelias and aloes. The evergreen woodland and forest found in ravines and along watercourses is dominated by the endemic Mulanje cedar (*Widdringtonia whytei*), a magnificent timber tree which can reach a height of over 40m.

Mulanje's fauna is less diverse than is its flora. In the open highlands, the only large mammal species seen with any regularity are klipspringer and rock hyrax. In the woodlands of the lower slopes and in forested areas, there is a good chance of seeing vervet and samango monkeys. Red duiker, bushbuck, leopard, bushpig and porcupine are present in wooded habitats

Organising a hike up Mulanje is straightforward. At Likhubula Forestry Station, you can book mountain huts and arrange porters and guides as required. A porter is recommended for the first day – the ascent is very steep. There is no entrance fee, the mountain huts cost US$1 per person, and a guide or porter shouldn't set you back more than US$3 per day.

Keep your luggage to the minimum – spare gear can be left at the forestry station or at Doogall's in Blantyre. A tent is dead weight, since camping is forbidden, but you need a sleeping bag or thick blanket and plenty of warm clothing for the nights. You should also bring food: stock up in Blantyre or at the well-stocked PTC supermarket and market in Chitikali.

A week is required to do a full circuit of the huts, but most visitors settle for a two- or three-day trip: a day each for the ascent and descent, and one for exploring part of the plateau. The most popular option is to loop using the Chambe Path one way and the Lichenya Path the other way, with a night each at Chambe and Lichenya Huts. You can also ascend and descend along the same route, allowing you to spend your day on the mountain without being hindered by a heavy pack. If you aren't carrying bedding, head for the CCAP hut on Lichenya Plateau.

Mulanje can be climbed at any time of year. The dry, cool months from April to September are generally regarded as the best for hiking, though there is a danger of treacherous mists (called *Chiperone*) enveloping the massif between May and July. If you are caught in *Chiperone* conditions, stay put – walking is very dangerous, even along marked trails. During the rainy season (November to early April), many paths become slippery and some may be temporarily impassable due to flooding. The Skyline path to Chambe is safe at all times of year as it only crosses one river, and there is a bridge.

Frank Eastwood's *Guide to the Mulanje Massif* (Lorton Communications), available from the tourist office in Blantyre for US$3, is recommended to casual ramblers and essential to serious hikers and climbers. It includes a wealth of background detail, as well as descriptions and times for hiking routes and rock climbs. The Map Sales Office in Blantyre stocks an excellent and current 1:40,000 contour map of the massif (US$1.50). Climbers and hikers who plan on using unusual routes should contact the Mountain Club of Malawi in Blantyre.

MULANJE MASSIF

To get to Thyolo Mountain, ask a country bus to drop you at Namabirizi, from where you'll probably have to walk along the 10km road through Satemwa Tea Estate to the base of the mountain. The tea estate has a constructive attitude to visitors, but you should still ask for permission to pass through. It will be a long round trip if you don't make arrangements to camp.

Where to stay and eat
Mulanje

Mulanje View Motel Clean spacious rooms **B**/**C** s/c sgl/dbl. Good meals US$2.
Council Resthouse Near bus station. Rooms **A** s/c dbl.
Chikiri Resthouse Cleanest of a couple of **A** hotels in Chitikali.

Likhubula Forest Station

CCAP and **Forestry Resthouses** Comfortable rooms **B** pp. Hot showers, kitchen.
Anonymous resthouse In Likhubula village at junction to forest station. **A**.

Mulanje Massif

There are seven mountain huts all **A** pp with firewood and water. The six forestry huts are run down, and have no bedding. The **CCAP Hut** is better maintained, and bedding is supplied. Bring food. Most frequently used are Chambe, Lichenya and CCAP Hut, all within a day's walk of Likhubula. Can book any hut at Likhubula the day before climbing.

Thyolo

Tione Motel Near bus station. Good value. Rooms **A** or **B** s/c dbl. Meals.

Thyolo Mountain

Satemwa Tea Estate Two guest cottages sleep six and eight people at a respective cost of US$50 and US$65 per cottage. With sufficient interest, a campsite is likely to be built as well. Contact the estate management for details; tel: 47 2256; fax: 47 2386; email: 113213.233@compuserve.com.

Namingomba Resthouse Close to the mountain and good value at **C** pp. Phone 47 2300/2492/2321 for bookings and directions.

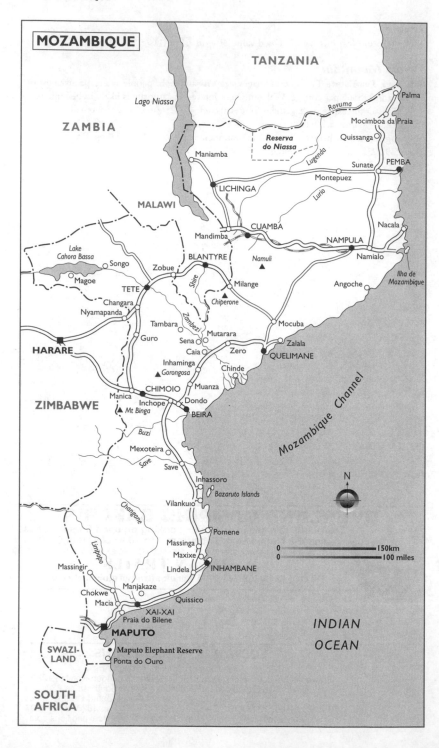

Mozambique

14

It's difficult to believe that a mere 25 years ago
Mozambique's convivial atmosphere and stunning
coastline attracted a greater volume of tourists than South
Africa and Zimbabwe combined. Like many South
Africans of my generation, I can barely remember a time
when Mozambique wasn't at war. To the rest of the world, I should
imagine that Mozambique is just another of those feuding African
nations which crawled briefly onto the lower rungs of the
newsworthiness scale before being consigned back to media
oblivion.

The remarkable thing about Mozambique today is how little it feels like a
country emerged from war. True, many roads are lined with bombed-out
buildings and pockmarked by gaping reminders of exploded mines. But the rate of
reconstruction since the 1992 Peace Accord has been extraordinary. And
Mozambique is not one of those countries which you sense might return to war at
the slightest provocation – perhaps because the so-called civil war was not truly
rooted in any internal ethnic or political difference, but a ghastly by-product of
what the South African apartheid government liked to term its 'destabilisation
policies'.

In travel terms, Mozambique might almost be two countries, until recently
linked only by a solitary motor ferry across the mighty Zambezi River, and divided
by 1,000km of rutted road. This division might gradually become less marked,
with the extensive upgrading of the road between Beira and Nampula in progress,
and the astounding 3.7km long Dona Anna Bridge between Sena and Mutarara
(built for the railway in 1934) recently converted to carry road traffic.
Nevertheless, the south and north of Mozambique share little in common other
than the widespread use of Portuguese in and around towns, and the beautiful
coastline.

FACTS AND FIGURES
Area: 801,600km² (16th in Africa)
Capital: Maputo (formerly Lourenço Marques)
Largest towns: Maputo, Beira, Nampula, Chimoio, Xai-Xai, Quelimane,
Pemba
Population: approx 19 million
Official language: Portuguese
Other languages: Makua-Lomwe, Tsonga, Shona
Currency: Metical
Head of State: President Joaquim Chissano

The south coast is the 'easy' bit, with ever-improving facilities and a ready tourist market in South Africa and Zimbabwe, not to mention a growing backpacker trade. The north, by contrast, cannot generally be recommended to independent travellers seeking comfort, predictability or packaged entertainment. Only Pemba and Mozambique Island have a reasonably dependable tourist infrastructure and can be accessed by air (LAM runs scheduled flights to Nampula, Lichinga and Pemba). Otherwise, the north of Mozambique offers the sort of challenging travel that recalls conditions in, say, Tanzania and Zambia in the mid-1980s, but exacerbated by linguistic barriers, intolerable summer humidity levels, relatively high costs, and a public transport system that often defies rational comprehension. Travelling through northern Mozambique regularly feels like travel for its own sake – a lot of bumpy motion punctuated by few highlights – but the area does boast two historical towns of compelling singularity, the former capital on Ilha de Mozambique and the remote, ancient island town of Ibo. No less important, it's one area which the adventurous traveller can truly experience for him or herself, without even a whiff of the distorting medium of a developed tourist industry.

BACKGROUND INFORMATION
Geography and climate
Eastern Mozambique consists of a low-lying coastal belt which widens from north to south to account for almost half of the country's surface area. This rises gradually towards the west to meet a plateau of 500–1,000m. Mozambique is generally rather flat, though much of the northwest is mountainous and several areas are dotted with isolated granite inselbergs known in southern Africa as koppies. Mount Binga in the Chimanimani Range on the Zimbabwe border is Mozambique's highest peak at 2,436m. Other notable mountains include the massive inselberg of Gorongosa (1,862m) in Sofala Province; Mount Chiperone (2,052m) near Milange; and Mount Namuli (2,419m) near Gurué. Mozambique is traversed from west to east by several major river systems, notably the Zambezi, Limpopo, Rovumo, Lurio and Save.

Mozambique has a tropical climate, with northern coastal regions in particular being very hot and humid. The dry winter runs from May to September and the wet summer from December to April, with weather during the in-between months often sharing elements of both seasons. Mozambique is more pleasant in winter, and there is less of a malaria risk.

History
The country Mozambique is a modern entity. Before 1890, Mozambique was not a country but a Portuguese-occupied island, and the country we know today as Mozambique was less a colony than a patchwork of endlessly mutating and fragmenting fiefdoms. Some of these fiefdoms did fall under the nominal or real rule of the Portuguese Crown, but a far greater number were lorded over by self-appointed despots, whether renegade Portuguese *mazungos*, indigenous chiefs or Muslim sheikhs.

Between 1650 and 1800, the Portuguese Crown took indirect control over the Zambezi Valley, formalising the existing *mazungo* chieftaincies into *prazo* leases. The *prazeros* (lease holders) ran their estates as small feudal empires, deriving their income from tributes extracted from the peasantry rather than by actively developing agriculture. The great drought of the early 19th century undermined the agricultural base of the Zambezi Valley, and many *prazeros* were forced to move on. By 1850, economic power in the Zambezi Valley was consolidated under five constantly feuding *mazungo* families, so that even this one part of the Mozambican interior to be extensively settled by the Portuguese fell under the full control of the Crown only after a minor civil war in 1887.

Even after the modern boundaries of Mozambique were agreed by the rival European powers, Portugal's hold was tenuous enough that Britain and Germany signed a secret treaty determining how the colony should be divided in the event of Portuguese withdrawal. In 1900, only Maputo, Inhambane, Gaza and Nampula of Mozambique's ten modern provinces were administered directly by Portugal. Of the other provinces, Niassa and Cabo Delgado were leased to the Niassa Company until 1929, Tete and Zambezia were chopped up into *prazos*, and Sofala and Manica were leased to the Mozambique Company until 1941.

A crucial trend during the first decade of formal colonisation was the economic rise of southern Mozambique. After 1894, when it was linked by rail to the gold mines of South Africa, Lourenço Marques grew to become the most important port in the region and in 1898 it replaced Mozambique Island in the north as the colonial capital. The South African mines also provided employment to between 50,000 and 100,000 Mozambican migrant labourers annually between the end of the Boer War and the start of World War II. In some years, the tax paid by the miners accounted for more than half the total revenue raised by the colonial government.

The process of shaping Mozambique into a coherent political unit started after 1926, when Portugal's Republican government was overthrown in a military coup which led to the foundation of the so-called 'New State' and the dictatorship of Antonio Salazar, Prime Minister of Portugal from 1932 to 1968. Salazar envisaged a future wherein Portugal and its colonies would form a self-sufficient closed economy with the mother country serving as the industrial core and the dependencies providing the agricultural produce and raw materials. Salazar outlawed the company concessions and *prazeros* which had until then practically ruled two-thirds of Mozambique, and he was largely successful in his efforts to create a more unitary administration.

Mozambique's first broad-based liberation movement, Frelimo, was formed in Dar es Salaam in 1963 under Eduardo Mondlane, a Mozambican academic living in the USA. Mondlane was assassinated by a letter-bomb in 1969, to be replaced by Samora Machel as party leader. Frelimo launched several military attacks on Mozambique, though their influence on Portuguese colonial policy is debatable bearing in mind concurrent political changes within Portugal. Upon entering the European Common Market in 1970, Portugal was compelled to dismantle its rigid trade agreements with Mozambique, resulting in the rapid realignment of the colony's economy. By 1974, South Africa was not only the main investor in Mozambique but also its principal trading partner. In April 1974, there was a left-wing coup in Lisbon; within six months the new Portuguese government had signed the Lusaka Accord, granting Mozambique independence nine months later and transferring power to Frelimo without even the pretence of a referendum or election.

It would be easy to portray the first 15 years of Frelimo rule as typical of the Marxist dictatorships that characterised post-independence Africa. It would also be simplistic. Frelimo assumed a dictatorial role largely through circumstance – there was no viable opposition – and its progressive ideals were a far cry from the self-serving policies of many of its peers. Frelimo had several successes on the social front. Primary school attendance doubled in its first years of rule, while enrolment at secondary schools increased sevenfold. An immunisation programme praised by the WHO as one of the most successful initiated in Africa resulted in a 20% drop in infant mortality. And Frelimo's abundant economic failures were at least partly due to factors beyond its control. Independence came during the depression that followed the 1973 Oil Crisis, which among other things forced the South African gold mines to lay off two-thirds of their Mozambican workers in 1976, resulting in an immense loss in foreign earnings. An exodus of skilled Portuguese settlers and related asset-stripping resulted in the collapse of secondary industry within a year of independence. Meanwhile, Frelimo's ambitious agricultural schemes were thwarted by disastrous floods in 1977/8, followed by four years of drought.

Frelimo had also to contend with South Africa's policy of 'destabilisation' through the medium of Renamo. This guerrilla organisation was conceived by the Rhodesian Special Branch as a fifth column to attack strategic bases in Mozambique, which at that time was allowing the Zimbabwean liberation movements to operate out of Manica. When Rhodesia became Zimbabwe, Renamo was retrained by South Africa to continue its campaign against Mozambique. On March 16 1984, Mozambique and South Africa signed the Nkomati Accord, an agreement that neither country would support elements hostile to the other. Mozambique abided by the accord. South Africa didn't. In September 1986, President Samora Machel's plane was diverted by a South African radio signal (whether by accident or design remains an open question). It crashed in South African territory, killing everybody on board.

Three months later, Malawi signed a mutual security agreement with Mozambique, forcing Renamo out of Malawi, where it had up until then been based. Renamo moved into Mozambique and took on a life of its own: war bands roamed through the countryside, supporting themselves with random raids on rural villages in what an official of the US State Department described as 'one of the most brutal holocausts against ordinary human beings since World War II'. It is estimated that, by 1990, at least 100,000 Mozambicans had been killed by Renamo war bands, and one-third of the population was displaced or exiled. In November 1990, pressured by overseas aid donors, Frelimo unveiled a new constitution allowing for multi-party elections, though civil war continued into 1992, when a Peace Accord was signed by Frelimo and Renamo in Rome. Mozambique remains under Frelimo rule following the first democratic election, held in October 1994, which achieved an 85% turn-out with Frelimo's Chissano obtaining 53% of the presidential vote and Renamo's Dhlakama 34%.

PRACTICAL INFORMATION
Accommodation
Outside Maputo City, where new ones seem to be opening every week, there are relatively few hotels in Mozambique and a basic double room generally costs in excess of US$10. Organised campsites are mainly restricted to beaches south of Beira, and prices tend to be high by African standards. Free camping away from towns and cities in small traditional villages is fine, ask for the *regulo* (chief), and show him your tent and where you want to pitch it. Firewood and water will be brought and food offered. Camping alone in the bush is dangerous due to landmines and opportunistic thieves. Resorts, hostels or campsites with facilities catering specifically for backpackers exist at (from south to north) Maputo, Bilene, Xai-Xai, Inhambane, Tofo, Barra Beach (Ponta da Barra), Maxixe, Linga-Linga, Vilankulo, Beira, Mozambique Island, Pemba and Lichinga.

Crime and safety
Theft and mugging appear to be less of a concern in Mozambique than in many other parts of the region. Even in Maputo we felt safe, but avoid shortcuts through

deserted parks and roads that pass through bush and, as always, it would be inadvisable to wander around after dark with more money than you need for the evening. Do carry a certified (notarised) copy of your passport at all times as the police are entitled to see some form of identification on demand. Armed banditry and car hijacks are a common occurrence and have resulted in fatalities in the last year or two, but they are of greater concern to people with private transport than those using public transport.

Never wander off established roads and footpaths, since, especially around bridges, deserted buildings and the old 'quartel' (garrison) in most villages, the countryside is littered with unexploded landmines.

Entry formalities

All visitors to Mozambique (except for Malawians) require a visa. This must be bought in advance; if you hear of anybody who was issued a visa at a border post it will not be legal and they were very lucky not to have to retrace their steps to the nearest city with Mozambican diplomatic representation, and to pay a US$100 per day fine. In most countries, a single-entry visa costs US$35 (in Malawi, Swaziland and South Africa US$8), while a transit visa allowing you to enter seven days from date of issue for a stay of only three days, costs US$10 (US$5 in Blantyre). You need a 30-day double-entry visa (multiple-entry visas are only issued against a letter from a Mozambican company, and allow only ten days on each entry). Upon arrival, you'll normally have a 30-day visitor's pass stamped in your passport, renewable if you need to spend longer there.

Food and drink

The Portuguese influence and presence of fresh seafood makes eating out a more pleasurable experience than it is in many other African countries. However, except in major cities, the adjectives vary and cheap won't often come into play. At the coast, it's mostly seafood, with fish (*peixe*), calamari (*lulas*) and crab (*caranguejo*) more affordable than lobster (*lagosta*) or prawns (*camarão*). Inland, you'll eat lots of chicken (*galinha* or *frango*), often dosed in delicious but searing hot *piripiri* sauce. Many restaurants quote a price for a whole chicken (*galinha enteiros*) but you can ask for a half (*maio*) chicken – and say whether you want it grilled (*grelhado*) or fried (*frita*). Near Zimbabwe, for instance in Tete and Chimoio, you'll see more meat dishes (*bife* or *carne*). In large towns, *pastelárias* serve sandwiches (*sandes*) in fresh rolls (*pão*), filled with eggs (*ovo*), cheese (*queijo*) or spicy sausage (*chouriço*). Many places serve steak rolls (*prego no pão*) and hamburgers (*amburque* or something similar). Most markets have stalls (*bancas*) where you can get a plate of fish or chicken stew for around US$1.50.

Locally bottled soft drinks are cheap, though you may have to specify you want the local variety (say, *Coca Cola nacionale*) or some clever soul will decide that you'd prefer to spend more on an imported can of the identical liquid. In the north, you'll sometimes find imported soft drinks only, and at a price. In the south, locally brewed beer (*cerveja nacionale*) is slightly cheaper than imported beer. The local brands, 2M (*dozyem*), Laurentina and Manica, come in 500ml and 340ml bottles (*garaffa*) and 450ml cans (*lata*). Beer is expensive in the north.

Getting around
By road

South of the Zambezi reliable bus services connect Maputo, Beira, Chimoio, Tete and points in between. The recommended lines for long-hauls between these towns are Oliveira's and Virginia, but there are also several local bus companies which connect the various towns between Maputo and Beira. The Mozambican word for bus is *machimbombo*, while a *chapa* (*shuppa*) is the equivalent of the East African *matatu*. In towns *chapas* are usually minibuses, but between towns (especially in the north) they are most often a large truck with caged sides, a plastic 'roof', and benches facing inwards. Note, if you want to get off a *chapa*, shout out 'Saida' (departing). In the south, *chapas* are one way to get along roads that connect places such as Bilene to the EN1. They become a more important form of transport in the north.

Getting around Mozambique is complicated by two things. The first is that people tend to tell you the last time at which public transport might leave – in other words when you are told that a bus or *chapa* leaves at 05.00, there's a good chance it will be gone if you don't arrive a few minutes early. The second is that few towns have a central bus terminal. Instead, there is an informally agreed departure point for vehicles going in any given direction, frequently 20 minutes from the town centre. If you're not a morning person, you can alleviate the stress slightly by locating the right spot to wait for transport on the afternoon before you travel.

By rail
The service between Maputo and Johannesburg in South Africa is efficient and well maintained, but buy a ticket only for the Komatipoort–Johannesburg leg, as Ressano Garcia to Maputo is very slow and almost everyone uses chapas. The one-class train between Beira and Mutare in Zimbabwe is slow and scruffy. An efficient daily service now connects Nampula to Cuamba, and a twice-weekly service connects Nayuchi (catch a *chapa* from Cuamba to Entre Lagos) to Liwonde in Malawi.

By boat
A regular ferry (06.00–22.00) connects Maputo to Catembe, while the Inhaca Island ship is often not available as it is the standby vessel for the Catembe ferry which often breaks down. Boats (dhows) must also be used to get to the island of Ibo, and to get between Vilankulo or Inhassoro and the Bazaruto Islands. In the north, private fishing dhows connect most ports north of Angoche, where they are a slow and uncomfortable alternative to travelling by road.

Language
English is spoken by very few people in Mozambique, so it's practically essential that you learn a few Portuguese phrases (see *Appendix 2*).

Money
The unit of currency is the metical (MT), plural meticais. The current exchange rate ranges from US$1=16,500MT to 18,500 MT, depending on where you change your money and whether you have cash or travellers' cheques. There are banks in all large towns, but private bureaux de change (*secundário de cámbios*) offer better rates for cash in Maputo, Beira, Tete, Nampula and Pemba. Banking hours are from 08.00 to 11.00. Cámbios keep normal shopping hours. Note that banks charge a hefty commission on travellers' cheques: 5% at all branches of the Banco Commercial Mozambique and a straight fee of US$7 at any Standard Bank.

There's an open black market for cash, one that you'll have to use if you arrive by land after 11.00. Do beware of professional cons, especially at borders, and don't expect a good rate. The US dollar always fetches a good rate, provided that you have note denominations of US$50 or smaller (there is a widespread suspicion about fake US$100 notes and some changers may not have enough local currency to change that much money in one go). The South African rand gets a good rate around Maputo, as does the Zimbabwe dollar in Chimoio, Beira or Tete, and the Malawi kwacha in Niassa.

As a rule, day-to-day expenses in Mozambique are twice what they would be in, say, Ethiopia, Malawi or Tanzania. That said, most travellers won't be embarking on expensive activities such as safaris or mountain climbs. And there are a few places – Vilankulo and Ibo spring to mind – where you could get by very cheaply indeed were you to settle in for a few days and cook seafood bought from fishermen.

Post and telephone
Mozambique's telephone system is reasonably efficient. From overseas, it's one of the easiest African countries to get through to first time. The international code is +258, and important area codes are Beira (03); Chimoio (051); Maputo (01); Nampula (06); Quelimane (04); Songo and Tete (052); and Xai-Xai (022).

Post from Mozambique is cheap and reasonably reliable, but it is often very slow. Poste restante letters can be collected in most large towns.

Public holidays
In addition to the following fixed public holidays, Good Friday and Easter Monday are recognised as public holidays in Mozambique.

January 1	New Year's Day	June 25	National Day
February 3	Heroes' Day		(Independence Day)
April 7	Women's Day	September 7	Victory Day
May 1	Labour Day	September 25	Armed Forces Day
		December 25	Family Day

Northern Mozambique
NIASSA PROVINCE
Niassa is Mozambique's most thinly populated province, and the driest (though parts are very wet from January to May), but it is also perhaps the most scenic and climatically pleasant part of the country. The western border is dominated by Lake Malawi – or Lago Niassa as it's known in Mozambique – and by the mountainous Rift Valley escarpment. Most backpackers entering Mozambique from Malawi will come through Niassa.

The most northerly entry point into Niassa is **Cóbuè**, a small port facing Likoma Island on a beautiful stretch of the lakeshore. Roughly 80km south of Cóbuè, **Metangula** is the largest settlement on the Mozambican shore of Lago Niassa. Formerly the main slave trading terminus on the eastern side of the lake, and now a naval base, Metangula is today somewhat out of the way, but it has a setting to rival famed Cape Maclear on the Malawian shore. The closest lakeshore settlement to Lichinga, the provincial capital, is **Meponda**, a glorified village set on a long sandy beach at the base of some low wooded hills.

Formerly known as Vila Cabral, **Lichinga**, the capital of Niassa, lies at an altitude of 1,277m on the plateau to the east of the lake. Surrounded by pine plantations and boasting a refreshingly breezy climate, Lichinga is markedly different in atmosphere to any other large town in Mozambique. Nevertheless, it's a rather poky little place, with poor and generally overpriced facilities and little in the way of tourist attractions. Lichinga has long been the best place to change US dollars cash into meticais – the going rate is currently around US$1=18,000MT as opposed to 16,500MT in Maputo, Beira or Nampula. You're safer changing money in an upmarket hotel or shop than on the street. It has become quite a boom-town but still has little in the way of tourist attractions.

Massangulo is an atmospheric small town lying about 2km off the main road south from Lichinga to Mandimba and Cuamba. Situated at the base of a pretty mountain and dominated by an extraordinary mission church, it could be an attractive place to spend a couple of nights, particularly if you like walking. Apart from having one of Mozambique's best markets, the same cannot be said of **Mandimba**, a dusty small town that sprawls uninvitingly along the main Lichinga–Cuamba road, but which is nevertheless of interest to travellers as the best and most accessible road border between Malawi and northern Mozambique. If heading for the coast from Blantyre, the Nayuchi/Entre Lagos route via Liwonde may be a better option, but note that a train runs (departs 05:00) Mondays, Wednesday and Friday between Balaka (near Liwonde) and Nayuchi, while Entre-Lagos to Cuamba is via *chapas*.

Niassa's second largest town and main route focus is **Cuamba**, situated at the junction of the railway line between Malawi and the coast, and the main roads north to Lichinga and south to Gurué. Cuamba is a humdrum place – a grid of flame-tree-lined avenidas salvaged from anonymity only by the surrounding granite hills. In its favour, Cuamba's proximity to Malawi means that it has the most affordable beers and sodas in northern Mozambique. Another notable feature of the town is a predominance of bicycle shops – presumably influenced by the quirky and mysterious trade patterns that characterise northern Mozambique.

Access and getting around

Access to Niassa from Malawi is covered under *Malawi to Mozambique* on pages 74–5. The only official road transport within the province is along the unsurfaced road connecting Cuamba and Lichinga via Mandimba. Two buses cover this 310km route daily in either direction, leaving at around 05.00 and taking up to eight hours. Buses to Cuamba leave Lichinga from the central market, while buses to Lichinga leave Cuamba from the opposite side of the railway line to the station and town centre. Several *chapas* and trucks also do this trip every day, leaving around midday.

Mandimba lies halfway between Lichinga and Cuamba, and buses travelling in either direction stop there between 09.00 and 10.00. Buses don't divert to Massangulo, but you can ask to be dropped at the signposted turn-off and then walk – it shouldn't take longer than 30 minutes.

Travellers heading between Lago Niassa and Lichinga will be dependent on *chapas* and trucks. The 60km unsurfaced road between Lichinga and Meponda is in excellent condition and covered by several *chapas* daily. North of Lichinga, a good surfaced road covers the 120km to Maniamba, which is connected to Metangula by a rough 28km dirt road. *Transportes Mundidelanji* buses and a few trucks cover this trip daily, generally leaving at around 05.00. Transport covering the 80km road between Metangula and Cóbuè is more erratic, but it's possible to use a fishing dhow between the two ports. All transport out of Lichinga leaves from the central market.

The new passenger train service between Cuamba and Nampula leaves at 06.00 daily in either direction, takes about eight hours and costs less than US$4. Cuamba is connected by road to Gurué in Zambezia Province, but there's not much transport along this route.

Where to stay and eat
Cóbuè
Hotel Santo Miguel Basic but clean. Rooms **C** pp.
Njafuwa Beach Camp 30-minute walk from the jetty. Meals and drinks. Camping **B** pp.

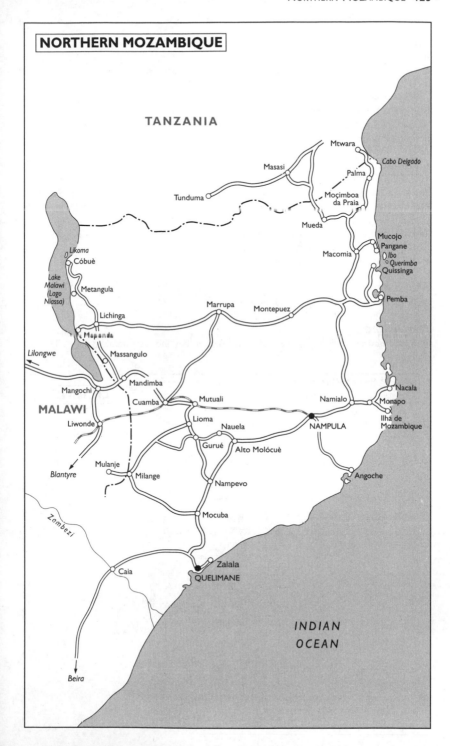

NORTHERN MOZAMBIQUE

Metangula

Chuianga Beach Resort On beach 5km north of town. Camping. Restaurant. Reed huts **C** pp.

Pensão Metangula Small, run-down *pensão* in town centre. **C**.

Meponda

Meponda Lodge Construction site signposted early 1997. No news of progress.

Salõa de Cha Restaurant on beach serving basic meals, beer, soft drinks. Camping permitted under the open-sided reed shelters.

Lichinga

Hotel Chiwindi Dingy, run-down rooms **C**/**E**.

Pousada Lichinga The most upmarket hotel and best restaurant in town. Rooms **F** dbl.

Quinta Capricornio 2km out on the Maniamba road. Camping **C** pp. Room **D** pp. Both rates include breakfast.

Loja Dona Luisa Cheap, bright blue family-run shop/restaurant/basic rooms next to market. Excellent meals. **B**/**C**.

Residencial Rival Good compromise between price and quality. **D** s/c dbl.

Massangulo

Yaileka Resthouse Basic place behind market. **C**.

Mandimba

Pensão Ngame Unsignposted behind petrol station. Bar and restaurant. **B** dbl.

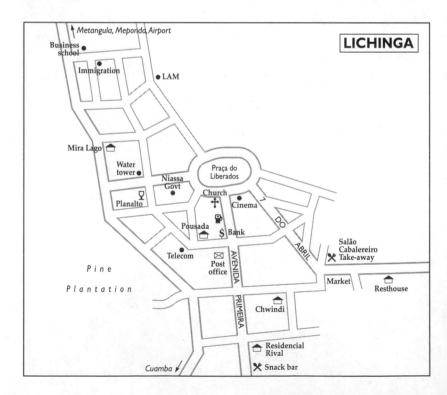

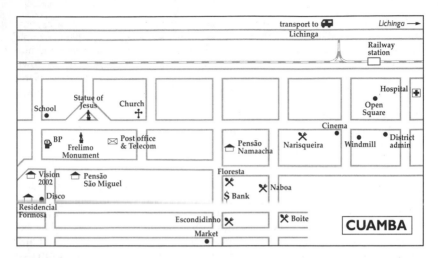

Cuamba

Hotel Vision 2002 Mid-range hotel. Rooms **F** a/c s/c dbl. Varied menu US$5–7.

Pensão São Miguel Best of a few *pensãos*. Meals around US$3.50. Room **E** s/c dbl.

Residencial Formosa Scruffy and potentially noisy, but cheapest for solo travellers. **C** pp.

CABO DELGADO

The northeastern province of Cabo Delgado is where travellers coming from Tanzania will enter Mozambique. The closest town to this border, **Quionga**, is fair-sized and lies on a pretty estuary 25km from the Rovuma River. The next town along the coast is **Palma**, which lies on an attractive palm-fringed lagoon, while further south the small port of **Moçimboa da Praia** offers access to **Mueda**, the principal town on the Mozambican part of the Makonde Plateau. On June 16 1960, Mueda became the setting of a massacre that's been called Mozambique's equivalent to Sharpeville, when Portuguese soldiers fired on an officially sanctioned meeting of peasant farmers, killing an estimated 600. Many Makonde carvers practise their famous craft in the villages around Mueda. Another attractive beach area, south of Moçimboa da Praia, is **Pangane**.

The **Quirimba Archipelago** is a string of 27 offshore islands which run roughly parallel to the coast between Pemba and the Tanzania border. Composed of fossil coral rock, the islands are lushly vegetated and the surrounding shallows support extensive mangrove swamps and a wide range of wading birds. The islands protect an important breeding colony of terns and a variety of turtles, while dolphins and a variety of colourful reef fish are frequently seen by snorkellers and from boats. The obvious base from which to explore the Quirimba Islands is **Ibo**, a small town situated on the island of the same name. Ibo is one of the most ancient towns in Mozambique, and after Mozambique Island it is arguably the most fascinating and atmospheric – the few travellers who make the effort to get there are likely to regard it as a highlight of their time in the country (see box *Around Ibo* on page 427).

Formerly known as Porto Amelia, **Pemba** is the capital of Cabo Delgado. It was founded in 1904 on the southern side of Pemba Bay, a semi-enclosed natural harbour which, depending on who you believe, is the second or third largest in the world. Pemba's modern town centre is very bland, but the old town near the port is more atmospheric and fringed by an attractive and remarkably neat reed-hut village called Paquite-Quete (pa kitty-cat). Instead of staying in the town centre, most travellers head to **Wimbe Beach**, 6km away, which has a tourist complex, a couple of restaurants, and a diving centre where you can arrange scuba excursions and hire snorkelling equipment. There is a small backpackers' campsite 2–3km further down the beach from Wimbe. Also of interest is the **Makonde wood-carving co-operative** about 1.5km from the town centre along the road to Wimbe Beach.

Access and getting around

The Rovuma River, which forms most of the border between Tanzania and Mozambique, has for many years been one of Africa's last great barriers to overland travel. This changed in June 2000, when a motorised ferry (able to carry four small vehicles or one overland truck) called *Mueda* started operating. Tickets cost US$0.50. No ticket is required for vehicles going in either direction, but if heading for Mozambique, get your visa in Dar Es Salaam.

From Singa, the immigration post 200m from the Mozambican side of the Rovuma ferry, the sandy track to Namoto, Quionga and Palma is serviced by 4x4 Tanzanian *chapas*. This road is sometimes swampy from January to May, and may then be impassable. Palma is connected to Moçimboa da Praia by an unsurfaced road that takes 3–4 hours by *chapa*. The whole trip from Singa to Moçimboa da Praia costs US$10. Trucks and *chapas* between Moçimboa da Praia and Mueda also take 3–4 hours. To get to Pangane, ask a vehicle heading between Moçimboa da Praia and Pemba to drop you at Macomia (accommodation available), from where there are a few *chapas* daily though to the small port of Mucojo. This lies two hours' walk from Pangane Beach, but is covered by at least one *chapa* in either direction daily, except for Sunday.

There are three ways of getting to Ibo. The first and most straightforward is to arrange the trip with a company called *Well Endhowed* in Pemba (tel: 3631), which runs dhow trips by arrangement at US$15 per person daily self-catering, or US$30 per person daily including meals. Group size must be a minimum of four and maximum of eight.

By public transport, the better option is probably by road from Pemba via Sunate and Bilibiza to Quissanga on the facing mainland. There is usually at least one *chapa* per day between Pemba or Macomia and Quissanga, or you could wait for a lift either at the bus stop on the Nampula road about 500m past the junction to Wimbe Beach, or else at Sunate which is the turn-off to Macomia, 87km from Pemba along the Nampula Road. Once at Quissanga, you'll need to walk for about 30 minutes to get to the small fishing village of Tandanhangui (Tandanyungy), where it's easy enough to arrange dhow transport to Ibo itself – expect to pay around US$20 per dhow for the round trip (haggle if on your own) and to be on the water for up to two hours each way.

The other way of getting to Ibo is with one of the dhows that run between Pemba and Moçimboa da Praia. The problem is that these depart to an erratic schedule dictated by the combination of tides, winds and demand, so you'll simply have to ask around – in Pemba, the best place to do this is Paquite Quete beach five minutes' walk from the old town. The trip from Pemba to Ibo will take at least 12 hours, quite possibly longer, and there will be no food, water, cover or toilet facilities on the dhow. Before trying anything else, it's definitely worth asking at the Complexo Nautilus on Wimbe Beach for a private lift to Quissanga or a motorboat to Ibo. For details of transport south from Pemba, see *Access and getting around* on page 434.

Heading south from Pemba, fancy new buses called '*flecha branca*' cover the route to Nampula now, at a cost of US$4 per person.

AROUND IBO

The Quirimba Islands were occupied by Muslims by the 15th century, and they became an important refuge for Muslim traders after Kilwa was occupied by Portugal in 1507. Portugal attacked the islands in 1523, killing some 60 people and looting large amounts of ivory and other trade goods; a report dating from 1609 tells us that seven of the nine largest islands were by that time ruled by Portuguese traders, and that Ibo itself was substantially fortified. After 1750, Ibo became the major supplier of slaves to the sugar plantation owners on the Île de France. It was granted municipal status in 1763, and soon rose to become the second most important Portuguese trading centre after Mozambique Island. Ibo was leased to the Niassa Company in 1897, but the shallow approach to the island wasn't suitable for modern ships, for which reason the Niassa Company relocated its base to Porto Amelia (Pemba) in 1904.

Ibo today is fantastically run down, chronically isolated and utterly compelling. The obvious point of comparison is Ilha de Mozambique, but the towns are very different in character. The cluttered alleyways of the former capital evoke the Muslim towns of the Swahili Coast more than anything European, whereas Ibo has an uncluttered and overwhelmingly Mediterranean character. The wide roads are lined with opulent high-roofed buildings boasting classical facades and expansive balconies supported by thick pillars. These abandoned palaces and villas have fallen into disrepair: the roofs are shedding their centuries-old cover of clay tiles while the moss-covered walls have been undermined by the vast sprawling tendrils of strangler figs. Exposed rag coral and fading whitewash gives the town a washed-out pastel air, one strangely at odds with the deep blue tropical sky and bright red flame trees that line the streets.

It is difficult to establish the antiquity of many of Ibo's buildings. Much of the town centre dates to the early nineteenth century, and the semi-fortified southern waterfront appears to be even older. The moderately sized Portuguese fort on the southwestern tip of the island was built in 1752–70; the large whitewashed Church of Our Lady of Rosaria next to it was reportedly erected in 1580, presumably by the Dominican missionaries who claimed to have made 16,000 converts on the Quirimbas by 1593. The most interesting building in Ibo, and one of the best preserved, is the large star-shaped fort to the northwest of the town centre, complete with a dozen or so cannons and ringed by a grove of tall palms. Built in 1791, this fort was used as a prison into the 1970s, and it is now occupied by traditional silversmiths who'll happily allow you to watch them at work without expecting you to buy anything. A nominal entrance fee is charged for entering the fort.

For those wishing to explore the water around the Quirimba Islands, the best option is to organise a dhow trip out of Ibo – this should cost around US$5 for a day and you stand a good chance of seeing dolphins, turtles and other large marine creatures. Quirimba Island, immediately to the south of Ibo, is the obvious target for a longer excursion – it's reputedly a very attractive place, and there are a couple of old Portuguese houses on a former prazo estate and a guesthouse run by the Gessners, third generation Germans on the island.

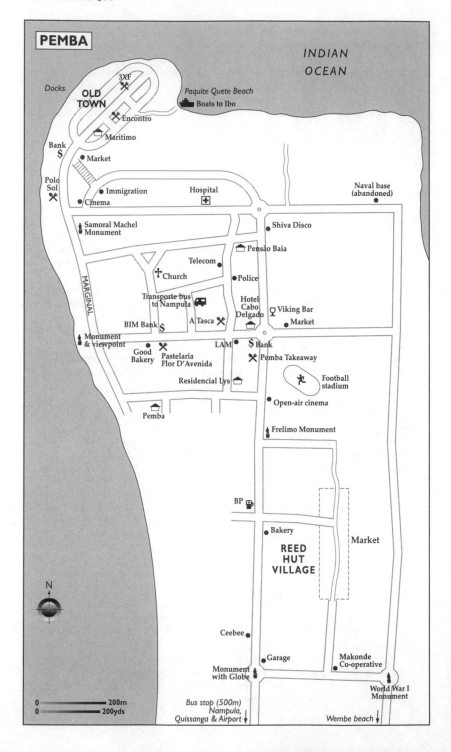

PEMBA

INDIAN OCEAN

Docks

3XF

OLD TOWN

Paquite Quete Beach
Boats to Ibo

Encontro

Maritimo

Bank
$

Market

Polo
Sol

Immigration

Hospital

Naval base
(abandoned)

Cinema

Samoral Machel
Monument

Shiva Disco

Pensão Baia

Telecom

MARGINAL

Church

Police

Transporte bus
to Nampula

Hotel
Cabo
Delgado

Viking Bar

Market

BIM Bank $

A Tasca

Monument
& viewpoint

Good
Bakery

Pastelaria
Flor D'Avenida

LAM

$ Bank

Pemba Takeaway

Residencial Lys

Football
stadium

Open-air cinema

Pemba

Frelimo Monument

BP

Bakery

REED
HUT
VILLAGE

Market

N

Ceebee

Garage

Makonde
Co-operative

Monument
with Globe

World War I
Monument

0 ——— 200m
0 ——— 200yds

Bus stop (500m)
Nampula,
Quissanga & Airport ↓

Wembe beach ↓

Where to stay and eat
From Tanzania to Moçimboa da Praia
There are very basic lodgings in Namoto, Namuiranga and Quiongoa (ie: no mattresses, nets or bedding). Marginally smarter guesthouses can be found in Palma, Mueda and Moçimboa da Praia, with prices spanning the **C** and **D** ranges.

Pangane
Pangane Acampamento Beautiful, secure campsite with good toilets and showers. Basic reed huts **B** pp. Camping **A** pp.
Casa Chung (also known as Casa Suki) Chinese-owned compound and shop near the fish market. Rooms with bedding **C** dbl. Good, inexpensive meals.

Ibo
Casa da Forino House with running water, kitchen, comfortable rooms with fan **E** dbl
Casa Janine (also known as Villa Ruben) Private house near the star-shaped fort which has been taking in travellers for years. Great setting and veranda, good meals prepared with two hours' notice. Camping **A** pp. Rooms **D** dbl with nets, fan, shared ablutions.
Wildlife Adventures Backpacker-friendly set-up in huge old Portuguese house on waterfront. **C** pp.

Pemba
CeeBee Good coffee bar and source of tourist information, also has email and international fax facilities.
Complexo Turístico Nautilus and **Cariaco Wimbe Beach** Upmarket hotels which no longer allow camping but do good food.
Caju Camping New backpackers campsite 2–3km along the track past Wimbe. Shady site under cashew trees, hot showers, cold beers, meals, kitchen. Nice spot but beware of petty theft. Own tent essential. **B** pp.
Indico Divers The owner of this diving centre at Nautalis can sometimes arrange camping.
Maritimo Only accommodation in old town centre. Run down. No fans. Room **C**/**D**.
Pemba Take-Away Nampula Rd. Inexpensive meals, eg: lobster US$3.50; burger US$1.50.
Pastelaria Flor D'Avenida Pavement tea garden serving coffee, cakes, good meals. The bakery a few doors up bakes great bread daily.
Pensão Baia Adequate accommodation in new town centre. Rooms **E** dbl with fan.
Restaurante A Tasca Near town centre. Tasty Portuguese dishes US$6. Coffee machine.
Viking Bar Popular drinking hole with expats, renowned for its burgers and seafood dishes.

NAMPULA
The province of Nampula is comprised largely of open savannah broken up by any number of isolated and imposing rocky outcrops, mesas and plateaux. The provincial capital, also called **Nampula**, is a modern city with good facilities for visitors, and an excellent museum of ethnology and attached Makonde carvers co-operative. The *câmbio* on Avenida Paolo Samuel Kamkomba offered the best rate for US dollar travellers' cheques we encountered in Mozambique.

The former Portuguese capital of **Ilha de Mozambique** on the small coral island of the same name was declared a UNESCO Cultural Heritage Site in 1992. Ilha de Mozambique – known locally as plain Ilha (pronounced ilia) – must surely rank as northern Mozambique's most alluring travel destination

EXPLORING ILHA DE MOZAMBIQUE

An important Muslim shipbuilding centre in the Shirazi trade era, Ilha de Mozambique was captured by Portugal in 1507 and, due to its defendable nature and position at the junction of the East African coast and the all-important spice route to India, it soon became the focus of Portuguese naval activities in East Africa. In 1530, the island effectively replaced Sofala as the capital of Portuguese East Africa, and it remained the economic hub of Portuguese East Africa until the late 19th century. Its modern slide into backwater status is rooted in two causes: the general southward drift of the economy towards Lourenço Marques and the Portuguese 'discovery' of the far superior natural harbour at nearby Nacala.

Ilha de Mozambique is one of the few towns in sub-equatorial Africa to have kept its historical appearance. The old town is a maze of narrow alleys lined with fading whitewashed buildings; it has barely changed shape in 200 years, and the mood is not unlike that of some of the older Swahili island towns of the Tanzanian and Kenyan coast – Lamu, say, or even more strikingly the old quarter of Mombasa. This might be because the old town has been almost entirely reoccupied by Muslims in recent years – creating a rather deceptive sense of historical continuity, one that has the effect of reducing four centuries of Portuguese occupation to something of a passing episode.

The old town was destroyed when the Dutch evacuated the island in 1607 and again in 1671 by the Omani. The only building actually in the old town to have survived all this is the former **Jesuit College of São Paulo**, constructed in 1619 and converted to a governor's palace in 1763. The original college church, opened in 1640, has a remarkably garish pulpit covered in a mixture of gargoyles, angels and dragons. The palace, now a museum, is a revelation: the 20-odd rooms are decorated in period style, presumably the furniture left behind when the governor moved to Lourenço Marques. Next door to this, the **Sacred Art Museum** is housed in the former Church of the Misericordia, built in 1700 and in use until the organisation was disbanded in 1915. The most unusual artefact here is a Makonde carving of Jesus – it would be interesting to know when and how this was acquired, since it is very different in style and subject from any other Makonde carving that I've seen.

both for its singular atmosphere and for its wealth of beautiful old buildings. Linked to the mainland by a 3.5km-long single lane causeway, the crescent-shaped island measures a mere 2.5km from north to south and is at no point more than 600m wide. Despite its small size, it supports a population of roughly 12,000 (1996) and, as the most important Portuguese settlement on the east African coast for the best part of four centuries, it boasts several of the oldest colonial buildings in the southern hemisphere (see box *Exploring Ilha de Mozambique*, above).

The modern port of **Nacala** is situated on the deep and attractive Bay of Fernão Veloso to the north of Ilha de Mozambique. Connected by rail to Malawi, Nacala is a port of some regional importance and it has been maintained largely through the use of Malawian and Zambian capital. The town is of little interest to travellers, though the relative bustle feels quite refreshing coming after the air of stagnation that envelops Ilha de Mozambique. Roughly 15km from Nacala, there is good snorkelling and diving off the beach at the entrance of the Bay of Fernão Veloso. There is also a small restaurant on the beach where you should be allowed to camp

Dominating the northern tip of the island, and older than any building in the town centre, the **Fortress of São Sebastião** has often been described as the most formidable fortress in Africa. Measuring up to 20m high, it was built with dressed limestone shipped from Lisbon between 1546 and 1583 as a response to the Turkish threat of 1538–53. There can be few other buildings which have played such a decisive role in shaping the course of history as has São Sebastião. In 1607, the Dutch navy landed on the island and occupied it for about a month, but they were unable to capture the fort and withdrew two months later. In 1608, the Dutch again seized the island and were again forced to withdraw as they were incapable of capturing the fort. Had São Sebastião been a less imposing fortress, it is almost certain that Mozambique Island would have become a Dutch property – this would not only have signalled the end of Portuguese influence in the region, but would also have given the Dutch little reason ever to have founded Cape Town. The **Church of Nossa Senhora Baluarte** within the fortress was built in 1522, making it the oldest standing European building in the southern hemisphere.

On the southern end of the island, not far from the causeway and separated from the old town by the more densely populated reed-hut part of town, the **Church of Senhora Saude** was founded in 1633 and extensively renovated in 1801. The attached cemetery is the oldest on the island, with many hundreds of tombstones marking Christian, Muslim and Hindu graves. Facing the Church of Senhora Saude, the 17-century **Fortress of São Lourenço** dominates a tiny, mushroom-shaped coral outcrop that can be reached on foot at low tide. If you want to walk across, check the tides in advance, since the island is accessible by foot for no longer than an hour. The best way to climb up to the island is through a gap in the coral overhang which can be reached by walking around the right side of the island for about 100m. Also of interest in this part of town is the whitewashed **Catholic cathedral**, an 18th-century building that stands on a palm-covered peninsula about 500m northeast of São Lourenço. On the beach in front of the cathedral, shipbuilders still practise the craft for which Ilha de Moçambique was famous even before the Portuguese arrived.

(though not, at the time of writing, a backpackers' lodge, despite persistent rumours over a couple of years).

Situated at the junction of the main Nampula–Pemba road and the turn-off to Ilha de Moçambique, **Namialo** might well provide an overnight stop to travellers heading between these towns. About 40km east of Namialo, **Monapo** lies 3km from the junction of the road to Nacala and the one to Ilha de Moçambique. Monapo is noted for its cashew factory, but unless using this route to Mogincual or Angoche, there's no reason why you'd want to spend the night. Near Mogincual, Fim do Mundo (World's End) is essentially a dive-camp for fly-in visitors, but if you have your own tent and food, the owner will welcome you to his beautiful spot and you may be able to get a cheap scuba-dive if he's not too busy.

Further south, **Angoche** was founded on the mouth of the Mluli River in the fifteenth century, probably by an offshoot of the ruling family of Kilwa. Like Ibo, Angoche became a refuge for Muslim traders in the early years of Portuguese influence. It enjoyed a trade boom between 1505 and 1511, at which

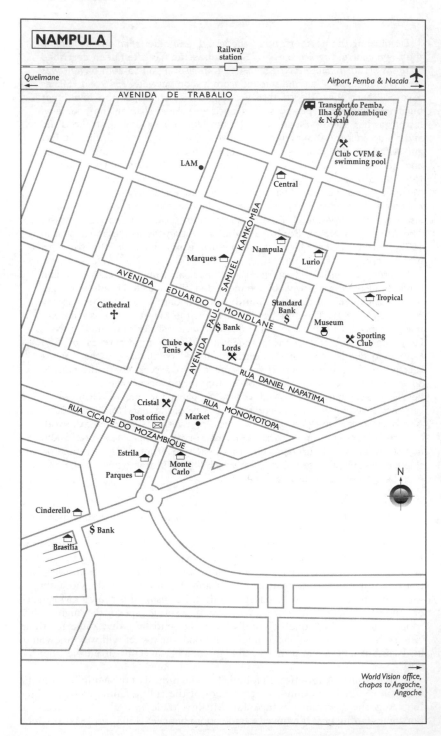

NAMPULA

Railway station

Quelimane

Airport, Pemba & Nacala

AVENIDA DE TRABALIO

Transport to Pemba, Ilha do Mozambique & Nacala

LAM

Club CVFM & swimming pool

Central

AVENIDA

SAMUEL KAMKOMBA

Marques

Nampula

Lurio

EDUARDO O MONDLANE

Cathedral

AVENIDA PAULO

Standard Bank

Tropical

Museum

Bank

Sporting Club

Clube Tenis

Lords

RUA DANIEL NAPATIMA

RUA CICADE DO MOZAMBIQUE

Cristal

Post office

RUA MONOMOTOPA

Market

N

Estrila

Monte Carlo

Parques

Cinderello

Bank

Brasilia

World Vision office, chapas to Angoche, Angoche

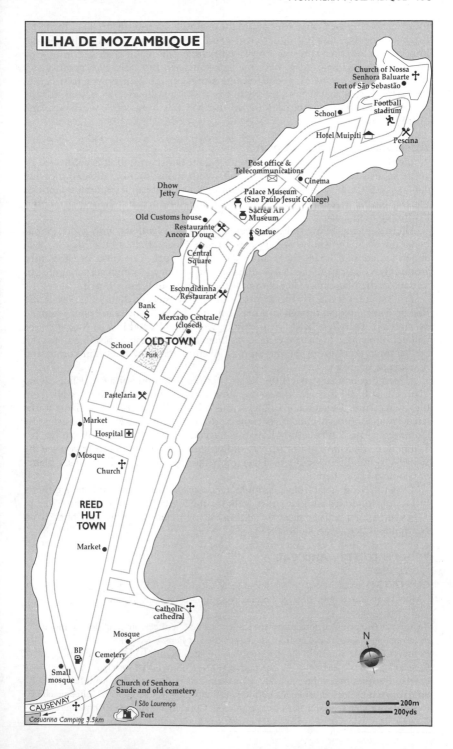

ILHA DE MOZAMBIQUE

Church of Nossa
Senhora Baluarte
Fort of São Sebastão

School

Football
stadium

Hotel Muipiti

Pescina

Post office &
Telecommunications

Cinema

Dhow
Jetty

Palace Museum
(Sao Paulo Jesuit College)

Old Customs house

Sacred Art
Museum

Restaurante
Ancora D'oura

Statue

Central
Square

Escondidinha
Restaurant

Bank

Mercado Centrale
(closed)

OLD TOWN

School

Park

Pastelaria

Market

Hospital

Mosque

Church

REED
HUT
TOWN

Market

Catholic
cathedral

Mosque

BP

Cemetery

Small
mosque

Church of Senhora
Saude and old cemetery

I São Lourenço

CAUSEWAY

Fort

Casuarina Camping 3.5km

N

0   200m
0   200yds

time it is estimated that the population stood at around 10,000. In 1511, Angoche was razed by Portuguese ships and its sheikh was captured. It then slid into relative obscurity, as ivory replaced gold as the major trading commodity on the coast, but enjoyed something of a revival in the early 19th century as a result of the slave trade. Angoche fell to Portugal in 1862, once again to sink into obscurity. It sees few visitors today, but is a worthwhile diversion, both for the atmospherically crumbling old town and for the long attractive beach and nearby islands.

Access and getting around

Nampula town is northern Mozambique's main transport hub. It is connected by an inexpensive railway service to Cuamba, with trains in either direction leaving daily at 06.00 and taking roughly eight hours. The seats are comfortable, though you risk having to stand for part of the way if you don't arrive at the station an hour before the train departs.

There is plenty of transport between Pemba and Nampula, with good options being the daily Transnorte or very comfortable Flecha Branca buses that leave in either direction at 05.00 sharp and take 10–12 hours. The buses leave Pemba around the corner from the Pensão Baia, and stop about 15 minutes later at the bus station on the Nampula road 500m past the turn-off to Wimbe Beach.

Trucks, buses and *chapas* run throughout the day between Nampula, Nacala and Ilha de Mozambique, though you may have to change vehicles at either Namialo or Monapo. Travellers heading directly between Pemba and Ilha de Mozambique will definitely have to change vehicles at Namialo. All transport heading north out of Nampula leaves from the junction of Avenida Paulo Samuel Kamkomba and Avenida de Trabalio.

At least one bus daily covers the 170km between Nampula and Angoche, leaving Nampula at 05.00 sharp from near the World Vision office 20 minutes' walk from the town centre. To get there, follow Avenida Paulo Kamkomba to the large traffic circle at its southern end, turn right and then immediately after passing the Commercial Bank turn left. Follow this curving road for 500m until you reach a T-junction where you must turn left and walk for another 1km before you see the World Vision office to your left. The stop is shortly after this and you'll see plenty of people waiting there.

To get to Mogincual from Nampula, take a *chapa* to Monapo and change there. From do Mondo it's an hour's easy walk from Mogincual – well worth it.

See *Access and getting around* for *Zambezia* for details of transport south from Nampula to Beira via Quelimane.

Where to stay and eat
Nampula
Club CVFM Restaurant with air conditioning. Meals around US$5. Swimming pool US$3.50.
Clube Tenis Smart outdoor place serving everything from steak to prawns. Meals from US$5.
Pastelaria Aurora Delicious pastries, excellent range of coffees, air conditioned, highly recommended. Two blocks up from the big circle past Pensão Marques.
Pensão Centrale Similar to the Marques, but no fans. Rooms **B/C**. Basic meals.
Pensão Marques The best of the cheap places. Large room **B/C** with fan.
Pensão Parques Best of the relatively upmarket pensãos. Rooms **E** dbl with fan.
Sporting Club Outdoor tables. Good food around US$3–4. Cheap beer. Coffee machine.
Restaurante Copacabana The place to be seen. Good food, fair prices. Opposite Hotel Tropical.

Namialo

Hotel Pousada Run-down but acceptable rooms at **C** dbl.
Restaurante Tropical Unsignposted green building two blocks from Pousada towards Nampula. Large, tasty helpings of fish or chicken US$4.

Ilha de Mozambique

Ancora d'Ouro Restaurant Cheap but good food opposite the Church of St Paul.
Camping Casuarinas A few steps from the mainland side of the causeway on a breezy clean beach, this is an exceptionally neat and efficiently-run campsite, with the disadvantage of being a 3.5km walk on the causeway from Ilha (easy to catch a lift on one of the frequent *chapas*). Facilities include a good restaurant and bar serving cold drinks. Camping **B** pp .
Hotel Muipiti The old Bauhaus-style Pousada Hotel, renovated and re-christened with the Macua name for Ilha. The grand opening has been repeatedly been postponed and it was still closed in July 2000.
Indico Restaurant On the seaward side of the old town. Good evening breeze but unreliable service and standards.
Private guesthouse In the Palace Museum, there is now an official tourist information centre with English-speaking guides and a wall map showing all of the guesthouses in town (at least a dozen in July 2000). There's plenty of choice to suit all budgets: for US$14 per person you can stay at the clean and breezy *Casa Blanca* which has foundations 400 years old, or for US$4 the other end of the scale is *Casa Luis* (also referred to as *The Private Garden*, though no-one on Ilha seems to know this name).
Relíquias Restaurant Close to the museum. Good service and seafood, view of the mainland.

Nacala

Carioca Pasteleria Burgers, ice-cream, fresh bread, imported sweets, cheap soft drinks.
Hotel Maiai (formerly Hotel Nacala) Clean upper-range hotel. Fair value. Renovated, a/c, US$40 per person.
Pensão Nacala From bus stop, walk downhill for a block past Carioca Pastelaria, turn into the road to your right, enter the first doorway to your left (next to a sign for a Video Club) and walk up two floors to reception. Scruffy and overpriced at **D** dbl.
Restaurante Boite Sandokan A contender for the best restaurant in the province. Meals

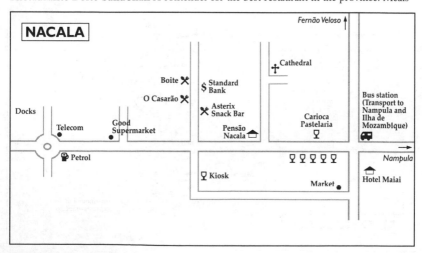

US$6–7. Plate of eight tiger prawns for US$10 will feed two. Minimum charge US$5 (man) or US$2 (woman)!

Restaurante O Casarão Next to the Boite Sandokan and cheaper.

Angoche

Pensão Oceania Basic rooms **©**. Staff can help organise dhows to nearby islands.

ZAMBEZIA

Mozambique's most populous and agriculturally rich province, Zambezia is generally passed through by travellers crossing overland from Malawi or heading from Nampula in northern Mozambique to Beira in the centre of the country.

The section of road from Nampula to Quelimane takes the best part of two days on public transport, with an overnight stop at either **Alto Molócuè** or **Mocuba**. Alto Molócuè sprawls around the Molócuè River, which separates the pretty administrative part of town, on a hill overlooking the north bank of the river, from the commercial centre, where a couple of hotels, restaurants and the municipal market are clustered around a triangular town 'square'. Mocuba lies at a sufficiently high altitude to stay relatively cool, and it is mostly of interest to travellers as the junction of the road between Nampula and Quelimane, and the road west to Milange on the Malawi border.

To the west of the Nampula–Quelimane road, the highland town of **Gurué** makes for an interesting off-the-beaten-track diversion. Situated amongst rolling hills and tea plantations at the base of the 2,419m-high Mount Namuli, Gurué has the highest rainfall figure of any town in the country and a fresh highland air that hardly feels like Mozambique at all. It is surrounded by promising walking country: the town centre sprawls along the higher contours of a small hill offering great views, while several dirt roads lead through the surrounding tea plantations and to the foot slopes of Namuli, where there are still a few well-maintained estate properties. One good day walk would be to follow the road to Alto Molócuè out of town for roughly 5km, where there is a large, isolated and apparently abandoned old church standing on a hill.

The provincial capital, **Quelimane**, is Mozambique's fourth largest town, situated on the north bank of the Bons Sinais (Good Omens), a waterway that

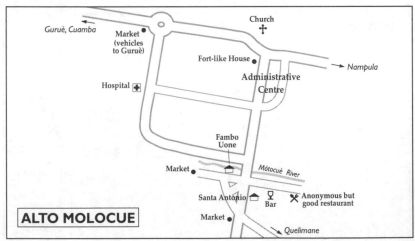

was linked to the Zambezi by a channel until it silted up in the 1820s. Quelimane was probably founded by Muslim traders at the same time as Tete and Sena; a Portuguese trading factory was established there in 1530, and reports from the 1590s depict an attractive small town surrounded by plantations and protected by a wooden fort. Given this sort of vintage, Quelimane is more modern in appearance than might be expected. We saw no trace of the old forts and customs house; the waterfront cathedral built in 1776 would appear to be the oldest extant building. The night market next to the cathedral is worth visiting – a couple of dozen reed-and-bamboo bars surrounding a rather incongruous and normally empty discotheque. Less than an hour from Quelimane by *chapa*, **Zalala Beach** is the best place to break up the slog between Beira and Nampula in relatively rustic surrounds.

Access and getting around

At least one bus daily in either direction covers the 525km road from Nampula to Quelimane, as do plenty of *chapas*. Vehicles in both directions leave at around 05.00, and those going from Quelimane to Nampula normally stop the night in Alto Molócuè, while those travelling from Nampula to Quelimane overnight in Mocuba. Transport heading towards Quelimane leaves Nampula from a stop 20 minutes' walk out of the town centre along the Quelimane road.

Gurué can be approached in two ways from the Nampula–Quelimane road. The first route goes from Alto Molócuè via Nauela along a little-used but very beautiful 80km road. The alternative route, which runs from Nampevo via Errego, is 125km long but reportedly carries more traffic. We found a lift along the direct route from Alto Molócuè via Nauela, but it's difficult to say how much this should be put down to luck. What is for sure is that you need to be waiting for a lift by 05.00 – the right place to wait lies 20 minutes' walk from the hotels, and about 500m past the church in the administrative part of Alto Molócuè.

Gurué can be approached from the north, by disembarking from the Cuamba–Nampula train at Mutuali, then using road transport to Gurué via Lioma, but there's not much traffic along this route. In the opposite direction, vehicles to Lioma and Cuamba leave from in front of Gurué market before 05.00.

There is no public transport along most of the road from Quelimane to Beira (plenty of chapas as far as the Zambezi), so you'll probably be dependent on getting a lift with a truck and you should expect this to take the best part of two days, with an overnight stop at Caia. People travelling from north to south should first take a bus from Quelimane to a small village near Nicuadala (I don't know the name of this village, but if you go to the bus station and ask for a vehicle heading to Beira you'll be put on the right bus) which is the conventional place to pick up vehicles heading further south. People travelling in the opposite direction should take any vehicle to Dondo, on the Chimoio road 28km west of Beira. Once you have found the huge crowd of people sitting by the northbound road that branches from the Beira Corridor at Dondo, you will know that you have found the right departure point. There is no bridge at Caia, but a vehicle ferry crosses back and forth throughout the day between 07.00 and 18.00, or you can cross in a dugout or rowing-boat. You will probably have to overnight at the river before picking up transport to Quelimane the next day. Either you can bed down in the huge truck yard with the other passengers, or else you can stay in the peculiar double-storey reed hotel on the north bank of the river.

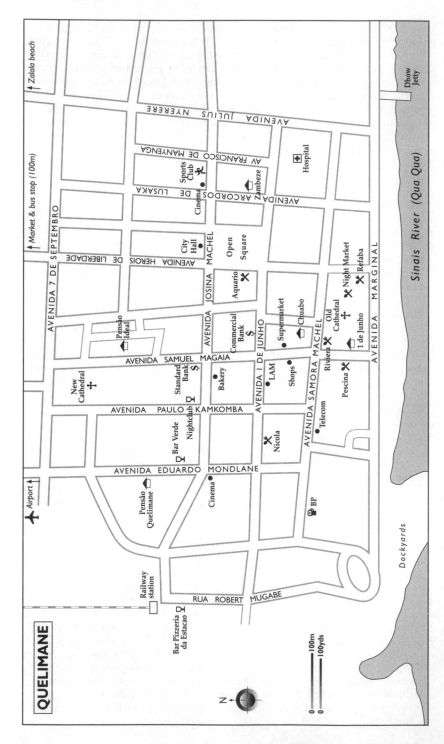

QUELIMANE

N

100m
100yds

Sinais River (Qua Qua)

Dhow Jetty

↑ *Zalala beach*

↑ Market & bus stop (100m)

AVENIDA JULIUS NYERERE

AV FRANCISCO DE MANYENGA

AVENIDA ARCORDOS DE LUSAKA

AVENIDA 7 DE SEPTEMBRO

AVENIDA HEROIS DE LIBERDADE

Hospital

Sports Club

Cinema

Zambeze

City Hall

Open Square

Aquario

OSINA

AVENIDA SAMORA MACHEL

AVENIDA

Commercial Bank

Supermarket

Chuabo

Night Market

Réfaba

Pensão Ideal

AVENIDA SAMUEL MAGAIA

Standard Bank

Bakery

LAM

Shops

Old Cathedral

1 de Junho

Riviera

Pescina

New Cathedral

AVENIDA PAULO KAMKOMBA

Bar Verde Nightclub

Nicola

AVENIDA I DE JUNHO

AVENIDA MARGINAL

Telecom

↑ Airport

AVENIDA EDUARDO MONDLANE

Pensão Quelimane

Cinema

BP

Railway station

RUA ROBERT MUGABE

Bar Pizzeria da Estacao

Dockyards

Where to stay and eat
Alto Molócuè
Pensão Fambo Uone Scruffy. No fans. **D** dbl.
Pensão Santa Antonio Clean and friendly. **D** dbl with fan. **F** s/c dbl. Poor food.
Restaurant Anonymous Good place 50m from main square (opposite direction to market).

Milange
Pensão Esplanada On the main road. **C** pp.

Mocuba
Pensão Cruzeiro Run-down and overpriced at **E** dbl.
O Sitio Restaurant Clean rooms and ablutions. On the wide avenue parallel to the main road.

Gurué
Complexo Turístico Sanzala Cramped and dingy rooms **D** s/c dbl. Flowering garden bar.
Pensão Gurué Large clean rooms **E** s/c dbl. Excellent meals US$3.50.

Quelimane
Café Riviera OK pastries, ice-cream, sandwiches, burgers and real coffee. Strictly halal so no alcohol. Not as good as it used to be.
Bar Pizzeria da Estacao Av Robert Mugabe. Excellent pizzas from US$3, seafood and great orange juice.
Cubanitos Restaurante New place on Av 7 de Septembro near market, good place for a drink, cheap snacks, and meals in US$3–7 range.

Zalala
Complexo Turístico Kassi-Kassi Beachfront resort named for the local word for evening mists. Tel: 21-2302. Often full at weekends, so call first. Four-bed chalet **F**. Camping **A** per tent. Restaurant and bar.

Central Mozambique
THE TETE CORRIDOR
The province of Tete, a northwestern extension of Mozambique surrounded on three sides by the former British territories of Malawi, Zambia and Zimbabwe, must rank as one of the most peculiar legacies of the colonial carve-up of Africa. It is also the part of Mozambique most frequently passed through by backpackers, since the so-called Tete Corridor – the road that bisects the province – forms the most direct route between Blantyre in Malawi and Harare in Zimbabwe. The Zóbuè border post, which lies between Blantyre and Tete, is the most accessible port of entry for travellers crossing between Malawi and southern Mozambique.

The provincial capital, also called **Tete**, is often and with some justification claimed to be the hottest town in Mozambique. Situated roughly 650km upriver from the mouth of the Zambezi, at an altitude of only 175m above sea level, the large suspension bridge at Tete is, remarkably, the only permanent crossing (the Sena bridge is due to return to rail traffic in a couple of years) of the Zambezi in Mozambique. Tete is thought to have been founded by Muslim gold traders in the 15th century, and it had been settled by Portuguese adventurers by 1531. The old part of town is not without a certain decrepit charm – there are some beautiful old

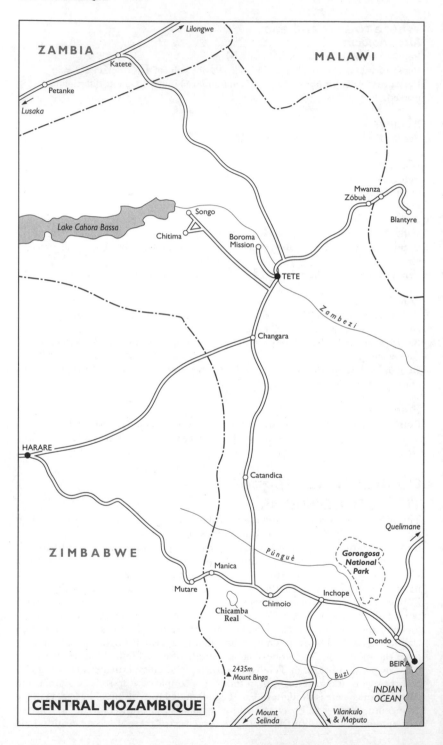

ZAMBIA

MALAWI

Lilongwe

Katete

Petanke

Lusaka

Mwanza
Zóbuè

Blantyre

Lake Cahora Bassa

Songo

Chitima

Boroma
Mission

TETE

Zambezi

Changara

HARARE

Catandica

Quelimane

ZIMBABWE

Púnguè

Gorongosa
National
Park

Manica

Mutare

Chimoio

Inchope

Chicamba
Real

Dondo

BEIRA

2435m
Mount Binga

Buzi

INDIAN
OCEAN

Mount
Selinda

Vilankulo
& Maputo

CENTRAL MOZAMBIQUE

houses, urgently in need of restoration – and the disused cathedral reportedly dates to 1563. The old slaving fort is situated above the municipal market, and there is a second fort on the riverfront below the bridge.

Apart from the **Massangano** citadel (accessible by hitching via Guro to Massangano village) which is on the south bank of the Zambezi 35km downstream of Tete city, the area around Tete is of relatively limited interest to travellers. The **Zambezi River** is certainly an attraction and it should be possible to arrange for a fisherman to paddle you a short way upriver, where you would stand a good chance of seeing hippos and crocs. More ambitiously, you could visit the **Boroma Mission**, about 60km upriver from Tete. Founded in 1891, the mission consists of a large and beautiful church on a hill overlooking the river, abandoned by the missionaries shortly after independence but recently reoccupied by an Italian priest.

The most obvious excursion from Tete is to Cahora Bassa, the world's fifth largest artificial lake. **Cahora Bassa** is potentially Africa's largest hydro-electric supplier; its five turbines – housed in a rock-hewn cavern of cathedralesque dimensions – boast a combined capacity of 2075MW, ten times the requirement for the whole of Mozambique. The dam was constructed in 1969–74 to export electricity to South Africa, but the external lines were damaged in the war, and only started to function properly in 1997. The closest town to the dam is Songo, built in the style of a Portuguese village in the cool, breezy highlands immediately south of the dam. The approach road to **Songo** is one of the most spectacular in Mozambique, and the well wooded, boulder-strewn hills that surround the town offer a refreshing contrast to the humid air and stark landscapes around Tete. Travellers cannot visit the dam without a *credencial*, which can be obtained from the HCB office on Avenida 25 de Junho in Tete, or by phoning Mr Nhamposa, HCB's chief of Public Relations at Songo, at 82221/2/3/4.

Access and getting around

For details of bussing directly from Malawi to Zimbabwe via Tete, see Chapter 6, page 75. Within Mozambique, the Virginia Bus Line runs daily buses between Tete, Chimoio and Beira, leaving Tete from the Virginia Bus terminal on Avenida 25 de Junho. Chapas to Beira and Chimoio leave Tete from in front of the Hotel Kassuende, while *chapas* to Songo and Chitima leave from opposite the Hotel Kassuende and *chapas* to Zóbuè on the Malawi border leave from in front of the market.

A few *chapas* run between Tete and Boroma daily, except after heavy rain. They generally leave Tete before 08.00, and they wait for passengers at a clearing which can be reached by walking out of town along Avenida 25 de Junho past the market for five to ten minutes. The clearing is roughly 100m past a large blue signpost to Boroma.

Songo lies 150km from Tete along an excellent surfaced road. Virginia Buses travel this route in either direction twice every day. In theory, buses leave Tete at 08.00 and 14.00, but this timetable is evidently not adhered to with any rigidity. Should you miss the bus, a few *chapas* leave for Songo daily from in front of the Hotel Kassuende. You could also take a *chapa* to Chitima (marked on some maps as Estima), a small town at the base of the mountains about 15km from Songo, and pick up a lift to Songo from there.

Where to stay and eat
Tete
A Piscina On riverfront. Rooms **F** a/c dbl. Camping **A** pp. Good food.
Complexo Turístico Pemba Good sundowner spot in flowering riverfront

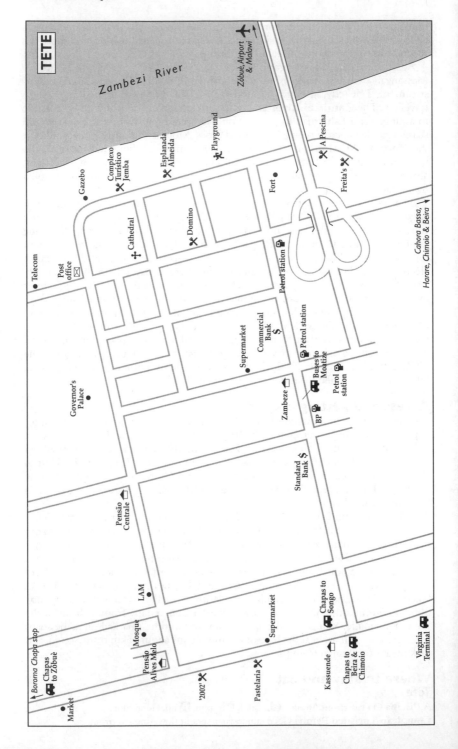

TETE

Zambezi River

Telecom

Gazebo

Complexo
Turístico
Jemba

Esplanada
Almeida

Playground

Zóbuè, Airport
& Malawi

A Pescina

Freita's

Fort

Post
office

Cathedral

Domino

Cahora Bassa,
Harare, Chimoio & Beira

Governor's
Palace

Petrol station

Supermarket

Commercial
Bank

Petrol station

Zambeze

Buses to
Moatize

Petrol
station

BP

Standard
Bank

Pensão
Centrale

LAM

Mosque

Supermarket

Chapas to
Songo

Boroma Chapa stop

Chapas
to Zóbuè

Pensão
Alves Melo

'2002'

Pastelaria

Kassuende

Chapas to
Beira &
Chimoio

Virginia
Terminal

Market

gardens. Meals US$3.50 (Galinha Pemba best meal I had in Mozambique).
Hotel Zambeze Acceptable, run-down high-rise hotel. **C** sgl with fan **E** a/c dbl.
Pastelaria Pastries, cheese sandwiches, fresh bread, burgers, fruit juice
and espresso coffee.
Pensão Alves Melo Best budget option. **B**/**C** sgl/dbl.
Pensão Central Good American-run place. Rooms **E** s/c a/c dbl.
Motel Tete Good views of river, air-conditioned rooms, excellent breakfasts.

Boromo
No formal accommodation. Should be allowed to pitch a tent near the mission.

Songo and Cahora Bassa
Pousada Sete Mentes Only hotel in Songo. Good restaurant. **D** dbl.
Dam Wall Camping allowed with written permission of HCB.
Chitima Basic, unsignposted resthouse behind the bar where *chapas* stop. **C**.

THE BEIRA CORRIDOR
The provinces of Sofala and Manica are of limited interest to travellers, but they
are crossed by one of the most important routes in Mozambique, the so-called
Beira Corridor, which connects Mutare in Zimbabwe to the Indian Ocean port of
Beira. The Beira Corridor assumed a high level of importance during the civil war,
when it was protected by Zimbabwe's army, and it remains the best way for
travellers to cross between Zimbabwe and Mozambique.
   The capital of Sofala province is **Beira**: Mozambique's second largest city and
most important port. A relatively modern city, Beira was founded in 1884 on the
sandy, marshy mouth of the Púnguè River and granted city status in 1894. In the
early days, it had the reputation of being Africa's most drunken, lawless settlement,
with 80 bars serving a population of 4,000. These days, it seems to be one of those
places that travellers either love or hate, and I must confess to being an admirer.
Beira has a definite atmosphere, determined by its sticky Indian Ocean air, a
preposterous mismatch of architectural styles, and a buzzing street and café life
focused around the attractive Praça da Municipalia and the grid of roads near the
railway station and port. The Praça da Municipalia is ringed by old colonial
buildings, notably the marble Municipal Hall and the old fort and jail, which now
serves as the city market. Other interesting buildings include the red-brick Casa
Portugal on Praça da Metical, the recently restored Casa Infante Sagres, the
adjacent railway station (described in the tourist literature as 'one of the most
beautiful modern buildings in Africa' and with more accuracy by a fellow traveller
as 'a hideous example of imperial overlord modern school architecture'), and the
gracious Beira Cathedral, built between 1907 and 1925 using stones taken from the
Portuguese fort at Sofala. There is a public swimming pool opposite the Hotel
Mozambique.
   The other sizeable town on the Beira Corridor is **Chimoio**, the capital of
landlocked Manica province. Superficially, Chimoio isn't somewhere you'd make
a special effort to see, but it's becoming a favoured stopover for backpackers,
mainly due to its friendly and vibrant people (Mike Slater regards it and
Inhambane as the nicest towns in Mozambique) and location 100km west of the
Zimbabwe border near Mutare. If you've just entered from Zimbabwe, you can
exchange foreign currency at the Commercial Bank on Avenido 25 de Setembro or
at the private *cambío* on the same road. Around the market, you'll find plenty of
people willing to change cash – Zimbabwe dollars fetch the best rate, but be
warned that there are some slick operators around.

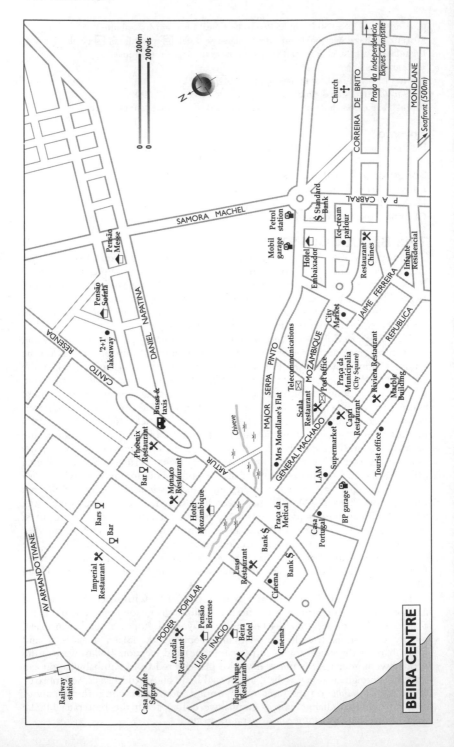

BEIRA CENTRE

Between Chimoio and the Zimbabwe border, **Chicamba Dam** lies in an area of thick brachystegia woodland and undulating hills offering good views of the Vumba Mountains to the south. The dam is popular with bass fishermen, and the surrounding hills would be of great interest to birdwatchers. Chicamba is a more inherently attractive stopover than Chimoio, and it would make for a welcome mid-altitude break from the sweaty coast for backpackers who are spending a while in Mozambique, but it offers little that couldn't be seen at dozens of similar places in Zimbabwe or South Africa.

The most obvious tourist attractions in this part of Mozambique are **Gorongosa National Park** and the nearby **Gorongosa Mountain**. Still little visited, Gorongosa National Park is now reasonably accessible to backpackers: there is a neat, shady campsite with good ablutions at Chitengo, and it's possible to get there by hitching from the junction at Inchope. Entrance is US$20, camping is US$10 per person and there is a Landrover Safari vehicle (bench seats on the back) which can be hired at a negotiable rate (starts at US$50 for half a day so it's best to do Gorongosa in a group). Note that there are no shops in the Reserve, so bring in whatever you will need for two or three days.

Access and getting around

The surfaced 300km road between Beira and Mutare is in reasonably good condition – poorer sections should have been resurfaced by the time you read this and the trip shouldn't take more than six hours by bus. The north–south road connecting Tete and Chimoio is in a similar condition. Regular buses and *chapas* connect Beira, Tete and Chimoio, with the Virginia Bus Line offering the most reliable and speedy service. Trains between Beira and Mutare run every other day, stopping at all stations en route. They're very slow, very cheap, and facilities are non-existent.

Arriving in Beira by bus, your trip will terminate either at the central bus station in the traffic island on Rua Artur Canto Resenda, or else at the market on the junction of Avenida Samora Machel and Avenida Armando Tivane. If the former, not only are you centrally positioned but there are also usually a few private taxis at this rank. If the latter, you'll feel like you've been abandoned in the middle of nowhere, but in fact you're only five minutes' walk from the town centre – walk across Samora Machel Avenue and follow Avenida Armando Tivane for about 100m and the first road to your left is Rua Artur Canto Resenda which, after an odd little kink and about 200m, will bring you to the central bus station.

Details of the route north from Beira to Quelimane are provided under the section on *Zambezia* on page 437. Details of buses travelling south from Beira towards Maputo are under the section on *The south coast* on page 449.

Where to stay and eat
Beira

Biques Campsite Popular site on the coast about 5km east of Praça da Independencia. Any *chapa* to Macuti can drop you there. Camping **B** pp. Four-bed caravans **F** per unit.
Café Riviera, Capri and **Scala** On or near Praça da Municipalia. Bread, pastries and tea.
Mrs Mandate Mozambican woman who will put up travellers. Flat no 103, on the tenth floor of a block on Rua General Machado facing Praça da Metical next to a bank. **B** pp.
Pensão Beirense Spacious but run-down rooms **C** dbl.
Pensão Messe The most popular place with backpackers. Rooms **D** dbl.
Pensão Sofala Near bus station. A dump but cheap. **B/C**.
Restaurante Pique-Nique Superlative service and great food in US$5–7 range.
Restaurante Arcadia One of Beira's top restaurants for three decades. Meals around US$4.
2+1 Take Away Opposite Pensão Sofala. Basic meals US$3. *Prego* rolls and burgers US$1.

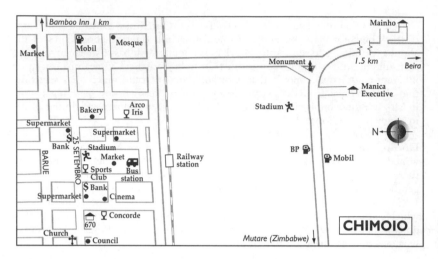

Chimoio

Centro do Cruz Vermelha (Red Cross) 4km from town centre, clean with communal bathrooms **D** pp.

Palhota de Chicoteco Open-air campsite around a huge tree 5km out on the road to Zimbabwe. Great ambience. Ask Senhor Santos where to camp. About **C** pp.

Flor de Vouga Rua Dr Araujo Lacerda, close to bus station US$20–30 dbl.

Arco Iris Salão da Cha Cheap ice-cream cones and fresh bread.

Maúa and **Ninucho restaurants** In the Feira over the Estrada Nacional 6 (bypass road), excellent food, lively and often crowded.

Bamboo Inn Basic but cheap. Ten minutes' walk from town centre. **B** dbl.

Moinho Motel Mill-shaped place 2km out of town off Beira road. Coming from Beira, ask to be dropped at the signposted turn-off, or else you face a 30-minute walk from the bus station. Rooms **E** s/c dbl with hot shower. Good meals around US$4.

Sports Club Bar Next to small stadium. Meat, fish and chicken dishes US$4.

Chicamba Dam

Casa Msika Motel An hour's walk from a turn-off signposted from Beira Corridor 47km east of Chimoio. Chalet **F** dbl. Camping **A** pp camping. Restaurant and bar.

Southern Mozambique
THE SOUTH COAST

The 1,000km stretch of coast between Beira and Maputo is the one part of Mozambique that has been significantly developed for tourism since the end of the civil war. Even then, facilities are almost without exception low-key and geared more to South African anglers and divers – or for that matter backpackers – than to fly-in tourists. Coming from Beira, the first substantial town you hit is **Inhassoro**, a rather sprawling place with an attractive beach that offers little you couldn't do or see further south, but which, equally, you could linger in for several days.

Roughly 500km south of Beira, the pretty coastal town of **Vilankulo** has become the focal point for backpackers passing through southern Mozambique, a status which is influenced less perhaps by its attractive coastline than by the presence of a couple of excellent backpackers' resorts along the beach north of the town centre. Vilankulo is also the main springboard for boat trips to the **Bazaruto Archipelago**, a string of small sandy islands lying roughly 20km from the mainland between Vilankulo and Inhassoro. The islands are one of Mozambique's most important habitats for marine animals – supporting, among other things, East Africa's last viable population of the endangered dugong, a large and exclusively marine herbivore related to the manatee of the Atlantic Ocean.

Although a casual glance at a map may have you believe otherwise, the EN1 (the main road connecting Beira and Maputo) actually runs about 50km or more inland for most of its length. The one place where it does skim the coast is at **Maxixe** (pronounced Masheesh), a popular stopover with people making their way between Maputo and Beira and the springboard for travellers heading to Inhambane, since the two towns lie on opposite sides of the same bay, separated by less than 4km of water and linked by a regular dhow service. Maxixe is not the most inherently interesting of places, with its stark grid-like layout and bustling African market-town atmosphere, but it lies on a pretty palm-lined stretch of coast with a pleasing view across the water to Inhambane at dusk.

Inhambane, capital of the synonymous province, is the oldest extant settlement on the south coast. Officially recognised as a Portuguese town in 1763, Inhambane was probably settled by Muslims before 1500 and it is thought to have been the most southerly port on the medieval trade network that stretched north to the Arabian Gulf. With its spacious layout of tree-lined avenues and several eye-pleasing colonial buildings, Inhambane has a decidedly Mediterranean character. It is also remarkably clean and orderly, with a subdued Old World atmosphere quite unlike anywhere else I've visited in Africa. Of particular interest is the beautiful 18th-century cathedral to the north of the main square (with what must surely be deliberate irony, the original cathedral and a more modern church are practically the only buildings on the block-long Rua Karl Marx!). The seafront itself is very pretty, particularly at sunset, though it isn't recommended for swimming. However, the peninsula on which Inhambane stands, noted for its seemingly endless stands of tall coconut palms, does boast several good beaches, of which **Praia do Tofo** and **Barra Reef** are readily accessible to backpackers.

Straddling the EN1 between Inhambane and Xai-Xai, **Quissico** lies inland of a stretch of coast noted for its several deep-blue freshwater lakes. One of the larger lakes lies immediately southeast of Quissico – there is a good view of it from the EN1 as you leave Quissico for Maxixe – and it can be reached along a 10km dirt road which leaves the EN1 just outside town. You could probably get there more directly by foot (the shore can't be more than 3km from town as the crow flies, but ask for local advice regarding footpaths – there's no danger of getting lost as the lake lies directly in front of you, but there may be a possibility of land mines if you stray off the established tracks).

Note that the Quissico lakes are brackish and give an unpleasant rotten-egg smell when the wind drops.

The capital of Gaza province, **Xai-Xai** (pronounced shy-shy) is a nondescript modern town situated on the north bank of the Limpopo River, which was very severely damaged by the floods of early 2000, and will perhaps never quite recover. Of interest only as a potential stopover along the EN1 (it's the last opportunity to hop off the bus if you're likely to reach Maputo after nightfall), it is also the springboard for visits to **Praia do Xai-Xai**, the sort of idyllic stretch of sand that's synonymous with Mozambique, though with facilities less suited to backpackers than some of the beaches further north. There are two points of interest near the beach: the ruined Motel Chonguene about 7km up the coast of the campsite, and Wenela tidepool 2km to the west. The tidepool is linked to the sea by an

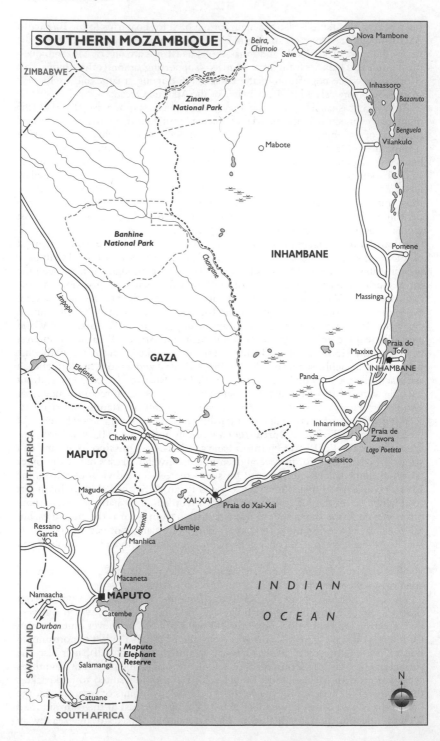

SOUTHERN MOZAMBIQUE

ZIMBABWE

Beira,
Chimoio

Save

Nova Mambone

Inhassoro

Bazaruto

Save

Zinave
National Park

Mabote

Benguela

Vilankulo

Pomene

Banhine
National Park

Chongane

INHAMBANE

Massinga

Limpopo

GAZA

Praia do
Tofo

Maxixe

INHAMBANE

Panda

Elefantes

Chokwe

Inharrime

Praia de
Zavora

Lago Poeteta

SOUTH AFRICA

MAPUTO

Quissico

Magude

XAI-XAI

Praia do Xai-Xai

Incomati

Uembje

Ressano
Garcia

Manhica

Macaneta

INDIAN

Namaacha

MAPUTO

OCEAN

Durban

Catembe

SWAZILAND

*Maputo
Elephant
Reserve*

Salamanga

N

Catuane

SOUTH AFRICA

underwater tunnel blowhole, which you should not even think about trying to swim through.

The next resort as you head south along the EN1 is **Bilene**, overlooking a pretty lagoon which is sometimes separated from the Indian Ocean by a sandbar. The calm lagoon is popular with water-sport enthusiasts, and offers safe swimming from white beaches. Though overrun by the Maputo crowd on weekends, Bilene offers quite a surprising array of places to stay, eat and drink.

Finally, the resort of **Macaneta** lies on the mouth of the Nkomati River, only 50km by road from the capital. The major attractions here are excellent game fishing and an attractive, clean beach – the sea isn't particularly suitable for snorkelling, diving or swimming – and the prolific birds to be seen along the river.

Access and getting around

The EN1 between Maputo and Beira is surfaced for most of its length, though the patch of road immediately north of the Save River does have some impressive potholes and there are several bad wash-aways from the floods, which are being repaired. Several bus companies run services between Maputo and Beira, stopping at all large towns along the way. For long hauls, the most reliable operators are the Virginia and Oliveira's buses which leave Maputo daily at 05.00 and arrive in Beira at around 09.00 the next morning following an overnight stop at the Save River. In the opposite direction, buses from Beira also leave at 05.00 but, because they can cross the road north of the Save in daylight, they arrive in Maputo late the same night. Virginia Bus Line also runs a bus service connecting Tete to Maputo via Chimoio.

For shorter hops, you can use Virginia and Oliveira's, but it might be as convenient to use the local buses and *chapas* which connect all towns along the south coast. Getting to Maxixe, Quissico and Xai-Xai is straightforward, since all these towns straddle the EN1. Inhassoro, Vilankulo, Inhambane and Bilene all lie between 20km and 40km east of the EN1, so you may have to change vehicles at the appropriate junction. All these places are connected to the EN1 by good surfaced roads and regular *chapas*, and the junctions are signposted.

Magaruque and Benguela, the most southerly islands in the Bazaruto Archipelago, can be visited from Vilankulo. The best place to organise a dhow across to the islands is at **Sail-Away** near the Dona Anna. You can arrange a boat on your own, but beware, you could be abandoned on one of the islands so ask around first. The boat and captain will cost around US$12 per day shared by up to six people. The trip takes around three to six hours each way, depending on the prevailing wind, and you should carry plenty of water, sunscreen and warm clothing – the combination of wet and wind can be surprisingly chilly.

Regular *chapas* cover the 33km road between the EN1 and Inhambane. It is far easier to reach Inhambane with the regular and inexpensive dhow service from Maxixe – avoid the motor-ferry which is quicker but is usually overloaded to the point of sinking. From Inhambane, there are a few *chapas* daily to Praia do Tofo, and you can pick up shared taxis that take you to within 3km of the backpacker's resort at Barra Reef. Chapas to Praia do Xai-Xai leave from the central square in Xai-Xai town. If you prefer to try to hitch to the beach, the signposted junction lies 2km from the town centre towards Maxixe.

Where to stay and eat
Inhassoro
Complexo Salema Mufundisse Chibique Filling meals US$3, double rooms US$12.
Complexo SETA Well-run hotel in wooded grounds above beach. Rooms **F** s/c dbl or **D** dbl. **B** pp camping. Good seafood restaurant.

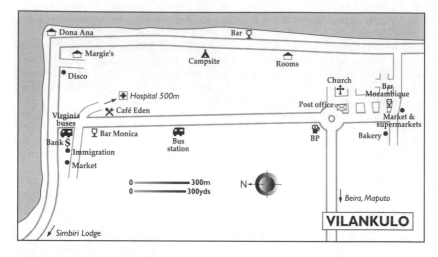

Hotel Inhassoro Stuffy, but friendly, and much better than camping (it's the same price) at SETA if it rains.

Vilankulo

Baobab Lodge and **New Last Resort** On beach 4km down from Dona Anna Hotel, ask for directions at *Mercado* (market). Rooms **C** pp. Camping **B** pp.

Bar Mozambique Near market. Chilled beers, wonky pool table. Only place in town with anything to eat other than seafood – *piri-piri* chicken, burgers and steaks US$4–6.

Bar Ti Zé On main road near market, good, basic Mozambican food, bad service, reasonable prices, disco weekends.

Campismo de Vilankulo Bland, uninviting but central camping **B** pp.

Casa Josef e Tine Nice *casas* (houses) with en-suite bathroom, go down to beach from *mercado*, then turn left, meals arranged. **E** per casa.

Disco Lino Mhe On main road near Ti Zé good disco weekends.

Dona Anna Hotel Bauhaus curiosity overlooking jetty. Pricey rooms, but worth visiting to buy a drink at the bar and climb up to the roof for sublime 'sundowners'. Rooms from **D/E**. Set-menu US$4.

Julião's On beach south of Dona Anna, directions at market, three-room house with beds. **C** pp.

Padaria Bakery near the ENH complex, run by a friendly Malawian, great pastries, excellent espresso.

Quisque Tropical On the beach down from Hotel Dona Anna. Breezy setting, popular evenings, poor ablutions. Basic huts **E** dbl.

Restaurant Na Sombra Unusual setting, good seafood. Rooms **F** dbl.

'Rooms' Unobtrusively signposted 500m from Campismo. Spotless rooms with shower and toilet facilities **B** pp.

Sam's Place On main road into Vilankulo, on the left-hand side just before arriving at the traffic circle. Basic huts with beds, space for tents. 45-minute walk to beach. **B** pp.

Maxixe

Campismo de Maxixe Excellent location and facilities. Rooms from **F** dbl. Camping **B** for two. Good meals (evenings only, lunches weekends, otherwise snacks only).

Hotel Golfinho Azul Opposite jetty. Adequate rooms **D** dbl.

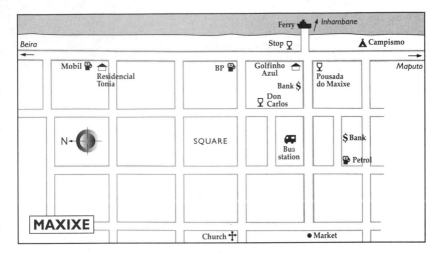

Restaurante Dom Carlos Similar menu at similar prices. Pleasant Mediterranean bar atmosphere.
Stop Snack Bar Open-air (and covered) restaurant. Great dhow-watching spot overlooking jetty. Excellent meals US$4–5.

Inhambane
Pensão Pachiça On the waterfront a few hundred metres from the jetty. Name is derived from the package slaves used to carry. Trips to Barra, Tofo and Linga Linga arranged. Great Italian food – real pizza! Dorm **C** pp. Room **D** dbl.
Escola Ferroviario Alojamento Pink building near railway station. Cheaper than hotel. **D**.
Inhambane Hotel Quiet, run-down, mid-range hotel. Rooms **E** s/c.
Maçarocca Restaurant One road away from bay near jetty, best in town.
Prima Vera Next to printing shop (antique presses) in Edwardian building. Good seafood.
Ti Jamu Snack Bar Good location overlooking jetty. Meals US$5–6.
Tic Tic Snack Bar Good, affordable meals – eg: fish and chips US$3.

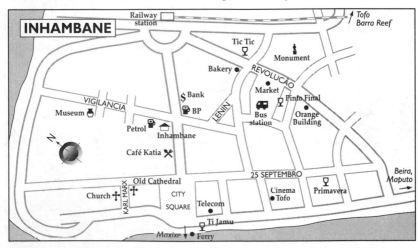

Praia do Tofo

Casa Azul Backpackers Right on the beach, run by Nick (formerly of Turtle Cove which burned down) – 200m south of Hotel Marinhos. **C** pp.

Bamoozy Beach Lodge Popular with backpackers, 20 minutes' walk north of Hotel Marinhos.

Diversity Dive In Casa Amarelha next to Ferroviario behind Marinhos, dive courses and good value dive packages, nice people.

Hotel Marinhos Quirky, convivial atmosphere, nice views, good food. Rooms **F** dbl.

Barra Reef

Barra Reef Backpackers Basic cabanas or camping **B** pp. Kitchen, flush toilets, hot showers and electricity. Snorkelling equipment, bar with cable TV and a dartboard at adjacent diving school.

Farol do Barra (Lighthouse Campsite) Run by Pachiça so get a ride with them or catch a *chapa* from Inhambane to within 3km of the site, then walk.

Quissico

Motel Pousada Restaurant and bar. Fair rooms **D** dbl.

Xai-Xai

Pastaleria Chaya Doura Fresh pastries, rolls, tea and coffee.

Pensão Africana Opposite market. Cheapest option in town. Rooms **E**/**F**.

Restaurante Zeje Good meals US$3–5.

Praia do Xai-Xai

Restaurante Golfinho Azul Best meals on the beach. US$5–6.

Xai-Xai Caravan Park Camping **C**/**D**. Good restaurant US$4–6.

Xai-Xai Diving and Fishing Camp Dormitory tents with beds, bedding and nets **C** pp.

Bilene

Complexo Turístico Parque Flora Attractive spot. Bungalows **E** dbl. Camping **B** pp.

Palm Tree Campsite Good but expensive. Reed huts **F** dbl. Camping **D** site.

Praia do Sol 2km south on lakeshore in duneforest. Backpackers' section with fixed tents, mattresses, kitchen and hot showers **C** pp.

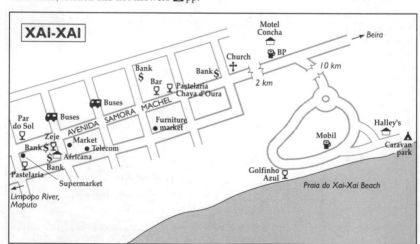

Complexo São Martinho Up the road from the *mercado*, well run and secure. Rooms **E** dbl. Chalets with kitchenette, two bedrooms (sleep four to six) US$35–50.

Macaneta
Jays Camp Take *chapa* to junction where there is a store and then walk 3km on sandy track. Standing tents **F** dbl. Expensive restaurant.
Complexo Turístico Macaneta Cheapest option. Chalet US$60. Camping **B** per site.

MAPUTO
Formerly called Lourenço Marques, Maputo is an attractive port, as safe as any African city, and with a good deal more character than most. Maputo's jacaranda, flame tree and palm-lined avenidas with their numerous street cafés have a relaxed Africa-meets-Mediterranean atmosphere that is distinctively Mozambican. Along the avenidas are any number of attractive old buildings in various states of renovation and disrepair, dwarfed at times by some rather incongruous Bauhaus relics of the 50s and 60s.

The Bay of Maputo was first visited by a Portuguese in 1502 and it was explored thoroughly by the trader Lourenço Marques in 1544, after which time it was regularly visited by Portuguese ivory traders. In 1721, the Dutch East India Company established a trading factory and fort on the site of modern-day Maputo, but it was abandoned as unprofitable in 1730. Only in 1781 did Portugal attempt to establish a permanent settlement on the bay, one which was several times abandoned before 1800 and razed by Dingane's Zulu army in 1833. Following the discovery of gold on the Witwatersrand in 1886, Portugal and the Transvaal decided to build a railway line between Pretoria and Lourenço Marques. By the turn of the century, the city centre had taken on its modern shape, the port handled roughly one-third of exports and imports from the Transvaal, and the railway line carried over 80,000 passengers annually. On November 12 1898, Lourenço Marques formally replaced Ilha de Moçambique as the capital of Portugal's East African colony. After independence, the city was renamed after the Rio Maputo.

Maputo lends itself to casual exploration. Among its more interesting buildings are the Natural History Museum, housed in a palace built in the Maunelini style (a sort of Portuguese Gothic); the old synagogue (now the Geological Museum); the Mercado Centrale (central market) a covered building constructed in 1901; the Victorian railway station on Praça dos Trabalhadores; and the sandstone 19th-century fortress on Praça dos 25 de Junho. Near the railway station is the old town, boasting several buildings constructed in the late 19th century, many of which still have either wood or iron filigree and covered balconies, reminiscent of the Creole style of Mauritius and La Réunion. On Avenida Samora Machel, the Jardim Tunduru (Botanical Garden) is a public park with many large shady trees. Perhaps the most surprising monument in Maputo is the Louis Trichardt Memorial Garden on Avenida Josina Machel, an anachronistic piece of 1960s apartheid chic which has, remarkably, been maintained with meticulous care throughout Mozambique's years of civil war and socialism.

There are several museums in Maputo. Aside from those already mentioned above, tourists interested in the revolutionary history of Mozambique should visit the Museu da Revolução on the Avenida 24 de Julho. More interesting, perhaps, is the Museu Nacional des Artes on the Avenida Ho Chi Minh with paintings and sculptures by Mozambique's most famous artists. There's also a cultural centre (Centro de Estudios Brasileiros) on Avenida 25 de Setembro, with regular exhibitions and performance arts on Fridays, and an irregular exhibition of various artists at the Nucleo de Arte, Rue da Argelia (just off Avenida Julius Nyerere).

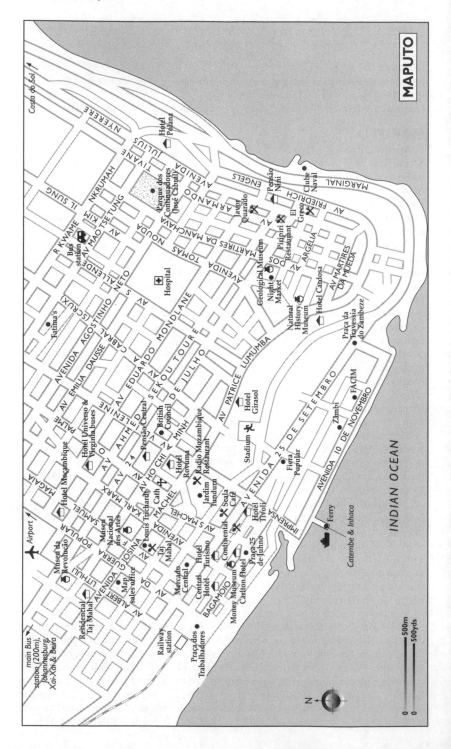

MAPUTO

Costa do Sol

Hotel Polana

Parque dos Combatentes (José Cabral)

AVENIDA JULIUS NYERERE

IL SUNG

NKRUMAH

Javor Quarado

Pensão Nini

Clube Naval

AV MARGINAL

AV FRIEDRICH ENGELS

R KWAME Bus station

AV KIM MAOTSETUNG

AV MARTIRES DA MACHAVA

El Greco

Pipiri Restaurant

ARGELIA

S ALLENDE

(SCRUX) CABRAL

S NETO

AVENIDA TOMAS NOUDA

Geological Museum

Night Market

SOC

Hospital

AV MARTIRES DA MUEDA

Hotel Cardosa

National History Museum

Fatima's

AV EMILIA DAUSSE

AVENIDA AGOSTINHO

EDUARDO MONDLANE

SEKOU TOURE

DE JULHO

AV PATRICE LUMUMBA

Praça da Travessia do Zambeze

PALME

Hotel Universo & Virginia buses

AMMED LENINE

AV HO CHI MINH

British Council

Pensão Central

Hotel Girasol

AVENIDA 25 DE SETEMBRO

Hotel Moçambique

AV KARL MARX

S MACHEL

AV JOSINA

Louis Trichardt

Radio Moçambique Restaurant

Hotel Rovdma

Stadium

MAGAIA

SAMUEL

POPULAR

Museu da Revolução

Museu Nacional des Artes

Cath

Taj Mahal

Jardim Tunduru

Scala Café

Hotel Tivoli

FACIM

Zambi

FACIM

AVENIDA 10 DE NOVEMBRO

Airport

GUERRA

AVENIDA ALBERT LITHULI

Map sales office

Hotel Turismo

Continental

Praça 25 de Julho

Hotel Carlton

Fiera Popular

IMPRENSA

INDIAN OCEAN

Residencial Taj Mahal

AV DA BAGAMOIO

Mercado Central

Central Hotel

Money Museum

Ferry

Catembe & Inhaca

Railway station

Praça dos Trabalhadores

main Bus station (200m), Johannesburg, Xai-Xai & Beira

N

0   500m
0   500yds

Separated by a kilometre-wide stretch of water, Catembe is Maputo's curiously downbeat twin, and the most obvious day trip from the capital. Decidedly low-rise, Catembe's dusty, unpaved streets could be those of practically any small Mozambican fishing village were it not for the skyscrapers dominating its northern skyline. To the left of the landing jetty at Catembe there is a pleasant restaurant and small beach.

Access and getting around

For travellers heading north, Oliveira's Bus depot is on Praça 16 de Junho on Avenida 24 de Julho, while the Virginia depot is on Avenida Karl Marx near the booking office on the first floor of the Hotel Universo. Most buses to Beira leave at 05.00 and overnight at the Save River, but others leave at 13.00 and overnight at Maxixe. If you are heading for Maxixe or destinations further south, it's probably easier to pick up a later bus, but if you want to go all the way to Beira in one trip then the earlier bus is recommended to avoid arriving in Beira after dark. Note that buses coming to Maputo all the way from Beira normally arrive after dark, which makes it advisable to disembark at Xai-Xai and continue to Maputo the next morning.

Taxi cabs are few and far between in Maputo, though you can rely on there always being some at the airport taxi rank, outside the central market, and outside the Hotel Cardosa and Hotel Polana. Catembe is reached from Maputo by a ten-minute ferry ride which leaves from the jetty on Avenida 10 de Novembro at 08.30 and every two hours thereafter, and in the opposite direction every alternate half-hour.

Where to stay

Campismo Maputo Part of the old, decrepit campsite on the Marginal (beach road) has been fenced off, good ablutions and security, but area is due for redevelopment (near the new Holiday Inn).

Carlton Hotel Rua da Bagamoio 200m from Central Hotel. Large, clean rooms **D/E**.

Central Hotel Rua do Bagamoio. Oldest hotel in Maputo. Central. Good rooms **F** dbl.

Fatima's Av Mao Tse Tung 1317. Highly recommended backpacker hostel 500m east of intersection with Av Vladimir Lenine. Good meals US$5. Multilingual staff, hot showers, lock-up safe. Dorm **C** pp. Room **E** dbl. Camping **B** pp.

Pensão Central Av 24 de Julho near intersection with Av Vladimir Lenine. Reliable long-standing favourite with backpackers. **D/E** sgl/dbl.

Pensão Nini Av Julius Nyerere. Acceptable rooms **E** dbl.

Hotel Girassol Circular high-rise block with fading signpost on Av Patrice Lumumba. Grotty, dank s/c rooms **B/C**. Only for the desperate.

Residencial Taj Mahal Av Ho Chi Minh near intersection with Av Albert Lithuli. Recently renovated and relatively good value at **E/F** sgl/dbl.

Where to eat

Coimbra Av V Lenine, rated highly by locals.

Snack-Bar Rossio Opposite Hotel Central, kick-ass prawns in butter sauce.

Café Scala and Continental Cnr Av 25 de Setembro and Samora Machel. Tea, coffee, *prego* rolls, hamburgers, fresh bread and pastries.

El Greco Pizzeria Around the corner from the Piri-Piri. Portuguese dishes and pizzas US$5.

Esplanada Tara Past the abandoned tall hotel on way to Costa do Sol. Where the locals eat and party at night.

Esplanada Gaby's Near Tara but has better view.

Pinha Paljota On the Marginal below Hotel Polana, reasonable prices, cool spot.

Feira Popular Av 25 de Setembro. Dozens of restaurants of which the Coquero, Felix and Bella Muchacha are particularly recommended.

Piri-Piri Restaurant Cnr Av Julius Nyerere and 24 de Junho. Reliable central option. Chicken *piri-piri*, prawn curry and steaks around US$5.

Mimmo's Pizzeria Av 24 de Julho a few blocks down from Julius Nyerere, nice pizza, reasonable prices, very popular.

Radio Mozambique Restaurant Shady veranda fringing Botanical Garden. Meals US$3–5.

Taj Mahal Av Samuel Magaia. Good Indian restaurant. Most dishes US$6.

Pastelaria Nautilus Delicious breakfasts and pasties, where the *Maputenses* drink coffee during the day on Av Julius Nyerere opposite Panthera Azul bus Terminal.

Practical listings

Books and newspapers English, American and South African newspapers are sold at inflated prices in the Hotel Polana. Sensaçoes next to Mundos is reasonably priced and sells Mozambican music CDs and tapes. The bookshop behind Jaron Quarado Restaurant on Avenida Julius Nyerere sells overpriced paperbacks, books about Mozambique and some second-hand novels.

Embassies Australia (49-3072); Belgium (49-0077); Denmark (42-0172); France (49-0444); Germany (49-2714); Malawi (49-1468); Netherlands (49-0031); Portugal (49-0316); South Africa (49-0059); Swaziland (49-2451); UK (42-0111/2/5/6/7); USA (49-2797); Zambia (49-2452); Zimbabwe (49-0404).

Foreign exchange The South African rand, Mozambican metical and to a lesser extent US dollar are widely interchangeable in Maputo. *i* and US dollars cash can be exchanged for local currency at any bank or *câmbio*, but rates vary greatly. Many hotels, restaurants and private individuals will informally change money, generally at a slightly better rate than the official one, which is useful since banks are open only on weekdays between 08.00 and 11.30. The private *câmbio* outside the Hotel Polana exchanges travellers cheques at a commission of 2% as opposed to the 5% or more that is deducted at banks. To get money (meticaís) with your credit card (Visa, Mastercard) the best bet are the branches of Banco Fomento, one is on Julius Nyerere.

Internet The most reliable and perhaps only internet café is Connection Time, which recently moved from Avenida 24 de Julho to Julius Nyerere one floor up in the Hotel Avenida business centre. US$6 per 30 minutes, fairly slow connection.

Maps The map sales office in the National Directorate of Geography and Cartography (DINAGECA) on Avenida Josina Machel sells a fair range of 1:250,000 sheets, but few more detailed maps. Hotel Polana Tabacaria has expensive tourist maps. Also try the Information Bureau (BIP) on Avenida Eduardo Mondlane, two blocks away from Avenida Julius Nyerere.

Nightlife Maputo is a particularly active city by night. Since the beginning of the century, Rua do Bagamoio near the railway station has been known to visiting sailors as 'Whisky Road' and the 'Street of Trouble', with ten to 15 bars congregated along its short length. Rua do Bagamoio is once again becoming a favoured place to find nocturnal diversions. An earthy place to hang out – whether you want to drink, eat, shoot pool, make friends, watch a strip show, or ride dodgem cars – is the Feira Popular on the east end of Avenida 25 de Setembro. The best of all places to drink are the night markets, of which the Mercado do Povo is the most central, though it is somewhat dwarfed in scale by the Barracas de Museu on Rua dos Lusiados, a warren-like conglomeration of perhaps 100 bars which must be one of the most extraordinary places to drink anywhere in Africa. For live music (if you're

INHACA ISLAND

Inhaca is the largest island in the Gulf of Maputo, lying about 35km from the city and 24km from the mainland. It has an archetypical tropical island atmosphere, with a couple of good beaches, a mangrove-lined north coast, and brightly coloured reefs off the west coast.

The island's main tourist focus is Inhaca village, a tiny settlement dominated by the recently refurbished Inhaca Hotel, which has a salt-water swimming pool, tree-lined paths, and a restaurant. If you have the time, a trip along the north coast to the lighthouse and the Indian Ocean beaches is most worthwhile – the beach directly in front of the hotel is not particularly attractive. In each direction the walk takes about two and a half to three hours.

You can get to Inhaca from Maputo by ferry (if it has not yet again had to do the Catembe crossing, as that boat breaks down frequently) for US$1.50 per person. The trip takes three to four hours. The ferry should leave Maputo for Inhaca at around 07.00 on Sunday, Tuesday and Thursday, and start the return trip at 03.00 on Monday, Wednesday and Friday. It crosses in either direction twice on Saturdays, leaving Maputo at 06.30 and 13.00, and returning at around 09.30 and 16.00. The ferry jetty is the same as the one for Catembe.

On the island Ribeiro's Place has basic reed huts (B pp) or you can go to Indigo Bay (arrange getting there through Fatimas) which has camping for US$6 per person or fixed tents for US$10 per person. You can eat at the Inhaca Hotel, but the food at nearby Lucas's (he also arranges accommodation) Restaurant is just as good and cheaper. Snorkelling equipment, diving trips and other excursions can be arranged at the hotel. There is a good natural history museum at the marine research centre.

going on a Friday, check the listings in the *Noticias* newspaper) note most clubs only start happening around midnight.

Arte Bar on Rua do Bagamoio is presently the most popular nightclub in town. Normally packed at weekends where the capital's youth gather to show off their skilful and passionate dancing skills.

Gypsies on Rua do Bagamoio is the second-most frequented bar, a short distance from Arte Bar. More of a pub than a nightclub, more relaxed ambience.

Bar Loko Avenida Julius Nyerere, small, brightly decorated bar/café with terrace, ideal for the hot summer nights.

Gil Vicente Bar and Café Avenida Samora Machel, Thursday night is when everyone is at Gil Vicente. Artists, young people, visitors come to listen to great traditional music, jazz, African drums and rhythms – all live.

Clube Txova Avenida Mateus Mutemba. African bands play every Wednesday, Friday and Saturday night.

Eagles Avenida Zedequias Manganhela. Live jazz at weekends.

Micaels Rua da Resistência off Vladimir Lenine near the Praça da OMM. Usually has some sort of music (live and disco) every night.

Esplanada Sanzala Avenida 25 de Setembro near Feira, usually very popular on weekends. On Saturday there is usually live jazz at the pizzeria in the Botanical Gardens.

Post and telephone The main post office on Avenida de 25 Setembro offers a poste restante service as well as an inexpensive *ultima hora* service where post is put on the next flight to Europe. There is reputedly a serious problem with postal workers opening mail in search of money, so it may be advisable to write your letters on locally printed aerogrammes or postcards. Direct international dialling is straightforward from the Telecommunicações on the ground floor of the '33' (trinte-trés) building on Avenida 25 de Setembro.

Tourist information office The Empresa Nacional de Turismo is on the first floor of the Trangilidere de Mozambique building at 1203 Avenida 25 de Setembro. The staff are helpful, though few of them speak English and no maps or pamphlets of any description are on sale. Much better to look at the info boards at Fatimas or to buy the *Time-Out* at the Tabacaria in Hotel Polana.

Zimbabwe

15

In many respects, Zimbabwe feels like the stepping stone between South Africa and the rest of the continent. For those coming from the south, the Zimbabwean landscape immediately seems wilder than South Africa, and uncompromisingly African by comparison. Travellers who arrive in Zimbabwe from the north, on the other hand, will probably experience something akin to a homecoming, the sensation that Africa has been crossed and they are now in more familiar surrounds – and if this sounds fanciful, then how else do you account for the number of southbound travellers who spend weeks huddled in the hostels of suburban Harare?

Tourism in Zimbabwe is centred on the magnificent Victoria Falls, an unmissable sight, and the base for the region's most spectacular bungee jump and most popular white-water rafting. Less popular with backpackers, but as impressive in its own right, the ruined city of Great Zimbabwe is the most haunting and interesting historical site this side of Lalibela in Ethiopia. There is also some great game viewing in any of several reserves, most notably Hwange and Mana Pools, though the little-known Kaburi Wilderness area near Kariba is of special interest to backpackers. The eastern highlands, meanwhile, offer some wonderfully scenic walking possibilities, ranging from serious hikes in the Chimanimani Range to some wonderful forest walks in Vumba and Chilinda.

BACKGROUND INFORMATION
Geography and climate

Zimbabwe is landlocked, though its northern and southern borders are formed by the major Zambezi and Limpopo rivers, and Lake Kariba on the Zambezi is one of the largest bodies of water in southern Africa. Zimbabwe consists of a mid-altitude plateau tilting up from the hot, dry Kalahari scrub of the west to the temperate highlands along the Mozambique border. A feature of Zimbabwe is the large

FACTS AND FIGURES

Area: 390,580km² (25th in Africa)
Capital: Harare
Largest towns: Harare, Bulawayo, Gweru, Mutare
Population: 11.5 million
Official language: English
Other languages: Shona, Matabele
Currency: Zimbabwe dollar
Head of State: President Robert Mugabe

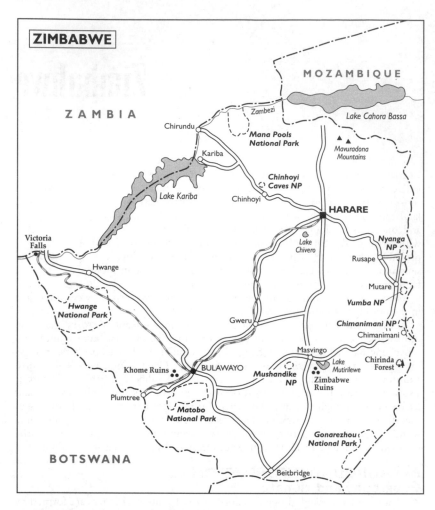

granite outcrops known as koppies. These often take one of two impressive forms – the weathered 'balancing rock' formations of the Matobo and Harare areas and the immense monolithic domes and whalebacks around Nyanga.

Temperatures are moderate to hot, with winter nights in some areas being surprisingly chilly. The hottest part of the country, not to say the most humid, is the Zambezi Valley. The coolest area is the highlands along the Mozambique border. Annual rainfall figures are low, and drought or semi-drought conditions regular. Rain falls in summer, from November to March. The winter months of May to September offer the best all-round travel conditions.

History

Central Zimbabwe was the source of the gold traded along the Swahili coast from AD1000 through to the Portuguese era. The medieval gold mining people of Zimbabwe are generally referred to as the Karanga, and they were almost certainly the precursors of the modern Shona people. At the heart of Karangaland lay the city now known as Great Zimbabwe, easily the most impressive pre-colonial architectural achievement in the African interior south of Ethiopia and, unlike contemporary Indian Ocean ports such as Kilwa and Gedi, one that shows no discernible external influences in architecture or execution.

Great Zimbabwe was abandoned in the mid-15th century, probably as a result of the environmental impact of a highly centralised society in this drought-prone region. The Karanga then split into several smaller empires, of which only the Torwa continued the architectural tradition by building Khame near modern Bulawayo, while the gold trade evidently fell under the control of the Mwene Matupa Empire, known to the Portuguese as Monomotapa.

In 1632, Portugal enjoyed its one successful military foray into the African interior, when Sousa de Menesis captured Mwene Matupa and effectively took control of Karangaland. Portuguese traders established several gold trading fairs in the interior, the most important of which was Dambarare near modern Harare. These Portuguese settlements were razed in 1693 by the Changamire chief Dongo, the founder of the Rozvi Empire which controlled the Zimbabwean plateau from 1700 until the 1830s, when it was overrun by Nguni refugees. In the fall-out from the Mfacane, western Zimbabwe was settled by the Matabele leader Mzilikazi, who died in 1868. Mzilikazi's son and successor Lobengula founded a new Matabele capital GuBulawayo (*The Place of Killing*) on the site of modern-day Bulawayo.

Rhodesia – as Zimbabwe was known up until independence – was not so much colonised by Britain as it was the personal acquisition of the South-African-based British businessman after whom it was named. The discovery of gold in the Witwatersrand in 1886 led Cecil John Rhodes to conclude that even richer pickings might lie further north. In 1888 he sent Leander Starr Jameson to Bulawayo, where he fraudulently secured a mineral rights and settlement treaty over Matabeleland from Lobengula. In 1899, Rhodes formed the British South Africa Company (BSAC) and obtained from the British government a concession to govern an area to the north of the Limpopo River. In 1890, Jameson led the BSAC 'Pioneer Column' up to Mashonaland to found the towns of Fort Victoria (Masvingo) and Umtali (Mutare).

Initially, Jameson met with little effective resistance from the Matabele and Shona. In 1896, however, after an abortive attempt to capture the Transvaal, orchestrated by Rhodes and led by Jameson, the Shona and Matabele recognised that their colonisers were not invincible and combined forces to launch the 'First Chimurenga', a rebellion that fizzled out after its leaders were executed in 1897. In a referendum held in 1922, Rhodesia's settler population of approaching 25,000 narrowly voted against becoming a fifth province of South Africa, and in 1923 the BSAC ceded control of Rhodesia for it to become a self-governing colony.

The years following World War II saw the emergence of a strong anti-colonial movement that evolved into two main groupings, the Matabele-dominated ZAPU and Shona-dominated ZANU, led respectively by Joshua Nkomo and Robert Mugabe. In 1963, amid a growing internal and international call for democracy, the two organisations were banned and their leaders jailed. Two years later, Prime Minister Ian Smith illegally announced Unilateral Declaration of Independence (UDI) from Britain. In 1968, the UN imposed sanctions on UDI Rhodesia, but these were rendered largely ineffective by the collaboration of South Africa and Mozambique in upholding Smith's government. Another result of UDI was that ZAPU and ZANU turned to violence: the ZANU attack on Chinhoyi on April 18 1966 is officially regarded to have been the start of the 'Second Chimurenga'.

The beginning of the end came in December 1974, when Smith was urged to open negotiations with ZANU and ZAPU by Prime Minister Vorster of South Africa and President Kaunda of Zambia in a famous meeting on the bridge at Victoria

Falls. Mugabe and Nkomo were released, and when negotiations broke down they fled to newly-independent Mozambique, from where they waged an intensified guerrilla war. The Smith government briefly fooled nobody except themselves by installing Bishop Muzerewa as a dummy prime minister. In late 1979, however, following the election of Thatcher's Conservatives to power, Smith was finally drawn into meaningful negotiations in Britain. The so-called 'Lancaster House Agreement' resulted in an electoral system which guaranteed whites 20 out of 100 seats, a significant concession on the part of Mugabe and Nkomo when you consider that whites made up a mere 3% of the population. In the election that followed, ZANU won 57 of the 'black' seats, ZAPU 20, and Muzerewa's discredited party a paltry three. Zimbabwe officially came into being on April 16 1980 with Robert Mugabe as Prime Minister and the Reverend Canaan Banana as president.

In power for almost two decades, Mugabe has proved to be an autocratic leader. Particularly abhorrent was the manner in which he treated ZAPU. In 1981, Nkomo was fired from the cabinet and a number of important ZAPU leaders were imprisoned, initiating a civil war which resulted in the pointless slaughter (and, it has recently emerged, brutal torture) of many thousands of Matabele by the predominantly Shona government troops. To Mugabe's credit, he averted total disaster in Matabeleland by declaring an amnesty, since when Zimbabwe has enjoyed a decade of peace and relative prosperity, marred tragically by the government mismanagement of food and water resources that surrounded the drought of the early 1990s, regarded to be the worst of the century.

Zimbabwe was a one-party state throughout the 1990s, and to all intents and purposes it remains one today: the country's first purportedly democratic election, in mid-2000, returned ZANU and Mugabe to power amid credible allegations of vote rigging from the opposition party. The early months of 2000 also saw renewed political instability after long years of peace, particularly in rural parts of Zimbabwe, where numerous white-owned farms were occupied by organisations led by veterans of the independence war, resulting in the deaths of some farm owners. This brought to a head the long-simmering issue of land redistribution: in mid-2000 Mugabe somewhat expediently decreed that hundreds of white-owned farms were to be appropriated by the state and resettled by subsistence farmers. At the time of writing, Zimbabwe is in a state of transition, and it is difficult to make any sensible predictions about how this will resolve itself over the next few years. It seems unlikely that Mugabe will be able to cling to power much longer, given his unpopularity both at home and abroad. So long as he remains, however, Zimbabwe seems unlikely to regain the political stability it enjoyed throughout the late 1980s and most of the 1990s.

PRACTICAL INFORMATION
Accommodation
The ubiquitous cheap local resthouses of East Africa are replaced in Zimbabwe by backpacker hostels. Most hostels have dormitory accommodation for US$3–5pp. Many also have double rooms for US$10–15 and allow camping for US$2–3pp. Hostels open, close and change hands with some frequency, so keep an eye on noticeboards and ask other travellers for current recommendations. Some hostel owners and managers are a good source of advice about accommodation in other towns; others are surprisingly ill-informed and unjustifiably bitchy. The other types of accommodation useful to backpackers are municipal or government caravan parks, which allow camping at cheaper rates than hostels and often offer some form of self-catering accommodation typically for around US$10 dbl.

The accommodation in the national parks warrants special attention. Most parks have a campsite costing US$3pp. Many also have cheap hutted accommodation with a fridge and cooking facilities – in 1997, chalets in Matabo, Lake Chivero and Hwange cost US$5 dbl, cottages in Hwange cost US$10 dbl, and lodges in Zambezi, Hwange, Matabo, Muturikwe, Chivero and Nyanga National Parks started at US$15. It's worth knowing there's a 50% discount on all accommodation and camping from Monday to Thursday during February, March, June, October and November. The problem with national parks is that accommodation other than camping must be booked through the reservations office in Harare or the branch office in Bulawayo. If you pitch up without a booking, you will only be accommodated at 17.00 (assuming that accommodation is available) and if you want to stay a second night you must vacate the room by 10.00 and try again that afternoon – even if the camp is empty. Bookings can be made on the spot in Harare or with a 24-hour delay in Bulawayo, and chances of getting a booking are always good for weekdays. If you arrive at a national park camp without a booking, you could offer to pay for a call to Harare, bearing in mind that the phone lines at headquarters are often jammed. I should stress that none of this applies if you plan to camp, since there's no need to book camping sites – the one exception being Mana Pools where camping is often fully booked.

The recent instability in Zimbabwe and resultant lull in backpacker trade meant that a great many backpacker hostels were struggling to run at a profit in mid-2000. Unless this situation resolves itself quickly it seems likely that a substantial number of the hostels listed in this chapter will have ceased to function by the time many readers travel in Zimbabwe. For this reason, it would be advisable to independently confirm the existence of any hostel before heading there – give the hostel a ring, check in *Coast to Coast*, or ask other travellers or hostel owners.

Books
Bookshops in Harare, Bulawayo and Mutare stock a reasonable range of books about Zimbabwe, southern African field guides and novels. Secondhand bookshops in the same cities are a good place to pick up cheap novels.

Crime and safety
Crime against tourists is on the increase, though largely confined to Harare and to a lesser degree Bulawayo and Victoria Falls. The usual rules apply, especially at night. Elsewhere, there's little cause for concern about crime. In Kariba town, for once, the risk of encountering an irate elephant or buffalo probably outranks any criminal threat.

The international headlines garnered by the ugly political events of 2000 have proved to be disastrous for Zimbabwe's tourist industry. We were in Victoria Falls in January 2000, and the town was busier than ever, yet reports from travellers who visited in June 2000 suggested that tourism had practically ground to a halt. Nevertheless, there is no reason to think that travel in Zimbabwe at the time of writing is any more risky than it would have been a few years ago, particularly if you stick to established tourist centres and to main roads. This could change, however, so it would be prudent to talk to other travellers and to hostels in neighbouring countries before heading to Zimbabwe.

Entrance fees
National park fees in Zimbabwe have shot up and down several times in recent years, at one point standing at US$20 per day, so it would be advisable to check in advance before heading to any national park. The mid-2000 fee is US$15 per person for Hwange and other popular parks, and US$10 per person for less popular parks.

All fees are currently valid for up to one week, rather than the 24 hours favoured by East African reserves, which makes visiting the parks in Zimbabwe very affordable by comparison to safaris in some other countries in the region.

Entrance fees to reserves other than national parks, for instance Chirinda Forest or Kuburi Game Reserve, are generally nominal. Entrance to Great Zimbabwe costs US$5 but this is good for several visits over a few days. Entrance to most other manned National Monuments such as the Khame and Ziwa Ruins costs US$2. There is no charge for visiting most rock art sites.

Entry formalities

Visas are not required by nationals of Commonwealth, European Union and Scandinavian countries or by nationals of the USA, Japan or South Africa. Visas must be bought in advance. Upon entry, you will normally be given up to three months without a problem. Zimbabwe is one country where you absolutely don't want to fly in on a one-way ticket, since immigration officials at the airport are very rigid about this and you may well be required to leave a cash or travellers' cheque deposit of US$1,000. You will get this back when you leave the country, but it could well be in the rather useless form of Zimbabwe dollars!

Overland border officials tend to be more officious than their counterparts elsewhere in the region. I've met a number of travellers over the years who were refused entry because they had insufficient funds. Assuming you have a flight out of Africa, a reasonable sum of money (in excess of US$1,500) or a credit card, you should be fine. If you expect problems, enter the country using an international train or coach service rather than on foot. Better still, buy a return ticket, assuming that you can use it or get a refund. Another possibility if your funds are very low would be to put your reason for entry as transit to any neighbouring country, ask for a week only to be stamped in your passport, and then to sort out an extension once you're in the country – you're much less likely to be asked questions if you appear just to be passing through.

Food and drink

You probably won't eat out much in Zimbabwe. Many hostels provide home cooked meals that compare favourably with any restaurant. Cooking for yourself is also an attractive option due to the well-stocked, cheap supermarkets, and the self-catering kitchens and barbecue facilities found in most hostels and campsites. Nevertheless, you can eat well at Zimbabwean restaurants, which are cheaper than in South Africa but better than in East Africa.

Getting around
By road

Most roads in Zimbabwe are excellent. Cheap local bus services cover just about every route, and they are generally quicker and safer than in East Africa. Drawbacks are the tendency towards antisocial early morning departures, and the fact that terminals are often situated some distance from the town centre. On major routes, it may be simpler in the end to pay more to use a faster and more comfortable coach, such as those operated by Express, Blue Arrow and Ajay's. Hitching is a realistic option on all but the most obscure routes, with the main risk undoubtedly coming from drunken driving.

By rail

Inexpensive overnight rail services with first- and second-class sleepers as well as economy booths connect Mutare to Harare, Harare to Bulawayo, and Bulawayo to

Victoria Falls. These trains run daily and you'll normally get a booking quite easily. International rail services connect Bulawayo and Harare to Johannesburg (South Africa), Bulawayo to Gaberone (Botswana), Victoria Falls to Livingstone (Zambia) and Mutare to Beira (Mozambique).

By ferry

The only ferry service of interest to backpackers is the DDF ferry between Kariba and Binga on Lake Kariba. This takes 50 hours, costs US$16 one way and leaves Kariba town every other Thursday at 09.00 and Binga at a similar time on the following Monday. Overnight stops are at Chalala and Sengwa. Another ferry service connects Kariba town to Mlibizi twice a week, taking 24 hours, but it's expensive at US$50 pp including three meals.

Taxis

These are available in most large towns, but many have two-tier metre systems, and you'll be put on the higher fare if you don't say anything.

Health

Zimbabwe is a healthy country. Within reasonable limits, you need have few concerns about what you eat or drink. Malaria is present, with the Zambezi Valley a particularly high-risk area. In most parts of the country, the risk of contracting malaria is negligible in the dry winter months.

Internet and email

There are good facilities in all large towns, especially Harare, Bulawayo, Victoria Falls and Masvingo. Many hostels offer cheap internet access, and those that don't will be able to point you to a nearby internet café where one exists.

Maps

Inexpensive commercially produced maps of Hwange National Park and the Victoria Falls and Nyanga area are available at most decent bookshops and in many hotel curio shops. A useful general map of Zimbabwe published by Globetrotter is widely available in South Africa and large towns in Zimbabwe.

Money

The unit of currency is the Zimbabwe dollar, which has plummeted against most international currencies over the last few years, particularly during the tumultuous events that characterised the country in 2000. In mid-1998, when the first edition of this guide went to print, the US dollar exchange rate stood at US$1=Z$11. In August 2000, the rate was around US$1=Z$50, and it shows no signs of stabilising.

Banking hours are between 08.30 and 14.00, except for Wednesdays (close 12.00), Saturdays (close 11.00) and Sundays. Forex bureaux are open for longer hours but generally give a lower rate or charge a high commission. In desperation, you can always change a small sum of foreign currency at a hotel. There is no real advantage to using the black market, and the risk of being scammed is considerable.

Zimbabwe is not especially cheap, but it does offer good value for money. Our experience was that quality is comparable with South Africa, but most things that backpackers are likely to spend money on work out at around 30% less in Zimbabwe.

Post and telephone

Zimbabwe's postal system is cheap, slow and as reliable as any in Africa. Poste restante facilities are available in all towns. Making international phone calls into

Zimbabwe is quite easy, but making calls out is a nightmare unless you can do it from a private phone or hotel.

The international dialling code for Zimbabwe is +263. Area codes all begin with a '1' which must be dropped if dialling from outside the country – in other words you'd dial 14 to reach Harare from elsewhere in Zimbabwe but +2634 from another country. Main area codes are as follows:

Beitbridge	186	Gweru	154	Masvingo	139
Binga	115	Harare	14	Mutare	120
Bulawayo	19	Juliusdale	129	Victoria Falls	113
Chimanimani	126	Kariba	161		
Dete	118	Kwekwe	155		

Public holidays

In addition to Christmas Day, Boxing Day and the Easter weekend, Zimbabwe recognises the following public holidays:

18 April	Independence Day	11 August	Heroes Day
1 May	Workers' Day	12 August	Defence Force Day
25 & 26 May	Africa Days		

Tourist information offices

There are very helpful and well-informed tourist offices in Harare, Bulawayo, Mutare, Victoria Falls, Nyanga and Masvingo.

Harare and the northeast

THE A1: CHIRUNDU AND KARIBA TO HARARE

Situated on the banks of the Zambezi along the main route between Lusaka and Harare, **Chirundu** is a predictably charmless border town, the sort of place where under normal circumstances you'd be hard pushed to find a reason to spend a night. An attraction to some, however, will be the amount of big game that haunts the riverine woodland here, though it's to be stressed that any thoughts of a DIY foot safari should be tempered by the real likelihood of encountering dangerous animals such as buffalo, elephant, hippo and some very large crocs practically within the town limits – *be careful!* Chirundu is also an important staging post for canoe trips on the Zambezi and, while overnight canoe safaris are best booked in advance in Harare, the Tiger Safari Lodge does reasonably priced day boat trips on request.

Heading south from Chirundu, Marongora is of interest mainly as the administrative centre and springboard for visits to **Mana Pools National Park**. Named after a group of four oxbow lakes lying close to the Zambezi River, Mana Pools is noted not only for its prolific big game (hippos, elephants and crocs are superabundant and it's a good place to see lions, black rhinos and a wide variety of antelope species), but also for being one of the few major African game reserves where there are practically no restrictions to exploration on foot. Sadly for backpackers, however, you do need a vehicle to enter the park and hitching is forbidden, a ruling that's indirectly enforced by the need to book accommodation in advance (which doesn't prevent you from hanging around the park headquarters at Marongora on the off-chance of a lift and a free campsite; it simply makes you an incurable optimist). The most realistic way of seeing Mana Pools is with an organised safari out of Harare.

About 10km south of Marongora, **Makuti** lies at the junction of the A1 and the

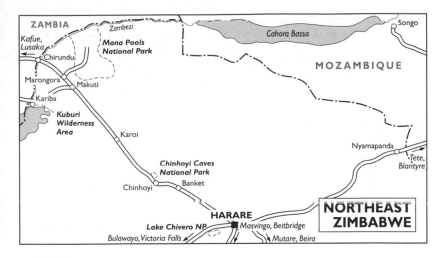

surfaced 65km road to **Kariba**, a small town which sprawls messily and without much focus over the hills on the eastern side of the synonymous man-made lake. Kariba has a rather marvellous setting, and the winding roads over the brachystegia-covered hills offer some stunning views over the lake. It also has the status of being one of the few African towns of comparable size where elephants regularly drink from suburban swimming pools. None of which can alter the reality that a combination of dispersed facilities, steep roads and sweaty climate makes Kariba rather enervating without your own vehicle. Aside from watersports, the main attraction in the town itself is the viewpoint over the 128m-high Kariba Dam wall, which forms a little-used border crossing between Zimbabwe and Zambia. Kariba town is also the eastern terminus for ferry services across the lake to Mlibizi and Binga (see box *Lake Kariba* on page 468).

If Kariba town barely qualifies as a tourist attraction, the same cannot be said for the little-known **Kaburi Wilderness Area** which practically borders it. Lying between the lakeshore and the main Kariba–Makuti road, and managed by the Wildlife Society of Zimbabwe, this wilderness area is both accessible and affordable to backpackers, since walking is permitted and fees are a fraction of those charged by the national parks. The floodplain in front of Kaburi Campsite is crossed by a steady stream of plains animals, notably zebra, elephant, warthog, impala and waterbuck, and it also hosts a profusion of birds (the gorgeous Lilian's lovebird nests in the camp). Better still, there's a good chance of seeing predators – we twice saw side-striped jackals trotting across the plain, heard lions roaring in the night, and were later told that a pair of lions had been seen sleeping almost exactly where our tent was positioned a week before!

The only tourist attraction between Makuti and Harare, **Chinhoyi Caves National Park** amounts to little more than a short walking trail into the flooded dolomite sinkhole after which it was named. It's a nice enough spot, and the incredibly clear water of the 90m-deep Chirorodzira Pool does have a certain haunting calm, but I would suspect it will attract a decreasing number of foreign visitors for so long as the same entrance fee is charged as for more substantial national parks. Only 8km south of the caves, **Chinhoyi** may be the largest town on the A1 north of Harare, but few travellers see more of it than is visible through a car or bus window. Not much more exciting is the town of **Karoi**, between Makuti and Chinhoyi.

Access and getting around

Several buses daily connect Mbare Musika in Harare to Chirundu and Kariba towns, stopping at all towns along the way. There are also plenty of private vehicles along these roads, so hitching is normally quite easy, though coming from Harare it would probably be worth taking a bus past the city outskirts. Directions to campsites around Kariba are given under the details for the individual site. For details of lake ferries, see box *Lake Kariba* above.

Where to stay and eat

Chirundu

Chirundu Campsite Riverside location. Limited facilities. Hippos, elephants and buffaloes are all regular visitors. **B** site.

Chirundu Valley Motel Pleasant small motel. Meals. Swimming pool. **E/F**.

Marongora

National Parks Office Camping permitted for free. Hot showers, toilets and braai places.

LAKE KARIBA

The construction of Kariba Dam, between 1955 and 1958, was dogged by climatic disasters which caused the coffer dam to be swept away twice and resulted in the death of 86 project workers. It was also a rather controversial project, resulting in the displacement of 50,000 Batonka people and – with a great deal more publicity! – numerous wild animals in the much-vaunted Operation Noah. Kariba is among Africa's largest artificial bodies of water, covering an area of roughly 5,000km², and it feeds one of the continent's largest hydro-electric stations.

Today, the shores of Kariba could be said to amount to one big wildlife sanctuary, with an image that's epitomised by photographs of a fish eagle sitting on a dead tree. Kariba town itself is frequently raided by elephants, and more remote parts of the shore, such as those protected in the Matusadona National Park, are among the most game-rich areas in the country. Unfortunately, however, few such places are readily accessible to backpackers. The obvious exception, the Kuburi Wilderness Area, is covered above, but most other parts of the lake are relatively expensive to visit.

One option open to backpackers is to take a ferry across the lake. The DDT ferry *Chaminuka* leaves Kariba town every Thursday at 09.00, arriving about 60 hours later at Binga on the western part of the lake. This service is very cheap and offers a high probability of seeing some wildlife, but facilities on the ferry are basic and you should take your own food. The alternative, Kariba Ferries' twice-weekly car ferry between Kariba and Mlibizi, is unlikely to be of interest to backpackers at around US$50 per head. For more details on Binga and Mlibizi, see *Northwestern Zimbabwe* on page 488.

Best of all, if you want to see some of the lake's best game viewing spots and can't afford to hire your own houseboat, is the excellent and affordable 'Backpackers' Cruise' which lasts for three days and costs a very reasonable US$100 per head. This is best organised a few days in advance, by calling Harare 66-5132.

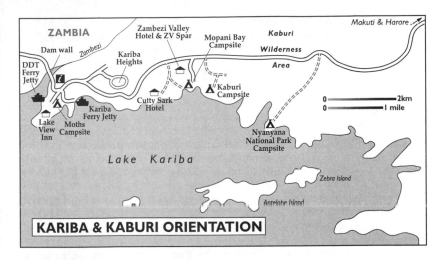

KARIBA & KABURI ORIENTATION

Mana Pools National Park
Nyamepi Camp The only campsite likely to be of interest to backpackers (other sites are for one group only). Good ablution facilities. Firewood for sale. No food or drink available. Camping **B** pp.

Makuti
Cloud's End Motel The only hotel in town. Rooms **F** pp.

Kariba and Kaburu Game Reserve
Kaburi Campsite Campsite near lakeshore run by Wildlife Society. Good game viewing and birds. The turn-off is signposted 15km out of Kariba town. You may have to walk the 6km from there to the lakeshore, keeping a very alert eye out for elephants, who needless to say have the right of way! Hot showers. Firewood and *braai* places but no food for sale. Camping **A** pp. The Wildlife Society Centre on the main Makuti Road about halfway between the turn-offs to Kuburi and Nyanyana campsites stocks maps and can give current information.

Mopani Bay Campsite Well wooded lakeshore site known for frequent hippo and elephant visits. To get there, bus or hitch along the main Makuti road out of Kariba for 9km, then follow the turn-off signposted for the 'Cutty Sark Hotel' for 2km. Meals 2km away at Cutty Sark Hotel. Hot showers. Camping **A** pp. Tent hire **A**.

MOTH Campsite The only affordable accommodation in Kariba town. Cramped, reasonably central waterfront site located 1km from Kariba Ferries jetty and 2km from the DDF ferry jetty. Nightly transfer to Lake View Inn for dinner. Large ablution blocks. Camp **A** pp. Standing tent **C** dbl. Room **D** dbl.

Nyanyana Campsite Campsite run by national parks, also in Kuburi Wilderness Area. Near lake and also good for game viewing. About 5km and signposted from the main Makuti road. Hot showers. Firewood. No food. Camping **B** pp.

ZV Spar Closest shop to the various out-of-town campsites. Very well stocked with fresh fruit, vegetables and meat. No more than 1km from the main road next to the Zambezi Valley Hotel. Turn off about halfway between those to the Mopani Bay and Kuburi campsites.

Karoi
Karoi Municipal Campsite On a small dam just outside town. **B** pp.

Chinhoyi and Chinhoyi Caves
Chinhoyi Caves National Park Campsite Sprawling and under-utilised site right outside the caves. Good meals at adjacent Caves Motel. No park entrance charged just for camping here. Camping **B** pp.
Orange Grove Motel In town centre. Rooms **F** pp (ask about backpackers' rates). Camping **A** pp.

HARARE
Zimbabwe's bustling capital city, known as Salisbury prior to independence, was founded in 1890. It was made the official capital of Southern Rhodesia in 1923 and granted city status in 1935. An important regional route focus, Harare is a well-organised city with an amenable mid-altitude climate and good facilities for the traveller; arrive there from countries to the north and you might well experience the minor culture shock associated with returning to a Western environment after a long period away from home. For all that, Harare offers little to travellers that couldn't be seen or done in any number of other cities; it's something of a mystery, at least to me, why you'll probably find a greater number of backpackers staying there on any given day than you will at any other place in Zimbabwe except perhaps Victoria Falls.

Definitely worth seeing in Harare is the **National Gallery of Zimbabwe**, one of the finest art museums on the African continent, with some excellent spiritual sculptures on the first floor. The **Queen Victoria Museum** is rather more mundane, dominated by natural history exhibits which do little more than replicate those you'll find in just about every other museum you visit in Africa. The largest park in the city centre, **Harare Gardens** boasts a swimming pool, an open-air restaurant and a rainforest-swathed model of Victoria Falls – worth a look, but not after dusk when there's a high incidence of rapes and muggings. Among the more interesting buildings in Harare are the **Market Hall** (built 1893), **Mother Patrick's Mortuary** (built 1895), the early 20th-century **Parliament Buildings**, and the **Anglican Cathedral**.

In the suburbs, the **Mukuvisi Woodland Nature Reserve** (tel: 74-7512) is a tract of indigenous woodland supporting a variety of introduced game species including elephant, giraffe, zebra and various large antelopes. In addition to a game-viewing platform overlooking a dam, there is a walk-in aviary and the reserve offers inexpensive horseback safaris at 08.30 and 15.00 as well as walking safaris at 14.30 daily. Another suburban attraction, one that's particularly worth visiting if you need to go to the nearby National Park Headquarters, is the **National Botanical Garden** off Sandringham Drive, where you can see tree species from all over Zimbabwe and elsewhere in Africa as well as a good variety of wild birds.

The area around Harare is noted for its many fantastic rock formations, the most famous of which are the **Epworth Balancing Rocks** 13km out of town on the Epworth Road. One of the formations here is depicted on Zimbabwe's banknotes, and the Museums Department levies a US$2 entrance fee, but otherwise there is little about the Epworth rocks that's any more special than a dozen other weird formations along the same road. Far more compelling, and free, are a number of outstanding **rock paintings** that lie within suburban Harare, most notably the 'Bridge' and 'Crocodile Men' sequences in Glen Norah. Accurate, detailed directions to these sites are included in the outstanding booklet *Tourist Guide to Rock Art Sites in Northern Zimbabwe*, which is available from the Queen Victoria Museum for around US$1.

For attractions further afield, see box *Short excursions from Harare* on pages 474–5.

Crime and safety

Harare used to be a very safe city but, so far as pickpocketing and muggings go, it has started to catch up with places like Johannesburg and Nairobi in the last few years. You should avoid walking around at night, particularly on relatively quiet roads, and keep your eyes open for pickpockets during the day. Harare is the one city covered in this book where you regularly hear of taxi-drivers conniving in scams – a popular trick is for the driver to drop you far enough from your hotel entrance for his friends to get the opportunity to mug you. That said, you should be safe if you stick to recognised taxi companies (such as Rixi and Cream Line), note down the taxi's registration number before you get in, and make sure you are dropped right at the entrance to where you are going.

Access and getting around

The international airport is 15km from the city centre. A regular express bus runs between Meikles Hotel in the city centre and the airport, or you can make use of a taxi for around US$5. The Backpackers & Overlanders Hostel (see *Where to stay*) is near the airport and offers a free pick-up service during the day.

Travellers coming by rail from Bulawayo, Mutare or South Africa will arrive at the centrally situated railway station on the corner of Second Street and Kenneth Kaunda Avenue.

Most cheap intercity buses, such as those run by the government ZUPCO, depart and arrive at the Mbare Musika bus station 5km from the city centre. The majority of buses leave Mbare Musika at around 06.00, though there are normally buses to major destinations such as Bulawayo, Masvingo and Mutare throughout the morning. For Mbare Musika, regular buses leave from the city centre at the bus terminal on Angwa Street between South and Robert Manyika Avenues, and a taxi will cost around US$1.50.

The more upmarket coach companies have scheduled departures to most large cities from their own terminal in the city centre. These include Express Motorways (cnr Baker and Rezende, tel: 72-0392) and the more expensive Blue Arrow (Chester House, Speke Ave, tel: 72-9514).

For getting around Harare itself, there is a good local bus network, though buses are often very crowded and you may have difficulty finding a seat unless you get on at one of the termini. Emergency taxis also run along most routes within the city. If you're not spending long in Harare, it may well be easiest to use private taxis on the few occasions when you need transport – the Rixi and Cream Line taxi companies have a good reputation and you'll rarely pay more than US$2 for a ride.

Where to stay

There are a great many hostels in Harare. About half of them are in the suburbs, while the rest are scattered around the compact grid of roads in the northern part of the city centre. Almost without exception, the better hostels are the suburban ones, and they all offer a free pick-up from the city centre. The more central hostels are generally run down and incidences of muggings in this area are on the increase, even in broad daylight. In Harare as elsewhere, hostels open and close with a high level of frequency, and the most reliable recommendations will come from travellers who've recently been in Harare.

Backpackers & Overlanders Hostel 932 Delport Rd; tel: 575715, email: conxshon@samara.co.zw. The one genuinely out-of-town (as opposed to suburban) hostel. In a lovely garden on a dam surrounded by pristine bush. Free pick-up 13.00 and 17.00 at Lido Café (cnr Union and Angwa St). Phone to arrange pick-up from airport. Good facilities, meals. Dorm **B** pp. Room **E** dbl. Camp **B** pp. Recommended.

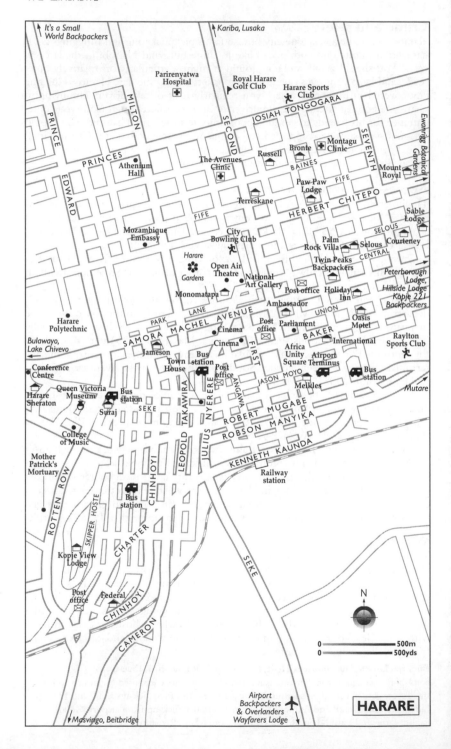

It's a Small World Backpackers

Kariba, Lusaka

Parirenyatwa Hospital

Royal Harare Golf Club

Harare Sports Club

MILTON

JOSIAH TONGOGARA

PRINCE

SEVENTH

Ewanrigg Botanical Gardens

PRINCES

Russell

Bronte

Montagu Clinic

BAINES

EDWARD

Athenium Hall

The Avenues Clinic

Paw Paw Lodge

FIFE

Mount Royal

HERBERT CHITEPO

Terreskane

SELOUS

Sable Lodge

FIFE

Mozambique Embassy

City Bowling Club

Palm Rock Villa

Selous

Courteney

CENTRAL

Harare Gardens

Open Air Theatre

National Art Gallery

Twin Peaks Backpackers

Peterborough Lodge, Hillside Lodge

Monomatapa

Post office

Holiday Inn

Kopje 221 Backpackers

Ambassador

UNION

Harare Polytechnic

PARK

MACHEL AVENUE

LANE

Post office

Parliament

BAKER

Oasis Motel

Bulawayo, Lake Chivevo

SAMORA

Cinema

FIRST

International

Raylton Sports Club

Conference Centre

Jameson

Cinema

Africa Unity Square

Airport Terminus

Bus station

Queen Victoria Museum

Bus Town House

station

Bus Post office

JASON MOYO

Meikles

Bus station

Mutare

Harare Sheraton

TAKAWIRA

office

NYERERE

LANGAWA

Suraj

SEKE

ROBERT MUGABE

College of Music

LEOPOLD

JULIUS

ROBSON MANYIKA

Mother Patrick's Mortuary

KENNETH KAUNDA

Railway station

ROTTEN ROW

SKIPPER HOSTEL

CHINHOYI

Bus station

CHARTER

SEKE

Kopje View Lodge

N

Post office

Federal

0 — 500m
0 — 500yds

CHINHOYI

CAMERON

Masvingo, Beitbridge

Airport Backpackers & Overlanders Wayfarers Lodge

HARARE

Coronation Park Camping Mutare Rd; tel: 486398. This out-of-town municipal site, formerly rather run down, is now an excellent, inexpensive place to pitch a tent. You can get here for a few Zimbabwe dollars on any minibus or bus heading from the city centre to Greendale; ask to get off in Msasa at the corner of Fourth St and Robert Mugabe Rd. Camping **A** pp.

Hillside Lodge 71 Hillside Rd; tel: 747961; email: hillside@samara.co.zw; web: www.zimweb.co.zw/hillside. Popular hostel set in an old colonial farmhouse on a well-wooded, two-acre property 20 minutes' walk from central Harare. Breakfast provided, kitchen, two supermarkets within walking distance. Free pick-up from Harare (when no car is available they will pay the taxi fare). Travel advice and outings. Camping **B** pp. Dorm **B** pp. Rooms **D** sgl or dbl.

It's a Small World Backpackers Lodge 72 King George Rd, Avondale; tel: 335341. Appalling name notwithstanding, this is one of the best hostels in Harare, busy but never crowded, and with good facilities including a swimming pool and internet café. Close to large shopping mall. Dorm **C** pp. Room **E** dbl. Camp **B** pp.

Palm Rock Villa Cnr Selous Av and Fifth St; tel: 700691 or 724550; email: square@cyberdude.com. Once rather run down, this has undergone something of a facelift in recent years and is now probably the best of the city centre hostels. Clean and well run, with internet facilities, yet in the heart of a lively (and mildly disreputable) part of the city. Dorm **C** pp. Rooms **D/F** sgl/dbl.

Peterborough Lodge 11 Peterborough Av, Eastlea; tel: 776145. Cosy. Avoid if you want a busy backpacker scene. Perfect for peace and quiet. Dorm **B** pp. Room **C/D** sgl/dbl.

Possum Lodge 7 Deary Av, Belgravia; tel: 726851; fax: 722803; email: possum@zol.co.zw. Set in an old colonial homestead, Possum is widely regarded to be one of the best hostels in the city, both for its busy, friendly atmosphere and its excellent facilities, which include a kitchen, restaurant and bar, internet café, travel agency, deposit boxes, swimming pool and pool table. Close to the city centre and embassies, free pick-up from town/airport by prior arrangement. Recommended. Camping **B** pp. Dorm **C** pp. Rooms **E** dbl.

Shoestring Resort Tel: 691966; email: shoestringhre@2000.co.zw. New backpackers' lodge, affiliated to its Victoria Falls namesake and with similar facilities, not very central but already becoming popular. Dorm **C** pp. Rooms **E** dbl.

The Rocks 18 Seke Rd; tel: 57-6309. Aimed mostly at overland trucks, this is a convivial place to hang out. Dorm **B** pp. Room **D** dbl. Camp **A** pp.

Wayfarers Lodge 47 Jesmond Rd, Hatfield; tel/fax: 572125; email: wayfarer@icon.co.zw. One of the oldest and most popular hostels. The claim that the accommodation has an 'African feel' is risible, but otherwise an excellent set up in large attractive gardens. Good, inexpensive tours. Twice-daily free shuttle into city centre. Phone for a free lift. Swimming pool. Good food. Camping **B** pp. Dorm **D** pp. Room **E** dbl.

Where to eat

Most backpackers stay at one of the out-of-town hostels, all of which provide inexpensive filling meals or have self-catering facilities, or both. If you're in the city centre by day, there are numerous restaurants and fast food outlets dotted around, with the greatest concentration on the First Street Mall – try the **Sidewalk Café** for a reasonably priced lunch. For dinner, a reliable, long-standing favourite for pasta, pizza and meat dishes is **Guido's** in the Montague Centre on the corner of Harare Street and Joseph Chinamano Avenue. More convenient if you're staying at one of the central hostels is **Coimbra**, a good Mozambican-style restaurant at 61 Selous Avenue.

Practical listings

Airlines Aeroflot (73-1971); Air India (70-0318); Air Zimbabwe (57-5021); American Airlines (73-3073); Balkan Airlines (75-9271); British Airways (75-9173); EgyptAir (72-8860); Ethiopian Airlines (79-0705); Kenya Airways (79-2181); KLM (73-1042); L.A.M (70-3338); Lufthansa (70-7606); Qantas (79-4676); South African Airways (73-8922).

Books and newspapers For field guides, travel literature and other new books, the best place to head for is one of the branches of Kingston's Book Shop – one is on the ground floor of the parking garage on the corner of Samora Machel Avenue and Second Street and the other is opposite the tourist information office on Second Street. The local *Daily Herald* newspaper is available from street vendors, while several bookshops stock international newspapers.

Cinemas If you've been exposed to the sorry parade of Indian singalongs and jingoistic sub-Rambo American drivel that passes for cinematic entertainment in most parts of Africa north of the Zambezi, you'll find that cinemas in Harare screen a thoroughly more enticing selection of fare. The main cinema complex is the Kine Centre on Union Avenue; for listings see the *Daily Herald*. Tickets are cheap.

Embassies Australia (75-7774); Austria (70-2921); Belgium (79-3306); Botswana (72-9551); Canada (73-3881); Denmark (75-8185); Ethiopia (72-5822); France (49-8096); Germany (73-1955); Israel (75-6808); Italy (49-7279); Japan (75-7868); Kenya (79-2901);

SHORT EXCURSIONS FROM HARARE

Ewanrigg National Park is best in winter when red, orange and yellow aloes attract a variety of beautiful sunbirds. The park lies 40km northeast of Harare; you can get within 30 minutes' walk of the entrance gate by catching a bus towards Shamva. Ewanrigg makes an attractive day excursion, but it's essentially a botanical garden and feels to be one of those national parks which don't justify a US$5 entrance fee. No overnight facilities exist.

Along the Bulawayo road, 23km from Harare, the **Lion and Cheetah Park** is surprisingly popular with backpackers, and day trips there are organised by several of the hostels. The first part of the park consists of two rather small drive-in enclosures which contain around ten cheetahs and lions respectively. The second part is a walk-through area near the restaurant and kiosk – essentially a zoo with representatives of more unusual species such as otter, caracal and serval. The largest part of the park is a drive-through game area, notable as much for its fantastic rock sculptures as for the opportunity to see large mammals such as elephant, giraffe, sable antelope, nyala and eland. Rather contrived, the lion and cheetah park's saving grace is the wonderfully authentic scenery. The nearby **Larvon Bird Gardens** will be of interest to those who want to learn more about Zimbabwe's varied birds.

A short distance further along the Bulawayo road, **Lake Chivero Recreational Park** encloses the reservoir after which it is named (formerly Lake Robert McIlwaine). The northern lakeshore, popular with Harare's watersport contingency, is of limited interest to travellers. All the same, it's difficult to think of a more aesthetically pleasing spot than the national parks campsite, which is situated in a patch of thick woodland right on the northern lake shore, 25 minutes' walk and signposted from the Shell Turnpike Garage about 30km out of Harare (camping **B** pp; no entrance fee charged). The southern lakeshore, which can be reached from a signposted turn-off 5km

Malawi (75-2137); Mozambique (79-0837); Namibia (72-2113); Netherlands (77-6701); New Zealand (75-9221); South Africa (77-6712); Sweden (79-0651); Switzerland (70-3997); Tanzania (72-4173); UK (79-3781); USA (79-4521); Zambia (79-0851).

Foreign exchange Changing money at banks is a simple procedure. Outside of banking hours, several upmarket hotels have foreign exchange kiosks, though rates are never as good as at banks.

Immigration The immigration office is in Liquenda House on Baker Avenue. Visa and visitor's pass extensions are normally obtained on the day of application.

Maps A useful variety of regional maps can be bought at branches of Kingston's Book Shop. The Department of Surveys map office is in Electra House on Samora Machel Avenue.

National Parks Office The reservations office is in the national parks headquarters at the northern end of the National Botanical Gardens. Any vehicle heading along Borrowdale Road can drop you five minutes' walk from the entrance to the national parks headquarters, which is on Sandringham Drive. Note that all accommodation in national parks *must* be booked in advance either here or at the reservations office in Bulawayo. You could also book by phone (tel: 70-6077) but it's easier to do it in person despite the hassle of getting out there. The office is open from 08.30 to 15.00.

further towards Bulawayo almost immediately after the road crosses the Manyame River, consists of a small but well-stocked game reserve. This is well worth visiting should you have access to a vehicle – white rhinos are very common, there are some remarkable rock paintings of dolphins at Bushman's Point, and the national parks' chalets are outstanding value for money at **C** dbl with cooker and fridge (plus the normal national parks entrance fee).

The **Chinamora Communal Land** to the north of Harare is notable for its spectacular boulderscapes and for a wealth of ancient rock art sites, at least two of which can easily be approached by using the bus service from Mbare Musika in Harare to Bindura via Chinamora. First up is **Domboshawa Cave**, where an extensive and reasonably well-preserved panel depicts several elephants and a group of humanoid figures called 'the rainmakers'. Domboshawa Cave lies 1km east of the bus route along a dirt road signposted 30km north of Harare and 4km past Domboshowa village. The other accessible site, and the better of the two, **Ngomakurira Shelter** consists of two extensive and well-preserved panels, and the rock outcrop on which they lie is revered locally for the reverberations it makes when you strike it. The shelter lies about 1km along the Sasa Road, signposted from the bus route about 10km north of Domboshawa Cave. If you prefer to do things as part of an organised trip, contact the Kopje 211 Hostel, which runs affordable excursions to this area every week or so.

If you feel like spending a few days in a relatively affordable wilderness atmosphere, a good bet is the **Hippo Pools Campsite** on the bank of the Mazowe River in the **Umfurudzi Wilderness Area** roughly 160km northeast of Harare. There's plenty of wildlife (hippos wander between the tents at night!), as well as good hiking and canoeing opportunities. Hippo Pools is easy to visit from Harare since the owners run a shuttle service there every Monday and Friday – for details contact the Bronte Hotel (132 Baines St; tel: 70-8843). Camping costs **C** pp and chalets **E** pp. Meals cost around US$7 or you can self-cater if you bring your own provisions.

Post and telephone The poste restante service at the main post office on Inez Terrace is reasonably efficient. The same cannot be said for the central telecommunications office in the same building – better to make any international calls from a private phone.

Tourist information office The tourist office on Unity Square in Second Street (tel: 70-7021) is well worth visiting, since it stocks a good range of leaflets and fliers for Harare and elsewhere in the country. Ask for a copy of the regularly updated booklet *Harare*, which has loads of useful contact numbers and ideas for things to do, as well as accommodation ads (though I should add that most of the hostels that advertised in the June 1997 edition have a bad name with travellers). The tourist office also keeps a regularly updated list of all hostels in Harare with addresses, telephone numbers and prices.

Western Zimbabwe
BULAWAYO AND SURROUNDS
Zimbabwe's second largest city, with a population approaching one million, **Bulawayo** has an altogether more relaxed, old world feel than the bustling capital, and it's widely regarded to be one of southern Africa's most pleasant large towns. The name Bulawayo derives from the Zulu expression 'GuBulawayo' (The Place of Killing), originally the name of Shaka's Zulu capital, and later adopted in 1881 by Lobengula of the Matabele, whose capital stood on the site of the modern State House until it was destroyed by Rhodes' troops in 1886. The name Bulawayo was retained when the settlers founded a city there in 1894. Significantly, Bulawayo is the country's only substantial town which retained its colonial name unaltered into the modern era.

Like most towns in Zimbabwe, Bulawayo is of interest less for its own sake than for some of the places that surround it. There are, however, a couple of worthwhile spots in the city, notably the **Natural History Museum** in Centenary Park, one of the best of its kind in Africa. For a relaxed stroll, the **Mabukuwene Nature Reserve** in Burnside boasts a large aloe garden, as well as supporting many interesting birds and small mammals, and it's very close by if you're staying at one of the hostels in Hillside or Burnside. You can also walk freely in the excellent **Tshabalala Sanctuary**, 8km out of town along the Matabo road, where pedestrians are likely to encounter a variety of large mammals including zebra and giraffe and several types of antelope.

Only 20km northeast of Bulawayo, and an important World Heritage Site, **Khami National Monument** consists of the attractive ruins of the former capital of the Torwa Empire, the dominant political force in western Zimbabwe from roughly 1450 until the rise of the Changamire/Rozvi in the 1690s. The centrepiece of Khami is the Hill Structure on the west bank of the Khami River, where stone walls several metres high are decorated in chevron patterns, a clear indication that this city was the most important archaeological successor to Great Zimbabwe itself. The Hill Structure was presumably the royal court, and several outlying ruins to its south may have protected the huts of lesser dignitaries. One of the more intriguing aspects of the ruins is the presence of a restored stone cross, perhaps 1m long which, according to the excellent pamphlet available at the site, 'is said to have been placed there by a Portuguese missionary, although there is little supporting evidence'.

About 50km south of Bulawayo, the landscape of **Matobo National Park** is one of the most memorable in Zimbabwe, noted for its immense granite domes and bizarre balancing rock formations. One of the best-known spots in the park is the 'View of the World' at Malindidzimu, where Rhodes' grave stands on a vast whaleback at the centre of a ring of giant boulders, home to dozens of colourful

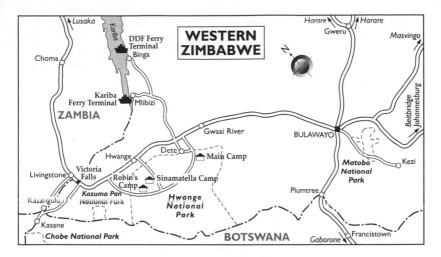

lizards. Matobo is also one of Zimbabwe's main repositories of rock art: of particular interest among the more accessible sites are several monochrome outlines of animals in the White Rhino Shelter near to the 'View of the World', and an extensive panel dominated by some outstanding figures of running giraffes at Nswatugi Cave. Matobo is well suited to backpackers because there are no restrictions on walking in the larger part of the national park, the area to the south and east of the Bulawayo–Kezi road. In this part of the national park, wildlife densities are low, though you stand a good chance of seeing klipspringer, rock hyrax, impala and many birds, including the magnificent black eagle, as common here as it is anywhere in Africa. To the west of this road, the Whovi Game Area supports a variety of big game species including introduced giraffe and white rhino, but it can only be entered in a vehicle.

An accurate map of Matobo National Park, complete with details of the various plants, mammals and birds recorded in the park, can be bought at the entrance gate for a nominal fee. For a geological and historical background, get hold of the inexpensive and informative booklet *The Matopo Hills: A Guide*, written by C K Cooke and published by the National Museums and Monuments of Zimbabwe.

Crime and safety

Bulawayo is generally a very safe, relaxed city, but the parks that separate the city centre from the caravan park have acquired a reputation for rapes and muggings. During the day, you should stick to main paths through these parks. Under no circumstances should campers walk through the parks after dark – a taxi to or from the city centre will cost less than US$2.

Access and getting around

The main bus stations in Bulawayo are the City Hall terminus on the corner of Eighth and Robert Mugabe, the Lobengula terminus on the corner of Sixth and Lobengula, and about ten minutes' walk away Renkini Musika along Sixth Avenue Extension. Long-distance buses to Victoria Falls, Harare, Beitbridge, Plumtree and Masvingo leave from Renkini Musika, generally in the early morning, so it's advisable to be there at around 06.00. Most ZUPCO buses leave from Lobengula Street terminal.

More comfortable coach services are run by Express Motorways twice daily to Harare, once daily to Johannesburg via Beitbridge, and on Thursday and Sunday to

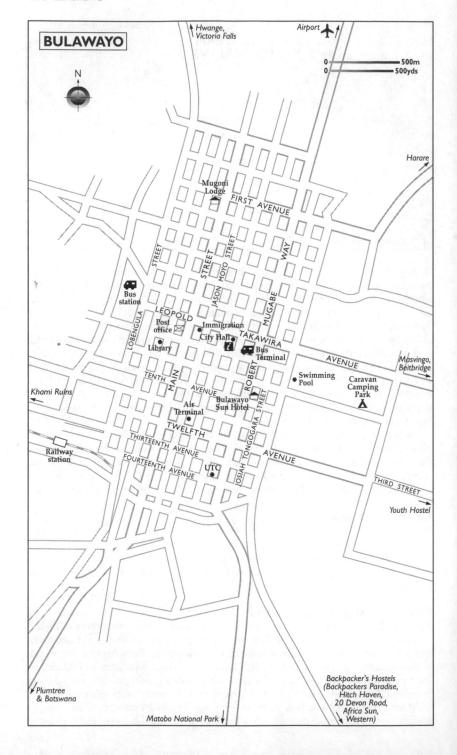

BULAWAYO

N

↑ Hwange,
Victoria Falls

Airport ✈

0 ⊢─────────── 500m
0 ⊢─────────── 500yds

→ Harare

Mugoni
Lodge

FIRST AVENUE

STREET

STREET

JASON MOYO STREET

MUGABE WAY

Bus
station

LEOPOLD

LOBENGULA

Post
office

Immigration
City Hall

TAKAWIRA

Library

i

Bus
Terminal

ROBERT

AVENUE

→ Masvingo,
Beitbridge

Khami Ruins ←

TENTH

MAIN

AVENUE

Swimming
Pool

Caravan
Camping
Park

Air
Terminal

Bulawayo
Sun Hotel

OSIAH TONGOGARA STREET

TWELFTH

THIRTEENTH AVENUE

UTC

AVENUE

Railway
station

FOURTEENTH AVENUE

THIRD STREET

→ Youth Hostel

↙ Plumtree
& Botswana

Backpacker's Hostels
(Backpackers Paradise,
Hitch Haven,
20 Devon Road,
Africa Sun,
Western)

↓ Matobo National Park ↓

Gaberone in Botswana. All Express Motorways buses leave from the City Hall; tickets can be booked through UTC/Hertz Office (cnr 14th and George Silundika, tel: 61402). Ajay's coaches to Victoria Falls and Harare leave from the Bulawayo Sun Hotel. Ajay's and most other coaches can be booked through Manica Travel on Tenth Avenue (tel: 62521). Minibuses to Johannesburg and Harare leave from the City Hall.

An overnight train service connects Harare to Bulawayo, leaving daily in either direction at 21.00 and taking ten hours. The overnight train service to Victoria Falls leaves at 19.00 daily in either direction, taking around 12 hours with a stop at Dete (for Hwange National Park) at around 01.00. There is also an overnight train service to Gaberone in Botswana.

Within Bulawayo, buses to the Hillside area (where many of the hostels are) leave from the City Hall. Taxis are inexpensive, and the safest way to get around after dark; a reliable company is Rixis (tel: 60666).

Most backpackers seem to visit Matobo National Park on a day tour from Bulawayo, which costs around US$25 per person including a drive in the game sanctuary. Reputable companies include Adventure Travel (tel: 66525) and Black Rhino (tel: 41662), though most of the backpackers' hostels can organise trips or make a recommendation. If you ask, most companies will drop you at Maleme Rest Camp and pick you up on another day. To get to Matobo National Park independently, catch a bus to Kezi from Renkini Musika in Bulawayo and ask to be dropped at one of the turn-offs to the park. From the first turn-off, it's a 3km walk to Sandspruit Campsite; from the second it's a similar distance to the Arboretum Campsite; and from the third (opposite the entrance to the game sanctuary) it's about 5km to Mezilume Dam. It shouldn't be difficult to hitch on to Maleme Rest Camp or Dam, assuming that you're on the road early enough – the first turn-off carries more traffic.

No public transport goes near the Khame Ruins, and the site is visited too rarely for hitching to be much of a prospect. The most realistic option would be to cycle there from Bulawayo – the road out is reasonably flat and you can find out about bicycle hire through any hostel or the tourist office. Alternatively, a half-day tour out of Bulawayo shouldn't be prohibitively expensive.

Where to stay
Bulawayo
Africa Sun Backpackers 398 Thurso Rd, Killarney; tel: 31528; email: zpn329@mweb.co.zw This pleasant and inexpensive hostel is one of the best in the city, and offers a free night's accommodation to anybody who does a Matobo safari with them (highly recommended). Swimming pool. Kitchen. Home-cooked meals. TV lounge. Free pick-up and shuttle to city centre. Dorm **B** pp. Room **D** dbl.
Berkeley Place 71 Josiah Tongogara St; tel: 67701. Smart and secure new hostel, attractively situated and relatively subdued atmosphere. Recommended for single women in particular. Rooms **C**/**D** sgl/dbl including breakfast.
Burke's Paradise 11 Inverleith Dve, Burnside; tel: 46481. Formerly Backpacker's Paradise, this is the oldest of the genuine backpackers' hostels and still one of the best. Large suburban property with swimming pool and *braai* places. TV and video. Good kitchen. Meat and provisions on sale. Laundry. Free pick-up from city centre. Budget tours to Hwange and Matobo. Double rooms **C** pp.
Hitch Haven Backpackers Lodge 7 Hillside Rd, Hillside; tel: 46274; email: hitchhaven_2000@yahoo.com or online@acacia.samara.co.zw. Popular and very cheap. Large garden. Good meals. Dorm **B** pp. Room **D** dbl. Camp **A** pp.
Mugoni Lodge Cnr Fort and First Av; tel: 64539. The only decent affordable accommodation in the city centre. Kitchen. Hot showers. Spacious furnished rooms with satellite TV **D**/**E**.

Municipal Caravan Park An excellent campsite and a reliable bet for longer than a decade. Ten minutes from the city centre, though you're urged not to walk there after dark. Good ablution blocks. Laundry. Firewood. Camping **A** pp. Chalets **C** pp.

Packers Rest 1 Oak Av; tel: 71111, 71132 or 540734; fax: 71124; email: packers@acacia.samara.co.zw. This new, centrally located hostel looks set to be real winner, with excellent rates, walking access to dozens of bars and restaurants, and good facilities including internet access, a variety of day tours, cheap mountain bike and car hire, and close proximity to a sports club. Kitchen, bar, fast food deliveries to lodge, free pick-up from anywhere in city, and drop-off when you leave. Dorm **B** pp. Room **C/D** sgl/dbl.

Shaka's Spear Cnr Jason Moyo Rd and Second Av; tel: 69923. Despite moving site a couple of years back, this long-serving hostel remains one of the most popular in Bulawayo, more for its energetically sociable atmosphere and rock-bottom rates than for any notable facilities. Dorm **A** pp. Rooms **C** dbl.

Western Backpackers' Lodge 5 Nottingham Rd, Hillcrest; tel: 44100; email: tourzim@telconet.co.zw. Garden with swimming pool and *braai* area. Close to shopping centre. Kitchen. Meals. Dorm **B** pp. Room **D** dbl.

White Hollows Youth Hostel Cnr Third and Townsend; tel: 76488. It's well established, the dorms are among the cheapest in town, and you no longer have to flee the property between 10.00 and 17.00. On the down side is the rigid 22.30 curfew and general mood of austerity. It has its devotees. Dorm **B** pp.

Matobo National Park

Maleme Rest Camp Set on a boulder-strewn slope in the heart of the national park, this beautiful camp is home to a variety of birds and lizards, as well as rock hyraxes and the peculiar little rock elephant-shrew, which emerges at dusk. All chalets have a fridge, kettle, electric cooker and *braai* place. Kiosk selling tinned food, frozen meat, soft drinks, beer and local wine. Chalets **C** dbl.

Campsites The main campsite is at Maleme Dam, only 1km from the rest camp; it's very spacious and attractive, with hot showers and *braai* places. There are several other campsites in the park, of which the Sandspruit, Arboretum and Mezilume Dam sites lie within easy walking distance of the main Bulawayo–Kezi bus route. Camping **B** pp.

Where to eat

As in Harare, most backpackers stay in a hostel and either cook for themselves or order the meal of the day. If you want to try eating out in the city centre, catch a taxi to the **Bulawayo Sun Hotel**, where a good dozen restaurants to suit most tastes and budgets are clustered within a block or two. The **Homestead Restaurant** in the hotel is excellent, but expensive. Other places you could try in this area include the **Cattleman** (for steaks), **Oriental Take Away** (Indian, sit down or takeaway), **La Gondola** (Italian) and the **Chicken**, **Pie** and **Ice-Cream Inns**.

Practical listings

Books and newspapers The best sources of new books and commercially produced maps are Kingston's Book Shop on Jason Moyo Street and the Book Centre on Eighth Avenue. There are a number of secondhand bookshops in Bulawayo – try Bookmart at 103 George Sindaluka Street.

Cinema The Kine 600 and Elite 400 Cinemas on Robert Mugabe Road normally show current Hollywood movies.

Immigration office CABS Building, Cnr Jason Moyo and Leopold Takawira; tel: 65621.

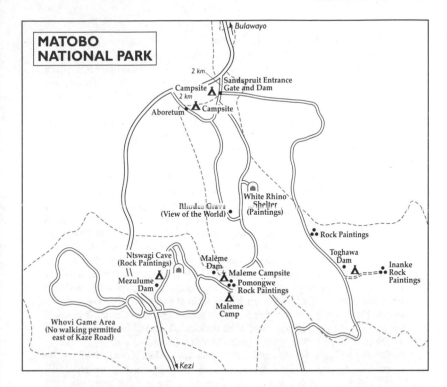

MATOBO NATIONAL PARK

Bulawayo

2 km

Campsite
2 km

Sandspruit Entrance
Gate and Dam

Aboretum

Campsite

White Rhino
Shelter
(Paintings)

Rhodes Grave
(View of the World)

Rock Paintings

Toghawa
Dam

Inanke
Rock
Paintings

Ntswagi Cave
(Rock Paintings)

Maleme
Dam

Mezulume
Dam

Maleme Campsite

Pomongwe
Rock Paintings

Maleme
Camp

Whovi Game Area
(No walking permitted
east of Kaze Road)

Kezi

Maps The official map sales office is in Tredgold House on the corner of Fort and Leopold Takawira.

National Park office The reservations office on the corner of Herbert Chitepo and Tenth Avenue (tel: 63646) is open from 08.30 to 15.00. It is more central and affable than its counterpart in Harare, although all bookings must be radioed through to Harare, so you'll probably have to wait 24 hours for confirmation.

Nightlife The Alabama Bar below the Bulawayo Sun is a relaxed place to drink, and popular with locals for the excellent jazz band which plays there on most nights.

Post and telephone Collect poste restante from the main GPO on the corner of Eighth and Main Street. International phone calls can be made from the same place.

Tourist office The tourist office behind the City Hall is exceptionally well organised and the people who work there are knowledgeable and helpful. It stocks a regularly updated list of budget accommodation in and around the city.

NORTHWESTERN ZIMBABWE

Zimbabwe's very own Wild West is a thinly populated and mostly rather flat region blanketed in dry mopane and brachystegia woodland and teeming with big game. The main backpacker focus in this region is **Victoria Falls**, or more accurately the small town of Victoria Falls, an overpriced tourist trap to which Africa's most spectacular waterfall is becoming something of a sideshow. Victoria Falls ranks high on any list of must-sees, and the small rainforest-swathed national park from which you view the 1,700m-wide waterfall still feels unspoilt, especially at sunrise when the light is stunning, bushbuck trot delicately between the trees, and the

THE A5: HARARE TO BULAWAYO

The trunk road connecting Zimbabwe's two largest cities offers little of interest to tourists, and most backpackers make the seven-hour bus trip or overnight train trip between Harare and Bulawayo without any noteworthy interruption. That said, two substantial towns lie along the A5 and it would seem remiss to ignore them entirely in this guide.

First up coming from Harare, **Kwekwe** lies at the heart of a gold-mining region which supplied prodigious quantities of ore to the trade ports of the east African coast during the Swahili and Portuguese eras. About the only point of interest in town is the Kwekwe National Mining Museum and the attached Mine Manager's House, a peculiar Victorian construction of papier mâché and wire mesh in which Rhodes is said to have slept at some point. About 5km out of town, the **Lower Zivagwe Dam** (formerly Dutchman's Pool) is a pretty, well-wooded spot known for prolific birds. If you don't have a tent, budget options in Kwekwe are limited, but campers have the choice of the run-down municipal site on the south side of town or the more attractive site at Lower Zivagwe Dam. Both cost **A** pp.

About 50km from Kwekwe, **Mopani Park Farm** (tel: 247822) is a small private game reserve of particular interest to backpackers with an equestrian bent. In addition to riding within the reserve, the owners can set up three-day horse safaris to nearby Sebakwe Dam. Camping costs **D** pp and rooms cost **E** pp, rates that include all meals. Ring them before 17.00 to arrange a cheap pick-up at the Wimpy in Kwekwe.

On the A5 between Kwekwe and Bulawayo, **Gweru** may well be the third largest city in Zimbabwe, but the atmosphere is emphatically small-town. If you get stuck, the Gweru Caravan Park amounts to a square of grass alongside an ablution block in the heart of the Sports Club. Camping rates are vague (we eventually paid in the lower **C** range for a small tent) and it's difficult to share the caretaker's enthusiasm for the free coffee that comes with paying a steep **E** for a tiny concrete double 'chalet'. On the plus side, you get access to the clubhouse, which has a good bar with jukebox and pool table and serves good cheap meals.

About 20km south of Gweru, the small highland town of **Shurugwe** has been bypassed not only by the A5 but by much else that's occurred since 1950. Charming or run-down, the choice is yours, but Shurugwe does lie at the heart of some great walking country, and it could make for a pleasant cheap break from the homogeneity of hostelry. The Ferny Creek Caravan Park lies 2km out of town on a thickly grassed slope ringed by brachystegia woodland. There are three scruffy but lockable two-bed huts with mattresses but no bedding (**A** dbl), and you can camp, though security might be suspect. The ablution block has cold running water.

South of the A5 between Gweru and Bulawayo, **Nalatale** and **Danangombe Ruins** are relics of Rozvi stone cities built in the seventeenth century. Nalatale is the more attractive of the two, with some excellent chevron patterning, but Danangombe is larger. The main obstacle to visiting either ruin is access – both lie about 20km from the main road and neither sees much traffic or has accommodation. There's no reason why a self-sufficient backpacker couldn't walk to either site and camp rough.

crowds are mostly still in bed. Many backpackers also make the day-trip into neighbouring Zambia to spend time at the falls, and travellers heading to Zimbabwe from Zambia are urged to linger on the northern side of the falls for a day or two before crossing the Zambezi. Once you've seen Victoria Falls, the waterfall (and at US$10 per entry on the Zimbabwean side this is likely to be a one-off event), you'll find that Victoria Falls the town, is a good base from which to organise all manner of activities, from the renowned bungee jump to a game drive in the lovely Zambezi National Park (see box *Passing time and spending money in Victoria Falls* on page 486–7).

Much of western Zimbabwe is protected in conservation areas, the most notable of which is undoubtedly **Hwange National Park**, the country's largest game reserve and most popular safari destination. Relatively inexpensive and easy of access, Hwange's Main Camp is a worthwhile goal for backpackers, especially as large herds of game tend to congregate in the surrounding area. Hwange is best known for elephants (up to 20,000 may be present at the height of the dry season) but the general game viewing is excellent. Lion, cheetah and hyena are regularly sighted in the roads around Main Camp, as are a variety of herbivores, most commonly giraffe, Burchell's zebra, wildebeest, impala and sable antelope. Several of the waterholes around Main Camp are worth spending time at; none more so than Nyamandhlovu with its wonderful viewing platform. Of great interest to backpackers are the daily game walks from Main Camp to Sedina Pan.

The main road through western Zimbabwe is the A8 between Bulawayo and Victoria Falls, and there are few urban centres of note along this. About 20km before the turn-off to Hwange National Park, there is little more to **Gwaai River** than its eponymous hotel, though the campsite 10km further north may be of interest to some backpackers. Of greater interest is **Dete**, about 15km to the west of the A8, since it has several backpackers' hostels and serves as the main springboard for budget trips into Hwange National Park. Much larger than Dete, but of no interest to travellers, **Hwange** is an important coal-mining town lying to the immediate west of the A8. Branching eastwards from the A8 at Dete Crossroads, a surfaced road leads to the western shores of Lake Kariba and the small ports of **Mlibizi** and **Binga**, the second of which, although visited by very few backpackers, is of interest not only as the western terminal of the fortnightly DDF ferry to Kariba town, but also as an excellent place to immerse yourself in the unusual culture of the remote Tonga people.

Access and getting around

Several buses and coaches daily run along the road between Bulawayo and Victoria Falls. An inexpensive and recommended service, Hwange Special Express, leaves three times daily from Renkini Musika in Bulawayo and Sopers Arcade in Victoria Falls. The most upmarket coach service, and the only one, so far as I'm aware, that actually diverts to Dete, is the daily Blue Arrow coach, which costs around US$22 one way – ring Bulawayo 65548 for timetable details. Hitching along the main road between Bulawayo and Victoria Falls is realistic; when leaving Victoria Falls you need only walk ten minutes to be clear of the town.

If you're bussing to Dete and don't use the Blue Arrow coach, then you should ask to be dropped at the signposted junction informally known as Dete Crossroads, where there are a couple of shops. Shared taxis cover the roughly 15km from the crossroads to Dete.

A more attractive option than bussing between Bulawayo and Victoria Falls, though it normally requires advance booking, is the inexpensive overnight rail

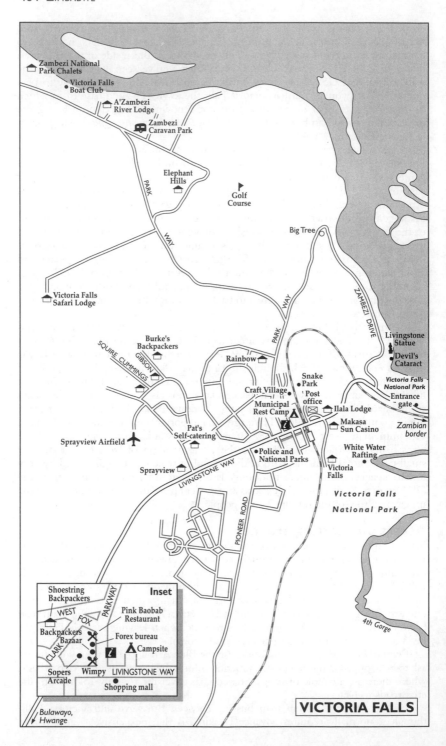

Zambezi National Park Chalets

Victoria Falls Boat Club

A'Zambezi River Lodge

Zambezi Caravan Park

Elephant Hills

Golf Course

Big Tree

PARK WAY

Victoria Falls Safari Lodge

Burke's Backpackers

SQUIRE CUMMINGS

GIBSON

Rainbow

Craft Village

Snake Park

Post office

Municipal Rest Camp

Ilala Lodge

Makasa Sun Casino

PARK WAY

ZAMBEZI DRIVE

Livingstone Statue

Devil's Cataract

Victoria Falls National Park

Entrance gate

Zambian border

Sprayview Airfield

Pat's Self-catering

Sprayview

LIVINGSTONE WAY

Police and National Parks

White Water Rafting

Victoria Falls

Victoria Falls National Park

PIONEER ROAD

4th Gorge

Inset

Shoestring Backpackers

WEST

PARKWAY

FOX

Pink Baobab Restaurant

Backpackers Bazaar

CLARK

Forex bureau

Campsite

Sopers Arcade

Wimpy

LIVINGSTONE WAY

Shopping mall

Bulawayo, Hwange

VICTORIA FALLS

service which leaves Bulawayo at 18.30 daily and Victoria Falls at 19.00. All trains stop at Dete in the early hours of the morning, so ring Wildside Hostel in advance to arrange to be met at the station; even if this isn't possible, it's only a two-minute walk from the station to the hostels and they're used to people arriving at these hours.

Several options are open to those who want to spend time in Hwange National Park. If you're carrying a tent, you can safely arrive at Main Camp without a booking, so the simplest option might be to bus along the Victoria Falls road as far as the turn-off to Main Camp and then hitch from there. However, there are advantages to booking accommodation in advance, in which case it would be safest to get yourself to Dete the night before your bookings start. If you organise a game drive out of Dete, you can be dropped at Main Camp at no extra charge.

There is one bus daily between Bulawayo and Binga. Travellers coming to or from Victoria Falls will have to change vehicles at the junction known as Dete Crossroads. The bus out of Binga leaves at 05.00 and the terminal is at least 30 minutes' walk from the nearest accommodation, so you may prefer to chance your arm hitching. The DDF ferry between Binga and Kariba town runs every two weeks, takes three days, and costs around US$16. If you want to head from Binga to Harare or Kariba town by road, the bus from Bulawayo continues on to Siabuwa, where you'll have to camp or ask around for informal accommodation before catching the bus to Karoi on the main Harare–Kariba road the next morning. There is no public transport along the turn-off to Mlibizi or to Deka Drum.

Where to stay and eat
Victoria Falls (town)
Burke's Backpackers 357 Gibson Rd; tel: 2209. Pleasant and popular, with a good swimming pool area, but arguably a touch overpriced. Dorm **D** pp. Rooms **F** dbl.
Club Shoestrings 12 West Dr; tel: 011 800 731. New and very popular hostel, in a large garden with a swimming pool only a few minutes' walk from the town centre. Recommended. Dorm **C** Room **E** dbl.
Council Rest Camp and Caravan Park Tel: 4210. Once the established backpackers' haunt in Victoria Falls, this place has dropped in popularity of late due to the stiff competition of more customised backpacker hostels. Still my first choice, however, not only as an escape from the hostel scene, but also because it is good value. Facilities include hot showers. The cheapest rooms cost fall into the **C** bracket sgl or dbl, while camping costs **A** pp.
Council Rest Camp Bar Cheap draught beer, tenderised steak to barbecue, noisy atmosphere. Contrary to expectations few backpackers drink here.
Explorer's Club Popular backpackers' bar with satellite TV and atmosphere that might briefly transport you to the trendier suburbs of Johannesburg. Good-value pub meals around US$4. Beers overpriced.
Jay's Spar One of the best supermarkets in the country. Good marinaded meat for barbecues – a prospect which makes Victoria Falls look a great deal more affordable.
Nahan's Take-away Good Indian and Western dishes; only place where you can eat for under US$3. Closed evenings.
Pizza Bistro Good pizzas but not cheap. Next to Explorer's Club.

Victoria Falls (out of town)
Zambezi Caravan Park This wonderful council run site lies on the Zambezi, 45 minutes' walk out of town towards Zambezi National Park. Plenty of wildlife passes through, and it's far less crowded than the town site. Firewood. Hot showers. Meals 500m upriver at A Zambezi Lodge. Camping **C** pp. The best place to camp, assuming that you'd rather explore the Zambezi than drink overpriced Zambezi lager at the Explorer's Club!

Zambezi National Park The string of lodges at the national park entrance an hour's walk from town is an excellent option for small groups. All lodges face the Zambezi, and elephant, buffalo, hippo and even lion are common. Equipped kitchen. Fridge. Each lodge has two bedrooms sleeping a maximum of four. US$35 per lodge, but bear in mind there's a 50% discount Monday to Thursday in low season and that no park entrance fee is charged if you stay in a lodge. Must book in advance in Bulawayo or Harare.

Jungle Junction Set on an island upstream of the falls, this is officially in Zambia but most often visited from the Zimbabwe side (and no visa is required since pick-up is from either side of the border). Highly recommended by all who stay there. Self-catering only. Safe swimming area, some wildlife and great birds. Lift from the border US$15 return. Camping **C** pp in own tent or **D** pp in hired tent. To make arrangements ring 832-4127 in Victoria Falls town, or 32-4127 in Livingstone, Zambia.

Hwange National Park

Main Camp At entrance gate, so accessible to hitchers. Restaurant meals US$4–6. Bar. Shop selling frozen meat, tinned and packaged foodstuffs, bread, cheese, cold meat, sodas, beer, maps, firewood and field guides. Game drives with private operators around US$25pp. Guided walks to Sedina Pan viewing platform US$30 per group of up to six people. All chalets and cottages have fridge, cooker and *braai* place. Ablution blocks have hot water. Chalet **C** dbl. Cottage **D** dbl. Camping **B** pp. Booking strongly advised unless you're camping.

Other camps Hwange's other camps aren't easily accessible without private transport. The

---

PASSING TIME AND SPENDING MONEY IN VICTORIA FALLS

Victoria Falls has established itself as the adrenaline-pumping heart of southern Africa's adventure tourism industry. Prospective bungee jumpers and white-water rafters will be in their element here, provided it's of little consequence that nothing comes cheaply. Travellers on a really tight budget will doubtless feel that the best approach they can take to Victoria Falls is to see what they have to see and then move on as quickly as possible.

The one thing you're bound to want to do is see the falls itself. This you can do for free: by lingering in the no-man's land of the bridge from Zambia to Zimbabwe (Zimbabwe's immigration officers will happily let you on to the bridge even if you don't enter Zambia); for a thoroughly reasonable US$3 per day on the Zambian side (a good deal provided that you belong to a nationality that doesn't require a visa to enter Zambia); for US$10 per visit on the Zimbabwe side; or for between US$45 and US$130 from the air, depending on how long you want to stay up there and whether you use a fixed-wing, seaplane, microlight or helicopter.

For those whose interests tend towards wildlife and birds, the Zambezi River upstream of the falls is well worth exploring. To the immediate north of the town, Zambezi Drive follows the river for about 2km passing the Livingstone Statue and 'Big Tree' (an impressive baobab) with a good possibility of encountering elephant, buffalo and hippo, sometimes even lion or leopard – needless to say, this isn't a walk to be taken lightly. There's also plenty of game to be seen by following the road out of town to the Zambezi Campsite and Zambezi National Park entrance gate.

More consistent game viewing, at a day entrance fee of US$5, is to be had within Zambezi National Park. You could see just about anything here, and will almost certainly encounter substantial herds of elephant and buffalo. Entry on foot is forbidden, but several other options exist – canoe safaris for US$50pp,

nicest, *Sinamatella*, stands on a cliff overlooking a waterhole and is frequented by honey badgers. *Robin's Camp* isn't as attractive but is regularly visited by lions and hyenas at night. Both these camps have camping and cottages at the same price as *Main Camp*, as well as a restaurant serving reasonably priced meals and a shop with a limited range of provisions.
Picnic sites An exciting and recommended alternative to staying at the camps, at least if you have a tent and transport, is to camp at one of six fenced picnic sites, most of which are close to water and allow for game viewing at night. *Masuma* and *Mandavu Dams* and *Kennedy Pan* are particularly recommended. Camping **C** pp. Book at one of the camps.

Gwaai River
Lions Den Campsite On the main road close to 'Hwange 80' signpost 10km north of Gwaai River and 10km south of the turn-off to Hwange Main Camp. Firewood. Hot showers. Plenty of wildlife in the area. Nearest meals 10km away at Gwaai River Hotel. Camping **C/D**.

Dete
Wildside Hostel One of a cluster of hostels in a leased block of the former rail workers' accommodation about 100m from the railway station. Game drives to Hwange start at US$20pp for three hours and transfer to Main Camp costs US$5pp; tel: 118-395 to arrange to be met if coming by train. Hot showers. Rooms **C** pp. If there's a problem here, try Paradise or SSET Lodge, both of which are also in the former rail workers' camp.
Railway Club Inexpensive meals, bar and pool table 200m from the hostels.

walking or horseback safaris for the same price, game drives for US$40pp, and even elephant-back safaris for an appropriately mammoth US$110pp. Since vehicles may only enter this reserve for the day, it might even be worth trying for a lift with a private vehicle. Finally, all-you-can-drink sundowner cruises start at US$18, and the focus is alcohol consumption not wildlife viewing – though elephants are commonly seen.

The series of more than 20 rapids below the falls is renowned for its excellent white-water rafting. Itineraries depend to some degree on season, but a day trip costs around US$95 and an overnight trip US$145. Another much publicised activity in Victoria Falls is the world's 'Highest Commercial Bridge Jump', a 110m bungee jump from the bridge below the falls that will set you back an astounding US$90.

Further afield, most tour operators in Victoria Falls can do trips to Hwange National Park and Chobe National Park in neighbouring Botswana. Typical prices range from US$150pp for a day trip to US$450 for a four-day, three-night safari to either reserve.

Major operators in Victoria Falls include Shearwater and Dabula Safaris, both of which have offices in the Parkway Shopping Centre opposite the Council Rest Camp. It's easy to arrange whatever activity appeals on the spot, but do shop around for prices.

A useful starting point for setting up trips in and around Victoria Falls is the recently opened **Backpackers Bazaar** (tel: 2208; email: backpack@ africaonline.co.zw), which is situated on Parkway immediately north of Soper's Arcade. The staff here provide good independent advice on everything from accommodation to day trips, as well as acting as a booking agent for most activities. For travellers newly arrived in Zimbabwe, they also stock a huge range of pamphlets for hostels and budget tours and activities all around the country.

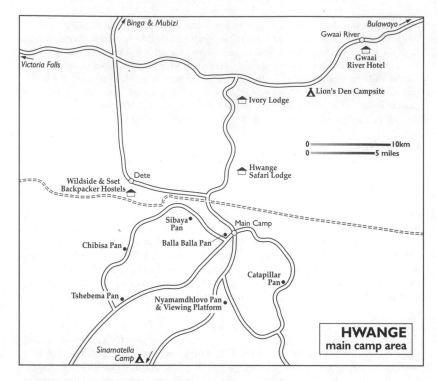

Binga & Mubizi
Bulawayo
Gwaai River
Victoria Falls
Gwaai
River Hotel
Lion's Den Campsite
Ivory Lodge
0 ———— 10km
0 ———— 5 miles
Hwange
Safari Lodge
Dete
Wildside & Sset
Backpacker Hostels
Sibaya
Pan
Main Camp
Chibisa Pan
Balla Balla Pan
Catapillar
Pan
Tshebema Pan
Nyamamdhlovo Pan
& Viewing Platform
Sinamatella
Camp

HWANGE
main camp area

Between Victoria Falls and Kariba

Deka Drum Resort Tel: 181-250524. At confluence of Deka and Zambezi rivers.
Reasonably priced resort of interest to anglers and birders. Access a problem, but you could
ring to see if anything's heading that way. Chalet **C** pp. Camping **A** pp.

Mlibizi

Mlibizi Resort Next to ferry terminal. Nice gardens. Hot showers. *Braai* packs and
firewood. Chalets **F** dbl. Camping **B** pp.

Binga

Binga Rest Camp Former District Commissioner's residence on lakeshore about 4km
from bus stop or ferry jetty. Restaurant and bar. Rooms **E** dbl. Camp **A** pp.
Chilangililo Cooperative About 5km from ferry jetty along Bulawayo road, but only
2km from bus stop. Accommodation in traditional Tonga stilted huts. Dorm **B** pp.

Eastern Zimbabwe

MUTARE AND SURROUNDS

Zimbabwe's fourth largest town, **Mutare**, is the principal town of the eastern
highlands and the springboard for the road and rail corridor to Beira in
Mozambique. Something of a southern African everytown, Mutare is not too big,
not too small, and it has all mod cons while retaining a strong aura of safety and
order. It is indisputably a pretty place, enclosed by a mountainous bowl from
which graciously wooded suburbs slope down to merge imperceptibly with the
grid of roads that forms the compact city centre. Mutare is worth a night – and

should you arrive there from Mozambique after completing the hard slog down the coast from Tanzania, you might never want to leave!

One good reason for prolonging a stay in Mutare is to spend a mellow day on the outskirts of town in the underrated **Cecil Kop Nature Reserve**. The main attraction here is the excellent viewing platform over the Tiger Kloof Dam, from where you can be pretty sure of seeing the reserve's three introduced elephants, particularly at around 16.00 when they're tempted from cover with a few favoured titbits. You might also see Daisy, a female white rhino whose nervous disposition I'm told can be put down to the amorous attentions of the male elephants. Cecil Kop is artificial, without doubt, but does it matter? The atmosphere is such that you'll quickly forget you're anywhere near a city; the entrance fee is nominal by comparison to the national parks; and observant visitors will see plenty of naturally occurring birds and small mammals in the riparian woodland behind the dam. You are, for instance, more likely to see the diminutive blue duiker here than perhaps anywhere in Zimbabwe.

Not much further afield, snucked up to the Mozambican border 20km southeast of Mutare, the misty forests of the **Vumba Mountains** are one of the loveliest parts of the eastern highlands, with plenty to occupy those who enjoy unstructured walks and rambles. The obvious focus of activity is the **Vumba National Botanical Reserves**, centred around an ornamental pool and beautiful landscaped gardens which give way to the natural forest and heath of the region. The recent increase in the entrance fee to US$5 puts off some, but I don't think that anyone with an interest in natural history will resent it – the birding is outstanding, samango monkeys are common, and in any case many travellers seem to be happy enough to spend a similar amount on a cup of coffee and slice of cake at the coffee shop near the entrance. That said, there are plenty of walking opportunities in the area which don't involve paying a fee: several footpaths through the Bunga Forest Reserve branch from the main road back towards Mutare, while the 5km trek from Vumba to the beautiful Leopard Rock Hotel passes through some fantastic scenery.

Access and getting around

Ordinary buses between Harare and Mutare leave hourly in either direction and take about six to seven hours. There are also several express coach services between these cities, and a nine-hour overnight train service which leaves Harare daily at 21.30 and Mutare daily at 21.00. First- and second-class train tickets are around the same price as buses, but coaches are rather more expensive.

Many backpackers visit Vumba on a guided day tour from Mutare; Ann Bruce or one of the other hostel owners will be able to recommend a guide with a vehicle. Otherwise, the best way to get to Vumba, assuming that you'll be staying at Cloud's Castle, is to ask about free pick-up times at the tourist information office in Mutare. Failing that, a few buses pass within 2km of the national park en route to the Leopard Rock Hotel over the weekends. With an early start, you shouldn't have much difficulty finding a lift to Vumba, though you may acquire a few grey hairs trying to get to a good hitching spot. Your best bet is to catch a bus or taxi between the central and Sakubva bus stations and ask to be dropped at the junction with Vumba Road.

A convenient service for backpackers, though double the price of the equivalent bus, the Foxtrot Minibus goes from Harare to Mutare on Monday, Mutare to Chimanimani on Tuesday and Thursday, Chimanimani to Mutare on Wednesday and Friday, and Mutare back to Harare on Saturday. Ring Harare 33-9469 or Mutare 67762 for further details.

Most buses to destinations south of Mutare (Vumba, Chimanimani, Chipinge and Masvingo) leave and arrive at the Sukubva bus terminal about 2km from the

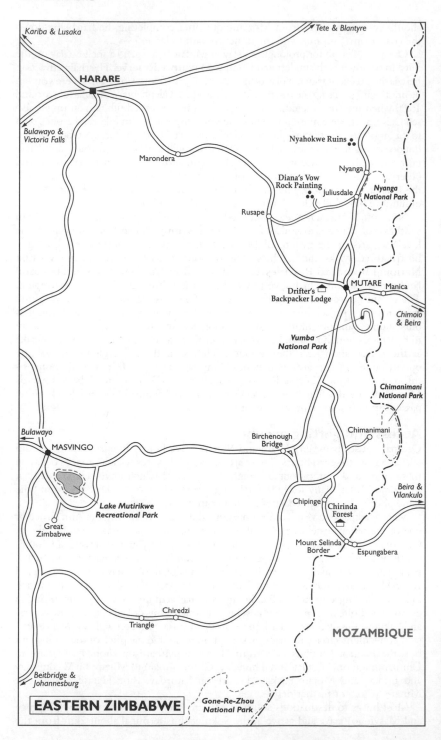

Kariba & Lusaka

Tete & Blantyre

HARARE

Bulawayo &
Victoria Falls

Marondera

Nyahokwe Ruins

Nyanga

Diana's Vow
Rock Painting

Juliusdale

Nyanga
National Park

Rusape

MUTARE Manica

Drifter's
Backpacker Lodge

Chimoio
& Beira

Vumba
National Park

Chimanimani
National Park

Bulawayo

Birchenough
Bridge

Chimanimani

MASVINGO

Lake Mutirikwe
Recreational Park

Chipinge

Beira &
Vilankulo

Chirinda
Forest

Great
Zimbabwe

Mount Selinda
Border

Espungabera

Chiredzi

Triangle

MOZAMBIQUE

Beitbridge &
Johannesburg

EASTERN ZIMBABWE

Gone-Re-Zhou
National Park

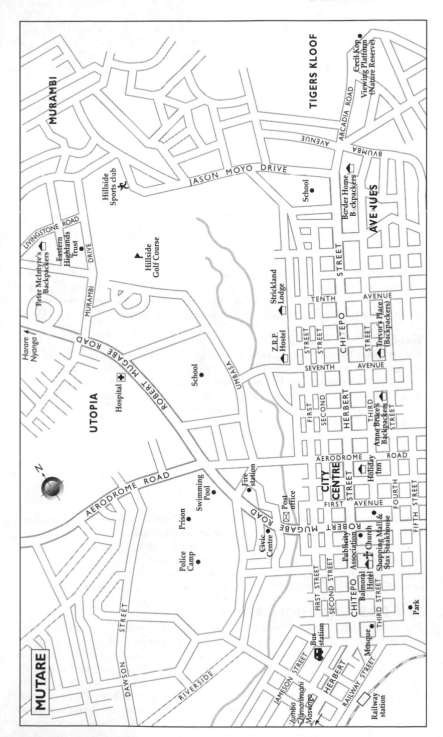

MUTARE

town centre along the Chimanimani road. Local buses and taxis connect this to the main bus terminal on the station end of Herbert Chitepo Avenue.

Where to stay and eat
Mutare
Ann Bruce's 99 Fourth St; tel: 63569. The oldest hostel in Mutare, and still the best. Central location. Inclusive atmosphere. Inexpensive home-cooking. Recommended. Room or dorm **B** pp.
Stax Steakhouse Norwich Union Arcade, Herbert Chitepo St. Reasonably priced and central place for steaks, burgers and the like.
Trevor's Place 119 Fourth St; tel: 67762. Two blocks from Ann Bruce's and a good second choice when her house is full. Rooms and dorm **C** pp.

Near Mutare
Drifters Tel: 62964. Excellent rural hostel, signposted alongside the Harare road 21km from Mutare. Large grounds in acacia woodland. Walking trail into adjacent game reserve (zebra, various antelope and prolific birds). Day trips to Chikanga Hill (rock art, stone ruins). Noticeboard. Meals and bar. Pizzas on Friday night. Camp **A** pp. Dorms and rooms **C** pp.
La Rochelle Estate The beautifully maintained, thickly vegetated grounds of this bizarre colonial relic, situated some 20km from Mutare, will be a treat for plant and bird lovers. To get there from Mutare, catch a bus to Penhalonga and hop off at the signposted turn-off, from where it's a 30-minute walk to the estate. Restaurant. Camp **C** site. Room from **E** pp.

Vumba
Ardroy Guest House Tel: 217121. Near the Hunga Forest about 10km from Vumba. To get there from Mutare catch the 06.00 bus to Mapofu or 11.00 bus to Burma Valley. Good meals. Laundry. Walks. Rooms **D** pp including breakfast.
Ndundu Lodge Tel: 63777; email: ndundulodge@yahoo.com. Formerly called Cloud Castle Lodge, this old thatched house lies in attractive grounds at the turn-off 2km from the national park entrance. Facilities include a lounge with fireplace, bar, music-corner, restaurant and self-catering kitchen. Bikes for hire. Pick-up from the tourist office in Mutare on Monday, Wednesday and Friday at around 12.00 (tel: 64711 for details). Camping **B** pp. Rooms **D/E** sgl/dbl.
Tony's Coffee Shop Next to Ndundu Lodge. Real coffee and sticky cakes in a deliciously kitsch thatched cottage set in a garden of king proteas. Don't think about it if you're trying to save money.
National Park Campsite Great setting in the botanical garden, though the walk is a slog with a backpack (ask for the back route). You must pay the weekly entrance fee to camp – worth it only if you settle in for a few days. Hot showers. Firewood. Camping **B** pp.
Seldomseen Farm About 1km and signposted from the main surfaced road between Mutare and Bvumba. Of particular interest to birdwatchers, as many unusual species are common. Guided bird walks US$5pp. Thatched self-catering cottages **E/F**.

THE EASTERN HIGHLANDS
The vast highland area straddling the Mozambique border defies every expectation of Zimbabwe with its cool moist climate, undulating scenery and sub-Alpine vegetation of rolling heath and lush forest. Traditionally, the main tourist focus in the highlands has tended to be Nyanga, to the north of Mutare, but these days more backpackers seem to head south from Mutare to Chimanimani; even further south, the wonderful Chirinda Forest has only recently been opened up to overnight visits.

The centrepiece of the highlands to the north of Mutare, **Nyanga National Park**, was at one time the personal property of Rhodes, hence its pre-independence name of Rhodes Inyanga. It is probably the most ecologically compromised of Zimbabwe's major reserves, with large areas given over to timber plantations and fruit cultivation. For all that, large areas of natural heath and woodland remain, and I've little ambition to add to that long list of descriptions of Nyanga which overstate its taming by northern hemisphere exotics to the point of tedium. Nyanga is stunningly beautiful, and to my eyes at least its boulder-strewn moonscapes, dominated by immense onion-peel granite domes that dwarf even their more publicised Matobo relations, have a mood and appearance that is unmistakably, defiantly Zimbabwean.

One problem for backpackers exploring the Nyanga area is that its most attractive spots are dispersed and in some cases almost inaccessible without private transport. Obvious bases are Nyangombe Campsite near the park headquarters at Nyanga Dam, or the towns of **Juliusdale** or **Nyanga**. Easy goals on foot are the Nyangombe Falls and ruins of Chawomera Fort. Less accessible, but worth making an effort to see, are the vast stone ruins at Ziwa, one of the most impressive sites of its kind in the country, and the bizarre rock paintings at Diana's Vow, 13km along a dirt road leading from the main road between Rusape and Juliusdale. Also worth looking at is the 762m-high Mtarazi Falls, the second highest in Africa, reached via a wonderful footpath through forest, heath and prehistoric cycad trees. There are many other beauty spots in the area, including Mount Nyangane, at 2,593m Zimbabwe's highest peak. Visitors are urged to make use of the clear, accurate and up-to-date *Nyanga Map and Tourist Guide* – I bought this for less than US$1 in Kingston's Book Shop in Harare and it's on sale locally at the tourist information office in Nyanga village.

More popular than Nyanga, at least with backpackers, is the village of **Chimanimani** (formerly Melsetter). Situated to the south of Mutare near the Mozambican border, at the base of the Chimanimani Mountains and synonymous national park, Chimanimani lies at the centre of some excellent walking country: popular excursions are to the Bridal Veil Falls, in a forested ravine 6km out of town, and the nearby Chimanimani Eland Sanctuary, home to zebra and a variety of antelope and birds including the rare blue swallow and peculiar Gurney's sugarbird. An excellent booklet *Chimanimani Milkmaps Guide*, sold by the tourist office in the village centre for next to nothing, contains maps and descriptions of these and six other day-walks emanating from the village. Chimanimani village is also the springboard for hiking excursions into Chimanimani National Park; see box *Hiking in Chimanimani National Park* on pages 496–7.

Chipinge is the southeastern highlands' largest town and main public transport hub. As things stand, the few backpackers who show their face there have generally strayed unwittingly from the direct road between Chimanimani and Masvingo. But this could change: Chipinge and the Mount Selinda border post are part of the shortest route between the backpacking meccas of Chimanimani and Vilankulo. It might only be a matter of time before improved road conditions and public transport make this route a popular alternative to the Beira Corridor.

Until then, the most convincing reason to pass through Chipinge is to get to **Chirinda Forest Reserve**, Africa's most southerly true rainforest. Botanically, Chirinda is noted for several massive specimens of the red mahogany *Khaya nyasica*, at least one of which is probably 1,000 years old. Even more remarkable are specimens of the strangler fig *Ficus chirindensis*: you can actually stand in the hollow formed by the matted aerial roots and look up for as much as 10m before they connect to support the large crown. Birdwatchers will be in their element in Chirinda, since it's the best place to see the dull but rare *Chirinda apalis* and altogether more striking Swynnerton's robin. Even those with no special interest in birds will enjoy the silvery-cheeked

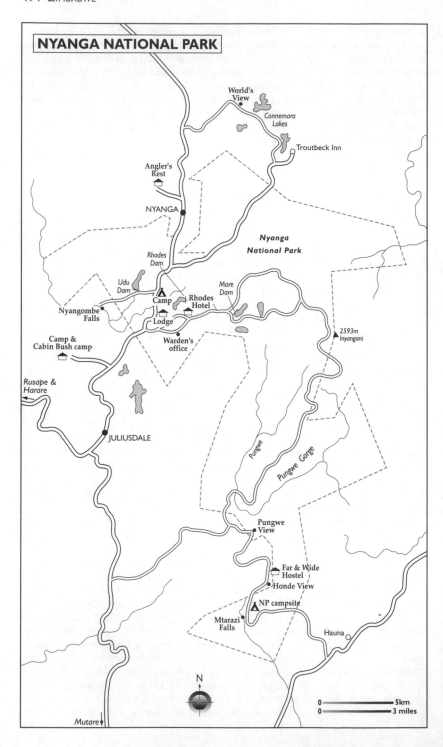

NYANGA NATIONAL PARK

World's View

Connemara Lakes

Troutbeck Inn

Angler's Rest

NYANGA

Nyanga National Park

Rhodes Dam

Udu Dam

Mare Dam

Camp

Rhodes Hotel

Nyangombe Falls

Lodge

2593m Inyangani

Warden's office

Camp & Cabin Bush camp

Rusape & Harare

JULIUSDALE

Pungwe

Pungwe Gorge

Pungwe View

Far & Wide Hostel

Honde View

NP campsite

Mtarazi Falls

Hauna

N

Mutare

0   5km
0   3 miles

hornbills, whose imbecile braying is a characteristic sound of Chirinda, as well as the truly beautiful Livingstone's loerie, a red, green and white resident of the forest canopy. The usual forest mammals are around, even leopards, but you're most likely to see samango monkeys, red squirrels and possibly blue duikers.

Access and getting around

Heading to Nyanga from Harare, the only direct bus service leaves at a rather inconvenient time and place. Far easier to take any Mutare-bound bus as far as Rusape, from where regular buses continue to Nyanga. Heading to Nyanga from Mutare, regular buses leave from the central bus station until midday. All buses to Nyanga stop at Juliusdale and Nyanga village.

Bus transport connects Mutare, Chimanimani, Chipinge and Masvingo and, provided that you don't attempt to hitch along any back routes, you'll have no difficulty getting between any two of these places in a day. At least two buses every morning leave Mutare for Chimanimani, and there are also direct buses between Mutare and Masvingo, some of which appear to make the diversion to

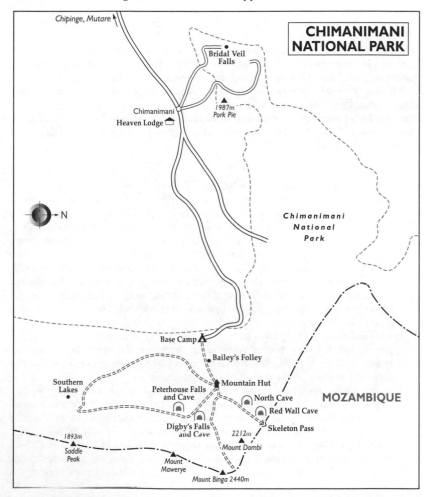

Chimanimani, as do the daily handful of buses that connect Chipinge to Mutare.

From Chipinge, regular buses cover the 30km road to Mount Selinda Mission on the fringe of the Chirinda Forest Reserve. These buses generally stop at Chaka village (where you should stay seated unless you want to buy provisions), before turning around to drive the last 2km to the mission. Two different dirt roads connect the main surfaced road and the rest camp. The first is roughly 3km long and is signposted for the rest camp about halfway between Chaka and the mission. The second, only 2km long, starts close to the mission and is signposted for the Swynnerton Memorial.

Wayfarer Adventures, based in the Harare hostel of the same name (tel: 47-0792), can organise a four-day tour of the eastern highlands for a daily rate of around US$35pp all inclusive. Minimum group size is five.

Where to stay and eat
Nyanga
Angler's Rest 20-minute walk from Nyanga Village. To get there continue on main tar road north of Nyanga for about 1km, then turn left at signpost reading 'Budget Accommodation'. Kitchen. Bicycle hire. Good supermarket in Nyanga village, and cheap, tasty bar meals at the Village Inn. Camping **A** pp. Dorm **C** pp. I'm unable to confirm rumours suggesting that it may have closed.

Far and Wide Hostel Beautifully situated in forest about 3km before Mtarazi Falls. Good base for adventure activities such as river rafting and kayaking (from US$50pp per day), mountain biking (from US$20pp per half-day), abseiling (from US$10pp) and fly fishing. Lift from office next to BP garage in Juliusdale. Accommodation feels overpriced. Camping **C** pp. Cabins **E** pp. Three meals US$17pp.

Mtarazi Falls Campsite Beautiful, little-used National Parks site about 15 minutes' walk from the waterfall. Rather difficult to reach without private transport. Camping **B** pp. Must pay national park entrance fee.

HIKING IN CHIMANIMANI NATIONAL PARK
Notable mostly for their scenic qualities, the Chimanimani Mountains support a variety of interesting sub-Alpine plants such as lobelias, heathers, orchids and aloes, as well as large mammals such as the chacma baboon, blue duiker, klipspringer and even a few leopards. The highest point in the range, Mount Binga, lies right on the Mozambican border at an altitude of 2,437m.

Over the last few years, this range has become one of the most popular hiking areas in Zimbabwe, thanks largely to the efforts of **Heaven Lodge** and the outstanding tourist office in Chimanimani village. The best base for organising a hike into the national park is Heaven Lodge, which runs a Land Rover shuttle along the 19km road to Base Camp daily at 08.00, returning at 17.00, and taking 45 minutes to an hour either way. The round trip costs US$5 per person. It's your choice whether to return on the same day or stay up longer, bearing in mind that the steep ascent to the plateau via Bailey's Folly takes at least two hours and more probably three.

Facilities on the mountain include a campsite with hot showers and firewood at **Base Camp**. On the plateau there is a beautifully situated hut about three hours' walk from Base Camp, but it's very overpriced and most people prefer to sleep in one of the caves designated for this purpose. The most popular caves are those closest to the mountain hut: **Digby's Falls** and **North Cave** (20–30 minutes) and **Peterhouse Cave** (about one hour). Camping or sleeping in a cave costs **B** pp. From Digby's Cave, it's no more than three hours' walk to the

Nyangombe Campsite National parks' site in pine forest. A lovely spot but few backpackers use it due to the weekly national park entrance fee being levied for an overnight stay. Facilities include hot showers and firewood. Meals are available at the nearby Rhodes Hotel. Camping **B** pp.

Chimanimani

Country Club Resthouse About 1km out of town. A sedate alternative to Heaven Lodge. Camping **A** pp. Rooms **D/E**.

Heaven Lodge About 500m from village along road to national park. One of the largest hostels in Zimbabwe, and probably the busiest, this place embodies everything that's conjured up by the phrase 'backpacker hostel'. It's also very friendly and well-run, even if at times you feel less a guest than an inmate. Good meals. Bar with log fire and music. Limited self-catering facilities. Hot showers. Sauna. Lifts to Chimanimani Base Camp. Camping **P** pp. Dorm **R** pp. Room or A-frame chalet **E** dbl.

Chipinge

Chipinge Hotel A run-down dump that would provide a powerful argument against arriving in Chipinge without a tent, even before knowing that the rooms cost in excess of US$30.

Municipal Campsite On a dam 500m from town along the Mount Selinda Road. Slight reservations about security aside, this has acceptable ablution facilities and looks to be a very mellow spot. Good value at **A** for up to two people.

Chirinda Forest

Forestry Commission Rest Camp Tel: 127-224116 or 126-24841. 3km from the tar road near Mount Selinda Mission and signposted. Wonderful setting on site of Swynnerton's old house. Cooking facilities. Hot showers. Accommodation is limited and there's nowhere

peak of Mount Binga, from where there are amazing views – on a clear day you might even see the Indian Ocean!

Hikers should be self-sufficient in food, and they must bring a gas cooker since the collection of firewood is explicitly and rightly forbidden. They should also bring enough warm clothes to cover temperatures dropping to freezing level during winter nights, and a poncho or similar protection against rain and wind. Other essentials are sunscreen and hat, torch, water bottle, sleeping bag and map. A useful annotated sketch map is available from Heaven Lodge or the tourist office in Chimanimani, and most other equipment can be hired from Heaven Lodge.

The usual national park entrance fee of US$5 per day entry or US$10 per week applies to hikers as well as visitors to **Chimanimani Eland Sanctuary** and **Bridal Veils Falls**, both of which lie in separate parts of the national park. Note, however, that we were unable to buy a weekly permit at the entrance to Bridal Veil, which doesn't matter if you're only going there for the day, but means that those who still plan to go up the mountain may end up paying total fees of US$15. In other words, it's best to visit the falls after you've been up the mountain.

Upon entering the national park, you should **advise park officials of your intended route and duration of stay**. If you do not return within 24 hours of this, a search party will be sent out. Do not stray off clear trails, particularly near the Mozambican border where there are still many unexploded landmines.

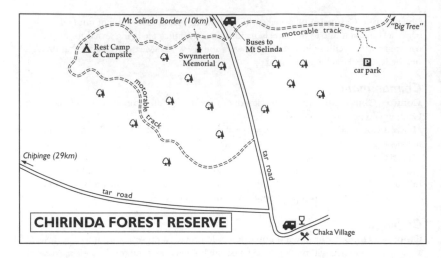

else to stay, so ring to check room availability if you don't have a tent. Nearest supermarkets in Chipinge; fresh bread, meat, vegetables, cold beers and sodas available in Chaka village 4km from the camp. Camping **A** site. Basic double hut **C** pp. Cottage **F** s/c dbl.

MASVINGO AND SURROUNDS

One of Zimbabwe's largest towns, with a population approaching 50,000, **Masvingo** is also an important route focus, lying at the junction of the A4 between Harare and Beitbridge and the A9 from Mutare to Bulawayo. Known as Fort Victoria prior to independence, Masvingo was the site of the first permanent encampment of the Pioneer Column, in August 1890, hence its rather tenuous claim to be the country's oldest town.

The name Masvingo derives from the Shona word for a stone enclosure, a reference to the ruined city of **Great Zimbabwe** which, lying less than 30km away by road, gives Masvingo its sole significance in tourist terms. The extensive stone remains of this medieval city, which supported a population in excess of 10,000 at its peak, lie close behind the Victoria Falls as the country's other absolute must-see. In architectural terms, Great Zimbabwe is the most impressive historical site in southern Africa. Its historical significance as the inland terminus of the Swahili gold trade is also considerable – see box *Exploring Great Zimbabwe* on pages 500–1.

Lying between Masvingo and Great Zimbabwe, **Lake Mutirikwe** (known as Lake Kyle until 1990) was formed in 1961 when a 300m-long wall was constructed to dam the Mutirikwe River. The entire lakeshore falls under the administration of the National Parks, though the southern lakeshore – the part closest to Great Zimbabwe – can be explored on foot and without paying entrance fees. The northern part of the lake shore, reached not from the Great Zimbabwe area but from the Mutare road, supports a fenced game reserve, where a large variety of antelope species can be seen along with white rhino, giraffe and a prolific population of warthogs. The game reserve is ideally explored with a vehicle, but it would also be worth trying to hitch to the rest camp enclosure. This lies on a large, well-wooded peninsula where walking is permitted along several kilometres of roads and there's a good chance of bumping into large mammals (we saw kudu, impala, warthog and hippo).

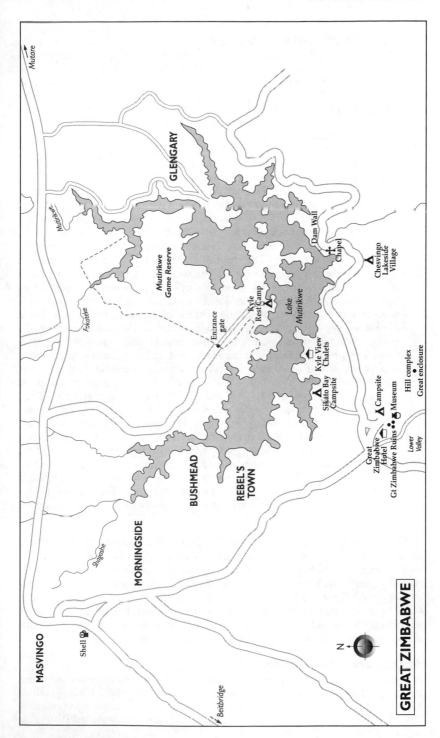

MASVINGO

Shell

Shagashe

MORNINGSIDE

BUSHMEAD

REBEL'S TOWN

Mutare

GLENGARY

Mutirikwe

Fikoteke

Mutirikwe Game Reserve

Entrance gate

Kyle Rest Camp

Lake Mutirikwe

Dam Wall

Chapel

Chesvingo Lakeside Village

Kyle View Chalets

Sikato Bay Campsite

Campsite

Museum

Great Zimbabwe Hotel

Gt Zimbabwe Ruins

Lower Valley

Hill complex

Great enclosure

Beitbridge

N

GREAT ZIMBABWE

EXPLORING GREAT ZIMBABWE

The absence of written records means that most of what is known about Great Zimbabwe is a result of archaeological detective work. Despite this, and notwithstanding the misguided claims of the former government of Rhodesia, the broad outline of Great Zimbabwe's history is well understood. No reputable archaeologist or historian has ever suggested that the ruins were constructed by anybody but indigenous Africans.

Great Zimbabwe was founded by the Karonga precursors of the modern-day Shona people. It would appear that in about AD900 the Karonga started trading ivory and alluvial gold with the East Coast and their leaders founded a stone-walled capital at Mapungubwe near the modern-day border of Zimbabwe and South Africa. This capital fell into disuse in around AD1270, at roughly the same time as the first wall building occurred at Great Zimbabwe.

From around 1270 until 1450, Great Zimbabwe lay at the centre of a vast trading empire, based around the gold and ivory that was exported via the Zambezi to ports such as Sofala near modern-day Beira, where it was traded for imported beads and cloth. The city had a population of between 10,000 and 20,000, and it also lay at the centre of a vast local trading network for goods such as salt, copper, iron, cattle and grain. The city was abandoned in the mid-15th century; evidently this was a rather sudden evacuation and there is no reason to suppose that it was prompted by an attack of any sort. More likely, Great Zimbabwe was evacuated due to a drought, which would have exacerbated the environmental degradation caused by years of overpopulation. The collapse of Great Zimbabwe coincided with a general devolution of Shona political power into several smaller rival empires spread across modern-day Zimbabwe and Mozambique, causing a northward realignment of trade routes which influenced Portuguese settlement patterns on the East African coast after 1500. Great Zimbabwe merits at least one day's exploration. Better, assuming that you are overnighting close to the ruins, split your explorations over an afternoon and the following morning. Most tours start at the **Site Museum**, where a useful booklet and route description can be bought for a nominal price. The centrepiece of the museum is the collection of seven soapstone birds, carved creatures of a mythical design that might well have been based on the bateleur eagle, regarded in Shona tradition to be a messenger of God and the ancestral spirits. The birds are thought by some to be dynastic totems and by others to commemorate specific ancestors.

The only other tourist attraction in the area is the **Mushandike National Park** on the Bulawayo road. A marvellous tract of brachystegia woodland sloping down to the attractive Mushandike Dam, this reserve is a good place to see hippos, crocodiles and a wide variety of terrestrial animals including zebra, kudu, sable antelope, wildebeest and impala. A perfect place for backpackers, you might think, but we were told that walking between the entrance gate and campsite is forbidden, an unfathomable ruling when you consider that there are no potentially threatening large mammals that you could encounter along the way.

Access and getting around

Masvingo is an important transport hub, with regular bus connections to Harare, Beitbridge, Bulawayo, Gweru, Chipinge and Mutare. If you're hitching out of Masvingo, it's easy enough to get to the outskirts of town on foot, and it isn't normally difficult to find a lift, particularly along the main road between Harare and Beitbridge.

The museum contains many other artefacts of aesthetic or historical interest, including a variety of imported goods demonstrating that Great Zimbabwe was not merely of regional importance but that it also served as the terminal of a gold trading network which extended across three continents.

The **Hill Complex**, built around a large granite whaleback, is the oldest part of Great Zimbabwe. Archaeological evidence suggests that it was settled by the Karanga in AD 1075, but it was obviously a rather minor settlement at this time since the first walls and gold objects date to around 200 years later. As was the tradition in Karonga cities, the stone wall enclosure on top of the hill was the royal residence, reachable only via the steep and easily defendable 'Ancient Path' through the boulders. Features of the Hill Complex include thin monoliths, which are thought to have represented horns or spears, and small stone towers representing grain bins – symbols of the royal duty to protect and provide for the people. Six of the seven stone birds displayed in the Site Museum were unearthed in the Eastern Enclosure of the Hill Complex.

Below the hill, numerous small walls emanate from the **Great Enclosure** with its 5m-thick and 11m-high outer wall which consists of roughly 900,000 blocks of stone – enough to build 45 ordinary houses. The Great Enclosure was probably built over the course of a century, and the main outer wall dates to around 1350. The purpose of the Great Enclosure remains open to speculation: it has been argued that it was the religious centre of the complex, or the house of the senior wife, but a more plausible theory, based on the many figurines that have been found there, is that it served as an education and premarital initiation centre for young men. Notable features of the Great Enclosure are the double chevron pattern on the top of the back outer wall and the massive 10m-high conical tower which, according to some theorists, represented a grain bin.

To the east of the Great Enclosure, the **Lower Valley Enclosures** are rather less striking than those already discussed. It is thought that the homesteads in this area were used by the royal harem – which may have numbered up to 1,000 women. The oldest enclosure in this area, thought to have been the home of the senior wife or vahozi, yielded a hoard of historically important artefacts including thousands of glass beads, bowls and dishes from Persia and China, and items made of gold, ivory and iron. A nearby residence is where the soapstone bird represented on the Zimbabwean flag was discovered. Of interest is the reconstructed *daga* hut village in this part of the complex.

There are at least three buses daily to Great Zimbabwe, leaving Masvingo from the Mucheke bus station at around 08.00, 12.00 and 13.30. The buses go all the way to Morgenster Mission, but the drivers will be able to drop you at the turn-off to the Great Zimbabwe Hotel, from where it's about 20 minutes' walk to the campsite. It's also quite easy to hitch to the ruins – the best place to wait is at the signposted turn-off opposite the Shell Garage and Restaurant complex 5km out of town along the Beitbridge road.

The signposted turn-off to Lake Mutirikwe National Park is about 20km from Masvingo along the Mutare road. From the turn-off, it's 19km to the entrance gate and a further 5km to the camp. Walking between the entrance gate and rest camp is forbidden, so it is probably best to wait at the turn-off for a lift. Hitching should be easy enough over weekends, but the reserve is quiet during the week.

The turn-off to Mushandike National Park is signposted '*Mushandike Camping and Caravan Park 11km*' about 25km from Masvingo along the Bulawayo road. In

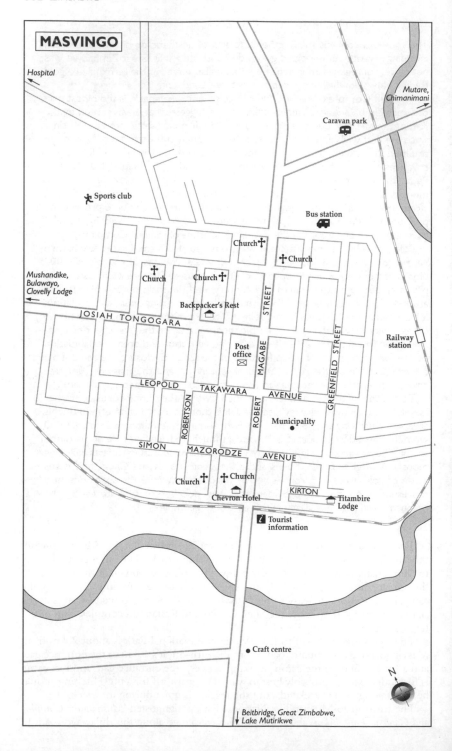

MASVINGO

Hospital

Mutare, Chimanimani

Caravan park

Sports club

Bus station

Mushandike, Bulawayo, Clovelly Lodge

Church

Church

Church

Church

STREET

Backpacker's Rest

Railway station

JOSIAH TONGOGARA

Post office

MAGABE

LEOPOLD

TAKAWARA

AVENUE

GREENFIELD STREET

ROBERTSON

ROBERT

Municipality

SIMON

MAZORODZE

AVENUE

Church

Church

KIRTON

Chevron Hotel

Titambire Lodge

Tourist information

Craft centre

N

Beitbridge, Great Zimbabwe, Lake Mutirikwe

theory, the walk from the main road to the campsite should be a relaxed three-hour stroll, but you may have to exercise considerable powers of persuasion to allow the ranger at the entrance gate (which lies about 2km along this road) to let you enter on foot. Hitching will be difficult unless you connect with a vehicle heading to the conservation college 1km from the campsite.

Where to stay and eat
Masvingo
Backpackers' Rest Dauth Building, cnr Robertson and Josiah Tongogara Av; tel: 65960. The most central accommodation, acceptable but nothing special. Vehicle and mountain bike hire. Dorm **B** pp. Room **D**/**E** including dinner and breakfast.
Clovelly Lodge 25 Glyn Tor Rd; tel: 64751. Well-established hostel in bush setting 6km out of town along the Bulawayo road. Ring for a free pick-up from town. Swimming pool. Horse-riding. Video. Dorm or double room **D** pp (this rate includes a good home-cooked dinner and substantial breakfast).
Hippo Lodge Tel/fax: 63659 or cell 011 208043; email: hippolodge@usa.net; web: www.hippolodge.com. Highly rated but rather pricey new lodge spread over a large well-wooded out-of-town plot near the lake. Features include a free guide to Great Zimbabwe, 15 minutes' free email access at an internet café in town, and a daily booze cruise for US$5. Kitchen, bar and restaurant. Free pick-up from the internet café in the Old Mutual Building on the Beitbridge Road. Rooms **E** pp.
Masvingo Caravan Park On the city outskirts along the Mutare road. Attractive setting on Shagashe River and adequate facilities. Camping **A** pp.
Sundowners Tel: 62718; email: sunbird@mvo.samara.co.zw. Popular new family-run hostel signposted from the Beitbridge Road near the Flamboyant Hotel. Camping **B** pp. Dorm **C** pp.

Great Zimbabwe and Lake Mutirikwe south shore
Chesvingo Lakeside Village Community-run project in an attractive bush setting on the south side of the main tar road about 5km past Kyle View chalets. Four-hour guided cave walk US$5pp and six-hour village tour US$7.50pp. Campsite with hot showers **A** pp. Ring Masvingo 7157 for more details.
Kyle View Chalets Attractive resort on wooded stretch of the lake shore, reached by continuing along main tar road for 7km past Great Zimbabwe. Swimming pool. Tennis court. Restaurant. Shop selling provisions. Camping **B** pp. Chalets **F** pp.
National Museums Rest Camp Campsite Large well-wooded site 200m from the ruins. Firewood for sale. Hot showers. Meals and bar less than 1km away at Zimbabwe Ruins Hotel. Camping **A** pp. There are also now rooms here for **D** pp.
Sikato Bay Campsite National Parks campsite on a thickly wooded slope next to the lake. About an hour's walk from the tar road along a dirt road signposted 300m past the entrance to Great Zimbabwe. Quiet spot, plenty of birds and hippos. Firewood. Hot showers. No entrance fee charged. Camping **B** pp.

Lake Mutirikwe National Park
Kyle Rest Camp On a fenced peninsula within the game reserve. Good views and some game to be seen. Campsite on hill, has hot showers, firewood, covered dining area with electric lights. Lodges have stove, fridge, cooking utensils, braai area, hot bath, sitting room. Camping **B** pp. Lodges **F** triple.

Mushandike National Park
National Parks Campsite Attractive but rather run-down site on lakeshore. Plenty of hippos, antelope and birds. Hot showers. Firewood. No food. Camping **B** pp.

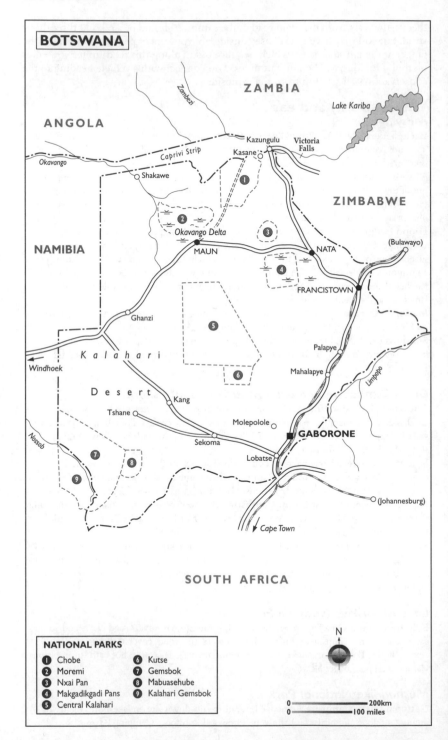

BOTSWANA

ZAMBIA

Zambezi

Lake Kariba

ANGOLA

Kazungulu

Victoria Falls

Kasane

Okavango

Caprivi Strip

Shakawe

ZIMBABWE

2

Okavango Delta

1

3

NAMIBIA

MAUN

NATA

(Bulawayo)

4

FRANCISTOWN

Ghanzi

5

K a l a h a r i

Palapye

Windhoek

Mahalapye

6

Limpopo

D e s e r t

Kang

Tshane

Molepolole

GABORONE

Nossob

Sekoma

7

8

Lobatse

9

(Johannesburg)

Cape Town

SOUTH AFRICA

N

NATIONAL PARKS

1	Chobe	**6**	Kutse
2	Moremi	**7**	Gemsbok
3	Nxai Pan	**8**	Mabuasehube
4	Makgadikgadi Pans	**9**	Kalahari Gemsbok
5	Central Kalahari		

0 ————— 200km
0 ————— 100 miles

Botswana
Philip Briggs and Chris McIntyre

This vast, thinly populated country is one of Africa's few economic success stories, in large part due to the immense mineral wealth that lies beneath its sandy soils. Botswana essentially consists of a flat, practically uninhabitable semi-desert known as the Kalahari, and is visited by relatively few backpackers due to the difficulty of getting around and widespread lack of affordable accommodation. It is included in this guide largely for the Okavango Swamps, a uniquely vast inland delta that is within practical reach of backpackers, and for the sake of travellers heading between Zimbabwe or Zambia and Namibia, who will probably pass through Botswana. Short as this chapter might be, it does provide thorough practical coverage for all parts of the country that can realistically be visited without private transport.

PRACTICAL INFORMATION
Accommodation
There is at least one affordable campsite anywhere that's likely to be visited by backpackers. Expect to pay an average of around US$5pp per night to camp. Other budget accommodation is virtually non-existent, and without a tent you can expect to average out at US$25 nightly.

Crime and safety
Crime against tourists is relatively unusual in Botswana – this is one African country where being eaten by lions or trampled by elephants is genuinely a greater concern than car accidents and armed theft. If you're camping in the Delta area or Chobe, be sensible!

Entrance fees
Non-resident national park fees in Botswana were recently increased to the equivalent of approximately US$25 per person per day for privately organised

FACTS AND FIGURES
Area: 581,730km² (21st in Africa)
Capital: Gaborone
Largest towns: Gaborone, Francistown, Selibi-Phikwe, Lobatse
Population: 1,350,000
Official languages: English, Setswana
Currency: Pula
Head of State: President Quett Masire

tours and around US$14 per person per day for guided tours by a local company. Unlike in East Africa, these fees are charged per calendar day rather than per 24 hours; in other words should you enter the park on one afternoon and leave the next morning you will be charged fees for two days. Camping in the parks now costs US$6 per person per night.

Entry requirements

Visas are not required by nationals of South Africa, the USA and most Commonwealth and European Union countries, who will have a 30-day entry permit stamped in their passport at the border. Other nationals should enquire about visas in advance – there are embassies in most of the countries covered in this guide.

Food and drink

Just about anything you could say about eating and drinking in Zimbabwe would apply equally well to Botswana.

Health

Standards of hygiene are comparable with those in Zimbabwe or Namibia. Malaria is rife in the Okavango and Chobe areas, but scarce elsewhere except after rain.

Money

The current rate of exchange is around US$1=Botswana pula 3.60. You can change foreign currency into pula at any bank. The South African rand is readily changed with pula, though you may find that you lose out at borders where a one-to-one rate tends to apply.

Public holidays

In addition to New Year's Day, the Easter weekend, Christmas Day and Boxing Day, Botswana recognises the third Monday and Tuesday of July as President's Day and September 30 and October 1 as Botswana Day.

AROUND THE COUNTRY

The part of Botswana that's most accessible to backpackers, the eastern corridor, is also the least interesting. The custom-built national capital **Gaborone**, little more than a village at independence in 1966, is today a charmless and expensive low-rise city which most travellers do their best to avoid. Less avoidable, because it lies on the main route between Zimbabwe and the Okavango Swamps, **Francistown** is Botswana's second largest city, a scaled-down version of the capital with a similar lack of tourist attractions. The other significant town on the eastern corridor is Nata, a dusty, formless little place notable mostly because it's situated on the junction with the road to Maun and the Okavango.

At the very north of the eastern corridor, **Kazangulu** is the name of a tiny settlement as well as the ferry which carries vehicles and passengers across the Chobe River into neighbouring Zambia. Only 10km to the west of Kazangulu, also on the elephant-infested banks of the Chobe, **Kasane** is a somewhat more substantial settlement from where you can organise game drives or sundowner cruises into **Chobe National Park**. One of Africa's great game reserves, but difficult to explore without your own 4x4, Chobe is an 11,700km^2 tract of pristine bush protecting the full range of southern Africa's large predators as well as the localised puku antelope and a migratory elephant population numbering up to 70,000.

Botswana's most popular wilderness area, accessible to backpackers at a price from the small town of **Maun**, is the 12,000km² **Okavango Swamp**. Essentially an inland delta, formed by the Kavango River as it is swallowed by the sands of the Kalahari, this vast swampland is noted for its peaceful, almost other-worldly atmosphere, not to say the prolific wildlife concentrated around **Moremi Game Reserve** and the astounding variety of birds. The best way to explore the delta is with a *mokoro*, a type of dugout canoe which local polers navigate through waters infested with crocs and hippos. Unfortunately, *mokoro* trips based out of camps in the heart of the delta are now prohibitively expensive for most backpackers, though less expensive trips can be arranged out of Maun itself. Another option, even more affordable, is to head out to the little-visited **Western Okavango** (see box *Western Okavango* on page 510).

The vast Kalahari Desert is generally inaccessible to backpackers, though the recently completed surfacing of the Trans-Kalahari Highway between Gaborone and Walvis Bay in Namibia will have an enormous impact on the region. It may also mean that a lot more travellers get to see **Ghanzi**, the self-proclaimed 'Capital of the Kalahari', a magnificently isolated and idiosyncratic small town which owes its existence to the plentiful water in the surrounding limestone ridges.

Getting around

A reasonably regular and efficient network of buses and minibuses runs along the main tar road through the eastern corridor, from Kazangulu in the north to Ramatlabana on the South African border, connecting Nata, Francistown, Gaborone and Lobatse. Hitching on this road is also possible: you may wait a while for a lift, but when something stops the odds are it's going a long way.

Useful public transport elsewhere is restricted to the daily Mahube Express bus along the surfaced road between Nata and Maun, and at least one bus daily from Francistown to Bulawayo via the Plumtree border. The daily overnight train service between Gaborone and Francistown is slow but comfortable, and a second-class sleeper costs US$25pp.

More useful than any of the above to most backpackers is the Route 49 minibus, similar in concept to the South Africa Baz Bus, and offering at least two services weekly in either direction connecting Maun, Gaborone and Francistown to each other, as well as to Johannesburg and Cape Town in South Africa and to Victoria Falls township in Zimbabwe. To give an idea of prices, a one-way ticket from Victoria Falls to Maun costs US$50. For full schedules and prices, ask at any backpackers' hostel in the relevant towns, or contact Route 49's head office in Cape Town directly; tel: +27 21 426 5593; fax: +27 21 423 0411; email: zimcaper@mweb.co.za.

Another shuttle service useful to backpackers connects Maun to Windhoek in Namibia via the recently surfaced Trans-Kalahari Highway. This door-to-door service is run by Audi Camp in Maun (see below for contact details).

Where to stay and eat
Gaborone and surrounds

Citi Camp Legolo Rd (next to the Bull and Bush Pub); tel/fax: 311912; email: citicamp@info.bw. Long overdue budget option in central Gaborone, close to several bars and restaurants, and with cooking facilities and *braai* area on site. Trips into the Kalahari and other destinations in Botswana can be arranged through agents in Gaborone. Camping **C** pp. Rooms **F** dbl.

Lion Park Tel: 37-2711. About 20km out of town along the Lobatse road. Any bus to Lobatse will drop you at the turn-off from where it's a 3km hitch or walk. Facilities include a swimming pool, restaurant and hot showers. Tents for hire. Camping **C** pp

Mokolodi Nature Reserve Tel: 35-3959. About 15km out of town along the Lobatse road. Good wildlife viewing. Cheap guided game walks. Restaurant. Call to check availability of dorms. Dorm **D** pp. Expensive chalets.

Francistown

Marang Hotel Tel: 21-3991. About 5km out of town past the golf course. Ring from town centre to arrange pick-up. Attractive acacia-dotted campsite with hot showers and affordable restaurant. Camping **C** pp. Thatched chalets around US$70 dbl.

Nata

Nata Lodge Tel: 61-1210. About 10km from town on the Francistown road. Friendly, pleasant site with good facilities and restaurant. Camping **B** pp. Standing tents work out at **D** pp for a group of four.

Kasane, Kazangulu and Chobe National Park

Chobe Safari Lodge Tel: 65-0336. On the outskirts of town bordering Chobe National Park. Popular busy campsite regularly visited by elephants. Sundowner cruises into the national park cost around US$12 to lodge residents and campers (plus entrance fee). Also does game drives for a similar price, and you'll pay only one set of park fees if you do a drive in the morning and cruise in the evening. Camping **C** pp. Rooms start at US$30/35.

Kubu Lodge Tel: 65-0312. In Kazangulu about 3km from ferry and 10km from Kasane. Not as convenient or good for wildlife as Chobe Safari Lodge. Camping **C** pp. Very expensive chalets.

Savuti Public Camp A basic site in the heart of the park, known for its uncomfortably close encounters with lions, elephants and hyenas. Ablutions long ago fell victim to thirsty elephants. Accessible in 4x4 only. Camping **C** pp (plus daily park entrance).

Serondela Public Campsite Quiet riverfront site 10km inside the entrance gate, reachable only in a 4WD, and teeming with game including aggressive, light-fingered baboons and elephants that go into tin-opener mode if they smell fruit in a car boot. Facilities limited to toilets and cold showers. Camping **C** pp (plus daily park entrance).

Thebe River President Av, plot 706; tel/fax: 650314; email: thebe@info.bw. Large new campsite in Kasane, aimed largely at backpackers. Bar and restaurant, game drives, boat cruises, micro-lighting. Camping **C** pp. Standing tents available.

Nata-Maun Road

Planet Baobab Tel: 212277; fax: 203575; email: unchart@info.bw; web: www.unchartedafrica.com. This promising new hostel is situated near to Gweta village, about 20km from the Makgadigadi Pans, and the management plans to set up fly-camping in Nxai and Makgadikgadi. Accommodation is in traditional huts, and meals and drinks are available. S/c huts **F** pp. Basic huts **D** pp. Camping **B** pp.

Maun

Audi Camp Tel: 660599/663005; fax: 660581; email: audicamp@info.bw; web: www.audi-delta.com. Situated 10km outside Maun on the road to Moremi Game Reserve on the banks of the Thamalakane River. Bar and restaurant, *braai* stands and firewood, laundry service, swimming pool, travel advice. Free transfer from Audi to Maun at 17.00 Monday to Friday; 12.00 Saturday. Drive-in *mokoro* trips: one-day US$60, two-day US$100, three-day US$130 per person. Mobile budget safaris to Moremi, Chobe, Kalahari and Pans, inclusive of food, equipment, park fees and vehicle and guide from US$75 per person per day. Runs a shuttle service between Maun and Windhoek (Namibia) US$50 per person one-way. Camping **B** pp. Bedded tents **F** dbl. Dome tents **D** dbl.

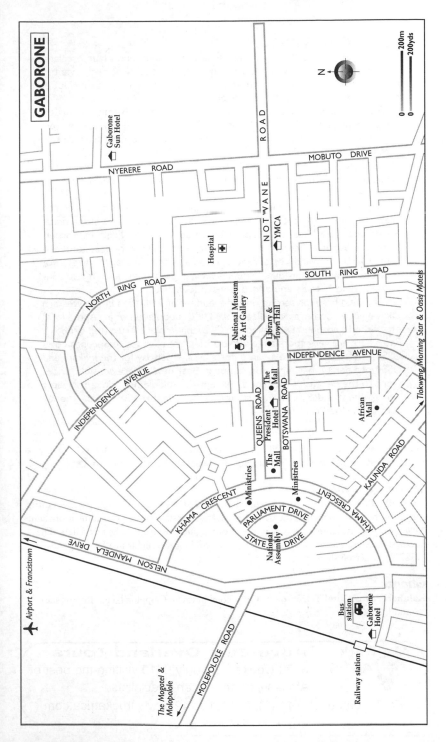

GABORONE

N

0 200m
0 200yds

Gaborone Sun Hotel

NYERERE ROAD

MOBUTO DRIVE

NOTWANE ROAD

Hospital

YMCA

SOUTH RING ROAD

NORTH RING ROAD

National Museum & Art Gallery

Library & Town Hall

INDEPENDENCE AVENUE

INDEPENDENCE AVENUE

The Mall

QUEENS ROAD

President Hotel

BOTSWANA ROAD

African Mall

The Mall

Ministries

Ministries

KHAMA CRESCENT

PARLIAMENT DRIVE

KAUNDA ROAD

KHAMA CRESCENT

STATE DRIVE

National Assembly

NELSON MANDELA DRIVE

Airport & Francistown

MOLEPOLOLE ROAD

The Mogotel & Molopolole

Bus station

Gaborone Hotel

Railway station

Tlokweng/Morning Star & Oasis Motels

WESTERN OKAVANGO

As prices for visiting the Okavango swamp in and around Maun escalate, adventurous travellers who are carrying camping equipment might want to look at exploring the more remote (and more affordable western side) of the swamp, also known as the Panhandle.

The main town in this area is Shakawe, close to the Namibian border, and easily hitched to from the Caprivi Strip, or from Maun by bus (at least two buses daily taking about eight hours). The most popular place to stay here is Drotsky's Cabins (tel: 675035; fax: 675043), situated on the banks of the Okavango about 10km south of town and 4km east of the main road. Camping costs **C** per person while rooms start at **F** per person. Facilities include a restauarnt, *braai* area and hot showers.

Unless you are coming from Namibia, there is no reason to go as far as Shakawe, since Sepuna, the springboard for exploring this part of the delta, lies on the main Maun road about 60km south of the Namibia border. Here, the Sepupa Swamp Stop is geared specifically to budget campers, with a large pub and restaurant overlooking the Okavango River, hot showers, secluded individual camping sites, and boats for hire. It also runs a variety of local tours and affordable sundowner trips.

The best base for setting up independent *mokoro* trips in the western Okavango is Seronga, a village of 3,000 people who in April 1998 established a co-operative called the Okavango Poler's Trust (tel: 676861). Rates here are very good: a *mokoro* transfer from Sepupa to Seronga costs US$6, while trips into the swamp costs US$24 per day for the *mokoro* and US$4 per person per night for camping. Best of all, these sensible prices work to the benefit of everybody except the middlemen, since travellers who get here under there own steam can be sure that 100% of the money goes to the local community.

Sedia Hotel Tel: 660177. About 5km from the centre of Maun, phone for a cheap transfer. Restaurant, bar and firewood. Hot showers. Camping **B** pp. Dorm **C** pp.

Okavango Swamps

Oddball's Palm Island Luxury Lodge Tel: 66-0220. Until recently, this excellent camp was the only budget option in the delta, but increased restrictions on the number of clients have pushed it into a price category well out of the range of many budget travellers. The cheapest package available is a four-night stay (including two nights in a fly camp) at US$720 per person sharing.

Ghanzi

Kalahari Arms Hotel Tel: 59-6298. Only hotel in town. Camping **B** pp. Rooms start at around US$45.

Namibia

17

Philip Briggs and Chris McIntyre

Like Botswana, Namibia is an arid and sparsely populated country, noted for its great mineral wealth and suited more to self-drive trips than to budget-conscious independent travellers. In recent years, the tendency has developed for backpackers to visit Namibia in a hired car or on an organised minibus trip out of Cape Town, and certainly it is difficult to see the full spectrum of this country's bizarre sandscapes, weird vegetation, isolated inselbergs and wonderful rock art, not to mention the outstanding Etosha National Park, using public transport. However, unlike Botswana, Namibia does boast a reasonable number of attractions accessible to backpackers, for instance the quaint German towns of Lüderitz and Swakopmund, or the immense flocks of flamingoes and waders at Walvis Bay. Even if the most fascinating parts of Namibia lie along far-flung 4x4 trails, you're unlikely to meet somebody who's backpacked through this country and not been deeply impressed by the unique beauty of its vast and desolate landscapes.

BACKGROUND INFORMATION
Geography and climate

The Namib Desert, which follows the 1,600km Atlantic coastal belt, is one of the driest places on earth. Inland, a deeply incised escarpment rises to an altitude of 2,000m before giving way to the mid-altitude plateau that merges with the Kalahari Desert of Botswana. The highest mountain in Namibia is the 2,573m Brandberg in the northwest. Apart from the Fish River, which has carved a spectacular canyon near the South African border, and the Orange River into which it flows. Namibia's only large rivers are the Cunene, Kavango, Linyanti and Zambezi in the far north. There are no substantial natural lakes in the country: the largest body of water is the artificial Hardap Dam near Mariental.

FACTS AND FIGURES
Area: 824,290km² (15th in Africa)
Capital: Windhoek
Largest towns: Windhoek, Keetmanshoop, Tsumeb, Swakopmund, Walvis Bay
Population: 2 million
Official language: English
Other languages: German, Afrikaans, Ovambo, Herero, Nama
Currency: Namibia dollar
Head of State: President Sam Nujoma

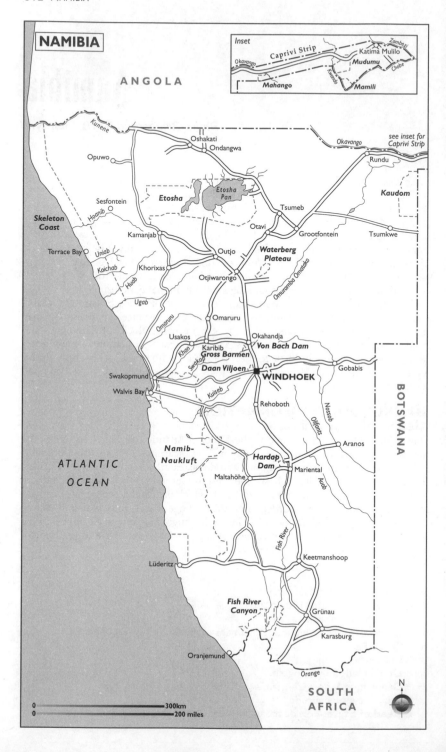

NAMIBIA

ANGOLA

Inset

Caprivi Strip

Okavango

Katima Mulilo

Zambezi

Mudumu

Mahango

Kwando

Chobe

Mamili

Kunene

Oshakati

Ondangwa

Okavango

see inset for
Caprivi Strip

Opuwo

Rundu

Kaudom

Sesfontein

Etosha

*Etosha
Pan*

Tsumeb

Hoanib

**Skeleton
Coast**

Kamanjab

Otavi

Grootfontein

Tsumkwe

Terrace Bay

Uniab

Khorixas

Outjo

**Waterberg
Plateau**

Koichab

Huab

Otjiwarongo

Omuramba Omatako

Ugab

Omaruru

Omaruru

Usakos

Okahandja

Karibib

Gross Barmen

Von Bach Dam

Khan

Swakop

Daan Viljoen

Gobabis

Swakopmund

■ **WINDHOEK**

Walvis Bay

Kuiseb

BOTSWANA

**ATLANTIC
OCEAN**

Rehoboth

**Namib-
Naukluft**

Aranos

Nossob

Olifants

**Hardap
Dam**

Mariental

Maltahöhe

Auob

Fish River

Keetmanshoop

Lüderitz

**Fish River
Canyon**

Grünau

Karasburg

Oranjemund

Orange

**SOUTH
AFRICA**

N

0   300km

0   200 miles

The climate is hot and dry with much colder night temperatures. Summer is from December to March, which is also when the country receives most of the average annual rainfall of below 250mm. The coast is frequently blanketed in overnight fog which persists into the morning.

History

Namibia is one of the most thinly populated countries in Africa as a result of its inhospitable climate. Probably for the same reason, it is also the last country in Africa to support a substantial number of Khoisan-speaking people, namely the Nama and Damara who together comprise some 10% of the population. Most Namibians are, however, Bantu-speakers, with the most significant groups being the Ovambo, Kavango and Herero.

The Portuguese navigator Diogo Cão became the first European to land on Namibian soil when he erected a cross at Cape Cross in 1496, but the harsh coast discouraged European settlement in the centuries that followed. From the mid-18th century onwards, hunters from the Cape Colony started to cross the Orange River into what is now Namibia. The first Europeans to settle in the area were missionaries such as Heinrich Schmelen of the London Missionary Society, who set up stall at Bethanie in 1814. The Rhenish missionaries who settled the region after 1840 founded many of Namibia's modern settlements.

Germany's colonial interest in the region was fuelled by Albert Lüderitz, who in 1883 bought a vast area of farmland around what is now the port of Lüderitz. Germany annexed the coastal strip in 1884, and the borders of German South West Africa were formally agreed with Britain and Portugal in the late 1890s. Britain retained its indirect ownership of the Walvis Bay enclave, part of the Cape Colony since 1793. In 1904, the mutually antagonistic Nama and Herero teamed up against colonial rule. Germany asserted its authority with genocidal brutality, claiming the lives of three-quarters of the country's Herero population, and many Nana people too.

After the outbreak of World War I, South Africa captured German South West Africa for the Allies and took over its governance, a situation that was formalised with a League of Nations mandate in 1921. In 1949, South Africa's newly elected Nationalist Party introduced an apartheid-style homeland policy on South West Africa, overstepping its mandate much to the chagrin of the UN, which nevertheless had difficulty imposing its view on the situation.

In 1966, the recently formed Swapo, a liberation movement founded by Sam Nujoma, appealed to the UN to take action against South Africa. When the UN failed to act, Swapo declared guerrilla war; within a year its leadership was either in jail or else, like Nujoma, forced into exile. In 1972, the UN finally declared the South African occupation of South West Africa to be illegal, but to little avail. After independence in Angola, which resulted in 15–20,000 Cuban troops being deployed to that country, South West Africa became an *ipso facto* military base from which South Africa waged its border war against Angola and Cuba. The decade of South African military occupation had a huge economic impact on the country as a whole and the north in particular.

As the Cold War drew to a close, Cuba, Angola, South Africa and Swapo finally huddled around the negotiating table. Cuba and South Africa signed a bilateral agreement to withdraw their troops from South West Africa and Angola. A democratic election took place in late 1989, and on March 21 1990 South West Africa became independent Namibia, with Sam Nujoma at the helm after his return from a three-decade period of exile. Namibia is widely regarded to be one of independent Africa's success stories, and Nujoma and Swapo were returned to power in the 1994 election with a 68% majority.

PRACTICAL INFORMATION
Accommodation

Travellers who want to cut costs should carry camping equipment, though there is now hostel accommodation in Windhoek, Lüderitz and Swakopmund. Elsewhere, you'll mostly stay in the excellent camping and chalet complexes run by Namibia Tourism and various municipalities – expect to pay US$5–8 per tent, or US$20 for the cheapest room or chalet. Accommodation and campsites in national parks and game and recreational reserves can be booked through the Ministry of Environment and Tourism in Windhoek. Tel: 23-6975.

Crime and safety

In Windhoek, pickpockets represent the major threat during daylight hours, but muggers move into the city centre at night. Some of the townships around Windhoek have a reputation for violent crime. Elsewhere in the country, the threat to life and limb is minimal, but property left unattended at urban campsites may well be gone when you return.

Entrance fees

A daily entrance fee of roughly US$2.25 is charged at all national parks and game and recreational reserves except for Etosha where the daily fee is around US$4.50.

Entry requirements

Visas are no longer required by nationals of the USA, all neighbouring countries, and most Commonwealth, European Union and Scandinavian countries, who will normally be issued with a 90-day temporary residence permit on arrival, extendable upon application at the Department of Home Affairs in Windhoek. Visas cannot be issued at land borders.

Food and drink

Supermarkets and restaurants are comparable with those in South Africa and Zimbabwe, though there is a far stronger German influence and various fish and crayfish dishes play an important part in coastal cuisine. South African wine is served in most restaurants and excellent local lager beer is widely available. Most backpackers will find themselves eating at their hostels as often as not, while campers will find the dry warm climate conducive to barbecues. As with South Africa and Zimbabwe, I have not included details of restaurants in this section, since most major towns have a good selection suitable for all budgets – if you're not comfortable following your nose, then backpacker hostels, campsite staff and tourist information offices will be able to make current recommendations.

Getting around
By road

Minibus and bus services cover the B1 (the main north–south road through Namibia) as well as sideroads to Swakopmund, Lüderitz and Katima Mulilo. The luxury Intercape Mainliner coaches (tel: 061 227847) connect Cape Town to Windhoek and points in-between four times per week (roughly US$50 one way), as well as offering thrice-weekly departures in either direction between Johannesburg and Windhoek, and twice-weekly departures in either direction between Windhoek and Victoria Falls via the Caprivi Strip. Except for the few trunk roads mentioned above, public transport is non-existent and hitching ranges from the slow to the impossible.

By rail

An overnight train service from Windhoek to Swakopmund and Walvis Bay runs six times a week in either direction. Trains from Windhoek to Tsumeb stop at all major towns along the way and leave three times a week in either direction. Along the B1 south to Keetmanshoop, an overnight service leaves Windhoek at 18.30 in either direction six times weekly. Trains are a comfortable way of getting around, and rarely crowded during the week when tickets for seated compartments work out at around US$1.50 per 100km and sleepers at around US$4 per 100km. Trains are much busier and ticket prices double on Friday, Saturday and Sunday.

Organised tour and car hire

There is a strong case for getting together a group to hire a car (some travellers buy a car on arrival and sell it before they leave) or for visiting the country as part of an organised tour. Four- to six-week tours through Namibia, Botswana and Zimbabwe generally start in Victoria Falls. Outside Namibia, the best place to organise a tour is Cape Town or Victoria Falls, where any backpacker hostel will be able to put you in touch with companies which run two-week camping trips for around US$35 per person per day inclusive. In the country, the Chameleon and Cardboard Box hostels in Windhoek run well-organised, inexpensive safaris to places like Etosha National Park, and they also rent vehicles at good rates.

If you decide to drive yourself around Namibia, do buy a travel guide with greater detail for out-of-the-way places, road conditions and other factors that assume importance on a self-drive safari. Chris McIntyre's *Namibia: The Bradt Travel Guide* is recommended.

Health

Namibia has a dry and largely disease-free climate. Malaria is a major threat on watercourses in the far north. The extreme sunshine experienced in much of Namibia demands that you pay extra attention to covering up. The high daytime temperatures and scarcity of ground water also make it essential to carry plenty of drinking water when you go for a walk or sit hitching.

Maps

A useful free map of the whole country is available from any Namibia Tourism office inside or outside the country. If you can't find a commercially printed map of a specific region, you'll find a survey map on sale at the Department of Surveys in Windhoek, just on the right of the main post office on Independence Avenue.

Money

The Namibia dollar replaced the South African rand as the currency at the time of independence, but it remains linked to the rand and interchangeable within Namibia. Banking hours are from 08.00 to 13.00 Monday to Saturday and 14.30 to 17.00 Monday to Friday.

Post and telecommunications

International post goes reasonably quickly provided that you post it from Windhoek. This is also the most reliable and quickest place to have your poste restante sent to. Post restante is free, but you will need some proof of identity. International phone services are efficient by African standards. The international telephone code is +264. Important regional dialling codes are:

Grootfontein	06731	Mariental	0661	Rundu	0671
Henties Bay	064	Okahandja	0621	Swakopmund	064
Karasburg	06342	Omaruru	064	Usakos	066
Katima Mulilo	0677	Otavi	06742	Walvis Bay	064
Keetmanshoop	0631	Otjiwarongo	0651	Windhoek	061
Lüderitz	06331	Outjo	0654		
Maltehohe	0663	Rehoboth	0627		

Public holidays

In addition to the variable Easter weekend and Ascension Day 40 days after that, the following days are celebrated as public holidays in Namibia:

1 January	New Year's Day	26 August	Heroes' Day
21 March	Independence Day	10 December	Human Rights Day
1 May	Workers' Day	25 December	Christmas Day
4 May	Cassinga Day	26 December	Boxing Day
25 May	Africa Day		

Tourist information offices

Namibia Tourism stocks an annually updated pamphlet of budget accommodation and campsites countrywide. Their phone number in Windhoek is 284-2411. They also have offices in South Africa (011 331 6281 or 021 419 3190), Germany (06172 406650) and Britain (020 7636 2924).

Northern Namibia

THE B8: THROUGH THE CAPRIVI STRIP

The Caprivi Strip is a 400km-long eastern appendage to the main body of Namibia, originally a part of British Bechuanaland (Botswana) but ceded to German South West Africa in 1900, so that Germany would have access to the Zambezi. The strip was named after the German Chancellor, Count von Caprivi, and a trading post called Schukmannsburg was established on the Zambezi. On September 22 1914, this small German outpost fell to what was probably the first successful Allied occupation of German territory in World War I. During the late 1970s and 1980s, the Caprivi Strip was in effect a South African buffer zone, the launching pad for the apartheid government's regular military forays into Angola. Today, the area is known for several remote game reserves, generally not accessible without a private 4x4. For backpackers, the road through the Caprivi Strip is the only viable route into Namibia from Botswana, Zambia or Zimbabwe.

For travellers entering Namibia, the gateway town to the Caprivi Strip is **Katima Mulilo**, which lies on the southern bank of the Zambezi on the border with Zambia. Founded by Britain in 1935 to replace Shuckmannsburg as the local capital, Katima Mulilo is a substantial town with good facilities and an attractive location. The stretch of the Zambezi on which it lies is teeming with hippos and crocs, and visited on occasion by elephants. It's easy enough to arrange to explore this part of the Zambezi by boat; rather more difficult, unless you have your own 4x4 vehicle, to get yourself to the game-rich Mamili and Mudumu National Park.

Once one of the most challenging trunk routes in southern Africa, the 500km B8 between Katima Mulilo and Rundu should have been surfaced in its entirety by the time you read this. Doubtless, the road will still often be covered in fresh elephant droppings, particularly on the stretch that passes through the largely undeveloped **Caprivi Game Reserve**. Within easy walking distance of the B8,

HITCHING THROUGH THE KAOKOVELD

The Kaokoveld, the name most often used to describe remote northwest of Namibia, is regarded as one of Africa's last true wilderness areas, sparsely populated by Himba pastoralists, and known for its wealth of rock art and as the home of the so-called 'desert elephants'. The region is not often visited by backpackers, due to a lack of public transport, but, as the following edited extracts from an email written by Italian reader Enrico Ferrari demonstrate, there is nothing to stop the truly determined and adventurous from giving it a go:

If you don't have a car and want to enjoy the environment, you have to walk. We tried to hitchhike, and found a lift from Ruacana to the Cunene River Lodge and then a lift towards Epupa. We decided to jump out after a while to enjoy walking, and for the next four days we kept on walking, because no cars passed, at all. It is a long way, I think about 110km from the Cunene River Lodge to Epupa, with nothing in the middle but Himba people. You can really enjoy the environment, drink the Cunene water if you have some disinfectant, but you have to carry your own backpack, filled with food. You must be careful of crocodiles when you wash in the Cunene. I just washed near the river's edge, without entering the water, but anyway I was a little afraid. I did not see any crocodiles, but I heard that there are plenty around.

With a tent, you should have no problem finding somewhere cheap to stay. In Ruacana I stayed at NamPower, where pitching a tent cost N$15 per day and rooms cost N$150/250 sgl/dbl; there is a restaurant, bathroom and *braai*, but no communal kitchen. Between Ruacana and Epupa Falls, about 50km from Ruacana, we stayed at Cunene River Lodge. Here, you can buy food, cook it on a *braai* or stove. There is a bar and restaurant, and camping cost N$30 per person. At Epupa, there are four camping spots: we slept in Epupa Camp which has cold showers and a *braai* and costs N$15 per person. There is just one shop in Epupa, where it is possible to find basic food, and a place where it is possible to buy hot bread, baked in a rough manner, but good and safe (because it is hot).

At Opuwo, we slept for free at the police station: we heard about this from other travellers and it seems to be customary, though facilities are limited to a toilet. Between Kamanjab (50km) and Outjo (110km) we slept in a hunting lodge owned by a nice woman, who gave us a generous discount for a room with kitchen and water as hitchhikers. This is the address: Jvan Vuuren, Ongaango Safaris, P/Bag 2670, Outjo, Namibia, 9000. You can buy basic food there.

Popa Falls is the one place where you might consider breaking this trip, not so much for the rather unspectacular set of rapids on the Kavango River as for the adjacent rest camp, a lushly vegetated haven which supports a large variety of birds as well as riverine animals such as the crocodile and water monitor.

The long drive west through the Caprivi Strip terminates at **Rundu**, a pleasant small town which effectively forms the bridge between Caprivi and the rest of Namibia. Rundu has an attractive situation on the Kavango River, and a strong Portuguese flavour has leaked across the border from Angola.

Access and getting around

The twice-weekly Intercape Coach which connects Victoria Falls to Windhoek stops at Kasane in Botswana as well as Katima Mulilo and Rundu (see *Zimbabwe to Namibia* on page 77). Local buses also cover the 60km road between Ngoma Bridge on the Botswana border and Katima Mulilo, leaving when they are full. A company called Egoli operates the only bus service between Katima Mulilo and Rundu, continuing on to Windhoek. Buses in either direction leave a few times every week from the local Shell Garage, which is also the best place to make enquiries about timetables and reservations.

Hitching between Katima Mulilo and Rundu is feasible enough. Admittedly, private vehicles are few and far between, but whatever does stop is almost certain to be going the whole way. If you want to stop at Popa Falls, the rest camp lies about 5km south of the B8 and the turn-off is signposted immediately to the west of the bridge across the Kavango River.

Where to stay and eat
Katima Mulilo
Guinea Fowl Inn Tel: 0677 3349. Seedy and run down, but great riverside location and very central and affordable. Rooms with net and fan **D**/**E**.
Hippo Lodge Tel: 067352 685. Good place to camp, though it's quite some walk out of town, so ring to ask about a lift. Rooms from US$30/45. Camping **B** pp.

Popa Falls
Popa Falls Rest Camp Great location next to the rapids. Camping **E** per site. Four-bed chalets US$30 per unit.

Rundu
Casa Mourisca Quality Portuguese restaurant in town centre.
Ngandu Safari Lodge Tel: 067 255910. New and central lodge with the most affordable rooms in Rundu area starting at **D**/**F**.
Sarasungu Lodge Tel: 067 255161. The longest-standing, best and most accessible of a few lodges lining the river outside town. A few kilometres from town centre; ring to arrange a lift. Good food. Mountain bike and canoe hire. Rooms US$50/60. Camping **B** pp.

THE B8 AND B1: FROM RUNDU TOWARDS WINDHOEK
Roughly 250km south of Rundu, the main road to Windhoek passes through **Grootfontein**, the most easterly of a trio of towns comprising the so-called 'Golden Triangle'. Grootfontein and the other two towns in the triangle, **Tsumeb** and **Otavi**, all lie about 50km apart from each other in the fertile, mineral-rich northern rim of the Namibian plateau. There is plenty to be seen in this area, notably Lake Otjikoto nestled in its sinkhole, Dragon's Breath Cave wherein lies the world's largest subterranean lake, and the massive Hoba Meteorite, but none of these sights are very accessible to backpackers. The B8 terminates at Otavi to meet the B1, the north–south road that connects Ondangwa near Angola to Noordoewer on the South African border.

Lying on the B1 about 100km south of Otavi, **Otjiwarongo** is an attractive town, founded as a staging post on the railway to Tsumeb, but these days of interest to travellers as the most important route focus in northern Namibia. To the east of Otjiwarango, the **Waterberg Plateau National Park** protects a large sandstone plateau which provides sanctuary to several large mammal species including giraffe, kudu, eland, roan antelope, sable, brown hyena, leopard, cheetah and the endangered white and black rhino and African wild dog. A major attraction of this park, at least for backpackers, is that exploration on foot is encouraged. Many trails emanate from the main camp, and because private vehicles aren't allowed you can easily arrange affordable game drives. The excellent four-day hiking trails (one accompanied and one not) must both be booked some time in advance which makes them less convenient for those on a flexible schedule.

To the northwest of Otjiwarango, reached along the B1 via the Golden Triangle towns of Otavi and Tsumeb, or else along a shorter route through **Outjo**, lies the game reserve which many regard to be the finest in southern Africa. The 22,270km² **Etosha National Park** is centred around the vast Etosha Pan, a remnant of a much larger lake, now dry most of the year round, but which partially fills in late summer depending on the amount of rain that's fallen. Flat, and largely consisting of open savannah, this national park's main attraction is the series of natural waterholes which line the southern shore of the pan, attracting large numbers of game in the dry season, not to say keen wildlife photographers from all over southern Africa. Visitors to the park can be pretty certain of seeing elephant, giraffe, springbok, roan antelope, red hartebeest, gemsbok, blue wildebeest, kudu, the highly localised black-faced impala, zebra and black rhino. It's also an excellent park for predators, with substantial populations of lion, leopard, cheetah, spotted and brown hyena, black-backed jackal and bat-eared fox.

Lying about 200km south of Otjiwarango, **Okahandja** is another important route focus, where the B1 meets the B2 running east to the Atlantic ports of Swakopmund and Walvis Bay. Okhandja is notable as the site of a cruel massacre in 1850, when more than 700 Herero people were killed by the Nama leader Jonker Afrikaner. Of interest in the town centre is the Rhenish church, completed in 1876, and the graveyard where several Herero leaders have been buried, as was Jonker Afrikaner in 1861. Local attractions include the **Gross Barmen Hot Springs**, a popular spa resort built around a dam about 25km southwest of town, and the **Von Bach Dam Resort**, a peaceful small reserve which lies 10km or so southeast of town, where it supports limited stocks of game including a reintroduced herd of Hartmann's mountain zebra, as well as offering some good fishing, walking and birding possibilities.

Access and getting around
Bus services connect the towns on the B8 between Rundu and Otavi, and the B1 between Tsumeb and Windhoek. South of Tsumeb and Grootfontein; these are supplemented by informal minibus services that whizz between towns. There are also four trains weekly in either direction between Windhoek and Tsumeb or Grootfontein, stopping at all major towns en route. Hitching along the B1 gets easier the closer you are to Windhoek.

To reach Etosha independently, your only practical option is to hitch. This is forbidden within the park, and the number of passengers is recorded when a vehicle enters the park and checked when it leaves. In effect, this means that you can only hitch into Etosha if your lift is prepared to take you out again! Hitching is also the best way to reach the Waterberg, Gross Barmen or the Von Bach Resort, though you could walk to the last of these with an earlyish start.

Where to stay and eat
Grootfontein
Lala Panzi Camp 6km south of Grootfontein, on the left coming from Otavi; tel/fax: 067 243648. Camping **A** pp. Rented camper **D** dbl. Rooms **F** pp. There is a restaurant.
Municipal Restcamp Tel: 067 313100. Small, spruce camp with good ablutions. Take precautions against theft. Camping **B** per site. Four-bed bungalow **F** per unit.
Roy's Camp On the B8 about 150km north of Grootfontein. Bush setting with plenty of small game. Rooms **F** pp. Camping **B** pp.

Tsumeb
Hikers Haven Tel: 067 221051. Run-down but clean backpackers' hostel behind the Makalani Hotel. Dorm or private room **C** pp. Bedding available.

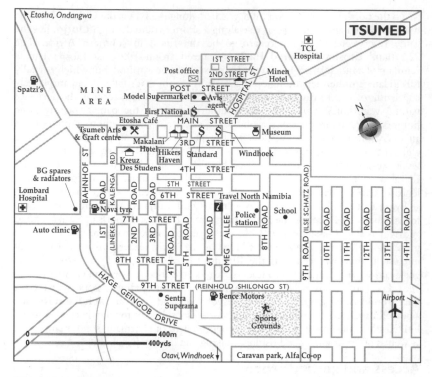

Punyu Tourist Park Tel: 067 22-0604. Adequate former municipal site 1km from town centre. Camping **B** site.

Tamboti Nature Park Tel: 067 220140 (may have closed so ring before heading this way), 22km from town. Walking trails. Swimming pool. Camping **C/D**.

Travel North Namibia Backpackers Allee St; tel: 067 220728; email: travelnn@tsumeb.nam.lia.net. Central tourist information office and hostel. Dorms **C** pp. Rooms **F** pp.

Otavi

Municipal Rest Camp Small, basic site. Camping **B** pp. Bungalows **E/F**.

Otjiwarongo

Municipal Campsite Tel: 0651 312231. Reasonable and very cheap campsite with clean ablutions next to a crocodile farm. Camping **A** pp.

Bed & Breakfast 21 Industria Av; tel: 0651 302616. Clean and pleasant rooms. **E** pp.

Waterberg National Park

Bernabe de la Bat Rest Camp Beautifully landscaped on slopes of Waterberg near site of former Rhenish Mission. Shop. Restaurant. Swimming pool. Day trails. Inexpensive game drives. Camping **D** per site. Triple chalets around US$40 per unit. Four-night unguided hiking trail **D** per person (minimum three people) including camping fees.

Outjo

Backpackers Lodge Tel: 067 313470. New lodge signposted from the museum. Dorm **C** pp.

Camp Setenghi Tel: 0654 313445; email: setenghi@iafrica.com.na. A few kilometres out of town along the C63. Excellent guided and unguided nature walks among striking rock formations. Drinks and firewood for sale. Rooms from US$50 pp. Camping in very well-equipped sites **B** pp.

Etosha National Park

Halali Camp Newest, smallest, and quietest of the three camps, situated about halfway between the other two. Restaurant. Shop. Swimming pool. Camping **F** per site. Rooms from US$45 dbl.

Namutoni Camp Largest camp, near to eastern gate. Based around a *Beau Geste*-style fort, a former police post, overlooking the palm-lined eastern edge of the pan. Restaurant. Shop selling tinned provisions as well as meat, bread, cheese and drinks. Swimming pool. Camping **F** per site. Rooms from US$32 dbl.

Okaukuejo Camp Oldest of Etosha's camps, near to the southerly Andersson Gate, and the camp at which you'd be most happy to be stranded as it overlooks a floodlit waterhole which routinely receives nocturnal visits from elephant, jackal, black rhino and lion. Restaurant. Shop. Swimming pool. Camping **F** per site. Bungalow from US$37 dbl.

Okahandja and surrounds

Gross Barmen Hot Springs Tel: 0621 501457. Swimming pool fed by springs. Shop. Restaurant. Camping **E** per site. Room or bungalow **E** dbl. Must book in advance.

Von Bach Dam Tel: 0621 501091. On edge of reservoir, good birdwatching and fishing. Camping **E** per site. Hut **F** dbl. Must book in advance.

Central and southern Namibia
WINDHOEK

Namibia's pleasant capital spreads across a wide valley between heavily bushed hills. With its picturesque German architecture and many pavement cafés, Windhoek's rather low-rise city centre is more European in appearance than any other similarly sized town in this part of Africa, an illusion that is undermined somewhat by the unmistakeably African curio kiosks and basket sellers lining the streets. Lying at an altitude of almost 1,800m in a region that rarely receives more than 350mm of rain in a year, Windhoek has a comfortable, healthy climate – and in case you're wondering, the name Windhoek, which translates from Afrikaans as Windy Corner, is not a climatic reference but a bastardisation of Winterhoek, the name of the South African farm on which the Nama leader Jonker Afrikaner was born.

Windhoek was an important Nama settlement in the early nineteenth century, but no tangible indications of this remain. The site was settled by Germans in the 1890s. Several interesting old buildings can still be seen in the city centre, concentrated around the intersection of Peter Muller Street and Robert Mugabe Avenue. The oldest buildings in town are the Alte Feste Fort (now the State Museum), construction of which started in 1890, and Ludwig von Estorff's house, built in 1891 as a military canteen and now a reference library. Also of interest are the original Lutheran Church (built 1896), the newer Lutheran Church (built 1907–10), the Hauptkasse (built 1898–99), and the former Officer's Mess (built 1906–7) which was restored in 1987.

Situated only 25km out of Windhoek, the **Daan Viljoen Game Reserve** offers an excellent network of day walking possibilities through the undulating Khomas Hochland Hills. The reserve supports a variety of large mammals including Hartmann's mountain zebra, blue wildebeest, red hartebeest, gemsbok, kudu, eland, klipspringer and baboon. It is also a good place to see a number of birds whose range

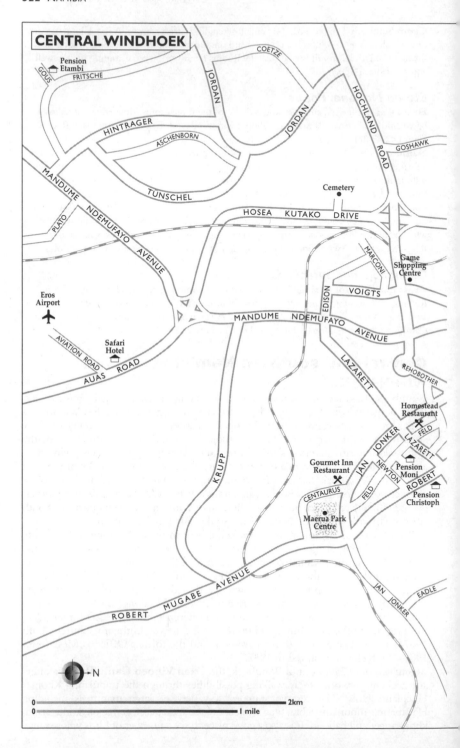

CENTRAL WINDHOEK

GOUS

Pension Etambi

FRITSCHE

COETZE

JORDAN

JORDAN

HOCHLAND ROAD

HINTRAGER

ASCHENBORN

GOSHAWK

TÜNSCHEL

Cemetery

MANDUME NDEMUFAYO AVENUE

PLATO

HOSEA KUTAKO DRIVE

MARCONI

Game Shopping Centre

Eros Airport

EDISON

VOIGTS

MANDUME NDEMUFAYO AVENUE

AVIATION ROAD

Safari Hotel

AUAS ROAD

LAZARETT

REHOBOTHER

Homestead Restaurant

FELD

LAZARETT

KRUPP

Gourmet Inn Restaurant

JONKER

JAN

NEWTON

Pension Moni

FELD

ROBERT

Pension Christoph

CENTAURUS

Maerua Park Centre

ROBERT MUGABE AVENUE

JAN JONKER

EADLE

N

0 —————————————— 2km
0 —————————————— 1 mile

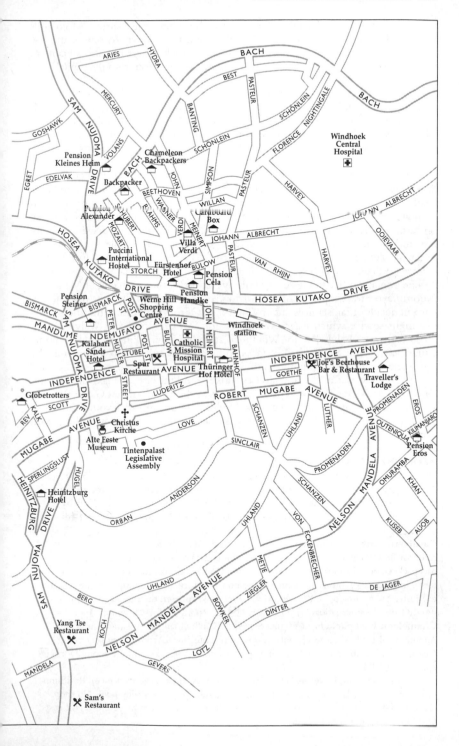

is largely restricted to Namibia, for instance the white-tailed shrike, Monteiro's hornbill, Ruppell's parrot, rosy-faced lovebird and rockrunner. As one of the few reserves in Namibia that is not only accessible to backpackers but also suitable to their needs, Daan Viljoen is a highly recommended excursion from the capital.

Access and getting around

A variety of bus and minibus services connect Windhoek to all towns along the B1, as well as to the coastal towns of Swakopmund and Walvis Bay. Minibuses work on a fill-up-and-go basis, and they leave from several points around the city depending on which direction they're heading in. If you're heading to destinations along the B1 south, or to Swakopmund or Walvis Bay, then your minibus will leave Windhoek from the stretch of Mandume Ndomufayo Street that lies between the Wernhill Shopping Mall and the main railway station. Less convenient, minibuses heading north along the B1 leave from the rather disreputable Katutura market, and it might be better to wait for a near-full minibus at the Independence Avenue on-ramp to the Western Bypass. Operators of more comfortable fixed-departure bus and coach services tend to come and go, but you'll be able to get current timetable details and make reservations at the Tourist Rendezvous Information Centre on Peter Muller Street. Hitching in and out of the capital is also quite easy.

The booking office in the central railway station on the north end of Mandume Ndomufayo Street, open until 16.00 Monday to Friday, is the best place to get current details of rail services out of Windhoek. Of most interest to travellers is the overnight service which leaves Windhoek for Swakopmund and Walvis Bay at 20.00 daily and Walvis Bay for Windhoek at 18.30 daily, taking around 11 hours either way. There are also rail services connecting Windhoek to Tsumeb in the north and Keetmanshoop in the south.

A reasonably useful network of buses runs around the city, and taxis are safe and cheap. There is, however, no public transport to the Daan Viljoen Game Reserve, so you'll have to hitch, which might take a while. Before you stick your thumb out, you'll first need to walk or catch a taxi some distance out of town along Sam Nujoma Drive.

Where to stay

BackPacker 5 Greig St; tel: 25-9485; cellphone: 081 124 4383 (day) or 081 125 9485 (eve). A fairly new hostel ten minutes from city centre. Swimming pool, sauna. Free pick-up from city. One- and two-day safaris to Sossusvlei US$75pp per night (leave Saturday). Two-night trips to Etosha cost US$160 and leave Tuesday. Dorm **B** pp. Room **E** dbl. Camp **B** pp.

Cardboard Box 15 Johann Albrecht St; tel: 22-8994; fax: 24-5587; email: cardboardbox@bigfoot.com; web: www.ahj.addr.com. Well-established and popular backpackers' hostel about 1km from city centre. Good noticeboard, booking agent for tours, internet café, and useful source of local travel information. Cheap car rental. Safaris to Etosha. Swimming pool. Kitchen. Meals. Free pick up from the bus station, shuttle service from the international airport. Dorm **C** pp. Room **D** dbl. Camping **B** pp.

Chameleon Backpackers 22 Wagner St; tel: 24-7668; email: chamnam@namib.com. Another well-established and popular hostel 15 minutes' walk from the city centre. Organises safaris and car hire. Swimming pool, kitchen, breakfast and TV room. Dorm **C** pp. Room **E** dbl.

Daan Viljoen Game Reserve Tel: 226806 (all visitors must ring in advance). Restcamp nicely situated on lakeshore. Day trails. Fishing. Restaurant. Swimming pool. No shop. Camping **E** per site. Chalets from US$40 dbl. The two-day, 32km Sweetthorn trail costs US$10pp including use of a basic overnight hut.

Puccini International Hostel 4 Puccini St; tel/fax: 23-6355; email: puccinis@mweb.com.na. Ten minutes' walk from the city centre. Swimming pool, sauna, kitchen. Free pick-up service from city. Tours and car hire arranged. Dorm **C** pp. Room **E** dbl. Light breakfast included.

Rivendell Guest House 40 Beethoven St; tel 061 25 0006; fax: 061 25 0010; email: rivendell@toothfairy.com; web: www.rivendell-namibia.com. Small, smart but affordable guesthouse under the same management as the Cardboard Box and only two minutes' walk away. Use of all facilities at the Cardboard Box. Free pick-up from bus station. Rooms **E** dbl or **F** s/c dbl.

Where to eat

Most backpackers eat or cook for themselves at one of the hostels. If you're in the city centre at lunch time, then have a snack or cup of coffee at the **Central Café** or **Schneider Café** which face each other in the Trip Arcade. There are also several proper restaurants in the city centre, most of which are open in the evening.

Practical listings

Airlines Air Namibia (22-9630); Air France (22-7688); Lufthansa (22-6662); SAA (23-7670); Zambia Airways (22-3623).

Books and newspapers There are branches of the South African news agency, CNA, in the Kalahari Sands and Wernhill shopping malls. There's also a book exchange on the corner of Garten and Tal Street.

Camping equipment A good range can be hired from Camping Hire Namibia at 12 Louis Raymond Street (tel/fax: 252995).

Embassies Angola (22-7535); Botswana (22-1942); Canada (22-2941); France (22-9021); Germany (22-9217); South Africa (tel: 22-9765); UK (22-3022); USA (22-1601); Zambia (23-7610); Zimbabwe (22-8134).

Foreign exchange Any of the several banks in the city centre can exchange foreign currency cash and travellers' cheques into Namibia dollars. There is no black market in Windhoek and outside banking hours your only options are the hotels or the international airport.

Immigration office The Ministry of Home Affairs in the Cohen Building (cnr Independence Avenue and Kasino Street) is open from 08.00 to 13.00 Monday to Friday.

Maps The Department of Surveys map sales office is in the Ministry of Justice on Independence Avenue, next to the main post office.

Ministry of Environment and Tourism Cnr John Meinart and Moltke St; tel: 23-6975. Until recently the Department of Nature Conservation, the MET office has information on all game reserves and national parks, and it is the only place to make advance bookings for accommodation and camping in all of Namibia's state conservation areas.

Post and telephone Collect your poste restante at the post office on Independence Avenue next to Verwoerd Park. International phone calls can be made at Telecommunications, practically next door to the post office.

Tourist information office The local tourist office in Post Street Mall and Namibia Tourist Bureau office on Independence Avenue are both worth a visit; the latter in particular since you can normally pick up a useful booklet listing most budget accommodation in Namibia and current prices. The Tourist Rendezvous Information Centre in Peter Muller Street (tel: 22-1225) serves as a booking agency for most bus and coach operators in Namibia.

THE B2: WINDHOEK TO WALVIS BAY

The twin ports of Swakopmund and Walvis Bay lie 35km apart on the Atlantic coast directly west of Windhoek, at a distance of roughly 300km from the capital as the crow flies, but 400km away by rail or along the surfaced B2 which branches from the B1 at Okahandja. Most travellers take a bus or train directly along the B2 as far as Swakopmund, but there are a couple of potentially interesting stops along the way.

First up, **Karabib** is a small town that's off-limits to backpackers due to a lack of affordable accommodation, though it does lie at the junction of the B2 and the C33, the short cut to Otjiwarango. The only substantial town along the C33, lying about 60km north of Karabib, is **Omaruru**, a green and rather picturesque settlement named after the river on which it lies. The town's small museum is housed in a former Rhenish mission building, built in 1872, but the most famous local landmark is Franke's Tower, erected in honour of the German Captain who relieved Omaruru after it had been captured by the Herero in 1904. Natural-history lovers should spend some time in the well-located hide in the Omaruru Bird Sanctuary 4km from town along the Otjiwarango road.

Back on the B2, only 30km past Karabib, **Usakos** is an important railway junction which also suffers a lack of affordable rooms, but it is worth stopping there to visit the **Amieb Ranch** in the Erongo Hills about 20km north of town. Founded as a Rhenish Mission in 1864, Amieb Ranch is well-known for its rock formations but most of all for the outstanding rock paintings in Philip Cave, made famous by Abbé Breuil's book of the same name, which was published in the 1950s and tendered the risible hypothesis that these and several other Namibian paintings were the work of European immigrants.

Swakopmund is the more attractive of the two ports on the B2: arriving from the desert, the pretty streets lined with palm trees and eye-catching colonial buildings give it the feel of a temperate oasis. Swakopmund owes its attempted development as a port to the fact that the far superior natural harbour of Walvis Bay ended up as an isolated British possession in the regional carve-up of 1884. Sadly for Germany, Swakopmund made for a lousy harbour. Since World War I, it's tended to serve as a holiday resort, while Walvis Bay has got on with the serious business of exporting and importing goods. In addition to many early 20th-century buildings, notably the railway station dating to 1901, Swakopmund boasts a good museum, a new aquarium and a pleasant if somewhat chilly swimming beach protected by a sandbank known as 'The Mole'.

Only 35km south of Swakopmund, **Walvis Bay**'s name dates to the era of Portuguese exploration when it was named the *Golfo da Baleia*, meaning 'Gulf of Whales'. The bay was frequented by American whalers from 1784, and claimed by the Dutch in 1793. Two years later, along with the Cape Colony, it was occupied by Britain. Of interest in the town centre is the old Rhenish Mission, built in 1880 and used until 1966. The wetland complex around Walvis Bay, which includes the sewage works and the lagoon, is among the most important avian habitats in southern Africa. Casual visitors are likely to be impressed by the flocks of thousands of greater and lesser flamingoes, which respectively account for 3% and 2% of the global population, while serious twitchers will be on the lookout for the localised Damara tern, chestnut-banded plover and any number of Palaearctic migrants that are rarely seen elsewhere in southern Africa.

To the north of Swakopmund, the so-called **Skeleton Coast**, one of the most bleak and remote stretches of tropical coast in the world, really isn't very accessible to backpackers. You might be lucky with a lift to **Henties Bay**, 80km north of Swakopmund, and possibly even to the remarkable breeding colony of up to 250,000

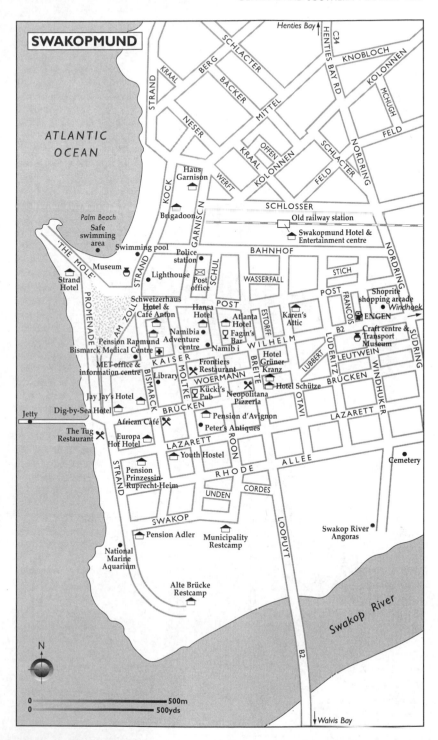

SWAKOPMUND

Henties Bay

ATLANTIC OCEAN

SCHLACTER
BERG
BACKER
KRAAL
STRAND
NESER
KNOBLOCH
KOLONNEN
MCHUGH
HENTIES BAY RD
C34
MITTEL
OFFEN
KRAAL
KOLONNEN
WERFT
SCHLACTER
FELD
NORDRING
FELD

Haus Garnison

GARNISCN
KOCK

Brigadoon

SCHLOSSER
Old railway station
Swakopmund Hotel & Entertainment centre

Palm Beach
Safe swimming area
Swimming pool
Police station
Museum
Lighthouse
Post office

BAHNHOF
WASSERFALL
STICH
POST
FRANCOIS
Shoprite shopping arcade
Windhoek
ENGEN
NORDRING

'THE MOLE'
PROMENADE
Strand Hotel
STRAND
AM ZOLL

Schweizerhaus Hotel & Café Anton
Hansa Hotel
POST
Atlanta Hotel
Fagin's Bar
ESTORFF
Karen's Attic
Namibia Adventure centre
Namib i
WILHELM
Hotel Grüner Kranz
B2
Craft centre & Transport Museum
Pension Rapmund
Bismarck Medical Centre
MET office & information centre
KAISER
BISMARCK
MOLTKE
Library
Frontiers Restaurant
WOERMANN
BREITE
Hotel Schütze
LÜBBERT
LÜDERITZ
LEUTWEIN
BRÜCKEN
WINDHUKER
SÜDRING

Jay Jay's Hotel
Jetty
Dig-by-Sea Hotel
BRÜCKEN
Kückl's Pub
Neopolitana Pizzeria
OTAVI
LAZARETT

The Tug Restaurant
African Café
Peter's Antiques
Pension d'Avignon
Europa Hof Hotel
LAZARETT
ROON
ALLEE
Cemetery
Youth Hostel
Pension Prinzessin-Ruprecht-Heim
RHODE
CORDES
UNDEN
STRAND
SWAKOP
LOOPUYT
Swakop River Angoras

Pension Adler
Municipality Restcamp
National Marine Aquarium
Alte Brücke Restcamp

Swakop River

N

0 ____ 500m
0 ____ 500yds

B2
Walvis Bay

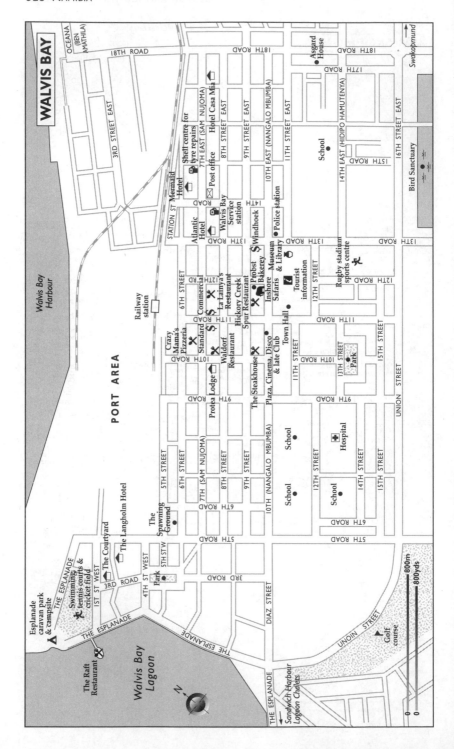

seals found at **Cape Cross**, also notable as the spot where the Portuguese navigator Diogo Cão placed his cross in 1486. Beyond that, you don't stand a chance.

Inland of the skeleton coast are several other remote places of interest, such as the 1,728m horn-shaped **Spitzkoppe Mountain** and the famous **Petrified Forest** to the west of Khorixas. Also of note is the 2,573m **Brandberg Massif**, Namibia's highest peak and site of the famous 'White Lady of the Brandberg' – a 40cm-high white rock painting of a human figure that only served to fuel Abbé Breuil's inventive speculation. The famous 'White Lady' (like other places mentioned in this paragraph) is inaccessible to backpackers; it's much easier to visit the similar but less publicised figure at Diana's Vow in the Nyanga region of Zimbabwe.

Access and getting around

The overnight train between Windhoek and Walvis Bay stops at Karabib, Usakos and Swakopmund. It leaves Windhoek at 20.00 daily except for Saturday, arriving in Swakopmund about nine hours later and in Walvis Bay 90 minutes after that. In the opposite direction it leaves Walvis Bay at 18.30 daily except for Sunday, stopping at Swakopmund at around 20.00 and arriving in Windhoek early the next morning. A seat between Windhoek and Walvis Bay costs US$6 Monday to Thursday and a sleeper costs US$15. These fares double over the weekend. This route is also covered by regular minibuses.

There is no public transport along the 200km road connecting Otjiwarongo to Karabib via Omaruru. Unless you are prepared to hitch, the best way to get to Omaruru is with the train service between Windhoek and Tsumeb. Hitching is the only viable way to get to points along the coast north of Swakopmund, and there isn't a great deal of traffic.

Where to stay and eat
Usakos
Usakos Hotel Only accommodation in town. Rooms **E** pp.

Omaruru
Omaruru Rest Camp Tel: 064 570516. Former municipal camp recently privatised. Pleasant setting near river. Camping **B** pp. Bungalows **E** pp.

Swakopmund
Alternative Space 46 Dr Alfons Weber St; tel: 064 402713; email: thespace@iwwn.com.na. Well-established and popular hostel 15 minutes from the city centre. Ring for free lift. Dorm **B** pp. Room **E** dbl.
Jay Jay's Hotel 8 Brucken St; tel: 40-2909. Central and friendly. Cheap meals and lively bar. Dorm **B** pp. Room **C**/**D**.
Karen's Attic Cnr Odavi and Post St; tel: 064 403057; email: kattic@iafrica.com.na. Comfortable new backpackers' with convenient central location. Dorm **C** pp.
Swakopmund Rest Camp Tel: 064 402807/8. Municipal resort near town centre and above beach. Accommodation starts with two-bed fisherman's cabin from **C** pp.

Walvis Bay
Langstrand Caravan Park Tel: 064 203134. Rather exposed municipal site about 15km from town on B2 to Swakopmund. Good restaurant. Rooms from **F** dbl. Camping **C** per site.
Esplanade Municipal Camp Tel: 064 205981. Sheltered campsite near town centre overlooking lagoon. Swimming pool and self-catering facilities. Camping **D** per site.

The Spawning Ground 55 Sixth St; tel: 064 205121. The best hostel in Walvis Bay, small but very relaxed. Dorms **C** pp. Camping **B** pp.

Henties Bay
Die Oord Holiday Cottages Tel: 064 500239. Self-catering cottages from **F** triple.
Eagle Holiday Flats Tel: 064 500032. Simple self-contained flats with TV. Flats **D** pp.
Jakkalsputz Campsite About 10km south of Henties Bay along road to Swakopmund.
Bleak, exposed site aimed mostly at anglers, not recommended for those without vehicles.
Camping **D** per site.

THE B1: SOUTH OF WINDHOEK
The first substantial settlement passed through by travellers heading south from Windhoek is **Rehoboth**, situated just north of the Tropic of Capricorn. Founded as a Rhenish mission in 1844, Rehoboth was abandoned in 1864 only to be reoccupied seven years later by the culturally cohesive group of mixed-race descendants of Dutch Settlers and Hottentots who call themselves Basters. Rehoboth remains the centre of Namibia's Baster community to this day, and the local museum recounts their history since they migrated from the Cape Colony in 1868. Also of interest to visitors is the Reho Spa on the outskirts of town, one of many thermal spring resorts in Namibia.

South of Rehoboth, **Mariental** serves as an important route focus and regional market town, but it is of limited interest to backpackers, not least because it lacks affordable accommodation options. Better, instead, to head to the **Hardap Dam Recreational Park** 20km northwest of town, where Namibia's largest reservoir forms the centrepiece of a game reserve which supports several large mammal species including Hartmann's mountain zebra, kudu, eland and gemsbok. The lake draws large numbers of water birds, including a breeding colony of white pelicans, while the surrounding arid scrub is a good place to see various dry country warblers, larks and chats. Best of all, walking is permitted anywhere in the reserve, which means that backpackers have some 80km of gravel roads and 20km of day trails to explore.

About 100km west of Mariental and the B1, **Maltohohe** is of interest as the springboard for visits to two places which, frankly, are almost impossible to visit without private transport. The first of these is **Duwasib Castle**, a bizarre and thoroughly misplaced example of German Baroque architecture, constructed quite literally in the middle of the desert for one Captain von Wolf in 1909. Less arcane but just as remote, **Namib-Naukluft National Park** is where those archetypical Namibian pictures of vast red dunes beneath a clear blue sky were snapped. The best-known spot in this park is Sossusvlei, where a group of particularly substantial dunes towers above a non-perennial pan which fills up with water every decade or so, most recently in 1997.

Back on the B1, lying some 230km south of Mariental, **Keetmanshoop** is the most populous town in southern Namibia. It was founded in 1866, and the church, which dates to 1895, now serves as a museum. On a private farm about 20km from Keetmanshoop, one of southern Namibia's most famous and accessible sights is the so-called **Kokerboom Forest**. Not a forest in any normal sense of the word, this is nevertheless thought to be the world's largest concentration of the kokerboom or 'quiver tree', a slow-growing variety of aloe which was used by Bushmen to make arrow quivers. The forest is especially worth visiting in mid-winter, when the trees burst into bright yellow bloom.

The **B4** is the surfaced road that connects Keetmanshoop to the port of Lüderitz. Roughly 350km long, the B4 is also known as the best locality for sighting Namibia's famous desert horses, a herd of almost 200 feral animals that

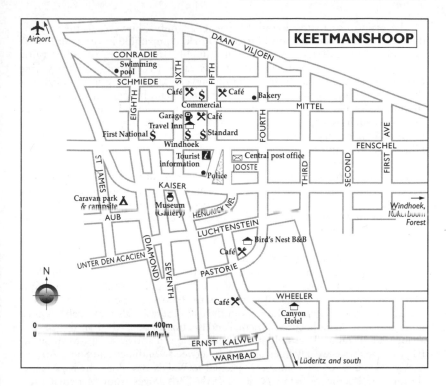

have adapted to some of the most arid conditions in the world. Nobody knows quite how these horses got to be where they are today – or perhaps more accurate to say that everybody seems to have a different explanation of their origin – but they are quite frequently seen in the vicinity of the Garub waterhole about 30km past the small town of Aus. Also worth looking out for along this road is a perfectly maintained picnic site that might just rank as the most isolated in Africa!

Lüderitz is a singularly surreal relic of German colonialism: a thoroughly remote small port which might almost have escaped from Bavaria with its impressive mixture of art nouveau and German Imperial architecture. The town itself is the main point of interest, but if you've come this far out of your way you'll probably want to stick around for a few days. Fortunately, there is plenty else to be seen in the area: it's easy to organise a boat trip to the large jackass penguin colony on Halifax Island, or to the Cape Seal Colony on Diaz Point (where Bartholomew Diaz raised a cross commemorating his visit to the harbour in 1498). Definitely worth a visit, the ghost town of Kolmanskop, 9km from Lüderitz, is a former diamond mining town which was abandoned in the 1950s, and despite some attempts at restoration it is now gradually being swallowed by the marching dunes.

The most notable settlements to the south of Keetmanshoop are **Grünau**, situated at the junction of the B1 south towards Cape Town and the B3 east towards Johannesburg, and the larger town of **Karasburg** on the B3 about 50km further east. There are a few points of interest in this area, but once again they are difficult to access without a private vehicle. One such place, lying about 50km south of Karasburg, is **Warmbad**, the site of a disused spa as well as of Namibia's oldest mission, founded in 1805 and currently being restored.

The main tourist attraction in this part of Namibia, however, is the vast and dramatic **Fish River Canyon National Park**, comparable in Africa only with Ethiopia's Blue Nile Gorge. Measuring roughly 160km from north to south, and up to 27km wide and 550m deep, this canyon is thought to have started forming along a large fault about 500 million years ago, and the river which runs through it is the only one in southern or central Namibia permanent enough to support fish. The canyon is notable mostly for its grand scenery, but large mammals such as klipspringer and baboon are frequently seen, as are several localised dry country birds, lizards and snakes. The five-day Fish River Canyon Hiking Trail, among the toughest and hottest in southern Africa, is recommended only to experienced, self-sufficient hikers, and it may only be done on production of a doctor's note proclaiming your fitness. Several shorter day trails can be undertaken from the rest camps at Ai-Ais and Hobas. Although the park is open throughout the year, the restcamp is closed from November 1 to the second Thursday in March due to the excessive heat and danger of flash floods in the canyon.

Access and getting around

The best way to get out of Windhoek along the B1 south is in one of the local minibuses which leave from the Wernhill Shopping Mall on Mandume Ndomufayo Street. A couple of minibuses to Rehoboth, about 100km south of Windhoek, leave every hour throughout the day. There are also reasonably regular minibuses from Windhoek to Mariental and Keetmanshoop, which lie respectively about 280km and 510km south of the capital. You can also get to any town on the B1 with the thrice-weekly Intercape coach between Windhoek and South Africa.

A weekly bus service connects Mariental to Walvis Bay along the back routes skirting the Namib-Naukluft National Park. This leaves from Mariental every Monday and from Walvis Bay on Tuesday, passing through Maltohohe; on alternate weeks only it also stops at Sesriem. While this isn't much use to travellers wanting to see Sossusvlei, since they would have to spend either just one night at Sesriem or a whole two weeks, it is the one affordable way for backpackers to see something of the Namib away from the B1.

A railways bus runs along the 350km surfaced road connecting Keetmanshoop to Lüderitz twice every week, leaving Keetmanshoop at 18.00 Friday and 14.00 Sunday and Lüderitz at 06.00 Saturday and 21.00 Sunday. To get to most other places lying off the B1 you're pretty much forced to hitch. One exception is Hardap Dam, which is only a 6km walk from the B1 along a turn-off signposted 15km north of Mariental. The best place to try for a lift to the Fish River Canyon is at the turn-off to Ai-Ais signposted 33km south of Grünau on the B1.

Where to stay and eat
Rehoboth
Oaneb Lake Resort Signposted a few kilometres west of Rehoboth. Bar, restaurant, water sports, hiking and horse trails. Camping **B** pp.
Reho Spa Tel: 0627 522774. Signposted on the southwest of town. Thermal pool. Busy weekends but quiet over the week. Good meals. Camping **C**/**D**. Four-bed bungalow from US$30 per unit.

Mariental
Engen Fuel Station Main road. Toilet, showers and guard. Free camping.
Guglhupf Restaurant Tel: 063 240718/9. Rooms **E**/**F** sgl/dbl. May allow camping in garden **A** pp.

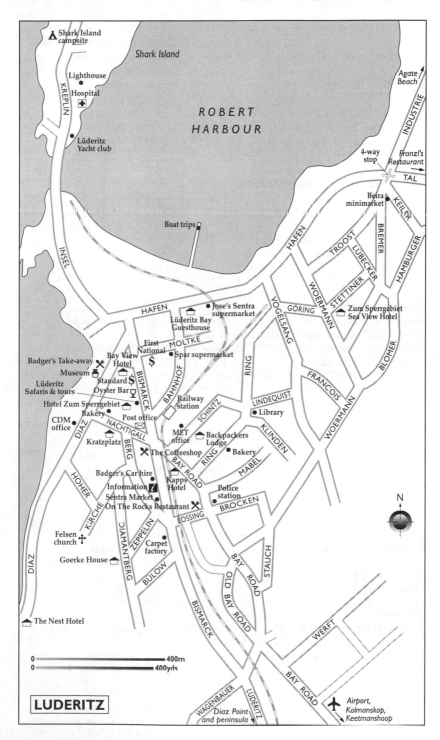

Shark Island campsite

Shark Island

Lighthouse
Hospital

Lüderitz Yacht club

ROBERT HARBOUR

Agate Beach

INDUSTRIE

4-way stop
Franzl's Restaurant

TAL

KEILO

Beira minimarket

Boat trips

INSEL

KREPLIN

HAFEN

Jose's Sentra supermarket

Lüderitz Bay Guesthouse

VOGELSANG

GÖRING

WOERMANN

STETTINER

TROOST

LÜBECKER

BREMER

HAMBURGER

Zum Sperrgebiet Sea View Hotel

BLOMER

First National

MOLTKE

Spar supermarket

Badger's Take-away
Museum
Bay View Hotel

Lüderitz Safaris & tours

Standard
Oyster Bar

Hotel Zum Sperrgebiet
Bakery

CDM office

BISMARCK

BAHNHOF

RING

FRANCOIS

WOERMANN

Railway station

SCHINTZ

LINDEQUIST

Library

Post office

DIAZ

NACHTIGALL

BERG

Kratzplatz

MET office

Backpackers Lodge

The Coffeeshop

RING

Bakery

KLINDEN

MABEL

Badger's Car hire

BAY ROAD

Information

Sentra Market
On The Rocks Restaurant

Kapps Hotel

Police station

BROCKEN

LOSSING

HOHER

KIRCHE

Felsen church

Goerke House

DIAMANTBERG

ZEPPELIN

Carpet factory

BÜLOW

BAY ROAD

OLD BAY ROAD

STAUCH

N

The Nest Hotel

0 ————— 400m
0 ————— 400yds

DIAZ

BISMARCK

WERFT

WAGENBAUER

LUDERITZ

BAY ROAD

Diaz Point and peninsula

Airport, Kolmanskop, Keetmanshoop

LUDERITZ

Hardap Dam Recreational Resort Turn-off from B1 signposted 15km north of Mariental. Overlooking dam close to entrance. Shop. Restaurant. Camping **E** per site. Bungalow **F** dbl.
Sandberg Hotel Tel/fax: 063 242291. Reasonable mid-range hotel. Rooms **F** dbl.

Maltohohe
Maltohohe Hotel Tel: 063 293013. Excellent country hotel, not too expensive at US$20/35. The owner can arrange Land Rover trips to Sossusvlei.

Duwasib
Duwasib Castle Kiosk selling drinks and snacks. Camping **D** per site.
Duwasib Farm Restcamp Private camp close to the castle. Meals available. Rooms **E** pp.

Namib Naukluft National Park
Nubib Adventures Lodge Tel: 06638 5713. Backpacker-friendly set-up 80km south of Sesriem. Superb hiking options include an unguided trail in the Nubib Mountains and a guided day trail through the dunes around Sossusvlei. Phone the owners for advice about getting there. Camping or dorm **B** pp. Rooms **E** pp B&B.
Sesriem Campsite The only public campsite that's vaguely accessible to backpackers. Booking advisable through MET in Windhoek. Meals available at nearby Karos Lodge. Camping **F** per site.

Keetmanshoop
Keetmanshoop Restcamp Grassy municipal site with excellent ablutions in the town centre. Laundromat. Camping **A** pp.
Kokerboom Campsite Tel: 063 222835. At kokerboom forest 20km from town. Rooms US$45/70. Camping **A** pp.
Lefanis Restcamp Tel/fax: 0631 24316. On the B1 next to a fuel station about 2km south of the junction with the B4 to Lüderitz. Far cheaper than any rooms in town. Swimming pool. Restaurant. Bungalows **E** dbl. Camping **A** pp.

Lüderitz
Backpackers Lodge 7 Schintz St; tel: 063 202000/202445; email: toya@ldz.namib.com. Spacious, central and popular hostel. Good local tourist information. Dorm **C** pp. Room **E** dbl.
Shark Island Rest Camp Exposed site ten minutes' walk along causeway north of town. Camping **D** per site. Bungalows available for around US$30 dbl.

Fish River Canyon and Ai-Ais
Ai-Ais Rest Camp Thermal swimming pool. Day walks. Shop. Restaurant. Camping **D** per site. Four-bed huts around US$30 per unit.
Fish River Lodge Friendly, attractively situated lodge signposted 22 km along a little gravelled road leading south from the main road between Grunau and Seeheim. Camping **C** pp. Dorm **C** pp. Huts **D** pp.
Hobas Campsite Swimming pool. Basic food supplies. Camping **D** per site.

Grünau
Grunau Motors Tel: 063 262026. Clean s/c bungalows next to garage on north end of town. Shop and take-away. Rooms **E/F**.
Vastrap Restcamp Tel: 06342 1322. Clean accommodation in restored farm buildings 5km out of town and 2km from the Karasburg Road. Affordable meals. Rooms **E/F**.

Karasburg
Van Riebeck Hotel Seedy, but the most affordable rooms in town at around **F** dbl. The slightly smarter and not much more expensive Kalkfontein Hotel is the only other option.

18

South Africa

South Africa is a country of stunning variety. Its landscapes encompass everything from the archetypal animal-rich acacia scrub of the Kruger Park to the majestic fynbos-clad slopes of Cape Town and the surrounding Winelands, from the picture-postcard beaches of the east coast to the starkly beautiful red dunes of the Kalahari in the west, and from the vast open grasslands of the Drakensberg to the intimate forests of the escarpment. South Africa may not be, as the Tourist Board is so fond of claiming, a 'World in One Country', but you could spend an incomparable three or four months establishing the invalidity of this claim. This entire chapter is little more than an introduction annotated with accommodation and public transport options – so read on…

BACKGROUND INFORMATION
Geography and climate
South Africa's most important topographical feature is the escarpment which runs around the country in a rough crescent between 50km and 250km inland and divides the country into three broad regions: the coastal belt, the highveld, and the escarpment itself. Most of South Africa has a temperate climate, though parts of the Northern Province and Northern Cape become very hot in summer, as does the humid coastal belt north of Durban. Summer falls between October and March, while winter falls between May and August. The western Cape has a winter rainfall pattern, but the rest of the country receives almost all its rain during summer. Rainfall is higher in the east, most of which averages around 1,000mm annually, while in the west coast area and Kalahari it drops to below 250mm.

History
After Portugal rounded Africa in 1488, European ships sailing to the East often stopped to trade for fresh produce with the Khoikhoi people of the Cape. The first

---

FACTS AND FIGURES
Area: 1,221,037 km² (10th in Africa)
Capital: Pretoria
Largest towns: Johannesburg, Cape Town, Durban, Pretoria, Bloemfontein, Port Elizabeth
Population: 45–50 million
Official languages: 11 including English, Zulu, Xhosa and Afrikaans
Currency: Rand
Head of State: President Thabo Mbeki

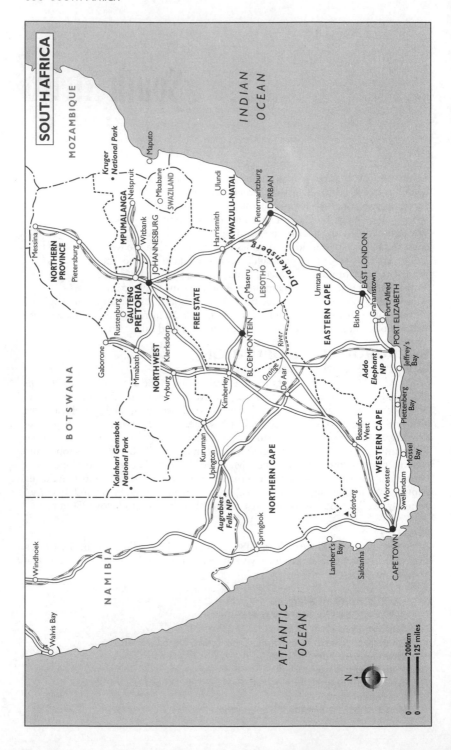

European settlement in the region was established by the Dutch East India Company (VOC) at Table Bay in 1652. By 1795, the settler population had grown to 15,000, and spread north to Stellenbosch and east to Port Elizabeth. The settlers were mostly Dutch farmers (Boers) who enslaved the unfortunate Khoikhoi as labourers. The Cape was formally colonised by Britain in 1815. New curbs on slavery initiated the northward migration of large numbers of Boers, the Voortrekkers, who were pivotal in shaping not only modern South Africa but also Afrikaner mythology. In 1836, a Voortrekker party led by Piet Retief was massacred by Dingane, Shaka's successor as king of the Zulu. Dingane in turn was defeated by Andries Pretorius's Voortrekker party, and in 1838 Pretorius established the Republic of Natalia with Pietermaritzburg as its capital. However, Britain occupied Durban in 1839 and four years later declared Natal a Crown Colony. The Voortrekkers moved on to establish the republics of the Transvaal and Orange Free State.

The discovery of the richest gold reefs known to man in the Transvaal in 1886 led to a territorial dispute that came to a head in 1899 with the outbreak of the Anglo-Boer War, the longest, bloodiest and most expensive war fought by Britain between 1815 and 1914. When conventional warfare failed, Britain razed Boer farms and crops, and herded civilians into concentration camps in which measles and dysentery claimed the lives of 30,000 Boers and 15,000 Africans. The Boers surrendered in 1902, and the Transvaal and OFS became British colonies. In 1910 the four colonies became the self-governing Union of South Africa.

The interests of the indigenous peoples were ignored during the colonial era. Most brutally affected were the Khoikhoi, who were forced from their traditional land into slavery or nomadism, and faced the twin scourges of superior settler firepower and exotic diseases such as smallpox. No 'pure' Khoikhoi survive in modern South Africa. Nor do San hunter-gatherers, who lived to the north of the colony, where they were hunted as vermin by European and Bantu alike. By the end of the nineteenth century, Britain had allocated pockets of southern Africa to various Bantu-speakers. Bechuanaland (Botswana), Basotholand (Lesotho), and Swaziland were never integrated into South Africa and remained British Protectorates until independence in 1962. Other areas, such as the Transkei and Zululand, became native reserves within the Union of South Africa.

Prior to World War II, parliamentary politics in South Africa dwelt myopically on the English-Afrikaans 'race' issue. Few whites took notice when the African National Congress (ANC) was founded in the 1920s, influenced by Gandhi's policy of passive resistance. Shortly after World War II, an ANC-backed miners' strike turned into a bloodbath when the police opened fire, for the first time bringing the broader race issue to the fore of parliamentary politics. The ruling United Party started talking about limited integration. The Nationalist Party (NP) responded with a campaign that focused on one word and one philosophy: Apartheid (separateness). In 1948, the NP was elected to government, a position it held until 1994.

The NP passed a series of bills enforcing apartheid. The Population Registration Act classified all South Africans into one of four racial groups (Asian, Black, Coloured, or White). The Immorality and Mixed Marriages Acts prevented people of different races from having sex or marrying. The Group Areas Act forced people to live in areas designated for their racial group. The State Aided Institutions Act banned Blacks from using facilities run by White institutions. Meanwhile, the Suppression of Communism Acts banned the Communist Party, a precursor of the draconian powers soon to be vested in the state. Then began the process of resettlement: areas of 'White' cities that had long been traditionally 'Black' or 'Coloured', most famously District Six in Cape Town and Sophiatown in Johannesburg, were razed and re-zoned for Whites. In 1960, South Africa was declared a republic and links with the Commonwealth were severed. In 1962, the pivotal Homelands Policy materialised when the Transkei became the first 'self-governing' black homeland, to be granted full 'independence' in 1976.

As the NP pursued its fantastic dogma, so the ANC grew in stature. In 1955, under Albert Lituli (later a Nobel Peace Prize winner), the ANC drew up a Freedom Charter asserting the ideal of a non-racial democracy. In 1959, a radical Africanist group split from the ANC to form the Pan African Congress (PAC). The turning point for both organisations was March 21 1960, when police opened fire on a peaceful protest in Sharpeville and 69 people were killed. The government reacted decisively. A state of emergency was declared, 18,000 people were detained, and the ANC and PAC were banned. Realising the futility of peaceful protest, the ANC turned to a policy of violent resistance. Nelson Mandela was called on to form the underground Umkonto we Sizwe (Spear of the Nation) and bomb 'soft' government targets such as police stations and post offices. The organisation's leaders were rounded up. In the 1963 Rivonia Trial, Mandela amongst others was sentenced to life imprisonment.

In Soweto, on June 16 1976, marchers protesting against the use of Afrikaans as a teaching medium were fired on by police and several children were killed. When the Soweto Riots subsided more than six months later, 700 people had died, thousands of children had been detained, 500 teachers had resigned, and hundreds of buses, schools, clinics, and other buildings in the townships had been gutted by angry protesters. Later that year, the Black Consciousness leader Steve Biko was killed in the custody of the police. Biko was not the first to die in this manner – numerous political detainees had previously contrived to kill themselves by jumping through barred windows or hanging themselves in their cells, and two even died after slipping on bars of soap in the shower. But he was the most prominent, and the international press jumped on the incident. The Minister of Justice said Biko's death left him cold. The police were exonerated in the official inquiry. The Soweto Riots and Biko's death galvanised the atmosphere in the townships, and South Africa would never be the same again.

In 1983, the NP drew up a new constitution giving Coloureds and Asians a limited say in the country's politics, but ignoring Blacks altogether. Put to a White referendum, it got a 66% 'yes' vote and was entrenched. The Conservative Party (CP) splintered from the NP, and the governing party had to contend with the unfamiliar risk of losing an election if it moved too quickly for the White electorate. Paralysis followed, and the government responded to growing international pressure for reform with every conceivable tactic to destabilise Black resistance. The house arrests, bannings and censorship of the 1960s and 1970s continued unabated, while the security forces, under the State of Emergency of 1986, used their unlimited powers with gay abandon. South Africa also dabbled destructively in the politics of its neighbours, funding and training resistance movements such as Renamo in Mozambique. The deadlock was broken only when the NP elected a new party leader, F W de Klerk, in 1989. On February 2 1990, de Klerk broke decisively with the past by lifting the bans on the ANC, PAC, and 20 other organisations, and unconditionally releasing Mandela from jail.

The next few years were to be something of an emotional roller-coaster for all South Africans. In an atmosphere of growing criminal and political violence, the NP, ANC and Zulu-based Inkatha Freedom Party (IFP) entered into a stop-start series of negotiations. At times, civil war seemed imminent and the only apparent response from politicians of all persuasions was to grandstand and point fingers. In early 1993, two pivotal events brought new focus to the negotiating table: the bilateral ANC-NP agreement on a five-year Government of National Unity, and the tragic assassination of Chris Hani, a leading figure in the ANC. In June 1993, the negotiators announced that April 27 1994 would be the date of South Africa's first all-party election. The IFP and right-wing CP walked out of negotiations.

An apocalyptic mood prevailed during the months before the election. The pivotal figure of this period was Mangasuthu Buthelezi of the IFP, whose nominal difference with the ANC and NP was its support of a federal constitution. The IFP formed the absurdly named Freedom Alliance with conservative Afrikaners and discredited former homeland leaders, and it threatened to boycott the election unless separate ballots were taken at national and provincial level. The ANC and NP agreed to this demand; yet on the cut-off date for registration a month before the election, the IFP announced it would not participate. Two weeks before the election, an Inkatha march on the ANC headquarters in Johannesburg led to a shoot-out in which dozens of people were killed. Equally ominously, the unpopular prime minister of the Bophuthatswana homeland threatened to retain power after the election. His civil service went on strike in protest, and so the security forces moved in with the approval of the ANC, only to be met by the AWB, an extreme right-wing 'army', who randomly killed dozens of Tswana people.

The first shaft of light in this gloomy scenario came about ten days before the election, when the IFP did a startling about-face by agreeing to participate in the election. This good news was tempered when, on the Sunday morning before the election, right wingers set off a bomb outside the ANC provincial headquarters in Johannesburg, killing seven people. Even more people were killed the next day in an explosion at an East Rand taxi rank.

The outcome of the election was hardly remarkable. The ANC won a 62% majority and, predictable as to be a formality, Nelson Mandela became the first black president of South Africa. The NP won 20% of the vote and Inkatha 10%, entitling de Klerk to a vice presidency and a seemingly reformed Buthelezi to a cabinet post. What was remarkable was the light, reconciliatory, almost unreal mood in which votes were cast. I doubt that anybody who settled in South Africa the day after the election could imagine what the country was like before. And nobody who flew out the day before could have a conception of how it has been since.

The period since 1994 has been remarkable for the normalisation of South African politics: overtly racial issues have largely retreated from centre stage, while the ANC has addressed with mixed success a cocktail of social problems bequeathed to them by the former government – inadequate healthcare, a housing shortage, inequalities of land distribution, unemployment and education. Contrary to many expectations, the country has held its ground economically, despite the dampening effects of an ailing currency and soaring crime rates. The octogenarian Mandela, whose charisma and drive for racial reconciliation gained him enormous popularity and respect both within South Africa and outside its borders, resigned from the presidency ahead of the country's second election in 1999, but he remains a figure of considerable influence. Under the leadership of former vice-president Thabo Mbeki, the ANC was returned to power in 1999, gaining 65% of the vote, an improvement on its 1994 showing, and one which underlines a worrying absence of credible opposition.

PRACTICAL INFORMATION
Accommodation

A large network of backpacker hostels has sprung up since 1991. Generally, hostels are the cheapest option in any given town, the best source of current travel information, and a good place to meet other backpackers. Large concentrations of hostels are found in Cape Town, Durban, Johannesburg, Port Elizabeth and the Garden Route, but there's a hostel in virtually every town of note. Dorms typically cost around US$7pp, and many hostels have private rooms and camping space. The inexpensive and regularly updated booklets *Coast to Coast* and *Jungle*, which can be picked up at any backpacker hostel, list most hostels countrywide with prices and contact numbers. Also very useful, with about 200 annotated hostel listings for southern Africa, is the fast and user-friendly Word of Mouth website (www.travelinafrica.co.za). The Just Backpacking Site (www.backpacking.co.za) is less easy to navigate and less critical, but has better details of hostels in countries neighbouring South Africa. The site for the Baz Bus (www.icon.co.za/~bazbus) includes listings of most hostels in South Africa, including all those at which it drops off passengers (or where it works in conjunction with a local shuttle), while highlighted entries link the user to the individual lodge website.

As this book went to print, the ongoing political dramas in Zimbabwe, coupled with the gang-rape of a backpacker in a hostel in Johannesburg had caused a lull in budget tourism to southern Africa and the closure of several well-established hostels.

Travellers who explore beyond the more popular parts of the country would do well to carry camping equipment, since every town has a municipal campsite where you can pitch a tent for around US$5. Campsites and self-catering accommodation can be found in most national parks and game reserves. Bed availability in backpacker hostels isn't affected by local school holidays, but other accommodation and campsites in resort areas tend to be booked solid and to double in price over these holiday periods.

Books and newspapers

In cities there are many bookshops, and you'll find an excellent range of historical works, field guides and travel guides covering sub-equatorial Africa. The South African press is arguably the most free and substantial in Africa. Good weekly papers include the *Mail & Guardian* (Friday), *Sunday Independent* and *British Weekly Telegraph* (Wednesday). The best local dailies are *The Star* (Johannesburg), *The Argus* (Cape Town), the *Natal Witness* and the *Natal Mercury*.

Crime and safety

South Africa has one of the highest crime rates in the world, and Johannesburg is the most dangerous city covered in this book. An increasingly large number of backpackers get robbed there, and it's the one place in the region where there's a significant risk of being killed for your possessions. Nearby Pretoria has much the same facilities as Johannesburg and is considerably safer, though muggings in Pretoria city centre are most definitely on the increase. If you survive Johannesburg and Pretoria, you're most of the way to avoiding becoming a victim of South Africa's fastest growing industry. Of course, crime does exist elsewhere in the country, with the greatest risk being in Durban city centre and parts of Cape Town. In any of the above cities, you can assume that muggers will know exactly what a money-belt is and where to find it. The important message, bearing in mind that the problem could spread to smaller cities during the lifespan of this edition, is never to walk in any city centre with your backpack and/or money-belt on. When you first arrive in town, use a taxi or phone a hostel to organise a lift. Once you're settled in, carry on your person only what you need. Nobody is above this advice – muggers will see right through any attempt to look poor, and they will have few qualms about mugging somebody in a group.

Entrance fees

A relatively negligible one-off entrance fee of around US$6 per vehicle plus US$3 per person is charged at all national parks. Most other game reserves charge an entrance fee, but this will rarely be more than US$3 per person. In South Africa, an entrance fee is normally exactly that – the fee is per entry, whether you spend an hour or a month in the reserve, not per day or 24 hours.

Entry formalities

Visas are not required by nationals of the USA, Israel, Japan and most EC, Scandinavian and Commonwealth countries. Other nationals can buy a visa from any South African Embassy or High Commission. All visitors will have a temporary residence permit stamped in their passport on arrival; insist on the full 90 days, since renewing it is a major hassle.

Before entering South Africa you may be asked to demonstrate you have an onward ticket and 'sufficient funds'. Immigration officials at overland borders are unlikely to raise this, though it can't hurt you to dress reasonably smartly. If you anticipate problems, you'll gain credibility if you arrive by coach or train with a return ticket (the return stub should be refundable with a minor deduction).

Immigration officials at international airports can be sticky to the point of irrationality about flying into South Africa on a one-way ticket. The technical requirement is an onward ticket *from South Africa to your country of origin*. You'll more than likely get through with an air ticket from somewhere like Kenya, but this can't be guaranteed. Bearing in mind that it's very much at the discretion of the individual official, travellers in this situation will help their case greatly if they can show an overland ticket out of South Africa (such as a rail ticket to Harare), at least US$2,000 in cash or travellers' cheques, and a credit card. When you buy a ticket to South Africa, bear in mind that the difference in price between a one-way and the cheapest return is often slight.

If you don't have an onward ticket, the worst-case scenario is that you'll have to either buy one on the spot or else leave a cash deposit with immigration. The former option is better assuming you can confirm the ticket will be refundable, since a deposit might be anything up to US$5,000 and, although it is refundable in full when you leave South Africa, this will be a bureaucratic nightmare.

Flying in

Many airlines fly to South Africa from Europe, North America and other African countries. Almost all international flights land at Johannesburg International Airport, though it's possible to book a flight straight on to Durban or Cape Town. See *Access and getting around* under *Johannesburg and Pretoria* for details of what to do when you arrive.

Food and drink

South Africa is very Westernised in this respect. In any large town you'll find several good supermarkets, fast food outlets and restaurants – the choice is large and varied, and any hostel manager or tourist office can make reliable suggestions. Groceries are cheap, and most hostels have kitchens while most campsites have fixed barbecues. If you want to eat out, a fast food meal costs US$2–3, while a main course in a proper restaurant costs around US$5–6.

Except in the Transkei, or unless you are specifically told otherwise, assume tap water is safe to drink. In addition to the usual canned beers and soft drinks, you can buy cartons of pure fruit juice for around US$1 per litre, and more than adequate red and white wines from US$3 per 750ml bottle. Drinkable 2-litre cartons of wine cost around US$5 – among the better 'box wines' are those produced by Drosdty Hof, Tassenberg and Cellar Cask.

Getting around
By road
The popular Baz Bus caters specifically to backpackers. It has changed its schedule slightly a few times over the years, and at present runs four times weekly anticlockwise through Pretoria, Johannesburg, the Drakensberg, Pietermaritzburg, Durban and Mbabane (in Swaziland), and then five times weekly in either direction between Durban and Cape Town, stopping at all large towns along the N2 on the way and connecting with local services to Coffee Bay, Port St John and Hermanus. It will normally drop you at the hostel of your choice, though in some towns it stops only at selected hostels. A full ticket from Pretoria or Johannesburg to Cape Town (with as many stops as you like) costs US$140. For further details of routes, stops, and bookings, ask at any hostel, ring 021 439-2323, or visit www.icon.co.za/~bazbus.

Similar local services aimed partly or entirely at backpackers include the Roller Coaster Taxi (tel: 011 857-2398 or 031 23-3706), which runs twice daily between Johannesburg and Durban. The Sani Pass Courier (tel: 033 701-1017) runs from Durban to Sani Pass every Monday, Wednesday and Friday. The Kwazintaba Tours bus (tel: 033 702-1228) travels between Sani Pass and Port St John every Thursday. It seems likely that new services of this sort will be up and running by the time you get to South Africa, so do check with one of the backpacker hostels.

More conventional and widespread coach services are run by Greyhound (tel: 011 838-3037) and Translux (tel: 011 774-3333). Between them, these two companies cover all the main routes in both directions at least three or four times a week. From Johannesburg or Pretoria, there are coaches to Hazyview, Durban, Richards Bay, East London, Bloemfontein, Port Elizabeth, Mossel Bay, Oudtshoorn, George, Kimberley and Cape Town. There are also coaches from Durban to Port Elizabeth via Port Shepstone, East London and Grahamstown, and from Durban to Upington via Bloemfontein and Kimberley. The fare from Johannesburg to Cape Town is US$60 one way and to Durban US$30. Intercape (tel: 021 386-4400) runs the only coach service connecting Johannesburg and Cape Town to Upington and Namibia.

Hitching is reasonably easy and there are areas where it is the only realistic option for backpackers, bearing in mind that the risks attached to hitching in any Western country are exacerbated in South Africa by the high crime rate. It's a difficult judgement call, but I think I'd be ducking the issue were I to advise against hitching entirely. Hitching in the vicinity of a large city is certainly foolhardy, as would be hitching through the former Transkei, and you should always plan ahead to ensure you don't risk being stuck on the roadside after nightfall. For the rest, I'd urge backpackers to use public transport where it's available, but I don't feel that there's a great risk attached to hitching through remote areas such as the Northern Cape.

Car hire is relatively affordable, especially for a group travelling together. In all major centres there are budget car rental companies with weekly rates starting at around US$250 for unlimited kilometres – any hostel will be able to make recommendations – and petrol costs around US$0.50 per litre. Backpacker hostels are the best places to find out about companies which run budget day tours and camping safaris to places such as the Kruger Park – don't think about booking a trip like this overseas or you'll pay a lot more.

By rail
Passenger trains connect Johannesburg and Pretoria to Komatipoort (via Nelspruit), Durban (via Pietermaritzburg), East London (via Bloemfontein and

Queenstown), Port Elizabeth (via Bloemfontein and Cradock), Cape Town (via Kimberley and Beaufort West) and Beitbridge (via Louis Trichardt). There are also passenger services between Cape Town and Port Elizabeth (via Swellendam and George) and between Cape Town and Durban (via Beaufort West, Bloemfontein and Pietermaritzburg). First- and second-class sleepers are generally slightly cheaper than the equivalent coach trip. The central reservations office can be contacted at 011 773-2944.

Health
South Africa is largely free of tropical diseases, though bilharzia is present in many lakes. Malaria is present during the rainy season only, when it is generally confined to low-lying parts of Zululand and Mpumalanga. Health facilities in South Africa are of a high standard, but they are expensive by comparison with those not only of neighbouring countries, but also of European countries with subsidised state health care. South Africa is definitely *not* the place to put together a medical kit.

Maps
Good map books of South Africa with colour town plans are readily available – buy one at a filling station, where you'll pay around US$3 for what will cost US$10 in a bookshop. Free maps of nature reserves and towns are normally stocked at the local tourist office.

Post and telephone
South Africa has a notoriously inefficient postal system. Not only is it very slow – up to two weeks for both internal and overseas mail – but letters frequently go missing. Anything of value should be couriered or sent using registered mail. By contrast, the local and international telephone system is as efficient as any in the world. Public telephone booths are to be found in most post offices, railway stations and shopping malls.

The international dialling code for South Africa is +27. Local codes (removing the leading zero for international calls) are included under the number given in the regional part of the guide. Codes for main cities are:

Bloemfontein	051	East London	0431	Port Elizabeth	041
Cape Town	021	Johannesburg	011	Pretoria	012
Durban	031	Nelspruit	013		

Money
The unit of currency is the rand, and the current exchange rate hovers around US$1=R6.50–7. This rate has dropped dramatically in recent years and might well again during the lifespan of this edition. Foreign currency can be changed into rands at any bank, most tourist class hotels, and at branches of Rennies Travel. Banking hours are 09.00 to 15.30 on weekdays and 08.30 to 11.00 on Saturday. There are 24-hour foreign exchange facilities at the international airports in Johannesburg, Cape Town and Durban. If you arrive overland in South Africa at the weekend, you'll have no choice but to change a small amount informally at the border – be discreet, because it's illegal, and watch out for con artists.

Public holidays
In addition to New Year's Day, the Easter weekend and Christmas and Boxing Day, the following public holidays are taken in South Africa.

21 March	Human Rights Day (anniversary of Sharpeville)
27 April	Freedom Day (anniversary of 1994 election)
1 May	Workers' Day
16 June	Youth Day (anniversary of Soweto Riots)
9 August	National Women's Day
24 September	Heritage Day
16 December	Day of Reconciliation

Tourist information

This chapter, one of the three longest in the book, may seem skeletal by comparison with other chapters. The number and diversity of South Africa's attractions are partly to blame for this, since they mean that a chapter of comparable depth with those on, say, Tanzania or Malawi would be hundreds of pages long. I also feel that backpackers in South Africa don't need the level of detail they might elsewhere – travel up the coast of Mozambique or Tanzania (or any other area where facilities and English-speakers are thin on the ground) and this book will be your sole source of reliable information. In South Africa by contrast, English literature on practically every aspect of the country is readily available, wherever you go there'll be a tourist office stocked with maps and pamphlets, and it's all held together by a network of backpacker hostels where staff and other travellers can offer more current practical advice than any book. South Africa will be the first or last country visited by most people using this book, and it is the only country in the region which boasts numerous decent bookshops. If you require a more detailed source of travel information, then supplement the overview in this chapter with one of several dedicated guides to South Africa (see *Appendix 3* for recommendations).

Johannesburg and Mpumalanga
JOHANNESBURG AND PRETORIA

Considering that it's southern Africa's largest city and the first port of call for a high proportion of visitors to South Africa, **Johannesburg** really couldn't have much less going for it as a tourist attraction. Founded in 1888 above what are the richest seams of gold yet to be discovered anywhere in the world, Johannesburg is an unabashedly modern city which offers little in the way of meaningful sightseeing. And the surrounding scenery is remarkable only for its monotony – unless perhaps you have an eye for the flat-topped mine dumps that dot the southern outskirts. On the sole basis of aesthetic merits, it's tempting to advise travellers to spend as little time as possible in Johannesburg. Take into account the ever-increasing number of visitors who find themselves on the wrong end of a gun or knife, and the temptation is to advise you to give it a miss completely.

Travel logistics alone mean that many backpackers end up in Johannesburg. Most if not all roads lead to the country's unofficial commercial capital and largest public transport hub, and Johannesburg remains the obvious place from which to arrange budget outings to places like the Kruger Park. And the city does have redeeming features: the climate, for starters, must rank as one of the most comfortable in the world. And those who are coming from countries further north will find Johannesburg to be almost shockingly Westernised, with its vast shopping malls, multi-screen cinema complexes and immense diversity of restaurants, bars and clubs.

Those who do decide to brave Johannesburg should think about which part of this vast urban sprawl they choose as a base. The city centre and other formerly popular areas such as Hillbrow are not so much dodgy as deadly, while the northern suburbs, though safer and dotted with backpacker hostels, have a sterile suburban atmosphere that makes for less than riveting travel. Probably the best base for travellers visiting Johannesburg is the relatively central suburb of Yeoville, which boasts a good cluster of backpacker hostels and is still reasonably safe even at night. The main drag through Yeoville, Rockey Street, boasts a string of cheap restaurants, relaxed nightspots, sleepy coffee-shops and idiosyncratic clothes and book stores. The suburb as a whole has a slightly Bohemian atmosphere, which dates to the 1980s when it was one of the few places in South Africa that attempted to subvert the apartheid ethic. That said, Yeoville *is* past its prime, and a spate of armed attacks on backpacker hostels in the area in mid-2000, one of which culminated in the brutal gang-rape of a female backpacker, might reasonably persuade most travellers to avoid the area altogether – assuming that it doesn't in any case force the closure of several or all of the Yeoville hostels through lack of business.

A recommended alternative to spending time in South Africa's undisputed crime capital is to base yourself in **Pretoria**. The capital of South Africa, situated only 60km north of Johannesburg and 47km from the international airport, is a considerably safer city and just as good a base from which to arrange things (better, in fact, if you need to trawl through the embassies). Pretoria is also considerably more pleasant on the eye, especially in October when the jacaranda trees are in bloom. Arguably, Pretoria lacks Joburg's cosmopolitan atmosphere, but this is more than compensated for by a clutch of notable buildings and low-key museums. The impressive Union Buildings, built in 1913 to a design by Sir Herbert Baker, will be a familiar sight to anybody who saw the televised broadcast of Nelson Mandela's presidential inauguration. Also of interest in the city centre are Melrose House (a Victorian abode decorated with period furniture), the original house of Paul Kruger, the Transvaal Museum (good fossil collection) and the Cultural Museum (cultural displays and rock art). The lovely Botanical Gardens and Wonderboom Nature Reserve (the latter protecting a thousand-year-old fig tree that has spread out over half a hectare) lie a mere 5km from the centre. Finally, there is the Voortrekker Monument: this granite monolith, perched on a hill to the south of the city centre, was constructed in 1936 as part of the Great Trek centenary celebration, and the adjoining museum has a superb collection of artefacts relating to the Voortrekker lifestyle.

Further afield, a fairly popular day excursion with backpackers is to **Sun City**, a vast and opulent casino and entertainment complex built in the former 'independent' homeland of Bophuthatswana as a way around the then draconian anti-gambling and anti-pornography laws of the Nationalist government. The Sun City complex does provide employment in a part of South Africa where jobs are thin on the ground, though a sceptic might reasonably dismiss it as little more than a comically grandiose monument to the hypocrisies of the former government and its supporters. Those who wish to make their own judgment about Sun City should definitely aim to spend time in the adjoining **Pilanesberg Game Reserve**. Proclaimed in 1979 on what was then farmland, the Pilanesberg now ranks as one of South Africa's best reserves. In addition to re-introduced lion, elephant, giraffe, zebra, buffalo and a wide range of antelope species, the Pilanesberg offers a better-than-even chance of a close encounter with rhinos, as well as some striking birds – crimson-breasted shrike and pied babbler for instance – that are otherwise unlikely to be seen unless you visit the western part of southern Africa.

Getting there and around

Whether you come by air, rail or road, you won't have a problem reaching the Johannesburg area (see *Access and getting around* on pages 549–51), and most public transport also stops in Pretoria. Of greater concern than getting to Johannesburg or

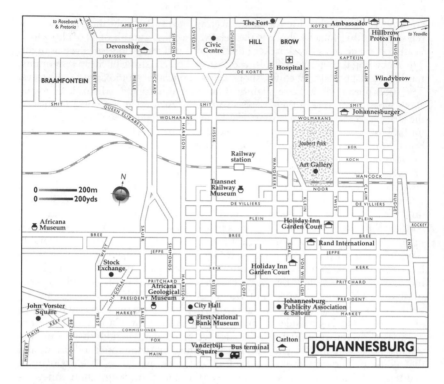

Pretoria is what to do once you arrive there. Walking around any part of Johannesburg with a pack on your back is positively courting disaster, as is walking around parts of central Pretoria. If you arrive in Johannesburg at the central railway station or the nearby Rotunda coach terminal, do not leave the building. Phone one of the hostels to arrange a free pick-up and follow their instructions about where to wait.

Most international flights to South Africa arrive at Johannesburg International Airport in the morning, when they will be met by representatives who will take backpackers directly to one of the Johannesburg hostels. There are also shuttle buses from the airport through to central Johannesburg, Sandton and Pretoria. Backpackers who want to go to Pretoria should use the shuttle which leaves from outside Terminal Three hourly between 07.00 and 20.00. This can drop you at the Word of Mouth Hostel on request, and backpackers heading to this hostel get a discount. If you're in any doubt, go to the *Info Africa* counter on the ground floor of the airport immediately facing the international arrival gate.

Once in a hostel, the staff will be able to give you current advice on getting around locally. They will also be able to recommend reliable companies offering day trips to Sun City, longer safaris and car hire. Regular game viewing trips run out of Sun City to the Pilanesberg.

Where to stay
Johannesburg
Airport Backpackers 3 Mohawk St, Rhodesfield, Kempton Park; email: airportbackpack@hotmail.com; web: home.mweb.co.za/ai/airbackp/. In a quiet suburb 2km from the airport, this new, spacious hostel is set in large grounds with a swimming pool and thatched *boma*. Close to shopping malls, restaurants, clubs and pubs. Owned by a former

overland truck diver who can offer expert travel advice. Day trips and tours to the Kruger and Kalahari. Free shuttle to and from Johannesburg International Airport. Dorm **C** pp. Rooms from **D** pp. Camping **C** pp (second night for new arrivals in the country free).
Backpackers Ritz 1A North Rd, Dunkeld West; tel: 011 325 7125; fax: 011 327 0233; email: ritz@iafrica.com; web: www.backpackers-ritz.co.za. Established in 1992, this is the oldest and one of the most popular hostels in the city, set in a historic mansion with a large garden. Facilities include a café, bar, pool table, swimming pool and *braai* area. Proximity to Rosebank shopping malls a bonus. Free pick-up from anywhere in Johannesburg. Travel desk arranges affordable day trips as well as three- to five-day Kruger Park trips from around US$150pp and overland trucks all over Africa. Dorms **C** pp. Rooms **E/F**. No camping.
Eastgate Backpackers 41 Hans Pirow Rd, Bruma; tel: 011 616 2741; fax: 011 615 1092; email: egatebp@netactive.co.za; web: www.web.netactive.co.za/~egatebp/index.html. Well-established, popular suburban hostel near vast Eastgate shopping mall and Bruma flea market. Email access, bar, equipped kitchen, meals, large garden with swimming pool, satellite TV with video. Booking for local and longer trips. Free pick-up always provided if needed. Room **E/F**. Dorm **C** pp. Camping **C** pp.
Rockey Street Backpackers Rockey St; tel: 011-648 8786; fax: 011 648 8423; email: bacpacrs@icon.co.za. One of the longest-standing backpacker hostels in the country, well positioned for exploring Yeoville and Rockey Street. Women-only dorm available. Self-catering kitchen, lively bar, weekend *braai*, free pick-up from airport or town between 08.00 and 19.00. Organise tours to Kruger Park, Mozambique, Cape Town, Victoria Falls, etc. Dorm **C** pp. Rooms **D/E**. No camping.
Ranch Hostel Inchanga Rd, Witkoppen; tel: 011 708-1304. Recommended semi-rural retreat on riverside farm only ten minutes from the bustling Fourways Shopping Mall (free pick-up from the mall). Swimming pool, tennis, horses, pool table, bar, jacuzzi. A little pricier than most of the more urban hostels. Cabins **E/F**. Dorms **C** pp. Camping **C** pp.

Pretoria
Hatfield Backpackers 1226 Park St, Hatfield; tel: 012 362 5501; fax: 012 362 1785; email: hatbackpackers@mweb.co.za; web: www.travelinafrica.co.za. New suburban hostel owned by the same people as Word of Mouth (see below) and likely to be similar in standard and offer similar facilities. Plenty of parking space. Accommodation will consist of 30 doubles. **F** dbl.
Kia Ora 257 Jacob Mare St; tel: 012 322 4803; fax: 012 322 4816; email: kia-ora@iafrica.com. The most central of Pretoria's hostels, close to the railway station and various historic buildings. Kitchen, bar, restaurant, tour desk, internet café. Free pick-up in Pretoria. Dorm **C** pp. Rooms from **E/F**.
North South Backpackers 355 Glyn Street, Hatfield; tel: 012 362 0989; fax: 012 362 0960; email: northsouth@mweb.co.za. Popular hostel in the buzzing suburb of Hatfield. Swimming pool, bar, satellite TV, kitchen, book exchange, spacious garden, cheap email/internet access, laundry, secure parking, regular barbecues. Free pick-up in Pretoria. Good travel centre runs several affordable day tours including Rietvlei Nature Reserve, Sterkfontein Caves and Rhino Park, Sun City, Soweto. Baz Bus and overland tour bookings. Room **F** dbl. Dorm **C** pp. Camping **B** pp.
Pretoria Backpackers 34 Bourke St, Sunnyside; tel 012 343 9754; fax: 012 343 2524; email: ptaback@hotmail.com. Well-established hostel in a a relaxed suburb with many bars and restaurants. Kitchen, bar, cheap laundry, internet. Free pick-up in Pretoria. Hourly shuttle to and from Johannesburg Airport. Cheap day tours to Soweto, Sun City, Pilanesberg, Ndebele Village, Pretoria City. Can book overland tours to Kruger Park, Victoria Falls, Nairobi, Botswana, as well as Baz Bus, Greyhound, Intercape tickets and flights. Camping and dorm **C** pp. Rooms **E/F**.

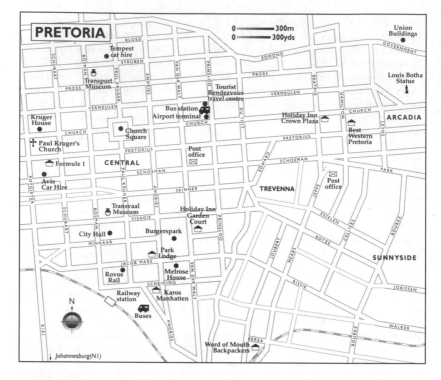

Word of Mouth 430 Reitz St; tel: 012 343 7499; email: wom@mweb.co.za; web: www.travelinafrica.co.za. Highly regarded and very comfortable, colourful hostel within easy walking distance of Sunnyside's bars and restaurants. The website is an excellent source of travel information for southern Africa. Excellent internet café. Lively bar, garden. Good travel desk with online booking for overland tours as well as several local day tour options. Free pick-up from anywhere in Pretoria (toll-free tel: 0800 108102). Hourly airport shuttle. New arrivals in South Africa get second night free. Dorm and camping **C** pp. Rooms **F** dbl.

Sun City and Pilanesberg
Manyane Camp Tel: 01465 56135. The only relatively affordable option in this area, situated at the Pilanesberg's Manyane Gate. Swimming pool, shop, restaurant, aviary with excellent photographic opportunities, walking trail in adjacent 'small game' area. Camping **B** pp (higher rates over weekends). Standing tents **E** pp.

Practical listings
There's little point in including extensive listings of embassies, public transport contacts, car hire firms, etc, since such information is rather more accessible in Johannesburg than in most other large African cities. The tourist offices in Johannesburg and Pretoria are currently in parts of the city you would be better avoiding with a pack on. Backpacker hostels, in any case, are a more reliable source of the sort of information that's of interest to their clientele. Informative entertainment listings are in the weekly *Mail & Guardian*. If you can't locate a phone number, dial enquiries at 1023.

MPUMALANGA

Formerly the Eastern Transvaal, Mpumalanga's tourist industry somewhat inevitably revolves around South Africa's best game reserve, the world-famous Kruger National Park. This scenic province, only four hours' drive from Johannesburg, is divided into the highveld and lowveld by the mountainous escarpment that runs through it from north to south. The provincial capital and main regional transport hub **Nelspruit** is a reasonably attractive and bustling town, and it has good facilities, though it's of interest to visitors primarily as a gateway to the rest of the province. That said, keen botanists should certainly pay a visit to the Lowveld Botanical Garden, on the Crocodile River 5km out of Nelspruit, while birdwatchers will find plenty to keep them occupied if they spend a day at the municipal campsite.

To the north of Nelspruit, a number of Mpumalanga's beauty spots lie between the town of Sabie and the northern end of the Blyde River Nature Reserve. **Sabie** itself is a compact and scenic highland town lying in the shadow of the 2,284m Mount Anderson, the forested slopes of which can be explored on the excellent 15km Lourie Trail. Along the R532 between Sabie and the altogether more humdrum town of **Graskop** lie a number of waterfalls, of which the Mac-Mac Falls are probably the prettiest. Another place in this area that's definitely worth a look is **Pilgrim's Rest**, a restored 1880s mining village on the R533 about 15km west of Graskop.

North of Graskop, a public road more-or-less follows the perimeter of the spectacular **Blyde River Canyon Nature Reserve**. There are several places where you can stop along this road: the bizarre Bourke's Luck Potholes, which lie at the confluence of the Blyde and Treur rivers; the panoramic viewpoint at God's Window, and the stunning Three Rondawels viewpoint over the canyon itself. To the north of the reserve, the Odendaal Camp is a lovely spot from where you can explore several short walking trails, notably the Kadashi Trail, which follows a stream through shady riverine forest passing a stalactite-like tufa waterfall on the way.

The **Kruger National Park** is the most accessible and affordable of Africa's major reserves (see box *Exploring the Kruger Park* on pages 552–3). Measuring 350km from north to south, and an average of 60km wide, this is one of Africa's largest reserves, and a total of 147 mammal, 507 bird, 114 reptile, 33 amphibian, and 49 fish species have been recorded within its boundaries. The dense bush that characterises most of the park means that game viewing isn't as easy as in somewhere like the Serengeti, but a visitor spending a few days in the reserve can reasonably expect to see five to ten varieties of antelope (impala, waterbuck, greater kudu, blue wildebeest, steenbok, bushbuck and common duiker are certain, while more localised species include sable, nyala, tsessebe, klipspringer, roan, and eland) as well as chacma baboon, vervet monkey, hippo, white rhinoceros, elephant, buffalo, Burchell's zebra, giraffe, warthog and a variety of mongooses. The most commonly seen large predators are lion and spotted hyena, but there is also a fair chance of seeing leopard, cheetah, black-backed jackal and – if you are very lucky – African hunting dog.

Access and getting around

Hitching is forbidden in the Kruger Park, and there is no public transport, so most travellers either hire a vehicle in Johannesburg or Pretoria or join an organised camping safari.

An organised camping safari out of Johannesburg and Pretoria can be arranged through any hostel. Alternatively, the Baz Bus runs between Johannesburg or Pretoria and Nelspruit four times a week, and there are also rail and coach

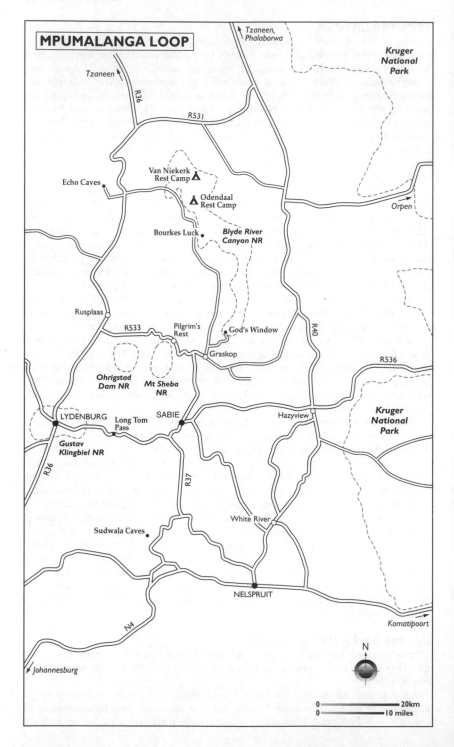

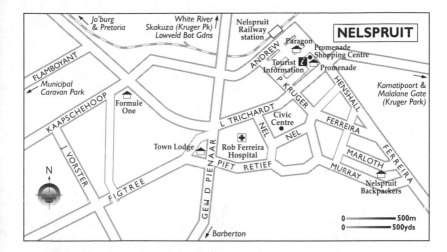

connections between these cities. The hostels in Nelspruit can also set up trips to the Kruger Park and elsewhere in the region.

Beyond that public transport options are limited, though Kruger Park Backpackers in Hazyview offers a free shuttle service from Nelspruit to connect with the Baz Bus, and once again they offer a variety of tours to the Kruger Park and elsewhere in the region. There is also a daily bus service from Johannesburg/Pretoria to Phalaborwa, a small town bordering the northern Kruger Park, where day trips can be arranged through the low-key Elephant Walk Backpackers (contact the North Link Bus at 015 291 1876).

Where to stay
Nelspruit
Formule One Hotel Junction N4 & Kaapsehoop St; tel: 013 44490. Rooms **F** triple.
Funky Monkeys Backpackers 102 Van Wijk St; tel: 083 310 4755 or 013 744 0534; email: funkymonkeys@yebo.co.za. New hostel with lively atmosphere next to a small nature reserve. The owner is a mine of local information and can arrange one- to four-day tours to Kruger Park, Blyde Canyon, etc. Laundry, meals, internet. Cabin **F** dbl. Dorm **C** pp. Camping **B** pp.
Nelspruit Backpackers 9 Andries Pretorius St; tel: 013 741 2237; email: nelback@hotmail.com. The oldest hostel in Nelspruit. Swimming pool. Bar with pool table. Close to nature reserve. Free pick-up from anywhere in town or airport. Very inexpensive Kruger Park safaris. Mozambique visas. Dorm **C** pp. Rooms **E/F**.
Nelspruit Municipal Campsite In a lovely piece of indigenous bush 20 minutes' walk from the Caltex Garage on the N4 towards Johannesburg. Chalet **F** dbl. Camping **C** site.

Sabie
Jock of the Bushveld Main St; tel: 013 764 2178. Pleasant, central, good facilities. Rooms **C** pp. Camping **C** pp.
Camel Rock Caravan Park Tel: 013 764-1241. Short walk from town centre. Next to a stream. Well positioned for starting the Loerie Trail. Camping **D** for two people.

Blyde River Canyon
Aventura Blydepoort Resort Tel: 031 769 8059. Beautiful location on edge of canyon. Entrance on the R532. Camping **B** for two people. Small youth hostel with rooms and

dorms 🅱pp. Expensive chalets. Rumours this resort will be bought by an upmarket hotel chain suggest it would be worth ringing for current prices in advance.

Kruger National Park

The rest camps from south to north are: **Berg-en-Dal**, **Crocodile Bridge**, **Pretoriuskop**, **Lower Sabie**, **Skukuza**, **Orpen**, **Satara**, **Balule**, **Olifants**, **Letaba**, **Shingwedzi**, **Mopani** and **Punda Maria**. Hutted accommodation exists at all camps, as does camping at all but Orpen, Olifants and Mopani (camping is available at Maroela 5km from Orpen). There are well-stocked shops at all camps except Balule, and restaurants at all except Crocodile Bridge, Orpen and Balule. Camping currently costs slightly more than US$10 per site for one or two people, and an extra US$2.50 for each additional person. Most huts are self-contained and cost

EXPLORING THE KRUGER PARK

Of the several factors that combine to make the Kruger Park the most affordable and accessible of Africa's major reserves, the fee structure is decisive. A couple who spent three nights in the Kruger would together pay around US$40 in camping and entrance fees. In most Tanzanian and Kenyan reserves, their combined fees would work out at US$240! A further consideration is the ease of organising a visit to the Kruger. You can get by in practically any car (main roads are surfaced!) and buy everything you're likely to need at a reasonable price from the rest camps' well-stocked shops.

One way to visit the park is make your way to **Hazyview** or **Nelspruit** and arrange a day trip with the local backpacker hostel. More straightforward and cheaper in the long run would be to take a budget camping safari out of **Johannesburg** or **Pretoria**. Companies that do this include **Bundu Bus** (tel: 011 693-1261), **To The Extreme** (tel: 011 452-2638), **Livingstone Trails** (tel: 011 867-2586) and **Wilderness Wheels** (tel: 011 648-5737). Trips range from four to six days and cost the equivalent of around US$40 per person daily all-inclusive.

You will almost certainly see more game with an experienced, knowledgeable guide on organised safari, but it won't be much more expensive and may even work out more cheaply to drive yourself to the park. The main advantage of this is that it gives you complete autonomy, something that's missing from any organised tour, no matter how backpacker-friendly it might be. Two or more people spending four or more days in the park should be able to stick to an average of under US$30 per head daily to cover such expenses as petrol, food, drink, camping costs and entrance fees. On top of this is the cost of hiring a car – around US$250 for a week with unlimited kilometres if you use a budget car hire company recommended by one of the hostels in Johannesburg. In other words, depending on group size, you'd be looking at somewhere between US$300 and US$400 per person for a seven-day self-drive trip to the Kruger Park.

If you decide to drive yourself, it's important that you book camping in advance and plan your itinerary so that you never have to cover more than 200km per day within the park. You're more likely to see well-camouflaged animals by driving slowly: allowing for stops, an average of around 15–20km/hour is about right. The park rules will be attached to your entrance voucher, as will the list of camp opening and closing times (these change from month to month depending on when the sun sets and rises, and late arrivals

around US$55 dbl, though there are basic huts costing around US$25 dbl at Orpen, Lower Sabie, Pretoriuskop, Balule, Letaba and Shingwedzi. Advance bookings should be made through a National Parks Board office. Campsites can normally be booked at short notice, except during school holidays. Booking huts at short notice could be a problem, though there is the possibility of entering the park as a day visitor and using the radio service between the camps to check what's available on a day-by-day basis – the reservation lists are passed to individual rest camps a day in advance.

Near the Kruger Park

Backpack Safari Lodge (Hazyview area) Tel/fax: 051 793 3816; email: backpack@gem.co.za; web: www.backpackers.co.za. This newish hostel, owned by the same people who run Cape Town's pioneering Backpack, lies in a private game reserve

are fined). An outstanding and inexpensive selection of maps and interpretative booklets is available at all camps and kiosks, as is the full range of field guides.

When you plan an itinerary, you should decide whether to stick to the southern half of the park or whether to head to the north. The area south of the Letaba River undoubtedly offers the best general game viewing, but it is also more crowded with visitors since it is closer to Johannesburg. The north of the park has more of a wilderness atmosphere, particularly the Punda Maria and Pafuri areas. If you opt to head north, I would suggest you enter at Melalane, spend your first two nights at Skukuza (using the spare day to loop through Lower Sabie to Crocodile Bridge, returning to Skukuza via the S25 and H6), your third night at Satara, your fourth at Letaba, and your last two nights at Punda Maria, using the spare day to explore the Pafuri River, then returning to Johannesburg via Louis Trichardt.

If you stick to the south, you can put together a more relaxed itinerary. It's worth knowing that the most attractive campsites south of the Sabie River are Berg-en-Dal, Skukuza and Crocodile Bridge, though most Kruger Park regulars agree that Lower Sabie is better positioned than the other camps for game drives. Two roads in the far south which offer reliably good game viewing are the tarred H4-1 between Skukuza and Lower Sabie, and the H4-2 between Lower Sabie and Crocodile Bridge (as well as the dirt roads to the east of this). The worst of the southern camps for overall atmosphere and location is probably Pretoriuskop – the roads round here are a good place for rhino and sable antelope, but otherwise you tend to see very little game.

Of the camps lying in the south-central region, Satara is the largest. Despite having a campsite with the atmosphere of a parking lot, Satara is an essential stop, as the surrounding plains are the best place to see lion and cheetah. The road between Satara and the Orpen Gate can be very rewarding, and the Maroela Campsite next to Orpen is one of the nicest in the park. Further north, Olifants has a commanding position on a cliff above the Olifants River, and it lies in an area where encounters with elephants are a virtual certainty. The nearest camping to Olifants is at Balule, a tiny and very attractive camp where you'll often see large animals strolling past. Also close to Olifants, Letaba is a very popular camp overlooking the Letaba River, and the surrounding mopane woodland offers good general game viewing as well as the best chance of seeing the rare roan antelope. I've yet to drive the dirt side-road between Olifants and Letaba without seeing something special.

bordering the Kruger Park near the Orpen Gate. Kitchen, bar, bush cuisine, swimming pool. Shuttles from the Baz Bus or from Nelspruit and Johannesburg/Pretoria can be arranged. Walking safaris, game drives, night drives, exclusive bush camps, visits to the Blyde River, river-rafting. Room **F**s/c dbl. Dorm **C**pp. Camping **B**pp.

Elephant Walk (Phalaborwa) 30 Anna Scheepers Av; tel/fax: 015 781 2758; cell: 082 495 0575; email: elephant.walk@nix.co.za. Small homely backpacker less than 1km from the Phalaborwa Gate to the Kruger National Park. Fully equipped kitchen, barbecue area, off-road parking and a lovely garden to relax in. Within walking distance of restaurants, pubs and a swimming pool. Kruger Park day trip from US$40pp, night drive US$15pp, game walks US$15pp, river safari US$8pp. Free pick up within Phalaborwa. Rooms or dorms **C** pp. Camping **B**pp.

Kruger Park Backpackers (Hazyview) Tel: 013 737 7224; fax: 013 737 7531; email: krugback@mweb.co.za; web: www.argo-navis.com/krugerpark. Well-established place near Hazyview, 40km from Numbi Gate. Ring from Nelspruit or Hazyview for directions. Good restaurant and pub. Kruger Park tours from US$125pp including two nights at the backpackers and one in the park. Dorm **C**pp. Hut **D** pp. Room **F**pp. Camping **C**pp.

KwaZulu-Natal
THE N3: JOHANNESBURG TO DURBAN

The N3 between Johannesburg and Durban is probably South Africa's busiest trunk route. Coming from Johannesburg, the first 300km of the road passes through the flat agricultural land that is characteristic of Free State Province, before coming to the town of **Harrismith** – an important route focus situated in pleasantly hilly countryside, but hardly – as one billboard rather optimistically proclaims – the Gem of the Free State.

For about 200km south of Harrismith, the N3 runs east of and roughly parallel to the Lesotho border and the Drakensberg, Southern Africa's most expansive mountain range (see *The Drakensberg* on page 559). The closest the N3 comes to passing through the Drakensberg is 30km south of Harrismith, where **Van Reenen's Pass** offers some fantastic views on a clear day and is quite terrifying on a misty one. The largest town along this stretch of the N3, **Estcourt**, is an unremarkable place, though it does have a couple of good nature reserves on its outskirts.

One of the most appealing stopovers along the N3 is **Howick**, a pretty small town set directly above the 95m-high Howick Falls. There are trails along the forested gorge beneath the falls, where you can see a variety of antelopes and birds – including cliff-nesting raptors such as crowned eagle and gymnogene. Close to Howick, **Midmar Dam** isn't anything special to look at but there are plenty of birds around, and the lake shore resort could be a convenient place to stop overnight.

Definitely worth a visit, **Pietermaritzburg**, the capital of KwaZulu-Natal, is an attractive and compact city ringed by forested hills. Founded by Voortrekkers but today a predominantly English and Zulu speaking city, Pietermaritzburg boasts several old buildings, most notably the Church of the Vow (built in 1841 and now a Voortrekker Museum), a Voortrekker House dating from 1846, and the Natal Museum (Loop Street), with displays relating to colonial history, as well as natural history and ethnographic sections. The tourist office on Commercial Road has details of walking trails through town and the surrounding hills.

South Africa's third largest city, and the busiest port on the subcontinent, **Durban** is also something of a resort town. The decidedly touristy beachfront has all the trappings you'd expect (an amusement park, a highly-rated aquarium

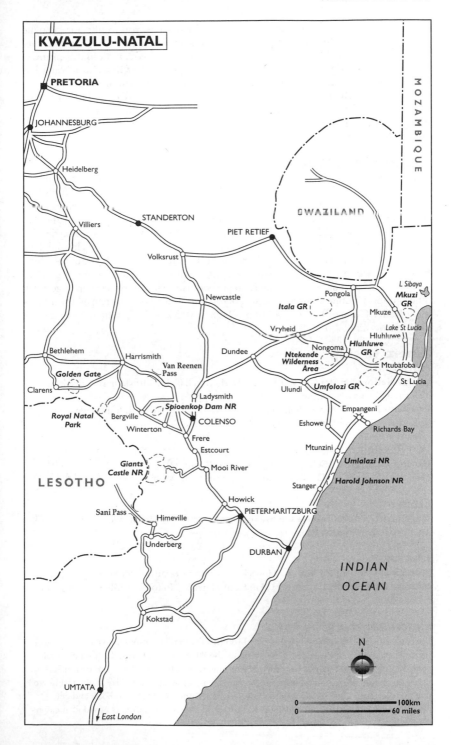

KWAZULU-NATAL

PRETORIA

JOHANNESBURG

Heidelberg

STANDERTON

Villiers

Volksrust

PIET RETIEF

MOZAMBIQUE

SWAZILAND

Newcastle

Itala GR

Pongola

L Sibaya

Mkuzi GR

Mkuze

Vryheid

Lake St Lucia

Hluhluwe

Hluhluwe GR

Bethlehem

Harrismith

Dundee

Nongoma

Ntekende Wilderness Area

Mtubafoba

St Lucia

Van Reenen Pass

Golden Gate

Ulundi

Umfolozi GR

Clarens

Ladysmith

Spioenkop Dam NR

COLENSO

Empangeni

Royal Natal Park

Bergville

Eshowe

Richards Bay

Winterton

Frere

Mtunzini

Estcourt

Giants Castle NR

Mooi River

Umlalazi NR

LESOTHO

Stanger

Harold Johnson NR

Howick

Sani Pass

Himeville

PIETERMARITZBURG

Underberg

DURBAN

INDIAN OCEAN

Kokstad

N

UMTATA

East London

0   100km

0   60 miles

and an endless string of restaurants and bars) and a few you might not (a snake park and colourfully dressed characters offering rickshaw rides). In the city centre, the Natural History Museum is one of the best of its kind in the country, and there's also a good local history museum. This part of KwaZulu-Natal has had a strong Asian presence for more than a century – the vibrant Indian Market is a must-see while the nearby Jumma Mosque is reputedly the largest in the southern hemisphere. The attractive resort town of Umhlanga Rocks, about 20km north of Durban, is worth a day trip for its beach and the Natal Sharks Board exhibition.

Access and getting around

Durban is an important public transport hub, with coach connections to Johannesburg (and of course Pretoria), Richards Bay, Bloemfontein, Upington, Port Shepstone, East London, Port Elizabeth and Cape Town (see *Getting around* on pages 559–60). Several Greyhound and Translux coaches run along the N3 between Johannesburg and Durban daily, a ten-hour trip with stops at Harrismith and Pietermaritzburg, costing US$30 one way. Another daily Greyhound Bus service connects Johannesburg to Durban via Richards Bay. The Baz Bus also runs between Johannesburg and Durban, stopping at all major centres along the N3 as well as at backpacker hostels in the Drakensberg (see *The Drakensberg* on page 559). The cheapest public transport between Johannesburg and Durban is the twice-daily Roller Coaster Taxi (tel: 011 857-2398 or 013 23-3706), which costs around US$17 one way.

Where to stay
Harrismith
Grand National Hotel Cnr Warden and Boshoff; tel: 05861 21060. Inexpensive hotel welcoming backpackers (ring for a lift). Rooms **F** pp.
President Brand Caravan Park Tel: 05861 21061. Shady site 2km from town centre on Wilge River. Camping **C** site.

Van Reenen Pass
Green Lantern Inn 7 Wragg St; tel: 05867 891. Rooms **D** pp.
Montrose Hotel On N3, 20km south of Harrismith. Expensive rooms. Camp **C** site.

Estcourt
Wagendrift Nature Reserve On road to Giant's Castle 5km from town centre near N3. Tel: 03631 22550. Camp **B** pp.

Howick
Municipal Caravan Park Above Howick Falls 500m from town centre. Camp **C** site.
Midmar Dam Resort Close to N3 5km from Howick. No food available. Cabin **E** dbl. Camp **B** pp.

Pietermaritzburg
Forest Lake Backpackers Tel: 033 569 1686 (no fax); email: info@forestlake.co.za; web: www.forestlake.co.za. Situated on the shore of the Albert Falls Dam and adjoining small game reserve, 20km north of Pietermaritburg, this rustic and little-known retreat offers many opportunities for outdoor activities such as canoeing, abseiling, day walks and horse trails in the game reserve, and Zulu cultural visits. Phone in advance to book and get directions or details of public transport to the hostel. Accommodation is in wooden cabins. Camping **B** pp. Dorms **C** pp. Rooms **D** dbl.

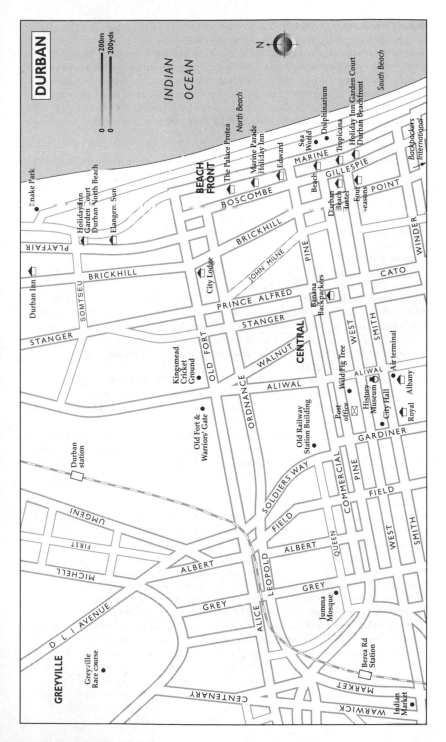

DURBAN

INDIAN OCEAN

N

0 200m
0 200yds

BEACH FRONT

Snake Park

Holiday Inn Garden Court Durban North Beach
Elangeni Sun

The Palace Protea
North Beach
Marine Parade Holiday Inn
Edward
Sea World
Dolphinarium
Tropicana
Holiday Inn Garden Court Durban Beachfront
South Beach

MARINE

Backpackers International

PLAYFAIR

Durban Inn

BRICKHILL

SOMTSEU

STANGER

BRICKHILL

BOSCOMBE

City Lodge

JOHN MILNE

PRINCE ALFRED

STANGER

WALNUT

GILLESPIE

Beach

Durban Beach Hostel

Four Seasons

POINT

WINDER

PINE

CATO

Banana Backpackers

WEST

SMITH

Kingsmead Cricket Ground

OLD FORT

ORDNANCE

ALIWAL

CENTRAL

Wild Fig Tree

ALIWAL

Air terminal

SMITH

Old Fort & Warriors' Gate

Durban station

Old Railway Station Building

Post office

History Museum
City Hall

Albany

Royal

GARDINER

UMGENI

FIRST

MICHELL

SOLDIERS WAY

FIELD

ALBERT

COMMERCIAL

PINE

FIELD

WEST

SMITH

ALBERT

LEOPOLD

QUEEN

GREY

GREY

ALICE

Jumma Mosque

Berea Rd Station

MARKET

WARWICK

CENTENARY

GREYVILLE

D L I AVENUE

Greyville Race course

Indian Market

Ngena Backpackers Lodge 293 Burger St; tel: 033 345 6237; fax: 033 345 6237; email: victoria1@cybertrade.co.za. New hostel. No rates available.

Sunduzi Backpackers and Bush Camp 140 Berg St; tel: 033 394 0072; fax: 033 395 6536; email: sunduzi@futurenet.co.za. Well-established, central hostel. Associated bush camp in nearby reserve with small mammals also recommended (the two are connected by a regular shuttle). Kitchen, bar, meals on request. Free pick-up from bus/train station. Day trips to game farm, Karkloof Falls (tubing), Midmar Dam (yachting) and townships (organised with local community). Room **C/F**. Dorm **C** pp. Camping **B** pp.

Durban

Angle Rock Backpackers On Warner Beach 30km south of Durban; tel: 031 916 7007; fax: 031 904 3812; email: anglerock@mweb.co.za; web: www.anglerock.co.za. Good beachfront hostel ideally suited for watersports such as surfing (free lessons), canoeing (day trip with lunch US$25pp) and scuba-diving (one dive US$30, two dives US$48, four-day course US$150). Kitchen, bar, pool table, swimming pool, volley ball, *braai* facilities. Restaurants, shops, travel agent, internet café within five minutes' walk. Free pick-up from anywhere in Durban. Dorm **C** pp. Rooms **F** dbl. No camping.

Banana Backpackers 108 Ambassador House, Cnr Pine and Prince Alfred St; tel: 031 368 4062; fax: 031 368 5783. Central and affordable, but many people who stay in this part of town get mugged. Dorm **C** pp. Rooms **D/E**

Beachbums Backpackers 65 Casuarina Dr, Tongaat; tel: 032 943 1907; fax: 032 943 1406; cell: 082 445 8951; email: bsbeach@iafrica.com. New hostel on attractive subtropical beach 40km north of Durban. Kitchen, bar, *braai*, laundry. Free pick-up to/from Durban daily. Activities include boat trip to swim with dolphins (US$15pp), microlight, swimming, surfing, exploring rock pools. Dolphins and whales often seen from the bar. Dorms and rooms **C** pp. Camping **C** pp.

Big J's Backpackers International 47 Essenwood Rd, Berea; tel: 031 202 3023; fax: 031 202 1738; email: bjbackpack@hotmail.com. Relaxed, colourfully decorated new hostel in a lively suburb close to the city centre. Dorms **C** pp. Rooms **E** dbl. Camping **B** pp.

Hippo Hide Guesthouse 2 Jesmond Rd, Berea; tel: 031 207 4366; fax: 031 207 4366; email: michelleh@hippohide.co.za; web: www.hippohide.co.za. Relaxed hostel run by an experienced traveller. Rock pool, poolside bar, kitchen, evening meals. Can assist with organising tours, safaris, car rental and day trips. Rooms **F** dbl. Dorm **C** pp. No camping.

Tekweni Backpackers Hostel 169 Ninth Av (off Florida Rd), Morningside; tel: 031 303 1433; email: tekwenihostel@global.co.za. Well-established and busy hostel in Morningside, close to a shopping mall and restaurants, 15 minutes' walk from the beach, and ten minutes by bus from the city centre. Kitchen, pool table, swimming pool, bar, off-road parking, good travel information centre. A related company, the commendable *Tekweni Ecotours* (www.tekweniecotours.co.za) runs several day trips (including two community-based tours), three-day Zululand safaris (depart Tuesday), three-day Drakensberg hikes (depart Saturday), and seven-day tours covering both areas. Overnight in a Zulu village on request. Dorm **C** pp (seventh night free). Rooms **F** dbl. Highly recommended.

Traveller's International Lodge 743 Currie Rd (off Florida Rd), Morningside; tel: 031 303 1064; fax: 031 303 1064; email: travelers-lodge@saol.com. Another hostel in Morningside close to the most 'happening' street in Durban. Ten minutes' bus ride to the city, 30-minute walk to the beach. Room **F** dbl. Dorm **C** pp. Recommended.

Valley Trust Tel: 031 777 1955; fax: 031 777 1114; email: vtrust@wn.apc.org; web: www.healthlink.org.za/valley. Unique rural development project offering down-to-earth cultural and social insights into traditional and contemporary Zulu lifestyles. Only 30 minutes from Durban; ring for details. Dorms **C** pp. Rooms **D/F**.

THE DRAKENSBERG

This extensive mountain range, often referred to as 'The Berg', is immensely popular with ramblers and hikers. Although the area is best-known for its superb scenery, it is also rich in rock art and supports a fair amount of wildlife as well as several birds endemic to South Africa and Lesotho. The Drakensberg extends into three South African provinces as well as the nation of Lesotho, but when people talk about the Drakensberg they usually mean the section in KwaZulu-Natal, which is entirely protected in nature reserves and wilderness areas.

The most northerly of these reserves and the most breathtaking, **Royal Natal Park** is dominated scenically by the 14km amphitheatre rising almost 2,000m above the surrounding hills. Other attractions include the 600m Tugela Falls, the 3,282m peak of Mont-aux-Sources, accessible rock art, a variety of antelope, and over 200 bird species. An informative 40-page pamphlet, available at the rest camp, describes more than 20 day trails ranging from 3km to 22km in length. The closest town to the Royal Natal Park, **Bergville**, is something of a route focus but of little inherent interest to backpackers. To the south of Bergville, the **Champagne Castle** area is beautiful and has good facilities for backpackers.

Lying off the R600 about 20km north of **Winterton**, the **Spioenkop Dam Nature Reserve** lies in the shadow of the Drakensberg at a low enough altitude to be a viable alternative to the mountains proper when the weather's playing up. The dense acacia woodland protected in this reserve is rich in bird and animal life and the campsite offers a lovely view across Spioenkop Dam to some low hills, with the Drakensberg as a backdrop. Of special interest is a small rustic camp which can be reached from the main camp either along a 10km walking trail or by motorboat.

The most important reserve in the southern Natal Drakensberg, **Giant's Castle**, was proclaimed in 1903 to protect a population of eland antelope. It is the most rewarding part of the Drakensberg for game viewing, and there are more than 500 rock paintings in a cave which lies an hour's walk from the rest camp. From Giant's Castle, a beautiful dirt road winds south to skirt the **Kamberg**, **Loteni** and **Vergelegen Nature Reserves** (not very accessible to backpackers) before arriving at the pretty town of Himeville, which has its own small nature reserve. Just outside Himeville is the turn-off to Sani Pass, the highest pass in South Africa and the one reliable entry point into eastern Lesotho (see box *Lesotho* on pages 562–3).

There are also a couple of places of interest in the part of the Drakensberg that lies in Free State province. The **Golden Gate National Park**, named after the pair of sandstone cliffs you pass through as you enter the reserve, is primarily of scenic interest, though it does protect several antelope species (including the endemic black wildebeest, blesbok and grey rhebok) which can be seen from any of several day trails or the popular two-day Rhebok Hiking Trail. Further west, 9km from Ficksburg, **Rustlers Valley Lodge** lies in a part of the Drakensberg foothills with plenty of potential for hiking, rambling and game-viewing. Rustlers Valley has for some years hosted South Africa's best known alternative music festival over the Easter weekend.

Access and getting around

The best way to reach the Drakensberg is with the Baz Bus from Johannesburg to Durban – ask to be dropped at Ntabeni Backpackers near Winterton or arrange for Berg Backpackers near Giant's Castle to meet you in Mooi River. The only other backpacker-specific transport into the Drakensberg is a minibus which runs between all hostels in Durban and Pietermaritzburg through to Sani Pass Lodge every Monday, Wednesday and Friday – ring 033 701-1017 to make sure you are collected.

Elsewhere in the region, you'll be reliant on hitching or minibus taxis. To give brief directions, the Royal Natal Park is reached on a good 20km tar road which is signposted from the R74 between Bergville and Oliviershoek Pass. Spioenkop Dam Game Reserve lies about 3km off the R600 north of Winterton. The best way to get to Champagne Castle is to turn south off the R74 into the R600 at Winterton, and continue for about 30km until you reach a fork in the road, where you should turn left to get to Inkosana, Dragon Peaks or Monk's Cowl.

Further information

The potential for hiking and climbing in the Drakensberg is endless and, while good maps and brochures showing day trails are readily available from the reserves, I would strongly urge anybody who wishes to undertake overnight hikes to buy a book called Drakensberg Walks by David Bristow. Recently revised and readily available at South African bookshops, this book describes, grades, and provides sketch maps for over 100 walks and hikes. It also gives a useful overview of the geology and natural history of the region, and contains potentially life-saving information on the dangers associated with hiking in an area that's notorious for its fickle weather.

Where to stay
Royal Natal Park and surrounds

Mahai Campsite In pine forest near park headquarters. Tel: 036 438-6303. Camp **B** pp.
Rugged Glen Nature Reserve Adjoins Royal Natal, entrances 3km apart. Camp **B** pp.
Hlalanathi Resort 10km outside entrance gate. Tel: 036 438-6308. Chalets from around US$40 per unit. Camp **B** pp.

Bergville, Winterton and Spioenkop

Bergville Caravan Park Tel: 036 448 1273. On R74 just south of Bergville. Free pick-up from town. Good value, accessible alternative to the hostel scene. Huts from **C/D**. Camp **A** pp.
Ntabeni Backpackers Tel: 036 488-1773. Recommended farm hostel about 5km from Winterton (pick-up from Winterton US$3). Dorm **C** pp.
Spioenkop Dam Nature Reserve Tel: 036 488 8157. Main camp about 30 minutes' walk from R600. Chalets US$30/unit. Camp **B** pp. Rustic camp 10km from main camp. Hut **F** dbl.

Champagne Castle area

Inkosana Lodge Signposted about 1km along left fork; tel/fax: 036 468 1202; email: inkosana@futurenet.co.za; web: www.inkosana.nf.net. Tranquil base from where to do dozens of day walks and hikes in scenic part of the Drakensberg. Kitchen, no bar (wine and juice available), meals. Free pick-up from Baz Bus in Winterton. Good trails, battle fields, rock paintings, horse-riding, overnight hikes. Rooms **D** pp. Dorms **D** pp. Camping **C** pp.
Monks Cowl Tel: 036 468-1103. Remote, beautiful campsite at end of road in nature reserve. Camping **B** pp.

Giant's Castle

Mount Lebanon Backpackers About 50km from Mooi River and 25km from Giant's Castle; tel: 0333 32214. Horse-riding, hiking, rock art, fishing, wildlife and rare birds (including wattled crane). Dorm **C** pp. Room **F** dbl. Free pick-up from Mooi River.
Hillside Camp In Giant's Castle. Dorm **C** pp. Overnight hiking (sleep in cave) **A** pp.

South of Giant's Castle

Kamberg Nature Reserve Bungalows **D** pp.

Loteni Nature Reserve Bungalows **E**/**F**. Camp **B** pp.

Himeville Nature Reserve Short walk from town. Camp **B** pp.

Drakensberg International Backpackers Lodge Tel: 033 263 7241. Highly rated new lodge in the Mooi River area. Hiking, horse-riding, rock art, trout fishing, wildlife. Meals, bar, satellite TV. Free pick-up from Wimpy on N3 near Mooi River. Daily shuttle from Durban. Camping **B** pp. Dorm **C** pp. Rooms **E** dbl.

Sani Lodge Near Underberg, 10km along Sani Pass near Underberg; tel/fax: 033 702 0330/1401; email: suchet@futurenet.co.za; web: www.sani-lodge.co.za. One of the oldest backpacker lodges in South Africa, with a spectacular setting, this forms an obvious springboard for trips to Lesotho (the owner is the author of a regularly updated booklet about travel there). Home-cooked meals, kitchen, beers on sale. Rock art, horse-riding, microlight flights, mountain-bike hire, self-guided day trails (maps provided), hikes of up two weeks' duration, 4x4 day and overnight tours up Sani Pass into Lesotho. Thrice-weekly shuttle to/from Durban. Free pick-up from Baz Bus in Himeville. Dorm **C** pp. Room **D** pp. Camping **B** pp.

Free State Drakensberg

Bokpoort Holiday Lodge Tel: 058 256 1181; email: horses@bokpoort.co.za. Signposted 3km from main road between Clarens and Golden Gate. Game viewing. Horse-riding. Hiking. Mountain-bike hire. Free pick-up from Clarens. Dorm **C** pp. Room **D** pp. Camping **B** per site

Glen Reenen Camp Straddles main road through Golden Gate National Park. Room **F** pp. Camping **C** site.

Rustlers Valley Lodge Tel: 051 933 3939; fax: 051 933 3286; cell: 082 854 8796; email: wemad@rustlers.co.za; web: www.rustlers.co.za. Legendary farm at foot of the Maluti Mountains, best known for the alternative music festivals hosted over New Year, Easter and in September. Great hiking possibilities, chilled atmosphere, regular workshops (see website for further details). Bar, restaurant and self-catering kitchen available. Internet access. Free pick-up from Ficksburg during the day (charge of US$3 for pick-up after hours. Rooms from **F** dbl. Dorm **C** pp. Camping **B** pp.

ZULULAND

Zululand is the informal name given to the lush, humid coastal belt that lies to the north of the Tugela River Mouth: the region that lay at the core of the nineteenth-century Zulu Empire and which even today has retained something of a wilderness atmosphere, boasting numerous fine game reserves that will be highly attractive to some backpackers.

Roughly 80km north of Durban, shortly before the N2 crosses the Tugela River, a short gravel turn-off leads to the **Harold Johnson Nature Reserve**, where a number of day trails run through an area of coastal forest noted for its bird life and epiphytic orchids, and home to a variety of small mammals including bushbuck and red and blue duiker. Fort Pearson, a relic of the Anglo-Zulu war, lies within the reserve.

The quiet and attractive town of **Eshowe**, 25km northwest of the N2, is fringed by the Dhlinza Forest Nature Reserve, the most accessible patch of mistbelt forest in Zululand and one of the few places where the rare blue duiker is easily seen. Also of interest in Eshowe is the unpretentious and well organised Zululand Historical Museum, housed in a 19th-century British fort.

Mtunzini is a modest resort town lying about 2km east of the N2 on the edge of the superb **Umlalazi Nature Reserve**. This coastal reserve protects a

LESOTHO

This small, mountainous kingdom is the only country in the world to lie entirely above 2,000m. Surrounded by South Africa, and heavily influenced by its larger neighbour both economically and politically, Lesotho was a made a British Protectorate in the late 19th century and remained one until 1966, when it was granted full independence. It is the home of the Basotho people, whose cohesive culture and friendliness, along with the wild mountainous scenery, make it a great destination for keen hikers and pony treks. It is, however, relatively impregnable, and since it lies off any main route it is visited by very few backpackers and you're only likely to pass through if you specifically choose to do so.

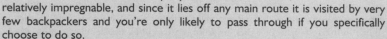

Visas are not required by nationals of South Africa, Ireland, Israel, the UK and Scandinavian countries. Everybody else must buy a visa from the Lesotho Embassy in Pretoria (tel: 012 322-6090). If you arrive at the border without a visa you'll get a three-day transit visa, which can only be extended in Maseru, the capital of Lesotho. Those who require a visa for South Africa should ensure it allows for multiple entries in order to return there.

The unit of currency in Lesotho is the loti (plural maloti), equivalent to the South African rand which is accepted freely in Lesotho, though maloti are rather less welcome in South Africa.

The main points of access to Lesotho are the N8 between Ladybrand and Maseru, and Sani Pass on the east of the country. Regular minibuses run between Bloemfontein in South Africa and Maseru. The only tarred roads are in the west near Maseru. Buses cover most but not all routes in the country. Hitching is slow, since vehicles are few and far between, but chances of a lift when something comes past are good.

Marco Turco's *Visitors' Guide to Lesotho* (Southern Book Publishers, 1995) costs US$12 in any South African bookshop, while the September 1999 edition of Russel Suchet's more backpack-friendly and cheaper (around US$2.50) *Backpackers' Guide to Lesotho* is written and sold by the manager of the Sani Pass Lodge. You'd do well to spend a night at either Taffy's Backpackers in Bloemfontein or Sani Lodge on Sani Pass before you visit.

You can hike and camp anywhere in Lesotho. Attractions include mountain scenery, remote traditional villages, rock art, waterfalls, and the sense of being well off any beaten trail. Lesotho isn't the place for novice hikers to break themselves in: experience, planning, and flexibility are prerequisite. Good 1:50,000 maps covering the whole country can be obtained from the Department of Planning and Surveys in Maseru.

Sani Pass

This is a popular entry point for backpackers visiting Lesotho, not least because there is a twice-weekly minibus shuttle from the major hostels in Durban to Sani Pass Lodge, a good backpackers' hostel near the base of the pass in South Africa (see page 561), and an outstanding source of travel information about Lesotho. From the lodge, a few trucks run to the top of the pass every day, as do a few Land Rovers serving as shared taxis. On the Lesotho side of the border, Sani Top Chalets has rooms for **D** dbl. There's good walking, and the staff organises hikes or horse treks to the top of the 3,482m Thabana Ntlenyana, the highest peak in southern Africa.

Sani Pass to Maseru

There is no public transport between Sani Pass and **Mokhotlong**, but a lift with a truck is easy to come by. The cheapest place to stay here is the Farmer Training Centre, where a bed costs **C** pp. There are two buses a day from Mokhotlong on to Leribe (formerly Hlotse), a former British outpost with a 19th-century tower. The cheapest rooms are, again, at the Farm Training College. From Leribe it's an easy trip on a tar road to Maseru.

Maseru

The Lesotho capital lies close to the South African border, 19km from Ladybrand in the Free State, and it is connected by regular minibuses to Bloemfontein in South Africa. The tourist office on Kingsway (tel: 32-2760) sells maps and organises pony treks. There isn't much cheap accommodation in Maseru: the Anglican Centre on Assisi Road (tel: 32-3046) has plenty of dormitory beds at **C** pp and rooms for **E** dbl. If you have a tent, the Motel Khali (tel: 32-5953) allows camping. Rooms here cost around R75pp.

Sehlabathebe National Park

Lesotho's only national park is a remote, unspoilt area dominated by a set of peaks known as the Three Bushmen and characterised by fantastic sandstone formations and caves. The main attraction is scenic, with sweeping views to the base of the escarpment, but antelope such as grey rhebok and eland may be seen, along with rare birds such as bald ibis and lammergeyer. Camping costs **A** pp and a bed in Jonathan's Lodge **B** pp. For more details ring the Conservation Department in Maseru at 32-3600 ext 18. For backpackers, one approach is from South Africa via **Bushmen's Nek Pass**, a 10km, six-hour hike. The base from which to start this hike and best source of information is Silver Streams Caravan Park (tel: 033701 1249) at the bottom of the pass in South Africa.

Pony treks

Ponies are the transport favoured by the rural Basotho, and the best way to visit remote areas. Popular bases for guided, equipped pony treks are **Malealea** and **Semonkong**, both of which are connected by a daily bus service to Maseru. The backpacker-friendly Malealea Lodge (tel: 051 447-3200; email: malealea@mweb.co.za; web: www.malealea.co.ls.) organises treks for around US$20 per day and hikes for US$5 per day. Transfers can be arranged through Taffy's Backpackers in Bloemfontein. Dorm **C** pp. Rooms **D** pp. Camping **B** pp.

Similar facilities at similar prices are offered by Fraser's Semonkong Lodge. Semonkong is Sesotho for 'Place of Smoke', a reference to the nearby Lebihan Falls, which at 190m are the highest in Lesotho and the country's most spectacular sight.

Cheaper guided pony treks can be organised with the Basotho Pony Project (tel: 31-4165) in Molimo Nthuse, two hours by bus from Maseru, but these will only be suitable for properly equipped people.

remarkable diversity of habitats, including the world's southernmost grove of raffia palms, one of only two places in South Africa where the striking palmnut vulture can be seen; the most accessible mangrove swamps in South Africa; a quiet, well-wooded lagoon and a near-perfect beach. There are a number of short trails in Umlalazi which can be combined to make a 10km day walk.

Two of Zululand's largest towns, **Empangeni** and **Richard's Bay**, lie about 20km apart on opposite sides of the N2 north of Mtunzini. Neither of these towns is of any great interest to travellers, and there are better backpacker facilities about 25km further north at **Kwa Mbonambi**.

The 350 km² **St Lucia Estuary**, the entire perimeter of which has been a nature reserve since 1895, has much to offer backpackers. The obvious base for exploring this area is **St Lucia Village** on the mouth of the estuary. Despite its slightly resort-like atmosphere, this attractive village offers numerous walking possibilities and it's only a 30-minute walk from the St Lucia Game Park, where three short nature trails (3–8km) offer the opportunity to see large mammals such as hippo, zebra, and wildebeest on foot. The Natal Parks Board Office in St Lucia can give further details of walking trails and they can radio through bookings and enquiries to most other rest camps in the area.

Elsewhere in the St Lucia area, the backpacker-friendly **False Bay** is the most northerly reserve on the western shore. Walking is permitted anywhere in the reserve, and there is a good chance of seeing crocodiles, hippos, nyala, warthog, red duiker, suni antelope and several localised birds. The 9km Dugandlovu trail leads to equipped rustic huts which are rarely full on weekdays.

The 100,000ha **Hluhluwe-Umfolozi Complex** is made up of two of South Africa's oldest and most important game reserves as well as a connecting corridor of state-owned land. Proclaimed in 1897, Umfolozi and Hluhluwe have been instrumental in the battle to save the black and white rhino from extinction. In addition to its dense rhino population, the complex protects populations of lion, leopard, cheetah, African hunting dog, elephant, buffalo, hippo, several antelope species and more than 400 birds.

Of several other good reserves in northern Zululand, the only one that can be considered accessible to backpackers is **Mkuzi Game Reserve**, known for its outstanding birds (over 400 species) and excellent system of hides. The central feature of the reserve, Nsumo Pan, is fringed by yellow-fever trees and ringed by low mountains, giving it a classically African feel. A short distance from the pan, the 3km Fig Forest Walk can be done unaccompanied. Mkuzi supports a wide range of large mammals including leopard, giraffe, both types of rhino, recently reintroduced elephants, and a variety of antelope species.

To the east of Mkuzi, snuggling up to the Mozambican border, the area broadly known as **Maputaland** is regarded to be one of South Africa's best-kept wilderness secrets. Little-visited game reserves such as **Ndumo** and **Tembe** are renowned for their profuse birdlife and big game, while the idyllic subtropical coastline is a haven for beach worshippers, fishermen and scuba-divers alike. Much of this region is difficult to travel in cheaply, but **Sodwana Bay** – routinely rated the best diving site in South Africa – does have one backpacker-friendly establishment that will be close to irresistible for underwater enthusiasts.

A somewhat remote but highly worthwhile excursion for backpackers with an interest in natural history, **Ntekende Wilderness Area** protects the extensive Ngome Forest in the hilly interior of northern Zululand. The unusual vegetation of this forest includes almost half of South Africa's epiphytic orchid species, as well as ferns with 3m long fronds, a variety of multi-coloured fungi and lichen, and the parasitic strangler fig. Wildlife includes both samango and vervet monkey, several small antelopes, highly vocal bushbabies, all manner of lovely butterflies and some localised forest birds. Roughly 40km of day trails radiate through the forest from the campsite.

Access and getting around
The Baz Bus now runs from Durban to Johannesburg via Zululand and Swaziland four times weekly, stopping at all towns along the N2 north of Durban. There are also Greyhound buses between Johannesburg and Durban via Zululand daily except Saturday, stopping at Richards Bay, Empangeni and Stanger. Translux coaches between Johannesburg and Richards Bay stop at Vryheid, Empangeni and Eshowe. The Amazulu Hostel in Kwa Mbonani will pick up travellers from Richards Bay, and they transfer people to and from the Durban hostels every Monday and Thursday.

There's no public transport off the main roads. Hitching is possible but rather slow, and you should be careful you aren't dropped off in the middle of nowhere. False Bay lies 13km from the N2 and 10km from Hluhluwe village. The entrance gate to Mkuzi Game Reserve lies about 15km from Mkuze town and the N2 (the campsite is outside the gate so you don't need your own vehicle to camp). Ntekende Forestry Station is 1km and signposted from the R618 between Vryheid and Nongoma, and it's a further 2km from the forest station to the campsite.

The only realistic way to see the Hluhluwe-Umfolozi complex without a private vehicle is on an organised day trip, which can be obtained affordably through any backpackers' hostel in the area, or as an overnight safari out of Durban (Tekwini Ecotours, based at the eponymous Durban hostel, is recommended).

Where to stay
Note that all accommodation in Zululand reserves should be booked through the KwaZulu-Natal Nature Conservation Service Reservations Office in Pietermaritzburg. Tel: 0331 845 1000/1067; fax: 0331 845 1001.

Camping should be booked through the individual reserve.

Harold Johnson Nature Reserve
Campsite Tel: 0324 61574. Camp **B** pp.

Eshowe
Inyezane Lodge In Gingindlovu near junction of N2 and R66 to Eshowe; tel: 035337 1326/1086; cell: 082 704 4766; email: inyezane@iphone.co.za. Easy access to Zulu cultural villages, game reserves, beaches. Cheap daily car rental rates. Phone from Gingindlovu Post Office for pick-up. Kitchen, bar, meals. Rooms with a/c **F** dbl. Dorms **C** pp. Camp **C** pp.
Municipal Caravan Park Next to Dhlinza Forest Reserve. Tel: 0354 41141. Camp **C** site.
Zululand Backpackers 36 Main St; tel: 035 474 4919; fax: 035 474 2894; email: eshowe@zululand.co.za; web: www.zululand.co.za/eshowe. Part of a small hotel whose owners are knowledgeable about the aera and keen to set up cultural and other activities at backpacker-friendly rates. Bar, kitchen, restaurants. Rooms from **D** pp. Dorm **C** pp. Camping **C** pp.

Mtunzini and Umlalazi
Umlalazi Restcamp On beach; tel: 0353 40-1836. Log chalet **E** pp. Camp **B** pp.
Xaxaza Caravan Park Tel: 0353 40-1843. Lush, shady grounds in village. Camp **B** pp.

Kwa Mbonambi
Amazulu Backpackers' Lodge 5 Killarney Place; tel: 035 580-1009. Pick-up from Richards Bay. Shuttle to/from Durban hostels Monday and Thursday. Cheap safaris. Swimming pool. Air-conditioned rooms. Dorm **C** pp. Rooms **E** dbl. Camp **B** pp.

SWAZILAND

This small kingdom, home to the Swazi people, is bordered by Mozambique to the east and South Africa to the other three sides. During the apartheid era, Swaziland's casinos and relaxed mood attracted a fair amount of tourism from South Africa, but the kingdom has never been visited much by backpackers, partly because it lies somewhat out of the way and partly because budget accommodation is limited. This could soon change, however, with the Baz Bus now passing through Swaziland between Durban and Johannesburg, and the pending establishment of a minibus service connecting Mbabane to Johannesburg and Mozambique.

The place to stay in **Mbabane** is The Chillage (18 Mission Street; tel: +268 605 8254; email: thechillage@flymail.com; web: www.thechillage.com) which offers camping at **B** pp, dorms at **C** pp and rooms at **E** dbl (discounts on advance bookings). The Chillage runs a regular minibus service between Durban, Johannesburg, Mbabane and Maputo (Mozambique), and its staff can also give good general advice and arrange customised trips into Mozambique. If you're coming on the Baz Bus, ring in advance to arrange to be met.

Mlilwane Game Reserve, south of Mbabane, has become popular with backpackers since the Baz Bus started stopping there overnight en route from Durban to Johannesburg (it no longer stops in the reserve overnight but a free shuttle connects the Baz Bus to Mlilwane). Not comparable to the best of the Zululand reserves, if only because it's been seriously infiltrated by exotic vegetation, Mlilwane supports plenty of game, including hippo, zebra, giraffe and various antelopes. Backpackers are catered for with night drives, horse treks, bicycle rental, rock paintings and a shop and restaurant. The place to stay here is Sonndzela Lodge (tel: +268 528 3117; fax: +268 528 3924; email: parksHQ@

Cuckoos Nest Backpackers 28 Albizia St; tel: 035 580 1001/2; email: cuckoos@mweb.co.za. The oldest hostel in Zululand, and still one of the best, set in large, lush grounds close to shops and banks. Swimming pool, volleyball, pool table. Good day tours to game reserves and traditional villages. Diving courses. Dinner only US$4. Breakfast free. Dorm **C** pp. Room **F** dbl. Camping **C** pp.

St Lucia Village

African Tale Backpackers About 10km from St Lucia town along road to Mtubatuba on the N2; tel: 035 550 4300; fax: 035 550 4300; email: africantale@hotmail.com; web: www.africantale.co.za. Good rustic hostel connected by regular shuttle to St Lucia. Accommodation in traditional beehive huts. Meals, bar with pool table, plunge pool, internet access. Various tours arranged. Free pick-up from Mtubatuba. Dorm **C** pp. Rooms **F** dbl. Camping **B** pp.

Bib's International Backpackers 310 Mackenzie St; tel/fax: 035 590 1056/1360; email: info@bibs.co.za; web: www.bibs.co.za. Busy, comfortable hostel on the main street through St Lucia Town within view of the estuary. Kitchen, bar with pool table, restaurant. Swimming pool, bureau de change, internet café. Free night drives, beach drives, fires on the beach at night. Free pick-up and drop-off at beach. Tours include Cape Vidal, snorkelling, Hluhluwe/Umfolozi in open vehicle, whale-watching, turtle tours. Dorm **C** pp. Rooms **E/F** twin/dbl. Camping **C** pp.

biggame.co.sz; web: www.biggame.co.sz.) which offers camping or dorms at **C** pp or rooms at **D**/**F** sgl/dbl.

There are several other small game and nature reserves in the kingdom, with the **Malolotja Nature Reserve** (tel: 61178) about 30km north of Mbabane being of particular interest to backpackers. The hiking here is excellent, and attractions include the beautiful mountain scenery, clear trails, wonderful flowers, more than 230 bird species and large mammals including wildebeest, hartebeest, blesbok, warthogs and leopards. There are several cheap campsites, the largest of which is close to the entrance gate on the main Pigg's Peak road. You will need to bring all your food requirements and a stove, since no fires are allowed.

Travellers heading to Mozambique might like to stop over at **Hlane National Park**, the entrance to which is on the main Manzani-Namaacha road about 5km south of Simunye. Set aside as the royal hunting ground by the late King Sobhuza, this lowveld reserve is home to a good range of big game species, including lion, elephant, white rhino, giraffe, zebra and various antelopes, and these can be seen by backpackers on affordable guided walks and open-top game drives. Huts from US$40/dbl. Camping **C** pp. Bring your own food.

Contact the central booking office in the Mbabane Mall (tel: 44541; fax: 40957) for bookings and further information for these and other reserves.

Most nationalities don't require a visa to enter Swaziland, and those who do will be issued one free at the border. A Mozambique visa issued at the embassy in Mbabane costs about half what it would in South Africa. The unit of currency in Swaziland is the *emalangeni*, tied to the *rand* and freely interchangeable with it in Swaziland but not South Africa. The international telephone code is +268. There are no regional codes. The best sources of information for Swaziland are Marco Turco's *Visitors Guide to Swaziland* (Southern Book Publishers) and the staff at Chillage House in Mbabane.

False Bay Game Reserve

NPB Campsite Tel: 035 562 0425. Near entrance gate **B** pp. There are also huts on the Dugandlovu Trail **D** dbl. The huts are rarely full out of season, but you're advised to ring to check availability if you are hitching out and don't have a tent. A limited range of foodstuffs is available from a shop 1km from the entrance.

Hluhluwe/Umfolozi area

Hilltop Camp (Hluhluwe) Tel: (031 845 1000). Brilliantly situated camp with modern huts, bar, shop and restaurant. Rooms from US$30 dbl.

Isinkwe Backpackers Tel/fax 035 562 2258; email: isinkwe@saol.com; web: isinkwe.hypermart.net. About 1km east of the N2 along Bushlands off-ramp, 30km north of Mtubatuba and 14km south of Hluhluwe Town. Rustic, family-run hostel set in a compelling patch of indigenous bush. Swimming pool. Kitchen. Meals served. Bar. 24-hour check-in. Free pick-up from Hluhluwe Town (also on Baz Bus route). Visit nearby Zulu Cultural Village or Cheetah Breeding Project. Full-day tours to Mkuze, Hluhluwe or Umfolozi. Rooms **F** dbl. Dorm **C** pp. Camping **C** pp.

Mpila Camp (Umfolozi) Tel: 031 845 1000. Relatively rustic self-catering camp with small shop. Great bush atmosphere, hyena and other animals pass through camp at night. Rooms from US$30 dbl.

Mkuzi Game Reserve

NPB Campsite At entrance gate. Call 0020 and ask for Mkuze 12. Camp **C** pp.
Main Camp 12km into the reserve. Shop. Huts from **E** pp.

Sodwana Bay

Coral Divers 80km from N2; tel: 082 556 2474; fax: 035 571 0042; email:
mmagic@iafrica.com; web: www.coraldivers.co.za. Good diving company based in
Sodwana Game Reserve with facilities for all budgets. Self-catering facilities and fridge
space. Meals provided on request. Bar, swimming pool, satellite TV. Single dive from
US$18. Five-dive package from US$75. Open Water Diver Courses start every Sunday
evening (US$200 pp). Backpacker safari tents **C** pp.

Ntekende Wilderness Area

Campsite Very basic and peaceful site in heart of forest. Facilities limited to cold running
water and long-drop toilet. Nearest shop 10km. Camp **B** pp.

The coast from Durban to Cape Town

FROM DURBAN TO PORT ELIZABETH

South of Durban, the N2 follows the coast for about 150km to Port Shepstone,
passing through South Africa's most developed beach resort area, with some 50-odd
campsites and dozens of self-catering establishments. During school holidays, this
stretch of coast is pure mayhem, and even out of season you'll find that the high level
of development has taken its toll environmentally. By contrast to the innumerable
resorts catering to South African holidaymakers, many of which offer affordable
camping facilities, backpacker-oriented accommodation in this area is restricted to
Umzumbwe and Port Shepstone – the latter an unexpectedly industrial-looking
town and the coastal terminus for the popular *Banana Express*, a steam train that
follows a 10-inch gauge line opened in 1911 to the small town of Paddock.

Port Shepstone lies at the junction of the N2 where it cuts inland towards
Kokstad, and the R61, which follows the so-called 'Hibiscus Coast' south to Port
Edward on the Eastern Cape border. Like the rest of the south coast, the stretch
between Port Shepstone and Port Edward is studded with a succession of resorts
which tend to be oppressively busy during school holidays and unexpectedly quiet
the rest of the time. And, once again, campers have a practically limitless choice of
sites catering mostly to the local market, but only the relative metropolis of
Margate and rather more low-key **Port Edward** area offer accommodation
aimed at backpackers. Port Edward is effectively the end of the road as far as public
transport goes, and most travellers heading this way will end up returning to Port
Shepstone and the N2.

At Port Shepstone, the N2 turns inland to skirt the **Oribi Gorge Nature
Reserve**. Easily explored on foot, the scenic gorge protected by this reserve
supports forest dwellers such as bushbuck and samango monkey as well as cliff
nesters like the black eagle. About 100km west of Port Shepstone, shortly before it
crosses into the Eastern Cape Province, the N2 bypasses **Kokstad**, an
unremarkable small town that's of interest mostly for the **Mount Currie Nature
Reserve**. Set in the Drakensberg foothills 5km from Kokstad, this small reserve is
crossed by footpaths from where a variety of antelope and birds can be seen.

The next large town along the N2 is **Umtata**, the pleasant but rather bland
former capital of what was once the nominally independent Transkei homeland.
This area has long been known for the remote reserves and hiking trails of the
little-developed **Wild Coast**, running roughly parallel to the inland N2. The

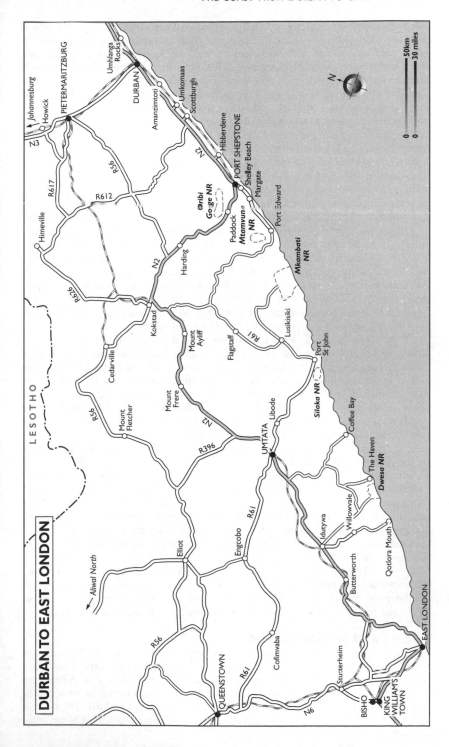

DURBAN TO EAST LONDON

closest thing the Wild Coast has to a resort town is **Port St John**, a low-key village with good backpacker facilities bordering the **Silaka Nature Reserve** in which a wide range of antelope and birds can be seen on foot. Another beautiful and accessible spot on the Wild Coast is **Coffee Bay**, from where a four-hour walk leads to the area's best-known geological feature, the so-called Hole in the Wall. The four- to five-day Wild Coast Hiking Trail between Port St John and Coffee Bay is one of the most attractive in South Africa; the hostel in either town can give you details of how to arrange the hike.

The N2 briefly skirts the coast again at **East London**. One of South Africa's largest cities, East London is somewhat lacking in character, though its beaches are highly rated by surfers. Far more appealing is **Grahamstown**, a university town with tangible 1820 Settler roots situated on the N2 180km west of East London. In addition to the excellent set of museums overseen by the Albany Museum (Somerset Street), Grahamstown boasts a number of old buildings and 40 churches. The Grahamstown Arts Festival every July is the major event of its kind in South Africa.

There's not much to be seen along the N2 between Grahamstown and Port Elizabeth: far better to cut across to the coastal town of **Port Alfred**, another 1820 settler town that has retained much of its charm. Sprawling along the coast around the Kowie River mouth, Port Alfred has a long and attractive beach. The inexpensive Kowie River Canoe Trail, which starts and ends in Port Alfred, can be done over two or three days stopping overnight at a small base camp on a horseshoe bend from where an optional 12km foot trail runs through the dense riverine vegetation of the Waters Meeting Nature Reserve.

Often referred to as PE, **Port Elizabeth** is South Africa's fifth-largest city and, although it's probably not worth making a special effort to see, it does have considerably more going for it than East London – notably the excellent museum and adjoining aquarium, dolphinarium and tropical bird and reptile house. The tourist office in Market Square (tel: 52-1315) can give further details. Situated about 50km north of Port Elizabeth, the **Addo Elephant National Park**, proclaimed in 1934, protects over 100 elephants, as well as 50 other mammal species (including buffalo and black rhino) and more than 150 birds.

The dry part of the Eastern Cape interior known as the Cambedoo isn't visited by too many backpackers, but it boasts at least one urban gem in the shape of **Graaff-Reinet**. This is South Africa's fourth oldest town, founded in 1769, and it contains numerous old Cape Dutch buildings of which roughly 200 are national monuments. There's an overnight hiking trail and several day walks in the adjoining **Karoo Nature Reserve**, noted for the spectacular Valley of Desolation and sanctuary to such large mammals as Cape mountain zebra and greater kudu.

Another old Cambedoo town that backpackers might visit is **Cradock**, noted as the burial place of the author Olive Schreiner and for the Spa on the outskirts of town. Cradock is also the gateway town to the **Mountain Zebra National Park**, an important stronghold for South African endemics such as blesbok, black wildebeest and Cape mountain zebra. Day trails and a three-day hiking trail loop out of the rest camp, and it's possible to organise game viewing on horseback.

Access and getting around

The most popular way for backpackers to explore this area is with the Baz Bus (see *Getting around* on page 542) which runs between Durban and Cape Town five times a week, stopping at Port Shepstone, Umtata, East London, Port Alfred and Port Elizabeth. The Baz Bus follows the N2 exactly from Durban as far south as East London (diverting to Cintsa just before it reaches East London). The hostels in Margate and Port Edward can meet travellers on the Baz Bus at Port Shepstone, while those in Port St John and Coffee Bay can meet the Baz Bus in Umtata, but this depends on demand so do let the hostel you want to visit know you are coming. Also worth mentioning is the daily Margate Mini Coach connecting Margate to Durban and towns inbetween (tel: 083 455 9736).

Between East London and Port Elizabeth, the Baz Bus follows the coastal R72 through Port Alfred and Kenton-on-Sea, stopping at most hostels en route. Greyhound buses cover the length of the N2 between Durban and Port Elizabeth, and unlike the Baz Bus they stick with the N2 between East London and Port Elizabeth, stopping at Grahamstown. Both Cradock and Graaff-Reinet lie around 200km inland. All trains between Port Elizabeth and Johannesburg stop at Cradock. Some Translux coaches between Port Elizabeth and Johannesburg stop at Cradock, while others stop at Graaff-Reinet.

Where to stay and eat
Umzumbwe
Mantis and Moon Backpackers Lodge Station Rd; tel: 039 684 6256; fax: 039 684 6256. Beachfront hostel in a small village with great surfing potential. Activities include ocean safaris (whales and dolphins), river cruises and abseiling. Room **F**dbl. Dorm **C**pp. Camping **C**pp.

Port Shepstone
The Spot International Backpackers Hostel 23 Ambleside Rd, North Beach, Umtentweni, 2km north of Port Shepstone; tel: 039 695 1318; fax: 039 695 0439; email: surfsa@icon.co.za. A good beachfront hostel that will appeal to keen surfers and sunworshippers. Rooms **E**dbl. Dorm **C**pp. Camping **C**pp.

Margate
Margate BackPackers 14 Collis Rd; tel/fax: 039 312 2176; email: ulrika@venturenet.co.za. Homely hostel close to beach and Margate's excellent selection of restaurants, bars and other amenities. Kitchen, bar, *braai* area, meals on request. Free pick-up from Baz Bus stop in Port Shepstone and the Margate area. Activities include day trips to Oribi Gorge (US$35pp), cultural tours (US$20pp), and diving in Protea Reef (plenty of sharks!). Room **E**dbl. Dorm **C**pp. Camping **C**pp.

Port Edward
Vuna Valley Backpackers 9 Old Pont Rd; tel: 039 313 2532; email: pitout@intekom.co.za. Relaxed, rustic hostel situated on the forested banks of the Umtamvuna River. Walking trails, birds and small mammals in the adjacent nature reserve. Horse trails. Kitchen. Meals on request. Ring to arrange pick-up from Baz Bus in Port Shepstone. Dorms **C**pp. Rooms **F** dbl. Camping **C**pp.

Oribi Gorge and Mount Currie
Mount Currie Nature Reserve Good campsite on dam. Camping **B**pp.
Oribi Gorge Nature Reserve Rest camp 1km from the N2 overlooking gorge. Huts **F** dbl.

Port St John
Mama Constance's Backpackers (bookings through Port St John Backpackers). Set in Mtambane Location, 30 minutes' walk from PSJ Backpackers, this Xhosa-run hostel offers a rare opportunity to experience indigenous African hospitality in a country where the backpacker industry is almost entirely dominated by white-run businesses. Accommodation is in mud huts, meals are supplied, and there are several local bars where you can enjoy a cold beer. Rooms cost **C**pp including dinner and breakfast.
Port St John Backpackers Berea Rd; tel: 047 564 1517; email: kirk@cdrive.co.za. This long-serving and consistently popular hostel is a good source of information about the Wild

Coast and the numerous rural hostels in the area. Pick-up from Baz Bus stop in Umtata. Stays at Mama Constance's (see above). Dorm **C** pp. Rooms **D**/**E**. Camping **B** pp.
Second Beach Backpackers Second Beach. Contact details as above. Beachfront hostel next to the lush Sileka Nature Reserve. Pick-up from Baz Bus stop in Umtata. Dorm **C** pp. Rooms **D**/**E**. Camping **B** pp.

Coffee Bay

Coffee Shack Backpackers Tel: 047 575 2048; fax: 083 631 7601; email: coffeeshack@ wildcoast.com. Good new hostel offering a great many activities for US$5–10 pp, eg: Hole in the Wall day trip, surf and beach day at Umdumbi point, Mpuzi cliff jumping, sacred falls, canoeing on Umtata River and Hluleka Game Reserve. Facilities include a kitchen, bar and good seafood meals. Camping **B** pp. Dorm **C** pp. Room **E** dbl. **Woodhouse Backpackers** Tel: 047 575 2029; cell: 083 639 1940. A rather new hostel with laidback atmosphere offering good day tours, meals and internet facilities. Dorm **C** pp. Rooms **E** dbl. Camping **B** pp.

East London

Areena Riverside Resort Tel: 043 734 3055; fax: 043 734 3312; email: areena@iafrica.com. Situated on the Kwelega River 25km east of East London. Nature-based activities include fishing, crabbing, swimming, hiking, birdwatching, canoeing. Floodlit tennis court, trampoline, volley ball, games room. Self-catering only. No meals or bar. On Baz Bus route. Rooms **F** dbl. Dorms **C** pp. Camping **B** pp.
Away With The Fairies Tel: 045 962 1031; email: sugarsk@iafrica.com. Recommended rural retreat in the wonderful Hogsback Mountains north of East London. Great rambling, hiking and horseback trips. Kitchen, laundry, bar, pool room, large campsite. Breathtaking

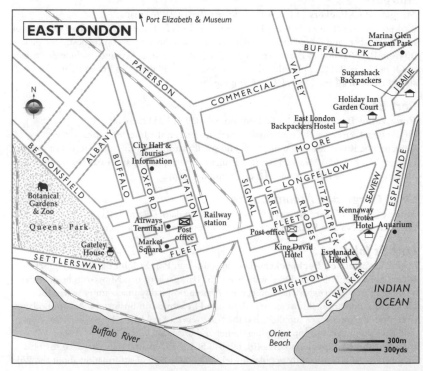

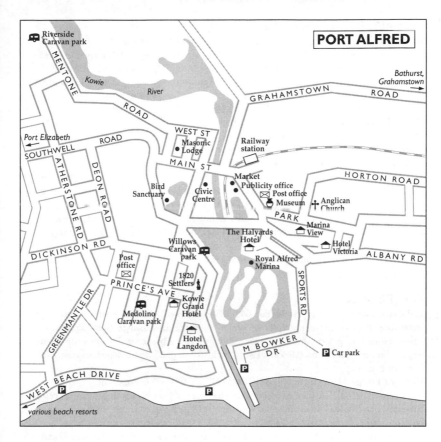

views from the lounge. Owned by the same people as Sugarshack in East London; shuttles between the two hostels every Monday, Wednesday and Friday. Rooms **E** dbl. Dorms **C** pp. Camping **B** pp.

Buccaneer's Retreat Tel: 043 734 3012; email: cintsabp@iafrica.com. Recommended coastal retreat and Baz Bus stop in Cintsa West roughly 40km from East London. Dorm **C** pp. Room **F** dbl. Camping **B** pp.

East London Backpackers 11 Quanza St; email: kaybeach@iafrica.com; web: elbackpackers.active3.co.za. New hostel located on the beachfront close to restaurants, clubs, pubs and supermarket. Facilities include TV, travel and tour desk, internet and email and secure off-road parking. Four-bed dorm **C** pp. Room **E** dbl.

Sugarshack Backpackers Eastern Beach, East London; tel/fax: 043 722 8240; email: sugarsk@iafrica.com. Well-established and organised hostel close to the city centre. Free surf lessons, surfboards, wetsuits, cliff jumping. Dolphin- and whale-watching platform. Cheap day trips include waterskiing US$10pp, coastal microlight over dolphins US$12pp. Horse-ride through game reserve US$20pp. Deep sea fishing US$12pp. Free pick-up from town. Dorms **C** pp. Rooms **E** dbl. Camping **B** pp.

Grahamstown

Old Goal Backpackers Somerset St; tel: 046 636 1001. Idiosyncratic hostel housed in a 19th-century prison. Dorm **C** pp. Rooms **E** dbl.

Municipal Caravan Park Grey St; tel: 046 603 6072. Camping **C** per site. Rooms **E** dbl.

Port Alfred and surrounds

Bushman's Backpackers Kenton on Sea; tel/fax: 046 648 2545; email: kellystours@imaginet.co.za; web: www.imaginet.co.za/kellystours. Recommended hostel at attractive small beach resort near Bushman's River Mouth 25km west of Port Alfred. Watersports, horseback trails, bird-watching, swimming, snorkelling. Addo Elephant day tours US$20pp. Self-catering kitchen. Restaurants and bars within walking distance. trails available at very reasonable prices. Room **C/E**. Dorm **C** pp. No camping.

Port Alfred Backpackers 29 Sports Rd; tel: 046 624 4011; fax: 046 624 2397; cell: 082 784 4028; email: backpackers@imaginet.co.za. Comfortable hostel 3km from the town centre, close to the beach. Self-catering kitchen, bar, TV lounge, pool table. Free pick-up from town. Dorm **C** pp. Room **E** dbl. No camping.

Sherwood Shack Situated 22km north east of Port Alfred just off the R72; tel/fax: 046 675 1090; email: src@imaginet.co.za; web: www.imaginet.co.za/sherwoodshack. Converted pig farm surrounded by nature reserves near Kleinemonde and Fish River beaches. Popular with birdwatchers and photographers. Self-catering kitchen (freezer and fridge), bar and restaurant. On Baz Bus route. Pick-up from Port Alfred. Room **F** dbl. Dorms **C** pp. Camping **B** pp.

Willows Caravan Park Albany Rd (next to bridge); tel 046 624 5201. Clean and central. Camping **C** site.

Port Elizabeth

Calabash Lodge 8 Dollery St; tel/fax: 041 585 6162; email: calabash@iafrica.com. Relatively upmarket lodge, tastefully decorated in ethnic African style. Specialised in cultural tourism, eg: township tour, evening *shebeen* (local bar) tour. Free pick-up from airport, bus and train station. Rooms **F** dbl inclusive of good homemade breakfast. No dorm or camping.

Jikeleza Lodge 44 Cuyler St; tel: 041 586 3721; fax: 041 585 6686; email: winteam@hinet.co.za. Clean, cosy hostel in the heart of Port Elizabeth's historical centre. Kitchens, bar, breakfast, *braai* area, TV lounge, gardens. Close to shops, cinema, restaurants, nightlife, pubs. At the start of a 14km nature trail. Free pick-up elsewhere in town. Day tours ranging from Addo Elephant Park to rock art to whale-watching. Free traditional

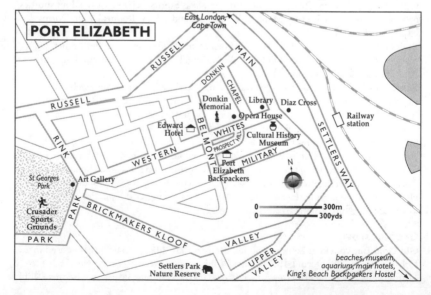

music and drama Tuesday and Friday night. Dorm **C** pp. Rooms **F** dbl. Camping **C** pp.
Kings Beach Backpackers 41 Windermere Rd; tel: 041 585 8113. Beachfront location.
Day tours to Addo. Free pick-up by arrangement. Dorm **C** pp. Rooms **E** dbl. Camp **B** pp.
Port Elizabeth Backpackers Hostel 7 Prospect Hill; tel: 041 586 0697; fax: 041 586
2032; email: pebakpak@global.co.za; web: www.welcome.to/pebakpak. Well-organised,
central hostel that's been popular for years. Dorm **C** pp. Room **D** dbl.

Addo Elephant National Park
Addo Rest Camp At entrance gate, 4km from R335 and 10km north of Addo Village; tel:
04252 140. Floodlit waterhole. Access to 6km Spekboom Day Trail. Restaurant and shop.
Camping **C** per site. Chalets around US$40 dbl. You can stay here without a vehicle, but
need to hitch into the reserve to stand much chance of seeing elephants.

Graaff Reinet
Urquhart Caravan Park Stockenstrom St; tel: 0491 22136. Rondawel **D** dbl. Chalet
F for up to four people. Camping **B** site.

Cradock
Cradock Spa 4km out of town. Tel: 0481 2709. Chalets from **E** dbl. Camping **B**/**C**.

Mountain Zebra National Park
Rest Camp 2km from entrance gate (walking and hitching permitted). Shop and
restaurant. Chalets from **E** pp. Camping **C** per site.

THE GARDEN ROUTE
The stretch of coast between Jeffrey's Bay and Mossel Bay, often referred to as the
Garden Route, boasts a string of unspoilt beaches and deep blue lagoons
interspersed with lush indigenous forests and fields of protea-rich fynbos. It is an
area well-suited to budget travel: compact, easily explored on foot, well equipped
with hostel accommodation, and serviced by a daily backpacker bus.

Coming from Port Elizabeth, the first Garden Route town is **Jeffrey's Bay**,
rated by enthusiasts to offer the best surfing in South Africa but otherwise
somewhat lacking in scenic qualities. To the south of Jeffrey's Bay, **Cape St
Francis** is arguably the more attractive of these towns, with a good beach,
excellent surfing, and a day trail connecting it to the Cape St Francis Nature
Reserve.

The scenic **Tsitsikama National Park** follows the coast for 80km between
Storms River Mouth and Nature's Valley. There are rest camps at both ends of the
park, but the only way of exploring the coast between the camps is along the Otter
Trail – South Africa's most popular hiking trail and as a consequence normally
booked solid. For backpackers, the best base in Tsitsikama is **Nature's Valley**, a
pretty residential village that lies within the national park. Overlooking a wide,
sandy beach, Nature's Valley merges into the surrounding indigenous forest and it
lies at the centre of a network of about 50km of day trails.

Plettenberg Bay is a large and reasonably attractive resort town boasting a
good beach. Possibly more interesting than the town itself are the nature reserves
and trails that lie near it. On the N2 only 4km east of Plettenberg Bay, in the
Keurbooms River Nature Reserve, there's an excellent and inexpensive canoe
trail, involving an easy 7km, two-hour paddle along the well-wooded river to a
simple 12-bed hut. Altogether different in character, the **Robberg Nature
Reserve** protects the rocky Robberg Peninsula 6km south of Plettenberg Bay by
road. The 11km trail through the reserve is a good place to see seals and

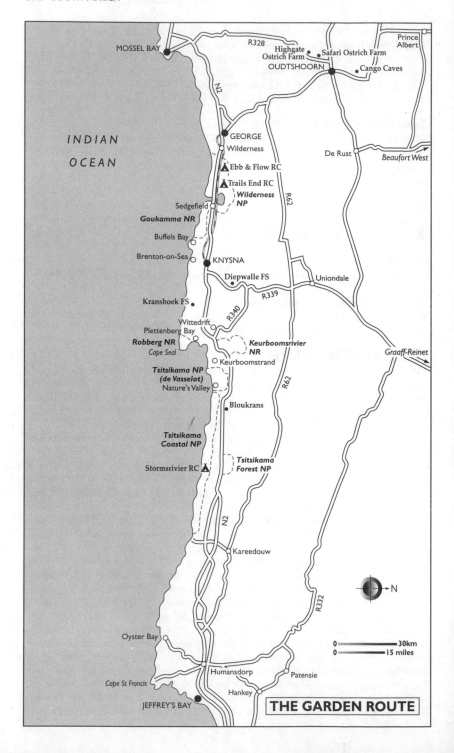

THE GARDEN ROUTE

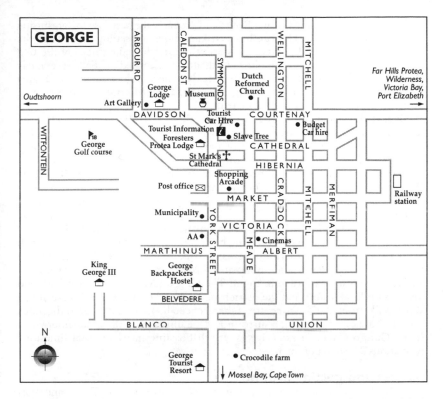

GEORGE

ARBOUR RD
CALEDON ST
SYMMONDS
WELLINGTON
MITCHELL

Oudtshoorn ←

Art Gallery •

George Lodge •

Museum 🏛

Dutch Reformed Church •

Far Hills Protea, Wilderness, Victoria Bay, Port Elizabeth →

DAVIDSON   Tourist Car Hire   COURTENAY

WITFONTEIN

🏌18
George Golf course

Tourist Information ℹ
Foresters •
Protea Lodge 🏠

• Slave Tree

Budget Car hire •

CATHEDRAL

St Mark's ✝
Cathedral

HIBERNIA

Post office ✉

Shopping Arcade •

CRADOCK
MITCHELL
MERRIMAN

Railway station

MARKET

Municipality •

YORK STREET

VICTORIA

AA •

MEADE

• Cinemas

MARTHINUS   ALBERT

King George III
🏛

George Backpackers Hostel 🏠

BELVEDERE

BLANCO   UNION

N

George Tourist Resort 🏠

• Crocodile farm

↓ Mossel Bay, Cape Town

humpbacked whales, as well as colonies of rare seabirds such as the black oystercatcher. Also of interest is the **Kranshoek Day Trail** (part of the overnight Harkerville Hiking Trail), which passes through an exceptional variety of habitats over the relatively short distance of 9km. The **Wittedrift Trail**, run by Wittedrift High School, is a loose collection of trails starting about 10km north of Plettenberg Bay and centred around an overnight hut on the forested banks of the Bitou River.

Overlooking the lagoon of the same name, **Knysna** has established itself as the most popular backpackers' resort on the Garden Route, and for good reason. In addition to having a lovely setting, Knysna bristles with old-world charm and it is a good base for a variety of watersports and walks. Many travellers visit Mitchell's Brewery, one of South Africa's few real ale breweries, while Jetty Tapas on the waterfront is popular for its good music and position as well as for cheap Mitchell's beer and plates of oysters. A popular walk in the Knysna area is the **Elephant Walk**, an 18km circular trail in Diepwalle State Forest, known for its giant yellowwood trees, excellent birdwatching, and as the last place in the Garden Route where elephants still occur naturally – all three of them! Another popular outing from Knysna is the inexpensive boat trip to **Featherbed Nature Reserve**, where a wander along a short guided trail can be followed by a fish *braai* or an oyster and champagne breakfast.

The stretch of the Garden Route delineated by the resort villages of **Sedgefield** and **Wilderness** is notable for a series of lakes and lagoons, protected in **Wilderness National Park**, where a variety of mammals and birds can be seen from the 12km Kingfisher Trail.

The largest town on the Garden Route and probably the best base for organising cheap tours and car hire, **George** has a striking mountain setting 12km from the coast. George has several points of historical interest including notably the Old Drosdty built in 1812 and an Anglican Cathedral consecrated in 1850. Several day trails radiate into the Groeneweide State Forest on the foot slopes of the Outeniqua Mountains. Only 10km from George, **Pacaltsdorp Mission** is the site of a Norman-style church constructed in 1813.

Mossel Bay is the most westerly town on the Garden Route. I thought it the least memorable of the Garden Route towns, but many travellers love it. It has in its favour a large, safe beach, a pretty market square, an excellent museum and several historical buildings. Also of interest are the day-trips to a nearby island which supports a 2,000-strong breeding colony of Cape seals. **Gouritz River Bridge** west of Mossel Bay is the site of one of South Africa's most popular bungee jumps, run daily in summer and every Saturday and Sunday during winter.

Situated in the Little Karoo, 60km inland of Mossel Bay and George, **Oudtshoorn** is best known for having been at the centre of the Victorian ostrich feather industry. Ostrich farming remains widely practised in the area: several ostrich farms are open to the public and related products such as ostrich meat and eggs are readily available in town. The CP Nel Museum in town has good displays on local history and the ostrich trade. Also of interest is Cheetahland, a short walk from the town centre, where cheetah, lion and other indigenous predators are caged in 'natural' surrounds. One must-see in the Oudtshoorn area is the **Cango Cave**, an extensive labyrinth boasting many unusual limestone formations 35km out of town.

Access and getting around
The Baz Bus stops at all towns along the N2 between Cape Town and Port Elizabeth five times weekly. The Intercape Bus (tel: 021 386-4400) between Cape Town and Port Elizabeth also stops at most towns on the N2. Don't miss out on the Outeniqua Choo-Tjoe (tel: 0441 68202 or 0445 82-5624), an inexpensive and scenic steam train service which travels twice-daily in either direction between George to Knysna, stopping at a number of small settlements en route.

Where to stay
Jeffreys Bay
Island Vibe Backpackers 10 Dageraad St; tel: 042 293 1625; fax: 042 293 3469; email: ivibe@lantic.co.za. Excellent beachfront hostel with stunning views and busy atmosphere. Bar, kitchen, *braai* lit every night, free surfboards and lifts to town. Free activity every evening with free wine. Sensibly prices tours to Addo Elephant, waterfall, township. Dorm **C** pp. Room **F** dbl. Camping **B** pp.

Jeffreys Bay Backpackers 12 Jeffrey St; tel: 042 293 1379; fax: 042 296 1763; email: backpac@netactive.co.za; web: www.hisa.org.za. A clean, well-organised, central and popular hostel that's been going for years. Communal kitchen, bar, internet access, swimming pool. Two minutes from beach, supermarkets, banks, surf factories and shops. Sandboarding, kloofing, tubing, horse-riding, trips to the waterfall. Tours to Shamwari Game Park, Addo Elephant Park and Scotia Game Park. Free pick-ups from within 20km radius. Every third night free. Rooms **D/E**. Dorm **C** dbl.

Supertubes Backpackers 6 Pepper St; tel/fax: 042 293 2957; email: supertubes@agnet.co.za. Overlooking the legendary 'Supertubes' waves, this has a prime surfer's setting and great ocean views. Dorms **C** pp. Prices rise during South African school holidays.

Cape St Francis

Sealpoint Backpackers Tel: 042 298 0054; fax: 042 298 0157; email: seals@iafrica.com. Large seafront resort complex 20km from town with attached backpacker lodge. Facilities within the complex include swimming pool, *braai* area, restaurant, pub. Free pick-up from the Baz Bus in Humansdorp and Jeffrey's Bay. Daily canal cruise (US$6pp), 4x4 safari (US$4pp), hiking, water-skiing, fishing, etc. Dorm **C** pp. Four-bed flat US$30 per unit. Bush camp in bird sanctuary **C** pp.

Tsitsikama

Storms Hikers House Cnr Darnell and Saffraan, Storms River Village; tel/fax: 042 5411 757; cell: 082 394 6441; email: rallus@mweb.co.za. Set in large grounds in the picturesque village of Storms River, this clean hostel is an excellent base from where to explore the scenic Tsitsikama coastline and embark on a daunting range of outdoor activities with Storms River Adventures (email: adventure@gardenroute.co.za). Self-catering kitchen and *braai* area. One of the cheapest hostels on the Garden Route. Dorms **C** pp. Camping **B** pp.

Nature's Valley

Hikers Haven 411 Patrick Rd; tel: 04457 6805. Bicycle hire. Booking recommended. Dorm **C** pp. Rooms **E** pp.
Garden Route Backpackers Close to junction of N2 and Nature's Valley turn-off. Tel: 044 534 8837; email: gardenroutebp@hotmail.com. New hostel on game farm. Free transport to Bloukrans bungee jump (reputedly the highest in the world) and plenty of walking and activities available. Dorm **C** pp. Room **F** dbl. Camping **C** pp.
Groot River Campsite Beautiful site in forest 1km from Nature's Valley. Camping **D** site.

Plettenberg Bay and surrounds

Albergo Backpackers 8 Church St; tel: 04457 34434. Central, popular, well-organised and plenty of activities. Free pick-up 08.00 to 20.00. Dorm **C** pp. Rooms **F** dbl.
Keurbooms River Nature Reserve Leafy riverside camp next to bridge on N2 4km east of Plettenberg Bay. Camping **C** site.
Nothando Travellers Lodge 5 Wilder St; tel/fax: 044 533 0220; email: deios@global.co.za. Comfortable, popular and central. Kitchen, bar, traditional meals. Can arrange whale and dolphin tours, day hikes in the Robberg, Kranshoek and Keurbooms reserves, surfing, sea-kayaking, diving, canoeing, abseiling, horse-riding, cycling, Knysna elephant visit, Bloukrans bungee jump, traditional theatrical and dance group. Free pick-up from bus station and local airport. Dorm **C** pp. Room **F** dbl.
Robberg Caravan Park Scenic location at entrance to Robberg Nature Reserve. Tel: 044 533 2571. Camping **C** site.
Weldon Kaya Backpackers Cnr N2 and Piesang Valley Rd, 2km from town; tel: 044 533 2437; fax: 044 533 4364; email: info@weldonkaya.co.za; web: www.weldonkaya.co.za. Colourful new hostel with African decor on a hill with great sea views. Kitchen, bar, restaurant (African dishes). Good travel centre arranges all sorts of tours and activities. Swimming pool, volleyball, pool table, pinball, live African entertainment Wednesday, live band at weekends. Free pick-up from town. Daily shuttle to beaches. Dorm **C** pp. Rooms **F** dbl.

Knysna

Overlanders Lodge 11 Nelson St; tel: 0445 82-5920. Dorm **C** pp. Rooms **E** dbl. Camp **B** pp.
Peregrin Backpackers 16 High St; tel/fax 044 382 3747; email: Peregrin@knysna.lia.net. Large hostel with great view over lagoon. Kitchen and meals. Satellite TV, swimming pool. Travel centre offers target shooting, horse rides, abseiling, sightseeing tours, sea-kayaking,

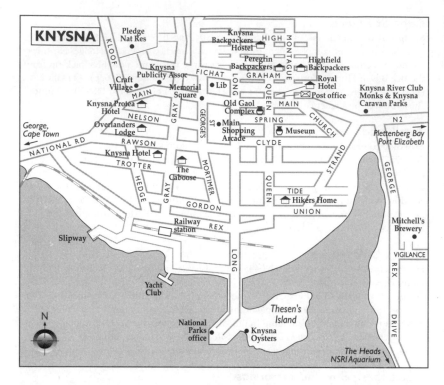

dolphin- and whale-watching, diving courses. Free pick-up anywhere in town. Discounts for second and third night. Free continental breakfast. Dorm **C** pp. Rooms **F** dbl. Camping **C** pp. **The Backpack Knysna Waterfront** 17 Tide St; tel: 044 382 4362; fax: 044 382 7766; email: backpack@gem.co.za; web: www.backpackers.co.za. Good new hostel under same ownership as The Backpack in Cape Town. Kitchen, bar, restaurant. Swimming pool, covered *braai* area, internet access. Travel centre arranges a wide selection of day trips. Free pick-up from anywhere in town. Competitive rates with discount for those who stayed at The Backpack in Cape Town. Dorms **C** pp. Rooms **F** dbl. Camping **B** pp.

Wilderness
Fairy Knowe Backpackers Tel: 044 877 1285; email:fairybp@mweb.co.za. Attractive situation near Fairy Knowe station (request stop for Outeniqua Choo-Tjoe). Space limited, so ring in advance. Dorm **C** pp. Room **F** dbl. Camping **C** pp

George
Sunshine Backpackers Hostel 103 Merriman St; tel: 044 873 0424. Dorm **C** pp. Rooms **F** dbl. Camping **B** pp.

Mossel Bay
Mossel Bay Backpackers 1 Marsh St; tel/fax: 044 691 3182; email: marquette@pixie.co.za. Cosy, spacious hostel close to The Point (one of the country's best surfing beaches) and within walking distance of restaurants, bars, banks and shops. Kitchen, bar, fish *braais* in the evening. Arranges a wide range of activities from bungee-jumps and mountain-biking to shark dives and whale-watching. Free pick-up from town. Room **F** dbl. Dorm **C** pp. Camping **C** pp. Ask about low season discounts in adjoining *Marquette Guesthouse* out of season.

Santos Express Santos Beach (town centre); tel/fax: 044 691 1995; email: trein@mb.lia.net. This refreshingly unconventional hostel consists of an old train parked on the beachfront within easy walking distance of the town, museums and harbour. Accommodation is in an authentic train compartment with a sea and mountain view. Kitchen, bar and restaurant specialising in seafood, traditional meals and *braai*. Room **F** dbl (includes breakfast). Dorm **C** pp.

Oudtshoorn
Backpackers Oasis 3 Church St; tel/fax: 044 279 1163; email: oasisbackpackers@yahoo.com. Well-established and popular hostel with good travel centre and internet access. Room **E** dbl. Dorm **C** pp. Camp **B** pp.
Backpackers Paradise 148 Baron van Reede St; tel: 044 272 3436; fax: 044 272 0877; email: jubilee@pixie.co.za. Clean, comfortable hostel in the shadow of the Swartberg Range. Kitchen, bar, ostrich *braai* and vegetarian meals, free ostrich egg breakfast. Arrange inexpensive mountain-biking, microlight trips, ostrich farm visits. Free pick-up from Oudtshoorn, or from George to tie in with Baz Bus and Outeniqua Choo-Tjoe. Rooms **F** s/c dbl. Dorms **C** pp. Camping **B** pp.
N A Smit Resort Park Rd; tel: 0443 22-4152. Municipal site. Rondawels from **D** dbl. Camping **C** site.

FROM MOSSEL BAY TO CAPE TOWN
The most significant town on the N2 between Mossel Bay and Cape Town is **Swellendam**, the third oldest town in South Africa. Oak-lined avenues and a few 18th-century buildings give Swellendam some character, but it is certainly less atmospheric than Stellenbosch or Graaff-Reinet, towns of a similar vintage –

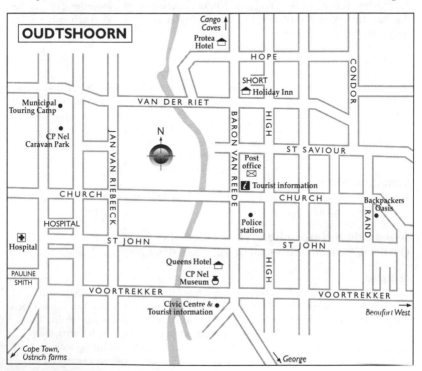

perhaps because much of the old town was destroyed by fire in 1865. Keen walkers will find much to occupy them in the Marloth Nature Reserve on the outskirts of town. The **Bontebok National Park** 6km from Swellendam protects the threatened bontebok and Cape mountain zebra as well as numerous birds.

Those who've come all the way overland from North Africa may find themselves irresistibly drawn down the R318 from Swellendam to **Cape Agulhas**, the southernmost point in Africa. Having looked at the obligatory plaque and established where you are, however, it must be said that this bleak and unwelcoming stretch of coast – more than 250 shipwrecks recorded since 1673 – is likely to prove somewhat anticlimactic. Only 6km from Agulhas and far more attractive for holiday making, **Struisbaai** has a 15km-long swimming beach and there are some restored whitewashed fishermen's cottages as you enter town.

Situated on Walker Bay, **Hermanus** is one of the most popular resort towns in the Cape, as much for its cobbled road and old world atmosphere as its near-perfect natural setting. Several walking trails run along the cliffs to the west of town and through the Fernkloof Nature Reserve in the Kleinrivier Mountains on its northern horizon. Hermanus is particularly famous for the Southern Right whales which come into Walker Bay every year during the calving season between June and December. The **Salmonsdam Nature Reserve** 40km east of Hermanus is one of the most underrated reserves in this part of the country, protecting an area of mountain fynbos dotted with giant proteas and home to a variety of small animals including bontebok, and fynbos specials such as Cape sugarbird and orange-breasted sunbird.

Access and getting around
All coaches between Cape Town and Port Elizabeth stop at Swellendam, as does the Baz Bus. You'll probably be dependent on hitching to reach other places mentioned in this section.

Where to stay
Swellendam
Swellendam Backpackers 5 Lichtenstein St; tel: 028 514 2648; fax: 028 514 1249; email: backpack@dorea.co.za. Long-standing and cosy hostel close to the town centre at the base of the Langeberg Range. Kitchen, bar, *braai*. Swimming pool, internet access, and evening campfires. Inexpensive activities include sunset cruise, canoe and mountain-bike hire, hikes, day trip to Bontebok National Park, Cape Agulhas and De Hoop Reserve. Baz Bus stop. Rooms **F** dbl. Dorm **C** pp. Camping **C** pp.

Bontebok National Park
Rest Camp Tel: 028 514 2735. Pleasantly situated overlooking a dam on the Breede River. Standing caravans **F** dbl. Camping **C** site.

Salmonsdam Nature Reserve
Rest Camp Rustic huts **C** pp. Camping **B** pp. Ring 02833 789 to check availability.

Arniston
South of Africa Backpackers Resort Tel: 028 445 9240; fax: 028 445 9254; email: info@southofafrica.co.za. Part of a three-star hotel, and more expensive than the average backpacker, though the facilities justify the price. Kitchen, bar, restaurant. Satellite TV, billiard and pool tables, table tennis, swimming pool, sauna, gym, squash courts, *braai* facilities, laundry. Activities include dune skiing, mountain-bike and hiking trails, snorkelling in tidal pools, day trips to Agulhas and De Hoop, whale-watching. Free pick-up

from Bredasdorp. All rooms with bedding and TV; rates include a good buffet. Rooms
E/**F**. No dorms or camping.

Agulhas area
Municipal campsites In Bredasdorp, Struisbaai and Agulhas, all with self-catering chalets.
For details ring Bredasdorp Municipality on 02841 41135.

Hermanus and surrounds
Great White Backpackers 13 Main Rd, Gansbaai; tel 028 384 1380; fax: 028 384 1381;
email: sharkdiv@itec.co.za; web: www.whitesharkdiving.com. Situated about 45km from
Hermanus in Gansbaai, one of the best whale-watching and shark-diving sites in the
country. Kitchen, internet access, close to restaurants and bars. Run by *White Shark
Adventures* who offer backpackers a discount on their five-hour shark cage dive trips to Dyer
Island (US$110pp). Rooms from **D** pp, Dorms **D** pp. Camping **B** pp.
Hermanus Backpackers 26 Flower St; tel: 028 312 4293; fax: 028 313 2727; email:
moobag@mweb.co.za. New but very promising hostel close to the town centre and some
of the best cliffs for whale-watching. Bar with pool table, kitchen, *braai* area, cheap evening
meals. Swimming pool, satellite TV, free bedding, bike hire. Pick-up from Baz Bus, drop-
off in Botriver. All rates include breakfast. Dorm **C** pp. Room **F** dbl.
Zoete Inval Traveller's Lodge 23 Main Rd; tel/fax: 028 312 1242; email:
zoetein@hermanus.co.za; web: www.zoeteinval.co.za. The central hostel was founded in
1993 and remains one of the best on this stretch of coast, with a strong eco-friendly ethic.
Kitchen, wine cellar, meals by arrangement. Offers all the conventional tours (whale
watching, shark cage diving, wine tours, mountain hikes) as well as township visits and
visits to a homeless shelter. Free pick-up from the tourist information office. Rooms **F** dbl.
Dorm **C** pp.

Cape Town and the Western Cape
CAPE TOWN
Founded in 1652 by the Dutch East India Company, **Cape Town** is not only
the oldest urban settlement in South Africa; it also ranks among the most
beautiful cities in the world. In many respects, Cape Town (along with the rest
of the Western Cape province of which it is capital) differs greatly from the rest
of South Africa. The predominant ethnic group, neither truly indigenous nor
exotic in origin, are the so-called 'Cape Coloureds', a cohesive group of mostly
Afrikaans-speaking people descended from a mixture of early European settlers,
the indigenous Khoikhoi and Malay slaves. Climatically, this region differs from
the rest of southern Africa in having a winter rainfall pattern, while the
vegetation – a heath-like cover known as *fynbos* – is so distinctive that the
Western Cape has come to be classified as a discrete floral kingdom, one of only
five on the planet.

Such are the number and variety of attractions in and around Cape Town that
the city would be worthy of a travel guide in its own right, and what follows is
inevitably rather cursory. Probably the single most important thing you need to
know about Cape Town is how well organised it is for backpackers – around 30
hostels at the last count, all of them able to offer sound and up-to-date advice on
everything from arranging budget day-trips and car or bicycle hire to public
transport, restaurants and nightlife.

The **city centre** is certainly worth exploring. The Castle of Good Hope,
completed in 1679, is the oldest extant European building in South Africa (there
are, of course, several older Portuguese buildings on Mozambique Island), while

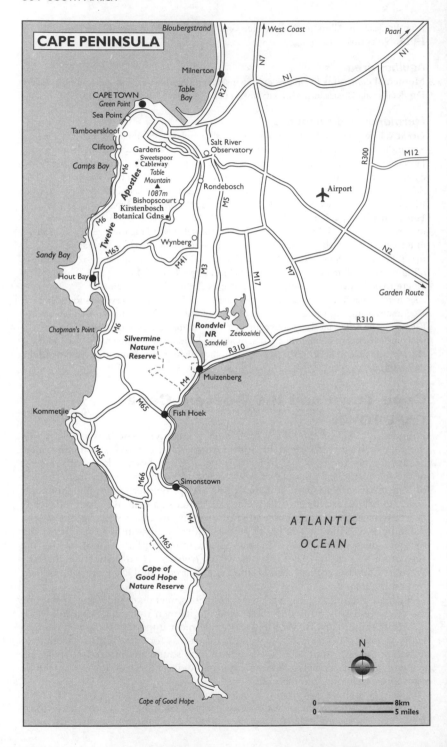

CAPE PENINSULA

Bloubergstrand

West Coast

Paarl

N1

Milnerton

N7

N1

Table
Bay

R27

CAPE TOWN
Green Point

Sea Point

Salt River
Observatory

R300

M12

Tamboerskloof

Clifton

Gardens
Sweetspoor
Cableway

Camps Bay

Table
Mountain
▲
1087m

Rondebosch

Airport

Bishopscourt

Kirstenbosch
Botanical Gdns

M5

Sandy Bay

M6
Twelve
Apostles

M63

Wynberg

M41

M3

N2

Hout Bay

Chapman's Point

M6

Silvermine
Nature
Reserve

Rondvlei
NR
Sandvlei

Zeekoeivlei

M17

M7

Garden Route

R310

R310

Kommetjie

M4

M65

Muizenberg

Fish Hoek

M65

M66

M4

Simonstown

ATLANTIC

OCEAN

M65

Cape of
Good Hope
Nature Reserve

N

Cape of Good Hope

0 — 8km
0 — 5 miles

the attractive Company Gardens also date to the earliest Dutch times – the Cultural History Museum that lies within the Gardens is the second oldest building in the city. The nearby South African Museum houses some impressive whale skeletons, a few exceptional examples of rock art, and a variety of prehistoric artefacts unearthed in Mpumalanga and Great Zimbabwe.

Immediately north of the city centre, the recently revitalised **Victoria & Albert Waterfront** has become the major tourist focus in central Cape Town – in addition to hosting dozens of curio shops, restaurants, bars and cinemas, it's also a good place to organise day tours, scuba-diving excursions and boat trips to Robben Island. Meanwhile, on the southwestern fringe of the city centre, **Table Mountain** offers stunning views over the city and its beach-lined suburbs – the cableway to the top of the mountain (currently under repair but expected to be operating by the time this goes to print) is an unmissable and affordable excursion, with cable cars leaving every 15 minutes when weather permits (ring 24-5148 to check weather conditions).

No less attractive than the city itself is the **Cape Peninsula** – the name given to the 50x10km sliver of mountainous terrain which officially divides the Atlantic and Indian Oceans immediately south of Cape Town. For anybody with an interest in natural history, the wonderfully scenic **Cape of Good Hope Nature Reserve** at the southern end of the peninsula is a must. Incredibly, more plant species occur naturally in this relatively small reserve than in the whole of the British Isles. It is also a good place to see a variety of marine birds as well as several *fynbos* animals, for instance the Cape mountain zebra, bontebok and birds such as the orange-breasted sunbird and Cape sugarbird. Also of interest for their bird and plant life are the **Kirstenbosch Botanical Garden** on the eastern slopes of Table Mountain and the **Rondevlei Nature Reserve** 4km from Muizenberg.

There are several good beaches on the peninsula. On the eastern side, **Muizenberg** is a long, sandy beach, easily reached on public transport. A short distance to the south of Muizenberg, **Simonstown** is a small village with a strong naval tradition and very English feel – worth visiting from central Cape Town or Muizenberg for the train ride alone. Two of the best beaches on the west of the peninsula are **Clifton** and **Llandudno**. Sandy Bay is an official beach 2km south of Llandudno.

Tourist information office

The Cape Tourist Board (CAPTOUR) is very efficient and helpful. The main office is on Adderley Street next to the railway station (tel: 418-5314, fax: 418-5228), but there are also offices in Muizenberg and on the Victoria & Albert Waterfront. Although these offices stock a useful range of pamphlets and leaflets, backpackers will find the hostels to be a better source of practical advice.

Access and getting around

For details of getting to Cape Town from other parts of the country, see *Getting around* on page 542. If you fly into Cape Town, your plane is bound to be met by a representative of one or other of the backpacker hostels. Arriving by intercity coach or train, you'll disembark at the very central Adderley Street Railway Station, from where most of the hostels will provide a free lift if you give them a ring.

The Cape Town area is unique in that it is the one part of South Africa which can be explored with relative ease using public transport. The Adderley Street Railway Station is the main terminal for most local bus and rail services. Regular

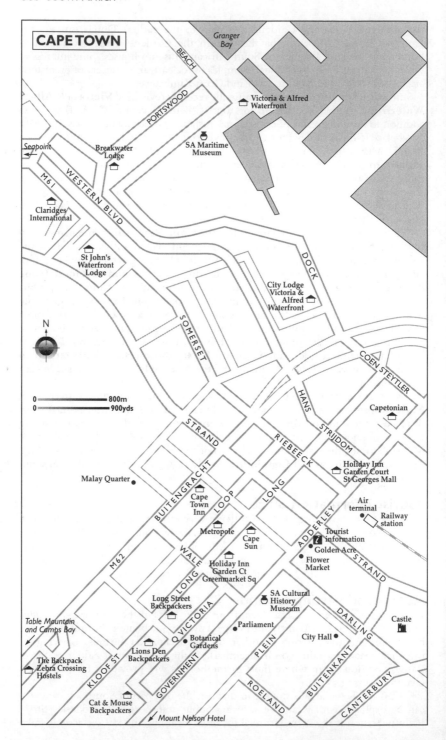

CAPE TOWN

Granger Bay

Victoria & Alfred Waterfront

SA Maritime Museum

Seapoint

Breakwater Lodge

M61

WESTERN BLVD

PORTSWOOD

BEACH

Claridges International

St John's Waterfront Lodge

DOCK

City Lodge Victoria & Alfred Waterfront

N

SOMERSET

COEN STEYTLER

0   800m
0   900yds

Capetonian

HANS

STRIJDOM

RIEBEECK

STRAND

Holiday Inn Garden Court St Georges Mall

Malay Quarter

BUITENGRACHT

LOOP

LONG

Cape Town Inn

Metropole

Cape Sun

ADDERLEY

Air terminal

Railway station

Tourist information

Golden Acre

Flower Market

STRAND

Holiday Inn Garden Ct Greenmarket Sq

LONG

WALE

Long Street Backpackers

VICTORIA

SA Cultural History Museum

M62

Table Mountain and Camps Bay

The Backpack Zebra Crossing Hostels

KLOOF ST

Lions Den Backpackers

Botanical Gardens

GOVERNMENT

Parliament

PLEIN

City Hall

DARLING

Castle

BUITENKANT

ROELAND

CANTERBURY

Cat & Mouse Backpackers

Mount Nelson Hotel

trains run from Adderley Street to Simonstown, a stunning trip with stops at Muizenberg and Vishoek. There are also efficient train services to the Wineland towns of Stellenbosch, Paarl, Worcester and Wellington, and to the Strand on the N2 east of Cape Town.

Public transport on the western side of the Cape Peninsula is restricted to buses and these only run as far as Camps Bay. The best way to explore the western and southern part of the peninsula is to join a day tour or to get a group together and hire a vehicle – neither option will be prohibitively expensive if you use a company geared to backpackers (ask your hostel for recommendations).

Where to stay

Cape Town boasts the greatest concentration of hostels in South Africa, at least 50, with new places opening and closing all the time. The following selection concentrates on the most convenient, popular and long-standing places, grouped by location. Travellers who arrive in Cape Town from elsewhere in southern Africa are bound to have heard numerous up-to-date reports.

City centre

Bob's Bistro 187 Long St; tel: 424 3584. The cheapest central hostel, adequate but a bit run down. Dorm **B** pp.

Cat and Moose Backpackers 305 Long St; tel/fax: 021 423 7638; email: catandmoose@hotmail.com; web: www.backpackafrica.co.za. One of the better central hostels, in a historical building with plenty of atmosphere. Facilities include a kitchen, bar, TV lounge, good travel desk, and free pick-up from bus/train station, airport or any other hostel in Cape Town. Dorm **C** pp. Rooms **E**/**F** dbl/tpl.

Elephant on Castle Backpackers 57 Castle St; tel/fax: 021 424 7524; email: castle@iafrica.com. Situated just off Long Street, this is a lively, relatively inexpensive new hostel with colourful decor and excellent facilities (kitchen, bar, pool table, TV, *braai*, meals, air conditioning, laundry). Pick-ups from town can be arranged, as can a variety of tours. Dorm **C** pp. Rooms **E** dbl.

Lion's Den Backpackers 255 Long St; tel: 021 423 9003; fax: 021 423 9166; email: lionsden@iafrica.co.za. Convenient, well-established hostel with two bars, and traditional South African food available at the Bar 'n' Yard Pub 50m away. They organise airport pick-ups and a variety of local and overland tours, eg: Winelands US$30pp, Bungee jump US$80. Caged snakes at reception include an anaconda and python. Dorm **C** pp. Rooms **D**/**F** sgl/dbl.

Long Street Backpackers 209 Long St; tel: 021 423 0615; fax: 021 423 1842; email: longstbp@mweb.co.za; web: www.nis.za/~longstbp/lodge.htm. Consistently popular for several years, and one of the only places in central Cape Town to offer a free pick-up from anywhere in town, this excellent hostel has a lively bar and good kitchen, and facilities include gym membership, internet access, satellite TV and free sunset trips to Signal Hill. There's a good in-house travel desk. Four-bed dorms **C** pp. Rooms **D**/**E** sgl/dbl.

Tamboerskloof
(very near city centre below Table Mountain cableway)

The Backpack 74 New Church St; tel: 021 423 5555; fax: 021 423 0065; email: backpack@gem.co.za; web: www.backpackers.co.za. This was the first backpackers' hostel to open in South Africa, back in 1990, and it remains one of the most consistently popular in the country. Facilities include a swimming pool and the excellent Africa Travel Centre, which offers a comprehensive range of budget trips ranging from day tours to overland trips throughout the region covered by this guide, as well as affordable car hire and airport shuttles. Highly recommended. Dorms **C** pp. Rooms **F** dbl.

Gardens
(immediately south of the city centre below Table Mountain)
Ambler's Backpackers 3 Upper Union St; tel: 021 424 2292; fax 021 424 4801; email: amblers@iafrica.com; web: www.amblers.com. This relative newcomer has a good location in gardens and offers a free pick-up from anywhere in the city centre. Facilities include a kitchen, TV lounge, pool table, swimming pool, bar, laundromat, and personalised local day tours and hikes. Dorm **C** pp. Rooms **F** dbl.
Ashanti Lodge and Travel Centre 11 Hof St; tel: 021 423 8721; fax: 021 423 8790; email: ashanti@iafrica.com; web: www.ashanti.co.za. Large, popular and central, this highly recommended hostel can sleep up to 100 people and also allows camping. Facilities include a self-catering kitchen, bar, café, email, travel centre, swimming pool, laundry service and baggage storage. They offer a free pick-up from the city centre and airport during business hours. Dorm **C** pp. Camping **B** pp. Rooms from **E/F** sgl/dbl.
Oak Lodge 21 Breda St; tel: 021 465 6182; fax: 021 465 6308; email: oaklodge@intekom.co.za; web: www.intekom.co.za/~oaklodge. Excellent hostel with 18 large and attractive double rooms, airy dorms, and slightly above par accommodation rates reflected by an extensive range of facilities, including self-catering kitchen, bar with pool table, free Sunday *braai* and free Tuesday *potjiekos* (a distinctly South African type of stew), washer and tumble-dryer, tv room with more than 550 videos, 24-hour internet access, and a good travel desk. Dorm **C** pp. Rooms from **F** dbl.

Greenpoint and Seapoint
(short bus-ride from city centre on Atlantic coastline)
Aardvark Backpackers 319 Main Road, Seapoint; tel: 021 434 4172; fax: 021 439 3813; email: aardbp@mweb.co.za; web: www.lions-head-lodge.co.za/aardvark.htm. A new and very smart hostel, with mixed and single-sex six-bed dormitories, each with a private kitchen and bathroom. Other facilities include two bars, a full restaurant, swimming pool, lounge with pool table, satellite TV and videos, internet café, secure parking and a good travel centre. Dorms **C** pp. Rooms around US$30 dbl.
St John's Lodge 9 St John's Rd, Seapoint; tel/fax: 021 439 9028; email: stjohnslodge@mweb.co.za. This is a well-established and consistently popular hostel, close to the beach, and boasting an olympic-size seawater swimming pool. Surrounded by restaurants, cafés, banks and shops. Dorm **C** pp. Rooms **E** sgl or dbl. Very reduced rates for winter.
Sunflower Stop 179 Main Rd, Greenpoint; tel: 021 434 6535; fax: 021 434 6501; email: devine@sunflowerstop.co.za; web: www.sunflowerstop.co.za. This new, brightly decorated hostel comes highly recommended and offers a free pick-up from the airport. Facilities include an indoor bar with pool table and fireplace, outdoor *braai* area next to swimming pool, cheap meals and laundry facilities. Dorm **C** pp. Room **F** dbl.

Southern suburbs
Boulders Beach Backpackers 4 Boulders Pl; tel: 786-1758. Recommended out-of-town hostel on a beach 2km from Simonstown railway station, close to a penguin breeding colony. Dorm **C** pp. Rooms **F** dbl.
Green Elephant Backpackers 57 Milton Rd, Observatory; tel: 0800-222722 (toll-free) or 021 448 6359; fax: 021 448 0510; email: greenelephant@iafrica.com. Set in the lively suburb of Observatory, which is dotted with trendy bars frequented by students, this long-standing favourite has the usual facilities (kitchen, bar, meals, travel desk) as well as fast internet service, jacuzzi, solar-heated swimming pool, large gardens, and a legendary tree-climbing dog. Free pick-up from airport or city centre. Camping **B** pp. Dorm **C** pp. Room **F** dbl.
Zandvlei Caravan Park Tel: 210-2507. Attractive municipal site 1km from Muizenberg Station. Five minutes from beach. Self-catering chalets **F** dbl. Camping **C** site.

THE CAPE WINELANDS

The mountainous area immediately northeast of Cape Town, often referred to as the Boland, has been Africa's premier wine-producing region since 1688 when the Franschoek Valley was settled by Huguenot refugees from France. Dominated by the rugged Cape Fold Mountains, the Boland is one of the most beautiful parts of South Africa, particularly in autumn when the vineyards turn deep purple. Best known for its wine farms, the Boland also has many great hiking and walking opportunities, and the towns are characterised by oak-lined avenues and graceful Cape Dutch architecture.

Founded less than 30 years after the Cape was settled by Europeans, **Stellenbosch** has retained its historical appearance to a far greater extent than Cape Town – Ryneveld and Dorp Streets in particular are dotted with buildings in the Cape Dutch style dating from as early as 1709. Stellenbosch is the only Boland town that currently caters for backpackers, and because it is a university town there are many cheap bars and restaurants. The helpful tourist office on Market Street (tel: 021 883-3584) stocks a pamphlet detailing important buildings and a map with details of the many wine estates in the area. It also sells maps and permits for the Vineyard Trail, a 12km to 24km day-walk through the surrounding hills and wine estates. About 10km from Stellenbosch, there are several day trails in the **Assegaaibosch Nature Reserve**, where several rare proteas can be seen in addition to typical *fynbos* birds and mammals.

Only 30km from Stellenbosch, and reached via a spectacular road, **Franschoek** is among the most beautifully situated villages in South Africa. The Franschoek area was settled by Huguenots in 1688 and it has retained something of a Gallic flavour. The Huguenot Museum and Monument on the outskirts of the village are worth a visit. There are 10 wine estates in the Franschoek Valley, most of which lie within 10km of the village along the Stellenbosch road – the 300-year-old Boschendal estate is particularly attractive. More sedentarily, you can taste local wines at the co-operative on the outskirts of the village. Roughly 30km southeast of Franschoek, in the small village of **Villiersdorp**, a nature reserve protects 500ha of montane *fynbos*, 60 protea species and a wide range of birds.

Paarl is the largest town in the Boland and, although it boasts several historical buildings, it has a far more modern feel than Stellenbosch. The Taal Monument was built just outside Paarl in 1975 to celebrate the Afrikaans language. On the outskirts of town, you can walk freely in the Paarl Mountain Nature Reserve, notable for the large granite domes which gave the town its name (early visitors thought they looked like pearls!). Other places of interest are the arboretum fringing the Berg River on the southern edge of town, and the several wine estates in and around town. The tourist office at 216 Main Street (tel: 02211 24842) can give further details.

Worcester is yet another historical town, situated close to the N1 about 100km from Cape Town. The publicity association (23 Baring Street, tel: 0231 71408) has pamphlets which cover the town's museums and national monuments, as well as the nearby Breede Valley Wine Route. Worcester lies in an area transitional to the *fynbos* of the Western Cape and the drier Karoo: the **Karoo National Botanical Garden** 4km from town protects a diverse collection of succulents and euphorbia, and it is known for outstanding wildflower displays in the spring.

There are several other towns worth visiting in the Boland. About 15km north of Paarl, **Wellington** is a quiet old town with a fair quota of Cape Dutch buildings. Further north, **Tulbagh** is little more than a village, but its Church Street boasts the highest concentration of national monuments in the country. Not strictly speaking a Boland town, **Ceres** is best-known for the Ceres Fruit Juice Factory (tel:

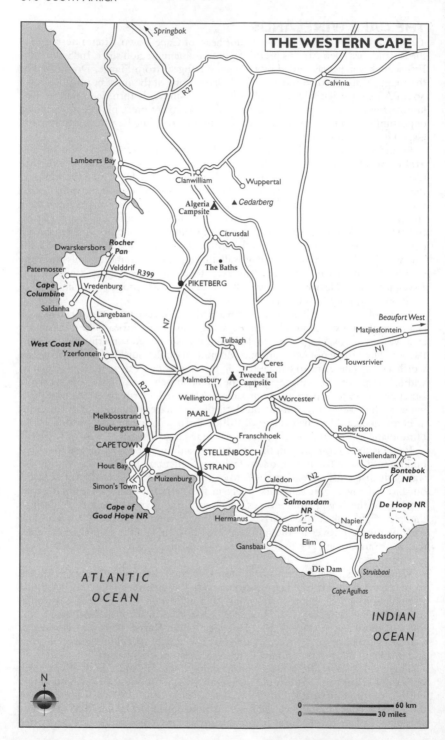

THE WESTERN CAPE

Springbok

Calvinia

R27

Lamberts Bay

Clanwilliam • Wuppertal

Algeria Campsite ▲ ▲ Cedarberg

Citrusdal

Rocher Pan
Dwarskersbors
Paternoster • The Baths
Cape Columbine Velddrif R399
Vredenburg PIKETBERG
Saldanha
Langebaan

Beaufort West
Matjiesfontein
West Coast NP
Yzerfontein N7 Tulbagh N1

Ceres Touwsrivier
R27 Malmesbury ▲ Tweede Tol Campsite
Wellington Worcester
Melkbosstrand PAARL Robertson
Bloubergstrand Franschhoek Swellendam
CAPE TOWN STELLENBOSCH Bontebok NP
Hout Bay STRAND
Simon's Town Muizenburg Caledon N2 De Hoop NR
Cape of Good Hope NR Salmonsdam NR Napier
Hermanus Stanford Bredasdorp
Gansbaai Elim

Die Dam Struisbaai
Cape Agulhas

ATLANTIC OCEAN

INDIAN OCEAN

N

0 ————— 60 km
0 ————— 30 miles

0223 23121 for a free tour). The Ceres Fynbos Reserve ten minutes out of town is worth a visit for its interesting rockscapes and profuse wild flowers and birds.

Access and getting around

Most of the towns in the Boland can be reached easily on public transport. There are regular metropolitan trains between Cape Town and Stellenbosch, and more infrequent services to Paarl and Wellington, while Worcester can be reached from Cape Town using any public transport heading towards Johannesburg. You will, however, have difficulty getting to the wine estates or to Franschoek and Ceres on public transport.

If you want to explore one of the wine circuits, the most popular option is to use one of the budget tour companies in Cape Town – any of the backpacker hostels can put you in touch with a reliable operator. For a group, hiring a car might work out more cheaply, bearing in mind that consuming vast amounts of alcohol and driving are mutually exclusive activities at least so far as the law is concerned. Best of all, head to the Stumble Inn in Stellenbosch, where you can arrange a wine-tasting tour for little more than US$10 per person.

Where to stay
Stellenbosch

Backpackers Inn De wet Centre, Cnr Bird and Church St; tel: 021 887 2020; fax: 021 887 2010; email: bacpac1@global.co.za. Central hostel with kitchen, laundry, TV lounge, pool table. Good local travel information and township tours. Dorm **C** pp. Rooms **F** dbl.
Stumble Inn 12 Market St, tel/fax: 021 887 4049; email: stumble@iafrica.com. Well-established and popular hostel close to the town centre. Excellent selection of day tours

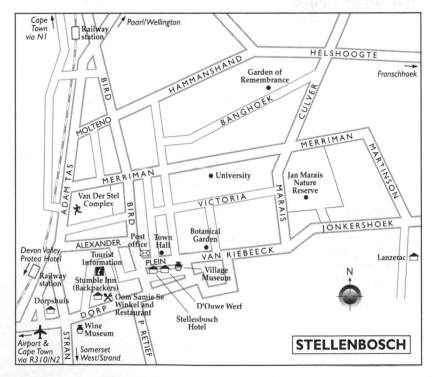

STELLENBOSCH

available. Bicycle hire. Horse-riding. Free pick-up from Baz Bus in Somerset West by prior arrangement. Camping **B** pp. Dorm **C** pp. Room **F** dbl.
Hillbilly's Haven 24 Dennesig Rd; tel: 887-8475. Dorm **C** pp. Rooms **E** dbl. Camping **B** pp.

Villiersdorp
Municipal Campsite At entrance to nature reserve. Very cheap and quiet.

Paarl
Winelands Backpackers Tel: 021 863 1378; email: portfoli@iafrica.com. New hostel, offering dorms only at **C** pp.

Worcester
Burger Caravan Park Cnr Roux and De la Bat; tel: 0231 71992. Central, shady municipal site. Camping **C** site.

Wellington
Pinnie Joubert Caravan Park Addey St; tel: 021 873-2603. Camping **C** pp.
Bloublommetjieskloof Farm Tel: 021 873-3696. Out of town in mountainous area. Dorm **C** pp. Rooms **F** dbl. Pick-up from railway station by prior arrangement.

Ceres
Pine Forest Resort Carson St; tel: 0233 21170. Central and shady. Huts **E** dbl. Camping **C** site. Note that prices double at weekends.

THE WEST COAST
The coast north of Cape Town sees relatively few visitors, but it is a lovely area, especially during August and September when the wild flowers are in bloom. This section follows the coast as far north as Lambert's Bay, then describes the return trip via the N7 and the Cedarberg Mountains, one of South Africa's most popular hiking destinations.

The first town of interest heading north from Cape Town is **Langebaan**, situated at the entrance to the synonymous lagoon, and the gateway to the West Coast National Park which was proclaimed in 1985. Langebaan is a rather resort-like place, but the lagoon offers good birding all year round. During the flower season, it is emphatically worth trying to get a lift into the Postberg section of the national park: the flowers are the best I saw anywhere in the country – field after field of pink, white, orange, yellow and blue – and you should see a variety of large mammals (eland, gemsbok and black wildebeest) as well as the localised black harrier.

Situated on the northern shore of Saldhana Bay, and named after the Portuguese navigator who explored the bay in 1503, **Saldhana** is an active fishing town and naval base with considerably more intrinsic character and appeal than Langebaan. An apparently nameless nature reserve run by the naval base lies within walking distance of the town – the day trails which run through the reserve offer a chance to see plenty of wild flowers in spring (amazing lilies!), large mammals such as springbok, and masses of breeding waterbirds. A pamphlet is available at the entrance to the naval base.

The stretch of coast between Saldhana and Lambert's Bay is marvellously unspoilt and isolated, with an atmosphere all of its own. The inland town of **Vredenburg** is the largest in the region and the main route focus, but there isn't much else that you can say about it. Far more interesting is **Paternoster**, a fishing village that lies 16km from Vredenburg, where several whitewashed houses reputed to be over 100 years old overlook a wide, deserted beach. A 30-minute walk from Paternoster, the **Cape Columbine Nature Reserve** is one of the most underrated in South Africa: set on a rocky stretch of coast, its attractions include wild flowers in spring, *fynbos*-covered dunes, rock pools, shell-strewn stretches of sand, varied birds, and the freedom to walk where you please. Overlooking the marshy mouth of the Berg River, **Velddrif** is a pleasant resort town, popular with fishermen. Situated on the coastal R27, 12km north of Velddrif, **Dwarskersbors** is a one-resort town, but its one resort is about the only place in this area that appears to be catering for backpackers. A further 10km north on the R27, **Rocher Pan Nature Reserve** is primarily a bird sanctuary – and a very good one, too – but large mammals such as steenbok, common duiker and water mongoose are also commonly seen.

The main attraction of the picturesque village of **Lambert's Bay** is Bird Island. Linked to the land by a breakwater, this small rocky island protects a large breeding colony of Cape gannets – it's nothing short of exhilarating to watch these large, strikingly marked birds swoop to the ground metres from the raised viewing platform – as well as a number of Cape cormorants and a flock of 50 or so jackass penguins which usually come to roost towards dusk. The town itself is a pleasant place to stroll through, with a good beach and pretty harbour frequented by Cape seals.

On the N7, almost directly 60km east of Lambert's Bay, **Clanwilliam** is one of South Africa's oldest towns (the former prison dates to 1808), and the small Ramskop Nature Reserve on its outskirts is definitely worth visiting during the wildflower season. Also on the N7, about 50km south of Clanwilliam, **Citrusdal** lies at the centre of a major fruit farming region, but otherwise it's an uninspiring place, salvaged somewhat by the idiosyncratic little resort called The Baths a few kilometres out of town.

The main turn-off to the **Cedarberg Wilderness Area** lies about halfway between Clanwilliam and Citrusdal. Traversed by 250km of footpaths which hikers can follow as they please. the Cedarberg is known for its bizarre natural rock sculptures, notably the 20m-high Maltese Cross, as well as a variety of rare plants, mammals such as rock hyrax, klipspringer and baboon, and several good rock painting sites. Whether you're a serious hiker or you simply want to spend some time doing day walks from the Algeria Forest Station or private Kromrivier Resort, this is a very beautiful area, highly recommended to those who want to break away from the towns.

Access and getting around

Aside from the Intercape bus to Springbok, which can drop you anywhere along the N7 (see *Getting around* on page 542), there is no formal public transport in this area. The options are hiring a vehicle, getting a group together to organise a tour out of Cape Town, or hitching. Provided that you're reasonably sensible, I don't feel that there is a high risk attached to hitching in this part of South Africa, though you may have to wait some time for lifts in out-of-the-way places. The way to get around this is only to accept lifts that will get you to another place where there is accommodation. If you want to hitch from Cape Town towards Langebaan, it would be advisable to use the city bus service as far as Melkbosstrand – there's a caravan park on the main road here should you get stuck. The 50km stretch of the R27 between Rocher Pan and Lambert's Bay often requires a 4x4 vehicle, and it will probably be very difficult to hitch – better to travel between these places via the N7.

The main base for hikes and walks in the Cedarberg is Algeria Forestry Station, 18km to the east of the N7 along a signposted dirt road. This isn't an easy hitch, so be prepared to walk. Nominal hiking fees must be paid to the rangers at Algeria, who will be able to supply hikers with maps and route advice. Bring sufficient supplies, and make an advance booking if you're going to arrive during school holidays (tel: 022921 3219). Those who are thinking of going on overnight hikes should be aware that the Cedarberg is not suitable for novice hikers – my advice is to arrange a hiking trip through Albergo Backpackers in Cape Town. For independent hikers, the best coverage of the Cedarberg is in Sandra & Willie Olivier's *Guide to Backpacking and Wilderness Trails* (Southern Books). Maps are available at Algeria.

Where to stay

This is another area with few facilities geared specifically to backpackers. With a tent, you'll be fine, except perhaps during school holidays when even the most obscure campsites tend to be overrun with fishermen and their families. Otherwise, you should be able to locate reasonably affordable self-catering or bed and breakfast accommodation through the various tourist offices, but you should probably resign yourself to the occasional expensive night. Prices tend to rocket during holiday periods.

Langebaan
Municipal Chalets and Campsite Tel: 02287 22115. The municipality runs a few groups of chalets as well as two caravan parks, of which the older one is cheaper and has better cover. Chalets **E** unit. Camping **C** site.

Saldanha Bay
Municipal Caravan Park Camp St; tel: 02281 42247. Centrally situated and pleasant, though campers will find it very exposed when the wind is up. Cottages **E** dbl. Camping **C** site.

Paternoster
Paternoster Hotel Tel: 02255 703. Only rooms in town. Not too expensive. Excellent crayfish.
Cape Columbine Nature Reserve Tel: 02281 32231. Sheltered campsite on beach. Facilities limited to running water and toilets. Camping **B** site.

Dwarskersbors
Dwarskersbors Holiday Resort Tel: 02288 40110. Good situation on beach. Huts **D** dbl. Camping **C** site. There are also campsites and chalets available at a few resorts in Velddrif.

Lambert's Bay
Eureka Apartments Tel: 027 432-1211. Central and well-run block. Expensive and normally full in season. Willing to negotiate at other times – expect to pay something in the **E** range.
Municipal Campsite Tel: 027 432-2238. Large site. Camping **C** site.

Clanwilliam
Clanwilliam Dam Resort Tel: 027 482-2133. On dam 1km out of town. Chalets from **F** dbl. Camping **B** pp.

Cedarberg
Algeria Forestry Station Beautiful wooded campsite **A** pp. Two old farm cottages **D** unit.

Kromrivier Resort Tel: 027 482-2807. Rooms **E** dbl. Camping **B**/**C** Organised drives, walks and horseback. About 25km past Algeria; access a problem without vehicle.

Citrusdal

Municipal campsite Cheap camping on a very bare site.
The Baths 16km from Citrusdal; tel: 022 921-3609. Attractively rambling piece of run-down Victoriana in well-wooded grounds surrounding supposedly therapeutic hot springs used by early Dutch explorers. Rooms from **F** dbl. Camping **B** pp.

Through routes from Cape Town to Johannesburg

THE N1 OR N12 VIA BLOEMFONTEIN OR KIMBERLEY

The 1,400km N1 connecting Cape Town to Johannesburg may be one of the most important routes through South Africa, but it offers little that's both of interest and accessible to the average backpacker. Much the same can be said of the N12, the road which runs roughly parallel to the N1 after splitting from it at Three Sisters about 540km from Cape Town, though the N12 does at least pass through Kimberley, formerly one of the world's most important diamond mining towns.

Coming from Cape Town, the N1 initially passes through the scintillating scenery of the Cape Winelands, skirting the towns of Paarl and Worcester (see *Cape Winelands* on page 589). After passing Worcester, you're more or less in the semi-desert **Karoo**, an area which some people regard as highly evocative and others dismiss as boring. Disregarding the archetypal small South African towns of Touws River and Laingsburg, the obvious place to stop along the 350km stretch of road between Worcester and Beaufort West would be **Matjiesfontein**, established as a health resort in 1883 when it was visited by such luminaries as Olive Schreiner and Cecil John Rhodes, then restored in 1979. More perverse options, but bound to appeal to somebody, are the isolated settlements of Prince Albert Road and Leeu-Gamka, dots on a map surrounded by the vast landscapes of the Karoo. As its name suggests, Prince Albert Road lies at the turn-off to **Prince Albert**, regarded by many to be one of the prettiest towns in this part of the world. Lying on the southern tip of the Karoo at the base of the Swartberg Mountains, Prince Albert is usefully positioned for anybody who is heading directly between the Garden Route and N1.

Founded in 1818, **Beaufort West** is the oldest town in the Karoo, and the largest. It is a convenient place to break up a long trip, and boasts a number of historical buildings (the publicity association in the city hall stocks useful maps and pamphlets) but it isn't somewhere that many people would choose to spend longer than a night. Altogether more alluring is the **Karoo National Park**, the entrance to which lies on the N1 5km south of Beaufort West. Crossed by several day trails, game-viewing roads, and the three-day, circular Springbok Hiking Trail, and supporting 61 mammal species (including bat-eared fox, Cape mountain zebra, springbok, gemsbok, kudu and red hartebeest) as well as numerous localised birds, this national park would be highly attractive to backpackers were it not that hitching or entering on foot are expressly forbidden. About 80km past Beaufort West, **Three Sisters** is where you get to choose between the N12 via Kimberley or N1 via Bloemfontein. There's not much more to this junction than the Shell Ultra City where hitchhikers and undecided motorists are at least guaranteed a hot meal and cold drink.

There is nothing about **Bloemfontein**, the capital of the Free State, that merits a special trip, but it is nevertheless one of the more attractive cities in the South

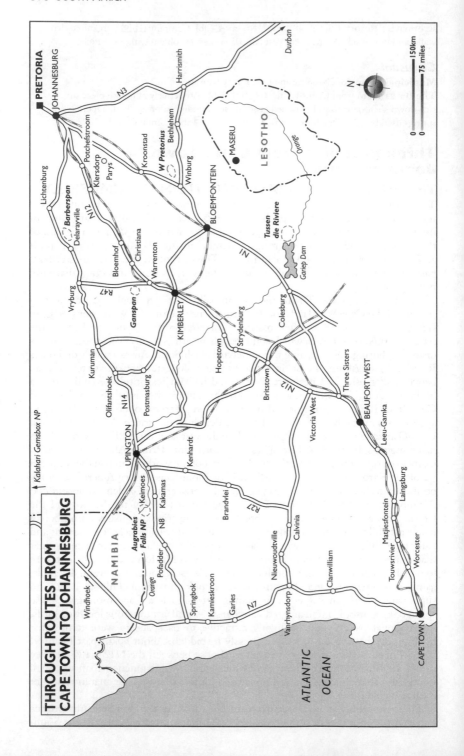

THROUGH ROUTES FROM
CAPE TOWN TO JOHANNESBURG

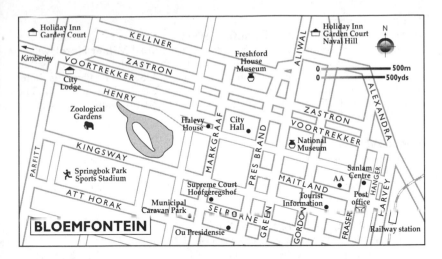

African interior. If you do drift into Bloemfontein, then the National Museum, Military Museum of the Boer Republic and Franklin Nature Reserve are worth a visit – the publicity association on President Hoffman Square can supply you with maps and other details. There is really very little of interest to backpackers between Bloemfontein and Johannesburg.

Kimberley is the capital of the Northern Cape but, because it lies on the eastern border of this vast province, it is more likely to be visited by travellers heading directly between Cape Town and Johannesburg than those who are exploring the Kalahari and Namaqualand. Established in the 1880s, Kimberley owes its existence to the Kimberlite Pipe, the richest diamond seam ever discovered. The town's major tourist attraction is still the 'Big Hole' that was dug around the pipe – until recently the largest man-made hole in the world, and a replica of old Kimberley that has been built around the hole. Of several museums, the McGregor Museum (Atlas St) and Duggan-Cronin Gallery (Egerton Rd) are particularly worth a visit, the latter offering a welcome glimpse into indigenous cultures with photographs of rural Africans that were taken all over the continent in the 1930s. For more details visit the publicity association on Old Main Road.

An interesting and little-known stop lying about 25km from the N12 between Kimberley and Johannesburg and 4km from the small town of Jan Kemp Dorp is the **Ganspan Waterfowl Reserve**. Centred around a pretty reed-lined pan, this reserve supports a prolific variety of birds, including greater and lesser flamingo, as well as small mammals such as ground squirrel, mongoose and marsh rat. You can walk along the 6km dirt road that encircles the pan.

Access and getting around

Most backpackers travel between Cape Town and Johannesburg in one go, either by rail or by bus. Buses and trains all stop at Beaufort West and, depending on the route they use, either Kimberley or Bloemfontein. For further details see *Getting around* on page 542. If you are thinking of stopping elsewhere, then you may have to hitch in places – though you should certainly take public transport to your first destination out of Cape Town or Johannesburg, since hitching out of either of these cities is both frustrating and dangerous.

Where to stay
Between Cape Town and Beaufort West
The only place to stay in Matjiesfontein, the restored **Lord Milner Hotel**, will be too expensive for backpackers, but the adjoining boarding house may be within reach of some budgets with rooms for around US$30/40. There is hotel accommodation at a similar price in Prince Albert Road and Leeu-Gamka. The **Wimpy Bar** in Laingsburg has the cheapest accommodation along this stretch of the N1: Rooms **D** pp and camping **C** site.

Prince Albert
Saxe-Coburg Lodge 60 Church St; tel: 04436 267. Guided hikes. Good source of local information. Rooms **D** pp.
Nuweplaas Farm 5km out of town; tel 04436 723. Good walking. Camping **B** pp.
Municipal Campsite Town centre. **B** site.

Beaufort West/Karoo National Park
Donkin House 14 Donkin St; tel: 0201 4287. Dorm **C** pp. Rooms **E** dbl.
Municipal Campsite Large shady site on Danie Theron St. Camping **C** site. Standing caravans **E** unit.
Karoo National Park Main camp with chalets at US$50/unit and camping **C** site.

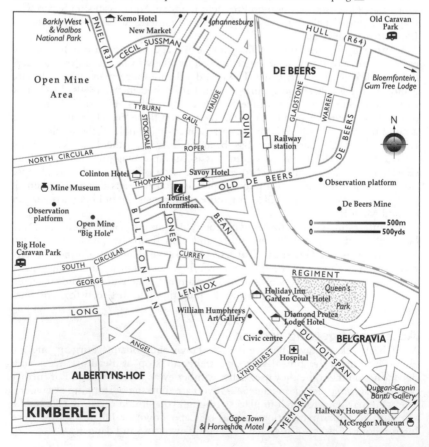

Colesburg
Colesburg Backpackers 39 Kerk St; tel: 051 753 0582. Set close to the N1 in a town almost midway between Johannesburg and Cape Town, this is a convenient and affordable, if not particularly inspiring, place to break the long drive. Camping **B** pp. Dorm **C** pp. Rooms **D** dbl.

Bloemfontein
Taffy's Backpackers 18 Louis Botha St, 3km from city centre; tel: 31-4533; email: taffys@global.co.za. Free pick-up 07.00 to 21.00. Info and daily shuttle to Malalea Lodge in Lesotho. Dorm **C** pp. Room **E** dbl. Camping **B** pp.
Municipal campsite Eerste St. Near to city centre. **C** site.

Kimberley
Gum Tree Lodge On Bloemfontein Rd, 5km from town centre; tel: 82-8577. No points for atmosphere or location, but the large grounds with swimming pool compensate. Dorm **C** pp. Rooms **D/E**.
Big Hole Campsite More attractive of two municipal sites and very centrally situated near the Big Hole. **C** site.

Ganspan Waterfowl Reserve
Camping Where you like, avoiding the rat infested reedbeds. Longdrop toilets. Cold water. **A** pp.

THE N7 AND N14 VIA THE NORTHERN CAPE
South Africa's largest and most thinly populated province, the Northern Cape is dominated by the vast and starkly beautiful semi-desert of the Kalahari, an area that some find more deeply impressive than any of South Africa's more popular and celebrated tourist attractions. Bisected by the Orange River, the Northern Cape can be divided into two broad ecosystems. Namaqualand is the name given to the stony region that lies to the south of the Orange, an area noted not only for its immense variety of succulent species, but also for the fantastic wildflower displays that erupt into colour following the first rains every August or September. To the north of the Orange, the Kalahari is more like a true desert in appearance: a land of red and white sand dunes interspersed with areas of dry acacia woodland.

The best way to explore the Northern Cape is to travel between Cape Town and Johannesburg following the N7 and N14 via the town of Springbok. Travellers coming from Cape Town will initially follow the N7 past Clanwilliam (see *The West Coast* on pages 592–3) through the lush Olifants River Valley to **Vanrhynsdorp**, a small town that is generally regarded to be the gateway to Namaqualand and which is noted for the nursery on its outskirts, said to have the largest succulent collection in the world.

Along the R27 about 50km east of Vanrhynsdorp, **Nieuwoudtville** is a good base for visiting several reserves and beauty spots. Just outside town, the Nieuwoudtville Wild Flower Reserve offers good day walks, especially during the wildflower season. About 6km along the Loeriesfontein road, the 100m high Doring River Waterfall is spectacular after rains, and a further 14km along this road is one of the largest forests of kokerbooms (quiver trees) in South Africa. To the south of Nieuwoudtville, the 5,070ha **Oorlogskloof Nature Reserve** protects a rugged escarpment area with flora and fauna that are transitional to the *fynbos* of the Western Cape and the drier Karoo. Camping areas have been cleared, and there's a 46km network of day and overnight trails – tel: 02726 81010 for details.

Straddling the N7 to the north of Vanrhynsdorp, **Garies** is an inherently rather dull small town but an excellent base from which to see spring wild flowers. The highest peak in the northern Cape, the Rooiberg, lies to the east of Garies, and it can be explored along a strenuous three-day hiking trail with overnight stays in a cave and in a hut – for further information and trail maps visit the Garies Town Clerk's Office. There are also some good unmapped trails in the vicinity of **Kamieskroon**, a small town on the N7 between Garies and Springbok – to find out about registered guides ring 0257 762.

Springbok is the principal town of Namaqualand, somewhat unmemorable in itself but an important route focus and the base for visits to the nearby **Goegap Nature Reserve**. Known for its superb spring wildflower displays, Goegap is worth visiting at any time of year for the Hester Malan Botanical Garden, where you'll see such bizarre northern Cape specials as the *kokerboom* and *halfmensboom* (half-human tree). The rugged terrain of the reserve can be explored on two-day trails, where you can expect to encounter a variety of localised birds and possibly even a few large mammals including the rare Hartmann's mountain zebra. Tel: 0251 21880 for details.

To the east of Springbok, a rather dull 250km drive along the N14 takes you through the entirely unmemorable town of Pofadder and then to **Kakamas** on the Orange River. As some indication of Kakamas's inherent lack of interest, the council has made a rather pathetic bid to attract tourism by claiming that their town is the same distance from the equator as Egypt! More convincing, perhaps, if they were to emphasise that there's a rather pleasant resort just out of town on the bank of the Orange River, or that Kakamas is the obvious springboard for backpackers heading up to one of South Africa's most underrated national parks...

Augrabies Falls National Park, proclaimed in 1966, is dominated by the 56m-high waterfall after which it is named and the granite ravine beneath it. What impresses most about this park is neither the height nor power of the waterfall itself, but the hauntingly bleak moonscape of massive granite outcrops that surrounds it. The vegetation is fascinating, dry-country birds and reptiles are prolific, and there is a fair amount of game to be seen. An attraction of the park for backpackers is that, in addition to the three-day Klipspringer Hiking Trail, there is a good day trail, you can walk freely on the roads, and the camp runs affordable night drives as well as day excursions to the wilderness area to the north of the river.

The next town along the N14 after Kakamas is **Keimoes**, where the Tierberg Nature Reserve protects a hill studded with kokerbooms and flowering Gariep aloes. It's a 4km walk from town to the top of the hill, which offers tremendous views over the Orange River and the irrigated land around it. Only 40km past Keimoes, **Upington** is the largest town in this region, with good facilities but few points of interest. It might be worth dropping into the Upington Tourist Office (tel: 054 26911) – very helpful and keen to promote tourism to this relatively obscure part of South Africa.

To the north of Upington, the **Kalahari Gemsbok National Park** is the second largest reserve in South Africa, a wedge of semi-desert sandwiched between the borders with Botswana and Namibia. Protecting the fragile ecosystem supported by the red dunes of the Kalahari Desert, this waterless habitat is bounded on either side by two river courses, the Auob and Nossob, neither of which runs more than once every two or three years. The Kalahari is memorable first for its isolated wilderness atmosphere, but it also offers surprisingly good game viewing – common antelopes are springbok, gemsbok, red hartebeest, eland, and steenbok, while predators such as lion, leopard, cheetah, black-backed jackal and bat-eared fox are easily spotted. Birdwatchers will find the park rewarding for its high raptor density and for several localised specials such as pygmy falcon, pririt batis, scaly-feathered and red-headed finch, tit-babbler, swallow-tailed bee-eater, crimson-breasted shrike and Kalahari robin. The park is also an animal photographer's dream: the contrast of red sand against blue sky is highly photogenic, the sparse vegetation allows you to get clear views of animals at a distance, and the light is so good that you can generally use low-speed films even with a zoom lens.

Kuruman is the most attractive town on the N14, and worth a stop for that reason alone. In the centre of town, 'The Eye' is a natural spring yielding over 50,000m³ of water a day, and the lily-covered pool it pours into. About 6km from Kuruman on the Hotazel road is the mission founded in 1821 by Robert Moffat. It's not to be missed, even if it's difficult to know whether to laugh or be touched at this English-village-like apparition in the middle of the desert. Meanwhile, those who've been stumbling over Livingstone-related landmarks throughout their East African travels will be pleased to know that the stone church in which Livingstone got married to Moffat's daughter Mary lies in the mission grounds (as does a plaque marking the stump of the pear tree under which Livingstone proposed!).

On the N14 east of Kuruman, you may find yourself stranded for a night in **Vryburg**, which has some historical pedigree as the former capital of the short-lived Boer Republic of Stellaland (1882–5) but is otherwise just another anonymous small town. A more inherently interesting stop, the entrance to which lies right on the N14 between Sannieshof and Delareyville, is the **Barberspan Nature Reserve**. One of South Africa's most important wetlands, Barberspan is of great interest to serious birders, but even casual visitors should be interested in seeing flocks of up to 20,000 flamingo as well as small mammals such as meerkat, mongoose, ground squirrel and reintroduced antelope. Visitors are free to walk in the reserve as they please.

Access and getting around
Although some coach services cover this part of the country (see *Getting around* on page 542), it would be difficult to co-ordinate your travels around them except as a way of getting out of Cape Town or Johannesburg to your first port of call. Otherwise you're likely to be dependent on hitching – which probably isn't as risky as in other parts of the country. Vehicles are thin on the ground, but when something does stop it will probably be going a long way. Hitching the 35km from Kakamas to Augrabies is feasible. The one unlikely hitch is the Kalahari Gemsbok (see box page 602).

Where to stay
Few backpackers visit the Northern Cape, so that the network of hostels found in most other parts of South Africa is entirely lacking. If you're carrying a tent, this won't be a problem, since almost every small town has a **municipal campsite** charging around 🄱 per site. For those without a tent, there's a one-star hotel in just about every town and, while rates are cheaper than elsewhere in the country, you'll still be looking at around US$40–50 for a double, though the tourist offices in most towns should be able to put you in touch with private bed-and-breakfasts in the US$20–30 range. Except during the flower season, it won't be a problem to find a room and you'll likely as not have most campsites to yourself. In season, rooms are hard to come by and campsites are generally crowded though not too full to fit in another small tent.

Aside from places covered in more detail below, there are campsites in the following towns: **Vanrhynsdorp, Garies, Nieuwoudtville, Kamieskroon,**

GETTING TO THE KALAHARI GEMSBOK

A round trip from Cape Town or Johannesburg (or starting at one and ending at the other) realistically requires a week. The reserve is 1,000km from either city, 300km of which is on dirt roads, so unless you start at about two in the morning and are an experienced rally driver, or are just plain crazy, you'll need two days each way.

Hitching could be slow and frustrating, and the only certain way of getting up is to hire a car. Backpackers' hostels in Johannesburg or Cape Town will be able to recommend good deals, though assuming that you can afford it you might be better off using one of the national operators, since they'll be better positioned to do something if you break down. Avis is represented in Upington, though rates here are very high (a six-day deal costs around R800 with 1,500km free – a limit you will almost certainly break, adding another 79c for each extra kilometre).

There are two ways to get to the reserve, one of which starts in Kuruman and the other in Upington. Coming from Johannesburg the Kuruman route is quicker, though both involve a 300km drive on well-maintained dirt roads. From Kuruman, take the R31 to Hotazel, where the tar ends. From here it is about 100km to Vanzylsrus, a dusty little centre with a cheap hotel, a shop, and a petrol station. You then continue through typical Kalahari scenery for 160km to Askham and Andriesvale.

Before you reach Andriesvale, about 110km past Vanzylsrus, there's a tempting little campsite on the farm at Gemsbokkie. It has ablution facilities, fireplaces and running water, and is about 500m from the road and clearly signposted. We only took a quick look around, but it has a marvellous setting amongst white dunes, and struck me as a perfect place to spend a night under the Kalahari sky. There is a small shop 7km further up the road. There is also a campsite at the Molopo Hotel (tel: 054902 916213) in Andriesvale, from where it's a 50km drive through lovely red dunes to the park entrance gate.

A company called Livingstone Trails recently started doing six-day camping trips to the Kalahari and Augrabies Falls out of Johannesburg or Pretoria. These cost around US$210pp at the time of writing. Tel 011 867-2568.

Springbok (at the Kokerboom Motel 5km south of town on the N7), **Kakamas** (the private campsite called **Die Mas** 4km out of town is far nicer than the municipal site – tel: 05542 3430 for directions), **Keimos**, **Olifantshoek**, **Vryburg** (5km out of town adjoining the Leon Taljaard Nature Reserve) and **Lichtenburg**. All of these towns have in addition at least one small hotel.

Augrabies Falls National Park

Kalahari Backpackers and Adventure Centre Roughly 10km from Augrabies Falls National Park; tel: 054 451 0177; fax: 054 451 0218; email: info@kalahari.co.za; web: www.kalahari.co.za. Possibly the most remote backpackers' in South Africa, this new hostel offers a welcome opportunity for adventurous travellers to explore the Northern Cape. In addition to a bar, kitchen and restaurant, they offer a variety of exciting excursions and tours including the Augrabies Rush (half-day river-rafting, Grade 3, US$25pp), a four-night canoe trail at around US$150pp), and a five-day Kalahari Back-road Safari taking in the Kalahari Gemsbok Park, Riemvasmaak Hot Springs, Augrabies Falls and Orange River Rafting at around US$250pp. Camping **B**pp. Dorm **C**pp. Room **E**dbl.

National Park Rest Camp Overlooking falls. Well-stocked shop. Restaurant. Shady campsite **C** site. Huts and cottages from **F** dbl.

Upington

Die Eiland Tel: 054 26911. Municipal resort on island in Orange River. Rondawels from **E** dbl. Camping **C** site.
Guest Lodge 14 Josling St; tel: 054 23133. Rooms **E**/**F**.
Youth Hostel 25km along N14 to Olifantshoek. Tel: 054 25468. Dorm **B** pp. Camp **A** pp.

Kuruman

Kuruman Guest House Cnr Seodin and Barnard; tel: 05373 21508. Rooms **E**/**F**.
Die Oog (The Eye) Resort Voortrekker St; tel: 05373 21479. Central, shady municipal resort. Rooms from **D** pp. Camping **C** site.

Barberspan Nature Reserve

Free camping Camp where you like at no charge in the reserve. No facilities other than longdrops.
Barberspan Hotel On lakeshore 3km from N14. Rooms around US$40. Cheap camping with ablution facilities. Restaurant.

Kalahari Gemsbok National Park

Twee Rivieren, **Mata-Mata**, and **Nossob camps** All three camps have campsites and self-contained huts, while Mata-Mata and Nossob also have a few basic huts using communal ablution facilities. All camps have fuel pumps and shops, and there's a restaurant at Twee Rivieren. Camping **C** site. Basic huts **E** dbl. Self-contained huts US$40–50/dbl.

Appendix 1

WILDLIFE GUIDE

This wildlife guide is designed in a manner that should allow you to put a name to practically every large mammal that you see in East and southern Africa. Fifty of the most widespread and common mammal species are described in detail, while less common or more localised species are featured under the heading *Similar species* beneath the species to which they are most closely allied or bear the strongest resemblance.

Cats and dogs

Lion *Panthera leo* Shoulder height 100–120cm. Weight 150–220kg.
Africa's largest predator, the lion is the animal that everybody hopes to see on safari. It is a sociable creature, living in prides of five to ten animals and defending a territory of between 20 and 200km². Lions hunt at night, and their favoured prey is large or medium antelope such as wildebeest and impala. Most of the hunting is done by females, but dominant males normally feed first after a kill. Rivalry between males is intense and takeover battles are frequently fought to the death, so two or more males often form a coalition. Young males are forced out of their home pride at three years of age, and male cubs are usually killed after a successful takeover. When not feeding or fighting, lions are remarkably indolent – they spend up to 23 hours of any given day at rest – so the anticipation of a lion sighting is often more exciting than the real thing. Lions naturally occur in any habitat but desert and rainforest, and they once ranged across much of the Old World, but these days they are all but restricted to the larger conservation areas in sub-Saharan Africa (one remnant population exists in India). South Africa's Kruger Park supports a population of 1,500 to 2,000 lions, but they are more easily observed in open country such as the Kalahari Gemsbok and Etosha national parks. One place where lion sightings are practically certain on a daily basis is Tanzania's vast Serengeti and Ngorongoro ecosystem, which extends into Kenya's Maasai Mara.

Leopard *Panthera pardus* Shoulder height 70cm. Weight 60–80kg.
The powerful leopard is the most solitary and secretive of Africa's large cat species. It hunts using stealth and power, often getting to within 5m of its intended prey before pouncing, and it habitually stores its kill in a tree to keep it from hyenas and lions. The leopard can be distinguished from the superficially similar cheetah by its rosette-like spots, lack of black 'tearmarks' and more compact, powerful build.

Leopards occur in all habitats, favouring areas with plenty of cover such as riverine woodland and rocky slopes, and there are many records of individuals living for years undetected in close proximity to humans. The leopard is the most common of Africa's large felines, yet a good sighting must be considered a stroke of extreme good fortune. Relatively reliable spots for leopard sightings are the Seronera Valley in the Serengeti, South Luangwa National Park in Zambia, the Nyika Plateau in Malawi, and the tarred road from Skakuza to Lower Sabie in South Africa's Kruger Park.

Cheetah *Acynonix jubatus* Shoulder height 70–80cm. Weight 50–60kg.

This remarkable spotted cat has a greyhound-like build, and is capable of running at 70km per hour in bursts, making it the world's fastest land animal. It is often seen pacing the plains restlessly, either on its own or in a small family group consisting of a mother and her offspring. A diurnal hunter, favouring the cooler hours of the day, the cheetah's habits have been adversely affected in areas where there are high tourist concentrations and off-road driving is permitted. Males are territorial, and generally solitary, though in the Serengeti they commonly defend their territory in pairs or trios. Despite superficial similarities, you can easily tell a cheetah from a leopard by the former's simple spots, disproportionately small head, streamlined build, diagnostic black tearmarks, and preference for relatively open habitats. Widespread, but thinly distributed and increasingly rare outside of conservation areas, the cheetah is most likely to be seen in savannah and arid habitats such as Serengeti, Etosha and Kalahari Gemsbok national parks.

Similar species: The **serval** (*Felis serval*) is smaller than a cheetah (shoulder height 55cm) but has a similar build and black-on-gold spots giving way to streaking near the head. Seldom seen, it is widespread and quite common in moist grassland, reedbeds and riverine habitats.

Caracal (*Felis caracal*) Shoulder height 40cm. Weight 15–20kg.

The caracal resembles the European lynx with its uniform tan coat and tufted ears. It is a solitary hunter, feeding on birds, small antelope and livestock, and ranges throughout the region favouring relatively arid savannah habitats. It is nocturnal and rarely seen.

Similar species: A West African species that occurs sparsely in a few forests in Uganda and western and central Kenya, the **golden cat** (*Felis aurata*) is rather like a caracal but lacks the ear tufts and has a spotted underbelly. The smaller **African wild cat** (*Felis sylvestris*) ranges from the Mediterranean to the Cape of Good Hope, and is similar in appearance to the domestic tabby cat. It has an unspotted torso, which should preclude confusion with the even smaller **small spotted cat**

(*Felis nigripes*), a thinly distributed resident of western South Africa, eastern Namibia and southern Botswana.

African hunting dog (*Lycaon pictus*) Shoulder height 70cm. Weight 25kg.
Also known as the wild or painted dog, the hunting dog is distinguished from other African dogs by its large size and cryptic black, brown and cream coat. Highly sociable, living in packs of up to 20 animals, the hunting dog is a ferocious hunter that literally tears apart its prey on the run. Threatened with extinction as a result of its susceptibility to diseases spread by domestic dogs, it is extinct in several areas where it was formerly abundant (the Serengeti for instance). The global population of fewer than 3,000 is concentrated in southern Tanzania, Zambia, Hwange National Park in Zimbabwe and the Kruger Park in South Africa.

Black-backed jackal (*Canis mesomelas*) Shoulder height 35–45cm. Weight 8–12kg.
The black-backed jackal is an opportunistic feeder capable of adapting to most habitats. Most often seen singly or in pairs at dusk or dawn, it is ochre in colour with a prominent black saddle flecked by a varying amount of white or gold. It is probably the most frequently observed small predator in Africa south of the Zambezi, and its eerie call is a characteristic sound of the bush at night. It is absent only from Malawi, Zambia and northern Mozambique.

Similar species The similar **side-striped jackal** (*Canis adustus*) is more cryptic in colour, and has an indistinct pale vertical stripe on each flank and a white-tipped tail. Nowhere very common, it is the only jackal found in northeast Zimbabwe, northern Mozambique, Malawi, Zambia and western Uganda, and it occurs alongside the black-backed jackal in the Kruger Park and most parts of East Africa. The **common jackal** (*Canis aureus*), also known as the Eurasian or golden jackal, is a cryptically coloured North African jackal, relatively pale and with a black tail tip. Its range extends as far south as the Serengeti, probably the best place to see it in the region. Africa's rarest carnivore, the **Simien wolf** (*Canis simensis*) is larger and bulkier than any jackal, with a striking foxy red coat and distinctive white throat that render it unmistakable. Endemic to the Ethiopian highlands, this once common canine has suffered a dramatic population drop in recent years, for similar reasons to the hunting dog. Most of the 300 to 500 surviving individuals are concentrated in the Alpine moorland of the Saneti Plateau in Ethiopia's Bale National Park, where they are surprisingly easy to locate.

Bat-eared fox *Otocyon megalotis* Shoulder height 30–35cm. Weight 3–5kg.
This small, silver-grey insectivore, unmistakable with its huge ears and black eye-mask, is most often seen in pairs or small family groups during the cooler hours of the day. Associated with dry

open country, it is abundant in the Kalahari Gemsbok and Serengeti national parks, and within the region is absent only from Zambia, Malawi, Mozambique and eastern parts of South Africa and Zimbabwe.

Similar species The **Cape fox** (*Vulpes chama*) is an infrequently seen dry country predator restricted to South Africa, Namibia and Botswana. The Cape fox lacks the prominent ears and mask of the bat-eared fox, and within its range it could be confused only with the larger black-backed jackal, though it lacks the jackal's black back. The **sand fox** (*Vulpes pallida*) is a tiny Sahelian canid which extends its range into northern Ethiopia, where a shoulder height of 25cm alone should preclude confusion with the common jackal, the other dog found there.

Spotted hyena (*Crocuta crocuta*) Shoulder height 85cm. Weight 70kg.

Hyenas are characterised by their bulky build, sloping back, brownish coat, powerful jaws and dog-like expression. Contrary to popular myth, hyenas are not exclusively scavengers: the spotted hyena in particular is an adept hunter capable of killing an animal as large as a wildebeest. Nor are they hermaphroditic, an ancient belief that stems from the false scrotum and penis covering the female hyena's vagina. Sociable animals, and fascinating to observe, hyenas live in loosely structured clans of about ten animals, led by females who are stronger and larger than males. The spotted hyena is the largest hyena, distinguished by its blotchily spotted coat, and common in most of East and southern Africa where it is most frequently seen at dusk and dawn in the vicinity of game reserve lodges, campsites and refuse dumps.

Similar species The North African **striped hyena** (*Hyaena hyaena*) is pale brown with several dark vertical streaks and a blackish mane. It occurs alongside the spotted hyena in dry parts of Tanzania, Kenya and Ethiopia, but is always relatively scarce and secretive. The equally secretive **brown hyena** (*Hyaena brunnea*) occurs locally in arid parts of South Africa, Botswana and Namibia, and has a shaggy, unmarked dark brown coat. Also dark, but with even darker stripes, the **aardwolf** (*Proteles cristatus*) is an insectivorous hyena, not much bigger than a jackal, which occurs in low numbers in most parts of South Africa, Namibia, Botswana, Zimbabwe, northern Tanzania, Kenya and eastern Ethiopia.

Primates

Gorilla (*Gorilla gorilla*) Standing height 150–170cm. Weight up to 200kg.

The mountain gorilla of East Africa is distinguished from the extralimital eastern and western lowland gorillas by several adaptations to living at high altitude, most visibly a longer and more luxuriant coat. It lives in troops of five or more, which unusually for mammals are focused around the dominant male (descriptively referred to as the silverback), who starts to acquire his harem at about 15 years and may continue to lead a troop into his 40s. The female gorilla reaches sexual

maturity at eight, and she often moves between troops several times before successfully giving birth; at which point she will normally stick with one silverback until he dies. She will help defend the troop against takeovers, motivated by the probability that a new male will kill nursing infants that aren't his. The gorilla is vegetarian, though insects form a major protein supplement. A troop spends most of its waking hours on the ground, moving into the trees at night when each individual builds a temporary nest. Surprisingly sedentary, a troop typically moves less than 1km in a day, though it will sometimes move much further after a stressful incident such as an aggressive encounter with another troop. Dian Fossey's *Gorillas in the Mist* is essential reading for anybody who wants to know more about mountain gorillas. Gorillas have few natural enemies and often live to be 50 years old. The long-term survival of the mountain gorilla, however, is critically threatened by deforestation and poaching. As few as 600 remain, all of them resident in Bwindi National Park (Uganda) or the volcanic Virunga range (on the border of Uganda, Rwanda and the Congo), where habituated troops can be visited on an organised gorilla tracking walk. Unlike the two lowland races, which together number around 50,000 wild animals, mountain gorillas have never been successfully reared in captivity.

Chimpanzee *Pan troglodytes* Standing height 100cm. Weight up to 55kg.
This distinctive black-coated ape is, along with the **bonobo** (*Pan paniscus*) of the southern Congo, more closely related to man than to any other living creature. The chimpanzee lives in large troops based around a core of related males dominated by an alpha male. Females aren't firmly bonded to their core group, so emigration between communities is normal. Primarily frugivorous, chimpanzees eat meat on occasion and, though most kills are opportunistic, stalking of prey is not unusual. The first recorded instance of a chimp using a tool was at Gombe Stream in Tanzania, where modified sticks were used to 'fish' in termite mounds. In West Africa, chimps have been observed cracking open nuts with a stone and anvil. In the USA, captive chimps have successfully been taught Sign Language and have created compound words such as 'rock-berry' to describe a nut. A widespread and common rainforest resident, the chimpanzee is thought to number 200,000 in the wild. In East Africa, chimps occur in Western Uganda and on the Tanzanian shore of Lake Tanganyika. They are seen easily and affordably in Uganda's Budongo and Kibale Forests and Chambura Gorge. It is possible to see chimps at the research centre founded by Jane Goodall in Tanzania's Gombe Stream, but by comparison with Uganda it's prohibitively expensive.

Common baboon *Papio cynocaphalus* Shoulder height 50–75cm. Weight 25–45kg.
This powerful terrestrial primate, distinguished from any other monkey by its much larger size, inverted 'U' shaped tail and distinctive dog-like head, is fascinating to watch from a behavioural perspective. It lives in large troops which boast a complex, rigid social structure characterised by matriarchal lineages and plenty of intertroop movement by males seeking social dominance. Omnivorous and at home in almost any habitat, the baboon is the most widespread primate in Africa, frequently seen in most

game reserves. There are three races, regarded by some authorities as full species. The chacma baboon (*P. c. ursinus*) is grey and confined largely to areas south of the Zambezi. The yellow baboon (*P. c. cynocephalus*) is a yellow-brown race occurring in Zambia, northern Mozambique, Malawi, southern and eastern Tanzania and eastern Kenya. The olive or anubis baboon (*P. c. anubis*) is a hairy green-to-brown baboon found in Ethiopia, Uganda, northern Tanzania and Kenya.

Similar species The male of the smaller **hamadryas baboon** (*Papio hamadryas*) is distinctive, with its naked pink face and ears and luxuriant silver-grey head and shoulder hair. Restricted to the Horn of Africa and Arabia, it is most common on rocky slopes and cliffs in eastern Ethiopia. The **gelada baboon** (*Theropithecus gelada*) is endemic to the northwestern highlands of Ethiopia, where it is very common, with troops of several hundred animals still recorded in the Simien Mountains. An exceptionally handsome animal, the gelada can be identified by the male's bright red chest patch and rather leonine mane.

Vervet monkey *Cercopithecus aethiops* Length (excluding tail) 40–55cm. Weight 4–6kg.

Also known as the green or grivet monkey, the vervet is probably the world's most numerous monkey and certainly the most common and widespread representative of the *Cercopithecus* guenons, a taxonomically controversial genus associated with African forests. An atypical guenon in that it inhabits savannah and woodland rather than true forest, the vervet spends a high proportion of its time on the ground and in most of its range it could be confused only with the much larger and heavier baboon. However, the vervet's light grey coat, black face and white forehead band should be diagnostic – as should the male's garish blue genitals. The Ethiopian race of vervet has white cheek tufts reminiscent of the blue monkey. The vervet is abundant in East Africa and eastern parts of South Africa, where it might be seen anywhere.

Similar species The terrestrial **patas monkey** (*Erythrocebus patas*), larger and more spindly than the vervet, has an orange-tinged coat and black forehead stripe. Essentially a monkey of the dry northwestern savannah, the patas occurs in parts of northern Kenya, northern Uganda and western Ethiopia, but it is most likely to be encountered by tourists in the Serengeti.

Blue monkey *Cercopithecus mitis* Length (excluding tail) 50–60cm. Weight 5–8kg. Known as the **samango monkey** in southern Africa, **Sykes monkey** in Kenya, and the **diademed** or **white-throated guenon** in some field guides, this most variable monkey is divided by some authorities into several species. It is the most common forest guenon in the region, occurring just about anywhere suitable in the eastern half of Africa. Unlikely to be confused with any other species through most of its range, the blue monkey has a uniformly dark blue-grey coat broken by a white throat which in some races extends all down the chest and in others around the collar. It lives in troops of up to ten animals and associates with other primates where their ranges overlap. Regarded by some authorities as a distinct species, the golden monkey is a localised resident of bamboo forest in the Western Rift region. The best place to see it is in the Virunga Mountains, where it is the most common monkey, though it also occurs in a few rather inaccessible parts of Nyungwe Forest, Rwanda.

Similar species The **red-tailed monkey** (*Cercopithecus ascanius*) is a small brown guenon with white whiskers, a red tail and a distinctive white heart on its nose. Common in several Ugandan forests, most visibly Kibale, it also occurs in the Kakamega Forest and Nyungwe Forest, and around northeastern Lake Tanganyika. **De Brazza's monkey** (*Cercopithecus neglectus*) is a thickset guenon with a shortish tail, rusty forehead patch and long, white beard. Associated with swamp and bamboo, it has a patchy distribution in East Africa, where it is likely to be seen only in the vicinity of Mount Elgon, Semoliki, Saiwa Swamp and Omo national parks. The relatively terrestrial **L'Hoest's monkey** (*Cercopithecus lhoesti*) is uniformly black except for the backward projecting white whiskers that partially cover its ears. The only guenon which habitually carries its tail in an upright position, it is a Western Rift endemic, with its main stronghold being Rwanda's Nyungwe Forest, where it is commonly seen from the road and in the campsite. It also occurs in Uganda's Kibale, Bwindi, Queen Elizabeth and possibly Ruwenzori national parks, though is rather uncommon.

Mangabeys are forest monkeys, similar in size to guenons. The **grey-cheeked mangabey** (*Cercocebus algigena*) is dark grey to black with few distinguishing features, though it has a shaggier coat than any guenon, as well as light grey cheeks and an indistinct pale mane. It is one of the more common monkeys in Uganda's Kibale Forest, and is known to occur in Semuliki and Nyungwe Forests. The **crested mangabey** (*Cercocebus galeritus*) is a yellow monkey of which two isolated races occur in East Africa, one in Tanzania's Udzungwa Mountains and another along Kenya's Tana River.

Black-and-white colobus (*Colobus guereza*) Length (excluding tail) 65cm. Weight 12kg.
This beautiful, jet-black monkey has bold white facial markings, a long white tail and in some races white sides and shoulders. Almost exclusively arboreal, it is capable of jumping up to 30m, a spectacular sight with its white tail streaming behind. Several races have been described, and most authorities recognise the similar but less boldly marked **Angola colobus** (*Colobus angolensis*) as a distinct species. The black-and-white colobus is common in most East African forests, particularly in southern and western Ethiopia where it is known as the guereza. The only place in the region where Angola colobus can be seen with ease is Rwanda's Nyungwe Forest, where a semi-habituated troop of 400 animals lives in the vicinity of the campsite.

Red colobus (*Procolobus badius*) Length (excluding tail) 60cm. Weight 10kg.
The status of this variable monkey is debatable, with between one and ten species recognised. Most populations have black on the upper back, red on the lower back, a pale tufted crown and a long-limbed appearance unlike that of any guenon or mangabey. Four populations are known in East Africa. Those in Uganda's Kibale Forest and Zanzibar's Jozani Forest are very accessible, those in Tanzania's Udzungwa Mountains and along Kenya's Tana River are less so. Some authorities

regard Kirk's red colobus of Zanzibar to be a full species *P. kirkii*, as do they the Uhehe red colobus *P. gordonorum* of the Udzungwa.

Lesser bushbaby (*Galago senegalensis*) Length (without tail) 17cm. Weight 150g.

The lesser bushbaby is the most widespread and common member of a group of small and generally indistinguishable nocturnal primates, distantly related to the lemurs of Madagascar. More often heard than seen, the lesser bushbaby can sometimes be picked out by tracing a cry to a tree and shining a torch into its eyes.

Similar species The most easily identified bushbaby due to its size, the **greater bushbaby** (*Galago crassicaudatus*) occurs on the eastern side of Africa as far south as East London. It produces a terrifying scream which you'd think was emitted by a chimpanzee or gorilla. The **potto** (*Perodicticus potto*), a sloth-like nocturnal primate of rainforest interiors, occurs in Kenya's Kakamega Forest and Uganda's Kibale, Bwindi and Queen Elizabeth national parks.

Large antelope

Roan antelope (*Hippotragus equinus*) Shoulder height 120–150cm. Weight 250–300kg.

This handsome, horse-like antelope is uniform fawn-grey with a pale belly, short decurved horns and a light mane. It could be mistaken for the female sable antelope, but this has a well-defined white belly, and lacks the roan's distinctive black-and-white facial markings. The roan is widespread but thinly distributed in Zambia, Malawi and western Tanzania – you can be pretty certain of seeing it on foot on the Nyika Plateau – and it occurs at Etosha in Namibia, Mana Pools in Zimbabwe and the Kruger Park in South Africa.

Sable antelope (*Hippotragus niger*) Shoulder height 135cm. Weight 230kg.

The striking male sable is jet black with a distinct white face, underbelly and rump, and long decurved horns. The female is chestnut brown and has shorter horns. Most common in the *miombo* woodlands of southern Tanzania, where a population of 30,000 is concentrated in Ruaha and Selous, the sable also occurs in several Zambian reserves, Kenya's Shimba Hills, the Pretoriuskop region of the Kruger Park, Hwange in Zimbabwe and Liwonde in Malawi.

Oryx or **gemsbok** (*Oryx gazella*) Shoulder height 120cm. Weight 230kg.

This regal dry-country antelope is unmistakable with its ash-grey coat, bold black facial marks and flank strip, and unique long, straight horns. The most handsome race is the gemsbok, which occurs in the western deserts and semi-deserts of southern Africa. Of the East African races, the fringe-eared oryx occurs in Amboseli, Tsavo and Tarangire national parks, while the Beisa oryx is common in the Samburu Reserve and Awash National Park.

Waterbuck (*Kobus ellipsiprymnus*) Shoulder height 130cm. Weight 250-270kg.

The waterbuck is easily recognised by its shaggy brown coat and the male's large lyre-shaped horns. The common race of southern Africa and areas east of the Rift Valley has a distinctive white ring around its rump, while the defassa race of the Rift Valley and areas further west has a full white rump. Especially common around Lake Nakuru, the waterbuck is frequently seen in small family groups grazing near water in all but the most arid national parks.

Blue wildebeest (*Connochaetes taurinus*) Shoulder height 130–150cm. Weight 180–250kg.

This ungainly antelope, also called the **brindled gnu**, is easily identified by its dark coat and bovine appearance. The superficially similar buffalo is far more heavily built. Immense herds of blue wildebeest occur in Tanzania's Serengeti Plains, where the annual migration of more than a million head into Kenya's Maasai Mara forms one of Africa's great natural spectacles. There are also significant populations in southern Tanzania, Namibia, Zambia, Botswana, Zimbabwe and the Kruger Park, Kalahari Gemsbok and Zululand regions of South Africa.

Similar species The **black wildebeest** (*Connochaetes gnou*), endemic to South Africa's central highveld, now numbers a mere 4,000 and is seen most easily at Golden Gate. It differs from the blue wildebeest in having a white tail, a defined black-on-white mane, and horns that slope sharply down then rise to form a 'U' when seen from the side.

Hartebeest (*Alcelaphus buselaphus*) Shoulder height 125cm. Weight 120–150kg.

Hartebeests are ungainly antelopes, readily identified by the combination of large shoulders, a sloping back, red-brown or yellow-brown coat and smallish horns in both sexes. Numerous races are recognised, all of which are generally seen in small family groups in reasonably open country. The races most likely to be seen by visitors are the red hartebeest in South Africa, Namibia and Botswana, the kongoni in northern Tanzania and southern Kenya; Swayne's and Lelwel's hartebeest in Ethiopia, and Liechtenstein's hartebeest in southern Tanzania, Zambia and Zimbabwe. Liechtenstein's hartebeest is often regarded as a full species, as is the extremely rare hirola of northeast Kenya.

Similar species The **topi** or **tsessebe** (*Damaliscus lunatus*) is basically a darker version of the hartebeest with striking yellow lower legs. Widespread but thinly and patchily distributed, the topi is most easily seen alongside the much yellower kongoni in the Serengeti and Maasai Mara. The **bontebok** (*Damaliscus dorcas*), a

South African endemic, is a hartebeest with a distinctive white face. The nominate race of the Western Cape *fynbos*, particularly striking with its chestnut back, black flanks and white belly and rump, and at one time·prolific within its limited range, was hunted close to extinction in the early 20th century. Roughly 2,000 bontebok are protected in a handful of reserves, most accessibly the Cape of Good Hope near Cape Town. The duller but more common **blesbok**, in essence the highveld race of bontebok, is frequently seen from the N3 between Johannesburg and Durban.

Greater kudu (*Tragelaphus strepsiceros*) Shoulder height 140–155cm. Weight 180–250kg.

The greater kudu is perhaps the most frequently observed member of the genus *tragelaphus*, a group of medium-sized to large antelopes characterised by the male's large spiralling horns and dark coat generally marked with several vertical white stripes; and normally associated with well-wooded habitats. The greater kudu is very large, with a grey-brown coat and up to ten stripes on each side, and the male has magnificent double-spiralled horns. A widespread animal occurring in most wooded habitats except for true forest, the greater kudu is most often seen in mixed or single-sex herds of up to ten animals.

Similar species The thinly distributed and skittish **lesser kudu** (*Tragelaphus imberbis*) is an East African species largely restricted to arid woodland. It often occurs alongside the greater kudu, from which it can be distinguished by its smaller size (shoulder height 100cm), two white throat patches and greater number of stripes (at least 11). The handsome male **nyala** (*Tragelaphus angasi*) has a shoulder height of 120cm and is unmistakable with its shaggy, off-black coat with roughly ten vertical white side stripes, reddish lower legs and heavy black horns. The smaller female might be confused with the bushbuck (see next plate) due to its lighter chestnut coat, but it has far more defined stripes. The nyala occurs in thick bush and near watercourses along the eastern coastal belt and Zambezi and Shire Valleys from Malawi south to Zululand, and it is quite common within this limited range, particularly in the Zululand reserves, the northern Kruger Park and Malawi's Lengwe National Park. The **mountain nyala** (*Tragelophus buxtoni*) looks less like the nyala than a shaggier and slightly smaller version of the greater kudu, with less distinct side stripes, smaller horns, and throat patches like those of the lesser kudu. First collected in 1908, the mountain nyala is endemic to Ethiopia's southwest highlands. More than half the estimated population of 2,500 animals lives in Bale National Park, where it is easily observed and might be confused only with the smaller bushbuck. The secretive and scarce **bongo** (*Tragelaphus euryceros*) is a large, stocky and clearly striped West African rainforest species, isolated populations of which occur in some of Kenya's montane forests. The semi-aquatic **sitatunga** (*Tragelaphus spekei*) is a widespread but infrequently observed inhabitant of west and central African swamps from the Okavango in Botswana to the Sudd in Sudan. It is most likely to be seen in Kenya's Saiwa Swamp, where suitable viewing platforms have been built. The male, with a shoulder height of up to 125cm and a shaggy fawn coat, is unmistakable in its habitat. The smaller female might be mistaken for a bushbuck (see opposite) but it has far more defined stripes.

Common eland (*Taurotragus oryx*) Shoulder height 150–175cm. Weight 450–900kg.

Africa's largest antelope, the common eland is light brown in colour, sometimes with a few faint white vertical stripes, and its somewhat bovine appearance is accentuated by relatively short horns and a large dewlap. It is widely distributed in East and southern Africa, and small herds may be seen almost anywhere in grassland or light woodland. The similar but more distinctly striped **Lord Derby's eland** (*Taurotragus derbianus*), also known as the giant eland (though it is no larger than the common eland), is a Sahelian species included on the official checklist for Uganda but almost certainly extinct in that country.

Medium and small antelope

Bushbuck (*Tragelaphus scriptus*) Shoulder height 70–80cm. Weight 30–45kg.
This attractive antelope, a member of the same genus as the kudus, shows great regional variation in colouring. The male is dark brown, chestnut or in parts of Ethiopia black, while the much smaller female is generally pale reddy brown. The male has relatively small, straight horns for a *tragelaphus* antelope. Both sexes have similar throat patches to the lesser kudu, and are marked with white spots and sometimes stripes, though the last are never as clear as the vertical white stripes on the otherwise similar female nyala or sitatunga. One of the most widespread antelope species in Africa, the bushbuck occurs in forest and riverine woodland, where it is normally seen singly or in pairs. The bushbuck tends to be secretive and skittish except where it is used to people, for instance in the rainforest above Victoria Falls and around Dinsho in Ethiopia's Bale National Park.

Thomson's gazelle (*Gazella thomsoni*) Shoulder height 60cm. Weight 20–25kg.
Gazelles are graceful, relatively small antelopes which generally occur in large herds in open country and have fawn-brown upper parts and a white belly. Thomson's gazelle is characteristic of the East African plains, where it is the only gazelle to have a black horizontal stripe. It is common in the Serengeti and surrounds, and a separate population occurs in southern Ethiopia and Sudan.

Similar species Occurring alongside Thomson's gazelle in many parts of East Africa, the larger **Grant's gazelle** (*Gazella granti*) lacks a black side-stripe and has comparatively large horns, particularly the race *G. g. raineyi* which occurs in Kenya's Samburu National Reserve. In addition to Grant's and Thomson's gazelles, four north African gazelle species have a restricted distribution in Ethiopia. Of these, **Soemmering's gazelle** (*Gazella soemmerringi*) might well be seen by tourists who visit the northern Rift Valley, where it can be distinguished by its bold black face mask and white rump. Less likely to be seen are the **red-fronted gazelle** (*Gazella rubifrons*) in the far northwest, the very rare **Speke's gazelle** (*gazella spekei*) in the southeast or the **dorcas gazelle** (*Gazella dorcas*) in the far northwest. Only one gazelle species occurs in southern Africa, the **springbok** (*Antidorcas marsupilis*), which looks very similar to Thomson's gazelle and is readily observed in most reserves in the dry west. An uncharacteristic gazelle, the **gerenuk** (*Litocranius walleri*) is a solitary, arid country species of Ethiopia, Kenya and northern Tanzania, similar in general colour to an impala but readily identified by its very long neck and singular habit of feeding from trees standing on its hind legs – good places to see it include Samburu in Kenya and Tarangire in Tanzania. The rather similar **ditabag** (*Ammodorcas clarkei*) is restricted to semi-deserts of eastern Ethiopia, where it may occur alongside the gerenuk but can be told apart reliably by the clear white mark running down the nose.

Impala (*Aepeceros melampus*) Shoulder height 90cm. Weight 45kg. This slender, handsome antelope is superficially similar to some gazelles, but in fact belongs to a separate family. Chestnut in colour, the impala has diagnostic black and white stripes running down its rump and tail, and the main has large lyre-shaped horns. One of the most widespread antelope species in East and southern Africa, the impala is normally seen in large herds in wooded savannah habitats, and it is the most common antelope in the Kruger Park, Hwange, and many other reserves. A discrete population, the so-called 'black-faced impala', occurs in the Etosha area of northern Namibia.

Reedbucks (*Redunca spp*) Shoulder height 65–90cm. Weight 30–65kg.
The three species of reedbuck are all rather nondescript fawn-grey antelopes generally seen in open grassland near water. The mountain reedbuck (*Redunca fulvorufula*) is the smallest and most distinctive, with a clear white belly, tiny horns, and an overall grey appearance. It has a broken distribution, occurring in mountainous parts of eastern South Africa, northern Tanzania, Kenya and southern Ethiopia. The Bohor reedbuck (*Redunca redunca*) and southern reedbuck (*Redunca arundinum*) are more fawn in general colour and the southern reedbuck has rather large horns. The Bohor reedbuck is essentially an East African species found in central Tanzania northwards to Ethiopia, whereas the southern reedbuck occurs only in southern Tanzania southwards.

Similar species The **grey rhebok** (*Palea capreolus*) is a South African endemic, particularly common in the Drakensberg and surrounds, and likely to be confused only with the mountain reedbuck from which it differs in having thin, straight horns and a woolly grey coat. The **kob** (*Kobus kob*), an attractive West African antelope similar in size and general colouration to the impala (but lacking any distinguishing markings), extends its range eastwards into Uganda, where it is the most common large mammal in Queen Elizabeth National Park. The golden-brown **puku** (*Kobus vardoni*) is similar in appearance to the kob, but the two are unlikely to be confused because the puku lives in marsh and moist grassland from Lake Rukwa in Tanzania to the Okavango in Botswana. The **lechwe** (*Kobus leche*) is another kob-like antelope restricted to moist open environments, predominantly in Zambia, where three distinct races have in common fawn to dark chestnut upper parts and clearly delineated white underparts in both sexes and reasonably large backward-sweeping horns in both sexes. A small population of the almost jet black **Nile lechwe** (*Kobus megaceros*) may occur near Gambela in western Ethiopia.

Klipspringer (*Oreotragus oreotragus*) Shoulder height 60cm. Weight 13kg.

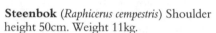

The klipspringer is a goat-like antelope, normally seen in pairs, and easily identified by its dark, bristly grey-yellow coat, slightly speckled appearance and unique habitat preference. Klipspringer means 'rockjumper' in Afrikaans and it is an apt name for an antelope which occurs exclusively in mountainous areas and rocky outcrops from Cape Town to the Red Sea.

Steenbok (*Raphicerus cempestris*) Shoulder height 50cm. Weight 11kg.

This rather nondescript small antelope has red-brown upper parts and clear white underparts, and the male has short straight horns. It is probably the most commonly observed small antelope, though it has a broken range, being absent from southern Tanzania, northern Zambia, Malawi and northern Mozambique. Like most other antelopes of its size, the steenbok is normally encountered singly or in pairs and tends to 'freeze' when disturbed.

Similar species Essentially plugging the gap between the eastern and southern populations of steenbok, **Sharpe's grysbok** (*Raphicerus sharpei*) is similar in size and appearance, though it has a distinctive white-flecked coat. It occurs alongside the steenbok in parts of Zimbabwe and the northeast of South Africa. The **Cape grysbok** (*Raphicerus melanotis*) is restricted to *fynbos* habitats in the Western Cape, where its white-flecked coat is diagnostic. Restricted to the eastern coastal belt and Zambezi Valley, the **suni** (*Neotragus moschatus*) has a shoulder height of 35cm, which makes it the smallest African antelope likely to be seen outside of forests, and a plain red-brown coat similar to that of the steenbok, from which it is most easily distinguished by its size and persistent habit of flicking its black and white tail. The **Oribi** (*Ourebia ourebi*) is a widespread but uncommon grassland antelope which looks much like a steenbok but stands about 10cm higher at the shoulder and has an altogether more upright bearing. **Kirk's dik-dik** (*Madoqua kirki*), smaller than the steenbok and easily identified by its large white eye circle, is restricted primarily to Tanzania and Kenya, where it is often the most commonly seen small antelope, though a discrete population occurs in northern Namibia. It is replaced by the outwardly very similar **Guenther's dik-dik** (*Madoqua guentheri*) in northern Kenya and southern Ethiopia and **Salt's dik-dik** (*Madoqua saltiana*) in northern and eastern Ethiopia.

Red duiker (*Cephalophus natalensis*) Shoulder height 45cm. Weight 14kg.
This is the most likely of Africa's 12 to 20 'forest duikers' to be seen by tourists. It is deep chestnut in colour with a white tail and, in the case of the East African race *C. n. harveyi* (sometimes considered to be a separate species), a black face. The red duiker occurs in most substantial forest patches along the eastern side of Africa from East London north to Bale in Ethiopia, though it is less often seen than heard crashing through the undergrowth. There is some debate as to whether the Weyn's, Peter's and black-fronted duiker (West African species which range into Uganda) should be regarded as races or full species.

Similar species The **blue duiker** (*Cephalophus monticola*) is widespread in Africa and the only other forest duiker to occur in countries south of Tanzania, and it can easily be told from the red duiker by its greyer colouring and much smaller size (it is the smallest forest duiker, about the same size as a suni). **Abbott's duiker** (*Cephalophus spadix*) is a large duiker, as tall as a klipspringer, restricted to a handful of montane forests in Tanzania, including those on Kilimanjaro and the Usambara, Udzungwa and Poroto Mountains. Another very localised species is **Ader's duiker** (*Cephalophus adersi*) which is found only in Kenya's Sokoke Forest (it's easily seen at Gedi Ruins) and on Zanzibar where it replaces the very similar red duiker. Most other forest duikers are essentially West African species but a few extend their range into Uganda – most notably the bushbuck-sized **yellow-backed duiker** (*Cephalophus leucogaster*), which has a blackish coat and yellow back patch, and occurs in Bwindi, Ruwenzori and Queen Elizabeth national parks.

Common duiker (*Sylvicapra grimmia*) Shoulder height 50cm. Weight 20kg.
This anomalous duiker holds itself more like a steenbok or grysbok and is the only member of its family to occur outside of forests. Generally grey in colour, the common duiker can most easily be separated from other small antelopes by the black tuft of hair that sticks up between its horns. It occurs throughout sub-Saharan Africa, and tolerates most habitats except for true forest and very open country.

Other large herbivores
African elephant (*Loxodonta africana*) Shoulder height 2.3–3.4m. Weight up to 6,000kg.
The world's largest land animal, the African elephant is intelligent, social and often very entertaining to watch. Female elephants live in closely knit clans in which the eldest female plays matriarch over her sisters, daughters and granddaughters. Mother-daughter bonds are strong and may last for up to 50 years. Males generally leave the family group at around 12 years to roam singly or form bachelor herds. Under normal circumstances, elephants range widely in search of food and water, but when concentrated populations are forced to live in conservation areas their habit of uprooting trees can cause serious environmental damage. Elephants are widespread and common in habitats ranging from desert to rainforest, and despite heavy poaching they are likely to be seen on a daily basis in most of the region's larger national parks.

Black rhinoceros (*Diceros bicornis*) Shoulder height 160cm. Weight 1,000kg.
This is the more widespread of Africa's two rhino species, an imposing and sometimes rather aggressive creature that has been poached to extinction in most

of its former range. It occurs in many southern African reserves, but is now very localised in East Africa, where it is most likely to be seen in Tanzania's Ngorongoro Crater.

Similar species More placid but bulkier, the **white rhinoceros** (*Ceratotherium simum*) typically weighs between 1,500 and 2,000kg. It is no paler in colour than the black rhino – the 'white' derives from the Afrikaans *weit* (wide) and refers to its flattened mouth, an ideal shape for cropping grass. This is the best way to tell the two rhino species apart, since the mouth of the black rhino, a browser in most parts of its range, is more rounded with a hooked upper lip. Aside from a relic population of some 30 animals in the northern Congo, the white rhino is now restricted to southern African reserves, notably the Kruger Park, Pilanesburg and Zululand Reserves, where it is generally seen more frequently than the black rhino.

Hippopotamus (*Hippopotamus amphibius*) Shoulder height 150cm. Weight 2,000kg.
Characteristic of Africa's large rivers and lakes, this large, lumbering animal spends most of the day submerged but emerges at night to graze. Strongly territorial, herds of ten or more animals are presided over by a dominant male who will readily defend his patriarchy to the death. Hippos are abundant in most protected rivers and water bodies, and they are still quite common outside of reserves, where they kill more people than any other African mammal.

African buffalo (*Syncerus caffer*) Shoulder height 140cm. Weight 700kg.
Frequently and erroneously referred to as a water buffalo (an Asian species), the African buffalo is a distinctive ox-like animal that lives in large herds on the savannah and occurs in smaller herds in forested areas. Common and widespread in sub-Saharan Africa, it is likely to be seen in most reserves. In Uganda's Queen Elizabeth National Park, you may well see hybrids between the familiar black savannah race of buffalo and the smaller, redder race of the West African rainforest.

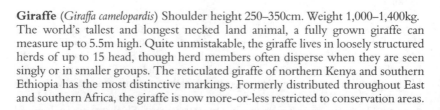

Giraffe (*Giraffa camelopardis*) Shoulder height 250–350cm. Weight 1,000–1,400kg.
The world's tallest and longest necked land animal, a fully grown giraffe can measure up to 5.5m high. Quite unmistakable, the giraffe lives in loosely structured herds of up to 15 head, though herd members often disperse when they are seen singly or in smaller groups. The reticulated giraffe of northern Kenya and southern Ethiopia has the most distinctive markings. Formerly distributed throughout East and southern Africa, the giraffe is now more-or-less restricted to conservation areas.

Common zebra (*Equus burchelli*) Shoulder height 130cm. Weight 300–340kg.
This attractive striped horse is common and widespread throughout most of East and southern Africa, where it is often seen in large herds alongside wildebeest. It is common in most conservation areas from northern South Africa, Namibia and Botswana all the way up to the southeast of Ethiopia. Southern races generally have paler 'shadow stripes' between the bold black stripes that are present in all races.

Similar species The localised **mountain zebra** (*Equus zebra*) is a southern species which lacks the 'shadow stripes' of the southern race of common zebra and is most easily observed in the South African national park to which it has lent its name. Two races are recognised: Hartmann's mountain zebra is confined to Namibia and the Cape mountain zebra to the Eastern and Western Cape. Another localised equine, **Grevy's zebra** (*Equus grevyi*), is confined to northern Kenya and southern Ethiopia. It is most easily seen in the Samburu complex of reserves, where it can be distinguished from the common zebra by its larger size (shoulder height 150cm) and much finer striping. Once widespread, the **African wild ass** (*Equus asinus*) has suffered massive range loss in recent times exacerbated by hybridisation with feral and domestic asses. A few hundred individuals survive in the northern Ethiopian Rift Valley, where only a few light black bands along the legs distinguish it from its domestic counterpart.

Walia ibex (*Capra ibex walie*) Shoulder height 70–100cm. Weight 50–70kg.
The only wild goat found in the region, the walia ibex is an Ethiopian endemic which some authorities regard as being a full species. Readily identified by its goat-like appearance and the male's immense horns, the walia ibex is one of the most endangered of African large mammals, with at most 400 individuals surviving in the Simien mountains where it is sometimes seen by hikers. People walking on Table Mountain in South Africa may come across the goat-like **tahr** (*Hemitragus jemlahicus*), an introduced Asian species.

Warthog (*Phacochoreus africanus*) Shoulder height 60–70cm. Weight up to 100kg.
This widespread and often conspicuously abundant resident of the African savannah is grey in colour with a thin covering of hairs, wart-like bumps on its face, and rather large upward curving tusks. Africa's only diurnal swine, the warthog is often seen in family groups, trotting off briskly with its tail raised stiffly (a diagnostic trait) and a determinedly nonchalant air.

Similar species Bulkier, hairier and browner, the **bushpig** (*Potomochoerus larvatus*) is as widespread as the warthog, but infrequently seen due to its nocturnal habits and preference for dense vegetation. Larger still, the **giant forest hog** (*Hylochoerus meinertzhageni*) can weigh up to 250kg. Primarily a species of the West African rainforest, it also occurs in western Ethiopia and in certain highland forests in northern Tanzania and western Kenya, where it is most frequently sighted at Mountain Lodge on Mount Kenya.

Small mammals
African civet (*Civettictis civetta*) Shoulder height 40cm. Weight 10–15kg.
This bulky, long-haired, rather feline creature of the African night is primarily carnivorous, feeding on small animals and carrion, but will also eat fruit. It has a similarly coloured coat to a leopard or cheetah, and this is densely blotched with large black spots becoming stripes towards the head. Civets are widespread and common in many habitats, but very rarely seen.

Similar species The smaller, more slender **tree civet** (*Nandinia binotata*) is an arboreal forest animal with a dark brown coat marked with black spots. The **small-spotted genet** (*Genetta genetta*) and **large-spotted genet** (*Genetta tigrina*) are the most widespread members of a group of similar small predators, all of which are very slender and rather feline in appearance, with a grey to gold-brown coat marked with black spots and an exceptionally long ringed tail. Most likely to be seen on nocturnal game drives or scavenging around game reserve lodges, the large-spotted genet is gold-brown with very large spots and a black-tipped tail, whereas the small-spotted genet is greyer with rather small spots and a pale-tipped tail.

Banded mongoose (*Mungos mungo*) Shoulder height 20cm. Weight around 1kg. The banded mongoose is probably the most commonly observed member of a group of small, slender, terrestrial carnivores. Uniform dark brown except for a dozen black stripes across its back, it is a diurnal mongoose occurring in family groups in most wooded habitats, absent only from the dry west of South Africa, Namibia and Botswana.

Similar species Another dozen mongoose species occur in the region, though several are too scarce and nocturnal to be seen by casual visitors. Of the rest, the **marsh mongoose** (*Atilax paludinosus*) is large, normally solitary and has a very scruffy brown coat, and it's widespread in the eastern side of Africa where it is often seen in the vicinity of water. The **white-tailed ichneumon** (*Ichneumia albicauda*) is another widespread, solitary, large brown mongoose, easily identified by its bushy white tail. The **slender mongoose** (*Galerella sanguinea*) is as widespread and also solitary, but it is very much smaller (shoulder height 10cm) and has a uniform brown coat and blackish tail tip. It is replaced in the western parts of South Africa by the **small grey mongoose** (*Galerella pulveruntela*), similar in size but grey with white flecks on its coat. Also restricted to the dry southwest, the **yellow mongoose** (*Cynitis penicillata*) is a small, sociable mongoose with a tawny or yellow coat. It often occurs alongside the similarly distributed **suricate** or **meerkat** (*Suricata suricatta*), a light grey mongoose with some dark bands on its back and the distinctive habit of sitting upright on its hind legs. Finally, the **dwarf mongoose** (*Helogate parvula*) is a diminutive (shoulder height 7cm), highly sociable light brown mongoose often seen in the vicinity of the termite mounds where it nests.

Ratel (*Mellivora capensis*) Shoulder height 30cm. Weight 12kg.
Also known as the honey-badger, the ratel is black with a puppyish face and grey-white back. It is an opportunistic feeder best known for its symbiotic relationship with a bird called the honeyguide which leads it to a bee hive, waits for it to tear it open, then feeds on the scraps. The ratel is among the most widespread of African carnivores, but it is thinly distributed and rarely seen except at Sinamatella Camp in Hwange National Park.

Similar species Several other mustelids occur in the region, including the **striped polecat** (*Ictonyx striatus*), a common but rarely seen nocturnal creature with black underparts and a bushy white back, and the similar but much scarcer **striped weasel** (*Poecilogale albincha*). The **Cape clawless otter** (*Aonyx capensis*) is a brown freshwater mustelid with a white collar, while the smaller **spotted-necked otter** (*Lutra maculicollis*) is darker with light white spots on its throat.

Aardvark (*Orycteropus afer*) Shoulder height 60cm. Weight up to 70kg.
This singularly bizarre nocturnal insectivore is unmistakable with its long snout and huge ears. It occurs practically throughout the region, but sightings are extremely rare.

Similar species Not so much similar as equally dissimilar to anything else, **pangolins** are rare nocturnal insectivores with distinctive armour-plating and a tendency to roll up in a ball when disturbed. Most likely to be seen in East and southern Africa is Temminck's pangolin (*Manis temmincki*). Also nocturnal, but spiky rather than armoured, several **hedgehog** and **porcupine** species occur in the region, the former generally no larger than a guinea pig, the latter generally 60–100cm long.

Rock hyrax (*Procavia capensis*) Shoulder height 35–30cm. Weight 4kg.
Rodent like in appearance, hyraxes are more closely related to
elephants. The rock hyrax and similar **bush hyrax** (*Heterohyrax brucei*) are often seen sunning in rocky habitats and become tame when used to people, for instance at Table Mountain, Zimbabwe Ruins and Seronera in the Serengeti. The less common **tree hyrax** (*Dendrohyrax arboreus*) is a nocturnal forest creature which often announces its presence with an unforgettable shrieking call.

Similar species The **elephant shrews** are rodents that look like miniature kangaroos with absurdly elongated noses. A number of species are recognised, but they are mostly secretive and nocturnal, so rarely seen. Two good places to see elephant shrews are at Rhodes Grave in Matabo National Park and at the Gedi Ruins.

Scrub hare (*Lepus saxatilis*)
This is the largest and commonest African hare or rabbit. In some areas a short walk at dusk or after nightfall might reveal three or four scrub hares. They tend to freeze when disturbed.

Ground squirrel (*Xerus inauris*)
A terrestrial animal of arid parts of South Africa, Namibia and Botswana, the ground squirrel is grey to grey-brown with a prominent white eye ring and silver-black tail. Within its range, it might be confused with the meerkat, which also spends much time on its hind legs, but unlike the meerkat it has a characteristic squirrel mannerism of holding food in its forepaws. The very similar unstriped ground squirrel (*X. rutilus*) occurs in arid parts of East Africa from the Serengeti northwards, and it is very common in Samburu in Kenya.

Bush squirrel (*Paraxerus cepapi*)
This is the typical squirrel of the eastern and southern savannah, rusty brown in colour with a silvery-black back and white eye rings. It is particularly common in Zimbabwe, where dozens of semi-tame individuals occur in rest camps. A great many other arboreal or semi-arboreal squirrels occur in the region – ten alone in Uganda – but most are difficult to tell apart in the field.

Appendix 2

COMMUNICATING IN EAST AND SOUTHERN AFRICA

Up to 100 languages are spoken in some of the individual countries covered in this guide, and the regional total is probably in excess of 500. The vast majority of these, especially those spoken south of the equator, belong to the Bantu group, of which the best-known tongues are Swahili, Kikuyu, Chichewa, Mashona, Xhosa, Sesotho and Zulu. Fortunately for most readers, however, the most widely spoken language in the region is English; in most circumstances anybody who can read this guide will have no problems getting around. The exception is Mozambique, where Portuguese is the language of education and business and very few people speak English. Travellers heading off the beaten track in Tanzania and Ethiopia may also hit linguistic barriers, but in other countries it would be remarkable to be unable to find somebody who speaks English.

The languages covered in this appendix are Portuguese, Amharigna (spoken throughout Ethiopia) and Swahili (the *lingua franca* of small-town and rural East Africa). Also included is a section on speaking English to Africans, and a glossary of Afrikaans and other words that have crept into southern African English, along with Afrikaans words that commonly occur on South African road signs.

Most place names are Bantu and are pronounced phonetically, often with the stress on the second last syllable, so that Same is pronounced SAR-may and Uganda oo-GUN-dah. Non-Bantu place names (mostly north of the Equator) are generally pronounced as for Bantu (for instance Robe is pronounced Row-bay) but with no stress on the second last syllable. In southern Africa, places with Afrikaans, Dutch or German names are generally pronounced as such by local English speakers, though there are exceptions (most notably Johannesburg which would start with a 'y' sound in Afrikaans).

Swahili

Swahili (or KiSwahili) is a coastal Bantu language which adopted several words from Arabic, Portuguese, Indian, German and English and spread into the interior along the nineteenth-century slave caravan routes. It is the official language of Tanzania, the *lingua franca* of Kenya, and spoken in bordering parts of Uganda, Malawi, Rwanda, Burundi, Congo, Zambia and Mozambique. Visitors to Tanzania and Kenya will find it helpful to master a few basic Swahili phrases and those heading off the beaten track in Tanzania will find it practically essential.

Pronunciation

Vowel sounds in Swahili and most other Bantu languages are as follows:

a   like the a in *father*
e   like the e in *wet*
i   like the ee in *free*, but less drawn-out

o   somewhere between the o in *no* and the word *awe*
u   similar to the oo in *food*

The double vowel in words like *choo* or *saa* is pronounced like the single vowel, but drawn out for longer. Consonants are in general pronounced as they are in English, though *l* and *r* are interchangeable in most Bantu languages (so *Kalema* is just as often spelt or pronounced *Karema*) as are *b* and *v*. You will be better understood if you speak slowly and avoid the common English-speaking habit of clipping vowel sounds – listen to how Swahili-speakers pronounce their vowels. In most Swahili words, pronunciation is phonetic with the emphasis on the second last syllable.

Grammar

Swahili is a simple language in that most words are built from a root word using prefixes. The main pronouns are *ni* (me), *u* (you), *tu* (us), *wa* (they) and *a* (he/she). Tense-related prefixes include *ku* (infinitive), *haku* (infinitive negative), *na* (present), *si* (present negative), *ta* (future) and *li* (past).

From a root word such as *taka* (want) you might thus build the following phrases:

Unataka soda	You want a soda
Tutataka soda	We will want a soda
Alitaka soda	He/she wanted a soda

In practice, *ni* and *tu* are often dropped from simple statements (it would be more normal to say *nataka soda* than *ninataka soda*). In many situations there is no interrogative mode in Swahili; the difference between a question and a statement lies in the intonation.

Greetings

There are several common greetings in Swahili. Although allowances are made for tourists, it is rude to start talking to someone without first using one or other formal greeting. The well-known greeting *Jambo* is perfectly adequate, though it is essentially a tourist greeting (the more correct *Hujambo*, to which the reply is *Sijambo*, is used in some areas). More widely used greetings generally start with the phrase *Habari*, for instance *Habari ya safari*, *Habari ako* or *Habari gani* (very loosely, *How is your journey*, *How are you* and *How are things* respectively). *Mzuri* is the polite reply to any such request. A more trendy greeting is *Mambo*, which few tourists recognise – reply *Safi* and you've made a friend. Another word often used in greeting is *Salama* (peace). When you enter a shop or hotel reception, you will often be greeted by a friendly *Karibu* (Welcome). *Asante sana* (thank you very much) seems an appropriate response.

It's polite to greet elders with the expression *Shikamu*. Children in Tanzania may greet you in this way, often with their heads bowed and so quietly it sounds like *Sh..oo* – a pleasant change from *Mzungu give me shilling*; and the polite answer is *Marahaba* (I'm delighted). It is respectful to address an old man as *Mzee*. *Bwana* means *Mister* and might be used to address a male who is equal or senior to you in age or rank, but who isn't a *Mzee*. Older women can be addressed as *Mama*.

The following phrases will come in handy for small talk:

Where have you just come from?	*(U)natoka wapi?*
I have come from Moshi	*(Ni)natoka Moshi*
Where are you going?	*(U)nakwenda wapi?*
We are going to Arusha	*(Tu)nakwende Arusha*

What is your name?	*Jina lako nani?*
My name is Philip	*Jina langu ni Philip*
Do you speak English?	*Unasema KiEngereze?*
I speak a little Swahili	*Ninasema KiSwahili kidigo*
Sleep peacefully	*Kulala salama*
Goodbye (for now)	*Kwaheri (sasa)*
Have a safe journey	*Safari njema*
Come again (welcome again)	*Karibu tena*
I don't understand	*Sielewi*
Say that again	*Sema tena*
No problem	*Hakuna matata*
Thanks very much	*Asante sana*

Day-to-day queries

The normal way of asking for something is *Ipo?*, which roughly means *Is there?*, so if you want a cold drink you would ask *Ipo soda baridi?* The response will normally be *Ipo* or *Kuna* (there is) or *Hamna* or *Hakuna* (there isn't). Once you've established the shop has what you want, you might ask *Nataka koka mbili* (I want two Cokes). To check the price, ask *Shillingi ngape?* The Swahili word for please, *tafadhali*, is rarely used in practice and it often provokes mirth coming from a foreigner. On the other hand, an *asante* (thank you) or *pole* (excuse me, sorry) will never go wrong in day-to-day conversation.

One way of getting around vocabulary limitations when you are shopping is to ask for a brand name such as *Omo* (washing powder) or *Blue Band* (margarine). Remember, too, that Swahili words for many modern things often derive from English: *resiti* (receipt), *gari* (car), *polisi* (police), *posta* (post office) and – my favourite – *stesheni masta* (station master). In desperation, it's always worth trying the English word with an *ee* sound on the end.

Where is there a guesthouse?	*Ipo wapi gesti?*
Do you have a room?	*Ipo chumba?*
Is there a bus to Moshi?	*Ipo basi kwenda Moshi?*
When does the bus depart?	*Basi ondoka saa ngapi?*
When will the vehicle arrive?	*Gari tafika saa ngapi?*
How far is it?	*Bale gani?*
I want to pay now	*Ninataka kulipa sasa*

Numbers

1	moja	10	kumi	90	tisini
2	mbili	11	kumi na moja	100	mia (moja)
3	tatu	20	ishirini	150	mia moja hamsini
4	nne	30	thelathini	155	mia moja hamsini
5	tano	40	arobaini		na tano
6	sita	50	hamsini	200	mia mbili
7	saba	60	sitini	1,000	elfu (moja) or
8	nane	70	sabani		mia kumi
9	tisa	80	themanini		

Swahili time

Many travellers to East Africa fail to come to grips with Swahili time, for which reason they hit serious misunderstandings when using public transport in remote parts of East Africa. The Swahili clock starts at the equivalent of 06.00, so that *saa moja asubuhi* (hour one in the morning) is 07.00, *saa mbili jioni* (hour two in the evening) is 20.00 etc. To ask the time in Swahili, say *Saa ngape?* If you are told in English that a bus leaves at nine, ask whether this is *saa tatu* or *saa tisa*, since some East Africans who speak English will convert to Western time and others won't. The days are Monday = *Jumatatu*, Tuesday = *Jumanne*, Wednesday = *Jumatano*, Thursday = *Alhamisi*, Friday = *Ijumaa*, Saturday = *Jumamosi* and Sunday = *Jumapili*.

Food and drink

avocado	*parachichi*	meat	*nyama*
bananas	*ndizi*	milk	*maziwa*
bananas (cooked)	*matoke*	onions	*vitungu*
beef	*(nyama ya) ngombe*	orange(s)	*(ma)chungwa*
bread (loaf)	*mkate*	pawpaw	*papai*
bread (slice)	*tosti*	pineapple	*nanasi*
chicken	*kuku*	potatoes	*viazi*
coconuts	*nazi*	rice (cooked plain)	*wali*
coffee	*kahawa*	rice (uncooked)	*mchele*
egg(s)	*(ma)yai*	salt	*chumvi*
fish	*samaki*	sauce	*mchuzi/supu*
food	*chakula*	sugar	*sukari*
fruit(s)	*(ma)tunda*	tea (without milk)	*chai (ya rangi)*
goat	*(nyama ya) mbuzi*	vegetables	*mbogo*
maize porridge	*ugali*	water	*maji*
mango(es)	*(ma)embe*		

Other useful words

again	*tena*	OK	*sawa*
big	*kubwa*	pay	*kulipa*
boat	*meli*	road	*barabara*
bus	*basi*	shop	*duka*
car	*gari*	slow	*pole pole*
cold	*baridi*	small	*kidogo*
come here	*njoo*	soon	*bado kidogo*
excuse me	*samahani*	stop	*simama*
European	*Mzungu*	there are	*zipo*
far away	*mbale kubwa*	there is	*ipo*
friend	*rafiki*	there isn't	*hamna*
good	*mzuri*	thief	*mwizi*
here	*hapa*	today	*leo*
hot	*moto*	toilet	*choo*
later	*bado*	tomorrow	*kesho*
me	*mimi*	very/many	*sana*
more	*ingine*	where	*wapi*
nearby	*karibu*	yes	*ndiyo*
no	*hapana*	yesterday	*jana*
now	*sasa*	you	*wewe*

Amharigna

Amharigna (pronounced *Amharinya* and often called Amharic) is a Semetic language spoken by the Amhara people of northwest Ethiopia. Amharigna was until recently the official language of Ethiopia and it remains the *lingua franca*. Most Ethiopian languages including Amharigna are written in a script unique to the country, for which there is no single correct English transcription. Hence the many different spellings of Ethiopian place names: Woldio or Weldiya, Mekele or Maqale, Zikwala or Zouquala, Addis Ababa or Adees Abeba. Generally, I spell Amharigna words as they sound to me. Vowel sounds are close to those in Swahili and pronunciation is phonetic – the town Bore is not pronounced 'Bor' but 'Bor-ay'.

Magic words
One word that every visitor to Ethiopia should know is *ishee* which roughly means 'OK' and can be used as an alternative to the myriad ways of saying hello or goodbye, to signal agreement, to reassure people etc. This is not just a foreigner's short cut – *ishee* is the single most spoken word in Ethiopia and I've often heard entire conversations which consisted of nothing more than two Ethiopians bouncing *ishee* backwards and forwards! A useful phrase, equivalent to the Swahili *kakuna matata*, is *chigger yelem*.

Greetings and farewells
Useful all-purpose greetings are *tenestalegn* (basically 'hello') and *selam* (identical in meaning to the Arabic *Salaam* and Swahili *Salama*). To enquire how somebody is, ask *denaneh?* to a male and *denanish?* to a female. The correct response to these and other greetings (of which there are dozens, invariably starting with the phrase *indemin-*) is *dehena*. There are just as many ways of saying good-bye or farewell; easiest to settle on *ciao* – preceded if you like with an *ishee*!

Questions and answers
The first barrier when you travel in unfamiliar linguistic surrounds is to learn a few basic questions and understand the answers. Answers first: *awoh* means yes, *aydelem* no, and in casual use these are often shortened to *aw* (pronounced as the 'ow' in 'how') and *ay* (pronounced 'eye'). Some Ethiopians use a rather startling inhalation of breath to signal assent.

You'll often use and hear the words *aleh* (there is) and *yelem* (there is not); for instance if you want to find out if a place serves coffee (*buna*), you would ask *buna aleh?* and the response should be *aleh* or *yelem*. Once you have established that what you want is in the *aleh* state, either say *falegalu* (I want) or state what you want and how many (for instance *and buna* (one coffee) or *hulet birra* (two beers). It's not customary to precede your request with *ibakih* or *ibakesh* (please to a male and female respectively), but you should say *ameseganalu* (thank you) when you get what you ask for.

The Amharigna word *no* means something roughly equivalent to 'is' and it is often interjected in a conversation much as we might say 'true' or 'really'. Needless to say, if you say *no* to somebody who isn't familiar with English they may well assume you mean 'yes'. If you don't want something, say *alfelagem*.

The word for 'where' is *yet*, from which derive the questions *yetno?* (where is?), *wedetno?* (to where?) and *keyetno?* (from where?). 'What' is *min*, which gives you *mindeno?* (what?), *lemin?* (why?), *minaleh?* (what is there?) and *indemin* (how?). *Mecheno?* is 'when?', *man?* is 'who?' and *sintno?* is 'how much?' .

Simple questions can be formed by prefixing the above phrases with a subject. Some examples:

Where is this bus going?	*Awtobus wedetno?*
What food is there?	*Migib minaleh?*
Is there a room?	*Alga aleh?*
(*alga* literally means bed)	

Where is the post office?	*Postabet yetno?*
How much does it cost?	*Waga sintno*
What (literally 'how much') is the time?	*Sa'at sintno?*
What is your name?	*Simu mindeno?*

Numbers
Ethiopian time

1	*and*	9	*zeten*	60	*silsa*
2	*hulet*	10	*asir*	70	*seba*
3	*sost*	11	*asir and*	80	*semagna*
4	*arat*	20	*haya*	90	*zetena*
5	*amist*	25	*haya amist (hamist)*	100	*meto*
6	*sidist*	30	*selasa*	200	*hulet meto*
7	*sabat*	40	*arba*	1,000	*shee*
8	*simint*	50	*amsa*	1,000,000	*meelyon*

Ethiopians measure time in 12-hour cycles starting at 6am and 6pm, in other words Ethiopian time works in the same way as Swahili time, and this can cause similar confusion as in Tanzania. To ask the time in Amharigna, say *sa'at sintno*. Times are from *and sa'at* (hour one) through to *assir hulet sa'at* (hour twelve). It is also worth noting that Ethiopia refers to the Julian Calendar, with New Year on September 11. The year falls seven or eight years behind Western time; in the year we consider to be 1999, it will be 1991 in Ethiopia from 1 January to 10 September and 1992 from 11 September to 31 December. There are 13 months in the calender of the Orthodox church: 12 are 30 days in length and the other is five days or six in a leap year. Most institutions likely to be used by tourists – banks, airline reservation offices – run on the Western calendar.

Food and drink
See also *Food and drink* in Chapter 7.

banana	*mus*	meat	*siga*
beef	*bure*	milk	*watat*
beer	*bira*	mutton	*bege*
coffee	*buna*	orange	*birtukan*
chicken	*doro*	salt	*chew*
egg	*inkulal*	sugar	*sukwar*
fish	*asa*	tea	*shai*
food	*migib*	water	*wuha*

Other useful words

before	*bifeet*	foreigner	*faranji*
bicycle	*bisikleet*	horse	*feres*
big	*tilik*	hospital	*hekim bet*
building	*bet*	hour	*sa'at*
bus	*awtobus*	key	*kolf*
car	*mekeena*	lake	*hayk*
cart	*gari*	later	*behwala*
church	*bet kirkos*	me	*inay*
cold	*kaskasa*	morning	*tiwat*
come	*na*	mountain	*terara*
cost	*waga*	much	*bizu*
dirty	*idfam*	near	*atageb*

enough	*beka*	now	*ahun*
Ethiopian	*habbishat*	problem	*chigger*
far	*ruk*	restaurant	*migib bet*
fast	*fetan*	river	*wenz*
first	*andegna*	road	*menged*
room	*Kifil*	toilet	*Shintabet*
small	*Tinish*	tomorrow	*Nege*
there	*Iza*	very	*Betam*
ticket	*Karnee*	yesterday	*Tilant*
today	*Zare*	you	*Ante/anchee*
			(male/female)

Portuguese
Sally Crook

Mozambicans speak Portuguese in a more sing-songy way than the Portuguese themselves, and their speech is much easier to understand than the guttural string of consonants Europeans use. There are two renderings of the verb 'to be'. *Ser* (*sou, é, somos, são*) is more or less for characteristics or permanent states, and *estar* (*estou, está, estamos, estão*) for temporary states. Many words can be guessed from English or Spanish and some Spanish speakers get along quite well with a mixture of *português* and *espanhol*, popularly known as *portanhol*. Examples include many words ending with -ion in English and -on in Spanish which are similar in Portuguese but end in -ão (plural usually -ões) – *televisão, razão* (reason), *verão* (summer).

Take care, though, for some similar Spanish and Portuguese words have completely different meanings: *Niño* (Spanish = child) versus *ninho* (Portuguese = nest); *pretender* means 'intend' rather than 'pretend' (*fingir*) and it is best not to describe an ordinary man as *ordinário* as this implies he is common or vulgar.

Asterisks (*) denote words derived in or specific to Mozambique or Africa.

ã + a followed by m	nasal (similar to 'ang').	o or ó	o when stressed (as in hot)
c	ss before i or e; k elsewhere	ou	o sound (as in both or window)
ç	ss	õ + o followed by m	nasal (similar to 'ong').
cc	ks	qu	k before i or e; kw elsewhere
ch	sh		
g	soft j before i or e; hard g elsewhere	s	z or sh (at end of syllable)
j	soft j (as in French)	x	sh or s
lh	ly (as in Spanish ll)	z	soft j
nh	ny (as Spanish ñ)		
o or ô	oo when unstressed		

Double vowels are pronounced separately:

compreendo	compree-endo
cooperação	coo-operassaoo

Greetings

Good morning	*Bom dia*	How are you?	*Como está* [komo
Good afternoon	*Boa tarde*		shta]
Good evening/ night	*Boa noite* (meeting as well taking leave)	I am well	*Estou bem* [shtow be(ng)] (or a reply to *como está*
Hello	*Hola*		might be *bom*
Goodbye	*Até logo* (until later)		*obrigado / boa obrigada* = I am
What is your name?	*Como sé chama?*		good, thank you)
My name is	*Chamou me* [shamow mu]		

Basic phrases

Please	*sé faz favor (or por favor)*	What's this (called)?	*Como se chama isso?*
Thank you	*obrigado/a* (I'm obliged)	Who?	*Quem?*
You're welcome	*de nada* (ie: 'it's nothing' – reply to thank-you)	When?	*Quando?*
		Where?	*Onde?*
		From where?	*Donde?* (contraction of *de onde*)
There is no	*não há* (or *falta*)		
Excuse me	*disculpe* (or *perdone me*)	Where is	*Onde fica /é / está?*
		Do you know	*Você sabe?*
give me	*dê me*	I don't know	*Não sei*
I like to	*eu gostou de...*	I don't understand	*Não compreendo* (also *não percebo*)
I would like	*(eu) queria*		
How?	*Como?*	Yes	*Sim*
How much?	*Quanto?*	No	*Não*
How much (cost)?	*Quanto custa / é isso?*	Perhaps	*Talvez* [talvej]
What?	*(O) Que?*	Good	*Bom / Boa* (m/f)

Food and drink

beef	*carne de vaca*	fish	*peixe* [payshy] or *pescado* (as food)
beer	*cerveja*		
bon appétit	*bom apetito*	fizzy soft drink	*refresco*
bread	*pão*	juice, squash	*sumo*
breakfast	*matabicho* (* lit. 'kill beast')		
		lunch	*almoço*
cake	*bolo*	maize beer	*byalwa* (*)
cassava, manioc	*mandioca*	maize, mealies	*milho*
coffee	*café*	maize porridge	*vuswa* (*) or
bean	*feijão (feijoada* = a dish of rice, beans and pork)		*nsima* (* in the north [nsheema])
		meat	*carne*
chicken	*frango* (as food)	milk	*leite*
chips, french fries	*batatas fritas*	pasta	*massa* (NB *pasta* =
dinner	*jantar*		file or briefcase)
drink (noun)	*uma bebida*	pork	*carne de porco*
drink (verb)	*beber*	potato	*batata*
eggs	*ovos*	restaurant	*restaurante*

rice	*arroz*	sweet potato	*batata doce*
rum (local)	*cachaça*	tea	*chá*
snack	*merenda* or *lanche* (elevenses)	to eat	*comer*
		water	*água*
spirits	*aguardente*		

Other useful words

a little (not much)	*pouco/a*	large	*grande*
a lot (very, much)	*muito/a*	lorry, truck	*camião*
aeroplane	*avião*	malaria	*malária, paludismo*
after	*depois (de)*	market	*mercado*
bank	*banco*	money	*dinheiro*
bathroom, toilet	*casa de banho*	mosque	*mesquita*
battery (dry)	*pilha*	mosquito net	*mosquiteiro*
bed	*cama*	mountain	*montanha*
before	*antes (de)*	never	*nunca*
block (of buildings)	*quarteirão*	night	*noite* [noyty]
boarding house	*pensão*	nightclub	*boite* [booat(y)]
book	*livro*	nothing	*nada*
bus	*machimbombo* (*) *autocarro* (Portuguese)	now	*agora* [agwara]
		on the beach	*na praia*
		railway	*caminho de ferro* (noun) *ferroviário/a* (adjective)
car	*carro*		
casualty department	*banco de socorros*		
change	*câmbio*	rain	*chuva*
child	*criança*	river	*rio*
church	*igreja*	road	*estrada* [shtrada]
city, town	*cidade*	sea	*mar*
cold/hot water	*água fria/quente*	shop	*loja*
(hard) currency	*devisas*	small	*pequenho/a*
day	*dia*	street, road, highway	*rua*
diarrhoea	*diarréia*	swamp, marsh	*pântano*
doctor	*médico*	today	*hoje*
dry season	*estação seca*	tomorrow	*amanhã*
enough	*bastante*	to hurt (or ache)	*doer*
fever	*febre*	to swim	*nadar*
film (roll of)	*película*	toilet paper	*papel higiênico*
hill	*colina*	too much	*demais/demasiado/a*
hospital	*hospital*	train	*comboio*
hotel	*hotel*	travellers cheques	*tcheques de viagem*
house	*casa*	village	*aldeia*
hut	*palhota*	yesterday	*ontem*
ill	*doente*	you	*você* (polite, formal), *tu* (familiar)
lake	*lago*		

Numbers

Each part of a cardinal number is changed to ordinal when referring to a place in a sequence (eg: 2112th = two thousandth hundredth tenth second), so it is simpler to call the 11th floor of a building *andar numero onze* than *o decimo primeiro andai*, for instance. For days of the month only the first is an ordinal number (first of May, but two of May etc). Therefore, one can get by with only the cardinal numbers and *primeiro/a* (= first).

1	um/uma	9	nove	60	sessenta
2	dois/duas	10	dez	70	setenta
3	três	11	onze	80	oitenta
4	quatro	20	vinte	90	noventa
5	cinco	21	vinte e um/uma	100	cem
6	seis	30	trinta	1000	mil
7	sete	40	quarenta	1,000,000	milhao
8	oito	50	cinquenta		

African English

When you learn a new language, you'll find that your skill at communicating depends greatly on the imagination and empathy of the person you are speaking to. The moment some people realise you speak a few words, they respond as if you are fluent and make you feel hopeless. Other people speak slowly and use common words, so you feel you're making real progress. Needless to say, this principle applies in reverse: as a result, many Africans find it easier to communicate in English with native French or Italian speakers than with English speakers.

Many Africans speak impeccable English, particularly in Zambia and countries further south. A greater number, however, have a limited vocabulary which they get little opportunity to use, and have acquired many idiosyncrasies in their use and pronunciation of those words with which they are familiar. In my opinion, the most useful communication skill for somebody moving through several countries is to recognise how well somebody speaks English and pitch their own use to that level.

Basic rules when dealing with somebody with limited English are to speak slowly and clearly, and to avoid colloquialisms. If you say to a waiter 'I think I'll have a Coke, mate' he may well not know what a 'cokemate' is. When you sense you are not being understood, don't repeat the same phrase or start shouting, but look for different, less complex ways of conveying the same idea – 'One Coke please'. Bear in mind, too, that it is normal for English speakers to prefix a question to a stranger with a phrase like 'I'm terribly sorry to disturb you but...'. This sort of thing can only create confusion when you talk to somebody with limited English; it would be as polite and more sensible to go through the litany of greetings that is customary in most African societies and then to ask for what you want in the most direct way possible – 'Coke?'.

Differences in pronunciation can obstruct communication. One way of acquiring a feel for African pronunciation is to look at the transcription of Amharigna words that were initially borrowed from English – meelyon (million), giroseri (grocery) or keelometer (kilometre). In most African languages, few words have paired consonants, so that Africans speaking English tend to drop things like the 'r' in import (it sounds more like eem-pot) and insert an 'ee' between consonants or at the end of words (so Coke becomes co-kah and penpal is pin-EE-pal).

Remember, too, that there is a tendency to use the grammatical phrasing of your home tongue when you speak a second language. Ethiopians often ask 'time how much?', a direct translation of sa'at sintno, while a speaker of Swahili or another Bantu language might ask 'you come from where?', again mimicking the normal Bantu phrasing. Without wanting to advocate that backpackers resort to Pidgin English as a matter of course, there are circumstances where it is useful to know the phrasing most likely to be understood.

You will find that certain common English words are readily understood in some countries while other equally common words draw a complete blank. As an example, the Amharigna word bet literally means house, but it is used to describe any building or even a room, so that a *postabet* is a post office, a *bunabet* is a coffee shop, and a *shintabet* is a toilet. Ethiopians thus use the English word 'house' in a much looser way than us: somebody might ask, for instance, 'where is your house?' meaning 'which hotel are you staying at?'; likewise, if, say, the word butcher isn't recognised, try asking for a 'meat house' – *sigabet*! One phrase which has caught on throughout the region is 'it is possible', so that 'It is possible to find a bus?' is more likely to be understood than 'do you know if there is a bus?'. Incidentally, Africans are most likely to tell you something is 'not possible' as opposed to 'impossible'. Words can also become completely distorted in their meaning in another country – the Swahili word *hoteli* derives from the English 'hotel' but means restaurant, while South African English-speakers call an artificial lake a dam and refer to the dam itself as a dam wall.

When you deal with officials and waiters, or ask directions or information of somebody whose English is limited, try to take things one point at a time and make sure that both parties are clear on each point before going on to the next one. When it comes to getting directions and information, you ought to allow for a cultural factor, which is that many African cultures find it rude to answer a question negatively – the experience of researching numerous African travel guides has taught me to avoid asking leading questions and on any important matter to canvas as many people as possible.

Doubtless there are a few readers who will see the above as condescending to both Africans and travellers. If that's the case, then my defence is the countless occasions on which I've watched travellers get offensively uptight and aggressive with an African who doesn't understand them, without it once occurring to them that the fault lay in their own inability to simplify their use of language to meet the occasion. When and to what extent you adjust your use of English is a matter of judgement.

Afrikaans and South African English

Several unfamiliar words are commonly used by English-speakers in southern Africa, and a few Afrikaans words regularly appear on signs in South Africa.

bakkie	a pick-up truck, one of the most popular vehicle types in southern Africa.
berg	mountain (range), as in *Drakensberg*, not to be confused with *burg* (town)
boma	traditional enclosure, but often also the communal area at a safari camp
boerewors	literally farmers' sausage. Good for *braaing*, often referred to as plain *wors*
braai	barbecue; many campsites sell *braai packs*, usually *boerewors* and steak
bush	loosely, any woodland or savannah, though '*The Bush*' implies a wild place
dame/here	ladies/gentlemen; toilets are often signposted *Dame* or *Here*
donga	small ravine, often once caused by water erosion
dorp	literally village, but applied vaguely insultingly to any small, quiet town
fynbos	the unique heath-like vegetation of the Western Cape
kantoor	any office
kloof	strictly speaking, a gorge, but often used to describe any rocky cliff or slope
koppie/kopje	a small hill or rocky outcrop. This word is used as far north as Kenya

kraal	traditional cattle enclosure, often used simply to mean a rural farm
lekker	used by English speakers rather slangily to mean nice or good
mielie	maize, the staple crop of the region, used to make *mieliepap* (porridge)
robot	a traffic light
rondawel	a traditional round hut of a design that's often mimicked at campsites
stad	city, as in *Kaapstad* (Cape Town); street signs for *Stad* point to city centre
trek	journey or travel
veld	often translated as grassland, but in practice use is broader, similar to 'bush'
vlei	shallow and often swampy lake, valley or floodplain
yebo	Zulu word literally meaning 'yes' but often used as a greeting

THE BRADT STORY
Hilary Bradt

The first Bradt travel guide was written by Hilary and George Bradt in 1974 on a river barge floating down a tributary of the Amazon in Bolivia. From their base in Boston, Massachusetts, they went on to write and publish four other backpacking guides to the Americas and one to Africa.

In the 1980s Hilary continued to develop the Bradt list in England, and also established herself as a travel writer and tour leader. The company's publishing emphasis evolved towards broader-based guides to new destinations – usually the first to be published on those countries – complemented by hiking, rail and wildlife guides.

Since winning The Sunday Times Small Publisher of the Year Award in 1997, we have continued to fill the demand for detailed, well-written guides to unusual destinations, while maintaining the company's original ethos of low-impact travel.

Travel guides are by their nature continuously evolving. If you experience anything which you would like to share with us, or if you have any amendments to make to this guide, please write; all your letters are read and passed on to the author. Most importantly, do remember to travel with an open mind and to respect the customs of your hosts – it will add immeasurably to your enjoyment.

Happy travelling!

19 High Street, Chalfont St Peter, Bucks SL9 9QE, England
Tel: 01753 893444 Fax: 01753 892333
Email: info@bradt-travelguides.com
Web: www.bradt-travelguides.com

Appendix

FURTHER READING
History and biography

Oliver and Fage's *Short History of Africa* (Penguin, 6th edition 1988) is rated as providing the best concise overview of African history, but it's too curt, dry, wide-ranging and dated to make for a satisfying read. A more focused book that will convey a strong historical perspective to the general reader, Richard Hall's *Empires of the Monsoon: A History of the Indian Ocean and its Invaders* (Harper Collins, 1996), is highly recommended for its storyteller's touch and for its largely successful attempt to place the last 1,000 years of east and southern African history in an international framework. Accessible and reliable historical accounts of individual countries include S Karugire's razor-sharp *Political History of Uganda* (Heinemann, 1980), B Zewde's eminently readable *History of Modern Ethiopia 1855-1974* (James Currey, 1991) and M Newitt's authoritative and stimulating 600-page *History of Mozambique* (Wits University Press, 1995).

Several books document specific periods and/or regions. One of the most up-to-date is the excellent 12-volume *Unesco General History of Africa*, each volume of which comes in a condensed paperback form covering a specific period region by region. For insight into the rise of the Shona and the gold trade out of Great Zimbabwe, a recommended read is D Beach's *The Shona and Zimbabwe 900-1850* (Heinemann, 1980). Good coverage of the coastal Swahili, who facilitated the trade between Zimbabwe and the Arab World, is provided in J de Vere Allen's *Swahili Origins* (James Currey, 1992). Among the better popular works on the early era of European exploration of the African interior are Hibbert's *Africa Explored: Europeans in the Dark Continent* (Penguin, 1982) and those well-known classics of the genre history-as-adventure-yarn Alan Moorehead's *The White Nile* and *The Blue Nile*, first published in 1960 and 1962 respectively and still available in Penguin paperback. An excellent biography pertaining to this era is Tim Jeal's *Livingstone* (Heinemann, 1973). Finally, for an erudite, compelling and panoramic account of the decade that turned Africa on its head, Thomas Pakenham's gripping 600-page tome *The Scramble for Africa* was aptly described by one reviewer as *Heart of Darkness* with the lights switched on. For a glimpse into the colonial era itself, just about everybody who sets foot in Kenya ends up reading Karen Blixen's autobiographical *Out of Africa* (Penguin, 1937).

You'll struggle to find many of the above books in any but the very best bookshops, but you'll have no such problem unearthing enough historical literature on South Africa to keep you reading for months. Among the best general accounts are L Thompson's *History of South Africa* (Yale, 1990) and the highly readable and balanced *Illustrated History of South Africa* (Reader's Digest, third edition 1993). Also worth looking at is D Hammond-Tooke's crisp and lavishly illustrated account of the country's pre-colonial history *The Roots of Black South Africa* (Jonathan Ball, 1993). Reliable accounts of the rise of Shaka Zulu and its aftermath include

D Morris' *Washing of the Spears* (Abacus, 1965; reprinted Pimlico, 1995) and S Taylor's *Shaka's Children* (Harper Collins, 1994), while the history of the Xhosa lies at the heart of N Mostert's highly regarded if discouragingly lengthy 800-page *Frontiers* (Pimlico 1992). Moving closer to the present time, Thomas Pakenham's self-explanatory *The Boer War* (Wiedenfeld and Nicholson, 1979) is as readable as it is authoritative. Among the better books written about events since the unbanning of the ANC in 1990 are Mike Nicol's *The Waiting Game* (Tortuga, 1995), Alistair Sparks' *Tomorrow is Another Country* (Struik, 1994) and Shaun Johnson's *Strange Days Indeed* (Bantam 1993 and 1994) — the last a particularly worthwhile collection of newspaper columns which serve as an impressionistic as-it-happened account of the uncoiling mood shifts of the early 1990s. Finally, Nelson Mandela's riveting autobiography *The Long Walk to Freedom* (Abacus, 1994) also serves as an incidental history of the struggle against apartheid, as does Emma Gibley's altogether more unsettling *The Lady: the Life and Times of Winnie Mandela* (Vintage, 1993).

Field guides and natural history

If you have difficulty finding South African natural history books at your local bookshop and you're not flying directly to South Africa (where you can pick them up easily) get hold of the Natural History Book Service, 2 Wills Road, Totnes, Devon TQ9 SXN (tel: 01803 865913) or Russel Friedman Books in South Africa (tel: 011 702 2300/1; fax: 011 702 1403).

Mammals

The standard mammal field guides for years, largely through lack of competition, have been Dorst & Dandelot's *Field Guide to the Larger Mammals of Africa* (Collins) and Haltennorth's *Field Guide to the Mammals of Africa (including Madagascar)* (Collins). These remain the most easily located books to get hold of in the UK, but both suffer from a ponderous style, outdated distribution and taxonomical information, and mediocre drawings.

Far better is Jonathon Kingdon's superb *Field Guide to African Mammals*, an essential purchase for anybody with a serious interest in mammal identification. The recent democratisation of South Africa has also led to this country's publishers of wildlife books spreading their coverage to countries further north, with excellent results. Chris and Tilde Stuart's *Field Guide to the Larger Mammals of Africa* (Struik 1997) is ideal for space-conscious travellers who are serious about putting a name to all they see. Better for most backpackers is the same authors' *Southern, Eastern and Central African Mammals: A Photographic Guide* (Struik, 1993), which is about 60% lighter but still gives adequate detail for 152 mammal species. The Stuarts have also written the coffee table format *Africa's Vanishing Wildlife* (Southern Book Publishers, 1996), the outstanding book of its sort and highly recommended as advance reading or a souvenir.

Not a field guide in the conventional sense so much as a guide to mammalian behaviour, Richard Estes' *The Safari Companion* (published in the UK by Green Books, in the USA by Chelsea Green and in South Africa by Russel Friedman Books) is well-organised and informative but impractically bulky for the purposes of most backpackers. Those with an interest in ape behaviour would do well to read Jane Goodall's books about chimpanzee behaviour, *In the Shadow of Man* (Collins, 1971) and *Through a Window* (Wiedenfeld and Nicholson, 1990), based on her acclaimed research in Tanzania's Gombe Stream National Park. Also recommended, the late Dian Fossey's *Gorillas in the Mist* (Hodder and Stoughton, 1983) relates the story of her conservation work and research with the mountain gorillas in the Rwandan part of the Virunga Mountains.

Birds

Ber Van Perlo's *Illustrated Checklist to the Birds of Eastern Africa* (Collins, 1995) is the best compact identification manual for East Africa (don't confuse it with John Williams' obsolete *Field Guide to the Birds of East Africa*, also by Collins), describing and illustrating all 1488 bird species recorded in Eritrea, Ethiopia, Kenya, Uganda and Tanzania with distribution maps. In a different league altogether, Zimmerman, Turner, Pearson, Willet & Pratt's *Birds of Kenya and Northern Tanzania* (Russel Friedman Books, 1996) is a contender for the best single volume field guide available to any African country or region, but it's too bulky, heavy and expensive to be of interest to any but the most bird-obsessed of backpackers.

A separate field guide will be necessary for identification in southern Africa, which in birding terms includes South Africa, Lesotho, Swaziland, Namibia, Botswana, Zimbabwe and Mozambique south of the Zambezi. This region is served by a number of comprehensive field guides. By no means the best, but probably the most useful in the context of travelling between East and southern Africa, Ber Van Perlo's *Illustrated Checklist to the Birds of Southern Africa* (Collins, 1999) has the advantage of serving as a companion to the same author's eastern Africa field guide, and is unique in that it covers the 'gap' region of Zambia, Malawi and northern Mozambique. For travellers sticking to areas south of the Zambezi, it would be better to buy one of the South African published guides, of which Gordon Maclean's Roberts' *Birds of Southern Africa* (John Voelcker Trust, 6th edition 1993) has the most detailed text, but Kenneth Newman's *Birds of Southern Africa* (Southern Book Publishers, 5th edition 1996) and Sinclair, Hockey and Tarboton's *Sasol Birds of Southern Africa* (Struik, 1993) are more useful in the field. For weight-conscious backpackers, the best option is the compact *Field Companion to Robert's Birds of Southern Africa* (John Voelcker Trust 1997), which reproduces the comprehensive plates from Roberts with concise identification notes, though regrettably no distribution maps.

Birderwatchers ought to be aware of the high level of inconsistency in English and sometimes even Latin names used in different field guides — not a problem in South Africa, where names are standardised, but confusing when you move between regions, to which end serious birdwatchers will be aided immensely by Phil Hockey's small and inexpensive *Sasol Checklist of Southern Africa: Checklist and Alternative Names* (Struik, 1994).

Other recommended titles are Ray Moore's *Where to Watch Birds in Kenya* (Trans Africa Press, Kenya, 1984); Hugh Chittendon's *Top Birding Spots in Southern Africa* (Southern Book Publishers, 1992) and Nigel Wheatley's *Where to Watch Birds in Africa* (A & C Black).

Other field guides

Struik Publishers in South Africa produce top-quality field guides to everything from trees to fish to reptiles and amphibians, but it's probably the case that such books are too esoteric to find their way into even a tiny proportion of backpacks. Readers with specific interests should contact one of the addresses above, or wait until they get to South Africa where all this literature is really easy to get hold of.

Travel
Travel guides

This aim of *The Backpacker's Manual* is to provide people who backpack through East and southern Africa with one thorough single-volume source of travel information for all the countries they are likely to visit. If I've succeeded in this aim, then the average reader won't need to buy another travel guide to any country. That said, a minority of readers might want to supplement this guide with one or more one-country guides: for instance, if they are spending a long time in one particular country. Given that no 'self-drive' guide to a comparable region exists, it's likely that *The Backpacker's Manual* will serve as a source of general travel information to some travellers who plan to drive through the region, and thus have fewer space restrictions and a greater interest in places that cannot be reached on public transport.

If you're looking for more detailed coverage on one or two countries, Bradt has published a dedicated travel guide to almost every country in the region (major exceptions are Zimbabwe and Kenya). In the case of Eritrea, Ethiopia, Zanzibar, Uganda, Malawi and Zambia, the Bradt guide is the only practical one-country title available. For background information, all these books are considerably more detailed than the relevant chapter here. The extent to which they add to the practical details is more variable: the guides to Zambia, Zanzibar, Ethiopia and Eritrea would top the list, while the Namibia guide would be most useful to motorised travellers, as would the Uganda guide.

Elsewhere, Richard Trillo's lively, enthusiastic and exhaustive *Kenya: The Rough Guide* (Rough Guides, 5th edition 1996) stands head-and-shoulders above any other Kenya guide aimed at backpackers, with an intelligent balance of practical and background information as well as good detail on off-the-beaten-track options. Worth considering for those who plan on doing some serious hiking is David Else's *Trekking in East Africa* (Lonely Planet).

For Zimbabwe, Barbara McRae and Tony Pinchuck's *Zimbabwe & Botswana: The Rough Guide* (Rough Guides, 3rd edition 1996) shares with the same publishers' Kenya guide a pithy writing style and good detail on major tourist spots, but it's disappointingly thin on less well-known areas. Lonely Planet's *Zimbabwe, Botswana and Namibia* (2nd edition 1995) is considerably more detailed.

The one country in the region where a more detailed dedicated travel guide is strongly recommended is South Africa, which has a vast tourist infrastructure and is the subject of several large travel guides. The new Bradt Guide – *South Africa: the Budget Travel Guide* – is aimed squarely at the traveller on a tight budget, with a range of options including South Africa for free. Equally good for backpackers is the annually updated *Let's Go South Africa*, which sticks almost exclusively to budget options and is incredibly on the ball and up to date. Also recommended are the Rough Guide and Lonely Planet guides to South Africa. For current accommodation information to South Africa, the best option is *Coast to Coast*, a regularly updated booklet which lists practically every hostel in the country and is sold at most hostels for next to nothing. (see *Accommodation* on pages 539–40). For detailed information about Swaziland or Lesotho, the best guides are Marco Turco's *Visitors' Guide to Swaziland* and *Visitor's Guide to Lesotho* (both Southern Book Publishers 1994), supplemented by the accommodation information in the booklets listed above.

Travel accounts
Hillaby, J *Journey to the Jade Sea* (Constable)
Marsden-Smedley, P *A Far Country* (Century 1990)
Middleton, N *Kalashnikovs and Zombie Cucumbers: Travels in Mozambique* (Phoenix 1994)
Murphy, D *The Ukimwi Road* (John Murray, 1993)
Murphy, D *In Ethiopia with a Mule* (John Murray, 1969)
Naipaul, S *North of South* (Penguin)
Thesiger, W *A Life of my Choice* (1987)

Maps

The map you want to buy beforehand is the *Michelin 955 Central and Southern Africa*, which covers all the countries in this guide except for Ethiopia (included on *Michelin 954 Northeastern Africa*). The Michelin map should be adequate for planning purposes, both before and during your trip and, if you want country or regional maps, these can be bought as you go along.

There are government map sales offices in most capital cities selling Survey maps useful to hikers. These are normally very cheap and in most countries they can be bought on the spot, though the map sales offices in Nairobi and Addis Ababa are very bureaucratic. For hiking on East Africa's larger mountains, good commercially produced maps are best bought in Nairobi. In South Africa, maps are supplied as proof of booking for most hiking trails.

Fiction

An enormous range of fiction has been written both by Africans and about Africa. A necessarily subjective shortlist of recommendations follows:

Bartlett, R (editor) *Short Stories from Mozambique*
Boyd, W *An Ice-cream War* or *Brazzaville Beach*
Brink, A *An Act of Terror* or *A Dry White Season*
Cartwright, J *Maasai Dreaming*
Coetzee, J *Waiting for the Barbarians*, *Age of Iron* or *Life and Times of Michael K*
Conrad, J *Heart of Darkness*
Dagarembga, T *Nervous Conditions*
Gordimer, N *July's People*
Lambkin, D *The Hanging Tree*
Lessing, D *The Grass is Singing*, *Children of Violence* (5 volumes), *Under my Skin* (autobiography)
Mazrui, A *The Trial of Christopher Okigbo*
Mungoshi, C *Coming of the Dry Season*
Mwangi, M *Going down River Road*
Mzamane, M (editor) *Hungry Flames* (anthology from South Africa)
Naipaul, V S *A Bend in the River*
Nkosi, L *Mating Birds*
Paton, A *Cry the Beloved Country*
Plaatjie, S *Native Life in South Africa*
Schreiner, O *The Story of an African Farm*
Sher, A *Middlepost*
Theroux, P *Jungle Lovers*
Thiong'o, N *Petals of Blood* or *A Grain of Wheat*
Van der Post, L *A Story like the Wind*

Health

Wilson-Howarth, Dr Jane *Healthy Travel: Bugs, Bites and Bowels*, Cadogan 1995
Wilson-Howarth, Dr Jane, and Ellis, Dr Matthew *Your Child's Health Abroad: A manual for travelling parents,* Bradt 1998

Index